COMPLETE BOOK OF
BUSINESS
SCHOOLS

The Princeton Review

COMPLETE BOOK OF

BUSINESS
SCHOOLS

2004 EDITION

NEDDA GILBERT

Random House, Inc.

New York

www.PrincetonReview.com

Princeton Review Publishing, L.L.C.
2315 Broadway
New York, NY 10024
E-mail: bookeditor@review.com

ISSN: 1014-7292
ISBN: 0-375-76346-5

Editorial Director: Robert Franek
Editor: Erica Magrey
Production Coordinator: Scott Harris
Account Manager: David Soto
Production Editor: Julieanna Lambert

Manufactured in the United States of America on partially recycled paper.

9 8 7 6 5 4 3 2 1

2004 Edition

Acknowledgments

This book absolutely would not have been possible without the help of my husband, Paul. With each edition of this guide, his insights and support have been invaluable—this book continues to be as much his as it is mine. That said, I also need to thank my nine-year-old daughter, Micaela, and her five-year-old sister, Lexi, for enduring all my time immersed in this project.

The following people were also instrumental in the completion of this book: Scott Harris, Julieanna Lambert, Erica Magrey, Erik Olson, David Soto, Ben Zelevansky, Miguel Lopez, Nathan Firer, Tiffany Titus, Michael Palumbo, Patrick Schmidt, Yojaira Cordero, Sarah Kruchko, Jeff Adams, and Chris Wujciak for putting all the pieces together; the sales staff at The Princeton Review: Tore Erickson, Nate Anderson, Eric Anderson, Ronan Campbell, Matt Doherty, Richard Strattner, Stephen Jordan, Josh Escott, and Thom MacLeod; Robert Franek and Young Shin, as well as Alicia Ernst and John Katzman, for giving me the chance to write this book; and to the folks at Random House, who helped this project reach fruition.

Thanks go to all those section-A mates, HBS-92, who lent a hand and provided valuable feedback when this project first got underway. And much appreciation to Kristin Hansen (Tuck '01) and Matt Camp (Tuck '02). Thanks must also go to Ramona Payne and all the folks at The Diversity Pipeline Alliance.

Special thanks go to the following members of the Harvard Business School, Class of '92: John Cattau, Clive Holmes, John Kim, Lionel Leventhal, Patricia Melnikoff, Jay O'Connor, Chiara Perry, and Steve Sinclair. I am also grateful for the unique insights provided by Cathy Crane-Moley, Stanford's Class of '92.

Thanks are also due to the business school folks who went far out of their way to provide essential information. They continue to make this book relevant and vital:

Linda Baldwin, director of admissions, The Anderson School, UCLA

Derek Bolton, assistant dean and director of admissions, Stanford University School of Business

Paul Danos, dean of the Tuck School of Business

Allan Friedman, University of Chicago

David Irons, University of California—Berkeley

Professor Mitch Knetter, associate dean of the Tuck School of Business

Steven Lubrano, assistant dean and director the MBA Program at the Tuck School of Business

Will Makris, Babson University

Rose Martinelli, director of admissions and financial aid of The Wharton School MBA Program

Julia Min, director of MBA admissions, Stern School of Business at New York University

Alysa Polkes, director of career management center, The Anderson School, UCLA

Carol Swanberg, director of admissions and financial aid, University of Chicago

Carol Tucker, interim director of media relations, The Anderson School, UCLA

Jeanne Wilt, assistant dean of admissions and career development at Michigan

The staff at the News and Publications Office, Stanford University

Contents

Part I

ALL ABOUT
BUSINESS SCHOOL

INTRODUCTION

PROVEN STRATEGIES FOR WINNING ADMISSION

Admission to the business school of your choice, especially if your choice is among the most selective programs, will require your absolute best shot. Thousands and thousands of prospective MBA candidates spend loads of time and money making sure they select, and are in turn admitted to, the "best" school. They spend their time working in jobs they think will impress a b-school; studying and preparing for the GMAT; writing essays; interviewing; visiting prospective schools; and buying guides like—but not as good as—this one.

This book is your best bet. It takes you into the secret deliberations of the admissions committees at the top schools. You get a firsthand look at who decides your fate. More important, you learn what criteria are used to evaluate applicants. As we found out, things aren't always the way you'd expect them to be. You also get straight talk from admissions officers—what dooms an application and how to ace the interview.

In addition to getting inside information on the application process, you learn when the best time to apply is, and what you can do before applying to increase your odds of gaining admission.

We also give you the facts—from the most up-to-date information on major curricula changes and placement rates to demographics of the student body—for the AACSB-accredited graduate business schools in the country. And we've included enough information about them—which we gather from admissions officers and administrators—to help you make a smart decision about where to go.

For eleven years, The Princeton Review has been publishing this book. We've always been able to chart the changes in the business school landscape—through the ups and downs, good times and bad. This year, things have been different and what is ahead is tough to predict. To help you navigate the waters, we've gone into greater depth and provided more analysis of recent business trends and their effect on b-school and b-school admissions. We've interviewed deans at several of the top schools to share with you their take on recent events. We also spoke with several Harvard MBAs on the eve of their tenth anniversary to find out what they had to say about their MBA experience and their lives after b-school. Reading all of this will give you added insight into the b-school world, which will, in turn, help you craft your applications, ace your interviews, and gain acceptance to the business schools you want.

HOW TO USE THIS BOOK

After learning what to expect at business school (Part I) and how to put together a winning application (Part II), you'll be able to research any and all of the 376 AACSB-accredited schools, both within the U.S. and abroad, that we feature in this book. You can check out our B-School Listing (Part III) to get the low-down on business school stats and offerings. Below, you'll find a breakdown of the details we offer in each school listing. But first, we'd like to answer some questions about Part III of the book.

How do we choose which b-schools to include in our B-School Listing (Part III)?

Any business school that is AACSB-accredited may be included in the book, as long as that school provides us with a sufficient amount of school-specific data. There is no fee to be included. If you're an administrator at an accredited business school and would like to have your school included, please send an email to surveysupport@review.com.

What's the AACSB, and by what standards are schools accredited?

The AACSB stands for The Association to Advance Collegiate Schools of Business. In April of 2003, the AACSB made some significant changes to its standards for accreditation. In fact, the actual number of standards went from 41 to 21. Some of the changes in accreditation include a shift from requiring a certain number of full-time faculty members with doctorates to a focus on teacher participation: schools may employ more part-time faculty members if they are actively involved in the students' business education. The onus of both the development of a unique curriculum and the evaluation of the success of that curriculum will fall on each b-school, and schools will be reviewed by the association every five years instead of every ten. As a result of the changes in accreditation standards, a number of schools have been newly accredited or re-accredited.

Here's what you'll find in each school listing:

CONTACT INFORMATION

Included in this shaded section at the top of each page is the admissions contact—that person to whom a possible applicant should address all correspondence—and his or her title. The school's physical address comes next, followed by the admission office's phone and fax numbers. Finally, this section includes the admission office's e-mail and Web addresses.

SCHOOL BLURB

Finally, we've offered a few words about what to expect at each school. We tell you if there is one particular attribute for which a program is renowned and we disclose details about the curriculum, student body, campus, or location to add a little flavor to your search. We've concocted these informative blurbs from both the schools' websites and our student surveys.

INSTITUTIONAL INFORMATION

This portion gives the nitty-gritty of the school's character. Is it a public or private school? Are evening classes available? How many total faculty does the school boast? What percent are female? Minority? Part time? What's the student/faculty ratio—important to know if you're one of those students who desire personal interaction with your professors—and how many other students (undergrads, other grad students) at the parent institution are you going to have to wade through to get to class? Finally, is the school on a semester, trimester, or quarter calendar?

PROGRAMS

In this section we tell you what single and joint degrees the school offers (MBA, EMBA, JD/MBA, etc.). For help cracking all those abbreviations, see the Decoding Degrees section on page 493. Each school has academic specialties—like finance, marketing, or accounting—and we include these so you can judge whether the school's programs fit your needs. Any special academic or extracurricular opportunities are also listed in this section. Finally, for those interested in studying abroad, we provide a list of countries in which the school sponsors a program.

STUDENT INFORMATION

The essentials of the student body are listed here. How many total business students are enrolled in this school? What percentage are full time? Female? Minority? Out of state? International? Finally, what's the average age of the b-school students?

COMPUTER AND RESEARCH FACILITIES

Because research and computer facilities are an absolute necessity for the modern b-school student, we present data on the facilities of each school. What libraries and special research centers or institutes are supported by the school? What percentage of b-school-dedicated classrooms are wired for laptops and provide Internet access? Does the school have a campuswide network? What type of computer (laptop, desktop, notebook) does the school recommend to or require of its students? Does the school have a purchasing agreement with any hardware companies? If so, with whom? Finally, will you have to pay a fee to be connected to the Internet?

EXPENSES/FINANCIAL AID

Don't worry, we didn't forget about money. We've tried to provide as much cost information as possible, including tuition (in and out of state, when applicable), room and board (on and off campus), and books and supplies. On the flip side, you'll find the amount of the average scholarship/grant (free money) and loan (not free money) awarded, as well as the percentages of first-year and total students who receive financial aid.

ADMISSIONS INFORMATION (OR, WHAT ARE YOUR CHANCES OF GETTING IN?)

This section lists all the various and sundry details you may want to know when applying to a particular b-school. What's the application fee? Does the school have an electronic application? Do they have an early decision program? When is the regular application deadline? How does the b-school notify its students; i.e., do they admit on a rolling basis or not? Can accepted students defer? If so, for how long? Can students apply for entry in the spring semester rather than the fall? Are transfer students accepted? If so, how many credits can he or she have transferred? Are admissions need-blind? How many applications did the school receive the previous year? Of that number, what percent were accepted? What percentage of accepted applicants actually enrolled? What was the average GPA of incoming students? GMAT scores? Average years of business experience? We also provide a section for the schools to highlight other factors they consider during the admissions process (e.g., communication and leadership skills). Finally, a list of other schools to which accepted and enrolled students applied is included.

INTERNATIONAL STUDENTS

This one's quick and easy. For those international students interested in applying, the b-school reports whether the Test of English as a Foreign Language (TOEFL) is required, and if it is, the minimum score the school will accept.

EMPLOYMENT INFORMATION

We've included some valuable information on post-grad employment expectations students might have. Here's where you will find whether each school has a placement office, the percentage of graduates who have jobs after three months, and the companies who frequently employ graduates. We also graph the most popular fields students enter upon graduation. Finally, in case you have seriously high aspirations, we list any prominent alumni.

AND JUST IN CASE YOU HAVE ANY ADDITIONAL QUESTIONS . . .

What's with the shaded profiles in School Says (Part IV)?

Part IV offers more detailed information about particular business schools authored by the schools themselves. The business schools included in this section pay a small fee for this space. These schools also have basic listings in Part III.

What about the nonaccredited b-schools?

Nonaccredited b-schools may pay a small fee to be included in the book. See page 477 for a peek at these schools.

Good luck!

CHAPTER 1

THIS ISN'T YOUR FATHER'S (OR MOTHER'S) B-SCHOOL ANYMORE

POST–SEPTEMBER 11: A CHANGED MBA LANDSCAPE

The MBA has always been seen as a golden passport, the trip-tik to romance and riches. The destination: career acceleration, power networks and recruiters, elite employers, and of course, generous paychecks.

But not everyone wants to make the trip. Several factors will always impact on the popularity of the MBA: 1) the state of the economy—interest in getting the MBA has generally waxed and waned with economic times; 2) trends and favorable or unfavorable press—in the 1980s, a rash of insider trading scandals in which MBAs were ensnared made the degree look smarmy and other graduate programs, notably law and medicine, look more appealing; 3) the immediacy of good professional opportunities—the collapse of the dot-com boom, followed by the severe retrenchment of traditional MBA destinations (such as investment banks and consulting firms) in this depressed economy, has left many current MBAs stranded; and 4) recruiter demand for newly minted MBAs—do employers see the skill sets of today's MBAs bringing measurable value to their companies?

RIDING OUT THE STORM: A WEAKENED ECONOMY SPURS NEAR-RECORD LEVELS OF APPLICANTS

"Applicants tend to seek shelter during a tumultuous time. They seek safe havens. Business schools are safe havens."

—Linda Baldwin,
director of admissions at the University of California
at Los Angeles's Anderson School of Business

So where does the MBA stand these days? Once again, it's in great demand. Recent events have made business school a great place to ride out the weakened economy.

Historically, the opportunity cost of leaving the work force for two years is minimized in a weak economy. During recessions, cutbacks in spending diminish opportunities to move up the corporate ladder, and waves of layoffs wash through corporate America. It's a no-brainer at times like these to look to b-schools to gain a key credential, develop networks of contacts, and even have some fun.

The "At-a-Glance" Version of the High-Tech Revolution

Head spinning from how fast the high-tech story unfolded? Need the abridged version? We did too, so here it is:

Early, high-visibility "liquidity events" such as initial public offerings (IPOs) showed that young people could gain extravagant wealth quickly by "scaling" their new Internet businesses and selling them to high bidders or by going public. Newly established techie business magazines competed with heavyweights like *Fortune* and *Forbes* in a race to get these stories out. The media blitz about this new unprecedented era of success stoked even greater interest in joining the dot-com race. Indifferent to gender, nationality, or race, the Nasdaq minted new millionaires daily. With all the hype, IPOs went right out of the gate to ravenous investor demand.

Continued

The increase in applications since September 11 is in sharp contrast to the numbers in recent years, when b-school applications trailed off. Between 1999 and 2000, the perceived value of the degree to potential applicants had dropped considerably in light of the booming economic climate, and according to the Graduate Management Admissions Council (GMAC), applications at full-time b-schools had decreased by 27 percent. In 2000, Rose Martinelli, director of admissions for the University of Pennsylvania Wharton MBA Program, commented on this drop: "Last year [2000], our applications fell by 11 percent. While we don't have accurate reasons for why this happened, we can point to certain indicators: a soaring economy, the lure to Internet companies, and people trying to pursue get-rich-quick strategies."

Of course, back in 2000, the hi-tech economy was roaring ahead. Economic experimentation occurred across a range of industries trying to make sense of the Internet. MBA or not, these companies needed brain power and bodies. Dot-coms hired extravagantly and paid obscene levels of salaries. With the dot-com boom, the very need for the MBA was questioned. How could two years at an MBA program keep up with the impact and rapid-fire changes of the Internet?

Unsurprisingly, professionals in their mid-twenties who would have followed the traditional path to b-school took that faster route to success. Rather than work their way up through a traditional organizational ladder, they become senior managers of newly formed dot-coms. Not even the most pedigreed program could compete with the immediacy and enormity of riches that the high-tech world offered.

Fast-forward to the present and the near future. The dot-com world has long fizzled. The economy hit the skids after the longest period of growth prosperity in history, and the September 11 attacks knocked the economy off its remaining leg. Most economists agree that we are finally nearing the end of a recession. Still, some skepticism remains.

Given all this, it's no surprise that the tough job market has influenced an unprecedented increase in the volume of applications. Applicants are worried about not only the economy and the threat of layoffs, but also their ability to remain competitive in the business world. Their survival strategy? They've decided to head back to b-school to acquire a degree that turbo-charges their future.

EXTREME APPLICATIONS

The spike in b-school applications in 2001 was far from normal, even in a time when a traditional business school education is once again perceived to be the best bet for many young professionals. At the Anderson School of Business, applications came in at an astounding rate in the first round. Admissions officers saw an increase of between 50 and 60 percent more applications than they had in the same round in the previous year. Notes Linda Baldwin, director of admission at the University of California at Los Angeles' Anderson School of Business, "What occurred for the past year [2001] for almost all the top schools occurred unusually early in the first three months. This absolutely coincided with two forces: September 11 and the economic downturn. The online application process became a true phenomenon in that it made it very easy to apply. Given what prospective applicants were hearing in terms of the recession, by the end of January the volume of applications was still high, at a time when we typically start to see a decline. In the last rounds it finally leveled off. This showed us how sensitive applications are to market trends and world events."

Stanford's School of Business saw a similar rise in applications, with an overall increase of about 10 to 15 percent. Derrick Bolton, director of admissions at Stanford, suggests another factor that may have impacted the less-than-normal first round: the feeling that b-school was the only option. "We saw a substantial change in the number of schools applicants applied to. Instead of a candidate applying to two schools, they applied to five."

Overall, application numbers in the past year have continued to rise despite increased hope for economic recovery. But, Anderson's Baldwin advises, "Looking ahead, the economy looks brighter, and there is more confidence. There are options. Now that things have come back to normalcy, people might say to themselves, 'Is this the right time to apply?' . . . I think about the people who started school in 2000. At that time everything looked bright. The peak was occurring at that point in terms of the economy, so timing is of the essence in terms of making a decision. You may not want to jump in when things are peaking. You really have to ask yourself how risk averse you are. But to reap great rewards, you have to risk."

As the economy recovers over the next year, app-happy candidates may simmer down, and b-school may lose its top spot in the hot destination rankings. For the near future however, it's likely that competition will remain stiff. Whatever tomorrow brings, one thing seems certain: in joining those who've chosen to pursue the MBA, you'll find yourself in stellar company.

YOUNGER MINDS

Although growing applicant pools may make admission seem impossibly competetive, there are now some unrecognized opportunities for candidates with less than the traditional two to four years of work experience to make a strong case for admittance.

Interest in turning to b-school after September 11 reinforced a small but notable trend toward re-thinking rigid admittance standards on work experience. Many schools had already begun to assess their emphasis on work experience as the be-all and end-all.

Continued

Starting with Netscape, the first high-profile Internet IPO, venture capitalists rushed their investment progeny ever faster into the hands of the investment bankers. In turn, these bankers put on "road shows" to explain the merits of their new company to analysts and investors at stops around the country. With the hype of the transformative power of the Internet, increasingly immature companies went public. Many were not even truly "revenue validated"—in other words, earning real sales dollars as opposed to just having a sizzling business concept.

As investors realized that much of the offerings coming through the pipeline were of low quality and that most of the hyped companies had little chance of earnings worthy of their valuations, the whole process came abruptly to a stop in March of 2000. The IPO window slammed shut. Companies started running out of funding from VCs and began folding in increasing numbers. And suddenly, the dot-com boom came to an ignominious end.

Admissions officers at large benchmark schools such as Stanford say that at their respective institutions this trend pre-dates the economic downturn. Stanford's Bolton notes, "The pendulum has gone too far in one direction in terms of the number of younger candidates applying to b-school. It has not kept pace with the overall pace of all applicants. We want more young applicants applying. The goal is to bring the average age down in the next couple of years."

"What's driving this is the willingness on the part of the b-schools to not be rigidly fixed on what's right for someone. We may not always be the best judge of when the best time is for a candidate to go to b-school," continues Bolton.

Wharton's Martinelli observed "a shift in that we became more tuned in to when students are ready in their leadership, professional, and personal development. We see so many nontraditional students that we don't want to have rules on when they can apply. We don't want to miss out on fabulous applicants because they don't think they can get in."

"When the applicant pool continues to get older and older, then we're closing out younger applicants who are on a fast track." Continues Martinelli, "Why should we wait? Why should they wait? We want to catch the human element in the application process."

At the Anderson School, there is a growing recognition that younger applicants can contribute as much in the classroom as their older counterparts. Baldwin notes, "We had already begun to consider, 'how much work experience do you really need?' Prior to September 11, we had done some experimenting in bringing in individuals who had less experience and we found they did very well. After September 11, we did see more students applying directly to the MBA program from undergraduate school and knew this was the result of recent events. Post–September 11 and even as the economy recovers, we'll be targeting our efforts at those undergraduates."

There may be more to the story. Because they may be less likely to be in committed relationships or have families, younger students are more active, generous alumni, and b-schools can't afford to ignore the market that these younger students represent. Despite the heightened competition, candidates with less experience are increasingly being deemed worthy of a coveted b-school seat.

FOREIGN MBA STUDENTS: WHAT HAS CHANGED

Opportunities to study abroad for part (or all) of an MBA program are considered highly relevant. U.S. schools stumble over each other to provide amazing overseas options in dozens of countries. Likewise, international enrollment at U.S. business schools has grown steadily. In 2002, non-U.S. students made up an average of 30 percent of the class at top business schools. Of course, that was before the new screening and tracking process for international applicants had gone into effect.

Previously, our position was clear: International students represent a win-win proposition for both U.S. business schools and the foreign industries that send them here. American business schools prize the global perspective and diversity international students bring into the classroom and community; foreign businesses operating in a global economy desire expertise in U.S. business practices, which are becoming the international standard.

So how has September 11 and subsequent wartime security upset this informal but critical partnership that we've established with foreign institutions?

The big change for foreign students appears to be in slogging through the new rules and procedures for obtaining and maintaining a visa under the Bureau of Citizenship and Immigration Services (BCIS). And the snags can be considerable.

As of January 2003, U.S. institutions must comply with the Student and Exchange Visitor Information System, or SEVIS, which tracks foreign students and exchange visitors, as well as some foreign professors. While there is hope that SEVIS will prevent potential terrorists from slipping through the cracks, critics fear that the intensified scrutiny will drive away many foreign applicants. The system may cause major delays in obtaining a student visa and additional delays whenever leaving or re-entering the country. In addition, compliance with SEVIS requires the staff of international student offices to perform a great deal of data entry, detracting from the face time advisors can spend with foreign students.

For the foreseeable future, students wishing to obtain a visa will not be able to escape the shadow of world events, but they should not be deterred. Most business schools stand firm on their commitment to foreign applicants throughout the entire process.

To those applying for a visa, Wharton's Martinelli offers this advice: "Emphasize plans to return home, rather than plans to immigrate to the United States." If a visa is denied, many schools will defer admission and hold that student's spot until the visa is obtained. Sums up Martinelli, "It may take a little longer for students from some countries to get their visas. But decisions here are not made based on whether they got a visa or not. Decisions are made based on what they'll do at our school and on the contributions they'll make."

Non-U.S. citizens should visit the BCIS website (www.bcis.gov) for the latest information on student visas.

THE CONTINUING RELEVANCE OF BUSINESS SCHOOL

> ## A Historical Perspective on B-School Curricula
>
> Revamped curricula are nothing new. Through the 1990s, three waves of change hit curricula across the country. First, in the early part of the decade, schools reeled from criticism that their graduates lacked ethics and were only out for themselves. The result? Major overhauls included Outward-Bound-type, touchy-feely orientation programs—which continue today—and loads of programs on ethics and diversity. Then, the concept of leadership broadened to include and eventually be founded on collaboration skills. Recruiters were demanding that graduating MBAs be team players, not command-and-control business warriors. Finally, to prepare graduates for the increasingly global nature of business, programs updated their materials and course structures to emphasize global commerce and decision-making in large and small countries around the world.
>
> The point of all this is that business schools are always going to change with the times. During times of great change, the pendulum will swing wildly. Inevitably, it will swing back to its point of equilibrium. Instead of schools focusing intensely on all the latest trends, they'll move to a more disciplined integration of what's new with what's basic.

The MBA is such an attractive option because it *does* confer huge value on the recipient. Business schools know how to keep pace with the rapidly changing face of business. After all, that's *their* business, so you're never really out of the game. In fact, if you look at the nation's top business programs, you'll find exciting innovations in curriculum that reflect all that's new and relevant. This includes unique opportunities for teamwork, internships, and laboratory simulations that replicate real-world, real-time business scenarios.

The integration of these real-world experiences into the basics produces better-trained, more well-rounded managers, as graduates are more adept at discerning the correlation between principle and reality. Even so, a turn from fad courses in search of business knowledge that is more widely applicable and more relevant long-term has caused a strong return to fundamentals.

BACKPEDALING TO THE BASICS

Many top schools are reviving the old classics: it's back to basics. Both schools and students now have enough of a perspective to look back at the frenzy of the last business cycle and understand that enduring values are rooted in a solid foundation. Gone is the frothy demand for trendy courses on e-commerce and other hype-driven topics. Just three years ago, a class at Stanford on the principles of Internet marketing was oversubscribed. Last year, only two people signed up for it.

So here's a sampler of the back-to-basics you'll get at b-school: an in-depth immersion in all of the key functional areas of an organization: marketing, management, sales, finance, operations, logistics, etc. And you'll look at these areas across dozens of industries and organizational types, from start-ups to Fortune 500 companies.

But the renewed focus on basics doesn't mean that you'll find yourself shorted on current events. Expect plenty of case study debate on corporate governance and the Enron debacle, and expect the themes of global perspective and technological competence to permeate many programs. You'll also find classes and seminars on leadership gaining popularity. "We're seeing a resurgence of leadership courses as students seek out professions and business models that are other-oriented," notes Stanford's Bolton. "This may be a new generation. But these are students who look at business as a positive force in the world, a more noble calling."

SURVIVOR POWER

Once you have your MBA, you can expect to hit the ground running. You'll start off your post b-school career with a load of contacts that you will periodically leverage over your career. Many graduates use the degree to embark on entirely new career paths than those that brought them to the school; consultants become bankers, entrepreneurs become consultants, marketers become financiers, and so on. The MBA has and will continue to be a terrific opportunity to reinvent oneself.

"An MBA is unlike any other professional degree because the breadth of knowledge poises you for a multitude of career choices," says Julia Min, director of MBA admissions for NYU Stern School of Business. "You can be an investment banker, yet two years from that point, segue into nonprofit work. You can move from banking to corporate finance to a venture-capital proposition to ultimately having an entrepreneurial experience. So it's a credential that allows you the flexibility to explore different industries; it's a long-term investment that will give you the tools to transition if you want to."

"What's wonderful about the MBA is that it provides fundamental skills that you can use whenever and wherever you need them," champions Martinelli. "I'm a cheerleader for the nontraditional because I feel the MBA is such a fundamental tool. It offers an ability to enter the business world and link passion with functionality."

"For example, for folks who want to go into public service or nonprofit, even the arts industry, they're very narrow fields. You need the passion and vision to be successful in them. But often credibility is undermined when you don't understand the business world's perspective," states Martinelli.

"You've got to know that industry if you're going to make it viable for the future. But you have to be able to know how to talk to the business world in order to get those investments to make it happen. And that's one of the reasons why an MBA is so valuable. It bestows credibility in the marketplace and helps us maintain these organizations in a world that doesn't often respect passion over the bottom line," she continues.

As a result of the weakened economy, companies continue to take a more cautious approach to hiring. That means even at the top schools recruiting has been deeply affected. Jeanne Wilt, assistant dean of admissions and career development at Michigan, says, "A weak economy, lay-offs, a year's worth of turmoil, the whole combination has made the job market for MBAs tougher, there's no question about that. That means that at the top schools, students maybe not getting the two or three offers they might have, but just one or two. Students are really having to use their networks to go after what they want."

Even so, hundreds of companies continue to visit and recruit from business school campuses. Many can ill afford the cost of bypassing campus recruiting for fear that when their hiring needs increase, MBA students will be less receptive to their offers. Thus, MBA programs remain one of the most effective means to get oneself in front of recruiters and senior managers from the most desirable companies. And while that may not grant you "immunity" from an economy of ups and downs, it will guarantee you survivor power.

GETTING INTO THE BEST SCHOOLS IS STILL TOUGH

With economic recovery at hand (and maybe well underway at the time of this book's publication) the opportunity to dive right into the corporate milieu may once again lure a percentage of young professionals away from the MBA, and application numbers may return to normal. Despite this possibility, if you want to be competitive, you'll need to develop a solid application strategy and apply to a diverse portfolio of schools.

LET US HELP YOU DECIDE

There are many factors to consider when deciding whether or not to pursue an MBA, and we'll help you make that decision in the following chapters. We'll also tell you a bit about each school in our profiles and prepare you for further research into the schools on your list. We've worked hard to provide you with thorough information on every angle of the MBA, but you don't have to take our word for it—see for yourself. Stanford's Bolton advises future applicants, "Start early. Visit as many schools as you can, because it's very hard to differentiate among programs from websites, books, and marketing materials. You need to get a feeling from walking down the halls."

After you decide to go, finding the right program can be extremely difficult. Bolton explains, "Applicants really have to dig beneath the programs they're looking at to determine what's going to make them happy. A lot of people wind up going to the wrong school. A lot of external factors contribute to that. People shouldn't worry about justifying the decision to others, but to themselves."

Chapter 2

Picking the Right Business School for You

MAKING THE DECISION TO GO

The next step for you may be b-school. Indeed, armed with an MBA you may journey far. But the success of your trip and the direction you take will depend on knowing exactly why you're going to b-school and just what you'll be getting out of it.

The most critical questions you need to ask yourself are the following: Do you really want a career in business? What do you want the MBA to do for you? Are you looking to gain crediblity, accelerate your development, or move into a new job or industry? Perhaps you're looking to start your own business, and entrepreneurial study will be important.

Knowing what you want doesn't just affect your decision to go, it also affects your candidacy; admissions committees favor applicants who have clear goals and objectives. Moreover, once at school, students who know what they want make the most of their two years. If you're uncertain about your goals, opportunities for career development—such as networking, mentoring, student clubs, and recruiter events—are squandered.

You also need to find a school that fits your individual needs. Consider the personal and financial costs. This may be the single biggest investment of your life. How much salary will you forego by leaving the workforce? What will the tuition be? How will you pay for it? If you have a family, spouse, or significant other, how will getting your MBA affect them?

If you do have a spouse, you may choose a program that involves partners in campus life. If status is your top priority, you should simply choose the most prestigious school you can get into.

The MBA presents many opportunities but no guarantees. As with any opportunity, you must make the most of it. Whether you go to a first-tier school or to a part-time program close to home, you'll acquire the skills that can jump-start your career. But your success will have more to do with you than with the piece of paper your MBA is printed on.

WHY THE RANKINGS AREN'T A USEFUL GUIDE TO SCHOOL SELECTION

All too many applicants rely on the magazine rankings to decide where to apply. Caught up with winners, losers, and whoever falls in between, their thinking is simply: Can I get into the top five? Top ten? Top fifteen?

But it's a mistake to rely on the rankings. Benjamin Disraeli once said, "There are lies, damn lies, and statistics." Today, he'd probably add b-school rankings. Why? Because statistics rarely show the whole picture. When deciding on the validity of a study, it's wise to consider how the study was conducted and what exactly it was trying to measure.

First, the rankings have made must-read news for several years. Not surprisingly, some of the survey respondents—current b-school students and recent grads—now know there's a game to play. The game is this: Give your own school the highest marks possible. The goal: that coveted number-one spot. Rumor has it that some schools even remind their students of how their responses will affect the stature of their program. This kind of self-interest is known as respondent bias, and b-school rankings suffer from it in a big way.

The rankings feature easy-to-measure differences such as selectivity, placement success, and proficiency in the basic disciplines. But these rankings don't allow for any intangibles—such as the progressiveness of a program, the school's learning environment, and the happiness of the students.

To create standards by which comparisons can be made, the rankings force an evaluative framework on the programs. But this is like trying to evaluate a collection of paintings—impressionist, modern, classical, and cubist—with the same criteria. Relying on narrow criteria to evaluate subjective components fails to capture the true strengths and weaknesses of each school.

The statistically measurable differences that the magazines base their ratings on are often so marginal as to be insignificant. In other words, it's too close to call the race. Perhaps in some years two schools should be tied for the number-one spot. What would the tie-breaker look lie? A rally cry of "We're number one" with the loudest school winning?

A designation as the number-one, number-five, or number-ten school is almost meaningless when you consider that it changes from year to year—and from magazine to magazine. (At least Olympic medalists enjoy a four-year victory lap.)

JUDGING FOR YOURSELF

Depending on what you're looking for, the rankings may tell you something about the b-schools. But it's wise to use them as approximations rather than the declarations of fact they're made out to be.

The rankings don't factor in your values or all of the criteria you need to consider. Is it selectivity? The highest rate of placement? The best starting salary? Surprise: The number-one school is not number one in all these areas. No school is.

The best way to pick a program is to do your homework and find a match. For example, if you have limited experience with numbers, then a program with a heavy quantitative focus may round out your resume. If you want to stay in your home area, then a local school that's highly regarded by the top regional companies may be best for you. If you know that you want to go into a field typified by cutthroat competition, or a field in which status is all-important . . . well, obviously, keep your eyes on those rankings.

You also need to consider your personal style and comfort zone. Suppose you get into a "top-ranked" school, but the workload is destroying your life, or the mentality is predatory. It won't matter how prestigious the program is if you don't make it through. Do you want an intimate and supportive environment, or are you happy to blend in with the masses? Different schools will meet these needs. Lecture versus case study, specialization versus broad-based general management curriculum, and heavy finance versus heavy marketing are other kinds of trade-offs.

One last thing to consider is social atmosphere. What is the spirit of the student body? Do students like each other? Are they indifferent? Perhaps a bit hostile? If you go through graduate school in an atmosphere of camaraderie, you'll never forget those two years. But if you go through school in an atmosphere of enmity . . . okay, you'll still remember those two years. It's up to you to decide how you want to remember them.

Remember when you applied to college? You talked to friends, alumni, and teachers. You visited the campus and sat in on classes (or should have). It's not all that different with b-school. Here are some of the things you should check out:

ACADEMICS

- Academic reputation
- International reputation
- Primary teaching methodology
- Renown and availability of professors
- General or specialized curriculum
- Range of school specialties
- Opportunities for global/foreign study
- Emphasis on teamwork
- Fieldwork/student consulting available
- Student support—extra study sessions, accessible faculty, tutoring
- Academic support—libraries, computer facilities, and expertise
- Grading/probation policy
- Workload/hours per week in class
- Class and section size
- Pressure and competition

CAREER

- Summer and full-time job placement (number of companies recruiting on and off campus)

- Placement rate

- Average starting salaries

- Salaries at five-year mark

- Career support—assistance with career planning, resume preparation, interview skills

- Networking with visiting executives

QUALITY OF LIFE

- Location

- Campus

- Orientation

- Range of student clubs/activities

- Diversity of student body

- Housing

- Social life

- Spouse/partner group

- Recreational facilities

EXPENSE

- Tuition

- Books, computer

- Cost of living

- Financial aid

CHAPTER 3

WHAT B-SCHOOL IS REALLY LIKE

AN ACADEMIC PERSPECTIVE

The objective of all MBA programs is to prepare students for a professional career in business. One business school puts it this way:

Graduates should be all of the following:

1. Able to think and reason independently, creatively, and analytically

2. Skilled in the use of quantitative techniques

3. Literate in the use of software applications as management tools

4. Knowledgeable about the world's management issues and problems

5. Willing to work in and successfully cope with conditions of uncertainty, risk, and change

6. Astute decision makers

7. Ethically and socially responsible

8. Able to manage in an increasingly global environment

9. Proficient in utilizing technology as a mode of doing business

Sound like a tall order? Possibly. But this level of expectation is what business school is all about.

Nearly all MBA programs feature a core curriculum that focuses students on the major disciplines of business: finance, management, accounting, marketing, manufacturing, decision sciences, economics, and organizational behavior. Unless your school allows you to place out of them, these courses are mandatory. Core courses provide broad functional knowledge in one discipline. To illustrate, a core marketing course covers pricing, segmentation, communications, product-line planning, and implementation. Electives provide a narrow focus that deepens the area of study. For example, a marketing elective might be entirely devoted to pricing.

Students sometimes question the need for such a comprehensive core program. But the functional areas of a real business are not parallel lines. All departments of a business affect each other every day. For example, an MBA in a manufacturing job might be asked by a financial controller why the company's product has become unprofitable to produce. Without an understanding of how product costs are accounted for, this MBA wouldn't know how to respond to a critical and legitimate request.

More Insider Lingo

Back of the Envelope: A quick analysis of numbers, as if scribbled on the back of an envelope.

Benchmarking: Comparing a company to others in the industry.

Burn Rate: Amount of cash a money-losing company consumes during a period of time.

Cycle Time: How fast you can turn something around.

Deliverable: Your end product.

Fume Date: Date the company will run out of cash reserves.

Low Hanging Fruit: Tasks or goals that are most easy to achieve (consultant jargon).

Net Net: End result.

Pro Forma: Financial presentation of hypothetical events, such as projected earnings.

Slice and Dice: Running all kinds of quantitative analysis on a set of numbers.

Value-Based Decision Making: Values and ethics as part of the practice of business.

At most schools, the first term or year is devoted to a rigid core curriculum. Some schools allow first-years to take core courses side by side with electives. Still others have come up with an entirely new way of covering the basics, integrating the core courses into one cross-functional learning experience, which may also include sessions on topics such as globalization, ethics, and managing diversity. Half-year to year-long courses are team-taught by professors who see you through all disciplines.

TEACHING METHODOLOGY

Business schools employ two basic teaching methods: case study and lecture. Usually, they employ some combination of the two. The most popular is the case study approach. Students are presented with either real or hypothetical business scenarios and are asked to analyze them. This method provides concrete situations (rather than abstractions) that require mastery of a wide range of skills. Students often find case studies exciting because they can engage in spirited discussions about possible solutions to given business problems and because they get an opportunity to apply newly acquired business knowledge.

On the other hand, lecturing is a teaching method in which—you guessed it—the professor speaks to the class and the class listens. The efficacy of the lecture method depends entirely on the professor. If the professor is compelling, you'll probably get a lot out of the class. If the professor is boring, you probably won't listen, which isn't necessarily a big deal since many professors make their class notes available on computer disc or in the library.

THE CLASSROOM EXPERIENCE

Professors teaching case methodology often begin class with a "cold call." A randomly selected student opens the class with an analysis of the case and makes recommendations for solutions. The cold call forces you to be prepared and to think on your feet.

No doubt, a cold call can be intimidating. But unlike law school, b-school professors don't use the Socratic method to torture you, testing your thinking with a pounding cross-examination. They're training managers, not trial lawyers. At worst, particularly if you're unprepared, a professor will abruptly dismiss your contribution.

Alternatively, professors ask for a volunteer to open a case, particularly someone who has had real industry experience with the issues. After the opening, the discussion is broadened to include the whole class. Everyone tries to get in a good comment, particularly if class participation counts heavily toward the grade. "Chip shots"—unenlightened, just-say-anything-to-get-credit comments—are common. So are "air hogs," students who go on and on because they like nothing more than to hear themselves pontificate.

Depending on the school, class discussions can degenerate into wars of ego rather than ideas. But for the most part, debates are kept constructive and civilized. Students are competitive, but not offensively so, and learn to make their points succinctly and persuasively.

A Glossary of Insider Lingo

B-school students, graduates, and professors—like most close-knit, somewhat solipsistic groups—seem to speak their own weird language. Here's a sampler of MBA jargon (with English translations):

B2B: "Business to Business"—a company that sells not to retail consumers, but to other enterprises. With the renewed focus on more traditional industries, this now stands for "Back to Basics."

B2C: "Business to Consumer"—a company that sells primarily to individual retail consumers. As with the above joke about B2B, business students occasionally say this really means "Back to Consulting."

Four Ps: Elements of a marketing strategy: Price, Promotion, Place, Product.

Rule of Three: You should not talk more than three times in any given class, but you should participate at least once over the course of three classes.

The Five Forces: Michael Porter's model for analyzing the strategic attractiveness of an industry.

Three Cs: The primary forces considered in marketing: Customer, Competition, Company.

THE TUCK INTERVIEW (WHAT MAKES TUCK SO SPECIAL)

In 2001, the Tuck School of Business at Dartmouth received the top ranking in a survey of 1,600 recruiters from around the globe conducted by *The Wall Street Journal*, in collaboration with Harris Interactive. We interviewed Paul Danos, dean of Tuck, to find out why recruiters value Tuck MBAs so much.

"What employers want from their top-performing people are leadership characteristics that relate to how you treat other people."

Q: **Dean Danos, in a study commissioned by** *The Wall Street Journal***, Tuck was lauded by corporate recruiters as the country's number-one business school. Congratulations. Recruiters said you are the school that most successfully graduates students with attributes such as: teamwork, communication, problem-solving skills, and the ability to drive results. Can you comment?**

A: Thank you. You know, a lot of people are on the side of the small school. For many, Tuck is an idealized image of what education should be. I don't think too many people would say, "Oh my idealized image of an education is to be with 2,000 other people in a class." We have worked hard to have this setting and this history. And we will stick to our philosophy, our program, and we are fortunate to have the resources that make our school exceptional.

There are many great schools in this world. But I think our model of a small-scale program, with very high-quality education, and still being competitive at the recruiter level, which is obvious from this *Wall Street Journal* study, is a viable alternative.

One of the categories in which we are very strong, and one which I thought was a clever question, asked the recruiters, "Where would you have liked to have gotten your MBA?" We beat the next school by something like thirty points. That says quite a lot about our program because the people surveyed were all highly experienced, selective recruiters.

Clearly, there is an experience at Tuck that you just can't make up and that is very hard to duplicate—the combination of our history, the personal scale of our program, the teamwork of our students. This place resonates with that idealized image of what an MBA education should be.

Q: **So is it the overall experience at Tuck that imbues students with characteristics that make them so highly valued?**

A: Absolutely. What I believe is this: You have to have a prestigious faculty, very good teaching, and a relevant and strong curriculum—we have all of that. So you have to be in a high-end, worldclass game in terms of all of that, and most of the top schools are. But then I think you have to distinguish yourself.

The way Tuck distinguishes itself is a combination of the way the students live here, the way they interact with each other, and their success with the major blue-ribbon employers of the world that hire MBAs.

If you listen to what those employers say, they say Tuck students meet the test for technical and analytical skills. But Tuck students have something special when it comes to working with other diverse people. And that something is very important.

Most companies want to hire people who can work well with other people. I think the biggest differential treatment people get when they come to Tuck is this ability to be sensitive to others. A very interesting comment we hear from recruiters is when we ask about what they thought about the class they just interviewed. They will say, "You know this is what's unusual about this school: You never hear a Tuck student putting down another just for personal advantage."

The other component to this is, I'll bet every MBA at a top school in the country would say, "I learned as much from my colleagues here as I learned from the faculty." Because the colleagues at a top school are an average of twenty-eight years old, they have had lots of business experience. I think Tuck is one of the best at bringing those people together, in creating teams that truly work together. The teamwork aspect is enhanced because of our location, because students learn to live together and work together a lot more closely.

Q: **But many schools, including those that are small and intimate like Tuck, have attempted to instill a genuine one-for-all feeling among their students. Why have you succeeded?**

A: Well, I believe that there is no school in the world that's better at it. I'm not saying there might not be a few that are close, but if you think about what you want from a business school, which is for all these diverse students to come together and work harmoniously in various teams and also as a whole class, I think we do it as well as, if not better than, anyone.

So to answer your question, Tuck students have an edge because they've been living in this community that fosters sensitivity, respect, communication, and working well with others. Even if you came to this community without such instincts, you have to develop some or else you're going to find you're not going to operate too well. Of course, there's self-selection too. The students who choose to come to Tuck are the ones who want this kind of experience.

But we operate and live as a family here. They all know each other and you will not find that closeness at every school.

Q: **All of this is somewhat surprising. I mean it runs counter-intuitive to what you think of business school. When you think about a business school student, you don't think of sensitivity training.**

A: There's no doubt in my mind that the number-one attribute the best employers want from MBAs beyond a high level of technical skill and knowledge is the ability to lead groups. MBAs must know how to be humane in their management styles; they must know how to be sensitive.

Even in the hardest–nosed industry, that's what people want, that's what the bankers want, that's what the consultants want.

This is something every company wants: What employers want from their top-performing people are leadership characteristics that relate to how you treat other people. This has a huge impact on how employers view and evaluate the people who will come into their organizations.

YOUR FIRST YEAR

The first six months of b-school can be daunting. You're unfamiliar with the subjects. There's a tremendous amount of work to do. And when you least have the skills to do so, there's pressure to stay with the pack. All of this produces anxiety and a tendency to over-prepare. Eventually, students learn shortcuts and settle into a routine, but until then much of the first year is just plain tough. The programs usually pack more learning into the first term than they do into each of the remaining terms. For the schools to teach the core curriculum (which accounts for as much as 70 percent of learning) in a limited time, an intensive pace is considered necessary. Much of the second year will be spent on gaining proficiency in your area of expertise and on searching for a job.

The good news is that the schools recognize how tough the first year can be. During the early part of the program, they anchor students socially by placing them in small sections, sometimes called "cohorts." You take many or all of your classes with your section-mates. Sectioning encourages the formation of personal and working relationships and can help make a large program feel like a school within a school.

Because so much has to be accomplished in so little time, getting an MBA is like living in fast-forward. This is especially true of the job search. No sooner are you in the program than recruiters for summer jobs show up, which tends to divert students from their studies. First-years aggressively pursue summer positions, which are linked with the promise of a permanent job offer if the summer goes well. At some schools, the recruiting period begins as early as October, at others in January or February.

Even More Insider Lingo

Air Hogs: Students who monopolize classroom discussion and love to hear themselves speak.

Case Study Method: Popular teaching method that uses real-life business cases for analysis.

Cold Call: Unexpected, often dreaded request by the professor to open a case discussion.

Functional Areas: The basic disciplines of business (e.g., finance, marketing, R&D).

HP12-C: A calculator that works nothing like a regular one, used by finance types when they don't have Excel handy.

Power Nap: Quick, intense, in-class recharge for the continually sleep deprived.

Power Tool: Someone who does all the work and sits in the front row of the class with his or her hand up.

Pre-enrollment Courses: Commonly known as MBA summer camp—quantitative courses to get the numerically challenged up to speed.

Quant Jock: A numerical athlete who is happiest crunching numbers.

Run the Numbers: Analyze quantitatively.

Soft Skills: Conflict resolution, teamwork, negotiation, oral and written communication.

Take-aways: The key points of a lecture or meeting that participants should remember.

A DAY IN THE LIFE
Matt Camp, First Year

Tuck School of Business, Dartmouth College

7:00 A.M.: Get dressed. Out of the door by 7:45 to head to the campus dining hall for breakfast. If I have time, I'll grab the *Financial Times* and *Wall Street Journal* and gloss over the front page. Today, I have an informal get-to-know-you-better meeting with marketing professor over breakfast.

8:30 A.M.: Core class in Corporate Finance. Grab any seat in a tiered classroom set-up. I'm usually in the middle toward the side. If possible, the front row stays empty.

10:00 A.M.: Go to e-mail kiosk on campus and check messages. Hang out or do a quick run to the library to read more of the *Times*.

10:30 A.M.: Macroeconomics lecture/case study class. Again, no assigned seating. Expect cold calls on case. Cold calls are not terrifying. Professors are supportive, not out to embarass you. Class discussion is lively, with a mix of people offering their view.

Noon: Back to the cafeteria. Tuck may be one of the few schools where everyone eats together at the same place. There isn't much in town, and you're tight on time, so it doesn't make sense to go back home or elsewhere. It's crowded, so I look for friends, but basically grab a seat anywhere at one of the large tables that seat six to seven. Professors, administrators, and students all eat at the same place. Food is above average.

1:15 P.M.: Classes are over for the day. From this point here, I begin to start homework; there's a lot of work to do. I can go to a study room on campus, but they get booked up pretty quickly for groups, so I head to the library. The majority of the people are doing work for tomorrow. It's rare to have someone working on a project that's due the following week. It's pretty much day-to-day.

4:00 P.M.: I head off to one of the scheduled sports I've signed up for. Today it's soccer, played about one mile from campus. I drive; friends hitch a ride with me. This is a big international scene, mostly men, but there's a small group of women too. It's definitely a game we play hard, but in a very congenial way.

6:00 P.M.: Head back to campus. I'm hungry. It's off to the dining hall again. Most first-years live in dorms, so home cooking is not an option. Almost all second-years live off-campus, so they head back for a home-cooked meal. Cafeteria is not crowded; I may eat alone.

7:00 P.M.: Head home for a quick shower and change. The night is just beginning.

7:30 P.M.: Meet with study group at school to flesh out rest of work that needs to be done in preparation for tomorrow's classes.

11:00 P.M.: Students and their wives/husbands or partners head out to play ice hockey at one of the two rinks here. Wives/husbands and partners play. Because there are different levels, there are different games going on for different skill levels. It's a lot of fun.

Midnight: Time to go and celebrate either a hard game or a sore butt, but everyone goes to get some wings and a beer. There are only two bars on campus, and they close at 1:00 A.M. so we head to one of them.

1:00 A.M.: After the bar closes, people head home.

1:15 A.M.: Exhausted, I go to bed. No TV. I've forgotten what that is.

YOUR SECOND YEAR

Relax, the second year is easier. By now, students know what's important and what's not. Second-years work more efficiently than first-years. Academic anxiety is no longer a factor. Having mastered the broad-based core curriculum, students now enjoy taking electives and developing an area of specialization.

Anxiety in the second year has more to do with the arduous task of finding a job. For some lucky students, a summer position has yielded a full-time offer. But even those students often go through the whole recruiting grind anyway because they don't want to cut off any opportunities prematurely.

Most MBAs leave school with a full-time offer. Sometimes it's their only offer. Sometimes it's not their dream job, which may be why most grads change jobs after just two years. One student summed up the whole two-year academic/recruiting process like this: "The first-year students collapse in the winter quarter because of on-campus recruiting. The second-years collapse academically in the first quarter of their second year because it's so competitive to get a good job. And when a second-year does get a job, he or she forgets about class entirely. That's why pass/fail was invented."

Just a Bit More Insider Lingo

Admissions Mistake: How each student perceives him or herself until getting first-year grades back from midterms.

Chip Shot: Vacant and often cheesy comments used not to truly benefit class discussion, but rather to get credit for participation.

Lingo Bingo: A furtive game of Bingo whereby he who "wins" must work a decided upon, often trite phrase (see "chip shot") into the class discussion. For example: "I didn't actually read the case last night, but the protagonist is two beers short of a six-pack." The winner also earns a prize and the admiration of classmates.

Skydeck: Refers to the back row of the classroom, usually when it's amphitheater style.

Monitize: To turn an idea into a moneymaking scheme.

Shrimp Boy: A student who comes to a corporate event just to scarf down the food.

A DAY IN THE LIFE
Kristin Hansen, Second-Year

Tuck School of Business, Dartmouth College

9:00 A.M.: Wake-up (my first class is at 10:30 A.M.) and finish work for Monday classes.

10:15 A.M.: Ride my bike to campus for 10:30 class.

10:30 A.M.: Head to International Economics class, an elective. I have only three classes this semester, my last. Prior to this I had four and a half classes each term. I front-loaded so I would have a light last semester. Grab a yogurt and juice on way in. Eat in class. We discuss a currency crisis case.

Noon: Head to study room to plug my personal computer into one of the many networked connections on campus to check e-mail. Finish work for next class.

1:00 P.M.: Grab a quick lunch in the dining hall. Will bring it to eat during class.

1:15 P.M.: Managerial Decision Making class, another elective. Today is the very last class that second-years will have at Tuck; we're off to graduation! Our professor brings in strawberries and champagne to celebrate. We all hang out and toast each other. This obviously doesn't happen everyday, but this is just the kind of thing a Tuck professor would do.

2:45 P.M.: I'm one of four Tuck social chairpersons, so I use this time to send e-mails to my co-chairs about the upcoming chili cook-off and farm party. Then I send a message to the school regarding other social events for the weekend. I get an e-mail from the New York office of CS First Boston, with whom I've accepted a job offer, with a calendar of the dates for my private client-services training.

3:00 P.M.: Go for a run, swim, or bike.

5:00 P.M.: Head home to shower and change. Usually I'd make dinner at home and eat, but tonight, I'm heading out to a social event. So I relax a bit and do an hour of preparation for the next day. On Monday, Tuesday, and Wednesday nights, the workload is heavier.

7:00 P.M.: Off to a Turkey Fry Dinner. This is a meal that will be prepared by my two Economics professors. They donated this "dinner" for the charity student auction. Friends of mine bid on it and won. Each of eight bidders gets to bring a guest, and I'm one of the guests. The professors are hosting this at one of their homes. Basically, they're taking three large turkeys and fry-o-lating them.

8:30 P.M.: We all head out to an "open-mic" night, led by the same two Economics professors that hosted the Turkey Fry. It's held at a local bar. Anyone in the audience can get onstage and perform. I'm a member of the Tuck band, so I get up on stage with my acoustic guitar and play various folk and bluegrass songs. This is a great warm-up for the Open Mic night at Tuck.

10:45 P.M.: We head out for Pub Night in downtown Hanover.

1:00 A.M.: The bar closes, so we head to "The End Zone," one of the second-year houses close to campus. All the second-year houses are named; these are names that have been passed down from generation to generation. On a typical Thursday night at Tuck, a small number of students will stay out until 3:00 A.M. I'm usually one of them.

3:00 A.M.: I walk home. My house, called "Girls in the Hood," is just a ten-minute stroll away. I may grab a 3:00 A.M. snack. Then, I quickly fall asleep, exhausted.

RECIPE FOR FRIED TURKEY AT TUCK

Prepared by Professor Andrew Bernard and Professor Michael Knetter, who was recently promoted to associate dean of the MBA Program.

From the chefs: "Students would say it's the best turkey they've ever had."

Equipment:

10-gallon aluminum pot with lid

Iron stand to sit pan in, Bunsen burner underneath

Large poultry syringe

Ingredients:

Coca-Cola

Bottle of onion juice

Couple of cans of beer

Garlic powder

Cajun spices

6 gallons peanut oil for frying

12-pound turkey

Directions:

The night before, combine the first four ingredients and bring to a boil. Let cool. Using a big poultry injector/syringe, inject bird with 16 to 20 ounces of marinade. Rub down the outside of the bird with the Cajun spices. Let sit overnight.

Heat the 6 gallons of oil in 10-gallon pot until bubbly. Carefully submerge turkey into 350-degree oil. Leave pot uncovered while turkey is cooking. Cook for about 4 minutes per pound. Repeat process as needed (once the oil is hot, it's easy to cook additional birds). *For a special treat:* try placing a chicken or duck in the cavity of your turkey.

LIFE OUTSIDE OF CLASS

Business school is more than academics and a big-bucks job. A spirited community provides ample opportunity for social interaction, extracurricular activity, and career development.

Much of campus life revolves around student-run clubs. There are groups for just about every career interest and social need—from "MBAs for a Greener America" to the "Small Business Club." There's even a group for Significant Others on most campuses. The clubs are a great way to meet classmates with similar interests and to get in on the social scene. They might have a reputation for throwing the best black-tie balls, pizza-and-keg events, and professional mixers. During orientation week, these clubs aggressively market themselves to first-years.

Various socially responsible projects are also popular on campus. An emphasis on volunteer work is part of the overall trend toward good citizenship. Perhaps to counter the greed of the 1980s, "giving back" is the b-school style of the moment. There is usually a wide range of options—from tutoring in an inner-city school to working in a soup kitchen to renovating public buildings.

Still another way to get involved is to work on a school committee. Here you might serve on a task force designed to improve student quality of life. Or you might work in the admissions office and interview prospective students.

For those with more creative urges there are always the old standbys: extracurriculars such as the school paper, yearbook, or school play. At some schools, the latter takes the form of the b-school follies and is a highlight of the year. Like the student clubs, these are a great way to get to know your fellow students.

Finally, you can play on intramural sports teams or attend the numerous informal get-togethers, dinner parties, and group trips. There are also plenty of regularly scheduled pub nights, just in case you thought your beer-guzzling days were over.

Most former MBA students say that going to b-school was the best decision they ever made. That's primarily because of nonacademic experiences. Make the most of your classes, but take the time to get involved and enjoy yourself.

CHAPTER 4

PALM PILOTS
AND POWER BREAKFASTS:
WHAT DOES AN MBA OFFER?

NUTS-AND-BOLTS BUSINESS SKILLS

Graduate business schools teach the applied science of business. The best business schools combine the latest academic theories with pragmatic concepts, hands-on experience, and real-world solutions.

B-schools also teach the analytical skills used to make complicated business decisions. You learn how to define the critical issues, apply analytical techniques, develop the criteria for decisions, and make decisions after evaluating their impact on other variables.

After two years, you're ready to market a box of cereal. Or prepare a valuation of the cereal company's worth. You'll speak the language of business. You'll know the tools of the trade. Your expertise will extend to many areas and industries. In short, you will have acquired the skills that open doors.

ACCESS TO RECRUITERS, ENTRÉE TO NEW FIELDS

Applicants tend to place great emphasis on "incoming" and "outgoing" statistics. First they ask, "Will I get in?" Then they ask, "Will I get a job?"

Obviously, the first is largely dependent on how selective the school is and the quality of your credentials. The latter question can almost assuredly be answered in the positive, "Yes, you will."

But the real question is how many offers will you receive? Again, that is dependent on the appeal of the school to recruiters (which is a readily available statistic you can get from each school) and the particular industry you elect to pursue. For example, investment banks and consulting firms are always going to come to the schools for formal recruiting periods, whereas more off-the-beaten-path choices will possibly require you to go off campus in search of opportunity.

GOODBYE GET-RICH-QUICK SCHEMES,
HELLO REALITY

Unhappily, the immediate, economic value of the MBA remains in flux. Although MBAs continue to be in demand, a weak economy and flat national job market have depressed recruiter appetite for new grads. The latest figures suggest a tough job market for newly minted MBAs. And first- and second-year business students are feeling the pinch of a tight job market as both full-time and summer positions become more difficult to obtain.

For the last several years, cash-heavy dot-coms and investment banks flush with business deals made a heavy play for MBAs. The loss of one of these recruitment sources and the downsizing of the other has further shrunk the recruiter pool and made for a more anxious recruiting period. Where once students were awash in three or more job offers apiece, the latest figures are more sobering: students are working hard to receive one or two offers. Of course with fewer offers, the jobs students get, and have to accept, may not be their first choice.

Although the stress of job hunting may be greater, that doesn't mean that hiring has come to a complete standstill. Steven Lubrano, assistant dean and director of the MBA Program at the Tuck School of Business, best summed up the career placement picture: "There are two issues at stake here: what the market has to offer students and what students come to expect when they enroll."

As we write this book, many schools still have a month or so to go until graduation. If past downturns offer us any insight, it is that students will continue to receive job offers up until and right past graduation into the summer months. Adds Lubrano, "Some of the best jobs come very late in the academic year. Our goal at Tuck is we don't rest until everybody has a job and is happy at that job."

At less prominent schools, the picture may not be as optimistic. Heavy hirers of MBAs who have few spots available during this recruiting go-around may bypass these schools.

The good news is that even in an uncertain economy, top schools will continue to produce in-demand MBAs for the marketplace. These schools tend to have an extensive history with big recruiting companies because the schools are a steady source of exceptional talent. Even during an economic downturn, big recruiters can't afford to lose face on these campuses. They need a constant presence at these schools to ensure that they'll have top picks when good times return. In fact, to cement that relationship, recruiters often have a partnership with the schools that includes sponsoring academic projects and hosting school club functions and informational cocktail hour events.

GOOD TIMES, BAD TIMES: GETTING THE MBA FOR THE LONG RUN

As you make plans to go to b-school, you need to accept that there is some risk that the labor market won't greet you with open arms at graduation. Consider the plight of this year's MBA graduates. When they entered b-school two years ago, the economy was roaring ahead. The immediate future looked exceptionally bright. Most MBAs probably thought that once they got in, they had it made, and they looked forward to generous starting salaries and bonuses. Few probably anticipated that tough times could hit so dramatically.

The best way to consider the value of the degree is by focusing on its long-lasting benefits. "When people come here for their MBA, they talk about re-tooling for their life. They think about the long term and recognize that there are some short term hurdles," says Rose Martinelli, director of admissions at the Wharton School. "Just out of business school, this is the very first job in a long career. This is really about building blocks and going for the long run. You may have to work harder to find a job now, but building your career is a lifelong process." The MBA gives you the tools, networking, and polish to meaningfully enhance your long-term prospects and earning potential.

"There is real opportunity here. The opportunity right now is to pursue your passion and perhaps not your wallet," continues Martinelli. "We're seeing more of an equalization in salary. Those high-paying jobs in finance, investment banking, and consulting are fewer and harder to find. So here you have an opportunity for a job with a true learning experience rather than one that just pays a lot. More people are going into nonprofit and government and making contributions back to the community."

SHOW ME THE MONEY

During the dot-com craze, e-commerce start-ups, as well as the more traditional industries, had to compete for students. To get their attention, hefty salaries and option packages were thrown at them. The hiring binge, career placement officers observe, and the over-inflated salaries that went with them, was an anomaly. This year, they argue, will be more typical, and students will have to re-adjust their expectations.

Ironically, salaries for new MBAs in the next few years will seem higher. But again, this is another remnant of the dot-com world that requires a closer look. Because dot-coms offered lower base pay and big options, dollar to dollar, the base salaries in other industries seem higher.

But not all the news is bad. A survey of placement offices reveals that salaries range from $60,000 to $130,000 for average first-year packages offered to MBA grads from top-flight schools.

The majority also receive a generous relocation package. Indeed, if you were fortunate enough to have spent the summer in between your first and second year at a consulting company, then you will, in all likelihood, also receive a "rebate" on your tuition. These companies pick up student's second-year tuition bill. The big enchilada, however, goes to those MBA students who worked at the firm before b-school. These lucky capitalists get their whole tuition paid for.

GETTING A JOB

For most would-be MBAs, b-school represents a fresh beginning—either in their current profession or in an entirely different industry. Whatever promise the degree holds for you, it's wise to question what the return on your investment will be.

As with starting salary, several factors affect job placement. School reputation and ties to industries and employers are important. At the top programs, the lists of recruiters read like a "Who's Who" of American companies. These schools not only attract the greatest volume of recruiters, but consistently get the attention of those considered "blue chip."

Not to be overlooked are lesser-known, regional schools that often have the strongest relationships with local employers and industries. Some b-schools (many of them state universities) are regarded by both academicians and employers as number one in their respective regions. In other words, as far as the local business community is concerned, these programs offer as much prestige and pull as a nationally ranked program.

Student clubs also play a big part in getting a job because they extend the recruiting efforts at many schools. They host a variety of events that allow you to meet leading business people, so that you can learn about their industries and their specific companies. Most important, these clubs are very effective at bringing in recruiters and other interested parties that do not recruit through traditional mainstream channels. For example, the high-tech, international, and entertainment student clubs provide career opportunities not available through the front door.

Your background and experiences also affect your success in securing a position. Important factors are academic specialization, academic standing, prior work experience, and intangibles such as your personal fit with the company. These days, what you did before b-school is particularly important; it helps establish credibility and gives you an edge in competing for a position in a specific field. For those using b-school to switch careers to a new industry, it's helpful if something on your resume ties your interest to the new profession. It's smart to secure a summer job in the new area.

Finally, persistence and initiative are critical factors in the job search. Since the beginning of this decade, many fast tracks have been narrowed. Increasingly, even at the best schools, finding a job requires off-campus recruiting efforts and ferreting out the hidden jobs.

MBA CAREERS: AN INTERVIEW WITH THE DIRECTOR OF THE MBA CAREER MANAGEMENT CENTER AT UCLA

The recruitment of MBAs has always been tied to the state of the economy. To better gauge the current tenor of MBA hiring, we spoke to Alysa Polkes, the director of the MBA Career Management Center at the Anderson School at UCLA. She shares with us her thoughts on the MBA job search process and provides insight into how things have evolved over the last few years.

Q: Alysa, I would think the Career Management Center is the epicenter of the MBA program. What's the mood on campus as students search for jobs? How have things changed from last year—for example, the number of offers students are getting?

A: The number of offers is always a tough one for me because I feel that we sometimes focus on it as the measuring stick of success. I think a student with just one offer that's exactly what he/she wanted to do is better off than the student with ten offers if none of those offers are what the student really wants to do.

So let me focus on the mood and how things are different from last year. When you look at the landscape of MBA career management over the last decade, I would say that overall, except for a little dip in 1991, we have a very stable thing going.

Then last year, we got a whack on the side of the head with the whole dot-com revolution. It created numerous challenges for those of us in the career management field. The primary one was that students were not taking the time for what we consider the necessary first step in this process: self-assessment. The market was so strong and the economy was so hot there really was no need to sit back and reflect on interests, skills, values, and strengths, all that stuff we believe is the foundation to a long-term successful career.

Of course it's true that we still had the bankers, consultants, and brand managers who followed their paths. But for the folks who were in the other categories of undecided or high-tech, they fell into the whole dot-com world.

It was interesting to watch this happen. Our traditional recruiters came in and asked us to help them attract top talent given what was happening. And we had dot-coms calling us who hadn't a clue about the MBA recruiting process, much less scheduling interviews six months in advance and reserving rooms.

Q: Did the more traditional companies up salaries to compete with the lure of the dot-coms?

A: That was one of the consequences. It was not completely out of control. We heard of one instance where a bank had offered a million dollars if you sign a contract that you'll stay for two or three years. But other than that, I didn't hear of anything that ludicrous.

Q: That's pretty ludicrous. But obviously I'm in the wrong field.

A: Exactly. You can suffer anything for two years if you're going to get a million dollars. But beyond that, we saw that what the traditional companies were offering was very competitive.

The problem was that you would think that students would be making a trade-off to go to a dot-com. You would think that, okay, there's a promise of all these options, but the base is not very high.

Q: What do you mean by a trade-off?

A: That the students who opted to go to a dot-com would trade off a strong base salary for the promise of rewards down the road. And they didn't, which made the whole thing more complicated.

They didn't have the trade-off. The dot-com base salaries were $75,000 to $80,000. No one was going to suffer at a salary like that, and then there was still the promise of the options.

The year before was a little different. The class of 1999 had to make some trade-offs for those packages. The dot-com salaries weren't yet what they were in 2000. In 1999, the salaries were fifties, sixties, and the promise of options. In 2000, the dot-com salaries were competitive. And then the lure was the millions.

Q: So . . . fast-forwarding to now . . .

A: Well, having done this for eleven years, you really get a big-picture perspective. Over the course of the summer, the dot-coms started to wind down, and then we heard about banks buying each other out and consolidating, so that raised some flags.

Students began to become cautious about banking opportunities and realized there were would be fewer spots. Then we started to see the demise of the e-commerce consulting firms, like March First. When they were on campus recruiting, the company filed bankruptcy, and they got a call to go home. Then the other dot-coms started going under, and that included the incubators. Then we started to see the venture capital money dry up. Then, we started hearing that the good old Fortune 500 companies had depressed earnings and were not making their targets.

At the same time, all these high-tech wannabe students realized they weren't going to be going to work for dot-coms or cool, new high-tech companies. So it seems that almost all at once they were going to hit companies like Intel, Dell, Hewlett Packard, Microsoft, and those kinds of companies. Sure enough, those companies turned around and said, "We're suffering too, and we're not going to be able to hire in the numbers that we thought." I've since that heard that some of these firms are pulling back offers.

Q: They rescinded them? I've never heard of that. How often have you?

A: Maybe three times in eleven years. It's not common, but they do get paid off.

Q: Oh, that's not bad.

A: It is if you turned down other offers. In any case, the Dells and Ciscos cut out recruiting. What this meant in the end is that we did have huge turnout for consulting and banking this year. And we do have more students at this time of year (April, May) without positions than last year. But again, last year was not normal.

I would say that we are down off an average year. But I wouldn't say it's dramatically so. People are just having to work harder to find their job

Q: Isn't entertainment a big draw at your school?

A: Yes. We are in a unique situation where we have a higher than average percentage of students who are interested in entertainment, real estate, entrepreneurial ventures, digital media, and optical networking. Where we stand now, three-quarters of each class has an offer.

Q: With the economic slump, the dot-com meltdown, and MBAs out there pounding the pavement hard, what would you say to someone trying to decide whether to go to business school?

A: I think if you look at how quickly things have changed in the past twenty-four to thirty-six months you can't possibly predict what the economy will be in twelve to twenty-four months. So making a decision based on the current state of the economy when you're looking at a two-year program is probably not a reasonable way to make a decision.

The better way to make a decision is to sit down and think about where you, as an individual, want to be in your career down the road. Draw a picture of what you already have in your portfolio to help you get there, and of what is missing. If you can say conclusively that you're missing a set of skills such as quantitative skills or leadership development skills that you would get from an MBA program, then waiting won't help propel your career.

There are always going to be jobs for the people who can't be turned down.

FRIENDS WHO ARE GOING PLACES,
ALUMNI WHO ARE ALREADY THERE

Most students say that the best part about b-school is meeting classmates with whom they share common goals and interests. Many students claim that the "single greatest resource is each other." Not surprisingly, with so many bright and ambitious people cocooned in one place, b-school can be the time of your life. It presents numerous professional and social opportunities. It can be where you find future customers, business partners, and mentors. It can also be where you establish lifelong friendships. And after graduation, these classmates form an enduring network of contacts and professional assistance.

Alumni are also an important part of the b-school experience. While professors teach business theory and practice, alumni provide insight into the real business world. When you're ready to interview, they can provide advice on how to get hired by the companies recruiting at your school. In some cases, they help secure the interview and shepherd you through the hiring process.

B-schools love to boast about the influence of their alumni network. To be sure, some are very powerful. But this varies from institution to institution. At the very least, alumni will help you get your foot in the door. A resume sent to an alum at a given company, instead of to "Sir or Madam" in the personnel department, has a much better chance of being noticed and acted on.

After you graduate, the network continues to grow. Regional alumni clubs and alumni publications keep you plugged in to the network with class notes detailing who's doing what, where, and with whom.

Throughout your career, an active alumni relations department can give you continued support. Post-MBA executive education series, fund-raising events, and continued job-placement efforts are all resources you can draw on for years to come.

CHAPTER 5

WHERE ARE THEY NOW?

HARVARD BUSINESS SCHOOL'S CLASS OF '92:
REFLECTIONS ON WHERE THEY'VE BEEN
AND WHERE THEY'RE HEADED, ELEVEN YEARS OUT

It takes a monumental leap of faith to go to business school, to take two years out of your professional life, go to zero income, and drop $60,000 or more on tuition. By contrast, making the decision to go to medical or law school is more straightforward. Of the three so-called primary professions—business, medicine, and law—business is the only one you can pursue without a degree. In fact, you can become highly successful (and may already be) without an MBA. So how do you decide?

Perhaps the best way to assess the value of the MBA is to talk to the people who have already gone through the program and can reflect on the experience and the credential.

This next section features tape-edited interviews with eight executives who are eleven years out of the MBA program. These interviews resonate with real-life lessons and insights. As these men and women reflect on their prospects out of business school and then bring us up to speed eleven years later, you get a personal and candid look at how the MBA has served them. *These* are the human stories behind all those big-number statistics.

What is most interesting about these MBAs is how what matters to them has broadened and deepened beyond money, immediate gratification, and career acceleration. Their experiences reflect the conflicts and yearnings that are natural to all striving professionals.

The one common element these interviewees share is an MBA from Harvard Business School, perhaps one of the most sought after business degrees in the world. These individuals are exceptionally intelligent, savvy, successful professionals. It is no accident they went to Harvard. As you will see, their life choices, experiences, and reflections on the value of the MBA are widely divergent, though all believe the MBA continues to serve them well in a variety of areas. Without a doubt, the MBA was a transforming experience in their lives.

As divergent as some of their paths have been, there are common themes to their stories:

- Where you go to school matters. A lot.

- Technical or knowledge-content learning at business school may be limited; the real learning is in how to approach a situation and think it through.

- Business school provides unimaginably rich social opportunities. Friendships made there offer a lifetime of personal and professional support.

- Like the network of friendships, the network of alumni offers continued social and professional opportunities.

- The desire for high level of achievement and success is great.

- They are highly competitive.

- There is some pressure to follow the money-making herd.

- Money is important, but its importance diminishes over time.

- Women often choose to disengage fromt he fast track and modify their career aspirations when they want to have a family.

- Family starts to matter, usually above all else.

- Time matters, and working 24/7 is a lifestyle all labor to leave behind.

- Over the years, the value of the MBA changes from the knowledge gained to the networks that can be leveraged.

- All agree, though not for all the same reasons, that the MBA was worth it.

Clive Holmes

Managing Director, Investment Banking Division, Deutsche Bank

"All this hype about everyone rushing off at twenty years old to become a billionaire and all that kind of stuff, that is a classic example of a very short-lived fad. You don't plan your career based on fads."

Q: Clive, fresh out of business school, what were your expectations about what your MBA could do for your business career?

A: I think I saw the degree as a way to open doors that weren't open before. I believe in optionality. You should have as many options in your career and in your life as possible open to you at all times. What I saw the MBA as doing is increasing that optionality because things I wouldn't have been able to do career-wise without the MBA would now be added to the list of things I could do. It was a great way to meet people, make contacts, network, and all that sort of stuff. The reach of the alumni network is amazing. But it's all part of the same increased optionality equation.

Q: How did you see the value of the degree at the five-year mark?

A: I think the degree itself was of declining value at that point because people were putting more emphasis on what your job experience is rather than your life experience. But without a doubt because of the field I went into, it was valuable. And the degree gives you credibility, meaning it allows you to skip questions that no longer need to be asked because you have that name on your resume.

Q: Did you use Harvard's alumni network in the first five years out to advance your career?

A: I really did not in any formal way. But without a shadow of a doubt, other Harvard people, when they know you're from Harvard, stick together. You just get treated differently. Things might be offered to you, or made available to you, that are not made available to people who did not go to that school by other people who did.

Q: Can you give an example?

A: There was a client company we were pursuing, and I was the junior guy on the deal. The client was choosing between our firm and a couple of other firms. At our first meeting, we went around the room for introductions, and the client wanted to know not only about our backgrounds, but where we went to school, that sort of stuff. I was the only one who had gone to Harvard. Well, so had he.

He was a big fan of Harvard, and he and I hit it off very well. He went on to award us the piece of business. I think quite a bit of that was a result of the personal relationship that he and I quickly developed. That goes to the spine of the Harvard alumni connection.

Q: Not a bad benefit of being a HBS alum.

A: Absolutely. And this stuff plays out subtly all the time in the financial world, and still plays out today, ten years later. People from HBS, even though you may not know each other personally, have an immediate kind of camaraderie. Now, you've got a slight leg up on someone you've never met before and know nothing about. That is an incredibly powerful business tool.

It really does work that way. Other grads from other schools have said, "Well on occasions this happens," or "There is some advantage that I feel I'm being afforded by being from Wharton or Duke or somewhere else." But this is not on occasion for Harvard. This happens all the time.

Q: Switching subjects, how many jobs did you hold in your first five years out of school?

A: Two.

Q: Both of them were in finance?

A: Yes.

Q: What was the reason for getting the second job?

A: Simply going to a better firm at the time. I went from Merrill Lynch to Morgan Stanley because I was doing mergers and acquisitions, and Merrill Lynch was number six or seven on the table while Morgan Stanley was number number one. Morgan Stanley approached me.

As someone relatively new to the business, exposure to deal flow and transactions and experience is what you want, and Morgan Stanley had more of that than anybody else.

Q: You went into finance, a discipline that can be studied in a school setting fairly well. Did you learn a lot about finance at Harvard? Did that impact on how well you did in business in the financial arena?

A: No. And no. Harvard is not a great finance school. I was an accountant before I went to Harvard, and there wasn't really a great deal about finance or the mechanical tools of finance that Harvard taught me.

What Harvard really taught me was a way to think. It taught me how to deal with vast amounts of information and to be able to discern what is important and what to focus on. Rather than giving me the tools to directly discern the answer, it gave me the tools to identify what 80 percent or 90 percent is just noise, and this is the piece you need to focus on. Focus your analysis in this area, and you'll get your answer. That sort of macro tool set was frankly more useful than something that you can pull out of a finance textbook and that you don't need to go to Harvard to get in the first place.

Q: On a scale of 1 to 10, how important would you say that learning "how to think" was in your first five years out?

A: A 9. That's the point I'm making. It really wasn't finance tools that they taught me. I knew a lot of that stuff. But the methodology of going about the problem solving, that was the key take-away from Harvard for me. And that I use every single day.

Q: **How has family or personal life impacted on your career choices?**

A: I think it's actually been the other way around for me in that my career choices have impacted family and personal life. To be honest, this wasn't a whole lot because at the time I was making those kinds of career choices, earlier on in my career, family and friends were sort of on the periphery for me. They followed what else was going on in my life.

That's why we came to New York, so I could work on Wall Street. My partner at the time, now my wife, followed me.

Q: **And now, ten years out, have your priorities changed?**

A: Absolutely. I think there comes a point for a lot of people where you reassess what your absolute priorities are in life.

I mean, I'm a banker by trade, so understand that, however you cut the pie, more money is better than less money. My instincts tell me more is better than less. That's the first thing I would tell you about priorities. But then after a while it becomes, well, just how much money is enough money, and what sacrifices are you willing to make to get more money.

The answer for me after a while was, I don't need to be a member of the BBC, the Billionaire Boys Club. But I need to be financially secure and comfortable, and I'm probably at that point in my career at this moment. And so that causes a reassessment, having reached that sort of critical level of what is acceptable in terms of sacrifice.

What has happened now is that the end does not in all instances justify the means, and by that I mean, when I didn't have that financial security, I would sacrifice everything to succeed in my job to make sure I got it. Having reached a level of financial security, I'm still very competitive, I want to do very well in my job, but I'm not prepared to work a hundred hours a week anymore.

So I guess my priorities have changed because that was not on the top of my mind right out of business school. You would simply do what it took to get the job done. Nowadays, you start to question what it takes to get the job done, and whether you're the best person to be doing it.

Q: **Speaking of nowadays, how many jobs have you held in the last five to ten years?**

A: Just one more.

Q: **You've stayed on a very straight course of banking?**

A: Correct. Now I've done things outside of banking as well; I'm not sure you're aware of that. I've started two or three companies, and I did private investing for my own accounts.

So I've done a little bit of this and that. We took a company public on the Nasdaq a couple of years back. We've had some fun. So if you look at my career, I've only had three jobs, yes.

Q: I'm curious, when you say "we" took a company public, who's the "we"? Are you talking about peers outside of work?

A: Yes. Six of us started a company in 1996, and in the following two years— now you know what I do with my weekends—we grew it from a start-up to four-and-a-half thousand employees and $100 million of revenue and $150 million of market capital as we sold it on the Nasdaq in '98.

Q: Are these business partners from Harvard?

A: No. None of these were. These were just good old-fashioned friends of mine that I went drinking with.

Q: Did any of these friends have MBAs?

A: Not all of them; half of them did. Three MBAs and three not MBAs.

Q: Would you say a side business is a common experience for a b-school grad like yourself?

A: Not really for investment banking. Other people were much more focused, which is not really the right word, but narrow maybe in their views.

My view was that investment banking would create another tool set that would be applicable across a wide range of opportunities of which this was one. And so I was the acting chief financial officer until we took it public, whereupon someone else stepped into that role, and I stepped back to just pure investment banking again until the next opportunity came up.

Q: There's that optionality again. Okay, so you're not part of the BBC. But you're part of the MMC, the Millionaire Men's Club.

A: Ah, thank you for that.

Q: There's a tremendous amount of uncertainty in the business world now about the state of the economy, the future of technology. What advice would you have for today's business school applicant?

A: I think I would say definitely go to business school. You still want to do that. And the answer is because all this hype about everyone rushing off at twenty years old to become a billionaire and all that kind of stuff, that is a classic example of a very short-lived fad.

You don't plan your career based on fads. You plan your career, as I've said, on optionality. You want to have as many options open to you and available to you throughout your professional career. You want to try and avoid the temptation to chase what's hot, what's there today, and really look to the future and say to yourself, "How will this opportunity, if it doesn't work out, prepare me for the rest of me career? "

To that I would say, first up, do go to business school. The reason is, you will meet people and learn processes that will benefit you throughout your career, no matter what you do, because of the network, the way of thinking, and the added maturity that you'll get during those couple of years interacting with some very, very, smart people. It's just good.

Coming out of business school think hard about what you want. Don't get revved up with what everyone else is doing. I went into investment banking because I liked finance. And I went into investment banking back in '92. Nineteen ninety-two was a terrible year on the street. They just weren't hiring, and everybody was going into consulting. I mean McKinsey was there interviewing 500 Harvard people. But the answer was, I didn't want to do that because it wasn't me, it wasn't what I was about. I'm not a consultant; that's not my nature. I like numbers. I'm facile with them. They're easy for me. So for me, going off and being an investment banker was what I really wanted to do, and I stuck to my goals, and I've stuck with it since. I've been very happy with my decision.

So I would tell MBAs coming out of school: Think hard about that you want to do. Don't do what everyone else is doing just cause it seems like a good idea. And if you go do what everyone else is doing, rather than what you really want to do, think hard about what happens next. Always be thinking one, two, three steps up the road. Because if you go off to start-up an Internet company at nineteen years old and it goes bust, and now you're a nineteen-year-old with no real business experience, no MBA, and no money in the bank, just exactly what are you going to do for the next twenty-five years? And how are you going to reach that level of financial security that everyone aspires to? Not the BBC, just that level of security that lets you know your kids will be able to go to good colleges and you'll be able to retire one day.

As for the young people that ran off and blew off getting their MBAs and everything else, for every one wonderful story you hear of going off and striking it rich in the millions, there are thousands that you don't hear about that crashed and burned. So unless you think you're that one special person, go out and do it properly. Go to business school and get it in the bag.

Jay O'Connor

Vice President, Marketing and Product Management for an Internet start-up

"The network value of my friends and classmates from business school increases with time."

Q: Jay, are you happy you got an MBA?

A: I'm very glad I went to business school. I felt that way when I graduated, and I continue to feel that way now. But I certainly don't think that everyone needs to get an MBA. There are some industries where an MBA is not that highly valued, and you might be better off getting two extra years of work experience rather than the MBA.

Q: Can you give us some examples?

A: Real estate, the entertainment industry, and perhaps the advertising business are examples of industries that may not place a high "credential" value on an MBA degree.

Q: What kinds of people get the most benefit from an MBA program?

A: Almost everyone learns something valuable. In terms of pure learning, I would say that the people who seem to learn relatively less from an MBA program are people who have been consultants or investment bankers, or who received an undergraduate business degree from a great undergrad business school like Wharton or Berkeley—anyone who already has had broad exposure to a range of different industries and who understands accounting and finance. People like this can still get lots of value from going to business school, but for them, the value is probably less about the "hard science" portion of the curriculum and more about the "soft sciences"—e.g., organizational behavior—the credential itself, and the network.

But if you think you might ever want the flexibility to shift industries or job functions, or if you feel you would learn a tremendous amount from the b-school curriculum, an MBA is very helpful.

Q: What about choosing a school?

A: I think it matters where you go. Not all MBAs are equal. This may sound elitist to some people, but over the years I've talked to lots of people who've attended different MBA programs. I consistently heard about much better experiences from people who went to, say, a top-five school, versus a lower-level school.

One of the biggest differences I hear people talk about is the quality of your fellow students. At a top-five school, you can be pretty sure that 90 percent of the people there are pretty darn sharp! Having case discussions can be much less interesting and educational if your fellow students aren't as sharp. And since some of the value of the MBA program is the network of friends and classmates you'll have access to over the years, going to school with a strong network will provide more long-term value.

I would say that if you're planning on going to a lower-ranked program, talk to some of their grads to find out what they got out of it.

Q: How did you feel about the value of your degree and career prospects upon graduation from Harvard?

A: Getting out of business school, I definitely felt that I had more career options than before. In fact, for me the MBA program at Harvard Business School (HBS) allowed me to make a seamless transition from one industry to another. My goal at Harvard was to develop a deep functional expertise in marketing and product management in the software industry.

Before business school, I had worked as an investment banker, a real estate developer, and a marketer. Afterwards, I went into the software industry as a marketing and product manager. I've stayed in that industry ever since and am now the vice president of marketing and product management for an Internet-based company in Silicon Valley.

Q: So you used the degree to make a significant career change?

A: A reasonably large percentage of people who went to HBS changed industries or functions after business school. Business school was a seamless way for them to do so without losing lots of valuable time in their career.

When they came to business school, many of my classmates didn't really know what they wanted to do *after* business school. They felt the MBA program would be a great way to help figure that out, by getting broad exposure to what industries are out there, interacting with lots of smart young people who've worked in different industries, and having tons of ready-made interview opportunities with the large number of companies that come to campus to interview.

Q: How helpful was getting the MBA in terms of finding a job in your specific area of interest—the software field?

A: For me, since I was interested in the software/technology industry, the career center wasn't very useful in my job search. Remember, this is ten years ago. But HBS did help my career search indirectly.

In business school, I was 100 percent focused on the software industry. At the same time, software and technology was not yet a big deal on campus, and only one or two software firms came to campus to interview people, either for summer jobs or full-time jobs. So I had to do a totally self-directed job search—had to figure out who the good companies were, find a contact at my target companies, and get someone to say yes to giving me an interview.

Since I didn't have any real background in software, I knew I would need to get some relevant experience during business school. So I worked hard to get a summer job with a software company, and during my second year, I did a four-month consulting project (field study) for a hot, local software company. Between these two experiences, I gained about seven months worth of experience in the field, had learned enough about business to be somewhat knowledgeable about it, and had demonstrated a commitment to the industry.

Getting out of business school, I felt confident that I would end up with an interesting job in my target industry. And I did. I went to work for Intuit, a leading financial software firm and the maker of Quicken, QuickBooks, and Turbo Tax. I loved my experience there.

Q: What else did you get out of the MBA?

A: The learning itself, especially the confidence that comes from exposure to so many different business situations through the case method at HBS. The case method builds your intuitive feel for business and your confidence. After two years, you've looked at literally thousands of different companies and business cases and scenarios.

It is a very useful synthesis of business knowledge, jam-packed into two years. The pace of the learning is so great, you learn about things you otherwise would not have been exposed to for a long time in the business world, for example production issues at a company. And you learn lots about what you don't know that you don't know, so you have fewer "blind spots" in future business situations.

I will say that the MBA program certainly doesn't teach you all the details about everything in business that there is to know. But you do get exposed to some very important ways of thinking about business and looking at business. You develop a set of helpful "tools," and you learn enough business basics across the spectrum of many subjects to develop an intuitive sense of what you need to know.

As a credential, an MBA can tell people you're pretty sharp and capable. Assuming there is some relevant experience on your resume, an MBA from a good school helps signal to people that you may be worth talking to.

Q: How did you feel about the value of your MBA degree at the five-year mark out of business school? Did anything change?

A: I would say the big difference was that at five years out, my career goals had changed. Upon leaving business school, my near-term career goal was to become a functional expert in marketing and product management in the software industry. By the five-year mark, I felt I had accomplished that goal.

At that point, I wanted to leverage the skills I had mastered and apply them to new businesses, and at a higher level of responsibility. I ended up staying at Intuit another year and a half, and had the chance to help create and to lead an interesting new Internet business at the company.

After six and a half years at Intuit, I developed a new career goal. I felt it was time for me to join a promising start-up where I would be the senior marketing person, would be on the senior management team, and would have a significant equity opportunity. So I left the company for the chance to apply what I'd learned at a higher level, and to have a real stake in the outcome.

Q: You stayed at your first job after business school for six and a half years. Was that unusually long compared to your peers?

A: Yes. I would guess that less than 20 percent of my graduating class stayed at one company six years or more out of business school. A lot of people changed jobs within two or three years of graduation. For me, I really enjoyed the company and the industry, and felt I was continually learning and developing important new skills, so I was happy to stay at one company for many years.

Q: And after ten years, how many jobs in total have you held?

A: I've worked for a total of three companies: Intuit and two different start-ups.

Q: As you approach the ten-year mark, how do you feel about the value of your business school training?

A: Ten years out, I'm still very glad I went to HBS. Over time, the relative importance of different aspects of the MBA change. In my experience, the value of the business network goes up over time, and the value of the learning goes down relative to when you first go out of school. The credential value is most useful early on. But the more senior you are, the more people are primarily concerned about your work experience and track record rather than your educational degrees.

Q: So the business network of friends and classmates matters more now?

A: Yes. I would say that the network value of my friends and classmates from HBS increases with time. There are a couple of examples that illustrate the point: A number of my HBS peers are now at prominent venture capital firms, and through them, I've heard about interesting start-up job opportunities. At my newest company, I'm now approaching those same contacts about investing in our company.

My HBS network provides many ongoing, useful contacts. All it takes is a quick call, or e-mail, to get a friendly introduction to the right person at a given company, as well as some inside perspective on how to best position a particular proposal to that company.

Q: Looking back, if you could do anything over again differently, what would it be?

A: I would have gotten my MBA a bit sooner. I went to business school about six years after college. I had been reluctant to get an MBA because I was skeptical about how much learning I would get out of the program. I thought most of the value would be from the getting the credential and the network aspects rather than the learning itself. I was pleasantly surprised by how much I learned at HBS.

Also, I would have spent more time getting to know more people outside of my section. HBS has a big class, so you need to make an effort to get to know most of your classmates. Unless you try hard, you may not get to know more than 30 percent of your classmates very well, 250 or 300 people. The way it works, you probably end up getting to know the same total number of people as at a smaller MBA program, but as a percentage of the class, it's a smaller number.

Q: Any regrets or complaints?

A: The two-year program was a bit long in my opinion. I think it could have been just as effective in about fifteen to eighteen months. By the end of the second year, it started feeling repetitive.

At the time, HBS didn't seem very attentive to student concerns, seemed to stick with tradition in response to a rapidly changing business environment, and was slow to innovate. The school seems to have responded and improved significantly in these areas in recent years, benefiting from more creative leadership.

Q: What advice do you have for today's MBA?

A: Focus on building your skills and developing a true, relevant expertise in a field that interests you.

If you want a senior-level role at a new company, know that hiring companies—especially early-stage companies—are looking for true experts in a given functional role. If they are looking to hire a vice president of a specific area—e.g., VP of marketing or business development—the vast majority of times they are NOT looking for well-rounded generalists. They want the expert. Being a generalist is a nice plus. But nine times out of ten, it won't get you the job you're looking for. If you are talking about a CEO or GM—general manager—role, it might be a different story.

Q: How has family or personal life affected your career development and the choices you've made?

A: You know, I'm still single. So compared to a lot of my peers who are married, it's been less of an issue so far. I worked really hard, really long hours. But family and personal issues have become more important to me over time, and I've definitely cut way back on the brutal hours.

John Kim

Co-Founder and CFO of an Internet start-up

"I think, without a question, my family is the priority in my life."

Q: What were your goals and ambitions as a newly minted MBA?

A: I have always had an entrepreneurial bent to my personality, and I didn't want to go the traditional investment banking or consulting route. I wanted to be involved in starting up a company or having some business of my own. So my primary goal in coming out of business school was to understand where there might be an opportunity in the future in terms of what industries would show significant areas of growth. I wanted to position myself within an operating unit to learn more about opportunities that might then actually arise from having been involved in that industry.

Coming out of business school, one of the areas I wanted to get involved in was called, at that point, "multi-media." This eventually evolved into the Internet space. I was fortunate enough to get a job working at Sony for one of the presidents of one of the operating units (within Sony).

Q: Did Harvard help you get your job with Sony?

A: I had worked the prior summer for Sony, (the summer between the first and second year of business school). That actually came through an alum of Harvard who worked at Sony. He saw my resume, and then he took me into Sony as a summer intern. That's how I networked within Sony to get a better position coming out of business school.

Q: What was the biggest surprise in your first couple of years about the value of your MBA?

A: My view on an MBA and a Harvard education was always that this was going to be about more than just the curriculum or education itself. What is really important about Harvard Business School is the network of people you meet while at school, as well as the network of alums outside of school. These are some of the advantages of going to HBS.

Business school gives you a pedigree and gives you access to a network. But to be honest, I assumed that was going to be the case, so I guess I had no real surprises.

Q: So the degree did for you what you thought it should?

A: Yeah, I think so. Again, I always thought that it's the network of people and friends that you meet that are the great lure, and permanent aspects that you take away from business school. My closest friends are the ones whom I met at HBS.

Q: How did your goals and ambitions change at the five-year mark out of business school?

A: I don't know if my goals changed all that dramatically. Basically, at the five-year mark, it's just a time to position yourself to see if you can really try to accomplish what you wanted to.

In my case, at the five-year mark I had the opportunity to go off and start a firm. I had the opportunity to go off with a handful of partners and start a merchant bank based in Asia. So I don't think the goals really necessarily changed; it was really just the opportunities were different at the five-year mark.

Q: **How different? They sound very different. You came out wanting to be in multi-media and wound up starting an investment fund.**

A: Well, I think some people are very good at taking a very long, slow, methodical approach and going step by step within an organization, or going step by step and trying to plan their life exactly. I think in my case, it was much more than trying to go from one step to another. It was trying to take advantage of opportunities that presented themselves to me.

So I started out in an operating unit in a media group, and then I had the opportunity to work more in an investment banking, advisory role for media companies pursuing cross-border transactions. From that I was able to raise a fund to invest in companies. It was not a direct progression of events, but kind of just taking advantage of opportunities.

In my case, I was much more opportunistic than methodical in my planning.

Q: **That leads to my next question. How many jobs did you have in your first five years out of school and what caused you to change jobs?**

A: I had three jobs in my first five years. Changing jobs was really a combination of trying to progress up, as well as address some personal issues in my life.

For example, my first job was at Sony, but it was on the West Coast. My wife was on the East Coast in a medical residency. So I decided that I had to move to the East Coast. That led me to my next job, which was in the investment space.

My next job change was a result of that investment job, which did not pan out to be what I expected it to be, so I didn't want to linger there too long. Within the first twelve months, I left for my third job.

Q: **How else has family and personal life continued to affect your career and the choices you make?**

A: Once you have a family your goals change. You not only have additional factors you want to take into consideration in your career plans, but there are other things which become a lot more important to you in life. I think, without a question, my family is the priority in my life.

In terms of career choices, I wouldn't say it's necessarily swayed me one way or the other. The only major move that we made as a family was to move back from Singapore to San Francisco. I wouldn't say that was the primary reason for that move. But in the back of my mind, I wanted my kids to grow up in a friendlier environment where they can play outside without suffering from the oppressive heat.

Q: **In terms of what you learned at business school, do you find that your learning was relevant to the work you do now?**

A: In the finance world, what I learned from HBS had minimal applicability since Harvard takes the case-study approach. I don't know whether that has changed dramatically, but my view on that has always been that certain tools have to be taught, and learning through the case-study method is not the best way to learn corporate finance. The case-study approach doesn't go deep enough. So at least in corporate finance, you learn much more on the job than you do at HBS.

Q: **What was the case study good for then?**

A: Arguably, it's very good for being able to assess a situation and problem and then to try to address it. More than anything else, it's great for learning how to try and communicate your viewpoint effectively to others.

Q: **What about analytical skills?**

A: I'm just not convinced. I don't know whether the people who were good at case studies were good before they were introduced to case studies, or whether they actually were able to progress and learn from the case studies.

Q: **Approaching the ten-year mark, where do you find yourself?**

A: I'm now involved in a start-up software company. I had a little bit of experience working in technology working in places like Sony and IBM. So when I moved back from San Francisco, I sought out an opportunity in technology. I met a good partner, who was a very strong engineer, and we started a software company. So the immediate goals are to position the company to be successful. I don't have any goals other than to try and make the company viable and succeed.

Q: **Sounds like you reached your goal of ten years ago, which was to start up a business?**

A: Yes.

Q: **What advice do you have for today's MBA?**

A: You have to be passionate about what you are doing. Since you'll be spending a significant portion of your time at work, try to be involved with something that you are truly excited about. Try to learn as much as you can from as many experiences as possible.

Chiara Perry

Senior Pricing Analyst, a division of United Technologies

"I think ten years later, it's very helpful to have Harvard up there on your resume. It will probably get you a least a second look if an employer is flipping through resumes. . . . [P]eople look at the school you've gone to and are impressed with you. And I have to be honest, that will make you feel good."

Q: **In 1992, the nation was in a recession. Jobs, even for Harvard B-School grads, were scarce. What was your mindset coming out of the program?**

A: Well, I was fortunate in that I had a job in place before graduating. And I was thinking about the opportunities and challenges I'd face in that position. The company that made me the offer was part of United Technologies, and they had come on campus looking for MBAs. I was really happy to already have the offer by graduation so I didn't have to worry about looking for some great job over the summer.

It's true that in 1992 the economy wasn't in great shape, so many people were heading into graduation without an offer yet. I had a lot of things going on in my life at that time: I got married and moved a thousand miles away from the east coast to the middle of the Midwest [Indiana].

In terms of my expectations about the degree, I think they were that it put me into an elevated position and salary compared to the people I would be working with at my new job.

Q: **Given your job offer, were you happy with what the MBA did for you?**

A: Oh, absolutely. The company was excited to have hired me, and I was excited to work for them. I still work for the same company in the same location.

Q: **For ten years straight?**

A: Yes. I'm probably not your typical Harvard MBA in that regard.

Q: **To what do you attribute having stayed with the same company for ten years?**

A: I think it's several things. It's a great place to work. They treat their employees really well. And I don't like to play the sexist card, but it's a wonderful company to work for if you're a woman. My husband and I also really love Bloomington, Indiana. We have two children, and this is a great place to raise a family. So it's been several factors, including having children come into the equation. I only work three days a week now, but I have a professional position.

Q: **Switching subjects, what kind of person is ideally suited for an MBA?**

A: I think the type of person that benefits from the MBA is someone who wants to learn a lot, but also realizes that this isn't rocket science. Yes, there are challenging courses, and I learned a tremendous amount when I was at school. But I thought it was hard because of the overwhelming amount of work, the perceived competitiveness within the class, at least the first year. It wasn't necessarily hard academically. There was only one class I felt a bit overwhelmed by. Mostly, I pretty much felt, "Oh, I can do this."

So, back to your question. Someone who can go into a business school program with the attitude that this is a good thing to have, that you're going to challenge yourself and expand your expertise is going to benefit the most. It's great if you can do it full-time because you can really devote yourself to the program and figure out what you want to do with your life. But don't think that afterwards you're going to be like this NASA engineer.

Q: Are you saying there are not huge intellectual gains, and that you shouldn't expect to be made into a great mind by the MBA?

A: Yes. From the intellectual point, I was challenged. It definitely broadened my thinking, and it was very interesting. I had some classes I didn't have as an undergrad, and so that was valuable. There were new concepts in my learning, but overall, I don't think it's the most cerebral experience in terms of content.

Q: But don't you think that's because for most people who go to a school like Harvard, there's a pre-selection factor, so they're already coming in so high above the bar . . .

A: Well, that's probably right to a certain degree. Someone who's going to get the MBA at a school like Harvard is probably going to be of higher caliber. They expect more. They not only want to further their development and education, but they also want to get the financial benefit.

Q: So how important is it to go to a really good school?

A: I think it is important because people look at the school you've gone to and are impressed with you. And I have to be honest, that will make you feel good. People will say, "Oh my gosh, you went to Harvard!" In a social setting, when people ask me where I went to school, I almost hesitate, because I know there will be this big reaction, especially out here in the Midwest. Not very many people out here went to Harvard.

But after that big reaction, I say, wait; I'm just a person here. But from a career perspective, it definitely helps for the recognition. There is somewhat of an expectation that you may be super intelligent or talented, so you have to tame them. But I have to say, one of the reasons I went to Harvard was that I got in. I said, 'Wow, I got into Harvard; I'm going to go.'

This may relate back to your other question, but right out of business school, I felt, you know, if this job doesn't work, I can go almost anywhere I want with this degree. I know that sounds kind of arrogant but I knew that with my business experience before I went to Harvard, and now with my MBA, I could take a risk. I could come out to this small town in the Midwest and if I needed to, I could leave and be okay.

Even ten years later, I think that's still true. A Harvard MBA certainly is helpful when you're trying to move to the next place or job. I don't think I can go anywhere I want now, because I've taken a little curve in my career track to be with my children. I've been working part time for three years now, three days a week. But the MBA from Harvard is going to be very helpful if we decide to leave.

Q: That's a Mommy "curve"?

A: Yes absolutely. And it's been great. The job, the flexibility, my schedule . . . I love every minute of it. It would be very hard for me to give it up.

Q: What, specifically?

A: The part-time schedule. Going back to full time.

Q: Do you ever anticipate re-entering the workforce as a full-time person or leaving your job? And if so, how do you think the opportunities will be enhanced with the MBA?

A: It's actually good you ask that question, because right now I'm grappling with that. Our factory is moving all of its manufacturing to Mexico. And so the question is, what will happen to the office staff? Will we go, have some role, or be laid off? That's an unanswered question right now.

Because we'd like to stay in the area, my husband and I have been thinking about different things I can do. So the MBA will be very beneficial as I face these issues.

Q: What else did you get out of the two years you were at school?

A: I met a lot of wonderfully diverse and interesting people. Many people were like Wall Street–Harvard–back to Wall Street, or consulting–Harvard–back to consulting. Or people were switching careers. There were people who had been in the Peace Corps, done public not-for-profit work, or come from the military. So from that perspective, it was just wonderful to meet all those incredible people.

And how many smart people can you put in a room? I mean students were just incredibly bright. It was impressive and added tremendously to the classes.

Q: As you approach the ten-year mark, how do you feel about the value of your business school training?

A: I absolutely still utilize it. I still think back on cases and situations and examples that I use to resolve issues going on in work. For example, we are moving some aspect of the business to Mexico, and I can remember that I did a case on that. Plus, with this colleague of mine who is currently getting his MBA, we'll chat even more about some of those issues from class.

But looking back, I can still remember comments I made in class, and my teachers and the classes themselves. It was a very valuable, memorable time in my life. But it wasn't always pleasant . . .

Q: Why wasn't it pleasant?

A: The first year class set-up and the overwhelming desire to make value-added comments was an immense amount of pressure on me. I mean I'm probably obsessive, but I even think of comments now!

Q: Someone reading this book might not understand what this comment thing is all about.

A: Comments you made to contribute to classroom discussion which, depending on the class, counted toward your grade. Comments could almost define the class—coming up with comments to be brilliant, or prove yourself to the others. I remember I was always second-guessing what I said in class. I could have said it better, or I could have said it a different way, that kind of thing.

Q: So you felt some pressure to prove yourself. Was it difficult to be a woman at Harvard?

A: No. I think it was hard to be a woman or man at Harvard. I didn't find that being a woman made it easier or harder. It had more to do with me, because I can be concerned about those kinds of things.

Q: How many women were in your section of ninety classmates?

A: You know, I want to say, twenty-three comes to mind, but I might be a little off on that. It was less than 50 percent for sure.

Q: Were your closest friends women?

A: No, I had women and men friends.

Q: We may have covered some of this, but how has family affected the career choices you've made?

A: Greatly. I'm totally off the fast track. I'm just on kind of a maintain track. I'm not a manger anymore; I'm a worker bee. I work about thirty hours a week, but I'm paid for twenty-four, which is fine because I love the work. I have a great boss, a flexible schedule. It all fits.

I don't feel like I'm wasting the MBA at all. I have a wonderful, challenging job that's very cerebral. I've managed exciting projects. I've trained people. I do a lot of great things at my job, that would typically be the province of a full-time person, but I get to do them as this part-timer. And that's very rewarding.

I feel extremely lucky. I don't make a pile of money, but I have a good balance. I have time with my kids, and then I get some time to go and work and be challenged at a very high level.

Q: Looking back, if you could do anything differently, what would it be?

A: Well, probably I would do a little better at networking and then keeping in touch with section mates, because I may need to call them at some point. I think if you have those networks in place, it's not really calling to ask for a job, it's talking about your situation, and then those people know what's going on and may be able to let you know about an opportunity.

Having been at the same job for ten years, and being out in the Midwest, I'm a little less connected to the pipeline of, "Hey, do you need someone like me at your company?" And that goes both ways. You know, time is a problem, and when kids come along, things change greatly. It's just hard to fit everything in.

Q: Summing up, what advice do you have for someone reading this book?

A: The MBA gives you an extra couple of years to go and figure out what you want to do. I liken it to what college does for you, but this is your second breath. And it's a very valuable one. I recommend you go full time, so you can really focus.

John Cattau

Vice-President, Inventory Management Services, PartMiner

"The herd mentality at a business school is very difficult to distance yourself from. . . . Think hard about what you really want. Don't get distracted by what's going on around you. Remember, you're the person that has to show up for work at the job that you accept."

Q: **John, what were your goals and ambitions right out of business school?**

A: I came out of business school looking at a general management position but with a focus on marketing. I specifically did not want to interview at any consulting firms and really avoided anything other than brand management and marketing positions.

The surprise that I had was that I thought coming out of Harvard Business School, I'd have a decent shot at switching from, say, a finance field to a marketing field. But in fact, when it came time to recruit, I had to force my way into the American Express recruiters lunch hour and make a hard sell on why I thought I would be the right person for the job.

Q: **What do you mean you had to force your way into a recruiter meeting?**

A: I wasn't allowed to get on the list because I was blocked out by all the people who had pre-business school work experience from P&G and McNeil Pharmaceuticals, and by all the students from the brand companies who wanted to switch from marketing soap to marketing credit cards. So they got on the recruiter sign-up list and I did not. I had to beg, borrow, and steal my way onto it.

I guess the guy running the session felt sorry for me, and so he said he had a few minutes to chat with me while he was eating his sandwich.

Q: **And you won him over.**

A: I guess. I basically told him, "Whatever you have, I'll take the job." And I got one; they were probably looking to pick up a couple of people. This was for a summer internship. So I was focused on making that career switch early on while I was at business school. And I stuck to it.

I ended up having a great experience at American Express. I stumbled into a great opportunity to the extent that I was able to move quickly though several different functional areas within American Express and in a number different settings.

Q: **Can I interupt for a moment and take you back to the comment you made about your focusing on marketing while at school? How does that work?**

A: Well, I guess if you're thinking about what you want to do, then you're focusing on particular opportunities. You're specifically not spending time interviewing or contemplating different directions from where you want to go. For me that meant not even considering the consulting firms.

Q: Did you focus your elective study on marketing?

A: Yes, I did, and I also pursued a group-study project that was in marketing. I went with three other students and did an extensive service-oriented marketing study for Steamboat Springs. It was also a great opportunity to travel all around the West and ski at all these mountains and ski resorts.

Q: Did that study help you when you went to get a job?

A: No, it didn't really have much of an impact. It was just a good learning opportunity.

Q: What made you so interested in American Express?

A: In my second year, I had some job opportunities in marketing in New Jersey and Philadelphia, but I was engaged and my fiancée was based in the New York area. So I focused my search on marketing positions in New York, where American Express is.

I wasn't about to jeopardize that kind of serious relationship by moving to Hong Kong or something.

Q: What happened at the five-year mark?

A: At the five-year mark I was openly questioning whether I should be staying at American Express.

It was '95 and a lot was just starting to happen with the Internet. But a lot was also happening inside of American Express. One opportunity in particular was focusing on a direct financial services unit that was a start-up within a large company. There was an opportunity for me to move into that unit, and it was a great fit for me. So faced with this new opportunity within American Express, versus going outside and starting over with a smaller company, I chose to stay.

So at the five-year mark I was contemplating leaving because obviously I had been there three years or so. Meanwhile, my business school colleagues had held at least two jobs by then, and some had held three after just three years out. I thought, "Am I really slow here or should I be moving on?"

But the opportunities just kept coming. After awhile, I was given some options on shares, so I started to get attached to the idea that if I stayed a little bit longer I might be able to reap some of those gains.

I stayed there long enough to get just a taste of that. Then they came more quickly after 1997, which made it even harder to leave.

Q: So how long were you there?

A: Eight years. The advantage to me was that I was able to cycle through a number of different areas. I was promoted and advanced rapidly through the organization and was made vice-president just after the five-year mark. Typically, the vice-president promotion takes six or seven years.

Q: **Having stayed at one job right out of business school for eight years, is that something you've felt you've had to defend to peers or recruiters?**

A: Well there were people with whom I was interviewing when I was considering leaving American Express who said, "What's taken you so long? What's wrong with you?" But I think that perspective was in the minority relative to others who said, "I'm looking for someone that really has demonstrated significant depth in one particular area."

What I found was that people were looking not so much for people who had done a year or two at this company, or a year or two at that company, and who had accumulated experiences at different places, as they were looking for someone who had sort of a spike if you will within a particular function.

Many of the opportunities both at small and larger companies were for someone who had eight to ten years of solid brand, service-marketing experience. So I really had very little difficulty interviewing with the American Express experience on my resume.

Q: **What was the biggest surprise in your first couple of years out of school about the value of your MBA?**

A: On selected occasions there were things that I was able to draw from early on right out of school. But everything that I started at American Express was so new there wasn't a whole lot that I was bringing from my business school training, especially from a marketing and branding perspective. I had to spend a lot of time learning the business.

And you ask yourself, "Gee, you know, I'm not really drawing on some of the things I learned at school." But what is true is you're not really aware of the learning you picked up at school and how it's impacting your thinking.

Even in my third or fourth year out and later on, there were many times I would go back to checklists and case notes and say, "Yeah, I've dealt with this issue before." I found that to be even more so after I moved into my different positions after American Express. It's particularly been the case in my current position here at PartMiner.

Q: **What do they do?**

A: We're an an electronic components distributor that has a market in semi-conductors.

Q: **So you left American Express. When?**

A: In May of 2000, I became quite ill. At the time I was working as the vice president of American Express in the brokerage unit, and I had to go on disability. It took two or three months to recover. While I was home recuperating, I thought through what I really wanted to do.

There were different opportunities to look at. One of them was PartMiner, which I officially joined in October of 2000. QTopics, a polling service that was Internet-dependent, was an opportunity that came up right when I was ready to return to work at American Express, though it turned out to be a short-lived opportunity.

In retrospect, with QTopics, I probably overlooked some things in my due diligence of the company. If I had looked at it with a case-study approach, I would have said something doesn't feel right. In fact, I did several role-plays with a Harvard business school friend, and he pointed out several flaws with the business plan.

Getting caught up in the hype of moving to a new job, I ignored my friend's advice and said thanks, but I took the job anyway.

Well, probably sixty days after I started, his insights and predictions came to be.

Q: So you went from a very stable, long-term employment situation to one which went south quickly?

A: Yes. Where I had decided to go after American Express was an important issue to share with my wife because of it's potential to impact on our finances and our lifestyle.

One of the things I remember in having that conversation with her—and I look to my wife as an equal and powerful voice—is: What is the downside if this blows up right away? You know what, not a lot of damage. Sometimes you need to take a risk, and you're not going to have complete information.

Well, basically, ninety days after I started at QTopics, the company imploded.

Q: Sounds like the fate of many Internet companies.

A: Yeah. The burn rate, things I should have picked up on but didn't, was crazy. We were not managing our cash appropriately, though there were many issues.

Q: Switching subjects, what would do differently with your two years at business school if you could do it again?

A: If I had an extra hour of time, which I didn't, I would have further deepened relationships with colleagues at school. Also, probably equally, I would have looked at what opportunities I could have pursued on my own, what areas might have made sense, and how I could have worked through a network to build that up.

Also, on that marketing study, it was a great experience, I learned a lot. But I might have looked at other opportunities in more entrepreneurial areas. I could have used all that research and legwork to give me a leg up on something more viable than the ski industry, something I really wanted to pursue.

But the reality is, from a financial standpoint, starting a company was a pipe dream. I was already significantly in debt from school. Just the thought of having to further borrow to fund a small start-up that really was not something I could have done.

But overall I would not have changed much.

Q: **What advice do you have for someone reading this book?**

A: The advice I typically give is to think very carefully about the balance they want between work and what they want to do personally, either relationships or the direction they want to go in. It won't happen by accident.

The herd mentality at a business school is very difficult to distance yourself from. And frankly, I felt pretty uncomfortable focusing on a marketing position when almost half the class was going into consulting.

Think hard about what you really want. Don't get distracted by what's going on around you. Remember, you're the person that has to show up for work at the job that you accept.

The best advice I ever heard was from two professors at Harvard. The first was from Robin Cooper, who said, "Every three months or so look in the mirror and ask yourself are you happy? And if you're not, go do something about it." It's pretty simple, but [it's] about the best advice I've ever gotten.

The other advice that sticks in my head is from Professor Michael Jansen. He basically said, "Look at yourself and accept the fact that you will fail." It may not be in five years. It may not be in ten years. But you will fail. You will be put in circumstances that you cannot overcome. So get over the fact that you may have a failure in your experiences.

My QTopics experience did not work out as well as I hoped. But that's an ongoing tension that I think people in MBA programs have, balancing risk and trying to understand what is the probability that I'm going to fail, relative to the potential reward that I might gain.

That is an ongoing tension you have to get comfortable with. Some MBAs have a risk tolerance that really is low, like mine was right out of school. It seems these days, people have higher tolerances. Either way, getting in touch with that is going to help you choose the right path.

Steve Sinclair

Operations Director for the Channel Sales Force, Cisco Systems

"I'm sure that competitiveness exists on an unpleasant level sometimes, but it is only competitive if you let it be. At the end of the day you need to compete more with yourself and think about what you're trying to achieve. If you do that, you're fine and on the right track."

Q: Coming out of business school, Steve, what were your expectations?

A: I guess when I was in business school and thinking about what would happen afterwards, I was hoping that it would do two key things: 1) It would help me in terms of knowledge, so I would have certain skill sets, and 2) it would open some doors for networking.

Q: How relevant has your learning been?

A: It's hard to take specific classes and attach them to specific things I do everyday. So I don't typically go, "Oh, I remember this from a marketing class," or "I should do this a certain way," especially because I'm in sales, and we really didn't have any classes in sales *per se.*

That said, I find myself often thinking back to specific discussions we might have had in classes, or to the way that people interacted together, and other learning experiences we had. It gives me a pretty good comfort level that there's a general base of knowledge that I don't doubt is helping me at some level, every day.

Q: How many jobs have you held since business school?

A: Well, I've been at two companies since business school. The first was for about nine months, which didn't work out. Then I've been at Cisco for a little over seven years, and at Cisco I've held a couple of different jobs.

Q: Is it unusual to stay at one company as long as you have compared to your peers?

A: Yeah, I think so. It's probably also unusual to still be at a fairly large company. I guess it's a combination of the fact that I ended up at a company that was at the sweet spot at the right place at the right time. I've been lucky enough to work for some good people here, so things have stayed interesting to me, and I've had room to grow and do different things.

It's kind of interesting. As I look at people who have changed jobs a lot, some of them have been very, very, happy, as they've done a bunch of different things. But I would say it's more the case that people are now at the point where they're a little frustrated that they've held four or five jobs and haven't found something yet that they really liked.

Q: You mean it's ten years out and they're still wondering when they're going to hit it?

A: Yes, and I don't know if "hit it" from a making-money perspective is the real issue, as much as it is finding something that they really enjoy. It's hard with jobs because often the first year or two, you're just getting your hands around it, figuring out the company, the industry, and the job, and so it really is years three through five when you feel like your hitting your stride, adding a lot of value, and having an impact, at least at a somewhat larger company.

Q: **How have your priorities changed in the last five years, if at all?**

A: I'm not sure that my priorities have changed that much. When I came out of business school, I didn't really understand what financial freedom would mean. I was living in a $1,000-a-month apartment in New York City, and I didn't even own a car, so except for a little debt from business school, there wasn't a lot to worry about.

Now that I'm a little further along, that would be a higher priority, though where I'm at is fine. The point is, had things not worked out at Cisco, which has enjoyed a great ride, I think that having financial freedom would be a lot higher on my mind than it is.

In terms of the salary you want to make coming out of business school, making a ton of money wasn't the highest priority for me. I wanted a job that I liked. Obviously, I wanted to be comfortable. But I didn't say, "Okay, I'm going to take this particular job because in five years I'm going to make a bazillion dollars."

If anything, I took my first job because I thought it would make sense for the family business and that was my immediate priority.

Q: **What happened with that job?**

A: Well, I went into an investment management job straight out of business school because I thought that I would take over my family's business eventually. But it turned out that I really didn't like it, although there were some other considerations as well. And I chose not to pursue that fairly quickly.

So again, I didn't really go into that first job with the idea of making a ton of money. I went into it to see if it was something I really wanted to do longer term.

So neither was it a higher priority to begin with, nor is it today, but for different reasons at both points.

The other comment I would make is that I went to business school pretty young, and that probably had an impact on my priorities. I was the first or second youngest person in our section I believe.

Q: **How old were you?**

A: I graduated when I was just a little over twenty-four.

Q: That's unusual. The average age is twenty-eight.

A: Yeah. So I think other people who were three and four years older had their priorities a little more worked out.

I think that was the difference. I think other people may have come out of business school with a little more specificity about where they were headed. And I was still in the mode of "Hey, I'm twenty-four years old. Let's party."

Being younger has its pluses and minuses. You can make an argument that it's a good thing to go to business school when you have an idea of exactly what you want to get out of it and where you're going. Because if you do, then you can be focused about the two years. And afterwards, I think folks that went in like myself, that were on the younger side, maybe weren't quite as determined or knew exactly what they wanted to do.

Q: Let's switch gears, Steve. If you could go back to business school and do your two years all over again, what would you do differently?

A: While I was at Harvard a lot of people said, "Gee, you really need to take the organizational behavior classes and the negotiation classes." I didn't do that that much. I took classes more like finance and marketing and very specific skill-set classes.

In retrospect, now that I'm managing a lot of people and having to work within a bigger organization, I wish I had done more of that kind of what we used to call "soft" or "fuzzy" classes. Because some of that stuff would have been pretty helpful the last few years here at Cisco. So, that's one thing.

Another is that I was kind of backwards at Harvard. By that I mean, during my first year at school, I didn't work very hard. I had been working my butt off in consulting prior to school, and so in the first year it was just like a big playground to me. In my second year, I worked a lot harder and didn't go out as much. In retrospect, I would probably have cranked up the focus a little bit more in year one because time is fleeting, and it's such a huge investment.

I would say that the biggest challenge to the whole place is clearly that there is so much that you can take advantage of, whether it's figuring out your career, making friends, getting in shape, taking classes, interacting with professors, or getting involved extracurricularly. And then there's Boston. The reality is, you just can't do everything well. You're probably better off picking three or four things and doing them well. Say to yourself, "Well, at least I did those well," rather than just taking a complete sampling, without achieving any depth.

Q: Do you have any regrets?

A: In my mind the experience I got out of Harvard was just great. It was well worth the investment, just for the two years alone, not even for what it would do for me afterwards.

If you can't justify the investment, and you don't think you're going to get enough out of it in those two years, then don't approach it just to justify the investment. I'm not sure the ROI will ever really be there. I think you can figure out a way to make more money, skip the two years of business school, and go right to what you want.

I justify the dollars I spent based on the fun I had, the friends I made, the experience I had. So I have no real regret about school—it was great.

Q: **Is the business school environment intimidating?**

A: One of the things about business school is that you have a lot of people with a lot of very diverse experience. They tend to be pretty self-confident, or at least they appear to be on the surface, and certainly people have one or two areas where they really excel. You can get into a situation where you kind of go, "Boy, how do I hang with everyone here?" But then, when you get to know people and understand where they're at, you realize that everyone has their challenges and their issues, and things they're good at and not so good at. And we're all kind of human as we go through this. Trying to work through that with people, and get through that façade, and not act like you know everything yourself, and being open about it, that's hard to do, but it's where you really break through barriers and learn.

Q: **Well what about the competitiveness you hear about business schools? Was that a problem for you?**

A: You know that's a funny one for me. People talk about how competitive Harvard is all the time. I didn't feel it, maybe because I had a study group of maybe seven or eight guys that I really got along with well who had a pretty balanced outlook on what was going on.

I remember the very first night of cases we had to do, four of us went to a Red Sox game because we wanted to see them play in Fenway Park, and so we sort of walked into class not very prepared on that first day of classes. And you know, we got away with it. And it was fine. And maybe that set a little bit of the tone in terms of not getting too stressed about the whole thing.

I'm sure that competitiveness exists on an unpleasant level sometimes, but it is only competitive if you let it be. At the end of the day you need to compete more with yourself and think about what you're trying to achieve. If you do that, you're fine and on the right track.

Patricia Melnikoff

Vice President, Marketing and Business Development,

Ariat International, a Manufacturer of Equestrian Footwear and Apparel

"Over a decade ago, I sat in a classroom and discussed for 90 minutes how to approach a crisis. Somehow that exercise of analyzing and debating potential scenarios left an impression on me that helped me years later . . . . I was told by several people that I would understand the true value of my MBA after 10 years. I would say that is mostly true."

Q: Patty, what kind of opportunities were you looking for post-MBA?

A: I was looking for an opportunity with a consumer-oriented company that sold goods and services. I was seeking product management, marketing, or strategic planning opportunities.

I was interested in working for a large multinational company, so I interviewed with companies like Disney and Sara Lee Corporation.

Q: Did they come on campus?

A: Yes they did.

Q: So you relied heavily on on-campus recruiters?

A: Very heavily. My second year I attended quite a few corporate presentations from different sectors: technology, packaged goods, and so forth.

At that time, we had the opportunity to attend recruiting presentations and the weekly Q&A sessions with well-known business leaders that are part of the second-year general management course. So by going to the more general presentations and learning about the companies or going to specific recruiting presentations, I actually came across quite a varied group of organizations.

Q: What was your summer position between your first and second year?

A: I participated in a fellowship in Eastern Europe. I worked with a group that was consulting with factories in Poland that were at risk of going out of business. It was 1991, so it was right after the fall of the communist system in Poland and there were a number of state-run factories and businesses that were in a state of collapse.

Q: How did you find your way to Poland?

A: I had worked previously with two of the founders of a consulting practice in Poland.

Q: You learned of this opportunity for a fellowship in Poland at Harvard? How did you unearth that?

A: Actually, it was a formalized program of doing nonprofit work. There were a number of HBS students who participated in the program.

I had to complete an application that explained the nature of the nonprofit work, and upon my return, I was required to write a summary report.

Q: Why did you seek out this particular opportunity in Europe for your summer job? A lot of MBAs expect that summer job to be the one that leads to a final job offer.

A: I'm always looking for interesting experiences in my life. I wanted to work overseas. I figured I probably wouldn't end up living my life in Eastern Europe, and so it was a unique opportunity at the time.

Q: How was Poland?

A: It was great fun. I ended up in a footwear factory, of all places, which is funny because now I work for a footwear company. It must have been fate.

Q: Okay, enough about Poland and you and shoes. What was your first position right out of school?

A: I took a position with the Sara Lee Corporation in Chicago. What drew me to them was that they were growing significantly in their international markets. Their largest revenue stream at the time was in apparel and accessories like Hanes, L'eggs, and Coach. While I was in business school, they were on an acquisition hunt in Europe and had acquired quite a few different brands. I thought that would be an interesting opportunity.

Coming out of Bain & Co. I had worked on quite a few acquisitions and big-picture European strategy projects. I had been in London with Bain before business school, so for me, there was a particular interest in working for a U.S.-based company with international interests.

Q: What was your title in that first job?

A: Senior Financial Analyst, Corporate Development.

Q: In plain English what does that mean?

A: That meant that I worked for a corporate staff group that reported to the CEO. We looked at acquisitions and divestitures and we also did long range and strategic planning. For example, I worked with the CEO of Coach on potential acquisitions and new business opportunities.

Q: How relevant were the things you learned at business school for your first job out?

A: I probably learned more basic analytical, communication, and process manage-ment skills from my experience at Bain & Co. My HBS education helped me to understand many of the big-picture issues facing the corporation.

Q: What did you learn at business school?

A: (Long pause) I can tell you more about how business school helps me today than how it helped me then. I was told by several people that I would understand the true value of my MBA after 10 years. I would say that is mostly true.

In the short term however, I did find that the finance courses I took helped me in my first job. I chose to take several finance courses at HBS because I wanted to develop a more in-depth understanding of that area. I did not plan on working in finance post-HBS, and I didn't think I would ever have another opportunity to learn about it.

Ten years out, it's all about the leadership and people issues. For example, my company was facing a potential product recall recently. I found myself drawing upon the case we studied on the Tylenol recall at J&J. I asked myself, what were the big picture decisions they had to make? How fast? How serious? What is the potential damage? What is the action plan and how will we communicate it? Being able to draw from that exposure to a crisis management situation was very helpful. Over a decade ago, I sat in a classroom and discussed for 90 minutes how to approach a crisis. Somehow that exercise of analyzing and debating potential scenarios left an impression on me that helped me years later.

Q: How long were you at Sara Lee?

A: Two years.

Q: Why did you change jobs?

A: I got married and moved out west.

Q: What did you do then?

A: I worked as a consultant while I looked for a position with a small company. I wanted an opportunity to work with a start-up company.

Q: Was that when you took the position at Ariat?

A: Yes. Three years out from HBS, I joined Ariat as a product manager and director of marketing.

Q: So you've been there now . . .

A: Seven years.

Q: So you've held only two jobs since school.

A: Yes, although I think I've held four different positions since I've been here.

Q: Do you think women switch jobs less so they can have more stability?

A: I can't speak to the experience of all women, but it has been true in my case. The organization has been very flexible in allowing me to make my family a priority, and at the same time, it has given me opportunities that keep me interested.

What has been critical for me as a mother of two young children is that I have a predictable work schedule while being professionally challenged. I am lucky to have found a company that offers that combination.

What I have found is that a lot of the women who aren't working feel like it's an either/or situation for them: "Either I work in a high-pressure, unpredictable job and never see my children, or I just quit altogether." I don't think it has to be that way, but you do have to be willing to make tradeoffs in compensation and promotions to strike the balance.

Q: If there were anything you could go back and do differently at business school what would it be?

A: I would take more of those organizational behavior classes that I laughed at.

Q: Because?

A: Oh you know, power, "group norms," and other people issues. None of those issues seemed that important to me at the time. I was still focused on mastering my knowledge in academic disciplines.

Q: Did you all laugh at them?

A: I don't think we valued those courses as much as other courses in the curriculum. But now I see the value, having managed so many people. In the second year, I might have taken more leadership courses and those organizational behavior courses.

Q: Do you have any regrets?

A: No, not at all.

Q: Do you think it was more intimidating for you to go to business school as a woman?

A: No. But I think I had to work harder in certain ways earlier on to establish myself as a credible voice in the class. Somehow I felt that if a woman was perceived to be too harsh or too focused, there was a natural tendency not to like her. And so I do think that women have to work harder at finding their place and fitting in.

Q: Overall would you say business school is an intimidating place?

A: No. I enjoyed it. I made great friends at HBS. I think the first week is terrifying for everyone, but overall, no.

Q: What would you say to someone who said, should I get my MBA today?

A: I think it depends on their circumstances. If they're very successful in business already and they are financially secure, I'm not sure business school is necessary. I meet incredible business people all the time who don't have MBAs.

But I think if you're younger in your career, or you're trying to make a career change, or you've found yourself limited, then I think it's a wonderful opportunity to go for two years and get the MBA.

Q: Do you think you went at the right time for the right reasons?

A: Absolutely. I was 25. It was perfect for a young woman with three years of business experience post-college, with my objectives, to go and get the MBA from the very best school I could.

Lionel Leventhal

Principal, $300 million private equity fund

"Spend every minute trying to think about how you get the most out of this experience, both in terms of content and people, but on content in particular. Try to understand how everything fits together because business school is not about taking however many courses you can in different subject areas. You go to business school to learn how businesses are built and run."

Q: Lionel, after graduating from Harvard Business School, what were your expectations about the value of your MBA at that time?

A: Having come from investment banking, like a lot of people in our class, what was interesting was that virtually none of them went back into that industry after graduating.

My objective for business school, from a curriculum perspective, had been to get exposure to the various elements of general management with a long-term goal of either starting a business or, in the private equity area, to be able to buy businesses and fix them up. So those were my expectations as to how to apply what I learned in school.

I didn't have any expectation about the period of time it would take to utilize everything I learned at business school or to network because I really was focused on that long-term goal.

But my first job out of school was amazing. With no experience in managing operations or people, I was given the opportunity to fix a $25 million business in New Jersey, at a can factory employing about 150 people that was losing money.

Q: Was that a manufacturing company?

A: Yes. I'm sure I was one of the few people in our year to do something as mundane as that. My summer in between my first and second year of business school was equally mundane because I worked in a plastics/chemical factory in Baton Rouge, Louisiana, to test whether being in that environment—maybe not in the long term—was something I would enjoy.

Q: Plastics and can companies, that doesn't sound like a typical MBA career path. How did you find those positions? Did Harvard help?

A: The summer job came from contacts at my investment banking job prior to business school. While at business school I wrote to some of the LBO groups that I had helped to buy businesses about working in the operations of some of the companies they had bought.

At the plastics company, I worked for two gentlemen who had previously been executives for a German chemical company. We had helped them buy a couple of plastics companies while I was at First Boston. They gave me a job in the summer of helping them to integrate two of these plastics businesses.

Q: Would you have been able to take on those positions without that business school experience?

A: No way, because I would say in particular the Operations Management class I had was critical to my understanding of these businesses.

I would think one of the major take-aways from business school is that management is not a science, but more a practical application of common sense and working with people to solve problems and set and reach goals. People always underestimate how important the working-with-people part is.

But again, my work that summer demonstrated to myself that someone without an engineering background could feel comfortable assessing how to change things in that environment.

Q: What about the can manufacturing business—how did you get that job?

A: Well, I had a very unique approach to looking for jobs at business school. Basically, the consulting firms came to me to interview. But I didn't really focus on that. I interviewed with Bain and got an open offer to join them whenever I wanted to.

My approach to interviewing was primarily focused on finding interesting smaller businesses where I could work for the owner with an objective of one time running the business.

I think it was the SBNE, the Small Business New Enterprise Club, at Harvard that sponsored a cocktail party with some of the people with YPO, The Young Presidents Organization.

I met this guy, started talking to him, and had dinner. After we spent some time talking, he offered me an opportunity. He was a steel trader who bought shiploads of steel. One of his customers was going bankrupt and offered him this can factory in lieu of the debt he owed him. So he ended up taking on this can factory even though it was in New Jersey and he lived in Boston. He had gone through three managers in five years. And the business wasn't doing any better.

We talked about common sense being more important than anything else in managing people and managing businesses. And he gave me the opportunity to fix the business.

It was overwhelming for the first few months because it involved renegotiating labor contracts, firing very senior people, and having people much older than I work for me, which was a new experience as well. At the factory, of the 150 people, I think two had gone to college. So, on a day-to-day basis I didn't really have a lot of people to bounce ideas off of. I did end up talking to a bunch of HBS professors, three in particular, during the first six months bouncing ideas off of them.

Q: Then the actual content learning at business school was very valuable to you?

A: Oh, yeah. It was essential. But I would say equally important to the content was the self-confidence that you could apply common sense to solve problems. And working with people is not something you can study.

Q: Are you saying you already had a style and a way of working with people that was effective?

A: I wouldn't say that because I had never managed anyone other than an analyst when I was at First Boston.

But one of the things business school did, outside of teaching actual course content, was expose us to many cases in which people with totally different backgrounds founded and managed businesses. Rather than having a technical background, such as engineering for example, they applied a common sense approach to solving problems.

Q: What caused you to leave that position and where did you go next?

A: We turned the can company around and went from losing money to breaking even to making money. And we sold the business to the largest company in the industry—US Can. That is what I was hired to do. It was a natural end to the job because I accomplished what I set out to accomplish.

I had an open-ended offer to join Bain, so I was keeping in touch with them as the process of selling the company started. Bain said, "Great! Sounds like you had a great experience, and come here when you are done. "

The fellow I worked for who owned the can factory became a great mentor of mine. He'll be a second father to me for life. He's an investor in the fund I manage now.

Q: Bring me up to speed from Bain to this fund you manage now.

A: It was all part of the same long-term plan. At Bain I spent thee years helping to manage case teams in various industries. Three quarters of the three years there was spent working on ten different projects for a $2.5 billion company that made various building products. But I would say I wasn't focused on a lifetime of consulting. I was focused on learning a lot and contributing a lot.

At the end of the three years the CEO of my primary client offered me the number-two marketing position at a $1.5 billion division, which made me feel pretty good. I had never held a marketing management job before, but they felt comfortable offering me the job.

Since that time, I have spent the last six years in the private equity area. Private equity is by definition providing equity privately to companies, both private and public. It's putting capital at risk that you've raised from investors. I spent a little over three years working at a small buyout fund in New York. It was a very small group, basically five of us. One of the guys, who I thought was a genius, taught me a ton about how to be very creative in terms of structuring transactions to protect the return to investors and provide money to companies.

A little more than two years ago, somebody I worked with fifteen years ago at First Boston invited me to join a very novel private equity fund that is focused on the pharmaceutical industry, on providing capital to companies that develop drugs. I came in to be the person who negotiated and structured the deals.

Q: Jumping around a bit, how valuable have your business school friendships been in your career?

A: I'd say extremely. I would never have had this first opportunity at the can factory without having been at business school and meeting the YPO people.

I would say the real value of your business school network starts to become apparent seven years out because that's when all your classmates are in positions where they have a lot of influence. I've worked on transactions with many classmates at various points and times. I've also served as an aide to a ton of my classmates from my year in an informal capacity.

Q: What do you mean by aide?

A: Just helping people to raise money for ventures they're starting, helping with their careers, helping people find jobs, and thinking through issues they face managing their businesses.

Q: How have your priorities changed since you got your MBA?

A: I'd say that every year I constantly have more control over my life. Even though I work hard, I try to have control over when I'm working and when I'm not working. I still spend an enormous amount of time with my parents and my brothers. I probably have dinner with them once a week. That's always been a priority. And when I get married it will be the same, that family will be a priority.

So the goal is more and more each year to get more control over my schedule. That's very important. My priorities haven't really changed, just the amount of control I have over my time and life have changed.

Q: Do you have any regrets?

A: Job-wise in terms of what I've done, I have zero regrets. I've been very lucky. You can never plan life. You can sort of say, "I'd like to do this, I'd like to do that," but you don't know when you turn around to the left who you're going to happen to meet.

I think life is setting goals, preparing to meet those goals, and reacting to chaos. Generally you have an objective of what you want to achieve, but you don't really control what opportunities are going to be created. What I'm trying to say is that if I got up one hour later, everything might be different, so there really isn't much I would change.

As for school, I had an outstanding group of people in my section and in my study group who I keep in contact with quite a bit. So I think the only thing I would have done a little differently would have been spending more time with people outside my section.

Q: **What advice do you have for someone considering going to business school?**

A: Well, a lot of people go to business school for the wrong reason. They go to a particular business school because someone else wants them to go or because they haven't thought it through. And it needs to be thought through. Where you go really impacts your career.

I've also seen people who've had completely different experiences at Harvard. Some people come away and haven't invested much of themselves in it and say, you know, it wasn't such an amazing experience. Well that's not a surprise. You get out what you put in.

Some people just go because they just got in, and that's not a reason to go. I saw a lot of mismatches that got through, and they just hated it.

My advice is this: I would spend every minute trying to think about how you get the most out of this experience, both in terms of content and people, but on content in particular. Try to understand how everything fits together because business school is not about taking however many courses you can in different subject areas. You go to business school to learn how businesses are built and run, which is understanding how everything has to fit together and be integrated. So, I would spend a lot of energy in all the classes trying to figure out, for example, if it's a marketing class, how things fit in with operations and finance and everything else.

Chapter 6

Money Matters

HOW MUCH WILL IT COST?

THE TRUTH

To say that business school is an expensive endeavor is an understatement. In fact, to really gauge how expensive business school is, you need to look not only at your tuition costs and living expenses, but also at the opportunity cost of foregoing a salary for the length of your program. Think about it: You'll have a net outflow of money.

But keep in mind that, unlike law school or medical school, business school is just a two-year program. And once those two years are over, you can expect to reap the rewards of your increased market value. Unfortunately, business school differs from law school and medical school in a much less desirable way as well—there are serious limitations on the amount of money available through scholarships and grants. Most of you will be limited to loans, and lots of them.

Try not to get too upset about borrowing the money for business school; think of it as an investment in yourself. But, like all investments, it should be carefully thought out and discussed with everyone (spouse, partner, etc.) concerned. This is especially important for those of you considering business school. You need a law degree to practice law, and a medical degree to practice medicine, but a business degree is not required to work in business. That said, certain professional opportunities may be tougher to pursue without an MBA on your resume.

THE COST OF B-SCHOOL

So get out some paper, a pencil, and a calculator, and figure out how much it will cost you to attend school. What should you include? Your opportunity cost (lost income) and your cost of attending b-school (tuition and fees). One more thing: For a more accurate assessment of your investment, you should figure taxes into the equation by dividing tuition cost by .65 (this assumes taxes of about 35 percent). Why? Because in order to pay tuition of $25,000, you would have to make a pre-tax income of about $38,500. If you are lucky enough to have a source of aid that does not require repayment, such as a grant, scholarship, or wealthy benefactor, subtract that amount from the cost of attending b-school.

For example, if you currently make $50,000 and plan to attend a business school that costs $25,000 per year, your investment would be approximately $177,000.

$$(50,000 \times 2) + [(25,000 \times 2)/.65] = 177,000$$

Now say you receive an annual grant of $5,000. Your investment would now be approximately $161,500.

$$(50,000 \times 2) + [(20,000 \times 2)/.65] = 161,500$$

HOW LONG WILL IT TAKE YOU TO RECOUP YOUR INVESTMENT?

To estimate this figure, you first need to estimate your expected salary increase post-MBA. Check out the average starting salaries for graduates of the programs you are looking at and adjust upward/downward based on the industry you plan to enter. Subtract your current salary from your expected salary and you'll get your expected salary increase.

Once you complete the step above, divide your investment (tuition and fees plus lost income) by your expected salary increase, and then add 2 (the length of a full-time MBA program). If you are contemplating a one-year MBA program, just add 1.

Going back to the example above, if your pre-MBA salary is $50,000 and you expect to make $75,000 when you graduate, your expected salary increase is $25,000 (a 50 percent increase). Let's assume you did not receive a grant and that your investment will be about $177,000.

$$(177,000/25,000) + 2 = 9.08$$

It will take you approximately nine years to earn back your investment.

Keep in mind, these are approximations and don't take into account annual raises, inflation, etc. But it is interesting, isn't it?

While business school is an expensive proposition, the financial rewards of having your MBA can be immensely lucrative as we discussed before. You won't be forced into bankruptcy if you finance it correctly. There are tried-and-true ways to reduce your initial costs, finance the costs on the horizon, and manage the debt you'll leave school with—all without selling your soul to the highest bidder.

COMPARISON SHOPPING

While cost shouldn't be the first thing on your mind when you are choosing a school, depending on your goals in getting an MBA, it might be fairly high on your list. Private schools aren't the only business schools. Many state schools have fantastic reputations. Regional schools may be more generous with financial aid. Tuition costs will vary widely between public and private schools, especially if you qualify as an in-state student. Keep in mind, however, that salary gains tend to be less dramatic at more regional schools.

HOW DO I FUND MY MBA?

The short answer: loans. Unless your company is underwriting your MBA, or you're able to pay your way in cash, you'll be financing your two years of business school through a portfolio of loans. Loans typically come in one of two forms: federal and private. Only a few of you will be lucky enough to qualify for, and get, grants and scholarships.

Anyone with reasonably good credit, regardless of financial need, can borrow money for business school. If you have financial need, you will probably be eligible for some type of financial aid if you meet the following basic qualifications:

- You are a United States citizen or a permanent U.S. resident.

- You are registered for Selective Service if you are a male, or you have documentation to prove that you are exempt.

- You are not in default on student loans already.

- You don't have a horrendous credit history.

International applicants to business school should take note: Most U.S. business schools will require all international students to pay in full or show proof that they will be able to pay the entire cost of the MBA prior to beginning the MBA program.

FEDERAL LOANS

The federal government funds federal loan programs. Federal loans are usually the "first resort" for borrowers since many are subsidized by the federal government and offer generous interest rates. Some do not begin charging you interest until after you complete your degree. Most federal loans are need-based, but some higher interest federal loans are available regardless of financial circumstances. Your business school's financial aid office will determine what, if any, your need is.

PRIVATE LOANS

Don't think private loans are available only from banks. There are programs that exist for the express purpose of lending money to business students. These loans are expensive and interest accumulates during your studies. You will also be responsible for many extra charges (guarantees and insurance fees).

ALTERNATIVE SOURCES OF FUNDING

We've already mentioned these in one form or other, but they are worthy of a bit more attention.

The first alternative is sponsorship of your employer or educational reimbursement. Not all companies treat this the same way, but if you are able to get your employer to kick in a portion of the cost, you are better off than before. But beware, this benefit also comes with strings attached. Most companies that pay for your MBA will require a commitment of several years upon graduation. If you renege, you could be liable for the full cost of your education. Others will require that you attend business school part time, which you may or may not want to do. Often, part-time students are ineligible to participate in on-campus recruiting efforts to the same extent as full-time students.

Educational reimbursement can come in another form as well. Some companies will provide sign-on bonuses to new MBAs that will cover the cost of a year's tuition. This is a fantastic development from the years of a robust economy, but it is by no means a guarantee during tougher times. Don't assume that you will have this option open to you just because it has been a common occurrence in past years.

The other "alternative" source of funding is a financial gift from family or another source. Either you have a resource that is willing and able to fund all or part of your MBA, or you don't. If you do, be thankful.

APPLYING FOR FINANCIAL AID

In order to become eligible for financial aid of any kind, you will need to complete the Free Application for Federal Student Aid, also known as the FAFSA. You complete and submit this form after January 1 of the year in which you plan to enter business school. You should aim to complete and submit this form as soon as possible after the first of the year to avoid any potential delays. The FAFSA is available from a school's financial aid office. You can also download the form directly from the website of the U.S. Department of Education at www.fafsa.ed.gov. A third option is to use the FAFSA Express software (also downloadable from the website) and transmit the application electronically.

It is important to note that the form requires information from your federal income tax returns. Plan to file your taxes early that year.

In addition to the FAFSA form, most schools will have their own financial aid form that you will be required to complete and submit. These often have their own deadlines, so it is wise to keep careful track of all the forms you must complete and all their respective deadlines. Yes, it's a lot of paperwork, but get over it. You'll be much happier when the tuition bill arrives.

LOAN SPECIFICS

GUIDE TO FEDERAL LOANS

Stafford Loans

Stafford loans require you to complete the FAFSA form in order to qualify. These are very desirable loans because they offer low-interest rates capped at 8.25 percent and are federally guaranteed. There is a limit to how much you can borrow in this program. The maximum amount per year you may borrow as a graduate student is $18,500 ($10,000 of this must be unsubsidized loans). The maximum amount you may borrow in total is $138,500 (only $65,500 of this may be in subsidized loans). The aggregate amount includes any Stafford loans you may have from your undergraduate or other graduate studies. One caveat: At the time of this writing, the Higher Ed Act is under review for reauthorization; loan limits may be affected.

The loans come in two types: subsidized and unsubsidized. Subsidized loans are need-based as determined by your business school. They do not charge interest while you are in school or in authorized deferment period (such as the first six months after graduation). This cost is picked up by the government (hence the name "subsidized"). Repayment begins at that time. Unsubsidized loans are not need-based and do charge interest from the time of disbursement to the time of full repayment. You can pay the interest while you are in school or opt for capitalization, in which case the interest is added to the principal. You will pay more in the long run if you choose capitalization. Interest payments may be tax deductible, so be sure to check. The standard repayment period for both is ten years.

You will pay a small origination and guarantee fee for each loan, but this is not an out-of-pocket expense. It is simply deducted from the loan amount. Some schools will allow you to borrow the money under the Stafford program directly from them, while others will require you to borrow from a bank. For more information on federal loans, call the Federal Student Aid Information Center at 1-800-433-3243.

Perkins Loans

Perkins loans are available to graduate students who demonstrate exceptional financial need. The financial aid office will determine your eligibility for a Perkins Loan. If you qualify for a Perkins Loan as part of your financial aid package, take it. The loans are made by the schools and are repaid to the schools, though the federal government provides a large portion of the funds. You can borrow up to $6,000 for each year of graduate study up to a total of $40,000 (this includes any money borrowed under this program during undergraduate study). The interest rates on this loan are low, usually 5 percent. There are no fees attached. The grace period is nine months upon graduation.

GUIDE TO PRIVATE/COMMERICAL LOANS

This is expensive territory. Not only are interest rates high, but terms are also quite different from those found with federal loans. You may not be able to defer payment of interest or principal until after graduation. Origination and guarantee fees are also much higher since these loans are unsecured. After all, banks and other specialized lenders exist to loan money to folks like you and, unlike the federal government, want to make money doing it. If you go this route, shop around diligently. Think of it as good practice for your post-MBA executive career.

Some of the more popular programs are listed below. *Please note, rates can vary and most programs require the borrower to be attending an approved graduate program at least halftime.* If you choose to investigate loans outside of the educational market, such as a personal line of credit, credit card, or a loan against an insurance plan, be aware that these can be quite costly.

The Access Group, Business Access Loan
Can borrow up to the amount certified by your school. Interest rate is the three-month London Interbank Offered Rates (LIBOR) + 2.7 percent. There is no guarantee or origination fee upon disbursement, but a guarantee fee between 7.5 and 12.9 percent is added to the principal at the time of repayment. Defer interest until repayment begins up to nine months after graduation. Repayment period can be as long as twenty years. For more information, call 1-800-282-1550 or go to www.accessgroup.org.

The Education Resources Institute (TERI) PEP Program
$15,000 annual limit. Prime rate for interest. Guarantee fee is 11 percent or 6.5 percent with a creditworthy cosigner. Repayment begins six months after graduation and can be up to twenty-five years. For more information go to www.teri.org.

Citibank CitiAssist® Loan
No minimum loan amount and no annual limit. Aggregate limit of $110,000. Prime rate + 0.5 percent. No guarantee or origination fees. Can defer interest while in school or make interest payments as you go. Repayment period up to fifteen years. Six-month grace period. For more information call 1-800-692-8200 or visit www.studentloan.citibank.com/slcsite/.

Nellie Mae EXCEL Grad Loan
Students can borrow up to $15,000 on their own or more with a qualified co-signer. Aggregate limit of $100,000 (without co-signer). No aggregate limit with co-signer. Guarantee fee is 6 percent (without co-signer) and 2 percent (with co-signer). Prime rate + 0 percent (monthly variable) or prime rate + 2 percent (annual variable). All loan payments may be deferred until six months following graduation. Interest payments may be made during school or capitalized. Repayment period up to twenty years. Call 1-800-9-TUITION or visit www.nelliemae.com.

Sallie Mae MBA Loans
Interest rates start at prime and depend on borrower's credit history. Disbursement fee from 0 to 4 percent based on credit rating. Repayment period up to twenty-five years. International students are eligible. For more information call 1-888-440-4622 or go to www.salliemae.com.

GUIDE TO SCHOLARSHIPS AND GRANTS

The usual sources for this type of funding are alumni groups and civic organizations. This funding is limited, and actual awards tend to be small. Even if you benefited from generous scholarship funding as an undergraduate, it would be unwise to assume you'll have the same experience as a graduate student. But do investigate. You never know what's out there. Schools will frequently list any scholarships and grants that are available at the back of their financial aid catalog.

Part II

HOW TO GET IN

CHAPTER 7

PREPARING TO BE
A SUCCESSFUL APPLICANT

GET GOOD GRADES

If you're still in school, concentrate on getting good grades. A high GPA says you've got not only brains, but also discipline. It shows the admissions committee you have what you need to make it through the program. If you're applying directly from college or have limited job experience, your grades will matter even more. The admissions committee will have little else on which to evaluate you.

It's especially important that you do well in courses such as economics, statistics, and calculus. Success in these courses is more meaningful than success in classes like "Monday Night at the Movies" film appreciation. Of course, English is also important; b-schools want students who communicate well.

STRENGTHEN MATH SKILLS

Number-crunching is an inescapable part of b-school. If your work experience has failed to develop your quantitative skills, take an accounting or statistics course for credit at a local college or b-school. If you have a liberal arts background and did poorly in math, or got a low GMAT math score, this is especially important. Getting a decent grade will go a long way toward convincing the admissions committee you can manage the quantitative challenges of the program.

WORK FOR A FEW YEARS—BUT NOT TOO MANY

Business schools have traditionally favored applicants who have worked full-time for several years. There are three primary reasons for this: 1) with experience comes maturity; 2) you're more likely to know what you want out of the program; 3) your experience enables you to bring real-work perspectives to the classroom. Since business school is designed for you to learn from your classmates, each student's contribution is important.

Until recently, b-schools preferred to admit only those students with two to five years of work experience. The rationale was that at two years you have worked enough to be able to make a solid contribution, while beyond four or five, you might be too advanced in your career to appreciate the program fully. However, as we noted earlier in this book, there is a new trend among top schools toward admitting "younger" applicants—that is, candidates with limited work experience as well as those straight from college.

Depending on the schools you're applying to and the strength of your resume of accomplishments, you may not need full-time, professional work experience. Of course, there's a catch: the younger you are, the harder you'll have to work to supply supporting evidence for your case as a qualified applicant. Be prepared to convince admissions committees that you've already done some incredible things, especially if you're hailing straight from college.

If you've targeted top-flight schools like Wharton, Columbia, or Stanford, applying fresh out of college is still a long shot. While your chances of gaining admission with little work experience have improved, your best shot is still to err on the conservative side and get a year or two of some professional experience under your belt.

If you're not interested in the big league or you plan on attending a local program, the number of years you should work before applying may vary. Research the admissions requirements at your target school. There's no doubt the MBA will jumpstart your career and have long-lasting effects on your business (and perhaps personal) outlook. If you're not ready to face the real world after college, plenty of solid b-schools will welcome you to another two years of academia.

There is one caveat to this advice, however. If your grades are weak, consider working at least three years before applying. The more professional success you have, the greater the likelihood that admissions committees will overlook your GPA.

LET YOUR JOB WORK FOR YOU

Many companies encourage employees to go to b-school. Some of these companies have close ties to a favored b-school and produce well-qualified applicants. If their employees are going to the kinds of schools you want to get into, these may be smart places to work.

Other companies, such as investment banks, feature training programs, at the end of which trainees go to b-school or leave the company. These programs hire undergraduates right out of school. They're known for producing solid, highly skilled applicants. Moreover, they're full of well-connected alumni who may write influential letters of recommendation.

Happily, the opposite tactic—working in an industry that generates few applicants—can be equally effective. Admissions officers look for students from underrepresented professions. Applicants from biotechnology, health care, not-for-profit, and even the Peace Corps are viewed favorably.

One way to set yourself apart is to have had two entirely different professional experiences before business school. For example, if you worked in finance, your next job might be in a different field, like marketing. Supplementing quantitative work with qualitative experiences demonstrates versatility.

Finally, what you do in your job is important. Seek out opportunities to distinguish yourself. Even if your responsibilities are limited, exceed the expectations of the position. B-schools are looking for leaders.

MARCH FROM THE MILITARY

A surprising number of b-school students hail from the military (although the armed forces probably had commanders in mind, not CEOs, when they designed their regimen). Military officers know how to be managers because they've held command positions. And they know how to lead a team under the most difficult of circumstances.

Because most have traveled all over the world, they also know how to work with people from different cultures. As a result, they're ideally suited to learn alongside students with diverse backgrounds and perspectives. B-schools with a global focus are particularly attracted to such experience.

The decision to enlist in the military is a very personal one. However, if you've thought of joining those few good men and women, this may be as effective a means of preparing for b-school as more traditional avenues.

CHECK OUT THOSE ESSAY QUESTIONS NOW

You're worried you don't have interesting stories to tell. Or you just don't know what to write. What do you do?

Ideally, several months before your application is due, you should read the essay questions and begin to think about your answers. Could you describe an ethical dilemma at work? Are you involved in anything outside the office (or classroom)? If not, now is the time to do something about it. While this may seem contrived, it's preferable to sitting down to write the application and finding you have to scrape for or, even worse, manufacture situations.

Use the essay questions as a framework for your personal and professional activities. Look back over your business calendar, and see if you can find some meaty experiences for the essays in your work life. Keep your eyes open for a situation that involves questionable ethics. And if all you do is work, work, work, get involved in activities that round out your background. In other words, get a life.

Get involved in community-based activities. Some possibilities are being a big brother/big sister, tutoring in a literacy program, or initiating a recycling project. Demonstrating a concern for others looks good to admissions committees, and hey, it's good for your soul, too.

It's also important to seek out leadership experiences. B-schools are looking for individuals who can manage groups. Volunteer to chair a professional committee or run for an office in a club. It's a wide-open world; you can pick from any number of activities. The bottom line is this: The extracurriculars you select can show that you are mature, multifaceted, and appealing.

We don't mean to sound cynical. Obviously, the best applications do nothing more than describe your true, heartfelt interests and show off your sparkling personality. We're not suggesting you try to guess which activity will win the hearts of admissions directors and then mold yourself accordingly. Instead, think of projects and activities you care about, that maybe you haven't gotten around to acting on, and act on them now!

PICK YOUR RECOMMENDERS CAREFULLY

By the time you apply to business school, you shouldn't have to scramble for recommendations. Like the material for your essays, sources for recommendations should be considered long before the application is due.

How do you get great recommendations? Obviously, good work is a prerequisite. Whom you ask is equally important. Bosses who know you well will recommend you on both a personal and professional level. They can provide specific examples of your accomplishments, skills, and character. Additionally, they can convey a high level of interest in your candidacy.

There's also the issue of trust. B-school recommendations are made in confidence; you probably won't see exactly what's been written about you. Choose someone you can trust to deliver the kind of recommendation that will push you over the top. A casual acquaintance may fail you by writing an adequate, yet mostly humdrum letter.

Cultivate relationships that yield glowing recommendations. Former and current professors, employers, clients, and managers are all good choices. An equally impressive recommendation can come from someone who has observed you in a worthwhile extracurricular activity.

We said before you won't see *exactly* what's being written about you, but that doesn't mean you should just hand a blank piece of paper to your recommender. Left to their own devices, recommenders may create a portrait that leaves out your best features. You need to prep them on what to write. Remind them of those projects or activities in which you achieved some success. You might also discuss the total picture of yourself that you are trying to create. The recommendation should reinforce what you're saying about yourself in your essays.

About "Big Shot" recommendations: Don't bother. Getting some professional golfer who's a friend of your dad's to write you a recommendation will do you no good if he doesn't know you very well, even if he is President of the Universe. Don't try to fudge your application—let people who really know you and your work tell the honest, believable, and impressive truth.

PREPARE FOR THE GRADUATE MANAGEMENT ADMISSION TEST (GMAT)

Most b-schools require you to take the GMAT. The GMAT is now a three-and-a-half-hour computer adaptive test (CAT) with multiple-choice math and verbal sections as well as an essay section. It's the kind of test you hate to take and schools love to require.

Why is the GMAT required? B-schools believe it measures your verbal and quantitative skills and predicts success in the MBA program. Some think this is a bunch of hooey, but most schools weigh your GMAT scores heavily in the admissions decision. If nothing else, it gives the school a quantitative tool to compare you with other applicants.

The test begins with the Analytical Writing Assessment (AWA) containing two essays questions. In the past, all questions that have appeared on the official GMAT have been drawn from a list of about 150 topics that appear in *The Official Guide to the GMAT* (published by the Educational Testing Service). Review that list and you'll have a pretty good idea of what to expect from the AWA. You will have thirty minutes to write each essay. By the way, you will be required to type your essay at the computer. Depending on how rusty your typing skills are, you may want to consider a bit of practice.

Next comes the multiple-choice section which has two parts: a seventy-five-minute math section and a seventy-five-minute verbal section. The math section includes problem-solving questions (e.g. "Train A leaves Baltimore at 6:32 A.M. . . .") and data-sufficiency questions. Data-sufficiency questions require you to determine whether you have been given enough information to solve a particular math problem. The good news about these types of questions is that you don't actually have to solve the problem; the bad news is that these questions can be very tricky. The verbal section tests reading skills (reading comprehension), grammar (sentence correction), and logic (critical reasoning).

For those unfamiliar with CAT exams, here's a brief overview of how they work: On multiple-choice sections, the computer starts by asking a question of medium difficulty. If you answer it correctly, the computer asks you a question that is slightly more difficult than the previous question. If you answer incorrectly, the computer asks a slightly easier question next. The test continues this way until you have answered enough questions that it can make an accurate (or so they say) assessment of your performance and assign you a score.

Most people feel they have no control over the GMAT. They dread it as the potential bomb in their application. But relax; you have more control than you think. You can take a test-preparation course to review the math and verbal material, learn test-taking strategies, and build your confidence. Test-prep courses can be highly effective. The Princeton Review offers what we think is the best GMAT course available. Even better, it offers two options for online preparation in addition to the traditional classroom course and one-on-one tutoring. Another option is to take a look at our book *Cracking the GMAT CAT*, which reviews all the subjects and covers all the tips you would learn in one of our courses.

How many times should you take the GMAT? More than once if you didn't ace it on the first try. But watch out: Multiple scores that fall in the same range make you look unprepared. Don't take the test more than once if you don't expect a decent increase, and don't even think of taking it the first time without serious preparation. Limiting your GMAT attempts to two is best. Three tries are okay if there were unusual circumstances or if you really need another shot at it. If you take it more than three times, the admissions committee will think you have an unhealthy obsession. A final note: If you submit more than one score, most schools will take the highest.

If you don't have math courses on your college transcript or numbers-oriented work experience, it's especially important to get a solid score on the quantitative section. There's a lot of math between you and the MBA.

CHAPTER 8

ADMISSIONS

HOW THE ADMISSIONS CRITERIA ARE WEIGHTED

Although admissions requirements vary among business schools, most rely on the following criteria: GMAT score, college GPA, work experience, your essays, letters of recommendation (academic and/or professional), an interview with an admissions representative, and your extracurriculars. The first four are generally the most heavily weighted. The more competitive the school, the less room there is for weakness in any area. Any component out of sync, such as a weak GMAT score, is potentially harmful.

Happily, the admissions process at business school is one where great emphasis is placed on getting to know you as a person. The essay component is the element that allows the schools to do just that. Your essays can refute weaknesses, fill in gaps, and in general, charmingly persuade an admissions board you've got the right stuff. They are the single most important criteria in business school admissions.

But as we've just said, they're not the only criteria. All pieces of your application must come together to form a cohesive whole. It is the *entire application* that determines whether you win admission.

ANTICIPATE AND COORDINATE

The application process is very time-consuming, so anticipating what you need to accomplish within the admissions time frame is critical. To make the best use of our advice, you should first contact each of the programs on your personal list of schools. Their standards and criteria for admission may vary, and you'll need to follow their specific guidelines. Please note that the less competitive a school is, the more easily you may be able to breeze through (or completely omit) the rigorous requirements we identify as crucial in the application process for the top programs.

In addition, business school applicants are often overwhelmed by how much they have to do to complete not only one, but several applications. Proper management of the process is essential, since there are so many factors to coordinate in each application.

Reminder:

We've done our best to give you solid advice on winning admission to *any* school in this book. But that doesn't mean these schools share the same standards for admission.

As you read through the next few sections, think about your personal list of schools. Contact each program directly to determine just how selective it is. This information will help you make the best use of our admissions advice.

Again, the less competitive the school is, the more easily you may be able to breeze through (or completely omit) the rigorous requirements we identify as crucial in the application process for top programs.

You'll have to prep for the GMAT, then actually take the test, round up some writers for your recommendations, follow up with those chosen to write recommendations, make sure the recommendations are mailed in on time, have your college transcript sent, and finally, write the essays. Of course, some schools require an interview as well. What makes all of this particularly challenging is that many applicants have to fit this in among the demands of a full-time job.

We know that it takes a supreme force of will to complete even one application. As grad school applications go, a top business school's is pretty daunting. So if you don't stay focused on the details and deadlines, you may drop the ball.

There are many common and incredibly embarrassing mistakes you can avoid with prudent early planning. They include allowing your recommendation writers to miss the deadline, submitting an application full of typos and grammatical errors, sending one school an essay intended for another, or forgetting to change the school name when using the same essay for several applications. Applicants who wind up cramming for the GMAT or squeezing their essay writing into several all-nighters seriously shortchange themselves.

APPLY EARLY

The best advice is this: Plan early and apply early. The former diminishes the likelihood of an accidental omission or a missed deadline. The latter increases your chances of acceptance.

The filing period ranges anywhere from six to eight months. The earlier you apply, the better your chances. There are a number of reasons for this:

First, there's plenty of space available early on. As the application deadline nears, spaces fill up. The majority of applicants don't apply until the later months because of procrastination or unavoidable delays. As the deadline draws close, the greatest number of applicants compete for the fewest number of spaces.

Second, in the beginning, admissions officers have little clue about how selective they can be. They haven't reviewed enough applications to determine the competitiveness of the pool. An early application may be judged more on its own merit than how it stacks up against others. This is in your favor if the pool turns out to be unusually competitive. Above all, admissions officers like to lock their classes in early; they can't be certain they'll get their normal supply of applicants. Admissions decisions may be more generous at this time.

Third, by getting your application in early you're showing a strong interest. The admissions committee is likely to view you as someone keen on going to their school.

To be sure, some admissions officers report that the first batch of applications tend to be from candidates with strong qualifications, confident of acceptance. In this case, you might not be the very first one on line; but closer to the front is still better than lost in the heap of last-minute hopefuls.

Of course, if applications are down that year at all b-schools or—thanks to the latest drop in its ranking—at the one to which you are applying, then filing later means you can benefit from admissions officers desperately filling spaces. But this is risky business, especially since the rankings don't come out until the spring.

Conversely, if the school to which you are applying was recently ranked number one or two, applying early may make only a marginal difference. Swings in the rankings from year to year send school applications soaring and sagging. From beginning to end, a newly crowned number-one or two school will be flooded with applications. Regardless, do not put in your application until you are satisfied that it is the best you can make it. Once a school has passed on your application, it will not reconsider you until the following year.

ROUNDS VS. ROLLING ADMISSIONS

Applications are processed in one of two ways: rounds or rolling admissions. Schools that use rounds divide the filing period into three or so timed cycles. Applications are batched into the round in which they are received and reviewed in competition with others in that round. A list of a b-school's round dates can be obtained by contacting their admissions office if they employ this method. Applications to schools with rolling admissions are reviewed on an ongoing basis as they are received.

GMAT AND GPA

The GMAT and GPA are used in two ways. First, they're "success indicators" for the academic work you'll have to slog through if admitted—will you have the brainpower to succeed in the program? Second, they're used as benchmarks to compare each applicant to other applicants within the pool. At the more selective schools, you'll need a higher score and average to stay in the game.

The Educational Testing Service (ETS) administers the GMAT. You'll need to register to take the exam by calling 800-GMAT-NOW (800-462-8669) or by registering online at www.mba.com. Many applicants take the exam more than once to improve their scores. Test preparation is also an option for boosting your numbers—call 800-2Review (800-273-8439) for more information about The Princeton Review's GMAT courses.

Your college transcript is a major factor in the strength of your candidacy. Some schools focus more closely on the junior- and senior-year grades than the overall GPA, and most consider the reputation of your college and the difficulty of your course selections. A transcript loaded with offerings like "Environmental Appreciation" and "The Child in You" won't be valued as highly as one packed with calculus and history classes.

THE ESSAYS

Admissions committees consider the essays the clincher, the swing vote on the "admit/deny" issue. Essays offer the most substance about who you really are. The GMAT and GPA reveal little about you, only that you won't crash and burn. Your work history provides a record of performance and justifies your stated desire to study business. But the essays tie all the pieces of the application together and create a summary of your experiences, skills, background, and beliefs.

The essays do more than give answers to questions. They create thumbnail psychological profiles. Depending on how you answer a question or what you present, you reveal yourself in any number of ways—creative, witty, open-minded, articulate, mature—to name a few. Likewise, your essay can reveal a negative side, such as arrogance, sloppiness, or an inability to think and write clearly.

LETTERS OF RECOMMENDATION

Letters of recommendation act as a reality check. Admissions committees expect them to support and reinforce what they're seeing in the rest of your application. When the information doesn't match up with the picture you've painted, it makes you look bad. Because you won't see the recommendation (it's sent in "blind"), you won't even know there's a problem. This can mean the end of your candidacy.

That's why you need to take extreme care in selecting your references.

Scan each application for guidelines on choosing your references—business schools typically request an academic or professional reference. The academic reference should be someone who can

THE TYPICAL COURSE A BUSINESS SCHOOL APPLICATION RUNS

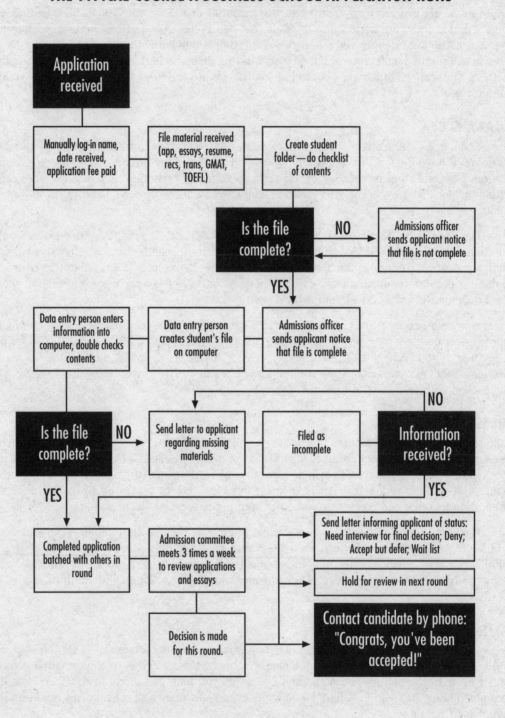

evaluate your performance in an academic environment. It's better to ask an instructor, teacher's aide, or mentor who knew you well than a famous professor who barely knew your name.

The same holds true for your professional reference. Seek out individuals who can evaluate your performance on many levels. The reference will be far more credible. Finding the right person to write your professional reference, however, can be trickier. You may not wish to reveal to your boss early on that you plan on leaving, and if the dynamics of your relationship are not ideal (hey, it happens once in a while), he or she might not make an appropriate reference. If this is the case, seek out a boss at a former job or someone who was your supervisor at your current job but has since moved to another organization. Avoid friends, colleagues, and clients as references unless the school explicitly says its okay.

Advise your writers on themes and qualities you highlighted in your application. Suggest that they include real-life examples of your performance to illustrate their points. In other words, script the recommendation as best you can. Your boss, even if he or she is your biggest fan, may not know what your recommendation should include.

A great recommendation is rarely enough to save a weak application from doom. But it might push a borderline case over to the "admit" pile. Mediocre recommendations can be damaging; an application that is strong in all other areas now has a weakness, an inconsistency.

A final warning on this topic: Procrastination is common here. Micromanage your references so that each recommendation arrives on time! If need be, provide packaging for an overnight letter, have your reference seal it up, and then ship it out yourself.

THE INTERVIEW

Not all business schools attach equal value to the interview. For some, it's an essential screening tool. For others, it's used to make a final decision on those caught somewhere between "admit" and "reject." Some schools may encourage, but not require, the interview. Others make it informative, with little connection to the admissions decision.

Like the letters of recommendation, an interview may serve as a reality check to reinforce the total picture. It may also be used to fill in the blanks, particularly in borderline cases.

If an interview is offered, take it. In person, you may be an entirely more compelling candidate. You can further address weaknesses or bring dull essays to life. Most important, you can display the kinds of qualities—enthusiasm, sense of humor, maturity—that often fill in the blanks and positively sway an admissions decision.

Act quickly to schedule your interview. Admissions departments often lack the time and staff to interview every candidate who walks through their doors. You don't want your application decision delayed by several months (and placed in a more competitive round or pool) because your interview was scheduled late in the filing period.

A great interview can tip the scale in the "admit" direction. How do you know if it was great? You were calm and focused. You expressed yourself and your ideas clearly. Your interviewer invited you to go rock climbing with him next weekend. (Okay, let's just say you developed a solid personal rapport with the interviewer.)

A mediocre interview may not have much impact, unless your application is hanging on by a thread. In such a case, the person you're talking to (harsh as it may seem) is probably looking for a reason not to admit you, rather than a reason to let you in. If you feel your application may be in that hazy, marginal area, try to be extra-inspired in your interview.

Approach this meeting as you would a job interview. Dress and act the part of a professional. But at the same time, remember: You're being sized up as a person in all of your dimensions. Avoid acting stiff or like a stuffed shirt. Limit your use of business jargon. Be personable. Gear yourself up for an enjoyable conversation where you may discuss your hobbies or recent cross-country trip. Talk about your passions or any areas in which you have achieved excellence—even something like gourmet cooking. Just avoid stunt-like gimmicks (we don't advise you to pull out a platter of peppercorn pâté sautéed in anchovy sauce). The idea is to get the interviewer thinking of you as someone who will contribute greatly to the quality of campus life. Try to be your witty, charming, natural self.

AN INTERVIEW WITH THE DIRECTOR OF MBA ADMISSIONS AT THE ANDERSON SCHOOL

To get some perspective on the most recent group of applicants, we sat down with Linda Baldwin, the director of MBA admissions at the Anderson School. We asked her to comment on the dot-com era, dispense some advice for prospective MBAs, and give out special words of wisdom for international applicants.

Q: What are some of your thoughts on the dot-com era?

A: The dot-com phenomenon allowed a number of individuals to dream in new ways. For some individuals, they pulled up their stake in very traditional jobs to work with entrepreneurial start-ups populated with other talented, educated, and skilled dreamers. For others, they began their career in the start-up environment never knowing traditional workplaces. For the most part, those who have worked for dot-coms enjoyed the high energy associated with these start-up organizations, the flow of ideas, the collaboration, the involvement in everything, and even the excitement of the uncertain payoff. They were young enough and strong enough to step out there and take on the risk associated with great reward or failure. They wanted a creative environment and in many cases they got that manifolds over.

I can't say they're any worse off, if they learned about themselves and have a better sense of what they need to know in the future. In fact we're now seeing a lot of those individuals saying, "Based on what I learned out there, I now know that I need to learn more, and an MBA will help me understand business fundamentals, and perhaps come up with better business models." Interestingly enough, these young people have plans of working in entrepreneurial environments whether it's with a start-up or within a larger organization.

Q: In a smaller entrepreneurial environment you have a huge impact; that's pretty heady stuff.

A: It's about having an impact, being able to see things take shape and knowing that you have contributed. Often in these environments there is a tremendous amount of collaboration and creativity; you're not alone in doing your work. That can be very exciting for individuals who may have worked in an organization where the daily work entailed mostly interacting with a monitor within a cubicle.

What's interesting in looking at the career aspirations of individuals who've left dot-coms is what they want to do with their lives after the MBA. They continue to have a strong preference for technology-related industries and they want to work within entrepreneurial environments.

Q: How does someone coming from a dot-com or entrepreneurial environment convince you that their prior experience was meaningful and that they're ready for the MBA?

A: Through essays and/or the interview process an applicant from a dot-com or entrepreneurial environment can persuasively position their work accomplishments by addressing the scope of their responsibilities; their assessment of their impact on their work environment/their company; they can address the business model driving their start-up, perhaps analyzing what went right and what went wrong.

  We're looking for their understanding of the bigger picture, and not just a description of their day-to-day activities. We ask open-ended questions to give them every opportunity to elaborate on their leadership experiences/challenges in these environments. If they are able to answer with a level of self-awareness about what occurred to them within that industry—that's great! Their understanding of the skills they developed, including soft skills; their role and how it evolved over time; as well as their rationale for MBA study—all can reveal a lot about the individual's readiness for MBA study.

Q: Are you wary of having an applicant pool for which the MBA is their only resort now?

A: I'm not wary at all. I've talked to many of these ex-dot-com prospectives and I think they've given the MBA a lot of thought. Their recent experiences have made them reflect on their situation. They have had numerous conversations with other ex-dot-com types about career directions. In most instances they have thought very carefully about their next step, having taken a risky one with questionable results.

Q: I guess these dot-com-ers are coming into your program more like mini-CEOs.

A: I believe they will come in with a greater desire to understand the business fundamentals because they were so personally impacted.

Q: In the next chapter we have a section called "Fifteen Sure-Fire Ways to Torpedo Your Application." What mistakes do you commonly see in applicants' essays or presentation?

A: Most candidates are quite savvy. However, I've seen a few individuals err in the interview or essays by denigrating others. When an applicant speaks poorly of a boss, a company, or colleagues in order to enhance him/herself it usually backfires.

Q: I bet it's hard not to, though. It's one of those things you slip into.

A: It's one of those things where you might start by describing a situation revealing the problems or errors, and suddenly the story is more about "what they did wrong," and "what they did not do," or "how they messed up" rather than your story. Venting is not a good way to impress anyone. Instead, my advice is to explain a failure objectively. Ask yourself what lessons you learned from the situation and how has that positioned you to take on future challenges.

Negative comments about employers—anyone—will get you nowhere. You can be critical, but also remember to be constructive. The moment you start to blame others, you're telling the admissions staff in a very obvious way that you may not be capable of working with people, and moreover you're not emotionally ready for the MBA. At Anderson you have to take responsibility for your behavior and the situation. We're always looking for the person who is the problem-solver as opposed to the person who is the naysayer/critic.

Q: We are frequently asked by readers, "How many times can someone take the GMAT before it's becomes a turn-off?"

A: Typically two times is acceptable. A third time might be acceptable if there's a good reason for it.

Q: Speaking of another admissions turn-off, when applicants describe their accomplishments, how easy is it to cross over into bragging?

A: In the application process you do have some leeway to toot your own horn. You should remember your recommenders are also on your side, so you need not go overboard.

Q: Well, that's assuming the recommenders did a decent job of recommending. It's a blind process.

A: Well you know, it isn't as blind as you might think. The applicant selects the recommenders and we would assume she or he would select someone who would have a balanced perspective of the applicant. You would not necessarily just leave your recommendation form without some discussion.

I would think that you would select a recommender with whom you have cultivated a relationship. You would spend some time with that person, perhaps discussing why you want to pursue an MBA degree, and maybe highlighting some of your accomplishments/achievements that relate to why you are now interested in pursuing an MBA. You manage that process of recommendations just like you manage the entire application process.

Q: What is a common mistake international applicants make?

A: Most international candidates don't make a lot of mistakes. However, among international candidates, two minor mistakes/misunderstandings occur from time to time.

First, they can be extremely persistent about wanting to communicate via e-mail or fax or phone about their accomplishments or unique situations. Our decision is based on the contents of the "completed application" and not these additional "lobbying" communications. All of these efforts to be familiar or to make a positive impression might be better spent doing an excellent job on the application.

Along this same line of thought, e-mailing information about one's background, test scores, accomplishments, and work experiences in order to get some feedback on one's viability in the applicant pool is a big no-no.

Q: So how do you answer that person? Do you re-direct them?

A: We tell the prospective applicant that it can't be done via a letter/e-mail. We do a comprehensive review of their application that requires submission of a completed application.

Q: This year the GMAC reported a big spike in the number of people taking the GMAT. Is the bulk of that increase international students?

A: Based on data provided by GMAC, I would say it certainly is. During the last five years, international test-takers have increased by 11 percent for men and 8 percent for women. U.S. men test-takers have declined by 21 percent, and U.S. women test-takers have declined by 16 percent.

Q: You said above that two or three is an acceptable number of times for domestic students to take the GMAT. What do you consider the acceptable number for international students?

A: Two times or three given special circumstances. Because the GMAT is offered monthly, we have noted that some international applicants are taking the GMAT every month, basically utilizing it as a practice test. This is not a good idea because the scores will be averaged, and all scores are reported to the school.

Q: Linda, what other advice would you give to someone considering business school today?

A: One piece of advice . . . in thinking about when to begin MBA study, each individual has a different timeframe. Each of us is ready at different points in time to pursue the MBA. One needs to think about how and why the MBA will serve them at this particular juncture. They should not be afraid of the fact that they have less than two years of work experience and they should not assume that just because the average is four years of work experience, that they're ready.

What is important to us is what you've accomplished in life thus far and how you see the MBA contributing to your further development . . . that is critical in deciding when to apply to The Anderson School at UCLA.

QUOTAS, RECRUITMENT, AND DIVERSITY

B-schools don't have to operate under quotas—governmental or otherwise. However, they probably try harder than most corporations to recruit diverse groups of people. Just as the modern business world has become global and multicultural, so too have b-schools. They must not only teach diversity in the classroom but also make it a reality in their campus population and, if possible, faculty.

Schools that have a diverse student body tend to be proud of it. They tout their success in profiles that demographically slice and dice the previous year's class by sex, race, and geographic and international residency. Prospective students can review this data and compare the diversity of the schools they've applied to.

But such diversity doesn't come naturally from the demographics of the applicant pool. Admissions committees have to work hard at it. In some cases, enrollment is encouraged with generous financial aid packages and scholarships.

While they don't have quotas per se, they do target groups for admission, seeking a demographic balance in many areas. Have they admitted enough women, minorities, foreign students, marketing strategists, and liberal arts majors? Are different parts of the country represented?

As we've said before, the best b-schools tend to attract top talent, students, and recruiters to their campus. Women and minorities are the most sought-after groups targeted for admission. So it's no surprise that programs that report higher-than-average female and minority enrollments tend to be among the very best.

FEMALES WANTED

The ratio of women to men enrolled in business school hasn't changed much in recent years, despite the attempts of b-schools to draw women to their campuses. A recent study by Michigan's Business School, Michigan's Center for the Education of Women, and Catalyst, Inc., found that women experience key barriers to b-school. Some of the reasons women shy away are the myth that the MBA is still really a male domain, lack of support from employers, lack of career opportunity and flexibility, lack of access to powerful business networks and role models, and concerns that b-school is overloaded with number-crunching. Armed with these findings, a new consortium has emerged whose sole focus is to attract more women to b-school.

"The mission of this new organization is to substantially increase the number of women business owners and leaders by increasing the flow of women into key education gateway and business networks," says Jeanne M. Wilt, executive director of the consortium and assistant dean of admissions and career development at the University of Michigan. A major area of activity for the consortium will be communication and education.

"One of the key barriers to business education is the lack of knowledge women have about the value and flexibility of business careers and education. There will be tremendous outreach about that. We also need to make more positive role models available to women and girls so that they can make good decisions about their career paths. So leadership development is a priority. This will involve mentorship and program internships for girls as sophomores and juniors in college," notes Wilt.

Also on the consortium's to-do list is to provide significant financial assistance to MBAs. To make all this happen, they've formed partnerships with market leaders Dell, Goldman Sachs, and Procter and Gamble. In the near future, they hope to expand these alliances to dozens of other b-schools and companies.

Women MBA Enrollments at Leading MBA Programs (1988–2000)
Top 20 Schools (as ranked by Business Week)

1988		1990		1992		1994		1996		1998		2000	
Kellogg	30%	Kellogg	30%	Kellogg	29%	Wharton	27%	Wharton	28%	Wharton	29%	Wharton	29%
Harvard	27%	Wharton	30%	Chicago	23%	Kellogg	30%	Michigan	25%	Kellogg	32%	Kellogg	31%
Dartmouth	26%	Harvard	28%	Harvard	29%	Chicago	20%	Kellogg	31%	Chicago	22%	Harvard	31%
Wharton	27%	Chicago	28%	Wharton	30%	Stanford	27%	Harvard	26%	Michigan	28%	MIT	27%
Cornell	23%	Stanford	31%	Michigan	23%	Harvard	29%	Virginia	34%	Harvard	30%	Duke	38%
Michigan	25%	Dartmouth	30%	Dartmouth	33%	Michigan	27%	Columbia	35%	Columbia	36%	Michigan	28%
Virginia	26%	Michigan	28%	Stanford	29%	Indiana	26%	Stanford	29.5%	Duke	33%	Columbia	37%
UNC	35%	Columbia	34%	Indiana	22%	Columbia	32%	Chicago	23%	Cornell	26%	Cornell	27%
Stanford	27%	Carnegie Mellon	19%	Columbia	32%	UCLA	29%	MIT	28%	Stanford	29%	Virginia	28%
Duke	25%	UCLA	33%	UNC	25%	MIT	25%	Dartmouth	29.7%	Dartmouth	29%	Chicago	23%
Chicago	23%	MIT	24%	Virginia	34%	Duke	30%	Duke	30%	Virginia	30%	Stanford	35%
Indiana	27.5%	UNC	30%	Duke	28%	Virginia	31%	UCLA	27%	UCLA	28%	UCLA	28%
Carnegie Mellon	21%	Duke	25%	MIT	25%	Dartmouth	31%	Berkeley	34%	NYU	38%	NYU	39%
Columbia	31%	Virginia	29%	Cornell	25%	Carnegie Mellon	20%	NYU	26%	Carnegie Mellon	24%	Carnegie Mellon	26%
MIT	20%	Indiana	30%	NYU	29%	Cornell	24%	Indiana	23%	MIT	27%	UNC	31%
UCLA	35%	Cornell	25%	UCLA	31%	NYU	28%	Washington	30%	Berkeley	38%	Dartmouth	32%
Berkeley	38%	NYU	31%	Carnegie Mellon	19%	Texas	31%	Carnegie Mellon	19.1%	Washington	26%	Texas	24%
NYU	39%	Texas	30%	Berkeley	30%	UNC	31%	Cornell	32%	Texas	25%	Berkeley	34%
Yale	37%	Berkeley	32%	Vanderbilt	23%	Berkeley	34%	UNC	36%	UNC	27%	Yale	30%
Rochester	30%	Rochester	30%	Washington	25%	Purdue	31%	Texas	25%	Yale	32%	Indiana	24%
Average	28.6%	Average	28.9%	Average	27.2%	Average	28.2%	Average	28.6%	Average	29.5%	Average	30.1%

If you're a woman, consider aiming high. You'll find yourself in solid company—almost 4 out of 10 classmates at top schools are female. At other programs, you may stick out. How much? That depends. The percentage of female MBAs at b-school can be as high as 38 percent, and in fact, at NYU's Stern School of Business, that's been the average for the last several years. Stern's director of admissions, Julia Min, notes, "We've been very proactive in our female representation. In the 1900s we were one of the very first schools to admit women."

Our advice: Look at the number of female MBA students attending your targeted school and evaluate whether you would feel comfortable there. Research the number and range of student organizations for women only and speak with female MBAs about school life.

AN INTERVIEW WITH CATHY CRANE-MOLEY, STANFORD GRADUATE SCHOOL OF BUSINESS, CLASS OF '92

While there remains a shortage of women in b-school, those who go the distance are not shorted on opportunity. We spoke with Cathy Crane-Moley, an outstanding MBA with the talent, passion, and drive that have made her one of America's most successful businesswomen. In fact, Entelos, Inc., which Cathy co-founded in 1996, has recently been named one of the 13 coolest companies in the nation by *Fortune* magazine.

Ten years out, Cathy is the co-founder and senior VP strategy, Entelos, Inc. and former CFO and head of corporate development.

Q: Cathy, as a newly minted MBA, what were your thoughts on what the degree could do for you?

A: At that point in time, I didn't have a 10-plus-year horizon in my view. My thoughts were more about the immediate future of my career. I was a molecular biology major as an undergrad. I had worked in sales and in the field and had a big passion for health care. So that's really why I went to get an MBA, to follow through on my passion and vision for a business career in the health care sector.

Q: How did you target Stanford as the school that would deliver on that vision?

A: That's an interesting question. I lived in Virginia at the time and I did a lot of research on schools. I had a number of goals, some of which changed once I got to business school, but one of the goals was to go to a top school—which Stanford is. And I was really interested in somehow combining international business and entrepreneurship, so another goal was to find an environment that would support my exposure to that. So I applied to Stanford and Harvard and Wharton and all the types of schools that would have recruiters coming on campus from an international background. And I chose Stanford as the best environment for my combined vision.

Q: But what was it about Stanford that fit with your career aspirations in particular?

A: What I really wanted from the MBA was to have the credibility to go build a company in health care. I had an expectation that business school would help me be a better businessperson in science. My goal was to be able to tie together the business and science and pursue a business career in biotechnology health care.

When I went to Stanford I was pretty nervous because all these investment bankers and consultants were using intimidating terms like "run the numbers." When I got to business school I learned that it just meant 2 + 2. So for me it was really about learning a whole new language.

Every domain has it's own jargon and half the battle is learning the language. Business isn't rocket science. It has some very pragmatic, practical, and even intuitive components to it. So putting a language to it was a critical step for me.

Q: Did you utilize Stanford's formal on-campus recruiting to get your first job or did you have to do a one-of-a-kind type of job search?

A: I did a little bit of both. The on-campus recruiting I did that was formalized was more for the sake of exposure. Mostly, I created my own job search, which touches on the MBA and how important the school's networks are. The Stanford community was pivotal to my getting the job. There is no question that if I hadn't come out of Stanford, I would not have had the job I had.

Q: Why?

A: A couple of things. Right out of school I went to become an entrepreneur-in-residence at the Mayfield Fund, a venture firm on Sand Hill Road [one of the most nationally prominent addresses for ventures funding]. The combination of my background and MBA was a big plus, but mostly getting my foot in the door was the result of befriending a wonderful woman who was from Stanford's Class of '87. She became a really strong mentor and made endless introductions in the venture community for me. She is now a dear friend of mine and was instrumental in my soul-searching.

Q: You met her while you were a student?

A: I did. She was panelist at a Stanford corporate event on biotech that was sponsored by a student-run club. She was extremely helpful.

Q: Who else influenced your path?

A: At Stanford, and I'm sure other schools are the same way, there were a number of visiting lecturers who came into class. During my second year, I took a venture capital class taught by Peter Wendell who was a partner at Sierra Ventures [a venture fund]. During that class, two of my classmates and I wrote a business plan for a scientist at [University of California at San Francisco]. This plan eventually became the biotech company Khepri Pharmaceuticals.

So interestingly enough, after I graduated I first became an entrepreneur-in-residence, working for a man at Mayfield Fund named Mark Levin who is now the CEO of Millennium Pharmaceuticals, but at that point was a very well-known health-care venture capitalist. I worked with him on a number of deals and then Mayfield, along with Sierra Ventures, ended up funding Khepri Pharmaceuticals, the company that I had written the plan for while at Stanford.

Q: What did you do at that point?

A: I went from doing the entrepreneur-in-residence to becoming the first business/operational person at Khepri.

Q: **And how long did you do that for?**

A: Until 1995, when we merged with a public company. Then I started my current company with my four co-founders in 1996, which is also in the biotechnology sector.

Q: **It sounds as though the Stanford networks were invaluable to this first experience out. What about this next stage?**

A: Absolutely invaluable. Not just because of the connections—that's one component—but in your own brainstorming about what you want to be in your life.

At business school, you are surrounded by people who have done everything. There were people in my environment that had been entrepreneurs, venture capitalists, investment bankers, and international marketers at pharmaceutical companies. There were incredibly helpful connected professors and alumni. It was all at your fingertips as you were solidifying your own vision.

Q: **I'm guessing that you would advise students beginning their MBA studies to think hard about why they're there and to take advantage of all the opportunities?**

A: Absolutely. What can happen is that it's easy to do it [pursue the opportunities], but it's also easy not to do it.

Stanford is a classic example. It's in such a beautiful location and people want to experience California; you can easily be distracted. But this is two years when anyone will return your call. You have heads of state, heads of corporations visiting, people in the nonprofit area showing up. And all you have to do is get on your bike and ride over there.

The other thing is, there are people who have come from a particular background, like investment banking and consulting, who know they intend to return to those careers after business school. But even if that is your goal, you still should use the two years to check everything out. You should use the two years to get more exposure and think about long term.

Q: **Would you have traveled this same road had you not gone to business school?**

A: Not a chance.

Q: **You knew that going in?**

A: I don't know if I knew that going in. My path as a molecular biology undergrad was more limited and linear; I couldn't have been exposed to all the things I could become. So I doubt I could have done all that I have post-MBA. I think that's what business school does for you. It gives you exposure to multiple pathways, all of which are attainable.

Q: You founded a second company, Entelos?

A: That's correct. Entelos is a leader in biosimulation and predictive biology. We work with major pharmaceutical companies to test out whether their drugs will work or not on virtual people in a computer before they are tested on real people in clinical trials.

Q: What is your role as a founder? How has it changed over the last several years?

A: For most of our company's growth, I was the CFO and head of corporate development. As you can imagine, in a start-up this role includes raising money, doing deals, hiring, and everything that's internal too.

About a year and a half ago I decided that I did not want to travel as much as I had when we started the company, so I migrated towards the role of strategy. At that point, we also brought in a CEO to help lead the company to its next level of operations and I ended up hiring two guys, one to take the CFO role and one to take the business development role.

Q: You scaled back on your responsibilities. I know you have children, so did that drive this change?

A: It did. My job now is really great, it's all the things I love: to help with strategy direction on where we take this revolutionary technology, to evaluate technology, to help our fundraising strategy, to do deal structure.

But what did I think I'd be when I left b-school? I thought I'd run a biotech company, or would be a CEO of a company; there was no question in my mind. I had the abilities.

But when kids came along, I thought, to be the CEO I want to be, I can't be that right now. I have a vision for what the CEO should be, and it's someone for whom the company is an all-encompassing focus. I have small children and for me, they are my top priority at this point in my life. Hence, at this point, I wouldn't be able to be the kind of CEO/leader that I believe a young company deserves.

Q: What was it like to go from leading a high growth start-up in your professional career to scaling back for personal reasons?

A: When you are passionate about what you do, it is hard to scale back. My transition has not been overnight. I have really migrated to a new role. I love leading-edge technologies and of course, Entelos, and I think I have created a role in which I can still make a significant contribution to our growth.

Q: So your priorities have changed?

A: There's no question in life, it may be kids, it may be your health, but there comes a time when you need to strike a balance. Ten years out I feel I have a really great base and a solid set of skills, so much so that I can now turn around and help other people out. This is one of the things I've started doing out over the last years, helping people who are at the same place I was ten years ago. And that's been very important to me.

Q: **Switching gears a bit, it's clear the networking opportunities were critical to your future career developments, but how important would you say actual content learning at school was?**

A: It actually was. But you'll see differences depending on people's backgrounds. For my husband, who was an undergrad at Wharton (I met him at Stanford), he could do corporate finance with his eyes closed. But for me, a molecular biology major as an undergrad, I had never taken business classes, so the academic training was critical. Take corporate finance, for example. I cannot imagine anyone being in the business world without formal corporate finance. Our strategy classes, entrepreneurial classes, small business classes were all great for me. Anything like cost accounting, I could have done without. Some of the options theory too. But the pragmatic fundamentals gave me the tools to build two businesses from nothing.

Q: **How was being a woman at Stanford?**

A: It was wonderful. The quality of people, male and female, was superb. I believe we have a ratio of 33 percent female. We had strong women and we did great. I never noticed any sort of difference in abilities based on gender.

Q: **Was the business school environment intimidating?**

A: I didn't think so. I felt very inspired by the people around me.

Q: **What advice do you have for someone thinking about going to business school now?**

A: I think it comes back to the theme we've already touched on: make the most of the community that you can, way over and above what the classes offer. Business school is a very unique opportunity—live it while you are there.

AN INITIATIVE FOR MINORITIES

Some schools report higher minority enrollments than others, so our advice is consistent: you need to thoroughly research the program you've set your sights on. Consider your goals. Do you simply want to attend the most prestigious program? How will social factors impact your goals and experiences on campus?

As you explore the schools in this book, you'll find that one program is especially noteworthy for it's unfaltering commitment to diversity. Unsurprisingly, it is the University of Michigan, which recently won the Outstanding Educational Institution of the Year Award from the National Black MBA Association (NBMBA). This award is presented to an institution that has made the greatest contribution toward encouraging African Americans to enter the field of business.

We don't want to single out just one school, as most business schools aspire to diversify their programs. It's the number of minorities applying to business school that has remained consistently low. The number of minorities taking the GMAT, a key indicator of how many will go on to b-school, was just roughly 14 percent of test administrations from 1999–2000.

An initiative of the Graduate Management Admissions Council called The Diversity Pipeline Alliance (www.diversitypipeline.org) was formed to reverse this trend and increase the number of African Americans, Hispanic Americans, and Native Americans pursuing a business career. Much like the initiative for women, this organization plans a powerful marketing campaign with a pro-business career message for students from middle school to graduate school. It offers information on current opportunities for mentorships, internships, and financial assistance and provides an impressive roster of member organizations, services, and educational opportunities.

Minority enrollment at business schools is still quite low, so in all likelihood, you will not experience the dramatic upward shift in b-school demographics in the near future that initiatives like the Diversity Pipeline Alliance hope to influence. However, by recognizing the disparity between the minority presence in the U.S. and minority involvement in business education and practice, we are working toward a solution.

As you make up your mind about where you want to go, know that the scenario is positive and that new infrastructures exist to support your business career.

Part III

B-School Listing

AMERICAN UNIVERSITY
Kogod School of Business

Admissions Contact: Sondra Smith, Director of Graduate Admissions and Financial Aid
Address: 4400 Massachusetts Avenue NW, Washington, DC 20016-8044
Admissions Phone: 202-885-1913 • Admissions Fax: 202-885-1078
Admissions E-mail: mbakogod@american.edu • Web Address: www.kogod.american.edu

Like many MBA programs, American University boasts an emphasis on the hot topics in today's MBA market: global business and information technology. But with its prime Washington, D.C., location and proximity to tech powerhouses in Virginia and Maryland such as AOL, American is well positioned to deliver that promise. Come ready for cultural interaction and leadership opportunities galore; in an unusual democratic twist, American expects its students to contribute to the running of the program. More than 40 percent of the student body is international.

INSTITUTIONAL INFORMATION

Public/Private: Private
Evening Classes Available? Yes
Total Faculty: 78
% Faculty Female: 14
% Faculty Minority: 8
% Faculty Part Time: 27
Student/Faculty Ratio: 6:1
Students in Parent Institution: 11,420
Academic Calendar: Semester

PROGRAMS

Degrees Offered: MBA with concentrations in Accounting, Entrepreneurship, Finance, International Business, Marketing Management, Marketing, Real Estate, International Finance, International Management, International Marketing, Management of Global Information Systems, and Design Your Own (full time or part time, 51 credits, minimum of 18 months); MSITM (part time, (full time or part time, 30 credits, 12 months to 2 years)
Combined Degrees: JD/MBA (4 years), MBA/MA in International Affairs (3 years)

STUDENT INFORMATION

Total Business Students: 451
% Full Time: 58
% Female: 42
% Minority: 7
% International: 57
Average Age: 28

COMPUTER AND RESEARCH FACILITIES

Campuswide Network? Yes
% of MBA Classrooms Wired: 100
Computer Model Recommended: Laptop
Internet Fee? No

EXPENSES/FINANCIAL AID

Annual Tuition: $22,116
Tuition Per Credit (Resident/Nonresident): $827
Room & Board (On/Off Campus): $11,346/$12,000
Books and Supplies: $800
Average Grant: $0
Average Loan: $0
% Receiving Financial Aid: 15
% Receiving Aid Their First Year: 15

ADMISSIONS INFORMATION

Application Fee: $60
Electronic Application? Yes

Regular Application Deadline: Rolling
Regular Notification: Rolling
Length of Deferment: 1 year
Non-fall Application Deadline(s): Spring, rolling admissions; for international studets, 6/1 for fall and 10/1 for spring
Transfer Students Accepted? Yes
Transfer Policy: Applicants must meet the same requirements as non-transfer students. Nine credits may be transferred into the program from an AACSB-accredited MBA program.
Need-Blind Admissions? Yes
Number of Applications Received: 529
% of Applicants Accepted: 63
% Accepted Who Enrolled: 42
Average GPA: 3.2
Average GMAT: 570
GMAT Range: 500-650
Average Years Experience: 6
Other Admissions Factors Considered: A resume and work experience are required for the application.
Other Schools to Which Students Applied: George Washington University, Georgetown University, University of Maryland at College Park

INTERNATIONAL STUDENTS

TOEFL Required of International Students? Yes
Minimum TOEFL: 600 (250 computer)

EMPLOYMENT INFORMATION

Placement Office Available? Yes
% Employed Within 3 Months: 82
Fields Employing Percentage of Grads: General Management (4%), Human Resources (4%), MIS (13%), Marketing (13%), Finance (29%), Consulting (37%)
Frequent Employers: AMS, Fannie Mae, Pricewaterhouse Coopers, U.S. Government, World Bank

See page 402.

APPALACHIAN STATE UNIVERSITY
Walker College of Business

Admissions Contact: T. Joseph Watts, Director
Address: ASU Box 32004, Boone, NC 28608
Admissions Phone: 828-262-2120 • Admissions Fax: 828-262-3296
Admissions E-mail: admissions@appstate.edu • Web Address: www.business.appstate.edu

With an enrollment of less than 50 students, the MBA program at Walker College of Business offers a more intimate education, especially for the prospective female students, who account for approximately half of the student body. Students are required to attend an "enrichment experience," an orientation that includes workshops, a "team-building outdoor experience," and plenty of downtime for social acclimation. Walker expects that its high-quality instruction will yield graduates that are competent in areas across the board, emphasizing information technology, global economy, communication, professional development, and ethical responsibility. The Distinguished CEO Lecture Series gives students a chance to learn from and engage with future employers, as a majority of Walker's graduates gain employment with North Carolina corporations.

INSTITUTIONAL INFORMATION

Public/Private: Public
Evening Classes Available? No

Total Faculty: 48
% Faculty Female: 20
Student/Faculty Ratio: 35:1
Students in Parent Institution: 12,500
Academic Calendar: Semester

PROGRAMS

Degrees Offered: MBA (64 credits, full time or part time, 2 years); MS in Accounting (30 credits, full time or part time, 1-2 years), with concentrations in Accounting, Taxation; MA in Industrial Organizational Psychology and Human Resources (30 credits, full time or part time, 1-2 years)

Academic Specialties: Case study, computer-aided instruction, computer analysis, computer simulations, field projects, group discussion, lecture, role playing, seminars by members of the business community, student presentations, team projects.

STUDENT INFORMATION

Total Business Students: 50
% Full Time: 80
% Female: 34
% Minority: 0
% Out of State: 2
% International: 10
Average Age: 25

COMPUTER AND RESEARCH FACILITIES

Computer Facilities: Carol Gotnes Belk Library plus 2 on-campus libraries, access to online bibliographic retrieval services
Campuswide Network? Yes
% of MBA Classrooms Wired: 100
Computer Model Recommended: Laptop
Internet Fee? No

EXPENSES/FINANCIAL AID

Annual Tuition (Resident/Nonresident): $1,590/$11,982
Room & Board (On/Off Campus): $3,836
Books and Supplies: $1,000

ADMISSIONS INFORMATION

Application Fee: $35
Electronic Application? No
Regular Application Deadline: 3/1
Regular Notification: 3/15
Deferment Available? Yes
Length of Deferment: 1 year
Non-fall Admissions? No
Transfer Students Accepted? Yes
Transfer Policy: Six credit hours can be transferred.
Need-Blind Admissions? No
Number of Applications Received: 77
% of Applicants Accepted: 79
% Accepted Who Enrolled: 61
Average GPA: 3.0
GPA Range: 2.0-3.0
Average GMAT: 484
GMAT Range: 250-690
Average Years Experience: 5
Other Admissions Factors Considered: Minimum GMAT 450; interview, résumé, work experience, and computer experience recommended
Other Schools to Which Students Applied: University of North Carolina-Greensboro

INTERNATIONAL STUDENTS

TOEFL Required of International Students? Yes
Minimum TOEFL: 550

EMPLOYMENT INFORMATION

Placement Office Available? Yes
% Employed Within 3 Months: 99

ARIZONA STATE UNIVERSITY
W. P. Carey School of Business

Admissions Contact: Judith Heilala, Director of Recruiting and Admissions
Address: PO Box 874906, Tempe, AZ 85287-4906
Admissions Phone: 480-965-3332 • **Admissions Fax:** 480-965-8569
Admissions E-mail: wpcareymba@asu.edu • **Web Address:** wpcarey.asu.edu/mba/

The "very quick" trimester academic calendar at affordable Arizona State University makes the MBA program a bit hectic, but "an enormous number of companies recruit here"—especially from the Southwest—and students leave "well equipped to work with top-level executives as well as loading dock or field representatives." Also, "living in Phoenix is great," and Computerworld recently ranked ASU's joint degree program in information management 15th in the nation.

INSTITUTIONAL INFORMATION

Public/Private: Public
Evening Classes Available? Yes
Total Faculty: 65
% Faculty Female: 15
% Faculty Minority: 11
Student/Faculty Ratio: 25:1
Students in Parent Institution: 45,693
Academic Calendar: Trimester

PROGRAMS

Degrees Offered: MBA (2 years), Master of Accountancy and Information Systems (1 year), MS in Economics (1 year), MS in Information Management (1 year), Master of Taxation (1 year), PhD in Economics (4 years), PhD in Business Administration (4 years)

Combined Degrees: MBA/MS in Economics (2 years), MBA/MS in Information Management (2 years), MBA/Master of Accountancy and Information Systems (2 years), MBA/Master of Taxation (2 years), MBA/Master of Health Services Administration (2 years), MBA/Master in International Management (AGSIM) (2 years), MBA/JD (3-4 years), MBA/Master in Architecture (3-4 years)

Academic Specialties: Economics, Financial Management and Markets, Health Services Administration, Information Management, Services Marketing and Management, Sports Business, Supply Chain Management

Study Abroad Options: ESC Toulouse, France; Universidad Carlos III de Madrid, Spain; Instituto Technologico Y De Estudios Superiores De Monterrey-Campus Estado de Mexico (ITESM-CEM), Mexico City, Mexico; Instituto Tecnologico Autonomo de Mexico (ITAM), Mexico City, Mexico; Escuela de Administracion de Negocios Para Graduados, Lima, Peru

STUDENT INFORMATION

Total Business Students: 450
% Full Time: 30
% Female: 19
% Minority: 11
% Out of State: 67
% International: 20
Average Age: 28

COMPUTER AND RESEARCH FACILITIES

Research Facilities: The L. William Seidman Research Institute at the W. P. Carey School of Business houses 8 research centers: Arizona Real Estate Center, Bank One Economic Outlook Center, CAPS Research (formerly Center For Advanced Purchasing Studies), Center for Advancing Business through Information Technology, Center for Business Research, Center for the Advancement of Small Business, Center for Services Leadership, Institute for Manufacturing Enterprise Systems.

Computer Facilities: The Ford Graduate Suite at the W. P. Carey School of Business is a multipurpose space dedicated for business graduate students only. The graduate suite houses 3 computer labs equipped with more than 100 IBM NetVista computers, each with a 1.8 GHz processor and 512 MB of RAM; all contain CD burners. The graduate suite includes 8 team rooms, each equipped with whiteboards, IBM NetVista computers that have video-capture and editing capabilities, and projectors for PC, videotape, or laptop use. The Ford Graduate Suite also has extra ports for laptops in all computer labs, team rooms, and in the Student Center, the open common area for students. The W. P. Carey School's committment to technology has lead to the implementation of wireless access capabilities within designated areas of the school of business complex. There are 4 wireless network nodes in the Ford Graduate Suite and 3 located near MBA classrooms, providing a large coverage area for immediate access to the Internet and licensed software.

The following software is available for use by W. P. Carey MBA students: Acrobat Reader; CLIPS; Compustat PC Plus; Dow Jones News Retrieval; DPL; Eviews; EWAN Winsock Telnet; Exceed Suite; Internet Explorer 5.0; Java Development Kit; Lexis-Nexis; Microsoft Developer Studio; Minitab; MS Office 2000; Excel Add-Ins: SPWSdde, CTI, Tree Plan; MS Project 2000; Network Associates Viruscan; Risk+ Add-In; People Express Flight Simulator; Principles of Marketing; Apple Quicktime; Real Player G2; SAILS; SAS System; SAS Enterprise Miner; Macromedia Shockwave; Smartdraw Professional Edition; SPSS; SPSS Production Facility; Synchrony Demo; Vensim PLE32; WinEdit; and Winzip. A new Bloomberg terminal with fast web connection is also available in the graduate suite allowing students access to up-to-date financial information.

Campuswide Network? Yes
% of MBA Classrooms Wired: 100
Computer Model Recommended: Laptop
Internet Fee? No

EXPENSES/FINANCIAL AID

Annual Tuition (Resident/Nonresident): $2,508/$11,028
Tuition Per Credit (Resident/Nonresident): $139/$460
Room & Board (On/Off Campus): $5,846/$7,236
Books and Supplies: $2,100
Average Grant: $6,750
Average Loan: $15,000
% Receiving Aid Their First Year: 90

ADMISSIONS INFORMATION

Application Fee: $45
Electronic Application? Yes
Regular Application Deadline: 5/1
Regular Notification: Rolling
Deferment Available? No
Non-fall Admissions? No
Transfer Students Accepted? No
Need-Blind Admissions? Yes
Number of Applications Received: 887
% of Applicants Accepted: 29
% Accepted Who Enrolled: 53
Average GPA: 3.4
GPA Range: 3.2-3.8
Average GMAT: 654
GMAT Range: 620-690
Average Years Experience: 4

Other Admissions Factors Considered: Amount and type of practical work experience, interest in W. P. Carey MBA specializations, leadership abilities, and community and professional involvement.
Minority/Disadvantaged Student Recruitment Programs: PepsiCo scholarships, graduate academic scholarships, graduate assistantships, and graduate fellowships
Other Schools to Which Students Applied: Indiana University, Michigan State University-Detroit College of Law, Ohio State University, University of Arizona, University of California-Los Angeles, University of Southern California, University of Texas-Austin

INTERNATIONAL STUDENTS

TOEFL Required of International Students? Yes
Minimum TOEFL: 580 (237 computer)

EMPLOYMENT INFORMATION

Placement Office Available? Yes
% Employed Within 3 Months: 86
Fields Employing Percentage of Grads: General Management (4%), Consulting (5%), Other (8%), Finance (13%), MIS (14%), Marketing (23%), Operations (33%)
Frequent Employers: Chevron Texaco, Dell Computer, Deloitte Consulting, DHL, Gateway, Honeywell, IBM, IBM Global Services, Intel Corp., Johnson & Johnson, McKesson Corp., Phelps Dodge, Planar Systems, Raytheon, Sprint Communications
Prominent Alumni: Craig Weatherup, chairman, The Pepsi Bottling Group; Steve Marriott, vice president of corporate marketing, Marriott Hotels; Wayne Doran, chairman of the board, Ford Motor Co.; Atul Vashistha, CEO, neoIT; Linda Brock-Nelson, president, LBN & Associates, Inc.

See page 404.

ARIZONA STATE UNIVERSITY WEST
School of Management

Admissions Contact: MBA Admissions, Sir or Madam
Address: PO Box 37100, Phoenix, AZ 85069-7100
Admissions Phone: 602-543-6201 • **Admissions Fax:** 602-543-6249
Admissions E-mail: mba@asu.edu • **Web Address:** www.west.asu.edu/som/mba

ASU West is a part-time, flexible MBA program designed specifically for working professionals. As expected, the average age of the student body, at 33, is considerably higher than that of the traditional, full-time MBA student, and admission emphasis is on the applicant's work experience. Through its new connectMBA program, ASU West offers an innovative, technology-based, weekend-only MBA program. Joint degrees with nearby Thunderbird lend an international flavor to the classroom.

INSTITUTIONAL INFORMATION

Public/Private: Public
Evening Classes Available? Yes
Total Faculty: 25
% Faculty Female: 28
% Faculty Minority: 12
% Faculty Part Time: 2
Student/Faculty Ratio: 20:1
Academic Calendar: Semester

PROGRAMS

Degrees Offered: MBA with 3 delivery options: scottsdaleMBA (27 months); connectMBA (24 months); and pmMBA (2.5 to 6 years)

Combined Degrees: MBA/MIM (jointly offered with Thunderbird, 3 years)
Academic Specialties: We are fully AACSB-accredited and so our faculty are research-qualified in their fields. Our curriculum provides a general business education rather than a specialty focused one.

STUDENT INFORMATION

Total Business Students: 445
Average Age: 34

COMPUTER AND RESEARCH FACILITIES

Research Facilities: The ASU West library has nearly 300,000 books; 3,400 journal subscriptions; and about 1.5 million microforms available locally. In addition, we are linked to the library on the main campus so that students have the full range of library support as do full-time students on the main campus.
Computer Facilities: ASU West has a state-of-the-art computing center with networked computers, laser printers, scanners, and other high quality peripherials available free of charge to students. In addition, we are linked to the main campus so that students have the full range of computer/technology support as do full-time students on the main campus.
Campuswide Network? Yes
% of MBA Classrooms Wired: 100
Internet Fee? No

EXPENSES/FINANCIAL AID

Tuition Per Credit (Resident/Nonresident): $126/$428
% Receiving Financial Aid: 20
% Receiving Aid Their First Year: 5

ADMISSIONS INFORMATION

Application Fee: $45
Electronic Application? No
Early Decision Application Deadline: 1/1
Early Decision Notification: 1/1
Regular Application Deadline: 6/1
Regular Notification: 7/1
Deferment Available? Yes
Length of Deferment: 1 year
Non-fall Admissions? Yes
Non-fall Application Deadline(s): 11/1, 4/1
Transfer Students Accepted? Yes
Transfer Policy: 9 credit hours of transfer credit from AACSB-accredited programs
Need-Blind Admissions? Yes
Number of Applications Received: 169
% of Applicants Accepted: 77
% Accepted Who Enrolled: 75
Average GPA: 3.5
GPA Range: 2.6-3.7
Average GMAT: 590
GMAT Range: 500-700
Average Years Experience: 8
Other Schools to Which Students Applied: Arizona State University

INTERNATIONAL STUDENTS

TOEFL Required of International Students? Yes
Minimum TOEFL: 600 (250 computer)

EMPLOYMENT INFORMATION

Placement Office Available? No
% Employed Within 3 Months: 100
Fields Employing Percentage of Grads: Consulting (2%), Operations (2%), MIS (2%), Human Resources (2%), Finance (5%), General Management (7%), Accounting (16%), Marketing (19%), Other (40%)

ARKANSAS STATE UNIVERSITY
College of Business

Admissions Contact: Dr. Thomas Wheeler, Dean, Graduate School
Address: PO Box 60, State University, AR 72467
Admissions Phone: 870-972-3029 • **Admissions Fax:** 870-972-3857
Admissions E-mail: gradsch@choctaw.astate.edu • **Web Address:** business.astate.edu

INSTITUTIONAL INFORMATION

Public/Private: Public
Evening Classes Available? No
Total Faculty: 33
% Faculty Female: 24
% Faculty Minority: 1
Student/Faculty Ratio: 25:1
Academic Calendar: Semester

PROGRAMS

Degrees Offered: MBA (12 months), MSE (12 months)
Academic Specialties: Certified Treasury Management
Study Abroad Options: Cyprus College

STUDENT INFORMATION

Total Business Students: 104

COMPUTER AND RESEARCH FACILITIES

Campuswide Network? Yes
Internet Fee? No

EXPENSES/FINANCIAL AID

Annual Tuition (Resident/Nonresident): $1,488/$3,744
Tuition Per Credit (Resident/Nonresident): $124/$312
Room & Board (On/Off Campus): $3,500
Books and Supplies: $2,100
Average Grant: $6,427

ADMISSIONS INFORMATION

Electronic Application? No
Regular Application Deadline: Rolling
Regular Notification: Rolling
Deferment Available? No
Non-fall Admissions? No
Transfer Students Accepted? No
Need-Blind Admissions? No
Number of Applications Received: 53
% of Applicants Accepted: 85
% Accepted Who Enrolled: 80

INTERNATIONAL STUDENTS

TOEFL Required of International Students? Yes
Minimum TOEFL: 550

EMPLOYMENT INFORMATION

Placement Office Available? Yes

AUBURN UNIVERSITY
College of Business

Admissions Contact: Director of Admissions, MBA Program
Address: 415 W. Magnolia Ave.; 503 Lowder Business Building, Auburn, AL 36849
Admissions Phone: 334-844-4060 • Admissions Fax: 334-844-2964
Admissions E-mail: mbainfo@auburn.edu • Web Address: www.mba.business.auburn.edu

Auburn is one of the better MBA values around. At less than one-tenth the price of other MBA programs, Auburn offers a flexible calendar (students can enter at four times during the year), a distance learning option (MBA via the Internet), and a curriculum that emphasizes teamwork and the fundamentals. A challenging team capstone project is required to get the degree.

INSTITUTIONAL INFORMATION

Public/Private: Public
Evening Classes Available? No
Total Faculty: 8
% Faculty Female: 11
% Faculty Minority: 2
% Faculty Part Time: 2
Student/Faculty Ratio: 35:1
Students in Parent Institution: 23,276
Academic Calendar: Semester

PROGRAMS

Degrees Offered: MBA (36-42 semester hours, 16 months to 2 years) with available concentration areas in Agribusiness, Aviation Management, Economic Development, Finance, Health Care Administration, Human Resource Development, Management Information Systems, Management of Technology, Marketing, Production/Operations Management, and Sports Management; EMBA (22 months), Physicians EMBA (22 months), Techno EMBA (22 months)
Combined Degrees: Dual degree program with Industrial and Systems Engineering
Academic Specialties: Business Strategy, Information Systems, Operations Management
Special Opportunities: Internship program for domestic as well as international placements is available. No formal study-abroad "exchange" programs are available. However, study-abroad programs are generally accommodated and approved on an individual student basis.
Study Abroad Options: Germany, Japan

STUDENT INFORMATION

Total Business Students: 377
% Full Time: 25
% Female: 32
% Minority: 5
% International: 12
Average Age: 25

COMPUTER AND RESEARCH FACILITIES

Research Facilities: Dedicated MBA computer lab and study room accessible 24/7
Computer Facilities: Access to online bibliographic retrieval services and online databases
Campuswide Network? Yes
% of MBA Classrooms Wired: 50
Internet Fee? No

EXPENSES/FINANCIAL AID

Annual Tuition (Resident/Nonresident): $3,650/$10,950
Tuition Per Credit (Resident/Nonresident): $151/$453
Room & Board (On/Off Campus): $9,000

Books and Supplies: $1,000
Average Grant: $1,000
Average Loan: $10,000
% Receiving Financial Aid: 50

ADMISSIONS INFORMATION

Application Fee: $25
Electronic Application? No
Regular Application Deadline: 3/1
Regular Notification: Rolling
Deferment Available? Yes
Length of Deferment: 1 year
Non-fall Admissions? Yes
Non-fall Application Deadline(s): 9/1, spring (Distance Learning MBA only)
Transfer Students Accepted? Yes
Transfer Policy: AACSB schools only; case-by-case basis and elective courses only
Need-Blind Admissions? Yes
Number of Applications Received: 148
% of Applicants Accepted: 52
% Accepted Who Enrolled: 75
Average GPA: 3.2
GPA Range: 3.0-3.4
Average GMAT: 578
GMAT Range: 530-610
Average Years Experience: 2
Other Admissions Factors Considered: Two years of full-time work experience is encouraged but not required.
Minority/Disadvantaged Student Recruitment Programs: Recruiting visits to minority campuses, particularly in-state

INTERNATIONAL STUDENTS

TOEFL Required of International Students? Yes
Minimum TOEFL: 550 (213 computer)

EMPLOYMENT INFORMATION

Placement Office Available? Yes
% Employed Within 3 Months: 64
Frequent Employers: AmSouth Bank, Colonial Bank, Home Depot, IBM, Milliken, Total Systems, WalMart
Prominent Alumni: Mohamed Mansour, CEO, Mansour Group in Egypt; Joanne P. McCallie, head coach, Michigan State University Women's Basketball; Wendell Starke, vice chairman of the board of EntreMed, Inc.

AUGUSTA STATE UNIVERSITY
College of Business Administration

Admissions Contact: Miyoko Jackson, Degree Program Specialist
Address: MBA Office, 2500 Walton Way, Augusta, GA 30904-2200
Admissions Phone: 706-737-1565 • Admissions Fax: 706-667-4064
Admissions E-mail: mbainfo@aug.edu • Web Address: www.aug.edu/coba/

Come to Augusta State's College of Business Administration ready to be called on—the outstanding student/faculty ratio of 9:1 makes class sizes uncommonly small. The MBA program is basically designed for working professionals—it offers only night classes for its students, and the average age of matriculation is 30. COBA's competitive curriculum provides core business knowledge and problem-solving solutions and addresses important global and ethical business perspectives.

INSTITUTIONAL INFORMATION

Public/Private: Public
Evening Classes Available? Yes
Total Faculty: 12
% Faculty Female: 42
Student/Faculty Ratio: 11:1
Students in Parent Institution: 5,317
Academic Calendar: Trimester

PROGRAMS

Degrees Offered: MBA (36 credit hours required, 16 months to 6 years to complete)

STUDENT INFORMATION

Total Business Students: 133
% Full Time: 29
% Female: 11
% Minority: 2
% International: 7
Average Age: 28

COMPUTER AND RESEARCH FACILITIES

Computer Facilities: Online bibliographic retrieval services
Campuswide Network? Yes
Internet Fee? No

EXPENSES/FINANCIAL AID

Annual Tuition (Resident/Nonresident): $2,096/$7,316
Tuition Per Credit (Resident/Nonresident): $97/$387
Room & Board (On/Off Campus): $9,500
Books and Supplies: $500

ADMISSIONS INFORMATION

Application Fee: $20
Electronic Application? No
Regular Application Deadline: Rolling
Regular Notification: Rolling
Deferment Available? Yes
Length of Deferment: 1 year
Non-fall Admissions? Yes
Non-fall Application Deadline(s): 11/15, spring; 4/15, summer; 7/15, fall
Transfer Students Accepted? Yes
Transfer Policy: Transfer students must meet our regular MBA admission standards. Up to 9 semester credit hours may be accepted for transfer.
Need-Blind Admissions? No
Number of Applications Received: 44
% of Applicants Accepted: 80
% Accepted Who Enrolled: 89
Average GPA: 3.1
GPA Range: 2.8-3.4
Average GMAT: 520
GMAT Range: 450-590
Average Years Experience: 6
Other Admissions Factors Considered: Computer experience required in word processing, spreadsheet, and database; work experience recommended; minimum 400 GMAT

INTERNATIONAL STUDENTS

TOEFL Required of International Students? Yes
Minimum TOEFL: 500 (173 computer)

EMPLOYMENT INFORMATION

Placement Office Available? Yes
% Employed Within 3 Months: 90

BABSON COLLEGE
F. W. Olin Graduate School of Business

Admissions Contact: Kate Klepper, Director of Admissions
Address: Olin Hall, Babson Park (Wellesley), MA 02457-0310
Admissions Phone: 781-239-4317 • **Admissions Fax:** 781-239-4194
Admissions E-mail: mbaadmission@babson.edu • **Web Address:** www.babson.edu/mba

Not for nothing is Babson College synonymous with entrepreneurial studies. Budding capitalists here enjoy "outstanding" course offerings, abundant opportunities for "in-the-field" learning, and access to the many perks of the "entrepreneurial incubator space" in newly built Olin Hall. Other highlights include a "tough, fun," and "committed" faculty and a Business Mentor program, which allows students to work as consultants for companies in the Boston area.

INSTITUTIONAL INFORMATION

Public/Private: Private
Evening Classes Available? Yes
Total Faculty: 153
% Faculty Female: 33
% Faculty Minority: 16
% Faculty Part Time: 30
Student/Faculty Ratio: 14:1
Students in Parent Institution: 3,407
Academic Calendar: Semester

PROGRAMS

Degrees Offered: 2-year MBA (21 months), 1-year MBA (12 months), Evening MBA (4 years), IntelMBA (2 years), Lucent MS in Finance (3 years), Fast Track MBA (27 months)
Academic Specialties: Babson has core strengths in entrepreneurship, marketing, finance (applied investments), high-tech, and consulting. Our highly integrated 2-year MBA program stresses opportunity recognition, innovation, and creative problem solving. Corporate leaders have recognized that a strictly functional approach to management education is no longer useful in today's complex global environment, where real business problems do not come in discrete functional blocks. In the second year of the 2-year MBA, defined career paths and intensity tracks provide an opportunity for students to focus in more depth in an area of their interest. Babson's field-based programs, mentor program, international internships, and management consulting programs provide opportunities for hands-on application of classroom learning.
Special Opportunities: Global Management Program, Management Consulting Field Experience (MCFE), international study programs, Babson Consulting Alliance Program, international independent study, MBA internships
Study Abroad Options: Semester abroad is offered in conjunction with partner schools in Asia, Europe, and Latin America: University of San Andres, Argentina; University of Adolfo Ibanez, Chile; Tsinghua University, China; L'Ecole Superieure de Commerce de Paris (ESCP), France; University of Erlangen, Germany; International University of Japan, Japan; University of St. Petersburg, Russia; University of Lausanne and University of St. Gallen, Switzerland; Cranfield School of Management, United Kingdom

STUDENT INFORMATION

Total Business Students: 1,656
% Full Time: 21
% Female: 29
% Minority: 1
% Out of State: 50
% International: 28
Average Age: 29

COMPUTER AND RESEARCH FACILITIES

Research Facilities: Arthur M. Blank Center for Entrepreneurial Studies,

Glavin Center for Global Entrepreneurial Leadership, Asian Institute of Business, Institute for Latin American Business, Center for Real Estate, Center for Information Management Studies, Center for Language and Culture, Center for Technology and Enterprise, Center for Women's Leadership

Computer Facilities: Babson offers 7 computer lab/classrooms (with 180 computers), including a 24-hour access lab, as well 47 networked public workstations in the Horn Library; all group study and mentor group rooms in the Horn Library and Computer Center and Olin Hall are equipped with computers. The Stephen D. Cutler Investment Management Center provides Babson students with the state-of-the-art online research tools used by leading investment management firms. Network access for student laptops is available everywhere in Olin Hall (home of the graduate school) and the Horn Centers; wireless access is available in various buildings across campus. Babson subscribes to more than 75 electronic online and CD-ROM subscriptions for periodicals, statistical data, electronic books, and reference. Fifty electronic services are available campuswide (20 of which are accessible when students are off campus as well). Accessible databases include Bloomberg Financial Markets, Lexis-Nexis, Dow-Jones Interactive, Dun's, Hoovers, ValueLine Investment Survey, and many more.

Campuswide Network? Yes
% of MBA Classrooms Wired: 100
Computer Model Recommended: Laptop
Internet Fee? No

EXPENSES/FINANCIAL AID

Annual Tuition: $27,124
Tuition Per Credit (Resident/Nonresident): $819
Room & Board (On/Off Campus): $11,796
Books and Supplies: $1,850
Average Grant: $15,570
Average Loan: $30,362
% Receiving Financial Aid: 59

ADMISSIONS INFORMATION

Application Fee: $75
Electronic Application? Yes
Regular Application Deadline: 4/15
Regular Notification: 5/31
Deferment Available? Yes
Length of Deferment: 1 year
Non-fall Admissions? Yes
Non-fall Application Deadline(s): 10/15; 1/31 for 1-year MBA
Transfer Students Accepted? Yes
Transfer Policy: We accept transfer credit from an AACSB-accredited program into our Evening MBA program.
Need-Blind Admissions? Yes
Number of Applications Received: 1,008
% of Applicants Accepted: 39
% Accepted Who Enrolled: 41
Average GPA: 3.1
GPA Range: 2.8-3.4
Average GMAT: 643
GMAT Range: 600-690
Average Years Experience: 5
Other Admissions Factors Considered: Admissions decisions are also influenced by candidate's fit with Babson's team orientation, modular curriculum, entrepreneurial focus, and global mindset.
Minority/Disadvantaged Student Recruitment Programs: Outreach through GMASS, scholarship program
Other Schools to Which Students Applied: Boston College, Boston University, Dartmouth College, Harvard University, Massachusetts Institute of Technology, New York University, Northwestern University

INTERNATIONAL STUDENTS

TOEFL Required of International Students? Yes
Minimum TOEFL: 600 (250 computer)

EMPLOYMENT INFORMATION

Placement Office Available? Yes
% Employed Within 3 Months: 84
Fields Employing Percentage of Grads: Operations (2%), General Management (5%), Consulting (17%), Entrepreneurship (23%), Marketing (23%), Finance (24%)
Frequent Employers: Adventis; A.T. Kearney; Bose Corp.; Boston Scientific Corp.; Charles River Associates; EMC Corp.; Fidelity Capital; Fidelity Investments; FleetBoston; Genuity; The Hartford; IBM; International Data Corpotation (IDC); Liberty Mutual Group; Merrill Lynch; Our Group; Philips Medical Systems; Pricewaterhouse Coopers; Staples, Inc.; Strategic Pricing Group, Inc.
Prominent Alumni: Robert Davis, founder, Lycos, and venture partner, Highland Capital; Mark Holowesko, president, Templeton Holdings Ltd.; Deborah A. McLaughlin, executive vice president, NSTAR; Akio Toyoda, managing director, Toyota Motor Group; Michael Smith, chairman and CEO, Hughes Electronics

See page 406.

BALL STATE UNIVERSITY
College of Business

Admissions Contact: Dr. Inga Hill, Assistant to the Dean for Graduate Business Programs
Address: WB 147, Muncie, IN 47306
Admissions Phone: 765-285-1931 • **Admissions Fax:** 765-285-8818
Admissions E-mail: mba@bsu.edu • **Web Address:** www.bsu.edu/mba

Best known as a leader in the jump to distance learning MBA programs, Ball State offers a fully accredited off-site MBA in four states. Ball State's other claim to fame is its nationally ranked Entrepreneurship Program.

INSTITUTIONAL INFORMATION

Public/Private: Public
Evening Classes Available? Yes
Total Faculty: 33
% Faculty Part Time: 0
Student/Faculty Ratio: 25:1
Students in Parent Institution: 20,113
Academic Calendar: Semester

PROGRAMS

Degrees Offered: MBA, general or with an Entrepreneurship concentration (30 credit hours; 1 year full time, 2 years part time); concentrations in Finance, Operations, and Information Systems (33 credit hours)
Academic Specialties: Dr. Donald Kuratko, the Jeff and Teri Stoops Distinguished Professor of Entrepreneurship, is the founding director of Ball State University's award-winning Entrepreneurship Program.

STUDENT INFORMATION

Total Business Students: 139
% Full Time: 30
% Female: 31
% Minority: 36
Average Age: 28

COMPUTER AND RESEARCH FACILITIES

Campuswide Network? Yes
% of MBA Classrooms Wired: 100
Internet Fee? No

EXPENSES/FINANCIAL AID

Annual Tuition (Resident/Nonresident): $6,050/$16,660
Room & Board (On/Off Campus): $7,200/$6,000
Books and Supplies: $1,300

ADMISSIONS INFORMATION

Application Fee: $35
Electronic Application? Yes
Regular Application Deadline: Rolling
Regular Notification: Rolling
Deferment Available? Yes
Length of Deferment: 2 years
Non-fall Admissions? Yes
Non-fall Application Deadline(s): Spring, 12/1; summer, 4/1
Transfer Students Accepted? Yes
Transfer Policy: A maximum of 9 credit hours may be considered for transfer.
Need-Blind Admissions? Yes
Number of Applications Received: 101
% of Applicants Accepted: 72
% Accepted Who Enrolled: 68
Average GPA: 3.2
GPA Range: 2.9-3.4
Average GMAT: 530
GMAT Range: 480-570
Average Years Experience: 7
Other Schools to Which Students Applied: Butler University, Indiana University—Kokomo, Indiana University-Purdue University—Fort Wayne, Indiana University-Purdue University—Indianapolis

INTERNATIONAL STUDENTS

TOEFL Required of International Students? Yes
Minimum TOEFL: 550 (213 computer)

EMPLOYMENT INFORMATION

Placement Office Available? Yes

BARRY UNIVERSITY
Andreas School of Business

Address: 11300 NE 2nd Avenue, Miami Shores, FL 33161
Admissions Phone: 305-899-3535 • **Admissions Fax:** 305-892-6412
Admissions E-mail: jpoza@mail.barry.edu • **Web Address:** www.barry.edu/business

Primarily serving students from Florida, Latin America, and the Caribbean, the Andreas School of Business at Barry University gives students a quality education in a friendly, caring environment. Strong ethics and a sense of social responsibility are key components of the instruction here, which is firmly rooted in the Dominican tradition. The school's international flavor is further bolstered by its location in culturally diverse South Florida.

INSTITUTIONAL INFORMATION

Evening Classes Available? Yes
Total Faculty: 24
% Faculty Female: 21
% Faculty Minority: 21
Student/Faculty Ratio: 12:1
Students in Parent Institution: 8,469
Academic Calendar: Semester

PROGRAMS

Degrees Offered: MBA (36 credit hours) available as general MBA or an MBA with the following specializations: Accounting, Health Services Administration, e-Commerce, Finance, Management, Management Information Systems and Marketing; MBA International Business (39 credit hours); MSA (30 credit hours)
Combined Degrees: MS/MBA (57 credit hours); MSN/MBA (69 credit hours); Doctor of Podiatric Medicine/MBA (205 credit hours)

STUDENT INFORMATION

Total Business Students: 75
% Full Time: 43
% Female: 47
% Minority: 66
% International: 59
Average Age: 29

COMPUTER AND RESEARCH FACILITIES

Campuswide Network? Yes
% of MBA Classrooms Wired: 100
Computer Model Recommended: No prefrence
Internet Fee? No

EXPENSES/FINANCIAL AID

Room & Board (On Campus): $7,200

ADMISSIONS INFORMATION

Application Fee: $30
Electronic Application? Yes
Regular Application Deadline: Rolling
Deferment Available? Yes
Length of Deferment: 1 year
Non-fall Admissions? Yes
Non-fall Application Deadline(s): Rolling
Transfer Students Accepted? Yes
Transfer Policy: Up to six graduate credit hours can be transferred
Need-Blind Admissions? Yes
Number of Applications Received: 125
% of Applicants Accepted: 25
% Accepted Who Enrolled: 71
Average GPA: 3.1
Average GMAT: 462

INTERNATIONAL STUDENTS

TOEFL Required of International Students? Yes
Minimum TOEFL: 550 (213 computer)

EMPLOYMENT INFORMATION

Placement Office Available? No

BARUCH COLLEGE/CITY UNIVERSITY OF NEW YORK
Zicklin School of Business

Admissions Contact: Frances Murphy, Director of Admissions
Address: One Bernard Baruch Way, Box H-0820, New York, NY 10010
Admissions Phone: 646-312-1300 • **Admissions Fax:** 646-312-1301
Admissions E-mail: ZicklinGradAdmissions@baruch.cuny.edu
Web Address: www.zicklin.baruch.cuny.edu

The Zicklin School of Business is the largest b-school in the United States, and it's the only CUNY school with AACSB-accredited programs. You've got three basic choices for pursuing your MBA at Baruch: the full-time MBA, which provides a broad-based education as well as a specialization; the accelerated part-time program, completed in about two years; and the flex-time program, which allows you to switch between full- and part-time studies as your schedule allows. (The full-time program is quite prestigious.) Baruch also offers an MBA in health care administration in conjunction with Mount Sinai and joint JD/MBA programs with Brooklyn and New York Law Schools.

INSTITUTIONAL INFORMATION
Public/Private: Public
Evening Classes Available? Yes
Total Faculty: 204
% Faculty Female: 28
% Faculty Minority: 29
% Faculty Part Time: 30
Student/Faculty Ratio: 40:1
Students in Parent Institution: 16,600
Academic Calendar: Semester

PROGRAMS
Degrees Offered: MBA (2 years full time, 4 years part time, 28 months accelerated part-time program); MS (1.5 years full time, 3 years part time); EMBA (2 years); EMS in Finance (1 year)
Combined Degrees: JD/MBA (4.5 years full time)
Academic Specialties: Large, diverse faculty holds 49 degrees from New York University, 44 from Columbia University, 14 from University of Pennsylvania, 7 from MIT, 7 from Harvard University, 5 from Cornell University, 5 from UC—Berkeley, 4 from Yale, 4 from Stanford, and other prestigious institutions; curriculum features deep 6-course specializations.
Study Abroad Options: Middlesex University, England; Lyon III (Jean Moulin), France; Leipzig University (HHL), Germany; Indian Institute of Management (Calcutta), India; Yonsei University, Korea; Iberoamericana, Mexico; University of Stockholm, Sweden

STUDENT INFORMATION
Total Business Students: 1,445
% Full Time: 12
% Female: 40
% Minority: 3
% Out of State: 80
% International: 55
Average Age: 28

COMPUTER AND RESEARCH FACILITIES
Research Facilities: Subotnick Financial Services Center, Weissman Center for International Business, Center for Financial Integrity, Center for Logistics and Transportation, Lawrence N. Field Center for Entrepreneurship and Small Business, Bernard L. Schwartz Communication Institute
Computer Facilities: The campus has new network infrastructure, 110 new smart classrooms, 30 new computer labs for students, and an innovative laptop loan program offered through the library. The library and the new vertical campus feature wireless networking. Outstanding business databases including Lexis-Nexis, CRSP, Compustat, S&P NetAdvantage, Business & Company Resource Center, Global Access, and Simmons Choices II. More than 8,000 full-text serials are available in over 100 end-user databases with remote access for faculty and students. The library offers an online reference chat service and electronic reserves.

Course information is offered through a web-based course information system; students are given e-mail addresses through a web-based e-mail system; and students register for classes online through a web-based registration system.

In collaboration with the Zicklin School, the library provides training on the use of the Reuters databases in the Subotnick Financial Services Center, a fully functioning trading floor and teaching facility.
Campuswide Network? Yes
% of MBA Classrooms Wired: 27
Internet Fee? No

EXPENSES/FINANCIAL AID
Annual Tuition (Resident/Nonresident): $6,000/$13,300
Tuition Per Credit (Resident/Nonresident): $265/$475
Room & Board (On/Off Campus): $15,000
Books and Supplies: $1,000
Average Grant: $3,429
Average Loan: $10,000
% Receiving Financial Aid: 50
% Receiving Aid Their First Year: 50

ADMISSIONS INFORMATION
Application Fee: $40
Electronic Application? Yes
Regular Application Deadline: 4/30
Regular Notification: 6/15
Deferment Available? Yes
Length of Deferment: 1 year
Non-fall Admissions? Yes
Non-fall Application Deadline(s): 10/31 spring
Transfer Students Accepted? Yes
Transfer Policy: Same application process as all applicants; maximum of 12 credits from an AACSB-accredited institution may be transferred
Need-Blind Admissions? Yes
Number of Applications Received: 654
% of Applicants Accepted: 22
% Accepted Who Enrolled: 58
Average GPA: 3.3
GPA Range: 2.8-4.0
Average GMAT: 650
GMAT Range: 590-700
Average Years Experience: 5
Other Admissions Factors Considered: TWE scores for international applicants
Minority/Disadvantaged Student Recruitment Programs: No specific programs; City University of New York affiliation and unusually low tuition rates make us well known to these groups.
Other Schools to Which Students Applied: Columbia University, Fordham University, Hofstra University, New York University, Pace University, Rutgers, The State University of New Jersey, St. John's University

INTERNATIONAL STUDENTS
TOEFL Required of International Students? Yes
Minimum TOEFL: 590 (243 computer)

EMPLOYMENT INFORMATION
Placement Office Available? Yes
% Employed Within 3 Months: 66
Fields Employing Percentage of Grads: General Management (5%), MIS (5%), Marketing (9%), Consulting (10%), Accounting (24%), Finance (47%)

Frequent Employers: Citigroup, Deloitte & Touche, Ernst & Young, Pricewaterhouse Coopers, Securities Industry Automation Corp.

Prominent Alumni: Larry Zicklin, chairman, Neuberger Berman; Mark Kurland, chairman and CEO, Bear, Stearns; Donald Marron, chairman and CEO, PaineWebber; Bernard Schwartz, chairman and CEO, Loral Space Corp.; Matthew Blank, chairman and CEO, Showtime Networks

See page 408.

BAYLOR UNIVERSITY
Hankamer School of Business

Admissions Contact: Laurie Wilson, Director, Graduate Business Admissions
Address: PO Box 98013, Waco, TX 76798-8013
Admissions Phone: 254-710-3718 • **Admissions Fax:** 254-710-1066
Admissions E-mail: mba@hsb.baylor.edu • **Web Address:** www.gradbusiness.baylor.edu

Dedicated professors, a strong Baptist influence, and a standout accounting program are the hallmarks of the Hankamer School of Business at Baylor University in Waco. Each semester, MBA students analyze a "focus firm" inside and out, giving students "the chance to solve real-world business problems from several aspects at once." In fall 1998, Baylor's focus firm was Dell Computers, headquartered in (relatively) nearby Austin.

INSTITUTIONAL INFORMATION

Public/Private: Private
Evening Classes Available? No
Total Faculty: 30
% Faculty Female: 20
% Faculty Minority: 2
Student/Faculty Ratio: 14:1
Students in Parent Institution: 14,159
Academic Calendar: Semester

PROGRAMS

Degrees Offered: MBA (16-21 months), MBA in Information Systems Management (16-21 months), MBA in International Management (16-21 months), MS in Economics (12 months), MACC (12 months), MTAX (12 months), MS in Information Systems (12-16 months)
Combined Degrees: JD/MBA (4 years), MBA/MS in Information Systems (2 years), JD/MTAX (4 years)
Academic Specialties: Baylor offers 2 specializations within the MBA program. The Customer Relationship Management (CRM) specialization features a series of elective courses, a CRM company-sponsored internship, and special CRM scholarships. The Healthcare Administration specialization includes a paid practicum in a hospital.
Special Opportunities: The Intergrated Management Seminar is a unique 1-semester seminar that satisfies all business prerequisites. It is offered for students without previous business training. Also, the Focus Firm serves as a special program within Baylor's MBA program. Each semester, 1 company volunteers to serve as the MBA's "focus firm." Its core issues become the centerpiece of the MBA curriculum. The focus-firm approach to learning provides students real-time delivery of theoretical applications, technological advances, global awareness, functional intergration, and team-centered learning.
Study Abroad Options: Australia, China, Cuba, England, France, Japan, Korea, Mexico, The Netherlands, Thailand

STUDENT INFORMATION

Total Business Students: 125
% Full Time: 100
% Female: 27

% Minority: 10
% Out of State: 26
% International: 29
Average Age: 25

COMPUTER AND RESEARCH FACILITIES

Research Facilities: MBA students enjoy wireless network access in their core MBA classes and in the Graduate Lounge. Distance learning and video conferencing are intergral parts of classroom activity. Video conferencing sessions with corporate executives are held regularly.
Computer Facilities: The Graduate Center houses a Graduate Computer Lounge with wireless network access. Printers and a scanner are available in the Graduate Lounge. Wireless networking is available in all MBA classrooms. The Casey Computer Center in the Hankamer School of Business contains approximately 100 desktop PCs as well as scanning equipment and color printers. Graduate students have free access to the Internet and e-mail service. Students have space to create a web page on the University server. The University has approximately 4,200 computers with more than 300 locations in five general-access computer labs.
Campuswide Network? Yes
% of MBA Classrooms Wired: 100
Computer Model Recommended: Laptop
Internet Fee? No

EXPENSES/FINANCIAL AID

Annual Tuition: $15,700
Room & Board (On/Off Campus): $10,000
Books and Supplies: $8,000
Average Grant: $16,128
Average Loan: $18,551
% Receiving Financial Aid: 80
% Receiving Aid Their First Year: 80

ADMISSIONS INFORMATION

Application Fee: $50
Electronic Application? Yes
Regular Application Deadline: 7/1
Regular Notification: Rolling
Deferment Available? Yes
Length of Deferment: 1 year
Non-fall Admissions? Yes
Non-fall Application Deadline(s): 11/1 spring, 4/1 summer
Transfer Students Accepted? Yes
Transfer Policy: A student who has been admitted to a graduate program at another university, and who desires admission to Baylor, must present a transcript that presents the student's active, satisfactory work toward the same degree. Only 6 hours may be transferred into the program.
Need-Blind Admissions? Yes
Number of Applications Received: 175
% of Applicants Accepted: 61
% Accepted Who Enrolled: 57
Average GPA: 3.1
GPA Range: 2.5-4.0
Average GMAT: 595
GMAT Range: 510-650
Average Years Experience: 3
Other Admissions Factors Considered: Work experience, leadership skills, community service
Other Schools to Which Students Applied: Babson College, Rice University, Southern Methodist University, Texas A&M University, Texas Christian University (TCU), Thunderbird, Wake Forest University

INTERNATIONAL STUDENTS

TOEFL Required of International Students? Yes
Minimum TOEFL: 600 (250 computer)

EMPLOYMENT INFORMATION

Placement Office Available? Yes

% Employed Within 3 Months: 70
Fields Employing Percentage of Grads: MIS (2%), Marketing (2%), General Management (4%), Finance (6%), Other (19%)
Frequent Employers: Accenture, Alltel, AT&T, Bank One, Cap Gemini, Chase, Conoco, Continental Airlines, Deloitte & Touche, Dynegy, ExxonMobil, HBK Investments, H.E.B. Grocery, IBM, Intecap, JP Morgan, Lockheed Martin, Microsoft, Raytheon, Shell, Southwest Airlines, SBC Communications, Sprint, Tivoli, Tucker Alan, TXU, VHA Inc.

See page 410.

BENTLEY COLLEGE
The Elkin B. McCallum Graduate School of Business

Admissions Contact: Paul J. Vaccaro, Director
Address: 175 Forest Street, Waltham, MA 02452
Admissions Phone: 781-891-2108 • **Admissions Fax:** 781-891-2464
Admissions E-mail: gradadm@bentley.edu • **Web Address:** www.bentley.edu

Bentley College offers three MBA tracks. The Information Age MBA is Bentley's answer to the traditional two-year multidisciplinary MBA. As expected, a heavy emphasis on information technology (IT) is included in the curriculum. IT is part of every course, and students utilize the hot technology of enterprise resource planning software to integrate the various disciplines of each lesson. Students can also choose from the popular part-time Self-Paced MBA or the One-Year MBA, designed to give those with an undergraduate business degree an intensive MBA education in one calendar year. Bentley is a hit with foreign students, giving the program a true international flavor.

INSTITUTIONAL INFORMATION

Public/Private: Private
Evening Classes Available? Yes
Total Faculty: 243
% Faculty Female: 35
% Faculty Minority: 14
% Faculty Part Time: 42
Student/Faculty Ratio: 14:1
Students in Parent Institution: 5,587
Academic Calendar: Semester

PROGRAMS

Degrees Offered: Flexible IAMBA (30-57 credits, 1-7 years), MS in Accountancy (30-60 credits, 1-7 years), MSIT (30-36 credits, 1-7 years), MS in Finance (30-57 credits, 1-7 years), MST (30-36 credits, 1-7 years), Cohort IAMBA (58 credits, 2 years), MSGFA (30-36 credits, 2-7 years), MSIAM (30 credits, 1-5 years), MSAIS (30-39 credits, 1-7 years), MSHFID (30 credits, 2-5 years)
Special Opportunities: Internship program, study electives in the summer
Study Abroad Options: Australia, Austria, Belgium, England, Estonia, France, Ireland, Italy, Mexico, Spain.

STUDENT INFORMATION

Total Business Students: 1,300
% Full Time: 20
% Female: 50
% Minority: 20
% Out of State: 6
Average Age: 27

COMPUTER AND RESEARCH FACILITIES

Computer Facilities: Access to online bibliographic retrieval services and online databases
Campuswide Network? Yes
Computer Model Recommended: Laptop
Internet Fee? No

EXPENSES/FINANCIAL AID

Annual Tuition: $24,240
Tuition Per Credit (Resident/Nonresident): $808
Room & Board (On/Off Campus): $3,880/$3,580
Books and Supplies: $1,000

ADMISSIONS INFORMATION

Application Fee: $50
Electronic Application? No
Regular Application Deadline: 6/1
Regular Notification: Rolling
Deferment Available? Yes
Length of Deferment: 1 year
Non-fall Admissions? Yes
Non-fall Application Deadline(s): 11/1 spring; 4/15 summer
Transfer Students Accepted? No
Need-Blind Admissions? No
Number of Applications Received: 516
% of Applicants Accepted: 57
% Accepted Who Enrolled: 62
Average GPA: 3.2
Average GMAT: 545
GMAT Range: 480-600
Average Years Experience: 6
Other Admissions Factors Considered: Interview, resume

INTERNATIONAL STUDENTS

TOEFL Required of International Students? Yes
Minimum TOEFL: 600 (250 computer)

EMPLOYMENT INFORMATION

Placement Office Available? Yes
Frequent Employers: Akamai Technologies, Deloitte & Touch LLP, Federal Express, Fleet, General Electric Co., IBM, Johnson & Johnson, KPMG Consulting, Nike, Pricewaterhouse Coopers LLP, Putnam Investments, Raytheon, Staples, State Street Corp., Teradyne Inc.
Prominent Alumni: Charles E. Peters, Jr., senior vice president and CFO, Burlington Industries; Ullas Naik, managing director, JAFCO Ventures; Thomas Venables, founder and CEO, Lighthousebank.com; Amy Hunter, executive vice president, Boston Private Bank and Trust

BINGHAMTON UNIVERSITY/STATE UNIVERSITY OF NEW YORK
School of Management

Admissions Contact: Alesia Wheeler, Asst. Director MBA/MS Program
Address: School of Management, Binghamton, NY 13902
Admissions Phone: 607-777-2317 • **Admissions Fax:** 607-777-4872
Admissions E-mail: somadvis@binghamton.edu • **Web Address:** som.binghamton.edu

Binghamton's MBA program builds on its excellent undergraduate reputation as one of the top 25 public universities in the United States. The four-semester program emphasizes general management skills with a special focus on teamwork. Binghamton stresses communication skills, understanding of group dynamics, and conflict resolution. Close ties with the local business community provide readily available internships and real-world expertise. A Fast-Track Program is available for those overachieving business undergraduates who want to be in and out in two semesters.

INSTITUTIONAL INFORMATION

Public/Private: Public
Evening Classes Available? No
Total Faculty: 33
% Faculty Female: 10
% Faculty Part Time: 5
Student/Faculty Ratio: 20:1
Students in Parent Institution: 13,099
Academic Calendar: Semester

PROGRAMS

Degrees Offered: MBA (2 years or 9 months), MS in Accounting (1 year), EMBA for Corporate Professionals (21 months), EMBA in Health Care (21 months)
Academic Specialties: World reknown leadership research center, one of the top 15% research institutions with regard to finance publications
Special Opportunities: Leadership certificate program, management development program

STUDENT INFORMATION

Total Business Students: 181
% Full Time: 88
% Female: 41
% Minority: 5
% Out of State: 5
% International: 64
Average Age: 25

COMPUTER AND RESEARCH FACILITIES

Computer Facilities: Access to online bibliographic retrieval services, AC-CESS, SQL server, Oracle
Campuswide Network? Yes
% of MBA Classrooms Wired: 100
Internet Fee? No

EXPENSES/FINANCIAL AID

Annual Tuition (Resident/Nonresident): $5,100/$8,416
Tuition Per Credit (Resident/Nonresident): $213/$351
Room & Board (On/Off Campus): /$10,077
Books and Supplies: $1,000
Average Grant: $13,556
Average Loan: $12,000
% Receiving Financial Aid: 20
% Receiving Aid Their First Year: 15

ADMISSIONS INFORMATION

Application Fee: $45
Electronic Application? Yes
Regular Application Deadline: 4/15
Regular Notification: Rolling
Deferment Available? Yes
Length of Deferment: 1 year
Non-fall Admissions? No
Transfer Students Accepted? No
Need-Blind Admissions? Yes
Number of Applications Received: 393
% of Applicants Accepted: 66
% Accepted Who Enrolled: 36
Average GPA: 3.3
GPA Range: 3.0-3.6

Average GMAT: 596
GMAT Range: 560-620
Average Years Experience: 3
Minority/Disadvantaged Student Recruitment Programs: Through the Clifford D. Clark Graduate Fellowship Program for Underrepresented Minority Students, the State University of New York has provided graduate fellowships for outstanding minority students from groups historically underrepresented (African American, Hispanic, Native American) in the University's graduate and professional programs. These fellowships are granted to students entering both master's and doctoral degree programs and carry stipends of between $6,800 and $12,750 (depending on discipline) for the academic year plus a full-tuition scholarship. Renewals or graduate assistantships may be awarded in subsequent years, depending on availability of funds.
Other Schools to Which Students Applied: University at Albany, Baruch College/City University of New York, Syracuse University, University at Buffalo/State University of New York

INTERNATIONAL STUDENTS

TOEFL Required of International Students? Yes
Minimum TOEFL: 580 (237 computer)

EMPLOYMENT INFORMATION

Placement Office Available? No
% Employed Within 3 Months: 71
Fields Employing Percentage of Grads: Human Resources (5%), Accounting (5%), General Management (10%), Marketing (15%), MIS (20%), Finance (40%)
Frequent Employers: BAE Systems, Deloitte & Touche, Ernst & Young, IBM, KPMG Peat Marwick, Lockheed Martin, Merrill Lynch, M&T Bank, Pricewaterhouse Coopers, United Health Services
Prominent Alumni: Managing director, Goldman Sachs; senior vice president, Paine Webber; senior partner, Arthur Andersen; president and CEO, Merrill Lynch/Japan; executive vice president, Disney Cruise Lines

BOISE STATE UNIVERSITY
College of Business and Economics

Admissions Contact: J Renee Anchustegui, Program Administrator
Address: 1910 University Drive B318, Boise, ID 83725-1600
Admissions Phone: 208-426-1126 • **Admissions Fax:** 208-426-1135
Admissions E-mail: ranchust@boisestate.edu
Web Address: cobe.boisestate.edu/graduate

Accountancy is at the forefront of Boise State's graduate business school, with two of its four programs focused on bottom lines. And new number-crunchers will be thrilled to calculate their own bottom-line tuition and fees at this bargain school. Boise State is unusually student-focused, as demonstrated by the Student of the Month awards it regularly gives to outstanding undergraduate and graduate students who the school believes "will represent the college well in their chosen profession." Each student chosen has his or her "photograph displayed in the foyer of the Business Building and are taken to lunch by the Dean to celebrate their award."

INSTITUTIONAL INFORMATION

Public/Private: Public
Evening Classes Available? Yes
Total Faculty: 55
% Faculty Female: 11
% Faculty Minority: 5
% Faculty Part Time: 1

Student/Faculty Ratio: 30:1
Students in Parent Institution: 17,883
Academic Calendar: Semester

PROGRAMS

Degrees Offered: MBA (37-49 credits, 18 months to 7 years), MSAT (30 credits, 12 months to 7 years), MSA (30 credits, 12 months to 7 years), MS in MIS (33 credits, 12 months to 5 years)
Academic Specialties: High-tech marketing, use of live business cases with local corporations, computer-aided instruction, computer analysis, computer simulations. Through their electives, students can specialize in accountancy/finance, engineering, health administration, high-tech marketing, information technology, instruction & performance technology, and public administration.
Special Opportunities: Internship program
Study Abroad Options: Finland, France, Germany, Italy, and Spain

STUDENT INFORMATION

Total Business Students: 128
% Full Time: 28
% Female: 42
% Minority: 11
% Out of State: 54
% International: 23
Average Age: 32

COMPUTER AND RESEARCH FACILITIES

Computer Facilities: Access to online bibliographic retrieval services and online databases
Campuswide Network? Yes
% of MBA Classrooms Wired: 10
Internet Fee? No

EXPENSES/FINANCIAL AID

Annual Tuition (Resident/Nonresident): $6,400
Room & Board (On/Off Campus): $6,000/$6,480
Books and Supplies: $1,800
Average Grant: $17,420
Average Loan: $6,000

ADMISSIONS INFORMATION

Application Fee: $30
Electronic Application? Yes
Regular Application Deadline: 3/1
Regular Notification: Rolling
Deferment Available? Yes
Length of Deferment: 1 year
Non-fall Admissions? Yes
Non-fall Application Deadline(s): 10/1 spring
Transfer Students Accepted? Yes
Transfer Policy: Limit of 9 graduate credits with grade of B or above from an AACSB-accredited institution
Need-Blind Admissions? Yes
Number of Applications Received: 146
% of Applicants Accepted: 79
% Accepted Who Enrolled: 62
Average GPA: 3.0
GPA Range: 2.8-3.5
Average GMAT: 576
GMAT Range: 470-680
Average Years Experience: 7
Other Admissions Factors Considered: Computer skills required in word processing, spreadsheet, and database; minimum GPA of 3.0 recommended; minimum 2 years of work experience recommended
Other Schools to Which Students Applied: University of Minnesota

INTERNATIONAL STUDENTS

TOEFL Required of International Students? Yes
Minimum TOEFL: 587 (240 computer)

EMPLOYMENT INFORMATION

Placement Office Available? Yes
% Employed Within 3 Months: 95
Prominent Alumni: Jan Packwood, president and COO, Idaho Power Co.; William Glynn, president, Intermountain Gas; Steve Heyl, vice president of strategic planning, Arby's; Norm Schlachter, vice president of finance, Micron Technology; Mary Schofield, controller, Boise Division, Hewlett-Packard

---

BOSTON COLLEGE
The Carroll School of Management

Admissions Contact: Shelley Conley, Director of Graduate Enrollment & MBA Admissions
Address: Fulton Hall 315, Chestnut Hill, MA 02467
Admissions Phone: 617-552-3920 • **Admissions Fax:** 617-552-8078
Admissions E-mail: BCMBA@bc.edu • **Web Address:** www.bc.edu\mba

With a median base salary of $80,000 for recent graduates and a rapid climb in the rankings, BC is an up-and-coming player in the MBA game. The program requires that all students participate in a team business plan competition as well as real-world consulting projects, thus focusing on the application of skills learned in the classroom. Combine this with a solid technical education and BC's traditional strength in finance, and BC graduates are being snapped up by the dotcom and financial worlds alike. Add in the prime Boston location and an even higher-ranked part-time MBA program, and BC begins to distinguish itself from the pack.

INSTITUTIONAL INFORMATION

Public/Private: Private
Evening Classes Available? Yes
Total Faculty: 90
Student/Faculty Ratio: 13:1
Students in Parent Institution: 14,297
Academic Calendar: Semester

PROGRAMS

Degrees Offered: MBA (2 years full time, 3.5 year part time), MSF (1 year full time, 2 years part time), MBA/MSF (2 years), PhD in Finance (4 years), PhD in Organizational Studies (4 years)
Combined Degrees: MBA/MSF (2 years); MBA/JD (4 years); MBA/MSW (3 years); MBA/MSN (3-4 years); MBA/MS in Biology, Geology, Geophysics (3 years); MBA/MA in Math, Slavic Studies, Russian, Linguistics (3 years)
Academic Specialties: Finance, Information Technology, Global Management, Consulting. Academic strengths: Blend of theory and practice; exposure to entrepreneurs and venture capitalists; consulting experience with industry clients; broad range of international opportunities; state-of-the-art concentrations including techno-MBA options.
Special Opportunities: Boston College MBA Program offers a dual degree program with the Robert E. Schuman University in Stratsbourg, France. Students earn both an MBA and the Diplome degree.
Study Abroad Options: Beijing International Management Center, Peking University, China; ESC Brest, ESC Bordeaux, and ESC Clermont, France; Smurfit Graduate School of Business, University College Dublin, Ireland; ITESM in Monterrey, Mexico; MSM in Maastricht, The Netherlands; ESADE in Barcelona, Spain

STUDENT INFORMATION

Total Business Students: 747
% Full Time: 33
% Female: 39

% **Minority:** 14
% **International:** 27
Average Age: 27

COMPUTER AND RESEARCH FACILITIES

Research Facilities: Retirement Research Center; Center for Corporate Community Relations; Small Business Development Center; Center for Work and Family

Computer Facilities: Among the more than 500 databases available through the library are the Dow Jones News Retrieval Service, Bloomberg Financial Services, Lexis-Nexis, abi/Inform, Compustat, crsp, dri/Basics Economics, and International Financial Statistics. There are a variety of computer resources available to students at the Boston College Graduate School of Management. Significantly expanded in 1998, the Graduate Computer Lab, located in the School of Management building, is dedicated solely to graduate students. The lab is accessible around the clock and is equipped with IBM workstations and laser printers. Lab workstations provide access to the Internet, e-mail accounts (available to all students), and EagleNet, Boston College's campuswide information network.

Campuswide Network? Yes
% **of MBA Classrooms Wired:** 100
Computer Model Recommended: Laptop
Internet Fee? No

EXPENSES/FINANCIAL AID

Annual Tuition: $27,244
Tuition Per Credit (Resident/Nonresident): $874
Books and Supplies: $1,500
Average Grant: $13,330
Average Loan: $9,999

ADMISSIONS INFORMATION

Application Fee: $50
Electronic Application? Yes
Early Decision Application Deadline: 12/1
Early Decision Notification: 1/31
Regular Application Deadline: 3/1
Regular Notification: Rolling
Deferment Available? Yes
Length of Deferment: 1 year
Non-fall Admissions? No
Transfer Students Accepted? Yes
Transfer Policy: Four courses are accepted (with a grade of B or higher) from other AACSB-MBA programs.
Need-Blind Admissions? Yes
Number of Applications Received: 1,093
% **of Applicants Accepted:** 15
% **Accepted Who Enrolled:** 63
Average GPA: 3.3
Average GMAT: 658
Average Years Experience: 4
Other Admissions Factors Considered: Match between applicant's interests and the school's core competencies
Minority/Disadvantaged Student Recruitment Programs: GMASS search mailings nationally to identify AHANA candidates; active participation in NBMBA case competitions, regional conferences, and national meetings

INTERNATIONAL STUDENTS

TOEFL Required of International Students? Yes
Minimum TOEFL: 600 (250 computer)

EMPLOYMENT INFORMATION

Placement Office Available? Yes
% **Employed Within 3 Months:** 79

BOSTON UNIVERSITY
School of Management

Admissions Contact: Evelyn Tate, Director of Graduate Admissions and Financial Aid
Address: 595 Commonwealth Avenue, Boston, MA 02215
Admissions Phone: 617-353-2670 • **Admissions Fax:** 617-353-7368
Admissions E-mail: mba@bu.edu • **Web Address:** management.bu.edu

The School of Management at Boston University is one of the largest in the country, and students here say it offers a "beautifully organized," "almost flawless" MBA program that stresses teamwork and practical, hands-on education. Professors are "extremely helpful, open for discussion," and "enthusiastic," and BU boasts a spiffy new building as well as a wide array of resources and dual degree programs.

INSTITUTIONAL INFORMATION

Public/Private: Private
Evening Classes Available? Yes
Total Faculty: 113
% **Faculty Female:** 24
Student/Faculty Ratio: 8:1
Students in Parent Institution: 28,981
Academic Calendar: Semester

PROGRAMS

Degrees Offered: MBA (2 years full time, 3-6 years part time), EMBA (17 months), MS in Investment Management (17 months), MS/MBA (21 months), DBA **Combined Degrees:** MBA/MS in Television Management, MBA/MA in International Relations, MBA/MS in Manufacturing Engineering, MBA/MA in Economics, MBA/MA in Medical Sciences (80 credits), MBA/JD (116 credits), MBA/MPH (85 credits), MBA/MD (114 credits), MS/MBA (dual degree MS in Information Systems and traditional MBA) (84 credits, 21 months)
Academic Specialties: Health Care Management, Finance, MIS, Entrepreneurship, Public and Nonprofit Management
Special Opportunities: Entrepreneurship; Health Care Management; Public and Nonprofit Management; Finance; Marketing; International Management Program, in either China or Japan program; international study in England and France
Study Abroad Options: International Management Program, Kobe, Japan; International Management Program, Shanghai, China; study abroad at University of Lyon, France, and University of Manchester, United Kingdom

STUDENT INFORMATION

Total Business Students: 846
% **Full Time:** 45
% **Female:** 35
% **Minority:** 16
% **International:** 39
Average Age: 27

COMPUTER AND RESEARCH FACILITIES

Research Facilities: Research centers and resources include: Systems Research Center, Entreprenurial Management Institute, Executive Development Roundtable, Center for Enterprise Leadership, Human Resources Policy Institute, Institute for Leading in a Dynamic Economy, Health Care Management Research Center, the Leadership Institute, the Center for Women's Entrepreneurship and Leadership, the Bronner e-Business Center and Hatchery, and the Center for Team Learning.

Computer Facilities: Our building houses more than 4,000 data ports; 5 computer labs, including a multimedia lab; and 28 classrooms with complete computing and audiovisual systems. A media control center connects all classrooms to the school's network, intranet, and the Internet. The Frederick S. Pardee Management Library, also located within our building, contains several computer terminals offering students access to a host of electronic databases (e.g., Lexis-Nexis, ABI Inform/Global, etc.). Many of these databases are also accessible remotely. In addition to our within-building resources, students can utilize the University public PC laboratory and main library (computer terminal access to various databases), both of which are situated on campus. Computer labs are also located in several dormitories on campus for use by residents.

Campuswide Network? Yes
% of MBA Classrooms Wired: 100
Internet Fee? No

EXPENSES/FINANCIAL AID

Annual Tuition: $27,042
Tuition Per Credit (Resident/Nonresident): $845
Room & Board (On/Off Campus): $10,030
Books and Supplies: $1,281
Average Grant: $10,511
Average Loan: $40,728
% Receiving Financial Aid: 80
% Receiving Aid Their First Year: 65

ADMISSIONS INFORMATION

Application Fee: $95
Electronic Application? Yes
Regular Application Deadline: 4/1
Regular Notification: 5/15
Deferment Available? Yes
Length of Deferment: 1 year
Non-fall Admissions? Yes
Non-fall Application Deadline(s): 11/15 spring (part time only)
Transfer Students Accepted? Yes
Transfer Policy: Part time only
Need-Blind Admissions? Yes
Number of Applications Received: 1,454
% of Applicants Accepted: 34
% Accepted Who Enrolled: 37
Average GPA: 3.1
Average GMAT: 632
Average Years Experience: 5
Other Admissions Factors Considered: Leadership skills, movement in professional career, team skills
Minority/Disadvantaged Student Recruitment Programs: Advertisements placed in periodicals that target specific communities, scholarships offered to minority students, partnership with the National Black MBA Association, student outreach to the ALANA community concerning NBMBAA and the National Hispanic MBA Association, attendance at minority recruiting events
Other Schools to Which Students Applied: Babson College, Boston College, Case Western Reserve University, Duke University, Georgetown University, New York University

INTERNATIONAL STUDENTS

TOEFL Required of International Students? Yes
Minimum TOEFL: 600 (250 computer)

EMPLOYMENT INFORMATION

Placement Office Available? Yes
% Employed Within 3 Months: 72
Frequent Employers: Akamai Technologies, Citizens Bank, Deloitte and Touche, Ernst and Young, Fidelity Investments, Hill Halliday, Home Depot, Johnson & Johnson (Jansen), JP Mogan Chase and Co., Liberty Mutual, Lockhead Martin Partners, Pricewaterhouse Coopers, Samsung, Sun Microsystems
Prominent Alumni: Jack E. Smith, Jr., chairman and CEO, Global Investment Management; Millard S. (Mickey) Drexler, chairman and CEO, J. Crew Group, Inc.; Jerald Fishman, CEO, Analog Devices, Inc.; Thomas Jones, president and CEO, Citigroup; Dr. Suzanne Cutler, executive vice president, New York Federal

BOWLING GREEN STATE UNIVERSITY
College of Business Administration

Admissions Contact: Carmen Castro-Rivera, Director, Graduate Studies in Business
Address: 369 Business Administration Building, Bowling Green, OH 43403
Admissions Phone: 419-372-2488 • **Admissions Fax:** 419-372-2875
Admissions E-mail: mba-info@cba.bgsu.edu • **Web Address:** www.bgsumba.com

It at first seems incongruous that you'd find a business school with a diverse range of graduate programs and student body in a small town in northern Ohio. But if you take time to look closely at Bowling Green State University's b-school, you'll find a student body that's 50 percent international and five very distinct graduate business programs. Practically any student with an interest in studying business will find a track of study appropriate to his or her skills and interests.

INSTITUTIONAL INFORMATION

Public/Private: Public
Evening Classes Available? Yes
Total Faculty: 42
% Faculty Female: 19
% Faculty Minority: 16
% Faculty Part Time: 10
Student/Faculty Ratio: 7:1
Students in Parent Institution: 20,480
Academic Calendar: Semester

PROGRAMS

Degrees Offered: MBA (14 months full time, 2.5 years part time), EMBA (18 months), MACC (1 year), Master of Organization Development (18 months), MS in Applied Statistics, MS in Computer Science (Operations Research), MA in Economics
Academic Specialties: The full-time program features a Leadership Assessment and Development component consisting of a series of workshops. The workshops lead students through an on-going process of reflection and self-discovery so that each obtains a better understanding of his- or herself in relation to a desired management career.
Special Opportunities: Specializations in MIS, Finance, and Accounting
Study Abroad Options: ESC Nantes, France

STUDENT INFORMATION

Total Business Students: 171
% Full Time: 30
% Female: 37
% Minority: 4
% Out of State: 8
% International: 60
Average Age: 28

COMPUTER AND RESEARCH FACILITIES

Research Facilities: Institute for Organizational Effectiveness, Statistical Consulting Center, Supply Chain Management Institute
Computer Facilities: The 9-story Jerome Library (the largest on campus) houses more than 5 million items. Through OhioLINK, students have access to an additional 31 million volumes held in Ohio's other state university libraries. The campus features a comprehensive network of digital academic computing resources on the new BGsupernet, a high-speed, state-of-the-art network with more than 34,319 access points across the campus. The campus also boasts Macintosh labs, a 24-hour computer lab in the student union, and a publicly acessible UNIX system. The Business Building contains several PC computer labs with a wide array of business, research, and statistical software loaded onto each workstation.
Campuswide Network? Yes
% of MBA Classrooms Wired: 100

Internet Fee? No

EXPENSES/FINANCIAL AID

Annual Tuition (Resident/Nonresident): $10,983
Tuition Per Credit (Resident/Nonresident): $339
Room & Board (On/Off Campus): $5,800
Books and Supplies: $800
% Receiving Financial Aid: 18
% Receiving Aid Their First Year: 38

ADMISSIONS INFORMATION

Application Fee: $30
Electronic Application? Yes
Regular Application Deadline: Rolling
Regular Notification: Rolling
Deferment Available? Yes
Length of Deferment: 1 year
Non-fall Admissions? Yes
Non-fall Application Deadline(s): 11/1 spring, 3/1 summer
Transfer Students Accepted? Yes
Transfer Policy: Students in the MBA programs (full time, evening, and executive) are limited to a maximum of 6 graduate credit hours of transfer credit from AACSB-accredited institutions. This policy limits transfer credit to the foundation courses (ECON 600, STAT 601, and MBA 600, 601, 602, and 603) and to the specialization. Transfer credit may be applied according to the following guidelines:

• Course equivalency will be determined by Graduate Studies in Business.
• No more than a total of 6 graduate credit hours of transfer credit shall be permitted to apply to the MBA program.
• Of the 6 hours, no more than 3 graduate credit hours shall be permitted to apply to the specialization courses.
• Of the 6 hours, up to 6 graduate credit hours shall be permitted to apply to the foundation courses.
• No transfer credit shall be permitted to apply to core or capstone courses.
• Credit may be transferred only for courses in which the student received the grades of A, B, or S if the grading school regards a grade of S to be a B or better (page 36 of 1998-2000 Graduate Catalog).
• Transferred courses shall not have been completed more than 3 years ago.

Need-Blind Admissions? Yes
Number of Applications Received: 159
% of Applicants Accepted: 69
% Accepted Who Enrolled: 75
Average GPA: 3.1
GPA Range: 2.3-4.0
Average GMAT: 565
GMAT Range: 320-710
Average Years Experience: 6
Other Admissions Factors Considered: Interview, work experience, undergraduate major
Minority/Disadvantaged Student Recruitment Programs: Project Search is a program in the Graduate College at BGSU that recruits students for University graduate programs (primarily full time) and then coordinates an array of services designed to lead these students from enrollment through graduation.

INTERNATIONAL STUDENTS

TOEFL Required of International Students? Yes
Minimum TOEFL: 550 (213 computer)

EMPLOYMENT INFORMATION

Placement Office Available? Yes
Frequent Employers: American Express, American Greetings, Ernst & Young, Marathon Ashland, National City Corp., Nationwide Insurance, Owens Corning, Plante & Moran, Progressive Insurance, State Farm Insurance

BRADLEY UNIVERSITY
Foster College of Business Administration

Admissions Contact: Dr. Edward Sattler, Director of Graduate Programs
Address: Baker Hall, Peoria, IL 61625
Admissions Phone: 309-677-2253 • **Admissions Fax:** 309-677-3374
Admissions E-mail: ade@bradley.edu • **Web Address:** www.bradley.edu/fcba/index.html

INSTITUTIONAL INFORMATION

Public/Private: Private
Evening Classes Available? Yes
Total Faculty: 51
% Faculty Part Time: 18
Student/Faculty Ratio: 1:1
Academic Calendar: Semester

PROGRAMS

Degrees Offered: MBA (1-5 years), MS in Accouting (18 months to 5 years)
Special Opportunities: Accounting, CIS or MIS, Finance (includes Banking), General Business, Health Services/Hospital Administration, Management, Marketing

COMPUTER AND RESEARCH FACILITIES

Campuswide Network? No
Internet Fee? No

EXPENSES/FINANCIAL AID

Annual Tuition: $8,832
Books and Supplies: $700

ADMISSIONS INFORMATION

Application Fee: $50
Electronic Application? No
Regular Application Deadline: Rolling
Regular Notification: Rolling
Deferment Available? Yes
Length of Deferment: 1 year
Non-fall Admissions? Yes
Non-fall Application Deadline(s): 1/1
Transfer Students Accepted? No
Need-Blind Admissions? Yes

INTERNATIONAL STUDENTS

TOEFL Required of International Students? Yes
Minimum TOEFL: 500

EMPLOYMENT INFORMATION

Placement Office Available? Yes

BRIGHAM YOUNG UNIVERSITY
Marriott School of Management

Admissions Contact: Debra Ruse, Program Administrator
Address: 640 TNRB, Provo, UT 84602
Admissions Phone: 801-422-3509 • **Admissions Fax:** 801-422-0513
Admissions E-mail: mba@byu.edu • **Web Address:** marriottschool.byu.edu/mba

Students at Brigham Young University's "remarkably" ethics-oriented Marriott School say their professors constantly emphasize the importance of character and the moral responsibilities of leadership. Marriott is also a tremendous place to study international business because many students have acquired foreign work experience, cross-cultural knowledge, and proficiency in a second (or third) language as missionaries for the Church of Jesus Christ of Latter-day Saints.

INSTITUTIONAL INFORMATION

Public/Private: Private
Evening Classes Available? No
Total Faculty: 160
% Faculty Female: 8
% Faculty Minority: 1
% Faculty Part Time: 20
Student/Faculty Ratio: 6:1
Students in Parent Institution: 32,242
Academic Calendar: Semester

PROGRAMS

Degrees Offered: EMBA (2 years), MBA (2 years), EMPA (3 years), MISM and MACC (5 years including undergraduate years), MPA (2 years)
Combined Degrees: MBA/JD (4 years); MBA/MS, IPD Program with Engineering Department (4 years); MBA/International (4 years); MACC/JD(4 years); MPA/JD (4 years)
Academic Specialties: Entrepreneurship, Corporate Finance, Investment Management, Management of Financial Institutions, Marketing Management, Information Systems, Organizational Behavior, Strategic Management, Production & Operations Management, Quantitative Methods, International Business, Accounting, White Collar Fraud, E-Business
Special Opportunities: The Executive Lecture Series, Entrepreneurship Lecture Series, International Business Series, Computer Summer Prep, Field Study Program, 9 business language programs, computer business simulation, faculty-hosted international business study in Asia and Latin America

STUDENT INFORMATION

Total Business Students: 265
% Full Time: 100
% Female: 15
% Minority: 4
% International: 11
Average Age: 28

COMPUTER AND RESEARCH FACILITIES

Research Facilities: Center for Entrepreneurship; Center for E-Business; Center for International Business Education and Research; Institute of Retail, Sales and Marketing; Financial Services Institute
Computer Facilities: Computer Labs, Lexis-Nexis, Bloomberg, EDGAR
Campuswide Network? Yes
% of MBA Classrooms Wired: 100
Computer Model Recommended: Laptop
Internet Fee? No

EXPENSES/FINANCIAL AID

Annual Tuition: $6,140
Tuition Per Credit (Resident/Nonresident): $342
Room & Board (On/Off Campus): $5,340/$5,640

Books and Supplies: $1,260
Average Grant: $4,146
Average Loan: $7,405
% Receiving Financial Aid: 84
% Receiving Aid Their First Year: 97

ADMISSIONS INFORMATION

Application Fee: $50
Electronic Application? Yes
Early Decision Application Deadline: 1/15
Early Decision Notification: 2/28
Regular Application Deadline: 3/1
Regular Notification: Rolling
Deferment Available? Yes
Length of Deferment: 2 years
Non-fall Admissions? No
Transfer Students Accepted? Yes
Transfer Policy: We accept 15 credit hours of graduate-level courses, no pass/fail grades, and a minimum grade of B.
Need-Blind Admissions? Yes
Number of Applications Received: 412
% of Applicants Accepted: 44
% Accepted Who Enrolled: 69
Average GPA: 3.6
GPA Range: 3.3-3.8
Average GMAT: 651
GMAT Range: 620-680
Average Years Experience: 3
Other Admissions Factors Considered: International experience, evidence of leadership skills
Minority/Disadvantaged Student Recruitment Programs: The diversity recruitment office is partnering with more than 10 companies through a diversity iniative to provide financial assistance to minority students. Other efforts include the Ford Motor Co. Extended Reach Scholarship, the Single Parent Scholarship, the International Student Support Program to provide financial assistance, and a focus on recruitment for minority students in large urban areas.

INTERNATIONAL STUDENTS

TOEFL Required of International Students? Yes
Minimum TOEFL: 580 (230 computer)

EMPLOYMENT INFORMATION

Placement Office Available? Yes
% Employed Within 3 Months: 90
Fields Employing Percentage of Grads: Human Resources (2%), Other (5%), Operations (5%), MIS (5%), Consulting (8%), General Management (9%), Marketing (12%), Finance (37%)
Frequent Employers: Bearsterns, Cigna, Citigroup, Daimler Chrysler, Dow Chemical, Ernst & Young, Ford Motor Co., General Electric, Hewlett-Packard, Honeywell, IBM, Intel, LexisNexis, Novell, Nutraceutical, Payless Shoes, Partners Group, SBC, The Church of Jesus Christ of Latter-day Saints, Union Pacific, Yellow Freight

BRYANT COLLEGE
School of Business Administration

Admissions Contact: Kristopher Sullivan, Director of Graduate Studies
Address: 1150 Douglas Pike, Smithfield, RI 02917-1284
Admissions Phone: 401-232-6230 • Admissions Fax: 401-232-6494
Admissions E-mail: gradprog@bryant.edu • Web Address: www.bryant.edu

INSTITUTIONAL INFORMATION
Public/Private: Private
Evening Classes Available? Yes
Total Faculty: 38
% Faculty Part Time: 29
Student/Faculty Ratio: 20:1
Students in Parent Institution: 3,365
Academic Calendar: Semester

PROGRAMS
Degrees Offered: MBA (48-54 credits, 19 months to, MS in Accounting (30-54 credits, 2-6 years), MST (30 credits, 2.5 to 6 years), MSIS (30-42 credits, 2-6 years)

STUDENT INFORMATION
Total Business Students: 318
% Full Time: 23
% Female: 38
% Minority: 1
% Out of State: 1
% International: 31
Average Age: 27

COMPUTER AND RESEARCH FACILITIES
Research Facilities: CD players available for student use.
Computer Facilities: The library offers Lexis-Nexis, Dialog (allows access to hundreds of databases), and the BRIDGE Information Systems Selective Ticker Service.
Campuswide Network? Yes
Internet Fee? No

EXPENSES/FINANCIAL AID
% Receiving Financial Aid: 5

ADMISSIONS INFORMATION
Application Fee: $60
Electronic Application? Yes
Regular Application Deadline: 7/15
Regular Notification: Rolling
Deferment Available? Yes
Length of Deferment: 1 year
Non-fall Admissions? Yes
Non-fall Application Deadline(s): 11/15 spring, 4/1 summer
Transfer Students Accepted? Yes
Transfer Policy: Transfer credits are limited to those taken within the last 3 years with a grade of B (3.0) or better from an AACSB-International-accredited master's program.
Need-Blind Admissions? No
Number of Applications Received: 103
% of Applicants Accepted: 55
% Accepted Who Enrolled: 98
Average GPA: 3.3
GPA Range: 3.1-3.6
Average GMAT: 521
GMAT Range: 480-590
Average Years Experience: 5
Other Admissions Factors Considered: Interview, work experience

INTERNATIONAL STUDENTS
TOEFL Required of International Students? Yes
Minimum TOEFL: 550 (215 computer)

EMPLOYMENT INFORMATION
Placement Office Available? Yes

BUTLER UNIVERSITY
College of Business Administration

Admissions Contact: Stephanie Judge, Director of Marketing
Address: 4600 Sunset Avenue, Indianapolis, IN 46208-3485
Admissions Phone: 317-940-9221 • Admissions Fax: 317-940-9455
Admissions E-mail: mba@butler.edu • Web Address: www.butler.edu/www/cba/mba

INSTITUTIONAL INFORMATION
Public/Private: Private
Evening Classes Available? Yes
Total Faculty: 35
% Faculty Female: 32
% Faculty Minority: 17
% Faculty Part Time: 23
Student/Faculty Ratio: 20:1
Students in Parent Institution: 3,700
Academic Calendar: Semester

PROGRAMS
Degrees Offered: MBA (30-58 credits; full time, part time, and evening programs available; 1-5 years), with concentrations in Finance, Marketing, Leadership, or customized concentration
Combined Degrees: PharmD/MBA (6 years full time)
Academic Specialties: The Butler MBA program offers a comprehensive, advanced business degree that includes not only business basics, but also a specialized focus on today's management trends and issues. The program is personalized and is ideal for early- and mid-career professionals. The program is flexible and convenient, not lockstep, and can be completed on a part-time or full-time basis. Butler MBA courses are held during the evening.

The curriculum is divided into three sections. Threshold courses (400-level courses) provide business basics, including an overview of accounting and quantitative methods. Foundation courses (400-level courses) prepare students for the graduate core. Coursework includes a variety of topics: organizational behavior, public policy, financial and managerial accounting, and statistics. The foundation also includes a broad emphasis on economics, finance, and marketing. The graduate core (500-level courses) offers an integrated framework based on contemporary leadership perspectives and management practice. This portion of the program is designed to prepare students to compete in a dynamic business environment and a growing international economy.

As students make progress in their self-paced programs, they choose a concentration in one of three focused areas: finance, leadership, or marketing. A specialized concentration may also be created based on a student's individual career path.

STUDENT INFORMATION
Total Business Students: 327
% Full Time: 9
% Female: 45
% Minority: 4
% International: 9
Average Age: 30

COMPUTER AND RESEARCH FACILITIES

Research Facilities: The Butler University Libraries contain more than 250,000 book volumes; 1,455 current periodical subscriptions; more than 60,000 bound periodicals; 185,000 microform volumes; and 115,000 government documents. Enhancing these collections is a strong array of services such as professional reference and research assistance, library instructional services, faculty reserve readings, interlibrary loan (including electronic transmission of many articles), and circulation. Students may do evening research in Irwin Library, where they can access numerous online catalogs, and CD-ROM and remote databases.

Computer Facilities: Two Windows-based labs—among Butler's 14 computer labs—are open in the evening. The labs in Atherton Union are open 24 hours a day and house both Macintosh and Windows-based platforms. Each student receives a Butler e-mail address upon admission to the University. The Butler e-mail may be forwarded to a primary e-mail address at work or home.

Campuswide Network? Yes
Internet Fee? No

EXPENSES/FINANCIAL AID

Annual Tuition: $11,300
Tuition Per Credit (Resident/Nonresident): $470
Books and Supplies: $1,400
Average Loan: $7,050

ADMISSIONS INFORMATION

Application Fee: $35
Electronic Application? Yes
Regular Application Deadline: 7/27
Regular Notification: 8/10
Deferment Available? Yes
Length of Deferment: 1 year
Non-fall Admissions? Yes
Non-fall Application Deadline(s): 11/27 spring, 4/27 summer
Transfer Students Accepted? Yes
Transfer Policy: Up to 9 credit hours, pending approval
Need-Blind Admissions? No
Number of Applications Received: 146
% of Applicants Accepted: 55
% Accepted Who Enrolled: 98
Average GPA: 3.0
Average GMAT: 550
Other Admissions Factors Considered: Butler takes a very holistic approach when looking at applicants. We consider undergraduate record, GMAT score, work experience, and letters of recommendation. Admittance to the program is a personalized process that involves more than an applicant's standardized minimum score on the GMAT.
Other Schools to Which Students Applied: Indiana University-Purdue University—Indianapolis, Indiana University
TOEFL Required of International Students? Yes
Minimum TOEFL: 550

EMPLOYMENT INFORMATION

Placement Office Available? Yes

CALIFORNIA POLYTECHNIC STATE UNIVERSITY—SAN LUIS OBISPO
Orfalea College of Business

Admissions Contact: Barry D. Floyd, Director, Graduate Programs
Address: 1 Grand Avenue, OCOB, San Luis Obispo, CA 93407
Admissions Phone: 805-756-2637 • **Admissions Fax:** 805-756-0110
Admissions E-mail: mba@calpoly.edu • **Web Address:** mba.calpoly.edu

This small MBA program (106 students) offers the requisite courses in all the usual suspects: finance, accounting, marketing, and so on. However, the program's competitive advantage lies in the opportunity it offers MBA students to focus on agribusiness. Cal Poly is an aggie school and it plays to this strength. Several other dual degrees are offered with other departments/schools ranging from architecture to engineering. The MBA/MS in Engineering program offers the option to concentrate on manufacturing management.

INSTITUTIONAL INFORMATION

Public/Private: Public
Evening Classes Available? No
Total Faculty: 61
% Faculty Female: 24
% Faculty Minority: 12
% Faculty Part Time: 16
Student/Faculty Ratio: 30:1
Students in Parent Institution: 17,890
Academic Calendar: Quarter

PROGRAMS

Degrees Offered: MBA (96 credits, 2 years full time); concentrations in Agribusiness, Management
Combined Degrees: MBA/MS in Engineering Management (96-98 credits, 2 years full time), MBA/MS in Computer Science (105 credits, 2-3 years full time), MBA/MS in Electrical Engineering (101 credits, 2-3 years full time), MBA/MS in Mechanical Engineering (101 credits, 2-3 years full time)
Academic Specialties: Excellent mix of theory and practice, strong business fundamentals coupled with excellent management skills, learn-by-doing environment with strong focus on career advancement and industry interaction
Special Opportunities: London Studies, Pacific Programs, Salamanca Study
Study Abroad Options: Australia (Swinburne University), China, Denmark (Copenhagen Business School, Aarhas School of Business, ESSAM), England, France (IFI Rouen, ESC Toulouse), Germany, Hungary, Israel, Italy, Korea, Mexicao (TEC de Monterrey), New Zealand, Spain, Sweden, Taiwan, Thailand, Zimbabwe

STUDENT INFORMATION

Total Business Students: 105
% Full Time: 99
% Female: 28
% Minority: 21
% Out of State: 12
% International: 8
Average Age: 26

COMPUTER AND RESEARCH FACILITIES

Research Facilities: Cisco Networking Lab, HP Projects Lab
Computer Facilities: A full range of facilities and resources
Campuswide Network? Yes
% of MBA Classrooms Wired: 100
Computer Model Recommended: Laptop
Internet Fee? No

EXPENSES/FINANCIAL AID

Annual Tuition (Resident/Nonresident): $1,650/$10,674

Room & Board (On/Off Campus): $7,119
Books and Supplies: $1,080
Average Grant: $2,073
Average Loan: $7,340
% Receiving Financial Aid: 45
% Receiving Aid Their First Year: 25

ADMISSIONS INFORMATION

Application Fee: $55
Electronic Application? Yes
Regular Application Deadline: 7/1
Regular Notification: Rolling
Deferment Available? Yes
Length of Deferment: 2 years
Non-fall Admissions? No
Transfer Students Accepted? Yes
Transfer Policy: 8 unit transfer
Need-Blind Admissions? No
Number of Applications Received: 130
% of Applicants Accepted: 53
% Accepted Who Enrolled: 64
Average GPA: 3.3
GPA Range: 2.1-3.6
Average GMAT: 598
GMAT Range: 540-620
Average Years Experience: 3
Other Admissions Factors Considered: April 1 is the fall deadline for international applicants. A minimum GPA of 3.0 is required of all applicants. A minimum of 3 years of work experience and computer experience are recommended.
Other Schools to Which Students Applied: California State Polytechnic University—Pomona, University of California—Davis, University of California—Los Angeles

INTERNATIONAL STUDENTS

TOEFL Required of International Students? Yes
Minimum TOEFL: 550 (213 computer)

EMPLOYMENT INFORMATION

Placement Office Available? Yes
% Employed Within 3 Months: 69
Frequent Employers: Deloitte Consulting, IBM, PG&E, Sun MicroSystems

CALIFORNIA STATE POLYTECHNIC UNIVERSITY—POMONA
College of Business Administration

Admissions Contact: Anyone, Administrative Coordinator
Address: 3801 West Temple Ave., Pomona, CA 91768
Admissions Phone: 909-869-3210 • Admissions Fax: 909-869-4529
Admissions E-mail: admissions@csupomona.edu
Web Address: www.csupomona.edu/~mba/

INSTITUTIONAL INFORMATION

Public/Private: Public
Evening Classes Available? Yes
Student/Faculty Ratio: 115:1
Students in Parent Institution: 16,304
Academic Calendar: Quarter

PROGRAMS

Degrees Offered: MBA (48 credits, full time or part time, up to 7 years to complete program), with concentrations in Accounting, Entrepreneurship, Finance, Human Resources, Information Management, International Business, Marketing, Operations Management, Production Management, Real Estate; MSBA (48 credits, full time or part time, up to 7 years), with concentration in Information Systems Auditing; general MBA (48 credits, full time or part time, up to 7 years); Professional MBA (EMBA) (48 credits, full time or part time, up to 7 years)

STUDENT INFORMATION

Total Business Students: 600
% Full Time: 25
% Female: 45
% Minority: 20
Average Age: 32

COMPUTER AND RESEARCH FACILITIES

Research Facilities: University Library, with total holdings of 592,433 volumes; 2,003,847 microforms; 2,964 current periodical subscriptions. CD players available for graduate student use; access provided to online bibliographic retrieval services and online databases
Computer Facilities: Various databases
Campuswide Network? Yes
% of MBA Classrooms Wired: 75
Computer Model Recommended: Laptop
Internet Fee? No

EXPENSES/FINANCIAL AID

Annual Tuition (Resident/Nonresident): $2,100/$4,100
Room & Board (On/Off Campus): $3,500/$8,000
Books and Supplies: $3,000
Average Grant: $18,500
Average Loan: $10,000

ADMISSIONS INFORMATION

Application Fee: $55
Electronic Application? Yes
Regular Application Deadline: Rolling
Regular Notification: Rolling
Deferment Available? Yes
Length of Deferment: 1-2 quarters
Non-fall Admissions? Yes
Non-fall Application Deadline(s): 9/1 winter, 1/2 spring, 3/1 summer
Transfer Students Accepted? Yes
Transfer Policy: Maximum of 3 transferrable classes
Need-Blind Admissions? No
Number of Applications Received: 163
% of Applicants Accepted: 30
% Accepted Who Enrolled: 59
Average GPA: 3.1
GPA Range: 2.7-4.0
Average GMAT: 520
GMAT Range: 450-720
Average Years Experience: 10
Other Admissions Factors Considered: A minimum of 3 years of work experience are required. A minimum GMAT score of 450 and GPA of 3.0 are required. Computer experience is recommended.

INTERNATIONAL STUDENTS

TOEFL Required of International Students? Yes
Minimum TOEFL: 580

EMPLOYMENT INFORMATION

Placement Office Available? Yes
% Employed Within 3 Months: 80

CALIFORNIA STATE UNIVERSITY—BAKERSFIELD

School of Business and Public Administration

Admissions Contact: Dr. Brian McNamara, MBA Director
Address: 9001 Stockdale Highway, Bakersfield, CA 93311-1099
Admissions Phone: 661-664-2326 • **Admissions Fax:** 661-664-2438
Admissions E-mail: admissions@csub.edu • **Web Address:** www.csubak.edu/BPA/

INSTITUTIONAL INFORMATION

Public/Private: Public
Evening Classes Available? No
Total Faculty: 25
% Faculty Part Time: 41
Students in Parent Institution: 4,820
Academic Calendar: Quarter

PROGRAMS

Degrees Offered: MBA (48 credits, full time or part time, 1-7 years), with concentration in Management; MPA (55 credits, full time or part time, 2-7 years); MS in Health Care Management (55 credits, full time or part time, 2-7 years)
Special Opportunities: General Business

STUDENT INFORMATION

Total Business Students: 718
% Female: 50
% Minority: 4
% Out of State: 1
% International: 6
Average Age: 30

COMPUTER AND RESEARCH FACILITIES

Campuswide Network? Yes
Internet Fee? No

EXPENSES/FINANCIAL AID

Annual Tuition (Resident/Nonresident): $1,700/$2,700

ADMISSIONS INFORMATION

Application Fee: $55
Electronic Application? No
Regular Application Deadline: 7/1
Regular Notification: 1/1
Deferment Available? No
Non-fall Admissions? Yes
Non-fall Application Deadline(s): 11/1 winter, 3/1 spring
Transfer Students Accepted? No
Need-Blind Admissions? No
Number of Applications Received: 80
% of Applicants Accepted: 84
% Accepted Who Enrolled: 96
Other Admissions Factors Considered: The minimum GMAT score accepted is 500. The minimum GPA accepted is 2.75. An interview and a minimum of 3 years of work experience are recommended.

INTERNATIONAL STUDENTS

TOEFL Required of International Students? Yes
Minimum TOEFL: 550

EMPLOYMENT INFORMATION

Placement Office Available? Yes

CALIFORNIA STATE UNIVERSITY—CHICO

College of Business

Admissions Contact: Sandy Jensen, Adviser, Business Graduate Programs
Address: BGAD@CSU, Chico 041, Chico, CA 95929
Admissions Phone: 530-898-4425 • **Admissions Fax:** 530-898-5889
Admissions E-mail: sjensen@csuchico.edu • **Web Address:** www.cob.csuchico.edu

The MBA program at CSU—Chico is designed for students with undergraduate study in any major or concentration. The program is traditional and comprehensive, and it fosters a strong intellectual focus on managerial preparation and real-world business skills. CSU—Chico's College of Business declares that its graduates have the "distinctive quality of 'extraordinary effectiveness'" that makes them appealing to recruiters.

INSTITUTIONAL INFORMATION

Public/Private: Public
Evening Classes Available? No
Total Faculty: 10
% Faculty Female: 20
% Faculty Minority: 5
% Faculty Part Time: 20
Student/Faculty Ratio: 35:1
Students in Parent Institution: 15,000
Academic Calendar: Semester

PROGRAMS

Degrees Offered: MBA (30 credits, full time or part time, 18 months to 5 years), with concentrations in Finance, Human Resources, Management; Management Information Systems, Marketing, Production Management; MSA (30 credits, full time or part time, 18 months to 5 years), with concentrations in Accounting, Management Information Systems
Combined Degrees: MBA with MIS emphasis (2 years)
Academic Specialties: Academic specialities: SAP, real-world consulting experience. Special strengths: team projects, project management, cutting-edge MIS applications

STUDENT INFORMATION

Total Business Students: 82
% Full Time: 70
% Female: 35
% Minority: 0
% Out of State: 0
% International: 45
Average Age: 27

COMPUTER AND RESEARCH FACILITIES

Computer Facilities: More than adequate computer facilities are available on campus.
Campuswide Network? Yes
% of MBA Classrooms Wired: 100
Internet Fee? No

EXPENSES/FINANCIAL AID

Annual Tuition (Resident/Nonresident): $2,500/$9,268
Room & Board (On/Off Campus): $8,000/$8,500
Books and Supplies: $1,200
Average Grant: $1,000
Average Loan: $7,500
% Receiving Financial Aid: 65
% Receiving Aid Their First Year: 50

ADMISSIONS INFORMATION

Application Fee: $55
Electronic Application? Yes
Regular Application Deadline: Rolling
Regular Notification: Rolling
Deferment Available? Yes
Length of Deferment: 1 year
Non-fall Admissions? Yes
Non-fall Application Deadline(s): Rolling
Transfer Students Accepted? Yes
Transfer Policy: Must meet our admissions criteria
Need-Blind Admissions? Yes
Number of Applications Received: 85
% of Applicants Accepted: 58
% Accepted Who Enrolled: 65
Average GPA: 3.3
GPA Range: 2.7-3.7
Average GMAT: 560
GMAT Range: 540-690
Average Years Experience: 3
Other Admissions Factors Considered: Computing skills are required (word processing, spreadsheet, database). A minimum score in the 50th percentile on the GMAT and a minimum GPA of 2.75 for the last 60 units are required. Three letters of recommendation are required. A minimum of 2 years of work experience are recommended.
Other Schools to Which Students Applied: California State University—Sacramento, San Francisco State University

INTERNATIONAL STUDENTS

TOEFL Required of International Students? Yes
Minimum TOEFL: 550 (213 computer)

EMPLOYMENT INFORMATION

Placement Office Available? Yes
% Employed Within 3 Months: 95
Fields Employing Percentage of Grads: General Management (1%), Finance (2%), Other (5%), Consulting (10%), Accounting (10%), MIS (70%)
Frequent Employers: Accenture, Apple, Chevron, Deloitte & Touche, Ernst & Young, Hewlett-Packard, Intel, Micron
Prominent Alumni: Prabhakar Kalavacharla, managing partner, KPMG; Ed Byers, managing partner, Deloitte & Touche; Masayuki Ishizaki, managing partner, Accenture; Bill Bales, CFO, Sierra Nevada Brewing Co.

CALIFORNIA STATE UNIVERSITY— FRESNO
Craig School of Business

Admissions Contact: Dr. Mark Keppler, Director of Graduate Studies
Address: 5245 North Backer Avenue, Fresno, CA 93740
Admissions Phone: 559-278-2107 • **Admissions Fax:** 559-278-4911
Admissions E-mail: nyeeg@csufresno.edu • **Web Address:** www.craigmba.com

INSTITUTIONAL INFORMATION

Public/Private: Public
Evening Classes Available? Yes
Total Faculty: 46
% Faculty Female: 33
% Faculty Part Time: 26
Student/Faculty Ratio: 6:1

Students in Parent Institution: 19,000
Academic Calendar: Semester

PROGRAMS

Degrees Offered: MBA
Academic Specialties: Faculty specialization: Financial Planning, Technology Management, Information Systems, Health Administration

STUDENT INFORMATION

Total Business Students: 218
% Full Time: 42
% Female: 45
% Minority: 7
% Out of State: 15
% International: 55
Average Age: 29

COMPUTER AND RESEARCH FACILITIES

Research Facilities: MBA students have full access to the Law Library.
Computer Facilities: MBA students have access to all computer facilities on the main campus in Chester and the Delaware Campus. Students can search databases from home through library website. There is also a specialized computer lab, including SAP software, for MIS/IS courses.
Campuswide Network? Yes
Internet Fee? No

EXPENSES/FINANCIAL AID

Room & Board (On/Off Campus): $10,700
Books and Supplies: $650

ADMISSIONS INFORMATION

Application Fee: $55
Electronic Application? Yes
Regular Application Deadline: 3/1
Regular Notification: Rolling
Deferment Available? Yes
Length of Deferment: 1 year
Non-fall Admissions? Yes
Non-fall Application Deadline(s): 10/1 spring
Transfer Students Accepted? Yes
Transfer Policy: All foundation courses may be waived through prior coursework. Up to 6 credits may be transferred into the core and elective portion of program. Transfer credit is granted on a case-by-case basis through syllabus review.
Need-Blind Admissions? Yes
Number of Applications Received: 148
% of Applicants Accepted: 62
% Accepted Who Enrolled: 72
Average GPA: 3.4
GPA Range: 3.1-3.7
Average GMAT: 593
GMAT Range: 560-630
Average Years Experience: 7
Other Schools to Which Students Applied: California Polytechnic State University—San Luis Obispo, Santa Clara University, University of California—Davis

INTERNATIONAL STUDENTS

TOEFL Required of International Students? Yes
Minimum TOEFL: 550 (213 computer)

EMPLOYMENT INFORMATION

Placement Office Available? Yes

CALIFORNIA STATE UNIVERSITY— FULLERTON

College of Business and Economics

Admissions Contact: Pre-Admission Advisor
Address: PO Box 6848, Fullerton, CA 92834
Admissions Phone: 714-278-2211 • **Admissions Fax:** 714-278-7101
Admissions E-mail: mba@fullerton.edu • **Web Address:** business.fullerton.edu

The Fullerton MBA offers three plans for the attainment of a Master in Business Administration. The MBA Generalist plan is constructed for those applicants who have little or no business course work or work experience; the MBA Specialist plan is designed for applicants who have recent business course work or experience and allows them to select an area of concentration; and the MBA International Business plan is designed for students with prior business education who wish to specialize in international business. Most Fullerton MBA students are working professionals, commuting to campus from work and attending afternoon or evening classes.

INSTITUTIONAL INFORMATION

Public/Private: Public
Evening Classes Available? Yes
Total Faculty: 44
% Faculty Female: 18
% Faculty Minority: 7
% Faculty Part Time: 7
Student/Faculty Ratio: 20:1
Students in Parent Institution: 30,000
Academic Calendar: Semester

PROGRAMS

Degrees Offered: MBA, Specialist (33 credits, part time, 1-5 years), with concentrations in Accounting, Finance, Management, Management Science, Management Information Systems, Marketing; MBA, distance learning option (57 credits, part time, 2-5 years); MST (30 credits, full time or part time, 1-5 years); MS in Management Science (33 credits, full time or part time, 1-5 years), with concentration in Management Information Systems; MSA (30 credits, full time or part time, 1-5 years)

Academic Specialties: Financial Accounting, Auditing, Managerial Accounting, Cost Accounting, Accounting Systems, Tax, Advanced Accounting, Governmental Accounting, International Economics, Macroeconomics, Money and Banking, International Trade, Economic Development, Economic Theory, Social Security, Financial Institutions, Corporate Finance, Real Estate, Business Law, Small Business Management, Strategic Management, Operations Management, Organizational Behavior, Human Resource Management, Strategic Management, Marketing Management, Marketing Analysis and Planning, Marketing Research, Marketing Technology, Computer Science, Micro-computers, Multivariate Analysis, Operations Research, Statistics, Information Systems, Supply Chain Management

STUDENT INFORMATION

Total Business Students: 351

COMPUTER AND RESEARCH FACILITIES

Research Facilities: SAP, XBRL, Center for Entrepreneurship, Center for the Study of Emerging Financial Markets, Center for Insurance Studies, Center for International Business Program, Family Business Council, Institute for Economic & Environmental Studies, Real Estate and Land Use Institute, Small Business Council
Computer Facilities: Computer labs, areas on campus of wireless Internet access, individual student portals for Internet access, numerous databases available through the library on the Internet
Campuswide Network? Yes

% of MBA Classrooms Wired: 100
Internet Fee? No

EXPENSES/FINANCIAL AID

Tuition Per Credit (Resident/Nonresident): $246
Room & Board (On/Off Campus): $9,056/$10,810
Books and Supplies: $810
Average Grant: $1,772
Average Loan: $8,750
% Receiving Financial Aid: 52
% Receiving Aid Their First Year: 18

ADMISSIONS INFORMATION

Application Fee: $55
Electronic Application? Yes
Regular Application Deadline: Rolling
Regular Notification: Rolling
Deferment Available? No
Non-fall Admissions? Yes
Non-fall Application Deadline(s): 11/1 spring
Transfer Students Accepted? Yes
Transfer Policy: Student must apply as a new student, and courses will be evaluted.
Need-Blind Admissions? No
Number of Applications Received: 456
% of Applicants Accepted: 39
% Accepted Who Enrolled: 56
Average GPA: 3.2
Average GMAT: 519
Other Admissions Factors Considered: Admission is competitive and depends on the applicant's personal information, letters of recommendation, GPA, and GMAT score. Admission is based on the caliber of applicants applying each semester, and the most qualified students are offered admission.

INTERNATIONAL STUDENTS

TOEFL Required of International Students? Yes
Minimum TOEFL: 570 (230 computer)

EMPLOYMENT INFORMATION

Placement Office Available? Yes
Frequent Employers: Ernst and Young, Home Depot, LLP, Mercury, Target
Prominent Alumni: Steve Charton, president and CEO; Kevin Costner, business man and actor; Robert Grant, managing partner; Maurice Myers, president and CEO; Shirley Reel Caldwell, president

CALIFORNIA STATE UNIVERSITY— HAYWARD

College of Business and Economics

Admissions Contact: Maria De Anda-Ramos, Director of Enrollment Services, Admissions and Recruitment
Address: 25800 Carles Bee Boulevard, Hayward, CA 94542
Admissions Phone: 510-885-2784 • **Admissions Fax:** 510-885-4059
Admissions E-mail: adminfo@csuhayward.edu • **Web Address:** cbegrad.csuhayward.edu

Hayward's MBA program proudly houses a student body with female and minority populations of more than 50 percent. The MBA has a multitude of concentrations, from new venture management and telecommunications to materials management and taxation. Hayward MBA students can participate

in a great selection of study abroad options, should they wish to leave Hayward, known locally as the "Heart of the Bay." Graduates of CSU—Hayward have been hired by Bay Area companies such as Chevron and Pacific Gas & Electric.

INSTITUTIONAL INFORMATION

Public/Private: Public
Evening Classes Available? Yes
Total Faculty: 75
% Faculty Part Time: 45
Students in Parent Institution: 10,952
Academic Calendar: Quarter

PROGRAMS

Degrees Offered: MBA (45 credits, part time, 1-5 years), with concentrations in Accounting, Economics, Computer Information Systems, E-Business, Finance, Human Resources, International Business, Management, Marketing, New Ventures/Small Business, Operations & Materials Management, Operations Research, Supply Chain Management, Strategic Management, Taxation, Telecommunications Management; MST (45 credits, part time, 1-5 years), with concentration in Taxation; MSBA: Computer Information Systems/Quantitative (45 credits, part time, 1-5 years), with concentrations in Decision Sciences, Management Information Systems; MA in Economics (45 credits, part time, 1-5 years), with concentration in Economics; MS in Telecommunication Systems (45 credits, part time, 1-5 years)
Study Abroad Options: Brazil, China, England, France, Germany, Hong Kong, Indonesia, Japan, Russia, and Singapore

STUDENT INFORMATION

Total Business Students: 763
% Full Time: 30
% Female: 47
% Minority: 67
% Out of State: 59
% International: 42
Average Age: 32

COMPUTER AND RESEARCH FACILITIES

Research Facilities: Alameda Center for Environmental Technologies (ACET); China America Business and Education Center (CABEC); Center for Business and Environmental Studies (CBES); Center for Economics Education (CEE); Center for Sustaining Development and Environmental Technologies (CSDET); California Urban Environmental Research Center (CUEREC); Center for Entrepreneurship; Environmental Finance Center, Region IX (EFC 9); Human Investment Research and Education Center (HIRE); Institute for Research and Business Development (IRBD); Small Business Institute (SBI); Smith Center for Private Enterprise Studies; Institute for Telecommunications Technologies
Campuswide Network? Yes
Internet Fee? No

EXPENSES/FINANCIAL AID

Annual Tuition (Resident/Nonresident): $2,808/$11,832
Room & Board (On/Off Campus): $6,435/$7,704
Books and Supplies: $10,000
Average Grant: $1,804
Average Loan: $10,304
% Receiving Financial Aid: 8
% Receiving Aid Their First Year: 8

ADMISSIONS INFORMATION

Application Fee: $55
Electronic Application? Yes
Regular Application Deadline: 6/1
Regular Notification: 6/21
Deferment Available? Yes
Length of Deferment: 1 quarter
Non-fall Admissions? Yes

Non-fall Application Deadline(s): 9/1 winter, 1/1 spring; international: 3/1 fall, 10/1 spring, winter 6/1
Transfer Students Accepted? No
Need-Blind Admissions? No
Number of Applications Received: 415
% of Applicants Accepted: 74
% Accepted Who Enrolled: 60
Average GPA: 3.2
Average GMAT: 540
Average Years Experience: 8
Other Admissions Factors Considered: Computer experience required: word processing, spreadsheet, database. GMAT score and letters of recommendation are recommended for application.
Minority/Disadvantaged Student Recruitment Programs: Educational Opportunity Program
Other Schools to Which Students Applied: San Jose State University, San Francisco State University, University of California—Berkeley

INTERNATIONAL STUDENTS

TOEFL Required of International Students? Yes
Minimum TOEFL: 550 (213 computer)

EMPLOYMENT INFORMATION

Placement Office Available? Yes
% Employed Within 3 Months: 99
Frequent Employers: Arthur D. Little, Bank of America, Chevron, Clorox, Hewlett-Packard, IBM, Intel, Mitsubishi, Oracle, Pricewaterhouse Coopers, SBC, Sony, Sun Microsystems, Sybase, Wells Fargo
Prominent Alumni: Georgeanne Proctor, vice president, Bechtel Corp.; Gary C. Wallace, senior partner, KPMG; Tom Coughlin, president and CEO, Wal-Mart; Hank Salvo, vice president and controller, Clorox; Scott Kriens, CEO, Juniper Networks

CALIFORNIA STATE UNIVERSITY— LONG BEACH
College of Business Administration

Admissions Contact: Paula Gloeckner, MBA Evaluator
Address: 1250 Bellflower Boulevard, Long Beach, CA 90840-0119
Admissions Phone: 562-985-7988 • **Admissions Fax:** 562-985-5590
Admissions E-mail: mba@csulb.edu • **Web Address:** www.csulb.edu/~cba/

INSTITUTIONAL INFORMATION

Public/Private: Public
Evening Classes Available? Yes
Total Faculty: 63
Student/Faculty Ratio: 25:1
Students in Parent Institution: 33,000
Academic Calendar: Semester

PROGRAMS

Degrees Offered: Fully employed MBA (2 years part time), MBA (36-50 credits, full time or part time, 18 months to 7 years), with concentrations in Finance, Human Resources, Management, Management Information Systems, Marketing, Accounting, Health Care

STUDENT INFORMATION

Total Business Students: 310
% Full Time: 35
% Female: 37

% Minority: 21
% Out of State: 1
% International: 30
Average Age: 28

COMPUTER AND RESEARCH FACILITIES

Campuswide Network? Yes
Internet Fee? No

EXPENSES/FINANCIAL AID

Annual Tuition (Resident/Nonresident): $5,076
Tuition Per Credit (Resident/Nonresident): $282

ADMISSIONS INFORMATION

Application Fee: $55
Electronic Application? No
Regular Application Deadline: 5/30
Regular Notification: 4/15
Deferment Available? Yes
Length of Deferment: 1 semester
Non-fall Admissions? Yes
Non-fall Application Deadline(s): 10/30 spring
Transfer Students Accepted? Yes
Transfer Policy: Must meet our admissions criteria
Need-Blind Admissions? No
Number of Applications Received: 289
% of Applicants Accepted: 52
% Accepted Who Enrolled: 75
Average GPA: 3.3
GPA Range: 2.7-4.0
Average GMAT: 560
GMAT Range: 480-710
Average Years Experience: 5
Other Admissions Factors Considered: A resume is required for admission, as is a minimum GPA of 2.75. Work experience and computer experience are recommended.
Other Schools to Which Students Applied: California State University—Fullerton, University of California—Irvine, Pepperdine University, California State University—Los Angeles

INTERNATIONAL STUDENTS

TOEFL Required of International Students? Yes
Minimum TOEFL: 550 (213 computer)

EMPLOYMENT INFORMATION

Placement Office Available? Yes

CALIFORNIA STATE UNIVERSITY— LOS ANGELES

College of Business and Economics

Admissions Contact: Cindy Leiby-Smith, Admissions Officer
Address: 5151 State University Drive, Los Angeles, CA 90032
Admissions Phone: 323-343-3901 • Admissions Fax: 323-343-6306
Admissions E-mail: admissions@calstatela.edu • Web Address: cbe.calstatela.edu/

INSTITUTIONAL INFORMATION

Public/Private: Public
Evening Classes Available? No
Total Faculty: 82

% Faculty Part Time: 33
Students in Parent Institution: 18,849
Academic Calendar: Quarter

PROGRAMS

Degrees Offered: MBA (2 years of work experience required; 48 credits, full time or part time, 18 months to 4 years), with concentrations in Accounting, Business Information Science, Economics, Finance, International Business, Management, Marketing, Health Care; MSBA (45 credits, full time or part time, 18 months to 4 years), with concentrations in Economics, Finance, International Business, Management, Management Information Systems, Marketing; MSA (45 credits, full time or part time, 18 months to 4 years), with concentration in Accounting; MS in Health Care Management (45 credits, full time or part time, 18 months to 4 years), with concentration in Health Care; MA in Economics (45 credits, full timeor part time, 18 months to 4 years), with concentrations in Financial Economics, International Economics
Special Opportunities: Accounting, CIS or MIS, Economics, Finance (includes Banking), Health Services/Hospital Administration, International Business, Management, Marketing

STUDENT INFORMATION

Total Business Students: 330
% Full Time: 0
Average Age: 31

COMPUTER AND RESEARCH FACILITIES

Research Facilities: John F. Kennedy Memorial Library: total holdings of 1,147,573 volumes; 814,721 microforms; 2,134 current periodical subscriptions. CD player(s) are available for graduate student use; access is provided to online bibliographic retrieval services and online databases.
Campuswide Network? Yes
Internet Fee? No

EXPENSES/FINANCIAL AID

Annual Tuition (Resident/Nonresident): $1,796/$5,732

ADMISSIONS INFORMATION

Electronic Application? No
Regular Application Deadline: 6/15
Regular Notification: 1/1
Deferment Available? No
Non-fall Admissions? Yes
Non-fall Application Deadline(s): 10/1 winter, 12/1 spring, 3/1 summer; international: 3/1 fall, 9/1 winter, 10/1 spring
Transfer Students Accepted? No
Need-Blind Admissions? No
Number of Applications Received: 388
% of Applicants Accepted: 43
% Accepted Who Enrolled: 52
Other Admissions Factors Considered: A minimum GMAT score of 550 and GPA of 3.0 is required. Three letters of recommendation and a minimum of 2 years of work experience are also required. An interview and computer experience are recommended.

EMPLOYMENT INFORMATION

Placement Office Available? Yes
% Employed Within 3 Months: 95

CALIFORNIA STATE UNIVERSITY— NORTHRIDGE

College of Business and Economics

Admissions Contact: Tammy Lee Tolgo, Assistant Director of Graduate Programs
Address: 18111 Nordhoff Street, Northridge, CA 91330-8380
Admissions Phone: 818-677-2467 • **Admissions Fax:** 818-677-3188
Admissions E-mail: mba@csun.edu • **Web Address:** csun.edu/mba

INSTITUTIONAL INFORMATION

Public/Private: Public
Evening Classes Available? Yes
Total Faculty: 34
% Faculty Female: 18
% Faculty Minority: 6
% Faculty Part Time: 3
Student/Faculty Ratio: 22:1
Students in Parent Institution: 30,000
Academic Calendar: Semester

PROGRAMS

Degrees Offered: Evening MBA (3 years average)
Academic Specialties: Family business studies, marketing to customer orientation (off-site with J.D. Power & Associates), strategic management, antitrust, labor and economics, computer-based learning and writing technologies, health industry
Special Opportunities: Small-business consulting in conjunction with the SBA and SBDC, tax and accounting programs in conjunction with the IRS, entertainment industry program in conjunction with university-wide center

STUDENT INFORMATION

Total Business Students: 275
% Full Time: 15
% Female: 50
% Minority: 50
Average Age: 29

COMPUTER AND RESEARCH FACILITIES

Research Facilities: Entertainment Industry (cross-discipline with College of Art, Media and Communication, and College of Engineering), Family Business Institute, Center for the Study of the San Fernando Valley, Small Business Institute, IRS-related programs providing tax form completion and audit assistance, Center for the Study of Insurance, Landlord-Tenant Clinic
Computer Facilities: Lexis-Nexis, Dow Jones, AMSPEC, Carl UnCover, and a myriad of other data and research resourses
Campuswide Network? Yes
% of MBA Classrooms Wired: 100
Internet Fee? No

EXPENSES/FINANCIAL AID

Annual Tuition (Resident/Nonresident): $2,000/$4,000
Books and Supplies: $200

ADMISSIONS INFORMATION

Application Fee: $55
Electronic Application? Yes
Regular Application Deadline: 5/1
Regular Notification: Rolling
Deferment Available? No
Non-fall Admissions? Yes
Non-fall Application Deadline(s): 10/1
Transfer Students Accepted? Yes
Transfer Policy: Maximum of 9 units transfer credit
Need-Blind Admissions? Yes

% Accepted Who Enrolled: 74
Average GPA: 3.3
Average Years Experience: 6

INTERNATIONAL STUDENTS

TOEFL Required of International Students? Yes
Minimum TOEFL: 550 (213 computer)

EMPLOYMENT INFORMATION

Placement Office Available? No
% Employed Within 3 Months: 90

CALIFORNIA STATE UNIVERSITY— SACRAMENTO

College of Business Administration

Admissions Contact: Jeanie Allam, Graduate Program Advisor
Address: 6000 J Street, Sacramento, CA 95819-6088
Admissions Phone: 916-278-6772 • **Admissions Fax:** 916-278-4979
Admissions E-mail: cbagrad@csus.edu • **Web Address:** www.csus.edu/cbagrad/index.html

Educated on the banks of the American River, Sacramento MBA students will thrive in this leadership-oriented program, not only from the high-quality education designed to meet the needs of working professionals, but also from the multiple degree options offered within the business school. CSU Sacramento is affiliated with many international business schools, affording the student several study abroad options, along with several additional educational opportunities at any of the Cal State universities in the region. New students will reap the benefits of an ambitious construction project involving a new alumni center and the expansion of the student union.

INSTITUTIONAL INFORMATION

Public/Private: Public
Evening Classes Available? Yes
Total Faculty: 26
% Faculty Female: 27
% Faculty Part Time: 7
Student/Faculty Ratio: 14:1
Students in Parent Institution: 26,923
Academic Calendar: Semester

PROGRAMS

Degrees Offered: MBA (33-55 credits; 1 year full time, 2 years part time), with concentrations in Accounting, Finance, Human Resources, Management Information Systems, Marketing, Urban Land Development; MSA (30-49 credits; 1 year full time, 2 years part time), with concentrations in Accounting, Taxation; MSBA (30-55 credits, 1.5 years full time, 2.5 years part time), with concentrations in Management Information Systems, Taxation
Combined Degrees: MBA/JD at McGeorge School of Law (approximately 4 years full time)
Academic Specialties: The faculty at CSUS are focused on teaching.
Special Opportunities: Certificate of Advanced Business Studies (19-21 units of general business studies; 1 year full or part time)
Study Abroad Options: None

STUDENT INFORMATION

Total Business Students: 385
% Full Time: 35
% Female: 46

% Minority: 22
% International: 20
Average Age: 28

COMPUTER AND RESEARCH FACILITIES

Research Facilities: In cooperation with the University, the College of Business has just finished installing the new CBA wireless network. This means that soon any faculty, staff, or student will be able to cruise the Internet or connect to the network with a wireless device connected to a laptop or personal digital assistant (PDA). Users will not not have to be "plugged in" anywhere: they can roam around the building or even outside (25-50 feet from the building) with a laptop and check e-mail. The technology works as does any household cordless phone, so the signal strength will vary depending on where one is in the building. Currently, the Student Union, the library, and Computer Engineering department are the only other organizations participating. Laptop users can access the wireless network in these locations without changing their laptop settings.

Campuswide Network? Yes
Internet Fee? No

EXPENSES/FINANCIAL AID

Annual Tuition (Resident/Nonresident): $2,197/$7,273
Room & Board (On/Off Campus): $8,400/$7,400
Books and Supplies: $2,000

ADMISSIONS INFORMATION

Application Fee: $55
Electronic Application? Yes
Regular Application Deadline: 4/1
Regular Notification: 5/30
Deferment Available? Yes
Length of Deferment: 1 semester
Non-fall Admissions? Yes
Non-fall Application Deadline(s): 10/1 spring
Transfer Students Accepted? No
Need-Blind Admissions? Yes
Number of Applications Received: 275
% of Applicants Accepted: 29
% Accepted Who Enrolled: 59
Average GPA: 3.2
Average GMAT: 585
Average Years Experience: 4
Other Admissions Factors Considered: The admission decision is based primarily on an actual calculation (index) of [200 × GPA + GMAT]. Two indices are used: Index 1—using the applicants overall undergraduate GPA, the Index must equal 1050 or above; Index 2—using the students last 60-semester (90-quarter) unit GPA, the Index must meet 1100 or above. The applicant must meet both indices to be admitted. The required GMAT score would vary based on the student's GPA. However, a minimum total GMAT score of 500 with 30 percent in both the quantitative and verbal sections, and an overall undergraduate GPA of 2.5 are required. A resume, letters of recommendation, and work experience are all optional (except for the MSBA/MIS program, for which these items are required). Computer experience (word processing, spreadsheet, database) and statistics are required.

INTERNATIONAL STUDENTS

TOEFL Required of International Students? Yes
Minimum TOEFL: 550 (213 computer)

EMPLOYMENT INFORMATION

Placement Office Available? Yes
Frequent Employers: Chevron, EDS Corp., Franchise Tax, Franklin Templeton, Hewlett Packard, Investors Bank & Trust, State Board of Equalization, State Controllers Office
Prominent Alumni: Dennis Gardemeyer, executive vice president, Zuckerman-Hertog; Tom Weborg, CEO, Cucina Holdings; William Keever, president, Vodafone Airtouch; Margo Murray, president and CEO, MMHA The Mangers' Mentors Inc.; Scott Syphax, president and CEO, Nehemiah Corp.

CALIFORNIA STATE UNIVERSITY— SAN BERNARDINO
College of Business & Public Administration

Admissions Contact: Director of Admissions and Recruitment
Address: 5500 University Parkway, San Bernardino, CA 92407
Admissions Phone: 909-880-5703 • **Admissions Fax:** 909-880-7582
Admissions E-mail: mba@csusb.edu • **Web Address:** www.csusb.edu

Another of the many California State system MBA programs, the San Bernardino MBA stands its ground with a student body that's a whopping 80 percent international students from 24 foreign countries and a sweeping view of the San Bernardino Mountains from any point on campus. The MBA program is known for its small class sizes, student/faculty relationships, and affordable in-state business education.

INSTITUTIONAL INFORMATION

Public/Private: Public
Evening Classes Available? Yes
Total Faculty: 62
% Faculty Female: 22
% Faculty Minority: 8
Student/Faculty Ratio: 22:1
Students in Parent Institution: 15,797
Academic Calendar: 2002-2003

PROGRAMS

Degrees Offered: MBA (approximately 1.5 years full time, 3-4 years part-time evenings)
Academic Specialties: Eight concentrations in specific areas of Accounting, Entrepreneurship, Finance, Information Systems, Management and Human Resources, Management of Conflict, Operations and Marketing

STUDENT INFORMATION

Total Business Students: 342
% Full Time: 72
% Female: 42
% Minority: 3
% Out of State: 1
% International: 51
Average Age: 33

COMPUTER AND RESEARCH FACILITIES

Campuswide Network? Yes
% of MBA Classrooms Wired: 50
Internet Fee? No

EXPENSES/FINANCIAL AID

Annual Tuition (Resident/Nonresident): $2,200/$6,600
Tuition Per Credit (Resident/Nonresident): $84/$182
Room & Board (On/Off Campus): $8,000/$12,000
Books and Supplies: $2,000
Average Grant: $1,000
Average Loan: $8,000

ADMISSIONS INFORMATION

Application Fee: $55
Electronic Application? Yes
Early Decision Application Deadline: February 1
Early Decision Notification: 6/1
Regular Application Deadline: 7/1
Regular Notification: 9/1

Deferment Available? Yes
Length of Deferment: 1
Non-fall Admissions? Yes
Non-fall Application Deadline(s): 10/1, 1/1
Transfer Students Accepted? Yes
Transfer Policy: Only 3 graduate courses may be transferred into the MBA program.
Need-Blind Admissions? Yes
Number of Applications Received: 204
% of Applicants Accepted: 67
% Accepted Who Enrolled: 44
Average GPA: 3.1
Average GMAT: 522
Average Years Experience: 4
Other Schools to Which Students Applied: California State Polytechnic University—Pomona, California State University—Fullerton, California State University—Los Angeles

INTERNATIONAL STUDENTS

TOEFL Required of International Students? Yes
Minimum TOEFL: 550 (213 computer)

EMPLOYMENT INFORMATION

Placement Office Available? Yes
Frequent Employers: Arrowhead Credit Union, Arthur Andersen, Citizens Bank, Community Bank, ESRI, GTE, Kaiser Permanente, Southern California Edison; almost all the regional accounting firms, banks, credit unions, etc.

CANISIUS COLLEGE
Richard J. Wehle School of Business

Admissions Contact: Laura McEwen, Director, Graduate Business Programs
Address: 2001 Main Street, 201 Bagen Hall, Buffalo, NY 14208-1098
Admissions Phone: 716-888-2140 • **Admissions Fax:** 716-888-2145
Admissions E-mail: gradubus@canisius.edu • **Web Address:** www.canisius.edu/business/

The Richard Wehle School of Business is a private institution, renowned for its strong Jesuit tradition of ethical responsibility and hard work; in fact, Canisius College is named for St. Peter Canisius, who established multiple colleges and seminaries in the United States and in Europe, fueled by "his zeal for education as an agent for change." The Canisius MBA offers both a full-time one-year MBA and a part-time evening MBA. Students can look forward to frequent intimate interactions with their professors, some of whom are consultants with prestigious corporations such as Fisher Price, Mattel, and Federal Express.

INSTITUTIONAL INFORMATION

Public/Private: Private
Evening Classes Available? Yes
Total Faculty: 42
% Faculty Female: 17
% Faculty Minority: 4
% Faculty Part Time: 25
Student/Faculty Ratio: 15:1
Students in Parent Institution: 4,538
Academic Calendar: Semester

PROGRAMS

Degrees Offered: MBA (2-5 years), MBA in Professional Accounting (3-5 years), 1-year MBA Program (12 calendar months), MSTM (2 years)

Combined Degrees: Bachelor's degree/MBA (5 years)
Academic Specialties: AACSB certified (only 30% of U.S. business schools have this certification); students can finish in as little 12 months or as long as 5 years; Jesuit tradition of engaging students as individuals
Special Opportunities: Accounting, Finance (includes Banking), IS, Human Resource Management (includes Labor Relations), Marketing, Other

STUDENT INFORMATION

Total Business Students: 304
% Full Time: 24
% Female: 34
% Minority: 10
% International: 7
Average Age: 28

COMPUTER AND RESEARCH FACILITIES

Computer Facilities: Library Lab, Wehle Lab, Amherst lab; many databases available in 400,000-volume library
Campuswide Network? Yes
% of MBA Classrooms Wired: 100
Internet Fee? No

EXPENSES/FINANCIAL AID

Annual Tuition: $29,841
Tuition Per Credit (Resident/Nonresident): $621
Room & Board (On/Off Campus): $5,000
Books and Supplies: $1,000

ADMISSIONS INFORMATION

Application Fee: $25
Electronic Application? Yes
Regular Application Deadline: Rolling
Regular Notification: Rolling
Deferment Available? Yes
Length of Deferment: 1 year
Non-fall Admissions? Yes
Non-fall Application Deadline(s): Spring, summer
Transfer Students Accepted? Yes
Transfer Policy: Case-by-case basis
Need-Blind Admissions? No
Number of Applications Received: 165
% of Applicants Accepted: 58
% Accepted Who Enrolled: 61
Average GPA: 3.1
GPA Range: 2.8-3.4
Average GMAT: 510
GMAT Range: 460-557
Average Years Experience: 6
Other Schools to Which Students Applied: University at Buffalo/State University of New York

INTERNATIONAL STUDENTS

TOEFL Required of International Students? Yes
Minimum TOEFL: 500 (200 computer)

EMPLOYMENT INFORMATION

Placement Office Available? Yes

CARNEGIE MELLON UNIVERSITY

Admissions Contact: Laurie Stewart, Director of MBA Admissions
Address: 5000 Forbes Avenue, Pittsburgh, PA 15213
Admissions Phone: 412-268-2272 • **Admissions Fax:** 412-268-4209
Admissions E-mail: gsia-admissions@andrew.cmu.edu • **Web Address:** www.gsia.cmu.edu

Carnegie Mellon's renowned Graduate School of Industrial Administration is "boot camp for the brain," and its innovative, Nobel Prize–winning faculty are excellent. Particularly noteworthy is the "real world–oriented" Management Game, in which students negotiate mock contracts with actual union reps and secure "financing" through Pittsburgh banks. Students say "no task is too complicated, intense, or daunting" if you have "already survived Management Game."

INSTITUTIONAL INFORMATION

Public/Private: Private
Evening Classes Available? Yes
Total Faculty: 147
% Faculty Female: 11
% Faculty Minority: 22
% Faculty Part Time: 37
Student/Faculty Ratio: 5:1
Students in Parent Institution: 8,500
Academic Calendar: Mini semester

PROGRAMS

Degrees Offered: MBA (2 years), PhD (4-5 years), MS in Computational Finance (1 year), MS in Electronic Commerce (1 year)
Combined Degrees: Computational Finance & MBA (dual degree, 2.5 years), Software Engineering & MBA (dual degree, 2.5 years), Law & MBA (dual degree, 3-4 years), Software Engineering & MBA (joint degree, 2 years), Environmental Engineering & MBA (joint degree, 2 years), Civil Engineering & MBA (joint degree, 2 years). Future dual degrees available in 2003: Robotics & MBA, Cyber Security & MBA, Biomedical Engineering & MBA, Healthcare Policy/Management & MBA (Contact the Admissions Office for more details regarding these four new dual-degree programs.)
Academic Specialties: Production/Operations Management, Management Information Systems, Entrepreneurship, Finance, Electronic Commerce, Economics, Quantitative Analysis, Corporate Strategy, Management & Strategy, Organizational Behavior. Carnegie Mellon business school faculty work closely with other campus colleges to fully integrate course curriculum throughout the campus community. This standard of complete integration—both inside and outside the business school—sets the benchmark among the top 25 MBA programs. Additionally, Carnegie Mellon faculty are consistently represented among the highest scoring ratings for Intellectual Capital reviews, attesting to their worldwide recognition for innovative research, peer-reviewed published papers, global consulting network, as well as government and association appointments.
Study Abroad Options: Otto Beisheim School of Management (WHU); Berlin and Koblenz, Germany; Prague, Czech Republic; Slovakia

STUDENT INFORMATION

Total Business Students: 753
% Full Time: 62
% Female: 24
% Minority: 5
% International: 36
Average Age: 28

COMPUTER AND RESEARCH FACILITIES

Research Facilities: Carnegie Bosch Institute, Center for E-Business Innovation, Center for Financial Markets, Center for Interactive Simulations, Center for the Management of Technology, Gailliot Center for Public Policy, Donald H. Jones Center for Entrepreneurship, Green Design Initiative, Institute for Electronic Commerce, Institute for Strategic Management, Technology Transfer Office, Center for Interactive Simulations, Center for Business Communication, Center for International Corporate Responsibility, Carnegie Mellon Electricity Industry Center
Computer Facilities: Business Dateline, Commerce Biz Daily, Dunn & Bradstreet's, EconLit, FISonline, Hoover's Online, Lexis-Nexis, INFORMS PubOnline, InfoTrac, Investext, Knowledge Max, Net Advantage, ProQuest Direct, Statistical Universe, STAT/USA, Wilson Business Abstracts, Worldscope Global, Ethnic Newswatch, NetFirst, NetLibrary, OCLC
Campuswide Network? Yes
% of MBA Classrooms Wired: 100
Computer Model Recommended: Laptop
Internet Fee? No

EXPENSES/FINANCIAL AID

Annual Tuition: $29,750
Tuition Per Credit (Resident/Nonresident): $329
Room & Board (On/Off Campus): $10,775
Books and Supplies: $3,965
Average Grant: $7,500
Average Loan: $25,000
% Receiving Financial Aid: 80
% Receiving Aid Their First Year: 78

ADMISSIONS INFORMATION

Application Fee: $100
Electronic Application? Yes
Regular Application Deadline: 3/31
Regular Notification: 5/15
Deferment Available? Yes
Length of Deferment: 2 years
Non-fall Admissions? No
Transfer Students Accepted? No
Need-Blind Admissions? Yes
Number of Applications Received: 1,781
% of Applicants Accepted: 26
% Accepted Who Enrolled: 54
Average GPA: 3.3
GPA Range: 3.0-3.6
Average GMAT: 661
GMAT Range: 620-700
Average Years Experience: 5
Minority/Disadvantaged Student Recruitment Programs: Challenge Weekend; member of the Consortium for Graduate Study in Management
Other Schools to Which Students Applied: Cornell University, Massachusetts Institute of Technology, New York University, University of Chicago, University of Michigan, University of Pennsylvania, Northwestern University

INTERNATIONAL STUDENTS

TOEFL Required of International Students? Yes
Minimum TOEFL: 600 (250 computer)

EMPLOYMENT INFORMATION

Placement Office Available? Yes
% Employed Within 3 Months: 79
Fields Employing Percentage of Grads: Other (3%), Strategic Planning (3%), Operations (6%), MIS (6%), General Management (8%), Consulting (12%), Marketing (14%), Finance (47%)
Frequent Employers: Alcoa, Bank of America, Citigroup, Ford Motor Co., Goodyear Tire and Rubber Co., Honeywell, IBM, Merck, M+T Bank, United Technologies Corp.
Prominent Alumni: Francois De Carbonnel, chief strategic officer, Citigroup, Inc.; Frank Risch, vice president and treasurer, ExxonMobil Corp. HQ; Dina Dublon, executive vice president and CFO, JP Morgan Chase; David Coulter, vice chairman, JP Morgan Chase & Co.; Yoshiaki Fujimori, president & CEO, GE (General Electric) Asia

CASE WESTERN RESERVE UNIVERSITY
Weatherhead School of Management

Admissions Contact: Christine L. Gill, Director of Marketing and Admissions
Address: 160 Peter B. Lewis Building, 10900 Euclid Avenue, Cleveland, OH 44106-7235
Admissions Phone: 216-368-2030 • **Admissions Fax:** 216-368-5548
Admissions E-mail: questions@exchange.cwru.edu
Web Address: www.weatherhead.cwru.edu

Outstanding aspects of Case Western Reserve's Weatherhead School of Management include its administrative "flexibility," a faculty "open to new course ideas and curriculum enhancements," and a cutting-edge, wavy-looking new building designed by Frank O. Gehry. The "team-oriented" classes here are "very challenging, but rewarding" as well, and "you'll be up to your ears in group projects with students from many other countries" from day one.

INSTITUTIONAL INFORMATION

Public/Private: Private
Evening Classes Available? Yes
Total Faculty: 96
% Faculty Female: 18
% Faculty Minority: 2
% Faculty Part Time: 2
Student/Faculty Ratio: 10:1
Students in Parent Institution: 9,530
Academic Calendar: Semester

PROGRAMS

Degrees Offered: EDM (3 years), EMBA (2 years), MBA (2 years), Accelerated MBA (11 months), MNO (2 years), MACC (1 year), MSM-Operations Research (1 year), MSM-Supply Chain (1 year), MOD (2 years), MEM (2 years)
Combined Degrees: MBA/JD (4 years), MD/MBA (5 years), MSN/MBA (2.5 years), MNO/JD (4 years), MNO/MA (2.5 years), MBA/MSSA (2.5 years), MBA/MIM (2.5 years), MACC/MBA (2 years), MBS/MPH (2.5 years)
Academic Specialties: Marketing, Finance, MIS, Entrepreneurship, Bioscience Management, Nonprofit Management, Health Systems Management, Operations Management, Organizational Behavior, Technology Management, Human Resource Management, International Management, E-Business, Leadership Assessment and Development, Emotional Intelligence, Competency-Based Learning, Appreciative Inquiry
Special Opportunities: Weatherhead Mentor Program, International Exchange Programs, International Institutes, Community Service Certificate, Public Policy Certificate, Health Systems Management Certificate, Nonprofit Management Certificate, E-Business Certificate, Professional Fellows Program, International Fest
Study Abroad Options: Exchange programs: Wirtschaftsuniversitat Wien, Austria; Instituto Centroamerico de Administracion de Empresas, Costa Rica; Copenhagen Business School, Denmark; Manchester Business School, England; University of Strasbourg, EM Lyon, France; Otto Beisheim Graduate School of Management, Germany; International Management Center, Hungary; Tel Aviv University, Israel; Instituto Tecnologico y de Estudios Superiores de Monterrey, Instituto Tecnologico Autonomo de Mexico, Mexico; Norwegian School of Management, Norway; Asian Institute of Management, Philippines; ESADE, Spain; WITS University, South Africa International institutes: Australia, Austria, China, Costa Rica, Czech Republic, France, Germany, Hungary, Mexico, Slovakia, South Africa, Spain

STUDENT INFORMATION

Total Business Students: 1,248
% Full Time: 35
% Female: 28
% Minority: 10

% Out of State: 60
% International: 43
Average Age: 28

COMPUTER AND RESEARCH FACILITIES

Research Facilities: Center for Regional Economic Issues; Enterprise Development, Inc.; Health Systems Management Center; Mandel Center for Nonprofit Organizations
Computer Facilities: Switched gigabit Ethernet connections in all classrooms, offices, study areas, meeting rooms, seminar rooms, and other common areas; pervasive wireless network access points; audiovisual facilities in classrooms, seminar, and meeting rooms; a state-of-the art teleconferencing classroom; a 24-seat Computer Lab and 24-seat, hands-on PC Training Lab, which is open to students more than 100 hours a week; an extensive suite of business and educational software on the Lab and Training Room machines; a help desk offering walk-in and phone support; faculty and student support for CWRU's Blackboard E-Learning system; free computer-familiarization workshops
Campuswide Network? Yes
% of MBA Classrooms Wired: 100
Computer Model Recommended: Laptop
Internet Fee? No

EXPENSES/FINANCIAL AID

Annual Tuition: $26,460
Tuition Per Credit (Resident/Nonresident): $1,103
Room & Board (On/Off Campus): $10,500/$14,355
Books and Supplies: $1,209
Average Grant: $9,351
Average Loan: $19,194
% Receiving Financial Aid: 79
% Receiving Aid Their First Year: 77

ADMISSIONS INFORMATION

Application Fee: $50
Electronic Application? Yes
Early Decision Application Deadline: 1/31
Early Decision Notification: 3/3
Regular Application Deadline: 3/22
Regular Notification: 4/15
Deferment Available? No
Non-fall Admissions? Yes
Non-fall Application Deadline(s): Full time accelerated: 4/19 summer; part time: 7/1 fall, 12/7 spring, 5/3 summer
Transfer Students Accepted? Yes
Transfer Policy: Maximum number of transferable credits is 6 semester hours from an AACSB-accredited program.
Need-Blind Admissions? Yes
Number of Applications Received: 707
% of Applicants Accepted: 45
% Accepted Who Enrolled: 49
Average GPA: 3.2
GPA Range: 2.8-3.4
Average GMAT: 608
GMAT Range: 540-690
Average Years Experience: 6
Other Admissions Factors Considered: Diversity of work and/or educational experience, demonstrated leadership abilities, demonstrated community involvement
Minority/Disadvantaged Student Recruitment Programs: On-campus scholars weekends, networking with minority professional associations and Weatherhead alumni
Other Schools to Which Students Applied: Ohio State University, University of Michigan, University of Notre Dame, University of Pittsburgh, University of Virginia, Vanderbilt University, Washington University of St. Louis

INTERNATIONAL STUDENTS

TOEFL Required of International Students? Yes
Minimum TOEFL: 600 (250 computer)

EMPLOYMENT INFORMATION

Placement Office Available? Yes
% Employed Within 3 Months: 68
Fields Employing Percentage of Grads: Human Resources (5%), Other (6%), Operations (6%), General Management (11%), Consulting (11%), Marketing (29%), Finance (32%)
Frequent Employers: In 2002: American Electric Power, Capital One, Emerson Electric, FBI, Johnson & Johnson, Johnson Controls, KeyCorp, McKinsey & Co., National City Corp., Progressive Corp., Samsung Electronics, TRW
Prominent Alumni: John Breen, CEO (ret.), Sherwin Williams; Clayton Deutsch, managing partner, McKinsey & Co.; David Daberko, chairman and CEO, National City Bank; John Neff, CEO (ret.), Vanguard Fund; Joseph Sabatini, managing director, JP Morgan

See page 412.

CENTRAL MICHIGAN UNIVERSITY
College of Business Administration

Admissions Contact: Pamela Stambersky, Director of Graduate Programs
Address: 105 Warriner Hall, Mount Pleasant, MI 48859
Admissions Phone: 517-774-3150 • **Admissions Fax:** 517-774-2372
Admissions E-mail: Pamela.Stambersky@cmich.edu • **Web Address:** www.cba.cmich.edu

INSTITUTIONAL INFORMATION

Public/Private: Public
Evening Classes Available? No
Total Faculty: 97
Students in Parent Institution: 16,613
Academic Calendar: Semester

PROGRAMS

Degrees Offered: MBA (30 credits, full time or part time; 1 to 4.2 years), with concentrations in Accounting, Finance, Human Resources, International Business, Management Information Systems, Marketing; MBE (36 credits, full time or part time, 1-7 years)
Special Opportunities: Accounting, Economics, Finance (includes Banking), General Business, Human Resource Management (includes Labor Relations), International Business, Marketing, Other

STUDENT INFORMATION

Total Business Students: 471
% Full Time: 50
% Female: 41
% Minority: 1
% International: 34
Average Age: 28

COMPUTER AND RESEARCH FACILITIES

Research Facilities: Park Library; total holdings of 697,546 volumes; 1,143,156 microforms; 5,285 current periodical subscriptions. CD player(s) available for graduate student use; access to online bibliographic retrieval services
Campuswide Network? Yes
Internet Fee? No

EXPENSES/FINANCIAL AID

Annual Tuition (Resident/Nonresident): $3,192/$5,818

ADMISSIONS INFORMATION

Application Fee: $30
Electronic Application? No
Regular Application Deadline: Rolling
Regular Notification: Rolling
Deferment Available? Yes
Non-fall Admissions? No
Transfer Students Accepted? No
Need-Blind Admissions? No
Number of Applications Received: 151
% of Applicants Accepted: 80
Other Admissions Factors Considered: Computer experience is required: spreadsheet, database, presentation graphics. A minimum GMAT score of 400 and GPA of 2.5 are required. Work experience is recommended.

INTERNATIONAL STUDENTS

TOEFL Required of International Students? Yes
Minimum TOEFL: 550

EMPLOYMENT INFORMATION

Placement Office Available? Yes

CENTRAL MISSOURI STATE UNIVERSITY
Harmon College of Business Administration

Admissions Contact: Terry Hazen, Admissions Evaluator, Graduate School
Address: Ward Edwards 1800, Warrensburg, MO 64093
Admissions Phone: 660-543-4621 • **Admissions Fax:** 660-543-4778
Admissions E-mail: thazen@cmsu1.cmsu.edu • **Web Address:** cis.cmsu.edu/hcba/

The average age of graduate students at the Harmon College of Business Administration is 35, as the MBA program is designed for the working professional. The students can expect a tightly knit educational community thanks to the MBA Association, a student-run organization that coordinates a renowned mentorship program, bridging MBA students with business managers in Kansas City and west central Missouri. The traditional MBA curriculum is complemented by a prestigious and competitive internship program.

INSTITUTIONAL INFORMATION

Public/Private: Public
Evening Classes Available? Yes
Total Faculty: 42
% Faculty Female: 29
% Faculty Minority: 1
% Faculty Part Time: 0
Student/Faculty Ratio: 2:1
Students in Parent Institution: 10,313
Academic Calendar: Semester

PROGRAMS

Degrees Offered: MBA (33 hours), with concentrations in Accounting, Information Systems, Finance, Marketing, Management; MSIT (33 hours); MA in Accountancy (33 hours)
Academic Specialties: Integration of core MBA courses
Study Abroad Options: Study abroad available based on student interest

STUDENT INFORMATION

Total Business Students: 52
% Full Time: 62
% Female: 38
% Minority: 22
% Out of State: 6
% International: 46
Average Age: 27

COMPUTER AND RESEARCH FACILITIES

Research Facilities: Institute for Entrepreneurial Studies and Development
Computer Facilities: On-campus computer facilities: Business Computing Center, Ward Edwards 2610; College of Education & Human Services Lab, Lovinger 402; College of Arts and Sciences Lab, Martin 231; Comp. U Center, Union 207; Harmon Computer Commons, James C. Kirkpatrick Library 1250; Learning Center, Humphreys 110; Safety Science and Technology Lab, Humphreys 312; Writing Center Lab, Humphreys 116; Psychology Lab, Lovinger 115. Databases available: Lexis-Nexis, Eric, Infotrak, MLA Bibliography, First Search, Ebsco Host, Criminal Justice Periodical Index, RSC (Checmistry Journals), Math Sci Net (Mathematics Journals), Shepard's Citations, CC Infoweb (Chemical Data), Gale Literary Index, College Source (College Catalogs)
Campuswide Network? Yes
% of MBA Classrooms Wired: 35
Internet Fee? No

EXPENSES/FINANCIAL AID

Annual Tuition (Resident/Nonresident): $3,580/$7,152
Tuition Per Credit (Resident/Nonresident): $160/$318
Room & Board (On/Off Campus): $4,000/$7,000
Books and Supplies: $500

ADMISSIONS INFORMATION

Application Fee: $25
Electronic Application? No
Regular Application Deadline: Rolling
Regular Notification: Rolling
Deferment Available? Yes
Length of Deferment: 2 semesters
Non-fall Admissions? Yes
Non-fall Application Deadline(s): Rolling
Transfer Students Accepted? Yes
Transfer Policy: A maximum of 8 hours may be transferred, and a B average or higher is required.
Need-Blind Admissions? Yes
Number of Applications Received: 98
% of Applicants Accepted: 59
% Accepted Who Enrolled: 60
Average GPA: 3.2
Average GMAT: 463
Other Admissions Factors Considered: None
Minority/Disadvantaged Student Recruitment Programs: None
Other Schools to Which Students Applied: University of Missouri—Kansas City, Southeast Missouri State University, Southwest Missouri State University, Widener University

INTERNATIONAL STUDENTS

TOEFL Required of International Students? Yes
Minimum TOEFL: 550 (213 computer)

EMPLOYMENT INFORMATION

Placement Office Available? Yes
Frequent Employers: Enterprise Rent-a-Car, Sherwin Williams, Sprint

CHAPMAN UNIVERSITY
The George L. Argyros School of Business and Economics

Admissions Contact: Debra Gonda, Associate Director
Address: Beckman Hall, One University Dr., Orange, CA 92866
Admissions Phone: 714-997-6745 • **Admissions Fax:** 714-997-6757
Admissions E-mail: gonda@chapman.edu • **Web Address:** www.chapman.edu/argyros/

If you're a mid-career manager or a senior level exec, you may want to get on board the Executive MBA program at the George L. Argyros School of Business and Economics. The EMBA offers a competitive, private education with a class size of about 50, and it takes only 22 months to complete. The program includes a trip to China to attend residential seminars and gain on-site education of the global economic community. The slightly younger applicants to the MBA program have the advantage of being under the tutelage of faculty with doctorates from prestigious institutions such as MIT and Cornell.

INSTITUTIONAL INFORMATION

Public/Private: Private
Evening Classes Available? Yes
Total Faculty: 22
% Faculty Female: 18
% Faculty Minority: 9
% Faculty Part Time: 0
Student/Faculty Ratio: 20:1
Students in Parent Institution: 4,591
Academic Calendar: Semester

PROGRAMS

Degrees Offered: MBA (2 years), EMBA (21 months)
Combined Degrees: JD/MBA (4 years)
Academic Specialties: The School has 3 centers that represent the strength of the School: the Anderson Center for Economic Research, the Ralph Leatherby Center for Entrepreneurship and Ethics, and the Walter Schmid Center for International Business.

STUDENT INFORMATION

Total Business Students: 131
% Full Time: 25
% Female: 51
% Minority: 5
Average Age: 27

COMPUTER AND RESEARCH FACILITIES

Computer Facilities: Computer labs with state-of-the-art IBM and MacIntosh computers
Campuswide Network? Yes
% of MBA Classrooms Wired: 100
Internet Fee? No

EXPENSES/FINANCIAL AID

Annual Tuition: $15,240
Tuition Per Credit (Resident/Nonresident): $635
Books and Supplies: $1,600
Average Grant: $3,500
Average Loan: $13,570
% Receiving Financial Aid: 35

ADMISSIONS INFORMATION

Application Fee: $40
Electronic Application? Yes
Regular Application Deadline: 7/1
Regular Notification: Rolling

Deferment Available? Yes
Length of Deferment: 1 year
Non-fall Admissions? Yes
Non-fall Application Deadline(s): 12/1 spring
Transfer Students Accepted? Yes
Transfer Policy: Up to 6 units of coursework
Need-Blind Admissions? Yes
Number of Applications Received: 118
% of Applicants Accepted: 54
% Accepted Who Enrolled: 58
Average GPA: 3.2
Average GMAT: 535
GMAT Range: 490-590
Average Years Experience: 0
Other Schools to Which Students Applied: California State University—Fullerton, Pepperdine University, University of California—Irvine, University of Southern California

INTERNATIONAL STUDENTS

TOEFL Required of International Students? Yes
Minimum TOEFL: 550 (213 computer)

EMPLOYMENT INFORMATION

Placement Office Available? Yes

CHINESE UNIVERSITY OF HONG KONG
MBA Programmes

Admissions Contact: Ms. Lauren Lee, Admissions Coordinator
Address: Rm. G01, Leung Kau Kui Building, CUHK, Shatin, New Territories, Hong Kong
Admissions Phone: 011-852-2609-7783 • **Admissions Fax:** 011-852-2603-6289
Admissions E-mail: cumba@cuhk.edu.hk • **Web Address:** www.cuhk.edu.hk/mba/

INSTITUTIONAL INFORMATION

Public/Private: Public
Evening Classes Available? Yes
% Faculty Female: 20
% Faculty Part Time: 7
Student/Faculty Ratio: 4:1
Students in Parent Institution: 15,071

PROGRAMS

Degrees Offered: Full-time MBA (51 credits, 18 months full time; 48 credits, 2-3 years part time evening or weekend); EMBA (48 credits, 2 years); MBA in Finance (2 years); MBA Global Program (21 months); MBA in Health Care (3 years); MS in Finance (30 credits, 2 years); Master of Philosophy in Business Administration (24 credits, 2-5 years); PhD in Business Administration (3-8 years); MACC (30 credits, 2-3 years); MS in Global Business Program (30 credits, 2-3 years); MSITM (33 credits, 18 months); MS in Business Economics (33 credits, 18 months); MS in E-Business (33 credits, 18 months); MS in Marketing (2 years)
Combined Degrees: Reciprocal recognition of credits program with HEC, France (2 years: 1 year at CUMBA and 1 year at HEC)
Academic Specialties: The No. 1 (Asia Inc. MBA Ranking, August 2002, and *BusinessWeek* EMBA ranking, October, 2001) Business School in Asia and the only Asian Business School ranked among the Top 20 (*Financial Times* EMBA ranking, October, 2002) in the world; consistently the premier business school in Hong Kong; accredited member of AACSB International; first chapter of Beta Gamma Sigma outside North America; long tradition of excellence in theory and practice; cross-cultural business education with special relevance to Hong Kong, Mainland China

and the world; student exchange programs with top business schools in the United States, Canada, Europe, Australia, and Asia; strong network with the business sector and the alumni; commitment to our society;a founding member of Global Workplace, which provides an exclusive online recruitment service for alumni
Study Abroad Options: Australia, Denmark, Canada, France, Japan, Spain, Switzerland, United Kingdom, United States

STUDENT INFORMATION

Total Business Students: 338
% Full Time: 20
% Female: 53
% International: 30
Average Age: 29

COMPUTER AND RESEARCH FACILITIES

Research Facilities: Office of China Research and Development: China's accession to the World Trade Organization and drive to develop her Western regions will facilitate further liberalization and opening of its economy. This presents both a challenge and opportunity for all the other economies in the region, Hong Kong and Taiwan in particular. Among the universities in the region, CUBA has the largest number of well-trained, proven researchers, multinational teaching staff, and bilingual publications in the areas of Chinese business and management to capitalize its comparative advantages. To further consolidate its strength, CUBA set up the Committee on China Research and Development (CCRD) in 1999 and the Office of China Research and Development (OCRD) in 2001. OCRD, as the operational arm of CCRD, is now directly managed by the Committee.
Computer Facilities: The University's state-of-the-art computer facilities are coordinated and networked at the University Information Technology Service Centre (ITSC), offering a vast array of Personal Computer Laboratory services to the academic, research, and administrative communities of the University. To cope with these different dimensions of services, ITSC has multiplexed its computer facility in recent years. This system is fully-networked—institutionally, locally, and internationally—and incorporates both high-powered mainframe computers as well as local area and personal computer systems. ITSC has recently established special-purpose laboratories furnished with high-tech facilities for multimedia development, optical mark scanning, color laser printing, image scanning, data visualization, and even user self-paced learning. Most of these facilities are accessible to the end user via the campus gigabit ethernet backbone network.

In addition to making the most of the general computing facilities of the University, the Faculty of Business Administration has also installed more than 100 microcomputers in a local area network (LAN) environment. These computing facilities are installed at the Personal Computer Laboratory of Fung King Hey Building for the use of faculty, students, and staff. On top of the many applications provided by the faculty, users of the PC Lab can also access all campuswide as well as Internet applications through the University's campuswide backbone network provided by the ITSC.

A LAN of Pentium-based PCs has also been installed at the Central MBA Town Centre for the use of the MBA and EMBA students. The PCs in the lecture rooms are integrated with contemporary audio/video systems to facilitate multimedia teaching. Access to the Internet and e-mail are also made available through a designated leased line.

Students of the MBA Programs are expected to be computer literate and are required to familiarize themselves with the use of computers in management. They are encouraged to use the above computer facilities for instruction and research purposes.
Campuswide Network? Yes
% of MBA Classrooms Wired: 100
Computer Model Recommended: Laptop
Internet Fee? No

EXPENSES/FINANCIAL AID

Annual Tuition (Resident/Nonresident):$16,385
Tuition Per Credit (Resident/Nonresident): $523
Room & Board (On/Off Campus): $3,000/$18,460
Books and Supplies: $10,974
Average Grant: $2,662
Average Loan: $1,282

ADMISSIONS INFORMATION

Application Fee: $25
Electronic Application? Yes
Regular Application Deadline: 2/28
Regular Notification: 5/10
Deferment Available? Yes
Length of Deferment: 1 year
Non-fall Admissions? No
Transfer Students Accepted? No
Need-Blind Admissions? Yes
Number of Applications Received: 912
% of Applicants Accepted: 47
% Accepted Who Enrolled: 61
Average GPA: 3.3
Average GMAT: 600
Average Years Experience: 4
Other Admissions Factors Considered: Consider all factors as a whole

EMPLOYMENT INFORMATION

Placement Office Available? Yes
% Employed Within 3 Months: 70
Fields Employing Percentage of Grads: Operations (2%), Other (3%), Human Resources (5%), General Management (11%), Marketing (13%), Accounting (14%), Consulting (20%), Finance (25%)
Frequent Employers: AMI Business Consulting, Citibank, DBS Kwong On Bank, Dah Sing Bank, Hong Kong & China Gas Co. Ltd., HKSAR Government, JP Morgan Chase Bank, KPMG, Mass Transit Railway Corp., Nestle (HK) Ltd., Park 'N Shop, Standard Chartered Bank
Prominent Alumni: Irving Koo, group marketing and corporate relations director, CLP Holdings; Rebecca Lai, permanent secretary for civil services, HKSARG; Roger Luk, managing director and deputy chief executive, Hang Seng Bank; Tat-lun Ng, managing director, Energizer Co. Inc.; Joseph Pang, executive director and deputy chief executive, Bank of East Asia Ltd.

See page 414.

THE CITADEL
College of Graduate and Professional Studies

Admissions Contact: Dr. Sheila Foster, MBA Director
Address: 171 Moultrie Street, Charleston, SC 29409
Admissions Phone: 803-953-5089 • **Admissions Fax:** 843-953-6764
Web Address: citadel.edu/citadel/otherserv/badm/

INSTITUTIONAL INFORMATION

Public/Private: Public
Evening Classes Available? Yes
Total Faculty: 18
Student/Faculty Ratio: 18:1
Academic Calendar: Semester

PROGRAMS

Degrees Offered: MBA (39 credits, 2-6 years)

STUDENT INFORMATION

Total Business Students: 143

COMPUTER AND RESEARCH FACILITIES

Campuswide Network? Yes
Internet Fee? No

EXPENSES/FINANCIAL AID

Tuition Per Credit (Resident/Nonresident): $150

ADMISSIONS INFORMATION

Application Fee: $25
Electronic Application? Yes
Regular Application Deadline: 1/1
Regular Notification: 1/1
Deferment Available? No
Non-fall Admissions? No
Transfer Students Accepted? No
Need-Blind Admissions? No
Number of Applications Received: 2
% of Applicants Accepted: 100
% Accepted Who Enrolled: 100
Other Admissions Factors Considered: Computer expereince

INTERNATIONAL STUDENTS

TOEFL Required of International Students? Yes
Minimum TOEFL: 550

EMPLOYMENT INFORMATION

Placement Office Available? Yes
% Employed Within 3 Months: 100

CLAREMONT GRADUATE UNIVERSITY
The Peter F. Drucker Graduate School of Management

Admissions Contact: Melanie C. Standridge, Assistant Director, MBA Admissions
Address: 1021 North Dartmouth Avenue, Claremont, CA 91711
Admissions Phone: 909-607-7811 • **Admissions Fax:** 909-607-9104
Admissions E-mail: drucker@cgu.edu • **Web Address:** www.drucker.cgu.edu

The chief draw of the Peter F. Drucker Graduate School of Management is the school's namesake. Mr. Drucker wrote The Practice of Management, *the sacred writ of MBAs the world over and the first book to recognize management as a distinct and important business skill. Students tell us there is a real "family atmosphere" here and a "super-high emphasis on hands-on learning," and "if you plan carefully, you can assemble a schedule of world-class professors."*

INSTITUTIONAL INFORMATION

Public/Private: Private
Evening Classes Available? Yes
Total Faculty: 12
% Faculty Female: 29
% Faculty Minority: 5
Student/Faculty Ratio: 12:1
Students in Parent Institution: 2,200
Academic Calendar: Semester

PROGRAMS

Degrees Offered: MBA (60 units), 4+1 accelerated program for undergraduates (48-60 units), MS in Financial Engineering (48 units), EMBA (48 units); PhD in Management (60 units)
Combined Degrees: Dual-degree programs in Human Resources, Information Sciences, Economics, Education, Psychology, and Public Policy, and by special arrangement in other disciplines

Academic Specialties: Strengths of faculty and curriculum in Strategic Management, Leadership/Ethics, Cost Management, Marketing, Finance, Risk Management

Special Opportunities: Strategic Management; International Fellows Program in Advanced English and Cultural Proficiency for Management

Study Abroad Options: England, France, Japan, Mexico, Switzerland

STUDENT INFORMATION

Total Business Students: 220
% Full Time: 65
% Female: 40
% Minority: 30
% Out of State: 10
% International: 35
Average Age: 28

COMPUTER AND RESEARCH FACILITIES

Research Facilities: Center for Advanced Studies in Leadership, New Venture Finance Institution, Quality of Life Research Center

Computer Facilities: Computer Lab in the Burkle Building dedicated to management students use with full range of software; academic computing lab accesible 24 hours per day; off-campus dial-in accounts available

Campuswide Network? Yes
% of MBA Classrooms Wired: 40
Computer Model Recommended: Laptop
Internet Fee? No

EXPENSES/FINANCIAL AID

Annual Tuition: $33,348
Tuition Per Credit (Resident/Nonresident): $1,099
Room & Board (On/Off Campus): $12,000
Books and Supplies: $810
Average Grant: $8,000
Average Loan: $18,500
% Receiving Financial Aid: 80
% Receiving Aid Their First Year: 60

ADMISSIONS INFORMATION

Application Fee: $50
Electronic Application? Yes
Regular Application Deadline: Rolling
Regular Notification: Rolling
Deferment Available? Yes
Length of Deferment: 2 semesters
Non-fall Admissions? Yes
Non-fall Application Deadline(s): 11/15 spring, 4/15 summer
Transfer Students Accepted? Yes
Transfer Policy: Maximum of 10 units
Need-Blind Admissions? Yes
Number of Applications Received: 350
% of Applicants Accepted: 71
% Accepted Who Enrolled: 48
Average GPA: 3.2
GPA Range: 2.8-3.7
Average GMAT: 610
GMAT Range: 550-680
Average Years Experience: 6
Other Admissions Factors Considered: Admissions decisions also influenced by leadership potential as indicated by experience and/or references
Minority/Disadvantaged Student Recruitment Programs: The Albrecht Endowed Fellowship is awarded to students who demonstrate academic and professional potential and financial need; other minority funding sources are available.
Other Schools to Which Students Applied: University of California—Los Angeles, University of Southern California, Pepperdine University

INTERNATIONAL STUDENTS

TOEFL Required of International Students? Yes
Minimum TOEFL: 600 (250 computer)

EMPLOYMENT INFORMATION

Placement Office Available? Yes
% Employed Within 3 Months: 85
Fields Employing Percentage of Grads: General Management (4%), Human Resources (5%), Operations (8%), Consulting (10%), MIS (10%), Marketing (18%), Other (20%), Finance (20%)
Frequent Employers: Accenture, Aerojet, Avery Deuison, Boeing, Deloitte and Touche, Rainbird
Prominent Alumni: Charles Emery, senior vice president and CEO, Horizon Blue CrossBlue Shield NJ; Stephen Rountree, executive vice president and COO, J. Paul Getty Trust; Rajiv Dutta, CFO, eBay, Inc.; Colin Forkner, president and CEO, California First National Bank; Brian Mulvaney, executive vice president, Aramark Corp.

See page 416.

CLARION UNIVERSITY
College of Business Administration

Admissions Contact: Dr. Robert S. Balough, Director of MBA Program
Address: 302 Still Hall, Clarion University, Clarion, PA 16214
Admissions Phone: 814-393-2605 • **Admissions Fax:** 814-393-1910
Admissions E-mail: mba@clarion.edu • **Web Address:** www.clarion.edu/mba

INSTITUTIONAL INFORMATION

Public/Private: Public
Evening Classes Available? No
Total Faculty: 22
% Faculty Female: 18
% Faculty Minority: 23
Students in Parent Institution: 6,541
Academic Calendar: Semester

PROGRAMS

Degrees Offered: MBA (33 credits, 11 months to 6 years)
Academic Specialties: Accreditation by AACSB International, the Association to Advance Collegiate Schools of Business

STUDENT INFORMATION

Total Business Students: 58
% Full Time: 93
% Female: 43
% Minority: 3
% International: 43
Average Age: 25

COMPUTER AND RESEARCH FACILITIES

Research Facilities: Data Analysis Research Center (DARC), Small Business Development Center (SBDC), Entrepreneurial Technology Center
Computer Facilities: Carlson Library, Still Hall Computer Lab. Databases: ABI Inform, Infotrac Business ASAP, EBSCO Business Databases, LexisNexis (Academic Universe), BRS, etc.
Campuswide Network? Yes
Internet Fee? No

EXPENSES/FINANCIAL AID

Annual Tuition (Resident/Nonresident): $5,254/$8,408

Tuition Per Credit (Resident/Nonresident): $256/$420
Room & Board (On/Off Campus): $4,344/$3,800
Books and Supplies: $3,000

ADMISSIONS INFORMATION

Application Fee: $30
Electronic Application? No
Regular Application Deadline: Rolling
Regular Notification: Rolling
Deferment Available? Yes
Length of Deferment: 1 year
Non-fall Admissions? Yes
Non-fall Application Deadline(s): Rolling
Transfer Students Accepted? Yes
Transfer Policy: May transfer up to 6 approved credits as electives
Need-Blind Admissions? Yes
Number of Applications Received: 74
% of Applicants Accepted: 89
% Accepted Who Enrolled: 48
Average GPA: 3.3
Average GMAT: 492
Average Years Experience: 2
Other Admissions Factors Considered: GMAT
Minority/Disadvantaged Student Recruitment Programs: Minority graduate assistantship positions are available.

INTERNATIONAL STUDENTS

TOEFL Required of International Students? Yes
Minimum TOEFL: 550 (213 computer)

EMPLOYMENT INFORMATION

Placement Office Available? Yes

COMPUTER AND RESEARCH FACILITIES

Campuswide Network? No
Internet Fee? No

EXPENSES/FINANCIAL AID

Annual Tuition: $13,237

ADMISSIONS INFORMATION

Application Fee: $40
Electronic Application? No
Regular Application Deadline: 4/1
Regular Notification: Rolling
Deferment Available? No
Non-fall Admissions? No
Transfer Students Accepted? No
Need-Blind Admissions? No
Number of Applications Received: 300
% of Applicants Accepted: 39
% Accepted Who Enrolled: 63
Average Years Experience: 99
Other Schools to Which Students Applied: Case Western Reserve University, Ohio State University, Bowling Green State University, Texas Tech University, John Carroll University, Ohio University, Brigham Young University

INTERNATIONAL STUDENTS

Minimum TOEFL: 500

EMPLOYMENT INFORMATION

Placement Office Available? Yes
% Employed Within 3 Months: 85

CLARK ATLANTA UNIVERSITY
School of Business Administration

Admissions Contact: Cele Echols, Director of Admissions and Financial Aid
Address: James P. Brawley Drive at Fair Street, Atlanta, GA 30314
Admissions Phone: 404-880-8447 • Admissions Fax: 404-880-6159
Web Address: www.cau.edu

INSTITUTIONAL INFORMATION

Public/Private: Private
Evening Classes Available? No
Total Faculty: 25
% Faculty Part Time: 3

PROGRAMS

Degrees Offered: MBA (60 credits, 21 months to 5 years), part-time MBA (minimum of 3 years work experience required; 54 credits, 21 months to 5 years); concentration in Finance and Marketing

STUDENT INFORMATION

Total Business Students: 155
% Full Time: 89
% Female: 60
% Minority: 92
% Out of State: 99
% International: 8
Average Age: 28

CLARK UNIVERSITY
Graduate School of Management

Admissions Contact: Patricia Tollo, Director of Admission, Graduate School of Management
Address: 950 Main Street, Worcester, MA 01610
Admissions Phone: 508-793-7406 • Admissions Fax: 508-793-8822
Admissions E-mail: clarkmba@clarku.edu • Web Address: www.clarku.edu/mba

INSTITUTIONAL INFORMATION

Public/Private: Private
Evening Classes Available? Yes
Total Faculty: 18
Student/Faculty Ratio: 14:1
Students in Parent Institution: 3,035
Academic Calendar: Semester

PROGRAMS

Degrees Offered: MBA (48 credits, 16 months to 6 years), MSF (30 credits, 1-6 years)
Study Abroad Options: Universite Laval, Canada; Vaxjo University, Sweden; Pantheon Sorbonne, Universite de Paris I, France

STUDENT INFORMATION

Total Business Students: 301
% Full Time: 36
% Female: 49
% Minority: 3
% International: 70
Average Age: 27

COMPUTER AND RESEARCH FACILITIES

Research Facilities: Access to more than 50 end-user subject-specific databases including ABI/Inform, InfoTrac Academic Index, Compustat, Lexis-Nexis, U.S. Census Material Social Sciences Index

Computer Facilities: Four on-campus computing laboratories, wireless network in main Business School building, extensive software library

Campuswide Network? Yes

Internet Fee? No

EXPENSES/FINANCIAL AID

Annual Tuition: $19,840

Tuition Per Credit (Resident/Nonresident): $826

Room & Board (On/Off Campus): $8,400/$9,000

Books and Supplies: $800

Average Grant: $8,816

% Receiving Financial Aid: 39

% Receiving Aid Their First Year: 39

ADMISSIONS INFORMATION

Application Fee: $50

Electronic Application? Yes

Regular Application Deadline: 6/1

Regular Notification: Rolling

Deferment Available? Yes

Length of Deferment: 1 year

Non-fall Admissions? Yes

Non-fall Application Deadline(s): 12/1 spring

Transfer Students Accepted? Yes

Transfer Policy: A maximum of 2 courses may be transferred into the program. Courses must have been taken at an AACSB-accredited school. Additional courses taken on the graduate level may be applicable to course waivers.

Need-Blind Admissions? Yes

Number of Applications Received: 302

% of Applicants Accepted: 77

% Accepted Who Enrolled: 36

Average GPA: 3.2

Average GMAT: 540

Average Years Experience: 5

Other Admissions Factors Considered: Resume, college transcripts, personal statement

Other Schools to Which Students Applied: Bentley College, Boston University, Suffolk University, Rochester Institute of Technology, Babson College

INTERNATIONAL STUDENTS

TOEFL Required of International Students? Yes

Minimum TOEFL: 550 (213 computer)

EMPLOYMENT INFORMATION

Placement Office Available? Yes

CLARKSON UNIVERSITY
School of Business

Admissions Contact: Brenda Kozsan, Associate Director of Graduate Programs
Address: CU Box 5770, Potsdam, NY 13699
Admissions Phone: 315-268-6613 • **Admissions Fax:** 315-268-3810
Admissions E-mail: busgrad@clarkson.edu
Web Address: www.clarkson.edu/business/graduate

This private school located in New York is renowned for its remarkable ratio of 32 faculty members to nearly 100 business students. Clarkson is proud of its "team-intensive learning communities," and it aims to "educate leaders who are energized by the entrepreneurial spirit and encouraged to serve the community." MBA students can participate in any of several experiential learning programs, including the Internet Consulting Group and the Corporate Partnership Program.

INSTITUTIONAL INFORMATION

Public/Private: Private

Evening Classes Available? No

Total Faculty: 34

% Faculty Female: 10

% Faculty Minority: 35

% Faculty Part Time: 6

Student/Faculty Ratio: 3:1

Students in Parent Institution: 3,000

Academic Calendar: August-May

PROGRAMS

Degrees Offered: MBA (1 year), with tracks in General MBA, Global Supply Chain Management, Innovation and New Venture Management, Operations and International Competitiveness; MBA (2 years); MS (1 year), with specializations in Manufacturing Management, Information Systems, Human Resources; MS in Engineering and Manufacturing Management (32 credits over 5 summers)

Combined Degrees: MBA/MS in Environmental Manufacturing (2 years)

Academic Specialties: Accounting & Law, Economics & Finance, Global Supply Chain Management, Entrepreneurship, Consulting, Marketing, Management Information Systems, Operations & Production Management, Organizational Studies, Strategy, Leadership

Strengths: Leadership Assessment & Development; experiential opportunities by participating in a consulting group, Corporate/Educational Partnership Program, or the International Summer Study Abroad Program in Reims, France

Special Opportunities: Reims Business School, Reims, France

Study Abroad Options: France

STUDENT INFORMATION

Total Business Students: 92

% Full Time: 86

% Female: 40

% Minority: 7

% Out of State: 22

% International: 11

Average Age: 25

COMPUTER AND RESEARCH FACILITIES

Research Facilities: Graduate Computer Lab, Graduate Student Lounge

Computer Facilities: State of the art labs and classrooms, network ports

Campuswide Network? Yes

% of MBA Classrooms Wired: 100

Internet Fee? No

EXPENSES/FINANCIAL AID

Annual Tuition: $25,970

Tuition Per Credit (Resident/Nonresident): $742

Room & Board (On/Off Campus): $9,315

Books and Supplies: $2,200

Average Grant: $7,500

Average Loan: $15,233

% Receiving Financial Aid: 93

% Receiving Aid Their First Year: 93

ADMISSIONS INFORMATION

Application Fee: $25

Electronic Application? Yes

Regular Application Deadline: Rolling

Regular Notification: Rolling

Deferment Available? Yes
Length of Deferment: 1 year
Non-fall Admissions? Yes
Non-fall Application Deadline(s): MS students: only for those applying to our MS in Management Systems program; MBA students: fall term only
Transfer Students Accepted? Yes
Transfer Policy: Graduate students who need to complete foundation coursework may enroll in the courses at Clarkson before entering the advanced MBA program. Students doing graduate work at another university may transfer in 9 credit hours of graduate work.
Need-Blind Admissions? Yes
Number of Applications Received: 205
% of Applicants Accepted: 65
% Accepted Who Enrolled: 62
Average GPA: 3.3
GPA Range: 2.8-3.9
Average GMAT: 552
GMAT Range: 480-730
Average Years Experience: 2
Other Admissions Factors Considered: Test of Spoken English (TSE) is required or it can be waived by the Graduate Office conducting a telephone interview. Students need to call our office at 315-268-6613 between 8 AM and 4 PM EST.
Other Schools to Which Students Applied: Rochester Institute of Technology, Syracuse University, Union College, Rensselaer Polytechnic Institute

INTERNATIONAL STUDENTS

TOEFL Required of International Students? Yes
Minimum TOEFL: 600 (250 computer)

EMPLOYMENT INFORMATION

Placement Office Available? Yes
% Employed Within 3 Months: 60
Fields Employing Percentage of Grads: Global Management (1%), Entrepreneurship (2%), Accounting (4%), MIS (6%), Consulting (7%), Operations (7%), Finance (7%), Marketing (19%), Other (21%), General Management (23%)
Frequent Employers: Accenture, Avnet, Carrier Corp., Cooper Industries, Frito-Lay, General Electric, Household International, IBM, Knowledge Systems and Research, Northwestern Mutual, Texas Instruments, Whiting-Turner
Prominent Alumni: William Harlow, vice president of corporate development; Paul Hoeft, president and CEO; Elizabeth Fessenden, president—flexible packaging; David Fisher, president; Vickie Cole, president and CEO

CLEMSON UNIVERSITY
Graduate School of Business and Behavioral Science

Admissions Contact: MBA Office–Admissions, Associate Director of MBA Programs
Address: 124 Sirrine Hall, Box 341315, Clemson University, Clemson, SC 29634-1315
Admissions Phone: 864-656-3975 • **Admissions Fax:** 864-656-0947
Admissions E-mail: mba@clemson.edu • **Web Address:** www.clemson.edu/business/mba/

The Clemson MBA provides a standard business education with a specific focus on the practical application of learned business knowledge, and students participate in computer-based simulations, role-playing scenarios, casework, and field study. The student body is 35 percent international, giving students a prime opportunity to learn about global business cultures and the true international marketplace of ideas. The part-time evening MBA program offers

flexibility for working professionals and a choice between two locations where Clemson faculty provide quality instruction: Greenwood and Greenville.

INSTITUTIONAL INFORMATION

Public/Private: Public
Evening Classes Available? Yes
Total Faculty: 93
% Faculty Female: 18
% Faculty Minority: 5
% Faculty Part Time: 8
Student/Faculty Ratio: 3:1
Students in Parent Institution: 16,900
Academic Calendar: August-May

PROGRAMS

Degrees Offered: PhD in Management (4 years), PhD in Management Science (4 years), PhD Applied Economics (4 years), MBA (2 years full time; 3 years part time, evening), MPACC (2 years), MECOM (1.5 years), MSIM (1 year), MA in Economics (2 years)
Combined Degrees: Dual degrees are allowed on the master's level. Up to one-sixth of the total hours in both programs combined may be double-counted. Dual degrees must be declared by the middle of the first semester of graduate school.
Academic Specialties: Entrepreneurship, Management Information Systems, Technology Management, Industrial Management, E-Commerce
Study Abroad Options: University of Newcastle, Australia (second masters can be earned); CIMBA, Itlay (summer program)

STUDENT INFORMATION

Total Business Students: 250
% Full Time: 31
% Female: 27
% Minority: 3
% Out of State: 55
% International: 23
Average Age: 27

COMPUTER AND RESEARCH FACILITIES

Research Facilities: Center for International Trade, Technology Transfer Institute, Spiro Center for Entrepreneurial Leadership, Strom Thurmond Institute of Government & Public Affairs
Campuswide Network? Yes
% of MBA Classrooms Wired: 100
Computer Model Recommended: Laptop
Internet Fee? No

EXPENSES/FINANCIAL AID

Annual Tuition (Resident/Nonresident): $5,764/$12,612
Tuition Per Credit (Resident/Nonresident): $356/$644
Room & Board (On/Off Campus): $8,985/$13,520
Books and Supplies: $1,770
Average Grant: $5,000
Average Loan: $11,000
% Receiving Financial Aid: 90
% Receiving Aid Their First Year: 85

ADMISSIONS INFORMATION

Application Fee: $40
Electronic Application? Yes
Regular Application Deadline: 4/15
Regular Notification: 5/15
Deferment Available? Yes
Length of Deferment: 1 year
Non-fall Admissions? No
Transfer Students Accepted? Yes

Transfer Policy: Must meet all admission requirements; can transfer a maximum of 6 semester hours of acceptable coursework
Need-Blind Admissions? Yes
Number of Applications Received: 387
% of Applicants Accepted: 45
% Accepted Who Enrolled: 65
Average GPA: 3.3
GPA Range: 3.1-3.7
Average GMAT: 615
GMAT Range: 570-640
Average Years Experience: 5

INTERNATIONAL STUDENTS

TOEFL Required of International Students? Yes
Minimum TOEFL: 580 (237 computer)

EMPLOYMENT INFORMATION

Placement Office Available? Yes
% Employed Within 3 Months: 91
Fields Employing Percentage of Grads: Human Resources (3%), General Management (12%), Consulting (12%), Operations (15%), MIS (15%), Marketing (16%), Finance (27%)
Frequent Employers: Avis, Accenture, Bank of America, First Union, Fluor Daniel, General Electric, Ingersol Rand, Michelin, Milliken

CLEVELAND STATE UNIVERSITY
James J. Nance College of Business Administration

Admissions Contact: Bruce M. Gottschalk, MBA Programs Administrator
Address: 1860 East 18th Street, BU 219, Cleveland, Oh 44114
Admissions Phone: 216-687-3730 • **Admissions Fax:** 216-687-5311
Admissions E-mail: cbacsu@csuohio.edu • **Web Address:** www.cba.csuohio.edu/index.htm

The James J. Nance College of Business Administration offers several MBA programs. The Accelerated Program is a "fast-paced weekend program, ideal for management-track professionals." The Executive MBA offers working professionals the opportunity to continue their careers while enhancing their knowledge and acquiring a degree. The Off-Campus Program allows students extreme schedule/location flexibility, enabling them to take courses at any of the four off-campus centers.

INSTITUTIONAL INFORMATION

Public/Private: Public
Evening Classes Available? Yes
Total Faculty: 75
% Faculty Female: 22
% Faculty Minority: 15
% Faculty Part Time: 17
Student/Faculty Ratio: 27:1
Students in Parent Institution: 16,479
Academic Calendar: Semester

PROGRAMS

Degrees Offered: MACC (2 years), MBA (1-2 years), MBA in Health Care Administration (2-3.5 years), Master of Computer and Information Science (2 years), Master of Labor Relations and Human Resouces (2 years), MPH (2 years)
Combined Degrees: JD/MBA 4 years

Academic Specialties: Comprehensive multidisciplinary method of instruction
Study Abroad Options: England, Germany

STUDENT INFORMATION

Total Business Students: 555
% Full Time: 23
% Female: 41
% Minority: 9
% Out of State: 53
% International: 51
Average Age: 29

COMPUTER AND RESEARCH FACILITIES

Research Facilities: Executive Development Center, Real Estate Institute, Small Business Institute
Computer Facilities: Networked laboratory of basic and advanced personal computers; networked laboratory of workstations including Sun Sparc, SGI Indy, and a DEC 3100/5100; graduate student lab with more than 75 Pentium IV desktop computers; SAS and SPSS databases for statistical research applications
Campuswide Network? Yes
% of MBA Classrooms Wired: 14
Internet Fee? No

EXPENSES/FINANCIAL AID

Annual Tuition (Resident/Nonresident): $6,936/$13,723
Tuition Per Credit (Resident/Nonresident): $289/$572
Room & Board (On/Off Campus): $8,100/$10,000
Books and Supplies: $1,100
% Receiving Financial Aid: 3
% Receiving Aid Their First Year: 7

ADMISSIONS INFORMATION

Application Fee: $30
Electronic Application? Yes
Regular Application Deadline: 7/1
Regular Notification: Rolling
Deferment Available? Yes
Length of Deferment: 12 months
Non-fall Admissions? Yes
Non-fall Application Deadline(s): 11/2 spring, 4/2 summer
Transfer Students Accepted? Yes
Transfer Policy: Must be in good academic standing
Need-Blind Admissions? Yes
Number of Applications Received: 408
% of Applicants Accepted: 75
% Accepted Who Enrolled: 70
Average GPA: 3.1
GPA Range: 2.8-3.3
Average GMAT: 500
GMAT Range: 460-590
Average Years Experience: 5
Other Admissions Factors Considered: None
Minority/Disadvantaged Student Recruitment Programs: None
Other Schools to Which Students Applied: Case Western Reserve University, John Carroll University, Kent State University, The University of Akron

INTERNATIONAL STUDENTS

TOEFL Required of International Students? Yes
Minimum TOEFL: 525 (197 computer)

EMPLOYMENT INFORMATION

Placement Office Available? No
% Employed Within 3 Months: 90
Fields Employing Percentage of Grads: Entrepreneurship (2%), MIS (2%), Human Resources (2%), Consulting (6%), Accounting (7%), General Management (8%), Marketing (17%), Finance (19%), Operations (24%)

Frequent Employers: Banc One, Cleveland Clinic, KeyCorp, MBNA, McDonald Investments, Medical Mutual, Moen Inc., National City Bank, Nestle, Progressive Insurance, Sherwin WIlliams, Steris, University Hospitals
Prominent Alumni: Monte Ahuja, chairman, president, and CEO, Transtar Industries; Michael Berthelot, chairman and CEO, Transtechnolgy Corp.; Ted Hlavaty, chairman and CEO, Neway Stamping & Manufacturing; Thomas Moore, president, Wolf Group; Kenneth Semelsberger, president, COO, and director, Scott Fetzer, Inc.

COLLEGE OF WILLIAM AND MARY
Graduate School of Business

Admissions Contact: Kathy Williams Pattison, Director, MBA Admissions
Address: PO Box 8795, Williamsburg, VA 23187
Admissions Phone: 757-221-2900 • **Admissions Fax:** 757-221-2958
Admissions E-mail: admissions@business.wm.edu • **Web Address:** www.business.wm.edu

A *"smaller program," "non-competitive attitude,"* and state-school prices attract MBAs to the College of William and Mary Graduate School of Business, where "very enthusiastic, very capable," and "very tough" professors offer "a great deal of personal attention." Incoming students here participate in an Outward Bound–style Orientation Week, during which they divide into teams and compete in, among other things, a high-ropes course and a raft-building exercise.

INSTITUTIONAL INFORMATION

Public/Private: Public
Evening Classes Available? Yes
Total Faculty: 55
% Faculty Female: 24
% Faculty Minority: 11
Student/Faculty Ratio: 4:1
Students in Parent Institution: 7,560
Academic Calendar: Semester

PROGRAMS

Degrees Offered: MBA (2 years full time, 3.5 years evening program), EMBA (20 months), MACC (1 year)
Combined Degrees: MBA/JD (4 years), MBA/MPP (3 years)
Academic Specialties: Finance, Operations Management, Information Technology, Marketing; leadership, team-building
Special Opportunities: Field studies (team consulting project in second year, 4.5 credits); international trip: Southeast Asia (winter break, 3 credits), Paris (spring break, 1 credit)
Study Abroad Options: INCAE, Costa Rica; ESCP-EAP, France; WHU—Koblenz, SIMT, Germany; IPADE, Mexico; NHH, Norway

STUDENT INFORMATION

Total Business Students: 322
% Full Time: 56
% Female: 32
% Minority: 10
% Out of State: 57
% International: 38
Average Age: 28

COMPUTER AND RESEARCH FACILITIES

Research Facilities: The Professional Resource Center is a state-of-the-art electronic-reference resource area. An Investment Management Center has a Bloomberg terminal and dedicated links to Baseline, an equity research service.
Computer Facilities: All classrooms are wired, and the MBA lounges, study

rooms, and common areas have wireless Internet receivers and networked laser printers. Databases include Lexis-Nexis, Compustat, CRSP, Proquest ABI-Inform, Stat-USA, Hoovers On Line, Piranhaweb and Global Access, and others. Every course has its own web page and news server.
Campuswide Network? Yes
% of MBA Classrooms Wired: 100
Computer Model Recommended: Laptop
Internet Fee? No

EXPENSES/FINANCIAL AID

Annual Tuition (Resident/Nonresident): $10,378/$21,658
Tuition Per Credit (Resident/Nonresident): $313/$634
Room & Board (On/Off Campus): $8,330
Books and Supplies: $1,500
Average Grant: $4,771
Average Loan: $16,829
% Receiving Financial Aid: 78
% Receiving Aid Their First Year: 73

ADMISSIONS INFORMATION

Application Fee: $80
Electronic Application? Yes
Early Decision Application Deadline: 11/15
Early Decision Notification: 1/1
Regular Application Deadline: 3/15
Regular Notification: Rolling
Deferment Available? Yes
Length of Deferment: 1 year
Non-fall Admissions? No
Transfer Students Accepted? No
Need-Blind Admissions? Yes
Number of Applications Received: 252
% of Applicants Accepted: 73
% Accepted Who Enrolled: 57
Average GMAT: 607
GMAT Range: 580-640
Average Years Experience: 4
Other Admissions Factors Considered: The Admissions Committee evaluates all aspects of a candidate's background: managerial and leadership potential, personal and professional achievements, communications skills, and academic promise. Decisions are based upon the applicant's academic record, recommendations, work experience, GMAT scores, interview, and other indications of aptitude for graduate study in business administration.
Other Schools to Which Students Applied: Babson College, Georgetown University, University of Maryland—College Park, University of North Carolina—Chapel Hill, University of Virginia, Wake Forest University

INTERNATIONAL STUDENTS

TOEFL Required of International Students? Yes
Minimum TOEFL: 600 (250 computer)

EMPLOYMENT INFORMATION

Placement Office Available? Yes
% Employed Within 3 Months: 85
Fields Employing Percentage of Grads: Human Resources (3%), Other (6%), Consulting (12%); Marketing (26%), Finance (53%)
Frequent Employers: BB&T, Bearing Point, Booz Allen Hamilton, Dominion Resources, GE, General Mills, IBM, Lehman Brothers, National City, Wachovia
Prominent Alumni: Charles Horner, lieutenant general; Steve Umberger, president, ValueClick International; Bill Fricks, chairman and CEO, Newport News Shipbuilding

See page 418 and page 420.

COLORADO STATE UNIVERSITY
College of Business

Admissions Contact: Linda Morita, MBA Advisor
Address: 1201 Campus Delivery, Fort Collins, MO 80523
Admissions Phone: 970-491-1499 • Admissions Fax: 970-491-0596
Admissions E-mail: gschool@grad.colostate.edu • Web Address: www.biz.colostate.edu

INSTITUTIONAL INFORMATION

Public/Private: Public
Evening Classes Available? Yes
Total Faculty: 61
Student/Faculty Ratio: 30:1
Students in Parent Institution: 22,782
Academic Calendar: August-May

PROGRAMS

Degrees Offered: MBA (11 months accelerated, 21 months part-time evening, 2-4 years distance program), EMBA (2 years)
Academic Specialties: Our program stresses globilization, technology, and team work.
Special Opportunities: General Business, Accounting, CIS, MIS

STUDENT INFORMATION

Total Business Students: 543
% Full Time: 8
% Female: 49
% Out of State: 28
% International: 14
Average Age: 36

COMPUTER AND RESEARCH FACILITIES

Campuswide Network? Yes
Internet Fee? No

EXPENSES/FINANCIAL AID

Annual Tuition (Resident/Nonresident): $4,146/$14,052
Books and Supplies: $1,800
Average Grant: $1,500
Average Loan: $2,500

ADMISSIONS INFORMATION

Application Fee: $30
Electronic Application? Yes
Early Decision Application Deadline: 12/15
Early Decision Notification: 2/15
Regular Application Deadline: Rolling
Regular Notification: Rolling
Deferment Available? Yes
Length of Deferment: 1 year
Non-fall Admissions? Yes
Non-fall Application Deadline(s): 10/1 distance
Transfer Students Accepted? No
Need-Blind Admissions? Yes
Number of Applications Received: 472
% of Applicants Accepted: 56
% Accepted Who Enrolled: 66
Average Years Experience: 8
Other Schools to Which Students Applied: University of Colorado—Boulder, University of Denver, University of Colorado—Denver

INTERNATIONAL STUDENTS

TOEFL Required of International Students? Yes
Minimum TOEFL: 565

EMPLOYMENT INFORMATION
Placement Office Available? No

COLUMBIA UNIVERSITY
Columbia Business School

Admissions Contact: Linda Meehan, Assistant Dean for Admissions
Address: 216 Uris Hall, 3022 Broadway, New York, NY 10027
Admissions Phone: 212-854-1961 • Admissions Fax: 212-662-5754
Admissions E-mail: apply@claven.gsb.columbia.edu
Web Address: www.gsb.columbia.edu

Columbia Business School's candle continues to burn brighter and brighter, thanks to its "truly outstanding professors" and a wealth of "very strong" resources and programs, especially in international business. Best of all, though, is Columbia's unbeatable New York City location. Internship opportunities are staggering and "several of the 'big guns' from Wall Street serve as adjunct faculty for many second-year courses."

INSTITUTIONAL INFORMATION

Public/Private: Private
Evening Classes Available? No
Total Faculty: 215
% Faculty Female: 14
% Faculty Minority: 1
% Faculty Part Time: 43
Student/Faculty Ratio: 6:1
Students in Parent Institution: 23,422
Academic Calendar: Trimester

PROGRAMS

Degrees Offered: PhD (5 years), EMBA (20 months), MBA (16-20 months)
Combined Degrees: MBA/MS in Urban Planning; MBA/MSN, MBA/MPH, MBA/EdD in Education Leadership/Management, MBA/MIA, MBA/MS in Industrial or Mining Engineering, MBA/MS in Social Work, MBA/MS in Journalism, MBA/JD, MBA/MD, MBA/DDS
Academic Specialties: The Columbia MBA equips students with the tools they need to be competitive and valuable in the international marketplace. The curriculum integrates the core disciplines of accounting, finance, management, marketing, and operations, and incorporates 4 overarching themes: total quality management, ethics, human resource management, and globalization. To increase the understanding of interdisciplinary concepts and practices, the faculty use combinations of lectures, group projects, and case studies. In addition, specialized programs—such as the entrepreneurship; media, entertainment and communications; public and non-profit management; and real estate programs—provide students with the opportunity to focus on cutting-edge issues. In fall 2002, a committee of senior faculty was appointed to evaluate the role of ethics in an MBA program while reviewing how ethics was currently integrated throughout the learning environment at Columbia Business School. After hundreds of hours of discussion with alumni, corporate leaders, and recruiters, the committee determined that graduate education should play a strong role in exposing MBA students to ethical dilemmas that they may encounter over the course of their careers. The committee also concluded that the School could best address ethical issues through a unique approach infusing ethics across the first-year core curriculum.
Special Opportunities: EMBA (New York-based, with London Business School, or with University of California—Berkeley), Executive Education Program (open enrollment and custom non-degree programs)
Study Abroad Options: Melbourne Business School, University of Melbourne, Australia; Wirtschaftuniversitat Wien, University of Vienna, Aus-

tria; Escola de Administracao de Empresas de Sao Paulo/Fundacao Getulio Vargas, Brazil; Chinese University of Hong Kong, Hong Kong University of Science and Technology, China; Helsinki School of Economics and Business Administration, Finland; HEC/ISA-Hautes Etudes Commerciales/Institut Superieur des Affaires, France; WHU—Koblenz, Otto Beisheim Graduate School of Management, and Ludwig-Maximilians Universitat Muchen, Germany; Leon Racanati Graduate School of Business Administration, Tel Aviv University, Israel; Scuola di Direzione Ariendale, Bocconi, Italy; Keio University, Graduate School of Business, Japan; IPADE-Instituto Panamericano de Alta Direccion de Empresa, Mexico; Rotterdam School of Management, Erasmus Universiteit Rotterdam, The Netherlands; Asian Institute of Management, Phillipines; National University of Singapore, Singapore; University of Cape Town, The Graduate School of Business, South Africa; IESE-International Graduate School of Management, Universidad de Navarra, Spain; Stockholm School of Economics, Sweden; Ecole des Hautes Etudes Commerciales, Universite de Lausanne and University of St. Gallen for Business Administration, Economics, Law and Social Sciences, Switzerland; London Business School, United Kingdom

STUDENT INFORMATION

Total Business Students: 1,188
% Full Time: 100
% Female: 34
% Minority: 23
% International: 28
Average Age: 27

COMPUTER AND RESEARCH FACILITIES

Research Facilities: Arthur J. Samberg Institute for Teaching Excellence; Center for International Business Education (CIBE); Center on Global Brand Leadership; Center on Japanese Economy and Business; Columbia Center for Excellence in E-Business (CEBiz); Columbia Institute for Tele-Information (CITI); Eugene M. Lang Center for Entrepreneurship; Financial Markets Laboratory; The Heilbrunn Center for Graham & Dodd Investing; Jerome A. Chazen Institute of International Business; MBNA Center for the Study of Banking and Financial Institutions; Paul Milstein Center for Real Estate; Sanford Bernstein Center for Leadership & Ethics; and the W. Edwards Deming Center for Quality, Productivity and Competitiveness

Computer Facilities: The School has developed initiatives to emphasize and implement technology throughout the MBA program. The Student Notebook Computer Initiative requires every student to own a notebook computer. An expanded number of network jacks—now totaling more than 1,800—allow students to log into the School's network, which provides access to the Internet, printers, electronic mail, and application software. Student computer kiosks also provide easy access to e-mail and web-browsing. The School has also implemented new web-based e-mail listservers for all courses, clusters, clubs, and administrative committees throughout the School, and has installed web-based instructional and administrative applications. A Trading Room utilizes real-time financial data trading simulation software for hands-on experience. The new business building, which opened in 1999, provides state-of-the-art multimedia classrooms modeled after recently renovated classrooms in Uris Hall. The classrooms include video-conferencing capability, allow for the delivery and /or recording of events in one classroom to be broadcasted to any other classroom via the Media Control Center, and allow Uris Hall to be connected to the classrooms in the new building. The amphitheater classrooms feature hubs for data and electric connectivity. Through the Thomas J. Watson Library of Business and Economics, students have access to more than 20 economic databases on the Web.

Campuswide Network? Yes
% of MBA Classrooms Wired: 90
Computer Model Recommended: Laptop
Internet Fee? No

EXPENSES/FINANCIAL AID

Annual Tuition: $32,154
Room & Board (On/Off Campus): $16,920
Books and Supplies: $1,138

Average Grant: $3,736
% Receiving Financial Aid: 70

ADMISSIONS INFORMATION

Application Fee: $180
Electronic Application? Yes
Early Decision Application Deadline: 10/15
Early Decision Notification: 11/30
Regular Application Deadline: 4/20
Regular Notification: Rolling
Deferment Available? No
Non-fall Admissions? Yes
Non-fall Application Deadline(s): 10/1 January entry
Transfer Students Accepted? No
Need-Blind Admissions? Yes
Number of Applications Received: 6,663
% of Applicants Accepted: 11
% Accepted Who Enrolled: 71
Average GPA: 3.5
GPA Range: 2.9-3.8
Average GMAT: 711
GMAT Range: 670-760
Average Years Experience: 4
Other Admissions Factors Considered: Columbia Business School selects applicants from varied business and other backgrounds who have the potential to become successful global leaders. Their common denominators are a record of achievement, demonstrated leadership, and the ability to work as members of a team.

Minority/Disadvantaged Student Recruitment Programs: Columbia Business School is not a cookie-cutter school. By design, efforts are made to admit students who add different perspectives to the learning experience. In this way, students are continually learning from the diverse professional experiences and cultural/geographical backgrounds of their classmates. Columbia Business School has also maintained, through a concerted strategic effort, one of the highest enrollments of women and underrepresented minorities among top business schools. There are fellowships available for minority students. In addition, the Office of Admissions, in conjuction with the School's Black Business Students Association, Hispanic Business Association, and African American Alumni Association, sponsors information sessions and receptions for prospective students.

Other Schools to Which Students Applied: Harvard University, Stanford University, University of Pennsylvania

INTERNATIONAL STUDENTS

TOEFL Required of International Students? Yes

EMPLOYMENT INFORMATION

Placement Office Available? Yes
% Employed Within 3 Months: 84
Fields Employing Percentage of Grads: Venture Capital (1%), Entrepreneurship (1%), Operations (1%), General Management (3%), Strategic Planning (3%), Marketing (10%), Consulting (15%), Finance (59%)
Frequent Employers: Bear, Stearns & Co., Inc.; Citigroup/Citicorp; Credit Suisse First Boston; Deutsche Bank; Goldman, Sachs & Co., Inc; J.P. Morgan Chase & Co.; Lehman Brothers, Inc.; McKinsey & Co.; Merrill Lynch; Morgan Stanley
Prominent Alumni: Warren Buffett, chairman, Berkshire Hathaway Inc.; Henry Kravis, kounding partner, Kohlberg, Kravis; Rochelle Lazarus, chairman and CEO, Ogilvy & Mather; Michael Gould, chairman and CEO, Bloomingdales; Benjamin Rosen, chairman emeritus, Compaq Computer

CONCORDIA UNIVERSITY
John Molson School of Business

Admissions Contact: Cynthia Law, MBA Program Admissions Officer
Address: 1455 de Maisonneuve Blvd. West, GM 710, Montreal, QC H3G 1M8
Admissions Phone: 514-848-2708 • **Admissions Fax:** 514-848-2816
Admissions E-mail: mba@jmsb.concordia.ca
Web Address: www.johnmolson.concordia.ca

Welcome to the John Molson School of Business, where you can attain an MBA and do just about anything else. The Concordia MBA opportunity comes packaged with an extravagant host of study abroad options, numerous academic specialties, and a growing number of degrees offered within the business school. Concordia is a private institution located in Quebec, so come prepared with your English-French dictionary.

INSTITUTIONAL INFORMATION

Public/Private: Public
Evening Classes Available? Yes
Total Faculty: 266
% Faculty Female: 26
% Faculty Part Time: 53
Student/Faculty Ratio: 12:1
Students in Parent Institution: 27,000
Academic Calendar: Trimester

PROGRAMS

Degrees Offered: MBA (16 months-5 years), EMBA (20 months), International Aviation MBA (12 months), Global e-Based Aviation MBA (2 years), MS in Administration (16 months-5 years), PhD (4-5 years), Diploma in Accountancy (1 year), Diploma in Administration (1 year), Diploma in Sport Administration (1 year), MBA in Investment Management (3-5 years), Master in Investment Management (3-5 years), Graduate Diploma in Investment Management (3-4 years), Graduate Certificate in e-Business (1 year)
Academic Specialties: Accounting, Finance, International Business, Aviation Management, Investment Management, E-Business, Portfolio Management, Not-for-profit and Sport Administration
Special Opportunities: CREPUQ University Agreements, John Molson MBA Bilateral Exchange Programs
Study Abroad Options: Australia, China, Denmark, France, Germany, Hungary, Italy, Mexico, New Zealand, Spain, Sweden, Switzerland, United Kingdom, United States

STUDENT INFORMATION

Total Business Students: 323
% Full Time: 44
% Female: 46
% Minority: 18
% Out of State: 68
% International: 52
Average Age: 29

COMPUTER AND RESEARCH FACILITIES

Research Facilities: Webster Library, Vanier Library: 1,700,000 holdings; 992,581 microforms; 6,070 current serials
Computer Facilities: Computer labs with Pentium computers; multiple databases: Lexis-Nexis, ABI Inform, Advertising Redbook, Compustat, Moody's, Standard & Poors, Stat-USA
Campuswide Network? Yes
% of MBA Classrooms Wired: 50
Computer Model Recommended: Laptop
Internet Fee? No

EXPENSES/FINANCIAL AID

Annual Tuition (Resident/Nonresident): $1,668/$12,500

Room & Board (On/Off Campus): $10,000/$11,000
Books and Supplies: $1,000
Average Grant: $9,000
Average Loan: $8,000
% Receiving Financial Aid: 15
% Receiving Aid Their First Year: 15

ADMISSIONS INFORMATION

Application Fee: $50
Electronic Application? Yes
Early Decision Application Deadline: 3 deadlines throughout the year
Early Decision Notification: 3/5
Regular Application Deadline: Rolling
Regular Notification: Rolling
Deferment Available? Yes
Length of Deferment: 1 year
Non-fall Admissions? Yes
Non-fall Application Deadline(s): 6/1 September, 10/1 January, 2/28 May
Transfer Students Accepted? Yes
Transfer Policy: Applicants may be eligible for advanced standing.
Need-Blind Admissions? Yes
Number of Applications Received: 660
% of Applicants Accepted: 17
% Accepted Who Enrolled: 81
Average GPA: 3.3
GPA Range: 3.0-4.0
Average GMAT: 650
GMAT Range: 600-780
Average Years Experience: 6
Other Admissions Factors Considered: Awards, career/leadership potential, personality and fit, level of maturity, communication skills
Minority/Disadvantaged Student Recruitment Programs: Non-credit courses and certificate programs for members of minority communities
Other Schools to Which Students Applied: University of Toronto, University of Western Ontario, McGill University, Queen's University

INTERNATIONAL STUDENTS

TOEFL Required of International Students? Yes
Minimum TOEFL: 550 (213 computer)

EMPLOYMENT INFORMATION

Placement Office Available? Yes
% Employed Within 3 Months: 93
Fields Employing Percentage of Grads: Global Management (2%), Consulting (2%), Human Resources (2%), Accounting (2%), Entrepreneurship (4%), MIS (11%), Finance (12%), General Management (16%), Marketing (20%), Other (27%)
Frequent Employers: Air Canada, Bombardier, Cap Gemini, Concordia University, Eicon Networks, Ernst & Young, Merck Frosst, Novartis, Royal Bank, TD Bank
Prominent Alumni: Brian Steck, former vice-chairman, Bank of Montreal; David Goldman, COO, Noranda Inc.; Jonathan Weiner, CEO, Canderel Inc.; Lawrence Bloomberg, former COO, National Bank; Christine Sirsley, executive vice president, Via Rail

CORNELL UNIVERSITY
Johnson Graduate School of Management

Admissions Contact: Natalie Grinblatt, Director, Office of Admissions and Financial Aid
Address: 111 Sage Hall, Ithaca, New York 14853, NY 14853
Admissions Phone: 607-255-4526 • **Admissions Fax:** 607-255-0065
Admissions E-mail: mba@johnson.cornell.edu • **Web Address:** www.johnson.cornell.edu

Selecting classes every semester is like attending a mile-long buffet table at Cornell University's Johnson School, where joint degree programs and specialized concentrations are legion. The "thrilling" pace of instruction here is "phenomenal," and students tell us "there hasn't been teaching this good since Socrates." Also noteworthy are the Johnson School's Immersion Learning courses, which come complete with "real-world" problems and time pressure.

INSTITUTIONAL INFORMATION

Public/Private: Private
Evening Classes Available? No
Total Faculty: 100
% Faculty Female: 24
% Faculty Minority: 26
% Faculty Part Time: 47
Student/Faculty Ratio: 6:1
Students in Parent Institution: 21,026
Academic Calendar: Semester

PROGRAMS

Degrees Offered: MBA (2 years; 12 months with advanced degree in science or technical field), EMBA (2 years), PhD (5 years)
Combined Degrees: MBA/MILR (5 semesters), MBA/MEng (5 semesters), MBA/MA in Asian Studies (6-7 semesters), JD/MBA (4 years)
Academic Specialties: Finance, Accounting, Entrepreneurship. Overall strenghts include the flexibility of the core program, "reality-based" education such as the immersion programs, and the Cayuga MBA Fund, as well as a collaborative community enjoying easy access and frequent interaction with faculty and a close connection to the vast resources of Cornell University.
Special Opportunities: 12-month option for scientists and engineers, Park Leadership Fellows Program, Leadership Skills Program, Joint Degree Program, PhD Program, EMBA Program, Executive Education, Brand Management Immersion, Semester in Manufacturing Immersion, Investment Banking Immersion, Managerial Finance Immersion, eBusiness Immersion, Entrepreneurship and Private Equity Immersion
Study Abroad Options: The International Exchange Program provides Johnson School students with options to study in 15 countries at 20 business school programs. These exchange programs are open to students who have completed 1 year of study at the Johnson School. The schools include: University of Melbourne Business School, Australia; Katholieke Universiteit te Leuven, Belgium; Copenhagen Business School, Denmark; London Business School and University of Manchester School of Management, England; Ecole Supérieure des Sciences Economiques et Commerciales (ESSEC) and Groupe HEC School of Management, France; Hong Kong University of Science & Technology, School of Business and Management, Hong Kong; Luigi Bocconi and SDA Bocconi, Italy; Groningen, The Netherlands; Norwegian School of Economics, Norway; Escuela Superior de Administración y Dirección de Empresas (ESADE) and University of Navarra International Graduate School of Management, Spain; WITS Business School, South Africa; Stockholm School of Economics, Sweden; St. Gallen, Switzerland; Sasin Graduate Institute of Business Administration of CHulalongkorn University, Thailand; IESA, Venezuela

STUDENT INFORMATION

Total Business Students: 561
% Full Time: 100
% Female: 27
% Minority: 22
% International: 28
Average Age: 28

COMPUTER AND RESEARCH FACILITIES

Research Facilities: Parker Center for Investment Research, Center for Leadership Development
Computer Facilities: 46-seat lab; 8 Quick Stations; MSOffice Suite; miscellaneous course software; Parker Center for Investment Research; Business Simulation Lab; business databases, including Bloomberg, Business and Industry, Datastream, Dow Jones Interactive, EIU Country Data, Global Access, Global Market Information Database, Lexis-Nexis Academic Universe, Market Insight, Marketresearch.com Academic, and Sourcebook America,
Campuswide Network? Yes
% of MBA Classrooms Wired: 100
Computer Model Recommended: Laptop
Internet Fee? No

EXPENSES/FINANCIAL AID

Annual Tuition: $30,975
Room & Board (On/Off Campus): $7,850
Books and Supplies: $1,100
Average Grant: $25,000
Average Loan: $31,800
% Receiving Financial Aid: 75
% Receiving Aid Their First Year: 85

ADMISSIONS INFORMATION

Application Fee: $200
Electronic Application? Yes
Regular Application Deadline: 3/15
Regular Notification: 5/31
Deferment Available? No
Non-fall Admissions? Yes
Non-fall Application Deadline(s): 11/15, 12/15, 1/15 for TMO only
Transfer Students Accepted? No
Need-Blind Admissions? Yes
Number of Applications Received: 2,434
% of Applicants Accepted: 22
% Accepted Who Enrolled: 57
Average GPA: 3.3
GPA Range: 2.8-3.9
Average GMAT: 673
GMAT Range: 600-730
Average Years Experience: 5
Other Admissions Factors Considered: Leadership, demonstrated record of achievement, creative problem-solving, team skills, interpersonal skills, analytical thinking
Minority/Disadvantaged Student Recruitment Programs: Toigo Fellowship; NSH MBA Membership; Johnson Means Business for Minority Students; MBA Alliance with Duke, Yale, New York University, and University of California—Berkeley; Prospective NMBAA membership; Office of Women & Minorities in Business; Black Graduate business Association; Hispanic American Business Leaders Association; Women's Management Council; Woman2Woman: Prospective Students—Women's Power Lunch
Other Schools to Which Students Applied: Columbia University, Dartmouth College, Harvard University, University of Michigan, University of Pennsylvania

INTERNATIONAL STUDENTS

TOEFL Required of International Students? Yes
Minimum TOEFL: 600 (250 computer)

EMPLOYMENT INFORMATION

Placement Office Available? Yes
% Employed Within 3 Months: 74

Fields Employing Percentage of Grads: Operations (2%), Consulting (9%), Marketing (18%), General Management (19%), Finance (44%)
Frequent Employers: Accenture, American Express, A.T. Kearney, Bain & Co., Goldman Sachs, Hewlett Packard, McKinsey and Co., PRTM, Pricewaterhouse Coopers, Solomon Smith Barney
Prominent Alumni: Jim Morgan , chairman & CEO, Applied Materials, Inc.; Daniel Hesse, president and CEO, Terabeam Corp.; Rick Sherlund, managing director, Goldman Sachs

CREIGHTON UNIVERSITY
College of Business Administration

Admissions Contact: Gail Hafer, Coordinator of Graduate Business Programs
Address: 2500 California Plaza, Omaha, NE 68178
Admissions Phone: 402-280-2829 • **Admissions Fax:** 402-280-2172
Admissions E-mail: cobagrad@creighton.edu • **Web Address:** cobweb.creighton.edu

Creighton University is a private Catholic school run by the Jesuits, so it's no surprise that the school prides itself on its awareness of ethics and its value-centered learning environment. With just over 100 MBA students per class, COBA's MBA program provides quality instruction and easy access to professors and community business leaders.

INSTITUTIONAL INFORMATION

Public/Private: Private
Evening Classes Available? Yes
Total Faculty: 35
% Faculty Female: 14
% Faculty Part Time: 11
Student/Faculty Ratio: 2:1
Students in Parent Institution: 6,297
Academic Calendar: August-July

PROGRAMS

Degrees Offered: MBA (2 years), MSITM, MBA/MSITM (3 years), MS in Electronic Commerce (2 years)
Combined Degrees: JD/MBA (3 years), MBA/Master of International Relations (3 years), JD/MS in Electronic Commerce (3 years), MSITM/Master of Computer Science(3 years), MBA/PharmD (4 years)
Academic Specialties: Investments, Leadership, Electronic Commerce
Special Opportunities: Mentor Program, Anna Tyler Waiter Graduate Leadership Fellow
Study Abroad Options: Beijing IMBA Program, China

STUDENT INFORMATION

Total Business Students: 111
% Full Time: 33
% Female: 30
% Minority: 10
% Out of State: 21
% International: 35
Average Age: 26

COMPUTER AND RESEARCH FACILITIES

Research Facilities: Carl Reinert Alumni Memorial Library
Computer Facilities: Seagate/Wad Labs Computer Center Lab
Campuswide Network? Yes
% of MBA Classrooms Wired: 100
Internet Fee? No

EXPENSES/FINANCIAL AID

Annual Tuition: $8,532
Tuition Per Credit (Resident/Nonresident): $474
Books and Supplies: $1,000
Average Grant: $1,422

ADMISSIONS INFORMATION

Application Fee: $40
Electronic Application? Yes
Regular Application Deadline: Rolling
Regular Notification: Rolling
Deferment Available? Yes
Length of Deferment: 1 year
Non-fall Admissions? Yes
Non-fall Application Deadline(s): 10/1
Transfer Students Accepted? Yes
Transfer Policy: Maximum of 6 hours of electives accepted from AACSB-accredited schools
Need-Blind Admissions? No
Number of Applications Received: 44
% of Applicants Accepted: 100
% Accepted Who Enrolled: 64
Average GPA: 3.2
Average GMAT: 550
Average Years Experience: 5
Other Admissions Factors Considered: 2-3 years work experience strongly preferred
Other Schools to Which Students Applied: University of Nebraska Medical Center

INTERNATIONAL STUDENTS

TOEFL Required of International Students? Yes
Minimum TOEFL: 550

EMPLOYMENT INFORMATION

Placement Office Available? Yes
Fields Employing Percentage of Grads: Other (8%)

DARTMOUTH COLLEGE
Tuck School of Business at Dartmouth

Admissions Contact: Kristine Laca, Director of Admissions
Address: 100 Tuck Hall, Hanover, NH 03755
Admissions Phone: 603-646-3162 • **Admissions Fax:** 603-646-1441
Admissions E-mail: Tuck.Admissions@dartmouth.edu
Web Address: www.tuck.dartmouth.edu

The workload is "humbling" and teamwork is essential at Tuck School of Business Administration, the world's first graduate school of management and the only top U.S. business school that offers an MBA and nothing else. The ridiculously happy students here report off-the-Richter-scale terrific teachers, an amazing array of resources, and "no such thing as not getting into a class." Also notable is Tuck's annual alumni giving rate of 63 percent (the highest in the country).

INSTITUTIONAL INFORMATION

Public/Private: Private
Evening Classes Available? No
Total Faculty: 66
% Faculty Female: 20

% Faculty Minority: 18
Student/Faculty Ratio: 7:1
Students in Parent Institution: 5,527
Academic Calendar: Quarter

PROGRAMS

Degrees Offered: MBA (21 months)
Combined Degrees: Tuck offers dual- and joint-degree programs and other creative curricular options. Tuck partners with the Fletcher School of Law and Diplomacy at Tufts University, the Kennedy School of Government at Harvard University, Vermont Law School, Dartmouth's Thayer School of Engineering, and Dartmouth Medical School.
Academic Specialties: A highlight of Tuck's core curriculum is the Tuck Leadership Forum. The Forum runs throughout all 3 terms of the first year. The Forum is a unique blend of traditional general management class sessions, experiential exercises (including a major field project focused on business development), and career-oriented instruction that connects Tuck students to industries, alumni, executives, and peers. More than half of Tuck's faculty have lived or taught abroad, and the low student-to-faculty ratio ensures students the best learning opportunities.
Special Opportunities: Alumnae Mentoring Program, International Field Study Program, Visiting Executive Program, Center for Asia and Emerging Economies, Foster Center for Private Equity, Center for Cooperative Governance, Achtmeyer Center for Global Leadership, Glassmeyer/McNamee Center for Digital Strategies, Allwin Initiative for Corporate Citizenship
Study Abroad Options: Tuck offers exchange programs for 1 term in the second year with the London Business School; the International University of Japan in Urasa; HEC School of Management in Paris; Instituto de Estudios Superiores de la Empresa in Barcelona, Spain; and Otto Beisheim Graduate School of Management at WHU in Koblenz, Germany.

STUDENT INFORMATION

Total Business Students: 464
% Full Time: 100
% Female: 32
% Minority: 19
% Out of State: 98
% International: 30
Average Age: 28

COMPUTER AND RESEARCH FACILITIES

Research Facilities: Feldberg Library and Bloomberg Professional Service, Center for Asia and Emerging Economies, Foster Center for Private Equity, Center for Coporate Governance, Achtmeyer Center for Global Leadership, Glassmeyer/McNamee Center for Digital Strategies, Initiative for Corporative Citizenship
Computer Facilities: Whittemore Wing of Information Technology, more than 450 powerports for computers on-campus. All classrooms and study rooms at Tuck are equipped with computers and network jacks, which provide access to library databases, online information services, the World Wide Web, e-mail, bulletin boards, file services, and high-speed laser printers. There are approximately 75 public access computers in Tuck's computer labs, study rooms, and library.
Campuswide Network? Yes
% of MBA Classrooms Wired: 100
Computer Model Recommended: Laptop
Internet Fee? No

EXPENSES/FINANCIAL AID

Annual Tuition: $32,490
Room & Board (On/Off Campus): $12,550/$13,700
Books and Supplies: $3,000
Average Grant: $10,000
Average Loan: $30,000
% Receiving Financial Aid: 79
% Receiving Aid Their First Year: 85

ADMISSIONS INFORMATION

Application Fee: $180
Electronic Application? Yes
Early Decision Application Deadline: 10/18
Early Decision Notification: 12/20
Regular Application Deadline: 4/18
Regular Notification: 5/19
Deferment Available? Yes
Length of Deferment: Case-by-case basis
Non-fall Admissions? No
Transfer Students Accepted? No
Need-Blind Admissions? Yes
Number of Applications Received: 3,266
% of Applicants Accepted: 14
% Accepted Who Enrolled: 51
Average GPA: 3.4
Average GMAT: 695
Average Years Experience: 4
Other Admissions Factors Considered: All data points of the application are important as is any information provided to us by the applicant.
Minority/Disadvantaged Student Recruitment Programs: Tuck is a member of the Consortium for Graduate Study in Management, a group of 14 member-schools that provide full-tuition fellowships to underrepresented minorities. Tuck is also a member school of the Robert F. Toigo Fellowship Foundation, which is open to U.S.minorities interested in pursuing careers in finance post-MBA. Additionally, a number of need-based and merit-based scholarships are available to minority students.
Other Schools to Which Students Applied: Columbia University, Harvard University, Northwestern University, Stanford University, University of Pennsylvania

INTERNATIONAL STUDENTS

TOEFL Required of International Students? Yes

EMPLOYMENT INFORMATION

Placement Office Available? Yes
% Employed Within 3 Months: 82
Fields Employing Percentage of Grads: MIS (4%), Venture Capital (7%), Marketing (10%), General Management (19%), Finance (26%), Consulting (32%)
Frequent Employers: Accenture, Bain & Co., BCG, Booz-Allen, Credit Suisse First Boston Corp., Goldman Sachs, JP Morgan Chase Co., McKinsey Consulting, Morgan Stanley, Parthenon Group
Prominent Alumni: William Achtmeyer, chairman and managing partner, The Parthenon Group; Alexander M. Cutler, chairman/CEO, Eaton Corp.; Akira Uehara, president, Taisho Pharmaceuticals; Peter R. Dolan, president/CEO, Bristol-Myers Squibb; Noreen Doyle, deputy vice president, European Bank

---

DEPAUL UNIVERSITY
Kellstadt Graduate School of Business

Admissions Contact: Christopher E. Kinsella, Director of Admission
Address: 1 East Jackson Blvd, Chicago, IL 60604
Admissions Phone: 312-362-8810 • **Admissions Fax:** 312-362-6677
Admissions E-mail: mbainfo@depaul.edu • **Web Address:** www.depaul.edu

You'll enjoy a solid education at the Kellstadt Graduate School of Business, one of the oldest b-schools in the United States. Kellstadt has earned national recognition for its MBA programs, which offer day, evening, and weekend classes. In addition, the MBA program in International

Marketing and Finance (MBA/IMF) is the only existing program of its kind. If the campus location near bustling Chicago doesn't satisfy, Kellstadt also offers MBAs in Hong Kong, Bahrain, and Prague.

INSTITUTIONAL INFORMATION

Public/Private: Private
Evening Classes Available? Yes
Total Faculty: 239
% Faculty Female: 17
% Faculty Minority: 15
% Faculty Part Time: 47
Student/Faculty Ratio: 53:1
Students in Parent Institution: 21,505
Academic Calendar: Quarter

PROGRAMS

Degrees Offered: MBA (full time: 80 credits, minimum of 18 months; part time: 60-80 total credits, 18 months-6 years), with concentrations in Accounting, E-Business, Economics, Entrepreneurship, Finance, Financial Analysis, Financial Management and Control, Health Care Management, Human Resources, International Business, International Marketing and Finance(full-time program only), Leadership and Change Management, Management Information Systems, Marketing, Operations Management; weekend MBA (60-80 credits), with concentrations in Strategic Management, Managerial Finance; MACC (45 credits, full time or part time, 18 months to 6 years); MSA (60-64 credits, full time or part time, 15 months to 6 years); MS in E-Business (48 credits, full time or part time, 18 months to 6 years); MS in Finance (48 credits, full time or part time, 18 months to 6 years); MS in Human Resources (48 credits, full time or part time, 18 months to 6 years), with concentration in Management; MS in Marketing Analysis (48 credits, full time or part time, 18 months to 6 years); MST (45-60 credits, full time or part time, 18 months to 6 years); MS in MIS (116 credits, full time or part time, 2-6 years to complete program)
Combined Degrees: MBA/JD (140 credits, full time or part time, 2.8 to 3.8 years), with concentrations in Accounting, Economics, Entrepreneurship, Finance, Human Resources, International Business, Management Information Systems, Marketing, Operations Management, E-Business

STUDENT INFORMATION

Total Business Students: 2,400
% Full Time: 3
% Female: 55
% Minority: 10
% Out of State: 20
% International: 40
Average Age: 27

COMPUTER AND RESEARCH FACILITIES

Research Facilities: Main library plus 3 additional on-campus libraries; total holdings of 738,072 volumes; 309,701 microforms; 10,136 current periodical subscriptions. CD players available for graduate student use; access to online bibliographic retrieval services
Campuswide Network? Yes
% of MBA Classrooms Wired: 100
Internet Fee? Yes

EXPENSES/FINANCIAL AID

Annual Tuition: $15,120
Books and Supplies: $7,200
Average Grant: $8,000
Average Loan: $18,500
% Receiving Financial Aid: 40
% Receiving Aid Their First Year: 40

ADMISSIONS INFORMATION

Application Fee: $60

Electronic Application? Yes
Regular Application Deadline: 7/1
Regular Notification: Rolling
Deferment Available? Yes
Length of Deferment: 1 year
Non-fall Admissions? Yes
Non-fall Application Deadline(s): 10/1 winter, 2/1 spring, 4/1 summer; international applicants: 6/1 fall, 9/1 winter, 1/1 spring, 3/1 summer
Transfer Students Accepted? Yes
Transfer Policy: Must apply as does any other applicant
Need-Blind Admissions? Yes
Number of Applications Received: 1,259
% of Applicants Accepted: 51
% Accepted Who Enrolled: 62
Average GPA: 3.1
Average GMAT: 561
Average Years Experience: 5
Other Admissions Factors Considered: Work experience recommended
Other Schools to Which Students Applied: Northwestern University, University of Chicago

INTERNATIONAL STUDENTS

TOEFL Required of International Students? Yes
Minimum TOEFL: 550 (213 computer)

EMPLOYMENT INFORMATION

Placement Office Available? Yes
% Employed Within 3 Months: 90
Fields Employing Percentage of Grads: Operations (4%), Consulting (12%), General Management (16%), Finance (28%), Marketing (32%)
Frequent Employers: Abbott Laboratories, ABN AMRO, Accenture, Bank One, Baxter, BP, Cigna, CNA, International Truck & Engine, KPMG, McDonald's Corp.
Prominent Alumni: Jaclyn Winship, director—strategy; Rosario Perrelli, executive vice president and CFO; Christopher Piesko, senior vice president; Frank Ptak, vice chairman; Jeffrey Rohr, managing partner

DRAKE UNIVERSITY
College of Business and Public Administration

Admissions Contact: Nancy Gabriel, Director of Graduate Programs
Address: 2507 University Avenue, Des Moines, IA 50311
Admissions Phone: 515-271-2188 • **Admissions Fax:** 515-271-4518
Admissions E-mail: cbpa.gradprograms@drake.edu
Web Address: www.drake.edu/cbpa/grad

INSTITUTIONAL INFORMATION

Public/Private: Private
Evening Classes Available? Yes
Total Faculty: 38
% Faculty Female: 21
% Faculty Minority: 16
Student/Faculty Ratio: 1:1
Students in Parent Institution: 4,646

PROGRAMS

Degrees Offered: MBA (32-47 hours), MPA (36 hours), MACC (30 hours)
Combined Degrees: MBA/Pharm D, MPA/JD
Special Opportunities: General Business, Accounting, Health Services/Hos-

pital Administration, Human Resource Management (includes Labor Relations), Other, Public Administration

STUDENT INFORMATION

Total Business Students: 336
% Full Time: 20
% Female: 12
% Minority: 6
% International: 32
Average Age: 28

COMPUTER AND RESEARCH FACILITIES

Campuswide Network? Yes
Internet Fee? No

EXPENSES/FINANCIAL AID

Annual Tuition: $16,200
Tuition Per Credit (Resident/Nonresident): $340
Books and Supplies: $400

ADMISSIONS INFORMATION

Application Fee: $25
Electronic Application? Yes
Regular Application Deadline: 1/1
Regular Notification: 1/1
Deferment Available? Yes
Length of Deferment: 1 term
Non-fall Admissions? Yes
Non-fall Application Deadline(s): Rolling
Transfer Students Accepted? Yes
Transfer Policy: Case-by-case evaluation
Need-Blind Admissions? Yes
Number of Applications Received: 89
% of Applicants Accepted: 94
% Accepted Who Enrolled: 94

INTERNATIONAL STUDENTS

TOEFL Required of International Students? Yes
Minimum TOEFL: 550 (213 computer)

EMPLOYMENT INFORMATION

Placement Office Available? Yes

DREXEL UNIVERSITY
The Bennett S. LeBow College of Business

Admissions Contact: Amanda Lutz, Assistant Director of Graduate Admissions
Address: 3141 Chestnut Street, Philadelphia, PA 19104-2875
Admissions Phone: 215-895-6705 • **Admissions Fax:** 215-895-5939
Admissions E-mail: acl28@drexel.edu • **Web Address:** www.lebow.drexel.edu/

INSTITUTIONAL INFORMATION

Public/Private: Private
Evening Classes Available? No
Total Faculty: 82
% Faculty Part Time: 26
Students in Parent Institution: 11,617
Academic Calendar: Quarter

PROGRAMS

Degrees Offered: MS in Marketing (48-72 credits, 1-7 years), MSA (48-72 credits, 1-7 years), MSF (48-72 credits, 1-7 years), MST (48-72 credits, 1-7 years), MS in Decision Sciences (48-72 credits, 1-7 years), MBA (48-72 credits, 1-7 years)
Special Opportunities: Accounting, CIS or MIS, E-Business (includes E-Commerce), Economics, Finance (includes Banking), Human Resource Management (includes Labor Relations), International Business, Marketing, Other, Production/Operations Management/Managerial Economics, Taxation

STUDENT INFORMATION

Total Business Students: 850
% Full Time: 37
% Female: 37
% International: 32
Average Age: 26

COMPUTER AND RESEARCH FACILITIES

Campuswide Network? Yes
Internet Fee? No

EXPENSES/FINANCIAL AID

Annual Tuition: $26,410
Tuition Per Credit (Resident/Nonresident): $511

ADMISSIONS INFORMATION

Application Fee: $35
Electronic Application? No
Regular Application Deadline: 8/31
Regular Notification: Rolling
Deferment Available? Yes
Non-fall Admissions? Yes
Non-fall Application Deadline(s): 11/30, 3/1, 5/31
Transfer Students Accepted? No
Need-Blind Admissions? No
Number of Applications Received: 858
% of Applicants Accepted: 55
% Accepted Who Enrolled: 43
Other Admissions Factors Considered: Resume

INTERNATIONAL STUDENTS

TOEFL Required of International Students? Yes
Minimum TOEFL: 570

EMPLOYMENT INFORMATION

Placement Office Available? Yes

DUKE UNIVERSITY
The Fuqua School of Business

Admissions Contact: Liz Riley, Director of Admissions
Address: 1 Towerview Drive, A-08 Academic Center, Durham, NC 27708
Admissions Phone: 919-660-7705 • **Admissions Fax:** 919-681-8026
Admissions E-mail: admissions-info@fuqua.duke.edu • **Web Address:** www.fuqua.duke.edu

Liberal arts majors with no experience in business courses should be prepared to hit the ground running at Duke University's Fuqua School of Business. Here, "the pace is very fast"—what with "six-week terms"—and students need a working knowledge of calculus just to survive the first year. Also, you heard it here first: The correct pronunciation of Fuqua is "few-kwa" and definitely not "foo-kwa." They really hate that.

INSTITUTIONAL INFORMATION

Public/Private: Private
Evening Classes Available? No
Total Faculty: 88
% Faculty Female: 13
% Faculty Minority: 1
% Faculty Part Time: 8
Student/Faculty Ratio: 18:1
Students in Parent Institution: 10,800
Academic Calendar: Terms

PROGRAMS

Degrees Offered: EMBA (global, 19 months; weekend, 20 months), MBA (daytime, 2 years; cross continent, 20 months), PhD (4-5 years)
Combined Degrees: MBA/JD (4 years), MBA/MPP (2-3 years), MBA/Master of Forestry (2-3 years), MBA/Master of Environmental Management (3 years), MBA/MS in Engineering (2-3 years), MBA/MD (5 years), MBA/MSN (3 years)
Academic Specialties: Fuqua's MBA Program is based on an integrative, general management curriculum that emphasizes cross-functional, strategic, and global perspectives. The Program is widely recognized for particular strength in the areas of Corporate Finance, Marketing Investments and General Management, Decision Science, and Operations.
Special Opportunities: International exchange programs, the MBA Enterprise Corps, Global Academic Travel Experiences (GATE) programs
Study Abroad Options: We currently have 25 reciprocal exchange programs with the following schools: Universidad Torcuato Di Tella, Beunos Aires, Argentina; Australian Graduate School of Management, Sydney, Australia; Melbourne Business School, Melbourne, Australia; Katholieke Universiteit, Leuven, Belgium; INCAE, Alajuela, Costa Rica; Copenhagen Business School, Copenhagen, Denmark; Ecole Supérieure des Sciences Economiques et Commerciales (ESSEC), Cergy-Pontoise, France; Hautes Etudes Commerciales (HEC), Jouy-en-Josas, France; Chinese University of Hong Kong and Hong Kong University of Science & Technology, China; Indian Institute of Management, Bangalore, India; SDA Bocconi, Milan, Italy; Instituto Panamericano de Alta Direccion de Empressa (IPADE), Mexico City, Mexico; Rotterdam School of Management at Erasmus University, Rotterdam, The Netherlands; Norwegian School of Economic and Business Administration, Bergen, Norway; Graduate School of Business, University of Cape Town, Cape Town, South Africa; Wits Business School, University of the Witwatersrand, Johannesburg, South Africa; IESE Business School at the University of Navarra and Escuela Superior de Administración y Dirección de Empresas (ESADE), Barcelona, Spain; Stockholm School of Economics, Stockholm, Sweden; Universitat St. Gallen, St. Gallen, Switzerland; SASIN Graduate Institute of Business Administration, Bangkok, Thailand; London School of Economics, Manchester Business School, and Warwick Business School, United Kingdom

STUDENT INFORMATION

Total Business Students: 696
% Full Time: 100
% Female: 34
% Minority: 12
% International: 34
Average Age: 28

COMPUTER AND RESEARCH FACILITIES

Research Facilities: Center for International Business Education and Research (CIBER), North Carolina Family Business Forum, Hartman Center, Accounting Research Center, Futures and Options Research Center (FORCE), Computer Mediated Learning Center
Computer Facilities: Fuqua's Student Computing Space includes 3 computing laboratories, 27 team rooms, 8 classrooms, and several special-purpose computing resource areas (library, student lounge, etc), which collectively provide students with access to 147 Pentium-class systems and 262 plug-in access points to FuquaNet for laptop systems. Via FuquaNet, students can access Fuqua's Computer-Mediated Learning Environment through FuquaWorld,

the intranet Web environment. Alumni have access to a similar intranet—Fuqua AlumniLink. These intranet environments enhance the sense of community that pervades Fuqua. These services are available 24 hours/day.
Campuswide Network? Yes
% of MBA Classrooms Wired: 11
Internet Fee? No

EXPENSES/FINANCIAL AID

Annual Tuition: $31,350
Books and Supplies: $13,720
Average Grant: $11,700
Average Loan: $28,875
% Receiving Financial Aid: 80
% Receiving Aid Their First Year: 77

ADMISSIONS INFORMATION

Application Fee: $175
Electronic Application? Yes
Regular Application Deadline: 12/2
Regular Notification: 2/3
Deferment Available? Yes
Length of Deferment: 1 year
Non-fall Admissions? No
Transfer Students Accepted? No
Need-Blind Admissions? Yes
Number of Applications Received: 3,382
% of Applicants Accepted: 19
% Accepted Who Enrolled: 53
Average GPA: 3.4
GPA Range: 2.8-3.8
Average GMAT: 701
GMAT Range: 640-760
Average Years Experience: 5
Other Admissions Factors Considered: We consider most of the above criteria equally.
Minority/Disadvantaged Student Recruitment Programs: Ford MBA Workshop for Minority Applicants; aggressive minority scholarship program includes Toigo Fellowship Partner

INTERNATIONAL STUDENTS

TOEFL Required of International Students? Yes
Minimum TOEFL: 600 (250 computer)

EMPLOYMENT INFORMATION

Placement Office Available? Yes
% Employed Within 3 Months: 89
Fields Employing Percentage of Grads: Operations (3%), MIS (8%), Other (10%), General Management (10%), Consulting (11%), Marketing (23%), Finance (35%)
Frequent Employers: More than 400 law firms annually offer positions to Duke Law students.
Prominent Alumni: Melinda Gates, philanthropist; Michael Crowley, president, Oakland Athletics Baseball Co.; George Morrow, president and CEO, Glaxo-Wellcom

DUQUESNE UNIVERSITY
John F. Donahue Graduate School of Business

Admissions Contact: Patricia Moore, Assistant Director
Address: 600 Forbes Avenue, Pittsburgh, PA 15282
Admissions Phone: 412-396-6276 • **Admissions Fax:** 412-396-1726
Admissions E-mail: grad-bus@duq.edu • **Web Address:** www.bus.duq.edu/grad/

INSTITUTIONAL INFORMATION

Public/Private: Private
Evening Classes Available? Yes
Total Faculty: 51
% Faculty Female: 10
% Faculty Part Time: 26
Student/Faculty Ratio: 27:1
Students in Parent Institution: 9,500
Academic Calendar: Semester

PROGRAMS

Degrees Offered: MBA (18-24 months full time, 36-42 months part time), MSISM (18-24 months full time, 36-42 months part time), MS in Taxation (12-18 months full time, 24 months part time)
Combined Degrees: MBA/MSISM (3 years full time, 4 years part time), MBA/JD (4 years full time, 5 years part time), MBA/MSN (3 years full time, 4 years part time), MBA/MS in Environmental Science and Management (2 years full time, 4 years part time), MBA/MS in Industrial Pharmacy (varies with changes in Pharmacy program)
Academic Specialties: E-Business (including electronic procurement and Internet Marketing), Supply Chain Management, Business Ethics, Production/Operations Management, Global Competition, Human Resource Management, Sports Marketing, Management Information Systems, Accounting, Finance and Investment Management, Marketing, International Business. Special strengths in the program: Incorporates the themes of globalization, ethics, technology, leading change, workforce diversity, and the value chain through specific courses in the core MBA curriculum; enables students to customize their programs of study with various areas of concentration; allows students to take up to 6 elective credits in other graduate programs on campus provided that the students can demonstrate relevance to the graduate business course of study. Customization is also possible through joint degree programs, independent study, and internship opportunities.
Special Opportunities: Accounting, Business Ethics, MIS, E-Business, Finance, Health Care Management , Human Resource Management, International Business, Management, Marketing,Supply Chain Management, Taxation, Environmental Science and Management; specialized master's: CIS or MIS, Taxation
Study Abroad Options: Northern Jiaotong University, China; University of Nancy, France; Sophia University, Japan

STUDENT INFORMATION

Total Business Students: 434
% Full Time: 20
% Female: 35
% Minority: 11
% Out of State: 5
% International: 8
Average Age: 30

COMPUTER AND RESEARCH FACILITIES

Research Facilities: The Donahue Graduate School of Business is also home to the Institute for Economic Transformation, a resource that provides economic development studies and assistance to the Western Pennsylvania Region. The Center is supported by grants from the various foundations in the region that focus on economic development. The School also supports the Center for Executive Education, which provides non-credit open enrollment and customized workshops for regional companies.
Computer Facilities: 4 computer laboratories. One laboratory is dedicated to personal computers and their applications across the business curriculum. Another laboratory consists of terminals that provide online access to software and applications associated with the University's mainframe computer system. The third laboratory is a teaching facility dedicated to multimedia applications. There is a 20-station Investment Management Lab utilizing the Bridge System for use by students in various courses. The fourth laboratory with 30 computers provides access to an ERP application used by the accounting students.The University library offers an online catalogue with remote access as well as 18 on-site stations and a CD-ROM Center that permits users to access the Library's data files. The CD-ROM system gives students access to hundreds of additional periodicals not physically housed in the Library. Students may also access other online resources through the Library.
Campuswide Network? Yes
% of MBA Classrooms Wired: 100
Internet Fee? No

EXPENSES/FINANCIAL AID

Annual Tuition: $16,767
Tuition Per Credit (Resident/Nonresident): $621
Room & Board (On/Off Campus): $7,170
Books and Supplies: $2,500
Average Grant: $16,767
Average Loan: $5,800
% Receiving Financial Aid: 70
% Receiving Aid Their First Year: 70

ADMISSIONS INFORMATION

Application Fee: $50
Electronic Application? No
Regular Application Deadline: 6/1
Regular Notification: 7/1
Deferment Available? Yes
Length of Deferment: 1 year
Non-fall Admissions? Yes
Non-fall Application Deadline(s): 11/1, 3/1
Transfer Students Accepted? Yes
Transfer Policy: Up to 15 transfer credits from an accredited college or university
Need-Blind Admissions? Yes
Number of Applications Received: 201
% of Applicants Accepted: 76
% Accepted Who Enrolled: 64
Average GPA: 3.1
Average GMAT: 510
Average Years Experience: 5
Other Admissions Factors Considered: Internship experiences, interviews when requested by applicants, quality of work experience. Although work experience is not required, it is highly preferred.
Other Schools to Which Students Applied: Carnegie Mellon, University of Pittsburgh

INTERNATIONAL STUDENTS

TOEFL Required of International Students? Yes
Minimum TOEFL: 550 (213 computer)

EMPLOYMENT INFORMATION

Placement Office Available? Yes
Frequent Employers: Alcoa, Deloitte and Touche, Federal Express Ground, H. J. Heinz Corp., Management Science Associates, Mellon Financial Corp., Mine Safety Appliance Corp., PNC Corp., U. S. Steel Corp.
Prominent Alumni: Robert Dickinson, president, Carnival Cruise Lines; James F. Will, president, St. Vincent College; Gail Gerono, director of investor relations, Calgon Carbon Corp.; William Lyons, CFO, Consol Energy; John Boscia, president and CEO, Lincoln National Corp.

EAST CAROLINA UNIVERSITY
School of Business

Admissions Contact: Frederick Niswander, Assistant Dean for Graduate Programs
Address: 3119 Bate Building, Greenville, NC 27858
Admissions Phone: 252-328-6966 • Admissions Fax: 252-328-2106
Admissions E-mail: norvillel@mail.ecu.edu • Web Address: www.business.ecu.edu/grad

INSTITUTIONAL INFORMATION
Public/Private: Public
Evening Classes Available? No
Total Faculty: 73
% Faculty Part Time: 3
Student/Faculty Ratio: 20:1
Students in Parent Institution: 17,799
Academic Calendar: Semester

PROGRAMS
Degrees Offered: MBA (30-60 credits, full time or part time, 8-20 months), MSA (30-60 credits, full time or part time, 8-20 months), MD/MBA (42 credits, full time or part time, 12 months; must be enrolled in an accredited medical school or be a medical resident)
Academic Specialties: Case study, computer-aided instruction, computer analysis, computer simulations, experiential learning, field projects, group discussion, lecture, research, role playing, student presentations, study groups, team projects
Special Opportunities: General Business, Accounting, Taxation

STUDENT INFORMATION
Total Business Students: 200
% Full Time: 64
% Female: 47
% Minority: 8
% International: 8
Average Age: 28

COMPUTER AND RESEARCH FACILITIES
Computer Facilities: Joyner Library plus 1 additional on-campus library; CD player available; access provided to online bibliographic retrieval services and online databases
Campuswide Network? Yes
Internet Fee? No

EXPENSES/FINANCIAL AID
Annual Tuition (Resident/Nonresident): $2,300/$10,162
% Receiving Financial Aid: 27

ADMISSIONS INFORMATION
Application Fee: $40
Electronic Application? No
Regular Application Deadline: Rolling
Regular Notification: Rolling
Deferment Available? No
Non-fall Admissions? No
Transfer Students Accepted? No
Need-Blind Admissions? No
Number of Applications Received: 330
% of Applicants Accepted: 82
% Accepted Who Enrolled: 74

INTERNATIONAL STUDENTS
TOEFL Required of International Students? Yes
Minimum TOEFL: 231

EMPLOYMENT INFORMATION
Placement Office Available? Yes
% Employed Within 3 Months: 83

EAST TENNESSEE STATE UNIVERSITY
College of Business

Admissions Contact: Dr. Martha Pointer, Director of Graduate Studies
Address: PO Box 70699, Johnson City, TN 37614
Admissions Phone: 423-439-5314 • Admissions Fax: 423-439-5274
Admissions E-mail: business@business.etsu.edu
Web Address: www.etsu.edu/gradstud/index.htm

INSTITUTIONAL INFORMATION
Public/Private: Public
Evening Classes Available? No
Total Faculty: 54
% Faculty Female: 10
Student/Faculty Ratio: 7:1
Students in Parent Institution: 11,347
Academic Calendar: Semester

PROGRAMS
Degrees Offered: MBA (39 credits, 16 months to 6 years), MACC (33 credits, 1-6 years), Master of Public Management (36 credits, 20 months to 6 years)
Special Opportunities: General Business, Accounting

STUDENT INFORMATION
Total Business Students: 211
% Full Time: 26
% Female: 43
% Minority: 14
% International: 9
Average Age: 32

COMPUTER AND RESEARCH FACILITIES
Campuswide Network? Yes
% of MBA Classrooms Wired: 25
Internet Fee? No

EXPENSES/FINANCIAL AID
Annual Tuition (Resident/Nonresident): $3,850/$10,808
Tuition Per Credit (Resident/Nonresident): $201/$502
Room & Board (On/Off Campus): $3,000/$6,000
Books and Supplies: $1,000
Average Grant: $6,000
Average Loan: $6,000
% Receiving Financial Aid: 25
% Receiving Aid Their First Year: 25

ADMISSIONS INFORMATION
Application Fee: $25
Electronic Application? Yes
Regular Application Deadline: 6/1
Regular Notification: Rolling
Deferment Available? Yes
Length of Deferment: 1 year
Non-fall Admissions? Yes
Non-fall Application Deadline(s): 11/1
Transfer Students Accepted? Yes
Transfer Policy: Up to 9 approved hours
Need-Blind Admissions? No
Number of Applications Received: 140
% of Applicants Accepted: 59
% Accepted Who Enrolled: 85
Average GPA: 3.2
Average GMAT: 530
Other Admissions Factors Considered: GMAT, work experience

INTERNATIONAL STUDENTS

TOEFL Required of International Students? Yes
Minimum TOEFL: 550 (213 computer)

EMPLOYMENT INFORMATION

Placement Office Available? Yes
% Employed Within 3 Months: 80

EASTERN ILLINOIS UNIVERSITY
Lumpkin College of Business and Applied Science

Admissions Contact: Dr. Cheryl Noll, Coordinator, Graduate Business Studies
Address: 600 Lincoln Avenue, 4009 Lumpkin Hall, Charleston, IL 61920-3099
Admissions Phone: 217-581-3028 • **Admissions Fax:** 217-581-7244
Admissions E-mail: mba@eiu.edu • **Web Address:** www.eiu.edu/~mba

INSTITUTIONAL INFORMATION

Public/Private: Public
Evening Classes Available? Yes
Total Faculty: 19
% Faculty Female: 2
Student/Faculty Ratio: 22:1
Students in Parent Institution: 11,000

PROGRAMS

Degrees Offered: MBA (1 year); MBA, with concentration in Accountancy (1 year)

STUDENT INFORMATION

Total Business Students: 163
% Full Time: 46
% Female: 43
% Minority: 2
% Out of State: 2
% International: 13
Average Age: 25

COMPUTER AND RESEARCH FACILITIES

Research Facilities: Booth Library—$22.5 million renovation completed spring 2002
Computer Facilities: 120 on-campus PCs are available for student use in Lumpkin Hall, and all are linked by a campuswide network with full access to the library system and other databases.
Campuswide Network? Yes
Internet Fee? No

EXPENSES/FINANCIAL AID

Annual Tuition (Resident/Nonresident): $4,111/$12,334
Tuition Per Credit (Resident/Nonresident): $114/$343
Room & Board (On/Off Campus): $6,000/$8,000
Books and Supplies: $325
Average Grant: $6,500
Average Loan: $1,500
% Receiving Aid Their First Year: 33

ADMISSIONS INFORMATION

Application Fee: $30
Electronic Application? Yes
Regular Application Deadline: Rolling

Regular Notification: Rolling
Deferment Available? Yes
Length of Deferment: 1 academic year
Non-fall Admissions? Yes
Non-fall Application Deadline(s): 12/1, 4/15, 6/1, 10/15, 4/1
Transfer Students Accepted? Yes
Transfer Policy: Maximum of 9 semester hours at grade of "B" or better
Need-Blind Admissions? Yes
Number of Applications Received: 105
% of Applicants Accepted: 93
% Accepted Who Enrolled: 85
Average GPA: 3.8
Average GMAT: 525
GMAT Range: 470-610
Average Years Experience: 4
Other Admissions Factors Considered: Applicants to the MBA Program must submit a program application, resume with references, and personal goal statement. To be admitted, applicants must score at least 1,000 points based on the following formula: 200 times the GPA of the last 60 hours of graded academic work plus the GMAT score. Minimum GMAT scores are: 400 overall, 18 verbal, 20 quantitative, and 2 analytical writing. Admission to the MBA Program also requires that applicants meet the following Graduate School admission requirements: application with $30 fee, official transcripts, and minimum GPA 2.75.

INTERNATIONAL STUDENTS

TOEFL Required of International Students? Yes
Minimum TOEFL: 550 (213 computer)

EMPLOYMENT INFORMATION

Placement Office Available? Yes

EASTERN MICHIGAN UNIVERSITY
College of Business

Admissions Contact: Christie Montgomery, Assistant Dean
Address: PO Box 970, Ypsilanti, MI 48197
Admissions Phone: 734-487-3060 • **Admissions Fax:** 734-487-1484
Admissions E-mail: graduate.admissions@emich.edu
Web Address: www.emich.edu/public/gradcatolog

The Eastern Michigan University MBA program has a trimester academic calendar, an intimate educational setting, and affordable tuition rates. The faculty members are nearly all full time, allowing the student body great accessibility to their professors, who are more than willing to lend a helping mind. EMU's Entrepreneurship Center is a fantastic resource for information, support for innovative ideas, and opportunities to interact with the entrepreneurial community.

INSTITUTIONAL INFORMATION

Public/Private: Public
Evening Classes Available? Yes
Total Faculty: 66
% Faculty Female: 24
% Faculty Minority: 8
% Faculty Part Time: 32
Student/Faculty Ratio: 25:1
Students in Parent Institution: 23,000
Academic Calendar: Trimester

PROGRAMS

Degrees Offered: MBA (1-6 years), MSIS (1-6 years), MSA (1-6 years), MS in Human Resources/Organizational Development (1-6 years)

Academic Specialties: Case study, computer-aided instruction, computer analysis, computer simulations, faculty seminars, field projects, group discussion, lecture, research, seminars by members of the business community, simulations, student presentations, team projects

Study Abroad Options: International exchange programs in Canada, France, Germany, Mexico, Spain

STUDENT INFORMATION

Total Business Students: 760
% Full Time: 36
% Female: 45
% Minority: 7
% International: 24
Average Age: 28

COMPUTER AND RESEARCH FACILITIES

Research Facilities: Alumni network, career counseling/planning, career fairs, career library, career placement, electronic job bank, job interviews arranged, job search course, resume referral to employers, resume preparation
Computer Facilities: Lexis-Nexis (EMU), WSJ Online (Web), Reference USA (EMU), Wilson Business Abstracts (Web)
Campuswide Network? Yes
Internet Fee? No

EXPENSES/FINANCIAL AID

Annual Tuition (Resident/Nonresident): $5,160/$10,560
Tuition Per Credit (Resident/Nonresident): $215/$440
Books and Supplies: $600

ADMISSIONS INFORMATION

Application Fee: $30
Electronic Application? Yes
Regular Application Deadline: 5/1
Regular Notification: 8/1
Deferment Available? No
Non-fall Admissions? Yes
Non-fall Application Deadline(s): 10/1, 3/1
Transfer Students Accepted? Yes
Transfer Policy: 6 credits may be accepted upon approval
Need-Blind Admissions? Yes
Number of Applications Received: 286
% of Applicants Accepted: 85
% Accepted Who Enrolled: 100
Average GPA: 3.0
Average GMAT: 495
GMAT Range: 410-590
Average Years Experience: 3
Other Admissions Factors Considered: Work experience, computer experience

Other Schools to Which Students Applied: Central Michigan University, Michigan State University-Detroit College of Law, Oakland University, University of Michigan, University of Michigan—Dearborn, Wayne State University, Western Michigan University

INTERNATIONAL STUDENTS

TOEFL Required of International Students? Yes
Minimum TOEFL: 550 (213 computer)

EMPLOYMENT INFORMATION

Placement Office Available? Yes
% Employed Within 3 Months: 98
Fields Employing Percentage of Grads: MIS (6%), Human Resources (7%), Consulting (9%), Other (13%), Marketing (16%), General Management (18%), Accounting (25%)

Frequent Employers: American Sun Roof, Arthur Andersen, Bank One, Com Share, Creative Solutions, Ford Motor Co., General Motors, Johnson Controls, Masco Corp, Pfizer Inc., Visteon Corp., Yakaki

EASTERN WASHINGTON UNIVERSITY
College of Business & Public Administration

Admissions Contact: Diana Teague, Program Assistant
Address: EWU 206 Showalter Hall, Cheney, WA 99004
Admissions Phone: 509-359-6297 • **Admissions Fax:** 509-359-6044
Admissions E-mail: gradprograms@ewu.edu • **Web Address:** www.cbpa.ewu.edu

The EWU College of Business and Public Administration is a small school with less than 100 students that provides an intimate classroom experience and an accessible faculty of "nationally renowned scholars with strong ties to the local business community." Much of the student body comes from out of state, allowing for a diversified learning experience. Unlike other graduate programs at EWU, the MBA program's courses are taught from within each of their respective departments at the business school. This approach benefits its students, enabling them to acquire "unique and interdisciplinary business expertise." Classes are available in the evenings and on weekends.

INSTITUTIONAL INFORMATION

Public/Private: Public
Evening Classes Available? Yes
Total Faculty: 36
% Faculty Female: 46
Student/Faculty Ratio: 15:1
Students in Parent Institution: 8,597
Academic Calendar: Quarter

PROGRAMS

Degrees Offered: MBA (49-60 credits, 1-1.5 years)
Combined Degrees: MBA/MPA (69 credits, 2 years)
Academic Specialties: Entrepreneurship, Non-Profit, Marketing, Health Services, AIS
Special Opportunities: Accounting, CIS or MIS, Economics, Finance (includes Banking), Human Resource Management (includes Labor Relations), Management, Marketing, Production/Operations Management/Managerial Economics, MBA (General Business)

STUDENT INFORMATION

Total Business Students: 82
% Full Time: 35
% Female: 45
% Minority: 8
% International: 55
Average Age: 28

COMPUTER AND RESEARCH FACILITIES

Campuswide Network? Yes
Internet Fee? No

EXPENSES/FINANCIAL AID

Annual Tuition (Resident/Nonresident): $4,470/$13,161
Tuition Per Credit (Resident/Nonresident): $149/$428
Room & Board (On/Off Campus): $5,567/$7,000
Books and Supplies: $1,200

ADMISSIONS INFORMATION

Application Fee: $35
Electronic Application? No
Regular Application Deadline: 1/1
Regular Notification: 1/1
Deferment Available? Yes
Length of Deferment: 1 year
Non-fall Admissions? Yes
Non-fall Application Deadline(s): 1/1
Transfer Students Accepted? Yes
Transfer Policy: Maximum of 12 credits
Need-Blind Admissions? Yes
Number of Applications Received: 44
% of Applicants Accepted: 50
% Accepted Who Enrolled: 91
Average GPA: 3.2
GPA Range: 2.9-3.7
Average GMAT: 479
GMAT Range: 420-600
Average Years Experience: 7
Other Admissions Factors Considered: Formula: GMAT (minimum = 450) + GPA (minimum = 3.0)

INTERNATIONAL STUDENTS

TOEFL Required of International Students? Yes
Minimum TOEFL: 580 (237 computer)

EMPLOYMENT INFORMATION

Placement Office Available? Yes

EMORY UNIVERSITY
Goizueta Business School

Admissions Contact: Julie R. Barefoot, Assistant Dean and Director of MBA Admissions
Address: 1300 Clifton Road, Atlanta, GA 30322
Admissions Phone: 404-727-6311 • **Admissions Fax:** 404-727-4612
Admissions E-mail: Admissions@bus.emory.edu • **Web Address:** www.goizueta.emory.edu

Students at Emory University's Goizueta Business School "love" its "up-and-coming" reputation, and they are thrilled about the "exceptional" as well as "brand-new and state-of-the-art business center" that houses the school. Goizueta includes a unique international business component in its core, and it offers several flexible programs of study. Students with an undergraduate business degree might consider Goizueta's intensive one-year accelerated MBA.

INSTITUTIONAL INFORMATION

Public/Private: Private
Evening Classes Available? Yes
Total Faculty: 98
% Faculty Female: 28
% Faculty Minority: 8
% Faculty Part Time: 15
Student/Faculty Ratio: 5:1
Students in Parent Institution: 11,600
Academic Calendar: Semester

PROGRAMS

Degrees Offered: MBA (1-2 years full time, 3 years evening), EMBA (16 months weekend program, 20 months modular program)
Combined Degrees: MBA/JD(4 years), MBA/MPH (5 semesters), MBA/

MDIV (4 years)
Academic Specialties: Marketing, Strategy/Entrepreneurship, Finance and Consulting
Special Opportunities: We offer our students Regional Studies Concentrations as one way to gain an in-depth understanding of tomorrow's emerging economies. Along with their MBA degree, students can earn a certificate of specialization in Latin American and Caribbean Studies or Russian/East European Studies.
Study Abroad Options: Australia, Chile, China, Costa Rica, Finland, France, Germany, Korea, Mexico, The Netherlands, Singapore, South Africa, Spain, Venezuela, United Kingdom

STUDENT INFORMATION

Total Business Students: 638
% Full Time: 74
% Female: 23
% Minority: 18
% International: 31
Average Age: 28

COMPUTER AND RESEARCH FACILITIES

Research Facilities: Goizueta Business Library
Computer Facilities: Computer lab
Campuswide Network? Yes
% of MBA Classrooms Wired: 100
Computer Model Recommended: Laptop
Internet Fee? No

EXPENSES/FINANCIAL AID

Annual Tuition: $30,580
Tuition Per Credit (Resident/Nonresident): $1,274
Room & Board (On/Off Campus): $11,700
Books and Supplies: $1,900
Average Grant: $15,873
Average Loan: $27,856
% Receiving Financial Aid: 85
% Receiving Aid Their First Year: 74

ADMISSIONS INFORMATION

Application Fee: $100
Electronic Application? Yes
Regular Application Deadline: 3/31
Regular Notification: Rolling
Deferment Available? Yes
Length of Deferment: 1 year
Non-fall Admissions? No
Transfer Students Accepted? No
Need-Blind Admissions? Yes
Number of Applications Received: 1,490
% of Applicants Accepted: 26
% Accepted Who Enrolled: 45
GPA Range: 3.0-3.7
Average GMAT: 675
GMAT Range: 610-740
Average Years Experience: 5
Other Admissions Factors Considered: Leadership
Minority/Disadvantaged Student Recruitment Programs: The School is a member of the Consortium of Graduate Study in Management. Additionally, the School hosts Inside Goizueta: A Conference for Prospective Minority Students.
Other Schools to Which Students Applied: Duke University, New York University, Northwestern University, University of Michigan, University of North Carolina—Chapel Hill, University of Pennsylvania, University of Virginia

INTERNATIONAL STUDENTS

TOEFL Required of International Students? Yes
Minimum TOEFL: 600 (250 computer)

EMPLOYMENT INFORMATION

Placement Office Available? Yes
% Employed Within 3 Months: 80
Fields Employing Percentage of Grads: MIS (2%), Strategic Planning (5%), Operations (5%), General Management (8%), Consulting (15%), Marketing (27%), Finance (38%)
Frequent Employers: Accenture, AT Kearney, Bank of America, Bear Stearns, Cap Gemini Ernst & Young, Credit Suisse First Boston, Deloitte Consulting, Eastman-Kodak, Equant, GE Capital, GlaxoSmithKline, Honeywell, IBM, IBM Consulting, ING, Johnson & Johnson, JP Morgan Chase, Kurt Salmon Associates, Lehman Brothers, McKinsey & Co., Mirant, Radiant, Reckitt Benckiser, Wachovia
Prominent Alumni: Alan Lacy, CEO, Sears; Michael Golden, vice chairman and senior vice president, New York Times Co.; Charles Jenkins Jr., CEO, Publik Super Markets, Inc.; C. Scott Mayfield, president, Mayfield Dairy Farms, Inc.; Andrew Conway, managing director, Credit Suisse First Boston

ERASMUS GRADUATE SCHOOL OF BUSINESS
Rotterdam School of Management

Admissions Contact: Mrs. Connie Tai, Director of Admissions
Address: Burgemeester Oudlaan 50, 3062 PA Rotterdam, The Netherlands
Admissions Phone: 011-31-10-408-2222 • **Admissions Fax:** 011-31-10-452-9509
Admissions E-mail: info@rsm.nl • **Web Address:** www.rsm.nl

The Erasmus Graduate School of Business is located in Rotterdam, home of the world's largest port, with access to a myriad of multinational businesses. The MBA program houses a mostly international student body, with more than 90 percent of the students coming from more than 50 countries around the globe. The classes are group-oriented, and there are study abroad opportunities in more than 30 countries. Erasmus offers multiple MBA options, including the Full-Time MBA, the Executive MBA, and the OneMBA program, "designed for achievement-oriented executives with increasing international responsibilities," with demanding admissions requirements.

INSTITUTIONAL INFORMATION

Public/Private: Private
Evening Classes Available? No
Total Faculty: 172
Students in Parent Institution: 16,000
Academic Calendar: Semester

PROGRAMS

Degrees Offered: IMBA (15 months full time), MBA/MBI (15 months full time), EMBA (24 months part time, weekend; 21 months part time, modular), MS in Financial Management (12 months full time), MS in Human Resources (18 months part time)
Academic Specialties: RSM offers broadly based MBA programs with functional strengths in Finance, Information Technology, and Strategy. The innovative MBA/MBI program offers the possibility to specialize in the managerial aspects of Information Technology.
Study Abroad Options: Australia, Canada, China, France, Germany, India, Italy, Japan, Mexico, Philippines, Republic of South Africa, Singapore, Spain, United Kingdom, United States, Thailand (36 schools in total)

STUDENT INFORMATION

Total Business Students: 700

% Full Time: 58
% Female: 21
% International: 96
Average Age: 29

COMPUTER AND RESEARCH FACILITIES

Research Facilities: Area010, a business 'incubator' for start-ups; Centre of Business History; Center for Technology and Innovation Management (CETIM); Econometric Institute; Erasmus Business Support Centre (EBSC); Erasmus Centre for Financial Research; Erasmus Institute for Philosophy and Economics (EIPE); Erasmus Research Institute of Management (ERIM); Erasmus University Research Institute for Decision and Information Systems (EURIDIS); European Institute for Comparative Urban Research (EURICUR); Institute for Sociologic Economic Research; Institute of Globalization, International Economic Law and Dispute Settlement (GLODIS); Research Centre for Economic Policy; The Netherlands Research School for Transport Infrastructure and Logistics; Research School Safety & Security in Society; Rotterdam Institute for Business Economic Studies (RIBES); Rotterdam Institute of Modern Asian Studies (RIMAS); Thomas Stieltjes Institute for Mathematics; Tinbergen Institute
Computer Facilities: In-building computer labs with 75 computers and 55 connections for laptop computers; databases include online access to Erasmus University's library databases and catalogues, plus online content providers such as Lexis-Nexis Academic Universe and Hoovers.com; trading room with simulation facilities, group systems, video conference
Campuswide Network? Yes
% of MBA Classrooms Wired: 100
Computer Model Recommended: Laptop
Internet Fee? No

EXPENSES/FINANCIAL AID

Annual Tuition: $16,250
Books and Supplies: $14,500

ADMISSIONS INFORMATION

Application Fee: $75
Electronic Application? Yes
Regular Application Deadline: 6/15
Regular Notification: Rolling
Deferment Available? No
Non-fall Admissions? No
Transfer Students Accepted? No
Need-Blind Admissions? Yes
Number of Applications Received: 770
% of Applicants Accepted: 39
% Accepted Who Enrolled: 57
Average GPA: 1.1
Average GMAT: 630
GMAT Range: 550-700
Average Years Experience: 5
Other Admissions Factors Considered: International outlook, leadership potential, motivation, contribution to the program, fun to work with

INTERNATIONAL STUDENTS

Minimum TOEFL: 600 (250 computer)

EMPLOYMENT INFORMATION

Placement Office Available? Yes
% Employed Within 3 Months: 83
Fields Employing Percentage of Grads: Venture Capital (1%), Accounting (1%), Other (2%), Entrepreneurship (2%), MIS (3%), Operations (5%), Strategic Planning (12%), General Management (15%), Consulting (15%), Marketing (21%), Finance (22%)
Frequent Employers: ABN Amro, AT Kearney, Bain & Co., Barclays Capital, Benson, Bertelsmann, Boston Consulting Group, Citibank, Citigroup, Eli Lilly, Ford Motor Co., General Electric, Hilti, Johnson and Johnson, Lehman Brothers, McKinsey, Novartis, Roland Berger Strategy Consultants, Royal Dutch Shell

Prominent Alumni: Durk Jager, former CEO, Proctor & Gamble; Bert van den Bergh, president, neuroscience products, Eli Lilly; Hans Ten Cate, member of executive board, Rabobank International; Johan Andresen, CEO, Ferd AS, Norway; Cees de Jong, managing director, Gist Brocades

See page 422.

ESADE

Admissions Contact: Nuria Guilera, MBA Admissions Director
Address: Av. d'Esplugues, 92-96, Barcelona, 08034
Admissions Phone: 011-34-934-952-088 • **Admissions Fax:** 011-34-934-953-828
Admissions E-mail: mba@esade.edu • **Web Address:** www.esade.edu

The ESADE MBA program is a "truly international education" with an incredible student/faculty ratio and study abroad opportunities at more than 30 schools. ESADE has a bilingual Spanish/English full-time MBA program and a part-time MBA available only in Spanish. Students can look forward to the professional demands of the curriculum, which requires each student to perform a filed consulting project and participate in an international corporate internship. ESADE is located in Barcelona, where the average temperature is 61 degrees Fahrenheit and the metropolitan population is 4,654,000.

INSTITUTIONAL INFORMATION

Public/Private: Private
Evening Classes Available? Yes
Total Faculty: 141
% Faculty Female: 21
% Faculty Part Time: 44
Student/Faculty Ratio: 3:1
Students in Parent Institution: 750
Academic Calendar: Annual

PROGRAMS

Degrees Offered: MBA (20 months part time; language is mainly Spanish), EMBA (18 months; language is mainly Spanish), PhD in Management Science (years)
Academic Specialties: Finance, Business Politics & Strategy, Marketing
Study Abroad Options: Australia, Belgium, Brazil, Canada, Chile, China, France, Germany, India, Israel, Italy, Japan, Korea, Malaysia, Mexico, the Netherlands, Norway, The Philippines, Singapore, South Africa, United Kingdom, United States, Venezuela

STUDENT INFORMATION

Total Business Students: 273
% Full Time: 42
% Female: 19
% International: 79
Average Age: 28

COMPUTER AND RESEARCH FACILITIES

Computer Facilities: Digital Library, European Documentation Centre, Coporate Information Centre; access to the following databases: ABI-Inform, Datastream, ProQuest, Stat-USA
Campuswide Network? Yes
% of MBA Classrooms Wired: 100
Computer Model Recommended: Laptop
Internet Fee? No

EXPENSES/FINANCIAL AID

Annual Tuition: $21,250

Room & Board (On/Off Campus): $7,200
Books and Supplies: $200
Average Grant: $18,474
Average Loan: $30,000

ADMISSIONS INFORMATION

Application Fee: $65
Electronic Application? Yes
Regular Application Deadline: 6/30
Regular Notification: Rolling
Deferment Available? Yes
Length of Deferment: 1 year
Non-fall Admissions? No
Transfer Students Accepted? No
Need-Blind Admissions? Yes
Number of Applications Received: 480
% of Applicants Accepted: 42
% Accepted Who Enrolled: 56
Average GPA: 3.5
Average GMAT: 640
GMAT Range: 600-680
Average Years Experience: 5
Other Admissions Factors Considered: Motivation of the candidate, potential for development and leadership
TOEFL Required of International Students? Yes
Minimum TOEFL: 600 (250 computer)

EMPLOYMENT INFORMATION

Placement Office Available? Yes
% Employed Within 3 Months: 85
Fields Employing Percentage of Grads: Operations (2%), Accounting (2%), MIS (3%), Human Resources (3%), Consulting (15%), Marketing (18%), Other (21%), Finance (30%)
Frequent Employers: Accenture, Bayer, BBVA, Citigroup, Danone, Deloitte&Touche, Dupont, General Electric, Intel, KPMG, L'Oreal, Nike, Novartis, PWC

FAIRFIELD UNIVERSITY
Charles F. Dolan School of Business

Admissions Contact: Colleen Doherty, Operations Assistant
Address: 1073 North Benson Road, Fairfield, CT 06824
Admissions Phone: 203-254-4180 • **Admissions Fax:** 203-254-4029
Admissions E-mail: mba@mail.fairfield.edu • **Web Address:** www.fairfield.edu/MBA

It's private, it's Jesuit, it's got an exceedingly high acceptance rate, and it's located on a beautiful 200-acre campus in Fairfield, Connecticut. The MBA program at the Charles F. Dolan School of Business requires that all students begin the full MBA at the same level. "Leveling" demands that students who do not have adequate grades or business course work take fundamental competency classes before commencing study at Fairfield. This process allows all students the chance to learn in an equal and ethical learning environment.

INSTITUTIONAL INFORMATION

Public/Private: Private
Evening Classes Available? Yes
Total Faculty: 44
% Faculty Female: 36

% Faculty Minority: 2
% Faculty Part Time: 9
Student/Faculty Ratio: 23:1
Students in Parent Institution: 5,154
Academic Calendar: Semester

PROGRAMS

Degrees Offered: MBA (1-5 years), MS in Finance (1-3 years)
Academic Specialties: Business Ethics, E-Marketing, Information Visualization, Supply Chain Management, gender differences in role modeling
Study Abroad Options: China, France, Germany, Japan, the Netherlands, United Kingdom

STUDENT INFORMATION

Total Business Students: 191
% Full Time: 12
% Female: 9
% Minority: 5
% International: 17
Average Age: 29

COMPUTER AND RESEARCH FACILITIES

Computer Facilities: Nyselius Library, Lexis-Nexis Academic Universe, Business and Company Resource Center (Gale), Disclosure Global Access (Primark), Stat-USA, ABI-Inform
Campuswide Network? Yes
% of MBA Classrooms Wired: 100
Internet Fee? No

EXPENSES/FINANCIAL AID

Annual Tuition: $19,100
Tuition Per Credit (Resident/Nonresident): $510
Books and Supplies: $1,000

ADMISSIONS INFORMATION

Application Fee: $55
Electronic Application? Yes
Regular Application Deadline: Rolling
Regular Notification: Rolling
Deferment Available? Yes
Length of Deferment: 1 year
Non-fall Admissions? Yes
Non-fall Application Deadline(s): Rolling
Transfer Students Accepted? Yes
Transfer Policy: 6 credits or Jesuit University
Need-Blind Admissions? No
Number of Applications Received: 72
% of Applicants Accepted: 78
% Accepted Who Enrolled: 100
Average GPA: 3.2
GPA Range: 2.9-3.8
Average GMAT: 548
GMAT Range: 490-650
Average Years Experience: 6
Other Admissions Factors Considered: Students are required to have taken an introductory course in computer information systems.
Other Schools to Which Students Applied: University of Connecticut

INTERNATIONAL STUDENTS

TOEFL Required of International Students? Yes
Minimum TOEFL: 550 (213 computer)

EMPLOYMENT INFORMATION

Placement Office Available? No
Frequent Employers: American Skandia, Bayer Corp., Cendant Corp., The Common Fund, Gartner, General Electric, People's Bank, Pfizer, Pitney Bowes, UBS Warburg, Unilever, United Technologies
Prominent Alumni: Dr. E. Gerald Corrigan, managing director, Goldman, Sachs

& Co.; Joseph Berardino, CEO, Andersen; Robert Murphy, Jr., senior vice president, The Walt Disney Co. Foundation; Christopher McCormick, president and CEO, LL Bean, Inc.; Dr. Francis Tedesco, president, Medical College of Georgia

FLORIDA ATLANTIC UNIVERSITY
College of Business

Admissions Contact: Fredrick Taylor, Graduate Advisor
Address: 777 Glades Road, Boca Raton, FL 33431
Admissions Phone: 561-297-3196 • **Admissions Fax:** 561-297-3684
Admissions E-mail: mba@fau.edu • **Web Address:** www.business.fau.edu

Boca Raton's Florida Atlantic University provides a suite of options for the MBA-hungry working professional. The most unique option is the Environmental MBA, which focuses on corporate responsibility with the belief that it's "possible for companies to create value for both society and shareholders." Other options include the Health Administration MBA; the MBASport, which aims to train sports executives and administrators; and the Executive MBA. Online programs are also available, including FAUMBA.net, the standard MBA course delivered both on campus and online.

INSTITUTIONAL INFORMATION

Public/Private: Public
Evening Classes Available? Yes
Total Faculty: 122
% Faculty Female: 30
% Faculty Part Time: 6
Student/Faculty Ratio: 12:1
Students in Parent Institution: 23,824
Academic Calendar: Semester

PROGRAMS

Degrees Offered: MBA (40-52 credits, 1-7 years), EMBA (48 credits, 20 months), Weekend MBA (39 credits, 15 months), Environmental MBA (40 credits, 15 months), MSIB (33 credits, 1 year), MACC (33 credits, 1-5 years), MTAX (33 credits, 1-5 years), Executive MTAX (30 credits, 2 years)
Study Abroad Options: Australia, Brazil, Chile, China, Denmark, Ecuador, Finland, France, Germany, Greece, Israel, Italy, Japan, Lithuania, Mexico, Russia, Spain, Sweden, United Kingdom

STUDENT INFORMATION

Total Business Students: 391
% Full Time: 29
% Female: 45

COMPUTER AND RESEARCH FACILITIES

Computer Facilities: FAU libraries offer more than 100 electronic databases and other computer resources to all FAU students.
Campuswide Network? Yes
% of MBA Classrooms Wired: 10
Internet Fee? No

EXPENSES/FINANCIAL AID

Annual Tuition (Resident/Nonresident): $4,468/$16,309
Tuition Per Credit (Resident/Nonresident): $187/$679
Books and Supplies: $2,500
Average Loan: $5,000

ADMISSIONS INFORMATION

Application Fee: $20
Electronic Application? No

Regular Application Deadline: 6/15
Regular Notification: Rolling
Deferment Available? Yes
Length of Deferment: Up to 1 year
Non-fall Admissions? Yes
Non-fall Application Deadline(s): 7/1 fall, 11/1 spring, 4/1 summer
Transfer Students Accepted? No
Need-Blind Admissions? Yes
Number of Applications Received: 359
% of Applicants Accepted: 53
% Accepted Who Enrolled: 63
Average GPA: 3.3
GPA Range: 3.0-3.6
Average GMAT: 525
GMAT Range: 474-568
Average Years Experience: 4
Other Admissions Factors Considered: GMAT score, GPA, PC literacy, work experience
Other Schools to Which Students Applied: Florida International University College of Business Administration, Florida State University, Miami University, University of Central Florida, University of Florida, University of South Florida

INTERNATIONAL STUDENTS

TOEFL Required of International Students? Yes
Minimum TOEFL: 600 (250 computer)

EMPLOYMENT INFORMATION

Placement Office Available? Yes

FLORIDA INTERNATIONAL UNIVERSITY COLLEGE OF BUSINESS ADMINISTRATION
Alvah H. Chapman, Jr., Graduate School of Business

Admissions Contact: Ellie Browner, Director, Admissions and Student Services
Address: 11200 S.W. 8th Street, RB 220, Miami, FL 33199
Admissions Phone: 305-348-3256 • **Admissions Fax:** 305-348-1221
Admissions E-mail: chapman@fiu.edu • **Web Address:** chapman.fiu.edu

It's no surprise that FIU's Global Executive MBA for managers in the Americas is so popular—not only is the College of Business Administration known for its expertise in Latin American commerce, it's been ranked the best business school for Hispanics in the United States by Hispanic Business magazine, with a student body that's 58 percent Hispanic American. Miami is a major center of international commerce, technology, travel and tourism, and real estate, but if you'd rather study abroad, you can get your Executive MBA in Kingston, Jamaica, your MIB in Cochabamba, Bolivia, or your International MBA in Saint-Etienne, France.

INSTITUTIONAL INFORMATION

Public/Private: Public
Evening Classes Available? Yes
Total Faculty: 127
% Faculty Female: 28
% Faculty Minority: 31
% Faculty Part Time: 1

Student/Faculty Ratio: 40:1
Students in Parent Institution: 32,712
Academic Calendar: Varies

PROGRAMS

Degrees Offered: EMBA (21 months), GEMBA (web-based, 13 months), Evening MBA (full time or part time, 2-3 years), IMBA (12 months full time), MACC (10 months), EMST (21 months), MS in Finance (21 months), MS in MIS (12 months), MS in Human Resource Management (16 months), Master of International Business (12 months full time, 15 months part time)
Academic Specialties: Faculty expertise and curriculum are strongest in global/international business (with emphasis on The Americas and links to the rest of the global economy) and in strategic uses/management of information technology (IT). We have eminent scholars and endowed professors in entreprise resource planning, e-business, informaiton systems, IT management, operations research, knowledge management, financial derivatives, international trade, international banking, consumer behavior, global management, global marketing, entrepreneurship, and corporate responsibilities.
Study Abroad Options: Bulgaria, France, Germany, Greece, Italy, Japan, Spain

STUDENT INFORMATION

Total Business Students: 416
% Full Time: 19
% Female: 49
% Minority: 75
% Out of State: 19
% International: 65
Average Age: 28

COMPUTER AND RESEARCH FACILITIES

Research Facilities: Center for International Business Education and Research, Knight Ridder Center for Excellence in Management, Ryder Center for Supply Chain Systems, Jerome Bain Real Estate Institute, Latin American and Caribbean Center; in development: Entrepreneurship Center. The University has a number of additional specialized research centers.
Computer Facilities: In the school, we have a number of business-related databases available for use in research. The FIU library has many more. In the graduate school, have hardwired all of our classrooms for at least 10Mbps access with direct connection to the Internet 2. Our classroom building, conference center, and additional classrooms on our University Park campus are covered for 11Mbps 803.11 wireless networking for students. Our 145-seat and 115-seat computer labs are equipped with multimedia projectors for instructors. Two 45-seat computer labs are equipped with multimedia projectors for instructors and video-conferencing over IP. All of our labs are equipped with instructor control over student computer stations for sharing operations on the projector screen. Our 120-seat auditorium is equipped with multimedia equipment and video-conferencing over IP, and our 60-seat-plus case rooms are equipped with multimedia projectors for instructor use. Plans are underway for construction of the Chapman Graduate School building (2005).
Campuswide Network? Yes
% of MBA Classrooms Wired: 100
Computer Model Recommended: Laptop
Internet Fee? No

EXPENSES/FINANCIAL AID

Annual Tuition (Resident/Nonresident): $26,000/$30,000
Tuition Per Credit (Resident/Nonresident): $177/$666
Room & Board (On/Off Campus): $12,000/$18,000
Books and Supplies: $1,800
Average Grant: $2,208
Average Loan: $7,818
% Receiving Financial Aid: 64
% Receiving Aid Their First Year: 96

ADMISSIONS INFORMATION

Application Fee: $20

Electronic Application? No
Regular Application Deadline: Rolling
Regular Notification: Rolling
Deferment Available? Yes
Length of Deferment: 1 year
Non-fall Admissions? Yes
Non-fall Application Deadline(s): Spring and Summer
Transfer Students Accepted? Yes
Transfer Policy: A student may receive permission to transfer up to six semester hours of graduate credit towards his or her degree program, if:

1) The courses were taken at the graduate level at an accredited college or university.

2) The courses were not introductory or "survey" in nature.

3) The student earned grades of B or higher in the courses.

4) The courses are judged by the department chair, college dean, and college advisor to be relevant to the student's degree program.

5) The courses were not core courses.

6) The credits were not used toward another degree.

All coursework, including transfer credits, must be completed within 6 years immediately preceding FIU's awarding of the MBA degree. Credits are not transferable, however, until the student has earned 15 semester hours of credit in a College of Business Administration graduate degree program. In addition, transfer credit will not be granted for "core" courses in the program.

Need-Blind Admissions? Yes
Number of Applications Received: 572
% of Applicants Accepted: 49
% Accepted Who Enrolled: 68
Average GPA: 3.3
GPA Range: 2.9-3.6
Average GMAT: 549
GMAT Range: 420-600
Average Years Experience: 5
Other Admissions Factors Considered: Admission criteria vary by program. In general, in addition to the standard minimum requirements and satisfactory exam scores, the Chapman School's admissions office seeks applicants who can demonstrate that they have played exceptional or distinctive roles in their work experiences (2 years minimum for Evening MBA, 8-plus years for EMBA/GEMBA). Successful applicants also will demonstrate a strong desire to learn new skills and to commit to graduate study. Chapman MBA programs also require applicants to articulate their motivation for pursuing the MBA in a statement of goals and to submit a current resume with the application. A personal interview is required for our EMBA and GEMBA programs. Applicants should demonstrate the motivation required to successfully complete the degree and to translate their new knowledge into career advancement.
Minority/Disadvantaged Student Recruitment Programs: The Chapman School serves a diverse ethnic community that reflects the international and demographics of South Florida. In 2002-2003, the graduate student distribution was as follows: Hispanic American 44%, African American 5.5%, Caucasian 21%, Non-Resident Alien 25%, and Asian 4.5%.
Other Schools to Which Students Applied: Florida State University, Thunderbird, University of Florida, University of Miami, University of South Carolina

INTERNATIONAL STUDENTS

TOEFL Required of International Students? Yes
Minimum TOEFL: 550 (213 computer)

EMPLOYMENT INFORMATION

Placement Office Available? No
% Employed Within 3 Months: 87
Fields Employing Percentage of Grads: Human Resources (2%), Global Management (6%), General Management (6%), Finance (8%), Consulting (11%), Marketing (27%) (Data provided here and in next section is for full-time MBA program only.)
Frequent Employers: Amadeus North America, Amerop Sugar Corp., Andrx Pharmaceuticals, AT&T, Bacardi USA Inc., Bank of America, Bechtel,

Bellsouth Telecommunications, Blue Cross & Blue Shield of Florida, Burdines, Citibank, The Corranino Group, Daimer-Chrysler Financial Services, Delta Consulting Group Inc., Exxon-Mobil, Florida Power and Light, Gomez-Acebo & Pombo, Harcos International, IBM-Lotus Latin America, Kroll Associates, Latin Venture Partners, Mercedez-Benz, Merrill Lynch, Morgan Stanley Dean Witter, Motorola, Nortel Networks, Ocean Bank, Pepsi-Cola, Ryder, Seagrams, Union Planters Bank, U.S. Coast Guard, U.S. Department of Commerce, Visa International, Yahoo! Latin America

Prominent Alumni: Augusto Vidaurreta, founder, Systems Consulting Group & Adjoined Techn; Carlos Migoya, president, Wachovia/First Union Bank, Miami; Anthony Argiz, managing partner, KPMG, LLP; Bob Bell, founder, Banana Boat and Sea & Ski; Anthony Rinconi, founder/president, Stratasys, Inc.

See page 424.

FLORIDA STATE UNIVERSITY
College of Business

Admissions Contact: Scheri L. Martin, Coordinator of Graduate Programs
Address: FSU College of Business, Tallahassee, FL 32306-1110
Admissions Phone: 850-644-6458 • **Admissions Fax:** 850-644-0915
Admissions E-mail: gradprog@cob.fsu.edu • **Web Address:** www.cob.fsu.edu

The MBA program at FSU's College of Business offers a full-time curriculum (1 year) and a part-time curriculum (2.5 years) at the Tallahassee campus and, if enrollment is high, a part-time evening curriculum (2.5 years) at the Panama City campus as well. FSU is home to the Jim Moran Institute of Global Entrepreneurship and the DeSantis Center of Executive Management Education, and is proud to announce its new Technology Center, equipped with three new computer labs and two computer classrooms.

INSTITUTIONAL INFORMATION

Public/Private: Public
Evening Classes Available? Yes
Total Faculty: 85
% Faculty Female: 13
Student/Faculty Ratio: 40:1
Students in Parent Institution: 35,000
Academic Calendar: Semester

PROGRAMS

Degrees Offered: MBA (43 credits, 12 months full time; 42 credits, 28 months part time), with concentrations in Finance, Global Entrepreneurship, Marketing & Supply Chain Management; JD/MBA (113 credits, 4 years); MACC (33 credits, 12 months full time; up to 7 years part time), with majors in Accounting Information Systems, Assurance Services, Corporate Accounting, Taxation; MSM in MIS (32 credits, 12 months full time; up to 7 years part time); MSM with a major in Risk & Insurance (33 credits, 24 months part time; half of credits taught distance-learning, half taught on site at the contracted insurance company's headquarters); MSM with major in Hospitality and Tourism (36 credits, 24 months part time); Corporate MBA (39 credits, 24 months; courses taught on the corporation site and are only for the contracted corporation's employees who have applied and been admitted); PhD in Business Administration (3-5 years), with majors in Accounting, Finance, Information & Management Sciences, Marketing, Organizational Behavior, Risk Management & Insurance, and Strategic Management
Combined Degrees: JD/MBA (113 credits, approximately 4 years)

STUDENT INFORMATION

Total Business Students: 178
% Full Time: 23

% Female: 30
% Minority: 18
% Out of State: 20
% International: 15
Average Age: 27

COMPUTER AND RESEARCH FACILITIES

Research Facilities: Jim Moran Institute for Entrepreneurship
Computer Facilities: Strozier Library
Campuswide Network? Yes
% of MBA Classrooms Wired: 100
Computer Model Recommended: Laptop
Internet Fee? No

EXPENSES/FINANCIAL AID

Room & Board (On/Off Campus): $10,000/$13,000
Books and Supplies: $4,750
Average Grant: $10,000
% Receiving Financial Aid: 37
% Receiving Aid Their First Year: 37

ADMISSIONS INFORMATION

Application Fee: $20
Electronic Application? Yes
Regular Application Deadline: 2/1
Regular Notification: Rolling
Deferment Available? Yes
Length of Deferment: 12 months
Non-fall Admissions? Yes
Non-fall Application Deadline(s): 10/1 spring, 2/1 summer
Transfer Students Accepted? Yes
Transfer Policy: Transfer applicants must complete the same application process as other applicants.
Need-Blind Admissions? No
Number of Applications Received: 153
% of Applicants Accepted: 42
% Accepted Who Enrolled: 63
Average GPA: 3.2
Average GMAT: 569
Average Years Experience: 5
Other Admissions Factors Considered: Bachelor's degree with minimum 3.0 GPA, applicant's statment, work experience and resume, college transcrpits, letters of recommendation, GMAT score, interview
Minority/Disadvantaged Student Recruitment Programs: FAMU Feeder Program, FAMU Graduate & Professional Days, PT-Program Seminars through the FSU Center for Professional Development, Minority Student Orientation Program, Leslie Wilson Assistantships, Delores Auzenne Minority Fellowship, University Fellowship

INTERNATIONAL STUDENTS

TOEFL Required of International Students? Yes
Minimum TOEFL: 600 (250 computer)

EMPLOYMENT INFORMATION

Placement Office Available? Yes
% Employed Within 3 Months: 77
Fields Employing Percentage of Grads: Other (4%), Operations (4%), MIS (4%), Human Resources (4%), Accounting (4%), General Management (19%), Consulting (19%), Marketing (19%), Finance (19%)
Frequent Employers: Accenture, Am South Banks, Bank of America
Prominent Alumni: Gary Rogers, president and CEO, GE Plastics; Craig Wardlaw, executive vice president and CIO, Bank of America; Craig Ramsey, partner, Accenture

FORDHAM UNIVERSITY
Graduate School of Business Administration

Admissions Contact: Frank Fletcher, Director
Address: 33 West 60th Street, 4th Floor, New York, NY 10023
Admissions Phone: 212-636-6200 • **Admissions Fax:** 212-636-7076
Admissions E-mail: admissions@fordham.edu • **Web Address:** www.bnet.fordham.edu

The Fordham MBA student needs only to step outside to begin his or her financial education in New York City, the corporate mecca of the twenty-first century. Offering a multitude of degree concentrations, an MBA student can specialize in areas ranging from accounting to media management to information and communications systems. Fordham also has a suburban campus located just a short train ride from the city campus, in Westchester County. A few big-time employers of Fordham MBA graduates are Ernst & Young, Chase Manhattan Bank, and G.E. Capital Citibank.

INSTITUTIONAL INFORMATION

Public/Private: Private
Evening Classes Available? Yes
Total Faculty: 180
% Faculty Part Time: 49
Student/Faculty Ratio: 4:1
Academic Calendar: Trimester

PROGRAMS

Degrees Offered: Deming Scholars MBA (60 credits); Global Professional MBA (69 credits); Transnational (Executive) MBA (69 credits); MBA (60 credits), with concentrations in Accounting, Professional Accounting, Communications and Media Management, Finance and Business Economics, Information and Communications Systems, Management Systems, Marketing; MBA (90 credits), with concentration in Taxation and Accounting; Beijing IMBA (60 credits); MST (54 Credits)
Combined Degrees: JD/MBA, American Graduate School of International Management "Thunderbird" Dual Degree
Special Opportunities: Dual Concentration Programs, Global Professional MBA Program, Masters in Taxation and Accounting
Study Abroad Options: Brazil, Chile, China, England, Finland, France, Holland, India, Ireland, Poland, Russia, Spain, Switzerland

STUDENT INFORMATION

Total Business Students: 1,534
% Full Time: 23
% Female: 38
% Minority: 16
% International: 26
Average Age: 28

COMPUTER AND RESEARCH FACILITIES

Campuswide Network? Yes
% of MBA Classrooms Wired: 3
Internet Fee? No

EXPENSES/FINANCIAL AID

Annual Tuition: $21,060
Tuition Per Credit (Resident/Nonresident): $585
Books and Supplies: $1,495
Average Grant: $3,000
Average Loan: $20,000

ADMISSIONS INFORMATION

Application Fee: $65
Electronic Application? Yes
Regular Application Deadline: 6/1

Regular Notification: 7/31
Deferment Available? Yes
Length of Deferment: 1 year
Non-fall Admissions? Yes
Non-fall Application Deadline(s): 11/1, 3/1
Transfer Students Accepted? Yes
Transfer Policy: ACCSB-sccredited school; only prerequisite and core courses can be waived
Need-Blind Admissions? Yes
Number of Applications Received: 822
% of Applicants Accepted: 62
% Accepted Who Enrolled: 63
Average Years Experience: 5
Other Schools to Which Students Applied: Columbia University, Baruch College, City University of New York, Babson College, Rensselaer Polytechnic Institute, Boston College

INTERNATIONAL STUDENTS

TOEFL Required of International Students? Yes
Minimum TOEFL: 250

EMPLOYMENT INFORMATION

Placement Office Available? Yes
% Employed Within 3 Months: 97
Fields Employing Percentage of Grads: Entrepreneurship (1%), Strategic Planning (1%), Global Management (2%), General Management (2%), Communications (2%), Operations (2%), MIS (5%), Consulting (10%), Marketing (10%), Accounting (10%), Finance (55%)
Frequent Employers: Block Drugs, Chase Manhattan Bank, Citibank, Ernst & Young, G.E. Capital, Rechetl

FRANCIS MARION UNIVERSITY
School of Business

Admissions Contact: Ben Kyer, Director
Address: Box 100547, Florence, SC 29501-0547
Admissions Phone: 843-661-1436 • **Admissions Fax:** 843-661-1432
Admissions E-mail: alpha1@fmarion.edu • **Web Address:** alpha1.fmarion.edu/~mba/

INSTITUTIONAL INFORMATION

Public/Private: Public
Evening Classes Available? No
Total Faculty: 21
Students in Parent Institution: 3,947
Academic Calendar: Semester

PROGRAMS

Degrees Offered: MBA (36 credits, 2-6 years), MBA in Health Management (36 credits, 2-6 years)

STUDENT INFORMATION

Total Business Students: 61
% Full Time: 5
% Female: 51
% Minority: 20
% International: 7
Average Age: 29

COMPUTER AND RESEARCH FACILITIES

Research Facilities: CD players
Computer Facilities: Online bibliographic retrieval services

Campuswide Network? Yes
Internet Fee? No

EXPENSES/FINANCIAL AID

Annual Tuition (Resident/Nonresident): $3,460/$6,920
% Receiving Financial Aid: 8

ADMISSIONS INFORMATION

Application Fee: $25
Electronic Application? No
Regular Application Deadline: Rolling
Regular Notification: Rolling
Deferment Available? Yes
Non-fall Admissions? No
Transfer Students Accepted? No
Need-Blind Admissions? No
Number of Applications Received: 33
% of Applicants Accepted: 85
% Accepted Who Enrolled: 93
Other Admissions Factors Considered: Computer experience

INTERNATIONAL STUDENTS

TOEFL Required of International Students? Yes
Minimum TOEFL: 550 (213 computer)

EMPLOYMENT INFORMATION

Placement Office Available? Yes

GEORGE MASON UNIVERSITY
School of Management

Admissions Contact: Carol Hoskins, MBA Program Coordinator
Address: 4400 University Drive, MSN 5A2, Enterprise Hall, Room 156, Fairfax, VA 22030
Admissions Phone: 703-993-2140 • **Admissions Fax:** 703-993-1778
Admissions E-mail: masonmba@som.gmu.edu • **Web Address:** www.som.gmu.edu

The George Mason University School of Management provides superb educational training in finance and leadership skills and acts as a supportive resource center for career information and placement. The George Mason MBA is generally completed over the course of two years and nine months, taking two classes per week, but students can opt for the accelerated course, completed in 24 months, taking three courses per semester. All MBA courses take place in the evening and utilize cohort groups of about 35 students. One unique feature of the program is that, prior to taking any MBA electives, students are required to pass an exam that tests their proficiency in the use of Web resources and knowledge of basic information technology.

INSTITUTIONAL INFORMATION

Public/Private: Public
Evening Classes Available? Yes
Total Faculty: 96
% Faculty Part Time: 24
Academic Calendar: Semester

PROGRAMS

Degrees Offered: EMBA (48credits, full time, up to 22 months); MBA (48 credits, full time, 2-6 years), with concentrations in Accounting, Decision Sciences, Entrepreneurship, Finance, International Business, Management, Management Information Systems, Marketing, Organizational Behavior/Development; Fast-Track MBA (48 credits, part time, 2.8 years), with concentrations in Entrepreneurship, International Finance, Accounting, Management,

Decision Sciences, Finance, International Business, Management Information Systems, Marketing, Organizational Behavior/Developement.

STUDENT INFORMATION

Total Business Students: 65
% Full Time: 22
% Female: 28
% Minority: 12
% International: 10
Average Age: 28

COMPUTER AND RESEARCH FACILITIES

Research Facilities: Fenwick Library plus 1 additional on-campus library; total holdings of 635,284 volumes; 1,683,847 microforms; 9,191 current periodical subscriptions. CD players available for graduate student use; access provided to online bibliographic retrieval services
Campuswide Network? Yes
Internet Fee? No

EXPENSES/FINANCIAL AID

Annual Tuition (Resident/Nonresident): $7,788/$12,696
Tuition Per Credit (Resident/Nonresident): $325/$529
% Receiving Financial Aid: 19

ADMISSIONS INFORMATION

Application Fee: $50
Electronic Application? Yes
Regular Application Deadline: 4/1
Regular Notification: 1/1
Deferment Available? Yes
Length of Deferment: 2 years
Non-fall Admissions? Yes
Non-fall Application Deadline(s): 11/1 spring; for international applicants: 3/1 fall, 9/1 spring
Transfer Students Accepted? Yes
Transfer Policy: Applicants must still submit all required application documents.
Need-Blind Admissions? No
Number of Applications Received: 210
% of Applicants Accepted: 54
% Accepted Who Enrolled: 58
Average GPA: 3.1
Average GMAT: 605
Average Years Experience: 6
Other Admissions Factors Considered: A minimum GPA of 3.1 and 2 years of work experience are required. Experience with PC software is recommended.

INTERNATIONAL STUDENTS

TOEFL Required of International Students? Yes
Minimum TOEFL: 600 (230 computer)

EMPLOYMENT INFORMATION

Placement Office Available? Yes
% Employed Within 3 Months: 90
Frequent Employers: Finnegan, Henderson, Farabow, Garret & Dunner, L.L.P.; Hunton & Williams; McGuire, Woods, Battle & Boothe; Shaw Pittman; Sterne, Kessler, Goldstein, and Fox; Sutherland, Asbill, and Brennan; U.S. Government; Wiley, Rein, and Fielding

THE GEORGE WASHINGTON UNIVERSITY
School of Business and Public Management

Admissions Contact: Tracy Widman, Director, Data and Enrollment Management
Address: 710 21st Street, NW Suite 301, Washington, DC 20052
Admissions Phone: 202-994-5536 • Admissions Fax: 202-994-3571
Admissions E-mail: mbaft@gwu.edu • Web Address: www.sbpm.gwu.edu

The location of GW's School of Business and Public Management in Washington, D.C., grants the MBA student the benefits of an international atmosphere and a continuous opportunity to interact with a truly global city. GW is a renowned academic institution that offers an outstanding financial education to working professionals and full-time students. Frequent employers of GW MBA graduates are Deloitte & Touche, Accenture, PricewaterhouseCoopers, and the U.S. government—Colin Powell is an alumnus of the program.

INSTITUTIONAL INFORMATION

Public/Private: Private
Evening Classes Available? Yes
Total Faculty: 120
% Faculty Female: 17
% Faculty Minority: 5
% Faculty Part Time: 9
Student/Faculty Ratio: 20:1
Students in Parent Institution: 23,019
Academic Calendar: Semester

PROGRAMS

Degrees Offered: MBA (21 months full time, 2-5 years part time, 24 months accelerated 24 months), EMBA (21 months), MACC (21 months), MPA (21 months), MPP (21 months), MS in Finance (1 year full time, 2 years part time), MS in Information Systems Technology (21 months), MS in Project Management (21 months), Master of Tourism Administration (21 months)
Combined Degrees: MBA/JD (4 years), MBA/MA in International Affairs (30 months)
Academic Specialties: Accountancy, Entrepreneurship and Small Business, Environmental Policy and Management, Finance and Investments, Health Services Administration, Human Resource Management, Information Systems Management, International Business, Management Decision-Making, Management of Science, Technology, and Innovation, Marketing, Non-Profit Organization Management, Organizational Behavior and Development, Public Administration, Real Estate and Urban Development, Strategic Management and Public Policy, Supply Chain Management, Tourism and Hospitality Management
Study Abroad Options: Brazil, France, Hungary, Korea, Spain, Sweden

STUDENT INFORMATION

Total Business Students: 891
% Full Time: 37
% Female: 45
% Minority: 17
% Out of State: 79
% International: 43
Average Age: 27

COMPUTER AND RESEARCH FACILITIES

Research Facilities: Institute for Global Management and Research, European Union Research Center, Financial Markets Research Institute, Center for Latin American Issues, Center for Real Estate and Urban Analysis, Council for the Advancement of Small Business, Council for Family Enterprise, NAFTA/ EU Project, Research Program in Social and Organizational Learning, International Institute of Tourism Studies, Center for Excellence in Municipal Management, Center for Law Practice Strategy and Management

Computer Facilities: MBA Computer Labs; GWU Computer Labs; various research databases: business, financial, social sciences; alumni databases
Campuswide Network? Yes
% of MBA Classrooms Wired: 75
Computer Model Recommended: Laptop
Internet Fee? No

EXPENSES/FINANCIAL AID

Annual Tuition: $19,464
Tuition Per Credit (Resident/Nonresident): $810
Room & Board (On/Off Campus): $14,400
Books and Supplies: $2,580
Average Grant: $10,000
Average Loan: $18,000
% Receiving Financial Aid: 75
% Receiving Aid Their First Year: 75

ADMISSIONS INFORMATION

Application Fee: $60
Electronic Application? Yes
Regular Application Deadline: 4/1
Regular Notification: Rolling
Deferment Available? No
Non-fall Admissions? Yes
Non-fall Application Deadline(s): 10/2
Transfer Students Accepted? Yes
Transfer Policy: Standard application procedures
Need-Blind Admissions? Yes
Number of Applications Received: 894
% of Applicants Accepted: 26
% Accepted Who Enrolled: 45
GPA Range: 3.2-3.5
Average GMAT: 620
GMAT Range: 580-660
Average Years Experience: 5
Other Admissions Factors Considered: Country diversity
Other Schools to Which Students Applied: Boston College, Boston University, Georgetown University, New York University, Thunderbird, University of Maryland—College Park, Vanderbilt University

INTERNATIONAL STUDENTS

TOEFL Required of International Students? Yes
Minimum TOEFL: 600 (250 computer)

EMPLOYMENT INFORMATION

Placement Office Available? Yes
% Employed Within 3 Months: 57
Fields Employing Percentage of Grads: Operations (7%), General Management (11%), Consulting (22%), Marketing (24%), Finance (29%)
Frequent Employers: BB&T Corp., Bearing Point, Corporate Executive Board, Cushman & Wakefield, General Services Administration, Johnson and Johnson, KPMG, Science Applications International Corp., World Bank Group
Prominent Alumni: Colin Powell, U.S. secretary of state; Henry Duques, president and CEO, First Data Corp.; Edward M. Liddy, chairman and CEO, Allstate Insurance; Darla A. Moore, president, Rainwater, Inc.; Clarence B. Rogers, Jr., chairman, president, and CEO, Equifax, Inc.

GEORGETOWN UNIVERSITY
The McDonough School of Business

Admissions Contact: Monica Gray, Director of Admissions
Address: Box 571148, Washington, DC 20057-1221
Admissions Phone: 202-687-4200 • **Admissions Fax:** 202-687-7809
Admissions E-mail: mba@georgetown.edu • **Web Address:** www.mba.georgetown.edu

Georgetown's School of Business has an "unbelievably dedicated" faculty and a tremendous Washington, D.C., location, but without a doubt, international business is its strong suit. Students here can take electives at the School of Foreign Service, and there is a strong "international flavor" among the students, as "nearly a quarter are foreign and almost everyone else has lived or worked abroad and speaks a second language."

INSTITUTIONAL INFORMATION

Public/Private: Private
Evening Classes Available? No
Total Faculty: 76
% Faculty Female: 23
% Faculty Minority: 9
% Faculty Part Time: 12
Student/Faculty Ratio: 8:1
Students in Parent Institution: 12,000
Academic Calendar: Module

PROGRAMS

Degrees Offered: MBA (21 months)
Combined Degrees: MBA/MSFS (3 years), MBA/MA in Physics (3 years), MBA/JD (4 years), MBA/MPP (3 years), MBA/MD (5 years), BS/MBA or BA/MBA (5 years), MBA/PhD in Physics (5 years)
Academic Specialties: Curriculum has integrated modules of varying legths. An international experience is required of all second years.
Special Opportunities: The International Business Diplomacy Certificate, Area Studies Certificate, Summer Study Abroad Opportunities, International Exchange Opportunities, Summer Pre-Enrollment "Prep" Workshops
Study Abroad Options: Summer Study Abroad programs available

STUDENT INFORMATION

Total Business Students: 502
% Full Time: 100
% Female: 33
% Minority: 66
% International: 35
Average Age: 28

COMPUTER AND RESEARCH FACILITIES

Research Facilities: Capital Markets Research Center
Computer Facilities: School maintains its own local area network, decision support center, Boland Information Systems Laboratory, and MBA Lounge computer centers. School maintains numerous databases (Georgetown U.) and full Internet services; school uses a Windows 2000 applications environment.
Campuswide Network? Yes
% of MBA Classrooms Wired: 100
Internet Fee? No

EXPENSES/FINANCIAL AID

Annual Tuition: $24,440
Room & Board (On/Off Campus): $14,000
Books and Supplies: $1,250
Average Grant: $12,500
Average Loan: $26,000
% Receiving Financial Aid: 90
% Receiving Aid Their First Year: 90

ADMISSIONS INFORMATION

Application Fee: $100
Electronic Application? Yes
Regular Application Deadline: 4/16
Regular Notification: 5/29
Deferment Available? No
Non-fall Admissions? No
Transfer Students Accepted? No
Need-Blind Admissions? Yes
Number of Applications Received: 2,816
% of Applicants Accepted: 21
% Accepted Who Enrolled: 45
Average GPA: 3.4
Average GMAT: 662
Average Years Experience: 5
Minority/Disadvantaged Student Recruitment Programs: Corporate-funded scholarship opportunities; specific, targeted marketing efforts made in this area

INTERNATIONAL STUDENTS

TOEFL Required of International Students? Yes
Minimum TOEFL: 600 (250 computer)

EMPLOYMENT INFORMATION

Placement Office Available? Yes
% Employed Within 3 Months: 88
Fields Employing Percentage of Grads: Human Resources (2%), General Management (4%), Strategic Planning (4%), Other (10%), Marketing (15%), Consulting (21%), Finance (44%)
Frequent Employers: Chase Manhattan, Citicorp, Cosmiar, Goldman Sachs, J&J, P&G, Pricewaterhouse Coopers, Toyota

GEORGIA COLLEGE & STATE UNIVERSITY
The J. Whitney Bunting School of Business

Admissions Contact: Maryllis Wolfgang, Director of Admissions
Address: GC&SU Campus Box 23, Milledgeville, GA 31061
Admissions Phone: 478-445-6289 • **Admissions Fax:** 478-445-1914
Admissions E-mail: lhardwic@gcsu.edu • **Web Address:** www.gcsu.edu

The J. Whitney Bunting School of Business allows in-state residents of Georgia to enjoy quality education with low tuition rates. Originally founded as a women's college, the Bunting School now has a student body that's 41 percent female. The part-time and full-time MBA programs emphasize practical financial knowledge and provide decision-making simulations to prepare MBA students for the real world.

INSTITUTIONAL INFORMATION

Public/Private: Public
Evening Classes Available? Yes
Total Faculty: 32
% Faculty Part Time: 2
Student/Faculty Ratio: 15:1
Students in Parent Institution: 5,079
Academic Calendar: Semester

PROGRAMS

Degrees Offered: MBA (30-57 credits, full time or part time, 1-7 years), MMIS (36-60 credits, full time or part time, 1-7 years), MACC (30-57 credits, full time or part time, 1-7 years)
Academic Specialties: AACSB-accredited
Study Abroad Options: Brazil, Hungary, Mexico, People's Republic of China, Spain, United Kingdom

STUDENT INFORMATION

Total Business Students: 144
% Full Time: 10
% Female: 46
% Minority: 17
% International: 14
Average Age: 27

COMPUTER AND RESEARCH FACILITIES

Research Facilities: Ina Dillard Russell Library, with total holdings of 170,834 volumes; 515,123 microforms; 1,137 current periodical subscriptions. CD player(s) available for graduate student use; access provided to online bibliographic retrieval services and online databases
Computer Facilities: Georgia Libraries Learning Online (GALILEO); JSTOR
Campuswide Network? Yes
% of MBA Classrooms Wired: 100
Internet Fee? No

EXPENSES/FINANCIAL AID

Annual Tuition (Resident/Nonresident): $4,329/$12,537
Tuition Per Credit (Resident/Nonresident): $131/$522
Room & Board (On/Off Campus): $9,000/$15,000
Books and Supplies: $1,080

ADMISSIONS INFORMATION

Application Fee: $25
Electronic Application? Yes
Regular Application Deadline: Rolling
Regular Notification: Rolling
Deferment Available? Yes
Length of Deferment: 1 year
Non-fall Admissions? Yes
Non-fall Application Deadline(s): 12/1 spring, 7/15 fall, 5/1 summer
Transfer Students Accepted? Yes
Transfer Policy: Minimum of 9 semester hours if equivalent to GC&SU curriculum
Need-Blind Admissions? No
Number of Applications Received: 90
% of Applicants Accepted: 50
% Accepted Who Enrolled: 71
Average GPA: 3.2
Average GMAT: 490
Other Admissions Factors Considered: Computer experience is recommended for application.
Minority/Disadvantaged Student Recruitment Programs: We recruit at seminars developed for minority students.

INTERNATIONAL STUDENTS

TOEFL Required of International Students? Yes
Minimum TOEFL: 500 (173 computer)

EMPLOYMENT INFORMATION

Placement Office Available? No

GEORGIA INSTITUTE OF TECHNOLOGY
DuPree College of Management

Admissions Contact: Paula Wilson, Assistant Director of Graduate Programs
Address: 755 Ferst Drive, Atlanta, GA 30332
Admissions Phone: 404-894-8722 • **Admissions Fax:** 404-894-4199
Admissions E-mail: mba@mgt.gatech.edu • **Web Address:** www.dupree.gatech.edu

Georgia Tech's DuPree School of Management offers an MSM, which is pretty much identical to an MBA. There is an "emphasis on analytic skills and technology" here—not surprising given Georgia Tech's prominence in engineering and the sciences—and "the operations faculty is one of the school's great strengths." Professors at DuPree all do extensive work in their industries" yet are "always available to students for support and advice."

INSTITUTIONAL INFORMATION

Public/Private: Public
Evening Classes Available? No
Total Faculty: 53
% Faculty Female: 20
Student/Faculty Ratio: 4:1
Students in Parent Institution: 15,576
Academic Calendar: Semester

PROGRAMS

Degrees Offered: MBA (60 credits, 2 years); EMSMOT (54 credits, 18 months); PhD in Management (4-5 years), with concentrations in Accounting, Finance, Information Technology Management, Marketing, Organizational Behavior, Operations Management, Strategic Management
Combined Degrees: Dual degree programs with any master's or PhD degree at Georgia Tech
Academic Specialties: Accounting, Finance, Information Technology Management, International Business, Marketing, Operations Management, Organizational Behavior, Strategic Management
Special Opportunities: Management of Technology, Electronic Commerce, Entrepreneurship and New Venture Development, International Business
Study Abroad Options: Argentina, Brazil, China, Colombia, Denmark, France, Germany, Japan, Mexico, the Netherlands, South Korea, Spain, Turkey

STUDENT INFORMATION

Total Business Students: 210
% Full Time: 100
% Female: 28
% Minority: 15
% Out of State: 26
% International: 26
Average Age: 27

COMPUTER AND RESEARCH FACILITIES

Research Facilities: MOT Program, Entrepreneurship Center, CIBER, Center for Quality.
Computer Facilities: Numerous on-campus computer labs, comprehensive online databases maintained by the University System of Georgia, SAP R/3 Lab
Campuswide Network? No
Computer Model Recommended: Laptop
Internet Fee? No

EXPENSES/FINANCIAL AID

Annual Tuition (Resident/Nonresident): $5,128/$18,040
Room & Board (On/Off Campus): $11,400
Books and Supplies: $1,400
Average Grant: $6,000
Average Loan: $20,845

ADMISSIONS INFORMATION

Application Fee: $50
Electronic Application? Yes
Regular Application Deadline: 3/20
Regular Notification: Rolling
Deferment Available? Yes
Length of Deferment: 1 year
Non-fall Admissions? No
Transfer Students Accepted? No
Need-Blind Admissions? Yes
Number of Applications Received: 470
% of Applicants Accepted: 39
% Accepted Who Enrolled: 61
Average GPA: 3.2
GPA Range: 2.6-3.8
Average GMAT: 645
GMAT Range: 600-700
Average Years Experience: 4
Other Admissions Factors Considered: We look at all of the above factors as well as many others in evaluating applicants.
Minority/Disadvantaged Student Recruitment Programs: FOCUS programs on campus, information sessions, Regent's Opportunity Scholarships', minority student outreach
Other Schools to Which Students Applied: Carnegie Mellon, Emory University, Indiana University, Massachusetts Institute of Technology, Purdue University, University of Georgia, University of Texas—Austin

INTERNATIONAL STUDENTS

TOEFL Required of International Students? Yes
Minimum TOEFL: 600 (250 computer)

EMPLOYMENT INFORMATION

Placement Office Available? Yes
% Employed Within 3 Months: 72
Fields Employing Percentage of Grads: Accounting (4%), Marketing (6%), MIS (12%), Operations (20%), Finance (20%), General Management (29%)
Frequent Employers: Assurant Group, BellSouth, Caterpiller,Coca-Cola Co., Dell, Disney, Earthlink, Ernst & Young, GE Supply, Georgia Pacific Corp., McKesson, NASD, Philip Morris, Southern Co., United Parcel Service
Prominent Alumni: Jimmy Carter, former U.S. president; Sam Nunn, former U.S. senator; Ivan Allen, Jr., former mayor of Atlanta, CEO of Ivan Allen Jr. Co.; David Dorman, CEO and president, AT&T; John Young, astronaut

GEORGIA SOUTHERN UNIVERSITY
College of Business Administration

Admissions Contact: Dr. John R. Diebolt, Associate Vice President, Graduate Studies
Address: PO Box 8113, Statesboro, GA 30460-8113
Admissions Phone: 912-681-5483 • **Admissions Fax:** 912-681-0740
Admissions E-mail: diebolt@gsvms2.cc.gasou.edu • **Web Address:** www2.gasou.edu/mba

Located in historic Statesboro, Georgia, GSU's College of Business has a high acceptance rate and a campus teeming with educational entertainment, ranging from a planetarium to a university museum and on to a botanic garden and wildlife education center. The GSU MBA provides working professionals with several part-time evening MBA program options, including the option to take classes at the Statesboro, Hinesville, Savannah, and Dublin campuses, depending on the program. GSU also offers a Web Exclusive Collaborative MBA, which began in the spring of 2002.

INSTITUTIONAL INFORMATION

Public/Private: Public
Evening Classes Available? Yes
Total Faculty: 50
% Faculty Female: 20
% Faculty Minority: 1
Student/Faculty Ratio: 7:1
Students in Parent Institution: 14,700

PROGRAMS

Degrees Offered: MBA (evening/part time, 2 years; web-based lockstep, 2 years; weekend lockstep, 2 years); MACC (2 years), rolling admission

STUDENT INFORMATION

Total Business Students: 313
% Full Time: 60
% Female: 47
% Minority: 10
% Out of State: 12
% International: 12
Average Age: 31

COMPUTER AND RESEARCH FACILITIES

Computer Facilities: Coastal Georgia Center computer labs (off-site teaching location)
Campuswide Network? Yes
% of MBA Classrooms Wired: 100
Internet Fee? No

EXPENSES/FINANCIAL AID

Annual Tuition (Resident/Nonresident): $1,702/$6,768
Tuition Per Credit (Resident/Nonresident): $94/$376
Room & Board (On/Off Campus): $4,154/$2,301
Books and Supplies: $950

ADMISSIONS INFORMATION

Electronic Application? Yes
Regular Application Deadline: 7/1
Regular Notification: 7/2
Deferment Available? Yes
Length of Deferment: 1 year
Non-fall Admissions? Yes
Non-fall Application Deadline(s): 11/15, 4/1
Transfer Students Accepted? Yes
Transfer Policy: No more than 6 semester hours of graduate credit may be transferred to a graduate program at GSU. Only grades of B or higher will be accepted for transfer.
Need-Blind Admissions? Yes
Number of Applications Received: 62
% of Applicants Accepted: 100
% Accepted Who Enrolled: 100
Average GPA: 3.0
GPA Range: 2.0-3.0
Average GMAT: 488
GMAT Range: 310-740
Average Years Experience: 3
Other Schools to Which Students Applied: Auburn University

INTERNATIONAL STUDENTS

TOEFL Required of International Students? Yes
Minimum TOEFL: 530

EMPLOYMENT INFORMATION

Placement Office Available? Yes
Frequent Employers: Great Dane Trucking, Inc.; Gulfstream Aerospace, Inc; Memorial Medical Hospital; Sun Trust Bank

GEORGIA STATE UNIVERSITY
J. Mack Robinson College of Business

Admissions Contact: Master's Admissions Counselors, Master's Counseling Staff
Address: MSC 4A0310, Georgia State University, 33 Gilmer Street SE, Atlanta, GA 30303
Admissions Phone: 404-651-1913 • **Admissions Fax:** 404-651-0219
Admissions E-mail: rcb-oaa@gsu.edu • **Web Address:** robinson.gsu.edu

The J. Mack Robinson College of Business is located in downtown Atlanta, a metropolis surrounded by financial corporations and elite businesses such as Coca-Cola, Home Depot, UPS, and BellSouth. Several options are available for the prospective MBA applicant: the Flexible MBA for working professionals, the Executive MBA for professionals with 7 to 10 years of business experience, and the Global e-Management Executive MBA, designed for working professionals with a concentration in e-commerce and technology. The GSU MBA program is well known for the excellence of its curriculum, faculty, and diverse student body.

INSTITUTIONAL INFORMATION

Public/Private: Public
Evening Classes Available? Yes
Total Faculty: 195
% Faculty Female: 27
% Faculty Minority: 10
Student/Faculty Ratio: 13:1
Students in Parent Institution: 27,500
Academic Calendar: Semester

PROGRAMS

Degrees Offered: MBA (39-75 credits, full time or part time, 1-5 years), MS (30-36 credits, full time or part time, 1-5 years), MAS (30 credits, full time, 1-5 years), MPACC (30 credits, full time or part time, 1-5 years), MSRE (36 credits, full time or part time, 1-5 years), MTAX (33 credits, full time or part time, 1-5 years), EMBA (66 credits, full time, 18 months), MSHA (36 credits, full time or part time, 1-5 years), MIB (33 credits, full time or part time, 1-5 years)
Combined Degrees: MBA/JD (63 credits, full time or part time, 2-6 years to complete the JD degree and 8 years to complete the MBA degree), MBA/MHA (51-63 credits, full time, 2.8 to 5 years)
Study Abroad Options: ESC-Toulouse, University of Nantes, France; EBS, Germany; Argentina, Brazil, China, Great Britain, Italy, Korea, Mexico, Russia, South Africa, Turkey

STUDENT INFORMATION

Total Business Students: 2,449
% Full Time: 37
% Female: 35
% Minority: 13
% Out of State: 48
% International: 28
Average Age: 28

COMPUTER AND RESEARCH FACILITIES

Research Facilities: William R. Pullen Library plus 1 additional on-campus library; total holdings of 1,215,397 volumes; 1,973,138 microforms; 11,283 current periodical subscriptions. CD player(s) available for graduate student use; access provided to online bibliographic retrieval services
Campuswide Network? Yes
Internet Fee? No

EXPENSES/FINANCIAL AID

Annual Tuition (Resident/Nonresident): $2,790/$11,160
Tuition Per Credit (Resident/Nonresident): $155/$620
Room & Board (On/Off Campus): $8,160
Books and Supplies: $3,840

ADMISSIONS INFORMATION

Application Fee: $25
Electronic Application? Yes
Regular Application Deadline: 5/1
Regular Notification: 6/15
Deferment Available? Yes
Length of Deferment: Up to 2 semesters
Non-fall Admissions? Yes
Non-fall Application Deadline(s): 9/1 spring, 2/1 summer
Transfer Students Accepted? No
Need-Blind Admissions? Yes
Number of Applications Received: 1,092
% of Applicants Accepted: 43
% Accepted Who Enrolled: 70
Average GPA: 3.2
GPA Range: 3.0-3.5
Average GMAT: 600
GMAT Range: 560-630
Average Years Experience: 5
Other Admissions Factors Considered: Letters of recommendation are permitted; work experience is recommended.
Other Schools to Which Students Applied: Baruch College/City University of New York, Clark Atlanta University, Emory University, Georgia Institute of Technology, Kennesaw State University, University of Florida, University of Georgia

INTERNATIONAL STUDENTS

TOEFL Required of International Students? Yes
Minimum TOEFL: 600 (250 computer)

EMPLOYMENT INFORMATION

Placement Office Available? Yes
% Employed Within 3 Months: 20
Fields Employing Percentage of Grads: Human Resources (1%), Communications (2%), Operations (4%), General Management (5%), Consulting (10%), Other (12%), Accounting (13%), Marketing (17%), MIS (18%), Finance (18%)
Frequent Employers: Top 10 Recruiters for 2002: IBM Global Services, Delta Air Lines, Bellsouth Telecommunications, Southern Co., Siemens, The Home Depot, Federal Reserve Bank, GE Power Systems, Sun Trust Banks, United Healthcare
Prominent Alumni: James E. Copeland, Deloitte & Touche/Tomats; A.W. Bill Dahlberg, chairman, Mirant; Kenneth Lewis, chairman and CEO, Bank of America; Richard H. Lenny, chairman, Hershey Foods; Mackey McDonald, chairman, president and CEO, VF Corp.

GOLDEN GATE UNIVERSITY
Edward S. Ageno School of Business

Admissions Contact: Cherron Hoppes, Director of Admissions
Address: 536 Mission Street, San Francisco, CA 94105-2968
Admissions Phone: 415-442-7800 • **Admissions Fax:** 415-442-7807
Admissions E-mail: admissions@ggu.edu • **Web Address:** www.ggu.edu

INSTITUTIONAL INFORMATION

Public/Private: Private
Evening Classes Available? Yes
Total Faculty: 400
% Faculty Female: 20
% Faculty Part Time: 80
Student/Faculty Ratio: 16:1

PROGRAMS

Degrees Offered: Executive Master of Business Administration (16 months); Executive Master of Public Administration (9 4-unit courses); Master of Accountancy (MAcc) (48 units); MA in Applied Psychology (36 units), with a concentration in Counseling; MA in Applied Psychology (36 units) with a concentration in Industrial/Organizational Management; MA in Psychology (48 units); Master of Business Administration (MBA) (30 units); MBA (48 units) with concentrations in Accounting, Electronic Business, Finance, Human Resource Management, Information Systems, International Business, Management, Marketing, Operations and Supply Chain Management, and Telecommunications; MS in Computer Information Systems (33 units); MS in Database Development and Administration (42 units); MS in Digital Security (30 units); MS in Electronic Business Systems and Technologies (33 units); MS in Enterprise Information Technology (48 units); MS in Finance (45 units); MS in Financial Planning (42 units); MS in Human Resource Management (33 units); MS in Integrated Marketing Communications (42 units) with a concentration in Public Relations; MS in Management of Technology (33 units); MS in Marketing (45 units); MS in Software Engineering (45 units); MS in Taxation (30 units); MS in Telecommunications Management (30 units); MS in Web Design and Development (36 units)
Joint Degrees: MBA/JD

COMPUTER AND RESEARCH FACILITIES

Campuswide Network? Yes
Internet Fee? No

ADMISSIONS INFORMATION

Application Fee: $55
Electronic Application? Yes
Regular Application Deadline: Rolling
Regular Notification: Rolling
Deferment Available? Yes
Length of Deferment: 1 year
Non-fall Admissions? Yes
Non-fall Application Deadline(s): Rolling
Transfer Students Accepted? Yes
Transfer Policy: May be able to transfer 6 units
Need-Blind Admissions? Yes
Number of Applications Received: 360
% of Applicants Accepted: 49
Other Schools to Which Students Applied: San Francisco State University, University of San Francisco, San Jose State University, California State University—Hayward, Santa Clara University, University of California—Berkeley

INTERNATIONAL STUDENTS

TOEFL Required of International Students? Yes
Minimum TOEFL: 550 (213 computer)

EMPLOYMENT INFORMATION

Placement Office Available? No
Frequent Employers: Arthur Andersen, Ernst & Young, Burr Pilger and Mayer, Franchise Tax Board
Prominent Alumni: Richard Belluzzo, president, Microsoft; George Christopher, former mayor, city and county of San Francisco; Richard Rosenberg, former CEO and chairman, Bank of America; Terence Henricks and Charles Precourt, NASA astronauts, Space Shuttle Columbia; Phillip Burton, former U.S. Representative, 8th District

See page 426.

GONZAGA UNIVERSITY
School of Business Administration

Admissions Contact: Dr. Gary Weber, Assistant Dean
Address: 502 East Boone Avenue, AD Box 9, Spokane, WA 99528
Admissions Phone: 509-323-3403 • **Admissions Fax:** 509-323-5811
Web Address: www.gonzaga.edu/mba-macc

INSTITUTIONAL INFORMATION

Public/Private: Private
Evening Classes Available? No
Total Faculty: 26
% Faculty Part Time: 14
Students in Parent Institution: 4,940

PROGRAMS

Degrees Offered: MBA, MACC
Combined Degrees: MBA/JD, MACC/JD
Special Opportunities: MBA with concentrations in CIS, MIS, General Business, MACC with concentrations in CIS, MIS, Taxation

STUDENT INFORMATION

Total Business Students: 158
% Full Time: 66
% Female: 35
% Minority: 9
% International: 47
Average Age: 27

COMPUTER AND RESEARCH FACILITIES

Campuswide Network? No
Internet Fee? No

EXPENSES/FINANCIAL AID

Annual Tuition: $5,340
Tuition Per Credit (Resident/Nonresident): $410
% Receiving Financial Aid: 22

ADMISSIONS INFORMATION

Application Fee: $40
Electronic Application? No
Regular Application Deadline: Rolling
Regular Notification: Rolling
Deferment Available? Yes
Length of Deferment: 1 year
Non-fall Admissions? No
Transfer Students Accepted? No
Need-Blind Admissions? No
Number of Applications Received: 206
% of Applicants Accepted: 59
% Accepted Who Enrolled: 60

INTERNATIONAL STUDENTS

TOEFL Required of International Students? Yes
Minimum TOEFL: 550

EMPLOYMENT INFORMATION

Placement Office Available? Yes
% Employed Within 3 Months: 90

GRAND VALLEY STATE UNIVERSITY
Seidman School of Business

Admissions Contact: Claudia Bajema, Graduate Business Programs Director
Address: 401 W. Fulton, Grand Rapids, MI 49504
Admissions Phone: 616-331-7400 • **Admissions Fax:** 616-331-7389
Admissions E-mail: go2gvmba@gvsu.edu • **Web Address:** www.gvsu.edu/ssb

The Seidman School of Business has a student body with an international population of 90 percent, giving the MBA program a global flavor. Classes are offered in four of the Greater Grand Rapids areas: Allendale, Muskegon, Downtown Grand Rapids, and Holland. Dual degrees are available with the MBA, including a Master of Science in Nursing (MSN). The unique MBA/MSN allows the student to fit the increasing need for managers who understand nursing and health care. Students may also obtain a JD/MBA via Grand Valley's partnership with nearby Michigan State University's Detroit College of Law.

INSTITUTIONAL INFORMATION

Public/Private: Public
Evening Classes Available? Yes
Total Faculty: 36
% Faculty Female: 11
% Faculty Minority: 3
% Faculty Part Time: 10
Student/Faculty Ratio: 25:1
Students in Parent Institution: 20,407
Academic Calendar: Semester

PROGRAMS

Degrees Offered: MBA (1.5 years), MST (1.5 years), MSA (1.5 years)
Combined Degrees: MSN/MB (4 years)
Academic Specialties: Operations, Accounting, Finance, Economics, Marketing, Organizational Behavior

STUDENT INFORMATION

Total Business Students: 320
% Full Time: 13
% Female: 26
% Minority: 3
% International: 44
Average Age: 31

COMPUTER AND RESEARCH FACILITIES

Computer Facilities: The IBM ES-9000 mainframe is accessible from 500 stations in 8 campus locations. These terminals are PCs that students also use for word processing and to run software packages. There are also PCs in residence halls.
Campuswide Network? Yes
% of MBA Classrooms Wired: 100
Internet Fee? No

EXPENSES/FINANCIAL AID

Annual Tuition (Resident/Nonresident): $4,356/$9,450
Tuition Per Credit (Resident/Nonresident): $242/$525
Room & Board (On/Off Campus): $5,000/$4,000
Books and Supplies: $1,500
Average Grant: $10,000
Average Loan: $5,000
% Receiving Financial Aid: 25

ADMISSIONS INFORMATION

Application Fee: $20
Electronic Application? Yes
Regular Application Deadline: 8/2
Regular Notification: Rolling
Deferment Available? Yes

Length of Deferment: 1 year
Non-fall Admissions? Yes
Non-fall Application Deadline(s): 11/1 January, 4/1 May
Transfer Students Accepted? Yes
Transfer Policy: Students may transfer up to 9 credits with B or better at the discretion of the program director.
Need-Blind Admissions? Yes
Number of Applications Received: 103
% of Applicants Accepted: 85
% Accepted Who Enrolled: 80
Average GPA: 3.3
GPA Range: 3.0-3.8
Average GMAT: 580
GMAT Range: 520-680
Average Years Experience: 9
Minority/Disadvantaged Student Recruitment Programs: Scholarship for African American and Hispanic students
Other Schools to Which Students Applied: Western Michigan University

INTERNATIONAL STUDENTS

TOEFL Required of International Students? Yes
Minimum TOEFL: 550

EMPLOYMENT INFORMATION

Placement Office Available? Yes
Fields Employing Percentage of Grads: Quantitative (10%), Global Management (10%), General Management (10%), Entrepreneurship (10%), Consulting (10%), Strategic Planning (10%), Operations (10%), Marketing (10%), Finance (10%), Accounting (10%)

GROUPE ESC TOULOUSE
Graduate School of Management

Admissions Contact: Director ESC Toulouse
Address: 20 bd Lascrosses-BP 7010, 31068 Tolouse Cedex 7 France
Admissions Phone: 05-61-29-49-49 • **Admissions Fax:** 05-61-29-49-94
Admissions E-mail: info.esc@esc-toulouse.fr • **Web Address:** www.esc-toulouse.fr

INSTITUTIONAL INFORMATION

Public/Private: Private
Evening Classes Available? No
Total Faculty: 111
% Faculty Part Time: 63
Students in Parent Institution: 1,424
Academic Calendar: Trimester

PROGRAMS

Degrees Offered: ESC Cycle Superieur (2-3 years), MS Audit Interne et Controle de Gestion (12-18 months), MS Banque et Ingenierie Financiere (12-18 months), MS Marketing et Communication Commerciale (12-18 months), MS Management de l'Innovation et de la Technologie (12-18 months), MS Management de la Sante (12-18 months), MS Management et Ingenierie des Organisations (12-18 months), MS Manager Public (12-18 months), MS Marketing et Technologie Agro-Alimentaires (12-18 months), Aerospace MBA (60 credits, 12-20 months)
Study Abroad Options: Canada, Colombia, Finland, Germany, Mexico, Ireland, Israel, Spain, United Kingdom, United States

STUDENT INFORMATION

Total Business Students: 850
% Full Time: 100
% Female: 48

% International: 16
Average Age: 23

COMPUTER AND RESEARCH FACILITIES

Campuswide Network? Yes
Computer Model Recommended: Laptop
Internet Fee? No

ADMISSIONS INFORMATION

Electronic Application? No
Regular Application Deadline: 7/30
Regular Notification: Rolling
Deferment Available? Yes
Non-fall Admissions? No
Transfer Students Accepted? No
Need-Blind Admissions? No
Number of Applications Received: 2,500
% of Applicants Accepted: 20
% Accepted Who Enrolled: 90
Other Admissions Factors Considered: GPA, interview, work experience

EMPLOYMENT INFORMATION

Placement Office Available? Yes
% Employed Within 3 Months: 85

HARVARD UNIVERSITY
Harvard Business School

Admissions Contact: Admissions Office, Admissions Office
Address: Soldiers Field, Boston, MA 02163
Admissions Phone: 617-495-6127 • **Admissions Fax:** 617-496-9272
Admissions E-mail: admissions@hbs.edu • **Web Address:** www.hbs.edu

Harvard Business School is indisputably the nation's most famous business school and arguably its best as well. HBS boasts more CEO alums than any other program, a nationally renowned faculty that have penned more than 90 percent of the case materials used worldwide, uncommonly loyal and generous alumni, and a ridiculously enormous endowment to boot. HBS students also get an average 3.8 job offers each—the highest average of any b-school.

INSTITUTIONAL INFORMATION

Public/Private: Private
Evening Classes Available? No
Total Faculty: 224
% Faculty Female: 20
Academic Calendar: September to May

PROGRAMS

Degrees Offered: MBA (4 15-week terms), DBA (4 years)
Combined Degrees: JD/MBA (4 years)
Academic Specialties: Entrepreneurship, General Management, Finance, Technology and Operations Management, Service Management

STUDENT INFORMATION

Total Business Students: 1,770
% Full Time: 100
% Female: 32
% Minority: 19
% International: 34

COMPUTER AND RESEARCH FACILITIES

Research Facilities: Research centers in Silicon Valley, Hong Kong, and Buenos Aires

Computer Facilities: Two on-campus computer labs containing 150 machines. Harvard Business School's library has more than 600,000 volumes and 7,001 periodicals as well as numerous databases and other electronic resources.

Campuswide Network? Yes

Internet Fee? No

EXPENSES/FINANCIAL AID

Annual Tuition: $28,500

% Receiving Financial Aid: 66

ADMISSIONS INFORMATION

Application Fee: $175

Electronic Application? Yes

Regular Application Deadline: 3/2

Regular Notification: Rolling

Deferment Available? No

Non-fall Admissions? No

Transfer Students Accepted? No

Need-Blind Admissions? Yes

Number of Applications Received: 8,124

Average GPA: 3.5

Minority/Disadvantaged Student Recruitment Programs: Summer Venture in Management Program for minority college juniors, minority open-house events

INTERNATIONAL STUDENTS

TOEFL Required of International Students? Yes

EMPLOYMENT INFORMATION

Placement Office Available? Yes

% Employed Within 3 Months: 99

Fields Employing Percentage of Grads: General Management (8%), Entrepreneurship (9%), Venture Capital (12%), Consulting (20%), Finance (27%)

HEC SCHOOL OF MANAGEMENT
HEC MBA Program

Admissions Contact: Valerie Gauthier, Associate Dean
Address: 1 Rue de la Liberation, Jouy-en-Josas Cedex, 78351 France
Admissions Phone: 011 33 0 1 39 67 71 67 • Admissions Fax: 011 33 0 1 39 67 74 65
Admissions E-mail: admissionmba@hec.fr • Web Address: www.hec.fr/hec/eng/mba/index.html

INSTITUTIONAL INFORMATION

Public/Private: Public

Evening Classes Available? No

Total Faculty: 157

% Faculty Female: 15

Students in Parent Institution: 1,144

PROGRAMS

Degrees Offered: English-language-only and bilingual (English/French) section (16 months)

Combined Degrees: 6 double-degree programs are available

Academic Specialties: Finance; international program, emphasis on interpersonal skills

Study Abroad Options: Australia, Austria, Brazil, Canada, Chile, Germany, Hong Kong, Israel, Italy, Japan, Mexico, the Netherlands, Philippines, Spain, United Kingdom, United States

STUDENT INFORMATION

Total Business Students: 198

% Female: 25

% International: 75

Average Age: 28

COMPUTER AND RESEARCH FACILITIES

Campuswide Network? Yes

Computer Model Recommended: Laptop

Internet Fee? No

EXPENSES/FINANCIAL AID

Annual Tuition (Resident/Nonresident): $30,000

Room & Board (On/Off Campus): $8,000/$11,000

Books and Supplies: $900

ADMISSIONS INFORMATION

Application Fee: $100

Electronic Application? Yes

Regular Notification: Rolling

Deferment Available? Yes

Length of Deferment: 1 year

Non-fall Admissions? Yes

Non-fall Application Deadline(s): September and January

Transfer Students Accepted? No

Need-Blind Admissions? No

Number of Applications Received: 750

% of Applicants Accepted: 35

% Accepted Who Enrolled: 76

Average GMAT: 633

GMAT Range: 570-730

Other Admissions Factors Considered: International exposure required; minimum 2-year work experience (6 years average), computer experience

INTERNATIONAL STUDENTS

TOEFL Required of International Students? Yes

Minimum TOEFL: 600 (250 computer)

EMPLOYMENT INFORMATION

Placement Office Available? Yes

% Employed Within 3 Months: 50

Frequent Employers: American Express, Cap Gemini, Ernst & Young, Hilti, L'oreal, Merrill Lynch, Mizuho Financial Group, PWC Counseling, Souere Generale, Total FinaElf, Valeo

Prominent Alumni: Sidney Taurel, president and CEO, Eli Lilly & Co; Fumiaki Maeda, managing director, Mitsubishi Bank; Daniel Bernard, CEO, Carrefour; Bruno Grob, CEO Europe, Otis Elevator International; Isabelle Guichot, CEO, Van Cleef & Arpels

HENDERSON STATE UNIVERSITY
School of Business Administration

Admissions Contact: Dr. Mike Watters, MBA Program Director
Address: HSU Box 7811, Arkadelphia, AR 71999
Admissions Phone: 870-230-5377 • Admissions Fax: 870-230-5286
Admissions E-mail: watterm@hsu.edu • Web Address: www.hsu.edu/dept/bus

INSTITUTIONAL INFORMATION

Public/Private: Public

Evening Classes Available? No

Students in Parent Institution: 3,754

PROGRAMS

Degrees Offered: MBA

COMPUTER AND RESEARCH FACILITIES

Campuswide Network? No
Internet Fee? No

ADMISSIONS INFORMATION

Electronic Application? No
Regular Application Deadline: 1/1
Regular Notification: 1/1
Deferment Available? No
Non-fall Admissions? No
Transfer Students Accepted? No
Need-Blind Admissions? No
Other Admissions Factors Considered: A minimum GPA/GMAT index of 1000 (formula: GPA _ 200 + GMAT score)

EMPLOYMENT INFORMATION

Placement Office Available? No

HOFSTRA UNIVERSITY
Frank G. Zarb School of Business

Admissions Contact: Thomas Rock, Dean for Graduate Admissions
Address: 126 Hofstra University, Hempstead, NY 11549
Admissions Phone: 866-472-3463 • **Admissions Fax:** 516-463-4664
Admissions E-mail: gradstudent@hofstra.edu • **Web Address:** www.hofstra.edu/Business

Students at Hofstra's "dynamic and intense" Zarb School of Business in parking-impaired Hempstead, New York (about 25 miles from New York City), are able to participate in consulting projects and engagements for companies ranging from small start-up shops to large, multinational firms. In addition, the faculty here receive great reviews for both brilliance and accessibility.

INSTITUTIONAL INFORMATION

Public/Private: Private
Evening Classes Available? Yes
Total Faculty: 43
% Faculty Female: 9
% Faculty Minority: 23
% Faculty Part Time: 16
Student/Faculty Ratio: 12:1
Students in Parent Institution: 13,412
Academic Calendar: Semester

PROGRAMS

Degrees Offered: MBA (2.5 years full time), MS (1 to 1.5 years), EMBA (20 months full time, 4 years part time)
Combined Degrees: JD/MBA (4 years)
Academic Specialties: Strengths of faculty and curriculum in Accounting, Finance, Marketing, International Business
Special Opportunities: The Hofstra University Consulting Group, The Association of Students of Economics and International Commerce, The Merrill Lynch Center for the Study of International Financial Markets, Investment Banking Association
Study Abroad Options: Helsinki School of Economics, Finland; Hong-ik University, Korea; Erasmus/Rotterdam School of Management, the Netherlands; University of Stockholm, Sweden

STUDENT INFORMATION

Total Business Students: 488
% Full Time: 25
% Female: 30
% Minority: 7
% Out of State: 34
% International: 28
Average Age: 27

COMPUTER AND RESEARCH FACILITIES

Research Facilities: Merrill Lynch Center for the Study of Financial Markets, Small Business Institute, Business Development Center
Computer Facilities: All of the databases and software proprietary to the McGraw-Hill companies (a gift of Hofstra alumnus Joseph Dionne, former CEO of McGraw-Hill); GIS (Geographic Information System); C.V. Starr Hall, a newly opened state-of-the-art instructional facility that provides Internet access at every seat in each team room, community area, and classroom through ports installed at all seats
Campuswide Network? Yes
% of MBA Classrooms Wired: 100
Internet Fee? No

EXPENSES/FINANCIAL AID

Annual Tuition: $14,877
Tuition Per Credit (Resident/Nonresident): $551
Room & Board (On/Off Campus): $8,450/$9,976
Books and Supplies: $1,910
Average Grant: $5,700
Average Loan: $8,500
% Receiving Financial Aid: 50
% Receiving Aid Their First Year: 50

ADMISSIONS INFORMATION

Application Fee: $40
Electronic Application? Yes
Early Decision Application Deadline: Rolling
Early Decision Notification: 1/1
Regular Notification: Rolling
Deferment Available? Yes
Length of Deferment: 1 year
Non-fall Admissions? Yes
Non-fall Application Deadline(s): Spring and summer
Transfer Students Accepted? Yes
Transfer Policy: Maximum of 9 credits
Need-Blind Admissions? Yes
Number of Applications Received: 384
% of Applicants Accepted: 56
% Accepted Who Enrolled: 61
Average GPA: 3.2
GPA Range: 2.8-3.4
Average GMAT: 518
GMAT Range: 470-560
Average Years Experience: 2
Other Admissions Factors Considered: Evidence of leadership, communications skills, analytical writing assessment of GMAT
Minority/Disadvantaged Student Recruitment Programs: Special consideration in the application process is given to minority students from disadvantaged backgrounds.
Other Schools to Which Students Applied: Baruch College/City University of New York, New York University, St. John's University, Pace University

INTERNATIONAL STUDENTS

TOEFL Required of International Students? Yes
Minimum TOEFL: 600

EMPLOYMENT INFORMATION

Placement Office Available? Yes
% Employed Within 3 Months: 82

Fields Employing Percentage of Grads: Consulting (2%), General Management (5%), MIS (6%), Other (10%), Accounting (11%), Operations (12%), Marketing (26%), Finance (28%)

Frequent Employers: Cablevision, Citigroup, Coca Cola, Credit Suisse First Boston, Deloitte & Touche, Ernst & Young, Fleet Bank, GE Consumer Finance, Glaxo Smith Kline, JP Morgan Chase, KPMG Peat Marwick, LIJ Health Systems, North Shore, The NPD Group Inc., Pricewaterhouse Coopers LLP, UBS Warburg

Prominent Alumni: Frank G. Zarb, former chairman and CEO, NASDAQ; Susan Axelrod, president, Love & Quiches Ltd.; Salvatore F. Sodano, chairman and CEO, American Stock Exchange; Norman Coleman, U.S. senator; Ala J. Bernon, COO, Dean Diary Group, Dean Food

---

HONG KONG UNIVERSITY OF SCIENCE & TECHNOLOGY
School of Business & Management

Admissions Contact: Pui Hung Mal, Executive Officer
Address: Clearwater Bay, Kowloon, Hong Kong
Admissions Phone: 852-2358-7539 • **Admissions Fax:** 852-2705-9596
Admissions E-mail: mba@ust.hk • **Web Address:** www.bm.ust.hk/mba

Since its official opening in October 1991, the Hong Kong University of Science and Technology has established itself as an intellectual powerhouse, an institution known for securing a spot on the academic world map in record-breaking time, and a great place for burgers (can we live without the comfort of fast food?). The campus occupies a 150-acre site of natural beauty on the Clear Water Bay peninsula in East Kowloon, less than 30 minutes away from central Hong Kong by car. HKUST's School of Business Management offers full-time and part-time programs taught in English by world-class faculty and an EMBA program that operates in conjunction with the renowned Kellogg Graduate School of Management at Northwestern University.

INSTITUTIONAL INFORMATION
Public/Private: Public
Evening Classes Available? No
Total Faculty: 127
% Faculty Female: 7
% Faculty Part Time: 1
Student/Faculty Ratio: 19:1

PROGRAMS
Degrees Offered: Master of Philosophy (2 years full time), PhD (4 years full time), MS in Investment Management (2 years part time), MSISM (2 years part time), MS in Electonic Commerce Management (16 months part time), EMBA (16 months part time)

Combined Degrees: MBA/MS in Investment Management (3 years part time), MBA/MSISM (3 years part time), MBA/MS in Electonic Commerce Management (3 years part time)

Academic Specialties: The HKUST Business School follows the highest international standards in its hiring of faculty, and the basic academic entry qualification for a faculty member is a doctorate. The quality of research produced by scholars of the Business School is judged according to international standards. Our MBA program's model is based on those at top business schools in North America that adopt a pedagogical approach combining scientfic and analytical methods with case studies. Students have the opportunity to concentrate in China Business. China-focused electives have been developed for this purpose. But more than course development, China business and management has been designated as a critical area for research and teaching at the HKUST Business School. Toward this end, the School has received strong support from the University as well as corporations in setting up supporting research centers such as the Hang Lung Center for Organization Research and the Shui-On Center for China Business and Management. In addition, Asia elements are built into individual courses and Asian cases are frequently used. For example, as part of curriculum development, a collection of Asian cases have been written and published in a book by a marketing faculty member.

Study Abroad Options: 37 MBA exchange partners from top business schools in Australia, Canada, China, Denmark, France, Germany, India, Israel, Japan, Singapore, Spain, United Kingdom, United States

STUDENT INFORMATION
Total Business Students: 196
% Full Time: 19
% Female: 50
% International: 42
Average Age: 29

COMPUTER AND RESEARCH FACILITIES
Research Facilities: The Business School runs 5 research centers to promote research in specific areas as well as multidisciplinary studies. These centers also serve as outreach centers for the coordination of faculty's involvement in consultancy or services to government, commercial, or professional organizations.

Computer Facilities: The campus is operated with powerful servers to provide campuswide network services such as e-mail, network printing, World Wide Web, and an electronic notice board. There are 3 computer barns all equipped with advanced computer and printing facilities. In addition to the central computing facilities, the Business School runs specialized laboratories with advanced computing facilities to serve different course purposes. Moreover, a number of online business databases are available through the University Library.

Campuswide Network? Yes
Internet Fee? No

ADMISSIONS INFORMATION
Application Fee: $45
Electronic Application? No
Regular Application Deadline: 3/15
Regular Notification: 5/15
Deferment Available? Yes
Length of Deferment: 1 year
Non-fall Admissions? No
Transfer Students Accepted? No
Need-Blind Admissions? No
Number of Applications Received: 718
% of Applicants Accepted: 36
% Accepted Who Enrolled: 76
Average Years Experience: 7

EMPLOYMENT INFORMATION
Placement Office Available? Yes
% Employed Within 3 Months: 92
Fields Employing Percentage of Grads: MIS (7%), Other (7%), Accounting (7%), Human Resources (7%), Operations (7%), Marketing (13%), Consulting (13%), Finance (39%)

Frequent Employers: ABN Amro, Citibank N.A., Coca-Cola, Exxon Mobil, Federal Express, Morgan Stanley, Salomon Smith Barney, UBS Warburg, Watson Wyatt

Prominent Alumni: Estella Ng, senior vice president, listing, HK Exchanges & Clearing Ltd.; Arthur Yuen, head, banking supervision, HK Monetary Authority; Terence Ma, director of business development & strategy, Motorola; Andy Yuen, vice president, head of warrants, HK, Citibank N.A.; Pascale Brunet, vice president, Morgan Stanley

HOWARD UNIVERSITY
School of Business

Admissions Contact: Donna Mason, Administrative Assistant
Address: 2600 Sixth Street NW, Washington, DC 20059
Admissions Phone: 202-806-1725 • **Admissions Fax:** 202-986-4435
Admissions E-mail: dmason@howard.edu • **Web Address:** www.bschool.howard.edu/mba

Where else would a highly accredited African American university reside but in Washington, D.C.? Here, Martin Luther King Jr. asked for something that Howard University is helping to deliver: freedom—that is, the freedom of education. The vision of the School of Business, Vision 21, is to "develop an agenda that reflects the needs of its core constituency (African Americans and people of color)." The MBA program offers a multitude of rigorous classes with professors who truly engage students with business material.

INSTITUTIONAL INFORMATION

Public/Private: Private
Evening Classes Available? Yes
Total Faculty: 37
% Faculty Female: 27
% Faculty Minority: 90
% Faculty Part Time: 5
Student/Faculty Ratio: 7:1
Students in Parent Institution: 1,618
Academic Calendar: Semester

PROGRAMS

Degrees Offered: MBA (2 years full time, 4 years part time)
Combined Degrees: JD/MBA (4 years)
Academic Specialties: Finance/International Business/Insurance, Accounting, Information Systems, Management (Human Resource Management), Marketing
Special Opportunities: Accounting, Finance, Marketing, Entrepreneurship, International Business, Supply Chain Management, Summer Enrichment Program, Federal Student Internship Program

STUDENT INFORMATION

Total Business Students: 49
% Full Time: 78
% Female: 50
% Minority: 73
% Out of State: 10
% International: 27
Average Age: 28

COMPUTER AND RESEARCH FACILITIES

Research Facilities: Small Business Development Center, Center for Banking Education, Center for Entrepreneurship, Center for Supply Chain Management, Center for Technology, Center for Professional Development, 21st Century Advantage Program
Computer Facilities: Howard University I-Lab, School of Business Computer Lab, wireless access in all dorms, SPSS, SAS, Access 97/2000
Campuswide Network? Yes
% of MBA Classrooms Wired: 53
Computer Model Recommended: Laptop
Internet Fee? No

EXPENSES/FINANCIAL AID

Annual Tuition: $11,590
Tuition Per Credit (Resident/Nonresident): $644
Room & Board (On/Off Campus): $9,000/$11,000
Books and Supplies: $1,000
Average Grant: $12,000
Average Loan: $14,363
% Receiving Financial Aid: 86
% Receiving Aid Their First Year: 76

ADMISSIONS INFORMATION

Application Fee: $45
Electronic Application? No
Regular Application Deadline: 4/1
Regular Notification: 5/31
Deferment Available? Yes
Length of Deferment: 2 semesters
Non-fall Admissions? Yes
Non-fall Application Deadline(s): 11/15 spring, part time
Transfer Students Accepted? No
Need-Blind Admissions? No
Number of Applications Received: 298
% of Applicants Accepted: 33
% Accepted Who Enrolled: 50
Average GPA: 3.0
GPA Range: 2.8-3.2
Average GMAT: 502
GMAT Range: 460-610
Average Years Experience: 3
Other Admissions Factors Considered: GMAT scores, undergraduate GPA, post-undergraduate work experience
Minority/Disadvantaged Student Recruitment Programs: Purchasing of mailing lists from GMAC, being a predominantly African American institution, recruiting at HBCU's and the National Association for Hispanic MBA Association
Other Schools to Which Students Applied: George Mason University, Georgetown University, University of Maryland—College Park

INTERNATIONAL STUDENTS

TOEFL Required of International Students? Yes
Minimum TOEFL: 550 (213 computer)

EMPLOYMENT INFORMATION

Placement Office Available? Yes
% Employed Within 3 Months: 5
Fields Employing Percentage of Grads: MIS (11%), Marketing (11%), Other (22%), Finance (56%)
Frequent Employers: Bank of America, Bayer, Dow Chemicals, General Motors, IBM, JP Morgan Chase, KPMG, Lucent, Pfizer, Philip Morris, Pricewaterhouse Coopers, SC Johnson, Securities & Exchange Commission, Travelers Insurance, United Technology Corp.,

IDAHO STATE UNIVERSITY
College of Business

Admissions Contact: Gordon Brooks, MBA Director
Address: Box 8020, Pocatello, ID 83209
Admissions Phone: 208-282-2966 • **Admissions Fax:** 208-236-4367
Admissions E-mail: broogord@isu.edu • **Web Address:** cob.isu.edu

INSTITUTIONAL INFORMATION

Public/Private: Public
Evening Classes Available? Yes
Total Faculty: 40
% Faculty Female: 20
% Faculty Part Time: 7
Students in Parent Institution: 11,935
Academic Calendar: Semester

PROGRAMS

Degrees Offered: MBA (30 credits, 1-3 years), MBA in Accounting (30 credits, 1-3 years)
Special Opportunities: Internship program, credit for military training programs

STUDENT INFORMATION

Total Business Students: 56
% Full Time: 32
% Female: 24
% Out of State: 64
% International: 23
Average Age: 34

COMPUTER AND RESEARCH FACILITIES

Research Facilities: CD players
Computer Facilities: Access to online bibliographic retrieval system
Campuswide Network? Yes
Internet Fee? No

EXPENSES/FINANCIAL AID

Annual Tuition (Resident/Nonresident): $4,318/$10,558
Tuition Per Credit (Resident/Nonresident): $189/$279
% Receiving Financial Aid: 8

ADMISSIONS INFORMATION

Application Fee: $35
Electronic Application? Yes
Regular Application Deadline: 7/1
Regular Notification: Rolling
Deferment Available? Yes
Length of Deferment: 2 years
Non-fall Admissions? Yes
Non-fall Application Deadline(s): 12/1 spring, 5/1 summer, 7/3 fall
Transfer Students Accepted? No
Need-Blind Admissions? No
Number of Applications Received: 64
% of Applicants Accepted: 72
Other Admissions Factors Considered: Minimum GPA of 3.0

INTERNATIONAL STUDENTS

TOEFL Required of International Students? Yes
Minimum TOEFL: 550 (213 computer)

EMPLOYMENT INFORMATION

Placement Office Available? Yes

ILLINOIS INSTITUTE OF TECHNOLOGY
Stuart Graduate School of Business

Admissions Contact: Lynn Miller, Associate Dean
Address: 565 W. Adams Street, Chicago, IL 60616
Admissions Phone: 312-906-6544 • **Admissions Fax:** 312-906-6549
Admissions E-mail: lmiller@stuart.iit.edu • **Web Address:** www.stuart.iit.edu

The Stuart MBA provides a "thorough grounding" in the major functional business areas, an understanding of technological and analytical approaches to business problem-solving, and a whole bunch of concentrations to choose from, all "within a holistic, global management perspective." Small classes allow for personal student-faculty and student-student

interaction, increasing the ability to network and inherit valuable personal lessons from experienced faculty who "bring a practical point of view to management issues."

INSTITUTIONAL INFORMATION

Public/Private: Private
Evening Classes Available? Yes
Total Faculty: 37
% Faculty Female: 8
% Faculty Part Time: 51
Student/Faculty Ratio: 15:1
Students in Parent Institution: 6,100
Academic Calendar: Quarter

PROGRAMS

Degrees Offered: MBA (72 credits, 12-20 months), Fast-Track MBA (58 credits, 12-15 months), MS in Environmental Management (50 credits, 12-15 months), MS in Finance (50 credits, 12-15 months), MS in Marketing Communication (50 credits, 12-15), PhD in Management (94 credits, 3-6 years)
Combined Degrees: JD/MBA (4-6 years), MBA/MS (2-3 years), JD/MS in Environmental Management (3-5 years)
Academic Specialties: Technology Management, Integrated Marketing Communication, Financial Markets, E-Business, Environmental Management, Quality Management, Entrepreneurial Management, Cross-Functional Teamwork, Mathematical and Computer Modeling, Strategic Marketing Planning, Project Financing, Impacts of Technology on Business Strategy, Information Management, Finance, International Business, Management Science, Marketing, Marketing Communication, Operations Management, Organization and Management, Strategic Management

STUDENT INFORMATION

Total Business Students: 284
% Full Time: 38
% Female: 24
% Minority: 5
% International: 73
Average Age: 30

COMPUTER AND RESEARCH FACILITIES

Research Facilities: Center for Research on the Impacts of Information Systems, Center for Research on Industrial Strategy and Policy, Center for Sustainable Enterprise, Center for the Management of Medical Technology
Computer Facilities: IIT was ranked number 27 in Yahoo!Internet Life magazine's 100 Most Wired Colleges. Stuart has 3 computer labs with more than 100 student workstations available to students. Labs include the Quantitative Research Lab (QRL), a state-of-the-art interactive teaching lab with real-time market feeds, financial industry databases, and a simulated trading environment. The QRL is considered among the nation's best resources for the study of financial markets. The QRL also supports other Stuart curricula with software in areas such as enterprise resource planning (ERP), marketing simulation, and simulated manufacturing environments. Stuart also offers a 45-workstation e-commerce lab equipped with leading edge software for developing e-commerce transactions and marketspaces.
Campuswide Network? Yes
Internet Fee? No

EXPENSES/FINANCIAL AID

Annual Tuition: $19,000
Tuition Per Credit (Resident/Nonresident): $585
Room & Board (On/Off Campus): $6,631/$13,866
Books and Supplies: $890
Average Grant: $10,000
Average Loan: $17,843
% Receiving Financial Aid: 32
% Receiving Aid Their First Year: 39

ADMISSIONS INFORMATION

Application Fee: $50

Electronic Application? Yes
Regular Application Deadline: 6/15
Regular Notification: Rolling
Deferment Available? Yes
Length of Deferment: 1 year
Non-fall Admissions? Yes
Non-fall Application Deadline(s): 10/1 winter, 1/5 spring, 4/15 summer
Transfer Students Accepted? Yes
Transfer Policy: With advisor approval, students may transfer up to 4 core courses and 2 elective courses.
Need-Blind Admissions? Yes
Number of Applications Received: 316
% of Applicants Accepted: 59
% Accepted Who Enrolled: 47
Average GPA: 3.0
Average GMAT: 568
GMAT Range: 490-650
Average Years Experience: 5

INTERNATIONAL STUDENTS

TOEFL Required of International Students? Yes
Minimum TOEFL: 550 (213 computer)

EMPLOYMENT INFORMATION

Placement Office Available? Yes
% Employed Within 3 Months: 45
Fields Employing Percentage of Grads: Operations (11%), Other (18%), Marketing (19%), Finance (19%), MIS (33%)
Frequent Employers: ABN-Amro, Akamal Trading, Bank of America, Bank One, Cantor Fitzgerald, JP Morgan, Lucent Technologies, McLagan Partners, Motorola, Inc., Navistar, Northern Trust, Reuters, U.S. Environmental Protection Agency, Vankampen, Zenith
Prominent Alumni: Robert Growney, president and COO, Motorola; John Calamos, president, CIO, and founder, Calamos Asset Management; Ajva Taulananda, president, TelecomASIA Corp.; Carl Spetzler, chairman and founder, Strategic Decisions Group; Les Jezuit, president, Quixote Corp.

ILLINOIS STATE UNIVERSITY
College of Business

Admissions Contact: Dr. Lee Graf, Director of MBA Program
Address: Williams Hall, Room 327, Campus Box 5500, Normal IL 61790
Admissions Phone: 309-438-8388 • Admissions Fax: 309-438-7255
Admissions E-mail: isumba@exchange.cob.ilstu.edu • Web Address: www.cob.ilstu.edu/

INSTITUTIONAL INFORMATION

Public/Private: Public
Evening Classes Available? Yes
Total Faculty: 93
% Faculty Part Time: 18
Student/Faculty Ratio: 17:1
Students in Parent Institution: 20,470
Academic Calendar: Semester

PROGRAMS

Degrees Offered: MBA (36 hours plus any required foundation courses), MSA (33 hours plus any required foundation courses)
Combined Degrees: Master of Professional Accountancy (30 hours beyond the undergraduate degree in accounting)
Special Opportunities: General Business, Accounting

STUDENT INFORMATION

Total Business Students: 214
% Full Time: 53
% Female: 17
% Minority: 4
% Out of State: 29
% International: 26
Average Age: 27

COMPUTER AND RESEARCH FACILITIES

Campuswide Network? Yes
Internet Fee? No

EXPENSES/FINANCIAL AID

Annual Tuition (Resident/Nonresident): $5,580/$13,377
Tuition Per Credit (Resident/Nonresident): $108/$325
Books and Supplies: $2,976

ADMISSIONS INFORMATION

Application Fee: $0
Electronic Application? Yes
Regular Application Deadline: 8/1
Regular Notification: 8/15
Deferment Available? Yes
Length of Deferment: 1 year
Non-fall Admissions? Yes
Non-fall Application Deadline(s): Spring: 10/1 priority, 1/1 regular; summer: 3/15 priority, 5/1 regular
Transfer Students Accepted? Yes
Transfer Policy: Must be in good academic standing and complete all regular application requirements; maximum 9 hours transfer credit accepted
Need-Blind Admissions? Yes
Number of Applications Received: 91
% of Applicants Accepted: 77
% Accepted Who Enrolled: 67
Average Years Experience: 6
Other Admissions Factors Considered: Work experience, community service
Minority/Disadvantaged Student Recruitment Programs: Graduate Minority Tuition Waivers, McNair Book Scholarships, McHenry Scholarship, Illinois Consortium for Educational Opportunity Program

INTERNATIONAL STUDENTS

TOEFL Required of International Students? Yes
Minimum TOEFL: 530

EMPLOYMENT INFORMATION

Placement Office Available? Yes

INCAE
Graduate Program

Admissions Contact: Sonia Jimenez, Representative
Address: Del Vivero Procesa #1, 2 Km al Oeste, La Garita Alajuela, Costa Rica
Admissions Phone: 506-433-9908 • Admissions Fax: 506-433-9989
Admissions E-mail: incaecr@mail.incae.cr • Web Address: www.incae.ac.cr

INSTITUTIONAL INFORMATION

Public/Private: Private
Evening Classes Available? No
Total Faculty: 31

Student/Faculty Ratio: 15:1
Students in Parent Institution: 441
Academic Calendar: Trimester

PROGRAMS

Degrees Offered: MBA (up to 2 years), Master of Business Economics (up to 2 years)
Study Abroad Options: Germany, Spain, United States

STUDENT INFORMATION

Total Business Students: 441
% Full Time: 80
% Female: 30
Average Age: 28

COMPUTER AND RESEARCH FACILITIES

Campuswide Network? Yes
Internet Fee? No

EXPENSES/FINANCIAL AID

Annual Tuition: $11,500
% Receiving Financial Aid: 3

ADMISSIONS INFORMATION

Application Fee: $50
Electronic Application? No
Regular Application Deadline: 7/15
Regular Notification: Rolling
Deferment Available? Yes
Non-fall Admissions? No
Transfer Students Accepted? No
Need-Blind Admissions? No
Number of Applications Received: 530
% of Applicants Accepted: 60
% Accepted Who Enrolled: 37
Other Admissions Factors Considered: Interview

EMPLOYMENT INFORMATION

Placement Office Available? No
% Employed Within 3 Months: 60

INDIANA STATE UNIVERSITY
School of Business

Admissions Contact: Dale Varble, Director, MBA Program
Address: Indiana State University, Terre Haute, IN 47802
Admissions Phone: 812-237-2002 • **Admissions Fax:** 812-237-8720
Admissions E-mail: mba@indstate.edu
Web Address: web.indstate.edu/schbus/mba.html

Indiana State's MBA program is designed for full-time or part-time students looking to obtain middle- or upper-management positions. The MBA curriculum uses an integrated approach to tackle the business fundamentals, teaching students the problem-solving, decision-making, and interpersonal skills that are vital to success. In a culminating experience, students act as top managers, using a corporate strategic management model and concepts learned in class to resolve problems, recognize opportunities, and "manage the implementation process to achieve the desired strategy." Most of Indiana State's MBA students leap into the fields of marketing, consulting, or finance upon graduation.

INSTITUTIONAL INFORMATION

Public/Private: Public
Evening Classes Available? Yes
Total Faculty: 32
% Faculty Part Time: 6
Student/Faculty Ratio: 18:1
Students in Parent Institution: 10,800
Academic Calendar: Trimester

PROGRAMS

Degrees Offered: MBA (35 credits, 16-32 months)
Academic Specialties: Finance, E-Commerce

STUDENT INFORMATION

Total Business Students: 105
% Full Time: 60
% Female: 40
% Minority: 3
% International: 55
Average Age: 30

COMPUTER AND RESEARCH FACILITIES

Computer Facilities: See http://panther.indstate.edu/dbalphalist.asp
Campuswide Network? Yes
% of MBA Classrooms Wired: 90
Internet Fee? No

EXPENSES/FINANCIAL AID

Annual Tuition (Resident/Nonresident): $2,720/$5,920
Tuition Per Credit (Resident/Nonresident): $105/$305
Room & Board (On/Off Campus): $7,404
Books and Supplies: $900
Average Grant: $6,210
% Receiving Financial Aid: 30
% Receiving Aid Their First Year: 30

ADMISSIONS INFORMATION

Application Fee: $35
Electronic Application? Yes
Regular Application Deadline: Rolling
Regular Notification: Rolling
Deferment Available? Yes
Length of Deferment: 2 years
Non-fall Admissions? Yes
Non-fall Application Deadline(s): Spring, summer
Transfer Students Accepted? Yes
Transfer Policy: Maximum of 6 credit hours from AACSB-accredited universities
Need-Blind Admissions? No
Number of Applications Received: 148
% of Applicants Accepted: 88
Average GPA: 3.0
GPA Range: 2.5-3.9
Average GMAT: 530
GMAT Range: 400-750
Average Years Experience: 4
Other Admissions Factors Considered: 3 letters of recommendation, a statement of intent for international students
Other Schools to Which Students Applied: Ball State University, Illinois State University, Indiana University—Kokomo, Indiana University-Purdue University—Indianapolis, Michigan State University-Detroit College of Law, Purdue University, University of Texas—Austin

INTERNATIONAL STUDENTS

TOEFL Required of International Students? Yes
Minimum TOEFL: 550 (213 computer)

EMPLOYMENT INFORMATION

Placement Office Available? Yes

INDIANA UNIVERSITY
Kelley School of Business

Admissions Contact: James Holmen, Director of Admissions and Financial Aid
Address: 1275 East Tenth Street, Suite 2010, Bloomington, IN 47405-1703
Admissions Phone: 812-855-8006 • **Admissions Fax:** 812-855-9039
Admissions E-mail: mbaoffice@indiana.edu • **Web Address:** www.kelley.indiana.edu/mba

Students at Indiana University's Kelley School of Business are well prepared "to analyze business issues from a broad perspective," and there is a strong emphasis on teamwork and collaborative learning. Professors at IU are "really absorbed," and the deans "make every effort to ensure that the business school is run like a small business" ("not a large bureaucracy").

INSTITUTIONAL INFORMATION

Public/Private: Public
Evening Classes Available? No
Total Faculty: 210
% Faculty Female: 25
% Faculty Minority: 10
% Faculty Part Time: 17
Student/Faculty Ratio: 24:1
Students in Parent Institution: 37,000
Academic Calendar: Semester

PROGRAMS

Degrees Offered: MBA (21 months)
Combined Degrees: MBA/JD (4 years), MBA/MS in Area Studies (3 years)
Academic Specialties: Finance and marketing are the most popular majors. Integrated approach gives the curriculum an applied force. Faculty emphasize teamwork and skill development. The program is taught by full-time, experienced faculty who are highly accessible to students.
Study Abroad Options: Australian Graduate School of Management and University of Melbourne, Australia; Wirtschaftuniversitat Wien, Austria; Universite Catholique de Louvain, Belgium; Pontificia Universidad Catolica (PUC), Chile; Hong Kong University of Science and Technology (HKUST), China; Copenhagen Business School, Denmark; Manchester Business School and Warwick Business School, England; Ecole Des Hautes Etudes Commerciales (HEC) and Ecole Superieure de Commerce de Rouen, France; Fachhochschule fur Wirtschaft, Pforzheim, Germany; University of Cologne, Germany; Wiso-Fakultat Universitat Erlangen-Nurnberg, Germany; Wissenschaftliche Hochschule Fur Unternehmensfuhrung (WHU—Koblenz), Germany; Universita Commerciale Luigi Bocconi, Italy; ITESM, Monterrey, Mexico; Norwegian School of Management, Norway; Nanyang Technological University, Singapore; Wits Business School, South Africa; Sun Kyun Kwan University, South Korea; Escuela Superior de Administration y Direccion de Empresas (ESADE), Barcelona, Spain; Hochschule St. Gallen, Switzerland

STUDENT INFORMATION

Total Business Students: 548
% Full Time: 100
% Female: 25
% Minority: 9
% Out of State: 84
% International: 30
Average Age: 29

COMPUTER AND RESEARCH FACILITIES

Research Facilities: Leadership Development Institute, Johnson Center for Entrepreneurship and Innovation, Center for Education and Research in Retailing, Center for International Business Education and Research, Center for Real Estate Studies, Global Business Information Network, Indiana Business Research Center, Institute for Urban Transportation, Indiana Center for Econometric Model Research, Center for Brand Leadership
Computer Facilities: Private lab with notebook-computer network connections and workstations; wireless network; more than 2,600 network connections available in classrooms and common areas
Campuswide Network? Yes
% of MBA Classrooms Wired: 100
Computer Model Recommended: Laptop
Internet Fee? No

EXPENSES/FINANCIAL AID

Annual Tuition (Resident/Nonresident): $11,204/$22,408
Room & Board (On/Off Campus): $8,000
Books and Supplies: $4,900
Average Grant: $9,305
Average Loan: $12,885
% Receiving Financial Aid: 69
% Receiving Aid Their First Year: 73

ADMISSIONS INFORMATION

Application Fee: $75
Electronic Application? Yes
Regular Application Deadline: 3/1
Regular Notification: 4/30
Deferment Available? Yes
Length of Deferment: 1 year
Non-fall Admissions? No
Transfer Students Accepted? No
Need-Blind Admissions? Yes
Number of Applications Received: 2,522
% of Applicants Accepted: 22
% Accepted Who Enrolled: 45
Average GPA: 3.3
Average GMAT: 651
Average Years Experience: 5
Minority/Disadvantaged Student Recruitment Programs: Member of the Consortium for Graduate Study in Management, which offers substantial support to underpresented minority students (www.cgsm.org).
Other Schools to Which Students Applied: University of Michigan, University of North Carolina—Chapel Hill, University of Texas—Austin, Vanderbilt University, Washington University in St. Louis

INTERNATIONAL STUDENTS

TOEFL Required of International Students? Yes
Minimum TOEFL: 580 (237 computer)

EMPLOYMENT INFORMATION

Placement Office Available? Yes
Fields Employing Percentage of Grads: MIS (1%), Human Resources (1%), General Management (3%), Operations (4%), Other (5%), Consulting (7%), Marketing (31%), Finance (48%)
Frequent Employers: Accenture, American Airlines, Banc of America Securities, Bristol Myers-Squibb, Brown & Williamson, Cisco Systems, Citibank, Deloitte Consulting, Eli Lilly & Co., Ford Motor Co., IBM, Pricewaterhouse Coopers, Procter & Gamble, Samsung, Sears
Prominent Alumni: John T. Chambers, president and CEO, Cisco Systems, Inc.; Ronald W. Dollens, president and CEO, Guidant Corp.; Jeff M. Fettig, president and COO, Whirlpool Corp.; Harold A. Poling, retired chairman and CEO, Ford Motor Co.; Frank P. Popoff, retired chairman and CEO, Dow Chemical Co.

INDIANA UNIVERSITY—KOKOMO
School of Business

Admissions Contact: Niranjan Pati, Dean of the School of Business
Address: PO Box 9003, Kokomo, IN 46904-9003
Admissions Phone: 765-455-9465 • **Admissions Fax:** 765-455-9348
Admissions E-mail: MBAdirector@iuk.edu • **Web Address:** www.iuk.edu/academics/business

INSTITUTIONAL INFORMATION
Public/Private: Public
Evening Classes Available? No
Total Faculty: 15
% Faculty Female: 40
% Faculty Minority: 20
Student/Faculty Ratio: 15:1
Students in Parent Institution: 2,796
Academic Calendar: Semester

PROGRAMS
Degrees Offered: MBA (30 credits, 2-4 years). Applicants may also need to take prerequisite courses, which are not included in the 30 credit hours.

STUDENT INFORMATION
Total Business Students: 235
% Full Time: 2
% Female: 25
% Minority: 13
% International: 13

COMPUTER AND RESEARCH FACILITIES
Computer Facilities: Indiana University has a wide variety of databases available to all IU students.
Campuswide Network? Yes
Internet Fee? No

EXPENSES/FINANCIAL AID
Annual Tuition (Resident/Nonresident): $4,206/$9,619
Tuition Per Credit (Resident/Nonresident): $142/$321
Books and Supplies: $800
Average Loan: $2,500

ADMISSIONS INFORMATION
Application Fee: $35
Electronic Application? No
Regular Application Deadline: 8/1
Regular Notification: Rolling
Deferment Available? Yes
Non-fall Admissions? Yes
Non-fall Application Deadline(s): 12/1, 4/1
Transfer Students Accepted? No
Need-Blind Admissions? No
Number of Applications Received: 50
% of Applicants Accepted: 100
% Accepted Who Enrolled: 88
Average GPA: 2.9
Average GMAT: 575
Other Admissions Factors Considered: Computer experience

INTERNATIONAL STUDENTS
TOEFL Required of International Students? Yes
Minimum TOEFL: 580

EMPLOYMENT INFORMATION
Placement Office Available? Yes
% Employed Within 3 Months: 100

INDIANA UNIVERSITY-PURDUE UNIVERSITY—FORT WAYNE
School of Business and Management

Admissions Contact: Sandy Franke, Secretary, MBA Program
Address: Neff 366, 2101 Coliseum Boulevard East, Fort Wayne, IN 46805-1499
Admissions Phone: 219-481-6145 • **Admissions Fax:** 260-481-6879
Admissions E-mail: mba@ipfw.edu • **Web Address:** www.ipfw.edu/bms

INSTITUTIONAL INFORMATION
Public/Private: Public
Evening Classes Available? No
Student/Faculty Ratio: 1:1
Students in Parent Institution: 10,749
Academic Calendar: Semester

STUDENT INFORMATION
Total Business Students: 191
% Full Time: 9
% Female: 35
Average Age: 32

COMPUTER AND RESEARCH FACILITIES
Research Facilities: Walter E. Helmke Library, with total holdings of 295,115 volumes; 428,570 microforms; 2,160 current periodical subscriptions. CD players available for graduate student use, access provided to online bibliographic retrieval services
Campuswide Network? No
Internet Fee? No

EXPENSES/FINANCIAL AID
Tuition Per Credit (Resident/Nonresident): $141

ADMISSIONS INFORMATION
Application Fee: $30
Electronic Application? No
Regular Application Deadline: 7/1
Regular Notification: 1/1
Deferment Available? Yes
Non-fall Admissions? Yes
Non-fall Application Deadline(s): 11/1, 4/1, 5/1
Transfer Students Accepted? No
Need-Blind Admissions? No
Number of Applications Received: 45
% of Applicants Accepted: 91
% Accepted Who Enrolled: 95

EMPLOYMENT INFORMATION
Placement Office Available? No

INDIANA UNIVERSITY—SOUTH BEND
School of Business and Economics

Admissions Contact: Dr. Katherine L. Jackson, Assistant Dean
Address: IUSB PO Box 7111, South Bend, IN 46634-7111
Admissions Phone: 574-237-4138 • **Admissions Fax:** 574-237-4866
Admissions E-mail: gradbus@iusb.edu • **Web Address:** www.iusb.edu/~gradbus

INSTITUTIONAL INFORMATION

Public/Private: Public
Evening Classes Available? Yes
Total Faculty: 29
% Faculty Female: 24
% Faculty Minority: 7
% Faculty Part Time: 5
Student/Faculty Ratio: 17:1
Students in Parent Institution: 7,162
Academic Calendar: Semester

PROGRAMS

Degrees Offered: MBA (36-57 credits, 2-3 years), MSA (2 years), MSIT (2-3 years)
Academic Specialties: More than 95 percent of our full-time faculty have terminal degrees. Our full-time faculty demonstrate the highest professional standards of research and scholarship.

STUDENT INFORMATION

Total Business Students: 182
% Full Time: 23
% Female: 48
% Minority: 2
% International: 95
Average Age: 31

COMPUTER AND RESEARCH FACILITIES

Research Facilities: We are members of SAP University Alliance Program and have a dedicated lab for the students.
Computer Facilities: We have 13 computer labs on campus. We have a number of data bases including Compustat, SPSS, CRSP, Hoovers, Lexis-Nexis Academic, Ebsco Host, Emerald Library, etc.
Campuswide Network? Yes
% of MBA Classrooms Wired: 100
Internet Fee? No

EXPENSES/FINANCIAL AID

Annual Tuition (Resident/Nonresident): $3,316/$7,918
Tuition Per Credit (Resident/Nonresident): $184/$440
Room & Board (On/Off Campus): $5,000/$8,000
Books and Supplies: $600

ADMISSIONS INFORMATION

Application Fee: $40
Electronic Application? No
Regular Application Deadline: 7/1
Regular Notification: Rolling
Deferment Available? Yes
Length of Deferment: 1 year
Non-fall Admissions? Yes
Non-fall Application Deadline(s): 11/1 spring, 4/1 summer
Transfer Students Accepted? No
Need-Blind Admissions? No
Number of Applications Received: 36
% of Applicants Accepted: 97
% Accepted Who Enrolled: 89
Average GPA: 3.0

GPA Range: 1.8-4.0
Average GMAT: 511
GMAT Range: 410-660
Average Years Experience: 3
Other Admissions Factors Considered: Professional work experience
Other Schools to Which Students Applied: University of Notre Dame, Western Michigan University

INTERNATIONAL STUDENTS

TOEFL Required of International Students? Yes
Minimum TOEFL: 550 (213 computer)

EMPLOYMENT INFORMATION

Placement Office Available? No

INSEAD
The European Institute of Business Administration

Admissions Contact: MBA Information Office
Address: Boulevard de Contstance, Fontainbleau, France 77305
Admissions E-mail: mbainfo@insead.fr
Web Address: www.insead.fr/mba

INSTITUTIONAL INFORMATION

Public/Private: Private
Evening Classes Available? No
Total Faculty: 166
% Faculty Female: 13
% Faculty Part Time: 35
Students in Parent Institution: 601

PROGRAMS

Degrees Offered: MBA (average 10 months), PhD (average 4 years)
Academic Specialties: General Management; intensive, 10-month MBA programs; truly international, and no dominant culture; teaching and reasearch are given equal weight, so pedagogical material is always realevant and up to date
Study Abroad Options: For 89 percent of our students, France is a foreign country and INSEAD is "study abroad." In addition, INSEAD will open a campus in Singapore in January 2000, and there will be exchange possibilities with the campus in Fontainbleau.

STUDENT INFORMATION

Total Business Students: 601
% Full Time: 100
% Female: 15
% International: 89
Average Age: 29

COMPUTER AND RESEARCH FACILITIES

Research Facilities: INSEAD Euro Asia Centre is a knowledge, information, and communication resource, created to enhance understanding among all communities doing business in Asia. The INSEAD EAC houses a dedicated library and documentation center. CEDEP is an independent center in partnership with INSEAD. The European Centre for Continuing Education is a consortium formed in 1971 by 6 European companies. Today, CEDEP has 23 member companies in the industry and service sector.
Computer Facilities: INSEAD (Fontainbleau): 150 PCs available for student use. INSEAD (Singapore) starting January 2000: 10 PCs will initially be available for 45 participants. Users on both campuses are connected to a messaging system for use on and off campus, and access to the Internet and Intranet is

available through Netscape. Access to the main online information providers (Reviers, MAID, Datastream, and Dialog)
Campuswide Network? No
Computer Proficiency Required? No
Special Purchasing Agreements? No

EXPENSES/FINANCIAL AID

Annual Tuition: $25,500
Room & Board (On Campus): $16,600
Average Grant: $10,000
% Receiving Aid Their First Year: 50

ADMISSIONS INFORMATION

Application Fee: $110
Electronic Application? Yes
Regular Application Deadline: Rolling
Regular Notification: Rolling
Deferment Available? Yes
Length of Deferment: 1 year
Non-fall Admissions? Yes
Non-fall Application Deadline(s): Rolling
Transfer Students Accepted? No
Need-Blind Admissions? Yes
Average GMAT: 677
GMAT Range: 550-800
Other Admissions Factors Considered: Computer experience
Minority/Disadvantaged Student Recruitment Programs: Everyone is a "minority," because there are 56 nationalities in attendance. The largest representation makes up only 12% of the student body.

INTERNATIONAL STUDENTS

TOEFL Required of International Students? Yes
Minimum TOEFL: 620

EMPLOYMENT INFORMATION

Placement Office Available? Yes
% Employed Within 6 Months: 93
Frequent Employers: McKinsey, Andersen, Booz-Allen & Hamilton, Credit Suisse, First Boston, Goldman Sachs, Morgan Stanley, Bertelsman, Pearson, F. Hoffman, La Roche
Prominent Alumni: Lord David Simon of Highbury, minister for trade and competitiveness, Department of Trade and Industry, London; Ms. Helen A. Alexander, chief executive, The Economist Group, London; Mr. Lindsay Owen-Jones, CEO L'Oreal, Paris

INSTITUTO DE EMPRESA

Admissions Contact: David Standen, Admissions Officer
Address: María de Molina 11-13-15, Madrid, Spain 28006
Admissions Phone: 011 34 91 568 9610 • **Admissions Fax:** 011 34 91 568 9710
Admissions E-mail: admissions-online@ie.edu • **Web Address:** www.ie.edu

INSTITUTIONAL INFORMATION

Public/Private: Private
Evening Classes Available? Yes
Student/Faculty Ratio: 11:1

PROGRAMS

Degrees Offered: IMBA (13 months), International EMBA (13 months)
Academic Specialties: Curriculum: Organizational Behaviour, Entrepre-

neurship, Information Systems and Technologies, General Management, Negotiation Skills. Faculty: Teaching quality, research
Study Abroad Options: Europe: Helsinki School of Economics, Finland; ESSEC, France; WHU Kolbenz, Germany; SDA Bocconi, Italy; Norwegian Business School, Norway; Manchester Business School, United Kingdom
North America: Loyola University, Louisiana; Southern Methodist University, Texas; University of California—Los Angeles; University of North Carolina—Chapel Hill; University of South Florida; University of Washington, Washington state; Instituto Technológico Autónoma de México and TEC de Monterrey, Mexico
South America: COPPEAD, Brazil; Universidad Pontificia Católica de Chile, Chile; Universidad de los Andes, Colombia; Universidad del Pacífico, Peru; IESA, Venezuela
Asia: China-Europe International Business School, China; Indian Institute of Management in Calcutta, India

STUDENT INFORMATION

Total Business Students: 292
% Full Time: 66
% Female: 40
% Minority: 26
% International: 84
Average Age: 29

COMPUTER AND RESEARCH FACILITIES

Research Facilities: International Centre for Entrepreneurship and Venture Development (ICEVED), Entrepreneurship Centre, Center for Development and Innovation of the Health Sector, Centre for Family Business, Euro-Latin America Centre, IMB-Airtel Human Resources Centre, Center for Negotiation and Mediation, Center for Innovation in the Production-Distribution Centre, Centre for Corporate Governance, Center for Diversity in Global Management, Ethics Chair
Computer Facilities: Global campus and the online library
Campuswide Network? Yes
% of MBA Classrooms Wired: 100
Computer Model Recommended: Laptop
Internet Fee? No

EXPENSES/FINANCIAL AID

Annual Tuition: $33,850
Books and Supplies: $350
Average Grant: $33,000
Average Loan: $20,000

ADMISSIONS INFORMATION

Application Fee: $120
Electronic Application? Yes
Regular Application Deadline: Rolling
Regular Notification: Rolling
Deferment Available? Yes
Length of Deferment: 2 years
Non-fall Admissions? Yes
Non-fall Application Deadline(s): Rolling
Transfer Students Accepted? No
Need-Blind Admissions? Yes
Number of Applications Received: 2,356
% of Applicants Accepted: 14
% Accepted Who Enrolled: 88
Average GPA: 3.7
Average GMAT: 670
Average Years Experience: 6
Other Admissions Factors Considered: Diversity of personal and professional experience, achievements, applicant's fit with IE norms and culture
Minority/Disadvantaged Student Recruitment Programs: Instituto de Empresa has agreements with 10 scholarship organizations offering various financial aid packages based on need, ethnicity, nationality, or field of study.

Other Schools to Which Students Applied: ESADE, International Institute for Management Development (IMD), INSEAD, University of Navarra

EMPLOYMENT INFORMATION

Placement Office Available? Yes
% Employed Within 3 Months: 82
Fields Employing Percentage of Grads: Operations (3%), Human Resources (3%), Venture Capital (4%), Other (5%), Global Management (7%), General Management (7%), Entrepreneurship (8%), Strategic Planning (9%), Marketing (10%), Communications (13%), Consulting (14%), Finance (17%)
Prominent Alumni: Fernando Barnuevo, head of global investment management, J.P. Morgan Chase; Pilar de Zulueta, Southern European director, Warner Bros.; José María Cámara, president, Sony Music, Spain; Juan PableSan Agustín, vice president, CEMEX; Isabel Aguilera, COO, NH Hoteles

INSTITUTO TECNOLOGICO Y DE ESTUDIOS SUPERIORES DE MONTERREY (ITESM)
EGADE School of Business

Admissions Contact: Raul Cardenas, Dean, MBA Program
Address: Avenida J. Oviedo 10 Parques Industrialrs, Queretaro, Mexico, 76000
Admissions Phone: 52-42-383-192 • **Admissions Fax:** 52-42-383-193
Admissions E-mail: contacto@itesm.mx • **Web Address:** www.itesm.mx

INSTITUTIONAL INFORMATION

Public/Private: Private
Evening Classes Available? No
Total Faculty: 13
% Faculty Part Time: 31
Students in Parent Institution: 3,000
Academic Calendar: Quarter

PROGRAMS

Degrees Offered: EMBA (180 credits, 15 months to 4 years), Master of Marketing (180 credits, 15 months to 4 years); MSF (180 credits, 15 months to 4 years)
Study Abroad Options: Canada, France, Germany, Norway, Spain, United States

STUDENT INFORMATION

Total Business Students: 140
% Female: 36
Average Age: 38

COMPUTER AND RESEARCH FACILITIES

Campuswide Network? Yes
Computer Model Recommended: Laptop
Internet Fee? No

ADMISSIONS INFORMATION

Electronic Application? No
Regular Application Deadline: 9/10
Regular Notification: Rolling
Deferment Available? Yes
Non-fall Admissions? Yes
Non-fall Application Deadline(s): 8/1, 4/10, 7/10
Transfer Students Accepted? No
Need-Blind Admissions? No
Number of Applications Received: 88

% of Applicants Accepted: 80
% Accepted Who Enrolled: 86
Other Admissions Factors Considered: Interview

INTERNATIONAL STUDENTS

TOEFL Required of International Students? Yes
Minimum TOEFL: 570

EMPLOYMENT INFORMATION

Placement Office Available? Yes
% Employed Within 3 Months: 95

INTERNATIONAL INSTITUTE FOR MANAGEMENT DEVELOPMENT

Admissions Contact: MBA Marketing Officer
Address: Chemin de Bellerive 23, PO Box 915, 1001 Lausanne, Switzerland CH-1001
Admissions Phone: 011-41-21-6180298 • **Admissions Fax:** 011-41-21-6180615
Admissions E-mail: mbainfo@imd.ch • **Web Address:** www.imd.ch/mba

INSTITUTIONAL INFORMATION

Evening Classes Available? No
Total Faculty: 50
Student/Faculty Ratio: 2:1
Academic Calendar: January-December

PROGRAMS

Degrees Offered: MBA in General Management (11 months), Executive MBA (16 months to 3 years)
Academic Specialties: Faculty is experienced and international with a strong sense of practical reality. Members remain close to management practice through their field-based research and consulting work. The curriculum is integrative, intensive, and international.
Special Opportunities: Executive Development Program

STUDENT INFORMATION

Total Business Students: 85
% Full Time: 100
% Female: 20
% International: 97
Average Age: 31

COMPUTER AND RESEARCH FACILITIES

Computer Facilities: Information center on campus provides access to online services including databases, CD-ROMs, and catologs.
Campuswide Network? Yes
Internet Fee? No

EXPENSES/FINANCIAL AID

Annual Tuition: $45,000
Average Grant: $28,000
Average Loan: $31,000

ADMISSIONS INFORMATION

Application Fee: $150
Electronic Application? Yes
Regular Application Deadline: Rolling
Deferment Available? No
Non-fall Admissions? Yes
Non-fall Application Deadline(s): 2/1, 4/1, 6/1, 8/1, 9/1
Transfer Students Accepted? No

Need-Blind Admissions? Yes
Number of Applications Received: 800
% of Applicants Accepted: 11
% Accepted Who Enrolled: 100
Average GMAT: 660
Average Years Experience: 5
Other Admissions Factors Considered: Professional achievement, intellectual ability, leadership potential, international outlook

EMPLOYMENT INFORMATION

Placement Office Available? Yes
Frequent Employers: Mckinsey & Co, Nestle, UBS, Fidelity Investrient, Hilt AG

Non-fall Admissions? No
Transfer Students Accepted? No
Need-Blind Admissions? No
Number of Applications Received: 125
% of Applicants Accepted: 62
% Accepted Who Enrolled: 84

INTERNATIONAL STUDENTS

TOEFL Required of International Students? Yes
Minimum TOEFL: 550

EMPLOYMENT INFORMATION

Placement Office Available? Yes
% Employed Within 3 Months: 96

IONA COLLEGE
Hagan School of Business

Admissions Contact: Tara Feller, Director of MBA Admissions
Address: 715 North Avenue, New Rochelle, NY 10801
Admissions Phone: 914-633-2288 • **Admissions Fax:** 914-637-7720
Admissions E-mail: hagan@iona.edu • **Web Address:** www.iona.edu/hagan

INSTITUTIONAL INFORMATION

Public/Private: Private
Evening Classes Available? No
Total Faculty: 51
% Faculty Part Time: 32
Students in Parent Institution: 4,645
Academic Calendar: Trimester

PROGRAMS

Degrees Offered: MBA, with concentrations in Finance, Management, Information and Decision Technology Management, Marketing, Human Resources

STUDENT INFORMATION

Total Business Students: 295
% Full Time: 12
% Female: 44
% Minority: 14
% International: 2
Average Age: 29

COMPUTER AND RESEARCH FACILITIES

Computer Facilities: Arrigoni Library, Ryan Library, McSpedon Hall (24 hours), Hagan Hall; computer resources: www.iona.edu/library.htm, ORION web-based online catalog, electronic databases
Campuswide Network? Yes
Internet Fee? No

EXPENSES/FINANCIAL AID

Tuition Per Credit (Resident/Nonresident): $480
% Receiving Financial Aid: 10

ADMISSIONS INFORMATION

Application Fee: $50
Electronic Application? No
Regular Application Deadline: Rolling
Regular Notification: Rolling
Deferment Available? Yes
Length of Deferment: 1 year

IOWA STATE UNIVERSITY
College of Business

Admissions Contact: Ronald J. Ackerman, Director of Graduate Admissions
Address: 218 Carver Hall, Ames, IA 50011
Admissions Phone: 515-294-8118 • **Admissions Fax:** 515-294-2446
Admissions E-mail: busgrad@iastate.edu • **Web Address:** www.bus.iastate.edu/grad/

Iowa State's Saturday MBA program, offering MBA classes on the weekends in Ames, Iowa, is an excellent option for busy working professionals who wish to maintain their full-time careers. ISU also offers employed professionals in the greater Des Moines area the option of earning their MBA in the evenings, right after work. These evening classes are held in downtown Des Moines, the financial aorta of Iowa. While researching schools, don't forget to check out the cartoon history of Iowa on the ISU website.

INSTITUTIONAL INFORMATION

Public/Private: Public
Evening Classes Available? Yes
Total Faculty: 65
% Faculty Female: 9
% Faculty Minority: 12
% Faculty Part Time: 9
Student/Faculty Ratio: 4:1
Students in Parent Institution: 27,898
Academic Calendar: Semester

PROGRAMS

Degrees Offered: MBA (48 credits, 2 years full time, 31 months part time Saturday), Evening MBA in Des Moines (48 credits, 31 months part time), MACC (32 credits, 1-3 years), MS in Information Assurance (30 credits, 1-2 years), MSIS (32 credits, 1-2 years), MS in Industrial Relations (30-36 credits, 1-3 years)
Combined Degrees: MBA/MS in Statistics (72 credits, 3 years), MBA/MS in Community and Regional Planning (73 credits, 3 years)
Academic Specialties: Accounting, Agribusiness, Finance, Human Resources, Information Systems, Marketing, Production and Operations, Sports Management, Transportation and Logistcs
Special Opportunities: IMBA Consortium, Asolo, Italy; Summer Internship Programs in the United Kingdom and Australia; European Summer School for Advanced Management; Asian Intensive School for Advanced Management
Study Abroad Options: Denmark Italy, Malaysia, Mexico, Scotland

STUDENT INFORMATION

Total Business Students: 232
% Full Time: 31

% Female: 31
% Minority: 3
% Out of State: 20
% International: 55
Average Age: 27

COMPUTER AND RESEARCH FACILITIES

Research Facilities: Pappajohn Center for Entrepreneurship, Murray G. Bacon Center for Ethics in Business, Center for Transportation Research and Education
Computer Facilities: Durham Computation Center, 2 College of Business Computer Labs
Campuswide Network? Yes
Internet Fee? No

EXPENSES/FINANCIAL AID

Annual Tuition (Resident/Nonresident): $4,388/$12,914
Tuition Per Credit (Resident/Nonresident): $244/$718
Room & Board (On/Off Campus): $9,800
Books and Supplies: $1,200
% Receiving Financial Aid: 50
% Receiving Aid Their First Year: 50

ADMISSIONS INFORMATION

Application Fee: $20
Electronic Application? Yes
Regular Application Deadline: Rolling
Regular Notification: Rolling
Deferment Available? Yes
Length of Deferment: 1 year
Non-fall Admissions? No
Transfer Students Accepted? No
Need-Blind Admissions? Yes
Number of Applications Received: 161
% of Applicants Accepted: 48
% Accepted Who Enrolled: 45
Average GPA: 3.3
Average GMAT: 622
Average Years Experience: 3
Minority/Disadvantaged Student Recruitment Programs: Graduate Minority Assistantship Program

INTERNATIONAL STUDENTS

TOEFL Required of International Students? Yes
Minimum TOEFL: 570 (230 computer)

EMPLOYMENT INFORMATION

Placement Office Available? Yes
% Employed Within 3 Months: 85
Fields Employing Percentage of Grads: General Management (7%), Operations (13%), Marketing (13%), Human Resources (13%), Finance (53%)
Frequent Employers: Wells Fargo, Principal Financial Group

JACKSON STATE UNIVERSITY
School of Business

Admissions Contact: Jesse Pennington, Director of Graduate Programs
Address: PO Box 18660, Jackson, MI 39217
Admissions Phone: 601-432-6315 • **Admissions Fax:** 601-987-4380
Admissions E-mail: gadmappl@ccaix.jsums.edu
Web Address: ccaix.jsums.edu/business/

INSTITUTIONAL INFORMATION

Public/Private: Public
Evening Classes Available? Yes
Students in Parent Institution: 6,292
Academic Calendar: Semester

PROGRAMS

Degrees Offered: MBA (1-8 years), MPACC (1-8 years), MBE (1-8 years), MS in Systems Management (1-8 years)
Academic Specialties: Case study, computer-aided instruction, experiential learning, faculty seminars, group discussion, lecture, research, seminars by members of the business community, student presentations, study groups, team projects, distance and Internet teaching

STUDENT INFORMATION

Total Business Students: 1,104

COMPUTER AND RESEARCH FACILITIES

Campuswide Network? Yes
Internet Fee? No

EXPENSES/FINANCIAL AID

Annual Tuition (Resident/Nonresident): $2,688/$2,858
Tuition Per Credit: $150
% Receiving Financial Aid: 8

ADMISSIONS INFORMATION

Application Fee: $20
Electronic Application? No
Regular Application Deadline: Rolling
Regular Notification: Rolling
Deferment Available? Yes
Non-fall Admissions? No
Transfer Students Accepted? No
Need-Blind Admissions? No
Number of Applications Received: 160
% of Applicants Accepted: 77
% Accepted Who Enrolled: 89
Other Admissions Factors Considered: Computer experience

INTERNATIONAL STUDENTS

TOEFL Required of International Students? Yes
Minimum TOEFL: 525

EMPLOYMENT INFORMATION

Placement Office Available? Yes
% Employed Within 3 Months: 84

JACKSONVILLE STATE UNIVERSITY
College of Commerce and Business Administration

Address: 700 Pelham Road North, Jacksonville AL 36265
Admissions Phone: 256-782-5329 • **Admissions Fax:** 256-782-5321
Admissions E-mail: graduate@jsucc.jsu.edu • **Web Address:** www.jsu.edu

Located at the foothills of the Appalachians, about an hour and a half northeast of Birmingham and two hours west of Atlanta, JSU offers a general MBA program with good accessibility to the faculty and absolutely no teaching assistants. The school is very open about its admissions policies, offering prospective students two different formulas that they can meet to receive automatic, unconditional admission.

INSTITUTIONAL INFORMATION

Public/Private: Public
Evening Classes Available? Yes
Total Faculty: 19
% Faculty Female: 33
Student/Faculty Ratio: 15:1
Students in Parent Institution: 8,400

PROGRAMS

Degrees Offered: MBA, general (1.5 years); MBA (2 years), with a concentration in Accounting

STUDENT INFORMATION

Total Business Students: 100
% Full Time: 30
% Female: 50
% Minority: 10
% Out of State: 10
% International: 75
Average Age: 37

COMPUTER AND RESEARCH FACILITIES

Campuswide Network? Yes
% of MBA Classrooms Wired: 20
Internet Fee? No

EXPENSES/FINANCIAL AID

Annual Tuition (Resident/Nonresident): $2,940/$5,880
Tuition Per Credit (Resident/Nonresident): $147/$294
Books and Supplies: $1,500
Average Grant: $1,000
Average Loan: $10,000

ADMISSIONS INFORMATION

Application Fee: $20
Electronic Application? Yes
Early Decision Application Deadline: 3 months prior to term
Early Decision Notification: 5/30
Regular Application Deadline: 6/30
Regular Notification: 7/31
Deferment Available? No
Non-fall Admissions? Yes
Non-fall Application Deadline(s): 3 months prior to term
Transfer Students Accepted? Yes
Transfer Policy: 6 hours of approved courses with grade of A or B
Need-Blind Admissions? Yes
Number of Applications Received: 40
% of Applicants Accepted: 80
% Accepted Who Enrolled: 78

Average GPA: 2.7
GPA Range: 2.2-4.0
Average GMAT: 470
GMAT Range: 250-650
Average Years Experience: 5
Other Admissions Factors Considered: A formula score of 200 × undergraduate degree GPA + GMAT score must be at least 950 for unconditional admission to the MBA program

INTERNATIONAL STUDENTS

TOEFL Required of International Students? Yes
Minimum TOEFL: 500

EMPLOYMENT INFORMATION

Placement Office Available? Yes

JAMES MADISON UNIVERSITY
College of Business

Admissions Contact: Deborah A. Mach, Administrative Assistant
Address: Zane Showker Hall, MSC 0206, Room 620, Harrisonburg, VA 22807
Admissions Phone: 540-568-3253 • **Admissions Fax:** 540-568-3587
Admissions E-mail: mba@mu.edu • **Web Address:** cob.jmu.edu/mba

INSTITUTIONAL INFORMATION

Public/Private: Public
Evening Classes Available? Yes
Total Faculty: 110

PROGRAMS

Degrees Offered: MBA, MBA in Information Security
Special Opportunities: MBA, General Business, Health Services/Hospital Administration, Accounting

STUDENT INFORMATION

Total Business Students: 180
% Full Time: 22
% Female: 9
% International: 5
Average Age: 35

COMPUTER AND RESEARCH FACILITIES

Campuswide Network? No
Internet Fee? No

EXPENSES/FINANCIAL AID

Annual Tuition (Resident/Nonresident): $4,554/$14,058
Tuition Per Credit (Resident/Nonresident): $138/$426

ADMISSIONS INFORMATION

Application Fee: $55
Electronic Application? Yes
Regular Application Deadline: 7/1
Regular Notification: Rolling
Deferment Available? Yes
Length of Deferment: 1 year
Non-fall Admissions? Yes
Non-fall Application Deadline(s): 7/1 fall at Harrisonburg; 11/1 spring at Charlottesville
Transfer Students Accepted? No
Need-Blind Admissions? No

Number of Applications Received: 70
% of Applicants Accepted: 87
% Accepted Who Enrolled: 89
Average GPA: 2.9
Average GMAT: 565
Average Years Experience: 8

INTERNATIONAL STUDENTS

TOEFL Required of International Students? Yes
Minimum TOEFL: 550

EMPLOYMENT INFORMATION

Placement Office Available? No
% Employed Within 3 Months: 100

JOHN CARROLL UNIVERSITY
John M. and Mary Jo Boler School of Business

Admissions Contact: Dr. James M. Daley, Associate Dean and Director, MBA Program
Address: 20700 North Park Boulevard, University Heights, OH 44118-4581
Admissions Phone: 216-397-4391 • Admissions Fax: 216-397-1728
Admissions E-mail: mmauk@jcu.edu • Web Address: bsob.jcu.edu

JCU offers the Mellen Series, where "chief executive officers of Ohio-headquartered, publicly traded firms meet with students and make a public presentation on the financial and strategic plans for their companies." John Carroll has agreements with 21 other American Jesuit business schools that allow for the transfer of graduate school credits. So if you started your MBA at the University of San Diego and your job transferred you from California to Ohio, you could complete your degree without having to start from scratch or agonize over lost credits.

INSTITUTIONAL INFORMATION

Public/Private: Private
Evening Classes Available? Yes
Total Faculty: 37
% Faculty Female: 19
% Faculty Minority: 2
% Faculty Part Time: 21
Student/Faculty Ratio: 16:1
Students in Parent Institution: 4,301
Academic Calendar: Semester

PROGRAMS

Degrees Offered: MBA (60 credits, 2-6 years)
Combined Degrees: Communications Management (33 credits, 2-3 years)
Special Opportunities: Beijing IMBA program
Study Abroad Options: University of Peking, China

STUDENT INFORMATION

Total Business Students: 256
% Full Time: 7
% Female: 26
% Minority: 11
Average Age: 26

COMPUTER AND RESEARCH FACILITIES

Computer Facilities: 5 computer labs on campus; online databases: ABI Inform, BNA HR Library, Business & Industry, CCH International Tax Research

Network, Compustat PC Plus, EconLit, EconLit Database, FIS Online, Global Access, International Financial Statistics, Moody's Company Data Direct, Moody's International, NBER Working Papers
Campuswide Network? Yes
% of MBA Classrooms Wired: 100
Internet Fee? No

EXPENSES/FINANCIAL AID

Annual Tuition: $11,304
Tuition Per Credit (Resident/Nonresident): $628
Books and Supplies: $600

ADMISSIONS INFORMATION

Application Fee: $25
Electronic Application? No
Regular Application Deadline: Rolling
Regular Notification: Rolling
Deferment Available? Yes
Length of Deferment: 1 year
Non-fall Admissions? Yes
Non-fall Application Deadline(s): Spring, summer A, summer B
Transfer Students Accepted? Yes
Transfer Policy: Applicants from members of the Network of MBA Programs at Jesuit Universities and Colleges will have all credits transferred. Otherwise, applications are reviewed on a case-by-case basis.
Need-Blind Admissions? Yes
Number of Applications Received: 84
% of Applicants Accepted: 74
% Accepted Who Enrolled: 82
Average GPA: 3.2
GPA Range: 2.2-3.9
Average GMAT: 504
GMAT Range: 390-640
Other Schools to Which Students Applied: Case Western Reserve University, Cleveland State University

INTERNATIONAL STUDENTS

TOEFL Required of International Students? Yes
Minimum TOEFL: 550 (215 computer)

EMPLOYMENT INFORMATION

Placement Office Available? Yes

KANSAS STATE UNIVERSITY
College of Business Administration

Admissions Contact: Lynn Waugh, Graduate Studies Assistant
Address: 110 Calvin Hall, Manhattan, KS 66506-0501
Admissions Phone: 785-532-7190 • Admissions Fax: 785-532-7216
Admissions E-mail: flynn@ksu.edu • Web Address: www.cba.ksu.edu

The Kansas State University MBA curriculum is designed to accommodate students who did not obtain an undergraduate degree in business; while a large percentage of students at KSU do possess a business degree, other MBAs have backgrounds as varied as food technology and modern language. The class size is capped to 70 full-time equivalent students and up to 35 new students each year to ensure a close-knit environment for students and faculty. The focus of the MBA program is simply "what you need to know to run a business."

INSTITUTIONAL INFORMATION

Public/Private: Public
Evening Classes Available? No
Total Faculty: 51
% Faculty Female: 22
% Faculty Minority: 4
% Faculty Part Time: 100
Student/Faculty Ratio: 5:1
Academic Calendar: Semester

PROGRAMS

Degrees Offered: MBA (52 credits, 2 years); Certificate of Business Administration (15 credits from Business core courses) offered to KSU graduate students in other fields
Academic Specialties: MBA Business Practicum, capstone to curriculum
Special Opportunities: Finance (includes Banking), Human Resource Management (includes Labor Relations), Production/Operations Management/Managerial Economics, Accounting
Study Abroad Options: Leipzig and Giessen, Germany; CIMBA, Italy (administered by University of Kansas)

STUDENT INFORMATION

Total Business Students: 91
% Full Time: 82
% Female: 30
% Minority: 9
% Out of State: 4
% International: 22
Average Age: 24

COMPUTER AND RESEARCH FACILITIES

Computer Facilities: KSU Library provides access to most major academic databases via any campus computer or home computer using the KSU as the ISP.
Campuswide Network? No
% of MBA Classrooms Wired: 100
Internet Fee? No

EXPENSES/FINANCIAL AID

Annual Tuition (Resident/Nonresident): $6,855/$19,340
Tuition Per Credit (Resident/Nonresident): $110/$350
Room & Board (On/Off Campus): $5,000/$6,000
Books and Supplies: $1,000
Average Grant: $2,500
Average Loan: $3,000
% Receiving Financial Aid: 18
% Receiving Aid Their First Year: 12

ADMISSIONS INFORMATION

Application Fee: $45
Electronic Application? Yes
Regular Application Deadline: 3/1
Regular Notification: 6/1
Deferment Available? Yes
Length of Deferment: 1 year
Non-fall Admissions? No
Transfer Students Accepted? Yes
Transfer Policy: Maximum of 9 graduate credit hours from an AACSB-accredited institution
Need-Blind Admissions? Yes
Number of Applications Received: 86
% of Applicants Accepted: 40
% Accepted Who Enrolled: 100
Average GPA: 3.4
Average GMAT: 548
Average Years Experience: 2

Other Admissions Factors Considered: Index created based on Adv GPA × 200 + GMAT = 1150 (minimum)
Minority/Disadvantaged Student Recruitment Programs: Exchange program with Grambling State University
Other Schools to Which Students Applied: Oklahoma State University, University of Kansas, University of Nebraska—Lincoln, University of Oklahoma, Wichita State University

INTERNATIONAL STUDENTS

TOEFL Required of International Students? Yes
Minimum TOEFL: 550 (213 computer)

EMPLOYMENT INFORMATION

Placement Office Available? Yes
Fields Employing Percentage of Grads: Entrepreneurship (8%), Communications (8%), MIS (8%), Marketing (8%), Human Resources (8%), Accounting (8%), Consulting (22%), Finance (30%)
Frequent Employers: Edward Jones, Hallmark, Payless ShoeSource, Phillips, Sprint, U.S. Military

KENNESAW STATE UNIVERSITY
Michael J. Coles College of Business

Admissions Contact: Tom Hughes, Director
Address: 1000 Chastain Road, Kennesaw, GA 30144
Admissions Phone: 770-420-4377 • **Admissions Fax:** 770-420-4435
Admissions E-mail: ksugrad@kennesaw.edu • **Web Address:** coles.kennesaw.edu/

INSTITUTIONAL INFORMATION

Public/Private: Public
Evening Classes Available? Yes
Total Faculty: 49
% Faculty Female: 36
% Faculty Minority: 6
% Faculty Part Time: 7
Student/Faculty Ratio: 19:1
Students in Parent Institution: 13,500
Academic Calendar: Semester

PROGRAMS

Degrees Offered: MBA (36 credits, 33 months to 6 years); MACC (36 credits, 33 months to 6 years)
Academic Specialties: Accounting, Economics, Finance, Business Administration, Business Information Systems Management, Entrepreneurship, Human Resource Management, Operations Management, International Business, Marketing, E-Business
Study Abroad Options: None

STUDENT INFORMATION

Total Business Students: 557
Average Age: 34

COMPUTER AND RESEARCH FACILITIES

Research Facilities: None
Computer Facilities: Computer labs, wireless Internet access, Galileo, Hoovers, 30-plus library databases
Campuswide Network? Yes
Internet Fee? No

EXPENSES/FINANCIAL AID

Annual Tuition (Resident/Nonresident): $1,160/$4,640

Tuition Per Credit (Resident/Nonresident): $97/$387
Books and Supplies: $750
Average Grant: $2,200

ADMISSIONS INFORMATION

Application Fee: $20
Electronic Application? Yes
Early Decision Application Deadline: Summer, fall, spring
Early Decision Notification: 5/1
Regular Application Deadline: Rolling
Regular Notification: Rolling
Deferment Available? Yes
Length of Deferment: 1 year
Non-fall Admissions? Yes
Non-fall Application Deadline(s): Rolling
Transfer Students Accepted? Yes
Transfer Policy: AACSB
Need-Blind Admissions? Yes
Number of Applications Received: 279
% of Applicants Accepted: 84
% Accepted Who Enrolled: 55
Average GPA: 3.2
GPA Range: 2.9-3.7
Average GMAT: 510
GMAT Range: 475-610
Average Years Experience: 11
Other Admissions Factors Considered: GMAT, work experience, letters of recommendation
Minority/Disadvantaged Student Recruitment Programs: None
Other Schools to Which Students Applied: Georgia State University

INTERNATIONAL STUDENTS

TOEFL Required of International Students? Yes
Minimum TOEFL: 550 (213 computer)

EMPLOYMENT INFORMATION

Placement Office Available? Yes

KENT STATE UNIVERSITY
Graduate School of Management

Admissions Contact: Louise Ditchey, Director, Master's Programs
Address: PO Box 5190, Kent, OH 44242-0001
Admissions Phone: 330-672-2282 • Admissions Fax: 330-672-7303
Admissions E-mail: gradbus@bsa3.kent.edu • Web Address: business.kent.edu/grad

The KSU Professional MBA program is designed for students who wish to obtain an advanced financial education on a part-time basis while holding on to their day jobs. The Kent State Traditional MBA program offers a comparable curriculum for full-time students but places greater emphasis on the internships. An Executive MBA is also offered, consisting of courses that alternate between Friday and Saturday for middle managers. Kent focuses on preparing students for management positions and recognizes that adjusting teaching methods to best serve the needs of each program group is key to providing relevant business experience.

INSTITUTIONAL INFORMATION

Public/Private: Public
Evening Classes Available? Yes
Total Faculty: 58
% Faculty Female: 21

% Faculty Minority: 5
% Faculty Part Time: 5
Student/Faculty Ratio: 15:1
Students in Parent Institution: 23,504
Academic Calendar: Semester

PROGRAMS

Degrees Offered: MBA (39-54 credits, 2 years), MA in Economics (30 credits, 1 year), MSA (32-55 credits, 1-2 years), PhD (4-5 years)
Combined Degrees: MBA/MSN (64 credits, 3 years), MBA/Master of Library Science (70 credits, 3 years), MBA/MARCH (70 credits, 3 years)
Academic Specialties: Finance, Marketing, Information Systems, Human Resource Management International Business, Accounting
Study Abroad Options: Groupe Ecole Superieure de Commerce de Rennes, France

STUDENT INFORMATION

Total Business Students: 336
% Full Time: 33
% Female: 47
% Minority: 6
% Out of State: 9
% International: 30
Average Age: 25

COMPUTER AND RESEARCH FACILITIES

Research Facilities: Trading Floor
Computer Facilities: The College of Business local area network supports e-mail, spreadsheets, graphics, word processing, various specialized packages, and Internet access. University buildings are networked via a high-speed ATM backbone. The University's Department of Academic Computing Technology supports computing on the IBM UNIX environment. It offers statistical packages such as SAS and SPSS and datasets such as CRSP, Compustat, and ICPSR.
Campuswide Network? Yes
% of MBA Classrooms Wired: 90
Internet Fee? No

EXPENSES/FINANCIAL AID

Annual Tuition (Resident/Nonresident): $6,780/$12,736
Tuition Per Credit (Resident/Nonresident): $309/$580
Room & Board (On/Off Campus): $5,860/$5,575
Books and Supplies: $950
% Receiving Financial Aid: 40
% Receiving Aid Their First Year: 30

ADMISSIONS INFORMATION

Application Fee: $30
Electronic Application? Yes
Regular Application Deadline: 4/1
Regular Notification: 4/15
Deferment Available? Yes
Length of Deferment: 1 year
Non-fall Admissions? Yes
Non-fall Application Deadline(s): 12/15 spring, 5/15 summer
Transfer Students Accepted? Yes
Transfer Policy: Credits must be from an AASCB-accredited program, less than 6 years old by the time Kent degree is conferred, and approved by the graduate committee and dean.
Need-Blind Admissions? Yes
Number of Applications Received: 145
% of Applicants Accepted: 79
% Accepted Who Enrolled: 41
Average GPA: 3.2
GPA Range: 2.9-3.5
Average GMAT: 519
GMAT Range: 460-570
Average Years Experience: 2

Other Schools to Which Students Applied: Bowling Green State University, Case Western Reserve University, Cleveland State University, John Carroll University, Ohio State University, University of Akron

INTERNATIONAL STUDENTS

TOEFL Required of International Students? Yes
Minimum TOEFL: 550 (213 computer)

EMPLOYMENT INFORMATION

Placement Office Available? No
% Employed Within 3 Months: 85
Fields Employing Percentage of Grads: MIS (3%), Human Resources (3%), Consulting (6%), Operations (9%), Accounting (9%), Other (10%), Finance (11%), General Management (17%), Marketing (26%)
Frequent Employers: Diebold Inc., Ernst and Young, FedEx Systems, Jo-Ann Stores Inc., Key Bank, Little Tikes, Progressive Insurance, Summa Health System, The Timken Co.
Prominent Alumni: Yank Heisler, CEO, Key Bank Corp.; Leigh Herington, Ohio state senator; M R Rangaswami, co-founder, Sand-Hill Venture Capital LLC; Richard Ferry, chairman, Korn-Ferry International; George Stevens, dean, College of Business, Kent State University

ADMISSIONS INFORMATION

Application Fee: $30
Electronic Application? No
Regular Application Deadline: 8/14
Regular Notification: Rolling
Deferment Available? Yes
Non-fall Admissions? Yes
Non-fall Application Deadline(s): 12/15, 4/15
Transfer Students Accepted? No
Need-Blind Admissions? No
Number of Applications Received: 142
% of Applicants Accepted: 85
% Accepted Who Enrolled: 89
Other Admissions Factors Considered: Undergraduate GPA, work experience, computer experience

INTERNATIONAL STUDENTS

TOEFL Required of International Students? Yes
Minimum TOEFL: 550

EMPLOYMENT INFORMATION

Placement Office Available? Yes
% Employed Within 3 Months: 99

LA SALLE UNIVERSITY
School of Business Administration

Admissions Contact: Kathy Bagnell, Director, Marketing and Graduate Enrollment
Address: 1900 West Olney Avenue, Philadelphia, PA 19141
Admissions Phone: 215-951-1057 • **Admissions Fax:** 215-951-1886
Admissions E-mail: ftmba@lasalle.edu • **Web Address:** www.lasalle.edu/academ/sba/sba.htm

INSTITUTIONAL INFORMATION

Public/Private: Private
Evening Classes Available? No
Total Faculty: 37
% Faculty Part Time: 31
Students in Parent Institution: 5,408
Academic Calendar: Trimester

PROGRAMS

Degrees Offered: MBA (33-48 credits, 1 to 5.3 years)
Special Opportunities: Accounting, CIS or MIS, Finance (includes Banking), Health Services/Hospital Administration, Human Resource Management (includes Labor Relations), International Business, Management, Marketing, Other, General Business

STUDENT INFORMATION

Total Business Students: 687
% Full Time: 10
% Female: 41
% Minority: 12
% International: 11
Average Age: 32

COMPUTER AND RESEARCH FACILITIES

Campuswide Network? Yes
Internet Fee? No

EXPENSES/FINANCIAL AID

Tuition Per Credit (Resident/Nonresident): $537

LAMAR UNIVERSITY
College of Business

Admissions Contact: Sandy Drane, Graduate Admissions Office
Address: PO Box I0009, Beaumont, TX 77710
Admissions Phone: 409-880-8350 • **Admissions Fax:** 409-880-8414
Admissions E-mail: dranesl@lub002.lamar.edu • **Web Address:** www.lamar.edu

INSTITUTIONAL INFORMATION

Public/Private: Public
Evening Classes Available? No
Total Faculty: 19
Student/Faculty Ratio: 14:1
Students in Parent Institution: 8,100
Academic Calendar: Semester

PROGRAMS

Degrees Offered: MBA (30-63 credits, 1-6 years)
Combined Degrees: MSN in Administration (42 hours)
Study Abroad Options: China, Estonia, France, Japan

STUDENT INFORMATION

Total Business Students: 77
% Full Time: 35
% Female: 40
% Minority: 19
% International: 13
Average Age: 32

COMPUTER AND RESEARCH FACILITIES

Campuswide Network? Yes
Internet Fee? No

EXPENSES/FINANCIAL AID

Annual Tuition (Resident/Nonresident): $1,200/$5,200
Tuition Per Credit (Resident/Nonresident): $176/$556
Room & Board (On/Off Campus): $4,000

Books and Supplies: $1,000
Average Grant: $7,000
Average Loan: $2,000
% Receiving Financial Aid: 10
% Receiving Aid Their First Year: 10

ADMISSIONS INFORMATION

Electronic Application? No
Regular Application Deadline: 5/1
Regular Notification: Rolling
Deferment Available? Yes
Non-fall Admissions? Yes
Non-fall Application Deadline(s): 10/1, 3/1
Transfer Students Accepted? No
Need-Blind Admissions? No
Number of Applications Received: 110
% of Applicants Accepted: 45
% Accepted Who Enrolled: 49
Other Admissions Factors Considered: Interview, letters of recommendation, personal statement, resume, computer experience

INTERNATIONAL STUDENTS

TOEFL Required of International Students? Yes
Minimum TOEFL: 525

EMPLOYMENT INFORMATION

Placement Office Available? Yes
% Employed Within 3 Months: 80

LEHIGH UNIVERSITY
College of Business and Economics

Admissions Contact: Mary Theresa Taglang, Director of Recruitment and Admissions
Address: 621 Taylor Street, Bethlehem, PA 18015
Admissions Phone: 610-758-5280 • Admissions Fax: 610-758-5283
Admissions E-mail: mba.admissions@lehigh.edu • Web Address: www.lehigh.edu/mba

Lehigh's College of Business and Economics is a private institution with decent tuition rates and an average student age of around 30. The Lehigh MBA program offers two unique joint programs: MBA/Master of Education (MBA & Ed), and MBA/Engineering (MBA & E). Frequent employers of Lehigh graduates are Lucent Technologies, Merrill Lynch, PricewaterhouseCoopers, and Andersen Consulting.

INSTITUTIONAL INFORMATION

Public/Private: Private
Evening Classes Available? Yes
Total Faculty: 55
% Faculty Female: 18
% Faculty Minority: 13
% Faculty Part Time: 8
Student/Faculty Ratio: 5:1
Students in Parent Institution: 6,437

PROGRAMS

Degrees Offered: MBA (36 credits), MS in Accounting and Information Analysis (30 credits), MS in Economics (30 credits), PhD in Business and Economics (72 credits
Combined Degrees: MBA and Engineering (45 crredits), MBA/MEd (45 credits)

STUDENT INFORMATION

Total Business Students: 288
% Full Time: 18
% Female: 29
% Minority: 7
% International: 49
Average Age: 30

COMPUTER AND RESEARCH FACILITIES

Computer Facilities: ABI-Inform, Compustat/Research Insight, CRSP, Dow Jones Interactive
Campuswide Network? Yes
% of MBA Classrooms Wired: 100
Internet Fee? No

EXPENSES/FINANCIAL AID

Annual Tuition: $14,640
Tuition Per Credit (Resident/Nonresident): $610
Books and Supplies: $1,300
Average Grant: $11,000

ADMISSIONS INFORMATION

Application Fee: $50
Electronic Application? Yes
Regular Application Deadline: 5/1
Regular Notification: Rolling
Deferment Available? Yes
Length of Deferment: 1 year
Non-fall Admissions? Yes
Non-fall Application Deadline(s): 4/30 summer I, 5/30 summer II, spring 12/1
Transfer Students Accepted? Yes
Transfer Policy: 6 credits from an AACSB-accredited school
Need-Blind Admissions? Yes
Number of Applications Received: 260
% of Applicants Accepted: 73
% Accepted Who Enrolled: 74
Average GPA: 3.2
Average GMAT: 601
Average Years Experience: 7

INTERNATIONAL STUDENTS

TOEFL Required of International Students? Yes
Minimum TOEFL: 600 (250 computer)

EMPLOYMENT INFORMATION

Placement Office Available? Yes
% Employed Within 3 Months: 70
Fields Employing Percentage of Grads: Finance (6%), Consulting (13%), Marketing (19%), Operations (25%), General Management (37%)
Frequent Employers: Aesculap, ALCOA, Aldi Inc., American Express, Arrow International, AT&T, AVAYA, Aventis Pasteur, B. Braun, Black & Decker, Boeing, Bristol-Myers Squibb, Computer Aid, Consolidated Edison, Hartford Insurance, Heartland Securities, Hennion & Walsh, IBM, Ingersoll-Rand, KPMG, Log-Net, Lutron, Metropolitan Life, Novartis, Ortho McNeil Pharmaceuticals, Pricewaterhouse Coopers, Standard & Poors, Tyco Flow

LOUISIANA STATE UNIVERSITY
E. J. Ourso College of Business Administration

Admissions Contact: Dr. P. David Shields, Director, Flores MBA Programs
Address: 3170 CEBA Building, Baton Rouge, LA 70803
Admissions Phone: 225-578-8867 • **Admissions Fax:** 225-578-2421
Admissions E-mail: busmba@lsu.edu • **Web Address:** www.bus.lsu.edu/mba

Small classes, incredible job placement, competitive internships—this is only the beginning of the list of great benefits of a Louisiana State University graduate business education. The E.J. Ourso College of Business Administration, located in the red-hot city of Baton Rouge, offers three different tracks (full-time, professional, and executive) leading to a distinctly LSU Flores MBA. Because many credits overlap curricula, students seeking a joint JD/MBA full time can expect to graduate in four years instead of the usual five.

INSTITUTIONAL INFORMATION

Public/Private: Public
Evening Classes Available? Yes
Total Faculty: 50
% Faculty Female: 20
% Faculty Minority: 10
Student/Faculty Ratio: 20:1
Students in Parent Institution: 32,228
Academic Calendar: August-May

PROGRAMS

Degrees Offered: PhD (4 years), MS (2 years), MPA (2 years), MBA (2 years full time), EMBA (22 months), Professional MBA (33 months)
Combined Degrees: JD/MBA (4 years; also awards a Bachelor of Science in Civil Law)
Academic Specialties: Finance, Internal Audit, Marketing, Information Systems and Decision Sciences (ISDS)
Special Opportunities: The Flores MBA Program Distinguished Speaker Series hosts 6 executives each year. These corporate CEOs, chairmen, and presidents expose MBA students to the latest ideas and forces shaping the global business world through a lecture and discussion format.

The Practice of Business Program offers workshops on career development, provides opportunities for students to tour corporate campuses, and advances the integration of curriculum with business skills that give students an edge in the corporate workplace.

The Visiting Business Executive Program brings practitioners from leading firms into the classroom to give instructional support and share their business experiences, best practices, and advice with students.

The Greer Series brings leaders of business, government, and academia to the Louisiana State University campus to address the E. J. Ourso College of Business Administration and members of the Baton Rouge community on current topics and issues. Past speakers have included Gerald R. Ford, 38th president of the United States (1992); David M. Brinkley, anchor of ABC's This Week with David Brinkley (1994); and Robert Novac, syndicated columnist and editor (1996).

The Flores MBA Advisory Program provides MBA student teams the opportunity to provide marketing and financial advisory assistance to local inner city businesses.
Study Abroad Options: Full-time students: France, Ecuador. EMBA students participate in a required 2-week resisdence abroad during the final semester of their studies. Trips have included England, France, Italy, and Germany.

STUDENT INFORMATION

Total Business Students: 309
% Full Time: 62
% Female: 34
% Minority: 12
% Out of State: 11
% International: 9
Average Age: 24

COMPUTER AND RESEARCH FACILITIES

Research Facilities: Louisiana Economic Development & Forecasting Center, Louisiana Institute for Entrepreneurial Education & Family Business Studies, Real Estate Research Institute, Louisiana Financial Services Education & Research Institute, Center for Virtual Organization & Commerce, Business & Technology Center, Small Business Development Center, SAP @LSU University Alliance Program
Computer Facilities: All MBA students have access to 2 computer labs and general access area housed in the Microcomputer Lab. MBA students also have access to all public access areas on the campus. The College of Business supports Compustat/Research Insight and the CRISP databases, as well as some accounting simulations.
Campuswide Network? Yes
Internet Fee? No

EXPENSES/FINANCIAL AID

Annual Tuition (Resident/Nonresident): $3,545/$8,845
Room & Board (On/Off Campus): $4,968/$4,800
Books and Supplies: $1,000
Average Grant: $5,000
Average Loan: $6,000
% Receiving Financial Aid: 50
% Receiving Aid Their First Year: 50

ADMISSIONS INFORMATION

Application Fee: $25
Electronic Application? Yes
Early Decision Application Deadline: 1/15
Early Decision Notification: 1/25
Regular Application Deadline: 5/15
Regular Notification: Rolling
Deferment Available? No
Non-fall Admissions? No
Transfer Students Accepted? No
Need-Blind Admissions? No
Number of Applications Received: 458
% of Applicants Accepted: 25
% Accepted Who Enrolled: 72
Average GPA: 3.4
GPA Range: 3.1-3.5
Average GMAT: 588
GMAT Range: 550-590
Average Years Experience: 2

INTERNATIONAL STUDENTS

TOEFL Required of International Students? Yes
Minimum TOEFL: 550 (213 computer)

EMPLOYMENT INFORMATION

Placement Office Available? Yes
% Employed Within 3 Months: 100
Fields Employing Percentage of Grads: Operations (1%), MIS (1%), Marketing (1%), Consulting (2%), Human Resources (4%), Accounting (10%), Finance (16%)
Frequent Employers: Accenture, ChevronTexaco, Eli Lilly, Entergy Corp., Ernst & Young, ExxonMobil, Fed Ex, IBM, KPMG Peat Marwick, Lockheed Martin, Pricewaterhouse Coopers, Shell

LOUISIANA STATE UNIVERSITY— SHREVEPORT

College of Business Administration

Admissions Contact: Susan Wood, MBA Director
Address: One University Place, Shreveport, LA 71115
Admissions Phone: 318-797-5213 • Admissions Fax: 318-797-5017
Admissions E-mail: swood@pilot.lsus.edu • Web Address: www.lsus.edu/ba/

INSTITUTIONAL INFORMATION

Public/Private: Public
Evening Classes Available? No
Total Faculty: 26
Student/Faculty Ratio: 20:1
Students in Parent Institution: 4,237
Academic Calendar: Semester

PROGRAMS

Degrees Offered: MBA (30-54 credits, 1-8 years)
Special Opportunities: General Business

STUDENT INFORMATION

Total Business Students: 150
% Full Time: 7
% Female: 53
% Minority: 10
% International: 5

COMPUTER AND RESEARCH FACILITIES

Campuswide Network? Yes
Internet Fee? No

EXPENSES/FINANCIAL AID

Annual Tuition (Resident/Nonresident): $3,245/$9,420
% Receiving Financial Aid: 60

ADMISSIONS INFORMATION

Electronic Application? No
Regular Application Deadline: 7/15
Regular Notification: Rolling
Deferment Available? No
Non-fall Admissions? Yes
Non-fall Application Deadline(s): 12/15, 5/1
Transfer Students Accepted? No
Need-Blind Admissions? No
Number of Applications Received: 70
% of Applicants Accepted: 71
% Accepted Who Enrolled: 80

INTERNATIONAL STUDENTS

TOEFL Required of International Students? Yes
Minimum TOEFL: 550

EMPLOYMENT INFORMATION

Placement Office Available? Yes
% Employed Within 3 Months: 98

LOUISIANA TECH UNIVERSITY

College of Administration and Business

Admissions Contact: Dr. Marc C. Chopin, Associate Dean of Graduate Studies & Research
Address: PO Box 10318, Ruston, LA 71272
Admissions Phone: 318-257-4528 • Admissions Fax: 318-257-4253
Admissions E-mail: gschool@cab.latech.edu • Web Address: www.cab.latech.edu

INSTITUTIONAL INFORMATION

Public/Private: Public
Evening Classes Available? Yes
Total Faculty: 41
Student/Faculty Ratio: 25:1
Students in Parent Institution: 10,708
Academic Calendar: Quarter

PROGRAMS

Degrees Offered: MBA (1-6 years), with concentrations in Accounting, Economics, Finance, Management, Marketing, Quantitative Analysis; Master of Professional Accountancy (1-6 years)
Academic Specialties: Case study, computer-aided instruction, computer analysis, computer simulation, field projects, group discussion, lecture, research, student presentations, team projects

STUDENT INFORMATION

Total Business Students: 101
% Full Time: 85
% Female: 40

COMPUTER AND RESEARCH FACILITIES

Campuswide Network? Yes
Internet Fee? No

EXPENSES/FINANCIAL AID

Annual Tuition (Resident/Nonresident): $3,504/$9,304
Tuition Per Credit (Resident/Nonresident): $476/$1,186
Books and Supplies: $800

ADMISSIONS INFORMATION

Application Fee: $20
Electronic Application? No
Regular Application Deadline: 8/1
Regular Notification: 1/1
Deferment Available? Yes
Length of Deferment: 1 year
Non-fall Admissions? Yes
Non-fall Application Deadline(s): 11/3, 2/3, 5/3
Transfer Students Accepted? Yes
Transfer Policy: Maximum of 6 graduate hours
Need-Blind Admissions? No
Number of Applications Received: 57
% of Applicants Accepted: 84
% Accepted Who Enrolled: 58
Average GPA: 3.2
Average GMAT: 500
Other Admissions Factors Considered: We use the following formula(s): Undergraduate GPA × 200 + GMAT = 1100 or above, or undergraduate GPA (last 60 hours) × 200 + GMAT = 1150 or above

INTERNATIONAL STUDENTS

TOEFL Required of International Students? Yes
Minimum TOEFL: 550 (213 computer)

EMPLOYMENT INFORMATION

Placement Office Available? Yes

LOYOLA COLLEGE IN MARYLAND
Sellinger School of Business and Management

Admissions Contact: Scott Greatorex, Graduate Admissions Director
Address: 4501 North Charles Street, Baltimore, MD 21210
Admissions Phone: 410-617-2000 • **Admissions Fax:** 410-617-2002
Admissions E-mail: mba@loyola.edu • **Web Address:** sellinger.loyola.edu

The Sellinger School of Business and Management is inspired by Jesuit values and guided by the principles of cura personalis (care for the whole person). The general MBA program is broad-based, and the graduate programs (Evening MBA, Executive MBA, and MBA Fellows Program) usually serve working professionals in the Baltimore/Washington region. Expect to pay very little for a quality, private-school business education.

INSTITUTIONAL INFORMATION

Public/Private: Private
Evening Classes Available? No
Total Faculty: 59
% Faculty Part Time: 17
Student/Faculty Ratio: 10:1
Students in Parent Institution: 6,181
Academic Calendar: Semester

PROGRAMS

Degrees Offered: MBA (51 credits (1-7 years), EMBA (21 months, 51 credits), MBA Fellows Program (51 credits, 2.8 months), MS in Finance (42 credits, 1-7 years)

STUDENT INFORMATION

Total Business Students: 948
% Minority: 14
% Out of State: 4
% International: 3
Average Age: 31

COMPUTER AND RESEARCH FACILITIES

Campuswide Network? Yes
Internet Fee? No

EXPENSES/FINANCIAL AID

Annual Tuition: $6,570
Tuition Per Credit (Resident/Nonresident): $365
% Receiving Financial Aid: 10

ADMISSIONS INFORMATION

Application Fee: $50
Electronic Application? No
Regular Application Deadline: 8/20
Regular Notification: Rolling
Deferment Available? Yes
Length of Deferment: 1 year
Non-fall Admissions? Yes
Non-fall Application Deadline(s): 11/20, 4/20
Transfer Students Accepted? No
Need-Blind Admissions? No
Number of Applications Received: 688
% of Applicants Accepted: 83
% Accepted Who Enrolled: 86
Average GMAT: 528
Other Admissions Factors Considered: Letters of recommendation, work experience

INTERNATIONAL STUDENTS

TOEFL Required of International Students? Yes
Minimum TOEFL: 550 (213 computer)

EMPLOYMENT INFORMATION

Placement Office Available? Yes

LOYOLA MARYMOUNT UNIVERSITY
MBA Program

Admissions Contact: Charisse Woods, MBA Program Coordinator
Address: One LMU Drive, Los Angeles, CA 90045-8387
Admissions Phone: 310-338-2848 • **Admissions Fax:** 310-338-2899
Admissions E-mail: mbapc@lmu.edu • **Web Address:** www.mba.lmu.edu

Most of Loyola Marymount's MBA students live in Los Angeles while attending school full time. The MBA education includes small classes with accessible professors and cutting-edge technology. Enabling the student to take courses catered to his or her current standing in the business world, LMU offers a general MBA, an Executive MBA, and an MBA for International Managers.

INSTITUTIONAL INFORMATION

Public/Private: Private
Evening Classes Available? Yes
Total Faculty: 45
% Faculty Female: 16
% Faculty Minority: 8
% Faculty Part Time: 20
Student/Faculty Ratio: 25:1
Students in Parent Institution: 7,151
Academic Calendar: Semester

PROGRAMS

Degrees Offered: MBA, EMBA (21 months)
Combined Degrees: MBA/JD (4 years)
Academic Specialties: Flexible program, evening classes, non-competitive environment, ethical issues throughout lesson plans, strong Entrepreneurship Program
Special Opportunities: Comparative Management Systems, EDHEC Master's in European Business, dual degree in 2 areas of emphasis
Study Abroad Options: EDHEC Graduate School of Management in Lille or Nice, France; Beijing, China; all other study abroad programs with which the consortium of Jesuit MBA Programs has exchange programs

STUDENT INFORMATION

Total Business Students: 400
% Full Time: 70
% Female: 38
% Minority: 12
% International: 9
Average Age: 27

COMPUTER AND RESEARCH FACILITIES

Computer Facilities: Computer labs on campus and various computers to check e-mail
Campuswide Network? Yes
% of MBA Classrooms Wired: 100
Internet Fee? No

EXPENSES/FINANCIAL AID

Annual Tuition: $13,608
Tuition Per Credit (Resident/Nonresident): $756
Room & Board (On/Off Campus): $6,500/$14,000
Books and Supplies: $500
Average Grant: $2,500
Average Loan: $12,000
% Receiving Financial Aid: 39
% Receiving Aid Their First Year: 50

ADMISSIONS INFORMATION

Application Fee: $35
Electronic Application? Yes
Regular Application Deadline: Rolling
Regular Notification: Rolling
Deferment Available? Yes
Length of Deferment: 1 year
Non-fall Admissions? Yes
Non-fall Application Deadline(s): Fall, spring, summer I or II
Transfer Students Accepted? Yes
Transfer Policy: Students from other Jesuit MBA Programs through the Jesuit Multilateral Agreement or students who attend an AACSB-accredited MBA Program with equivalent coursework of B or better may transfer in only 6 units of upper-division course credit.
Need-Blind Admissions? Yes
Number of Applications Received: 331
% of Applicants Accepted: 67
% Accepted Who Enrolled: 58
Average GPA: 3.2
GPA Range: 2.4-3.9
Average GMAT: 565
GMAT Range: 450-760
Average Years Experience: 4
Other Admissions Factors Considered: Work experience is not required but could help an application.

INTERNATIONAL STUDENTS

TOEFL Required of International Students? Yes
Minimum TOEFL: 600 (250 computer)

EMPLOYMENT INFORMATION

Placement Office Available? Yes

LOYOLA UNIVERSITY CHICAGO
Graduate School of Business

Admissions Contact: Alan Young, Director of Enrollment and Recruitment
Address: 820 North Michigan Avenue, Chicago, IL 60611
Admissions Phone: 312-915-6120 • Admissions Fax: 312-915-7207
Admissions E-mail: mba-loyola@luc.edu • Web Address: www.gsb.luc.edu

Great facilities abound for MBA students at Loyola University Chicago, a school with a strong "Jesuit tradition" and an emphasis on "ethics in business." The student body includes "part-time students with significant work experience," "international students," and people who generally "differ greatly in age, work experience, and cultural backgrounds." Beyond the campus is Chicago, one of the world's most active financial trading centers and a great American city.

INSTITUTIONAL INFORMATION

Public/Private: Private
Evening Classes Available? Yes
Total Faculty: 64
% Faculty Female: 17
% Faculty Minority: 10
% Faculty Part Time: 11
Student/Faculty Ratio: 11:1
Students in Parent Institution: 11,864
Academic Calendar: Quarter

PROGRAMS

Degrees Offered: MBA (14-18 courses, 2 years full time, 3.5 years part time), MSA (12 courses, 1 year full time, 2 years part time), MSIS (14 courses, 1 year full time, 2 years part time), MSIMC (14 courses, 1 year full time, 2 years part time), MS in Human Resources (14 courses, 1 year full time, 2 years part time), MS in Organizational Development (14 courses, 1 year full time, 2 years part time), MS in Industrial Relations (14 courses, 1 year full time, 2 years part time)
Combined Degrees: MBA/JD (4 years full time, 6 years part time), MBA/MSISM (2 years full time, 4 years part time), MBA/MSIMC (2 years full time, 4 years part time), MBA/MSN (2 years full time, 4 years part time), MBA/MS in Pharmacology (2 years full time, 4 years part time), MS Industrial Relations/JD (4 years full time, 6 years part time), MS in Organizational Development/MS in Human Resources (2 years full time, 3 years part time), MS in Organizational Development/MS in Industrial Relations (2 years full time, 3 years part time)
Academic Specialties: Finance, Derivatives, Business Ethics, Information Systems Management, Integrated Marketing Communications, Health Care Administration, E-Commerce, International Business, Strategic Management, Accountancy, Legal Environment, Economics
Special Opportunities: International study at Loyola's Rome Center Campus, multicultural advisors for minority students
Study Abroad Options: Loyola programs in Rome, Italy; Athens, Greece; Bangkok, Thailand

STUDENT INFORMATION

Total Business Students: 599
% Full Time: 25
% Female: 44
% Minority: 15
% Out of State: 53
% International: 46
Average Age: 28

COMPUTER AND RESEARCH FACILITIES

Research Facilities: Family Business Center, Center for Information Management & Technology, Center for Business Ethics, Center for Financial & Policy Studies
Computer Facilities: 3 computer classrooms, wide range of applications software available via network
Campuswide Network? Yes
% of MBA Classrooms Wired: 50
Internet Fee? No

EXPENSES/FINANCIAL AID

Annual Tuition: $18,648
Tuition Per Credit (Resident/Nonresident): $777
Room & Board (On/Off Campus): $7,550/$10,000
Books and Supplies: $900
Average Grant: $9,900
Average Loan: $10,100

ADMISSIONS INFORMATION

Application Fee: $40
Electronic Application? Yes
Regular Application Deadline: 7/1
Regular Notification: Rolling

Deferment Available? Yes
Length of Deferment: 1 year
Non-fall Admissions? Yes
Non-fall Application Deadline(s): 10/1 winter, 1/15 spring, 4/1 summer
Transfer Students Accepted? Yes
Transfer Policy: While applicants from other MBA programs may apply at any time for transfer admission consideration, only those from AACSB-accredited institutions will be eligible to receive transfer credit for up to 3 courses with grades of B or higher.
Need-Blind Admissions? Yes
Number of Applications Received: 512
% of Applicants Accepted: 81
% Accepted Who Enrolled: 53
Average GPA: 3.1
GPA Range: 2.7-3.0
Average GMAT: 540
GMAT Range: 490-670
Average Years Experience: 5
Other Admissions Factors Considered: Applicants are evaluated on the basis of academic grade point average, GMAT score, professional work experience, personal statement/essays, letters of recommendation and their written responses to the questions on our application.
Other Schools to Which Students Applied: DePaul University, University of Chicago, Northern Illinois University, University of Illinois, Northwestern University, University of Illinois—Chicago, Illinois Institute of Technology

INTERNATIONAL STUDENTS

TOEFL Required of International Students? Yes
Minimum TOEFL: 550 (213 computer)

EMPLOYMENT INFORMATION

Placement Office Available? Yes
% Employed Within 3 Months: 48
Fields Employing Percentage of Grads: General Management (3%), Operations (6%), Accounting (6%), Other (9%), Consulting (9%), MIS (9%), Finance (18%), Marketing (33%)
Frequent Employers: Accenture, Allstate, American Medical Association, Bank One, Boeing, Citicorp, Deloitte & Touche, FBOP, Kraft Foods, McDonald's, Merrill Lynch, National City, Ortho-McNeil Pharmaceuticals, Pricewaterhouse Coopers, RR Donnelley, Sara Lee
Prominent Alumni: Michael Quinlan, chairman of the board, McDonald's Corp.; Robert Parkinson, former president and CEO, Abbott Laboratories; John Menzer, president and CEO, Wal-Mart International; Carl Koenemann, executive vice president and CFO, Motorola; John Rooney, president and CEO, US Cellular

LOYOLA UNIVERSITY NEW ORLEANS
The Joseph A. Butt, S.J. College of Business Administration

Admissions Contact: Jan Moppert, Coordinator of Graduate and External Programs
Address: 6363 St. Charles Avenue, Campus Box 15, New Orleans, LA 70118
Admissions Phone: 504-864-7965 • **Admissions Fax:** 504-864-7970
Admissions E-mail: jamopper@loyno.edu • **Web Address:** cba.loyno.edu

The Jesuit-centered tradition of Loyola University New Orleans offers the MBA student a solid business education in a great southern city. The curriculum is strengthened by the school's dedication to ethical responsibility and critical thinking. The school's mission statement indicates that Loyola aims to produce graduates who "possess a love for, the critical intelligence to pursue, and the eloquence to articulate truth."

INSTITUTIONAL INFORMATION

Public/Private: Private
Evening Classes Available? Yes
Total Faculty: 25
% Faculty Female: 32
% Faculty Minority: 12
% Faculty Part Time: 15
Student/Faculty Ratio: 14:1
Students in Parent Institution: 5,396
Academic Calendar: Semester

PROGRAMS

Degrees Offered: MBA (1-7 years), traditional or concentrations in Finance, International Business, Marketing
Combined Degrees: MBA/JD (5 years)
Academic Specialties: Adhering to the Jesuit tradition of education, Loyola University New Orleans graduates individuals with the capability and motivation to become effective and socially responsible business leaders. The program focuses on critical reasoning, discernment, business ethics, leadership, entrepreneurship, and international business.
Study Abroad Options: Catholic University of Louvain, Belgium; Peking University, Beijing, China; Instituto de Empresa, Madrid, Spain; Escola Superior d'Administracio I Direccio d'Empreses (ESADE), Barcelona, Spain; others available through multi-lateral agreement with JEBNET, a consortium of 28 Jesuit universities

STUDENT INFORMATION

Total Business Students: 83
% Full Time: 45
% Female: 40
% Minority: 24
% Out of State: 37
% International: 20
Average Age: 26

COMPUTER AND RESEARCH FACILITIES

Computer Facilities: The College of Business Administration houses a lab for business students. Additionally, the library has several computer labs available 24 hours a day while school is in session. The library has multiple computer-based resources available to students.
Campuswide Network? Yes
Internet Fee? No

EXPENSES/FINANCIAL AID

Annual Tuition: $13,632
Tuition Per Credit (Resident/Nonresident): $568
Room & Board (On/Off Campus): $5,000
Books and Supplies: $2,500
Average Grant: $5,000
Average Loan: $10,000

ADMISSIONS INFORMATION

Application Fee: $50
Electronic Application? Yes
Regular Application Deadline: 6/30
Regular Notification: Rolling
Deferment Available? Yes
Length of Deferment: 1 academic year
Non-fall Admissions? Yes
Non-fall Application Deadline(s): 11/30 spring
Transfer Students Accepted? Yes

Transfer Policy: If the applicant comes from an AACSB-accredited program, the foundation work may apply to our program. Also, a maximum of 6 credit hours may be applied to the advanced level. Only B's or better are accepted.

Need-Blind Admissions? Yes

Number of Applications Received: 74

% of Applicants Accepted: 72

% Accepted Who Enrolled: 62

Average GPA: 3.2

GPA Range: 2.3-3.8

Average GMAT: 545

GMAT Range: 470-680

Average Years Experience: 3

Other Admissions Factors Considered: Work experience, though not required, is strongly recommended. The interview is optional.

Other Schools to Which Students Applied: Tulane University, Louisiana State University, University of New Orleans

INTERNATIONAL STUDENTS

TOEFL Required of International Students? Yes

Minimum TOEFL: 580 (237 computer)

EMPLOYMENT INFORMATION

Placement Office Available? Yes

% Employed Within 3 Months: 97

MARQUETTE UNIVERSITY
College of Business Administration

Admissions Contact: Dr. Jeanne Simmons, Assistant Dean

Address: PO Box 1881, Milwaukee, WI 53201-1881

Admissions Phone: 414-288-7145 • **Admissions Fax:** 414-288-1660

Admissions E-mail: mba@Marquette.edu • **Web Address:** www.busadm.mu.edu/mba

INSTITUTIONAL INFORMATION

Public/Private: Private

Evening Classes Available? Yes

Total Faculty: 65

% Faculty Female: 17

% Faculty Minority: 2

% Faculty Part Time: 5

Student/Faculty Ratio: 9:1

Academic Calendar: Semester

PROGRAMS

Degrees Offered: MBA (1-6 years), EMBA (17 months), MS in Human Resources (1-6 years), MS in Applied Economics (1-6 years), MS in Engineering Management (1-6 years)

Combined Degrees: MBA/JD (4 years), MBA/JD in Sport Business (4 years), MBA/MSN (4-6 years)

Special Opportunities: An internship program is available.

Study Abroad Options: Australia, Austria, Belgium, Canada, Denmark, Spain, England, France, United Kingdom

STUDENT INFORMATION

Total Business Students: 575

% Full Time: 15

% Female: 30

% Minority: 1

Average Age: 30

COMPUTER AND RESEARCH FACILITIES

Computer Facilities: On-campus 24-hour University facility; College Lab; off-campus access to library databases and college network

Campuswide Network? Yes

Internet Fee? No

EXPENSES/FINANCIAL AID

Annual Tuition: $11,340

Tuition Per Credit (Resident/Nonresident): $630

Books and Supplies: $750

ADMISSIONS INFORMATION

Application Fee: $40

Electronic Application? Yes

Regular Application Deadline: Rolling

Regular Notification: Rolling

Deferment Available? Yes

Length of Deferment: Usually 1 year

Non-fall Admissions? Yes

Non-fall Application Deadline(s): January and May

Transfer Students Accepted? Yes

Transfer Policy: We accept transfers from other Jesuit schools (JEBNET agreement—see www.jebnet.org). We will also accept up to 12 approved credits from AACSB schools.

Need-Blind Admissions? No

Number of Applications Received: 281

% of Applicants Accepted: 95

% Accepted Who Enrolled: 64

Average GPA: 3.3

Average GMAT: 547

Average Years Experience: 6

Other Admissions Factors Considered: Letters of recommendation, work experience, computer experience

Other Schools to Which Students Applied: Loyola University Chicago, University of Wisconsin—Milwaukee, University of Wisconsin—Madison

INTERNATIONAL STUDENTS

TOEFL Required of International Students? Yes

Minimum TOEFL: 550

EMPLOYMENT INFORMATION

Placement Office Available? Yes

% Employed Within 3 Months: 100

MARSHALL UNIVERSITY
College of Business

Admissions Contact: Dr. Michael A. Newsome, MBA Director

Address: Corby Hall 217, 400 Hal Greer Boulevard, Huntington, WV 25755-2305

Admissions Phone: 304-696-2613 • **Admissions Fax:** 304-696-3661

Admissions E-mail: e-mail@school.edu • **Web Address:** lcob.marshall.edu/

The Marshall University Elizabeth McDowell Lewis College of Business has a long name, a great school song titled "Sons of Marshall," and a long list of educational amenities like technological sophistication and a delightful campus. Named for U.S. Supreme Court Chief Justice John Marshall, MU allows its students to obtain a solid education without having to sacrifice their souls to pay the bill.

INSTITUTIONAL INFORMATION

Public/Private: Public
Evening Classes Available? Yes
Total Faculty: 20
% Faculty Female: 10
% Faculty Minority: 10
% Faculty Part Time: 25
Student/Faculty Ratio: 5:1
Academic Calendar: Semester

PROGRAMS

Degrees Offered: MBA (36 credits, 1-5 years), EMBA (18 months to 2 years)
Special Opportunities: Interships are available.

STUDENT INFORMATION

Total Business Students: 80
% Full Time: 75
% Female: 60
% Minority: 15
% International: 30

COMPUTER AND RESEARCH FACILITIES

Research Facilities: Center for Business and Economic Research (CBER), Marshall University Research Corp.
Computer Facilities: College of Business Computer Libaratories, Library Computer Labs, Student Center Computer Labs
Campuswide Network? Yes
% of MBA Classrooms Wired: 25
Internet Fee? No

EXPENSES/FINANCIAL AID

Annual Tuition (Resident/Nonresident): $2,884/$8,158
Tuition Per Credit (Resident/Nonresident): $150
Room & Board (On/Off Campus): $4,000
Books and Supplies: $1,000
% Receiving Financial Aid: 50
% Receiving Aid Their First Year: 50

ADMISSIONS INFORMATION

Application Fee: $20
Electronic Application? No
Regular Application Deadline: Rolling
Regular Notification: Rolling
Deferment Available? No
Non-fall Admissions? Yes
Non-fall Application Deadline(s): Rolling
Transfer Students Accepted? Yes
Transfer Policy: When a student's plan of study is approved, credit may be transferred with the approval of the graduate dean. The work must have been completed at another regionally accredited graduate institution and must be appropriate to the student's program. Grades earned must be at the grade level of B or better, and acceptable to the advisor and the graduate dean. A maximum of 12 hours will be accepted, provided that they meet time limitation requirements. Graduate credit transferred from other institutions will not become part of the Marshall University grade point average and will simply meet credit hour requirements toward graduation.
Need-Blind Admissions? No
Number of Applications Received: 100
% of Applicants Accepted: 84
% Accepted Who Enrolled: 95
Average GPA: 3.5
Average GMAT: 530
Average Years Experience: 2
Other Admissions Factors Considered: Interview, letters of recommendation, and resume are recommended.

INTERNATIONAL STUDENTS

TOEFL Required of International Students? Yes
Minimum TOEFL: 525 (195 computer)

EMPLOYMENT INFORMATION

Placement Office Available? No
% Employed Within 3 Months: 90
Fields Employing Percentage of Grads: Accounting (75%)
Frequent Employers: BB&T, CSX Transportation, Ernst & Young, Steel of West Virginia

MASSACHUSETTS INSTITUTE OF TECHNOLOGY
Sloan School of Management

Admissions Contact: Rod Garcia, Admissions Director
Address: E52-118, Cambridge, MA 02139
Admissions Phone: 617-258-5434 • **Admissions Fax:** 617-253-6405
Admissions E-mail: mbaadmissions@sloan.mit.edu • **Web Address:** mitsloan.mit.edu

You know that the vaunted Sloan School of Management is home to arguably "the best" economics department "in the world" and "high-tech business" galore (including a nifty $3.5 million virtual trading floor). We bet you didn't know that "entrepreneurial spirit and activities pervade" Sloan. For example, the annual $50K Entrepreneurship Competition here "has spawned such successful companies as Direct Hit Technologies," the power behind the Lycos search engine.

INSTITUTIONAL INFORMATION

Public/Private: Private
Evening Classes Available? No
Total Faculty: 97
% Faculty Female: 17
% Faculty Minority: 8
% Faculty Part Time: 1
Student/Faculty Ratio: 10:1
Students in Parent Institution: 9,947
Academic Calendar: Semester

PROGRAMS

Degrees Offered: MBA (2 years), MS (2 years), PhD (5 years)
Combined Degrees: SM in Management/SM in Engineering (1 of 6 departments) (2 years)
Academic Specialties: Financial Engineering, Financial Management, Strategic Management/Consulting, Product and Venture Development, Strategic Information Technology, Operations Management/Manufacturing
Special Opportunities: The MIT-Japan Program in Science, Technology, and Management
Study Abroad Options: London Business School and IESE

STUDENT INFORMATION

Total Business Students: 733
% Full Time: 100
% Female: 27
% Minority: 3
% Out of State: 81
% International: 41
Average Age: 28

COMPUTER AND RESEARCH FACILITIES

Research Facilities: Dewey Library plus 14 additional on-campus libraries; 2,532,175 volumes; 2,225,281 microforms; 18,359 current periodicals; access provided to online bibliographic retrieval services and online databases
Campuswide Network? No
Internet Fee? No

EXPENSES/FINANCIAL AID

Annual Tuition: $31,200

ADMISSIONS INFORMATION

Application Fee: $175
Electronic Application? Yes
Regular Application Deadline: 1/31
Regular Notification: 3/30
Deferment Available? No
Non-fall Admissions? No
Transfer Students Accepted? No
Need-Blind Admissions? Yes
Number of Applications Received: 4,100
% of Applicants Accepted: 12
% Accepted Who Enrolled: 63
Average GPA: 3.5
GPA Range: 3.2-3.9
Average GMAT: 663
GMAT Range: 610-740
Average Years Experience: 5
Other Admissions Factors Considered: Previous coursework in calculus and economics

INTERNATIONAL STUDENTS

Minimum TOEFL: 600

EMPLOYMENT INFORMATION

Placement Office Available? Yes
% Employed Within 3 Months: 90
Fields Employing Percentage of Grads: Other (5%), General Management (8%), Marketing (8%), Operations (9%), Finance (30%), Consulting (40%)
Frequent Employers: Accenture, AT Kearney, Bain and Co., Booz-Allen and Hamilton, Boston Consulting Group, Citigroup, Intel Corp., McKinsey and Co., Microsoft Corp., Merrill Lynch, Siebel Systems Inc.

MCNEESE STATE UNIVERSITY
MBA Program

Admissions Contact: Physsis Hanagriff, University Admissions
Address: PO Box 92495, Lake Charles, LA 70609-2495
Admissions Phone: 337-475-5153 • **Admissions Fax:** 337-475-5189
Admissions E-mail: info@mail.mcneese.edu
Web Address: www.mcneese.edu/colleges/business/mba

INSTITUTIONAL INFORMATION

Public/Private: Public
Evening Classes Available? Yes
Total Faculty: 15
% Faculty Female: 1
% Faculty Minority: 45
Student/Faculty Ratio: 15:1
Students in Parent Institution: 8,142
Academic Calendar: Semester

PROGRAMS

Degrees Offered: MBA (18 months to 4 years)
Combined Degrees: None
Academic Specialties: Case study, computer-aided instruction, computer analysis, computer simulations, group discussion, lecture, research, seminars by members of the business community, student presentations, team project
Special Opportunities: None
Study Abroad Options: None

STUDENT INFORMATION

Total Business Students: 91
% Full Time: 20
% Female: 10
% Minority: 10
% Out of State: 45
% International: 10
Average Age: 28

COMPUTER AND RESEARCH FACILITIES

Campuswide Network? Yes
Internet Fee? No

EXPENSES/FINANCIAL AID

Annual Tuition (Resident/Nonresident): $1,987/$3,530
Tuition Per Credit (Resident/Nonresident): $540/$882
Room & Board (On/Off Campus): $3,000
Books and Supplies: $1,000

ADMISSIONS INFORMATION

Application Fee: $20
Electronic Application? No
Regular Application Deadline: Rolling
Regular Notification: Rolling
Deferment Available? Yes
Length of Deferment: 1 year
Non-fall Admissions? Yes
Non-fall Application Deadline(s): Spring, fall
Transfer Students Accepted? No
Need-Blind Admissions? No
Number of Applications Received: 36
% of Applicants Accepted: 72
% Accepted Who Enrolled: 69
Average GPA: 3.6
GPA Range: 2.4-4.0
Average GMAT: 459
GMAT Range: 250-630
Average Years Experience: 6

INTERNATIONAL STUDENTS

TOEFL Required of International Students? Yes
Minimum TOEFL: 550

EMPLOYMENT INFORMATION

Placement Office Available? Yes
% Employed Within 3 Months: 90

MIAMI UNIVERSITY
Richard T. Farmer School of Business

Admissions Contact: Judy Barille, MBA Director
Address: Laws Hall, Oxford, OH 45056
Admissions Phone: 513-529-6643 • **Admissions Fax:** 513-529-2487
Admissions E-mail: miamimba@muohio.edu
Web Address: www.sba.muohio.edu/mbaprogram

INSTITUTIONAL INFORMATION

Public/Private: Public
Evening Classes Available? No
Total Faculty: 32
% Faculty Female: 35
% Faculty Minority: 10
% Faculty Part Time: 10
Student/Faculty Ratio: 9:1
Students in Parent Institution: 16,000
Academic Calendar: Semester

PROGRAMS

Degrees Offered: MBA (36 credits, 1-3 years)
Academic Specialties: Entrepreneurship, Human Resource Management
Special Opportunities: Agribusiness, Entrepreneurship, Finance (includes Banking), General Management, Human Resource Management, International Business, Marketing, MIS

STUDENT INFORMATION

Total Business Students: 55
% Full Time: 45
% Female: 35
% Minority: 4
% Out of State: 36
% International: 20
Average Age: 26

COMPUTER AND RESEARCH FACILITIES

Campuswide Network? Yes
% of MBA Classrooms Wired: 100
Internet Fee? Yes

EXPENSES/FINANCIAL AID

Annual Tuition (Resident/Nonresident): $6,560/$15,284
Tuition Per Credit (Resident/Nonresident): $273/$637
Room & Board (On/Off Campus): $6,000
Books and Supplies: $1,000
Average Grant: $2,000
Average Loan: $1,500
% Receiving Financial Aid: 25
% Receiving Aid Their First Year: 80

ADMISSIONS INFORMATION

Application Fee: $35
Electronic Application? Yes
Regular Application Deadline: 3/1
Regular Notification: Rolling
Deferment Available? Yes
Length of Deferment: 2 years
Non-fall Admissions? Yes
Non-fall Application Deadline(s): 4/15 summer
Transfer Students Accepted? No
Need-Blind Admissions? No
Number of Applications Received: 102
% of Applicants Accepted: 41
% Accepted Who Enrolled: 74

Average GPA: 3.2
GPA Range: 3.0-3.5
Average GMAT: 552
GMAT Range: 520-580
Average Years Experience: 2
Other Admissions Factors Considered: Personal statment, resume, work experience, computer experience
Other Schools to Which Students Applied: Bowling Green State University, Indiana University, Ohio State University, University of Cincinnati, University of Dayton

INTERNATIONAL STUDENTS

TOEFL Required of International Students? Yes
Minimum TOEFL: 550 (220 computer)

EMPLOYMENT INFORMATION

Placement Office Available? Yes
% Employed Within 3 Months: 75
Fields Employing Percentage of Grads: MIS (16%), Marketing (42%), Finance (42%)
Frequent Employers: AMS, Deloitte & Touche, Ernst& Young, 5th 3rd Bank
Prominent Alumni: John Smale, brand management (retired), Proctor & Gamble; Richard Farmer, CEO and chairman of board (retired), Cintas; Michael Armstrong, former chairman, AT&T; Art Reimers, partner (retired), Goldman Sachs; Tom Stallkamp, former president, Daimler/Chrysler

MICHIGAN STATE UNIVERSITY
The Eli Broad Graduate School of Management

Admissions Contact: Jennifer Chizuk, Director, Full Time MBA Program
Address: 215 Eppley Center, East Lansing, MI 48824-1121
Admissions Phone: 517-355-7604 • **Admissions Fax:** 517-353-1649
Admissions E-mail: mba@msu.edu • **Web Address:** mba.bus.msu.edu

A strong national reputation, low tuition, "approachable" professors, and "a solid alumni base around the world" are a few reasons to consider the Eli Broad Graduate School of Management. Also notable is the Leadership Alliance Program, which provides students with "firsthand knowledge about a specific industry." Students say East Lansing "is a great place to live," too, thanks to its "very social atmosphere" and "shockingly beautiful" campus.

INSTITUTIONAL INFORMATION

Public/Private: Public
Evening Classes Available? No
Total Faculty: 109
% Faculty Female: 21
% Faculty Minority: 10
% Faculty Part Time: 19
Student/Faculty Ratio: 2:1
Students in Parent Institution: 44,937
Academic Calendar: Semester

PROGRAMS

Degrees Offered: MBA (21 months full time, day program), MSA (5 years: 4 + 1), Weekend MBA Program in Intergrative Management (17 months), MS in Manufacturing Engineering/Management (5 years: 4 + 1), EMBA (21 months), MS in Foodservice Management, 8 PhD programs

Combined Degrees: JD/MBA in conjunction with MSU-Detroit College of Law (4 years), MBA/MIM in conjuction with Thunderbird—The American School of International Management (25 months)

Academic Specialties: Supply Chain Management (emphasis in Logistics, Purchasing, Operations, Production, and Transportation); Finance (emphasis in Corporate Finance: corporate and divisional valuation, project and risk analysis, hedging strategies, and instruments); revised Marketing curriculum (focus on Marketing in Technology-Intensive Environments, including e-commerce systems, new product development, and relationship marketing systems); Human Resource Management (includes Labor Relations); Information Systems (secondary concentration); Corporate Accounting; Hospitality Business; International Management

Special Opportunities: Leadership Alliance Program, Integrative Case Experience, Big 10 Case Competition, Simon School (Rochester) Case Competition, National Black MBA Case Competition, Council of Logistics Management Case Competition, International Study Trip

Study Abroad Options: International University, Germany; International University of Japan; ITESM, Monterrey, Mexico; Norwegian School of Management BI, Norway

STUDENT INFORMATION

Total Business Students: 218
% Full Time: 100
% Female: 23
% Minority: 15
% International: 34
Average Age: 28

COMPUTER AND RESEARCH FACILITIES

Research Facilities: Center for International Business and Education Research-(CIBER), Business and Technology Center, Executive Education Center, Troy Management Education Center, International Student Center

Computer Facilities: MBA students have access to an MBA computer lounge with Pentium computers, laptop ethernet connections, and laser printers. All entering MBA students are expected to own their own laptop computer. All students have free access to the Internet and full access to MSU's main library, business library, and affiliated online research. The Business Library has extensive collections of print, online, and CD-ROM business volumes and subcriptions. The Business School has high-technology classrooms with laptop and ethernet connections for MBA classes. The Business School also has a dedicated Information Systems Microlab for MBA BIS courses and a Financial Analysis Laboratory for advanced courses in finance, investing, and risk management.

Campuswide Network? Yes
% of MBA Classrooms Wired: 100
Computer Model Recommended: Laptop
Internet Fee? No

EXPENSES/FINANCIAL AID

Annual Tuition (Resident/Nonresident): $13,400/$19,400
Books and Supplies: $1,500
Average Grant: $5,101
Average Loan: $17,611
% Receiving Financial Aid: 77
% Receiving Aid Their First Year: 77

ADMISSIONS INFORMATION

Application Fee: $40
Electronic Application? Yes
Early Decision Application Deadline: 12/16, 1/31, 3/14
Early Decision Notification: 5/1
Regular Application Deadline: 6/2
Regular Notification: 7/15
Deferment Available? Yes
Length of Deferment: 1 year
Non-fall Admissions? No
Transfer Students Accepted? No

Need-Blind Admissions? Yes
Number of Applications Received: 919
% of Applicants Accepted: 22
% Accepted Who Enrolled: 53
Average GPA: 3.3
Average GMAT: 639
GMAT Range: 570-710
Average Years Experience: 5
Other Admissions Factors Considered: Good understanding of the program and curriculum, good career fit with our programmatic and curricular offerings, aptitude to perform well in teams
Minority/Disadvantaged Student Recruitment Programs: Academic Achievement Graduate Assistantship Program, Educational Opportunity Fellowship Program, Multicultural Business Programs Scholarships. Also, Broad School and MSU Graduate School sponsor qualified minority candidates to visit the Broad School during the admissions process.
Other Schools to Which Students Applied: Arizona State University, Indiana University, Ohio State University, Penn State University—Great Valley Campus, Purdue University, University of Michigan, University of Wisconsin—Madison

INTERNATIONAL STUDENTS

TOEFL Required of International Students? Yes
Minimum TOEFL: 600 (250 computer)

EMPLOYMENT INFORMATION

Placement Office Available? Yes
Fields Employing Percentage of Grads: Consulting (4%), MIS (6%), Human Resources (6%), General Management (9%), Marketing (15%), Finance (27%), Operations (33%)
Frequent Employers: Applied Materials, The Dow Chemical Co., Federal-Mogul Corp., Ford Motor Co., Guidant Corp., General Electric Co., Johnson & Johnson, International Truck & Engine Corp., Raytheon Co., Standard & Poor's Corporate Value Consulting, United Technologies Corp., Visteon Corp., Whirlpool
Prominent Alumni: Eli Broad, chairman and CEO, SunAmerica, Inc.; Drayton McClane, CEO, McClane Group, and owner of the Astros; James Miller, president, Mazda Motor Corp.

MILLSAPS COLLEGE
Else School of Management

Admissions Contact: Anne McDonald, Director of Graduate Business Admissions
Address: 1701 North State Street, Jackson, MS 39210
Admissions Phone: 601-974-1253 • **Admissions Fax:** 601-974-1224
Admissions E-mail: mbamacc@millsaps.edu • **Web Address:** www.millsaps.edu/esom

INSTITUTIONAL INFORMATION

Public/Private: Private
Evening Classes Available? Yes
Total Faculty: 18
% Faculty Female: 39
% Faculty Minority: 5
% Faculty Part Time: 1
Student/Faculty Ratio: 12:1
Students in Parent Institution: 1,374
Academic Calendar: Semester

PROGRAMS

Degrees Offered: MBA (1-6 years), with concentrations in Finance, Marketing, Management, Accounting, International; MACC (1-6 years)

Academic Specialties: Case study, computer-aided instruction, computer analysis, computer simulations, experiential learning, field projects, group discussions, lecture, research, role playing, seminars by members of the business community, stimulations, student groups, team projects

Study Abroad Options: England, German, Italy, Mexico

STUDENT INFORMATION

Total Business Students: 90
% Full Time: 40
% Female: 38
% Minority: 14
% Out of State: 30
% International: 6
Average Age: 28

COMPUTER AND RESEARCH FACILITIES

Research Facilities: Millsaps-Wilson Library, dedicated computer lab
Computer Facilities: Computer facilities on campus, EBESCO, AICPA
Campuswide Network? Yes
% of MBA Classrooms Wired: 100
Internet Fee? Yes

EXPENSES/FINANCIAL AID

Annual Tuition: $19,140
Tuition Per Credit (Resident/Nonresident): $638
Room & Board (On/Off Campus): $10,000
Books and Supplies: $550
% Receiving Financial Aid: 85
% Receiving Aid Their First Year: 100

ADMISSIONS INFORMATION

Application Fee: $25
Electronic Application? No
Regular Application Deadline: 7/1
Regular Notification: 7/15
Deferment Available? Yes
Length of Deferment: 1 year
Non-fall Admissions? Yes
Non-fall Application Deadline(s): 11/15 spring, 4/15 summer
Transfer Students Accepted? Yes
Transfer Policy: Must be student in good standing; 6 hours from a non-AACSB-program, 12 hours from an AACSB-accredited program
Need-Blind Admissions? Yes
Number of Applications Received: 81
% of Applicants Accepted: 75
% Accepted Who Enrolled: 77
Average GPA: 3.4
GPA Range: 3.0-3.7
Average GMAT: 570
GMAT Range: 510-640
Average Years Experience: 4

INTERNATIONAL STUDENTS

TOEFL Required of International Students? Yes
Minimum TOEFL: 550 (230 computer)

EMPLOYMENT INFORMATION

Placement Office Available? Yes
% Employed Within 3 Months: 15

MISSISSIPPI STATE UNIVERSITY
College of Business and Industry

Admissions Contact: Dr. Barbara Spencer, Director of Graduate Studies in Business
Address: PO Drawer 5288, Mississippi State, MS 39762
Admissions Phone: 662-325-1891 • **Admissions Fax:** 662-325-8161
Admissions E-mail: gsb@cobilan.msstate.edu
Web Address: www.cbi.msstate.edu/cobi/gsb/index2.html

Due to its strong leadership-oriented approach, the new MBA in project management at Mississippi State attracts many applicants. Mississippi State University's emphasis on technology management is fitting, as the school offers interactive video courses to students in Columbus, Meridian, Vicksburg, and Gautier. Most students attend full time and are Mississippi natives.

INSTITUTIONAL INFORMATION

Public/Private: Public
Evening Classes Available? Yes
Total Faculty: 68
% Faculty Female: 18
% Faculty Minority: 6
Student/Faculty Ratio: 4:1
Students in Parent Institution: 16,500
Academic Calendar: Semester

PROGRAMS

Degrees Offered: MBA (30 credits, 1-6 years), MSBA (30 credits, 1-6 years), Master of Professional Accountancy (30 credits, 1-6 years), MTAX (30 credits, 1-6 years), MSIS (30 credits, 1-6 years), MBA in Project Management (32 credits, 1-6 years), PhD in Business Administration(3-10 years), Ph.D. in Applied Economics (3-10 years), MA in Applied Economics (1-6 years)
Academic Specialties: Strategic Management, Human Resource Management, Leadership, Taxation, Real Estate, Insurance, Marketing Management, Internet Marketing

STUDENT INFORMATION

Total Business Students: 134
% Full Time: 70
% Female: 36
% Minority: 16
% Out of State: 48
% International: 10
Average Age: 26

COMPUTER AND RESEARCH FACILITIES

Research Facilities: The MSU Libraries support research through the provision of a state-of-the art instructional media center. Multimedia software and computer terminals are available to students; workshops are offered free of charge.The MSU Libraries also offer a large collection of government depository material, including a large number of statistical CD-ROMs.
Computer Facilities: ABI/Inform, BNA Environmental Library, Business Source Elite, CCH Internet Tax Research, Choices II (Simmons Market Research), Compustat, Disclosure Corporate Snapshots, Dissertation Abstracts, EconLit, General Business File ASAP, Journal Citation Reports, Lexis-Nexis Academic Universe, NBER Online Reports, Predicasts PROMPT, PsycINFO, Reference USA, Social Sciences Citation Index, Statistical Universe, ValueLine, Worldscope GLOBAL. Fee-based search services are available for DIALOG.
Campuswide Network? Yes
% of MBA Classrooms Wired: 100
Internet Fee? No

EXPENSES/FINANCIAL AID

Annual Tuition (Resident/Nonresident): $3,874/$4,906
Tuition Per Credit (Resident/Nonresident): $215/$488
Room & Board (On/Off Campus): $5,250/$7,250
Books and Supplies: $750
Average Grant: $920
Average Loan: $9,461
% Receiving Financial Aid: 66
% Receiving Aid Their First Year: 68

ADMISSIONS INFORMATION

Application Fee: $0
Electronic Application? Yes
Regular Application Deadline: 7/1
Regular Notification: Rolling
Deferment Available? Yes
Length of Deferment: 1 year
Non-fall Admissions? Yes
Non-fall Application Deadline(s): 11/1 spring, 4/1 summer
Transfer Students Accepted? Yes
Transfer Policy: 6 hours of transfer credit from accredited institutions
Need-Blind Admissions? Yes
Number of Applications Received: 275
% of Applicants Accepted: 51
% Accepted Who Enrolled: 69
Average GPA: 3.4
GPA Range: 3.1-3.7
Average GMAT: 527
GMAT Range: 490-560
Average Years Experience: 1
Other Admissions Factors Considered: GMAT score
Minority/Disadvantaged Student Recruitment Programs: We visit several minority schools.

INTERNATIONAL STUDENTS

TOEFL Required of International Students? Yes
Minimum TOEFL: 575

EMPLOYMENT INFORMATION

Placement Office Available? Yes
% Employed Within 3 Months: 80
Fields Employing Percentage of Grads: Human Resources (3%), MIS (6%), Accounting (6%), Marketing (9%), Operations (14%), General Management (17%), Finance (19%), Other (26%)
Frequent Employers: Amsouth Bank, BellSouth, Cintas, Exxon Mobil,International Paper, JC Penny, Shell Oil, U.S. General Accounting Office
Prominent Alumni: Jerry Thames, former CEO at GTS, currently at Lehman Bros.; Cynthia A. Tucker, manager of strategy and portfolio management

---

MONMOUTH UNIVERSITY
School of Business Administration

Admissions Contact: Kevin Roane, Director, Graduate Admission
Address: 400 Cedar Avenue, West Long Branch, NJ 07764-1898
Admissions Phone: 732-571-3452 • **Admissions Fax:** 732-263-5123
Admissions E-mail: gradadm@monmouth.edu • **Web Address:** www.monmouth.edu

The School of Business Administration is one of the seven colleges of Monmouth University, located on a 147-acre campus only five minutes by car from the Atlantic Ocean. Monmouth's MBA comes in the broad-based, general format or with a concentration in accounting or health care management, and all classes are offered in the evening for part-time students. Emphasis is placed on ethical, global, and technological perspectives in an MBA program that "combines management practice and theory in a contemporary managerial context." One of the highlights of the School of Business Administration is the Business Council, which acts as a student resource for training and consulting, while also working to ensure that business students at the university can reciprocate these services and act as a resource for the community.

INSTITUTIONAL INFORMATION

Public/Private: Private
Evening Classes Available? Yes
Total Faculty: 27
% Faculty Female: 15
Student/Faculty Ratio: 10:1
Students in Parent Institution: 6,032
Academic Calendar: Semester

PROGRAMS

Degrees Offered: MBA (30-48 credits, 1-years), MBA with a concentration in Health Care Management (33-54 credits, 1-5 years), MBA with a track in Accounting (30-48 credits, 1-5 years)

STUDENT INFORMATION

Total Business Students: 311
% Full Time: 15
% Female: 42
% Minority: 6
% Out of State: 8
% International: 31
Average Age: 28

COMPUTER AND RESEARCH FACILITIES

Campuswide Network? Yes
% of MBA Classrooms Wired: 18
Internet Fee? No

EXPENSES/FINANCIAL AID

Annual Tuition: $9,882
Tuition Per Credit (Resident/Nonresident): $549
Books and Supplies: $800
Average Grant: $1,933
Average Loan: $12,658
% Receiving Financial Aid: 90
% Receiving Aid Their First Year: 92

ADMISSIONS INFORMATION

Application Fee: $35
Electronic Application? Yes
Regular Application Deadline: 8/1
Regular Notification: Rolling
Deferment Available? Yes
Length of Deferment: 1 year
Non-fall Admissions? Yes
Non-fall Application Deadline(s): spring 12/15, summer 5/15
Transfer Students Accepted? Yes
Transfer Policy: Must complete at least 30 credits at Monmouth; transfer credits must be within 7 years and with acceptable grade
Need-Blind Admissions? Yes
Number of Applications Received: 185
% of Applicants Accepted: 84
% Accepted Who Enrolled: 66
Average GPA: 3.2
GPA Range: 2.8-3.6
Average GMAT: 505
GMAT Range: 460-555

Other Admissions Factors Considered: Resume; letters of recommendation required of students who have graduated 8 or more years ago.

INTERNATIONAL STUDENTS

TOEFL Required of International Students? Yes
Minimum TOEFL: 550 (213 computer)

EMPLOYMENT INFORMATION

Placement Office Available? Yes

See page 428.

MONTANA STATE UNIVERSITY
College of Business

Admissions Contact: Marc A. Giullian, MPAC Director
Address: 338 Reid Hall, PO Box 173040, Bozeman, MT 59717-3040
Admissions Phone: 406-994-4681 • **Admissions Fax:** 406-994-6206
Admissions E-mail: mgiullian@montana.edu • **Web Address:** www.montana.edu/cob/

INSTITUTIONAL INFORMATION

Public/Private: Public
Evening Classes Available? No
Total Faculty: 9
% Faculty Female: 33
Student/Faculty Ratio: 20:1
Academic Calendar: Semester

PROGRAMS

Degrees Offered: Master of Professional Accountancy (1-4 years)
Academic Specialties: Computer-aided instruction, computer analysis, research, seminars by members of the business community, student presentations, team projects, fraud examination, accounting information systems

STUDENT INFORMATION

Total Business Students: 40
% Full Time: 80
% Female: 75
Average Age: 25

COMPUTER AND RESEARCH FACILITIES

Computer Facilities: Financial Accounting Research System
Campuswide Network? Yes
% of MBA Classrooms Wired: 100
Internet Fee? No

EXPENSES/FINANCIAL AID

Annual Tuition (Resident/Nonresident): $3,080/$8,352
Tuition Per Credit (Resident/Nonresident): $103/$278
Average Grant: $5,000
% Receiving Financial Aid: 50

ADMISSIONS INFORMATION

Application Fee: $50
Electronic Application? No
Regular Application Deadline: 3/15
Regular Notification: Rolling
Deferment Available? Yes
Length of Deferment: 1 year
Non-fall Admissions? Yes
Non-fall Application Deadline(s): 11/15 spring, 3/15 summer, 6/30 fall
Transfer Students Accepted? Yes

Transfer Policy: Limited number of graduate credits can be transferred
Need-Blind Admissions? No
Number of Applications Received: 50
% of Applicants Accepted: 62
% Accepted Who Enrolled: 94
Average GPA: 3.5
Average GMAT: 520

INTERNATIONAL STUDENTS

TOEFL Required of International Students? Yes
Minimum TOEFL: 550

EMPLOYMENT INFORMATION

Placement Office Available? Yes
% Employed Within 3 Months: 85
Fields Employing Percentage of Grads: Accounting (85%)
Frequent Employers: Deloitte & Touche, Ernst & Young, KPMG, Pricewaterhouse Coopers

MONTCLAIR STATE UNIVERSITY
School of Business

Admissions Contact: Dr. Eileen Kaplan, Assistant Dean
Address: Partridge Hall 454, Upper Montclair, NJ 07043
Admissions Phone: 973-655-4306 • **Admissions Fax:** 973-655-5312
Admissions E-mail: sbus@mail.montclair.edu • **Web Address:** www.montclair.edu/mba

INSTITUTIONAL INFORMATION

Public/Private: Public
Evening Classes Available? Yes
Total Faculty: 60
% Faculty Female: 20
Student/Faculty Ratio: 25:1
Students in Parent Institution: 15,000
Academic Calendar: Year-round

PROGRAMS

Degrees Offered: MBA (54 credits)
Academic Specialties: All PhDs; many have significant businesses
Special Opportunities: Accounting, CIS or MIS, Economics, Finance (includes Banking), International Business, Management, Marketing
Study Abroad Options: France

STUDENT INFORMATION

Total Business Students: 370
% Full Time: 24
Average Age: 26

COMPUTER AND RESEARCH FACILITIES

Research Facilities: Center for International Business
Campuswide Network? No
% of MBA Classrooms Wired: 10
Internet Fee? No

EXPENSES/FINANCIAL AID

Annual Tuition (Resident/Nonresident): $10,646/
Tuition Per Credit (Resident/Nonresident): $354/$462
Room & Board (On/Off Campus): $8,250
Books and Supplies: $850

ADMISSIONS INFORMATION

Application Fee: $40

Electronic Application? Yes
Deferment Available? Yes
Length of Deferment: 1 year
Non-fall Admissions? No
Transfer Students Accepted? No
Need-Blind Admissions? Yes
Average GPA: 3.1
Average GMAT: 520
Other Admissions Factors Considered: Work experience
Other Schools to Which Students Applied: Rutgers/The State University of New Jersey, Seton Hall University, Fairleigh Dickinson University

INTERNATIONAL STUDENTS

TOEFL Required of International Students? Yes
Minimum TOEFL: 550 (213 computer)

EMPLOYMENT INFORMATION

Placement Office Available? No

MORGAN STATE UNIVERSITY
Earl Graves School of Business and Management

Admissions Contact: Dr. Mildred Glover, Director
Address: 1700 E. Cold Spring Lane, McMechen Building, Baltimore, MD 21251
Admissions Phone: 443-885-3160 • **Admissions Fax:** 443-885-8253
Admissions E-mail: mba@morgan.edu
Web Address: www.morgan.edu/academics/sbm/academic/sbm.htm

INSTITUTIONAL INFORMATION

Public/Private: Public
Evening Classes Available? No
Total Faculty: 47
% Faculty Part Time: 9
Student/Faculty Ratio: 12:1
Students in Parent Institution: 5,900
Academic Calendar: Semester

PROGRAMS

Degrees Offered: MBA (30-60 credits, 16 months to 5 years)
Special Opportunities: CIS or MIS, Finance (includes Banking), Management, Marketing

STUDENT INFORMATION

Total Business Students: 103

COMPUTER AND RESEARCH FACILITIES

Research Facilities: Soper Library
Campuswide Network? Yes
Internet Fee? No

EXPENSES/FINANCIAL AID

Tuition Per Credit (Resident/Nonresident): $193/$364
Room & Board (On/Off Campus): $2,990

ADMISSIONS INFORMATION

Application Fee: $20
Electronic Application? No
Regular Application Deadline: Rolling
Regular Notification: Rolling
Deferment Available? Yes

Non-fall Admissions? No
Transfer Students Accepted? No
Need-Blind Admissions? No
Other Admissions Factors Considered: Interview, resume

INTERNATIONAL STUDENTS

TOEFL Required of International Students? Yes
Minimum TOEFL: 600

EMPLOYMENT INFORMATION

Placement Office Available? Yes
% Employed Within 3 Months: 86

MURRAY STATE UNIVERSITY
College of Business and Public Affairs

Admissions Contact: MBA Coordinator
Address: PO Box 9, Murray, KY 42071
Admissions Phone: 270-762-6970 • **Admissions Fax:** 270-762-3482
Admissions E-mail: gerry.muuka@murraystate.edu
Web Address: www.mursuky.edu/qacd/cbpa/mba/index.htm

INSTITUTIONAL INFORMATION

Public/Private: Public
Evening Classes Available? No
Total Faculty: 26
Student/Faculty Ratio: 20:1
Students in Parent Institution: 9,000
Academic Calendar: Semester

PROGRAMS

Degrees Offered: MBA, distance learning option (67 credits,1-8 years); MS in Economics (30 credits, 18 months to 8 years); MPA, distance learning option (36 credits, 18 months to 8 years); Telecommunications Systems Management (TSM) (36 credits, 18 months to 8 years)
Study Abroad Options: Australia, Belize, China, Finland, France, Germany, United Kingdom

STUDENT INFORMATION

Total Business Students: 160
% Full Time: 47
Average Age: 31

COMPUTER AND RESEARCH FACILITIES

Research Facilities: Waterfield Library plus 2 additional on-campus libraries; total holdings of 375,952 volumes; 179,044 microforms; 2,361 current periodical subscriptions. CD player(s) available
Campuswide Network? Yes
Internet Fee? No

EXPENSES/FINANCIAL AID

Annual Tuition (Resident/Nonresident): $2,852/$7,980
Room & Board (On/Off Campus): $3,800

ADMISSIONS INFORMATION

Application Fee: $20
Electronic Application? No
Regular Application Deadline: Rolling
Regular Notification: Rolling
Deferment Available? Yes
Non-fall Admissions? Yes
Non-fall Application Deadline(s): Rolling

Transfer Students Accepted? Yes
Transfer Policy: None
Need-Blind Admissions? No
Number of Applications Received: 121
% of Applicants Accepted: 75
% Accepted Who Enrolled: 52
Other Admissions Factors Considered: For international applicants, proof of adequate funds are required. Financial aid is not available to international students.

INTERNATIONAL STUDENTS

TOEFL Required of International Students? Yes
Minimum TOEFL: 525

EMPLOYMENT INFORMATION

Placement Office Available? Yes

NATIONAL UNIVERSITY OF SINGAPORE
NUS Business School

Admissions Contact: Mr. Gary Chan, MBA Programs Office
Address: BIZ 2 Building, 1 Business Link, Level 5, Singapore, 117592, Singapore
Admissions Phone: 011 68 74 2068 • Admissions Fax: 011 68 72 4423
Admissions E-mail: nusmba@nus.edu.sg • Web Address: www.fba.nus.edu.sg/

Cultures converge in Singapore, where market capitalism brought by English colonists dances with the customs, traditions, and language of the city-state's ethnically Chinese majority. NUS Business School's programs mirror their unique surroundings—in the IMBA program, a joint effort with China's Peking University, half of the classes are conducted in English while the rest are taught in Mandarin or bilingually. The MBA program focuses on case studies and group projects and is usually completed in two years; under certain circumstances, though, it can be completed in 16 months. The Executive MBA program is rigorous and intensive, consisting of six two-week residential periods that involve nine hours of classes, six days a week, over a span of 18 months.

INSTITUTIONAL INFORMATION

Public/Private: Public
Evening Classes Available? Yes
Total Faculty: 108
% Faculty Female: 25
% Faculty Minority: 0
% Faculty Part Time: 4
Student/Faculty Ratio: 2:1
Academic Calendar: Trimester

PROGRAMS

Degrees Offered: MBA (16-22 months full-time, 28-48 months part-time); Asia-Pacific Executive MBA in both English and Chinese (18 months)
Combined Degrees: NUS-Peking University IMBA dual degree (24 months)

STUDENT INFORMATION

Total Business Students: 254
% Full Time: 70
% Female: 40
% Minority: 20
% International: 70
Average Age: 29

COMPUTER AND RESEARCH FACILITIES

Campuswide Network? Yes
% of MBA Classrooms Wired: 100
Computer Model Recommended: Laptop
Internet Fee? No

EXPENSES/FINANCIAL AID

Annual Tuition (Resident/Nonresident): $10,500/$11,550
Room & Board (On/Off Campus): $9,600/$5,000
Books and Supplies: $600
% Receiving Financial Aid: 100

ADMISSIONS INFORMATION

Electronic Application? Yes
Regular Application Deadline: 2/28
Regular Notification: 5/1
Deferment Available? Yes
Length of Deferment: 1 year
Non-fall Admissions? No
Transfer Students Accepted? Yes
Transfer Policy: Must be a reputable MBA school
Need-Blind Admissions? No
Number of Applications Received: 952
% of Applicants Accepted: 13
% Accepted Who Enrolled: 73
Average GMAT: 672
GMAT Range: 620-700
Average Years Experience: 5
Other Admissions Factors Considered: Attitude and aptitude of applicant, leadership, entrepreneurial quality, and value to alumni.

INTERNATIONAL STUDENTS

TOEFL Required of International Students? Yes
Minimum TOEFL: 620 (260 computer)

EMPLOYMENT INFORMATION

Placement Office Available? Yes
% Employed Within 3 Months: 75
Fields Employing Percentage of Grads: Accounting (5%), Consulting (15%), Finance (5%), General Management (40%), Global Management (5%), Marketing (2%), Management Information Systems (5%), Operations (5%), Quantitative (2%), Strategic Planning (5%)
Frequent Employers: ExxonMobil Asia Pacific, Hewlett-Packard Singapore, International Interprise Singapore, KPMG International, Ministry of Trade and Industry, National Computer Board, NEC Singapore Ltd, P & G, Philips Electronics, Shell Eastern Petroleum, Singapore Police Force, Sony Systems Design International, Swiss Bank Corporation, WorldCom

NEW JERSEY INSTITUTE OF TECHNOLOGY
School of Management

Admissions Contact: Stuart J. Lipper, Director of Graduate Programs
Address: University Heights, Newark, NJ 07102
Admissions Phone: 973-596-3248 • Admissions Fax: 973-596-3074
Admissions E-mail: lipper@njit.edu • Web Address: management.njit.edu/

All graduate business energy at NJIT is tunneled into its single MBA program: the MBA in Management of Technology. MBA students are trained to increase the productivity and competitiveness of technology-based organizations, while recognizing the importance of ethical business standards and a global perspective. The future technology managers of the MBA program can specialize in e-commerce, infrastructure management, financial management, or management information systems, and can attend courses at the main Newark campus or at three other convenient locations. The quality of all educational programs at NJIT, undergrad or graduate, is enhanced by its 17 state-of-the-art research centers.

INSTITUTIONAL INFORMATION

Public/Private: Public
Evening Classes Available? No
Total Faculty: 38
% Faculty Part Time: 54
Student/Faculty Ratio: 13:1
Students in Parent Institution: 7,504
Academic Calendar: Semester

PROGRAMS

Degrees Offered: EMSM (39 credits, 14 months), MSM (30-48 credits, 1-7 years), MBA in Management of Technology (48-60 credits, 18 months to 7 years)

STUDENT INFORMATION

Total Business Students: 442
% Full Time: 15
Average Age: 32

COMPUTER AND RESEARCH FACILITIES

Campuswide Network? Yes
Internet Fee? No

EXPENSES/FINANCIAL AID

Annual Tuition (Resident/Nonresident): $4,033/$6,184
Tuition Per Credit (Resident/Nonresident): $434/$597
Room & Board (On/Off Campus): $7,050/$8,100
Books and Supplies: $1,000

ADMISSIONS INFORMATION

Application Fee: $50
Electronic Application? No
Regular Application Deadline: Rolling
Regular Notification: Rolling
Deferment Available? No
Non-fall Admissions? Yes
Non-fall Application Deadline(s): Rolling
Transfer Students Accepted? No
Need-Blind Admissions? No
Number of Applications Received: 150
% of Applicants Accepted: 87
% Accepted Who Enrolled: 75
Average Years Experience: 5
Other Admissions Factors Considered: For international students: proof of adequate funds, proof of health/immunizations required

INTERNATIONAL STUDENTS

TOEFL Required of International Students? Yes
Minimum TOEFL: 525

EMPLOYMENT INFORMATION

Placement Office Available? Yes
% Employed Within 3 Months: 100

NEW MEXICO STATE UNIVERSITY
College of Business Administration and Economics

Admissions Contact: Dr. Wayne Hendrick, Director, MBA Program
Address: PO Box 173040, Dept 3GSP, La Cruces, NM 88003-8001
Admissions Phone: 505-646-8003 • **Admissions Fax:** 505-646-7977
Admissions E-mail: mba@nmsu.edu • **Web Address:** cbae.nmsu.edu/~mba/

INSTITUTIONAL INFORMATION

Public/Private: Public
Evening Classes Available? No
Total Faculty: 77
% Faculty Part Time: 2
Students in Parent Institution: 15,409
Academic Calendar: Semester

PROGRAMS

Degrees Offered: MBA (36-55 credits, 18 months to 3.3 years)
Special Opportunities: General Business

STUDENT INFORMATION

Total Business Students: 125
% Full Time: 56
% Female: 41
% Minority: 24
% International: 14
Average Age: 26

COMPUTER AND RESEARCH FACILITIES

Campuswide Network? Yes
Internet Fee? No

EXPENSES/FINANCIAL AID

Annual Tuition (Resident/Nonresident): $2,994/$9,402
Tuition Per Credit (Resident/Nonresident): $104/$340

ADMISSIONS INFORMATION

Application Fee: $15
Electronic Application? No
Regular Application Deadline: 7/1
Regular Notification: Rolling
Deferment Available? Yes
Non-fall Admissions? Yes
Non-fall Application Deadline(s): 11/1, 4/1
Transfer Students Accepted? No
Need-Blind Admissions? No
Number of Applications Received: 92
% of Applicants Accepted: 74
% Accepted Who Enrolled: 49
Other Admissions Factors Considered: College transcripts

INTERNATIONAL STUDENTS

TOEFL Required of International Students? Yes
Minimum TOEFL: 530

EMPLOYMENT INFORMATION

Placement Office Available? Yes
% Employed Within 3 Months: 40

NEW YORK UNIVERSITY LEONARD N. STERN SCHOOL OF BUSINESS

Admissions Contact: Julia Min, Assistant Dean, MBA Admissions
Address: 44 West 4th Street, Suite 6-70, New York, NY 10012
Admissions Phone: 212-998-0600 • **Admissions Fax:** 212-995-4231
Admissions E-mail: sternmba@stern.nyu.edu • **Web Address:** www.stern.nyu.edu

INSTITUTIONAL INFORMATION

Public/Private: Private
Evening Classes Available? Yes
Total Faculty: 210
Student/Faculty Ratio: 8:1
Students in Parent Institution: 51,901
Academic Calendar: Semester

PROGRAMS

Degrees Offered: PhD (4-5 years average, but must be completed in 6 years)
Combined Degrees: JD/MBA, with the School of Law (4 years); MA/MBA, with the Institute of French Studies (GSAS, 3 years); MA/MBA, with the Department of Politics (GSAS, 3 years); MPA/MBA, with the School of Public Administration (3 years); MS/MBA, with the Department of Biology (3 years)
Academic Specialties: Finance, Entrepreneurship and Innovation, Management, Marketing, Global Business
Special Opportunities: Majors: Accounting, Economics, Finance, Information Systems, Management and Organizational Behavior, Marketing, Operations Management, Statistics; Co-Majors: Entrepreneurship and Innovation; Program Initiatives: Digital Economy; Entertainment, Media and Techonology; Law and Business; Quantitative Finance; Real Estate Finance
Study Abroad Options: Argentina, Australia, Austria, Belgium, Brazil, Chile, China, Costa Rica, Czech Republic, England, France, Germany, Hong Kong, India, Israel, Italy, Japan, Mexico, The Netherlands, Norway, Singapore, South Africa, South Korea, Spain, Sweden, Switzerland, Venezuela

STUDENT INFORMATION

Total Business Students: 2,551
% Full Time: 32
% Female: 37
% Minority: 13
Average Age: 27

COMPUTER AND RESEARCH FACILITIES

Research Facilities: Salomon Center for the Study of Financial Institutions, Glucksman Institute for Research in Securities Markets, Center for Japan-U.S. Business and Economic Studies, Vincent C. Ross Institute of Accounting Research, Berkley Center for Entrepreneurial Studies, Center for Digital Economy Research, New York University Center For Law and Business
Computer Facilities: Computer labs and electronic classrooms offer approximately 200 Pentium PCs. All PCs are networked and provide access to time-sharing and the Internet. All classroom spaces and some public study/lounge areas offer wireless Internet access.
Campuswide Network? Yes
% of MBA Classrooms Wired: 100
Computer Model Recommended: Laptop
Internet Fee? No

EXPENSES/FINANCIAL AID

Annual Tuition: $30,600
Tuition Per Credit (Resident/Nonresident): $1,130
Books and Supplies: $2,163
Average Grant: $7,600
Average Loan: $35,000
% Receiving Financial Aid: 85
% Receiving Aid Their First Year: 80

ADMISSIONS INFORMATION

Application Fee: $150
Electronic Application? Yes
Early Decision Application Deadline: 12/1
Early Decision Notification: 2/15
Regular Application Deadline: 3/15
Regular Notification: Rolling
Deferment Available? No
Non-fall Admissions? Yes
Non-fall Application Deadline(s): Part-time program only: 9/15 spring
Transfer Students Accepted? No
Need-Blind Admissions? Yes
Number of Applications Received: 4,962
% of Applicants Accepted: 15
% Accepted Who Enrolled: 52
Average GPA: 3.4
GPA Range: 3.0-3.8
Average GMAT: 700
GMAT Range: 650-750
Average Years Experience: 5
Other Admissions Factors Considered: Applicants should have some progressive work experience. Admissions decisions are influenced by academic potential, involvement in community, professional progression, goals in pursuing an MBA, and letters of recommendation.
Minority/Disadvantaged Student Recruitment Programs: NYU Stern is a member of the Consortium for Graduate Study in Management, which sponsors underrepresented minorities in business schools. Stern is a member of the Robert A. Toigo Foundation, which provides financial assistance, mentoring, summer internships, and job placement services to the top minority candidates in the country. There are minority scholarship programs that have been sponsored by Merril Lynch, JP Morgan Chase, and Credit Suisse First Boston. Stern also participates in workshops for Management Leadership for Tomorrow (MLT).

INTERNATIONAL STUDENTS

TOEFL Required of International Students? Yes
Minimum TOEFL: 600 (250 computer)

EMPLOYMENT INFORMATION

Placement Office Available? Yes
% Employed Within 3 Months: 86
Fields Employing Percentage of Grads: MIS (1%), Entrepreneurship (1%), Entrepreneurship (1%), MIS (1%), Operations (1%), Quantitative (2%), Strategic Planning (5%), Other (6%), Consulting (8%), Marketing (14%), Finance (57%)
Frequent Employers: American Express; Bear Stearns; Booz Allen & Hamilton; Citigroup; Credit Suisse First Boston; Deloitte & Touche; Deutsche Bank; Goldman Sachs; IBM; Johnson & Johnson; JP Morgan Chase; Lehman Brothers; McKinsey & Co.; Merrill Lynch; Morgan Stanley; Nabisco; Pfizer; Pricewaterhouse Coopers; Salomon Smith Barney; Standard's & Poor; UBS Warburg; Unilever
Prominent Alumni: Richard Fuld, Chairman and CEO, Lehman Brothers Holdings, Inc.; Thomas E. Freston, Chariman and CEO, MTV Networks; Abby F. Kohnstamm, senior vice president of marketing, IBM

NEW YORK UNIVERSITY STERN EXECUTIVE MBA PROGRAM

Admissions Contact: Peter Todd, Admissions Coordinator
Address: 44 West 4th Street, Suite 10-66, New York, NY 10012
Admissions Phone: 212-998-0789 • **Admissions Fax:** 212-995-4222
Admissions E-mail: executive@stern.nyu.edu
Web Address: www.stern.nyu.edu/executive/emba

The "street-smart, focused" students at NYU's Stern School of Business love its location near "the heart of" diverse and glittering New York City's "bustling financial, consumer-products, and media industries." With nearly 30 exchange programs and international research centers, international business is especially noteworthy at Stern, as is the Management Consulting Program, in which corporations like Reebok and IBM hire teams of students to do consulting work.

INSTITUTIONAL INFORMATION

Public/Private: Private
Evening Classes Available? No

STUDENT INFORMATION

% Female: 25
% Minority: 11
% International: 14
Average Age: 34

ADMISSIONS INFORMATION

Application Fee: $150
Electronic Application? Yes
Regular Application Deadline: 2/28
Deferment Available? Yes
Length of Deferment: 1 year
Non-fall Admissions? Yes
Non-fall Application Deadline(s): See website
Transfer Students Accepted? No
Need-Blind Admissions? No
Number of Applications Received: 600
% of Applicants Accepted: 25
% Accepted Who Enrolled: 67
Average GPA: 3.6
Average GMAT: 660
Average Years Experience: 9

NICHOLLS STATE UNIVERSITY
College of Business Administration

Admissions Contact: Becky LeBlanc-Durocher, Director of Admissions
Address: PO Box 2004, Thibodaux, LA 70310
Admissions Phone: 877-642-4655 • **Admissions Fax:** 985-448-4929
Admissions E-mail: esai-bl@nicholls.edu • **Web Address:** www.nicholls.edu

Nicholls State University takes its name from Francis T. Nicholls, governor of Louisiana in the late nineteenth century and later chief justice to the Louisiana Supreme Court, who is known for reestablishing Louisiana's "Home Rule" political status and campaigning against the corrupt Louisiana State lottery. Nicholls is primarily an undergraduate institution, but it offers select graduate programs and insists that all students across the board be

encouraged to lead responsible lives and be given the opportunity to develop character through advanced education. The MBA program, available full time or part time, emphasizes an ethical and technological approach to problem solving, critical thinking, effective communication, and maintaining a global perspective.

INSTITUTIONAL INFORMATION

Public/Private: Public
Evening Classes Available? Yes
Total Faculty: 26
% Faculty Female: 27
Student/Faculty Ratio: 15:1
Students in Parent Institution: 7,206

PROGRAMS

Degrees Offered: MBA (33-69 semester hours)
Study Abroad Options: France: Ecole Superieure du Commerce Exterier, Paris; Ecole Superieure de Commerce, Saint Etienne; University of Paris IX, Dauphine

STUDENT INFORMATION

Total Business Students: 105
% Full Time: 26
% Female: 41
% Minority: 3
% Out of State: 6
% International: 14

COMPUTER AND RESEARCH FACILITIES

Campuswide Network? Yes
Internet Fee? No

EXPENSES/FINANCIAL AID

Annual Tuition (Resident/Nonresident): $2,400/$7,800
Room & Board (On/Off Campus): $3,902
Books and Supplies: $2,000
% Receiving Financial Aid: 20

ADMISSIONS INFORMATION

Application Fee: $20
Electronic Application? Yes
Regular Application Deadline: 6/30
Regular Notification: Rolling
Deferment Available? Yes
Length of Deferment: 1 semester
Non-fall Admissions? Yes
Non-fall Application Deadline(s): Spring, summer
Transfer Students Accepted? Yes
Transfer Policy: Maximum of 9 hours may be transferred from an accredited institution.
Need-Blind Admissions? Yes
Number of Applications Received: 55
% of Applicants Accepted: 100
% Accepted Who Enrolled: 58
Average GPA: 3.1
Average GMAT: 469

INTERNATIONAL STUDENTS

TOEFL Required of International Students? Yes
Minimum TOEFL: 550 (213 computer)

EMPLOYMENT INFORMATION

Placement Office Available? Yes
Prominent Alumni: Barry Melancon, president, AICPA

NORTH CAROLINA STATE UNIVERSITY
College of Management

Admissions Contact: Pam Bostic, Director of Admissions
Address: MBA Program Office /Campus Box 7229, Raleigh, NC 27695-7229
Admissions Phone: 919-515-5584 • **Admissions Fax:** 919-515-5073
Admissions E-mail: mba@ncsu.edu • **Web Address:** www.mba.ncsu.edu

INSTITUTIONAL INFORMATION

Public/Private: Public
Evening Classes Available? Yes
Total Faculty: 81
Student/Faculty Ratio: 1:1
Students in Parent Institution: 29,637

PROGRAMS

Degrees Offered: MBA (52 credits, 2 years full tim; 45 credits, 3 years part time), with concentrations in Electronic Commerce, Financial Management, Information Technology Management, Operations and Supply Chain Management, Product Innovation Management, Marketing Management, Technology Commercialization

STUDENT INFORMATION

Total Business Students: 92
% Full Time: 34
% Female: 35
% Minority: 3
% Out of State: 6
% International: 26
Average Age: 29

COMPUTER AND RESEARCH FACILITIES

Research Facilities: D.H. Hill Library, located near the center of campus, offers access to millions of volumes of books and journals and an extensive and growing collection of CD-ROM and electronic databases.
Computer Facilities: The College of Management's compuer lab houses 100 microcomputers connected to a campuswide network. Students have access to a wide range of spreadsheet, word processing, database, statistical, and econometric software, as well as several large databases.
Campuswide Network? Yes
% of MBA Classrooms Wired: 90
Computer Model Recommended: Laptop
Internet Fee? No

EXPENSES/FINANCIAL AID

Annual Tuition (Resident/Nonresident): $8,012/$19,661
Tuition Per Credit (Resident/Nonresident): $377/$1,833
Books and Supplies: $1,300
Average Grant: $16,800
Average Loan: $10,829

ADMISSIONS INFORMATION

Application Fee: $55
Electronic Application? Yes
Regular Application Deadline: 4/4
Regular Notification: 5/4
Deferment Available? Yes
Length of Deferment: 1 year
Non-fall Admissions? No
Transfer Students Accepted? Yes
Transfer Policy: The NC State MBA Program can accept up to 12 hours of transfer credit from another AACSB-accredited MBA program The grade received for a transfer class must be a B or better, and the class must have been taken in the last 6 years.
Need-Blind Admissions? Yes
Number of Applications Received: 228

% of Applicants Accepted: 57
% Accepted Who Enrolled: 70
Average GPA: 3.3
Average GMAT: 625
Average Years Experience: 6

INTERNATIONAL STUDENTS

TOEFL Required of International Students? Yes
Minimum TOEFL: 620 (260 computer)

EMPLOYMENT INFORMATION

Placement Office Available? Yes
% Employed Within 3 Months: 78
Frequent Employers: Accenture, American Airlines, Bayer, BB&T, Caterpillar, Channel Master, Cisco Systems, Corning, Duke Energy, Duke University, Ericsson, GE Capital, GlaxoSmithKline, HAHT Commerce, IBM, Intel, John Deere, Kimberly-Clark, KPMG Consulting, Lord Corp., Milliken & Co., Motorola, Nortel Networks, Parker Hannifin Corp., Pfizer, Porivo Technologies, Progress Energy, Red Hat, Research Triangle Institute, Wachovia

See page 430.

NORTH DAKOTA STATE UNIVERSITY
College of Business Administration

Admissions Contact: Paul Brown, MBA Director
Address: Putnam Hall, Fargo, ND 58105
Admissions Phone: 701-231-8651 • **Admissions Fax:** 701-231-7508
Admissions E-mail: NDSUAdmission@ndsu.nodak.edu • **Web Address:** www.ndsu.edu/cba/

INSTITUTIONAL INFORMATION

Public/Private: Public
Evening Classes Available? No
Total Faculty: 76
% Faculty Part Time: 28
Student/Faculty Ratio: 19:1

PROGRAMS

Degrees Offered: MBA (30-52 credits, 1-5 years)
Combined Degrees: MBA/JD (105-127 credits, 3.5 to 5 years)

STUDENT INFORMATION

Total Business Students: 537
% Full Time: 11
% Female: 40
% International: 8
Average Age: 29

COMPUTER AND RESEARCH FACILITIES

Campuswide Network? Yes
Internet Fee? No

EXPENSES/FINANCIAL AID

Annual Tuition (Resident/Nonresident): $7,632
Tuition Per Credit (Resident/Nonresident): $424

ADMISSIONS INFORMATION

Application Fee: $30
Electronic Application? No
Regular Application Deadline: Rolling
Regular Notification: Rolling
Deferment Available? Yes
Non-fall Admissions? Yes

Non-fall Application Deadline(s): Rolling
Transfer Students Accepted? No
Need-Blind Admissions? No
Number of Applications Received: 162
% of Applicants Accepted: 90
% Accepted Who Enrolled: 80
Other Admissions Factors Considered: Essay, letters of recommendation, personal statement, resume, work experience, computer experience

INTERNATIONAL STUDENTS

TOEFL Required of International Students? Yes
Minimum TOEFL: 550

EMPLOYMENT INFORMATION

Placement Office Available? Yes
% Employed Within 3 Months: 95

NORTHEASTERN UNIVERSITY
Graduate School of Business Administration

Admissions Contact: Jennifer Kott, Manager, Full-Time MBA Programs
Address: 360 Huntington Avenue, Boston, MA 02115
Admissions Phone: 617-373-5992 • **Admissions Fax:** 617-373-8564
Admissions E-mail: gsba@neu.edu • **Web Address:** www.cba.neu.edu/gsba

The competitive MBA students at Northeastern in "intellectually exciting" Boston have many options. There is a part-time program, an Executive MBA, a two-year full-time MBA, an "excellent" High Technology MBA for technical professionals, and the fast-paced, popular, unique, and "challenging and rewarding" Cooperative Education MBA, which provides "invaluable," paid, MBA-level employment during part of the program. After graduation, most students go into finance or consulting.

INSTITUTIONAL INFORMATION

Public/Private: Private
Evening Classes Available? Yes
Total Faculty: 113
% Faculty Part Time: 13
Student/Faculty Ratio: 12:1
Students in Parent Institution: 24,501
Academic Calendar: Quarter

PROGRAMS

Degrees Offered: Cooperative MBA (21 months full time), Part-time MBA (30-84 months), EMBA (16 months), High Technology MBA (20 months), MS in Finance (12-21 months), MST (24-27 months), MSA
Combined Degrees: MSA/MBA, JD/MBA, MS/MBA in Nursing Administration
Academic Specialties: Finance, Accounting, Marketing, International Business, Enterpreneurship, Management Information Systems, Management, Production/Operations Management, Transportation, Supply Chain Management
Special Opportunities: EMBA Program, Cooperative MBA Program
Study Abroad Options: Eastern Europe, France, Southeast Asia

STUDENT INFORMATION

Total Business Students: 621
% Full Time: 37
% Female: 40

% Minority: 5
% International: 34
Average Age: 27

COMPUTER AND RESEARCH FACILITIES

Computer Facilities: Snell Library plus 4 additional libraries; 870,475 volumes; 2,057,538 microforms; 8,417 current periodicals. CD players available; access provided to online bibliographic retrieval services
Campuswide Network? Yes
% of MBA Classrooms Wired: 100
Internet Fee? No

EXPENSES/FINANCIAL AID

Annual Tuition: $28,670
Tuition Per Credit (Resident/Nonresident): $610
Books and Supplies: $950
Average Grant: $20,000
Average Loan: $13,000

ADMISSIONS INFORMATION

Application Fee: $50
Electronic Application? Yes
Regular Application Deadline: Rolling
Regular Notification: Rolling
Deferment Available? Yes
Length of Deferment: 1 year
Non-fall Admissions? Yes
Non-fall Application Deadline(s): Rolling
Transfer Students Accepted? Yes
Transfer Policy: Please visit website for transfer policy.
Need-Blind Admissions? Yes
Number of Applications Received: 298
% of Applicants Accepted: 44
% Accepted Who Enrolled: 51
Average GPA: 3.1
Average GMAT: 560
Average Years Experience: 4
Minority/Disadvantaged Student Recruitment Programs: Provost Minority Scholarship Program, Association of Latino Accounting & Finance Professionals' Scholarship

INTERNATIONAL STUDENTS

TOEFL Required of International Students? Yes
Minimum TOEFL: 600 (250 computer)

EMPLOYMENT INFORMATION

Placement Office Available? Yes
% Employed Within 3 Months: 57
Frequent Employers: EMC Corp., Fidelity, State Street Bank, W.R.Grace

NORTHERN ARIZONA UNIVERSITY
College of Business Administration

Admissions Contact: Joe Anderson, Director, MBA Program
Address: PO Box 15066, Flagstaff, AZ 86011-5066
Admissions Phone: 928-523-7342 • **Admissions Fax:** 928-523-7331
Admissions E-mail: MBA@nau.edu • **Web Address:** www.cba.nau.edu/mbaprogram

Flagstaff, home of Northern Arizona University, has a comfortable climate and an average of 288 sunny days each year, creating "excellent conditions for study and recreation." The MBA program has several different options: full time (10 months), half time (2 years), or quarter time (4 years). Frequent employers of NAU graduates are IBM, Motorola, Andersen, and Ernst & Young.

INSTITUTIONAL INFORMATION

Public/Private: Public
Evening Classes Available? No
Total Faculty: 54
% Faculty Part Time: 2
Student/Faculty Ratio: 22:1
Students in Parent Institution: 19,728

PROGRAMS

Degrees Offered: MBA (31 credits, full time or part time, 10 months to 4 years), with concentrations in Management Information Systems, Finance, Customs

STUDENT INFORMATION

Total Business Students: 68
% Full Time: 80
% Female: 33
% Minority: 5
% International: 26
Average Age: 25

COMPUTER AND RESEARCH FACILITIES

Research Facilities: Counseling and Testing Center
Computer Facilities: MBA Lab, Online Library, NAU Learning Assistance Centers
Campuswide Network? Yes
% of MBA Classrooms Wired: 100
Internet Fee? No

EXPENSES/FINANCIAL AID

Annual Tuition (Resident/Nonresident): $3,906/$13,268
Tuition Per Credit (Resident/Nonresident): $126/$428
Room & Board (On/Off Campus): $7,216
Books and Supplies: $1,115

ADMISSIONS INFORMATION

Application Fee: $45
Electronic Application? Yes
Regular Application Deadline: 3/1
Regular Notification: 4/1
Deferment Available? Yes
Length of Deferment: 1 year
Non-fall Admissions? Yes
Non-fall Application Deadline(s): 10/15 spring, 1/15 summer
Transfer Students Accepted? Yes
Transfer Policy: 9 hours toward electives only
Need-Blind Admissions? No
Number of Applications Received: 86
% of Applicants Accepted: 51
% Accepted Who Enrolled: 95
Average GPA: 3.4
Average GMAT: 540
Average Years Experience: 4
Other Admissions Factors Considered: Computer experience

INTERNATIONAL STUDENTS

TOEFL Required of International Students? Yes
Minimum TOEFL: 600 (250 computer)

EMPLOYMENT INFORMATION

Placement Office Available? Yes
% Employed Within 3 Months: 80
Frequent Employers: Arthur Andersen, Ernst and Young, IBM, Motorola

NORTHERN ILLINOIS UNIVERSITY
College of Business, Office of MBA Programs

Admissions Contact: Mona Salmon, Assistant Director
Address: Wirtz 140, Dekalb, IL 60115
Admissions Phone: 800-323-8714 • **Admissions Fax:** 815-753-3300
Admissions E-mail: cobgrads@niu.edu • **Web Address:** www.cob.niu.edu/grad/grad.html

Northern Illinois University offers two MBA programs: an Evening MBA curriculum, designed for part-time students, and an Executive MBA curriculum, offered on Saturdays and designed for mid-career working professionals. NSU has a professional, cooperative learning environment and a student body comprised of motivated part-time students—full-time professionals who wish to advance their education and gain more experience. The evening program offers study abroad options in Italy, China, and Korea as well as international business seminars that tour Europe.

INSTITUTIONAL INFORMATION

Public/Private: Public
Evening Classes Available? Yes
Total Faculty: 86
% Faculty Female: 19
% Faculty Minority: 4
Student/Faculty Ratio: 24:1
Students in Parent Institution: 23,248

PROGRAMS

Degrees Offered: AACSB-Accredited: MBA (30-48 hours, 10-18 courses), MAS (30-67 hours, 10-25 courses), MSMIS (30-51 hours, 10-20 courses). Not AACSB-Accredited: MST (30 hours, 10 courses)
Academic Specialties: Accounting, Finance, MIS, International Business
Special Opportunities: International Business Seminars in Europe, Business and Culture in China and Korea; offer short-term international experience for part-time students
Study Abroad Options: Shanghai University of Finance & Economics, China; Kyung Hee University, Seoul, Korea

STUDENT INFORMATION

Total Business Students: 528
% Full Time: 1
Average Age: 32

COMPUTER AND RESEARCH FACILITIES

Computer Facilities: Computer labs at each campus: Hoffman Estates, Naperville, Rockford
Campuswide Network? Yes
Computer Model Recommended: Desktop
Internet Fee? No

EXPENSES/FINANCIAL AID

Annual Tuition (Resident/Nonresident): $6,632/$8,972
Tuition Per Credit (Resident/Nonresident): $401

ADMISSIONS INFORMATION

Application Fee: $30
Electronic Application? No
Regular Application Deadline: 6/1
Regular Notification: Rolling
Deferment Available? Yes
Length of Deferment: 24 months
Non-fall Admissions? Yes
Non-fall Application Deadline(s): 11/1 spring, 4/1 summer; for international students: 5/1 fall, 10/1 spring

Transfer Students Accepted? Yes
Transfer Policy: A limit of 9 semester-hours are accepted for phase-two credit from AACSB-accredited schools only.
Need-Blind Admissions? Yes
Number of Applications Received: 262
% of Applicants Accepted: 97
% Accepted Who Enrolled: 70
Average GPA: 3.2
Average GMAT: 535
Average Years Experience: 9

INTERNATIONAL STUDENTS

TOEFL Required of International Students? Yes
Minimum TOEFL: 550 (213 computer)

EMPLOYMENT INFORMATION

Placement Office Available? No

NORTHERN KENTUCKY UNIVERSITY
College of Business

Admissions Contact: Nina Thomas, Assitant Dean/MBA Program Director
Address: PO Box 9, Highland Heights, KY 41099
Admissions Phone: 859-572-5165 • **Admissions Fax:** 859-572-6177
Admissions E-mail: mbusiness@nku.edu • **Web Address:** www.nku.edu/~mbusiness

INSTITUTIONAL INFORMATION

Public/Private: Public
Evening Classes Available? No
Total Faculty: 39
% Faculty Part Time: 8
Student/Faculty Ratio: 20:1
Students in Parent Institution: 11,799

PROGRAMS

Degrees Offered: MBA (21 months to 8 years), JD/MBA (minimum 2.8 years)

STUDENT INFORMATION

Total Business Students: 192
% Full Time: 7
Average Age: 34

COMPUTER AND RESEARCH FACILITIES

Campuswide Network? Yes
Internet Fee? No

EXPENSES/FINANCIAL AID

Annual Tuition (Resident/Nonresident): $2,600/$7,800

ADMISSIONS INFORMATION

Application Fee: $25
Electronic Application? No
Regular Application Deadline: 8/1
Regular Notification: Rolling
Deferment Available? Yes
Non-fall Admissions? Yes
Non-fall Application Deadline(s): 12/1, 5/1
Transfer Students Accepted? Yes
Transfer Policy: None
Need-Blind Admissions? No
Number of Applications Received: 61

% of Applicants Accepted: 79
% Accepted Who Enrolled: 71
Average Years Experience: 2

INTERNATIONAL STUDENTS

TOEFL Required of International Students? Yes
Minimum TOEFL: 550

EMPLOYMENT INFORMATION

Placement Office Available? Yes

NORTHWESTERN UNIVERSITY
Kellogg School of Management

Admissions Contact: Beth Flye, Director of Admissions and Financial Aid
Address: 2001 Sheridan Road, 2nd Floor, Evanston, IL 60208
Admissions Phone: 847-491-3308 • **Admissions Fax:** 847-491-4960
Admissions E-mail: MBAadmissions@kellogg.northwestern.edu
Web Address: www.kellogg.northwestern.edu

Northwestern University's Kellogg Graduate School of Management has a strong reputation in marketing and finance, and it offers many areas of professional specialization including health services, transportation, and real estate. The "very friendly and helpful" students here are "generally laid-back about life, but somewhat serious about school," and they rate Kellogg "great in every respect." Employment prospects for Kellogg grads are tremendous. More than 300 firms conduct more than 13,000 on-campus interviews annually.

INSTITUTIONAL INFORMATION

Public/Private: Private
Evening Classes Available? Yes
Total Faculty: 226
% Faculty Female: 17
% Faculty Minority: 18
% Faculty Part Time: 36
Student/Faculty Ratio: 10:1
Students in Parent Institution: 17,000
Academic Calendar: Quarter

PROGRAMS

Degrees Offered: PhD (4-plus years)
Combined Degrees: MBA/MD (medical school, 5 years), MBA/JD (law school, 3 years), MEM/MBA (engineering school, 2 years)
Academic Specialties: Entrepreneurship, Finance, General Management, Marketing and Strategy
Study Abroad Options: Exchange programs within the following countries: Australia, Chile, China, Denmark, France, Hong Kong, Israel, India, Italy, Japan, the Netherlands, Norway, Spain, Thailand, United Kingdom

STUDENT INFORMATION

Total Business Students: 2,320
% Full Time: 46
% Female: 31
% Minority: 19
% International: 33
Average Age: 28

COMPUTER AND RESEARCH FACILITIES

Computer Facilities: Visit N.U. homepage on the World Wide Web at www.northwestern.edu.

Campuswide Network? Yes
% of MBA Classrooms Wired: 100
Computer Model Recommended: Laptop
Internet Fee? No

EXPENSES/FINANCIAL AID

Annual Tuition: $32,040
Tuition Per Credit (Resident/Nonresident): $3,204
Books and Supplies: $12,726
Average Grant: $7,000
Average Loan: $30,000
% Receiving Financial Aid: 60

ADMISSIONS INFORMATION

Application Fee: $185
Electronic Application? Yes
Regular Application Deadline: 3/14
Regular Notification: 5/9
Deferment Available? Yes
Length of Deferment: Case by case
Non-fall Admissions? Yes
Non-fall Application Deadline(s): 3/15
Transfer Students Accepted? No
Need-Blind Admissions? Yes
Number of Applications Received: 6,719
% of Applicants Accepted: 13
% Accepted Who Enrolled: 63
Average GPA: 3.4
Average GMAT: 700
Average Years Experience: 5
Minority/Disadvantaged Student Recruitment Programs: Annual conference sponsored by the Black Management Association includes activities intended to recruit minorities. Admission minority recruitment counselor on staff

INTERNATIONAL STUDENTS

TOEFL Required of International Students? Yes

EMPLOYMENT INFORMATION

Placement Office Available? Yes
% Employed Within 3 Months: 88
Fields Employing Percentage of Grads: Other (9%), General Management (16%), Marketing (21%), Consulting (26%), Finance (28%)
Frequent Employers: A.T. Kearney; Bain and Co.; Banc of America Securities; Boston Consulting Group; Citigroup; Deloitte Consulting; Eli Lilly and Co.; GE Capital; Goldman, Sachs and Co.; J.P. Morgan Chase; Lehman Brothers; McKinsey and Co.; Merrill Lynch; Quaker Oats Co.; ZS Associates
Prominent Alumni: Betsey Holden, co-CEO, Kraft Foods Inc.; Philip Marineau, president and CEO, Levi Strauss; Christopher Galvin, chairman and CEO, Motorola

OAKLAND UNIVERSITY
School of Business Administration

Admissions Contact: Donna D. Free, Coordinator of Graduate Business Programs
Address: 432 Elliott Hall, Rochester, MI 48309-4493
Admissions Phone: 248-370-3287 • Admissions Fax: 248-370-4964
Admissions E-mail: gbp@oakland.edu • Web Address: www.sba.oakland.edu

The MBA program at Oakland University's School of Business and Administration emphasizes information technology and international business and has an almost all-male student body. The OU MBA curriculum is designed for undergraduate majors from any discipline. Internships with many major corporations are available, including DaimlerChrysler Corporation, which has a brand-new Tech Center close by.

INSTITUTIONAL INFORMATION

Public/Private: Public
Evening Classes Available? Yes
Total Faculty: 51
% Faculty Female: 16
% Faculty Minority: 5
Student/Faculty Ratio: 19:1
Students in Parent Institution: 16,059
Academic Calendar: Semester

PROGRAMS

Degrees Offered: MACC (2-6 years), MBA (2-6 years), MSITM (1-6 years), EMBA in Health Care (21 months to 6 years)
Academic Specialties: Case study, computer-aided instruction, computer analysis, group discussion, lecture, research, role playing, seminars by members of the business community, student presentations, study groups, team projects

STUDENT INFORMATION

Total Business Students: 523
% Full Time: 5
% Female: 2
% Out of State: 5
% International: 5
Average Age: 29

COMPUTER AND RESEARCH FACILITIES

Research Facilities: Alumni network, career counseling/planning, career fairs, career library, career placement, electronic job bank, job interviews arranged, resume referral to employers, resume preparation
Computer Facilities: Open computer lab with 40 PCs and 2 printers
Campuswide Network? Yes
Internet Fee? No

EXPENSES/FINANCIAL AID

Annual Tuition (Resident/Nonresident): $4,833/$9,144
Tuition Per Credit (Resident/Nonresident): $269/$508
Room & Board (On/Off Campus): $7,500
Books and Supplies: $800
Average Grant: $3,600

ADMISSIONS INFORMATION

Application Fee: $30
Electronic Application? Yes
Regular Application Deadline: 8/3
Regular Notification: Rolling
Deferment Available? Yes
Length of Deferment: 1 year
Non-fall Admissions? Yes
Non-fall Application Deadline(s): 4/3, 6/3, 12/3
Transfer Students Accepted? Yes
Transfer Policy: Up to 9 credits (grade of 3.0 or better)
Need-Blind Admissions? Yes
Number of Applications Received: 222
% of Applicants Accepted: 79
% Accepted Who Enrolled: 64
Average GPA: 3.2
Average GMAT: 546
Average Years Experience: 5
Other Admissions Factors Considered: Resume, minimum of 2 years of work experience
Other Schools to Which Students Applied: Wayne State University

INTERNATIONAL STUDENTS

TOEFL Required of International Students? Yes
Minimum TOEFL: 550 (213 computer)

EMPLOYMENT INFORMATION

Placement Office Available? Yes
% Employed Within 3 Months: 98
Frequent Employers: DaimlerChrysler, General Motors

OHIO STATE UNIVERSITY
Fisher College of Business

Admissions Contact: Associate Director, Graduate Programs Office
Address: 100 Gerlach Hall 2108 Neil Avenue, Columbus, OH 43210
Admissions Phone: 614-292-8511 • **Admissions Fax:** 614-292-9006
Admissions E-mail: cobgrd@osu.edu • **Web Address:** fisher.osu.edu

Students entering the MBA program at Ohio State's Fisher College of Business must complete a pre-enrollment review of accounting, economics, statistics, and computer literacy. It's a rigorous start to a tightly integrated and fairly exhaustive program that remains extremely challenging throughout the first-year core curriculum. Campus life is "fun," though, especially during football season, and "the campus is beautiful during spring and summer." Golf facilities are "fantastic" as well, and unmarried students report an active and satisfying social life.

INSTITUTIONAL INFORMATION

Public/Private: Public
Evening Classes Available? Yes
Total Faculty: 100
% Faculty Female: 16
% Faculty Minority: 16
Student/Faculty Ratio: 5:1
Students in Parent Institution: 54,989
Academic Calendar: Quarter

PROGRAMS

Degrees Offered: PhD in Business (4 years), PhD in Accounting and MIS (4 years), PhD in Labor and Human Resources (4 years), MACC (1 year), Master of Labor and Human Resources (5 Quarter)
Combined Degrees: MBA/JD, 4 years; MBA/MHA, 3 years; MBA/MD, 5 years
Academic Specialties: Accounting, Finance, Consulting, Human Resources, International Business, Logistics, MIS, Marketing, Operations, Real Estate
Special Opportunities: Business Solution Team, Student Investment Management, Executive Luncheon Series: Mentoring Program
Study Abroad Options: Chile, China, Germany, Italy, Mexico, South Korea

STUDENT INFORMATION

Total Business Students: 578
% Full Time: 50
% Female: 30
% Minority: 35
% Out of State: 39
% International: 32
Average Age: 30

COMPUTER AND RESEARCH FACILITIES

Research Facilities: Center for International Business & Research, Center for Real Estate Education & Research, Supply Chain Management Research Group
Computer Facilities: MBA classrooms allow access to college and university

networks through laptops. Computer labs in Gerlach and Mason include state-of-the-art hardware, software, and databases. The college has more than 3,000 computer ports.
Campuswide Network? Yes
% of MBA Classrooms Wired: 100
Internet Fee? No

EXPENSES/FINANCIAL AID

Annual Tuition (Resident/Nonresident): $12,531/$23,106
Tuition Per Credit (Resident/Nonresident): $447/$800
Room & Board (On/Off Campus): $9,528/$11,000
Books and Supplies: $1,500
Average Grant: $4,000
Average Loan: $9,000
% Receiving Financial Aid: 70
% Receiving Aid Their First Year: 35

ADMISSIONS INFORMATION

Application Fee: $30
Electronic Application? Yes
Early Decision Application Deadline: 1/15
Early Decision Notification: 2/28
Regular Application Deadline: 4/30
Regular Notification: 5/30
Deferment Available? Yes
Length of Deferment: 1 year
Non-fall Admissions? No
Transfer Students Accepted? No
Need-Blind Admissions? Yes
Number of Applications Received: 990
% of Applicants Accepted: 29
% Accepted Who Enrolled: 58
Average GPA: 3.3
GPA Range: 3.1-3.7
Average GMAT: 655
GMAT Range: 620-710
Average Years Experience: 5
Other Admissions Factors Considered: Caliber of undergraduate institution/major, quality of work experience, evidence of leadership and teamwork, recommendations, GPA, GMAT score, essay questions, communication skills
Minority/Disadvantaged Student Recruitment Programs: Graduate and Professional Schools Visitation Day, Graduate Enrichment Fellowship Program, Targeted Minority Recruitment Initiative, Minority Student Visitation Weekend
Other Schools to Which Students Applied: Case Western Reserve University, Indiana State University, Michigan State University-Detroit College of Law, Northwestern University, Purdue University, University of Michigan

INTERNATIONAL STUDENTS

TOEFL Required of International Students? Yes
Minimum TOEFL: 600 (250 computer)

EMPLOYMENT INFORMATION

Placement Office Available? Yes
% Employed Within 3 Months: 98
Fields Employing Percentage of Grads: Accounting (1%), General Management (2%), Human Resources (3%), MIS (12%), Finance (12%), Operations (13%), Consulting (19%), Marketing (21%)
Frequent Employers: Andersen Consulting, Bank One, Cinergy, Ford Motor Co., Hewlett Packard, IBM, John Deere, Kimberly Clark, Lexmark, National City Bank, Owens Corning, Procter and Gamble, The Scotts Co., 3M, Wells Fargo
Prominent Alumni: Leslie Wexner, chairman and CEO, The Limited, Inc.; Alan J. Patricof, chairman, Patricof & Co. Ventures, Inc.; Lionel Nowell, executive vice president and CFO, Pepsi Bottling; Ray Groves, chairman, Legg Mason Merchant Banking; Max Fisher, industrialist and philanthopist

OHIO UNIVERSITY
College of Business

Admissions Contact: Jan Ross, Assistant Director, Graduate Program
Address: 514 Copeland Hall, Athens, OH 45701
Admissions Phone: 740-593-4320 • Admissions Fax: 740-593-1388
Admissions E-mail: rossj@Ohio.edu • Web Address: www.cob.ohiou.edu/grad/

Ohio University offers a Full-Time MBA, an Executive MBA for busy working professionals, foreign MBAs, and the MBA Without Boundaries program (MBAWB), created for working professionals who wish to earn their master's degree through a combination of residential experiences and Internet-based learning. The traditional MBA requires an intensive 10-week prerequisite educational training for those without an undergrad degree in business.

INSTITUTIONAL INFORMATION

Public/Private: Public
Evening Classes Available? No
Total Faculty: 12
% Faculty Female: 10
% Faculty Minority: 10
Student/Faculty Ratio: 10:1
Students in Parent Institution: 19,000
Academic Calendar: Quarter

PROGRAMS

Degrees Offered: MBA (12 months)
Combined Degrees: MBA/MSpAd (24 months), MBA/MA in International Affairs (24 months)
Academic Specialties: Interactive, problem-based curriculum with 6-8 client-based experiences
Study Abroad Options: Brazil, China, Hungary, India, South Africa

STUDENT INFORMATION

Total Business Students: 105
% Full Time: 100
% Female: 45
% Minority: 7
% Out of State: 50
% International: 20
Average Age: 25

COMPUTER AND RESEARCH FACILITIES

Campuswide Network? Yes
% of MBA Classrooms Wired: 100
Computer Model Recommended: Laptop
Internet Fee? Yes

EXPENSES/FINANCIAL AID

Annual Tuition (Resident/Nonresident): $10,340/$19,150
Room & Board (On/Off Campus): $10,000
Books and Supplies: $4,700
Average Grant: $8,000
Average Loan: $15,000
% Receiving Financial Aid: 70
% Receiving Aid Their First Year: 70

ADMISSIONS INFORMATION

Application Fee: $30
Electronic Application? No
Regular Application Deadline: 3/1
Regular Notification: 4/1
Deferment Available? Yes

Length of Deferment: 1 year
Non-fall Admissions? No
Transfer Students Accepted? No
Need-Blind Admissions? Yes
Number of Applications Received: 264
% of Applicants Accepted: 64
% Accepted Who Enrolled: 63
GPA Range: 3.0-3.8
Average GMAT: 555
GMAT Range: 470-670
Average Years Experience: 2

INTERNATIONAL STUDENTS

TOEFL Required of International Students? Yes
Minimum TOEFL: 600 (250 computer)

EMPLOYMENT INFORMATION

Placement Office Available? Yes

OKLAHOMA STATE UNIVERSITY
College of Business Administration

Admissions Contact: Brooks Thomas, Assistant Director, MBA Program
Address: 102 Gundersen Hall, Stillwater, OK 74078-4011
Admissions Phone: 405-744-2951 • Admissions Fax: 405-744-7474
Admissions E-mail: mba-osu@okstate.edu • Web Address: mba.okstate.edu

The Oklahoma State University MBA program makes no assumptions about the previous business experience of its applicants, so students from any undergraduate discipline are encouraged to apply. Thanks to a generous donation from Dynegy and its CEO, Chuck Watson, MBA students can learn on a professional-quality trading floor with 36 workstations; this is the only one of its kind in Oklahoma and one of only a few nationally. OSU also offers a Certificate in International Studies as an addition to an MBA degree, as well as a part-time study option at the Tulsa campus.

INSTITUTIONAL INFORMATION

Public/Private: Public
Evening Classes Available? Yes
Total Faculty: 20
% Faculty Female: 15
% Faculty Minority: 5
Student/Faculty Ratio: 7:1
Students in Parent Institution: 21,750
Academic Calendar: Semester

PROGRAMS

Degrees Offered: MBA (49-55 credits, 2 years full time; 39-45 credits, 3-5 years part time), MSTM (33-35 credits, 12-18 months); MSA (24-32 credits, (1-5 years), MS in Economics (30-33 credits, 1-5 years), MSMIS (33-35 credits, 12-18 months), MSAIS (33-35 credits, 12-18 months)
Combined Degrees: MBA/MSTM (60 credits, 2 years)
Academic Specialties: Finance, MIS, Accounting, Marketing, E-Bbusiness, Telecommunications, Venture Management, International Business
Study Abroad Options: England, Canada, China, Italy, France, Mexico

STUDENT INFORMATION

Total Business Students: 386
% Full Time: 32
% Female: 34

% Minority: 6
% Out of State: 8
% International: 30
Average Age: 27

COMPUTER AND RESEARCH FACILITIES

Research Facilities: Dynegy Trading Floor, Center for Research on Information Technology Transfer
Computer Facilities: Computer labs, Dow Jones
Campuswide Network? Yes
% of MBA Classrooms Wired: 80
Computer Model Recommended: Laptop
Internet Fee? Yes

EXPENSES/FINANCIAL AID

Annual Tuition (Resident/Nonresident): $2,576/$5,752
Tuition Per Credit (Resident/Nonresident): $92/$205
Room & Board (On/Off Campus): $11,000/$12,500
Books and Supplies: $1,000
Average Grant: $1,000
Average Loan: $4,000
% Receiving Financial Aid: 40
% Receiving Aid Their First Year: 45

ADMISSIONS INFORMATION

Application Fee: $25
Electronic Application? Yes
Regular Application Deadline: 7/1
Regular Notification: Rolling
Deferment Available? Yes
Length of Deferment: 1 year
Non-fall Admissions? Yes
Non-fall Application Deadline(s): 11/1 spring; for international students, 8/1 spring
Transfer Students Accepted? Yes
Transfer Policy: Applicants must be a student in good standing at an AACSB-accredited university.
Need-Blind Admissions? Yes
Number of Applications Received: 170
% of Applicants Accepted: 69
% Accepted Who Enrolled: 47
Average GPA: 3.5
GPA Range: 2.6-4.0
Average GMAT: 602
GMAT Range: 500-720
Average Years Experience: 5
Other Admissions Factors Considered: Work experience, undergraduate institution, letters of recommendation
Minority/Disadvantaged Student Recruitment Programs: Minority scholarships
Other Schools to Which Students Applied: University of Arkansas—Fayetteville, University of Kansas, University of Oklahoma, University of Tulsa

INTERNATIONAL STUDENTS

TOEFL Required of International Students? Yes
Minimum TOEFL: 575

EMPLOYMENT INFORMATION

Placement Office Available? Yes
% Employed Within 3 Months: 85
Fields Employing Percentage of Grads: Entrepreneurship (2%), Human Resources (2%), Communications (3%), Consulting (3%), Other (4%), General Management (5%), MIS (7%), Marketing (8%), Accounting (13%), Finance (47%)
Frequent Employers: Accenture; American Airlines; Bank of Oklahoma; Bearing Point; Cargill; Dynegy; Eli Lilly; Ernst & Young; ExxonMobil; Federal Reserve Bank; Halliburton; Hilti; IBM; Koch Industries; Midfirst Bank;

Payless Shoe Source; Phillips Petroleum; Williams, Inc.; Samson
Prominent Alumni: Mike Holder, head golf coach, Oklahoma State University; Jim Alcock, controller, ExxonMobil; Bill Hobbs, senior vice president—energy marketing and trading, Williams; T. Boone Pickens, fonder, MESA Petroleum

OLD DOMINION UNIVERSITY
College of Business and Public Administration

Admissions Contact: Ms. Jean Turpin, MBA Program Manager
Address: Constant Hall 1026, Norfolk, VA 23529
Admissions Phone: 757-683-3585 • **Admissions Fax:** 757-683-5750
Admissions E-mail: mbainfo@odu.edu • **Web Address:** www.odu-cbpa.org

Old Dominion University offers its MBA students the chance to study year-round at any of four different locations in the greater Norfolk area, taking classes full time or part time. Currently, there are about 10 specializations within the MBA program, ranging from accounting to decision science to maritime and port management, and Old Dominion plans to add an e-commerce specialization in the near future.

INSTITUTIONAL INFORMATION

Public/Private: Public
Evening Classes Available? Yes
Total Faculty: 85
% Faculty Part Time: 6
Student/Faculty Ratio: 14:1
Students in Parent Institution: 20,500

PROGRAMS

Degrees Offered: MBA (48 credits), MSA (30 credits), MA in Economics (30 credits), MPA (39 credits), Master of Urban Studies (36 credits), PhD in Business (48 credits), PhD in Urban Studies
Academic Specialties: Finance, Marketing, International Business, Econometrics
Study Abroad Options: Belgium, China, Denmark, England, Korea, Philippines

STUDENT INFORMATION

Total Business Students: 373
% Full Time: 39
% Female: 55
% Minority: 13
% Out of State: 70
% International: 60
Average Age: 28

COMPUTER AND RESEARCH FACILITIES

Campuswide Network? Yes
% of MBA Classrooms Wired: 100
Internet Fee? No

EXPENSES/FINANCIAL AID

Annual Tuition (Resident/Nonresident): $3,700/$10,300
Tuition Per Credit (Resident/Nonresident): $216/$574
Room & Board (On/Off Campus): $5,232/
Books and Supplies: $1,000
Average Grant: $5,000

ADMISSIONS INFORMATION

Application Fee: $30

Electronic Application? No
Regular Application Deadline: 7/1
Regular Notification: Rolling
Deferment Available? Yes
Length of Deferment: 1 year
Non-fall Admissions? Yes
Non-fall Application Deadline(s): 4/1, 11/1, 7/1
Transfer Students Accepted? Yes
Transfer Policy: Credits accepted from AACSB-accredited schools only.
Need-Blind Admissions? Yes
Number of Applications Received: 255
% of Applicants Accepted: 71
% Accepted Who Enrolled: 69
Average GPA: 3.0
Average GMAT: 540
Average Years Experience: 6

INTERNATIONAL STUDENTS

TOEFL Required of International Students? Yes
Minimum TOEFL: 550 (550 computer)

EMPLOYMENT INFORMATION

Placement Office Available? Yes
% Employed Within 3 Months: 33

OREGON STATE UNIVERSITY
School of Business Administration

Admissions Contact: Fran Saveriano, MBA Program Coordinator
Address: 200 Bexell Hall, Corvallis, OR 97330
Admissions Phone: 541-737-6031 • Admissions Fax: 541-737-4890
Admissions E-mail: osumba@bus.orst.edu • Web Address: www.bus.orst.edu

OSU's MBA is an accelerated management program heavy on technology. It aims to enable students not only to recognize situations where advanced technology is appropriate but also to know "which technologies are viable in various business contexts." Although the program is ideal for those students with technical backgrounds wishing to boost their biz savoir faire, other students looking for an education in technology management will find that the "practical value-added content" of the program suits their needs as well. Hewlett-Packard, Nike, and Procter & Gamble are just a few of the major corporations that provide great internship opportunities for Oregon State MBA students.

INSTITUTIONAL INFORMATION

Public/Private: Public
Evening Classes Available? Yes
Total Faculty: 33
% Faculty Female: 15
% Faculty Minority: 24
% Faculty Part Time: 0
Student/Faculty Ratio: 3:1
Students in Parent Institution: 18,396
Academic Calendar: Quarter

PROGRAMS

Degrees Offered: MBA (45 credits, 3 terms)
Academic Specialties: Technology focus

STUDENT INFORMATION

Total Business Students: 81
% Full Time: 94

% Female: 3
% Minority: 1
% Out of State: 1
% International: 25
Average Age: 28

COMPUTER AND RESEARCH FACILITIES

Computer Facilities: College of Business and other colleges on campus
Campuswide Network? Yes
% of MBA Classrooms Wired: 100
Internet Fee? No

EXPENSES/FINANCIAL AID

Annual Tuition (Resident/Nonresident): $7,413/$12,465
Tuition Per Credit (Resident/Nonresident): $445/$633
Room & Board (On/Off Campus): $5,000
Books and Supplies: $3,763

ADMISSIONS INFORMATION

Application Fee: $50
Electronic Application? No
Regular Application Deadline: 3/1
Regular Notification: Rolling
Deferment Available? Yes
Non-fall Admissions? Yes
Non-fall Application Deadline(s): 50 days before term starts
Transfer Students Accepted? Yes
Transfer Policy: Up to 15 credits of approved coursework (AACSB-accredited)
Need-Blind Admissions? Yes
Number of Applications Received: 212
% of Applicants Accepted: 38
% Accepted Who Enrolled: 58
Average GPA: 3.3
GPA Range: 3.0-3.6
Average GMAT: 552
GMAT Range: 510-590
Average Years Experience: 3
Other Admissions Factors Considered: Resume, work experience, computer experience
Other Schools to Which Students Applied: Portland State University, University of Oregon

INTERNATIONAL STUDENTS

TOEFL Required of International Students? Yes
Minimum TOEFL: 575 (233 computer)

EMPLOYMENT INFORMATION

Placement Office Available? Yes
% Employed Within 3 Months: 95

PACE UNIVERSITY
Lubin School of Business

Admissions Contact: Joanne Broda, Director of Graduate Admission
Address: 1 Martine Avenue, White Plains, NY 10606-1909
Admissions Phone: 914-422-4283 • Admissions Fax: 914-422-4287
Admissions E-mail: grapwp@pace.edu • Web Address: www.pace.edu/lubin/lubmain.html

The Lubin School of Business, one of Pace's six schools, is located within a half hour of New York City, providing the "opportunity for all" that Pace's motto, "Opportunitas," promises. Alumni employed by leading corporations nearby know that graduates of the "practitioner-oriented" Lubin MBA program will be prepared for responsible management positions from the get-go. Established as an accounting school in 1906, the Lubin School of Business prepares its students for positions in a global economy at multiple NYC and Westchester County campus locations.

INSTITUTIONAL INFORMATION

Public/Private: Private
Evening Classes Available? No
Total Faculty: 126
% Faculty Female: 13
% Faculty Minority: 19
% Faculty Part Time: 25
Student/Faculty Ratio: 22:1
Students in Parent Institution: 13,461
Academic Calendar: Semester

PROGRAMS

Degrees Offered: MBA, MBA in Finance (1 year), MS, APC, DPS, EMBA
Combined Degrees: JD/MBA
Academic Specialties: Finance, Management, Manangement Science, Marketing, Tax. Finance majors have proximity to Wall Street.
Special Opportunities: Accounting, Behavioral Science/Organizational Behavior, CIS or MIS, Economics, Finance (includes Banking), Health Services/Hospital Administration, Human Resource Management (includes Labor Relations), International Business, Management, Marketing, Operations Research, Other, Strategic Management, Taxation
Study Abroad Options: China; ESC, Grenoble, France; Karl Rubrechts University, Heidelberg, Germany

STUDENT INFORMATION

Total Business Students: 1,473
% Full Time: 32
% Female: 48
% Minority: 18
% International: 47
Average Age: 29

COMPUTER AND RESEARCH FACILITIES

Research Facilities: Center for Global Finance
Campuswide Network? Yes
% of MBA Classrooms Wired: 10
Computer Model Recommended: Laptop
Internet Fee? No

EXPENSES/FINANCIAL AID

Annual Tuition: $23,508
Tuition Per Credit (Resident/Nonresident): $625
Books and Supplies: $540
Average Grant: $5,038
Average Loan: $12,663
% Receiving Financial Aid: 28
% Receiving Aid Their First Year: 35

ADMISSIONS INFORMATION

Application Fee: $60
Electronic Application? No
Regular Application Deadline: 8/1
Regular Notification: Rolling
Deferment Available? No
Non-fall Admissions? No
Transfer Students Accepted? No
Need-Blind Admissions? No
Number of Applications Received: 1,307
% of Applicants Accepted: 61
% Accepted Who Enrolled: 47

INTERNATIONAL STUDENTS

TOEFL Required of International Students? Yes
Minimum TOEFL: 550

EMPLOYMENT INFORMATION

Placement Office Available? Yes
% Employed Within 3 Months: 95

PACIFIC LUTHERAN UNIVERSITY
School of Business

Admissions Contact: Catherine Pratt, Associate Dean, School of Business
Address: Office of Admissions, Tacoma, WA 98447
Admissions Phone: 253-535-7151 • **Admissions Fax:** 253-536-5136
Admissions E-mail: business@plu.edu • **Web Address:** www.plu.edu/~busa/mba

INSTITUTIONAL INFORMATION

Public/Private: Private
Evening Classes Available? Yes
Total Faculty: 9
% Faculty Female: 33
% Faculty Minority: 11
% Faculty Part Time: 7
Student/Faculty Ratio: 15:1
Students in Parent Institution: 3,385
Academic Calendar: 4-1-4

PROGRAMS

Degrees Offered: MBA (2 years), MBA with emphasis in Technology/Innovation Management (2 years)
Academic Specialties: Technology/Innovation Management, International Business, Management, Finance/Accounting, Organization Development, Marketing

STUDENT INFORMATION

Total Business Students: 94
% Full Time: 57
% Female: 33
% Minority: 5
% Out of State: 21
% International: 16
Average Age: 29

COMPUTER AND RESEARCH FACILITIES

Research Facilities: E-commerce & Technology Management Center, with faculty interactions and graduate fellowships; see http://eplu.plu.edu
Computer Facilities: School of Business Lab, Library databases, General Student Computer Lab
Campuswide Network? Yes
% of MBA Classrooms Wired: 100
Internet Fee? No

EXPENSES/FINANCIAL AID

Annual Tuition: $13,872
Tuition Per Credit (Resident/Nonresident): $578
Room & Board (On/Off Campus): $5,780
Books and Supplies: $850
Average Grant: $1,604
Average Loan: $8,269

ADMISSIONS INFORMATION

Application Fee: $35
Electronic Application? No
Regular Application Deadline: Rolling
Regular Notification: Rolling
Deferment Available? Yes
Length of Deferment: 1 year
Non-fall Admissions? Yes
Non-fall Application Deadline(s): Spring, summer (rolling deadlines)
Transfer Students Accepted? Yes
Transfer Policy: Minimum of 24 semester hours in residence
Need-Blind Admissions? Yes
Number of Applications Received: 47
% of Applicants Accepted: 89
% Accepted Who Enrolled: 71
Average GPA: 3.3
GPA Range: 2.9-3.6
Average GMAT: 529
GMAT Range: 480-570
Average Years Experience: 8
Other Admissions Factors Considered: Applicants are evaluated individually based on a presentation of factors indicating equivalence to admission standards, a promise of success in graduate school, qualities of good character, and potential contributions to the education mission of the graduate program and university.
Minority/Disadvantaged Student Recruitment Programs: Graduate scholarships and assistantships are available by application from all students.
Other Schools to Which Students Applied: Seattle University, University of Washington, Seattle Pacific University

INTERNATIONAL STUDENTS

TOEFL Required of International Students? Yes
Minimum TOEFL: 550 (213 computer)

EMPLOYMENT INFORMATION

Placement Office Available? No

PENNSYLVANIA STATE UNIVERSITY IMBA

Admissions Contact: Dusty Hasselman, Program Specialist
Address: 207 Mitchell Building, University Park, PA 16802-3601
Admissions Phone: 814-898-6527 • **Admissions Fax:** 814-898-6528
Admissions E-mail: imba@psu.edu • **Web Address:** www.worldcampus.psu.edu/imba

Professors are "very accessible and willing to offer help"; team teaching and seven-week "blocks" keep things fast-paced and dynamic; and "everybody knows everybody" within the tiny, affordable confines of the MBA program at Penn State. Meanwhile, Smeal also provides "the resources of one of the largest universities in the nation." Students also laud the finance department and its "strong Wall Street alumni network," which is especially worth investigating "if you are interested in investment banking but don't want to pay $35,000 a year to get there."

INSTITUTIONAL INFORMATION

Public/Private: Public
Evening Classes Available? No

PROGRAMS

Degrees Offered: IMBA(2 years part time online)

Study Abroad Options: IMBA is online so students may complete program from anywhere in the world.

STUDENT INFORMATION

Total Business Students: 30
Average Age: 33

COMPUTER AND RESEARCH FACILITIES

Campuswide Network? Yes
Internet Fee? No

ADMISSIONS INFORMATION

Application Fee: $75
Electronic Application? Yes
Early Decision Application Deadline: 12/15
Early Decision Notification: 1/15
Regular Application Deadline: 5/15
Regular Notification: 6/1
Deferment Available? Yes
Length of Deferment: GMAT scores must be less than 5 years old.
Non-fall Admissions? No
Transfer Students Accepted? Yes
Transfer Policy: Maximun of 6 credits with content-consistent IMBA program.
Need-Blind Admissions? Yes
Average GPA: 3.1
Average GMAT: 602
Average Years Experience: 8

INTERNATIONAL STUDENTS

TOEFL Required of International Students? Yes
Minimum TOEFL: 600 (250 computer)

PENNSYLVANIA STATE UNIVERSITY
Smeal College of Business Administration

Admissions Contact: Ms. Michele (Mitch) Kirsch, Director, MBA Admissions
Address: 106 Business Administration Building, University Park, PA 16802-3000
Admissions Phone: 814-863-0474 • **Admissions Fax:** 814-863-8072
Admissions E-mail: msk11@psu.edu • **Web Address:** www.smeal.psu.edu/mba

Professors are "very accessible and willing to offer help"; team teaching and seven-week "blocks" keep things fast-paced and dynamic; and "everybody knows everybody" within the tiny, affordable confines of the MBA program at Penn State. Meanwhile, Smeal also provides "the resources of one of the largest universities in the nation." Students also laud the finance department and its "strong Wall Street alumni network," which is especially worth investigating "if you are interested in investment banking but don't want to pay $35,000 a year to get there."

INSTITUTIONAL INFORMATION

Public/Private: Public
Evening Classes Available? No
Total Faculty: 91
% Faculty Female: 20
% Faculty Minority: 19
Student/Faculty Ratio: 2:1
Students in Parent Institution: 41,445
Academic Calendar: 7-1-7 modules

PROGRAMS

Degrees Offered: MBA (21 months), MS in most disciplines (1-2 years), PhD (4 years)

Combined Degrees: BS/MBA (5 years), Quality and Manufacturing Management (3 years), MHA/MBA (3 years), JD/MBA (5 years), MBA/HRIM (2 years)

Academic Specialties: Corporate Financial Analysis and Planning, Corporate Innovation and Entrepreneurship, E-Business/Information Technology for Management, Investment Management and Portfolio Analysis, Product and Market Development, Supply Chain Management, Strategic Management and Consulting. Special strengths: Communications, Corporate Finance, Financial Statement Analysis, Strategic Leadership, Strategy Implementation and Organizational Change, Venture Capital

Special Opportunities: E.M. Lyon, France (1-month session) and ESC Reims, France (1-month session), but program takes place in China; Koblenz School of Corporate Management, Germany (1-month session)

Study Abroad Options: E.M. Lyon and ESC Reims, France; Koblenz School of Corporate Management, Germany

STUDENT INFORMATION

Total Business Students: 199
% Full Time: 100
% Female: 26
% Minority: 8
% Out of State: 50
% International: 36
Average Age: 28

COMPUTER AND RESEARCH FACILITIES

Research Facilities: Smeal College Trading Room, Center for Global Business Studies, Center for the Management of Technological and Organizational Change, Center for Research in Conflict and Negotiation, Center for Supply Chain Research, Center for the Study of Business and Public Issues, Institute for Real Estate Studies, Institute for the Study of Business Markets, Risk Management Research Center, eBusiness Research Center, Farrell Center for Entrepreneurship, Garber Venture Capital Center

Computer Facilities: ABI Inform, Bloomberg Financial, CCH-Tax Database, Compustat, Corporate Affiliations, CRSP, Data Stream, Dialog, Disclosure, Dissertation Abstracts, Dow Jones, Ebsco, EconLit, Economic Census, Economist Intelligence Unit, ExecuComp, First Search, FISCOnline, Hoover's Online, I/B/E/S, ISI Emerging Markets, Lexis-Nexis, Lexis-Nexis Academic Universe, Morningstar, Multex, Periodicals Abstracts Research, Philadelphia Options Exchange, ProQuest, Public Affairs Info Service, Simmons Study of Media & Markets, Sports Business Research Network, Standards & Poors, Stat-USA, TableBase, TAQ, Wharton Research Data Service, and Zacks University Analyst Watch

Campuswide Network? Yes
% of MBA Classrooms Wired: 100
Computer Model Recommended: Laptop
Internet Fee? No

EXPENSES/FINANCIAL AID

Annual Tuition (Resident/Nonresident): $10,304/$19,682
Room & Board (On/Off Campus): $6,230/$13,140
Books and Supplies: $1,500
Average Grant: $15,900
Average Loan: $14,779
% Receiving Financial Aid: 78
% Receiving Aid Their First Year: 72

ADMISSIONS INFORMATION

Application Fee: $60
Electronic Application? Yes
Early Decision Application Deadline: 12/1
Early Decision Notification: 2/1
Regular Application Deadline: 4/15
Regular Notification: 6/1
Deferment Available? Yes

Length of Deferment: 1 year
Non-fall Admissions? No
Transfer Students Accepted? No
Need-Blind Admissions? Yes
Number of Applications Received: 880
% of Applicants Accepted: 24
% Accepted Who Enrolled: 43
Average GPA: 3.4
GPA Range: 3.0-3.7
Average GMAT: 645
GMAT Range: 610-680
Average Years Experience: 5
Other Admissions Factors Considered: Demonstrated leadership, communication skills
Minority/Disadvantaged Student Recruitment Programs: Program awarding graduate assistantships (tuition waiver plus stipend) each year to incoming minority students
Other Schools to Which Students Applied: Purdue University, University of Illinois, University of Maryland—College Park, Indiana University, Michigan State University Detroit College of Law, Ohio State University

INTERNATIONAL STUDENTS

TOEFL Required of International Students? Yes
Minimum TOEFL: 600 (250 computer)

EMPLOYMENT INFORMATION

Placement Office Available? Yes
% Employed Within 3 Months: 86
Fields Employing Percentage of Grads: Other (2%), General Management (5%), Consulting (5%), Operations (16%), Marketing (28%), Finance (44%)
Frequent Employers: Air Products & Chemicals, Inc.; American Express; Apple Computer; Black & Decker Corp.; Fisher Scientific; Ford Motor Co.; ExxonMobil; General Electric Co.; The Hartford Financial; IBM; Johnson & Johnson; S.C. Johnson; PNC Financial Services; W.W. Grainger, Inc.
Prominent Alumni: Ian A. MacKinnon, managing director, corporate, Vanguard Group, Inc.; Lt. General William G. Pagonis, senior executive vice president of supply chain, Sears; J. David Rogers, chairman and CEO, JD Capital Management

PENNSYLVANIA STATE UNIVERSITY— ERIE, THE BEHREND COLLEGE
School of Business

Admissions Contact: Ann M. Burbules, Graduate Admissions Counselor
Address: 5091 Station Road, Erie, PA 16563
Admissions Phone: 814-898-6100 • **Admissions Fax:** 814-898-6044
Admissions E-mail: behrend.admissions@psu.edu • **Web Address:** www.pserie.psu.edu

Small classes on a small campus are emphasized at the recently-named Sam and Irene Black School of Business, where a $30 million Research and Economic Development Center is scheduled to house the MBA program in a couple of years. The MBA faculty at this Penn State satellite campus in northwestern Pennsylvania pride themselves on developing strong problem-solving skills in their students. The city of Erie has more than 280,000 residents, while Buffalo, Cleveland, and Pittsburgh, the closest big cities, are roughly two hours away.

INSTITUTIONAL INFORMATION

Public/Private: Public
Evening Classes Available? Yes

Total Faculty: 23
% Faculty Female: 26
% Faculty Minority: 26
Student/Faculty Ratio: 4:1
Students in Parent Institution: 3,500
Academic Calendar: Semester

PROGRAMS

Degrees Offered: MBA (48 credits, 18 months to 8 years)
Academic Specialties: Penn State—Erie has an exceptional faculty with PhDs from major research universities. They are actively conducting research in their fields, writing journal articles and books, and are also noted for their teaching. In addition, most of the faculty members have corporate management experience in various functions including information systems, marketing, entrepreneurship, human resources, international management, and project management in industries ranging from financial services to manufacturing to utilities. PSU—Erie is in the process of adding focus areas in international business, project management, leadership, finance, and marketing.

STUDENT INFORMATION

Total Business Students: 97
% Full Time: 11
% Female: 36
% Minority: 9
% International: 9
Average Age: 33

COMPUTER AND RESEARCH FACILITIES

Research Facilities: Knowledge Park, Economic Research Institute of Erie, Center for E-Commerce, Small Business Institute, Center for Organizational Research and Evaluation (CORE), Center for Corporate & Adult Learning, Pennsylvania Sea Grant
Computer Facilities: The General Electric Foundation Computer Center has 5 class-sized computer labs in the Hammermill Building. In addition, there are 2 satellite labs—one is located in the Library and the other is in the Nick Building. The labs are equipped with personal computers, which are connected to the Computer Center's local area network. These networked computers have access to the Internet and to a wide variety of application and instructional software packages. The computing facilities are available to faculty, staff, and students during regularly scheduled hours. The Behrend campus also has access to the University's resources: Information Technology Services and Penn State Computing Resources. Penn State students utilize the Library Information Access System.
Campuswide Network? Yes
Internet Fee? No

EXPENSES/FINANCIAL AID

Annual Tuition (Resident/Nonresident): $7,884/$14,976
Tuition Per Credit (Resident/Nonresident): $438/$832
Room & Board (On/Off Campus): $6,444
Books and Supplies: $584
Average Grant: $1,400
Average Loan: $8,723
% Receiving Financial Aid: 28
% Receiving Aid Their First Year: 3

ADMISSIONS INFORMATION

Application Fee: $45
Electronic Application? Yes
Regular Application Deadline: 8/3
Regular Notification: Rolling
Deferment Available? Yes
Length of Deferment: 2 years
Non-fall Admissions? Yes
Non-fall Application Deadline(s): 12/15 spring, 4/14 summer
Transfer Students Accepted? Yes
Transfer Policy: Up to 10 credits of relevant graduate work completed at any accredited institution may be applied toward the Penn State—Erie MBA.

Credits earned to complete a previous graduate degree may not be used to fulfill MBA degree requirements. Transferred graduate work must have been completed no more than 5 years before the student is fully admitted as a degree candidate at Penn State—Erie. Coursework must be of at least a B quality and appear on the graduate transcript of a regionally accredited institution. Pass/Fail grades are not transferable.

Need-Blind Admissions? No
Number of Applications Received: 34
% of Applicants Accepted: 79
% Accepted Who Enrolled: 85
Average GPA: 3.3
Average GMAT: 514
Average Years Experience: 11

INTERNATIONAL STUDENTS

TOEFL Required of International Students? Yes
Minimum TOEFL: 550 (213 computer)

EMPLOYMENT INFORMATION

Placement Office Available? Yes
% Employed Within 3 Months: 10
Fields Employing Percentage of Grads: Finance (12%), MIS (13%), Other (25%), Operations (25%)
Frequent Employers: Erie Insurance Group, General Electric Transportation Systems, Pennsylvania State University

---

PENNSYLVANIA STATE UNIVERSITY— HARRISBURG CAMPUS
School of Business Administration

Admissions Contact: Dr. Thomas Streveler, Director of Enrollment Services
Address: 777 West Harrisburg Pike, Middletown, PA 17057
Admissions Phone: 717-948-6250 • **Admissions Fax:** 717-948-6325
Admissions E-mail: hbgadmit@psu.edu • **Web Address:** www.hbg.psu.edu/sbus

Most of Penn State Harrisburg's MBA students reside in south central Pennsylvania and are part-time students. Courses are offered primarily in the evening to allow working professionals to maintain their careers. MBA applicants will need to prove their proficiency in mathematics, composition, and computer skills before they can write out the check for their education. Penn State Harrisburg has designed its MBA curriculum not only to satisfy the immediate educational needs of its students but also to promote lifelong learning.

INSTITUTIONAL INFORMATION

Public/Private: Public
Evening Classes Available? Yes
Total Faculty: 28
Student/Faculty Ratio: 12:1
Students in Parent Institution: 3,239
Academic Calendar: Semester

PROGRAMS

Degrees Offered: MBA (30 credits, 18 months to 6 years); MSIS (30 credits, 18 months to 6 years)

STUDENT INFORMATION

Total Business Students: 207
% Full Time: 12
% Female: 36

% Minority: 7
% Out of State: 5
% International: 5
Average Age: 27

COMPUTER AND RESEARCH FACILITIES

Campuswide Network? Yes
% of MBA Classrooms Wired: 100
Computer Model Recommended: Laptop
Internet Fee? No

EXPENSES/FINANCIAL AID

Annual Tuition (Resident/Nonresident): $9,264/$17,592
Books and Supplies: $4,170
Average Grant: $4,200
Average Loan: $6,873

ADMISSIONS INFORMATION

Application Fee: $50
Electronic Application? Yes
Regular Application Deadline: 7/18
Regular Notification: Rolling
Deferment Available? Yes
Length of Deferment: 3 years
Non-fall Admissions? Yes
Non-fall Application Deadline(s): 11/18, 4/18
Transfer Students Accepted? Yes
Transfer Policy: Maximum of 10 credits
Need-Blind Admissions? Yes
Number of Applications Received: 76
% of Applicants Accepted: 91
% Accepted Who Enrolled: 90
Average GPA: 3.0
Average GMAT: 520
Average Years Experience: 3
Other Admissions Factors Considered: Prior business experience

INTERNATIONAL STUDENTS

TOEFL Required of International Students? Yes
Minimum TOEFL: 550 (213 computer)

EMPLOYMENT INFORMATION

Placement Office Available? Yes
% Employed Within 3 Months: 100

PEPPERDINE UNIVERSITY
The Graziadio School of Business and Management

Admissions Contact: Darrell Eriksen, Director of Admissions
Address: 24255 Pacific Coast Highway, Malibu, CA 90263
Admissions Phone: 310-568-5535 • Admissions Fax: 310-568-5779
Admissions E-mail: gsbm@pepperdine.edu • Web Address: www.Bschool.pepperdine.edu

The "brilliant, eccentric," and eclectic students at Pepperdine's Graziadio School of Business love its "conservative curriculum" that stresses "practical knowledge." Students in the "very effective" Master in International Business program are especially happy (perhaps because they get to spend a year overseas). Stateside, Pepperdine offers a "wonderful alumni network" and a "very fast-paced" one-year program to students who qualify.

To top everything off, Pepperdine's paradise location in Malibu provides "one of the most beautiful settings in the world."

INSTITUTIONAL INFORMATION

Public/Private: Private
Evening Classes Available? Yes
Total Faculty: 176
% Faculty Female: 20
% Faculty Minority: 10
% Faculty Part Time: 56
Student/Faculty Ratio: 20:1
Students in Parent Institution: 7,637
Academic Calendar: Trimester

PROGRAMS

Degrees Offered: MBA (12-15 months full time; 6 trimesters, evening program; 2-year programs available), EMBA (5 trimesters), Presidential/Key EMBA (5 trimesters), MSOD (6 trimesters), MIB (5 trimesters)
Combined Degrees: JD/MBA (4 years), MBA/MPP (3 years)
Academic Specialties: Strategic Management (ranked among top executive programs in the United States), Organization Development (also ranked among top programs in the discipline), Marketing, Finance, Global/International Business, Technology
Special Opportunities: MBA concentrations in Finance, Marketing, Global Business, Technology; additional programs/options include: mentorship program; internships; non-profit consulting projects; business fluency in French, German, or Spanish; communication workshop; business strategy simulation; integration and application seminars.
Study Abroad Options: Europe: University of Antwerp (UFSIA), Belgium; ESC Marseille-Provence (ESCMP), ESC Montpellier, and ESC Rouen, France; IECS Strasbourg, Robert Schuman University, France; European Business School (EBS), Germany; University of Mannheim, Germany; TSM Business School, The Netherlands; IESE University of Navarra, Spain; The University of Birmingham, United Kingdom

Latin America: Escola de Administracao de Empressas de Sao Paulo da Fundacao Getulio Vargas (EAESP/FGV), Brazil; Universidad Adolfo Ibanez, Chile; Instituto Tecnologico y de Estudios Superiores de Monterrey (ITESM), Mexico

Asia: Fudan University, School of Management, China; Tsinghua University, School of Economics and Management, China; Hong Kong University of Science and Technology (HKUST), Hong Kong; Asian Institute of Management (AIM) Philippines; Assumption Univeristy Graduate School of Business (ABAC), Thailand

STUDENT INFORMATION

Total Business Students: 1,664
% Full Time: 12
% Female: 42
% Minority: 39
% International: 37
Average Age: 26

COMPUTER AND RESEARCH FACILITIES

Research Facilities: Teleconferencing unit for students to conduct video interviews with companies or organizations anywhere in the world
Computer Facilities: 6 computer facilities; research through more than 700 online journals and electronic databases, including Lexis-Nexis, Dow Jones Interactive, General Business File, Infotrac, ABI/Inform, etc. The Graziadio School has implemented an Intranet portal to provide an online community for students and faculty as well as staff and alumni. Students can collaborate with their student teams on classroom projects and have access to online research and other vital information.
Campuswide Network? Yes
% of MBA Classrooms Wired: 100
Computer Model Recommended: Laptop
Internet Fee? No

EXPENSES/FINANCIAL AID

Annual Tuition: $26,280
Tuition Per Credit (Resident/Nonresident): $890
Room & Board (On/Off Campus): $12,709
Books and Supplies: $1,000
Average Loan: $27,662
% Receiving Financial Aid: 43
% Receiving Aid Their First Year: 50

ADMISSIONS INFORMATION

Application Fee: $45
Electronic Application? Yes
Early Decision Application Deadline: 12/15
Early Decision Notification: 1/15
Regular Application Deadline: 5/1
Regular Notification: Rolling
Deferment Available? Yes
Length of Deferment: 1 year
Non-fall Admissions? No
Transfer Students Accepted? Yes
Transfer Policy: A maximum of 2 courses may be transferred, contingent upon approval of policy committee.
Need-Blind Admissions? Yes
Number of Applications Received: 462
% of Applicants Accepted: 56
% Accepted Who Enrolled: 43
Average GPA: 3.1
GPA Range: 2.7-3.4
Average GMAT: 640
GMAT Range: 580-665
Average Years Experience: 4
Other Admissions Factors Considered: Leadership qualities, professional portfolio, managerial experience, promotions. Full-time work experience is required for the 12- and 15-month MBA programs.

INTERNATIONAL STUDENTS

TOEFL Required of International Students? Yes
Minimum TOEFL: 550 (213 computer)

EMPLOYMENT INFORMATION

Placement Office Available? Yes
% Employed Within 3 Months: 78
Fields Employing Percentage of Grads: Other (12%), Operations (12%), Consulting (13%), MIS (19%), Marketing (19%), Finance (25%)
Frequent Employers: Allergan, Bank of America, Boeing, EMI Music Distribution, Ernst & Young, Infonet, Merrill Lynch, Oracle, Pacific Bell, Pricewaterhouse Coopers, Warner Bros.
Prominent Alumni: David Mount, chairman and CEO, WEA Inc.; Dirk Gates, chairman, president, and CEO, Xircom Inc.; James Q. Crowe, president and CEO, Level 3 Communications; Shirley Choi, CEO, Seapower Group

PITTSBURG STATE UNIVERSITY
Gladys A. Kelce College of Business

Admissions Contact: Marvene Darraugh, Administrative Officer–Graduate Studies
Address: 1701 South Broadway, Pittsburg, KS 66762-7540
Admissions Phone: 620-235-4222 • **Admissions Fax:** 620-235-4219
Admissions E-mail: grad@pittstate.edu • **Web Address:** www.pittstate.edu/kelce/

The Kelce College of Business in Pittsburg, Kansas, offers an affordable education and boasts sizable populations of women, minorities, and international students. An interesting aside: Pittsburg State University is the only college in the country with a gorilla as its mascot; in 1920, at the time of the mascot's inception, "gorilla" was a slang term for roughnecks.

INSTITUTIONAL INFORMATION

Public/Private: Public
Evening Classes Available? Yes
Total Faculty: 33
% Faculty Female: 15
% Faculty Minority: 10
Student/Faculty Ratio: 4:1
Students in Parent Institution: 6,300
Academic Calendar: Semester

PROGRAMS

Degrees Offered: MBA (34 semester hours, 1 year full time), with concentrations in General Administration, Accounting
Academic Specialties: Finance, Marketing, Management, Accounting, MIS, Economics
Special Opportunities: Accounting, General Business
Study Abroad Options: Australia, China, Finland, France, Korea, Paraguay, Russia

STUDENT INFORMATION

Total Business Students: 110
% Full Time: 80
% Female: 40
% Out of State: 53
% International: 53
Average Age: 25

COMPUTER AND RESEARCH FACILITIES

Research Facilities: Axes Library, with total holdings of 350,000 volumes; 624,000 microforms; 1,600 current periodical subscriptions. CD player(s) available
Computer Facilities: ABI Inform, Dialogue, Compact Disclosure, Accounting and Tax Index, Infotrac, Lexis-Nexis
Campuswide Network? Yes
% of MBA Classrooms Wired: 100
Internet Fee? No

EXPENSES/FINANCIAL AID

Annual Tuition (Resident/Nonresident): $2,922/$7,496
Tuition Per Credit (Resident/Nonresident): $124/$315
Room & Board (On/Off Campus): $4,570/$6,000
Books and Supplies: $1,200
Average Grant: $3,500
Average Loan: $8,500
% Receiving Financial Aid: 50
% Receiving Aid Their First Year: 25

ADMISSIONS INFORMATION

Electronic Application? No
Regular Application Deadline: 7/15
Regular Notification: 8/1

Deferment Available? Yes
Length of Deferment: 1 year
Non-fall Admissions? Yes
Non-fall Application Deadline(s): 12/15, 5/1
Transfer Students Accepted? Yes
Transfer Policy: Up to 9 semester hours may be transferred from another accredited program.
Need-Blind Admissions? Yes
Number of Applications Received: 250
% of Applicants Accepted: 78
% Accepted Who Enrolled: 57
Average GPA: 3.5
GPA Range: 2.7-4.0
Average GMAT: 510
GMAT Range: 400-710
Average Years Experience: 1

INTERNATIONAL STUDENTS

TOEFL Required of International Students? Yes
Minimum TOEFL: 550 (213 computer)

EMPLOYMENT INFORMATION

Placement Office Available? Yes
Fields Employing Percentage of Grads: MIS (15%), Marketing (17%), Accounting (30%), General Management (38%)
Frequent Employers: AllState, Cessna, Core-Mark, Deloitte & Touche, Hallmark, Kock\h, Payless Shoe Source, Pricewaterhouse Coopers, Sprint, Wal-mart
Prominent Alumni: Lee Scott, president and CEO Wal-mart; John Lampe, president and CEO, Firestone/Bridgestone; John Lowe, executive vice president, ConocoPhillips; Orvil Bicknell, CEO, NPC International; Richard Colliver, executive vice president, American Honda

PORTLAND STATE UNIVERSITY
School of Business Administration

Admissions Contact: Pam Mitchell, Graduate Programs Administrator
Address: 631 SW Harrison St, Portland, OR 97201
Admissions Phone: 503-725-3712 • **Admissions Fax:** 503-725-5740
Admissions E-mail: info@sba.pdx.edu • **Web Address:** www.sba.pdx.edu

MBA students at Portland State can choose from programs in innovation and technology, finance, and international business, as well as an online program, the eMBA, that parallels Portland's on-site education. The Master of International Management, focusing on the Pacific Rim markets, is also available. The support of the business community allows the School of Business Administration to combine "academic integrity with practical, hands-on experience," and the school strives to serve the community in return.

INSTITUTIONAL INFORMATION

Public/Private: Public
Evening Classes Available? Yes
Total Faculty: 35
% Faculty Female: 23
% Faculty Minority: 9
Student/Faculty Ratio: 35:1

PROGRAMS

Degrees Offered: MBA (2 years full time, 3 years part time/online), MSFA (5-6 Quarter), MIM (1 year full time, 2 years part time)
Academic Specialties: PSU's Online MBA Program was listed in *U.S. News and World Report*'s Top 25 List. PSU accounting students ranked 5th in the nation on the CPA exam in 1999.
Special Opportunities: There are 3 options offered in conjunction with the MBA program—Management of Innovation and Technology, Finance, International Business—as well as specialized studies in food industry.
Study Abroad Options: Denmark, France, Italy

STUDENT INFORMATION

Total Business Students: 363
% Full Time: 23
% Female: 44
% Minority: 13
% Out of State: 12
% International: 41
Average Age: 30

COMPUTER AND RESEARCH FACILITIES

Computer Facilities: On-campus, 30-station MBA computer lab for MBA students; databases: Compustat, Standard & Poors's Research Insight, all PSU Library databases (including Infotrac, Edgar, GlobalAccess, etc.)
Campuswide Network? Yes
Internet Fee? No

EXPENSES/FINANCIAL AID

Annual Tuition (Resident/Nonresident): $6,834/$11,613
Tuition Per Credit (Resident/Nonresident): $259
Room & Board (On/Off Campus): $14,268
Books and Supplies: $1,200

ADMISSIONS INFORMATION

Application Fee: $50
Electronic Application? Yes
Regular Application Deadline: 3/1
Regular Notification: 6/30
Deferment Available? No
Non-fall Admissions? No
Transfer Students Accepted? Yes
Transfer Policy: Maximum of 1/3 of the total number of PSU credits may transfer from an accredited university in the United States.
Need-Blind Admissions? No
Number of Applications Received: 340
% of Applicants Accepted: 39
% Accepted Who Enrolled: 88
Average GPA: 3.2
Average GMAT: 598
Average Years Experience: 6
Other Admissions Factors Considered: 2 years of business work experience preferred
Other Schools to Which Students Applied: Oregon State University, University of Oregon, University of Portland

INTERNATIONAL STUDENTS

TOEFL Required of International Students? Yes
Minimum TOEFL: 550 (213 computer)

EMPLOYMENT INFORMATION

Placement Office Available? No
% Employed Within 3 Months: 67
Fields Employing Percentage of Grads: Other (17%), Operations (33%), Marketing (50%)
Frequent Employers: Arthur Andersen, IBM (Sequent), Intel, Mentor Graphics, Nike
Tektronix, U.S. Bancorp, Wells Fargo, Xerox

PURDUE UNIVERSITY—CALUMET
School of Management

Admissions Contact: Paul McGrath, Coordinator, Graduate Management Programs
Address: Anderson Building, Room 356, 2200 169th Street, Hammond, IN 46323-2094
Admissions Phone: 219-989-2425 • **Admissions Fax:** 219-989-3158
Admissions E-mail: pmcgrat@calumet.purdue.edu
Web Address: www.calumet.purdue.edu

Located just 25 miles southeast of downtown Chicago, Purdue University Calumet's School of Management accommodates students with a variety of undergraduate backgrounds. The MBA program consists of three stages: foundation course work, the core program, and electives, and together they form a strong foundation of financial knowledge. Purdue's MBA program has a curriculum that fosters managerial growth in each of the functional areas and accommodates students from a multitude of undergraduate and professional backgrounds.

INSTITUTIONAL INFORMATION

Public/Private: Public
Evening Classes Available? No
Total Faculty: 52
% Faculty Part Time: 6
Students in Parent Institution: 23,676
Academic Calendar: Semester

PROGRAMS

Degrees Offered: MBA (31-52 credits, full time or part-time, up to 7 years), with concentrations in Accounting, Finance, Human Resources, Management Information Systems, Marketing, Real Estate; MSA (30-49 credits, full time or part time, up to 7 years), with concentrations in Accounting, Taxation; MSBA(30-49 credits, full time or part time, up to 7 years), with concentrations in Management Information Systems, Taxation

STUDENT INFORMATION

Total Business Students: 539
% Full Time: 24
% Female: 45
% Minority: 23
% International: 14
Average Age: 32

COMPUTER AND RESEARCH FACILITIES

Research Facilities: Total library holdings of 205,000 volumes; 1,361 current periodicals subscriptions. Access to online bibiliographic retrieval services
Campuswide Network? Yes
Internet Fee? No

EXPENSES/FINANCIAL AID

Tuition Per Credit (Resident/Nonresident): $128/$280

ADMISSIONS INFORMATION

Application Fee: $30
Electronic Application? No
Regular Application Deadline: 5/1
Regular Notification: 1/1
Deferment Available? Yes
Non-fall Admissions? Yes
Non-fall Application Deadline(s): 11/1 spring
Transfer Students Accepted? No
Need-Blind Admissions? No
Number of Applications Received: 296
% of Applicants Accepted: 60
% Accepted Who Enrolled: 61

Other Admissions Factors Considered: Computer experience is required: word processing, spreadsheet, database. A minimum GMAT score of 420 and GPA of 2.5 are required. A GRE score, personal statement, resume, and work experience are all recommended.

INTERNATIONAL STUDENTS

TOEFL Required of International Students? Yes
Minimum TOEFL: 550

EMPLOYMENT INFORMATION

Placement Office Available? No

PURDUE UNIVERSITY— WEST LAFAYETTE
Krannert Graduate School of Management

Admissions Contact: Ward Snearly, Director of Admissions
Address: KCTR 104, 425 W State Street, West Lafayette, IN 47907
Admissions Phone: 765-494-4365 • **Admissions Fax:** 765-494-9841
Admissions E-mail: krannert_ms@mgmt.purdue.edu
Web Address: www.mgmt.purdue.edu

The "state-of-the-art" Krannert Graduate School of Management offers its small "technically oriented, hardworking, focused" student body "an intense program leading to a great technology MBA" and arguably "the strongest" program "in the country when it comes to using computers for quantitative analysis." There is an intimate atmosphere here, which means you'll "know everyone," and few students anywhere graduate with more job offers on average than Krannert MBAs.

INSTITUTIONAL INFORMATION

Public/Private: Public
Evening Classes Available? No
Total Faculty: 106
% Faculty Female: 16
% Faculty Minority: 10
% Faculty Part Time: 9
Student/Faculty Ratio: 4:1
Students in Parent Institution: 38,208
Academic Calendar: Semester

PROGRAMS

Degrees Offered: MS in Industrial Administration (11 months), MS in Human Resource Management. (2 years), MBA (2 years), EMSM (2 years), PhD in Economics and Management
Academic Specialties: E-Business, Operations, Corporate Finance, Manufacturing and Technology Management, Marketing, Organizational Behavior and Human Resource Management, Strategic Management, Total Quality Management, Services Operations, Corporate Finance, Inforamtion Technology. All major functional areas represented. In addition, programs in Entrepreneurship and International Management are available. Especially strong in Operations/Manufacturing Management, Corporate Finance, and Applications of Information Technology, including E-Commerce.
Special Opportunities: Washington Campus Program, Plus Leadership Program, Management Volunteer Program, Burton Morgan Entrepreneruship Competition, Innovation Realization Lab, Dauch Center for the Management of Manufacturing Enterprises, SAP Alliance Program, Center for International Business Education and Research, Business Opportunity Program, Student Managed Investment Fund, MBA Enterprise Corps

Study Abroad Options: German International School of Management and Administration (GISMA), Hannover, Germany; ISC Paris and ESC-EAP, Paris, France

STUDENT INFORMATION

Total Business Students: 150
% Full Time: 100
% Female: 17
% Minority: 5
% Out of State: 73
% International: 39
Average Age: 28

COMPUTER AND RESEARCH FACILITIES

Research Facilities: Dauch Center for the Management of Manufacturing Enterprises, Center for International Business Economics Research and Education, Center for Research on Contracts and the Structure of Enterprises. Institute of Industrial Compulsiveness, SEAS, SAP Initiatives, Technology Transfer Initiative, Catalyst (an online system in which course registration, grades, class discussions, syllabi, directories, and calendars are available)
Computer Facilities: Agricola, ARTFL, ArticleFirst, Beilstein, Biological & Agricultural Index, Business Periodicals Index, Compendex, Current Contents, ERIC, GPO Index, Humanities Index, MathSci Index, MathSci Net, MedLine, Social Sciences Index, WorldCat, CRSP, Compustat, Berkeley Options database, First Call, Datastream, among others. There are hundreds available. We also support all PDA's.
Campuswide Network? Yes
% of MBA Classrooms Wired: 100
Computer Model Recommended: Laptop
Internet Fee? No

EXPENSES/FINANCIAL AID

Annual Tuition (Resident/Nonresident): $12,248/$23,032
Room & Board (On/Off Campus): $6,720
Books and Supplies: $1,900
Average Grant: $11,012
Average Loan: $11,000
% Receiving Financial Aid: 79

ADMISSIONS INFORMATION

Application Fee: $55
Electronic Application? Yes
Early Decision Application Deadline: 11/1
Early Decision Notification: 12/15
Regular Application Deadline: 5/15
Regular Notification: 6/15
Deferment Available? Yes
Length of Deferment: 2 years
Non-fall Admissions? No
Transfer Students Accepted? No
Need-Blind Admissions? Yes
Number of Applications Received: 1,378
% of Applicants Accepted: 100
% Accepted Who Enrolled: 11
Average GPA: 3.2
GPA Range: 3.1-3.4
Average GMAT: 642
GMAT Range: 610-680
Average Years Experience: 4
Minority/Disadvantaged Student Recruitment Programs: Business Opportunity Program
Other Schools to Which Students Applied: Indiana University, Ohio State University, University of Chicago, University of Michigan, University of North Carolina—Chapel Hill, University of Southern California, University of Texas—Austin

INTERNATIONAL STUDENTS

TOEFL Required of International Students? Yes
Minimum TOEFL: 575 (230 computer)

EMPLOYMENT INFORMATION

Placement Office Available? Yes
% Employed Within 3 Months: 78
Fields Employing Percentage of Grads: Other (5%), Human Resources (5%), Consulting (6%), MIS (6%), Operations (11%), General Management (14%), Marketing (14%), Finance (39%)
Frequent Employers: Air Products & Chemicals, Barclays Capital, Capital One Services, Convergys, Eli Lilly, General Electric, Guidant, IBM, Owens Corning, Procter & Gamble, United Technologies, Whirlpool
Prominent Alumni: Albert Nahmad, chairman and CEO, Watsco, Inc.; Joseph Forehand, managing partner and CEO, Accenture; Marshall Larsen, president and COO, Goodrich; Jerry Rawls, CEO, Finisar; Marjorie Magner, COO, Global Consumer Group, Citigroup

QUEEN'S UNIVERSITY
Queen's School of Business

Admissions Contact: Program Coordinator
Address: Goodes Hall, Queen's University, Kingston, ON K7L 3N6 Canada
Admissions Phone: 613-533-2302 • **Admissions Fax:** 613-533-6281
Admissions E-mail: admin@mbast.queensu.ca
Web Address: www.business.queensu.ca/mbast

An interesting program option at Queen's University is the MBA for Science and Technology, which prepares students for management positions in areas as wide-ranging as pharmaceutical industries and aerospace. Another option is the Queen's Executive MBA, which is earned in two years and can be taken in person in downtown Ottawa or via real-time interactive videoconference by executives in other major metropolitan areas throughout Canada.

INSTITUTIONAL INFORMATION

Public/Private: Public
Evening Classes Available? No
Total Faculty: 24
Student/Faculty Ratio: 3:1
Students in Parent Institution: 17,510
Academic Calendar: 12 month

PROGRAMS

Degrees Offered: MBA for Science and Technology (minimum of 12 months), EMBA (minimum of 2 years), NEMBA (minimum of 2 years)
Special Opportunities: Bachelor of Commerce (4 years, undergraduate degree)
Study Abroad Options: Australia, Belgium, Canada, Chile, China, Denmark, Finland, France, Germany, Japan, Mexico, Norway, Scotland, Singapore, Sweden, Switzerland, Taiwan

STUDENT INFORMATION

Total Business Students: 78
% Full Time: 100
% Female: 25
% Minority: 5
% International: 20
Average Age: 30

COMPUTER AND RESEARCH FACILITIES

Research Facilities: Queen's Centre for Enterprise Development, Queen's Centre for Knowledge-Based Enterprise, Queen's Executive Decision Centre, CGA Ontario International Business Research Centre
Campuswide Network? Yes
% of MBA Classrooms Wired: 100
Computer Model Recommended: Laptop
Internet Fee? No

EXPENSES/FINANCIAL AID

Annual Tuition (Resident/Nonresident): $48,000
Room & Board (On/Off Campus): $15,000
Average Loan: $48,000

ADMISSIONS INFORMATION

Application Fee: $100
Electronic Application? Yes
Regular Application Deadline: 1/31
Regular Notification: 12/22
Deferment Available? Yes
Length of Deferment: 1 year
Non-fall Admissions? Yes
Non-fall Application Deadline(s): May
Transfer Students Accepted? No
Need-Blind Admissions? Yes
Number of Applications Received: 297
% of Applicants Accepted: 27
% Accepted Who Enrolled: 75
Average GPA: 3.2
Average GMAT: 675
GMAT Range: 630-700
Average Years Experience: 6
Other Admissions Factors Considered: Demonstrated desire to participate in a challenging, team-based learning environment
Other Schools to Which Students Applied: University of Toronto, University of Western Ontario

INTERNATIONAL STUDENTS

TOEFL Required of International Students? Yes
Minimum TOEFL: 600 (250 computer)

EMPLOYMENT INFORMATION

Placement Office Available? Yes
% Employed Within 3 Months: 95
Frequent Employers: Accenture, AT Kearney, Bell Canada Enterprises, Deloitte Consulting, JDS Uniphase, Nortel Networks, Parke-Davis (New Jersey), PRTM (Boston)
Prominent Alumni: Mel Goodes, retired chair and CEO, Warner-Lambert Co.; Don Carty, chair, president, and CEO, AMR Corp. and American Airlines; Michael Ball, president, Allergan Inc.

RADFORD UNIVERSITY
College of Business and Economics

Admissions Contact: Dr. Duncan Herrington, Director, MBA Program
Address: MBA Office, Box 6956, Radford, VA 24142
Admissions Phone: 540-831-5258 • **Admissions Fax:** 540-831-6655
Admissions E-mail: rumba@radford.edu. • **Web Address:** www.radford.edu/~cobe-web/

INSTITUTIONAL INFORMATION

Public/Private: Public
Evening Classes Available? Yes
Total Faculty: 34
% Faculty Female: 25
% Faculty Minority: 10
Student/Faculty Ratio: 3:1
Students in Parent Institution: 8,368

PROGRAMS

Degrees Offered: MBA (12-24 months)

STUDENT INFORMATION

Total Business Students: 83
% Full Time: 20
% Female: 45
% Minority: 5
% International: 12
Average Age: 29

COMPUTER AND RESEARCH FACILITIES

Computer Facilities: McConnel Library with many Internet-accessible databases, dedicated computers in all off-campus facilities
Campuswide Network? Yes
% of MBA Classrooms Wired: 100
Internet Fee? No

EXPENSES/FINANCIAL AID

Annual Tuition (Resident/Nonresident): $3,600/$6,570
Books and Supplies: $600

ADMISSIONS INFORMATION

Application Fee: $40
Electronic Application? Yes
Regular Application Deadline: Rolling
Regular Notification: Rolling
Deferment Available? Yes
Length of Deferment: 1 year
Non-fall Admissions? Yes
Non-fall Application Deadline(s): 3/1 summer, fall; 10/1 spring
Transfer Students Accepted? Yes
Transfer Policy: Maximum of 6 credit hours
Need-Blind Admissions? Yes
Number of Applications Received: 75
% of Applicants Accepted: 60
% Accepted Who Enrolled: 51
Average GPA: 3.1
Average GMAT: 480
Other Schools to Which Students Applied: Virginia Polytechnic Institute and State University

INTERNATIONAL STUDENTS

TOEFL Required of International Students? Yes
Minimum TOEFL: 550 (230 computer)

EMPLOYMENT INFORMATION

Placement Office Available? No

RENSSELAER POLYTECHNIC INSTITUTE
Lally School of Management and Technology

Admissions Contact: Mr. Frank J. Mendelson, Director of MBA/MS Admissions
Address: 110 Eighth St. Pittsburgh Building, Troy, NY 12180-3590
Admissions Phone: 518-276-6586 • **Admissions Fax:** 518-276-2665
Admissions E-mail: lallymba@rpi.edu • **Web Address:** lallymba.mgmt.rpi.edu

Rensselaer's intimate Lally School of Management and Technology is not for technophobes or the fainthearted. Nearly everyone here has an extensive background in computers and engineering, and the "friendly but busy" students study like crazy. RPI boasts small classes, great computing facilities, and a lot of student/faculty interaction, and its "top-notch" professors "have a wealth of both academic and professional experience."

INSTITUTIONAL INFORMATION

Public/Private: Private
Evening Classes Available? Yes
Total Faculty: 68
% Faculty Female: 19
% Faculty Minority: 13
% Faculty Part Time: 7
Student/Faculty Ratio: 15:1
Students in Parent Institution: 9,145
Academic Calendar: Semester

PROGRAMS

Degrees Offered: MBA (2 years), MS (1 year), PhD (3-5 years)
Combined Degrees: MBA/MS (2.5 to 3 years), MBA/MS in Engineering (2.5 to 3 years), MBA/JD (3-4 years), MBA/MSIT (2.5 to 3 years)
Academic Specialties: Management and Technology; emphasis on innovation and entrepreneurship, with strengths in Value Creation (New Product Development & Management, Technological Entrepreneurship, Production & Operations Management), Systems (MIS, Manufacturing), Finance, and Environmental Management & Policy; customized management and technology concentrations available
Special Opportunities: International Exchange in 9 countries, EMBA

STUDENT INFORMATION

Total Business Students: 593
% Full Time: 13
% Female: 31
% Minority: 12
% Out of State: 75
% International: 31
Average Age: 29

COMPUTER AND RESEARCH FACILITIES

Research Facilities: The Lally School of Management and Technology is linked with the Design and Manufacturing Institute (searches out solutions to productivity problems), the Severino Center for Technological Enterpreneurship (provides focus for research in new ventures), the Radical Innovation Project, the Center for Services Research and Education Study of Financial Technology (focuses on financial engineering, the impact of information technology on financial markets, and entrepreneurial finance), the Office of Commercialization of Technology, and the Lighting Research Center. Other research areas include biotechnology and entrepreneurship, and nanotechnology.
Computer Facilities: The library systems allow access to collections, databases, and Internet resources from campus terminals, and the Rensslear Computing System, which permeates the campus with a coherent array of advanced workstations, a shared toolkit of applications for interactive learning and re-

search, and high-speed Internet connectivity. MBA project teams use state-of-the-art Information Technology Tools that include development tools, enterprise databases (Microsoft SQL server), IIS web servers, and Visual Intedev and MS Access to build hands-on technical solutions to real-world business problems. Many of the core courses use computing intensively. The Rensselaer Computing System (RCS) has more than 500 public IBM, Sun, and Silicon Graphic workstations and personal computers. *Yahoo! Internet Life* has consistently ranked Rensselaer as one of the top most wired campuses.
Campuswide Network? Yes
% of MBA Classrooms Wired: 100
Computer Model Recommended: Laptop
Internet Fee? No

EXPENSES/FINANCIAL AID

Annual Tuition: $27,700
Tuition Per Credit (Resident/Nonresident): $1,320
Room & Board (On/Off Campus): $9,000
Books and Supplies: $1,580

ADMISSIONS INFORMATION

Application Fee: $45
Electronic Application? Yes
Early Decision Application Deadline: 1/15 fall
Early Decision Notification: 2/15
Regular Application Deadline: Rolling
Regular Notification: Rolling
Deferment Available? Yes
Length of Deferment: 1 year
Non-fall Admissions? No
Transfer Students Accepted? Yes
Transfer Policy: Maximum of 6 credits
Need-Blind Admissions? Yes
Number of Applications Received: 186
% of Applicants Accepted: 73
% Accepted Who Enrolled: 90
Average GPA: 3.2
Average GMAT: 611
Average Years Experience: 4
Other Admissions Factors Considered: Quality work experiences; demonstrated desire to integrate business, management, and technology; a passion for innovation; an entrepreneurial spirit
Minority/Disadvantaged Student Recruitment Programs: Rensselaer Graduate Fellowship Program, Herman Family Fellowship for Women in Entrereneurship
Other Schools to Which Students Applied: Babson College, Boston University, Carnegie Mellon, Case Western Reserve University, Cornell University, Massachusetts Institute of Technology, University of Illinois—Chicago

INTERNATIONAL STUDENTS

TOEFL Required of International Students? Yes
Minimum TOEFL: 600 (250 computer)

EMPLOYMENT INFORMATION

Placement Office Available? Yes
% Employed Within 3 Months: 70
Fields Employing Percentage of Grads: Entrepreneurship (4%), MIS (4%), Finance (9%), Accounting (9%), General Management (14%), Other (18%), Operations (18%), Marketing (24%)
Frequent Employers: American Express, American Management Systems, Diversified Technologies, EMC Corp., Fusion Technologies, General Electric, IBM Corp., PriceWaterhouse Coopers, Parexel International, Quest Diagnostics, Rockwell Automation, Texas Instruments

See page 432.

RICE UNIVERSITY
Jesse H. Jones Graduate School of Management

Admissions Contact: Peter Veruki, Executive Director of Career Planning & Admissions
Address: 6100 Main Street , MS 531, Jones School Ste. 109, Houston, TX 77005-1892
Admissions Phone: 713-348-4918 • **Admissions Fax:** 713-348-6147
Admissions E-mail: ricemba@rice.edu • **Web Address:** www.jonesgsm.rice.edu

Thanks to an "excellent faculty" and a "challenging curriculum," Rice University's Jones School enjoys a well-deserved reputation as an excellent place to get an MBA, albeit one that draws students primarily from its immediate region. Rice's surprisingly tranquil and beautiful 300-acre campus is located in a residential section of Houston, and the "highly intelligent," "competitive" students call themselves "mostly very friendly, sociable, and fun."

INSTITUTIONAL INFORMATION

Public/Private: Private
Evening Classes Available? No
Total Faculty: 90
% Faculty Female: 19
% Faculty Minority: 11
Student/Faculty Ratio: 8:1
Students in Parent Institution: 4,367
Academic Calendar: Semester

PROGRAMS

Degrees Offered: MBA (21 months)
Combined Degrees: MBA/Master of Electrical Engineering (24 months), MBA/Master of Computer Science, MBA/Master of Chemical Engineering, MBA/Master of Civil Engineering, MBA/Master of Environmental Engineering, MBA/MS in Mechanical Engineering, MBA/Master of Engineering, MBA/ MD (with Baylor College of Medicine)(60 months)
Academic Specialties: Finance, Entrepreneurship (part of the core curriculum), Marketing. Action Learning Project: As part of the core curriculum, first-years are placed in companies to perform specific projects. Classes are broken into 5-and 10-week modules throughout the MBA program. The program emphasizes an intergrated curriculum with both leadership and communications skills development coordinated throughout as well.
Study Abroad Options: INCAE, Costa Rica

STUDENT INFORMATION

Total Business Students: 359
% Full Time: 100
% Female: 36
% Minority: 12
% Out of State: 23
% International: 24
Average Age: 28

COMPUTER AND RESEARCH FACILITIES

Research Facilities: Rice Alliance for Technology and Entrepreneurship, Center on Management Information Technology (COMIT)
Computer Facilities: Global Researcher, SEC/Worldscope, Business Dateline, Bloomberg, ABI/INFORM, Wall Street Journal, Infotrack EF, PAIS, Business ASAP, Lexis, Dow Jones News Retrieval, RDS, S & P Dialog, Compustat PC Plus, Market Guide, Morningstar (Mutual Funds & VS Stock Tools), Investext, Datastream, Bridge, Insite 2, Reference USA, Disclosure Co. Select, Global Access, FIS Co. Data Direct, Hoovers, Prompt, StatUSA, Statistical Universe, Kalorama, Valueline, Doing Business In...
Campuswide Network? Yes
% of MBA Classrooms Wired: 100
Computer Model Recommended: Laptop
Internet Fee? No

EXPENSES/FINANCIAL AID

Annual Tuition: $28,000
Room & Board (On/Off Campus): $9,500/$13,500
Books and Supplies: $1,240
Average Grant: $5,000
Average Loan: $18,500
% Receiving Financial Aid: 65
% Receiving Aid Their First Year: 65

ADMISSIONS INFORMATION

Application Fee: $100
Electronic Application? Yes
Early Decision Application Deadline: 10/3
Early Decision Notification: 11/3
Regular Application Deadline: 4/4
Regular Notification: 5/4
Deferment Available? Yes
Length of Deferment: 2 years
Non-fall Admissions? No
Transfer Students Accepted? No
Need-Blind Admissions? Yes
Number of Applications Received: 767
% of Applicants Accepted: 36
% Accepted Who Enrolled: 67
Average GPA: 3.3
GPA Range: 3.0-3.6
Average GMAT: 630
GMAT Range: 580-660
Average Years Experience: 5
Other Admissions Factors Considered: Leadership experience and team-based experiences; unique qualities that the candidate will contribute to the program
Minority/Disadvantaged Student Recruitment Programs: An independent organization, RICE-TMS, offers merit-based scholarships for underrepresented minority students completing an MBA at Rice.
Other Schools to Which Students Applied: University of Texas—Austin, Southern Methodist University, University of California—Los Angeles, Columbia University, Vanderbilt University, Harvard University, Northwestern University

INTERNATIONAL STUDENTS

TOEFL Required of International Students? Yes
Minimum TOEFL: 600 (250 computer)

EMPLOYMENT INFORMATION

Placement Office Available? Yes
% Employed Within 3 Months: 95
Fields Employing Percentage of Grads: Other (8%), General Management (9%), Consulting (10%), Marketing (11%), Finance (62%)
Frequent Employers: BP, Conoco Phillips, Credit Suisse First Boston, Deutsche Bank Alex. Brown, Duke Energy, Ernst & Young, Exxon Mobil Corp., J.P. Morgan Chase & Co., Merrill Lynch, Morgan Stanley, Kellogg's, Kraft, Pantellos, Shell Oil
Prominent Alumni: James S. Turley, chairman, Ernst & Young LLP, Worldwide; Abby Rodgers, vice president of innovation, Coca-Cola; Flint Brenton, vice president of E-Commerce, Compaq Computer Corp; Doug Foshee, chairman, president, and CEO, Nuevo Energy Co.; Caroline Caskey, founder and CEO, Identigene

See page 434.

RIDER UNIVERSITY
College of Business Administration

Admissions Contact: Christine Zelenak, Director, Graduate Admissions
Address: SC 237, 2083 Lawrenceville Road, Lawrenceville, NJ 08648-3099
Admissions Phone: 609-896-5033 • **Admissions Fax:** 609-895-5680
Admissions E-mail: grdsrv@rider.edu
Web Address: www.rider.edu/academic/ccs/gradbus/index.htm

The Rider University MBA program has a flexible curriculum, whereby students may choose to pursue a general program, a concentration in the basic functional business disciplines, or an interdisciplinary concentration; if none of these options seems suitable, students may mix courses to accommodate their specific needs and interests. Rider also boasts great computer facilities and small classes in the evenings and on weekends, taught by a faculty composed almost entirely of PhD-holding scholars and researchers. Rider's main campus in Lawrenceville, New Jersey, is conveniently located between New York and Philadelphia.

INSTITUTIONAL INFORMATION

Public/Private: Private
Evening Classes Available? Yes
Total Faculty: 27
% Faculty Female: 23
% Faculty Minority: 7
% Faculty Part Time: 23
Student/Faculty Ratio: 14:1
Students in Parent Institution: 5,469
Academic Calendar: Semester

PROGRAMS

Degrees Offered: MBA (30-51 semester hours), MACC (30-57 credit hours)
Combined Degrees: BS/BA/MBA (5 years), BS/BA/MACC (5 years)
Academic Specialties: Faculty: Accounting, Finance, Management; curriculum: Leadership, Interpersonal Skills

STUDENT INFORMATION

Total Business Students: 356
% Full Time: 14
% Female: 47
% Out of State: 7
% International: 12
Average Age: 26

COMPUTER AND RESEARCH FACILITIES

Computer Facilities: Labs, Bloomberg and full complement of major databases via library
Campuswide Network? Yes
% of MBA Classrooms Wired: 100
Internet Fee? No

EXPENSES/FINANCIAL AID

Annual Tuition: $9,360
Tuition Per Credit (Resident/Nonresident): $520
Room & Board (On/Off Campus): $8,830
Books and Supplies: $700
Average Grant: $6,122
Average Loan: $11,171
% Receiving Financial Aid: 21
% Receiving Aid Their First Year: 37

ADMISSIONS INFORMATION

Application Fee: $40
Electronic Application? No
Regular Application Deadline: 8/1
Regular Notification: 1/1
Deferment Available? Yes
Length of Deferment: 1 year
Non-fall Admissions? Yes
Non-fall Application Deadline(s): 12/1 spring, 5/1 summer
Transfer Students Accepted? Yes
Transfer Policy: Each case is evaluated individually. No more than 24 transferred credits against 51 required maximum; maximum of 6 credits against 30 in the advance portion
Need-Blind Admissions? Yes
Number of Applications Received: 147
% of Applicants Accepted: 71
% Accepted Who Enrolled: 71
Average GPA: 3.3
GPA Range: 3.1-3.7
Average GMAT: 495
GMAT Range: 440-590
Average Years Experience: 5
Other Admissions Factors Considered: Experience, as demonstrated via resume and interview, may positively affect admit/deny decision and potential waiver of requirements.
Other Schools to Which Students Applied: Drexel University, Fairleigh Dickinson University, La Salle University, Monmouth University, Rutgers/The State University of New Jersey, Rutgers/The State University of New Jersey—Camden, Seton Hall University

INTERNATIONAL STUDENTS

TOEFL Required of International Students? Yes
Minimum TOEFL: 585 (240 computer)

EMPLOYMENT INFORMATION

Placement Office Available? No
Frequent Employers: We are a part-time program focused on career advancement support of the already employed and successful.
Prominent Alumni: Dennis Longstreet, company group chairman, Johnson and Johnson; Robert Christie, president and CEO, Thomson Corp.; Bernard V. Vonderschmitt, chairman of the board, Xilinx, Inc.; Anne Sweigart, chair, president, and CEO, D & E Communications; Kenneth Burenga, former president and CEO, Dow Jones & Co.

ROCHESTER INSTITUTE OF TECHNOLOGY
College of Business

Admissions Contact: Nancy Woebkenberg, Marketing Manager
Address: 105 Lomb Memorial Drive, Rochester, NY 14623
Admissions Phone: 585-475-2229 • **Admissions Fax:** 585-475-5476
Admissions E-mail: gradinfo@rit.edu • **Web Address:** www.ritmba.com

RIT is a national leader in classroom technology, it has an MBA program in Prague to bolster students' global exposure, and RIT's philosophy of quality translates into treating its students "as partners and customers." Flexible part-time and full-time curricula are taught in classrooms of only about 25 heads and feature almost as many concentration options.

INSTITUTIONAL INFORMATION

Public/Private: Private
Evening Classes Available? Yes
Total Faculty: 39

% Faculty Female: 13
% Faculty Minority: 5
Student/Faculty Ratio: 9:1
Students in Parent Institution: 15,000
Academic Calendar: Quarter

PROGRAMS

Degrees Offered: MBA (6 Quarter), MS in Finance (4 Quarter), MSIB (4 Quarter), EMBA (2 years)
Study Abroad Options: U.S. Business School, Prague,Czech Republic

STUDENT INFORMATION

Total Business Students: 462
% Full Time: 39
% Female: 30
% Minority: 4
Average Age: 28

COMPUTER AND RESEARCH FACILITIES

Research Facilities: Center for International Business and Economic Growth, Technology Management Center
Computer Facilities: Wallace Library, extensive database
Campuswide Network? Yes
% of MBA Classrooms Wired: 100
Internet Fee? No

EXPENSES/FINANCIAL AID

Annual Tuition: $21,870
Tuition Per Credit (Resident/Nonresident): $613
Room & Board (On/Off Campus): $6,500
Books and Supplies: $1,500
Average Grant: $10,000
% Receiving Financial Aid: 26

ADMISSIONS INFORMATION

Application Fee: $50
Electronic Application? Yes
Regular Application Deadline: 8/1
Regular Notification: Rolling
Deferment Available? Yes
Length of Deferment: 1 year
Non-fall Admissions? Yes
Non-fall Application Deadline(s): 10/31, 1/31, 5/1
Transfer Students Accepted? Yes
Transfer Policy: Transfer up to 3 courses if relevant to program; grade of B or better
Need-Blind Admissions? Yes
Number of Applications Received: 363
% of Applicants Accepted: 79
% Accepted Who Enrolled: 35
Average GPA: 3.2
GPA Range: 3.0-3.7
Average GMAT: 576
GMAT Range: 530-630
Average Years Experience: 4

INTERNATIONAL STUDENTS

TOEFL Required of International Students? Yes
Minimum TOEFL: 580 (237 computer)

EMPLOYMENT INFORMATION

Placement Office Available? Yes
% Employed Within 3 Months: 67
Fields Employing Percentage of Grads: Other (6%), Operations (6%), MIS (6%)
Frequent Employers: Deloitte & Touche, LLP; Eastman Kodak Co.; IBM Corp.; Johnson & Johnson, Inc.; Pricewaterhouse Coopers, LLP; Xerox, Inc.

Prominent Alumni: Daniel Carp, chairman and CEO, Eastman Kodak Co.; Thomas Curley, president and publisher, USA Today

ROLLINS COLLEGE
Crummer Graduate School of Business

Admissions Contact: Craig Domeck, Director of Full-time MBA Programs
Address: 1000 Holt Ave. - 2722, Winter Park, FL 32789-4499
Admissions Phone: 407-646-2405 • **Admissions Fax:** 407-646-2522
Admissions E-mail: crummer@rollins.edu • **Web Address:** www.crummer.rollins.edu

Arguably Florida's most prestigious MBA program, the Crummer Graduate School of Business offers four MBA options: a one-year program, a two-year program, a part-time take-your-time program, and an Executive MBA program designed for business professionals with 10 or more years of experience. Rollins College is located on the shores of Lake Virginia in Winter Park, a lovely upscale suburb of Orlando, Florida.

INSTITUTIONAL INFORMATION

Public/Private: Private
Evening Classes Available? Yes
Total Faculty: 20
% Faculty Female: 5
% Faculty Minority: 10
Student/Faculty Ratio: 20:1
Students in Parent Institution: 2,500
Academic Calendar: Semester

PROGRAMS

Degrees Offered: EMBA (for middle to senior level executives; 20 months), Professional MBA (2.5 years evening part time), Accelerated MBA 11 months full time), Early Advantage MBA (program designed especially for younger students with little work experience; 20 months)
Academic Specialties: Our experienced faculty has developed an international reputation for teaching through a "hands-on" method of applying business concepts. Our most popular concentrations are electronic commerce, finance, and international business.
Special Opportunities: Global Business Consulting Projects, National Business Consulting Projects, Crummer SunTrust Portfolio, 10-hour service requirement to a not-for-profit organization
Study Abroad Options: Brazil; China; Croatia; Nottingham University, England; Vaxjo University, Sweden

STUDENT INFORMATION

Total Business Students: 416
% Full Time: 44
% Female: 35
% Minority: 10
% Out of State: 26
% International: 25
Average Age: 26

COMPUTER AND RESEARCH FACILITIES

Research Facilities: The College's Olin Library has a 24-hour computer lab for Internet research and study.
Computer Facilities: Olin Online Catalog; electronic databases: ProQuest Direct, Wilson Web, Academic Universe, DialogWeb, FIS Online, Hoover's Online, ValueLine, Stat-USA, Hispanic American Periodials Index, JSTOR, Orlando Sentinel via Newsbank, Westlaw
Campuswide Network? Yes

% of MBA Classrooms Wired: 100
Computer Model Recommended: Laptop
Internet Fee? No

EXPENSES/FINANCIAL AID

Annual Tuition: $23,400
Tuition Per Credit (Resident/Nonresident): $723
Room & Board (On/Off Campus): $14,520
Books and Supplies: $1,500
Average Grant: $12,000
Average Loan: $12,500
% Receiving Financial Aid: 50
% Receiving Aid Their First Year: 50

ADMISSIONS INFORMATION

Application Fee: $50
Electronic Application? Yes
Regular Application Deadline: Rolling
Regular Notification: Rolling
Deferment Available? Yes
Length of Deferment: 1 year
Non-fall Admissions? Yes
Non-fall Application Deadline(s): Spring, Professional MBA program; June,
Accelerated MBA program
Transfer Students Accepted? Yes
Transfer Policy: Up to 6 credits from an AACSB-accredited MBA program
Need-Blind Admissions? Yes
Number of Applications Received: 305
% of Applicants Accepted: 62
% Accepted Who Enrolled: 65
Average GPA: 3.2
GPA Range: 3.1-3.7
Average GMAT: 599
GMAT Range: 540-640
Average Years Experience: 3
Other Admissions Factors Considered: Admissions to the Crummer School
is selective and based on an evaluation of all application materials. This includes
previous academic records, test scores, recommendations, and evidence of
maturity and motivation.
Minority/Disadvantaged Student Recruitment Programs: Scholarships
and graduate assistantships
Other Schools to Which Students Applied: Florida State University, University of Queensland, Stetson University, University of Central Florida, University of Florida, University of Miami, University of South Florida

INTERNATIONAL STUDENTS

TOEFL Required of International Students? Yes

EMPLOYMENT INFORMATION

Placement Office Available? Yes
% Employed Within 3 Months: 80
Fields Employing Percentage of Grads: MIS (2%), Entrepreneurship
(3%), Operations (5%), Consulting (15%), General Management (16%), Marketing (24%), Finance (33%)
Frequent Employers: AT&T, Andersen Consulting, CIA, Citigroup, CNL
Group, Darden Restaurant Group, Dyntech, Federal Express, General Mills,
Harris Corp., Johnston & Johnston, Marriott International, Radiant, Seimens
Westinghouse, Tupperware, SunTrust Bank, Universal Studios, Walt Disney
Prominent Alumni: Al Weiss, president; Thomas Jones, senior vice president,
operations; Steve Grune, publisher; Charles Rice, president; F. Duane
Ackerman, president and CEO

RUTGERS/THE STATE UNIVERSITY OF NEW JERSEY
Rutgers Business School

Admissions Contact: Glenn S. Berman, Assistant Dean for Admissions
Address: 190 University Avenue, Newark, NJ 07102-1813
Admissions Phone: 973-353-1234 • Admissions Fax: 973-353-1592
Admissions E-mail: admit@business.rutgers.edu • Web Address: business.rutgers.edu

Rutgers Graduate School of Management has a large student body, a host of research centers catered to various business disciplines, and many options for MBA study, including a number of joint degrees. The MBA program is rigorous, especially for those students who need to compensate for deficiencies in calculus and/or statistics. MBA applicants are greatly discouraged from working during their first year of studies, but can expect a solid education in return for their diligence and academic labor.

INSTITUTIONAL INFORMATION

Public/Private: Public
Evening Classes Available? Yes
Total Faculty: 123
% Faculty Part Time: 14
Student/Faculty Ratio: 15:1
Students in Parent Institution: 50,000
Academic Calendar: Trimester

PROGRAMS

Degrees Offered: MBA in Management (60 credits, 15 months to 2 years);
MACC (30 credits, 10 months to 2.5 years), with concentrations in Governmental Accounting, Taxation; PhD in Management (72 credits, 2-6 years);
MBA in Professional Accounting (62 credits, 14 months); EMBA (20 months);
Master of Quantitative Finance (30 credits, 1 year)
Combined Degrees: MPH/MBA, MD/MBA, JD/MBA, MS/MBA in Biomedical Sciences

STUDENT INFORMATION

Total Business Students: 1,215
% Full Time: 17
% Female: 40
% Minority: 11
% International: 36
Average Age: 27

COMPUTER AND RESEARCH FACILITIES

Research Facilities: Center for Entrepreneurial Management; Center for
Governmental Accounting Education and Research; Center for Information
Management, Integration, and Connectivity; Center for Middle East/North Africa Business Studies; Center for Research in Regulated Industries; Center for
Supply Chain Management; Global Financial Market Center; Whitcomb Center
for Research in Financial Services; Rutgers Accounting Research Center; Technology Management Research Center; Rutgers Center for Operations Research;
University Ventures; Rutgers University Technical Assistance Program
Computer Facilities: Blackboard course management system provides such features as posted course materials and announcements, discussion boards, virtual chat
sessions with whiteboard functionality, e-mail functionality, a digital drop box for
students to submit assignments, and online assessments. Approximately 90 percent of
RBS courses use this system. Rutgers Business School has also deployed extensive
wireless networking infrastructure. The school has an instance of SAP R/3, through
its inclusion in the SAP University Alliance program. Global Financial Market Research Center (trading room) is a 40-seat smart classroom containing Wall Street data
feeds and financial research databases. RBS also manages a number of specialized
computing labs that offer more than 150 networked computers and 6 high-speed
networked printers, supplemented by additional systems and facilities available
through the Rutgers University Computing Services Department. This department

provides students with e-mail accounts, web space, a number of volume licensed software applications, and over 25 general-access computing labs.
Campuswide Network? Yes
Computer Model Recommended: Laptop
Internet Fee? No

EXPENSES/FINANCIAL AID
Annual Tuition (Resident/Nonresident): $11,382/$16,972
Tuition Per Credit (Resident/Nonresident): $471/$705
Books and Supplies: $3,000
Average Grant: $3,000
Average Loan: $8,604

ADMISSIONS INFORMATION
Application Fee: $50
Electronic Application? Yes
Regular Application Deadline: 6/1
Regular Notification: Rolling
Deferment Available? Yes
Length of Deferment: 1 year
Non-fall Admissions? Yes
Non-fall Application Deadline(s): 11/15 spring (part time only), 5/1 summer,5/1(MBA in Professional Accounting only)
Transfer Students Accepted? Yes
Transfer Policy: Students may transfer credits with a grade of B or better from an AACSB-accredited school.
Need-Blind Admissions? Yes
Number of Applications Received: 910
% of Applicants Accepted: 58
% Accepted Who Enrolled: 66
Average GPA: 3.2
Average GMAT: 591
Average Years Experience: 5
Other Admissions Factors Considered: Work experience is strongly recommended as it is a major factor in admissions decisions. Also considered are community activities and awards or honors.
Other Schools to Which Students Applied: Baruch College/City University of New York, Columbia University, Fordham University, New York University, Seton Hall University

INTERNATIONAL STUDENTS
TOEFL Required of International Students? Yes
Minimum TOEFL: 600 (250 computer)

EMPLOYMENT INFORMATION
Placement Office Available? Yes
% Employed Within 3 Months: 82
Fields Employing Percentage of Grads: Consulting (1%), Accounting (1%), Human Resources (3%), Marketing (16%), Finance (18%)
Frequent Employers: AT&T, Bear Stearns, Citigroup, Commerce Bank, Federal Reserve Bank of New York, Goldman Sachs, Health Products Research, Hoffman-La Roche, Johnson & Johnson, Kraft, Mass Mutual, Novartis, Organon, Prudential, Raytheon
Prominent Alumni: Tom Renyi, chairman and CEO, Bank of New York; Gary Cohen, president, Becton-Dickinson Medical; Irwin Lerner, CEO, Hoffmann-La Roche; John D. Finnegan, president and CEO, The Chubb Corp.

RUTGERS/THE STATE UNIVERSITY OF NEW JERSEY—CAMDEN
School of Business

Admissions Contact: Dr. Izzet Kenis, MBA Program Director
Address: MBA Program, 227 Penn Street, Camden, NJ 08102-1401
Admissions Phone: 856-225-6452 • **Admissions Fax:** 856-225-6231
Admissions E-mail: mba@camden-sbc.rutgers.edu • **Web Address:** camden-sbc.rutgers.edu/

The MBA curriculum asserts that its broad educational strategy provides students with comprehensive business knowledge as well as the critical thinking skills necessary to make it in today's evolving economy. Strategically located within minutes of Center City in the heart of Philadelphia, Rutgers offers the benefits of a small campus environment with big-city options. Concentrations are available in health care management and international business, and courses are also offered in Atlantic City.

INSTITUTIONAL INFORMATION
Public/Private: Public
Evening Classes Available? No
Total Faculty: 38
% Faculty Part Time: 16
Students in Parent Institution: 5,052
Academic Calendar: Semester

PROGRAMS
Degrees Offered: MBA (60 credits, 18 months to 2 years)
Combined Degrees: MBA/JD (108-120 credits, 3 to 5 years)

STUDENT INFORMATION
Total Business Students: 264
% Full Time: 15
% Female: 28
% Minority: 9
% International: 15
Average Age: 28

COMPUTER AND RESEARCH FACILITIES
Campuswide Network? Yes
Internet Fee? No

ADMISSIONS INFORMATION
Application Fee: $40
Electronic Application? No
Regular Application Deadline: Rolling
Regular Notification: Rolling
Deferment Available? No
Non-fall Admissions? No
Transfer Students Accepted? No
Need-Blind Admissions? No
Number of Applications Received: 158
% of Applicants Accepted: 85
% Accepted Who Enrolled: 62
Other Admissions Factors Considered: Work experience, computer experience

INTERNATIONAL STUDENTS
TOEFL Required of International Students? Yes
Minimum TOEFL: 550

EMPLOYMENT INFORMATION
Placement Office Available? Yes
% Employed Within 3 Months: 98

SAGINAW VALLEY STATE UNIVERSITY
College of Business and Management

Admissions Contact: Barbara Sageman, Director of Graduate Admissions
Address: 136 Wickes Hall, University Center, MI 48710
Admissions Phone: 989-964-6096 • **Admissions Fax:** 989-964-7497
Admissions E-mail: gradadm@svsu • **Web Address:** www.svsu.edu/gradadm/mba

Working professionals will appreciate the flexible scheduling at SVSU's College of Business and Management, offering the opportunity to take two classes in one evening and the potential to complete the 12-course program in two years or less. Small classes with an emphasis on international business, team building and student presentations prepare students to take on the global work force. Earning your MBA in Curtiss Hall's state-of-the-art classrooms doesn't have to break the bank, either; several private scholarships from the College of Business and Management as well as graduate assistantships and fellowships are available.

INSTITUTIONAL INFORMATION

Public/Private: Public
Evening Classes Available? Yes
Total Faculty: 14
% Faculty Female: 7
% Faculty Minority: 36
% Faculty Part Time: 0
Student/Faculty Ratio: 6:1
Students in Parent Institution: 9,189
Academic Calendar: Semester

STUDENT INFORMATION

Total Business Students: 101
% Full Time: 24
% Female: 33
% Minority: 13
% International: 42
Average Age: 30

COMPUTER AND RESEARCH FACILITIES

Campuswide Network? Yes
% of MBA Classrooms Wired: 100
Computer Model Recommended: No prefrence
Internet Fee? No

EXPENSES/FINANCIAL AID

Annual Tuition (Resident/Nonresident): $6,982/$13,263
Tuition Per Credit: $858
Room & Board (On Campus): $5,485
Books and Supplies: $1,500
% Receiving Financial Aid: 42
% Receiving Aid Their First Year: 50

ADMISSIONS INFORMATION

Application Fee: $25
Electronic Application? Yes
Deferment Available? Yes
Length of Deferment: 7 semesters
Non-fall Admissions? Yes
Transfer Students Accepted? Yes
Transfer Policy: 6 credits transfer
Need-Blind Admissions? Yes
Number of Applications Received: 41
% of Applicants Accepted: 83
% Accepted Who Enrolled: 71
Average GPA: 3.3
Average GMAT: 517

GMAT Range: 450-570
Average Years Experience: 6
Other Schools to Which Students Applied: Central Michigan University, Northwood University

INTERNATIONAL STUDENTS

TOEFL Required of International Students? Yes
Minimum TOEFL: 525 (197 computer)

EMPLOYMENT INFORMATION

Placement Office Available? Yes

ST. CLOUD STATE UNIVERSITY
Herberger College of Business

Admissions Contact: Graduate Studies Office, Graduate Admissions Manager
Address: 720 4th Ave. South, Business Building 116, St. Cloud, MN 56301-4498
Admissions Phone: 320-255-2113 • **Admissions Fax:** 320-654-3986
Admissions E-mail: grads@stcloudstate.edu • **Web Address:** cob.stcloudstate.edu

Located on the banks of the Mississippi River, St. Cloud State University is 131 years old and is Minnesota's second largest university. The MBA program at St. Cloud involves two phases: In the first, a set of foundation-type business courses must be completed, and in the second, students move on to advanced graduate course work. The MBA program has a broad-based curriculum that aims to educate students on all of the functional areas of business and teaches students how to quantify, analyze, interpret, and communicate effectively. If on-campus facilities are a major concern on your list of prospective b-school features, have a peek at the new $32.5 million high-tech James W. Miller Learning Resources Center.

INSTITUTIONAL INFORMATION

Public/Private: Public
Evening Classes Available? Yes
Total Faculty: 90
% Faculty Female: 20
% Faculty Part Time: 11
Student/Faculty Ratio: 20:1
Students in Parent Institution: 15,000
Academic Calendar: Semester

PROGRAMS

Degrees Offered: MBA (18 months to 5.3 years), with Accounting, Business Information Science, Economics, Finance, Insurance, International Business, Management, Marketing, Real Estate, Taxation
Academic Specialties: Case study, computer-aided instruction, group discussion, lecture, research, student presentations, team project.
Special Opportunities: Economics, Human Resource Management (includes Labor Relations), Taxation

STUDENT INFORMATION

Total Business Students: 98
% Full Time: 76
% Female: 26
% Minority: 35
% Out of State: 37
% International: 35

COMPUTER AND RESEARCH FACILITIES

Campuswide Network? Yes

% of MBA Classrooms Wired: 10
Internet Fee? No

EXPENSES/FINANCIAL AID

Annual Tuition (Resident/Nonresident): $8,815
Tuition Per Credit (Resident/Nonresident): $245
Books and Supplies: $500

ADMISSIONS INFORMATION

Application Fee: $20
Electronic Application? No
Early Decision Application Deadline: 4/15, 6/15
Early Decision Notification: 1/1
Regular Application Deadline: Rolling
Regular Notification: Rolling
Deferment Available? No
Non-fall Admissions? Yes
Non-fall Application Deadline(s): 4/15, 6/15
Transfer Students Accepted? No
Need-Blind Admissions? No
Number of Applications Received: 49
% of Applicants Accepted: 73
% Accepted Who Enrolled: 53
Average GPA: 3.2
GPA Range: 2.8-4.0
Average GMAT: 546
GMAT Range: 470-700
Other Admissions Factors Considered: Personal statement, recommendation letters
Minority/Disadvantaged Student Recruitment Programs: Recruiting events

INTERNATIONAL STUDENTS

TOEFL Required of International Students? Yes
Minimum TOEFL: 550 (213 computer)

EMPLOYMENT INFORMATION

Placement Office Available? No
% Employed Within 3 Months: 80
Frequent Employers: Andersen Consulting, Bankers Systems, Cargill, Federated Insurance, General Mills, IBM, Target

---

ST. JOHN'S UNIVERSITY
The Peter J. Tobin College of Business

Admissions Contact: Sheila Russell, Assistant Director of MBA Admissions
Address: 8000 Utopia Parkway, Jamaica, NY 11439
Admissions Phone: 718-990-1345 • **Admissions Fax:** 718-990-5242
Admissions E-mail: mbaadmissions@st.johns.edu
Web Address: www.tobincollege.stjohns.edu

A private Catholic university, St. John's provides several New York campuses—historic Queens, the financial district of Manhattan, eastern Long Island, and Staten Island. In addition to these campuses, students wishing to pursue an MBA in international finance and marketing have the option of doing so in Rome. The Peter J. Tobin College of Business Administration is proud of the progressive technology found in its classrooms and research centers. The Financial Services Institute, with its courses, seminars, conferences, and publications, aims to prepare students for careers in the global financial industry after graduation.

INSTITUTIONAL INFORMATION

Public/Private: Private
Evening Classes Available? Yes
Total Faculty: 101
% Faculty Female: 18
% Faculty Minority: 10
% Faculty Part Time: 15
Student/Faculty Ratio: 9:1
Students in Parent Institution: 18,621
Academic Calendar: Semester

PROGRAMS

Degrees Offered: MBA (1-2 years), with concentrations in Accounting, CIS for Managers, Decision Sciences, Executive Management, Financial Services, International Business, International Finance, Marketing Management, Taxation, Risk Management, Risk Financing, Insurance Management; MS in Forecasting and Planning (33-60 credits); MST (33-60 credits); MSA (33-60 credits)
Combined Degrees: JD/MBA (4 years, full-time enrollment required)
Academic Specialties: Our curriculum is focused on development of managers who are well prepared for the many challenges of business in a globally focused environment. The core of our mission is to provide students with an excellent grounding in business and leadership while emphasizing our core values of integrity, commitment, and ethical behavior.
Study Abroad Options: Rio de Janeiro, Brazil; Rome, Italy; London, United Kingdom;

STUDENT INFORMATION

Total Business Students: 672
% Full Time: 25
% Female: 37
% Minority: 15
% Out of State: 40
% International: 40
Average Age: 26

COMPUTER AND RESEARCH FACILITIES

Research Facilities: The Main Library of the University is in St. Augustine's Hall, located on the Queens Campus, which hosts a "Graduate Commons" specifically dedicated to our graduate population. Together with the collections of the Loretto Memorial Library on the Staten Island Campus, the Law School Library, the Oakdale Campus Library, and the Rome Campus Library, the total University Libraries collections number 1.7 million volumes and include more than 6,000 periodic subscriptions. These materials support course offerings as well as student cultural and recreational interests. Collections include government documents and audiovisual materials. There is also an extensive collection of indexes, abstracts, and full text databases.
Computer Facilities: Students have access to four newly upgraded microcomputer laboratories, over 100 multimedia classrooms, microcomputer classrooms, library patron computers, and a newly added cyber lounge for resident students. Deployment of desktop computers to these facilities now total more than 825 Intel-based workstations and more than 125 high-end Macintosh computers. A variety of educational, business, statistical, and other electronic information resources are accessible through the campus's high-speed 310Mbps ATM backbone with 100Mbps switched Ethernet to each desktop computer. Internet connectivity is provided through a fractional T3 @ 3MB link to NYSERNET, and remote 56K dial-in access.
Campuswide Network? Yes
% of MBA Classrooms Wired: 85
Computer Model Recommended: Laptop
Internet Fee? No

EXPENSES/FINANCIAL AID

Annual Tuition: $15,120
Tuition Per Credit (Resident/Nonresident): $630
Room & Board (On/Off Campus): $12,000/$15,000
Books and Supplies: $3,000
Average Grant: $1,812

Average Loan: $6,937
% Receiving Financial Aid: 55
% Receiving Aid Their First Year: 47

ADMISSIONS INFORMATION

Application Fee: $40
Electronic Application? Yes
Regular Application Deadline: 5/1
Regular Notification: Rolling
Deferment Available? Yes
Length of Deferment: 1 year
Non-fall Admissions? Yes
Non-fall Application Deadline(s): 3/1 spring, 5/1 summer
Transfer Students Accepted? Yes
Transfer Policy: Must use regular application; individual review of transfer credits
Need-Blind Admissions? Yes
Number of Applications Received: 565
% of Applicants Accepted: 62
% Accepted Who Enrolled: 43
Average GPA: 3.0
GPA Range: 2.7-3.6
Average GMAT: 515
GMAT Range: 440-630
Average Years Experience: 4
Other Admissions Factors Considered: Work experience, leadership in extracurricular or community activities
Other Schools to Which Students Applied: Fordham University, Hofstra University, New York University

INTERNATIONAL STUDENTS

TOEFL Required of International Students? Yes
Minimum TOEFL: 550

EMPLOYMENT INFORMATION

Placement Office Available? Yes
% Employed Within 3 Months: 89
Frequent Employers: Accenture, American Express, Citi Group, City of New York, JP Morgan Chase, Merrill Lynch, Revlon

See page 436.

SAINT JOSEPH'S UNIVERSITY
The Erivan K. Haub School of Business

Admissions Contact: Susan Kassab, Director
Address: 5600 City Avenue, Philadelphia, PA 19131
Admissions Phone: 610-660-1101 • Admissions Fax: 610-660-1224
Admissions E-mail: gradstaff@sju.edu • Web Address: www.sju.edu

The Erivan K. Haub School of Business is a nationally recognized private Jesuit university in Philadelphia that promises to teach the ideals and philosophies of Jesuit education. The MBA program is a part-time program designed for working professionals and guarantees faculty concerned with each individual student. Other MBAs offered are two different Executive MBAs (one is a two-year program, and the other is completed in only one year) and the industry-specific Pharmaceutical Marketing MBA. More than 40 percent of graduates have a starting salary higher than $65,000 per year.

INSTITUTIONAL INFORMATION

Public/Private: Private

Evening Classes Available? Yes
Total Faculty: 80
% Faculty Female: 20
% Faculty Minority: 10
% Faculty Part Time: 20
Student/Faculty Ratio: 20:1
Students in Parent Institution: 3,550

PROGRAMS

Degrees Offered: Professional MBA, MSFS, MS in Human Resource Management, EMBA (21 month), EMBA (1 year), MS in International Marketing, Executive Pharmaceutical Marketing MBA, Executive Online Pharmaceutical Marketing MBA
Combined Degrees: DO/MBA with Philadelphia College of Osteopathic Medicine

STUDENT INFORMATION

Total Business Students: 552
% Full Time: 10
% Female: 40
Average Age: 29

COMPUTER AND RESEARCH FACILITIES

Research Facilities: Francis A. Drexel Library, Campbell Collection in Food Marketing
Computer Facilities: ABI/Inform Global, Business Source Elite, EconLit, FirstSearch, FISonline, Hoover's Online, Lexis-Nexis Academic Universe, NetLibrary (e-books collection), New York Times, Political Risk Yearbook, Polling the Nations (survey database), The Red Books Online, Stat-USA, TableBase, Wall Street Journal
Campuswide Network? Yes
% of MBA Classrooms Wired: 67
Internet Fee? No

EXPENSES/FINANCIAL AID

Annual Tuition: $10,260
Tuition Per Credit (Resident/Nonresident): $570
Books and Supplies: $800
Average Loan: $7,200
% Receiving Financial Aid: 12

ADMISSIONS INFORMATION

Application Fee: $35
Electronic Application? No
Regular Application Deadline: Rolling
Regular Notification: Rolling
Deferment Available? No
Non-fall Admissions? Yes
Non-fall Application Deadline(s): 4/1 summer I, 5/1 summer II, 11/15 spring
Transfer Students Accepted? Yes
Transfer Policy: Applicants must provide a completed application, including original test scores.
Need-Blind Admissions? Yes
Number of Applications Received: 267
% of Applicants Accepted: 70
% Accepted Who Enrolled: 51
Average GPA: 3.3
Average GMAT: 520
Average Years Experience: 4
Other Schools to Which Students Applied: La Salle University, Pennsylvania State University—Great Valley Campus, Temple University, Villanova University

INTERNATIONAL STUDENTS

TOEFL Required of International Students? Yes
Minimum TOEFL: 550 (213 computer)

EMPLOYMENT INFORMATION

Placement Office Available? No

SAINT LOUIS UNIVERSITY
John Cook School of Business

Admissions Contact: Janell Kiel Nelson, Manager of Admissions and Recruitment
Address: 3674 Lindell Blvd., St. Louis, MO 63108
Admissions Phone: 314-977-2013 • **Admissions Fax:** 314-977-1416
Admissions E-mail: mba@slu.edu • **Web Address:** mba.slu.edu

Located just west of downtown St. Louis, the John Cook School of Business offers a private, Jesuit-centered business education that is well worth the investment. To top that off, SLU provides nearly half of its students with financial assistance. The MBA curriculum allows the student to choose from many concentrations, including less common areas such as decision sciences and industrial/labor relations and the more standard management information systems.

INSTITUTIONAL INFORMATION

Public/Private: Private
Evening Classes Available? Yes
Total Faculty: 60
% Faculty Female: 15
% Faculty Minority: 2
Student/Faculty Ratio: 22:1
Students in Parent Institution: 11,274
Academic Calendar: Semester

PROGRAMS

Degrees Offered: MBA (2 years full time), with areas of emphasis in Accounting, E-Commerce, Operations and Supply Chain Management, Entrepreneurial Studies, Economics, Finance, International Business, Management, Management Information Systems, Marketing; Professional Evening MBA (2-5 years part time); MSF (18 months to 5 years); MACC (1-5 years); EMIB (2 years)
Combined Degrees: JD/MBA (3.5 to 4 years), MHA/MBA (3 years), MD/MBA (5 years)
Academic Specialties: Case study, computer-aided instruction, experiential learning, field projects, group discussion, lecture, research, simulations, student presentations, study groups, team projects, capstone consulting projects
Study Abroad Options: Hong Kong, China; Madrid, Spain

STUDENT INFORMATION

Total Business Students: 271
% Full Time: 20
% Female: 32
% Minority: 7
% International: 28
Average Age: 26

COMPUTER AND RESEARCH FACILITIES

Research Facilities: Boeing Institure of International Business, Firstar Women's Leadership Suite, Emerson Center for Business Ethics, Jefferson Smurfit Center for Entrepreneurial Studies, Consortium for Supply Chain Management.
Computer Facilities: Busines School computer lab open 7 days a week (for business students only); additional labs available throughout campus for all students

Campuswide Network? Yes
% of MBA Classrooms Wired: 100
Computer Model Recommended: Laptop
Internet Fee? No

EXPENSES/FINANCIAL AID

Annual Tuition: $25,500
Tuition Per Credit (Resident/Nonresident): $725
Room & Board (On/Off Campus): $11,000
Books and Supplies: $750
Average Grant: $8,500
% Receiving Financial Aid: 75
% Receiving Aid Their First Year: 85

ADMISSIONS INFORMATION

Application Fee: $75
Electronic Application? Yes
Regular Application Deadline: 3/1
Regular Notification: 3/28
Deferment Available? Yes
Length of Deferment: 1 year
Non-fall Admissions? No
Transfer Students Accepted? Yes
Transfer Policy: Maximum of 6 credit hours from another AACSB-accredited school
Need-Blind Admissions? Yes
Number of Applications Received: 124
% of Applicants Accepted: 41
% Accepted Who Enrolled: 55
Average GPA: 3.0
Average GMAT: 603
Average Years Experience: 4
Other Admissions Factors Considered: Work experience plays a large role. For applicants with limited or no work experience, the GMAT and GPA become very important. Interviews are recommended for all applicants but are required for applicants with no work experience.
Other Schools to Which Students Applied: Washington University in St. Louis

INTERNATIONAL STUDENTS

TOEFL Required of International Students? Yes
Minimum TOEFL: 600 (250 computer)

EMPLOYMENT INFORMATION

Placement Office Available? Yes

SAINT MARY'S UNIVERSITY, CANADA
Frank H. Sobey Faculty of Commerce

Admissions Contact: Jennifer Johnson, MBA Program Manager
Address: 923 Robie Street, Halifax, NS B3H 3C3
Admissions Phone: 902-420-5729 • **Admissions Fax:** 902-420-5119
Admissions E-mail: mba@stmarys.ca • **Web Address:** www.stmarys.ca/mba

INSTITUTIONAL INFORMATION

Public/Private: Public
Evening Classes Available? Yes
Students in Parent Institution: 8,000
Academic Calendar: Semester

PROGRAMS

Degrees Offered: MBA (1-2 years), EMBA (up to 2 years)
Academic Specialties: Human Resources, Finance, General Management
Study Abroad Options: Brazil, Denmark

STUDENT INFORMATION

Total Business Students: 225
% Full Time: 58
% Female: 56
% Out of State: 34
% International: 23
Average Age: 29

COMPUTER AND RESEARCH FACILITIES

Campuswide Network? Yes
% of MBA Classrooms Wired: 50
Internet Fee? No

EXPENSES/FINANCIAL AID

Annual Tuition (Resident/Nonresident): $5,500/$11,000
Tuition Per Credit (Resident/Nonresident): $925
Room & Board (On/Off Campus): $6,000/$8,000
Books and Supplies: $1,500
Average Grant: $3,000
% Receiving Financial Aid: 20
% Receiving Aid Their First Year: 10

ADMISSIONS INFORMATION

Application Fee: $35
Electronic Application? No
Regular Application Deadline: Rolling
Regular Notification: Rolling
Deferment Available? Yes
Length of Deferment: 12 months
Non-fall Admissions? No
Transfer Students Accepted? Yes
Transfer Policy: Must submit full application and suppporting documents
Need-Blind Admissions? Yes
Number of Applications Received: 305
% of Applicants Accepted: 57
% Accepted Who Enrolled: 59
Average GPA: 3.3
Average GMAT: 600
Average Years Experience: 4
Other Admissions Factors Considered: Years of full-time work experience

INTERNATIONAL STUDENTS

TOEFL Required of International Students? Yes
Minimum TOEFL: 550 (220 computer)

EMPLOYMENT INFORMATION

Placement Office Available? No

SAINT MARY'S UNIVERSITY, SAN ANTONIO

School of Business and Administration

Admissions Contact: Dr. Thomas Hamilton, MBA Program Director
Address: One Camino Santa Maria, San Antonio, TX 78228-8507
Admissions Phone: 210-431-2027 • **Admissions Fax:** 210-436-3620
Admissions E-mail: mba@stmarytx.edu • **Web Address:** www.stmarytx.edu/acad/business

INSTITUTIONAL INFORMATION

Public/Private: Private
Evening Classes Available? No
Total Faculty: 28
% Faculty Part Time: 29
Students in Parent Institution: 4,243
Academic Calendar: Semester

PROGRAMS

Degrees Offered: MBA (33-39 credits, full time or part time, 18 months to 5 years), MACC (30 credits, full time or part time, 18 months to 5 years)
Study Abroad Options: Finance (includes Banking), General Business, International Business, Management, Accounting

STUDENT INFORMATION

Total Business Students: 128
% Full Time: 16
% Female: 41
% Minority: 49
% International: 3
Average Age: 29

COMPUTER AND RESEARCH FACILITIES

Research Facilities: Academic Library plus 1 additional on-campus library; total holdings of 525,000 volumes; 17,000 microforms; 1,400 current periodical subscriptions. CD player(s) available for graduate student use; access provided to online bibliographic retrieval services
Campuswide Network? Yes
Internet Fee? No

EXPENSES/FINANCIAL AID

Annual Tuition: $14,300
Tuition Per Credit (Resident/Nonresident): $383

ADMISSIONS INFORMATION

Application Fee: $30
Electronic Application? No
Regular Application Deadline: Rolling
Regular Notification: Rolling
Deferment Available? Yes
Length of Deferment: 2 years
Non-fall Admissions? No
Transfer Students Accepted? Yes
Transfer Policy: On recommendation of the Graduate Program director, may accept a maxium of 6 semester hours
Need-Blind Admissions? No
Number of Applications Received: 50
% of Applicants Accepted: 90
Average GPA: 2.7
GPA Range: 1.7-4.0
Average GMAT: 470
GMAT Range: 430-530
Other Admissions Factors Considered: A minimum GMAT score of 400 and GPA of 2.5 are required. An essay, interview, personal statement, and computer experience are recommended.

Number of Applications Received: 198
% of Applicants Accepted: 39
% Accepted Who Enrolled: 100
Other Admissions Factors Considered: Computer expereince

INTERNATIONAL STUDENTS

TOEFL Required of International Students? Yes
Minimum TOEFL: 550

EMPLOYMENT INFORMATION

Placement Office Available? No
% Employed Within 3 Months: 95

ST. MARY'S UNIVERSITY OF MINNESOTA

School of Business and Social Sciences

Admissions Contact: Carolyn Verret, Director, School of Graduate Studies
Address: 2500 Park Avenue, Minneapolis, MN 55404-4403
Admissions Phone: 612-728-5135 • **Admissions Fax:** 612-728-5135
Admissions E-mail: tc-admission@smumn.edu • **Web Address:** www.smumn.edu

INSTITUTIONAL INFORMATION

Public/Private: Private
Evening Classes Available? Yes
Total Faculty: 41
Student/Faculty Ratio: 15:1
Students in Parent Institution: 4,350
Academic Calendar: Trimester

PROGRAMS

Degrees Offered: MA in Management (35 credits, 2-5 years); MAIB, with concentrations in International and Area Business Studies, International Business, International Management (41 credits, 15 months to 5 years); MA in Management/Health Human Services Administration (48 credits, 2.3 to 5 years), with concentrations in Management, Technology Management, Public Policy and Administration, Public Management, Public Management, Health Care; MA in Management/MS in Telecommunications (57 credits, 2.3 to 5 years), with concentrations in Management, Technology Management, Telecommunications Management
Academic Specialties: Case study, computer analysis, experiential learning, faculty seminars, field projects, group discussion, lecture, research, role playing, simulations, student presentations, study groups, team projects

STUDENT INFORMATION

Total Business Students: 300
Average Age: 32

COMPUTER AND RESEARCH FACILITIES

Campuswide Network? Yes
Internet Fee? No

EXPENSES/FINANCIAL AID

Tuition Per Credit (Resident/Nonresident): $205

ADMISSIONS INFORMATION

Application Fee: $20
Electronic Application? No
Regular Application Deadline: Rolling
Regular Notification: Rolling
Deferment Available? No
Non-fall Admissions? No
Transfer Students Accepted? No
Need-Blind Admissions? No

SALISBURY UNIVERSITY

Franklin P. Perdue School of Business

Admissions Contact: Janine Vienna, Director, Graduate Business Programs
Address: 1101 Camden Avenue, Salisbury, MD 21801-6837
Admissions Phone: 410-548-3983 • **Admissions Fax:** 410-548-2908
Admissions E-mail: jmvienna@salisbury.edu
Web Address: www.salisbury.edu/Schools/Perdue/MBA

INSTITUTIONAL INFORMATION

Public/Private: Public
Evening Classes Available? Yes
Total Faculty: 20
% Faculty Female: 10
Student/Faculty Ratio: 22:1
Students in Parent Institution: 6,700
Academic Calendar: Semester

PROGRAMS

Degrees Offered: MBA (30-63 credits, 1-7 years)
Academic Specialties: Strategic Management
Special Opportunities: Management, Accounting
Study Abroad Options: Chile, France

STUDENT INFORMATION

Total Business Students: 107
% Full Time: 45
% Female: 55
% Minority: 6
% Out of State: 31
% International: 13
Average Age: 26

COMPUTER AND RESEARCH FACILITIES

Research Facilities: Outreach Centers (primarily business consulting), including Business Economic and Community Outreach Network (BEACON), Small Business Development Center (SBDC)
Computer Facilities: 8 student computer labs (1 dedicated to business students) with 234 PCs and 20 MAC computers; database access includes: Business Source Premier, EconLit, ABO/Inform, Lexis-Nexis, Berkeley Wire News, Datapro Research, FIS Online, Gartner Research, Regional Business News, Science Direct
Campuswide Network? Yes
Internet Fee? Yes

EXPENSES/FINANCIAL AID

Annual Tuition (Resident/Nonresident): $5,520/$11,400
Tuition Per Credit (Resident/Nonresident): $184/$380

Room & Board (On/Off Campus): $8,000
Books and Supplies: $750
Average Grant: $37,560
Average Loan: $125,368

ADMISSIONS INFORMATION

Application Fee: $45
Electronic Application? Yes
Regular Application Deadline: 3/1
Regular Notification: 4/1
Deferment Available? Yes
Length of Deferment: 1 semester
Non-fall Admissions? Yes
Non-fall Application Deadline(s): 10/1 spring
Transfer Students Accepted? Yes
Transfer Policy: Maximum of 9 credit hours of approved transfer credit; transfer candidate must complete all application requirements.
Need-Blind Admissions? Yes
Number of Applications Received: 55
% of Applicants Accepted: 93
% Accepted Who Enrolled: 82
Average GPA: 3.2
Average GMAT: 459
Average Years Experience: 3
Other Admissions Factors Considered: Work experience, computer experience

INTERNATIONAL STUDENTS

TOEFL Required of International Students? Yes
Minimum TOEFL: 550 (213 computer)

EMPLOYMENT INFORMATION

Placement Office Available? No

SAM HOUSTON STATE UNIVERSITY
College of Business Administration

Admissions Contact: Dr. Mitchell Muehsam, MBA Director
Address: PO Box 2056, Huntsville, TX 77341-2056
Admissions Phone: 936-294-1246 • Admissions Fax: 936-294-3612
Admissions E-mail: gbamsq@shsu.edu • Web Address: coba.shsu.edu/

INSTITUTIONAL INFORMATION

Public/Private: Public
Evening Classes Available? No

PROGRAMS

Degrees Offered: MBA (1-6 years)

STUDENT INFORMATION

Total Business Students: 164
% Full Time: 29
% Female: 51
% Minority: 7
% International: 5

COMPUTER AND RESEARCH FACILITIES

Campuswide Network? Yes
Internet Fee? No

EXPENSES/FINANCIAL AID

Annual Tuition (Resident/Nonresident): $2,301/$7,317
Tuition Per Credit (Resident/Nonresident): $238/$447

ADMISSIONS INFORMATION

Application Fee: $20
Electronic Application? No
Regular Application Deadline: Rolling
Regular Notification: Rolling
Deferment Available? No
Non-fall Admissions? No
Transfer Students Accepted? No
Need-Blind Admissions? No
Number of Applications Received: 58
% of Applicants Accepted: 86
% Accepted Who Enrolled: 60

EMPLOYMENT INFORMATION

Placement Office Available? Yes

SAMFORD UNIVERSITY
School of Business

Admissions Contact: Dr. Douglas L. Smith, Director of Graduate Studies
Address: DBH 344, School of Business, 800 Lakeshore Dr., Birmingham, AL 35209
Admissions Phone: 205-726-2931 • Admissions Fax: 205-726-2464
Admissions E-mail: business.graduate.studies@samford.edu
Web Address: www.samford.edu

INSTITUTIONAL INFORMATION

Public/Private: Private
Evening Classes Available? Yes
Total Faculty: 19
% Faculty Female: 20
% Faculty Minority: 10
% Faculty Part Time: 5
Student/Faculty Ratio: 12:1
Students in Parent Institution: 4,377
Academic Calendar: 9-week terms

PROGRAMS

Degrees Offered: MBA (30-48 credits, full time or part time, 1-7 years), with concentration in Management; MACC (30 credits, full time or part time, 1-7 years), with concentration in Accounting
Combined Degrees: MBA/MACC (45-63 credits, full time or part time, 18 months to 7 years), with concentrations in Management, Accounting; MBA/JD (99-117 credits, 3-7 years full time,); MACC/JD (99 credits, 3-4 years full time); MBA/MDIV (106-118, 3-7 years part time); MBA/MSN (106-118 credits, 2-7 years part time)
Academic Specialties: Entrepreneurship, Accounting, Finance, Marketing, Information Technology, Leadership, Organizational Behavior, Operations Management; case-based format
Study Abroad Options: Czech Republic, United Kingdom

STUDENT INFORMATION

Total Business Students: 172
Average Age: 31

COMPUTER AND RESEARCH FACILITIES

Research Facilities: Public Interest Research Council, Alabama Center for Law and Civic Education, London Study Center
Computer Facilities: Computer Classroom dedicated to School of Business; computer labs for students; all major online business databases: ABI Inform, Academic Universe, etc.
Campuswide Network? Yes

% of MBA Classrooms Wired: 100
Internet Fee? No

EXPENSES/FINANCIAL AID

Annual Tuition: $9,840
Tuition Per Credit (Resident/Nonresident): $410
Books and Supplies: $600
Average Loan: $4,000

ADMISSIONS INFORMATION

Application Fee: $25
Electronic Application? No
Regular Application Deadline: Rolling
Regular Notification: Rolling
Deferment Available? Yes
Length of Deferment: 1 year
Non-fall Admissions? Yes
Transfer Students Accepted? Yes
Transfer Policy: Must submit complete application and meet admissions deadlines; limited number of credits may transfer
Need-Blind Admissions? Yes
Number of Applications Received: 70
% of Applicants Accepted: 93
% Accepted Who Enrolled: 97
Average GPA: 3.0
Average GMAT: 510
Average Years Experience: 7
Other Admissions Factors Considered: All applicants must have at least 3 years of full-time work experience to be eligible for admission.
Other Schools to Which Students Applied: University of Alabama—Birmingham

INTERNATIONAL STUDENTS

TOEFL Required of International Students? Yes
Minimum TOEFL: 550

EMPLOYMENT INFORMATION

Placement Office Available? Yes
% Employed Within 3 Months: 100

SAN DIEGO STATE UNIVERSITY
Graduate School of Business

Admissions Contact: S. Scott, MBA Program Coordinator; or S.Temores-Valdez, MSBA Program Coordinator
Address: 5500 Campanile Drive, San Diego, CA 92182
Admissions Phone: 619-594-8073 • Admissions Fax: 619-594-1863
Admissions E-mail: sdsumba@mail.sdsu.edu • Web Address: www.sdsu.edu

SDSU is located in the heart of San Diego, "a hotbed of entrepreneurship in biotech, telecommunications, software, and several other high-growth industries." The SDSU MBA is designed for students who do not have an undergraduate business degree. In addition to a broad range of courses in the curriculum, students are required to take one class in each of four themes: interpersonal skills, the environment, information and technology, and globalization. For the older, more experienced crowd, an EMBA is also offered.

INSTITUTIONAL INFORMATION

Public/Private: Public
Evening Classes Available? Yes

Total Faculty: 97
% Faculty Female: 14
% Faculty Minority: 3
% Faculty Part Time: 25
Student/Faculty Ratio: 35:1
Students in Parent Institution: 33,285
Academic Calendar: Semester

PROGRAMS

Degrees Offered: MBA (2-4 years),MSBA (1-2 years), MSA (1-2 years)
Combined Degrees: MBA/MA in Latin American Studies (2-4 years), MBA/JD (4 years)

STUDENT INFORMATION

Total Business Students: 727
% Full Time: 55
% Female: 40
% Minority: 15
% Out of State: 14
% International: 40
Average Age: 28

COMPUTER AND RESEARCH FACILITIES

Campuswide Network? No
Internet Fee? No

EXPENSES/FINANCIAL AID

Annual Tuition (Resident/Nonresident): $2,176/$8,944
Room & Board (On/Off Campus): $8,307/$8,149
Books and Supplies: $800

ADMISSIONS INFORMATION

Application Fee: $55
Electronic Application? Yes
Regular Application Deadline: 4/15
Regular Notification: 6/15
Deferment Available? No
Non-fall Admissions? Yes
Non-fall Application Deadline(s): 11/1 spring
Transfer Students Accepted? Yes
Transfer Policy: Transfer applicants apply through the normal admissions process, and then will transfer in courses at our discretion.
Need-Blind Admissions? Yes
Number of Applications Received: 801
% of Applicants Accepted: 42
% Accepted Who Enrolled: 58
Average GPA: 3.3
GPA Range: 2.7-3.6
Average GMAT: 602
GMAT Range: 560-620
Average Years Experience: 5
Other Admissions Factors Considered: Reputation of undergraduate institution, major GPA
Other Schools to Which Students Applied: University of San Diego

INTERNATIONAL STUDENTS

TOEFL Required of International Students? Yes
Minimum TOEFL: 570 (230 computer)

EMPLOYMENT INFORMATION

Placement Office Available? Yes

SAN FRANCISCO STATE UNIVERSITY
Graduate School of Business

Admissions Contact: Albert Koo, Admissions Coordinator
Address: 1600 Holloway Avenue, San Francisco, CA 94132
Admissions Phone: 415-338-1279 • **Admissions Fax:** 415-405-0495
Admissions E-mail: mba@sfsu.edu • **Web Address:** www.sfsu.edu/~mba

Rolling hills, trolleys, Fisherman's Wharf, perpetual spring/autumn—all of this could be yours for a great low price while obtaining an MBA from San Francisco State. The most popular program is the straight-up MBA, geared toward students working full time, but SF State also offers the Alliance MBA, delivered partially online, and the Accelerated MBA. The San Francisco State MBA aims to equip students with a broad understanding of management and a balanced knowledge base and encourages creativity, imagination, and lifelong learning.

INSTITUTIONAL INFORMATION

Public/Private: Public
Evening Classes Available? Yes
Total Faculty: 150
% Faculty Female: 36
% Faculty Minority: 40
% Faculty Part Time: 35
Student/Faculty Ratio: 25:1
Students in Parent Institution: 26,500

PROGRAMS

Degrees Offered: MBA (2 years), MSBA (2 years)
Academic Specialties: Accounting, Business Analysis, Computer Information System, Electronic Commence, Finance, Hospitality Management, Human Resources Management, International Business, Mangement, Marketing, Transportation/Logistics
Special Opportunities: Accelerated MBA
Study Abroad Options: France, Germany, Japan, Korea

STUDENT INFORMATION

Total Business Students: 900
% Full Time: 35
% Female: 51
% Minority: 25
Average Age: 30

COMPUTER AND RESEARCH FACILITIES

Campuswide Network? No
Internet Fee? No

EXPENSES/FINANCIAL AID

Annual Tuition (Resident/Nonresident): $1,904/$7,808
Room & Board (On/Off Campus): $7,000
Books and Supplies: $1,500

ADMISSIONS INFORMATION

Application Fee: $1,904
Electronic Application? Yes
Regular Application Deadline: 5/15
Regular Notification: 6/15
Deferment Available? No
Non-fall Admissions? Yes
Non-fall Application Deadline(s): 11/15
Transfer Students Accepted? Yes
Transfer Policy: Applicants need to apply to the program and waive out our requirements.
Need-Blind Admissions? No

Number of Applications Received: 1,017
% of Applicants Accepted: 53
% Accepted Who Enrolled: 46
Average GPA: 3.2
GPA Range: 2.7-4.0
Average GMAT: 536
GMAT Range: 470-700
Average Years Experience: 4

INTERNATIONAL STUDENTS

TOEFL Required of International Students? Yes
Minimum TOEFL: 550 (213 computer)

EMPLOYMENT INFORMATION

Placement Office Available? Yes

SAN JOSE STATE UNIVERSITY
Collge of Business

Admissions Contact: Amy Kassing, Admissions Coordinator
Address: One Washington Square, San Jose, CA 95192-0162
Admissions Phone: 408-924-3420 • **Admissions Fax:** 408-924-3426
Admissions E-mail: mba@cob.sjsu.edu • **Web Address:** www.cob.sjsu.edu/graduate

San Jose State University is situated in illustrious Silicon Valley. SJSU offers a few MBA program options, including an accelerated off-campus Evening MBA with classes in Rose Orchard Tech Center; an on-campus, traditional MBA program; and MBA One, a full-time day program. SJSU is a branch of the California State university system.

INSTITUTIONAL INFORMATION

Public/Private: Public
Evening Classes Available? Yes
Student/Faculty Ratio: 40:1
Academic Calendar: Semester

PROGRAMS

Degrees Offered: MBA (12 months), On-Campus MBA (18-48 months, variable), Off-Campus MBA (30 months, variable), MS in Transportation Management (24-36 months), MST (9-48 months), MSA (12 months)
Combined Degrees: MBA/MSE (32 months, lock step)

STUDENT INFORMATION

Total Business Students: 546
% Full Time: 8
% Female: 52
% Minority: 40
Average Age: 33

COMPUTER AND RESEARCH FACILITIES

Campuswide Network? No
Internet Fee? No

EXPENSES/FINANCIAL AID

Annual Tuition (Resident/Nonresident): $22,560
Tuition Per Credit (Resident/Nonresident): $125/$406
Books and Supplies: $2,000

ADMISSIONS INFORMATION

Application Fee: $55
Electronic Application? Yes
Regular Application Deadline: 5/1
Regular Notification: 7/1
Deferment Available? No
Non-fall Application Deadline(s): 9/15 spring
Transfer Policy: Applicant must meet admission requirements; up to 6 units may be transferred from an AACSB-accredited institution.
Need-Blind Admissions? No
Number of Applications Received: 461
% of Applicants Accepted: 44
% Accepted Who Enrolled: 66
Average GPA: 3.3
Average GMAT: 556

INTERNATIONAL STUDENTS

TOEFL Required of International Students? Yes
Minimum TOEFL: 550 (213 computer)

EMPLOYMENT INFORMATION

Placement Office Available? No

See page 438.

SANTA CLARA UNIVERSITY
Leavey School of Business

Admissions Contact: Jana Hee, Director, Graduate Business Admissions
Address: MBA Office, Kenna Hall #223, Santa Clara, CA 95053-0001
Admissions Phone: 408-554-4539 • **Admissions Fax:** 408-544-2332
Admissions E-mail: mbaadmissions@scu.edu • **Web Address:** Business.scu.edu

Calling itself "the premier business program for Silicon Valley," SCU, a Jesuit business school, emphasizes the education of the whole person, along with establishing managerial leadership skills and critical thinking capabilities. One unique degree offered is an MBA in agribusiness, available through Santa Clara U's Food and Agribusiness Institute. Silicon Valley business leaders are frequent contributors to classroom discussions and are frequent employers of Santa Clara MBA graduates.

INSTITUTIONAL INFORMATION

Public/Private: Private
Evening Classes Available? Yes
Total Faculty: 68
% Faculty Female: 20
% Faculty Minority: 15
% Faculty Part Time: 15
Student/Faculty Ratio: 34:1
Students in Parent Institution: 7,368
Academic Calendar: Quarter

PROGRAMS

Degrees Offered: MBA (2-6 years), EMBA (17 months)
Combined Degrees: JD/MBA (4 years)
Academic Specialties: Entrepreneurship; Consulting, High-Tech, Finance, Leadership

STUDENT INFORMATION

Total Business Students: 988
% Full Time: 19

% Female: 38
% Minority: 13
% Out of State: 1
% International: 18
Average Age: 29

COMPUTER AND RESEARCH FACILITIES

Computer Facilities: 5 general purpose computer labs with 200 networked computers; multitude of software options including library research packages
Campuswide Network? Yes
Computer Model Recommended: Laptop
Internet Fee? No

EXPENSES/FINANCIAL AID

Annual Tuition: $16,200
Tuition Per Credit (Resident/Nonresident): $594
Room & Board (On/Off Campus): $12,000
Books and Supplies: $500
% Receiving Financial Aid: 50

ADMISSIONS INFORMATION

Application Fee: $75
Electronic Application? Yes
Early Decision Application Deadline: 3/1 fall
Early Decision Notification: 5/1
Regular Application Deadline: 5/1
Regular Notification: Rolling
Deferment Available? Yes
Length of Deferment: 2 quarters
Non-fall Admissions? Yes
Non-fall Application Deadline(s): 8/1 winter, 11/1 spring
Transfer Students Accepted? Yes
Transfer Policy: Apply as all others
Need-Blind Admissions? Yes
Number of Applications Received: 468
% of Applicants Accepted: 68
% Accepted Who Enrolled: 74
Average GPA: 3.3
GPA Range: 2.7-3.7
Average GMAT: 615
GMAT Range: 540-710
Average Years Experience: 7
Other Admissions Factors Considered: Level of work experience, undergraduate institution and major, level of commitment determined by essay responses
Other Schools to Which Students Applied: San Jose State University, University of California—Berkeley, University of California—Davis, Pepperdine University, University of San Francisco

INTERNATIONAL STUDENTS

TOEFL Required of International Students? Yes
Minimum TOEFL: 250

EMPLOYMENT INFORMATION

Placement Office Available? No

SEATTLE PACIFIC UNIVERSITY
School of Business & Economics

Admissions Contact: Debbie Wysomierski, Associate Graduate Director
Address: 3307 Third Ave. W., Seattle, WA 98119
Admissions Phone: 206-281-2753 • Admissions Fax: 206-281-2733
Admissions E-mail: mba@spu.edu • Web Address: www.spu.edu/sbe

INSTITUTIONAL INFORMATION

Public/Private: Private
Evening Classes Available? Yes
Total Faculty: 19
% Faculty Female: 21
% Faculty Minority: 5
% Faculty Part Time: 10
Student/Faculty Ratio: 17:1
Students in Parent Institution: 3,684
Academic Calendar: Quarter

PROGRAMS

Degrees Offered: MBA (72 credits/24 courses if no business undergraduate degree), MSISM (51 credits/17 courses, including background courses)
Academic Specialties: General Management from a strategic perspective, Human Resources Management, Information Systems Management/E-Commerce

STUDENT INFORMATION

Total Business Students: 124
% Full Time: 15
% Female: 50
% Minority: 4
% International: 100
Average Age: 30

COMPUTER AND RESEARCH FACILITIES

Research Facilities: Center for Applied Learning (mentor program, entrepreneurship, live-case field studies)
Computer Facilities: School of Business & Economics computer lab, SPU Library computer lab
Campuswide Network? Yes
% of MBA Classrooms Wired: 100
Internet Fee? No

EXPENSES/FINANCIAL AID

Annual Tuition: $13,014
Tuition Per Credit (Resident/Nonresident): $482
Books and Supplies: $1,200

ADMISSIONS INFORMATION

Application Fee: $50
Electronic Application? Yes
Regular Application Deadline: 8/1
Regular Notification: 8/15
Deferment Available? Yes
Length of Deferment: 1 year
Non-fall Admissions? Yes
Non-fall Application Deadline(s): 11/1, 2/1, 5/1
Transfer Students Accepted? Yes
Transfer Policy: Regular admission process
Need-Blind Admissions? Yes
Number of Applications Received: 49
% of Applicants Accepted: 69
% Accepted Who Enrolled: 65
Average GPA: 3.5
GPA Range: 3.2-3.7

Average GMAT: 508
GMAT Range: 470-550
Average Years Experience: 7
Other Schools to Which Students Applied: Seattle University, University of Washington

INTERNATIONAL STUDENTS

TOEFL Required of International Students? Yes
Minimum TOEFL: 565 (225 computer)

EMPLOYMENT INFORMATION

Placement Office Available? Yes
Frequent Employers: Boeing, Microsoft, Safeco, Starbucks

SEATTLE UNIVERSITY
Albers School of Business and Economics

Admissions Contact: Janet Shandley, Director, Graduate Admissions
Address: 900 Broadway, Seattle, WA 98122
Admissions Phone: 206-296-2000 • Admissions Fax: 206-296-5656
Admissions E-mail: grad-admissions@seattleu.edu
Web Address: www.seattleu.edu/asbe

Facing ethical issues in business and completing service projects are priorities in the MBA curriculum at Seattle University, one of 28 Jesuit colleges in the United States. The learning environment at Seattle U is "diverse and culturally rich" with "a wide range of religious and ideological viewpoints" and nurturing faculty who dedicate personal attention to students. A noteworthy on-campus landmark is the Chapel of St. Ignatius, a scale model of which has been selected for inclusion in the permanent collection of the Museum of Modern Art in New York City. Architect Steven Hull's concept for the chapel was "A Gathering of Different Lights," as it refers to the "consolations and desolations" St. Ignatius believed comprised spiritual life and describes the mission of Seattle University.

INSTITUTIONAL INFORMATION

Public/Private: Private
Evening Classes Available? Yes
Total Faculty: 43
% Faculty Female: 31
Student/Faculty Ratio: 11:1
Students in Parent Institution: 6,337
Academic Calendar: Quarter

PROGRAMS

Degrees Offered: MBA, MIB, MPACC, MSF
Combined Degrees: JD/MBA (4 years)
Academic Specialties: We have faculty members that specialize in Fnance, Accounting, Economics, Management, Marketing, and ECIS, along with master's programs in Finance, Accounting, and International Business.

STUDENT INFORMATION

Total Business Students: 519
% Full Time: 20
% Female: 38
% Minority: 1
% Out of State: 6
% International: 7
Average Age: 31

COMPUTER AND RESEARCH FACILITIES

Research Facilities: ECIS computer lab
Computer Facilities: There are several computer labs situated around the campus that MBA students can utilize. The following databases are available: ABI inform, Compustat, CRSP, Dialog, Disclosure, Dissertation Abstracts, Ebsco, FirstSearch, Lexis/Nexis Academic Universe, ProQuest, Public Affairs Info Service, Stat-USA
Campuswide Network? Yes
% of MBA Classrooms Wired: 100
Internet Fee? No

EXPENSES/FINANCIAL AID

Annual Tuition: $14,688
Tuition Per Credit (Resident/Nonresident): $544
Room & Board (On/Off Campus): $6,627
Books and Supplies: $1,500
Average Grant: $8,527
Average Loan: $16,932
% Receiving Financial Aid: 34
% Receiving Aid Their First Year: 55

ADMISSIONS INFORMATION

Application Fee: $55
Electronic Application? Yes
Regular Application Deadline: 8/20
Regular Notification: 9/1
Deferment Available? Yes
Length of Deferment: 1 year
Non-fall Admissions? Yes
Non-fall Application Deadline(s): 11/20 winter, 2/20 spring, 5/20 summer
Transfer Students Accepted? Yes
Transfer Policy: Applicants must meet standard admission requirements (GMAT 500 or greater, 1-year work experience, undergrad GPA of 3.0 or greater). University will accept 9 quarter credits.
Need-Blind Admissions? Yes
Number of Applications Received: 243
% of Applicants Accepted: 63
% Accepted Who Enrolled: 72
Average GPA: 3.2
GPA Range: 3.0-3.4
Average GMAT: 562
GMAT Range: 525-605
Average Years Experience: 6
Other Schools to Which Students Applied: Pacific Lutheran University, San Francisco State University, Seattle Pacific University, University of Washington, Washington State University, Western Washington University

INTERNATIONAL STUDENTS

TOEFL Required of International Students? Yes
Minimum TOEFL: 580 (237 computer)

EMPLOYMENT INFORMATION

Placement Office Available? Yes
Prominent Alumni: Leo Hindery, CEO, Yankee Entertainment & Sports Network; Frank Murkowski, U.S. senator, Alaska; Gary P. Brinson, president, GP Brinson Investments; Carolyn Kelly, COO and president, Seattle Times; William Foley, Jr., chairman and CEO, Fidelity National Financial

SETON HALL UNIVERSITY
Stillman School of Business

Admissions Contact: Lorrie Dougherty, Director of Graduate Admissions
Address: 400 South Orange Avenue, South Orange, NJ 07079-2692
Admissions Phone: 973-761-9262 • **Admissions Fax:** 973-761-9208
Admissions E-mail: stillman@shu.edu • **Web Address:** www.business.shu.edu

Seton Hall is a Catholic university, located in South Orange, New Jersey, just a train ride away from New York City. The Stillman School of Business at Seton Hall offers four joint degrees, including the MBA/MADIR, a Master in Business Administration coupled with a Master of Arts in Diplomacy and International Relations. Frequent employers of Seton Hall grads are AT&T, Pfizer, and Deloitte & Touche. Applicants to the Stillman School of Business also apply to Fordham University, New York University, and Pace University.

INSTITUTIONAL INFORMATION

Public/Private: Private
Evening Classes Available? Yes
Total Faculty: 94
% Faculty Female: 23
% Faculty Minority: 24
% Faculty Part Time: 38
Student/Faculty Ratio: 6:1
Students in Parent Institution: 8,324
Academic Calendar: Semester

PROGRAMS

Degrees Offered: MBA (42 credits, 2-5 years), MSIB (33 credits, 18 months to 5 years), MST (30 credits, 1-5 years), MSA (30 credits, 1-5 years), MS in Professional Accounting (30 credits, 1-5 years)
Combined Degrees: MBA/MSIB (63 credits, 3-5 years), MBA/JD (105 credits, 4 years), MBA/MSN (54 credits, 2.5 to 5 years), MSIB/MA in Diplomacy and International Relations (57 credits, 2.5 to 5 years), MBS/MA in Diplomacy and International Relations (63 credits, 2.5 to 5 years)
Academic Specialties: We offer the premier MBA in Sport Management in the country. Each student has the opportunity to acquire an internship in the field of Sport Management and can receive up to 6 graduate/elective credits during the summer semester. For more information regarding this program, please contact Dr. Ann Mayo, Director of the Center for Sport Management at: mayoann@shu.edu.
Study Abroad Options: University of International Business and Economics, Beijing, China; Centro Universitario Marianum, Rome, Italy; Ireland; University of Warsaw, Poland

STUDENT INFORMATION

Total Business Students: 522
% Full Time: 15
% Female: 34
% Minority: 12
% Out of State: 14
% International: 10
Average Age: 29

COMPUTER AND RESEARCH FACILITIES

Computer Facilities: ABI Inform-Business (VALE); Academic Journals (ProQuest); Academic Universe (Lexis-Nexis); America: History and Life; Anthropological Index; Art Dictionary (the Grove Dictionary of Art); Art Index (SilverPlatter); ATLA Religion (VALE); Biological Abstracts (SilverPlatter); CINAHL-Allied Health/Nursing Index (VALE); Classical Literature (Perseus); Criminal Justice Abstracts; Criminal Justice: NCJRS Abstracts; Dissertation Abstracts (ProQuest); EBSCO Online (Search full-text articles of selected library subscription journals); Encyclopaedia Britannica Online; Environment Information; ERIC Education; ERIC Education (SilverPlatter); Ethnic NewsWatch; FISonline— Company Data Direct; Gender NewsWatch; Grants Research Database; JSTOR: The Scholarly Journal Archive ; Lexis-Nexis; Literature Resource Center (Galenet); MathSciNet; MEDLINE (Medical) 1966- ; MEDLINE (NLM); MLA Bibliography 1963- (VALE); Music Literature (IIMP); Newspapers (ProQuest); Nursing Index - CINAHL (VALE); Oxford English Dictionary; Patrologia Latina Database (provided by the Immaculate Conception Seminary); Philosopher's Index; Project Gutenberg; Project Muse (Humanities); Project Perseus; PsycInfo (VALE); PubSCIENCE; RIA Checkpoint Tax (obtain a remote password); ScienceDirect; Social Work Abstracts (VALE); Sociological Abstracts 1963- (SilverPlatter); UnCover; Wall Street Journal

Campuswide Network? Yes
% of MBA Classrooms Wired: 100
Computer Model Recommended: Laptop
Internet Fee? Yes

EXPENSES/FINANCIAL AID

Annual Tuition: $19,380
Tuition Per Credit (Resident/Nonresident): $646
Room & Board (On/Off Campus): $10,200
Books and Supplies: $1,100
Average Grant: $20,904
Average Loan: $12,500
% Receiving Financial Aid: 22
% Receiving Aid Their First Year: 17

ADMISSIONS INFORMATION

Application Fee: $75
Electronic Application? Yes
Regular Application Deadline: 6/1
Regular Notification: Rolling
Deferment Available? Yes
Length of Deferment: 1 year
Non-fall Admissions? Yes
Non-fall Application Deadline(s): 11/1 spring, 3/15 summer
Transfer Students Accepted? Yes
Transfer Policy: Student must submit a formal application, which is reviewed by the dean. This review determines how many credits will transfer into the program; a maximum of 12 credits can be transferred.
Need-Blind Admissions? Yes
Number of Applications Received: 255
% of Applicants Accepted: 58
% Accepted Who Enrolled: 78
Average GPA: 3.3
GPA Range: 3.0-4.0
Average GMAT: 527
GMAT Range: 510-640
Average Years Experience: 5
Other Admissions Factors Considered: Interview, computer experience
Minority/Disadvantaged Student Recruitment Programs: Graduate Access Program for Business (GAP-B) (For information please contact Ms. Carol McMillan at mcmillca@shu.edu or (973) 761-9162.)
Other Schools to Which Students Applied: Fordham University, New York University, Pace University, Rutgers/The State University of New Jersey, Boston College, Villanova University, Columbia University

INTERNATIONAL STUDENTS

TOEFL Required of International Students? Yes
Minimum TOEFL: 550 (213 computer)

EMPLOYMENT INFORMATION

Placement Office Available? Yes
Frequent Employers: Arthur Andersen, AT&T, Deloitte & Touche, KPMG, Lucent Technologies, Pfizer, Prudential
Prominent Alumni: L. Dennis Kozlowski, CEO, Tyco International; Gerald P. Buccino, chairman and CEO, Buccino & Associates; Joseph D. Abruzzese, president of network sales, CBS; Joseph M. LaMotta, chairman emeritus, Oppenheimer Capital; Thomas Spagnolia, president/CEO, AskmeLaw

SIMMONS COLLEGE
Simmons Graduate School of Management

Admissions Contact: Andrea Bruce, Director of Admissions
Address: 409 Commonwealth Avenue, Boston, MA 02215
Admissions Phone: 617-521-3840 • **Admissions Fax:** 617-521-3880
Admissions E-mail: gsmadm@simmons.edu • **Web Address:** www.simmons.edu/gsm

INSTITUTIONAL INFORMATION

Public/Private: Private
Evening Classes Available? Yes
Total Faculty: 16
% Faculty Part Time: 25
Student/Faculty Ratio: 16:1
Students in Parent Institution: 3,000

PROGRAMS

Degrees Offered: MBA (1, 1.5, 2 years, 2.5 years, 3, or 3.5 years)
Academic Specialties: Gender Dynamics, Leadership, Negotiations

STUDENT INFORMATION

Total Business Students: 250
% Female: 100
% Minority: 15
% International: 30
Average Age: 32

COMPUTER AND RESEARCH FACILITIES

Research Facilities: Simmons Graduate School of Management houses the Center for Gender in Organizations (CGO), an innovative research center that analyzes gender dynamics in organizations and focuses on the conditions required for women's success.
Computer Facilities: Microcomputer lab, additional microcomputing terminals in the undergraduate computing facility, the Business Periodical Index, Business News Abstracts, Wilson Business Abstracts, and Paperchase (medical information). ABI/Inform, Business Dateline, Morningstar Mutual Funds, SEC/Disclosure, and the National Trade Data Bank are all available on CD-ROM computer workstations. Simmons is a member of the Fenway Library Consortium.
Campuswide Network? Yes
Computer Model Recommended: No
Internet Fee? No

EXPENSES/FINANCIAL AID

Annual Tuition: $31,000
Tuition Per Credit: $686
Room & Board (On Campus): $10,980
Books and Supplies: $3,000
Average Grant: $8,600
Average Loan: $10,000
% Receiving Aid Their First Year: 25

ADMISSIONS INFORMATION

Application Fee: $75
Electronic Application? Yes
Regular Application Deadline: 6/30
Regular Notification: Rolling
Deferment Available? Yes
Length of Deferment: 1 year
Non-fall Admissions? Yes
Non-fall Application Deadline(s): 11/15 (January entry)
Transfer Students Accepted? Yes
Transfer Policy: Reviewed on case-by-case basis
Need-Blind Admissions? Yes

Number of Applications Received: 120
% of Applicants Accepted: 88
% Accepted Who Enrolled: 91
Average GPA: 3.0
Average GMAT: 550
Average Years Experience: 8
Other Schools to Which Students Applied: Babson College, Bentley College, Boston College, Boston University

INTERNATIONAL STUDENTS

TOEFL Required of International Students? Yes
Minimum TOEFL: 550 (213 computer)
Placement Office Available? Yes
% Employed Within 3 Months: 80
Prominent Alumni: Gail Snowden, executive VP, Fleet Boston Financial; Maryann Tocio, president and COO, Bright Horizon; Donna Fernandes, director, Buffalo Zoo; Gail Deegan, former CFO and executive VP, Houghton Mifflin; Sue Paresky, senior VP, Dana Farber Cancer Institute

SOUTHEAST MISSOURI STATE UNIVERSITY

Donald L. Harrison College of Business

Admissions Contact: Dr. Kenneth Heischmidt, Director, MBA Program
Address: MBA Office, Cape Girardeau, MO 63701
Admissions Phone: 573-651-5116 • **Admissions Fax:** 573-651-5032
Admissions E-mail: mba@semo.edu • **Web Address:** www.semo.edu

Southeast Missouri State University is the proud home of the internationally recognized Golden Eagles Marching Band. More important, it's the home of Harrison College of Business, where tuition rates are low and 99 percent of graduates are placed within a year of graduation. SMSU emphasizes the strength of its assistantship opportunities, which enable a graduate student to teach, research, or assist with administrative duties in the business school; for the student's services, the school will provide a stipend and a waiver of all fees. Most applicants to the MBA program possess an undergrad degree in business, although without one, admission is possible under certain circumstances.

INSTITUTIONAL INFORMATION

Public/Private: Public
Evening Classes Available? Yes
Total Faculty: 45
Student/Faculty Ratio: 20:1
Students in Parent Institution: 9,000
Academic Calendar: Semester

PROGRAMS

Degrees Offered: MBA (33-63 credits, 1-6 years part time), with concentrations in Accounting, Management, International Business, Environmental Management
Academic Specialties: Case study, computer analysis, computer simulations, experiential learning, field projects, group discussion, lecture, research, seminars by members of the business community, student presentations, study groups, team projects
Study Abroad Options: International exchange program in various counrties in Western Europe

STUDENT INFORMATION

Total Business Students: 100
% Full Time: 68
% Female: 45
% Minority: 5
% International: 44
Average Age: 27

COMPUTER AND RESEARCH FACILITIES

Computer Facilities: Several campuswide computer labs
Campuswide Network? Yes
Internet Fee? No

EXPENSES/FINANCIAL AID

Annual Tuition (Resident/Nonresident): $3,000/$5,000
Tuition Per Credit (Resident/Nonresident): $164/$289
Room & Board (On/Off Campus): $4,500
Books and Supplies: $500
Average Grant: $6,200
Average Loan: $1,000
% Receiving Financial Aid: 38

ADMISSIONS INFORMATION

Application Fee: $20
Electronic Application? Yes
Regular Application Deadline: Rolling
Regular Notification: Rolling
Deferment Available? Yes
Length of Deferment: 1 year
Non-fall Admissions? Yes
Non-fall Application Deadline(s): Spring, summer
Transfer Students Accepted? Yes
Transfer Policy: May transfer 9 hours authorized by director of MBA Program
Need-Blind Admissions? No
Number of Applications Received: 53
% of Applicants Accepted: 79
% Accepted Who Enrolled: 93
Average GPA: 3.2
Average GMAT: 510
Average Years Experience: 2
Other Admissions Factors Considered: GMAT test scores
Other Schools to Which Students Applied: Saint Louis University, Southern Illinois University—Carbondale, Southwest Missouri State University, University of Missouri—Columbia

INTERNATIONAL STUDENTS

TOEFL Required of International Students? Yes
Minimum TOEFL: 550 (213 computer)

EMPLOYMENT INFORMATION

Placement Office Available? Yes
% Employed Within 3 Months: 100
Fields Employing Percentage of Grads: Consulting (10%), MIS (15%), Accounting (15%), Finance (20%), General Management (40%)
Frequent Employers: Accenture, Bausch and Lomb, Dow Jones, Pricewaterhouse Coopers, Texas Instruments, TG Missouri

SOUTHEASTERN LOUISIANA UNIVERSITY
College of Business and Technology

Admissions Contact: Sandra Meyers, Graduate Admissions Specialist
Address: SLU 10752, Hammond, LA 70402
Admissions Phone: 800-222-7358 • **Admissions Fax:** 985-549-5632
Admissions E-mail: smeyers@selu.edu
Web Address: www.selu.edu/Academics/Business

The MBA program at Southeastern Louisiana University's College of Business stresses the practical aspects of business leadership and prepares students for leadership positions in both business and government. Every classroom is wired for laptop use, and the MBA curriculum has recently expanded to include new courses on international business and e-commerce. Graduation from the MBA program is contingent upon the completion of 30 hours of undergraduate business prerequisites in addition to 33 hours of MBA course work. Apart from a general MBA, SLU also offers an Executive MBA, which meets on Saturdays and includes frequent interaction with Hammond County business managers.

INSTITUTIONAL INFORMATION

Public/Private: Public
Evening Classes Available? Yes
Total Faculty: 34
% Faculty Female: 18
Student/Faculty Ratio: 7:1
Students in Parent Institution: 14,522
Academic Calendar: Semester

PROGRAMS

Degrees Offered: MBA (1-6 years), with concentrations in Accounting, Marketing; EMBA (17-month lock-step program meeting mainly on weekends)
Academic Specialties: Case study, computer-aided instruction, computer-analysis, experiential learning, faculty seminars, field projects, group discussion, lecture, research, role playing, seminars by members of the business community, simulations, study groups, team projects
Special Opportunities: Study abroad program
Study Abroad Options: Costa Rica, Germany

STUDENT INFORMATION

Total Business Students: 248
% Full Time: 63
% Female: 48
% Minority: 48
% Out of State: 1
% International: 37
Average Age: 28

COMPUTER AND RESEARCH FACILITIES

Research Facilities: Business Research Center
Computer Facilities: On-campus computer labs, St. Tammany Center (EMBA program)
Campuswide Network? Yes
% of MBA Classrooms Wired: 100
Internet Fee? No

EXPENSES/FINANCIAL AID

Annual Tuition (Resident/Nonresident): $2,457/$6,453
Room & Board (On/Off Campus): $3,440
Average Grant: $1,909
Average Loan: $8,916
% Receiving Financial Aid: 24
% Receiving Aid Their First Year: 8

ADMISSIONS INFORMATION

Application Fee: $20
Electronic Application? Yes
Regular Application Deadline: 7/15
Regular Notification: Rolling
Deferment Available? Yes
Length of Deferment: 1 year
Non-fall Admissions? Yes
Non-fall Application Deadline(s): 12/1, 5/1
Transfer Students Accepted? Yes
Transfer Policy: The student must earn 12 hours of graduate credit at Southeastern before applying for any transfer credit from another university. That university must be an accredited institution that regularly grants the master's degree, or an equivalent foreign institution. The student must be eligible for readmission to the institution from which the credits are to be transferred and must have earned a minumun grade of B in each course to be transferred. No more than one-third of the hours required for graduation may be transferred.
Need-Blind Admissions? No
Number of Applications Received: 124
% of Applicants Accepted: 69
% Accepted Who Enrolled: 73
Average GPA: 2.9
Average GMAT: 470

INTERNATIONAL STUDENTS

TOEFL Required of International Students? Yes
Minimum TOEFL: 525 (195 computer)

EMPLOYMENT INFORMATION

Placement Office Available? Yes
Prominent Alumni: Robin Roberts, ESPN sportscaster; Russell Carollo, Pulitzer Prize winner; Harold Jackson, president (retired), Sunsweet Products; James J. Brady, former president, National Democratic Party; Carl Barbier, federal judge

SOUTHERN ILLINOIS UNIVERSITY— CARBONDALE
College of Business Admnistration

Admissions Contact: Joe Pineau, Coordinator, MBA Program
Address: Rehn Hall 133, Carbondale, IL 62901-4625
Admissions Phone: 618-453-3030 • **Admissions Fax:** 618-453-7961
Admissions E-mail: mbagp@cba.siu.edu • **Web Address:** www.cba.siu.edu

The focus of Southern Illinois University—Carbondale's MBA program is to prepare students for managerial positions in profit and nonprofit organizations and in business, government, education, and health sectors. Whether or not a student possesses an undergrad business degree, SIU is willing to impart upon him or her problem-solving and decision-making skills that lead to success in management. SIU is proud to provide a comprehensive business education focusing on the political, social, legal, and economic forces at work in business environments.

INSTITUTIONAL INFORMATION

Public/Private: Public
Evening Classes Available? No
Total Faculty: 40
Student/Faculty Ratio: 6:1
Students in Parent Institution: 22,250
Academic Calendar: Semester

PROGRAMS

Degrees Offered: MBA (33 credits, 1-2 years), EMBA (33 credits, 18 months)

Combined Degrees: MBA/JD (105 credits, 3-4 years), MBA/MS in Agribusiness Economics (51 credits, 1 to 2.5 years), MBA/MA in Communication (51 credits, 1 to 2.5 years)

Study Abroad Options: ESC Grenoble and Sup de Co Montpellier, France.

STUDENT INFORMATION

Total Business Students: 128
% Full Time: 88
% Female: 43
% Minority: 8
% Out of State: 11
% International: 50
Average Age: 26

COMPUTER AND RESEARCH FACILITIES

Research Facilities: Pontikes Center
Computer Facilities: 3 University computer labs, including 1 in the College of Business.
Campuswide Network? No
% of MBA Classrooms Wired: 100
Computer Model Recommended: Laptop
Internet Fee? No

EXPENSES/FINANCIAL AID

Annual Tuition (Resident/Nonresident): $4,000/$8,200

ADMISSIONS INFORMATION

Application Fee: $35
Electronic Application? No
Regular Application Deadline: 6/15
Regular Notification: 1/1
Deferment Available? Yes
Length of Deferment: 1 year
Non-fall Admissions? Yes
Non-fall Application Deadline(s): 11/15, 4/15, 9/15, 2/15
Transfer Students Accepted? Yes
Transfer Policy: Maximum of 6 transfer credits accepted for core curriculum
Need-Blind Admissions? No
Number of Applications Received: 278
% of Applicants Accepted: 52
% Accepted Who Enrolled: 46
Average GPA: 3.3
GPA Range: 2.4-3.7
Average GMAT: 533
GMAT Range: 470-590
Average Years Experience: 4
Other Schools to Which Students Applied: Eastern Illinois University, University of Illinois, University of Missouri—Columbia, Western Illinois University

INTERNATIONAL STUDENTS

TOEFL Required of International Students? Yes
Minimum TOEFL: 550 (220 computer)

EMPLOYMENT INFORMATION

Placement Office Available? Yes

SOUTHERN ILLINOIS UNIVERSITY— EDWARDSVILLE
School of Business

Admissions Contact: Dr. Kathryn Martell, Associate Dean for Academic Affairs
Address: Campus Box 1051, Edwardsville, IL 62026
Admissions Phone: 618-650-3840 • **Admissions Fax:** 618-650-3979
Admissions E-mail: mba@siue.edu • **Web Address:** www.siue.edu/BUSINESS

The SIU—Edwardsville MBA education encompasses "the social, economic, political, regulatory, and cultural forces that shape the external environment in which an organization operates." MBA students at Southern Illinois—Edwardsville can choose between a general MBA and an MBA specializing in either e-commerce or management information systems. SIU also hosts a notable lecture series called Executive Business Hour, which grants students the opportunity to meet and learn from successful business leaders and then bring their enriching lessons back to class, where they may be applied to the curriculum.

INSTITUTIONAL INFORMATION

Public/Private: Public
Evening Classes Available? Yes
Total Faculty: 56
% Faculty Female: 19
% Faculty Minority: 12
Student/Faculty Ratio: 19:1
Students in Parent Institution: 12,442

PROGRAMS

Degrees Offered: MBA (1-6 years), MSA (1-6 years), MS in Economics and Finance (1-6 years), MA in Economics and Finance (1-6 years), MS in CIS (1-6 years), MS in Marketing Research (1-6 years), MBA with MIS Specialization (1-6 years), MBA with E-Business Specialization (1-6 years)

Special Opportunities: The calendar is divided into 10-week semesters beginning in August, November, February, and May.

Study Abroad Options: Europe, Mexico

STUDENT INFORMATION

Total Business Students: 255
% Full Time: 32
% Female: 45
% Minority: 5
% International: 16
Average Age: 32

COMPUTER AND RESEARCH FACILITIES

Research Facilities: Lovejoy Library; 20 million items at 45 member libraries and 800 other Illinois libraries can be identified and borrowed.

Computer Facilities: 400 on-campus computer terminals/PCs are available for student use, and all or some are linked by a campuswide network. The network has full access to the Internet.

Campuswide Network? No
Internet Fee? No

EXPENSES/FINANCIAL AID

Annual Tuition (Resident/Nonresident): $2,034/$4,068
Tuition Per Credit (Resident/Nonresident): $339
Room & Board (On/Off Campus): $4,552
Books and Supplies: $1,000

ADMISSIONS INFORMATION

Application Fee: $30
Electronic Application? Yes
Regular Application Deadline: 7/15
Regular Notification: 1/1
Deferment Available? Yes
Non-fall Admissions? Yes
Non-fall Application Deadline(s): 30 days prior to first day of class
Transfer Students Accepted? Yes
Transfer Policy: Maximum of 9 hours from an accredited school
Need-Blind Admissions? No
Average GPA: 3.2
Average GMAT: 520
Average Years Experience: 9
Other Admissions Factors Considered: Bachelor's degree, minimum GPA of 2.5, college transcripts
Other Schools to Which Students Applied: Saint Louis University, Washington University in St. Louis, University of Missouri—St. Louis

INTERNATIONAL STUDENTS

TOEFL Required of International Students? Yes
Minimum TOEFL: 550 (213 computer)

EMPLOYMENT INFORMATION

Placement Office Available? Yes
Prominent Alumni: Robert Baer, president and CEO, United Van Lines; Wilton Heylinger, dean, School of Business, Morris Brown College; Ralph Korte, president, Korte Construction Co.; Mitch Meyers, president, Zipatoni Co.; James Milligan, president (retired), Spalding Sports Center

---

SOUTHERN METHODIST UNIVERSITY
Cox School of Business

Admissions Contact: Arrion Rathsack, Director, MBA Admissions
Address: PO Box 750333, Dallas, TX 75275
Admissions Phone: 214-768-1214 • **Admissions Fax:** 214-768-3956
Admissions E-mail: mbainfo@mail.cox.smu.edu • **Web Address:** mba.cox.smu.edu

"Open-door policy" doesn't even describe the amount of attention that the faculty at SMU's "state-of-the-art" Cox School of Business heap on the MBA students. "We can meet with our professors at any time," gloats one student. "We often have happy hours together." Cox students also laud the tremendously popular mentor program and the Business Leadership Center, and they tell us that "Dallas is an incredible resource for jobs and a great lifestyle."

INSTITUTIONAL INFORMATION

Public/Private: Private
Evening Classes Available? Yes
Total Faculty: 95
% Faculty Part Time: 25
Student/Faculty Ratio: 4:1
Students in Parent Institution: 10,000
Academic Calendar: Modular/Semester

PROGRAMS

Degrees Offered: MBA (2 years full time), Professional MBA (2.5 years part time), EMBA (21 months), MSA (2 years)

Combined Degrees: JD/MBA (4 years plus 1 semester), MA/MBA in Arts Administration (24 months)
Academic Specialties: General Management, Accounting, Financial Consulting, Finance, Telecommunications and Electronic Commerce, Management Consulting and Strategy, Marketing Strategy and Entrepreneurship
Special Opportunities: Executive Mentor Program, Business Leadership Center, International Exchange Opportunities, Business Information Center, Global Leadership Program, Career Management Training Program, Caruth Institute, Maguire Institute, FINA Foundation Business Leaders Spotlight Series, Management Briefing Series
Study Abroad Options: Australia, Belgium, Brazil, China, Denmark, England, France, Germany, Japan, Mexico, Singapore, Spain, Venezuela

STUDENT INFORMATION

Total Business Students: 897
% Full Time: 27
% Female: 27
% Minority: 10
% Out of State: 52
% International: 20
Average Age: 28

COMPUTER AND RESEARCH FACILITIES

Research Facilities: Caruth Institute of Owner-Managed Business, Business Leadership Center, Finance Institute, Maguire Oil and Gas Institute, Business Information Center, Center for Research in Real Estate and Land Use Economics
Computer Facilities: Center for Media and Instructional Technology, Patterson; Business Information Center, Bradfield; Hamon Fine Arts Library; Dialog, Bloomberg, Lexis-Nexis, CRISP, CompuStat, Dow Jones Interactive, Datastream, Economist Intelligence Unit Viewswire, S+P Net Advantage, Disclosure Global Access; numerous busness-related CD-ROM products and subscription Internet databases
Campuswide Network? Yes
% of MBA Classrooms Wired: 100
Computer Model Recommended: Laptop
Internet Fee? No

EXPENSES/FINANCIAL AID

Annual Tuition: $26,808
Room & Board (On/Off Campus): $10,000
Books and Supplies: $1,650
Average Grant: $28,000

ADMISSIONS INFORMATION

Application Fee: $75
Electronic Application? Yes
Early Decision Application Deadline: 11/30
Early Decision Notification: 1/30
Regular Application Deadline: 5/1
Regular Notification: 6/15
Deferment Available? Yes
Length of Deferment: 1 year
Non-fall Admissions? No
Transfer Students Accepted? No
Need-Blind Admissions? Yes
Number of Applications Received: 772
% of Applicants Accepted: 30
% Accepted Who Enrolled: 50
Average GPA: 3.2
GPA Range: 2.7-3.7
Average GMAT: 660
GMAT Range: 590-720
Average Years Experience: 5
Other Admissions Factors Considered: The Cox MBA Admissions Committee seeks a diverse group of candidates who demonstrate strong academic

capabilities, significant professional and life experiences, strong leadership potential, and personal qualities such as maturity, self-confidence, motivation, and strong interpersonal and communication skills. Finally, and most importantly, all of these attributes should be complemented by a strong commitment to learning and achieving.

Minority/Disadvantaged Student Recruitment Programs: Steve Denson, Cox MBA Director of Diversity, develops relationships with organizations that promote the recruitment of underrepresented minority groups and international students.

Other Schools to Which Students Applied: Duke University, Emory University, Georgetown University, Rice University, University of Texas—Austin, Vanderbilt University, Washington University in St. Louis

INTERNATIONAL STUDENTS

TOEFL Required of International Students? Yes
Minimum TOEFL: 600 (250 computer)

EMPLOYMENT INFORMATION

Placement Office Available? Yes
Fields Employing Percentage of Grads: Other (5%), Operations (5%), General Management (6%), Consulting (9%), Marketing (26%), Finance (49%)
Frequent Employers: America Airlines, Citigroup, Deloitte Consulting, ExxonMobil Corp., Sabre Inc., Samsung, Stanley Works, Texas Instruments, TXU, Wells Fargo
Prominent Alumni: Thomas W. Horton, senior vice president/CFO, American Airlines; David B. Miller, managing director, El Paso Energy; Ruth Ann Marshall, president, MasterCard; James MacNaughton, managing director, Rothschild, Inc.; C. Fred Ball, CEO, Bank of Texas

See page 440.

SOUTHWEST MISSOURI STATE UNIVERSITY
College of Business Administration

Admissions Contact: Tobin Bushman, Graduate College Coordinator
Address: 901 S. National, Springfield, MO 65804
Admissions Phone: 417-836-5335 • **Admissions Fax:** 417-836-6888
Admissions E-mail: GraduateCollege@smsu.edu • **Web Address:** www.coba.smsu.edu

Breakfast of Champions is a lecture series at Southwest Missouri State's College of Business Administration, where local business executives speak and interact with the students, allowing connections to be made and opportunities to multiply. The long list of on-campus recruiters on SMSU's website further attests to the school's close ties to the business community. SMSU offers a general MBA and a Techno-MBA, designed for students seeking an MBA with a concentration in computer information systems. The quality and low cost of living in Springfield, located near the beautiful Ozark area, provides students with a comfortable arrangement and easy access to incredible recreational activities.

INSTITUTIONAL INFORMATION

Public/Private: Public
Evening Classes Available? Yes
Total Faculty: 70
% Faculty Female: 24
Student/Faculty Ratio: 20:1
Students in Parent Institution: 18,932

PROGRAMS

Degrees Offered: MBA (1-2 years), MACC (1-2 years), MHA (1-2 years), Master of CIS (1-2 years)
Academic Specialties: Accounting, CIS, Management, Marketing, Finance and General Business, Human Resource Management, International Management, Logistics

STUDENT INFORMATION

Total Business Students: 329
% Full Time: 31
% Female: 17
% Minority: 2
% International: 24
Average Age: 29

COMPUTER AND RESEARCH FACILITIES

Research Facilities: Meyer Libraray
Computer Facilities: Computer Lab, Glass Hall; Computer Lab, Cheek Hall; Computer Lab, Public Affairs; computer facilities in dormitories
Campuswide Network? Yes
% of MBA Classrooms Wired: 100
Internet Fee? No

EXPENSES/FINANCIAL AID

Annual Tuition (Resident/Nonresident): $3,552/$7,104
Tuition Per Credit (Resident/Nonresident): $148/$296
Room & Board (On/Off Campus): $5,200
Books and Supplies: $900
Average Grant: $5,000
Average Loan: $12,000

ADMISSIONS INFORMATION

Application Fee: $25
Electronic Application? Yes
Regular Application Deadline: Rolling
Regular Notification: Rolling
Deferment Available? Yes
Length of Deferment: 1 semester
Non-fall Admissions? Yes
Non-fall Application Deadline(s): 3 weeks before term begins
Transfer Students Accepted? Yes
Transfer Policy: With advisor permission
Need-Blind Admissions? No
Number of Applications Received: 361
% of Applicants Accepted: 88
% Accepted Who Enrolled: 104
Average GPA: 3.4
GPA Range: 2.2-4.0
Average GMAT: 520
GMAT Range: 430-630
Average Years Experience: 2
Other Schools to Which Students Applied: Arkansas State University, Central Missouri State University, Southeast Missouri State University, University of Arkansas—Little Rock, University of Missouri—Kansas City, University of Missouri—Columbia, University of Missouri—St. Louis

INTERNATIONAL STUDENTS

TOEFL Required of International Students? Yes
Minimum TOEFL: 550

EMPLOYMENT INFORMATION

Placement Office Available? Yes
% Employed Within 3 Months: 79
Frequent Employers: AG Edwards; Anheuser Busch; Archer Daniels Midland; Baird Kurtz & Dobson; Boeing; Caterpillar; Cerner; DataTronics;

Deloitte & Touche; Edward Jones; Enterprise; FedEx; Federal Reserve Bank; Federated Insurance; Gateway Financial; Hallmark; John Hancock; Kirkpatrick, Phillips & Miller, CPAs; Koch Industries; KPMG; Occidental Petroleum; Payless; Renaissance Financial; Samson; Sherwin Williams; State Farm; State Street; Target; Toys R Us; Wal-Mart; Yellow

Prominent Alumni: David Glass, former CEO, Wal-Mart, and CEO, KC Royals; Todd Tiahrt, 4-term congressman; Richard McClure, president, Uni Group, Inc.; Jim Smith, president ABA, 2001-02; Terry Thompson, president, Jack Henry

SOUTHWEST TEXAS STATE UNIVERSITY
Graduate School of Business

Admissions Contact: Dr. Robert Olney, Director of Graduate Business Programs
Address: 601 University Drive, San Marcos, TX 78666
Admissions Phone: 512-245-2581 • **Admissions Fax:** 512-245-8365
Admissions E-mail: gradcollege@swt.edu • **Web Address:** www.business.swt.edu

INSTITUTIONAL INFORMATION
Public/Private: Public
Evening Classes Available? Yes
Total Faculty: 52
% Faculty Female: 23
% Faculty Minority: 8
Student/Faculty Ratio: 12:1
Students in Parent Institution: 22,500
Academic Calendar: Semester

PROGRAMS
Degrees Offered: MBA (1-6 years), MACC (1-6 years)
Combined Degrees: MBA with Technology Emphasis (1-6 years)

STUDENT INFORMATION
Total Business Students: 343
% Full Time: 10
% International: 10
Average Age: 33

COMPUTER AND RESEARCH FACILITIES
Research Facilities: Center for Latin American Business, Center for Entrepreneurial Studies
Campuswide Network? Yes
% of MBA Classrooms Wired: 80
Internet Fee? No

EXPENSES/FINANCIAL AID
Annual Tuition (Resident/Nonresident): $5,552/$15,872
Tuition Per Credit (Resident/Nonresident): $318/$530
Books and Supplies: $550
Average Grant: $5,000

ADMISSIONS INFORMATION
Application Fee: $25
Electronic Application? No
Regular Application Deadline: 6/15
Regular Notification: 7/1
Deferment Available? Yes
Length of Deferment: 1 year
Non-fall Admissions? Yes

Non-fall Application Deadline(s): 10/15 spring, 4/15 summer
Transfer Students Accepted? Yes
Transfer Policy: Maximum of 6 semester hours
Need-Blind Admissions? Yes
Average GPA: 3.2
GPA Range: 2.5-3.8
Average GMAT: 550
GMAT Range: 450-710
Average Years Experience: 7
Other Schools to Which Students Applied: Texas A&M University, Texas Tech University, University of Texas Health Science Center—San Antonio

INTERNATIONAL STUDENTS
TOEFL Required of International Students? Yes
Minimum TOEFL: 550 (213 computer)

EMPLOYMENT INFORMATION
Placement Office Available? Yes
% Employed Within 3 Months: 100

STANFORD UNIVERSITY
Stanford Graduate School of Business
MBA Program

Admissions Contact: Derrick Bolton, Director of MBA Admissions
Address: 518 Memorial Way, Stanford, CA 94305-5015
Admissions Phone: 650-723-2766 • **Admissions Fax:** 650-725-7831
Admissions E-mail: mba@gsb.stanford.edu • **Web Address:** www.gsb.stanford.edu

Feeling lucky? Got credentials out the wazoo? Check out Stanford's Graduate School of Business, home to an "entrepreneurial spirit," a "supportive and comfortable atmosphere," a great social life, and a Nobel Prize–winning faculty. Stanford MBAs are sane again after the demise of the heady days of the Silicon Valley rush, but this is still CEO training ground. Students graduate as stellar general managers (Stanford doesn't produce specialists) with a proclivity for networking and landing leadership posts.

INSTITUTIONAL INFORMATION
Public/Private: Private
Evening Classes Available? No
Total Faculty: 130
Student/Faculty Ratio: 6:1
Academic Calendar: Quarter

PROGRAMS
Degrees Offered: Sloan Program(10 months), leads to MS degree; PhD (4 years)
Combined Degrees: It is possible to earn dual degrees with other departments; common dual degrees: JD/MBA and MBA/MA in Education.
Academic Specialties: General Management-includes all majors disciplines. Finance, Economics, Strategic Management, Marketing, Accounting, Human Resources/Organizational Behavior, Operations, Information and Technology, Political Science, Entrepreneurship
Special Opportunities: Global Management Program, Public Management Program

STUDENT INFORMATION
Total Business Students: 749
% Full Time: 100

% Female: 37
% Minority: 23
Average Age: 27

COMPUTER AND RESEARCH FACILITIES

Research Facilities: Center for Entrepreneurial Studies at Stanford, Center for Electronic Business and Commerce, Center for Social Innovation, Global Supply Chain Management Forum, Stanford Project on Emerging Companies
Computer Facilities: School of Business computer center, state-of-the-art networking, online and CD ROM databases in BusinessSchool Library, full network at Schwab residence for first-year MBA students
Campuswide Network? Yes
% of MBA Classrooms Wired: 100
Computer Model Recommended: Laptop
Internet Fee? No

EXPENSES/FINANCIAL AID

Annual Tuition: $36,252
Room & Board (On/Off Campus): $17,646/$19,275
Books and Supplies: $3,051
Average Grant: $11,787
% Receiving Financial Aid: 67

ADMISSIONS INFORMATION

Application Fee: $200
Electronic Application? Yes
Deferment Available? Yes
Length of Deferment: Very limited
Non-fall Admissions? No
Transfer Students Accepted? No
Need-Blind Admissions? Yes
Number of Applications Received: 5,864
Average Years Experience: 5
Other Admissions Factors Considered: Leadership potential, strong academic aptitude, diversity among students
Minority/Disadvantaged Student Recruitment Programs: Partnership for diversity program offers financial support and professional experience to selected minority admits.
Other Schools to Which Students Applied: Harvard University

INTERNATIONAL STUDENTS

TOEFL Required of International Students? Yes
Minimum TOEFL: 600 (250 computer)

EMPLOYMENT INFORMATION

Placement Office Available? Yes
% Employed Within 3 Months: 94
Fields Employing Percentage of Grads: Operations (1%), Entrepreneurship (6%), General Management (8%), Marketing (8%), Other (18%), Finance (22%), Consulting (37%)
Frequent Employers: Accenture; Bain & Co.; The Boston Consulting Group; Booz Allen & Hamilton Inc.; The Bridgespan Group; Cisco Systems Inc.; Deloitte Consulting; Goldman, Sachs & Co.; McKinsey & Co.; Merrill Lynch; Monitor Co.; Siebel Systems, Inc.
Prominent Alumni: Phil Knight, chairman/CEO, Nike Inc.; Charles Schwab, chairman/CEO; Henry McKinnell, chairman/CEO, Pfizer Co.; Mads Ovlisen, president/CEO, Novo Nordisk A/S Denmark; Dominick Cadbury, chairman, Schwepps PLC

STATE UNIVERSITY OF WEST GEORGIA
Richards College of Business

Admissions Contact: John R. Wells, Director, Director, MBA Program
Address: 1600 Maple Street, Carrollton, GA 30118-3000
Admissions Phone: 770-836-6467 • **Admissions Fax:** 770-836-6774
Admissions E-mail: jwells@westga.edu • **Web Address:** www.westga.edu

The Richards College of Business is proud to offer the Georgia Web MBA, an online degree opportunity available through a consortium of five University System of Georgia member institutions. The Web MBA is a 10-course distance learning program, designed for middle- and upper-management professionals who wish to attain an education without interrupting their careers. The general AACSB-accredited MBA is a nonthesis program with a broad-based curriculum designed to serve a whole range of students: those looking for a terminal degree to increase their competencies, those looking for in-service training, and those looking to prepare for doctoral studies in business.

INSTITUTIONAL INFORMATION

Public/Private: Public
Evening Classes Available? Yes
Total Faculty: 28
Student/Faculty Ratio: 19:1
Students in Parent Institution: 9,675
Academic Calendar: Semester

PROGRAMS

Degrees Offered: General MBA (12 months), MPACC (12 months)
Academic Specialties: Case study, computer-aided instruction, computer analysis, computer simulations, experiential learning, group discussion, lecture, research, seminars by members of the business community, simulations, student presentations, study groups, team projects

STUDENT INFORMATION

Total Business Students: 65
% Full Time: 51
% Female: 34
% Minority: 38
% Out of State: 46
% International: 50
Average Age: 26

COMPUTER AND RESEARCH FACILITIES

Research Facilities: Ingram Library
Computer Facilities: Computer labs with 100-plus seats, databases, Microsoft applications
Campuswide Network? Yes
% of MBA Classrooms Wired: 100
Internet Fee? No

EXPENSES/FINANCIAL AID

Annual Tuition (Resident/Nonresident): $4,440/$15,296
Tuition Per Credit (Resident/Nonresident): $154/$454
Room & Board (On/Off Campus): $6,156/$7,000
Books and Supplies: $1,200
Average Grant: $1,000
% Receiving Financial Aid: 24
% Receiving Aid Their First Year: 15

ADMISSIONS INFORMATION

Application Fee: $20
Electronic Application? Yes
Regular Application Deadline: 7/2
Regular Notification: 8/2
Deferment Available? Yes
Length of Deferment: 1 year
Non-fall Admissions? Yes
Non-fall Application Deadline(s): 12/10 spring, 5/28 summer
Transfer Students Accepted? Yes
Transfer Policy: 2 courses from an accredited program
Need-Blind Admissions? No
Number of Applications Received: 41
% of Applicants Accepted: 88
% Accepted Who Enrolled: 81
Average GPA: 3.2
GPA Range: 2.5-3.8
Average GMAT: 510
GMAT Range: 450-710
Other Admissions Factors Considered: Computer experience, resume, GPA for last 2 years

INTERNATIONAL STUDENTS

TOEFL Required of International Students? Yes
Minimum TOEFL: 550 (213 computer)

EMPLOYMENT INFORMATION

Placement Office Available? Yes
% Employed Within 3 Months: 99

STEPHEN F. AUSTIN STATE UNIVERSITY
College of Business

Admissions Contact: Violet Rogers, MBA Director
Address: PO Box 13004, Nacogdoches, TX 75962
Admissions Phone: 936-468-3101 • **Admissions Fax:** 936-468-1560
Admissions E-mail: mba@sfasu.edu • **Web Address:** www.cob.sfasu.edu

Make sure you can pronounce "Nacogdoches," the name of the city that Stephen F. Austin State University calls home, before you apply to the College of Business MBA program. The MBA program is designed primarily for part timers, as most classes are scheduled during evening hours, but full-time students may enroll as well. An SFASU MBA education provides advanced training in the theory and practice of management and exposes students to a wide assortment of fundamental business disciplines. At the host institution, business majors currently account for about 22 percent of the more than 11,000 students. Applicants to the College of Business also apply to Texas A&M and University of Texas at Tyler.

INSTITUTIONAL INFORMATION

Public/Private: Public
Evening Classes Available? Yes
Total Faculty: 25
% Faculty Female: 50
% Faculty Minority: 5
Student/Faculty Ratio: 16:1
Students in Parent Institution: 11,500

PROGRAMS

Degrees Offered: MPACC (36 hours), MBA (36 hours), MS in Computer Science (36 hours)

STUDENT INFORMATION

Total Business Students: 65
% Full Time: 10
% Female: 40
% Minority: 11
% Out of State: 2
% International: 2
Average Age: 28

COMPUTER AND RESEARCH FACILITIES

Computer Facilities: Library research databases
Campuswide Network? Yes
Computer Model Recommended: Desktop
Internet Fee? No

EXPENSES/FINANCIAL AID

Annual Tuition (Resident/Nonresident): $432/$2,976
Tuition Per Credit (Resident/Nonresident): $120/$744
Room & Board (On/Off Campus): $4,500/$6,000
Books and Supplies: $1,000
Average Grant: $3,300
Average Loan: $3,300
% Receiving Financial Aid: 9
% Receiving Aid Their First Year: 9

ADMISSIONS INFORMATION

Electronic Application? Yes
Regular Application Deadline: 7/1
Regular Notification: 8/1
Deferment Available? Yes
Length of Deferment: 1 year
Non-fall Admissions? Yes
Non-fall Application Deadline(s): 12/1, 5/1
Transfer Students Accepted? Yes
Transfer Policy: 6 hours graduate credit from an AACSB-International-accredited school
Need-Blind Admissions? Yes
Number of Applications Received: 56
% of Applicants Accepted: 89
% Accepted Who Enrolled: 78
Average GPA: 3.0
GPA Range: 2.6-3.3
Average GMAT: 482
GMAT Range: 440-530
Average Years Experience: 5
Other Admissions Factors Considered: None
Minority/Disadvantaged Student Recruitment Programs: Minority scholarships posted on bulletin board

INTERNATIONAL STUDENTS

TOEFL Required of International Students? Yes
Minimum TOEFL: 550 (213 computer)

EMPLOYMENT INFORMATION

Placement Office Available? Yes
% Employed Within 3 Months: 100
Frequent Employers: Andersen, Exxon-Mobil, Haliburton, Temple Inland

STETSON UNIVERSITY
School of Busines Administration

Admissions Contact: Dr. Frank A. DeZoort, Director, Graduate Business Programs
Address: 421 North Woodland Boulevard, Unit 8398, DeLand, FL 32720-7413
Admissions Phone: 386-822-7410 • **Admissions Fax:** 386-822-7413
Admissions E-mail: jbosco@stetson.edu • **Web Address:** business.stetson.edu/

INSTITUTIONAL INFORMATION

Public/Private: Private
Evening Classes Available? No
Total Faculty: 39
% Faculty Female: 25
% Faculty Part Time: 4
Student/Faculty Ratio: 15:1
Students in Parent Institution: 2,700
Academic Calendar: Semester

PROGRAMS

Degrees Offered: MBA (5 semesters), MALL (5 semesters)
Combined Degrees: MBA/JD (3 years)
Academic Specialties: Human Resourse Management, Finance, Accounting, Marketing, Information Systems
Special Opportunities: General Business, Accounting

STUDENT INFORMATION

Total Business Students: 160
% Full Time: 50
% Female: 46
% Minority: 2
% Out of State: 1
% International: 5
Average Age: 24

COMPUTER AND RESEARCH FACILITIES

Campuswide Network? Yes
% of MBA Classrooms Wired: 6
Computer Model Recommended: Laptop
Internet Fee? No

EXPENSES/FINANCIAL AID

Tuition Per Credit (Resident/Nonresident): $430
Books and Supplies: $1,200

ADMISSIONS INFORMATION

Application Fee: $25
Electronic Application? Yes
Early Decision Application Deadline: 1/1
Early Decision Notification: 1/1
Regular Application Deadline: 1/1
Regular Notification: 1/11
Deferment Available? Yes
Length of Deferment: 1 year
Non-fall Admissions? Yes
Non-fall Application Deadline(s): 7/15, 10/15, 3/15
Transfer Students Accepted? Yes
Transfer Policy: Maximum 6 credit hours from AACSB-accredited shool
Need-Blind Admissions? Yes
Number of Applications Received: 100
% of Applicants Accepted: 150
% Accepted Who Enrolled: 120
Average Years Experience: 2

INTERNATIONAL STUDENTS

TOEFL Required of International Students? Yes
Minimum TOEFL: 550

EMPLOYMENT INFORMATION

Placement Office Available? No
Frequent Employers: Small to medium firms in the greater Tampa Bay area, state attorney's offices, public defender's office

---

SUFFOLK UNIVERSITY
Frank Sawyer School of Management

Admissions Contact: Judith L. Reynolds, Director of Graduate Admissions
Address: 8 Ashburton Place, Boston, MA 02108
Admissions Phone: 617-573-8302 • **Admissions Fax:** 617-523-0116
Admissions E-mail: grad.admission@admin.suffolk.edu
Web Address: www.sawyer.suffolk.edu

It would be nearly impossible for a prospective b-school student not to find a suitable MBA program at the Frank Sawyer School of Management. Students may enroll part time or full time, and classes are offered mostly at night but also during the day, on Saturdays, and during two summer sessions. Suffolk offers 13 MBA programs to choose from, including a general MBA and ranging from the MBA for pharmacists to the Accelerated MBA for music management majors at Berklee College of Music, as well as MBA programs at three other campuses and a summer session in Senegal. Frequent employers of Suffolk grads include Fidelity Investments, State Street Bank, and Fleet Financial.

INSTITUTIONAL INFORMATION

Public/Private: Private
Evening Classes Available? Yes
Total Faculty: 148
% Faculty Female: 26
% Faculty Minority: 5
% Faculty Part Time: 53
Student/Faculty Ratio: 12:1
Students in Parent Institution: 7,078
Academic Calendar: Semester

PROGRAMS

Degrees Offered: Acelerated MBA for attorneys (1 year full time), EMBA (15-21 months), MBA (10-16 months full time), MBA/Entreprenuership (10-16 months full time)
Combined Degrees: JD/MPA (4 years full time), JD/MBA (5 years part time), MBA/MSA (2 years full time), MBA/MST (2 years full time), MBA/GDPA (1-2 years)
Academic Specialties: Entrepreneurship, International Business, Finance
Study Abroad Options: 1- to 2-week seminars in Argentina, China, France, Ireland, Italy, Prague, Spain

STUDENT INFORMATION

Total Business Students: 774
% Full Time: 21
% Female: 41
% Minority: 4
% Out of State: 4

% International: 61
Average Age: 33

COMPUTER AND RESEARCH FACILITIES

Computer Facilities: Lexis-Nexis, Info Track, AbInform, Compustat, Dunn & Bradstreet, PredicastsProut, General Business File ASAP, Wall Street Journal, Academic Universe, FIS online, Reference USA
Campuswide Network? Yes
% of MBA Classrooms Wired: 8
Computer Model Recommended: Laptop
Internet Fee? No

EXPENSES/FINANCIAL AID

Annual Tuition: $20,440
Room & Board (On/Off Campus): $9,500
Books and Supplies: $700
Average Grant: $3,270
Average Loan: $14,259
% Receiving Financial Aid: 22

ADMISSIONS INFORMATION

Application Fee: $50
Electronic Application? No
Regular Application Deadline: 6/15
Regular Notification: Rolling
Deferment Available? Yes
Length of Deferment: 1 year
Non-fall Admissions? Yes
Non-fall Application Deadline(s): 11/15 spring, 4/15 summer
Transfer Students Accepted? Yes
Transfer Policy: Same as for regular applicants
Need-Blind Admissions? Yes
Number of Applications Received: 498
% of Applicants Accepted: 79
% Accepted Who Enrolled: 57
Average GPA: 3.2
GPA Range: 2.8-3.4
Average GMAT: 505
GMAT Range: 430-550
Average Years Experience: 3
Other Admissions Factors Considered: Length and quality of work experience
Minority/Disadvantaged Student Recruitment Programs: Attendance at under-represented students college fairs
Other Schools to Which Students Applied: Bentley College, Boston College, Boston University, Northeastern University, University of Massachusetts at Amherst

INTERNATIONAL STUDENTS

TOEFL Required of International Students? Yes
Minimum TOEFL: 550 (213 computer)

EMPLOYMENT INFORMATION

Placement Office Available? Yes
% Employed Within 3 Months: 95
Fields Employing Percentage of Grads: Quantitative (2%), Human Resources (2%), Operations (5%), Accounting (7%), Consulting (9%), MIS (9%), General Management (10%), Marketing (24%), Finance (24%)
Frequent Employers: Fidelity Investments, Fleet Financial, State Street Bank

SYRACUSE UNIVERSITY
School of Management

Admissions Contact: Carol J. Swanberg, Director of Admissions and Financial Aid
Address: 900 South Crouse Avenue, Suite 100, Syracuse, NY 13244-2130
Admissions Phone: 315-443-9214 • **Admissions Fax:** 315-443-9517
Admissions E-mail: MBAinfo@som.syr.edu • **Web Address:** www.som.syr.edu

Syracuse University's School of Management is, by its own account, "driven by the entrepreneurial spirit," and students say the "entrepreneurship professors are exceptional." The faculty in other areas are "spotty," though, and Syracuse winters can be brutal. Weather permitting, the generally "young" MBA students here enjoy a beautiful 200-acre campus replete with grassy lawns and historic buildings by day and a decent downtown bar and restaurant scene by night.

INSTITUTIONAL INFORMATION

Public/Private: Private
Evening Classes Available? Yes
Total Faculty: 58
% Faculty Female: 18
% Faculty Part Time: 10
Students in Parent Institution: 18,072
Academic Calendar: Semester

PROGRAMS

Degrees Offered: MBA (2 years), MSA (1 year), MS in Media Management (1 year)
Combined Degrees: MBA/JD, MBA/MS in Nursing Management
Academic Specialties: Accounting, Finance, Global Entrepreneurship, Marketing Management, Innovation Management, Management of Technology, Supply Chain Management, General Management
Special Opportunities: Full-time MBA, Evening MBA, Independent Study MBA, EMBA, MSA, MS in Media Management.
Study Abroad Options: International campuses: London, England; Shanghai, China; Harare, South Africa; Madrid, Spain; Singapore
Exchange Programs:University of Shanghai for Science and Technology, Sahnghai; National Chengchi University, Taipei, China; Kyung Hee University; Sejong University, Seoul, Korea; University of Limerick, Limerick, Ireland

STUDENT INFORMATION

% Full Time: 36
% Female: 30
% Minority: 15
% International: 32
Average Age: 27

COMPUTER AND RESEARCH FACILITIES

Research Facilities: Ballentine Center (Securities), Falcone Center (Entrepreneurship), Kiebach Center (International Business), Franklin Salzberg (Logistics), Brethen Center (Operations)
Computer Facilities: Library CD-ROM databases, electronic teaching stations, free dial-up Internet access, computers in group study areas, marketracks MX (stock market feed), high-performance Internet access, e-mail accounts
Campuswide Network? Yes
Computer Model Recommended: Laptop
Internet Fee? No

EXPENSES/FINANCIAL AID

Annual Tuition: $20,580
Tuition Per Credit (Resident/Nonresident): $647
Room & Board (On/Off Campus): $11,820

Books and Supplies: $1,270
Average Grant: $10,000
Average Loan: $17,000
% Receiving Financial Aid: 50
% Receiving Aid Their First Year: 50

ADMISSIONS INFORMATION

Application Fee: $50
Electronic Application? Yes
Regular Notification: Rolling
Deferment Available? Yes
Length of Deferment: 1 year
Non-fall Admissions? No
Transfer Students Accepted? No
Need-Blind Admissions? Yes
Number of Applications Received: 475
% of Applicants Accepted: 29
% Accepted Who Enrolled: 42
Average GPA: 3.2
Average GMAT: 636
GMAT Range: 570-700
Average Years Experience: 4
Other Admissions Factors Considered: Quality of full-time work experience, appropriateness for Syracuse's program, evidence of leadership potential, motivation, teamwork ability, perseverance
Minority/Disadvantaged Student Recruitment Programs: We have a feeder program with Florida A & M.
Other Schools to Which Students Applied: Boston University, Cornell University, New York University, Pennsylvania State University—Harrisburg Campus, University of Illinois, University of Rochester, University of Wisconsin—Madison

INTERNATIONAL STUDENTS

TOEFL Required of International Students? Yes
Minimum TOEFL: 580 (237 computer)

EMPLOYMENT INFORMATION

Placement Office Available? Yes
% Employed Within 3 Months: 88
Fields Employing Percentage of Grads: General Management (2%), Human Resources (2%), Consulting (5%), Marketing (7%), Operations (10%), Finance (21%)
Frequent Employers: American Airlines, Cannon, Cisco Systems, Goldman Sachs, IBM, Intel, Kodak, Lockheed Martin, United Technologies

TCU
M. J. Neeley School of Business

Admissions Contact: Peggy Conway, Director of MBA Admissions
Address: PO Box 298540, Fort Worth, TX 76129
Admissions Phone: 817-257-7531 • Admissions Fax: 817-257-6431
Admissions E-mail: mbainfo@tcu.edu • Web Address: www.mba.tcu.edu

Thanks to its prime location in the Dallas/Fort Worth Metroplex, students at TCU's very affordable Neeley School of Business have "great connections" all over the region. Neeley also offers a unique finance elective that allows students to manage the $1.3 million William C. Connor Educational Investment Fund. If you are looking for an affordable place to get your MBA, you will be hard-pressed to beat Neeley, especially if you want a career in Dallas.

INSTITUTIONAL INFORMATION

Public/Private: Private
Evening Classes Available? Yes
Total Faculty: 83
% Faculty Female: 17
% Faculty Minority: 11
% Faculty Part Time: 17
Student/Faculty Ratio: 5:1
Students in Parent Institution: 8,074
Academic Calendar: Semester

PROGRAMS

Degrees Offered: MBA (21 months full time); Professional MBA (28-33 months evenings); Accelerated MBA (12 months full time), for applicants with a BBA, at least 3 years of postgraduate work experience, and minimum GMAT of 620; EMBA (21 months); MACC (1 year)
Combined Degrees: Educational Leadership, MBA/EdD (3 years), Physics PhD/MBA (6 years, including dissertation), MIM (2 years)
Academic Specialties: Finance, Corporate Finance, Investment Management, Marketing, Value-Chain Marketing, International Business, E-Business, Entrepreneurship, Management
Special Opportunities: Professional Development Program: a series of personal and career assessments and workshops to help build key managerial skills and a stronger sense of professionalism; Educational Investment Fund: student-managed investment portfolio valued in excess of $1.8 million; MBA Enterprise Program: teams of MBA students are hired by corporate clients for consulting projects on a wide range of business issues; Center for Professional Communication: communication specialist and high-tech facilities available to help students develop more effective communication skills; Global Experiences: elective courses taught in English by TCU faculty in France and Germany; semester abroad options also available in France, Germany, or Mexico for students with adequate language skills
Study Abroad Options: France, Germany, Hungary, Mexico

STUDENT INFORMATION

Total Business Students: 259
% Full Time: 45
% Female: 28
% Minority: 8
% International: 31
Average Age: 27

COMPUTER AND RESEARCH FACILITIES

Research Facilities: Charles Tandy American Enterprise Center: executive education center that attracts hundreds of mid- and senior-level executives to campus each year; Ryffel Entrepreneurship Center: center to bring entrepreneurial experiences and expertise to students, funded by recent $8 million gift; Supply-Chain Management Institute: newly announced resource center to foster research and experiential learning opportunities in supply-chain management
Computer Facilities: 2 on-site labs with more than 80 PCs, 8 other labs, Internet access, Dow Jones News Retrieval Service, Infotrac, Disclosure, ABI Inform, Valuline Investment, Hoover's Online, Wilson Select Plus, Compustat, BNA Tax Management Portfolios, O'Neil Database, Marketguide, Mood's International Company Data
Campuswide Network? Yes
% of MBA Classrooms Wired: 100
Computer Model Recommended: Laptop
Internet Fee? No

EXPENSES/FINANCIAL AID

Annual Tuition: $14,700
Tuition Per Credit (Resident/Nonresident): $490
Books and Supplies: $1,000
Average Grant: $10,244

Average Loan: $14,885
% Receiving Financial Aid: 88
% Receiving Aid Their First Year: 91

ADMISSIONS INFORMATION

Application Fee: $50
Electronic Application? Yes
Early Decision Application Deadline: Rolling; applications accepted as early as 9/1
Early Decision Notification: 12/1
Regular Application Deadline: 4/30
Regular Notification: Rolling
Deferment Available? Yes
Length of Deferment: 1 year
Non-fall Admissions? No
Transfer Students Accepted? Yes
Transfer Policy: Maximum of 6 semester hours from an AACSB-accredited institution
Need-Blind Admissions? Yes
Number of Applications Received: 203
% of Applicants Accepted: 63
% Accepted Who Enrolled: 46
Average GPA: 3.1
GPA Range: 2.0-3.0
Average GMAT: 613
GMAT Range: 580-650
Average Years Experience: 4
Other Admissions Factors Considered: A holistic admissions approach is used to assess the applicant's fit with the program. In addition to academic ability, applicants must demonstrate the desire and ability to perform in a highly interactive, team-based environment.
Minority/Disadvantaged Student Recruitment Programs: Scholarships to recognize the achievements of Henry B. Gonzalez and Martin Luther King, Jr. are made available to TCU MBA students by the PepsiCo Foundation.
Other Schools to Which Students Applied: Baylor University, Southern Methodist University, Texas A&M University, Tulane University, University of Texas—Arlington, University of Texas—Austin

INTERNATIONAL STUDENTS

TOEFL Required of International Students? Yes
Minimum TOEFL: 550 (213 computer)

EMPLOYMENT INFORMATION

Placement Office Available? Yes
% Employed Within 3 Months: 77
Fields Employing Percentage of Grads: Consulting (7%), General Management (11%), Marketing (30%), Finance (52%)
Frequent Employers: BHA/Novation, Burlington Northern Santa Fe, Deloitte & Touche, Campbell's Soup, ECDI, Johnson & Johnson International, Lockheed Martin Aeronautics, Lufthansa, SBC, UBS Warburg
Prominent Alumni: John Roach, Roach Investments/Field Electronics; Luther King, Luther King Capital Management; Roger Ramsey, Investments; John Davis III, CEO and chairman, Pegasus Systems; Vivian Noble Dubose, president, Noble Properties

See page 442.

TEL AVIV UNIVERSITY
Leon Recanati Graduate School of Business Administration

Admissions Contact: Ms. Orit Mendelson, Shoham Program Director
Address: P.O.B. 39010 Ramat Aviv, Tel Aviv, 69978 Israel
Admissions Phone: 011-640-6065
Admissions E-mail: oritm@tauex.tau.ac.il • Web Address: www.tau.ac.il/gsba

Graduates from Israel's largest business school are not only the first recruiting choice for Israel's top corporations, banks, and consulting firms— they also attract recruiters among a growing number of multinationals, such as L'Oreal and Procter & Gamble. If your Hebrew isn't up to snuff, you may want to skip the Executive MBA program; rest assured, though, that the full-time Kellogg-Recanati International Executive MBA Program is taught in English. Partnerships with schools in the U.S., Great Britain, Germany, China, and throughout the Middle East give students the multinational business experience they could only read about elsewhere.

INSTITUTIONAL INFORMATION

Public/Private: Private
Evening Classes Available? No
Total Faculty: 260
% Faculty Part Time: 69
Student/Faculty Ratio: 45:1
Students in Parent Institution: 26,000
Academic Calendar: Semester

PROGRAMS

Degrees Offered: MBA (30 credits, 2-5 years); EMBA (30 credits, 16 months); Kellogg-Recanati International EMBA (30 credits, 2 years); MHA (30 credits, 2-5 years); MS in Management Sciences (22 credits, 2-5 years), with concentrations in Operations Research, Information Systems, Organizational Behavior, Finance
Study Abroad Options: Australia, Canada, Denmark, Finland, France, Holland, Hong Kong, Italy, Norway, Spain, Turkey, United States

STUDENT INFORMATION

Total Business Students: 2,196
Average Age: 29

COMPUTER AND RESEARCH FACILITIES

Campuswide Network? Yes
Internet Fee? No

ADMISSIONS INFORMATION

Application Fee: $160
Electronic Application? No
Regular Application Deadline: 2/1
Regular Notification: Rolling
Deferment Available? No
Non-fall Admissions? Yes
Non-fall Application Deadline(s): 11/1
Transfer Students Accepted? No
Need-Blind Admissions? No
% Accepted Who Enrolled: 100
Other Admissions Factors Considered: GMAT

EMPLOYMENT INFORMATION

Placement Office Available? Yes

TEMPLE UNIVERSITY
Richard J. Fox School of Business and Management

Admissions Contact: Natale A. Butto, Director, Graduate Admissions
Address: 1810 North 13th Street, Speakman Hall, Room 5, Philadelphia, PA 19122
Admissions Phone: 215-204-5890 • **Admissions Fax:** 215-204-1632
Admissions E-mail: masters@sbm.temple.edu • **Web Address:** www.sbm.temple.edu

Temple University's Fox School of Business and Management, among the largest comprehensive business schools in the world, has 13 MBA programs available in the evening to part-time students. Fox promises a "results-oriented" and "student-centered" education to all students, although only 35 percent are registered as full timers. One of the Fox options is the unique International MBA, an 11-month tricontinent learning experience in the world's major economic regions—four months in Paris, six months in Philadelphia, and one month in Tokyo.

INSTITUTIONAL INFORMATION

Public/Private: Public
Evening Classes Available? Yes
Total Faculty: 153
% Faculty Female: 18
% Faculty Minority: 20
% Faculty Part Time: 17
Student/Faculty Ratio: 8:1
Students in Parent Institution: 29,872

PROGRAMS

Degrees Offered: MBA (12-18 months), with concentrations in Accounting, Business Administration, E-Business, Economics, Finance, General and Strategic Management, Healthcare Management, Human Resource Administration, International Business Administration, International Business (Tri-Continent), MIS, Management Science/Operations Management, Risk Management and Insurance; EMBA (Tokyo and Philadelphia; 2 years); MA in Economics; MS in Accounting, Actuarial Sciences, Finance, Healthcare Financial Management, MIS, Management Science/Operations Management, Marketing, Statistics
Combined Degrees: JD/MBA; MD/MBA; DMD/MBA; MBA/MS in E-Business (2 years); MBA/MS in Healthcare Management/Healthcare Financial Management (2 years)
Academic Specialties: Empirical/archival financial accounting, accounting information systems/technology; Executive compensation, financial accounting, earnings manipulation; Valuation of small businesses; Labor economics and economics of personnel: examining incentive effects of compensation mechanisms, exploring promotion structures in large corporations, conducting empirical tests of theories of executive compensation; Small businesses, entrepreneurship, consumer credit, economic policy/forecasting, performance of the economy (inflation, federal policy, etc.), financial regulation; Economics of sports; Public finance; telecommunications; Mergers and acquisitions; Banking and financial institutions; International business; Entrepreneurship; Business ethics; Cyber law; E-commerce; Databases, data warehousing, knowledge management, data mining, application service providers, systems development, IT outsourcing, IT implementation; Healthcare management and healthcare financial management; Risk management; Property and liability insurance; Biostatistics; Multivariate statistical inference, multiple comparisons, inequalities in statisitcs, pharmaceutical statistics, competing risks models
Special Opportunities: EMBA offered in Japan and Philadelphia
Study Abroad Options: France, India, Italy, Japan

STUDENT INFORMATION

Total Business Students: 868
% Full Time: 35
% Female: 35
% Minority: 13
% Out of State: 57
% International: 47
Average Age: 30

COMPUTER AND RESEARCH FACILITIES

Research Facilities: Irwin Gross eBusiness Institute, Innovation and Entrepreneurship Institute, Institute for Global Management Studies, Small Business Development Center
Computer Facilities: Computer labs in Business School buildings with a total of 170 computers; Palley Library has 170 databases, which are available through the Internet; IBM-server lab
Campuswide Network? Yes
% of MBA Classrooms Wired: 100
Computer Model Recommended: Laptop
Internet Fee? No

EXPENSES/FINANCIAL AID

Annual Tuition (Resident/Nonresident): $8,760/$14,040
Tuition Per Credit (Resident/Nonresident): $365/$585
Room & Board (On/Off Campus): $8,250/$11,000
Books and Supplies: $1,100
Average Grant: $5,000
Average Loan: $18,500

ADMISSIONS INFORMATION

Application Fee: $40
Electronic Application? Yes
Regular Application Deadline: 4/15
Regular Notification: Rolling
Deferment Available? Yes
Length of Deferment: 1 year
Non-fall Admissions? Yes
Non-fall Application Deadline(s): 9/30, 3/15
Transfer Students Accepted? Yes
Transfer Policy: Up to 6 upper-level credits if applicable to the program
Need-Blind Admissions? Yes
Number of Applications Received: 574
% of Applicants Accepted: 63
% Accepted Who Enrolled: 50
Average GPA: 3.1
GPA Range: 2.9-3.5
Average GMAT: 565
GMAT Range: 530-600
Average Years Experience: 3
Other Admissions Factors Considered: Work experience, statement of goals. Prospective students should have a statement of goals that expresses the direction in which they wish to move their career and how an MBA will serve that goal.
Minority/Disadvantaged Student Recruitment Programs: Participate in an annual statewide conference for minority undergraduate students looking to further their education; participate with KPMG in their diversity recruiting
Other Schools to Which Students Applied: Drexel University, Saint Joseph's University, Villanova University

INTERNATIONAL STUDENTS

TOEFL Required of International Students? Yes
Minimum TOEFL: 575 (230 computer)

EMPLOYMENT INFORMATION

Placement Office Available? Yes
% Employed Within 3 Months: 100
Fields Employing Percentage of Grads: General Management (10%), Operations (10%), MIS (10%), Accounting (10%), Finance (11%), Consulting (14%), Marketing (14%), Other (21%)
Frequent Employers: Cigna, Eli Lilly, First Union, GlaxoSmithKline, IBM, Independence Blue Cross, J.P. Morgan, KPMG, Lands End, Mass Mutual, Merck, Subaru of America, Unisys, Vanguard, William M. Mercer, Wyeth Ayerst

TENNESSEE STATE UNIVERSITY

Admissions Contact: Dr. G.B. Hartman, Coordinator of MBA Program
Address: 3500 John Merritt Blvd., Nashville, TN 37209-1561
Admissions Phone: 615-963-7137 • **Admissions Fax:** 615-963-7139
Admissions E-mail: mwalters@tnstate.edu • **Web Address:** www.cob.tnstate.edu

INSTITUTIONAL INFORMATION

Public/Private: Public
Evening Classes Available? Yes
Total Faculty: 35

STUDENT INFORMATION

Total Business Students: 250
% Full Time: 25
Average Age: 28

COMPUTER AND RESEARCH FACILITIES

Campuswide Network? Yes
% of MBA Classrooms Wired: 5
Internet Fee? No

EXPENSES/FINANCIAL AID

Annual Tuition (Resident/Nonresident): $3,884/$10,356
Tuition Per Credit (Resident/Nonresident): $191/$461

ADMISSIONS INFORMATION

Application Fee: $25
Electronic Application? Yes
Regular Application Deadline: 1/1
Regular Notification: 1/1
Deferment Available? Yes
Length of Deferment: 1
Non-fall Admissions? Yes
Non-fall Application Deadline(s): Rolling
Transfer Students Accepted? Yes
Transfer Policy: 6 credits from non-AACGB college; 12 credits from AACGB college
Need-Blind Admissions? Yes
Number of Applications Received: 39
% of Applicants Accepted: 79
% Accepted Who Enrolled: 100
Average GPA: 3.2
Average GMAT: 510
Average Years Experience: 4

INTERNATIONAL STUDENTS

TOEFL Required of International Students? Yes
Minimum TOEFL: 500

EMPLOYMENT INFORMATION

Placement Office Available? Yes

TENNESSEE TECHNOLOGICAL UNIVERSITY
College of Business Administration

Admissions Contact: Dr. Virginia Moore, Director of MBA Studies
Address: Box 5023, Cookeville, TN 38505
Admissions Phone: 931-372-3600 • **Admissions Fax:** 931-372-6249
Admissions E-mail: mbastudies@tntech.edu • **Web Address:** www2.tntech.edu/mba/

The Tennessee Technological University MBA program has a case method–based curriculum, and all applicants who haven't taken undergrad business prerequisites must take the Pre-MBA Foundation modules before getting started. TTU's one-year MBA program focuses on the advancement of written and oral communication skills and offers concentrations in accounting and management information. MBA students may start interviewing for jobs as soon as they matriculate, and should they happen to secure dream jobs while enrolled, they may simply complete the degree via Tennessee Tech's Distance MBA program.

INSTITUTIONAL INFORMATION

Public/Private: Public
Evening Classes Available? Yes
Total Faculty: 30
% Faculty Female: 23
% Faculty Minority: 5
Student/Faculty Ratio: 24:1
Students in Parent Institution: 8,800

PROGRAMS

Degrees Offered: MBA (36 credits, 1-6 years)

STUDENT INFORMATION

Total Business Students: 122
% Full Time: 48
% Female: 12
% Minority: 7
% Out of State: 4
% International: 10
Average Age: 27

COMPUTER AND RESEARCH FACILITIES

Computer Facilities: ABI Inform, Disclosure, Dissertation Abstracts, InfoTrak, Morningstar, ProQuest
Campuswide Network? Yes
% of MBA Classrooms Wired: 100
Internet Fee? No

EXPENSES/FINANCIAL AID

Annual Tuition (Resident/Nonresident): $6,958
Tuition Per Credit (Resident/Nonresident): $301
Room & Board (On/Off Campus): $3,600/$4,800
Books and Supplies: $1,500
Average Grant: $1,125
Average Loan: $5,000
% Receiving Financial Aid: 33
% Receiving Aid Their First Year: 17

ADMISSIONS INFORMATION

Application Fee: $25
Electronic Application? Yes
Regular Application Deadline: Rolling
Regular Notification: Rolling
Deferment Available? Yes
Length of Deferment: 1 year
Non-fall Admissions? Yes
Non-fall Application Deadline(s): Rolling
Transfer Students Accepted? Yes
Transfer Policy: TTU will transfer 9 hours or less from an AACSB-accredited school.
Need-Blind Admissions? Yes
Number of Applications Received: 80
% of Applicants Accepted: 89
% Accepted Who Enrolled: 59
Average GPA: 3.1
GPA Range: 2.5-4.0
Average GMAT: 528
GMAT Range: 450-580
Average Years Experience: 3
Other Admissions Factors Considered: Interview, computer experience
Minority/Disadvantaged Student Recruitment Programs: Special minority fellowships, graduate assistantsips

INTERNATIONAL STUDENTS

TOEFL Required of International Students? Yes
Minimum TOEFL: 550 (220 computer)

EMPLOYMENT INFORMATION

Placement Office Available? Yes
% Employed Within 3 Months: 87
Prominent Alumni: Harry Stonecipher, president/COO, Boeing; Lark Mason, vice president, Sotheby's Inc.; Jimmy Bedford, master distiller, Jack Daniel's; Roger Crouch, astronaut; C. Stephen Lynn, former CEO, Shoney's Inc.

TEXAS A&M UNIVERSITY— COLLEGE STATION

Mays College and Graduate School of Business

Admissions Contact: Wendy Flynn, Assistant Director, Mays MBA
Address: TAMU 4117, College Station, TX 77845
Admissions Phone: 979-845-4714 • **Admissions Fax:** 979-862-2393
Admissions E-mail: MaysMBA@tamu.edu • **Web Address:** http://mba.tamu.edu

Texas A&M University's MBA program emphasizes extensive teamwork training and offers a great deal of program benefits, including business

lectures with local business leaders and professional internship opportunities at home and abroad. Texas A&M is one of the few schools that offer students the chance to combine an MBA with a foreign business degree, available in conjunction with schools in Europe, Latin America, or the Pacific Rim. If you dazzle your professors, you may be chosen to participate in the Aggies on Wall Street program, which involves a three-week "immersion experience" or an enrichment experience in Washington, D.C.

INSTITUTIONAL INFORMATION

Public/Private: Public
Evening Classes Available? No
Total Faculty: 131
% Faculty Female: 35
% Faculty Minority: 10
Student/Faculty Ratio: 10:1
Students in Parent Institution: 43,000
Academic Calendar: Semester

PROGRAMS

Degrees Offered: MBA (54 credit hours, 16-21 months), with concentrations in Accounting, Banking and Financial Markets, Consulting and Strategic Planning, E-Commerce, Finance, Human Resources Management, Information Technology, International Business, Marketing, Operations, Real Estate, Individualized Concentration (choose the courses that are most logical for your career goals)
Combined Degrees: Dual Degree program (3 years)
Academic Specialties: Outstanding training in teamwork; other strengths include: E-Business, Finance, Marketing, Information Systems, Human Resources, International Business, Management
Special Opportunities: Aggies on Wall Street, a 2-week intensive Wall Street Program; The Washington Campus, a 1-week program to explore business and government; multiple short-term study abroad programs in between semester breaks; Graduate Certificate in International Business
Study Abroad Options: Texas A&M is a Center for International Business and Research (CIBER) school. We aggressively pursue exchange opportunities for our students and provide significant scholarship support to students who participate in study abroad programs. Countries include: Austria, China, England, France, Germany, Japan, Korea, Mexico, the Netherlands, and Switzerland.

STUDENT INFORMATION

Total Business Students: 208
% Full Time: 100
% Female: 22
% Minority: 10
% Out of State: 30
% International: 27
Average Age: 29

COMPUTER AND RESEARCH FACILITIES

Research Facilities: Reliant Energy Securities and Commodities Trading Center, Real Estate Center, Center for International Business Study, Center for Retailing Management, Center for Human Resources Development, Center for New Venture Capital
Computer Facilities: Fully furnished master's-student-only computer lab with 90-plus Pentium computers, available 24 hours a day/7 days a week; exceptional dial-up capabilities for the university. MBA classrooms reserved are for MBA-only use and are equipped with the most current presentation technologies.
Campuswide Network? Yes
% of MBA Classrooms Wired: 100
Internet Fee? No

EXPENSES/FINANCIAL AID

Annual Tuition (Resident/Nonresident): $3,828/$10,055
Room & Board (On/Off Campus): $8,892
Books and Supplies: $818
Average Grant: $8,000

% Receiving Financial Aid: 90
% Receiving Aid Their First Year: 90

ADMISSIONS INFORMATION

Application Fee: $50
Electronic Application? Yes
Early Decision Notification: 3/1
Regular Application Deadline: 5/1
Regular Notification: 6/1
Deferment Available? Yes
Length of Deferment: 1 year
Non-fall Admissions? No
Transfer Students Accepted? No
Need-Blind Admissions? Yes
Number of Applications Received: 669
% of Applicants Accepted: 29
% Accepted Who Enrolled: 63
Average GPA: 3.3
GPA Range: 3.0-3.9
Average GMAT: 628
GMAT Range: 550-710
Average Years Experience: 5
Other Admissions Factors Considered: Strongest emphasis is on work experience. GMAT quantitative and verbal sections must have scores at least at the 50th percentile for consideration.
Minority/Disadvantaged Student Recruitment Programs: We agressively seek to enhance diversity on all levels in our program and have programs in place to recruit all students who will bring diversity to our program.
Other Schools to Which Students Applied: University of Maryland—College Park, Vanderbilt University, University of Notre Dame, Rice University, Michigan State University-Detroit College of Law, Arizona State University

INTERNATIONAL STUDENTS

TOEFL Required of International Students? Yes
Minimum TOEFL: 600 (250 computer)

EMPLOYMENT INFORMATION

Placement Office Available? Yes
% Employed Within 3 Months: 98
Fields Employing Percentage of Grads: Human Resources (4%), Operations (5%), MIS (7%), General Management (14%), Marketing (18%), Consulting (21%), Finance (31%)
Frequent Employers: Accenture, AT&T, Chevron, Compaq, Coral Energy, Dell, Deloitte and Touche, Duke Energy, Entergy, Ericsson, Ernst & Young, ExxonMobil, Fed Ex, FMC Corp., Ford Motor Co., Halliburton, Hewlett Packard, IBM, Marathon Oil, Motorola, Nortel Networks, Pricewaterhouse Coopers, Raytheon, Reliant Energy, Texas Instruments, 3M

TEXAS A&M UNIVERSITY—COMMERCE
Graduate Programs in Business

Admissions Contact: Tammi Thompson, Admissions Advisor
Address: PO Box 3011, Commerce, TX 75429
Admissions Phone: 903-886-5167 • **Admissions Fax:** 903-886-5165
Admissions E-mail: graduate_school@tamu-commerce.edu
Web Address: www.tamu-commerce.edu/graduateprograms

Texas A&M—Commerce offers three MBA program options: the Fast-Track MBA for students with an undergraduate background in business; the Comprehensive MBA for students without substantial prior business course

work; and the Weekend MBA for 9-to-5ers, with cohort-style Saturday classes. Students can also check out the MBA British summer study option at King's College in London for a change of pace and some invaluable international insight.

INSTITUTIONAL INFORMATION

Public/Private: Public
Evening Classes Available? Yes
Total Faculty: 23
% Faculty Female: 33
% Faculty Minority: 28
% Faculty Part Time: 4
Student/Faculty Ratio: 35:1
Students in Parent Institution: 8,991
Academic Calendar: Semester

PROGRAMS

Degrees Offered: MBA (30-48 hours, 1-6 years), MSM (30-36 hours), MS in Marketing (30-36 hours), MS in Electronic Commerce (30-54 hours)
Combined Degrees: BPA/MBA, with emphasis in Accounting (4 years + 1 year)
Academic Specialties: Entrepreneurship, Strategy, Human Resources, Finance, Economics, International Business, Accounting. The curriculum has a general management (strategic management) orientation.
Study Abroad Options: China (CUG), France, Germany, Italy, Jamaica, Mexico (ITESM), United Kingdom

STUDENT INFORMATION

Total Business Students: 576
% Full Time: 46
% Female: 35
% Minority: 12
% Out of State: 27
% International: 35
Average Age: 31

COMPUTER AND RESEARCH FACILITIES

Computer Facilities: Business PC Lab with 60 Pentium-class PCs; 120 PCs in other parts of the campus; www.tamu-commerce.edu/geelibrary; various databases such as Lexis-Nexis plus Internet resources; 25 Pentium-class computers, Mesquite, Texas; graphics arts lab, downtown Dallas
Campuswide Network? Yes
% of MBA Classrooms Wired: 60
Internet Fee? No

EXPENSES/FINANCIAL AID

Annual Tuition (Resident/Nonresident): $3,600/$8,832
Tuition Per Credit (Resident/Nonresident): $188/$406
Room & Board (On/Off Campus): $4,100
Books and Supplies: $800
Average Grant: $4,798
% Receiving Financial Aid: 8

ADMISSIONS INFORMATION

Application Fee: $35
Electronic Application? Yes
Regular Application Deadline: 6/1
Regular Notification: Rolling
Deferment Available? Yes
Length of Deferment: 2 semesters
Non-fall Admissions? Yes
Non-fall Application Deadline(s): 11/1, 3/15
Transfer Students Accepted? Yes
Transfer Policy: Students can transfer up to 12 semester hours in the 36- to 48-hour program and 9 semester hours for the 30- to 33-hour program.
Need-Blind Admissions? No

Number of Applications Received: 425
% of Applicants Accepted: 94
% Accepted Who Enrolled: 92
Average GPA: 3.0
GPA Range: 2.5-3.6
Average GMAT: 460
GMAT Range: 380-620
Average Years Experience: 7
Other Admissions Factors Considered: Graduate coursework with an overall 3.0 GPA
Other Schools to Which Students Applied: Southern Methodist University, Texas Christian University (TCU), University of Dallas, University of Texas—Arlington

INTERNATIONAL STUDENTS

TOEFL Required of International Students? Yes
Minimum TOEFL: 500 (173 computer)

EMPLOYMENT INFORMATION

Placement Office Available? No

TEXAS A&M UNIVERSITY— CORPUS CHRISTI

College of Business Administration

Admissions Contact: Betsy O'Lavin, Director of Master's Programs
Address: 6300 Ocean Drive, Corpus Christi, TX 78412
Admissions Phone: 361-825-2655 • Admissions Fax: 361-825-2725
Admissions E-mail: eolavin@cob.tamucc.edu • Web Address: www.cob.tamucc.edu

Deep in southern Texas lies Texas A&M—Corpus Christi, with a broad-based curriculum, churning out graduates who primarily go on to the fields of finance and consulting. Texas A&M offers a working model of a real business organization called Society for Advancement of Management, providing exceptional hands-on experience in multiple business disciplines and a personal introduction to practicing managers in the local community.

INSTITUTIONAL INFORMATION

Public/Private: Public
Evening Classes Available? Yes
Total Faculty: 31
% Faculty Part Time: 16
Students in Parent Institution: 6,161
Academic Calendar: Semester

PROGRAMS

Degrees Offered: MBA (36-60 credits, 1-6 years); MACC (36-60 credits, 1-6 years)
Special Opportunities: General Business, Accounting

STUDENT INFORMATION

Total Business Students: 150
% Full Time: 30
% Female: 44
% Minority: 25
% International: 1
Average Age: 32

COMPUTER AND RESEARCH FACILITIES

Campuswide Network? Yes
Internet Fee? No

EXPENSES/FINANCIAL AID

Annual Tuition (Resident/Nonresident): $2,878/$9,328

ADMISSIONS INFORMATION

Application Fee: $30
Electronic Application? Yes
Regular Application Deadline: Rolling
Regular Notification: Rolling
Deferment Available? Yes
Length of Deferment: 1 year
Non-fall Admissions? Yes
Non-fall Application Deadline(s): 7/15, 11/15, 4/15, 5/15
Transfer Students Accepted? Yes
Transfer Policy: Possibility of transferring in 6 credits from accredited school with grade of B or above
Need-Blind Admissions? Yes
Number of Applications Received: 45
% of Applicants Accepted: 89
% Accepted Who Enrolled: 83
Average GPA: 3.1
GPA Range: 2.3-4.0
Average GMAT: 500
GMAT Range: 410-600
Average Years Experience: 7
Other Admissions Factors Considered: Undergraduate cumulative GPA, GPA from last 60 hours, work experience

INTERNATIONAL STUDENTS

TOEFL Required of International Students? Yes
Minimum TOEFL: 550 (213 computer)

EMPLOYMENT INFORMATION

Placement Office Available? Yes

TEXAS TECH UNIVERSITY

Jerry S. Rawls College of Business Administration

Admissions Contact: Sheila Dixon, Academic Program Advisor
Address: Box 42101, Lubbock, TX 79409-2101
Admissions Phone: 806-742-3184 • Admissions Fax: 806-742-3958
Admissions E-mail: mba@ba.ttu.edu • Web Address: grad.ba.ttu.edu

Texas Tech University's MBA program is populated mostly by native Texans and offers a choice of academic concentrations to complement its general degree. A number of joint degrees are also offered, including MBAs coupled with MAs in French, German, and Spanish and the MBA/MD in health organization management, for physicians-to-be looking to gain advanced management know-how for use in the workplace. Student Naeem Malik comments that his team-building and critical thinking experiences at Texas Tech "reinforce the excellence and achievement that have always been in my vocabulary, and attending the Jerry S. Rawls College of Business adds them to my résumé."

INSTITUTIONAL INFORMATION

Public/Private: Public
Evening Classes Available? Yes
Total Faculty: 68
% Faculty Female: 7
% Faculty Minority: 2
% Faculty Part Time: 1
Student/Faculty Ratio: 4:1
Students in Parent Institution: 25,573
Academic Calendar: Rolling

PROGRAMS

Degrees Offered: MBA (1.5 years), MSBA (2 years or less), PhD (4 years), MSA (2 years or less)
Combined Degrees: MD/MBA (4 years); JD/MBA (3 years); BA in foreign language/MBA (5 years); MA in foreign language/MBA (2 years); MA in Architecture/MBA (2.5 years); dual MBA programs with Universidad Anahuac, Mexico (2 years), Sup ce Co Montpellier, France (2 years)
Academic Specialties: Taxation, Accounting, Controllership, Health Organization Management, High-Performance Management, Marketing, Entrepreneurship, Agribusiness, E-Business, Finance, International Business, Management Information Systems
Study Abroad Options: Helsinki School of Economics, Finland; Maximilians Universitaet Munich, Germany; University of Nottingham, United Kingdom; Sup ce Co Montpellier, France; Universidad Anahuac, Mexico

STUDENT INFORMATION

Total Business Students: 213
% Full Time: 86
% Female: 27
% Minority: 13
% Out of State: 6
% International: 12
Average Age: 23

COMPUTER AND RESEARCH FACILITIES

Computer Facilities: Microcomputers: Pentium II, III, IV; I-Macs. Operating systems: Windows NT and Workstation, Red Hat Linux 7.1, Unix. Databases: MS Access, Oracle 8i, 11i, JD Edwards. Software: MSDN; Internet Explorer; Netscape Navigator; Adobe Photoshop, Illustrator, Reader, Writer. High-performance computer: SGI Origin 2400 with 56 nodes; works on Irix Operating system and enables rendering, imaging, animation using Maya, VIS 5, and virtual reality theater. Other computing services: online computer-based training(CBT) classes; reference materials, eRaider account, personal web pages, web mail, interactive log-ons with open VMS cluster
Campuswide Network? Yes
% of MBA Classrooms Wired: 100
Internet Fee? No

EXPENSES/FINANCIAL AID

Annual Tuition (Resident/Nonresident): $1,920/$6,984
Tuition Per Credit (Resident/Nonresident): $80/$291
Room & Board (On/Off Campus): $4,500/$6,000
Books and Supplies: $1,500
Average Grant: $1,000
Average Loan: $9,210
% Receiving Financial Aid: 21
% Receiving Aid Their First Year: 31

ADMISSIONS INFORMATION

Application Fee: $25
Electronic Application? Yes
Regular Application Deadline: Rolling
Regular Notification: Rolling
Deferment Available? Yes

Length of Deferment: 1 Year
Non-fall Admissions? Yes
Non-fall Application Deadline(s): 9/1 spring, 3/1 fall
Transfer Students Accepted? Yes
Transfer Policy: Up to 6 hours
Need-Blind Admissions? No
Number of Applications Received: 209
% of Applicants Accepted: 50
% Accepted Who Enrolled: 57
Average GPA: 3.4
GPA Range: 3.2-3.6
Average GMAT: 580
GMAT Range: 540-600
Average Years Experience: 3
Other Admissions Factors Considered: Work experience, research, awards, leadership positions held in college and/or industry, likelihood of bringing a unique perspective to the program, civic and volunteer activities, motivation, past success, letters of recommendation
Minority/Disadvantaged Student Recruitment Programs: Advertise in minority magazines, recruit in minority colleges in New Mexico and Texas, Attend and recruit at minority forums and conferences such as the National Black Graduate Student Conference
Other Schools to Which Students Applied: Texas A&M University

INTERNATIONAL STUDENTS

TOEFL Required of International Students? Yes
Minimum TOEFL: 550 (213 computer)

EMPLOYMENT INFORMATION

Placement Office Available? Yes
% Employed Within 3 Months: 78
Fields Employing Percentage of Grads: Consulting (9%), Marketing (9%), MIS (12%), Other (15%), Finance (19%), General Management (23%)
Frequent Employers: Accenture, Andersen, Cap Gemini, CINTAS, Comerica, Covenant Health Systems, Dell, Deloitte&Touche, KPMG, National Instruments, PNB Financial, Pricewaterhouse Coopers, Ryan and Co., SBC, Wells Fargo Financial

THUNDERBIRD
American Graduate School of International Management

Admissions Contact: Judy Johnson, Dean of Admissions
Address: 15249 North 59th Avenue, Glendale, AZ 85306-6000
Admissions Phone: 602-978-7100 • **Admissions Fax:** 602-439-5432
Admissions E-mail: admissions@t-bird.edu • **Web Address:** www.thunderbird.edu

Like a great steak house that serves one dish exceedingly well, Thunderbird focuses on one thing: international business. Students here—who refer to themselves as T-Birds—study international economy and overseas markets, modern languages, and world business. That's pretty much it. Though the local area is "in need of a charm transfusion," T-Birds can easily head for nearby Phoenix or take "bonding trips to California and Vegas" to let off steam.

INSTITUTIONAL INFORMATION

Public/Private: Private
Evening Classes Available? No

% Faculty Female: 26
% Faculty Minority: 35
% Faculty Part Time: 27
Student/Faculty Ratio: 11:1
Students in Parent Institution: 1,475
Academic Calendar: Trimester

PROGRAMS

Degrees Offered: MBA in International Management (48-60 credits, varies by track/specialization; 1-3 years full time), with concentrations in Global Marketing, Global Finance, Global Development and Policy; EMBA in International Management (50 credits, up to 2 years; program offered in Arizona; Sao Paolo, Brazil; Taipei, Taiwan); MIM Latin America (50 credits, minimum of 22 months full time; distance-learning option available); Post-MBA MIM Program (30 hours, 7-16 months full time)
Combined Degrees: MBA/MIM (30 credits, full time or distance-learning, 18 months to 5 years), with concentration on International Management, in conjunction with Arizona State University, Arizona State University West, University of Arizona, Case Western Reserve University, University of Colorado—Denver, Drury College, University of Florida, University of Houston, University of Texas—Arlington
Academic Specialties: All aspects of International Management (Cross-Cultural Communication, Global Strategy, Emerging Market, Regional Market Development); Corporate Marketing and Finance
Special Opportunities: On campus: Winterim; Off campus: Chile; Cuba; Geneva; India; Kenya; London; New York; Paris; Peru; San Francisco/Silicon Valley; South Africa; Vietnam; Washington, DC
Study Abroad Options: China, Czech Republic, France/Geneva, Japan, Mexico, Russia

STUDENT INFORMATION

Total Business Students: 1,100
% Full Time: 100
% Female: 32
% Minority: 4
% International: 65
Average Age: 28

COMPUTER AND RESEARCH FACILITIES

Research Facilities: CIBER and IF&T, MyThunderbird, on line
Computer Facilities: IBIC-42 databases; 1,200 periodicals; ITS-Taping facilities
Campuswide Network? Yes
% of MBA Classrooms Wired: 15
Computer Model Recommended: Laptop
Internet Fee? Yes

EXPENSES/FINANCIAL AID

Annual Tuition: $26,800
Room & Board (On/Off Campus): $8,000/$9,500
Books and Supplies: $1,500
Average Grant: $2,500
Average Loan: $20,000
% Receiving Financial Aid: 67
% Receiving Aid Their First Year: 70

ADMISSIONS INFORMATION

Application Fee: $125
Electronic Application? Yes
Regular Application Deadline: 8/15
Regular Notification: Rolling
Deferment Available? Yes
Length of Deferment: 1 year
Non-fall Admissions? Yes

Non-fall Application Deadline(s): 1/15 spring, 4/15 summer
Transfer Students Accepted? No
Need-Blind Admissions? Yes
Number of Applications Received: 1,126
% of Applicants Accepted: 78
% Accepted Who Enrolled: 49
Average GPA: 3.3
GPA Range: 3.1-3.9
Average GMAT: 600
GMAT Range: 545-725
Average Years Experience: 5
Other Admissions Factors Considered: Work experience, computer experience: Microsoft Office
Other Schools to Which Students Applied: Arizona State University, Georgetown University, University of California—Los Angeles, University of South Carolina, University of Southern California, University of Texas—Austin, Vanderbilt University

INTERNATIONAL STUDENTS

TOEFL Required of International Students? Yes
Minimum TOEFL: 600 (250 computer)

EMPLOYMENT INFORMATION

Placement Office Available? Yes
% Employed Within 3 Months: 75
Fields Employing Percentage of Grads: Other (1%), MIS (1%), Operations (5%), General Management (6%), Consulting (9%), Finance (17%), Marketing (25%)
Frequent Employers: Citibank, General Motors, IBM, Intel, Merck, Johnson & Johnson
Prominent Alumni: John Lampe, CEO, Firestone Tire; Olga Reisler, regional vice president-Infitiniti Division, Nissan; Sir Bruce Harris, executive director-Latin America, Covenant House; Sam Garvin, founder and CEO, Continental Promotion Group; Louis Moreno, Colombian Ambassador to the United States

TRUMAN STATE UNIVERSITY
Division of Business and Accountancy

Admissions Contact: Dr. Jeff Romine, Master of Accountancy Coordinator
Address: VH 2400, 100 East Normal, Kirksville, MO 63501-4221
Admissions Phone: 660-785-4378 • Admissions Fax: 660-785-7471
Admissions E-mail: jromine@truman.edu • Web Address: www.truman.edu

INSTITUTIONAL INFORMATION

Public/Private: Public
Evening Classes Available? No
Total Faculty: 16
Students in Parent Institution: 6,200
Academic Calendar: Semester

PROGRAMS

Degrees Offered: MACC (30-42 credits, 1-2 years)

STUDENT INFORMATION

Total Business Students: 16
% Full Time: 100
% Female: 25
% Minority: 8

% **International:** 13
Average Age: 23

COMPUTER AND RESEARCH FACILITIES

Campuswide Network? Yes
Internet Fee? No

EXPENSES/FINANCIAL AID

Annual Tuition (Resident/Nonresident): $4,072/$7,400
Books and Supplies: $500
Average Grant: $8,000
% Receiving Financial Aid: 63

ADMISSIONS INFORMATION

Electronic Application? No
Regular Application Deadline: 6/1
Regular Notification: Rolling
Deferment Available? Yes
Non-fall Admissions? Yes
Non-fall Application Deadline(s): 11/1
Transfer Students Accepted? No
Need-Blind Admissions? No
Number of Applications Received: 18
% of Applicants Accepted: 78
% Accepted Who Enrolled: 71
Average GPA: 3.5
Average GMAT: 600

INTERNATIONAL STUDENTS

TOEFL Required of International Students? Yes
Minimum TOEFL: 560

EMPLOYMENT INFORMATION

Placement Office Available? Yes
% Employed Within 3 Months: 100
Fields Employing Percentage of Grads: Accounting (100%)
Frequent Employers: Andersen; Baird, Kurtz,and Dobson; Ernst and Young; KPMG

TULANE UNIVERSITY
Freeman School of Business

Admissions Contact: Bill D. Sandefer, Director of Admissions and Financial Aid
Address: 7 McAlister Drive, Suite 401, New Orleans, LA 70118
Admissions Phone: 504-865-5410 • **Admissions Fax:** 504-865-6770
Admissions E-mail: freeman.admissions@tulane.edu • **Web Address:** freeman.tulane.edu

Tulane University's "blissfully challenging" Freeman School of Business offers a wealth of excellent programs and a "superb," seven-story facility with computers galore and a laboratory for simulating manufacturing processes. The especially notable finance department is "filled with superstars" who share a "tremendous ability to articulate ideas." Beyond campus, of course, is the great city of New Orleans, America's preeminent party town.

INSTITUTIONAL INFORMATION

Public/Private: Private
Evening Classes Available? Yes
Total Faculty: 96

% Faculty Female: 15
% Faculty Minority: 15
% Faculty Part Time: 37
Student/Faculty Ratio: 22:1
Students in Parent Institution: 13,330
Academic Calendar: Semester

PROGRAMS

Degrees Offered: MACC (1 year, with undergraduate business courses), MSF (1 year), PhD (5 years), MBA (2 years)
Combined Degrees: MBA/JD (4 years), MBA/MA in Latin American Studies (2.5 years), MBA/MPH (3 years), MBA/Master of Political Science (3 years), MACC/JD (3-4 years), MACC/MBA (2 years)
Academic Specialties: At Freeman, institutes augment the traditional classroom discussion with centers for specific interest. Burkenroad Reports develop student analyst teams to research publicly traded companies; Burkenroad inspires a small cap mutual fund (HYBUX). Burkenroad Reports-Latin America recently began research in conjunction with the Goldring Institute. The Goldring Institute focuses on international business and coordinates the efforts of the Center for Research on Latin American Financial Markets; the Levy-Rosenblum Institute focuses on entrepreneurship; and the Burkenroad Institute centers around the study of leadership and ethics in management. The Energy Trading Center is a major feature of the new business school expansion.
Special Opportunities: Study Abroad, Semester Abroad, faculty development doctoral program (Bolivia, Colombia, Mexico, Venezuela), joint-venture executive education programs (Chile, China, Ecuador, Taiwan)
Study Abroad Options: Argentina, Australia, Austria, Brazil, Chile, Czech Republic, Denmark, Ecuador, Finland, France, Germany, Hong Kong, Hungary, Mexico, Spain, Venezuela

STUDENT INFORMATION

Total Business Students: 200
% Full Time: 100
% Female: 28
% Minority: 12
% Out of State: 92
% International: 35
Average Age: 28

COMPUTER AND RESEARCH FACILITIES

Research Facilities: Burkenroad Institute for the Study of Ethics and Leadership in Management; Goldring Institute of International Business; Levy-Rosenblum Institute for Entrepreneurship; Stewart Center for Executive Education; Burkenroad Reports, the student-written investment analysis program; wireless Ethernet network; Center for Research on Latin American Financial Markets; Fenner Fund; Burkenroad Mutual Fund
Computer Facilities: 50-workstation Pentium-based computer lab; 20-workstation Pentium-based computer lab; 42-workstation Pentium-based computer classroom; 4 Pentium-based electronic mail workstations. All computers are connected to an internal Windows 2000 server network and are also connected to the campus fiber-optic backbone for access to campus-side shared systems and the Internet. Ethernet network drops located throughout the building (72 in the atrium, 20 in the library, 16 in breakout rooms, 180 in classrooms) allow connectivity to the local network, the campus network, and the Internet from student notebook computers. Wireless network provides building-wide access to network services. Research databases include Bloomberg, Standard & Poor's Compustat, Center for Research on Securities Pricing (CRSP), Lexis-Nexis, ABI-Inform, IBES, and others.
Campuswide Network? Yes
% of MBA Classrooms Wired: 60
Computer Model Recommended: Laptop
Internet Fee? No

EXPENSES/FINANCIAL AID

Annual Tuition: $27,480
Tuition Per Credit (Resident/Nonresident): $916

Room & Board (On/Off Campus): $7,545
Books and Supplies: $1,600
Average Grant: $16,000
Average Loan: $15,000
% Receiving Financial Aid: 85
% Receiving Aid Their First Year: 80

ADMISSIONS INFORMATION

Application Fee: $40
Electronic Application? Yes
Regular Application Deadline: 3/15
Regular Notification: 4/15
Deferment Available? No
Non-fall Admissions? No
Transfer Students Accepted? No
Need-Blind Admissions? Yes
Number of Applications Received: 438
% of Applicants Accepted: 64
% Accepted Who Enrolled: 44
Average GPA: 3.3
GPA Range: 2.9-3.8
Average GMAT: 663
GMAT Range: 620-710
Average Years Experience: 6
Other Admissions Factors Considered: Given that applications are evaluated in 3 main rounds, candidates are encouraged to apply in the earliest round possible.
Minority/Disadvantaged Student Recruitment Programs: Destination MBA, National Black MBA Association Career Fair, targeted GMASS searches, minority fellowships
Other Schools to Which Students Applied: Emory University, Georgetown University, New York University, University of Maryland—College Park, University of Texas—Austin, Vanderbilt University, Washington University in St. Louis

INTERNATIONAL STUDENTS

TOEFL Required of International Students? Yes
Minimum TOEFL: 600 (250 computer)

EMPLOYMENT INFORMATION

Placement Office Available? Yes
% Employed Within 3 Months: 81
Fields Employing Percentage of Grads: Accounting (4%), Other (8%), Consulting (8%), General Management (11%), Marketing (14%), Finance (55%)
Frequent Employers: Banc of America, Citibank, Credit Suisse First Boston, D&T Management Solutions, Dynegy, El Paso Energy, Entergy, Federal Express, First Union Securities, Jackson & Rhodes, JP Morgan Chase, Mirant, PA Consulting, Reliant Energy, Towers Perrin, TXU
Prominent Alumni: Berdon Lawrence, chairman, Kirby Corp. (nation's largest tank barge operator); Wayne A. Downing, national coordinator—counterterrorism, Homeland Security Council; Ray Nagin, mayor, City of New Orleans; Daniel F. Packer, president, Entergy Corp.

UNION COLLEGE
MBA @ Union

Admissions Contact: Rhonda Sheehan, Director of Graduate Admissions and Registration
Address: Lamont House, 807 Union St., Schenectady, NY 12308
Admissions Phone: 518-388-6238 • Admissions Fax: 518-388-6686
Admissions E-mail: gradeducation@union.edu
Web Address: www.gradeducation.union.edu

Union College is a private institution in upstate New York with a small but diverse palette of MBA options. Classes with an average of 15 students "ensure that your education is not a 'spectator sport'" and the "global curriculum within a 'small college' environment" undoubtedly enhance the learning atmosphere. Union College also offers an MBA in health systems administrations, accelerated MBA courses, and a joint JD/MBA in conjunction with Albany Law School. Frequent employers of Union College MBA graduates are PricewaterhouseCoopers, IBM, and General Electric.

INSTITUTIONAL INFORMATION

Public/Private: Private
Evening Classes Available? Yes
Total Faculty: 11
% Faculty Female: 30
% Faculty Part Time: 20
Student/Faculty Ratio: 15:1
Students in Parent Institution: 2,371
Academic Calendar: Trimester

PROGRAMS

Degrees Offered: MBA (2 years full time, 4 years part time), MBA in Health Systems Administration (2 years full time, 4 years part time)
Combined Degrees: JD/MBA (4 years), Accelerated MBA: BA/MBA or BS/MBA (5 years), PharmD/MS (6 years)
Academic Specialties: Accounting, Economics, Finance, Health Care Management, Organization Behavior, Operation Sciences, Statistics

STUDENT INFORMATION

Total Business Students: 220
% Full Time: 50
% Female: 37
% Minority: 4
% Out of State: 18
% International: 19
Average Age: 26

COMPUTER AND RESEARCH FACILITIES

Campuswide Network? Yes
% of MBA Classrooms Wired: 90
Internet Fee? No

EXPENSES/FINANCIAL AID

Annual Tuition: $16,200
Tuition Per Credit (Resident/Nonresident): $545
Room & Board (On/Off Campus): $8,800
Books and Supplies: $1,200
Average Grant: $5,500
Average Loan: $12,000

ADMISSIONS INFORMATION

Application Fee: $50
Electronic Application? No
Regular Application Deadline: Rolling
Regular Notification: Rolling
Non-fall Application Deadline(s): All terms—rolling admissions
Transfer Policy: Up to 8 courses (20 required)
Need-Blind Admissions? Yes
Number of Applications Received: 205
% of Applicants Accepted: 54
% Accepted Who Enrolled: 75
Average GPA: 3.3
GPA Range: 2.7-4.0
Average GMAT: 545
GMAT Range: 470-680
Average Years Experience: 2
Other Admissions Factors Considered: A phone interview may be requested.
Other Schools to Which Students Applied: Rensselaer Polytechnic Institute, University at Albany/State University of New York

INTERNATIONAL STUDENTS

TOEFL Required of International Students? Yes
Minimum TOEFL: 550 (213 computer)

EMPLOYMENT INFORMATION

Placement Office Available? Yes
% Employed Within 3 Months: 80
Fields Employing Percentage of Grads: Consulting (6%), Operations (6%), MIS (6%), Human Resources (6%), Other (8%), Finance (12%), General Management (18%), Accounting (18%), Marketing (20%)
Frequent Employers: Andersen Consulting, IBM, General Electric, KPMB Peat Maverick, Lehrman Bros., Pricewaterhouse Coopers
Prominent Alumni: Michael Keegan, president, M&T Bank, Albany, NY; Wayne McDougall, DFO-MapInfo, Troy, NY; James Mandell, president, Boston Children's Hospital; Lauretta Chrys, senior vice president, Charter One Bank, Albany, NY; James Figge, medical director, CDPHP-HMO, Albany, NY

See page 444.

UNIVERSIDAD PANAMERICANA
IPADE Business School

Admissions Contact: Oscar Carbonell, Director of Admissions
Address: Floresta 20 Col Claveria, Mexico City 02080, Mexico
Admissions Phone: 52 55 53 54 18 00 ext. 4157 • **Admissions Fax:** 52 55 53 99 76 82
Admissions E-mail: oscarbonell@ipade.mx • **Web Address:** www.ipade.mx

The Instituto Panamericano de Alta direccion de Empresa (IPADE) was founded in Mexico City in 1967 by a group of Mexican businessmen, with the assistance of faculty members from the Harvard Graduate School of Business Administration and Barcelona's Instituto de Estudios Superiores de la Empresa (IESE), in an attempt to bring business management in Mexico to a higher level. Professors from both Harvard and IESE still regularly serve as guest lecturers. Well-financed by the private sector and free from government control, the school is also free from many of the economic constraints that plague much of Mexico's educational system. IPADE's MBA program takes only 130 students per annum, keeping classes small and personal. These chosen students have a significant networking advantage in Mexican business, as most top businessmen in the country have attended the school in some capacity.

INSTITUTIONAL INFORMATION

Public/Private: Private
Evening Classes Available? No
Total Faculty: 58
% Faculty Female: 5
% Faculty Part Time: 0
Student/Faculty Ratio: 3:1

PROGRAMS

Degrees Offered: Advanced Management Programs and General Management Programs (9 months), MBA and Executive MBA (2 years)

STUDENT INFORMATION

Total Business Students: 78
% Full Time: 100
% Female: 15
% International: 11
Average Age: 26

COMPUTER AND RESEARCH FACILITIES

Campuswide Network? Yes
% of MBA Classrooms Wired: 100
Internet Fee? Yes

EXPENSES/FINANCIAL AID

Room & Board (Off Campus): $8,400
% Receiving Financial Aid: 75
% Receiving Aid Their First Year: 75

ADMISSIONS INFORMATION

Application Fee: $50
Electronic Application? Yes
Regular Application Deadline: 7/31
Regular Notification: 8/31
Deferment Available? Yes
Length of Deferment: 1 year
Non-fall Admissions? No
Transfer Students Accepted? No
Need-Blind Admissions? No
Number of Applications Received: 672
% of Applicants Accepted: 23
% Accepted Who Enrolled: 51
Average GPA: 3.0
Average Years Experience: 3

INTERNATIONAL STUDENTS

TOEFL Required of International Students? Yes
Minimum TOEFL: 570 (230 computer)

EMPLOYMENT INFORMATION

Placement Office Available? Yes
% Employed Within 3 Months: 76
Fields Employing Percentage of Grads: Finance (18%), Entrepreneurship (17%), Marketing (14%), Operations (13%), Accounting (9%), General Management (9%)
Frequent Employers: CEMEX, Comercial Mexicana, Walmart, Tyco, Grupo Financiero Bital, Banamex Citigroup, Eli Lilly, Sanyo, AutomotrizTame, Bayer, GE, Deloitte Consulting, Bristol Mayer, Dominos Pizza, Grupo Mabe, Marsh & Mclennon, Unilever

UNIVERSITE LAVAL
Faculte Des Sciences De L'Administration

Admissions Contact: Andre Gascon, Director of the MBA Program
Address: Universite Laval, Quebec, QC G1K 7P4 Canada
Admissions Phone: (418) 656-3080 • **Admissions Fax:** (418) 656-5216
Admissions E-mail: reg@reg.ulaval.ca
Web Address: www.fsa.ulaval.ca/formation/2ecycle.html

INSTITUTIONAL INFORMATION

Public/Private: Private
Evening Classes Available? No
Total Faculty: 80
% Faculty Part Time: 8
Student/Faculty Ratio: 25:1
Students in Parent Institution: 36,628
Academic Calendar: Semester

PROGRAMS

Degrees Offered: MBA (45 credits, 16 months to 4 years)
Study Abroad Options: Belgium, France, Sweden, United Kingdom, United States

STUDENT INFORMATION

Total Business Students: 1,107
% Full Time: 49
% Female: 43
% International: 20
Average Age: 29

COMPUTER AND RESEARCH FACILITIES

Campuswide Network? Yes
% of MBA Classrooms Wired: 98
Computer Model Recommended: Laptop
Internet Fee? No

EXPENSES/FINANCIAL AID

Annual Tuition: $2,469
Room & Board (On/Off Campus): $2,400
Books and Supplies: $3,000

ADMISSIONS INFORMATION

Application Fee: $30
Electronic Application? Yes
Regular Application Deadline: 8/14
Regular Notification: Rolling
Deferment Available? Yes
Length of Deferment: 1 year
Non-fall Admissions? Yes
Non-fall Application Deadline(s): 9/1
Transfer Students Accepted? No
Need-Blind Admissions? No
Number of Applications Received: 1,707
% of Applicants Accepted: 52
% Accepted Who Enrolled: 48
Average GPA: 3.2
Other Admissions Factors Considered: Computer experience, French language

EMPLOYMENT INFORMATION

Placement Office Available? Yes

UNIVERSITY AT ALBANY/ STATE UNIVERSITY OF NEW YORK
School of Business

Admissions Contact: Albina Y. Grignon, Assistant Dean
Address: UAB 121 1400 Washington Ave., Albany, NY 12222
Admissions Phone: 518-442-4961 • **Admissions Fax:** 518-442-4975
Admissions E-mail: a.grignon@albany.edu • **Web Address:** www.albany.edu/business

University at Albany is a branch of the State University of New York (SUNY) system, known for its academic excellence and experienced faculty. Full-time and part-time MBA schedules are available for completing the MBA program at SUNY Albany, where the tuition is affordable and the educational return on your investment is high. The curriculum is "focused on the information age," enabling graduates to enter the working world equipped with the skills of a confident manager who is comfortable with the various applications of technology in a business environment.

INSTITUTIONAL INFORMATION

Public/Private: Public
Evening Classes Available? Yes
Total Faculty: 45
% Faculty Female: 10
% Faculty Minority: 6
% Faculty Part Time: 20
Student/Faculty Ratio: 4:1
Students in Parent Institution: 17,000
Academic Calendar: September-May

PROGRAMS

Degrees Offered: MBA (2 years), with concentrations in MIS, Human Resources/IS; MSA (1 year); MST (1 year); MSA (2 years); MBA (2 years full time); MBA (2-6 years part time)
Academic Specialties: Albany's MIS program was ranked top 10 in a ComputerWorld survey of corporate recruiters. MIS Faculty specialities: Decision Support Systems, Knowledge Management, E-Commerce, Finance, Public Finance. Human Resources/IS specialties: Compensation and Benefits Design, Entrepreneurship, Change Management
Study Abroad Options: Fudan University in China

STUDENT INFORMATION

Total Business Students: 148
% Full Time: 35
% Female: 40
% Minority: 8
% Out of State: 46
% International: 44
Average Age: 25

COMPUTER AND RESEARCH FACILITIES

Research Facilities: Center for Environmental Technology and Science, Small Business Development Center, Health Care Institute
Computer Facilities: A new library was built in 1999, completely wired for Internet access. Students have free access to Lexis-Nexis and Ebsco databases for research. There are 3 new computer labs available to MBA students in the business building that were donated by prominent consulting firms that recruit from the program. Morethan 35 new systems with state-of-the-art application software are available.
Campuswide Network? Yes
% of MBA Classrooms Wired: 100
Computer Model Recommended: Laptop
Internet Fee? No

EXPENSES/FINANCIAL AID

Annual Tuition (Resident/Nonresident): $2,550/$4,208
Tuition Per Credit (Resident/Nonresident): $213/$351
Room & Board (On/Off Campus): $3,255
Books and Supplies: $500
Average Grant: $10,500
Average Loan: $10,000
% Receiving Financial Aid: 90
% Receiving Aid Their First Year: 52

ADMISSIONS INFORMATION

Application Fee: $50
Electronic Application? Yes
Regular Application Deadline: 5/2
Regular Notification: 5/15
Deferment Available? Yes
Length of Deferment: 1 year or 9 credits
Non-fall Admissions? No
Transfer Students Accepted? No
Need-Blind Admissions? Yes
Number of Applications Received: 535
% of Applicants Accepted: 57
% Accepted Who Enrolled: 17
Average GPA: 3.3
GPA Range: 2.8-3.8
Average GMAT: 528
GMAT Range: 450-620
Average Years Experience: 3
Other Schools to Which Students Applied: University at Buffalo/State University of New York

INTERNATIONAL STUDENTS

TOEFL Required of International Students? Yes
Minimum TOEFL: 580 (237 computer)

EMPLOYMENT INFORMATION

Placement Office Available? Yes
% Employed Within 3 Months: 84
Fields Employing Percentage of Grads: Entrepreneurship (2%), Accounting (4%), Human Resources (7%), Finance (8%), Marketing (13%), MIS (17%), Consulting (47%)
Frequent Employers: Private law firms, government agencies, business and industry
Prominent Alumni: Herbert Lurie, managing director, co-head of investment banking, Merrill Lynch; Jeffrey Black, managing partner, Assurance, Andersen LLP; Michael Weiss, CEO, Access Oncology, Inc.; Thomas Connnolly, senior vice president and controller, SUNY Music; David Light, managing director, fixed income securities, SSBarney

UNIVERSITY AT BUFFALO/STATE UNIVERSITY OF NEW YORK
School of Management

Admissions Contact: Jaimie Taylor, MBA Admissions
Address: 206 Jacobs Management Center, Buffalo, NY 14260
Admissions Phone: 716-645-3204 • **Admissions Fax:** 716-645-2341
Admissions E-mail: som-mba@buffalo.edu • **Web Address:** www.mgt.buffalo.edu

The University at Buffalo, a SUNY system school, has an "increasingly global business environment" and is dedicated to team-oriented learning.

UAB offers an evening MBA, a three-year program structured for working professionals with at least one year of professional work experience under their belts. Any students itching to escape Buffalo for an academic stint elsewhere can travel to Singapore or Beijing on one of UB's international Executive MBA programs. UB's LEAP program provides an opportunity for graduate students to enroll in a practicum for formal real-world business exposure in a chosen area of concentration.

INSTITUTIONAL INFORMATION

Public/Private: Public
Evening Classes Available? Yes
Total Faculty: 61
% Faculty Female: 18
% Faculty Minority: 2
Student/Faculty Ratio: 8:1
Students in Parent Institution: 26,000
Academic Calendar: Semester

PROGRAMS

Degrees Offered: MBA (2 years full time), MSA (1 year with undergraduate accounting degree), MSMIS (1 year), MS in Supply Chains and Operations Management (1 year)
Combined Degrees: JD/MBA, MD/MBA, Architecture/MBA, Pharmacy/MBA, Geography/MBA, BS/MBA Business or Engineering
Academic Specialties: Information Systems, Market Research, International, Competency Development
Study Abroad Options: Study abroad is offered in 20 countries.

STUDENT INFORMATION

Total Business Students: 831
% Full Time: 79
% Female: 32
% Minority: 5
% International: 75
Average Age: 25

COMPUTER AND RESEARCH FACILITIES

Computer Facilities: Wireless network on 2 floors of Management building, large number of fully equipped computer labs, study rooms with computers, technically equipped classrooms across campus, Compustat PC Plus/Research Insight database, SPSS, Microsoft Software Suite free to students
Campuswide Network? Yes
% of MBA Classrooms Wired: 66
Computer Model Recommended: Laptop
Internet Fee? No

EXPENSES/FINANCIAL AID

Annual Tuition (Resident/Nonresident): $5,100/$8,416
Tuition Per Credit (Resident/Nonresident): $500
Room & Board (On/Off Campus): $7,100
Books and Supplies: $1,000
Average Grant: $5,100
Average Loan: $12,000

ADMISSIONS INFORMATION

Application Fee: $50
Electronic Application? Yes
Regular Application Deadline: 7/1
Regular Notification: Rolling
Deferment Available? No
Non-fall Admissions? No
Transfer Students Accepted? No
Need-Blind Admissions? Yes
Number of Applications Received: 767
% of Applicants Accepted: 62
% Accepted Who Enrolled: 29

Average GPA: 3.3
GPA Range: 2.9-3.5
Average GMAT: 601
GMAT Range: 540-650
Average Years Experience: 3
Other Admissions Factors Considered: Work experience, prior academic record, essay
Minority/Disadvantaged Student Recruitment Programs: The University at Buffalo offers competitive fellowships and assistantships to highly qualified minority applicants.
Other Schools to Which Students Applied: Baruch College/City University of New York, George Washington University, Syracuse University, University at Albany/State University of New York, University of Illinois, University of Rochester

INTERNATIONAL STUDENTS

TOEFL Required of International Students? Yes
Minimum TOEFL: 550 (220 computer)

EMPLOYMENT INFORMATION

Placement Office Available? Yes
% Employed Within 3 Months: 56
Fields Employing Percentage of Grads: Operations (6%), MIS (7%), Human Resources (9%), Marketing (18%), Accounting (18%), Finance (42%)
Frequent Employers: Aravali HiTech, Bank of Tokyo-Mitsubishi, Delphi Harrison, Dopkins & Co. CPA, Ernst & Young, ExxonMobil, Fisher Price, Ford Motor Co., ITOCHU/USA, Johnson Controls, JC Penney, Kalieda Health, Kyobo Securities, Lumsden & McCormick CPA, M&T Bank, National Fuel, New England Financial, Rich Products, Russer Foods, Praxair, Samsung Capital, SKTelecom
Prominent Alumni: William H. Lichtenberger, chairman and CEO (retired), Praxair; James M. Ringler, vice chairman, Illinois Tool Works Inc.; James L. Gray, former chairman, president, and CEO, PrimeStar; Ajit Pendse, president, CEO, and founder, Fusion

UNIVERSITY COLLEGE DUBLIN
The Michael Smurfit Graduate School of Business

Admissions Contact: Vicki Samootin, MBA Admissions Officer
Address: University College Dublin, Carysfort Avenue, Blackrock, Co. Dublin, Ireland
Admissions Phone: 011 1 7168862 • Admissions Fax: 011 1 7168965
Admissions E-mail: pba@ucd.ie • Web Address: www.ucd.ie/smurfitschool

INSTITUTIONAL INFORMATION

Public/Private: Public
Evening Classes Available? Yes
Total Faculty: 106
% Faculty Part Time: 17

PROGRAMS

Degrees Offered: Master of Business Studies (1 year), Master of Management Science (1 year), MS in Marketing Practice (1 year), MACC (1 year), MS in Quantitative Finance (2 years)
Combined Degrees: Community of European Management Schools (CEMS) Master's (1 year)
Study Abroad Options: 17 CEMS schools throughout Europe; Reims Management School, France; Tsinghua University, Beijing, China; and others

STUDENT INFORMATION

Total Business Students: 330
% Full Time: 34
% Female: 23
% International: 35
Average Age: 31

COMPUTER AND RESEARCH FACILITIES

Research Facilities: Hatchery
Computer Facilities: ABI Inform, European Intelligence Wire, Infotrac, Euromonitor, Swersnet
Campuswide Network? Yes
% of MBA Classrooms Wired: 100
Computer Model Recommended: Laptop
Internet Fee? No

EXPENSES/FINANCIAL AID

Annual Tuition: $14,860

ADMISSIONS INFORMATION

Application Fee: $32
Electronic Application? Yes
Regular Application Deadline: 3/31
Regular Notification: Rolling
Deferment Available? Yes
Length of Deferment: 1 year
Non-fall Admissions? Yes
Non-fall Application Deadline(s): All terms, no deadlines
Transfer Students Accepted? No
Need-Blind Admissions? Yes
Number of Applications Received: 299
% of Applicants Accepted: 60
% Accepted Who Enrolled: 60
Average GPA: 1.0
Average GMAT: 614
GMAT Range: 530-700
Average Years Experience: 7
Other Admissions Factors Considered: In the absence of GMAT or TOEFL (where required) scores, applicants should include proof of a testing date confirmed.

INTERNATIONAL STUDENTS

TOEFL Required of International Students? Yes

EMPLOYMENT INFORMATION

Placement Office Available? Yes
% Employed Within 3 Months: 76
Fields Employing Percentage of Grads: Human Resources (2%), Entrepreneurship (4%), Other (5%), Marketing (7%), Consulting (15%), General Management (17%), Operations (17%), Accounting (24%)
Frequent Employers: A&L Goodbody, Citibank, Elan, Eli Lilly, GE, KMPG, Riverdeed
Prominent Alumni: Patrick Haren, group chief executive, Viridian; Cathal McGloin, CEO and founder, Perform; JP Donnelly, managing director, Ogilvy & Mather

UNIVERSITY OF AKRON
Graduate Programs in Business

Admissions Contact: Dr. James J. Divoky, Assistant Dean and Director
Address: University of Akron, CBA 412, Akron, OH 44325-4805
Admissions Phone: 330-972-7043 • **Admissions Fax:** 330-972-6588
Admissions E-mail: gradcba@uakron.edu • **Web Address:** www.uakron.edu/cba/grad

The University of Akron houses a student body that's half international and has an average age of 31, so expect a diverse, mature, and dedicated class of MBA business students. The College of Business Administration offers the unique IE-MBA program for midlevel executives involved in international finance, where students visit the headquarters of multinational corporations in the United States, in the UK, and throughout Europe, touring factories, interacting with executives, and attending presentations by internationally recognized business speakers. UA also offers the 1+1 MBA program, which involves one year of Web-based MBA classes followed by one year on campus.

INSTITUTIONAL INFORMATION

Public/Private: Public
Evening Classes Available? Yes
Total Faculty: 65
% Faculty Female: 11
% Faculty Minority: 25
Student/Faculty Ratio: 12:1
Students in Parent Institution: 23,400
Academic Calendar: Fall

PROGRAMS

Degrees Offered: MBA (34-58 credits), with concentrations in E-Business, Accounting, Finance, International Business, Internatial Finance, Health Services Administration, Management of Technology and Innovation, Management, Marketing, Global Sales Management, Supply Chain Management; MSM (33-57 credits), with concentrations in Human Resources, Information Systems; MTAX (30-48 credits); MSA (30-63 credits), with options in Professional Accounting, Accouting Information Systems; EMBA (58 credits, 1 year)
Combined Degrees: MBA/JD, MTAX/JD, MSM in Human Resources/JD
Study Abroad Options: Copenhagen Business School, Denmark; ESC Rennes, ESC Marseilles, and ESC Lille, France; Stuttgart, Germany; Korea; ITESM: Cuernavaca, UVM, AU Guadalajara, Mexico; St. Ignacio Loyola, Peru; Ubon, Thailand; United Kingdom

STUDENT INFORMATION

Total Business Students: 268
% Full Time: 43
% Female: 45
% Minority: 7
% Out of State: 2
% International: 41
Average Age: 27

COMPUTER AND RESEARCH FACILITIES

Research Facilities: Member of Oracle DBMS Academic Initiative; Fisher Sales Laboratory (sales simulation and skills practice facility), Fitzgerald Institute of Entrepreneurial Studies
Computer Facilities: Web-based MBA courses, Standard & Poor's Research Insight, CRSP Financial Database, ABI/Inform, Disclosure Global Access, Lexis-Nexis, Zach's University Analyst Watch
Campuswide Network? Yes
% of MBA Classrooms Wired: 100
Internet Fee? No

EXPENSES/FINANCIAL AID

Annual Tuition (Resident/Nonresident): $10,280/$16,529
Tuition Per Credit (Resident/Nonresident): $279/$459
Room & Board (On/Off Campus): $8,050
Books and Supplies: $600
Average Grant: $10,567
% Receiving Financial Aid: 20
% Receiving Aid Their First Year: 12

ADMISSIONS INFORMATION

Application Fee: $40
Electronic Application? No
Regular Application Deadline: 8/1
Regular Notification: 8/15
Deferment Available? Yes
Length of Deferment: 2 years
Non-fall Admissions? Yes
Non-fall Application Deadline(s): 12/1 spring, 5/1 summer
Transfer Students Accepted? Yes
Transfer Policy: Up to 24 credits of foundation courses may be waived; 9 credits of the core may transfer from AACSB-accredited schools.
Need-Blind Admissions? Yes
Number of Applications Received: 91
% of Applicants Accepted: 66
% Accepted Who Enrolled: 67
Average GPA: 3.3
GPA Range: 3.0-3.5
Average GMAT: 565
GMAT Range: 500-600
Average Years Experience: 4
Other Admissions Factors Considered: Previous graduate and post-baccalaureate performance, professional associations and student organization memberships
Minority/Disadvantaged Student Recruitment Programs: Graduate School provides a minority recruitment program with Dr. Lathardus Goggins.
Other Schools to Which Students Applied: Case Western Reserve University, Cleveland State University, John Carroll University, Kent State University, Ohio State University, University of Cincinnati, Youngstown State University

INTERNATIONAL STUDENTS

TOEFL Required of International Students? Yes
Minimum TOEFL: 550 (213 computer)

EMPLOYMENT INFORMATION

Placement Office Available? Yes
Fields Employing Percentage of Grads: Other (1%), Entrepreneurship (2%), Operations (2%), Human Resources (2%), Accounting (3%), Marketing (7%), Global Management (9%), General Management (17%), Finance (23%), MIS (27%)
Frequent Employers: Arthur Andersen; Brouse & McDowell; Buckingham, Doolittle, & Burroughs; City of Akron Law Department; County Prosecutor Offices; CSFA; Ernst & Young; Jones, Day, Reavis & Pogue; 9th District Court of Appeals; Roetzel & Andress; Stark & Summit Counties Courts of Common Pleas; U.S. Army JAG Corps
Prominent Alumni: Peter Burg, chairman and CEO, First Energy; James McCready, chairman of Cypress Companies; John Piecuch, retired president & CEO, LaFarge Coppee; Joanne Rohrer, secretary/treasurer, Rohrer Corp.; Ernest Pouttu, vice president of finance and CFO, Harwick Standard Distribution

UNIVERSITY OF ALABAMA— BIRMINGHAM
Graduate School of Management

Admissions Contact: Melody Lake, MBA Program Coordinator
Address: 1530 3rd Avenue South HUC 511, Birmingham, AL 35294-1150
Admissions Phone: 205-934-8817 • **Admissions Fax:** 205-934-8413
Admissions E-mail: inquire@gradschool.huc.uab.edu
Web Address: www.business.uab.edu

INSTITUTIONAL INFORMATION

Public/Private: Public
Evening Classes Available? Yes
Total Faculty: 47
% Faculty Part Time: 6
Student/Faculty Ratio: 40:1
Students in Parent Institution: 16,000
Academic Calendar: Semester

PROGRAMS

Degrees Offered: MBA (36-48 credits, 1-7 years part time), with concentrations in Finance, Itechnology Management, Accounting, Health Care Management; MACC (30 credits, 1-7 years part time), with concentrations in Practice, Infomation Systems
Combined Degrees: MBA/MPH (72 credits, full time or part time, 2-7 years), MBA/MSHA (72 credits, 2-8 years full time)
Study Abroad Options: Germany

STUDENT INFORMATION

Total Business Students: 334
% Female: 37
% Minority: 9
% International: 11
Average Age: 27

COMPUTER AND RESEARCH FACILITIES

Research Facilities: Mervyn Sterne Library plus 1 additional on-campus library; total holdings of 1,476,168 volumes; 416,175 microforms; 5,390 current periodical subscriptions. CD player(s) available for graduate student use; access provided to online bibliographic retrieval services and online databases
Campuswide Network? Yes
% of MBA Classrooms Wired: 100
Computer Model Recommended: Desktop
Internet Fee? No

EXPENSES/FINANCIAL AID

Tuition Per Credit (Resident/Nonresident): $112/$224

ADMISSIONS INFORMATION

Application Fee: $50
Electronic Application? Yes
Regular Application Deadline: 7/1
Regular Notification: 8/1
Deferment Available? Yes
Length of Deferment: 1 year
Non-fall Admissions? Yes
Non-fall Application Deadline(s): 11/1 spring, 3/1 summer
Transfer Students Accepted? No
Need-Blind Admissions? Yes
Number of Applications Received: 240
% of Applicants Accepted: 79
% Accepted Who Enrolled: 74
Average GPA: 3.2
Average GMAT: 525

Other Admissions Factors Considered: A formula score (GPA × 200 + GMAT = 1050 or higher), minimum GMAT score of 450

INTERNATIONAL STUDENTS

TOEFL Required of International Students? Yes
Minimum TOEFL: 550

EMPLOYMENT INFORMATION

Placement Office Available? Yes
% Employed Within 3 Months: 92

UNIVERSITY OF ALABAMA— HUNTSVILLE
College of Administrative Science

Admissions Contact: Dr. J. Daniel Sherman, Associate Dean
Address: ASB 102, Huntsville, AL 35899
Admissions Phone: 256-824-6024 • **Admissions Fax:** 256-890-7571
Admissions E-mail: msmprog@email.uah.edu
Web Address: www.uah.edu/colleges/adminsci

INSTITUTIONAL INFORMATION

Public/Private: Public
Evening Classes Available? Yes
Total Faculty: 30
% Faculty Female: 23
% Faculty Minority: 10
% Faculty Part Time: 6
Student/Faculty Ratio: 5:1
Academic Calendar: Semester

PROGRAMS

Degrees Offered: MSMOT (2 years), MACC (2 years), MSMIS (2 years)
Academic Specialties: Management of Technology

COMPUTER AND RESEARCH FACILITIES

Research Facilities: Center for the Management of Science & Technology
Campuswide Network? Yes
Internet Fee? No

EXPENSES/FINANCIAL AID

Tuition Per Credit (Resident/Nonresident): $190/$386
Books and Supplies: $527

ADMISSIONS INFORMATION

Application Fee: $35
Electronic Application? No
Regular Application Deadline: 8/1
Regular Notification: 1/1
Deferment Available? No
Non-fall Admissions? Yes
Non-fall Application Deadline(s): Rolling
Transfer Students Accepted? Yes
Transfer Policy: Transfer credit evaluated by program advisor
Need-Blind Admissions? Yes
Number of Applications Received: 2
% of Applicants Accepted: 100
% Accepted Who Enrolled: 100

INTERNATIONAL STUDENTS

TOEFL Required of International Students? Yes
Minimum TOEFL: 600

UNIVERSITY OF ALABAMA— TUSCALOOSA

Manderson Graduate School of Business

Admissions Contact: Ms. Burch Barger, Coordinator of Admission & Recruiting
Address: Box 870223, Tuscaloosa, AL 35487-0223
Admissions Phone: 205-348-6517 • Admissions Fax: 205-348-4504
Admissions E-mail: mba@cba.ua.edu • Web Address: www.cba.ua.edu/mba

The Manderson Graduate School of Business has a unique student body, as it encourages students with varied, nonbusiness undergrad degrees as well as students with little or no work experience to apply to its MBA program. Manderson's MBA class has only about 65 students, so as you can imagine, students and faculty intermingle in a comfortable and personal learning environment. Aiming to provide a solid academic foundation, the Manderson MBA curriculum focuses on team-building skills, real-world experience, community involvement and networking, and achieving a "balance between personal and professional activities."

INSTITUTIONAL INFORMATION

Public/Private: Public
Evening Classes Available? No
Total Faculty: 86
% Faculty Female: 12
% Faculty Minority: 7
% Faculty Part Time: 3
Student/Faculty Ratio: 13:1
Students in Parent Institution: 19,000

PROGRAMS

Degrees Offered: MA (1 year) in Banking and Finance, Economics, Human Resources Management, Management Science, Marketing, or Statistics; MS (1 year); MACC (1 year); EMBA (1.5 years); PhD (4 to 5 years
Combined Degrees: MBA/JD (4 years), 3+2 MBA/BA or BS (5 years), MBA/MA in Modern Languages (3 years), MBA/MSN (3 years)
Academic Specialties: Systems Consulting, Strategic Planning and Implementation, Strategic Business Management, Marketing, Statistics, Finance, Economics, Real Estate, MIS, Accounting
Study Abroad Options: Belgium, Chile, Denmark, France, Germany, Italy, Spain, South Africa

STUDENT INFORMATION

Total Business Students: 120
% Full Time: 100
% Female: 34
% Minority: 9
% Out of State: 34
% International: 15
Average Age: 26

COMPUTER AND RESEARCH FACILITIES

Research Facilities: Center for Business and Economic Research, Alabama Institute for Manufacturing Excellence, Alabama International Trade Center, Alabama Productivity Center, Alabama Real Estate Research and Education Center, Center for Economic Education, Enterprise Integration Lab, Small Business Development Center

Computer Facilities: Sloan Y. Bashinsky Computer Center, all campus libraries, computer labs, Enterprise Integration Lab
Campuswide Network? Yes
% of MBA Classrooms Wired: 100
Computer Model Recommended: Laptop
Internet Fee? No

EXPENSES/FINANCIAL AID

Annual Tuition (Resident/Nonresident): $3,556/$9,624
Room & Board (On/Off Campus): $8,800
Books and Supplies: $800
Average Grant: $6,956
Average Loan: $13,000
% Receiving Financial Aid: 70
% Receiving Aid Their First Year: 100

ADMISSIONS INFORMATION

Application Fee: $25
Electronic Application? Yes
Early Decision Application Deadline: Fall (rolling up to 1/5)
Early Decision Notification: 2/4
Regular Application Deadline: 4/15
Regular Notification: Rolling
Deferment Available? Yes
Length of Deferment: 1-year renewable
Non-fall Admissions? No
Transfer Students Accepted? Yes
Transfer Policy: Up to 24 credit hours accepted from AACSB-accredited programs subject to committee approval
Need-Blind Admissions? Yes
Number of Applications Received: 207
% of Applicants Accepted: 44
% Accepted Who Enrolled: 55
Average GPA: 3.4
GPA Range: 2.2-3.8
Average GMAT: 603
GMAT Range: 520-680
Average Years Experience: 2
Other Admissions Factors Considered: Each Alabama MBA class is selected to represent a diversity of academic, work, cultural, and international experiences that reflects today's workplace. An applicant's background that has the potential to make a unique or missing contribution to an incoming MBA class' make-up can be the deciding admissions factor that supercedes other factors.
Minority/Disadvantaged Student Recruitment Programs: Capstone MBA Fellows program seeks to place underrepresented students in the private sector for 10-20 hours per week for the duration of the 2-year MBA program. Financial aid support is also available to recruit high achieving, high potential students.
Other Schools to Which Students Applied: University of Georgia, Vanderbilt University, Tulane University, University of Tennessee—Knoxville, Emory University, Wake Forest University, University of South Carolina

INTERNATIONAL STUDENTS

TOEFL Required of International Students? Yes
Minimum TOEFL: 575 (575 computer)

EMPLOYMENT INFORMATION

Placement Office Available? Yes
% Employed Within 3 Months: 72
Fields Employing Percentage of Grads: Other (3%), Operations (4%), Accounting (5%), Consulting (8%), MIS (11%), Marketing (12%), Finance (18%)
Frequent Employers: AEA Group, Cap Gemini E&Y, Federal Express, International Paper, Lithonia Lighting, Mercedes, Proctor & Gamble, Southern Co.
Prominent Alumni: Thomas Cross, managing partner, Pricewaterhouse Coopers; Samuel D. DiPiazza, vice chairman, Pricewaterhouse Coopers

UNIVERSITY OF ALASKA—ANCHORAGE
College of Business and Public Policy

Admissions Contact: Michael Smith, MBA Program Assistant
Address: 3211 Providence Drive, Anchorage, AK 99508-8060
Admissions Phone: 907-786-4100 • **Admissions Fax:** 907-786-4119
Admissions E-mail: anmbs1@uaa.alaska.edu • **Web Address:** www.cbpp.uaa.alaska.edu

INSTITUTIONAL INFORMATION

Public/Private: Public
Evening Classes Available? Yes
Total Faculty: 43
Student/Faculty Ratio: 20:1
Academic Calendar: September-May

PROGRAMS

Degrees Offered: MPA (2 years), MBA (2 years)
Academic Specialties: Economics, Accounting, Business Administration, Global Logistics Management, Management Information Systems
The College of Business and Public Policy is fully accredited by the Commission on Colleges of the Northwest Association of Schools and Colleges. It is also separately accredited by the International Association for Management Education.
Special Opportunities: Management; Supply Chain Management, Transportation, Logistics

STUDENT INFORMATION

Total Business Students: 27
% Full Time: 42
% Female: 7
% Minority: 11
% International: 22

COMPUTER AND RESEARCH FACILITIES

Research Facilities: Institute of Social and Economic Research, Institute for Circumpolar Health Studies, American Russian Center, Biomedical Program, Center for Alcohol and Addiction Studies, Center for Economic Development, Center for Economic Education, Small Business Development Center
Campuswide Network? Yes
% of MBA Classrooms Wired: 12
Internet Fee? No

EXPENSES/FINANCIAL AID

Annual Tuition (Resident/Nonresident): $3,375/$6,327
Tuition Per Credit (Resident/Nonresident): $172/$336
Books and Supplies: $500
Average Grant: $6,057
Average Loan: $7,116

ADMISSIONS INFORMATION

Application Fee: $45
Electronic Application? No
Regular Application Deadline: Rolling
Regular Notification: Rolling
Deferment Available? Yes
Length of Deferment: 1 semester
Non-fall Admissions? Yes
Non-fall Application Deadline(s): Rolling
Transfer Students Accepted? Yes
Transfer Policy: Applicants must meet all UAA and MBA admissions requirements. Up to 9 semester credits not previously used to obtain any other degree or certificate bay be transferred to UAA from a regionally accredited institution and accepted toward a graduate degree or certificate.
Need-Blind Admissions? Yes
Number of Applications Received: 27

% of Applicants Accepted: 59
% Accepted Who Enrolled: 94

INTERNATIONAL STUDENTS

TOEFL Required of International Students? Yes
Minimum TOEFL: 550

EMPLOYMENT INFORMATION

Placement Office Available? No
Frequent Employers: British Petrolium, Fedex, Unocal, UPS

UNIVERSITY OF ALBERTA
School of Business

Admissions Contact: Joan White, Executive Director, MBA Programs
Address: 2-30 Business Building, Edmonton, AB T6G 2R6 Canada
Admissions Phone: 780-492-3946 • **Admissions Fax:** 780-492-7825
Admissions E-mail: mba.programs@ualberta.ca
Web Address: www.bus.ualberta.ca/MBA

Edmonton, the capital of Alberta, is home to a dynamic and evolving business center. The class size at U of A's Faculty of Business is deliberately small, allowing for an intense amount of class interaction and access to faculty, and professors encourage participation in summer internships in Edmonton to exercise skills learned in the classroom. The Faculty of Business offers several unique joint degrees, including an MBA/Master of Agriculture, an MBA/Master of Forestry, and an MBA/Master of Engineering. UA also offers several interesting MBA concentrations, ranging from natural resources and energy to technology commercialization.

INSTITUTIONAL INFORMATION

Public/Private: Public
Evening Classes Available? Yes
Total Faculty: 105
% Faculty Female: 14
% Faculty Part Time: 17
Student/Faculty Ratio: 3:1
Students in Parent Institution: 31,000

PROGRAMS

Degrees Offered: MBA (20 months); EMBA (21 months); MBA (20 months), with specializations in International Business, Leisure and Sport Management, Natural Resources and Energy, Technology Commercialization; MBA/LLB (4 years); MBA/Meng (2 years); MBA/Mag (2 years); MBA/MF (2 years)
Combined Degrees: MBA/LLB (4 years), MBA/MEng (2 years), MBA/MAg (2 years), MBA/MF (2 years)
Academic Specialties: Specializations offered in International Business, Leisure and Sport Management, Natural Resources and Energy, Technology Commercialization
Special Opportunities: Specializations offered in International Business, Leisure and Sport Management, Natural Resources and Energy, Technology Commercialization
Study Abroad Options: Australia, Austria, Chile, Denmark, Finland, France, Germany, Hong Kong, Japan, Mexico, Scotland, Sweden, Switzerland, Thailand, United Kingdom, United States

STUDENT INFORMATION

Total Business Students: 240
% Full Time: 55

% **Female:** 42
% **International:** 43
Average Age: 28

COMPUTER AND RESEARCH FACILITIES

Research Facilities: Centre for Applied Business Research in Energy and the Environment (CABREE), Centre for Entrepreneurship and Family Enterprise (CEFE), Centre for Executive and Management Development, (CEMD), Centre for Excellence in Operations (CEO), Centre for International Business Studies (CIBS), Centre for Professional Service Firm Management (PSFM), Chartered Accountants Centre, Canadian Institute of Retailing & Services (CIRAS), Canadian Centre for Social Entrepreneurship (CCSE), Cultural Industries Research Centre (CIRC), Environmental Research Studies Centre (ERSC), Institute for Financial Research, Western Centre for Economic Research (WCER)
Computer Facilities: MBA Computer Lab equipped with 25 computers, a scanner, and high speed printer; database access for students through University of Alberta Library Systems
Campuswide Network? Yes
% **of MBA Classrooms Wired:** 100
Internet Fee? No

EXPENSES/FINANCIAL AID

Annual Tuition (Resident/Nonresident): $3,100/$6,100
Room & Board (On/Off Campus): $3,100
Books and Supplies: $1,000
Average Grant: $2,600

ADMISSIONS INFORMATION

Electronic Application? Yes
Regular Application Deadline: 4/30
Regular Notification: Rolling
Deferment Available? Yes
Length of Deferment: 1 year
Non-fall Admissions? No
Transfer Students Accepted? No
Need-Blind Admissions? Yes
Number of Applications Received: 452
% **of Applicants Accepted:** 25
% **Accepted Who Enrolled:** 50
Average GPA: 3.4
Average GMAT: 627
GMAT Range: 570-710
Average Years Experience: 5

INTERNATIONAL STUDENTS

TOEFL Required of International Students? Yes
Minimum TOEFL: 600 (250 computer)

EMPLOYMENT INFORMATION

Placement Office Available? Yes
% **Employed Within 3 Months:** 93
Fields Employing Percentage of Grads: General Management (6%), Communications (6%), Finance (6%), Consulting (10%), Operations (31%), Other (35%)
Frequent Employers: Alberta Department of Environment, Alberta Economic Development, Aquila Energy, BP Energy, Canadian Imperial Bank of Commerce, EPCOR, Imperial Oil, KPMG Consulting, Perforex, PetroCanada, Pricewaterhouse Coopers, Suncor Energy Inc., Telus, University of Alberta, University of Alberta Hospital
Prominent Alumni: Guy Kerr, vice president; Gay Mitchell, executive vice president, Ontario; Guy Turcotte, chairman and CEO; Eric Morgan, president

UNIVERSITY OF ARIZONA
Eller Graduate School of Management

Admissions Contact: Misty Salinas, Associate Director for Full-Time MBA Admissions
Address: McClelland Hall 210, 1130 E Helen, Tucson, AZ 85721-0108
Admissions Phone: 520-626-9455 • **Admissions Fax:** 520-621-2606
Admissions E-mail: mba_admissions@eller.arizona.edu
Web Address: ellermba.arizona.edu

The tuition is dirt cheap at the University of Arizona's Eller School of Management, home to a nationally renowned information technology department, which draws substantial financial support from tech behemoths like IBM and Hewlett-Packard. U of A also boasts a "very well-respected entrepreneurial program," and MBA students here tell us that "Tucson is a great place to live" because "the cost of living is low and it has a laid-back environment."

INSTITUTIONAL INFORMATION

Public/Private: Public
Evening Classes Available? Yes
Total Faculty: 105
% **Faculty Female:** 17
% **Faculty Minority:** 7
Student/Faculty Ratio: 40:1
Students in Parent Institution: 35,000
Academic Calendar: Semester

PROGRAMS

Degrees Offered: MBA (21 months), MIS (10-21 months), MACC (10 months)
Combined Degrees: JD/MBA (4 years), MBA/MIM (2-4 years), MIS/MBA (3 years), MBA/PharmD (5 years)
Academic Specialties: Entrepreneurship, Management Information Systems, Finance
Study Abroad Options: None

STUDENT INFORMATION

Total Business Students: 137
% **Full Time:** 49
% **Female:** 28
% **Minority:** 4
% **Out of State:** 50
% **International:** 24
Average Age: 29

COMPUTER AND RESEARCH FACILITIES

Research Facilities: None
Computer Facilities: Graduate Computer Lab, Park Street Lab, Economics Lab (There are additional computer facilities on campus, but these are specifically for Business and MBA students.)
Campuswide Network? Yes
% **of MBA Classrooms Wired:** 100
Internet Fee? No

EXPENSES/FINANCIAL AID

Annual Tuition (Resident/Nonresident): $13,258/$22,028
Tuition Per Credit (Resident/Nonresident): $556
Room & Board (On/Off Campus): $10,000
Books and Supplies: $1,500
Average Grant: $16,582
Average Loan: $18,500
% **Receiving Financial Aid:** 100
% **Receiving Aid Their First Year:** 100

ADMISSIONS INFORMATION

Application Fee: $50
Electronic Application? Yes
Early Decision Application Deadline: 11/15
Early Decision Notification: 12/15
Regular Application Deadline: Rolling
Regular Notification: Rolling
Deferment Available? Yes
Length of Deferment: 1 year
Non-fall Admissions? No
Transfer Students Accepted? No
Need-Blind Admissions? Yes
Number of Applications Received: 356
% of Applicants Accepted: 67
% Accepted Who Enrolled: 58
Average GPA: 3.4
GPA Range: 3.1-3.6
Average GMAT: 636
GMAT Range: 600-660
Average Years Experience: 4
Other Admissions Factors Considered: Quality of work experience, performance on the quantitative and analytical sections of the GMAT, quality of application essays
Other Schools to Which Students Applied: Arizona State University, Cornell University, Purdue University, University of California—Berkeley, University of California—Los Angeles, University of Maryland—College Park, University of Texas—Austin

INTERNATIONAL STUDENTS

TOEFL Required of International Students? Yes
Minimum TOEFL: 600 (250 computer)

EMPLOYMENT INFORMATION

Placement Office Available? Yes
% Employed Within 3 Months: 77
Fields Employing Percentage of Grads: Human Resources (5%), MIS (7%), Other (9%), General Management (9%), Consulting (9%), Operations (13%), Marketing (16%), Finance (32%)
Frequent Employers: America West Airlines, Avery Dennison, Deloitte Consulting, E & J Gallo Winery, First Magnus Financial Corp., Ford Motor Co., Honeywell, IBM, Intel Corp., Raytheon Co., Target Corp.—Mervyn's Division
Prominent Alumni: Mark Hoffman, CEO, Commerce One; Robert Eckert, chairman, CEO, Mattel, Inc.; Jim Whims, managing partner, Tech Fund; Stephen Forte, senior vice president, flight operations, United Airlines; Tom Hennings, president and CEO, OrderFusion

UNIVERSITY OF ARKANSAS— FAYETTEVILLE

Sam M. Walton College of Business

Admissions Contact: Michele Halsell, Managing Director, Graduate School of Business
Address: 475 Business Building, Fayetteville, AR 72701
Admissions Phone: 479-575-2851 • **Admissions Fax:** 479-575-8721
Admissions E-mail: gsb@walton.uark.edu • **Web Address:** gsb.uark.edu

The Sam M. Walton College of Business Administration offers an accelerated one-year MBA program and a part-time managerial MBA program, and short preparatory courses are available to students who fail to meet the business admission requisites or score above 70 percent on the sample exams. A special feature of UA's business program takes place in mid-October

of each year, when the MBA class travels to the Southwest MBA Fair, a regional career fair in Dallas that attracts big-name companies such as Intel, Nortel Networks, Deloitte & Touche, American Express, and Sprint. Applicants to UA Fayetteville also apply to East Tennessee State University, Arkansas State, Kansas State, Oklahoma State, and Vanderbilt, among others.

INSTITUTIONAL INFORMATION

Public/Private: Public
Evening Classes Available? Yes
Total Faculty: 85
% Faculty Female: 27
% Faculty Minority: 9
Student/Faculty Ratio: 20:1
Students in Parent Institution: 16,035
Academic Calendar: July-June

PROGRAMS

Degrees Offered: MBA (1 year), MACC (1 year), MAECON (18 months), MTLM (1 year), MIS (1 year)
Combined Degrees: MBA/JD (4 years)
Academic Specialties: 1-year program (38 hours lock-step), consulting projects, Retailing, Logistics, Supply-Chain Management, Marketing
Study Abroad Options: China, France, Italy, Japan; NAFTA

STUDENT INFORMATION

Total Business Students: 148
% Full Time: 56
% Female: 39
% Minority: 10
% Out of State: 10
% International: 21
Average Age: 25

COMPUTER AND RESEARCH FACILITIES

Research Facilities: Students Aquiring Knowledge through Enterprise (SAKE), a non-profit organization; Center for Retailing Excellence, a major site for consumer packaged goods (CPG) and retailing industry (hosts a major conference each fall with attendance by industry giants)
Computer Facilities: More than 200 general-access lab computers; Graduate Student Lab with 20 computers; all computers have Internet access; the only school in the country with access to all 3 major commercial data services (AC Nielson, Spectra, IRI); wireless network through the Business Building and several other locations throughout campus
Campuswide Network? Yes
% of MBA Classrooms Wired: 100
Internet Fee? No

EXPENSES/FINANCIAL AID

Annual Tuition (Resident/Nonresident): $10,435/$21,409
Tuition Per Credit (Resident/Nonresident): $28/$563
Room & Board (On/Off Campus): $9,979
Books and Supplies: $1,000
Average Grant: $8,623
Average Loan: $12,911
% Receiving Financial Aid: 84
% Receiving Aid Their First Year: 84

ADMISSIONS INFORMATION

Application Fee: $40
Electronic Application? Yes
Regular Application Deadline: 2/15
Regular Notification: 3/15
Length of Deferment: 1 year
Non-fall Application Deadline(s): Summer only

Transfer Policy: Maximum of 6 hours of electives from an AACSB-accredited school, A or B grades
Need-Blind Admissions? Yes
Number of Applications Received: 200
% of Applicants Accepted: 75
% Accepted Who Enrolled: 73
Average GPA: 3.3
GPA Range: 2.9-3.6
Average GMAT: 593
GMAT Range: 550-620
Average Years Experience: 2
Other Admissions Factors Considered: Candidates with significant business experience are given preference.
Minority/Disadvantaged Student Recruitment Programs: Underrepresented minorities are encouraged to apply. Special financial assistance is available to minority students.
Other Schools to Which Students Applied: University of Texas—Austin, University of Oklahoma, Texas A&M University, University of Tennessee—Knoxville, Southern Methodist University, University of Georgia

INTERNATIONAL STUDENTS

TOEFL Required of International Students? Yes
Minimum TOEFL: 550 (213 computer)

EMPLOYMENT INFORMATION

Placement Office Available? Yes
% Employed Within 3 Months: 48
Fields Employing Percentage of Grads: Operations (7%), Marketing (7%), Consulting (13%), Accounting (13%), Other (26%), Finance (27%)
Frequent Employers: Accenture, J.B Hunt, LAM, Tyson Foods, Unilever, Wal-Mart Stores Inc.
Prominent Alumni: S. Robson Walton, chairman, Wal-Mart Stores Inc.; William Dillards Sr., chairman, Dillards Inc.; Frank Fletcher, entrepreneur; Jack Stephens, Stephens Inc.; Thomas F. McLarty, former U.S. presidential advisor

See page 446.

STUDENT INFORMATION

Total Business Students: 225
% Full Time: 13
% Female: 42
% Minority: 8
% Out of State: 1
% International: 15
Average Age: 29

COMPUTER AND RESEARCH FACILITIES

Campuswide Network? Yes
Internet Fee? No

EXPENSES/FINANCIAL AID

Annual Tuition (Resident/Nonresident): $4,937/$10,037

ADMISSIONS INFORMATION

Electronic Application? No
Regular Application Deadline: Rolling
Regular Notification: Rolling
Deferment Available? Yes
Non-fall Admissions? No
Transfer Students Accepted? No
Need-Blind Admissions? No
Number of Applications Received: 87
% of Applicants Accepted: 66
% Accepted Who Enrolled: 74
Other Admissions Factors Considered: The GMAT is recommended (minimum score of 450); a minimum GPA of 2.7 is required.
Other Schools to Which Students Applied: University of Florida, Babson College, Rensselaer Polytechnic Institute, University of Pennsylvania, University of Texas—Austin, Florida International University, Florida State

INTERNATIONAL STUDENTS

TOEFL Required of International Students? Yes
Minimum TOEFL: 550

EMPLOYMENT INFORMATION

Placement Office Available? Yes
% Employed Within 3 Months: 95

UNIVERSITY OF ARKANSAS— LITTLE ROCK
College of Business Administration

Admissions Contact: Dr. Ken Glachus, MBA Advisor
Address: 2801 South University Avenue, Little Rock, AR 72204
Admissions Phone: 501-569-3048 • **Admissions Fax:** 501-569-8898
Admissions E-mail: • **Web Address:** www.cba.ualr.edu

INSTITUTIONAL INFORMATION

Public/Private: Public
Evening Classes Available? No
Total Faculty: 42
% Faculty Part Time: 19
Students in Parent Institution: 9,925
Academic Calendar: Semester

PROGRAMS

Degrees Offered: MBA (30-66 credits; full time, part time, or distance learning; 1-5 years), with concentrations in Accounting, Finance, Management, Marketing, MIS; EMBA (46 credits, 17 months part time; 5 years work experience required)
Special Opportunities: General Business

UNIVERSITY OF BALTIMORE
Merrick School of Business

Admissions Contact: Jeffrey Zavronty, Assistant Director of Admissions
Address: 1420 North Charles Street, Baltimore, MD 21201
Admissions Phone: 877-277-5982 • **Admissions Fax:** 410-837-4793
Admissions E-mail: Admissions@ubmail.ubalt.edu • **Web Address:** www.ubalt.edu

"The career-minded university," University of Baltimore is 1 of 13 schools under the umbrella of the University System of Maryland. The Robert G. Merrick School of Business offers a multitude of MBA program options. The Advantage MBA is a one-year full-time track; the Saturday MBA is a two-year track designed for busy executives and managers; the Web MBA is designed for an online educational experience; and the Custom Track allows students to mix and match courses from the Advantage, Saturday, and Web MBA tracks to create a more personalized degree experience. To kick up the global perspective a notch, UB also offers the Executive MBA program in China and Chile.

INSTITUTIONAL INFORMATION

Public/Private: Public
Evening Classes Available? Yes
Total Faculty: 53
% Faculty Female: 25
% Faculty Minority: 34
Student/Faculty Ratio: 15:1
Students in Parent Institution: 4,639
Academic Calendar: Semester

PROGRAMS

Degrees Offered: Advantage MBA (30-48 credits, 12 months), Flex MBA (30-51 credits, 1-7 years), MS in Finance (30-42 credits, 1-7 years), MSIS (33-45 credits, 1-7 years), MST (30 credits, 1-7 years), Professional MBA (48 credits, 23 months), MSA (30-51 credits, 1-7 years), Chinese EMBA (48 credits, 12 months), Web MBA (48 credits, 2 years), MS in Marketing and Venturing (48 credits, 2-4 years)
Combined Degrees: MBA/MSN (66 credits, 2-7 years), MBA/PhD in Nursing (85 credits, 2-7 years), MBA/PharmD (155 credits, 2-7 years), MBA/JD (102-123 credits, 3-7 years)
Academic Specialties: International Business, Entrepreneurship, Finance, Information Systems, Accounting, Human Resource Management, Decision Technologies, Service and Manufacturing Operations, Marketing

STUDENT INFORMATION

Total Business Students: 506
% Full Time: 46
% Female: 43
% Minority: 18
% Out of State: 16
% International: 33
Average Age: 29

COMPUTER AND RESEARCH FACILITIES

Research Facilities: MBNA Information Systems Institute, which includes the Information Systems Research Center (ISRC) and the E-Learning Center.
Campuswide Network? Yes
% of MBA Classrooms Wired: 100
Internet Fee? No

EXPENSES/FINANCIAL AID

Annual Tuition (Resident/Nonresident): $5,941/$8,533
Tuition Per Credit (Resident/Nonresident): $294/$438
Books and Supplies: $900

ADMISSIONS INFORMATION

Application Fee: $30
Electronic Application? Yes
Regular Application Deadline: Rolling
Regular Notification: Rolling
Deferment Available? Yes
Length of Deferment: 1 year
Non-fall Admissions? Yes
Non-fall Application Deadline(s): 12/1 spring, 4/1 summer
Transfer Students Accepted? Yes
Transfer Policy: Maximun of 6 credits from an AACSB-accredited MBA program
Need-Blind Admissions? Yes
Number of Applications Received: 376
% of Applicants Accepted: 62
% Accepted Who Enrolled: 63
Average GPA: 3.0
GPA Range: 2.8-3.1
Average GMAT: 500
GMAT Range: 470-520
Other Admissions Factors Considered: Work experience
Other Schools to Which Students Applied: Loyola College in Maryland,

University of Maryland—College Park

INTERNATIONAL STUDENTS

TOEFL Required of International Students? Yes
Minimum TOEFL: 550 (213 computer)

EMPLOYMENT INFORMATION

Placement Office Available? Yes
Frequent Employers: Governement agencies, corporations
Prominent Alumni: William Donald Schaeffer, govenor, State of Maryland; Peter Angelos, owner, Baltimore Orioles; Joseph Curran, attorney general, State of Maryland; Vernon Wright, vice chairman, MBNA America Bank

UNIVERSITY OF BATH
School of Management

Admissions Contact: Ruth Cooper, MBA Admissions and Marketing Manager
Address: MBA Office, School of Management, Claverton Dewr., Bath, BA2 7AY, United Kingdom
Admissions Phone: 011 44 (0) 225 383432 • **Admissions Fax:** 011 44 (0) 225 386210
Admissions E-mail: mba-info@management.bath.ac.uk • **Web Address:** www.bath.ac.uk/management

INSTITUTIONAL INFORMATION

Evening Classes Available? No
Total Faculty: 51
% Faculty Female: 22
% Faculty Part Time: 7
Student/Faculty Ratio: 8:1
Students in Parent Institution: 8,000

PROGRAMS

Degrees Offered: MBA (full time, 1 year); Executive MBA (Bath) (part time, 2 years); Executive MBA (Swindon) (part time, 3 years); Modular MBA (part time, 2 to 8 years, 3 or 4 average); MS in Management (full time, 1 year); MS in Responsibility and Business Practice (part time, 2 years)
Joint Degrees: BS in International Management and Modern Languages (IMML): French, German, Spanish (4 years)
Academic Specialties: The programs cover all the key quantitative techniques and subject areas, while the behavioral and values-based aspects of management are also key components. Academic areas of expertise include Accounting and Finance, Business Economics and Strategy, Decision and Information Systems, Higher Education Management, Human Resource Management, International Business, Marketing, Operations Management and the Management of Supply, Organizational Behavior, and Risk Management.
Study Abroad Options: Czech Republic, Denmark, France, Germany, Netherlands, Canada, United States

STUDENT INFORMATION

Total Business Students: 293
% Female: 43
% International: 34
Average Age: 30

COMPUTER AND RESEARCH FACILITIES

Research Facilities: The centres currently based within the school are Centre for Action Research in Professional Practice, Centre for Technology and Innovation Management, Centre for Information Management, Centre for Research in Strategic Purchasing and Supply, Centre for the Study of Regulated Industries, Industrial Marketing and Purchasing Centre, International Centre for Higher Education Management, and Work and Employment Research Centre.

Computer Facilities: The Library and Learning Center is one of the few in the United Kingdom to offer 24-hour service during term time.
Campuswide Network? Yes
% of MBA Classrooms Wired: 50
Computer Model Recommended: No
Internet Fee? No

EXPENSES/FINANCIAL AID
Room & Board: $8,000

ADMISSIONS INFORMATION
Electronic Application? Yes
Regular Application Deadline: 1/6
Length of Deferment: 2 years
Non-fall Application Deadline(s): All terms
Transfer Policy: Normal application process
Need-Blind Admissions? No
Number of Applications Received: 400
% of Applicants Accepted: 23
% Accepted Who Enrolled: 87
Average GMAT: 580
GMAT Range: 450-710
Average Years Experience: 8
Other Admissions Factors Considered: Our selection process is designed to identify those students for whom the MBA represents more than just a "means to an end" and are able and willing to contribute their views and ideas to enrich the learning experience for all concerned. Although around 90 percent of participants hold a first degree, we believe experience, motivation, and commitment are just as important. Therefore, candidates without a degree or professional qualification but with valuable business experience are welcome to apply.
Other Schools to Which Students Applied: Manchester Business School, University of Warwick

INTERNATIONAL STUDENTS
TOEFL Required of International Students? Yes
Minimum TOEFL: 500 (250 computer)

EMPLOYMENT INFORMATION
Placement Office Available? Yes
% Employed Within 3 Months: 80
Frequent Employers: BP Castrol, Lucent, Nortel Networks, Orange, Penna Change Consulting, Siemens

---

UNIVERSITY OF CALGARY
Faculty of Management

Admissions Contact: Penny O'Hearn, Admissions Officer
Address: 2500 University Drive, NW, Calgary, AB T2N 1N4 Canada
Admissions Phone: 403-220-3808 • **Admissions Fax:** 403-282-0095
Admissions E-mail: mbarequest@mgmt.ucalgary.ca
Web Address: www.ucalgary.ca/mg/mba

UC touches on Thornton May's rules about learning in the new economy by placing emphasis on conversation among workers, synergy, and meeting deadlines with efficiency and cooperation. Faculty members at U of Calgary also stress international finance, as well as the oh-so-necessary MBA requirements of a global perspective and a grasp on the ever-changing techno-economy. An especially unique feature of the MBA program is the presence of managers from a wide range of companies and industry sectors, who work in class alongside students as on-site mentors and consultants. An

Executive MBA is also available, thanks to the combined forces of the University of Calgary and the University of Alberta.

INSTITUTIONAL INFORMATION
Public/Private: Public
Evening Classes Available? Yes
Total Faculty: 85
% Faculty Female: 27
Students in Parent Institution: 25,500
Academic Calendar: Semester

PROGRAMS
Degrees Offered: 2 years full time; up to 6 years part time (average 4 to 4.5 years); thesis (2-5 years); PhD (4-6 years)
Combined Degrees: MBA/LLB (4 years), MBA/MSW
Academic Specialties: Finance, Entrepreneurship, E-Business
Study Abroad Options: Europoen Summer School for Advanced Management, North American Summer School for Advanced Management, Asian Intensive School for Advanced Management, numerous exchange programs (see our web page)

STUDENT INFORMATION
Total Business Students: 398
% Full Time: 33
% Female: 43
% International: 35
Average Age: 30

COMPUTER AND RESEARCH FACILITIES
Research Facilities: Energy Centre, Centre for International Business, Canadian Association of Family Enterprise (CAFÉ)
Computer Facilities: Business management databases include: Bloomberg's Online Service; Canadian Buisness and Current Affairs; Canadian Labour Law Library; Canadian Newsdisc; Canadian Periodical Index; Candian Research Index; Cancorp Financials; CCH; Tax Works; CRSP Database; DRI PRO Global Economics; Dun & Bradstreet Industry Norms and Key Business Ratios; Econlit; Expanded Academic ASAP; FP Analyser; Fund Profiler; Globe and Mail; Insite2; International Hospitality & Tourism Database; Investext; Lodging, Restaurant and Tourism Index; Moody's Co. Data (FIS Online); Public Affairs Information Services (PAIS) International; Political Risk Services; Proquest Direct; Research Insight; Stat-USA; TableBase; Tax Partner; Tour CD; T.S.E.; Wall Street Journal on disc. Remote access (off campus) is available for Internet subscription databases.
Campuswide Network? Yes
% of MBA Classrooms Wired: 25
Computer Model Recommended: Laptop
Internet Fee? No

EXPENSES/FINANCIAL AID
Annual Tuition (Resident/Nonresident): $6,000/$12,000
Tuition Per Credit (Resident/Nonresident): $528/$1,056
Books and Supplies: $1,500

ADMISSIONS INFORMATION
Application Fee: $60
Electronic Application? No
Regular Application Deadline: 5/1
Regular Notification: Rolling
Deferment Available? Yes
Length of Deferment: 1 year
Non-fall Admissions? No
Transfer Students Accepted? No
Need-Blind Admissions? No
Number of Applications Received: 299
% of Applicants Accepted: 81
% Accepted Who Enrolled: 65

Average GPA: 3.2
GPA Range: 3.0-4.0
Average GMAT: 598
GMAT Range: 550-740
Average Years Experience: 6

INTERNATIONAL STUDENTS

TOEFL Required of International Students? Yes
Minimum TOEFL: 600

EMPLOYMENT INFORMATION

Placement Office Available? Yes
% Employed Within 3 Months: 95
Fields Employing Percentage of Grads: Other (3%), Human Resources (3%), General Management (8%), Marketing (17%), Finance (25%), Consulting (36%)
Frequent Employers: Adculture Group; AEC; Alliance Pipeline; ANGLE Technology Ltd.; AT&T Canada; Bell Intrigna; Bennett Jones LLP; Burlington Resources; Calgary Catholic School Board; Canada Customs; Canada Energy Ltd.; Canada Safeway; Canadian Natural Resources Limited; Canadian Pacific Railway; Canadian Western Bank; CAP; CIBC; City of Calgary
Prominent Alumni: Al Duerr, CEO, Emergo Projects International; Charlie Fisher, president and CEO, Nexen; Hal Kvisle, president and CEO, Trans. Canada Pipelines; Brett Wilson, managing director, First Energy Capital; Byron Osing, chairman, Launchworks Inc.

UNIVERSITY OF CALIFORNIA— BERKELEY
Haas School of Business

Admissions Contact: Peter Johnson, Director of International Admissions, Full-Time MBA Program
Address: 440 Student Services Building #1902, Berkeley, CA 94720-1902
Admissions Phone: 510-642-1405 • Admissions Fax: 510-643-6659
Admissions E-mail: mbaadms@haas.berkeley.edu • Web Address: haas.berkeley.edu

A strong international presence and "smart people" with "a wide variety of backgrounds" and "great stories to tell" are present in abundance at Berkeley's Haas School of Business. Students here laud their "top-notch" and "personable" professors, as well as the "challenging and demanding" course work and the "emphasis on learning, not grades." The San Francisco Bay Area location is also "superb"; students claim it "cannot be topped for climate and lifestyle."

INSTITUTIONAL INFORMATION

Public/Private: Public
Evening Classes Available? Yes
Total Faculty: 106
% Faculty Female: 18
% Faculty Minority: 16
% Faculty Part Time: 36
Student/Faculty Ratio: 8:1
Students in Parent Institution: 29,000
Academic Calendar: Semester

PROGRAMS

Degrees Offered: MBA (2 years), Joint degrees with full-time MBA (3 years), Evening MBA (3 years part time)
Combined Degrees: Concurrent degree programs: JD/MBA (3 years), MBA/MPH (3 years), MBA/MA in Asian Studies (3 years), MBA/MIAS (3 years)

Academic Specialties: E-Business, Entrepreneurship, International Business, Management of Technology, Finance, Marketing, Real Estate, Health Care Management, Organizational Behavior, Corporate Strategy
Special Opportunities: Certificate in Entrepreneurship & Innovation, Certificate in Global Management, Certificate in Management of Technology, Certificate in Health Services Management
Study Abroad Options: London Business School (LBS), London, England; L'Ecole Des Hautes Etudes Commerciales (HEC), Jouy-en-Josas, France; Hong Kong University of Science and Technology (HKUST), Hong Kong; Scuola di Direzione Aziendale (SDA), Bocconi, Milan, Italy; Rotterdam School of Management (RSM), Rotterdam, the Netherlands; Instituto des Estudios Superiores de la Empresa (IESE), Barcelona, Spain

STUDENT INFORMATION

Total Business Students: 840
% Full Time: 56
% Female: 30
% Minority: 7
% Out of State: 49
% International: 33
Average Age: 28

COMPUTER AND RESEARCH FACILITIES

Research Facilities: Lester Center for Entrepreneurship and Innovation, Fisher Center for Strategic Use of Information Technology, Clausen Center for International Business and Policy, Fisher Center for Real Estate and Urban Economics
Computer Facilities: OneSource, Nexis, ABI Inform, Disclosure, Compustat, CRSP, InfoTrak, Dow Jones Interactive, WRDS, IBIS, ZACKS, Forrester, Datastream, World Data, TSM Global Economic Data Base, World Resources Data Base, National Trade Data Bank, International Financial Statistics, Zacks Investment Research Database, Econometrics Laboratory (EML)
Campuswide Network? Yes
% of MBA Classrooms Wired: 9
Computer Model Recommended: Desktop
Internet Fee? No

EXPENSES/FINANCIAL AID

Annual Tuition (Resident/Nonresident): $10,704
Tuition Per Credit (Resident/Nonresident): $1,581
Room & Board (On/Off Campus): $11,258
Books and Supplies: $2,000
Average Grant: $15,320
Average Loan: $15,000
% Receiving Financial Aid: 60
% Receiving Aid Their First Year: 60

ADMISSIONS INFORMATION

Application Fee: $125
Electronic Application? Yes
Early Decision Application Deadline: November, December, February, March
Early Decision Notification: 2/1
Regular Application Deadline: 3/15
Regular Notification: 5/31
Deferment Available? No
Non-fall Admissions? No
Transfer Students Accepted? No
Need-Blind Admissions? Yes
Number of Applications Received: 3,265
% of Applicants Accepted: 14
% Accepted Who Enrolled: 50
Average GPA: 3.4
GPA Range: 3.1-3.7
Average GMAT: 690
GMAT Range: 640-710
Average Years Experience: 5

Other Admissions Factors Considered: Demonstration of quantitative ability; quality of work experience, including depth and breadth of responsibilities; opportunities to demonstrate leadership, etc.; strength of letters of recommendation; depth and breadth of extracurricular and community involvement; stength of short answer and essays, including articulation of clear focus and goals

Minority/Disadvantaged Student Recruitment Programs: We are members of the Consortium for Graduate Study in Management and the Toigo Fellowships Program, as well as the Diversity Alliance.

Other Schools to Which Students Applied: Columbia University, Harvard University, New York University, Northwestern University, Stanford University, University of California—Los Angeles, University of Pennsylvania

INTERNATIONAL STUDENTS

TOEFL Required of International Students? Yes
Minimum TOEFL: 570 (230 computer)

EMPLOYMENT INFORMATION

Placement Office Available? Yes
% Employed Within 3 Months: 87
Fields Employing Percentage of Grads: Venture Capital (2%), Entrepreneurship (2%), Strategic Planning (2%), General Management (14%), Marketing (16%), Consulting (30%), Finance (34%)
Frequent Employers: Accenture, A.T. Kearney, The Clorox Co., Credit Suisse First Boston, Dain Rauscher Wessels, Deloitte Consulting Goldman Sachs & Co., Hewlett-Packard & Co., McKinsey & Co., Siebel Systems, Inc.
Prominent Alumni: Donald Fisher, chairman and founder, The Gap; Rodrigo Rato, deputy prime minister and minister of economy, Spain; Barbara Desoer, executive vice president, Bank of America; Bengt Baron, president, Absolut Vodka; Jorge Montoya, president, Procter & Gamble Latin America

See page 448.

UNIVERSITY OF CALIFORNIA—DAVIS
Graduate School of Management

Admissions Contact: Donald A. Blodger, Assistant Dean of Admissions
Address: One Shields Ave., Davis, CA 95616
Admissions Phone: 530-752-7658 • **Admissions Fax:** 530-752-2924
Admissions E-mail: admissions@gsm.ucdavis.edu • **Web Address:** www.gsm.ucdavis.edu

The Graduate School of Management provides a positive learning environment for the business-minded in northern California, as well as a cooperative and enthusiastic student spirit and an emphasis on management in high-tech environments. The MBA program options range from a Full-Time MBA to a Working MBA for busy daytime professionals to a Full-Time Interdisciplinary MBA, a dual degree program that requires serious dedication. The most notable dual degree programs available at UC Davis include an MBA/Juris Doctor, MBA/Doctor of Medicine, MBA/Master of Engineering, and an MBA/Master of Agricultural and Resource Economics.

INSTITUTIONAL INFORMATION

Public/Private: Public
Evening Classes Available? Yes
Total Faculty: 46
% Faculty Female: 13
% Faculty Minority: 11
% Faculty Part Time: 52
Student/Faculty Ratio: 10:1
Students in Parent Institution: 27,292
Academic Calendar: Quarter

PROGRAMS

Degrees Offered: MBA (2 years full time, 3-4 years Working Professional Program)
Combined Degrees: JD/MBA (4 years), MD/MBA (6 years), Engineering/MBA (2 years), Agricultural Economics/MBA (2 years)
Academic Specialties: Finance, Marketing, Technology Management
Special Opportunities: HKUST, ITAM, ERASMUS, Heinrich Heine, Helsinki School of Economics and Business Administration, HEC, Manchester Business Schol, University of Lyon, Bocconi
Study Abroad Options: England, Finland, France, Germany, Holland, Hong Kong, Italy, Mexico

STUDENT INFORMATION

Total Business Students: 131
% Full Time: 98
% Female: 42
% Minority: 4
% Out of State: 6
% International: 27
Average Age: 29

COMPUTER AND RESEARCH FACILITIES

Computer Facilities: The Graduate School of Management has a wireless local area network with high-speed Internet access; 2 student PC labs with standard Microsoft Office XP applications; Internet access; and access to school and university UNIX workstations. The school maintains access to CRSP and Compustat databases and several general databases such as ABI, Lexis-Nexis; systemwide access to more than 1,000 scholarly and trade journals; other data available thru the University's California Digital Library project.
Campuswide Network? Yes
% of MBA Classrooms Wired: 100
Computer Model Recommended: Laptop
Internet Fee? No

EXPENSES/FINANCIAL AID

Annual Tuition (Resident/Nonresident): $10,782/$21,027
Room & Board (On/Off Campus): $10,500/$10,300
Books and Supplies: $1,500
Average Grant: $7,200
Average Loan: $14,000
% Receiving Financial Aid: 73
% Receiving Aid Their First Year: 70

ADMISSIONS INFORMATION

Application Fee: $40
Electronic Application? Yes
Early Decision Application Deadline: 12/1
Early Decision Notification: 1/31
Regular Application Deadline: 4/1
Regular Notification: 5/31
Length of Deferment: 1 year
Non-fall Admissions? No
Transfer Students Accepted? No
Need-Blind Admissions? Yes
Number of Applications Received: 449
% of Applicants Accepted: 29
% Accepted Who Enrolled: 47
Average GPA: 3.3
GPA Range: 3.0-3.6
Average GMAT: 662
GMAT Range: 630-710
Average Years Experience: 6
Other Admissions Factors Considered: Motivation, leadership potential
Minority/Disadvantaged Student Recruitment Programs: The Michael Maher Scholarship is offered to assist in preparing to enter the Graduate School of Management. The GSM Fellows Program is designed to assist disadvantaged students in preparing for graduate-level business education.

Other Schools to Which Students Applied: Stanford University, University of Arizona, University of California—Berkeley, University of California—Los Angeles, University of Southern California, University of Texas—Austin, University of Washington

INTERNATIONAL STUDENTS

TOEFL Required of International Students? Yes
Minimum TOEFL: 600 (250 computer)

EMPLOYMENT INFORMATION

Placement Office Available? Yes
% Employed Within 3 Months: 82
Fields Employing Percentage of Grads: Entrepreneurship (2%), MIS (2%), Accounting (2%), General Management (3%), Strategic Planning (3%), Operations (7%), Consulting (15%), Marketing (15%), Finance (46%)
Frequent Employers: Agilent, Barclay's Global Investors, California State Auditors, CalPERS, Cisco, Deloitte & Touche, E&J Gallo Winery, Gartner Group, GATX Capital, Hewlett Packard, Intel, KPMG, Lam Research, Mervyn's-Dayton Hudson, Morgan Stanley, National Parks Conservation Association, Sun Microsystems,Wells Fargo
Prominent Alumni: David H. Russ, UC treasurer and vice president of investments; Christine Smith, Global Catalyst Partners; Gordon C. Hunt, Jr., MD, senior vice president, Clinical Integration/Chief

See page 450.

UNIVERSITY OF CALIFORNIA—IRVINE
Graduate School of Management

Admissions Contact: Bryan McSweeney, Associate Director, MBA Admissions
Address: 110 MPAA, Irvine, CA 92697-3125
Admissions Phone: 949-824-9647 • **Admissions Fax:** 949-824-2944
Admissions E-mail: gsm-mba@uci.edu • **Web Address:** www.gsm.uci.edu

UC Irvine is part of the 10-campus California university system. "It works and sprawls like Silicon Valley, but looks and lives like Mediterranean Europe," bubbles the website. How can you blame them, when you can kick back California-style and still have access to nearby big-city business opportunities? UC Irvine MBA programs are offered for full-time and part-time students, and Information Technology for Management is a theme that's integrated into every core class and many electives, including an extensive series of e-commerce courses.

INSTITUTIONAL INFORMATION

Public/Private: Public
Evening Classes Available? Yes
Total Faculty: 90
% Faculty Female: 26
% Faculty Minority: 13
% Faculty Part Time: 43
Student/Faculty Ratio: 8:1
Students in Parent Institution: 21,550
Academic Calendar: September-June

PROGRAMS

Degrees Offered: MBA (2 years full time), EMBA (2 years), Health Care EMBA (2 years), Fully-Employed MBA (3 years), PhD (4 years)
Combined Degrees: MD/MBA (5 years)
Academic Specialties: Our full-time program is widely recognized for integrating the principles of information and technology into the MBA curriculum. For example, GSM is ranked first among business schools worldwide by *Finan-*

cial Times for its focus on Information Technology for Management (ITM). Full-time MBA students can gain hands-on experience in our ITM labs with the tools they will need to lead change, whether they are reinventing an established firm or launching a new one. In ITM labs or electives across all the business disciplines, students learn how technology and information transform business functions and business models.
Special Opportunities: Students choose elective courses based on individual educational and professional goals. Elective coursework is offered in: Accounting, Business and Government, Economics, Finance, Health Care Management, Information Systems, Marketing, Operations and Decisions Technologies, Organization and Strategy, Real Estate Management, and Management of Innovation and Growth.
Study Abroad Options: Wirtschafts Universitat Wien, Austria; Katholieke University, Belgium; Chinese European International Business School, China; ESSEC Graduate School of Management, France; Budapest University of Economic Sciences, Hungary; Hong Kong University of Science and Technology, Hong Kong; National University of Singapore, Singapore

STUDENT INFORMATION

Total Business Students: 328
% Full Time: 41
% Female: 26
% Minority: 3
% International: 22
Average Age: 29

COMPUTER AND RESEARCH FACILITIES

Research Facilities: Center for Research on Information Technology and Organizations (CRITO), a National Science Foundation-supported center to develop research ideas to understand the impacts of information and technology; Irvine Innovation Initiative, program in which teams of students submit proposals to win space, resources, and mentoring to develop business ideas
Computer Facilities: Standard & Poor's Compustat; CRSP Data; Wharton Research Data Services; Disclosure Global Access; Investext Plus; Lexis-Nexis; Moody's Company Data Direct
Campuswide Network? Yes
% of MBA Classrooms Wired: 100
Computer Model Recommended: Laptop
Internet Fee? No

EXPENSES/FINANCIAL AID

Annual Tuition (Resident/Nonresident): $11,132
Room & Board (On/Off Campus): $10,342/$11,587
Books and Supplies: $4,320
Average Grant: $7,000
Average Loan: $18,000
% Receiving Financial Aid: 85
% Receiving Aid Their First Year: 70

ADMISSIONS INFORMATION

Application Fee: $90
Electronic Application? Yes
Regular Application Deadline: 5/16
Regular Notification: 6/30
Deferment Available? Yes
Length of Deferment: 1 year
Non-fall Admissions? Yes
Non-fall Application Deadline(s): There is a spring section of the Fully Employed Program.
Transfer Students Accepted? No
Need-Blind Admissions? Yes
Number of Applications Received: 849
% of Applicants Accepted: 31
% Accepted Who Enrolled: 51
Average GPA: 3.3
GPA Range: 3.0-3.8
Average GMAT: 681

GMAT Range: 640-730
Average Years Experience: 5
Other Admissions Factors Considered: Career progression, well-articulated educational and professional goals, clear understanding of MBA programs, presentation skills, leadership potential
Minority/Disadvantaged Student Recruitment Programs: Educational Opportunity Program (EOP): The EOP was established for highly motivated students from non-traditional backgrounds. Students are required to submit an additional application describing economic, social, or educational factors that have adversely affected their opportunity for academic achievement.
Other Schools to Which Students Applied: University of California—Berkeley, University of California—Los Angeles, University of Southern California, University of Texas—Austin, University of Washington

INTERNATIONAL STUDENTS

TOEFL Required of International Students? Yes
Minimum TOEFL: 600 (250 computer)

EMPLOYMENT INFORMATION

Placement Office Available? Yes
% Employed Within 3 Months: 71
Fields Employing Percentage of Grads: General Management (4%), Other (6%), Operations (7%), MIS (9%), Consulting (16%), Marketing (26%), Finance (26%)
Frequent Employers: Accenture, ARES, Bechman Coulter, Bristol Myers Squibb, Conexant, Deloitte & Touche, Gateway, Intel, Microsoft, Nissan, PacifiCare, Pricewaterhouse Coopers, Taco Bell, Wells Fargo
Prominent Alumni: Darcy B. Kopcho, executive vice president, Capital Group Companies; George W. Kessinger, president and CEO, Goodwill Industries International; Norman Witt, vice president, community development, The Irvine Co.

UNIVERSITY OF CALIFORNIA— LOS ANGELES
The Anderson School at UCLA

Admissions Contact: Linda Baldwin, Director of Admissions
Address: 110 Westwood Plaza , Gold Hall, Suite B201, Los Angeles, CA 90095-1481
Admissions Phone: 310-825-6944 • Admissions Fax: 310-825-8582
Admissions E-mail: mba.admissions@anderson.ucla.edu
Web Address: www.anderson.ucla.edu

You just can't beat living on the beach with an ocean view, contend the "very active and entrepreneurial" MBA students at UCLA's Anderson School, where "life is good" thanks to an "unbeatable location" and, of course, "February beach parties." The Career Center is fabulous as well, but students sing their highest praises for Anderson's entrepreneurship program, which gives MBAs a chance to study under professors like "Wild Bill" Cockrum—arguably "the top entrepreneurial professor in the nation"—and "Big Al" Osborne.

INSTITUTIONAL INFORMATION

Public/Private: Public
Evening Classes Available? No
Total Faculty: 112
% Faculty Female: 15
% Faculty Minority: 16
% Faculty Part Time: 10
Student/Faculty Ratio: 8:1

Students in Parent Institution: 37,494
Academic Calendar: Quarter

PROGRAMS

Degrees Offered: MBA(2 years), EMBA (2 years), Fully-Employed MBA (3 years), PhD (4 years)
Combined Degrees: MBA/JD, MBA/MD, MBA/MPH, MBA/Master of Latin American Studies, MBA/Master of Urban Planning, MBA/Master of Computer Science
Academic Specialties: Finance, Marketing, Economics, General Management, Operations Management, Manufacturing and Technology Management, Organizational Behavior, Strategy and Policy, Information Systems Management
Special Opportunities: International Business, Real Estate, Entrepreneurial Studies, Business Forecasting, Technology Management, Entertainment Management
Study Abroad Options: Argentina, Australia, Austria, Belgium, Brazil, Chile, China, Czech Republic, Denmark, England, France, Germany, Italy, Japan, Mexico, the Netherlands, New Zealand, Norway, Peru, Philippines, South Africa, Spain, Sweden, Switzerland, Venezuela

STUDENT INFORMATION

Total Business Students: 1,233
% Full Time: 54
% Female: 29
% Minority: 19
% International: 22
Average Age: 28

COMPUTER AND RESEARCH FACILITIES

Research Facilities: Harold Price Center for Entrepreneurial Studies, UCLA Anderson Forecast, Center for International Business Education and Research (CIBER), Center for Management in the Information Economy (CMIE), Center for Communication Policy/Entertainment Media, Richard S. Ziman Center for Real Estate
Campuswide Network? Yes
% of MBA Classrooms Wired: 100
Computer Model Recommended: Laptop
Internet Fee? No

EXPENSES/FINANCIAL AID

Annual Tuition (Resident/Nonresident): $11,820/$22,952
Room & Board (On/Off Campus): $9,500
Books and Supplies: $5,400
Average Grant: $7,500
Average Loan: $24,500
% Receiving Financial Aid: 62

ADMISSIONS INFORMATION

Application Fee: $150
Electronic Application? Yes
Early Decision Application Deadline: 11/6
Early Decision Notification: 1/16
Regular Application Deadline: 4/4
Regular Notification: 6/6
Deferment Available? No
Non-fall Admissions? No
Transfer Students Accepted? No
Need-Blind Admissions? Yes
Number of Applications Received: 4,570
% of Applicants Accepted: 15
% Accepted Who Enrolled: 49
Average GPA: 3.6
GPA Range: 3.2-3.9
Average GMAT: 710
GMAT Range: 640-750
Average Years Experience: 5

Other Admissions Factors Considered: Evidence of managerial potential, leadership qualities, interpersonal skills, personal values, special character
Minority/Disadvantaged Student Recruitment Programs: The Anderson School actively seeks highly qualified minority applicants for the MBA Program. Our graduate advisors play an important role in providing information and counseling for prospective minority applicants. Advisors assist in arranging visits to the campus and annually organize an MBA Information Day for applicants. Anderson also sponsors the LEAD Program for high school students and the Riordan Programs for college-aged and post-graduate students.
Other Schools to Which Students Applied: Harvard University, Northwestern University, Stanford University, University of Pennsylvania

INTERNATIONAL STUDENTS

TOEFL Required of International Students? Yes
Minimum TOEFL: 600 (260 computer)

EMPLOYMENT INFORMATION

Placement Office Available? Yes
% Employed Within 3 Months: 74
Fields Employing Percentage of Grads: Communications (1%), MIS (1%), Operations (2%), Venture Capital (4%), Entrepreneurship (4%), Strategic Planning (4%), Other (7%), General Management (9%), Consulting (15%), Marketing (17%), Finance (36%)
Frequent Employers: Baxter, BEA Systems, Boston Consulting Group, Deloitte Consulting, Deutsche Bank, Diamondcluster, General Mills, Goldman Sachs, Guidant Corp., Lehman Brothers, McKinsey & Co., Merrill Lynch, Morgan Stanley, Toyota
Prominent Alumni: Jeff Henley, CFO, Oracle; Mark Zoradi, president, Buena Vista International; Chris Zyda, international CFO, Amazon; Lisa Brummel, vice president of home products, Microsoft; William Gross, CEO, PIMCO/Investment Management

UNIVERSITY OF CALIFORNIA— RIVERSIDE

A. Gary Anderson Graduate School of Management

Admissions Contact: Charlotte Weber, Assistant Dean, Student Affairs
Address: Anderson Hall, University of California–Riverside, Riverside, CA 92521-0203
Admissions Phone: (909) 787-4551 • **Admissions Fax:** (909) 787-3970
Admissions E-mail: mba@agsmmail.ucr.edu • **Web Address:** www.agsm.ucr.edu

Located about 50 miles east of Los Angeles, the A. Gary Anderson Graduate School of Management teaches the "art and science" of management. Quantitative and analytical skills—among them the savvy to deal with the latest technological advances—are taught alongside the ability to solve complex problems and communicate ideas effectively. A twelve-course core curriculum and an internship experience are required of students, just under half of which hail from foreign countries.

INSTITUTIONAL INFORMATION

Public/Private: Public
Evening Classes Available? Yes
Total Faculty: 42
% Faculty Female: 17
% Faculty Minority: 10
% Faculty Part Time: 7
Student/Faculty Ratio: 15:1

Students in Parent Institution: 14,000
Academic Calendar: Quarter

PROGRAMS

Degrees Offered: MBA (18 to 24 months)
Academic Specialties: Accounting, Corporate Environmental Management, Entrepreneurial Management, Finance, Human Resources Management/Organizational Behavior, International Management, Management Information Systems, Management Science, Marketing, Production and Operations Management
Special Opportunities: University of California Education Abroad Program

STUDENT INFORMATION

Total Business Students: 130
% Full Time: 82
% Female: 49
% Minority: 15
Average Age: 26

COMPUTER AND RESEARCH FACILITIES

Research Facilities: Center for Entrepreneurial Management, UCR Forecasting Center, Electronic Economy Management Center
Computer Facilities: Compustat Research Insight, Datastream, Securities Data Worldwide Global News Issues, CRSP Security Prices
Campuswide Network? Yes
% of MBA Classrooms Wired: 100
Internet Fee? No

EXPENSES/FINANCIAL AID

Annual Tuition (Resident/Nonresident): $10,704
Tuition Per Credit (Resident/Nonresident): $5,352
Room & Board (On/Off Campus): $10,105
Books and Supplies: $900
Average Grant: $5,000

ADMISSIONS INFORMATION

Application Fee: $40
Electronic Application? Yes
Regular Application Deadline: 5/2
Regular Notification: 6/2
Deferment Available? No
Non-fall Admissions? Yes
Non-fall Application Deadline(s): Winter, spring
Transfer Students Accepted? Yes
Transfer Policy: A maximum of 2 graduate courses taken in residence may transfer.
Need-Blind Admissions? Yes
Number of Applications Received: 257
% of Applicants Accepted: 50
% Accepted Who Enrolled: 39
Average GPA: 3.4
GPA Range: 3.0-3.8
Average GMAT: 594
GMAT Range: 540-660
Average Years Experience: 3
Other Admissions Factors Considered: Academic reputation of the undergraduate and graduate institutions attended
Other Schools to Which Students Applied: University of California—Irvine

INTERNATIONAL STUDENTS

TOEFL Required of International Students? Yes
Minimum TOEFL: 550 (213 computer)

UNIVERSITY OF CENTRAL ARKANSAS
College of Business Administration

Admissions Contact: Rebecca Gatlin-Watts, MBA Director
Address: Burdick Business Building, Room 224, Conway, AR 72035
Admissions Phone: 501-450-5316 • **Admissions Fax:** 501-450-5302
Admissions E-mail: mba@mail.uca.edu • **Web Address:** www.business.uca.edu

INSTITUTIONAL INFORMATION

Public/Private: Public
Evening Classes Available? No
Total Faculty: 43
Students in Parent Institution: 9,000
Academic Calendar: Semester

PROGRAMS

Degrees Offered: MBA (30 credits, full time or part time, 1-6 years)
Combined Degrees: IMBA
Special Opportunities: General Business, International Business
Study Abroad Options: University of Luton, England; The Haagse Hoge School, the Netherlands

STUDENT INFORMATION

Total Business Students: 60
% Full Time: 40
% Female: 38
% Minority: 8
% Out of State: 1
% International: 25
Average Age: 27

COMPUTER AND RESEARCH FACILITIES

Campuswide Network? Yes
Internet Fee? No

EXPENSES/FINANCIAL AID

Tuition Per Credit (Resident/Nonresident): $159/$170
Room & Board (On/Off Campus): $6,000
Books and Supplies: $1,500

ADMISSIONS INFORMATION

Application Fee: $25
Electronic Application? Yes
Regular Application Deadline: Rolling
Regular Notification: Rolling
Deferment Available? Yes
Non-fall Admissions? Yes
Non-fall Application Deadline(s): Rolling for all domestic applicants; $40 international application fee and deadline of 6/15 fall, 11/1 spring, 4/15 summer
Transfer Students Accepted? No
Need-Blind Admissions? No
Number of Applications Received: 122
% of Applicants Accepted: 68
% Accepted Who Enrolled: 37
Other Admissions Factors Considered: A minimum GMAT score of 400 and GPA of 2.7 are required.

INTERNATIONAL STUDENTS

TOEFL Required of International Students? Yes
Minimum TOEFL: 550 (213 computer)

EMPLOYMENT INFORMATION

Placement Office Available? Yes
% Employed Within 3 Months: 85
Frequent Employers: Acxiom, Alltell, Kimberly Clark

UNIVERSITY OF CENTRAL FLORIDA
College of Business Administration

Admissions Contact: Judy Ryder, Director of Graduate Studies
Address: POBox 161400, Orlando, FL 32816
Admissions Phone: 407-823-2412 • **Admissions Fax:** 407-823-6206
Admissions E-mail: cbagrad@bus.ucf.edu • **Web Address:** www.bus.ucf.edu

The University of Central Florida is located just 13 miles east of downtown Orlando, a huge center of international commerce and culture that's home of some of the world's best and most popular theme parks. The UCF curriculum is designed to develop a student's analytical, problem-solving, and decision-making capabilities instead of just focusing on the theoretical concepts of finance. Prospective MBA students may choose from a selective one-year daytime MBA program for honors students, an evening MBA program for part-time and full-time students, and an Executive MBA program, composed of 13 Friday or Saturday courses and two off-campus residencies.

INSTITUTIONAL INFORMATION

Public/Private: Public
Evening Classes Available? Yes
Total Faculty: 40
% Faculty Female: 5
% Faculty Minority: 1
Student/Faculty Ratio: 35:1
Students in Parent Institution: 38,795
Academic Calendar: Semester

PROGRAMS

Degrees Offered: MBA (39 credits, 4 years part time), MBA (39 credits, 1 year full time, cohort program), MAAE (30 credits, up to 2 years), MSA (30 credits, up to 2 years), MST (30 credits, up to 2 years), EMBA (39 credits, up to 21 months), MSM/Human Resources and Change Management (30 credits, up to 2 years), MSMIS (30 credits, up to 2 years), Master of Sport Business Management (46.5 credits, up to 21 months)
Combined Degrees: MBA/Sport Business Management (24 months)
Academic Specialties: Applied Economics, Management Information Systems, Hi-Tech Marketing
Study Abroad Options: N/A

STUDENT INFORMATION

Total Business Students: 592
% Full Time: 25
% Female: 42
% Minority: 5
% Out of State: 13
% International: 20
Average Age: 31

COMPUTER AND RESEARCH FACILITIES

Research Facilities: Small Business Development Center, UCF Incubator, Executive Development Center
Computer Facilities: Access to more than 100 data sources such as Lexis, Academic Universe available online to all students
Campuswide Network? Yes
% of MBA Classrooms Wired: 100
Internet Fee? No

EXPENSES/FINANCIAL AID

Annual Tuition (Resident/Nonresident): $4,400/$16,000
Tuition Per Credit (Resident/Nonresident): $181/$667
Room & Board (On/Off Campus): $5,000
Books and Supplies: $1,200

ADMISSIONS INFORMATION

Application Fee: $20
Electronic Application? Yes
Regular Application Deadline: 6/15
Regular Notification: Rolling
Deferment Available? Yes
Length of Deferment: 1 semester
Non-fall Admissions? Yes
Non-fall Application Deadline(s): 11/1 spring, 3/15 summer
Transfer Students Accepted? Yes
Transfer Policy: Transfer applicants must be from an AACSB-accredited university.
Need-Blind Admissions? Yes
Number of Applications Received: 268
% of Applicants Accepted: 50
% Accepted Who Enrolled: 64
Average GPA: 3.3
GPA Range: 3.0-3.5
Average GMAT: 556
GMAT Range: 500-600
Average Years Experience: 7
Minority/Disadvantaged Student Recruitment Programs: Recruiting at local minority venues
Other Schools to Which Students Applied: Rollins College, University of Florida, Florida State University, University of South Florida

INTERNATIONAL STUDENTS

TOEFL Required of International Students? Yes
Minimum TOEFL: 575 (233 computer)

EMPLOYMENT INFORMATION

Placement Office Available? Yes
% Employed Within 3 Months: 98

UNIVERSITY OF CHICAGO
Graduate School of Business

Admissions Contact: Don Martin, Associate Dean for Enrollment Management
Address: 6030 South Ellis Avenue, Chicago, IL 60637
Admissions Phone: 773-702-7369 • **Admissions Fax:** 773-702-9085
Admissions E-mail: admissions@gsb.uchicago.edu • **Web Address:** gsb.uchicago.edu

"I would pit my instructors against any other faculty in the nation, bar none," boasts one confident student at the University of Chicago's Graduate School of Business Administration where Nobel laureates abound and social life takes a back seat to "business, business, business!" Though Chicago is best known for finance and economics and is considered "numbers-heavy," it offers much more, including an International MBA, which "builds truly global management skills."

INSTITUTIONAL INFORMATION

Public/Private: Private
Evening Classes Available? Yes
Total Faculty: 172
Student/Faculty Ratio: 17:1
Students in Parent Institution: 12,989
Academic Calendar: Quarter

PROGRAMS

Degrees Offered: PhD (5.5 years)
Combined Degrees: MBA/AM Area Studies and Business, MBA/AM International Relations and Business, JD/MBA, MD/MBA, MBA/MPP, MBA/AM Social Service Administration
Academic Specialties: Economics, Finance, Marketing, General Management, International Business, Accounting, Organizational Behavior and Strategy, Entrepreneurship
Special Opportunities: IMBA, Business Exchange Program
Study Abroad Options: Australia, Austria, Belgium, Brazil, Chile, China, France, Germany, Hong Kong, Israel, Italy, Japan, Mexico, the Netherlands, Singapore, South Africa, South Korea, Spain, Sweden, Switzerland, United Kingdom

STUDENT INFORMATION

Total Business Students: 3,017
% Full Time: 33
% Female: 26
% Minority: 6
% Out of State: 92
% International: 29
Average Age: 29

COMPUTER AND RESEARCH FACILITIES

Research Facilities: Center for Research in Security Prices, Center for Decision Research, Center for the Study of the Economy and State, Center for Population Economics, Center for Statistics Research, Management Labs, Polsky Center for Entrepreneurship, Kilts Center for Marketing
Computer Facilities: Students have access to both mainframe and personal computers through the schools computing services department and student labs. Databases include: Center for Research in Security Prices, Compustat, and DRI. Online services include Bloomberg, DataStream, Investex, and One Source, as well as most electronic services provided through the University library.
Campuswide Network? Yes
Internet Fee? Yes

EXPENSES/FINANCIAL AID

Annual Tuition: $32,500
Room & Board (On/Off Campus): $14,850
Books and Supplies: $1,650
Average Grant: $10,000
Average Loan: $44,128
% Receiving Financial Aid: 78

ADMISSIONS INFORMATION

Application Fee: $200
Electronic Application? Yes
Early Decision Application Deadline: 11/8, 1/8, 3/21
Early Decision Notification: 1/1
Regular Application Deadline: 12/6
Regular Notification: 3/23
Deferment Available? Yes
Length of Deferment: 1 year
Non-fall Admissions? Yes
Non-fall Application Deadline(s): Winter, spring
Transfer Students Accepted? No
Need-Blind Admissions? Yes
Number of Applications Received: 4,732
% of Applicants Accepted: 15
% Accepted Who Enrolled: 67
Average GPA: 3.4
GPA Range: 3.0-3.8
Average GMAT: 687
GMAT Range: 610-710
Average Years Experience: 5
Minority/Disadvantaged Student Recruitment Programs: Co-sponsored Minority Scholarship Program, Offfice of Diversity Affairs, receptions, recruiting forums

Other Schools to Which Students Applied: Harvard University, University of Pennsylvania, Stanford University

INTERNATIONAL STUDENTS

TOEFL Required of International Students? Yes
Minimum TOEFL: 600 (250 computer)

EMPLOYMENT INFORMATION

Placement Office Available? Yes
% Employed Within 3 Months: 82
Frequent Employers: Bear, Stearns & Col, Inc.; Booz-Allen & Hamilton Inc.; The Boston Consulting Group; Credit Suisse; Deloitte Consulting; Goldman, Sachs & Co.; J.P. Morgan Chase & Co.; Lehman Brothers; McKinsey & Co., Inc.; Merrill Lynch; Morgan Stanley; Salomon Smith Barney
Prominent Alumni: Basil L. Anderson, vice chairman, Staples, Inc.; Judith G. Boynton, CFO, The Royal Dutch/Shell Group; Arthur Velasquez, chairman, presidents, and CEO, Azteca Foods Inc.; James Kilts, chairman and CEO, The Gillette Co.; R. Philip Purcell, chairman and CEO, Morgan Stanley

UNIVERSITY OF CINCINNATI
College of Business Administration

Admissions Contact: Valerie O. Robinson, Associate Director, Graduate Programs
Address: Carl H. Lindner Hall, Suite 103, Cincinnati, OH 45221
Admissions Phone: 513-556-7020 • **Admissions Fax:** 513-558-7006
Admissions E-mail: graduate@uc.edu • **Web Address:** www.business.uc.edu/mba

"An MBA is a business investment," declares the University of Cincinnati's website, and it means business. The MBA curriculum at Cincinnati's Graduate School of Business Administration is as solid as the walls of Carl H. Linder Hall, where its classes are held. UC offers an excellent opportunity for working professionals to earn an MBA in the evenings and on Saturdays, as well as a full-time program and an MBA that combines on-campus course work with online instruction. The UC MBA student will benefit from the Graduate School's close ties to Cincinnati's business leaders through field studies, job placement services, and many other hands-on opportunities within the community.

INSTITUTIONAL INFORMATION

Public/Private: Public
Evening Classes Available? Yes
Total Faculty: 45
% Faculty Female: 13
% Faculty Part Time: 2
Student/Faculty Ratio: 7:1
Students in Parent Institution: 37,000
Academic Calendar: Quarter

PROGRAMS

Degrees Offered: MBA (12 months full time, 24 months part time); MS in Quantitative Analysis (12 months); MSBA in Accounting (12-15 months); MST (12 months); PhD (5 years), with concentrations in Accounting, Finance, Marketing, Quantitative Analysis, Management, Information Systems, Operations Management
Combined Degrees: MBA/JD (4 years), MBA/MA in Arts Administration (3 years), MBA/MD (5 years), MBA/Nursing (3 years)
Academic Specialties: The UC MBA programs have strong faculty across all areas, with special emphasis in: Marketing, Supply Chain, Quantitative Analysis, General Management, and International. Also, the full-time program at UC MBA is offered in an efficient and innovative 12-month format, which enables students to see a quick return on their investment.

Special Opportunities: International seminars available to both full- and part-time UC MBA students. Students travel abroad for 7-10 days to our partnership schools for courses taught by their faculty and visits to companies located in the area. Also, we offer weekend courses taught by visiting international faculty. This enables our students to experience an international course without leaving Cincinnati.
Study Abroad Options: Johannes Kepler University, Linz, Austria, and Prague, Czech Republic; Universidad del Desarrollo, Santiago, Chile; ESC Toulouse, Toulouse, France, and Barcelona, Spain; Rheinisch-Westfalische Technische Hochschule (RWTH), Aachen, Germany; Chiang Mai University, Chiang Mai, Thailand

STUDENT INFORMATION

Total Business Students: 319
% Full Time: 19
% Female: 33
% Minority: 20
% Out of State: 40
% International: 27
Average Age: 31

COMPUTER AND RESEARCH FACILITIES

Research Facilities: Cincinnati Center for Management & Executive Development, Goering Center for Family & Private Businesses, Center for Entrepreneurship Education and Research, Total Quality Management Center, Center for Global Competitiveness
Computer Facilities: The UC Business College has 5 computer labs available to our MBA students and numerous computer labs across the campus. Corporate and industry research databases include wetfeet.com, Bizweb, Vault Reports, Hoovers Online, Bradynet Inc, Internationalist, and the Bloomberg Personnel.
Campuswide Network? Yes
% of MBA Classrooms Wired: 80
Computer Model Recommended: Laptop
Internet Fee? No

EXPENSES/FINANCIAL AID

Annual Tuition (Resident/Nonresident): $14,216/$17,976
Tuition Per Credit (Resident/Nonresident): $365
Room & Board (On/Off Campus): $6,500/$5,400
Books and Supplies: $3,136
Average Grant: $10,468
Average Loan: $12,000
% Receiving Financial Aid: 100
% Receiving Aid Their First Year: 100

ADMISSIONS INFORMATION

Application Fee: $30
Electronic Application? Yes
Early Decision Application Deadline: 2/15 summer
Early Decision Notification: 3/30
Regular Application Deadline: 3/30
Regular Notification: Rolling
Deferment Available? Yes
Length of Deferment: 1 year
Non-fall Admissions? Yes
Non-fall Application Deadline(s): 3/30 summer
Transfer Students Accepted? Yes
Transfer Policy: No more than 3 classes from an AACSB-accredited institution
Need-Blind Admissions? Yes
Number of Applications Received: 326
% of Applicants Accepted: 79
% Accepted Who Enrolled: 78
Average GPA: 3.2
GPA Range: 2.9-3.5
Average GMAT: 592

GMAT Range: 550-640
Average Years Experience: 4
Other Admissions Factors Considered: Optional interview, leadership, extracurricular activites
Minority/Disadvantaged Student Recruitment Programs: UC offers the Albert C. Yates Scholarships and Fellowships to candidates from underrepresented ethnic groups. The scholarships cover full tuition and fees, and the fellowship additionally provides a stipend each quarter.
Other Schools to Which Students Applied: Miami University, Northern Kentucky University, Ohio State University, Xavier University

INTERNATIONAL STUDENTS

TOEFL Required of International Students? Yes
Minimum TOEFL: 600 (250 computer)

EMPLOYMENT INFORMATION

Placement Office Available? Yes
% Employed Within 3 Months: 50
Fields Employing Percentage of Grads: Other (3%), General Management (10%), Consulting (10%), MIS (10%), Operations (13%), Marketing (20%), Finance (28%)
Frequent Employers: Accenture, Cincinnati Bell, Cintas, Eli Lilly, Ethicon Endo Surgery, Executive Benefits, Fidelity Investments, Fifth Third Bank, Johnson Investments, Kroger, Northlich, Procter and Gamble, Sara Lee, Steak n' Shake
Prominent Alumni: Robert Taft, governor of Ohio; John F. Barrett, president and CEO, Western-Southern Life; Myron E. Ullman, III, group managing director, LVMH Moet Hennessy; Dr. Candace Kendle Bryan, chairman and CEO, Kendle International; Richard E. Thornburgh, vice chairman, Credit Suisse First Boston

UNIVERSITY OF COLORADO—BOULDER
Leeds School of Business

Admissions Contact: Toby Hemmerling, Acting Associate Director
Address: Business 204, UCB 419, Boulder, CO 80309
Admissions Phone: 303-492-8397 • **Admissions Fax:** 303-492-1727
Admissions E-mail: LeedsMBA@colorado.edu • **Web Address:** leeds.colorado.edu

Students at the "well-run" Leeds School of Business can boast one of "the best" entrepreneurship programs in the nation, as well as enjoy the benefits that accompany a sizable school endowment. Said endowment is primarily the result of the sixth largest donation ever ($35 million) to an American b-school, made by Michael Leeds (hence the school's re-christening), former president and CEO of CMP Media. And "if you enjoy balancing social life with a solid academic life" and skiing, "Boulder offers the perfect mix."

INSTITUTIONAL INFORMATION

Public/Private: Public
Evening Classes Available? Yes
Total Faculty: 74
% Faculty Female: 19
% Faculty Minority: 23
% Faculty Part Time: 41
Student/Faculty Ratio: 10:1
Students in Parent Institution: 26,035
Academic Calendar: Semester

PROGRAMS

Degrees Offered: MBA (2 years full time), Professional Evening MBA (33 months)
Combined Degrees: JD/MBA (4 years full time), MBA/MS in Telecommunications (3-3.5 years full time), MBA/MA in Fine Arts, Germanic Languages, or Anthropology (3 years full time)
Academic Specialties: Small class sizes optimize opportunities for students to network with each other, the faculty members, and program guests. The School's close ties to the Colorado business community facilitate the practical application of academic coursework through class projects, internships, and mentor programs. To further specialize their MBA degree, students are also allowed to enroll in as many as 12 units of "free electives" in other graduate programs on the University of Colorado—Boulder campus. The University has a nationally ranked entrepreneurship program
Special Opportunities: Summer course held in London studies international finance and economics of the European community. Study tour courses are 2-week visits overseas that focus on business topics in other countries, and include visiting companies and talking with business executives.
Study Abroad Options: Tilburg University, the Netherlands

STUDENT INFORMATION

Total Business Students: 176
% Full Time: 64
% Female: 28
% Minority: 10
% Out of State: 37
% International: 19
Average Age: 28

COMPUTER AND RESEARCH FACILITIES

Research Facilities: Business Research Division, Real Estate Center, Center for Entrepreneurship, Burridge Center for Securities Analysis & Valuation
Computer Facilities: Lexis-Nexis, ABI/INFORM, Compact Disclosure, Infotrac PC, Compustat, Dun & Bradstreet, Corp Tech, Disclosure Select; MBA Business Center—a dedicated facility for MBA students that provides computer workstations, fax, phone, conference facilities
Campuswide Network? No
% of MBA Classrooms Wired: 100
Computer Model Recommended: Laptop
Internet Fee? No

EXPENSES/FINANCIAL AID

Annual Tuition (Resident/Nonresident): $4,992/$19,748
Room & Board (On/Off Campus): $13,000
Books and Supplies: $3,000
Average Grant: $2,500
Average Loan: $5,500
% Receiving Financial Aid: 60
% Receiving Aid Their First Year: 60

ADMISSIONS INFORMATION

Application Fee: $52
Electronic Application? Yes
Early Decision Application Deadline: 12/1
Early Decision Notification: 2/15
Regular Application Deadline: 4/1
Regular Notification: 5/29
Deferment Available? No
Non-fall Admissions? No
Transfer Students Accepted? No
Need-Blind Admissions? Yes
Number of Applications Received: 293
% of Applicants Accepted: 47
% Accepted Who Enrolled: 44
Average GPA: 3.0
GPA Range: 2.5-3.7

Average GMAT: 636
GMAT Range: 590-710
Average Years Experience: 5
Other Admissions Factors Considered: Ability to add diversity to the student body, to work well with a team/group focus, and to make unique contributions to the program
Other Schools to Which Students Applied: Arizona State University, University of California—Berkeley, Thunderbird, University of Colorado—Denver, University of Denver, University of Southern California, Southern Methodist University

INTERNATIONAL STUDENTS

TOEFL Required of International Students? Yes
Minimum TOEFL: 600 (250 computer)

EMPLOYMENT INFORMATION

Placement Office Available? Yes
% Employed Within 3 Months: 94
Fields Employing Percentage of Grads: Consulting (3%), MIS (3%), Marketing (17%), General Management (20%), Other (28%), Finance (29%)
Frequent Employers: Agilent Technologies, Cap Gemini, Gartner Solista, Hewlett Packard, IBM Global Services, IBM Printing Systems, Intel, Millennium Venture Group, Qwest, Softsource, Sun Microsystems
Prominent Alumni: Kevin Burns, managing principle, Lazard Technology Partners; John Puerner, president and CEO, Los Angeles Times; Patrick Tierney, president and CEO, Thompson Financial; Jeanne Jackson, CEO, Walmart.com

UNIVERSITY OF COLORADO— COLORADO SPRINGS
Graduate School of Business Administration

Admissions Contact: Maureen Cathey, MBA Program Director
Address: 1420 Austin Bluffs Parkway, Colorado Springs, CO 80918
Admissions Phone: 719-262-3408 • Admissions Fax: 719-262-3100
Admissions E-mail: busadvsr@uccs.edu • Web Address: web.uccs.edu/business

Exercising a focus on new technology, University of Colorado at Colorado Springs offers a Distance MBA program, where students learn about the evolving tech economy and discuss class material via chat rooms. This virtual classroom setting allows for quite a bit of scheduling flexibility, as students are not required to be online at any specific time as long as they check in regularly and participate in discussions. UC Colorado Springs also offers an Executive MBA Program, designed for mid-career professionals who wish to acquire an advanced education in less than two years. Exchange programs are available for MBA students with the Helsinki School of Economics and Business in Finland and the Vaxjo University in Sweden.

INSTITUTIONAL INFORMATION

Public/Private: Public
Evening Classes Available? Yes
Total Faculty: 34
% Faculty Female: 15
% Faculty Minority: 3
% Faculty Part Time: 6
Student/Faculty Ratio: 8:1
Students in Parent Institution: 7,407
Academic Calendar: Semester

PROGRAMS

Degrees Offered: MBA (1.5 to 5 years, 2-3 years average)
Combined Degrees: NA
Academic Specialties: We offer the MBA program both on campus and via a web-based distance program.

STUDENT INFORMATION

Total Business Students: 273
Average Age: 29

COMPUTER AND RESEARCH FACILITIES

Research Facilities: Small Business Development Center
Computer Facilities: All library databases, Oracle lab
Campuswide Network? Yes
% of MBA Classrooms Wired: 25
Internet Fee? No

EXPENSES/FINANCIAL AID

Tuition Per Credit (Resident/Nonresident): $227/$824
Room & Board (On/Off Campus): $8,000

ADMISSIONS INFORMATION

Application Fee: $60
Electronic Application? No
Regular Application Deadline: 6/1
Regular Notification: Rolling
Deferment Available? Yes
Length of Deferment: 1 year
Non-fall Admissions? Yes
Non-fall Application Deadline(s): Rolling, 11/1 spring, 4/1 summer
Transfer Students Accepted? Yes
Transfer Policy: 6 hours from an AACSB-accredited MBA program
Need-Blind Admissions? Yes
Number of Applications Received: 79
% of Applicants Accepted: 90
% Accepted Who Enrolled: 76
Average GPA: 3.2
GPA Range: 2.8-3.6
Average GMAT: 540
GMAT Range: 490-560
Average Years Experience: 7
Other Admissions Factors Considered: Work experience, letters of recommendation; GRE also accepted

INTERNATIONAL STUDENTS

TOEFL Required of International Students? Yes
Minimum TOEFL: 550 (213 computer)

EMPLOYMENT INFORMATION

Placement Office Available? No

UNIVERSITY OF COLORADO—DENVER
College of Business and Administration

Admissions Contact: Graduate Admissions Coordinator
Address: Campus Box 165, PO Box 173364, Denver, CO 80217-3364
Admissions Phone: 303-556-5900 • Admissions Fax: 303-556-5904
Admissions E-mail: grad.business@cudenver.edu.
Web Address: www.business.cudenver.edu

Located in the heart of Denver's business community, UC Denver offers several MBA programs. The 11-Month MBA program meets during the day in the historic Masonic Temple Building on the 16th Street Mall in Denver, and the Individualized MBA allows students to advance at their own pace. Students can also choose from the Cohort MBA or the On-Site MBA. The curriculum of each MBA program includes case studies, computer simulations, and interaction with Colorado businesses, and the MBA programs are self-contained, requiring no preliminary course work. UC Denver encourages its students to participate in Mentor Programs, where students learn from those who've already been there, done that.

INSTITUTIONAL INFORMATION

Public/Private: Public
Evening Classes Available? Yes
Total Faculty: 66
Student/Faculty Ratio: 35:1
Students in Parent Institution: 11,050
Academic Calendar: Semester

PROGRAMS

Degrees Offered: MBA (16 months to 5 years), EMBA (up to 22 months), MBA/MS (2-3 years), MBA/MIM (2-3 years), MS (9 months to 5 years); 11-Month MBA
Academic Specialties: Technology-Global, Entrepreneurship
Special Opportunities: An intership is available.
Study Abroad Options: Belgium, France, Spain

STUDENT INFORMATION

Total Business Students: 1,249
% Full Time: 29
% Female: 11
% Minority: 10
% Out of State: 1
% International: 14
Average Age: 25

COMPUTER AND RESEARCH FACILITIES

Research Facilities: Bard Center for Entrepreneurship, Center for Information Technology Innovation
Computer Facilities: J.D. Edward
Campuswide Network? Yes
Internet Fee? No

EXPENSES/FINANCIAL AID

Annual Tuition (Resident/Nonresident): $4,244/$13,818
Tuition Per Credit (Resident/Nonresident): $237/$828
Average Grant: $1,000
% Receiving Financial Aid: 29

ADMISSIONS INFORMATION

Application Fee: $50
Electronic Application? No
Regular Application Deadline: 6/15
Regular Notification: Rolling
Deferment Available? Yes
Length of Deferment: 1 year
Non-fall Admissions? Yes
Non-fall Application Deadline(s): 11/1 spring, 4/1 summer
Transfer Students Accepted? Yes
Transfer Policy: Varies by student and program
Need-Blind Admissions? Yes
Number of Applications Received: 547
% of Applicants Accepted: 74
% Accepted Who Enrolled: 64
Other Admissions Factors Considered: GRE score accepted; resume, work experience, computer experience

INTERNATIONAL STUDENTS

TOEFL Required of International Students? Yes
Minimum TOEFL: 525 (197 computer)

EMPLOYMENT INFORMATION

Placement Office Available? Yes
% Employed Within 3 Months: 90

UNIVERSITY OF CONNECTICUT
School of Business

Admissions Contact: Richard N. Dino, Associate Dean
Address: 2100 Hillside Road Unit 1041, Storrs, CT 06269-1041
Admissions Phone: 860-486-2872 • **Admissions Fax:** 860-486-5222
Admissions E-mail: uconnmba@business.uconn.edu
Web Address: www.business.uconn.edu

Reasonable tuition and a variety of programs attract MBAs to the University of Connecticut's School of Business Administration. The top brass here is "constantly seeking ways to improve" the school, and professors—though they "pile the work up"—are "well respected," especially in management, operations, and finance. UConn also boasts a "tremendous number of international students" and an "excellent," "rural and quaint" location "between New York and Boston."

INSTITUTIONAL INFORMATION

Public/Private: Public
Evening Classes Available? Yes
Total Faculty: 102
% Faculty Female: 19
% Faculty Minority: 27
% Faculty Part Time: 27
Student/Faculty Ratio: 13:1
Students in Parent Institution: 25,842
Academic Calendar: Semester

PROGRAMS

Degrees Offered: MBA (2 years), EMBA (21 months), PhD (4 years), MSA (1 year), Professional MBA (3-6 years part time)
Combined Degrees: JD/MBA, MD/MBA, MSW/MBA, MBA/MA in International Studies, MBA/MIM, MBA/MSN (2.5 years)
Academic Specialties: Information Technology, Finance, Management Consulting, Marketing Intelligence and Interactivity, Accounting, Health Systems, Real Estate. Our curriculum emphasizes information technology and globalization as themes that cut across all disciplines. We require a laptop computer as a "tool of the trade" and have integrated its use into the curriculum.
Special Opportunities: Edgelab, Student Managed Fund, Wolff Program in Entrepreneurship, Health Care Management, Advanced Business Certificates, MBA Business Plan Competition, Mentor Program
Study Abroad Options: EM Lyon, France

STUDENT INFORMATION

Total Business Students: 837
% Full Time: 12
% Female: 42
% Minority: 6
% Out of State: 12
% International: 47
Average Age: 28

COMPUTER AND RESEARCH FACILITIES

Research Facilities: Edgelab; Center for International Business, Education and Research (CIBER); GE Global Learning Center; Real Estate Center; Health Systems Center

Computer Facilities: 10 labs, 8 databases, Academic Universe, DowJones, UCONN Online Catalog, Survey of Current Business, ABI Global, ABI/Inform, National Trade Data Bank, CCH Internet Tax Research, D&B Millennium Dollar Database, Primark Global Access, Dow Jones Interactive, Infotrac, Econlit, Lexis-Nexis, Standard & Poor's, ValueLine, Academic Universe

Campuswide Network? Yes

% of MBA Classrooms Wired: 100

Computer Model Recommended: Laptop

Internet Fee? No

EXPENSES/FINANCIAL AID

Annual Tuition (Resident/Nonresident): $5,692/$14,784

Tuition Per Credit (Resident/Nonresident): $490

Room & Board (On/Off Campus): $7,780/$8,800

Books and Supplies: $2,500

% Receiving Financial Aid: 64

% Receiving Aid Their First Year: 52

ADMISSIONS INFORMATION

Application Fee: $52

Electronic Application? Yes

Regular Application Deadline: 4/1

Regular Notification: Rolling

Deferment Available? Yes

Length of Deferment: 11 months

Non-fall Admissions? No

Transfer Students Accepted? Yes

Transfer Policy: All students requesting to transfer are required to meet with the director of the MBA Program. A maximum of 15 credits are accepted.

Need-Blind Admissions? Yes

Number of Applications Received: 200

% of Applicants Accepted: 63

% Accepted Who Enrolled: 50

Average GPA: 3.4

GPA Range: 3.1-3.7

Average GMAT: 628

GMAT Range: 580-660

Average Years Experience: 6

Other Admissions Factors Considered: Quality of undergraduate institution, quality and length of professional work experience

Minority/Disadvantaged Student Recruitment Programs: Specialized recruiting by the MBA Program and the Office of Diversity Initiatives

Other Schools to Which Students Applied: Arizona State University, Boston College, Ohio State University, Pennsylvania State University, University of Illinois, University of Wisconsin—Madison

INTERNATIONAL STUDENTS

TOEFL Required of International Students? Yes

Minimum TOEFL: 575 (233 computer)

EMPLOYMENT INFORMATION

Placement Office Available? Yes

% Employed Within 3 Months: 74

Fields Employing Percentage of Grads: Other (4%), Accounting (4%), Marketing (6%), Consulting (7%), General Management (13%), MIS (20%), Finance (44%)

Frequent Employers: Aetna, Cartesis, CIGNA, CitiGroup, ESPN, GE, General Dynamics The Hartford, IBM, Travelers, United Technologies

Prominent Alumni: Robert E. Diamond, chief executive, Barclays Capital; John Y. Kim, president, CIGNA Retirement and Investment Service; Christopher P.A. Komisarjevsky, president and CEO, Burston-Marsteller Worldwide; Penelope A. Dobkin, portfolio manager, Fidelity Investments; Janet A. Alpert, president, Land America Financial Group

UNIVERSITY OF DAYTON
School of Business Aministration

Admissions Contact: Janis Glynn, Director
Address: 300 College Park Avenue, Dayton, OH 45469
Admissions Phone: 937-229-3733 • **Admissions Fax:** 937-229-3882
Admissions E-mail: mba@udayton.edu • **Web Address:** www.sba.udayton.edu/mba

UD's School of Business Administration's catchphrase is "Integrating Technology Across the School of Business Administration." The Catholic University of Dayton boasts university centers and state-of-the-art computer and research facilities that grant students the opportunity to meet local business leaders and potential future employers, as well as participate in experiential learning through the use and application of cutting-edge technology. Full timers and part timers alike will find a place in UD's MBA program, where internships, capstone consulting projects, fellowships, assistantships, and study abroad opportunities abound.

INSTITUTIONAL INFORMATION

Public/Private: Private

Evening Classes Available? Yes

Total Faculty: 38

% Faculty Female: 11

Students in Parent Institution: 10,180

Academic Calendar: Semester

PROGRAMS

Degrees Offered: MBA (1-2 years full time, 2-3 years part time)

Combined Degrees: JD/MBA (3-5 years)

Academic Specialties: Accounting, Finance, International Business, Managemenet Information Systems, Operations Management, Marketing, Technology-Enhanced Business. Special strength: Integrative, team-teaching

Special Opportunities: We also offer a Post-Master's Certificate Program for students holding an MBA or similar graduate degree.

Study Abroad Options: China; Czech Republic; Finland; University of Toulouse, France; University of Augsburg, Germany

STUDENT INFORMATION

Total Business Students: 431

% Full Time: 21

% Female: 46

Average Age: 29

COMPUTER AND RESEARCH FACILITIES

Research Facilities: U.D. Center for Portfolio Management and Security Analysis, U.D. Center for Business and Economic Research (CBER), Center for Leadership and Executive Development

Computer Facilities: Lexis-Nexis, U.D. Ryan C. Harris Learning-Teaching Center

Campuswide Network? Yes

Computer Model Recommended: Laptop

Internet Fee? No

EXPENSES/FINANCIAL AID

Annual Tuition: $8,658

Tuition Per Credit (Resident/Nonresident): $481

Books and Supplies: $600

ADMISSIONS INFORMATION

Electronic Application? Yes
Regular Application Deadline: Rolling
Regular Notification: Rolling
Deferment Available? Yes
Length of Deferment: 1 year
Non-fall Admissions? Yes
Non-fall Application Deadline(s): Rolling
Transfer Students Accepted? Yes
Transfer Policy: Students may request up to 12 semester hours of approved graduate transfer credit of coursework with a grade of B or better.
Need-Blind Admissions? Yes
Number of Applications Received: 368
% of Applicants Accepted: 80
% Accepted Who Enrolled: 80
Average GPA: 3.2
Average GMAT: 543
Average Years Experience: 7
Other Admissions Factors Considered: Trend in GPA, GPA average within major, possible work experience
Other Schools to Which Students Applied: Xavier University, University of Cincinnati, Wright State University, Miami University

INTERNATIONAL STUDENTS

TOEFL Required of International Students? Yes
Minimum TOEFL: 550 (213 computer)

EMPLOYMENT INFORMATION

Placement Office Available? Yes
% Employed Within 3 Months: 95
Prominent Alumni: Allen Hill, president and CEO, Dayton Power and Light; Phil Parker, president and CEO, Dayton Area Chamber of Commerce; Mike Turner, former mayor, City of Dayton

---

UNIVERSITY OF DELAWARE
MBA Programs, College of Business and Economics

Admissions Contact: Ronald I. Sibert, Director of MBA Programs
Address: 103 MBNA America Hall, Newark, DE 19716
Admissions Phone: 302-831-2221 • **Admissions Fax:** 302-831-3329
Admissions E-mail: mbaprogram@udel.edu • **Web Address:** www.mba.udel.edu

University of Delaware students are enraptured with their campus, "absolutely the most gorgeous campus anywhere." The College of Business and Economics offers full- and part-time MBA programs, with a self-contained curriculum requiring no specific prerequisites as well as the unique MBA concentration in museum leadership and management. Most MBA students go into finance upon graduation, and many are employed by companies like Citibank, JPMorgan Chase, and IBM.

INSTITUTIONAL INFORMATION

Public/Private: Public
Evening Classes Available? Yes
Total Faculty: 64
% Faculty Female: 14
% Faculty Minority: 3
% Faculty Part Time: 5
Student/Faculty Ratio: 30:1

Students in Parent Institution: 20,949
Academic Calendar: Semester

PROGRAMS

Degrees Offered: MBA (48 credits, 16 months to 5 years), EMBA (48 credits, 19 months), MSA (48 credits, 16 months to 5 years)
Combined Degrees: MA in Economics/MBA (57 credits)
Academic Specialties: 20% faculty are also members of company boards of directors or boards of advisors; corporate governance, DE Audit Institute
Special Opportunities: MIB/MBA (57 credits)
Study Abroad Options: Groupe ESC Grenoble, France

STUDENT INFORMATION

Total Business Students: 302
% Full Time: 24
% Female: 51
% Minority: 5
% Out of State: 27
% International: 50
Average Age: 27

COMPUTER AND RESEARCH FACILITIES

Research Facilities: Center for Corporate Governance, Small Business Development Center (SBDC)
Computer Facilities: 800 databases (major resources related to business and economics), top national award for Excellence in Campus Networking (CAUSE), ranked Number 2 Most Wired College (2000) by *Yahoo!*, state-of-the-art technology in case rooms, newly outfitted computer labs, ERP software and site server, web server for classrooms applications, wireless networking
Campuswide Network? Yes
% of MBA Classrooms Wired: 100
Internet Fee? No

EXPENSES/FINANCIAL AID

Annual Tuition (Resident/Nonresident): $6,020/$13,860
Tuition Per Credit (Resident/Nonresident): $334/$770
Room & Board (On/Off Campus): $6,200/$7,200
Books and Supplies: $1,400
Average Grant: $3,940
% Receiving Financial Aid: 60
% Receiving Aid Their First Year: 26

ADMISSIONS INFORMATION

Application Fee: $50
Electronic Application? Yes
Regular Application Deadline: 5/1
Regular Notification: Rolling
Deferment Available? Yes
Length of Deferment: 1 academic year
Non-fall Admissions? Yes
Non-fall Application Deadline(s): 11/1 spring, part time only
Transfer Students Accepted? Yes
Transfer Policy: Up to 9 semester hours (12 by special request) of graduate credit earned at another institution may be accepted toward the University of Delaware MBA degree. The courses must have completed with grades of B or better and within 5 years of the date of the requested transfer. Only those credits earned at an AACSB-accredited institution are transferable and only after the candidate has completed at least 9 credit hours as a matriculated MBA Program student at the University of Delaware. The student must submit a written request for credit evaluation, and a waiver examination may be required. (Only the credits—not the grades—are transferable.)
Need-Blind Admissions? Yes
Number of Applications Received: 259
% of Applicants Accepted: 75
% Accepted Who Enrolled: 65
Average GPA: 3.0
GPA Range: 2.1-3.9

Average GMAT: 555
GMAT Range: 330-750
Average Years Experience: 5
Other Admissions Factors Considered: Work experience, undergrad and graduate work, GMAT/TOEFL scores, letters of recommendation, statement of objectives
Other Schools to Which Students Applied: Temple University, University of Pennsylvania, Villanova University

INTERNATIONAL STUDENTS

TOEFL Required of International Students? Yes
Minimum TOEFL: 587 (240 computer)

EMPLOYMENT INFORMATION

Placement Office Available? Yes
% Employed Within 3 Months: 2
Fields Employing Percentage of Grads: Human Resources (4%), Other (9%), MIS (9%), Operations (10%), General Management (14%), Consulting (18%), Marketing (18%), Finance (18%)
Frequent Employers: Agilent Technologies, Cigna, Citicorp, Dade Behring, Deloitte Consulting, FMC, FNX, IBM, Johnson and Johnson, JP Morgan, MIDI, Morgan Chase, The Siegfried Group, TransUnion LLC, Wilmington Trust, W.L. Gore and Associates
Prominent Alumni: Thomas R. Carper, governor, State of Delaware, candidate for U.S. Senate; Leonard Quill, CEO and chairman of the board, Wilmington Trust Corp.; Howard Cosgrove, chairman and CEO, Conectiv; Dennis Sheehy, partner, Deloitte and Touche

UNIVERSITY OF DENVER
Daniels College of Business

Admissions Contact: Admissions Staff, Admissions Staff
Address: 2101 South University Blvd. #255, Denver, CO 80208
Admissions Phone: 303-871-3416 • **Admissions Fax:** 303-871-4466
Admissions E-mail: daniels@du.edu • **Web Address:** www.daniels.du.edu

A *"great city, great mountains,"* and *"great outdoor life"* are a few of the perks available at the University of Denver's Daniels College of Business, *"one of the nation's most technologically advanced business schools"* and home to a sizable international student contingent. Scheduling is *"flexible"* and the range of courses is broad, though the academic pressure can be *"intense"* thanks largely to a *"hectic"* quarter system.

INSTITUTIONAL INFORMATION

Public/Private: Private
Evening Classes Available? Yes
Total Faculty: 83
% Faculty Female: 15
% Faculty Minority: 5
% Faculty Part Time: 5
Student/Faculty Ratio: 10:1
Students in Parent Institution: 9,300
Academic Calendar: Quarter

PROGRAMS

Degrees Offered: EMBA (60 quarter hours, 18 months), Accelerated MBA (60 quarter hours, 12-18 months), MBA (48-72 quarter hours, 12-21 months full time or evening), IMBA (48-78 quarter hours, 15-24 months full time or evening), MACC (48-plus quarter hours, depending on previous coursework completed; 12-21 months), MS in Finance (48-64 quarter hours, 12-21

months), MS in Real Estate and Construction Management (48-64 quarter hours, 12-21 months), MSM (48-64 quarter hours, 12-21 months), MS in Marketing (48-64 quarter hours, 12-21 months). Note: Some coursework for each of these programs (with the exception of the EMBA) may be waived depending on previous academic background and/or work experience.
Combined Degrees: JD/MBA, JD/IMBA, JD/MS in Real Estate and Construction Management (all approximately 3-4 years); Flexible Dual Degree with any other University of Denver degree (varies); Combined Degree with other Daniels College of Business degrees (varies)
Academic Specialties: MBA and IMBA specializations: Accounting, Electronic Commerce, Entrepreneurship, Finance, Hospitality Property Development and Asset Management, Hospitality Information Technology and E-Business, Information Technology, Integrated Marketing Communications, Integrated Marketing Strategy, Real Estate and Construction Management, Software Engineering, XML, Customized Specialization
MSM industry-specific concentrations: Training and Development, Cable Telecommunication, Applied Communication, Sports Management, etc.
Special Opportunities: EMBA (full time Friday and Saturday), Accelerated MBA, MBA, IMBA, MACC, MS in Finance, Master of Real Estate and Construction Management, MSM, MS in Marketing, MSIT. All programs are available in flexible full-time or part-time format (except EMBA cohort, which is alternating Fridays and Saturdays for 18 months.)
Study Abroad Options: Varies

STUDENT INFORMATION

Total Business Students: 482
% Full Time: 71
% Female: 32
% Minority: 7
% Out of State: 40
% International: 22
Average Age: 27

COMPUTER AND RESEARCH FACILITIES

Research Facilities: Daniels College of Business Building provides an outstanding learning environment with wired classrooms, study rooms, and lounges, as well as access to Daniels College of Business server for class notes, discussion, and updates and provides students access to new technologies through the Technology Center. The WebCentral portal provides access to MyWeb, the Daniels e-net, university e-mail, and Blackboard classroom support.
Computer Facilities: Computer lab/resource center specific to Daniels College of Business students; other campus computer labs available to MBA students; access to Internet, e-mail, Lexis-Nexis statistical software; numerous other databases available through University of Denver e-resources, real estate/construction management software, Microsoft Office Suite
Campuswide Network? Yes
% of MBA Classrooms Wired: 100
Computer Model Recommended: Laptop
Internet Fee? No

EXPENSES/FINANCIAL AID

Annual Tuition: $22,680
Tuition Per Credit (Resident/Nonresident): $630
Room & Board (On/Off Campus): $8,000
Books and Supplies: $1,000
Average Grant: $3,500
Average Loan: $19,500
% Receiving Financial Aid: 60
% Receiving Aid Their First Year: 60

ADMISSIONS INFORMATION

Application Fee: $50
Electronic Application? Yes
Regular Application Deadline: 5/15
Regular Notification: 7/1
Length of Deferment: 1 year
Non-fall Application Deadline(s): 12/15

Transfer Policy: 12 quarter hours (9 semester hours) toward electives
Need-Blind Admissions? Yes
Number of Applications Received: 462
% of Applicants Accepted: 75
% Accepted Who Enrolled: 55
Average GPA: 3.0
GPA Range: 2.6-3.6
Average GMAT: 560
GMAT Range: 470-630
Average Years Experience: 7
Other Admissions Factors Considered: Community service
Minority/Disadvantaged Student Recruitment Programs: Limited amount of need-based scholarships
Other Schools to Which Students Applied: Arizona State University, Colorado State University, Southern Methodist University, Thunderbird, University of Arizona, University of Colorado, University of Colorado—Denver

INTERNATIONAL STUDENTS

TOEFL Required of International Students? Yes
Minimum TOEFL: 550 (213 computer)

EMPLOYMENT INFORMATION

Placement Office Available? Yes
% Employed Within 3 Months: 71
Fields Employing Percentage of Grads: Other (2%), MIS (2%), Human Resources (2%), Operations (7%), Marketing (10%), General Management (22%), Consulting (22%), Finance (30%)
Frequent Employers: Accenture, AIMCO, Citigroup, Coors Brewing Co., First Data Corp., IBM, J.D. Edwards, Johnson Controls, Keane Consulting Group, Lockheed Martin, Pricewaterhouse Coopers, Qwest Communications
Prominent Alumni: Peter Coors, CEO, Coors Brewing Co.; Andrew Daly, president, Vail Resorts; Michael Enzi, U.S. senator, Wyoming; Gale Norton, secretary of interior, United States; Carol Tome, executive vice president and CFO, Home Depot

See page 452.

UNIVERSITY OF DETROIT MERCY
College of Business Administration

Admissions Contact: Dr. Bahman Mirshab, Director of Graduate Business Programs
Address: College of Business Administration, Detroit, MI 48219-0900
Admissions Phone: 313-993-1202 • **Admissions Fax:** 313-993-1673
Admissions E-mail: admissions@udmercy.edu • **Web Address:** www.business.udmercy.edu

The University of Detroit—Mercy, Michigan's largest and most comprehensive Catholic university, boasts small class sizes and a strong dedication to the education of the whole person. Some proud themes of the MBA program include "teaching students self-reflection, teamwork with diverse peoples, and responsible stewardship for the common good." The student body is composed of nearly all part-time MBA students. Intensive courses with an emphasis on global business are offered during the summer in England, Ireland, China, Brazil, and Mexico.

INSTITUTIONAL INFORMATION

Public/Private: Private
Evening Classes Available? Yes
Total Faculty: 53
% Faculty Part Time: 38
Student/Faculty Ratio: 30:1

Students in Parent Institution: 5,843
Academic Calendar: Semester

PROGRAMS

Degrees Offered: MBA (37-55 credits, 1-5 years), MS in Computer and Information Systems (33-36 credits, 1-5 years), MS in Product Development (45 credits, 2 years)
Combined Degrees: JD/MBA
Study Abroad Options: China, Brazil, France, Mexico, United Kingdom

STUDENT INFORMATION

Total Business Students: 235
% Full Time: 9
% Female: 35
% Minority: 26
% Out of State: 1
% International: 8
Average Age: 29

COMPUTER AND RESEARCH FACILITIES

Campuswide Network? Yes
% of MBA Classrooms Wired: 12
Computer Model Recommended: Laptop
Internet Fee? No

EXPENSES/FINANCIAL AID

Tuition Per Credit (Resident/Nonresident): $640

ADMISSIONS INFORMATION

Application Fee: $30
Electronic Application? Yes
Regular Application Deadline: 7/15
Regular Notification: 8/1
Deferment Available? Yes
Length of Deferment: 2
Non-fall Admissions? Yes
Non-fall Application Deadline(s): 10/15, 3/15, 4/15
Transfer Students Accepted? Yes
Transfer Policy: Up to 12 credits from AACSB programs
Need-Blind Admissions? No
Number of Applications Received: 65
% of Applicants Accepted: 94
% Accepted Who Enrolled: 59
Average GPA: 3.1
Average GMAT: 513
Average Years Experience: 6
Other Schools to Which Students Applied: University of Pittsburgh, University of Scranton

EMPLOYMENT INFORMATION

Placement Office Available? Yes
% Employed Within 3 Months: 95

UNIVERSITY OF FINDLAY
College of Business

Admissions Contact: MBA Program Director
Address: 1000 N. Main Street, Findlay, OH 45840
Admissions Phone: 419-434-4676 • Admissions Fax: 419-434-6781
Admissions E-mail: obenour@findlay.edu
Web Address: www.findlay.edu/academic_programs/business/index.html

INSTITUTIONAL INFORMATION

Public/Private: Private
Evening Classes Available? Yes
Total Faculty: 18
% Faculty Female: 17
% Faculty Minority: 39
% Faculty Part Time: 25
Student/Faculty Ratio: 25:1
Students in Parent Institution: 4,405
Academic Calendar: Semester

PROGRAMS

Degrees Offered: MBA (33 credits, 18 months to 5 years)
Academic Specialties: Program blends theory, research, problem solving, and decision making; PhD in Marketing Management, Finance, Accounting, Operations, Strategy, and International Business

STUDENT INFORMATION

Total Business Students: 450
% Full Time: 12
% Female: 19
% Minority: 80
% Out of State: 95
% International: 90
Average Age: 32

COMPUTER AND RESEARCH FACILITIES

Research Facilities: Center for Management Development
Computer Facilities: Website and numerous computer labs on campus
Campuswide Network? Yes
% of MBA Classrooms Wired: 70
Computer Model Recommended: No
Internet Fee? Yes

EXPENSES/FINANCIAL AID

Annual Tuition: $13,572
Tuition Per Credit: $377
Books and Supplies: $2,000
Average Grant: $5,000
Average Loan: $10,000

ADMISSIONS INFORMATION

Application Fee: $25
Electronic Application? Yes
Regular Application Deadline: Rolling
Regular Notification: Rolling
Deferment Available? Yes
Length of Deferment: Varies upon reason
Non-fall Admissions? Yes
Non-fall Application Deadline(s): Winter, spring, summer
Transfer Students Accepted? Yes
Transfer Policy: May transfer up to 9 credits of similar courses of the program
Need-Blind Admissions? No
Number of Applications Received: 282
% of Applicants Accepted: 83
% Accepted Who Enrolled: 165

Average GPA: 3.3
Average GMAT: 550
Average Years Experience: 6
Other Schools to Which Students Applied: Bowling Green State University, University of Toledo

INTERNATIONAL STUDENTS

TOEFL Required of International Students? Yes
Minimum TOEFL: 525

EMPLOYMENT INFORMATION

Placement Office Available? Yes
% Employed Within 3 Months: 95

UNIVERSITY OF FLORIDA
Warrington College of Business

Admissions Contact: Amanda Moore, Admissions Coordinator
Address: 134 Bryan Hall, POBox 117152, Gainesville, FL 32611-7152
Admissions Phone: 352-392-7992 • Admissions Fax: 352-392-8791
Admissions E-mail: floridamba@notes.cba.ufl.edu • Web Address: www.floridamba.ufl.edu

Strong programs in entrepreneurship and finance, diverse course offerings, and a paradise-like atmosphere draw future MBAs to the "practical" University of Florida Graduate School of Business. It's also "a bargain financially"—particularly for in-staters—and the sweltering, hopping, activity-laden college town of Gainesville "is probably unparalleled socially."

INSTITUTIONAL INFORMATION

Public/Private: Public
Evening Classes Available? No
Total Faculty: 91
% Faculty Female: 13
% Faculty Minority: 14
Student/Faculty Ratio: 6:1
Students in Parent Institution: 45,000
Academic Calendar: Semester

PROGRAMS

Degrees Offered: MBA (14-33 months); MSM (1 year); MA in International Business (1 year); MA in Real Estate (1 year); MS in Decision and Information Sciences (1 year); MACC (1 year); MS in Finance (1 year); PhD (3-6 years), with programs in Marketing, Finance, Management, DIS, Economics
Combined Degrees: MBA/JD (4 years), MBA/Master of Exercise and Sport Science (3 years), MBA/MS in Biotechnology, MBA/PharmD, MBA/PhD in Medical Sciences, MBA/MD
Academic Specialties: Electronic Commerce, Supply Chain Management, Entrepreneurship, Management of Technology, Financial Services, Decision and Information Sciences
Special Opportunities: Traditional MBA; EMBA; MBA for Professionals (1- and 2-year options); Internet MBA (1 and 2-year options); IMBA; MBA for Engineers and Scientists
Study Abroad Options: Belgium, Chile, China (Hong Kong), Denmark, Finland, France, Germany, Great Britain, Italy, the Netherlands, Norway, Spain, Turkey, Venezuela, Japan

STUDENT INFORMATION

Total Business Students: 457
% Full Time: 76

% **Female:** 24
% **Minority:** 10
% **Out of State:** 52
% **International:** 21
Average Age: 27

COMPUTER AND RESEARCH FACILITIES

Research Facilities: Bureau of Economic & Business Research, Business Ethics Education & Research Center, Center for Accounting Reserch & Professional Education, Center for International Economic & Business Studies, Center for Public Policy Research, Consumer Research, Decision & Information Sciences Forum, Enterpreneurship & Innovation Center, Florida Insurance Research Center, Human Resource Research Center, Public Utilities Researh Center, Real Estate Research Center, Retailing Education & Research Center

Computer Facilities: Technology Assistance Center

Campuswide Network? Yes

% **of MBA Classrooms Wired:** 100

Computer Model Recommended: Laptop

Internet Fee? No

EXPENSES/FINANCIAL AID

Annual Tuition (Resident/Nonresident): $4,620/$16,018

Room & Board (On/Off Campus): $6,800

Books and Supplies: $2,935

Average Grant: $4,750

Average Loan: $10,000

ADMISSIONS INFORMATION

Application Fee: $20

Electronic Application? Yes

Early Decision Application Deadline: 12/15 fall

Early Decision Notification: 2/15

Regular Application Deadline: 4/15

Regular Notification: 6/15

Deferment Available? No

Non-fall Application Deadline(s): 10/15 spring programs for working professionals, 6/1 fall programs for working professionals

Transfer Students Accepted? No

Need-Blind Admissions? Yes

Number of Applications Received: 491

% **of Applicants Accepted:** 22

% **Accepted Who Enrolled:** 46

Average GPA: 3.3

GPA Range: 2.8-3.5

Average GMAT: 655

GMAT Range: 600-680

Average Years Experience: 4

Other Admissions Factors Considered: Leadership potential

Minority/Disadvantaged Student Recruitment Programs: Graduate Minority Campus Visitation Program

Other Schools to Which Students Applied: University of Texas—Austin, University of Georgia, University of Miami, Arizona State University, Emory University, Georgetown University, Texas A&M University

INTERNATIONAL STUDENTS

TOEFL Required of International Students? Yes

Minimum TOEFL: 600 (250 computer)

EMPLOYMENT INFORMATION

Placement Office Available? Yes

% **Employed Within 3 Months:** 93

Fields Employing Percentage of Grads: Other (10%), Consulting (19%), Finance (29%), Operations (42%)

Frequent Employers: Deloitte & Touche, ExxonMobil, General Electric, Arthur Andersen, Ford Motor, Pricewaterhouse Coopers, Samsung, SunTrust Bank

Prominent Alumni: John Dasburg, president and CEO, Burger King; Don

McKinney, venture capitalist, partner, Watershed Capital; William R. Hough, president, William R. Hough & Co. & WRH Mortgage

See page 454.

UNIVERSITY OF GEORGIA
Terry College of Business, Graduate School of Business Administration

Admissions Contact: Anne C. Cooper, Director, MBA Admissions
Address: 346 Brooks Hall, Athens, GA 30602-6264
Admissions Phone: 706-542-5671 • **Admissions Fax:** 706-542-5351
Admissions E-mail: terrymba@terry.uga.edu • **Web Address:** www.terry.uga.edu/mba

What with "state-of-the-art" facilities and flexible degree programs, the University of Georgia's Terry College of Business is "an excellent value" and one of the nation's best public business schools. You certainly can't beat its location; students say the "comfortable" environs of Athens provide "a broad spectrum of individuals and culture" and "epitomize what a college town should be." As an added bonus, Atlanta—the "Capital of the New South"—is a mere 70 miles away.

INSTITUTIONAL INFORMATION

Public/Private: Public

Evening Classes Available? Yes

Total Faculty: 132

Student/Faculty Ratio: 25:1

Students in Parent Institution: 32,500

Academic Calendar: Semester

PROGRAMS

Degrees Offered: MBA (41-66 credits, 11- 22 months), with concentrations in Accounting, Economics, Entrepreneurship, Finance, Insurance, International Business, Real Estate, Risk Manangement, Organizational Consulting, Productivity/Quality Management; MBA/JD (26 credits, 3.3 years); MACC (30 credits, 9 months to 2 years), with concentrations in Economics, Financial Economics, International Economics; MA in Economics (30-36 credits, 9 months to 2 years); MMR (40 credits, 18 months)

Combined Degrees: JD/MBA (4 years), MACC (5 years)

Academic Specialties: One of the program's greatest strengths is the opportunity to specialize in many areas, including Entrepreneurship, Real Estate, Risk Management, MIS, Corporate Finance, Investments, Marketing, Productivity/Quality Management, Accounting, Organizational Consulting, and International Business.

Study Abroad Options: Nyenrode University, the Netherlands

STUDENT INFORMATION

Total Business Students: 368

% **Full Time:** 50

% **Female:** 21

% **Minority:** 9

% **Out of State:** 54

% **International:** 31

Average Age: 27

COMPUTER AND RESEARCH FACILITIES

Research Facilities: Institute for Leadership Advancement, Center for Enterprise Risk Management, Center for Information Systems Leadership, Ramsey Center for Private Enterprise, Coca-Cola Center for International Business, Coca-Cola Center for Marketing Studies, Bonbright Utilities Center,

Selig Center for Economic Growth

Computer Facilities: GALIN online library search service; sizeable library of software provided by professors from their classes; 900-plus seats in new classroom; Sanford Hall, with laptop connectivity to the campus network (LAN)

Campuswide Network? Yes

% of MBA Classrooms Wired: 100

Computer Model Recommended: Laptop

Internet Fee? No

EXPENSES/FINANCIAL AID

Annual Tuition (Resident/Nonresident): $3,348/$14,392

Room & Board (On/Off Campus): $4,870/$6,825

Books and Supplies: $900

Average Grant: $2,500

% Receiving Financial Aid: 65

% Receiving Aid Their First Year: 54

ADMISSIONS INFORMATION

Application Fee: $50

Electronic Application? Yes

Regular Application Deadline: 5/1

Regular Notification: Rolling

Deferment Available? Yes

Length of Deferment: 1 year

Non-fall Admissions? Yes

Non-fall Application Deadline(s): 2/1 summer, for 11-month MBA

Transfer Students Accepted? No

Need-Blind Admissions? Yes

Number of Applications Received: 631

% of Applicants Accepted: 29

% Accepted Who Enrolled: 61

Average GPA: 3.3

GPA Range: 2.8-3.5

Average GMAT: 658

GMAT Range: 580-660

Average Years Experience: 5

Other Schools to Which Students Applied: Emory University, Vanderbilt University, University of North Carolina—Chapel Hill

INTERNATIONAL STUDENTS

TOEFL Required of International Students? Yes

Minimum TOEFL: 577 (233 computer)

EMPLOYMENT INFORMATION

Placement Office Available? Yes

% Employed Within 3 Months: 93

Frequent Employers: Andersen Consulting, BellSouth, Cintas, Coca-Cola, Delta Airlines, Fannie Mae, Federal Express, International Paper, Pricewaterhouse-Coopers, Shopping Center Properties, SunTrust, Wachovia

---

UNIVERSITY OF HAWAII—MANOA
College of Business Administration

Admissions Contact: Marsha Anderson, Assistant Dean

Address: 2404 Maile Way B201, Honolulu, HI 96822

Admissions Phone: 808-956-8266 • **Admissions Fax:** 808-956-2657

Admissions E-mail: osasgrad@cba.hawaii.edu • **Web Address:** www.cba.hawaii.edu

INSTITUTIONAL INFORMATION

Public/Private: Public

Evening Classes Available? Yes

Total Faculty: 65

% Faculty Female: 5

% Faculty Minority: 10

% Faculty Part Time: 22

Student/Faculty Ratio: 25:1

Students in Parent Institution: 17,532

Academic Calendar: Semester

PROGRAMS

Degrees Offered: MBA (42-48 credits, 2 years), EMBA (48 credits, 22 months), MACC (30 credits, 12 months), Japan-focused EMBA (48 credits, 15 months), China-focused EMBA (48 credits, 15 months), PhD in International Management (4-5 years)

Combined Degrees: MBA/JD (122-128 credits, 4 years)

Academic Specialties: International Business, Entreprenuership, Information Technology Management

Special Opportunities: Entrepreneurship and Internship program

Study Abroad Options: China, Denmark, Finland, France, Germany, Hong Kong, Japan, Korea, Singapore, Taiwan, Thailand

STUDENT INFORMATION

Total Business Students: 319

% Full Time: 52

% Female: 39

% Minority: 18

% Out of State: 8

% International: 21

Average Age: 29

COMPUTER AND RESEARCH FACILITIES

Research Facilities: Instructional Resource Center, Behavior Research Laboratory, Sunset Reference Center, Asia-Pacific Center for Executive Development, Academy of International Business, Asia Pacific Economic Corporation Study Center, Center for Japanese Global Investment and Finance, Pacific Asian Management Institute, Center for International Business Education and Research, Hawaii Real Estate Research and Education Center, Pacific Business Center, Pacific Research Institute for Information Systems and Management

Computer Facilities: 2 computer labs at the College of Business Administration; 10 computers in the graduate reading room area; access to online bibliographic retrieval systems and online databases, includingABI Inform, Disclosure, Dissertation Abstracts, Lexis-Nexis, Periodicals Abstracts Research, Public Affairs Info Service

Campuswide Network? Yes

% of MBA Classrooms Wired: 5

Computer Model Recommended: Laptop

Internet Fee? No

EXPENSES/FINANCIAL AID

Annual Tuition (Resident/Nonresident): $8,928/$14,544

Tuition Per Credit (Resident/Nonresident): $305/$552

Room & Board (On/Off Campus): $12,000/$14,000

Books and Supplies: $950

Average Grant: $25,000

Average Loan: $10,900

% Receiving Financial Aid: 25

ADMISSIONS INFORMATION

Application Fee: $25

Electronic Application? Yes

Regular Application Deadline: 5/1

Regular Notification: Rolling

Deferment Available? Yes

Length of Deferment: 1 semester

Non-fall Admissions? Yes

Non-fall Application Deadline(s): 11/1 spring

Transfer Students Accepted? Yes

Transfer Policy: Credits may be transferred into the MBA program from other AACSB-accredited business schools, from other University of Hawaii graduate programs, or by petition as follows: Up to half of the program's requirements may be transferred. Transfer credit is appropriate for both core (upon approval) and electives.
Need-Blind Admissions? No
Number of Applications Received: 313
% of Applicants Accepted: 39
% Accepted Who Enrolled: 55
Average GPA: 3.3
GPA Range: 2.7-3.9
Average GMAT: 575
GMAT Range: 500-710
Average Years Experience: 4
Other Admissions Factors Considered: Computer experience required: ICS 101 or equivalent

INTERNATIONAL STUDENTS

TOEFL Required of International Students? Yes
Minimum TOEFL: 550 (220 computer)

EMPLOYMENT INFORMATION

Placement Office Available? Yes
% Employed Within 3 Months: 80
Fields Employing Percentage of Grads: Consulting (5%), Human Resources (5%), Accounting (5%), General Management (10%), MIS (10%), Finance (15%), Global Management (25%), Marketing (25%)
Frequent Employers: AdWorks, Andersen Consulting, Bank of Hawaii, City and County of Honolulu, City Bank, First Hawaiian Bank, Hewlett Packard, KPMG LLP, Microsoft, Star Supermarket, Starr-Siegal Advertising, StarrTech, State of Hawaii
Prominent Alumni: Robin Campaniano, pres and CEO, Insurance; Brenda Lei Foster, executive assistant to the governor, State of Hawaii; Sharon Weiner, vice president, DFS, Hawaii; C. Dudley Pratt, Jr., former trustee, Campbell Estate; David McCoy, CEO, Campbell Estate

UNIVERSITY OF HOUSTON
C.T. Bauer College of Business

Admissions Contact: Amy L. Rice, Admissions Coordinator
Address: 334 Melcher Hall, Suite 275, Houston, TX 77204-6021
Admissions Phone: 713-743-5936 • **Admissions Fax:** 713-743-4368
Admissions E-mail: houstonmba@uh.edu • **Web Address:** www.bauer.uh.edu/mba

INSTITUTIONAL INFORMATION

Public/Private: Public
Evening Classes Available? Yes
Total Faculty: 82
% Faculty Female: 23
% Faculty Minority: 24
Student/Faculty Ratio: 10:1
Students in Parent Institution: 34,443
Academic Calendar: Semester

PROGRAMS

Degrees Offered: MBA (48 credits, 2-5 years), MSA (36-51 credits, 1.5 to 5 years), EMBA (48 credits, 18-24 months)
Combined Degrees: MBA/JD (111 credits, 4-6 years), MBA/MIE (72 credits, 2-5 years), MBA/MA in Spanish (64 credits, 2-5 years), MBA/Master's in Hospitality Management (78 credits, 2-5 years), MBA/MSW (87 credits, 3-5 years), MBA/Master's in International Management (66 credits, 3-5 years)

Academic Specialties: Certificate Programs (optional groupings of elective courses targeting a particular area of interest; for Fall 2003 these include Energy Risk Management, Energy Accounting, Management of Financial Services, IT Project Management)
Special Opportunities: The Berlin International Study Program and Prague International Study Program, along with the India Study Abroad Program, are held during the summer, while the Chile International Study Program takes place over the winter break.
Study Abroad Options: Chile, Czech Republic, Germany, India

STUDENT INFORMATION

Total Business Students: 818
Average Age: 28

COMPUTER AND RESEARCH FACILITIES

Research Facilities: AIM Center for Investment Management (state-of-the-art trading floor with multiple workstations and extensive data feeds; utilized by select MBA students to manage actual mutual fund), Global Energy Management Institute; Institute for Energy, Law and Enterprise; Center for Executive Development
Computer Facilities: 150 networked PCs with printing capabilities and Internet access; wireless access to network throughout building; same capabilities available in University library
Campuswide Network? Yes
% of MBA Classrooms Wired: 100
Computer Model Recommended: Laptop
Internet Fee? No

EXPENSES/FINANCIAL AID

Annual Tuition (Resident/Nonresident): $2,376/$6,300
Tuition Per Credit (Resident/Nonresident): $132/$350
Room & Board (On/Off Campus): $7,920
Books and Supplies: $1,000
Average Grant: $1,750

ADMISSIONS INFORMATION

Application Fee: $75
Electronic Application? No
Regular Application Deadline: 5/1
Regular Notification: 6/1
Deferment Available? Yes
Length of Deferment: 1 year
Non-fall Admissions? Yes
Non-fall Application Deadline(s): 10/1 spring
Transfer Students Accepted? No
Need-Blind Admissions? Yes
Number of Applications Received: 583
% of Applicants Accepted: 48
% Accepted Who Enrolled: 71
Average GPA: 3.3
GPA Range: 3.0-3.6
Average GMAT: 590
GMAT Range: 560-620
Average Years Experience: 4
Other Admissions Factors Considered: Essay, personal statement, work experience
Other Schools to Which Students Applied: Rice University, Texas A&M University, University of Houston—Clear Lake, University of Texas—Austin

INTERNATIONAL STUDENTS

TOEFL Required of International Students? Yes
Minimum TOEFL: 620 (260 computer)

EMPLOYMENT INFORMATION

Placement Office Available? Yes
% Employed Within 3 Months: 91
Frequent Employers: AIM Management Group, Inc.; Dell Computer Corp.; ExxonMobil; Hewlett-Packard; Shell Services International

Prominent Alumni: Bruce Williamson, president and CEO, Dynegy, Inc.; Sam DiPiazza, global CEO, Pricewaterhouse Coopers; Fran Keeth, president and CEO, Shell Chemical, LP; Lt. Col. Barrye Price, PhD, executive officer to Deputy Secretary of the Army; Karen Katz, president and CEO, Neiman Marcus

UNIVERSITY OF HOUSTON—CLEAR LAKE
School of Business and Public Administration

Admissions Contact: Rose Sklar, Registrar
Address: 2700 Bay Area Blvd., Houston, TX 77058-1098
Admissions Phone: 281-283-2500 • **Admissions Fax:** 281-283-2530
Admissions E-mail: admissions@cl.uh.edu • **Web Address:** www.cl.uh.edu/bpa/index.html

INSTITUTIONAL INFORMATION
Public/Private: Public
Evening Classes Available? Yes
Total Faculty: 55
% Faculty Female: 38
% Faculty Minority: 12
Student/Faculty Ratio: 18:1
Students in Parent Institution: 7,753
Academic Calendar: Semester

PROGRAMS
Degrees Offered: MBA (36-57 credits, 2-5 years), MS in Finance (36-57 credits, 2-5 years), MSA (36-69 credits, 2-5 years), MSMIS (36-57 credits, 2-5 years), MA in Human Resources (42-54 credits, 2-5 years), MS in Environmental Management (36-54 credits, 2-5 years), MSHA (48-66 credits, 2-5 years)
Combined Degrees: MHA/MBA (60-81 credits, 3 years)

STUDENT INFORMATION
Total Business Students: 533
% Full Time: 36
% Female: 39
% Minority: 24
% International: 12
Average Age: 34

COMPUTER AND RESEARCH FACILITIES
Campuswide Network? Yes
Internet Fee? No

EXPENSES/FINANCIAL AID
Annual Tuition (Resident/Nonresident): $3,168/$9,432
Tuition Per Credit (Resident/Nonresident): $88/$262
Room & Board (On/Off Campus): $18,520
Books and Supplies: $1,800
Average Grant: $1,000
Average Loan: $8,000
% Receiving Financial Aid: 20

ADMISSIONS INFORMATION
Application Fee: $35
Electronic Application? Yes
Regular Application Deadline: 8/1
Regular Notification: Rolling
Deferment Available? Yes

Length of Deferment: 12 months
Non-fall Admissions? Yes
Non-fall Application Deadline(s): 12/1, 5/1
Transfer Students Accepted? Yes
Transfer Policy: Final 24 semester hours earned at UHCL-SBPA
Need-Blind Admissions? Yes
Number of Applications Received: 214
% of Applicants Accepted: 79
% Accepted Who Enrolled: 77
Average GPA: 3.1
Average GMAT: 523
Average Years Experience: 5

INTERNATIONAL STUDENTS
TOEFL Required of International Students? Yes
Minimum TOEFL: 550 (213 computer)

EMPLOYMENT INFORMATION
Placement Office Available? Yes

UNIVERSITY OF ILLINOIS—CHICAGO
UIC MBA Program

Admissions Contact: Rita Rackauskas, Recruitment and Admissions Counselor
Address: 815 West Van Buren, Suite 220, Chicago, IL 60607
Admissions Phone: 312-996-4573 • **Admissions Fax:** 312-413-0338
Admissions E-mail: mba@uic.edu • **Web Address:** www.uic.edu/cba/mba

University of Illinois at Chicago caters to the demands of students' varying schedules and offers both full-time and part-time MBA programs. In addition, UI sends 8 to 12 students per semester off to foreign countries, including Germany, Mexico, France, and Malaysia, for unforgettable experiences working with companies such as Kellogg's, American Express, Deutsche Bank, and Nestle. Such foreign business opportunities may or may not be in conjunction with study abroad and typically last from six to nine months. Dual degrees, including an MBA/Master in Public Health and MBA/Doctor of Medicine, are also available.

INSTITUTIONAL INFORMATION
Public/Private: Public
Evening Classes Available? Yes
Student/Faculty Ratio: 30:1
Students in Parent Institution: 24,865
Academic Calendar: Semester

PROGRAMS
Degrees Offered: MBA (54 credits, full time or part time, 2-6 years)
Combined Degrees: MBA/MSA (68 credits, full time or part time, 2.5-6 years), MBA/MPH (70 credits, full time or part time, 2.5-6 years), MBA/MSN (67 credits, full time or part time, 2-6 years), MBA/MA in Economics (72 credits, full time or part time, 2.5-6 years), MBA/MSMIS (70 credits, 2.5-6 years), MBA/MD (medical curriculum and 48 MBA credits, 5 years)
Academic Specialties: Same professors teaching full- and part-time programs; flexible pace for students; can switch between full and part time to accommodate individual schedule; day, evening, and online courses available
Special Opportunities: WU WEIN, Austria; ESC Normandie, France; Leeds Metropolitan University, United Kingdom. Summer programs: Know Europe, Doing Business in Brazil, Know Korea
Study Abroad Options: Austria, Brazil, France, Korea, United Kingdom

STUDENT INFORMATION

Total Business Students: 499
% Full Time: 40
% Female: 39
% Minority: 19
% International: 30
Average Age: 28

COMPUTER AND RESEARCH FACILITIES

Research Facilities: Center for Urban Business, Family Business Council, Insitute for Entrepreneurial Studies, Thursday Business Forum
Computer Facilities: Multiple on-campus computer labs; UIC website that offers access to much individual class information from remote locations as well; on-campus labs that offer: SPSS, OmniPro, all current Office software
Campuswide Network? Yes
Internet Fee? No

EXPENSES/FINANCIAL AID

Annual Tuition (Resident/Nonresident): $11,078/$18,334
Tuition Per Credit (Resident/Nonresident): $462/$764
Room & Board (On/Off Campus): $9,900
Books and Supplies: $1,290

ADMISSIONS INFORMATION

Application Fee: $40
Electronic Application? Yes
Regular Application Deadline: 6/1
Regular Notification: Rolling
Deferment Available? Yes
Length of Deferment: 1 year
Non-fall Admissions? Yes
Non-fall Application Deadline(s): 10/15 spring, 4/1 summer; international applicants: 4/1 fall, 9/15 spring, 3/1 summer
Transfer Students Accepted? Yes
Transfer Policy: Need to apply and be accepted to the UIC MBA Program; can submit transcripts from previous coursework with a grade of B or better and a course description; must be from an AACSB-accredited institution; maximum of 24 semester hours may transfer
Need-Blind Admissions? Yes
Number of Applications Received: 568
% of Applicants Accepted: 59
% Accepted Who Enrolled: 53
Average GPA: 3.1
Average GMAT: 580
Average Years Experience: 5
Other Schools to Which Students Applied: DePaul University, Northwestern University, University of Chicago

INTERNATIONAL STUDENTS

TOEFL Required of International Students? Yes
Minimum TOEFL: 570 (230 computer)

EMPLOYMENT INFORMATION

Placement Office Available? Yes
% Employed Within 3 Months: 82

UNIVERSITY OF ILLINOIS— URBANA-CHAMPAIGN
College of Business

Admissions Contact: Brian Deverman, Assistant Director of Admissions and Marketing
Address: 410 David Kinley Hall, Urbana, IL 61820
Admissions Phone: 217-244-7602 • **Admissions Fax:** 217-333-1156
Admissions E-mail: mba@uiuc.edu • **Web Address:** www.mba.uiuc.edu

Because the University of Illinois's MBA program boasts a "huge international population," one benefit of coming here is that you can almost "study abroad without going abroad." At the least, students tell us you'll come away with "very cool global business experience." Illinois's "integrated" first-year curriculum allows for seriously "hands-on" learning, and the Office for the Study of Business Issues allows MBAs to work with engineers and entrepreneurs to evaluate the commercial potential of their innovations.

INSTITUTIONAL INFORMATION

Public/Private: Public
Evening Classes Available? No
Total Faculty: 139
% Faculty Female: 21
% Faculty Minority: 21
% Faculty Part Time: 6
Student/Faculty Ratio: 3:1
Students in Parent Institution: 36,936
Academic Calendar: Semester

PROGRAMS

Degrees Offered: PhD (4-5 years), with programs in Accountancy, Information Systems, International Business, Management Science/Process Management, Marketing, Organizational Behavior, Strategic Management and Policy, Economics, Finance
Combined Degrees: MBA/MA in Architecture (2 years), MBA/MS in Computer Science (2.5 years), MBA/MS in Civil and Environmental Engineering (2.5 years), MBA/MS in Electrical Engineering (2.5 years), MBA/MSIE (2.5 years), MBA/MS in Mechanical Engineering (2.5 years), MBA/MS in Medicine (5 years), MBA/MS in Journalism (2.5 years), MBA/MS in Law (4 years), MBA/MS in Human Resource Education (2.5 years), Custom-Designed joint degree (2.5 years)
Academic Specialties: Finance, Marketing, MIS; adding Business Management and Operations for Fall 2003. Completely intergrated 1st year; both Global Tycoon computer simulation "game" and team-consulting competition (ABP) during first year; Techno-MBA program; Office for Strategic Business Initiatives offers students hands-on consulting experience; nationally recognized Food & Brand Lab; study abroad
Special Opportunities: Custom Executive Development Program
Study Abroad Options: Brazil; Canada; Denmark; Ecole Superieure des Sciences Economiques et Commerciales (ESSEC), France; Graduate School of Management, Leipzig, Germany; the Netherlands; Norway; Phillippines; Escuela Superior de Admin. y Direccion de Empresas (ESADG), Spain; Manchester, United Kingdom. Students can study in virtually any country through university-to-university agreements arranged through the University Study Abroad Office. The MBA program has formalized agreements with MBA programs in the partnering countries listed.

STUDENT INFORMATION

Total Business Students: 367
% Full Time: 100
% Female: 30
% Minority: 29
% Out of State: 45
% International: 45
Average Age: 27

COMPUTER AND RESEARCH FACILITIES

Research Facilities: NSCA, RTMO (technology transfer), OIM, LIS, CCSO, Commerce Reference Library

Computer Facilities: Each MBA student is required to have a laptop computer, for which high-speed ethernet ports are available in all MBA classrooms and in a variety of computer labs in the College of Commerce and Business Administration (CCBA) and across campus. In addition, there is an MBA Computer Lab, a College of Commerce and Business Administration Computer LAB (OIM), and a large variety of all-campus computer labs. Students also have access to the extensive University modem pool.

Databases and resources available online: ABI/Inform Global Edition, AICPA-JAATP, AICPA-Prof Standards, AICPA-AAG, Business & Industry, CitiBase, Disclosure Database, EconLit, FAST-FARS, Pricewaterhouse-Researcher, Lexis-Nexis, RIA OnPoint, World Data, World Development Indicators. Full-text article databases are available through the Commerce WWW: ABI/Inform, EconLit, Wilson. Bridge systems are available throughout OIM and in selected spots within CCBA. Web-based resources: OneSource (http://www.onesource.com, US Business Browser), Zack's Financial Database. Mainframe databases: Compustat, CRSP, Global Vantage, IBES, NIKKEI, PACAP Database for Japan

Campuswide Network? Yes

% of MBA Classrooms Wired: 100

Computer Model Recommended: Laptop

Internet Fee? No

EXPENSES/FINANCIAL AID

Annual Tuition (Resident/Nonresident): $13,764/$22,688

Room & Board (On/Off Campus): $8,200

Books and Supplies: $1,250

Average Grant: $7,000

Average Loan: $18,000

ADMISSIONS INFORMATION

Application Fee: $40

Electronic Application? Yes

Early Decision Application Deadline: 12/15

Early Decision Notification: 2/15

Regular Application Deadline: 4/1

Regular Notification: Rolling

Deferment Available? Yes

Length of Deferment: 1 year

Non-fall Admissions? No

Transfer Students Accepted? Yes

Transfer Policy: A student can transfer up to 3 units or 12 hours, subject to review.

Need-Blind Admissions? Yes

Number of Applications Received: 1,157

% of Applicants Accepted: 31

% Accepted Who Enrolled: 46

Average GPA: 3.3

GPA Range: 2.9-3.5

Average GMAT: 640

GMAT Range: 550-660

Average Years Experience: 4

Other Admissions Factors Considered: Work experience, interships, military experience

Minority/Disadvantaged Student Recruitment Programs: Preview Weekends, MBA Saturdays, Value the an MBA program

Other Schools to Which Students Applied: Indiana University, Northwestern University, Purdue University, University of Chicago, University of Michigan, University of Wisconsin—Madison, Washington University in St. Louis

INTERNATIONAL STUDENTS

TOEFL Required of International Students? Yes

Minimum TOEFL: 620 (260 computer)

EMPLOYMENT INFORMATION

Placement Office Available? Yes

% Employed Within 3 Months: 96

Fields Employing Percentage of Grads: MIS (3%), Human Resources (4%), Other (8%), Operations (8%), General Management (11%), Accounting (11%), Consulting (12%), Marketing (17%), Finance (26%)

Frequent Employers: Accenture, Agilent Technologies, Aquila, AT&T, Deloitte Consulting, Dynegy, Ford Motor Co., Samsung

Prominent Alumni: Mike Tokarz, general partner, Kohlberg, Kravis & Roberts; Tom Siebel, founder, chairman and CEO, Siebel Systems, Inc.; Jan Klug, vice president, global marketing, Ford Motor Co.; Mark Hogan, president, E-GM, group vice president, General Motors Corp.; Steve Vivian, investment manager, Prism

UNIVERSITY OF IOWA
Henry B. Tippie School of Management

Admissions Contact: Admissions Office, Director of MBA Admissions and Financial Aid
Address: 108 John Pappajohn Business Building, Iowa City, IA 52242-1000
Admissions Phone: 319-335-1039 • **Admissions Fax:** 319-335-3604
Admissions E-mail: iowamba@uiowa.edu • **Web Address:** www.biz.uiowa.edu/mba

The "immensely talented and cooperative" students at the University of Iowa say theirs is "an MBA program on the rise." Iowa boasts an "incredibly advanced" facility complete "with the latest multimedia," a "fantastic" administration, and an "ever-improving atmosphere." Finance is probably the strongest discipline here, thanks to innovative programs like "the Applied Securities Management program, which allows students to apply classroom ideas to manage real portfolios."

INSTITUTIONAL INFORMATION

Public/Private: Public

Evening Classes Available? Yes

Total Faculty: 142

% Faculty Female: 21

% Faculty Minority: 15

% Faculty Part Time: 30

Student/Faculty Ratio: 5:1

Students in Parent Institution: 29,697

Academic Calendar: Semester

PROGRAMS

Degrees Offered: MBA (21 months), MACC (9-21 months, depending on undergraduate degree), PhD in Business Administration (4 years), PhD in Economics (4 years)

Combined Degrees: MBA programs with Law (4 years), Hospital and Health Administration (2.5 years), Library Science (3 years), Nursing (3 years), Medicine (5 years)

Academic Specialties: Finance/Investments, Marketing, Enterpreneurship, Accounting, Management Information Systems. The curriculum effectively combines lecture, case analyses, and field projects. The curriculum is designed to give students the opportunity during the second semester to begin coursework in their area of concentration.

Special Opportunities: Summer internship programs, consulting projects (in United States and abroad)

Study Abroad Options: Wirtschafts University, Vienna, Austria; Johann Wolfgang Goethe University, Germany; American College of Thessaloniki, Greece; Budapest University of Economic Sciences & Public Administration, Hungary; programs developing in Germany; the Netherlands; and Mt. Eliza Business School, Australia

STUDENT INFORMATION

Total Business Students: 856

% Full Time: 17
% Female: 19
% Minority: 3
% Out of State: 68
% International: 43
Average Age: 27

COMPUTER AND RESEARCH FACILITIES

Research Facilities: Pappajohn Enterpreneurial Center, Iowa Electronic Markets, Behavioral Research Laboratory, Small Business Development Center, Iowa Institute for International Business, Pomerantz Business Library, Economic Research Institute, Hawkinson Institute of Business Finance, Stead Technology Services Group
Computer Facilities: Computing laboratories are available in the John Pappajohn Business Building as well as throughout the campus. A computer laboratory is set aside for MBA students within the building. Extensive software and hardware is provided, including Bloomberg, Lexis-Nexis, Dow-Jones News Retrieval, Wharton Research Data Services (WRDS).
Campuswide Network? Yes
% of MBA Classrooms Wired: 100
Internet Fee? No

EXPENSES/FINANCIAL AID

Annual Tuition (Resident/Nonresident): $10,050/$18,362
Tuition Per Credit (Resident/Nonresident): $387
Room & Board (On/Off Campus): $8,000/$11,000
Books and Supplies: $1,400
Average Grant: $2,598
% Receiving Financial Aid: 53
% Receiving Aid Their First Year: 49

ADMISSIONS INFORMATION

Application Fee: $30
Electronic Application? Yes
Early Decision Application Deadline: 12/15
Regular Application Deadline: 7/15
Regular Notification: Rolling
Length of Deferment: 1 year
Non-fall Application Deadline(s): 11/1 spring evening
Transfer Policy: Maximum of 9 credits from AACSB-accredited program
Need-Blind Admissions? Yes
Number of Applications Received: 501
% of Applicants Accepted: 38
% Accepted Who Enrolled: 41
Average GPA: 3.3
GPA Range: 3.0-3.6
Average GMAT: 638
GMAT Range: 610-680
Average Years Experience: 3
Other Admissions Factors Considered: Management and business experience, demonstrated leadership abilities
Minority/Disadvantaged Student Recruitment Programs: Financial aid, Minority MBA Association; financial aid available due to a FIPSE grant to the Iowa Electronic Markets' initiative to promote knowledge of markets among minority students
Other Schools to Which Students Applied: Indiana University, Purdue University, University of Illinois, University of Minnesota, University of Wisconsin—Madison

INTERNATIONAL STUDENTS

TOEFL Required of International Students? Yes
Minimum TOEFL: 600 (250 computer)

EMPLOYMENT INFORMATION

Placement Office Available? Yes
% Employed Within 3 Months: 94

Fields Employing Percentage of Grads: Other (4%), General Management (4%), MIS (4%), Consulting (7%), Marketing (33%), Finance (48%)
Frequent Employers: AEGON, USA, Inc; Allstate Corp., Allsteel Inc.; Best Buy Co.; CitCards; General Electric Co.; International Truck & Engine Corp.; John Deere Credit Co.; Kimberly-Clark Corp.; Kraft Foods Inc.; Maytag Corp.; NCS Pearson; Principal Financial Group Inc.; Procter & Gamble Co.; Rockwell-Collins, Inc.
Prominent Alumni: Steven L. Caves, president, Firstar Bank Iowa (banking); Kathleen A. Dore, president, The Bravo Networks (entertainment); Kerry Killinger, chairman, president, and CEO, Washington Mutual Savings Bank; Michael Maves, M.D., CEO, American Medic; Ted E. Ziemann, Cargill Health & Food

See page 456.

UNIVERSITY OF KANSAS
School of Business

Admissions Contact: Dee Steinle, Associate Director of Master's Programs
Address: 206 Summerfield Hall, Lawrence, KS 66045
Admissions Phone: 785-864-3844 • **Admissions Fax:** 785-864-5328
Admissions E-mail: bschoolgrad@ku.edu • **Web Address:** www.business.ku.edu

The management program is king at the University of Kansas School of Business, and the "highly competitive" and "ambitious" students here tell us that "the KU MBA program provides a great education for the money." The campus is "beautiful" as well, and Lawrence is by all accounts an "ideal college town." When life gets dull, students can head to the more bustling metropolis of Kansas City, "which is only 30 minutes away and has a lot to offer."

INSTITUTIONAL INFORMATION

Public/Private: Public
Evening Classes Available? Yes
Total Faculty: 55
% Faculty Female: 16
% Faculty Minority: 12
% Faculty Part Time: 3
Student/Faculty Ratio: 8:1
Students in Parent Institution: 26,894
Academic Calendar: Semester

PROGRAMS

Degrees Offered: MBA (2 years full time, 3 years part time), MS in Human Resources Management (1 year), MS in Organizational Behavior (1 year), MSIS (1 year with BS in Business, 2 years without BS in Business), MAIS (1 year with Bachelor's degree in Accounting, 2 years without Bachelor's degree in Accounting)
Combined Degrees: JD/MBA (4 years)
Academic Specialties: Strengths of faculty include strong research and consulting records and a genuine commitment to teaching.
Study Abroad Options: Brazil, England, France, Italy, Japan

STUDENT INFORMATION

Total Business Students: 477
% Full Time: 21
% Female: 31
% Minority: 1
% Out of State: 33
% International: 25
Average Age: 28

COMPUTER AND RESEARCH FACILITIES

Research Facilities: Watson Library plus 12 additional on-campus libraries, with total holdings of 3,292,923 volumes; 2,797,658 microforms; 33,051 current periodical subscriptions. CD player(s) available for graduate student use; access provided to online bibliographic retrieval services and online databases
Campuswide Network? Yes
Internet Fee? No

EXPENSES/FINANCIAL AID

Annual Tuition (Resident/Nonresident): $3,434/$11,212
Books and Supplies: $800
Average Grant: $1,200

ADMISSIONS INFORMATION

Application Fee: $60
Electronic Application? Yes
Regular Application Deadline: 4/1
Regular Notification: Rolling
Deferment Available? Yes
Length of Deferment: 1 year
Non-fall Admissions? Yes
Non-fall Application Deadline(s): 10/1 spring
Transfer Students Accepted? Yes
Transfer Policy: Maximum of 6 credit hours
Need-Blind Admissions? Yes
Number of Applications Received: 124
% of Applicants Accepted: 73
% Accepted Who Enrolled: 64
Average GPA: 3.3
GPA Range: 3.1-3.5
Average GMAT: 606
GMAT Range: 540-690
Average Years Experience: 1
Minority/Disadvantaged Student Recruitment Programs: Some scholarship money is available to minority students. Recruiting is conducted at MBA Forums, local employer fairs, and paid ads in certain minority magazines, such as *Minority MBA Magazine*.
Other Schools to Which Students Applied: University of Iowa, University of Missouri—Columbia, Iowa State University, University of Oklahoma, University of Nebraska—Lincoln

INTERNATIONAL STUDENTS

TOEFL Required of International Students? Yes
Minimum TOEFL: 600 (250 computer)

EMPLOYMENT INFORMATION

Placement Office Available? Yes
% Employed Within 3 Months: 86
Fields Employing Percentage of Grads: General Management (6%), MIS (6%), Marketing (6%), Finance (19%), Other (29%), Consulting (32%)
Frequent Employers: Accenture, Andersen Consulting, Aquila, Cap Gemini, Cerner, Deloitte Consulting, Payless ShoeSource, Sprint

UNIVERSITY OF KENTUCKY
Gatton College of Business and Economics

Admissions Contact: Dr. Fred Morgan, MBA Director
Address: 145 Carol Martin Gatton College of Business and Economics, Lexington, KY 40506-0034
Admissions Phone: 859-257-5889 • **Admissions Fax:** 859-323-9971
Admissions E-mail: fwmorg1@uky.edu • **Web Address:** gatton.uky.edu

The MBA program at the University of Kentucky offers two distinct tracks: a business track for students with undergraduate business degrees and a nonbusiness track for everybody else. Each can be completed in three semesters, but the business track is a lot more flexible. Students here say one of the main advantages of UK is its location: a "safe" college town in a region of strong economic growth. When monotony sets in, more metropolitan Louisville is a short drive away.

INSTITUTIONAL INFORMATION

Public/Private: Public
Evening Classes Available? Yes
Total Faculty: 73
% Faculty Female: 25
Student/Faculty Ratio: 5:1
Students in Parent Institution: 32,549
Academic Calendar: Semester

PROGRAMS

Degrees Offered: PhD in Business Administration (4 years), PhD in Economics (4 years), MS in Economics (2 years), MSA (1 year)
Combined Degrees: MBA/JD (4 years), BS in Engineering/MBA (5 years), MD/MBA (5 years), PharmD/MBA (4 years)
Academic Specialties: School of Management: DSIS, Finance, Management/Organizational Behavior, Marketing; School of Accountancy, Department of Economics: concentrations in International Business, Management Information Systems, Marketing Distribution, Finance, Real Estate and Banking, Accounting, Corporate Finance
Special Opportunities: Internships, Summer Study Abroad
Study Abroad Options: RMIT Melbourne, Australia; Wu-Wien, Austria; Lancaster University, England; ESC-Grenoble and ESC-Dijon, France; Heidelburg, Germany; Italy; ISEP schools worldwide (200 through Study Abroad Office)

STUDENT INFORMATION

Total Business Students: 233
% Full Time: 64
% Female: 31
% Minority: 14
% Out of State: 24
% International: 10
Average Age: 26

COMPUTER AND RESEARCH FACILITIES

Research Facilities: 7 centers: Center for Business and Economics Research, Center for Business Development, Small Business Development Center, Center for Labor Educaton and Research, Real Estate Studies, International Business and Management Center, Center for Entrepreneurial Studies
Computer Facilities: On-campus Computing Center has several high-level systems supporting research and networking; the College Business Information Center offers state-of-the-art business-database access and terminals. Various sites around campus offer students computer access.
Campuswide Network? Yes
% of MBA Classrooms Wired: 100
Internet Fee? No

EXPENSES/FINANCIAL AID

Annual Tuition (Resident/Nonresident): $3,610/$10,830
Tuition Per Credit (Resident/Nonresident): $201/$602
Room & Board (On/Off Campus): $6,500/$7,100
Books and Supplies: $800
Average Grant: $3,615
% Receiving Financial Aid: 35
% Receiving Aid Their First Year: 33

ADMISSIONS INFORMATION

Application Fee: $30
Electronic Application? Yes
Early Decision Notification: 4/1
Regular Application Deadline: 7/15
Regular Notification: Rolling
Deferment Available? Yes
Length of Deferment: 3 years
Non-fall Admissions? No
Transfer Students Accepted? Yes
Transfer Policy: Maximum of 9 hours
Need-Blind Admissions? Yes
Number of Applications Received: 296
% of Applicants Accepted: 45
% Accepted Who Enrolled: 80
Average GPA: 3.3
GPA Range: 3.1-3.7
Average GMAT: 613
GMAT Range: 580-670
Average Years Experience: 3
Other Admissions Factors Considered: Communication skills, international experience, work experience; TWE for foreign applicants: minimum score 4.5
Minority/Disadvantaged Student Recruitment Programs: Kentucky Scholars Program, Lyman T. Johnson Fellowships, Commonwealth Minority Scholarship Program, Academic Excellence
Other Schools to Which Students Applied: University of Tennessee—Knoxville, Ohio State University, Indiana University, Vanderbilt University, University of Georgia, University of Alabama—Birmingham, University of—Austin

INTERNATIONAL STUDENTS

TOEFL Required of International Students? Yes
Minimum TOEFL: 550 (213 computer)

EMPLOYMENT INFORMATION

Placement Office Available? Yes
% Employed Within 3 Months: 94
Fields Employing Percentage of Grads: Accounting (7%), General Management (9%), Consulting (9%), Operations (9%), Finance (9%), MIS (12%), Other (17%), Marketing (28%)
Frequent Employers: Accenture; Aegon; Aeronatautical Systems; Alcoa; Alltech; Analysts International; Arthur Andersen; ASAP Automation; Ashland Oil, Inc.; Bank One; Baird, Kurtz and Dobson; Black and Decker; Branch Banking and Trust; Brown Foreman; Brown & Williamson; Burke Research; Carpenter, Mountjoy & Bressler; Central Bank & Trust Co.; Central Baptist Hospital
Prominent Alumni: Paul Chellgren, CEO/chairman, Ashland, Inc.; Kim Hatch Burse, president/CEO, Louisville Devel-Bancorp; Edward Breathitt, former governor or Kentucky, politics/education; Bambang Sudibyo, former finance minister, Indonesia; Warren Rosenthal, restaurants/franchising

See page 458.

UNIVERSITY OF LOUISIANA—MONROE
College of Business Administration

Admissions Contact: Jacqueline O'Neal, Director, MBA Program
Address: 700 University Avenue, Monroe, LA 71209-0100
Admissions Phone: 318-342-1100 • Admissions Fax: 318-342-1101
Admissions E-mail: econeal@ulm.edu • Web Address: ele.ulm.edu/MBA/

Small class sizes, less than 100 students enrolled in the MBA program, and a diverse student makeup that's nearly one-third international: This is the UL Monroe experience. MBA applicants can enroll during any semester, take day or night classes, and study full time or part time, while full-time students will enjoy the benefit of completing their MBA program in only one year. UL Monroe offers standard academic concentrations in e-commerce, health care administration, and entrepreneurship and also makes the unique offer to study business with a concentration in gerontology. Located between Dallas, Texas, and Jackson, Mississippi, the university is accessible to all neighboring states and their businesses.

INSTITUTIONAL INFORMATION

Public/Private: Public
Evening Classes Available? Yes
Total Faculty: 34
Student/Faculty Ratio: 2:1
Students in Parent Institution: 10,942
Academic Calendar: Semester

PROGRAMS

Degrees Offered: MBA (1 year full time, 2 years part time), with concentrations in Entrepreneurship, Health Care Administration, E-Commerce, Gerontology
Academic Specialties: Case studies, computer-aided instruction, computer analysis, computer simulations, faculty seminars, group discussion, research, student presentations, study groups, team projects

STUDENT INFORMATION

Total Business Students: 78
% Full Time: 81
% Female: 40
% Minority: 5
% Out of State: 14
% International: 32
Average Age: 27

COMPUTER AND RESEARCH FACILITIES

Campuswide Network? Yes
Internet Fee? No

EXPENSES/FINANCIAL AID

Annual Tuition (Resident/Nonresident): $1,900/$7,858
Room & Board (On/Off Campus): $2,560
Books and Supplies: $600
Average Grant: $5,000
Average Loan: $5,000

ADMISSIONS INFORMATION

Application Fee: $20
Electronic Application? No
Regular Application Deadline: 7/1
Regular Notification: 7/15
Deferment Available? Yes
Length of Deferment: 1 year
Non-fall Admissions? Yes
Non-fall Application Deadline(s): 11/1 spring, 4/1 summer I, 5/1 summer II
Transfer Students Accepted? Yes
Transfer Policy: Varies according to individual

Need-Blind Admissions? No
Number of Applications Received: 57
% of Applicants Accepted: 79
% Accepted Who Enrolled: 78
Average GPA: 3.0
GPA Range: 2.2-4.0
Average GMAT: 500
GMAT Range: 390-710
Other Admissions Factors Considered: Work experience

INTERNATIONAL STUDENTS

TOEFL Required of International Students? Yes
Minimum TOEFL: 480 (157 computer)

EMPLOYMENT INFORMATION

Placement Office Available? Yes

UNIVERSITY OF LOUISVILLE
College of Business and Public Administration

Admissions Contact: Dr. Audrey Kline, Associate Dean for Academic Programs
Address: CBPA Dean's Office, Louisville, KY 40292
Admissions Phone: 502-852-6440 • Admissions Fax: 502-852-7557
Admissions E-mail: audrey.kline@louisville.edu • Web Address: cbpa.louisville.edu/

INSTITUTIONAL INFORMATION

Public/Private: Public
Evening Classes Available? No
Total Faculty: 75
% Faculty Female: 19
% Faculty Minority: 25
% Faculty Part Time: 15
Student/Faculty Ratio: 30:1
Students in Parent Institution: 21,089
Academic Calendar: Semester

PROGRAMS

Degrees Offered: MBA (1-6 years), ME/MBA (minimum 3 years),Integrative MBA (2 years), JD/MBA (4 years)
Study Abroad Options: Germany

STUDENT INFORMATION

Total Business Students: 675
% Full Time: 32
% Female: 37
% Minority: 12
% Out of State: 38
% International: 36
Average Age: 30

COMPUTER AND RESEARCH FACILITIES

Campuswide Network? Yes
% of MBA Classrooms Wired: 100
Computer Model Recommended: Laptop
Internet Fee? No

EXPENSES/FINANCIAL AID

Annual Tuition (Resident/Nonresident): $8,884/$24,472
Tuition Per Credit (Resident/Nonresident): $247/$680
Books and Supplies: $900

Average Grant: $2,000
% Receiving Financial Aid: 2

ADMISSIONS INFORMATION

Application Fee: $25
Electronic Application? No
Regular Application Deadline: Rolling
Regular Notification: Rolling
Deferment Available? Yes
Non-fall Admissions? No
Transfer Students Accepted? No
Need-Blind Admissions? No
Number of Applications Received: 345
% of Applicants Accepted: 74
% Accepted Who Enrolled: 97
Average GPA: 3.5
Average GMAT: 564

INTERNATIONAL STUDENTS

TOEFL Required of International Students? Yes
Minimum TOEFL: 550

EMPLOYMENT INFORMATION

Placement Office Available? Yes

UNIVERSITY OF MAINE
Maine Business School

Admissions Contact: Mary Cady, Assistant to the Director of Graduate Programs
Address: 5723 DP Corbett Business Building, Orono, ME 04469-5723
Admissions Phone: 207-581-1973 • Admissions Fax: 207-581-1930
Admissions E-mail: mba@maine.edu • Web Address: www.umaine.edu/business

The University of Maine's MBA class size is less than 100 students, enabling the university's focus on student-centered learning to hold true. MBA applicants to the Maine Business School, who come from a great variety of backgrounds, can matriculate in the fall, spring, or summer, allowing for flexibility with the student's schedule. The MBA program provides students with a business education that's both broad and deep and is designed to "equip the candidate with concepts, analytical tools, and supervisory skills" necessary to hold responsible management positions.

INSTITUTIONAL INFORMATION

Public/Private: Public
Evening Classes Available? Yes
Total Faculty: 20
% Faculty Female: 50
Student/Faculty Ratio: 12:1
Students in Parent Institution: 10,282
Academic Calendar: Semester

PROGRAMS

Degrees Offered: MBA (12-24 months full time, up to 6 years part time), MSA (12-24 months full time, up to 6 years part time)
Academic Specialties: Electives continually change with current business trends; small classes with group work and presentations; small faculty-student ratio; latest classroom technology

STUDENT INFORMATION

Total Business Students: 95
% Full Time: 42

% Female: 52
% Minority: 18
% Out of State: 40
% International: 30
Average Age: 30

COMPUTER AND RESEARCH FACILITIES

Computer Facilities: Computer lab exclusively for business students is located in Business Building where all classes meet and is open at convenient hours for graduate students; other computer facilities in library, student union
Campuswide Network? Yes
% of MBA Classrooms Wired: 50
Internet Fee? No

EXPENSES/FINANCIAL AID

Annual Tuition (Resident/Nonresident): $3,780/$10,728
Tuition Per Credit (Resident/Nonresident): $210/$596
Room & Board (On/Off Campus): $5,728
Books and Supplies: $600
Average Grant: $2,500

ADMISSIONS INFORMATION

Application Fee: $50
Electronic Application? No
Regular Application Deadline: 2/1
Regular Notification: 3/1
Deferment Available? Yes
Length of Deferment: 1 year
Non-fall Admissions? Yes
Non-fall Application Deadline(s): 12/1 spring
Transfer Students Accepted? Yes
Transfer Policy: A maximum of 6 hours accepted from accredited schools with approval
Need-Blind Admissions? Yes
Number of Applications Received: 23
% of Applicants Accepted: 100
% Accepted Who Enrolled: 96
Average GPA: 3.2
Average GMAT: 530
Average Years Experience: 6

INTERNATIONAL STUDENTS

TOEFL Required of International Students? Yes
Minimum TOEFL: 550 (213 computer)

EMPLOYMENT INFORMATION

Placement Office Available? No

Student/Faculty Ratio: 24:1
Students in Parent Institution: 22,000
Academic Calendar: 11-month

PROGRAMS

Degrees Offered: MBA (11 months full time, 3-6 years part time)

STUDENT INFORMATION

Total Business Students: 102
% Full Time: 16
% Female: 37
% Minority: 1
% Out of State: 1
% International: 3
Average Age: 31

COMPUTER AND RESEARCH FACILITIES

Campuswide Network? Yes
Internet Fee? No

EXPENSES/FINANCIAL AID

% Receiving Financial Aid: 6

ADMISSIONS INFORMATION

Application Fee: $50
Electronic Application? No
Regular Application Deadline: 5/1
Regular Notification: Rolling
Deferment Available? No
Non-fall Admissions? No
Transfer Students Accepted? No
Need-Blind Admissions? No
Number of Applications Received: 94
% of Applicants Accepted: 50
% Accepted Who Enrolled: 64
Other Admissions Factors Considered: Computer experience
Other Schools to Which Students Applied: California State Polytechnic University—Pomona, University of Missouri—Kansas City, California State University—Los Angeles

INTERNATIONAL STUDENTS

TOEFL Required of International Students? Yes
Minimum TOEFL: 550

EMPLOYMENT INFORMATION

Placement Office Available? Yes
% Employed Within 3 Months: 100

UNIVERSITY OF MANITOBA
Asper School of Business

Admissions Contact: Charlene Okell, MBA Program Manager
Address: 268 Drake Center, Winnipeg, MB R3T 5V4 Canada
Admissions Phone: 204-474-8448 • **Admissions Fax:** 204-474-7529
Admissions E-mail: Asper_Grad@UManitoba.ca
Web Address: www.umanitoba.ca/management/mbapage.html

INSTITUTIONAL INFORMATION

Public/Private: Public
Evening Classes Available? No
Total Faculty: 70

UNIVERSITY OF MARYLAND— COLLEGE PARK
Robert H. Smith School of Business

Admissions Contact: Sabrina White, Director MBA & MS Admissions
Address: 2308 Van Munching Hall, University of Maryland, College Park, MD 20742-1871
Admissions Phone: 301-405-2278 • **Admissions Fax:** 301-314-9862
Admissions E-mail: mba_info@rhsmith.umd.edu • **Web Address:** www.rhsmith.umd.edu

Registration, billing, and everything else is online at the University of Maryland's state-of-the-art School of Business, where there is a "strong technology emphasis." The "intelligent, fun, and personable" students here "are of exceptional character," and "the business school is like a campus in itself: tight-knit, easy to get to know others," and boasting many of the assets of a smaller school. Nearby Washington, D.C., "Mecca for high tech" and government, "provides plenty of cultural, political, and nightlife activities."

INSTITUTIONAL INFORMATION

Public/Private: Public
Evening Classes Available? Yes
Total Faculty: 177
% Faculty Female: 19
% Faculty Minority: 19
% Faculty Part Time: 31
Student/Faculty Ratio: 11:1
Students in Parent Institution: 33,000
Academic Calendar: Semester

PROGRAMS

Degrees Offered: MBA (54 credits, 18 months to 5 years), MS (30 credits, 1-5 years)
Combined Degrees: MBA/MS (66 credits, 21 months to 5 years), MBA/JD (108 credits, 3-5 years), MBA/Master of Public Management (66 credits, 2.3 to 5 years), MBA/MSW (88 credits, 2.3 to 5 years)
Academic Specialties: Recognizing technology's role in all business practices in today's digital economy, the Smith MBA program integrates technology across the curriculum—from the foundational business areas to the e-related areas. The Smith School faculty is grouped into 6 academic areas: Accounting and Information Assurance; Finance; Supply Chain Management, Logistics & Transportation; Decision & Information Technologies; Management & Organization (includes Entrepreneurship); and Marketing. Smith MBA elective areas include: Accounting and Information Assurance, Change and Organizational Management, E-Commerce, Entrepreneurship, Finance, Financial Engineering, Information Systems, International Business, Leadership Skill Development, Management and Consulting, Management of Human Capital, Management Science, Marketing, Strategy, and Supply Chain Management/Logistics. In addition, the Smith School offers the Netcentricity Laboratory, Center for e-Service, Netcentric Financial Markets Laboratory, MBA Consulting Program, Venture Fund Experience, Dingman Center for Entrepreneurship, Experiential Learning Modules (ELMs), and Marketing Curriculum.
Special Opportunities: The Smith School's Center for Global Business sponsors 7-10 day programs that combine seminars at a leading business school in a foreign country with visits to executives heading multinational companies and global organizations. In addition, the school is a member of the MBA Enterprise Corps, a consortium of leading U.S. business schools that recruits recently graduated MBAs to work in developing and transitional markets providing technical and managerial assistance to private enterprises. Smith graduates may apply through our Center for Global Business to the corps for 15-month assignments in Eastern Europe, the Commonwealth of Independent States, and Asia.
Study Abroad Options: Australia, China, Denmark, France, Germany, India, Italy, Norway, Spain, United Kingdom

STUDENT INFORMATION

Total Business Students: 1,258
% Full Time: 33
% Female: 31
% Minority: 16
% International: 37
Average Age: 26

COMPUTER AND RESEARCH FACILITIES

Research Facilities: In addition to those listed above: Office of Career Management, Office of Executive Education, Dingman Center for Entrepreneurship, Center for Global Business
Computer Facilities: The Smith School's computer facilities and resources include computing laboratories; Netcentricity Laboratory; Netcentric Financial Markets Laboratory; Supply Chain Management Laboratory; Center for e-Service; Center for Electronic Markets and Enterprises; Center for Human Capital, Innovation, and Technology; a dual-display advanced teaching theater; IT wire-

less access in the student lounges and public areas; and the Virtual Business Information Center (a collection of electronic and print business resources).
Campuswide Network? Yes
% of MBA Classrooms Wired: 100
Internet Fee? No

EXPENSES/FINANCIAL AID

Annual Tuition (Resident/Nonresident): $12,564/$20,700
Tuition Per Credit (Resident/Nonresident): $698/$1,150
Room & Board (On/Off Campus): $10,000
Books and Supplies: $5,000
Average Grant: $17,875
% Receiving Financial Aid: 39
% Receiving Aid Their First Year: 41

ADMISSIONS INFORMATION

Application Fee: $50
Electronic Application? Yes
Regular Application Deadline: Rolling
Regular Notification: Rolling
Deferment Available? Yes
Length of Deferment: 1 year
Non-fall Admissions? No
Transfer Students Accepted? No
Need-Blind Admissions? No
Number of Applications Received: 2,418
% of Applicants Accepted: 35
% Accepted Who Enrolled: 68
Average GPA: 3.4
GPA Range: 3.1-3.6
Average GMAT: 656
GMAT Range: 610-710
Average Years Experience: 5
Other Admissions Factors Considered: GMAT, GRE, work experience, letters of recommendation, essay response
Minority/Disadvantaged Student Recruitment Programs: Kaliedoscope: Advancing Diversity@Smith, a fall semester recruitment event for underrepresented minority students; online chats for prospective Latino students; presentations for various groups, including Society for Hispanic Professional Engineers, Women's Information Network, Graduate Women in Business, National Society for Black Engineers, and Black MBA Association events.
Other Schools to Which Students Applied: Carnegie Mellon, Georgetown University, University of North Carolina—Chapel Hill, University of Texas—Austin, Vanderbilt University

INTERNATIONAL STUDENTS

TOEFL Required of International Students? Yes
Minimum TOEFL: 600

EMPLOYMENT INFORMATION

Placement Office Available? Yes
% Employed Within 3 Months: 71
Fields Employing Percentage of Grads: Human Resources (1%), Operations (4%), General Management (5%), MIS (7%), Other (10%), Consulting (17%), Marketing (21%), Finance (33%)
Frequent Employers: Booz Allen Hamilton, Campbell Soup Co., Capital One, Citigroup/Citibank, Ernst & Young, Honeywell International, Intel, McKinsey, PepsiCo, SAIC, UBS Warburg, Washington Gas, World Bank
Prominent Alumni: Carly Fiorina, chairman and CEO, Hewlett Packard; James F. O'Brien, head coach, Boston Celtics; Harold Kahn, CEO, Macy's East; Thomas J. Healy, partner, Accenture

UNIVERSITY OF MASSACHUSETTS— AMHERST

Isenberg School of Management

Admissions Contact: MaryBeth Harris, Admissions Coordinator
Address: 305 Isenberg School of Management, UMASS, Amherst, MA 01003
Admissions Phone: 413-545-5608 • **Admissions Fax:** 413-577-2234
Admissions E-mail: gradprog@som.umass.edu • **Web Address:** www.umass.edu/mba

Professors are excellent and administrators are very supportive at the intimate Isenberg School of Management at the University of Massachusetts. "There's a good team spirit within the classes" here, and students who choose to specialize in finance and operations management have access to the Center for International Security and Derivatives Markets, a real-time trading room.

INSTITUTIONAL INFORMATION

Public/Private: Public
Evening Classes Available? Yes
Total Faculty: 55
% Faculty Female: 22
% Faculty Minority: 11
Student/Faculty Ratio: 8:1
Students in Parent Institution: 24,129
Academic Calendar: Semester

PROGRAMS

Degrees Offered: MBA (2 years), PhD (4 years), Professional MBA (2-4 years)
Combined Degrees: MBA/MS in Sport Management (2 years)
Academic Specialties: Research orientation of the faculty; the small, intimate nature of the program; the quality of educational material; presentation of a very committed faculty
Study Abroad Options: Rouen, France; Baden-Wurttemberg, Germany; Lund and Linkeoping, Sweden

STUDENT INFORMATION

Total Business Students: 312
% Full Time: 24
% Female: 43
% Minority: 7
% Out of State: 40
% International: 33
Average Age: 27

COMPUTER AND RESEARCH FACILITIES

Research Facilities: Massachusetts Small Business Development Center (MSBDC), Family Business Center, Center for International Security and Derivations Markets (CISDM), Massachusetts Institute for Social and Economic Research (MISER), Strategic Information Technology Center (SITEC), Electronic Enterprise Center (EEC), Graduate Business Association (GBA), Nonprofit Center
Computer Facilities: Facility completely rewired to category 6 Internet access; wireless network access points are available; 2 new Computer Labs have been added; a Video Conferencing Center is in place; 3 Case Classrooms with Internet connections at each seat are available; all classrooms are connected to the Internet; communications with students are further enhanced using flat-screen televisions located throughout the Isenberg School; a portal for all Isenberg School of Management undergraduate curriculum has been built; the MBA Professional Program curriculum is available online; portions of the undergraduate curriculum are online as well. Windows 2000, Office Professional 2000, and XP; InfoTrac; Compu-Stat; SAS; Lexis-Nexis; American Business Information-Company Directory; Standard & Poor's Corp.; SPSS; Systat; Minitab; and Peachtree Accounting are used throughout the school.
Campuswide Network? Yes
% of MBA Classrooms Wired: 100
Internet Fee? No

EXPENSES/FINANCIAL AID

Annual Tuition (Resident/Nonresident): $3,025/$11,385
Tuition Per Credit (Resident/Nonresident): $490
Room & Board (On/Off Campus): $5,215/$8,500
Books and Supplies: $2,000
Average Grant: $17,768
Average Loan: $9,832
% Receiving Financial Aid: 93
% Receiving Aid Their First Year: 88

ADMISSIONS INFORMATION

Application Fee: $40
Electronic Application? Yes
Regular Application Deadline: 2/1
Regular Notification: 3/15
Deferment Available? Yes
Length of Deferment: 1 year
Non-fall Admissions? No
Transfer Students Accepted? No
Need-Blind Admissions? Yes
Number of Applications Received: 214
% of Applicants Accepted: 32
% Accepted Who Enrolled: 62
Average GPA: 3.2
GPA Range: 3.0-3.4
Average GMAT: 615
GMAT Range: 560-740
Average Years Experience: 4
Other Admissions Factors Considered: We like to see at least 3 to 5 years of professional work experience, with 2 professional (rather than academic) letters of recommendation.
Minority/Disadvantaged Student Recruitment Programs: Diversity Recruitment Committee, including current Isenberg School students and administrators, meets regularly to design and implement effective strategies to continue development of diversity in the program.

INTERNATIONAL STUDENTS

TOEFL Required of International Students? Yes
Minimum TOEFL: 600 (250 computer)

EMPLOYMENT INFORMATION

Placement Office Available? Yes
% Employed Within 3 Months: 84
Fields Employing Percentage of Grads: Other (5%), Communications (5%), Human Resources (5%), Operations (10%), Accounting (10%), Marketing (14%), General Management (23%), Finance (28%)
Frequent Employers: Accenture; Avery Dennison; Baystate Health System; IBM; MassMutual; Morgan Stanley Dean Witter; Frito-Lay; Pricewaterhouse Coopers; Siemens, Inc.; Teradyne; Tillion, Inc.; United Technologies Corp.
Prominent Alumni: John P. Flavin, chaiman of the board, Flavin, Blake & Co. Inc.; Eugene M. Isenberg, chairmain and CEO, Nabors Industries, Inc.; Jayne A. McMellen, vice president, fund administration, State Street Bank & Trust Co. Inc.; John F. Smith, Jr., chairman of the board, General Motors Corp.; Michael Philipp, chairman and CEO, Deutsche Asset Management

UNIVERSITY OF MASSACHUSETTS— BOSTON
Graduate College of Management

Admissions Contact: Daniel Robb, Assistant Dean/Director of Graduate Programs
Address: 100 Morrissey Boulevard, Boston, MA 02125-3393
Admissions Phone: 617-287-7720 • **Admissions Fax:** 617-287-7725
Admissions E-mail: mba@umb.edu • **Web Address:** www.mgmt.umb.edu

INSTITUTIONAL INFORMATION
Public/Private: Public
Total Faculty: 49
% Faculty Female: 29
% Faculty Minority: 33
% Faculty Part Time: 5
Student/Faculty Ratio: 16:1
Academic Calendar: Semester

PROGRAMS
Degrees Offered: MBA (2 years full time, 3 years part time)
Combined Degrees: MBA/MS (joint degree with nursing; 3 years full time, 4 years part time)
Academic Specialties: Accounting, Finance, Human Resources, International Management, Environmental Management, Marketing, Information Systems, Operations, Internet Marketing
Study Abroad Options: Students can create study abroad opportunities in any country in collaboration with our International Office.

COMPUTER AND RESEARCH FACILITIES
Research Facilities: Environmental Business Technology Center, Center for Collaborative Leadership, Manufacturing Parntership, Small Business Development Center
Computer Facilities: Students have access to applicable and desired programs through license-sharing agreements owned by the University.
Campuswide Network? Yes
% of MBA Classrooms Wired: 15
Internet Fee? No

EXPENSES/FINANCIAL AID
Annual Tuition (Resident/Nonresident): $6,624/$14,488
Tuition Per Credit (Resident/Nonresident): $108/$367
Room & Board (On/Off Campus): $10,000
Books and Supplies: $900
Average Loan: $10,000

EMPLOYMENT INFORMATION
Placement Office Available? Yes

UNIVERSITY OF MASSACHUSETTS— LOWELL
College of Management

Admissions Contact: Duncan G. LaBay, PhD, Management Graduate Programs Director
Address: 1 University Avenue, Lowell, MA 01854-2881
Admissions Phone: 978-934-2848 • **Admissions Fax:** 978-934-4017
Admissions E-mail: mba_mms@uml.edu
Web Address: www.uml.edu/college/management/

INSTITUTIONAL INFORMATION
Public/Private: Public
Evening Classes Available? No
Total Faculty: 35
% Faculty Part Time: 11
Student/Faculty Ratio: 25:1
Students in Parent Institution: 12,350

PROGRAMS
Degrees Offered: MBA (42 credits, full time or part-time, 2.5 to 4 years), MMS in Manufacturing (33 credits, full time or part time, 2-4 years)
Academic Specialties: Case study, lecture, seminars by members of the business community, student presentations, team projects

STUDENT INFORMATION
Total Business Students: 322
% Full Time: 9
% Female: 32
% Minority: 4
% International: 6
Average Age: 28

COMPUTER AND RESEARCH FACILITIES
Research Facilities: Lydon Library plus 1 additional on-campus library; 388,712 volumes; 611,799 microforms; 3,425 current periodicals. CD players available; access provided to online bibliographic retrieval services
Campuswide Network? Yes
% of MBA Classrooms Wired: 100
Internet Fee? No

EXPENSES/FINANCIAL AID
Annual Tuition (Resident/Nonresident): $1,600/$6,400
Tuition Per Credit (Resident/Nonresident): $91/$357
Books and Supplies: $1,000
% Receiving Financial Aid: 5
% Receiving Aid Their First Year: 2

ADMISSIONS INFORMATION
Application Fee: $20
Electronic Application? No
Regular Application Deadline: Rolling
Regular Notification: Rolling
Deferment Available? No
Non-fall Admissions? Yes
Non-fall Application Deadline(s): 11/1 spring
Transfer Students Accepted? No
Need-Blind Admissions? No
Number of Applications Received: 181
% of Applicants Accepted: 83
% Accepted Who Enrolled: 84
Average GPA: 3.3
Average GMAT: 525
Average Years Experience: 5

INTERNATIONAL STUDENTS

TOEFL Required of International Students? Yes
Minimum TOEFL: 550

EMPLOYMENT INFORMATION

Placement Office Available? Yes
% Employed Within 3 Months: 90

UNIVERSITY OF MEMPHIS
Fogelman College of Business and Economics

Admissions Contact: Carol Danehower, Director of Master's Programs
Address: Graduate School Administration Building, Room 216, Memphis, TN 38152-3370
Admissions Phone: 901-678-2911 • **Admissions Fax:** 901-678-5023
Admissions E-mail: gradsch@memphis.edu • **Web Address:** www.fcbe.memphis.edu

INSTITUTIONAL INFORMATION

Public/Private: Public
Evening Classes Available? No
Total Faculty: 130
% Faculty Female: 22
% Faculty Minority: 24
% Faculty Part Time: 27
Student/Faculty Ratio: 30:1
Students in Parent Institution: 20,332
Academic Calendar: Semester

PROGRAMS

Degrees Offered: MBA (33-54 credits, 1-6 years), EMBA (48 credits, 22 months), International MBA (56 credits, 22 months), MSBA (33 credits, 1-6 years), MSA (30-51 credits, 1-6 years), MA in Economics (33 credits, 1-6 years), MS in Electronic Commerce (33 credits, 1-6 years)
Combined Degrees: MBA/JD (54 credits, 4 years)

STUDENT INFORMATION

Total Business Students: 645
% Full Time: 54
% Female: 2
% Minority: 43
% International: 77
Average Age: 29

COMPUTER AND RESEARCH FACILITIES

Campuswide Network? Yes
Internet Fee? No

EXPENSES/FINANCIAL AID

Annual Tuition (Resident/Nonresident): $3,964/$8,968
Tuition Per Credit (Resident/Nonresident): $228/$506
Room & Board (On/Off Campus): $3,000/$8,000
Books and Supplies: $10,000

ADMISSIONS INFORMATION

Application Fee: $25
Electronic Application? No
Regular Application Deadline: 8/1
Regular Notification: Rolling
Deferment Available? Yes
Non-fall Admissions? Yes
Non-fall Application Deadline(s): 12/1, 5/1

Transfer Students Accepted? No
Need-Blind Admissions? No
Number of Applications Received: 694
% of Applicants Accepted: 64
% Accepted Who Enrolled: 73
Average GPA: 3.2
GPA Range: 2.7-3.0
Average GMAT: 530
GMAT Range: 430-500
Other Admissions Factors Considered: Essay, undergraduate GPA (transcripts), personal statement

INTERNATIONAL STUDENTS

TOEFL Required of International Students? Yes
Minimum TOEFL: 550 (213 computer)

EMPLOYMENT INFORMATION

Placement Office Available? Yes
% Employed Within 3 Months: 90

UNIVERSITY OF MIAMI
School of Business Administration

Admissions Contact: Susan Gerrish, Associate Director
Address: PO Box 248505, Coral Gables, FL 33124-6524
Admissions Phone: 305-284-4607 • **Admissions Fax:** 305-284-1878
Admissions E-mail: mba@miami.edu • **Web Address:** www.bus.miami.edu

"Diversity" is the catchword at the University of Miami Business School. Enjoying a location "in the midst of one of the most dynamic areas of international business growth in the western hemisphere," relishing the fact that one-third of its student body is international, and offering 27 specializations from which MBA candidates can choose, the Business School has a pretty apt catchword. The Global Master of Science for Business Executives and Professionals is a unique 13-month track designed to develop the skills necessary to analyze "issues and policies affecting the relations of states and world regions" while allowing candidates to hold on to their regular jobs.

INSTITUTIONAL INFORMATION

Public/Private: Private
Evening Classes Available? Yes
Total Faculty: 131
% Faculty Female: 5
% Faculty Minority: 6
Student/Faculty Ratio: 13:1
Students in Parent Institution: 13,715
Academic Calendar: August-May

PROGRAMS

Degrees Offered: MBA (1-2 years full time), MS (1-2 years full time), PhD (4 years)
Combined Degrees: JD/MBA, MBA/MS in CIS
Academic Specialties: The University of Miami School of Business takes pride in being a solid traditional school, offering full-time MBA programs as well as extensive EMBA programs throughout Florida. The effectiveness of these programs sharpens the skills of the faculty. Because of the experience and adaptability of the faculty, the school has adapted quickly to the changing complexity of the practice of management. A few of the more popular specializations are currently being offered in E-Commerce, Enterprise and Resource Planning, and International Business.

STUDENT INFORMATION

Total Business Students: 529
% Full Time: 75
% Female: 35
% Minority: 15
% Out of State: 34
% International: 42
Average Age: 26

COMPUTER AND RESEARCH FACILITIES

Campuswide Network? Yes
Internet Fee? No

EXPENSES/FINANCIAL AID

Tuition Per Credit (Resident/Nonresident): $1,010
Books and Supplies: $700
Average Grant: $12,730
Average Loan: $18,520
% Receiving Financial Aid: 50
% Receiving Aid Their First Year: 61

ADMISSIONS INFORMATION

Application Fee: $50
Electronic Application? Yes
Regular Application Deadline: Rolling
Regular Notification: Rolling
Deferment Available? Yes
Length of Deferment: 1 year
Non-fall Admissions? Yes
Non-fall Application Deadline(s): Rolling admissions
Transfer Students Accepted? Yes
Transfer Policy: 6 credits
Need-Blind Admissions? Yes
Number of Applications Received: 730
% of Applicants Accepted: 48
% Accepted Who Enrolled: 42
Average Years Experience: 3
Minority/Disadvantaged Student Recruitment Programs: Florida A&M University Program

INTERNATIONAL STUDENTS

TOEFL Required of International Students? Yes
Minimum TOEFL: 213

EMPLOYMENT INFORMATION

Placement Office Available? No
% Employed Within 3 Months: 92

UNIVERSITY OF MICHIGAN— ANN ARBOR
Business School

Admissions Contact: Cynthia Shaw, Office of Communications
Address: 701 Tappan Street, Ann Arbor, MI 48109
Admissions Phone: 734-763-5796 • Admissions Fax: 734-763-7804
Admissions E-mail: umbsmba@umich.edu • Web Address: www.bus.umich.edu

The University of Michigan Business School—possibly "the world's most innovative business school"—"has strength across all business disciplines." Consequently, according to the "down-to-earth, humble, smart risk-takers" here, "you cannot say Michigan is just a 'fill in the blank: finance, marketing,

etc.' school." When they begin their job searches, Michigan Business School alums can cash in on an alumni network that numbers some 30,000.

INSTITUTIONAL INFORMATION

Public/Private: Public
Evening Classes Available? Yes
Total Faculty: 174
% Faculty Female: 25
% Faculty Minority: 19
% Faculty Part Time: 20
Student/Faculty Ratio: 17:1
Students in Parent Institution: 38,100
Academic Calendar: Semester

PROGRAMS

Degrees Offered: MBA, PhD, EMBA, BBA, Master's of Accounting
Combined Degrees: Manufacturing, Environmental Management, Public and Nonprofit Management, plus joint degree programs in: Architecture, Chinese Studies, Construction and Engineering Management, Industrial and Operations Engineering, Public Policy Studies, Japanese Studies, Law, Manufacturing Engineering, Modern Middle Eastern and North African Studies, Music, Natural Resources and Environment, Naval Architecture and Marine Engineering, Patient Care Administration, Public Health, Russian and East European Studies, Social Work, South and Southeast Asian Studies, Urban Planning
Academic Specialties: Michigan's real strength and value comes from combining across-the-board academic prowess·with a set of special programs of management development. These programs develop students' skills and capabilities for standout effectiveness and leadership. Michigan is not only a management education institution but also an innovative, high-impact leadership development institution. It is a powerful, career-enhancing distinction. This makes for a particularly strong general management program but also provides the depth of expertise that allows students to specialize in any field of functional area of their choosing confident in the knowledge that any department meets the very highest standards.
Special Opportunities: Executive Skills Seminars; Leadership Development Program; international in-company learning (Europe, Asia, Africa, South America); required in-company immersion/development experience; international network of corporate partnerships
Study Abroad Options: Australia, Austria, Costa Rica, Denmark, Finland, France, Hong Kong, Italy, the Netherlands, Singapore, Spain, Sweden, Switzerland, United Kingdom

STUDENT INFORMATION

Total Business Students: 1,860
% Full Time: 48
% Female: 28
% Minority: 21
% International: 29
Average Age: 28

COMPUTER AND RESEARCH FACILITIES

Research Facilities: Of particular note: The Business School houses the world headquarters of the William Davidson Institute, which is a creator and repository of knowledge of emerging markets and provides practical business assistance (often involving MBAs) to companies operating in those markets. Special institutes for environmental management, manufacturing, and entrepreneurship also yield exceptional opportunities for students in those areas. The School also houses a center for developing and deploying technologies related to "distance learning." Of further note is that the Business School has its own superb business library, one of the largest such libraries in the United States. University of Michigan MBA students also have access to the following resources: Electronic Library, Financial Trading Floor, eCommerce Research Lab, Global Learning Center, Career Resource Center, M-Track.
Computer Facilities: Statistics and Computation Service provides the resources for high performance research computing, including large volume statistical, mathematical, and geographic information system data analysis.

Instructional Education Services works with faculty, staff, or students to prepare them to teach workshops to their groups. Included are instructor materials, student materials, and consultation. University of Michigan Television (UMTV) is a 60-channel campus cable television system. Wolverine Access allows students direct access to their own records. Conferencing on the Web (COW), which students can access from the Internet using a regular Web browser, works as a kind of bulletin board service.

University Library Systems: The Media Union provides University students, faculty, and staff with traditional and digital libraries, computer training rooms, an advanced visualization laboratory, a virtual reality laboratory, video and audio performance studios, lab space for special projects, an exhibition gallery, a teleconference suite, and more than 500 workstations in open areas. Student Organization Resource Center (SORC) has 5 "Creation Stations" available for student organization access. The New Media Center (NMC) is a site with resources to help students complete multimedia class projects. An Adaptive Technology Computing Site (ATCS) is an ergo-assistive work-study environment designed to accommodate the information technology needs of physically, visually, learning, and ergonomically impaired students, faculty, and staff.

Campuswide Network? Yes
% of MBA Classrooms Wired: 85
Computer Model Recommended: Laptop
Internet Fee? No

EXPENSES/FINANCIAL AID

Annual Tuition (Resident/Nonresident): $27,500/$32,500
Tuition Per Credit (Resident/Nonresident): $900
Room & Board (On/Off Campus): $15,246
Books and Supplies: $1,100
Average Grant: $16,026
Average Loan: $37,500

ADMISSIONS INFORMATION

Application Fee: $125
Electronic Application? Yes
Early Decision Application Deadline: 11/1
Early Decision Notification: 1/15
Regular Application Deadline: 1/7
Regular Notification: 3/15
Deferment Available? No
Non-fall Admissions? No
Transfer Policy: Transfer applicants are welcome to apply, but no credits will transfer into our program.
Need-Blind Admissions? Yes
Number of Applications Received: 4,048
% of Applicants Accepted: 19
% Accepted Who Enrolled: 56
Average GPA: 3.4
GPA Range: 2.9-4.0
Average GMAT: 681
GMAT Range: 620-730
Average Years Experience: 6
Other Admissions Factors Considered: Track record of success, clarity of goals, management and leadership potential
Minority/Disadvantaged Student Recruitment Programs: Member of Consortium for Graduate Study in Management; UpClose Program, a weekend for prospective minority students; Robert F. Toigo Fellowships in Finance; Management Leadership for Tomorrow (MLT), which provides mentorship opportunities; National Society of Hispanic MBA Conference; National Black MBA Conference; faculty and alumni outreach; student phonathon
Other Schools to Which Students Applied: Duke University, Northwestern University, University of Chicago, University of Pennsylvania

INTERNATIONAL STUDENTS

TOEFL Required of International Students? Yes
Minimum TOEFL: 600 (250 computer)

EMPLOYMENT INFORMATION

Placement Office Available? Yes
% Employed Within 3 Months: 77
Fields Employing Percentage of Grads: Strategic Planning (3%), Other (4%), General Management (7%), Consulting (16%), Marketing (27%), Finance (43%)
Frequent Employers: Accenture; American Express; A.T. Kearney; Banc of America Securities; Bear, Stearns, & Co.; Booz Allen & Hamilton; The Boston Consulting Group; Bristol-Myers Squibb Co.; Citigroup/Citibank; Dell Computer Corp.; Deloitte Consulting; DiamondCluster International; Eli Lilly & Co.; Ford Motor Co.; General Motors Corp.; Goldman, Sachs, & Co.; International Business Machines Corp.; Kraft Foods, Inc.; Lehman Brothers Inc.; McKinsey & Co; Mercer Management Consulting; Morgan Stanley; Pittiglio Rabin Todd & McGrath; Pricewaterhouse Coopers, LLP; Salomon Smith Barney, Inc.; S.C. Johnson & Son., Inc.; Siebel Systems; UBS Warburg

UNIVERSITY OF MICHIGAN— DEARBORN
School of Management

Admissions Contact: Janet McIntire, Graduate Programs Advisor
Address: School of Management, 4901 Evergreen Road, Dearborn, MI 48128-1491
Admissions Phone: 313-593-5460 • **Admissions Fax:** 313-593-4071
Admissions E-mail: gradbusiness@umd.umich.edu
Web Address: www.som.umd.umich.edu

The University of Michigan—Dearborn School of Management is a solid choice for business school students looking to build a career in Michigan. UM—Dearborn offers a unique dual Master of Business Administration/ Master of Science in Industrial and Systems Engineering. Developed to produce management- and technology-savvy MBAs for "the corporate/ manufacturing/industrial center that is southeast Michigan," the program is popular and pretty selective. Dearborn also offers a WebMBA (entirely online course work), which takes most candidates two to four years to complete.

INSTITUTIONAL INFORMATION

Public/Private: Public
Evening Classes Available? Yes
Total Faculty: 30
% Faculty Female: 20
% Faculty Minority: 30
Student/Faculty Ratio: 22:1
Students in Parent Institution: 8,386
Academic Calendar: Semester

PROGRAMS

Degrees Offered: MBA (2-4 years part time), with concentrations in Accounting, Finance, International Business, Marketing, Workforce Management, Management Information Systems; Web-MBA (2-4 years part time, entirely online); MSA (1 year full time, 2 years part time); MS in Finance (1 year full time, 2 years part time)
Combined Degrees: Dual MBA/MSIE (4-5 years part time)
Academic Specialties: Accounting, Finance, Marketing, Strategy, Management Information Systems, Organizational Behavior and Human Resources, Operations Management
Study Abroad Options: Hong Kong (MS in Finance offered);Germany; University of Oviedo, Spain

STUDENT INFORMATION

Total Business Students: 396
% Full Time: 5
% Female: 26
% Minority: 20
Average Age: 29

COMPUTER AND RESEARCH FACILITIES

Research Facilities: Mardigian Library: total holdings of 299,792 volumes; 432,298 microforms; 1,169 periodical subscriptions. CD players available for graduate students, access provided to online bibliographic retrieval services and online databases, alumni network, career counsling/planning, career fairs, career library, career placement, job interviews arranged, resume referral to employers, resume preparation
Campuswide Network? Yes
Internet Fee? No

EXPENSES/FINANCIAL AID

Annual Tuition (Resident/Nonresident): $10,700/$19,955
Tuition Per Credit (Resident/Nonresident): $370/$826
Books and Supplies: $1,200
Average Grant: $1,500
Average Loan: $5,000

ADMISSIONS INFORMATION

Application Fee: $55
Electronic Application? No
Regular Application Deadline: 8/1
Regular Notification: 8/20
Deferment Available? Yes
Length of Deferment: 1 year
Non-fall Admissions? Yes
Non-fall Application Deadline(s): Fall, winter, summer
Transfer Students Accepted? Yes
Transfer Policy: For equivalent courses to our MBA core courses, waivers will be given. Up to 6 credits of transfer may be given for other MBA courses.
Need-Blind Admissions? Yes
Number of Applications Received: 143
% of Applicants Accepted: 69
% Accepted Who Enrolled: 76
Average GPA: 3.2
Average GMAT: 565
Average Years Experience: 5
Other Admissions Factors Considered: 2 years full-time professional work experience is required.
Other Schools to Which Students Applied: University of Michigan, Wayne State University, Oakland University, University of Detroit Mercy, Eastern Michigan University, Michigan State University-Detroit College of Law

INTERNATIONAL STUDENTS

TOEFL Required of International Students? Yes
Minimum TOEFL: 560 (222 computer)

EMPLOYMENT INFORMATION

Placement Office Available? Yes

UNIVERSITY OF MICHIGAN—FLINT
School of Management

Admissions Contact: Cheryl Tabachki, MBA, NetPlus! MBA Coordinator
Address: UM–F, MBA Office, 364 French Hall, 303 E. Kearsley, Flint, MI 48502-1950
Admissions Phone: 810-761-3163 • **Admissions Fax:** 810-762-0736
Admissions E-mail: ctabachk@umflint.edu
Web Address: www.flint.umich.edu/departments/som/MBA

Whether you're a resident or not, the tuition song remains the same, and it's a pretty good deal either way you slice it. Most UM—Flint students are from the upper central states, and that's where most Flint MBAs expect to work when they graduate. If cold winters don't entice you, how does a 100 percent chance of snagging a job within three months of graduation sound?

INSTITUTIONAL INFORMATION

Public/Private: Public
Evening Classes Available? Yes
Total Faculty: 23
% Faculty Female: 26
% Faculty Minority: 39
% Faculty Part Time: 35
Student/Faculty Ratio: 35:1
Academic Calendar: Semester

PROGRAMS

Degrees Offered: Traditional MBA (3 years), NetPlus! MBA (mixed mode delivery; 2 years)

STUDENT INFORMATION

Total Business Students: 225

COMPUTER AND RESEARCH FACILITIES

Computer Facilities: Labs and classrooms contain 140 computers. LANs provide additional storage; UNIX machines provide e-mail services. Campus users connect to the Internet thorough the MichNet Computer System.
Campuswide Network? Yes
% of MBA Classrooms Wired: 6
Internet Fee? Yes

EXPENSES/FINANCIAL AID

Annual Tuition (Resident/Nonresident): $8,420
Tuition Per Credit (Resident/Nonresident): $370
Books and Supplies: $1,200
Average Grant: $1,000
Average Loan: $5,700

ADMISSIONS INFORMATION

Application Fee: $50
Electronic Application? No
Regular Application Deadline: 7/1
Regular Notification: 8/1
Deferment Available? Yes
Length of Deferment: 3 years
Non-fall Admissions? Yes
Non-fall Application Deadline(s): 11/1 winter
Transfer Students Accepted? Yes
Transfer Policy: Maximum of 6 graduate-level credit hours with a grade of B or better from an AASCB-accredited program; cannot be part of any other degree
Need-Blind Admissions? Yes
Number of Applications Received: 71
% of Applicants Accepted: 96
% Accepted Who Enrolled: 76
Average GPA: 3.1
Average GMAT: 530

INTERNATIONAL STUDENTS

TOEFL Required of International Students? Yes
Minimum TOEFL: 550 (213 computer)

EMPLOYMENT INFORMATION

Placement Office Available? No
% Employed Within 3 Months: 100

UNIVERSITY OF MINNESOTA—DULUTH
School of Business and Economics

Admissions Contact: Candy Furo, MBA Director
Address: 431 Darland Administration Building, Duluth, MN 55812-2496
Admissions Phone: 218-726-7523 • Admissions Fax: 218-726-6970
Admissions E-mail: grad@d.umn.edu • Web Address: sbe.d.umn.edu/SBEHome/

U of M—Duluth offers one track: a part-time evening program that takes most students between two and seven years to complete. For those anti–standardized test activists, U of M—Duluth can waive the GMAT requirement for admission if you're a CPA or have obtained some other graduate degree from a regionally accredited institution.

INSTITUTIONAL INFORMATION

Public/Private: Public
Evening Classes Available? Yes
Total Faculty: 35
Students in Parent Institution: 10,000
Academic Calendar: Semester

PROGRAMS

Degrees Offered: Evening MBA (2-7 years)
Academic Specialties: Case study, computer-aided instruction, computer simulations, field projects, group discussion, lecture, simulations, student presentations, team projects

STUDENT INFORMATION

Average Age: 30

COMPUTER AND RESEARCH FACILITIES

Campuswide Network? Yes
Internet Fee? No

EXPENSES/FINANCIAL AID

Annual Tuition (Resident/Nonresident): $12,660
% Receiving Financial Aid: 35

ADMISSIONS INFORMATION

Application Fee: $50
Electronic Application? No
Regular Application Deadline: 7/15
Regular Notification: 1/1
Deferment Available? Yes
Non-fall Admissions? Yes
Non-fall Application Deadline(s): 11/1, 5/1
Transfer Students Accepted? No
Need-Blind Admissions? No
Number of Applications Received: 730
% of Applicants Accepted: 10
% Accepted Who Enrolled: 71
Other Admissions Factors Considered: GRE scores, work experience, word processing, spreadsheet

INTERNATIONAL STUDENTS

TOEFL Required of International Students? Yes
Minimum TOEFL: 550

EMPLOYMENT INFORMATION

Placement Office Available? Yes

UNIVERSITY OF MINNESOTA—MINNEAPOLIS
Curtis L. Carlson School of Management

Admissions Contact: Sandra Kelzenberg, Director of Admissions
Address: 321 19th Avenue South, Minneapolis, MN 55455
Admissions Phone: 612-625-5555 • Admissions Fax: 612-626-7785
Admissions E-mail: Full-TimeMBAInfo@csom.umn.edu
Web Address: www.CarlsonSchool.umn.edu

Winters are "too long and too cold" at the University of Minnesota's Carlson School of Management. Other than that, though, the "mature, helpful, friendly" midwesterners here have practically no complaints. They say the "small and comfortable" Carlson School has "accessible professors" and "a very cooperative learning environment." Also, student life here is particularly "active." There are "regular happy hours" and "many clubs and organizations," and "classmates enjoy being in activities with each other."

INSTITUTIONAL INFORMATION

Public/Private: Public
Evening Classes Available? Yes
Total Faculty: 140
% Faculty Female: 21
Student/Faculty Ratio: 10:1
Students in Parent Institution: 46,597
Academic Calendar: Semester

PROGRAMS

Degrees Offered: BSB (4 years), MBA (2 years), Carlson EMBA (2 years), MA in Human Resources in Industrial Relations (2 years), MHA 2 years), Master of Business Taxation (1 year), MS in Management of Technology (2 years), PhD in Business (4 years), PhD in Human Recources and Industrial Relations (4 years), PhD in Health Services Administration (4 years)
Combined Degrees: JD/MBA (4 years), MHA/MBA (2 years), MD/MBA (6 years), MPH/MBA (3 years)
Academic Specialties: Accounting, Finance, Information Systems, Marketing, Entrepreneurship, Operations, International Business, Supply Chain Management, Strategic Management, Healthcare Management; ranked Number 1 in MIS and Operations, Number 7 in Strategy, Number in Marketing, and Number 7 overall in Research Productivity.
Special Opportunities: Doing Business in Central and Eastern Europe (Austria); Vienna Summer Program (Austria); Lyon Summer Program (France); Business and the Environment: Lessons from Central America (Costa Rica); Ethical Environment of International Business (Brussels); MBA Enterprises Program: Student-run businesses/experiential learning opportunities: Carlson Funds Enterprise, Carlson Consulting Enterprise, Carlson Ventures Enterprise, Carlson Brand Management Enterprise
Study Abroad Options: University of Melbourne Graduate School of Management, Australia; Universite Catholique de Louvain-la-Neuve, Belgium; Escola de Administracao de Empresas de Sao Paulo, Brazil; Instituto Centroamericano de Administracion De Empresas (INCAE), Costa Rica; Manchester Business School, England; Haute Etudes Commerciales (HEC),

France; Keio University Graduate School of Business, Japan; University of Otago, New Zealand; Norwegian School of Management, Norway; Escuela Superior de Administracion y Direccion de Empresas (ESADE), Spain; Stockholm School of Economics, Sweden; University of St. Gallen, Switzerland

STUDENT INFORMATION

Total Business Students: 1,356
% Full Time: 17
% Female: 27
% Minority: 10
% Out of State: 30
% International: 30
Average Age: 30

COMPUTER AND RESEARCH FACILITIES

Research Facilities: Student-run businesses/experiential learning opportunities include Carlson Funds Enterprise, Carlson Consulting Enterprise, Carlson Ventures Enterprise, and Carlson Brand Management Enterprise. Resources include Financial Markets Lab (Investments), Juran Center (Quality Management), Center for Corporate Responsibility (Ethics), Center for Industrial Relations, Strategic Management Research Center, Center for Entrepreneurial Studies, and MIS Research Center.
Computer Facilities: 2 computer labs for MBA students in the Carlson School, networked and wireless classrooms and breakout rooms, MIS Lab, Financial Markets Lab for "live" trading, Bridge and Rueters databases, access to Center for Research in Security Prices (CRSP) from University of Chicago, NY Stock Exchange TAQ, Alcar, Dow Jones, FDIC, Philidelphia Stock Exchange, Subscribe and Wharton School Research Data Services, Compustat, University of Minnesota Library Research databases, programming support for research projects
Campuswide Network? Yes
% of MBA Classrooms Wired: 100
Computer Model Recommended: Laptop
Internet Fee? No

EXPENSES/FINANCIAL AID

Annual Tuition (Resident/Nonresident): $16,500/$23,500
Tuition Per Credit (Resident/Nonresident): $562/$822
Room & Board (On/Off Campus): $7,500/$9,750
Books and Supplies: $2,000
Average Grant: $16,000
Average Loan: $17,000

ADMISSIONS INFORMATION

Application Fee: $60
Electronic Application? Yes
Early Decision Application Deadline: 1/1
Early Decision Notification: 2/15
Regular Application Deadline: 4/1
Regular Notification: 5/15
Deferment Available? Yes
Length of Deferment: 1 year
Non-fall Admissions? No
Transfer Students Accepted? No
Need-Blind Admissions? Yes
Number of Applications Received: 765
% of Applicants Accepted: 40
% Accepted Who Enrolled: 42
Average GPA: 3.2
GPA Range: 2.9-3.5
Average GMAT: 645
GMAT Range: 610-690
Average Years Experience: 6
Other Admissions Factors Considered: Interview recommended; international applicants must pay a $90 application fee
Minority/Disadvantaged Student Recruitment Programs: Minnesota Blvd, a program in which Minnesota-based companies work jointly with

Carlson School to bring minority MBA candidates to Twin Cities for jobs, mentoring, and MBA; minority scholarships; close ties with NBMBAA (National Black MBA Association)and NSHMBA, for example, help call students for recruiting, scholarships, and retention

INTERNATIONAL STUDENTS

TOEFL Required of International Students? Yes
Minimum TOEFL: 580 (240 computer)

EMPLOYMENT INFORMATION

Placement Office Available? Yes
% Employed Within 3 Months: 88
Fields Employing Percentage of Grads: Other (1%), General Management (4%), Operations (5%), MIS (9%), Consulting (12%), Marketing (28%), Finance (41%)
Frequent Employers:, Cargill, Carlson Companies, Deloitte Consulting, Ecolab, General Mills, Guidant, HB Fuller, Honeywell, Kimberly-Clark, Medtronic, Northwest Airlines, Royal Bank of Canada, Target Corp., 3M, US Bancorp
Prominent Alumni: Fredrick Kappel, late chairman, AT&T; Charles W. Mooty, CEO, International Dairy Queen; William G. Van Dyke, chairman, president and CEO, Donaldson Co., Inc.; Curtis C. Nelson, president and CEO, Carlson Hospitality Worldwide; Barbara J. Mowry, president and CEO, TMC Consulting

UNIVERSITY OF MISSISSIPPI
School of Business Administration

Admissions Contact: Dr. John Holleman, Director of MBA Adminstratrion
Address: 319 Conner Hall, University, MS 38677
Admissions Phone: 662-915-5483 • **Admissions Fax:** 662-915-7968
Admissions E-mail: jholleman@bus.olemiss.edu • **Web Address:** www.mba.olemiss.edu

When your business school is in the hometown of Faulkner, you're expected to master people skills. Indeed, the School of Business Administration, one of the oldest in the United States, encourages students to build relationships with the faculty, the surrounding community, and one another. Even though "no academic regimen has [a] better grasp of today's new technology," Ole Miss knows that some things never change, including the fact "that leaders achieve success by gaining the cooperation of those who work with them." Fittingly, many an MBA candidate cites "the importance of balancing work and play." So if you've got the technical skills but don't know how to schmooze—or vice versa—you'll leave Ole Miss as the total package: a dealmaker and a code breaker.

INSTITUTIONAL INFORMATION

Public/Private: Public
Evening Classes Available? No
Total Faculty: 49
% Faculty Female: 18
Student/Faculty Ratio: 30:1
Students in Parent Institution: 13,500
Academic Calendar: Semester

PROGRAMS

Degrees Offered: MBA (18 months to 2.2 years), with concentrations in Management, Accounting, Banking, Economics, Finance, International Business, Management Information Systems, Marketing, Operations Management, Organizational Behavior/Development, Quantitative Analysis, Real Estate, Financial Management/Planning, Human Resources, Information Management, Insurance, Managerial Economics System Management

Academic Specialties: Case study, computer analysis, computer simulations, experiential learning, field projects, group discussion, lecture, seminars by members of the business community, student presentations, study groups, team projects
Special Opportunities: Accounting, CIS or MIS, Economics, Finance (includes Banking), Human Resource Management (includes Labor Relations), International Business, Management, Marketing, Other, Production/Operations Management/Managerial Economics, Quantitative Methods, Real Estate

STUDENT INFORMATION

Total Business Students: 96
% Full Time: 100
% Female: 41
% Minority: 4
% Out of State: 41
% International: 8
Average Age: 26

COMPUTER AND RESEARCH FACILITIES

Campuswide Network? Yes
% of MBA Classrooms Wired: 100
Computer Model Recommended: Laptop
Internet Fee? No

EXPENSES/FINANCIAL AID

Annual Tuition (Resident/Nonresident): $7,094/$15,899
Room & Board (On/Off Campus): $8,800/$10,000
Books and Supplies: $5,000
Average Grant: $1,469
Average Loan: $10,000

ADMISSIONS INFORMATION

Electronic Application? Yes
Regular Application Deadline: 4/1
Regular Notification: 5/1
Deferment Available? No
Non-fall Admissions? Yes
Non-fall Application Deadline(s): 4/1 summer
Transfer Students Accepted? No
Need-Blind Admissions? Yes
Number of Applications Received: 225
% of Applicants Accepted: 45
% Accepted Who Enrolled: 55
GPA Range: 3.0-3.8
Average GMAT: 550
GMAT Range: 500-610
Average Years Experience: 2

INTERNATIONAL STUDENTS

TOEFL Required of International Students? Yes
Minimum TOEFL: 600

EMPLOYMENT INFORMATION

Placement Office Available? Yes
% Employed Within 3 Months: 100
Fields Employing Percentage of Grads: General Management (5%), Entrepreneurship (5%), Accounting (5%), Consulting (10%), Marketing (15%), Finance (15%), MIS (20%)
Frequent Employers: Top regional employers from across the South and Southeast

UNIVERSITY OF MISSOURI—COLUMBIA
College of Business

Admissions Contact: Barbara Schneider, Coordinator Recruiting and Admissions
Address: 213 Cornell Hall, Columbia, MO 65211
Admissions Phone: 573-882-2750 • **Admissions Fax:** 573-882-6838
Admissions E-mail: mba@missouri.edu • **Web Address:** mba.missouri.edu

INSTITUTIONAL INFORMATION

Public/Private: Public
Evening Classes Available? No
Total Faculty: 48
% Faculty Part Time: 8
Student/Faculty Ratio: 20:1
Students in Parent Institution: 22,723
Academic Calendar: Semester

PROGRAMS

Degrees Offered: MBA (33-55 credits, 1-2 years)
Combined Degrees: MBA/MSIE, MBA/JD (4 to 4.5 years), MBA/MHA
Special Opportunities: Accounting, Business Ethics, Business Law/Legal Environment, CIS or MIS, Economics, Finance (includes Banking), General Business, Health Services/Hospital Administration, Human Resource Management (includes Labor Relations), International Business, Management, Marketing, Other, Public Administration
Study Abroad Options: Italy, Romania

STUDENT INFORMATION

Total Business Students: 121
% Full Time: 100
% Female: 38
% Minority: 5
% International: 25
Average Age: 27

COMPUTER AND RESEARCH FACILITIES

Campuswide Network? Yes
Internet Fee? No

EXPENSES/FINANCIAL AID

Annual Tuition (Resident/Nonresident): $1,719/$4,856
Tuition Per Credit (Resident/Nonresident): $173/$521
% Receiving Financial Aid: 62

ADMISSIONS INFORMATION

Application Fee: $25
Electronic Application? No
Regular Application Deadline: 8/1
Regular Notification: Rolling
Deferment Available? Yes
Non-fall Admissions? Yes
Non-fall Application Deadline(s): 12/1, 5/1
Transfer Students Accepted? No
Need-Blind Admissions? No
Number of Applications Received: 828
% of Applicants Accepted: 16
% Accepted Who Enrolled: 71
Other Admissions Factors Considered: Work experience, computer experience

INTERNATIONAL STUDENTS

TOEFL Required of International Students? Yes
Minimum TOEFL: 550

EMPLOYMENT INFORMATION

Placement Office Available? Yes
% Employed Within 3 Months: 92

UNIVERSITY OF MISSOURI— KANSAS CITY

Henry W. Bloch School of Business & Public Administration

Admissions Contact: Director of Admissions
Address: 5100 Rockhill Road, Kansas City, MO 64110
Admissions Phone: 816-235-1111 • **Admissions Fax:** 816-235-5544
Admissions E-mail: admit@umkc.edu • **Web Address:** www.umkc.edu/bloch

To budding entrepreneurs from the state of Missouri, hark! You will find an environment ripe with opportunity to hone the skills you'll need to make your own business thrive at the Bloch School of Business and Public Administration. Students with an emphasis in entrepreneurship (one of six options) can give themselves a baptism of fire with the Entrepreneurial Growth Resource Center, which basically outsources undergraduate and graduate business students to small businesses to help them with their needs, whether it be "business plan[s], a website, [or] assistance in getting government contracts."

INSTITUTIONAL INFORMATION

Public/Private: Public
Evening Classes Available? Yes
Total Faculty: 42
% Faculty Female: 28
% Faculty Minority: 11
% Faculty Part Time: 12
Student/Faculty Ratio: 21:1
Students in Parent Institution: 10,016
Academic Calendar: Semester

PROGRAMS

Degrees Offered: MBA (1-7 years), with concentrations in Entreneurship, Finance, Management, Management Information Systems, Marketing, Operations Management, Leadership, Change in Human Systems; MSA (1-7 years); MPA (1-7 years), with concentrations in Nonprofit Management, Organizational Behavior, Human Resources, Urban Administration, Health Care, Early Childhood Leadership, Information Operations; EMBA (21 months)
Combined Degrees: JD/MBA (4 years), JD/MPA (4 years)
Academic Specialties: Case study, computer-aided instruction, computer analysis, computer simulations, experiential learning, faculty seminars, field projects, group discussion, lecture, research, seminars by members of the business community, simulations, student presentations, study groups, team projects
Study Abroad Options: Numerous; contact Office of International Academic Programs www.umkc.edu/intl

STUDENT INFORMATION

Total Business Students: 403
% Full Time: 31
% Female: 40
% Minority: 9
% International: 29
Average Age: 31

COMPUTER AND RESEARCH FACILITIES

Research Facilities: Entrepreneur Growth Resource Center, Direct Marketing, Small Business Development Center
Computer Facilities: Compustat, Bloomberg, CRSP
Campuswide Network? Yes
Internet Fee? No

EXPENSES/FINANCIAL AID

Annual Tuition (Resident/Nonresident): $3,553/$10,572
Tuition Per Credit (Resident/Nonresident): $194/$584
Room & Board (On/Off Campus): $7,040/$6,860
Books and Supplies: $606
Average Grant: $11,227
Average Loan: $5,569
% Receiving Financial Aid: 69
% Receiving Aid Their First Year: 72

ADMISSIONS INFORMATION

Application Fee: $25
Electronic Application? No
Regular Application Deadline: 5/1
Regular Notification: Rolling
Deferment Available? Yes
Length of Deferment: 1 year
Non-fall Admissions? Yes
Non-fall Application Deadline(s): 10/1 winter, 3/1 summer
Transfer Students Accepted? Yes
Transfer Policy: Up to 6 hours of graduate credit from an AACSB-accredited institution
Need-Blind Admissions? Yes
Number of Applications Received: 349
% of Applicants Accepted: 54
% Accepted Who Enrolled: 74
Average GPA: 3.3
Average GMAT: 559
Average Years Experience: 5

INTERNATIONAL STUDENTS

TOEFL Required of International Students? Yes
Minimum TOEFL: 550

EMPLOYMENT INFORMATION

Placement Office Available? No
% Employed Within 3 Months: 90
Fields Employing Percentage of Grads: Entrepreneurship (5%), Consulting (5%), Operations (5%), Human Resources (5%), General Management (10%), MIS (10%), Other (14%), Marketing (14%), Finance (29%)
Frequent Employers: DST, Federal Reserve Bank, Hallmark, Sprint
Prominent Alumni: Kay Waldo Barnes, mayor, Kansas City, Missouri; Terry Dunn, president and CEO, Dunn Industries; Dave Thomas, executive director, Sprint Foundation; Tom Holcom, president, Pioneer Financial Services; Bob Regnier, president, Bank of Blue Valley

UNIVERSITY OF MISSOURI—ST. LOUIS
College of Business Administration

Admissions Contact: Karl W. Kottemann, Provisional Director, Graduate Programs in Business
Address: 8001 Natural Bridge Road, 461 Social Science and Business, St. Louis, MO 63121-4499
Admissions Phone: 314-516-5885 • **Admissions Fax:** 314-516-7202
Admissions E-mail: mba@umsl.edu • **Web Address:** mba.umsl.edu

INSTITUTIONAL INFORMATION

Public/Private: Public
Evening Classes Available? Yes
Total Faculty: 37
% Faculty Female: 16
% Faculty Minority: 5
% Faculty Part Time: 14
Student/Faculty Ratio: 21:1
Students in Parent Institution: 15,000
Academic Calendar: Semester

PROGRAMS

Degrees Offered: PhD (4-6 years); Traditional MBA (2-4 years); Professional MBA (2 years online); MSMIS (2-4 years); MSA (2-4 years); MACC (18 months to 6 years), with concentrations in Accounting, Taxation
Academic Specialties: Case study, computer-aided instruction, computer analysis, computer simulations, faculty seminars, field projects, group discussion, lecture, research, role playing, seminars by members of the business community, simulations, student presentations, study groups, team projects, Internet based communication

STUDENT INFORMATION

Total Business Students: 353
% Full Time: 39
% Female: 44
% Minority: 15
% Out of State: 38
% International: 48
Average Age: 30

COMPUTER AND RESEARCH FACILITIES

Research Facilities: Center for Business and Industrial Studies, Center for Transportation Studies, Bank Data Institute, Student Investment Trust
Computer Facilities: Compustat, CRSP, various economic and social science databases
Campuswide Network? Yes
% of MBA Classrooms Wired: 80
Computer Model Recommended: Laptop
Internet Fee? No

EXPENSES/FINANCIAL AID

Annual Tuition (Resident/Nonresident): $5,823/$17,520
Tuition Per Credit (Resident/Nonresident): $194/$584
Room & Board (On/Off Campus): $7,170
Books and Supplies: $1,000
Average Grant: $7,600
Average Loan: $10,541
% Receiving Financial Aid: 25
% Receiving Aid Their First Year: 23

ADMISSIONS INFORMATION

Application Fee: $25
Electronic Application? Yes
Regular Application Deadline: 7/1
Regular Notification: Rolling
Deferment Available? Yes
Length of Deferment: 1 year

Non-fall Admissions? Yes
Non-fall Application Deadline(s): 12/1, 5/1(earlier for international applicants)
Transfer Students Accepted? Yes
Transfer Policy: Transcripts are evaluated for relevant coursework. Maximum of 9 hours acceptable graduate credit allowed to transfer in.
Need-Blind Admissions? Yes
Number of Applications Received: 272
% of Applicants Accepted: 78
% Accepted Who Enrolled: 72
Average GPA: 3.1
GPA Range: 2.8-3.5
Average GMAT: 546
GMAT Range: 490-590
Average Years Experience: 4
Other Admissions Factors Considered: Professional experience since graduation, motivation, other indicators of ability

INTERNATIONAL STUDENTS

TOEFL Required of International Students? Yes
Minimum TOEFL: 550 (213 computer)

EMPLOYMENT INFORMATION

Placement Office Available? Yes
% Employed Within 3 Months: 66
Fields Employing Percentage of Grads: MIS (14%), Communications (29%), Other (43%)
Frequent Employers: Citimortgage, Edward Jones, May Co.

UNIVERSITY OF MONTANA— MISSOULA
School of Business Administration

Admissions Contact: Kathleen Spritzer, Administrative Officer
Address: School of Business Administration, University of Montana–Missoula, MT 59812
Admissions Phone: 406-243-4983 • **Admissions Fax:** 406-243-2086
Admissions E-mail: kathleen.spritzer@business.umt.edu
Web Address: www.mba-macct.umt.edu

You can work toward a UM—Missoula MBA from just about any big city in Big Sky country, including Billings, Bozeman, Butte, Helena, Great Falls, Kalispell, and Missoula, with the Off-Campus MBA. A low cost of living and low tuition make UM—Missoula a terrific choice for in-state and out-of-state students alike. No matter which city you choose to do your course work in, bring a serious jacket. And gloves. And lip balm.

INSTITUTIONAL INFORMATION

Public/Private: Public
Evening Classes Available? Yes
Total Faculty: 33
% Faculty Female: 33
% Faculty Minority: 1
% Faculty Part Time: 10
Student/Faculty Ratio: 21:1
Students in Parent Institution: 13,058
Academic Calendar: Semester

PROGRAMS

Degrees Offered: MBA (1 calendar year), MACC (1 calendar year)
Combined Degrees: JD/MBA (3 years), MBA/PharmD (5 years)

Academic Specialties: The general MBA, with 10 semester credits of electives available, allows students to specialize in an area of their interest. Faculty academic specialities include Accounting Theory, Banking, Business Law, Corporate Finance, Entrepreneurship, Financial Accounting, Human Resource Management, Income Taxation, Information Systems, International Management, Investments, Management, Communications, Marketing, Operations Management, Research Methods, Strategic Marketing

STUDENT INFORMATION

Total Business Students: 96
% Full Time: 75
% Female: 49
% Minority: 6
% International: 10
Average Age: 29

COMPUTER AND RESEARCH FACILITIES

Research Facilities: Bureau of Business and Economic Resources, Montana World Trade Center, American Indian Business Leaders, Montana Business Connections
Computer Facilities: The Gallagher Business Building has 2 open computer labs of 50 stations each, a 50-station computer classroom, 3 interactive distance-learning classrooms, as well as 8 additional classrooms equipped with computers, VCRs, projectors, and audio systems for classroom presentations. Microsoft and Hewlett-Packard have partnered to provide the building with the latest software and hardware on an on-going basis.
Campuswide Network? Yes
% of MBA Classrooms Wired: 65
Internet Fee? No

EXPENSES/FINANCIAL AID

Annual Tuition (Resident/Nonresident): $4,920/$12,360
Tuition Per Credit (Resident/Nonresident): $208/$518
Room & Board (On/Off Campus): $8,250
Books and Supplies: $1,500
Average Grant: $8,850
Average Loan: $8,500

ADMISSIONS INFORMATION

Application Fee: $45
Electronic Application? No
Regular Application Deadline: 5/1
Regular Notification: 5/15
Deferment Available? Yes
Length of Deferment: 1 year
Non-fall Admissions? Yes
Non-fall Application Deadline(s): 11/1 spring, 5/1 summer
Transfer Students Accepted? Yes
Transfer Policy: Up to 9 semester credit hours
Need-Blind Admissions? Yes
Number of Applications Received: 135
% of Applicants Accepted: 81
% Accepted Who Enrolled: 88
Average GPA: 3.3
Average GMAT: 565
Average Years Experience: 3
Minority/Disadvantaged Student Recruitment Programs: One graduate assistantship is restricted to an enrolled member of a Native American tribe.
Other Schools to Which Students Applied: Montana State University, University of Colorado, University of Oregon, University of Washington, Washington State University

INTERNATIONAL STUDENTS

TOEFL Required of International Students? Yes
Minimum TOEFL: 580 (237 computer)

EMPLOYMENT INFORMATION

Placement Office Available? Yes
Frequent Employers: Andersen Consulting, Arthur Andersen, Cargill, Deloitte Consulting, Ernst & Young, GTE, Hewlett-Packard, KPMG, Microsoft, Pricewaterhouse Coopers, Safeco, U.S. Bank, Wells Fargo Bank, U.S. Marines

UNIVERSITY OF NAVARRA
IESE International Graduate School of Management

Admissions Contact: Alberto Arribas, Director of MBA Admissions
Address: Av. Pearson 21, Barcelona, Spain 08034
Admissions Phone: 011-34-93-253-4227 • **Admissions Fax:** 011-34-93-253-4343
Admissions E-mail: mbainfo@iese.edu • **Web Address:** www.iese.edu

INSTITUTIONAL INFORMATION

Public/Private: Private
Evening Classes Available? No
Total Faculty: 111
% Faculty Part Time: 34
Student/Faculty Ratio: 5:1
Students in Parent Institution: 16,000
Academic Calendar: Trimester

PROGRAMS

Degrees Offered: MBA (2 years), PhD in Management (3 years)
Academic Specialties: General Management, Entrepreneurship, IT Management, Organizational Behavior, Business Ethics
Study Abroad Options: University of California—Berkeley, USA; China Europe International Business School, China; University of Chicago, USA; Columbia Business School, USA; Cornell University, USA; Chinese University of Hong Kong, Hong Kong; University of Virginia, USA; Duke University, USA; Georgetown University, USA; Instituto Centroamericano de Administración de Empresas, Costa Rica; Instituto Panamericano de Alta Dirección de Empresa, Mexico; Keio University, Japan; Northwestern University, USA; University of London, U.K.; University of Michigan, USA; Massachusetts Institute of Technology, USA; Erasmus University, The Netherlands; Dartmouth College, USA; Univeristy of California—Los Angeles, USA; University of Western Ontario, Canada; University of Pennsylvania, USA

STUDENT INFORMATION

Total Business Students: 220
% Full Time: 100
% Female: 22
% International: 59
Average Age: 27

COMPUTER AND RESEARCH FACILITIES

Research Facilities: The International Center for Financial Investigation, The Center for Operations Excellence, The Center for Entrepreneurship and Family-Owned Business, The International Research Center on Organizations, The Center for Enterprise in Latin America, The International Research Center on Logistics
Computer Facilities: Databases include Proquest Direct, BOENET, DOGC, Lexis-Nexis Academic Universe, Hoover's Online, International Financial Statistics, SABE, Snapshots, WorldScope among others.
Number of Computer Labs: 10
Number of Student Computers: 90
Campuswide Network? Yes
% Who Own Computers: 95

Computer Proficiency Required? No
Special Purchasing Agreements? No
Internet Fee? No

EXPENSES/FINANCIAL AID

Annual Tuition: $17,000
Books and Supplies: $500
Average Grant: $9,100
Average Loan: $32,000

ADMISSIONS INFORMATION

Application Fee: $60
Electronic Application? Yes
Regular Application Deadline: 4/3
Regular Notification: Rolling
Deferment Available? Yes
Length of Deferment: 1 year
Non-fall Admissions? No
Transfer Students Accepted? No
Need-Blind Admissions? No
Number of Applications Received: 1,289
% of Applicants Accepted: 21
% Accepted Who Enrolled: 75
Average GMAT: 640
Average Years Experience: 4

INTERNATIONAL STUDENTS

TOEFL Required of International Students? Yes
Minimum TOEFL: 600
Placement Office Available? Yes
% Employed Within 6 Months: 100
Frequent Employers: Cluster Consulting, Arthur D. Little, Andersen Consulting, McKinsey & Company
Prominent Alumni: Jan Oosterveld, Philips; vice president for corporate strategy; Harry Anderson; vice president, The Boston Consulting Group; David Stead, partner, Andersen Consulting

UNIVERSITY OF NEBRASKA—LINCOLN
College of Business Administration

Admissions Contact: Judy Shutts, Graduate Adviser
Address: CBA 126, Lincoln, NE 68588-0405
Admissions Phone: 402-472-2338 • Admissions Fax: 402-472-5180
Admissions E-mail: cgraduate@unlnotes.unl.edu • Web Address: www.cba.unl.edu

Present at the creation? UN—Lincoln was a charter member (along with Harvard, Northwestern, and the University of Texas) of the AACSB. Entrepreneurial then and entrepreneurial now, UN—Lincoln's Center for Entrepreneurship was recently named tops in the nation by the U.S. Association for Small Business and Entrepreneurship. UN—Lincoln isn't sitting on its laurels, though. Plans for the inauguration of a PhD specialization in leadership, to be offered in partnership with the Gallup Organization, are currently in the works.

INSTITUTIONAL INFORMATION

Public/Private: Public
Evening Classes Available? No
Total Faculty: 58
% Faculty Female: 19
% Faculty Minority: 12
% Faculty Part Time: 1

Student/Faculty Ratio: 6:1
Students in Parent Institution: 22,764
Academic Calendar: Semester

PROGRAMS

Degrees Offered: MA (2 years), MBA (2 years), MPACC (2 years)
Combined Degrees: MBA/JD (4 years), MBA/MArch (3 years)
Special Opportunities: Consortium of International MBA (CIMBA), Italy; Oxford University Summer Program, United Kingdom; Senshu University, Senshu, Japan
Study Abroad Options: Australia, England, France, Germany, Italy, Japan, Mexico

STUDENT INFORMATION

Total Business Students: 149
% Full Time: 50
% Female: 29
% Out of State: 7
% International: 9
Average Age: 27

COMPUTER AND RESEARCH FACILITIES

Research Facilities: Nebraska Center for Entrepreneurship, Bureau of Business Research, Public Policy Center, Center for Economic Education
Computer Facilities: CRSP, Research Insight, ExecuComp
Campuswide Network? Yes
% of MBA Classrooms Wired: 100
Internet Fee? No

EXPENSES/FINANCIAL AID

Annual Tuition (Resident/Nonresident): $3,540/$9,540
Tuition Per Credit (Resident/Nonresident): $148/$398
Room & Board (On/Off Campus): $5,110/$6,100
Books and Supplies: $750
Average Grant: $1,603
Average Loan: $9,973
% Receiving Financial Aid: 30
% Receiving Aid Their First Year: 50

ADMISSIONS INFORMATION

Application Fee: $35
Electronic Application? Yes
Regular Application Deadline: 6/15
Regular Notification: Rolling
Deferment Available? No
Non-fall Admissions? Yes
Non-fall Application Deadline(s): 11/15 spring, 4/15 summer
Transfer Students Accepted? Yes
Transfer Policy: 12 credit hours may be accepted from an AACSB-accredited institution if approved by the Graduate Committee.
Need-Blind Admissions? Yes
Number of Applications Received: 127
% of Applicants Accepted: 55
% Accepted Who Enrolled: 63
Average GPA: 3.5
GPA Range: 3.1-3.7
Average GMAT: 603
GMAT Range: 560-640
Average Years Experience: 6
Minority/Disadvantaged Student Recruitment Programs: Fellowships for minority students

INTERNATIONAL STUDENTS

TOEFL Required of International Students? Yes
Minimum TOEFL: 550 (213 computer)

EMPLOYMENT INFORMATION

Placement Office Available? Yes
% Employed Within 3 Months: 10

Fields Employing Percentage of Grads: Global Management (10%), MIS (20%), Marketing (20%), Other (40%)

Frequent Employers: Archer Daniels Midland, Intel, Ondeo Nalco, Union Pacific

Prominent Alumni: Marsha Lommel, president/CEO, Madonna Rehabilitation Hospital; Vinod Gupta, founder/chairman, InfoUSA; David Maurstad, director, Federal Emergency Management Agency (FEMA); Bernard Reznicek, national director, Central States Indemnity Co.; William Ruud, policy director, State of Idaho

UNIVERSITY OF NEBRASKA—OMAHA
College of Business Administration

Admissions Contact: Lex Kaczmarek, Director, MBA Program
Address: 6001 Dodge Street, Omaha, NE 68182-0048
Admissions Phone: 402-554-2303 • **Admissions Fax:** 402-554-3747
Admissions E-mail: mba@unomaha.edu • **Web Address:** cba.unomaha.edu/mba

INSTITUTIONAL INFORMATION

Public/Private: Public
Evening Classes Available? Yes
Total Faculty: 40
% Faculty Female: 23
% Faculty Minority: 5
Student/Faculty Ratio: 30:1
Students in Parent Institution: 15,423
Academic Calendar: Semester

PROGRAMS

Degrees Offered: MBA (36-51 credits, 15 months to 6 years), EMBA (48 credits, 2 years), MACC (36 credits, 15 months to 6 years), MS in Economics (36 credits, 15 months to 6 years), MA in Economics (30 credits, 15 months to 5 years)

STUDENT INFORMATION

Total Business Students: 345
Average Age: 27

COMPUTER AND RESEARCH FACILITIES

Research Facilities: Investment Science Lab
Computer Facilities: MBA students have access to a 40-PC lab, 7 days a week. Also, DTN, Research Insight, Webstract, CCH Electronic Library
Campuswide Network? Yes
% of MBA Classrooms Wired: 100
Internet Fee? No

EXPENSES/FINANCIAL AID

Tuition Per Credit (Resident/Nonresident): $155/$400
Room & Board (On/Off Campus): $5,840/$6,300

ADMISSIONS INFORMATION

Application Fee: $40
Electronic Application? Yes
Regular Application Deadline: 7/1
Regular Notification: Rolling
Deferment Available? Yes
Length of Deferment: 1 year
Non-fall Admissions? Yes
Non-fall Application Deadline(s): 11/1, 4/1
Transfer Students Accepted? Yes

Transfer Policy: Up to 9 hours of transfer credit from another AACSB-accredited institution; requires submission of course syllabi and relevant catalog information

Need-Blind Admissions? Yes
Number of Applications Received: 89
% of Applicants Accepted: 72
% Accepted Who Enrolled: 83
Average GPA: 3.4
Average GMAT: 535
Average Years Experience: 5

INTERNATIONAL STUDENTS

TOEFL Required of International Students? Yes
Minimum TOEFL: 550 (213 computer)

EMPLOYMENT INFORMATION

Placement Office Available? No

UNIVERSITY OF NEVADA—LAS VEGAS
College of Business

Admissions Contact: Nasser Daneshvary, MBA Director/Associate Dean
Address: 4505 Maryland Parkway, Box 456031, Las Vegas, NV 89154-6031
Admissions Phone: 702-895-3655 • **Admissions Fax:** 702-895-4090
Admissions E-mail: cobmba@ccmail.nevada.edu • **Web Address:** business.unlv.edu

For MBAs who want an edge in the hospitality industry, take a look at the recently initiated combined MBA/Master of Hotel Administration program at UNLV. And it can't hurt that the school happens to be in one of the most popular vacation cities in the world. (Vegas, baby. Vegas!) While the school wants to graduate "visionary...executive leaders," accountants who want to audit evil companies in dark, quiet rooms and economists who want to pontificate from ivory towers will find master's degree programs to prepare them to achieve their dreams.

INSTITUTIONAL INFORMATION

Public/Private: Public
Evening Classes Available? Yes
Total Faculty: 75
% Faculty Female: 10
% Faculty Minority: 5
Student/Faculty Ratio: 25:1
Students in Parent Institution: 24,965
Academic Calendar: Semester

PROGRAMS

Degrees Offered: MBA (2 years full time evening, 3-4 years part time evening), EMBA (18 months block attendance)
Combined Degrees: MS Hotel Administration/MBA (2.5 years)
Academic Specialties: Teamwork emphasis, case study approach

STUDENT INFORMATION

Total Business Students: 179
% Full Time: 40
% Female: 36
% Minority: 6
% Out of State: 52
% International: 13
Average Age: 28

COMPUTER AND RESEARCH FACILITIES

Research Facilities: Center for Business and Economic Research, Nevada Small Business Development Center

Computer Facilities: Lied Library, Campus Computer Labs, ABI, Inform, Compustat,CRSP, dissertation abstracts, Ebsco, First Search, Infotrack, Lexis-Nexis, Moody's, PAIS, Simmons Study Media/Markets, Stat/USA

Campuswide Network? Yes

Internet Fee? No

EXPENSES/FINANCIAL AID

Annual Tuition (Resident/Nonresident): $7,785

Tuition Per Credit (Resident/Nonresident): $107/$220

Room & Board (On/Off Campus): $5,000/$7,000

Books and Supplies: $600

Average Grant: $2,500

Average Loan: $9,180

% Receiving Financial Aid: 49

% Receiving Aid Their First Year: 10

ADMISSIONS INFORMATION

Application Fee: $40

Electronic Application? No

Regular Application Deadline: 6/1

Regular Notification: 7/1

Deferment Available? Yes

Length of Deferment: 1 semester

Non-fall Admissions? Yes

Non-fall Application Deadline(s): 6/1 fall, 11/15 spring

Transfer Students Accepted? Yes

Transfer Policy: Total of 6 credits from an AACSB-accredited school

Need-Blind Admissions? Yes

Number of Applications Received: 186

% of Applicants Accepted: 41

% Accepted Who Enrolled: 75

Average GPA: 3.7

GPA Range: 3.0-4.0

Average GMAT: 588

GMAT Range: 530-600

Average Years Experience: 5

INTERNATIONAL STUDENTS

TOEFL Required of International Students? Yes

Minimum TOEFL: 550 (213 computer)

EMPLOYMENT INFORMATION

Placement Office Available? Yes

% Employed Within 3 Months: 4

Fields Employing Percentage of Grads: Consulting (5%), Accounting (5%), Other (10%), General Management (10%), MIS (10%), Marketing (20%), Finance (40%)

Frequent Employers: Bechtel SAIC, Pulte Homes, US Bank

UNIVERSITY OF NEVADA—RENO
College of Business Administration

Admissions Contact: Associate Director of Graduate Studies

Address: Mailstop 326, Reno, NV 89557

Admissions Phone: 775-784-6869 • **Admissions Fax:** 775-784-6064

Admissions E-mail: gradadmissions@unr.edu • **Web Address:** www.coba.unr.edu/MBA/

INSTITUTIONAL INFORMATION

Public/Private: Public

Evening Classes Available? Yes

Total Faculty: 47

Student/Faculty Ratio: 30:1

Students in Parent Institution: 1,128

Academic Calendar: Semester

PROGRAMS

Degrees Offered: MBA (2-6 years), MA in Economics (2-6 years), MS in Economics (2-6 years)

Academic Specialties: Cae study, faculty seminars, group discussion, lecture, research, student presentations, team projects

Special Opportunities: Accounting, Business Law/Legal Environment, Finance (includes Banking), Hotel/Restaurant/Tourism, International Business, Management, Marketing, Production/Operations Management/Managerial Economics, Supply Chain Management/Transportation/Logistics

STUDENT INFORMATION

Total Business Students: 167

% Full Time: 26

Average Age: 29

COMPUTER AND RESEARCH FACILITIES

Campuswide Network? Yes

Internet Fee? No

EXPENSES/FINANCIAL AID

Annual Tuition (Resident/Nonresident): $1,986/$7,094

Tuition Per Credit (Resident/Nonresident): $96

ADMISSIONS INFORMATION

Application Fee: $40

Electronic Application? No

Regular Application Deadline: 2/1

Regular Notification: Rolling

Deferment Available? Yes

Length of Deferment: 1 year

Non-fall Admissions? Yes

Non-fall Application Deadline(s): 10/1

Transfer Students Accepted? No

Need-Blind Admissions? No

Number of Applications Received: 72

% of Applicants Accepted: 93

% Accepted Who Enrolled: 76

Other Admissions Factors Considered: Computer expereince

INTERNATIONAL STUDENTS

TOEFL Required of International Students? Yes

Minimum TOEFL: 550

EMPLOYMENT INFORMATION

Placement Office Available? Yes

% Employed Within 3 Months: 99

UNIVERSITY OF NEW HAMPSHIRE
Whittemore School of Business and Economics

Admissions Contact: George Abraham, Director, Graduate and Executive Programs
Address: 116 McConnell Hall, 15 College Road, Durham, NH 03824
Admissions Phone: 603-862-1367 • **Admissions Fax:** 603-862-4468
Admissions E-mail: wsbe.grad@unh.edu • **Web Address:** www.mba.unh.edu

UNH offers your basic garden variety of graduate business degrees. A new master's in the management of technology brings candidates who pursue it through a teamwork-focused curriculum. Three-quarters of graduates end up working in New England making not too shabby a salary, so if you're looking to make a life in the region, Whittemore is a solid choice.

INSTITUTIONAL INFORMATION

Public/Private: Public
Evening Classes Available? Yes
Total Faculty: 40
% Faculty Female: 23
% Faculty Minority: 5
% Faculty Part Time: 23
Student/Faculty Ratio: 3:1
Students in Parent Institution: 14,248
Academic Calendar: Trimester

PROGRAMS

Degrees Offered: MBA (19 months full time), Evening MBA 2.5 to 3 years part time), EMBA (19 months), MSA (1 year full time, 2.5 years part-time), MA in Economics (1.5 years), PhD in Economics (4-5 years)
Combined Degrees: BA/MA in Economics (5 years)
Academic Specialties: The full-time MBA program begins with a month-long residency in September devoted to team development and pre-class seminars. The remainder of the first year is devoted to completion of core courses. The second year requires a corporate field-based project with electives/specializations. Currently specializations are offered in Marketing and Supply Chain Management, Entrepreneurship, Financial Management, and General Management.

The part-time MBA program allows students employed full-time to puruse the degree in the evenings. It typically takes 3 years to complete the part-time program. The part-time program is offered in both Durham and Manchester, New Hampshire. In addition to the specializations offered in the full-time program, there is also an option in Health Administration that part-time students in Manchester can pursue.

The EMBA is designed to provide a flexible full-time program for professionals or managers with a minimum of 7 years of work experience. The 19-month program meets alternating Fridays and Saturdays so students can continue to work while enrolled.

STUDENT INFORMATION

Total Business Students: 249
% Full Time: 30
% Female: 29
% Minority: 1
% Out of State: 39
% International: 15
Average Age: 31

COMPUTER AND RESEARCH FACILITIES

Computer Facilities: All graduate students are able to utilize computers and printers in the Graduate Conference Room. In addition, there are several computer clusters open to all university students throughout the campus.
Campuswide Network? Yes

Computer Model Recommended: Laptop
Internet Fee? No

EXPENSES/FINANCIAL AID

Annual Tuition (Resident/Nonresident): $6,640/$16,340
Tuition Per Credit (Resident/Nonresident): $443/$523
Room & Board (On/Off Campus): $6,184
Books and Supplies: $1,250

ADMISSIONS INFORMATION

Application Fee: $50
Electronic Application? Yes
Early Decision Application Deadline: April 1
Early Decision Notification: 5/15
Regular Application Deadline: 7/1
Regular Notification: Rolling
Deferment Available? Yes
Length of Deferment: 1 year
Non-fall Admissions? Yes
Non-fall Application Deadline(s): 11/15 winter term, part-time program only, on a space-available basis
Transfer Students Accepted? Yes
Transfer Policy: A maximum of 3 courses from an AACSB institution may be considered for transfer credit.
Need-Blind Admissions? Yes
Number of Applications Received: 156
% of Applicants Accepted: 76
% Accepted Who Enrolled: 76
Average GPA: 3.1
GPA Range: 2.8-3.3
Average GMAT: 552
GMAT Range: 510-620
Average Years Experience: 7
Other Schools to Which Students Applied: Babson College, Bentley College, University of Massachusetts—Amherst

INTERNATIONAL STUDENTS

TOEFL Required of International Students? Yes
Minimum TOEFL: 550 (213 computer)

EMPLOYMENT INFORMATION

Placement Office Available? Yes
Prominent Alumni: Dan Burnham, president, Raytheon, Defense; Michael Baldwin, president and COO, Cheesecake Factory; Terry Tracy, managing director, Salomon Smith Barney; John Hollowell, president, Colonial Williamsburg; David Cote, chairman, president, CEO, Honeywell

UNIVERSITY OF NEW MEXICO
Robert O. Anderson Graduate School of Management

Admissions Contact: Loyola Chastain, MBA Program Manager
Address: University of New Mexico, Albuquerque, NM 87131
Admissions Phone: 505-277-3147 • **Admissions Fax:** 505-277-9356
Admissions E-mail: chastain@mgt.unm.edu • **Web Address:** asm.unm.edu

Hispanic Magazine ranked Anderson's MBA program as one of the top 10 nationally for Hispanic students. With a starting salary well above the region's average, more than a quarter of its students of minority status, and more than 40 percent of its students women, Anderson is sitting pretty. Its

MBA candidates are sure to have a dynamic academic experience and one that pays off nicely after graduation.

INSTITUTIONAL INFORMATION

Public/Private: Public
Evening Classes Available? Yes
Total Faculty: 86
% Faculty Female: 33
% Faculty Part Time: 46
Student/Faculty Ratio: 30:1
Students in Parent Institution: 23,956
Academic Calendar: Semester

PROGRAMS

Degrees Offered: MBA (48 credits, 18 months to 3 years), MSA (33 credits, 2-5 years), EMBA (50 credits, 2 years)
Combined Degrees: MBA/MA in Latin American Studies (72 credits, 4.4 to 6 years), MBA/JD (129 credits, 5-8 years)
Study Abroad Options: France, Hong Kong, Mexico, United Kingdom, Western Europe

STUDENT INFORMATION

Total Business Students: 431
% Full Time: 57
% Female: 43
% Minority: 26
% Out of State: 4
% International: 9
Average Age: 31

COMPUTER AND RESEARCH FACILITIES

Research Facilities: Bureau of Business and Economic Research
Computer Facilities: ASM has 2 computer pods available for students to use.
Campuswide Network? Yes
% of MBA Classrooms Wired: 100
Internet Fee? No

EXPENSES/FINANCIAL AID

Annual Tuition (Resident/Nonresident): $3,301/$11,737
Tuition Per Credit (Resident/Nonresident): $139/$491
Room & Board (On/Off Campus): $10,200
Books and Supplies: $1,200
Average Grant: $4,500
Average Loan: $18,000
% Receiving Financial Aid: 75

ADMISSIONS INFORMATION

Application Fee: $40
Electronic Application? No
Regular Application Deadline: 6/1
Regular Notification: Rolling
Deferment Available? Yes
Length of Deferment: 1 year
Non-fall Admissions? Yes
Non-fall Application Deadline(s): 11/1, 4/1, 6/1
Transfer Students Accepted? Yes
Transfer Policy: Up to 6 credit hours
Need-Blind Admissions? No
Number of Applications Received: 129
% of Applicants Accepted: 57
% Accepted Who Enrolled: 100
Average GPA: 3.2
GPA Range: 2.7-3.8
Average GMAT: 562
GMAT Range: 420-740

INTERNATIONAL STUDENTS

TOEFL Required of International Students? Yes
Minimum TOEFL: 550 (213 computer)

EMPLOYMENT INFORMATION

Placement Office Available? Yes
% Employed Within 3 Months: 86
Fields Employing Percentage of Grads: Other (3%), Marketing (5%), Human Resources (5%), Accounting (6%), Operations (8%), Finance (10%), General Management (24%), MIS (31%)
Frequent Employers: Ford Motor Co., IBM, Intel, KPMG, Sandia National Laboratories

UNIVERSITY OF NEW ORLEANS
College of Business Administration

Admissions Contact: Roslyn Sheley, Director of Admissions
Address: Admin Building, Room 103, New Orleans, LA 70148
Admissions Phone: 504-280-6595 • **Admissions Fax:** 504-280-5522
Admissions E-mail: admissions@uno.edu • **Web Address:** www.uno.edu

The student body of UNO's College of Business Administration reflects the changing face of the MBA: women and minorities each comprise more than half of the overall population. The recently introduced EMBA-Kinston (Jamaica) is drawing applications by the score. It's no wonder. What MBA candidate wouldn't want to enjoy the Mai Tai life most other already made MBAs are working long hours to achieve? The tuition is low, the temperature is high, and there's no city that makes it easier to network than the Big Easy.

INSTITUTIONAL INFORMATION

Public/Private: Public
Evening Classes Available? Yes
Total Faculty: 33
% Faculty Female: 30
% Faculty Minority: 18
% Faculty Part Time: 3
Student/Faculty Ratio: 25:1
Students in Parent Institution: 17,320
Academic Calendar: Semester

PROGRAMS

Degrees Offered: MBA (16 months to 8 years), with concentrations in Finance, International Business, Marketing, Real Estate, Human Resources, Travel Industry/Tourism Management, Management Information Systems, Technology Management, Health Care; EMBA (18 months); MSA (16 months to 8 years); MST (16 months to 8 years); Master of Philosophy in Financial Education (3-10 years); Master in Health Care Management (18 months to 8 years), Master of Science in Health Care Management (13 months)
Academic Specialties: Case study, computer analysis, computer simulations, faculty seminars, field projects, group discussion, lecture, research, seminars by members of the business community, student presentations, study groups, team projects
Study Abroad Options: International exchange program in Austria

STUDENT INFORMATION

Total Business Students: 845
% Full Time: 44
% Female: 49
% Minority: 28

% Out of State: 28
% International: 24
Average Age: 31

COMPUTER AND RESEARCH FACILITIES

Computer Facilities: University Computing and Communications Lab, Library Lab, Business Lab
Campuswide Network? Yes
Internet Fee? No

EXPENSES/FINANCIAL AID

Annual Tuition (Resident/Nonresident): $2,876/$9,920
Tuition Per Credit (Resident/Nonresident): $455/$1,793
Room & Board (On/Off Campus): $3,900
Books and Supplies: $1,150
Average Grant: $4,200
Average Loan: $5,000

ADMISSIONS INFORMATION

Application Fee: $20
Electronic Application? Yes
Regular Application Deadline: 8/30
Regular Notification: 9/1
Deferment Available? Yes
Length of Deferment: 1 semester
Non-fall Admissions? Yes
Non-fall Application Deadline(s): 11/15, 5/1
Transfer Students Accepted? Yes
Transfer Policy: Maximum of 12 credit hours
Need-Blind Admissions? No
Number of Applications Received: 643
% of Applicants Accepted: 78
% Accepted Who Enrolled: 72
Average GPA: 3.0
Average GMAT: 473
GMAT Range: 420-530
Other Admissions Factors Considered: Computer experience

INTERNATIONAL STUDENTS

TOEFL Required of International Students? Yes
Minimum TOEFL: 550 (213 computer)

EMPLOYMENT INFORMATION

Placement Office Available? No
Prominent Alumni: Dr. James Clark, chairman of the board, Netscape Communications; Michael Fitzpatrick, CEO, Rohm & Haas; Erving Johnson, starting center, Milwaukee Bucks; Mike Kettenring, president and general manager, Gillett Broadcasting; Dr. Reuben Arminana, president, Sonoma State University

UNIVERSITY OF NORTH CAROLINA— CHAPEL HILL

Kenan-Flagler Business School

Admissions Contact: Sherry Wallace, Director, MBA Admissions
Address: CB #3490, McColl Building, Chapel Hill, NC 27599-3490
Admissions Phone: 919-962-3236 • **Admissions Fax:** 919-962-0898
Admissions E-mail: mba_info@unc.edu • **Web Address:** www.kenan-flagler.unc.edu

The "pace is very fast and sometimes stressful," but "the faculty are outstanding, jobs are plentiful, students are intelligent, and everyone loves one another" at the Kenan-Flagler Business School at the University of North Carolina at Chapel Hill. Seriously. Students also appreciate the "global focus throughout the curriculum," and the surrounding area provides a "relaxed atmosphere" and a good social scene.

INSTITUTIONAL INFORMATION

Public/Private: Public
Evening Classes Available? Yes
Total Faculty: 139
% Faculty Female: 19
% Faculty Minority: 3
% Faculty Part Time: 28
Student/Faculty Ratio: 4:1
Students in Parent Institution: 23,000
Academic Calendar: Semester

PROGRAMS

Degrees Offered: MBA; EMBA (24 months evening, 20 months weekend); OneMBA, a global program (21 months); PhD (4 years); MACC (12 months)
Combined Degrees: MBA/JD (4 years), MBA/Master of Regional Planning (3 years), MBA/MHA (3 years), MBA/MSIS
Academic Specialties: UNC Kenan-Flagler faculty are known for excellence in teaching and research in Marketing; Finance; Accounting; Operations, Technology, and Innovation Management (OTIM); Management; and Information Technology and E-Commerce. We offer second-year MBA concentrations in Corporate Finance, Customer and Product Management, Investment Management, Management Consulting, Real Estate, Global Supply Chain Management, Entrepreneurship and Venture Development, Electronic Business and Digital Commerce, Sustainable Enterprise, and International Business.
Special Opportunities: Office of International Programs; Frank Hawkins Kenan Institute of Private Enterprise; Center for Sustainable Enterprise; Center for Community Capitalism; Center for Economic Development; Center for Entrepreneurship and Technology Venturing and its Venture Capital Investment Competition; Center for Logistics & Digial Strategy; Center for Real Estate Development; Center for Technology & Advanced Commerce; Urban Investment Strategies Center; Global Immersion electives; The Washington Campus; Center for International Business Education and Research (CIBER); Center for Innovation in Learning; Launcher, a business incubator; international internships

Through our Global Center, MBAs may take a course called "Working Spanish" (www.globalcenter.org/workingspanish1.htm). Students learn Spanish and Spanish-speaking business culture using a unique combination of interactive technology, distance learning, instructor-led workshops, conversation hours, and an in-country immersion to create culturally sensitive Spanish speakers who can function comfortably and effectively in the Spanish-speaking workplace.
Study Abroad Options: Australia, Austria, Belgium, Brazil, Chile, China, Czech Republic, Denmark, England, France, Germany, Hungary, INCAE, India, Israel, Italy, Mexico, the Netherlands, Norway, Peru, the Philippines, Singapore, South Africa, Spain, Sweden, Switzerland, Thailand, Turkey, Venezuela

STUDENT INFORMATION

Total Business Students: 560
% Full Time: 100
% Female: 30
% Minority: 15
% Out of State: 76
% International: 26
Average Age: 28

COMPUTER AND RESEARCH FACILITIES

Research Facilities: Frank Hawkins Kenan Institute of Private Enterprise, which includes: Center for Entrepreneurship and Technology Venturing, Center for Sustainable Enterprise, Center for Real Estate Development, Center for Community Capitalism, Center for Logistics and Digital Strategy, Center for Technology and Advanced Commerce, Center for Economic Development, Urban Investment Strategies Center; other centers: Center for Tax Excellence

Computer Facilities: In addition to UNC Kenan-Flagler's technology center, our faculty, staff, and students have wireless access to the School's wireless network. Students can access UNC Kenan-Flagler's network from other parts of campus covered by wireless access. UNC Kenan-Flagler maintains more than 2,800 Internet connections in our McColl Building. A state-of-the-art Trading Room facility allows finance students to gain exposure to the latest technologies used in finance and trading. We have a 40-workstation multimedia classroom to facilitate computer-enabled training and instruction. Other labs available are on the UNC campus. The library has access to a number of online resources including Lexis-Nexis, UMI Proquest, Hoover's, and Stat-USA databases, as well as CD-ROM and electronic databases.

Campuswide Network? Yes
% of MBA Classrooms Wired: 100
Computer Model Recommended: Laptop
Internet Fee? No

EXPENSES/FINANCIAL AID

Annual Tuition (Resident/Nonresident): $11,794/$26,749
Room & Board (On/Off Campus): $9,299
Books and Supplies: $4,700
Average Grant: $26,454

ADMISSIONS INFORMATION

Application Fee: $100
Electronic Application? Yes
Regular Application Deadline: 4/4
Regular Notification: 5/15
Deferment Available? Yes
Length of Deferment: 1 year (emergency only)
Non-fall Admissions? No
Transfer Students Accepted? No
Need-Blind Admissions? Yes
Number of Applications Received: 2,016
% of Applicants Accepted: 30
% Accepted Who Enrolled: 47
Average GPA: 3.2
Average GMAT: 61
GMAT Range: 600-740
Average Years Experience: 5
Other Admissions Factors Considered: Achieving a well-balanced class
Minority/Disadvantaged Student Recruitment Programs: At UNC Kenan-Flagler, current minority students play an active role in recruiting other high-achieving students of color. Each fall, the Alliance of Minority Students hosts Inside Kenan-Flagler, a weekend workshop designed to give prospective, top minority candidates an in-depth, personal experience with our MBA Program. UNC Kenan-Flalger is an exhibitor at the National Black MBA Association annual conference and at the National Society of Hispanic MBAs annual conference. UNC Kenan-Flagler is a member of the Consortium for Graduate Study in Management (CGSM), an alliance of 14 business schools working in partnership with corporate America to facilitate the entry of minorities into managerial positions in business. The CGSM recruits college-trained African American, Hispanic American, and Native American U.S. citizens and invites them to compete for merit-based fellowships for graduate study leading to an MBA (www.cgsm.org). Student organizations of interest include Latin American Student Association and the Alliance of Minority Business Students.
Other Schools to Which Students Applied: Duke University, Northwestern University, University of Michigan, University of Virginia

INTERNATIONAL STUDENTS

TOEFL Required of International Students? Yes
Minimum TOEFL: 600 (250 computer)

EMPLOYMENT INFORMATION

Placement Office Available? Yes
% Employed Within 3 Months: 95
Fields Employing Percentage of Grads: Operations (2%), Strategic Planning (3%), General Management (4%), Consulting (23%), Finance (29%), Marketing (33%)

Frequent Employers: Accenture, Bank of America, Bear Stearns, Bristol-Myers Squibb, Chase Bank, Dell Computer, Deloitte Consulting, Dupont, Eli Lilly, Ericsson, First Union, GlaxoSmithKline, Goldman Sachs, Hewlett-Packard, IBM, JP Morgan Chase & Co., Johnson & Johnson, Kraft Foods, Lehman Brothers, McKinsey & Co., Merrill Lynch, Nabisco, Nortel Networks, Procter & Gamble, Salomon Smith Barney, UPS, Walt Disney
Prominent Alumni: Lee S. Ainslie III, managing partner, Maverick Capital; Richard L. Michaux, executive chairman of the board (retired), Avalo; Michael Parekh, managing director, Goldman, Sachs & Co

UNIVERSITY OF NORTH CAROLINA— CHARLOTTE

Belk College of Business Administration

Admissions Contact: Johnna Watson, Assistant Dean for Enrollment Services
Address: 9201 University City Boulevard, Charlotte, NC 28223-0001
Admissions Phone: 704-687-3366 • **Admissions Fax:** 704-687-3279
Admissions E-mail: gradadm@email.uncc.edu • **Web Address:** www.belkcollege.uncc.edu/

If you're a North Carolina resident looking to stay in the region and make some good money for low opportunity costs, you'd better take a look at UNC—Charlotte. The Bank of America, a perennially high-placing company on the Fortune 500, is one of the major employers of UNC—Charlotte MBAs, which is fitting, since its world headquarters happen to be in Charlotte.

INSTITUTIONAL INFORMATION

Public/Private: Public
Evening Classes Available? Yes
Total Faculty: 68
% Faculty Female: 26
% Faculty Minority: 9
% Faculty Part Time: 3
Student/Faculty Ratio: 6:1
Students in Parent Institution: 18,916
Academic Calendar: Semester

PROGRAMS

Degrees Offered: MBA (2-3 years), MACC (1-2 years), MS in Economics (2 years)
Academic Specialties: UNC—Charlotte's MBA Program is designed to suit working professionals so that students can earn their degree by attending evening classes without interrupting their careers. The program provides a balance of lectures, case studies, and projects, and a balance between individual and team assignments. Students have the option of pursuing areas of concentration such as Business Finance, Information and Technology Management, E-Business, Management, Marketing, Economics, Real Estate Finance and Development, and Financial Institutions/Commercial Banking. Students may also self-structure their area of concentration in consultation with the MBA director. A new concentration in International Business will be available in 2003-2004.
Study Abroad Options: Germany (pending); Mexico

STUDENT INFORMATION

Total Business Students: 365
% Full Time: 21
% Female: 27
% Minority: 13
% Out of State: 4
% International: 43

Average Age: 30

COMPUTER AND RESEARCH FACILITIES

Computer Facilities: Compact Disclosure, Dow Jones News Retrieval, National Trade Bank, FirstSearch, Academic Universe, CCH Tax Research Network, Choices II, MasterFile Full Test 1500, Pro Quest Direct, Research Bank Web, Stat USA

Campuswide Network? Yes

% of MBA Classrooms Wired: 50

Internet Fee? No

EXPENSES/FINANCIAL AID

Annual Tuition (Resident/Nonresident): $3,022/$12,748

Tuition Per Credit (Resident/Nonresident): $168/$776

Room & Board (On/Off Campus): $5,100/$5,600

Books and Supplies: $950

Average Grant: $9,500

Average Loan: $11,469

ADMISSIONS INFORMATION

Application Fee: $35

Electronic Application? No

Regular Application Deadline: 7/1

Regular Notification: Rolling

Deferment Available? Yes

Length of Deferment: 1 year

Non-fall Admissions? Yes

Non-fall Application Deadline(s): 7/1 fall, 11/1 spring

Transfer Students Accepted? Yes

Transfer Policy: All students have to complete the graduate application materials and submit official test scores. With permission, it may be possible to transfer 12 credit hours of graduate-level work from an AACSB-accredited university. This will be considered when the application materials are officially reviewed.

Need-Blind Admissions? Yes

Number of Applications Received: 231

% of Applicants Accepted: 63

% Accepted Who Enrolled: 57

Average GPA: 3.2

GPA Range: 3.0-3.6

Average GMAT: 569

GMAT Range: 530-600

Average Years Experience: 7

Other Admissions Factors Considered: Work experience, extracurricular activities, professional designations, international experience

Minority/Disadvantaged Student Recruitment Programs: Information sessions

INTERNATIONAL STUDENTS

TOEFL Required of International Students? Yes

Minimum TOEFL: 550 (220 computer)

EMPLOYMENT INFORMATION

Placement Office Available? Yes

% Employed Within 3 Months: 91

Fields Employing Percentage of Grads: General Management (2%), Consulting (5%), Accounting (5%), Other (9%), MIS (10%), Marketing (12%), Operations (19%), Finance (38%)

Frequent Employers: Accenture, Bank of America, BB&T, Duke Energy, IBM, KPMG Peat Marvick, Potter and Co., Royal and SunAlliance, The Vanguard Group, Wachovia

Prominent Alumni: David Hauser, executive vice president and treasurer, Duke Energy; Dr. Robert Rucho, DDS, senator, North Carolina General Assembly; Manuel Zapata, president, Zapata Engineering; Verl Purdy, president, AGDATA

UNIVERSITY OF NORTH CAROLINA— GREENSBORO

Joseph M. Bryan School of Business & Economics

Admissions Contact: Dr. Catherine Holderness, Associate Director, MBA Program

Address: PO Box 26165, Greensboro, NC 27402-6165

Admissions Phone: 336-334-5390 • **Admissions Fax:** 336-334-4209

Admissions E-mail: mba@uncg.edu • **Web Address:** www.uncg.edu/bae/mba

The study abroad opportunities are fat and the tuition is thin at the Bryan School. And even if you don't go international, that's okay. Bryan has brought international to you with a student body that's 50 percent non-American. You can take only evening MBA classes here, so if you're a late riser, welcome home. But if you're a nighttime social bug, you'd better clear your schedule.

INSTITUTIONAL INFORMATION

Public/Private: Public

Evening Classes Available? Yes

Total Faculty: 45

% Faculty Female: 17

% Faculty Minority: 9

% Faculty Part Time: 12

Student/Faculty Ratio: 9:1

Students in Parent Institution: 14,300

Academic Calendar: Semester

PROGRAMS

Degrees Offered: Evening MBA (36-48 credits, 1.5 to 2 years full time, 2-4 years part time), MSITM (36 credits, 2 years full time), MSA (30 credits, 1.5 years full time)

Combined Degrees: MSN/MBA (42-54 credits, 2-5 years)

Academic Specialties: The Bryan School has the largest number of graduate degrees among the business schools in the state of North Carolina. MBA students and students in other graduate programs may take elective courses in Advanced Accounting, Management Information Systems, and Economics, as well as the usually offered MBA electives in Finance, Marketing, and International Business. The School has internationally recognized faculty in the areas of International Business, Operations Management, and Economics. Students may also take graduate electives in related programs such as the Master's of Textile Design and Marketing Program. The evening format allows maximum flexibility for working students and allows daytime internship opportunities for full-time students.

Special Opportunities: Week-long study abroad courses each fall; spring semester and summer abroad options for full-time students

Study Abroad Options: Australia, Austria, Canada, Estonia, Finland, France, Germany, Israel, Japan, Mexico, Poland, Spain, Sweden, United Kingdom

STUDENT INFORMATION

Total Business Students: 227

% Full Time: 40

% Female: 65

% Minority: 15

% International: 65

Average Age: 27

COMPUTER AND RESEARCH FACILITIES

Research Facilities: SAP Alliance, Center for Global Business Research and Education, Center for Applied Research

Computer Facilities: There are 3 computer labs in the Business School and several other labs across campus, including a computing superlab in the Library. An extensive assortment of databases, as well as software, is available to students. We are a SAP Alliance School, and SAP software is loaded in our labs and utilized in classroom instruction. Each classroom is equipped with a computer and projection system.

Campuswide Network? Yes
% of MBA Classrooms Wired: 100
Internet Fee? No

EXPENSES/FINANCIAL AID

Annual Tuition (Resident/Nonresident): $1,798/$12,362
Tuition Per Credit (Resident/Nonresident): $225/$1,545
Room & Board (On/Off Campus): $7,000
Books and Supplies: $1,200
Average Grant: $14,000

ADMISSIONS INFORMATION

Application Fee: $35
Electronic Application? Yes
Regular Application Deadline: 7/1
Regular Notification: Rolling
Deferment Available? Yes
Length of Deferment: 1 year
Non-fall Admissions? Yes
Non-fall Application Deadline(s): 11/1
Transfer Students Accepted? Yes
Transfer Policy: Transfer applicants must be in good standing at a fellow AACSB-accredited MBA Program and may transfer no more than 12 semester credit hours of approved coursework.
Need-Blind Admissions? Yes
Number of Applications Received: 176
% of Applicants Accepted: 65
% Accepted Who Enrolled: 92
Average GPA: 3.0
Average GMAT: 570
Average Years Experience: 4
Other Admissions Factors Considered: Maturity achieved through work or other experience post-baccalaureate, demonstrated ability to succeed academically
Other Schools to Which Students Applied: University of North Carolina—Chapel Hill, Wake Forest University

INTERNATIONAL STUDENTS

TOEFL Required of International Students? Yes
Minimum TOEFL: 550 (213 computer)

EMPLOYMENT INFORMATION

Placement Office Available? Yes
% Employed Within 3 Months: 85
Fields Employing Percentage of Grads: Entrepreneurship (2%), Human Resources (2%), Accounting (2%), Communications (4%), Quantitative (5%), Other (6%), Global Management (8%), Consulting (10%), Operations (10%), Marketing (10%), Finance (10%), General Management (12%), MIS (15%)
Frequent Employers: American Express; Arthur Andersen & Co.; AT&T; Burlington Industries; Cameron-Brown Co.; Carolina Steel Corp.; Center for Creative Leadership; Dow Corning; Duke Power Co.; Ernst & Young; Eveready Battery Co.; Guilford Mills; IBM Corp.; Jefferson-Pilot; Kayser-Roth; Konica; North Carolina Baptist Hospital; Proctor & Gamble; RJR Nabisco; Roche Biomedical; SaraLee; Stockhausen, Inc.; Syngenta; Unifi
Prominent Alumni: Nido R. Qubein, founder, chairman, and CEO, Creative Services, Inc.; Sue W. Cole, president, U.S. Trust Co. of North Carolina; Joe K. Pickett, chairman and CEO, HomeSide International, Inc.; Lee McGehee Porter III, managing director, Weiss, Peck & Greer, L.L.C.

UNIVERSITY OF NORTH CAROLINA—WILMINGTON
Cameron School of Business

Admissions Contact: MBA Director
Address: 601 South College Road, Wilmington, NC 28403
Admissions Phone: 910-962-3777 • **Admissions Fax:** 910-962-3815
Admissions E-mail: gradstudies@uncwil.edu • **Web Address:** www.csb.uncwil.edu

INSTITUTIONAL INFORMATION

Public/Private: Public
Evening Classes Available? No
Total Faculty: 11
Students in Parent Institution: 9,300

PROGRAMS

Degrees Offered: MBA (49 credits, 2 years part time)

STUDENT INFORMATION

Total Business Students: 120
% Female: 39
% Minority: 3
Average Age: 32

COMPUTER AND RESEARCH FACILITIES

Computer Facilities: Randall Library: 389,611 volumes; 837,013 microforms; 4,998 current periodicals
Campuswide Network? Yes
Internet Fee? No

EXPENSES/FINANCIAL AID

Tuition Per Credit (Resident/Nonresident): $256/$1,286

ADMISSIONS INFORMATION

Electronic Application? No
Regular Application Deadline: 3/15
Regular Notification: Rolling
Deferment Available? No
Non-fall Admissions? No
Transfer Students Accepted? No
Need-Blind Admissions? No
Number of Applications Received: 147
% of Applicants Accepted: 44
% Accepted Who Enrolled: 92
Other Admissions Factors Considered: GMAT score, resume

INTERNATIONAL STUDENTS

TOEFL Required of International Students? Yes
Minimum TOEFL: 500

EMPLOYMENT INFORMATION

Placement Office Available? Yes
% Employed Within 3 Months: 100

UNIVERSITY OF NORTH DAKOTA
College of Business Administration

Admissions Contact: Dr. Jacob Wambsganss, MBA Director
Address: Gamble Hall, PO Box 8098, Grand Forks, ND 58202
Admissions Phone: 701-777-2135 • **Admissions Fax:** 701-777-5099
Admissions E-mail: gradschool@mail.und.nodak.edu
Web Address: bpa.und.nodak.edu/mba/

INSTITUTIONAL INFORMATION

Public/Private: Public
Evening Classes Available? No
Total Faculty: 60
% Faculty Part Time: 21
Students in Parent Institution: 11,300

PROGRAMS

Degrees Offered: MBA (60 credits, 2-7 years)
Special Opportunities: Internship program

STUDENT INFORMATION

Total Business Students: 90
% Full Time: 17
% Female: 31
% Minority: 4
% International: 7
Average Age: 27

COMPUTER AND RESEARCH FACILITIES

Computer Facilities: Access to online bibliographic retrieval services
Campuswide Network? Yes
Internet Fee? No

EXPENSES/FINANCIAL AID

Annual Tuition (Resident/Nonresident): $1,649/$3,999

ADMISSIONS INFORMATION

Electronic Application? No
Regular Application Deadline: Rolling
Regular Notification: Rolling
Deferment Available? No
Non-fall Admissions? No
Transfer Students Accepted? No
Need-Blind Admissions? No
Number of Applications Received: 275
% of Applicants Accepted: 28
% Accepted Who Enrolled: 73
Other Admissions Factors Considered: GMAT accepted, 450 minimum

INTERNATIONAL STUDENTS

TOEFL Required of International Students? Yes
Minimum TOEFL: 550

EMPLOYMENT INFORMATION

Placement Office Available? Yes
% Employed Within 3 Months: 95

UNIVERSITY OF NORTH FLORIDA
College of Business Administration

Admissions Contact: Graduate Studies Coordinator
Address: 4567 St John's Bluff Road S., Building 42, Jacksonville, FL 32224
Admissions Phone: 904-620-2590 • **Admissions Fax:** 904-620-2832
Admissions E-mail: cmoore@unf.edu • **Web Address:** www.unf.edu/coba/

INSTITUTIONAL INFORMATION

Public/Private: Public
Evening Classes Available? Yes
Total Faculty: 59
Student/Faculty Ratio: 3:1
Students in Parent Institution: 12,240

PROGRAMS

Degrees Offered: MBA (36 semester hours), MHRM (36 semester hours), MACC (36 semester hours)

STUDENT INFORMATION

Total Business Students: 388
% Full Time: 25
% Female: 50
% Minority: 15
% Out of State: 32
% International: 24
Average Age: 29

COMPUTER AND RESEARCH FACILITIES

Computer Facilities: UNF computer labs; computer classrooms; library databases for research, which can be accessed via UNF computers or dial-in from home computer
Campuswide Network? Yes
% of MBA Classrooms Wired: 15
Internet Fee? No

EXPENSES/FINANCIAL AID

Annual Tuition (Resident/Nonresident): $6,137/$20,909
Books and Supplies: $600
Average Grant: $1,177
Average Loan: $6,365
% Receiving Financial Aid: 30
% Receiving Aid Their First Year: 37

ADMISSIONS INFORMATION

Electronic Application? Yes
Regular Application Deadline: 7/7
Regular Notification: Rolling
Deferment Available? Yes
Length of Deferment: 1 semester
Non-fall Admissions? Yes
Non-fall Application Deadline(s): 11/3, 3/10
Transfer Students Accepted? Yes
Transfer Policy: Case-by-case basis
Need-Blind Admissions? Yes
Number of Applications Received: 232
% of Applicants Accepted: 49
% Accepted Who Enrolled: 79

INTERNATIONAL STUDENTS

TOEFL Required of International Students? Yes
Minimum TOEFL: 550

EMPLOYMENT INFORMATION

Placement Office Available? Yes

UNIVERSITY OF NORTH TEXAS
College of Business Administration

Admissions Contact: Denise Galubenski or Konni Stubblefield, Graduate Degree Program Advisors
Address: PO Box 311160, Denton, TX 76203
Admissions Phone: 940-369-8977 • **Admissions Fax:** 940-369-8978
Admissions E-mail: MBA@cobaf.unt.edu • **Web Address:** www.coba.unt.edu

Offering more graduate business degrees and degree combos than your average b-school, UNT maintains a people-oriented approach to the MBA. Specializations within the MBA program are operations management science, human resource management, and administrative management, all designed "to present a realistic, relevant, and thorough view of people working in organizations." Denton lies about 25 miles northwest of the so-called Dallas/Fort Worth Metroplex near the shores of one of the many lakes in the area.

INSTITUTIONAL INFORMATION

Public/Private: Public
Evening Classes Available? Yes
Student/Faculty Ratio: 30:1
Students in Parent Institution: 27,000
Academic Calendar: Semester

PROGRAMS

Degrees Offered: MBA (up to 6 years),MSA (up to 6 years), MS (up to 6 years), EMBA (up to 20 months)
Combined Degrees: MBA in Operations Management Science/MS in Engineering Technology (48 hours), MBA (any professional field)/MS in Merchandising (54 hours), MBA (any professional field)/MS in Hospitality Management (54 hours)
Study Abroad Options: Mexico, United Kingdom

STUDENT INFORMATION

Total Business Students: 412
% Full Time: 45
% Female: 37
% Minority: 8
% Out of State: 1
% International: 15

COMPUTER AND RESEARCH FACILITIES

Computer Facilities: More computers per student than other comparable Texas institutions; 14 general-access computer labs with more than 550 microcomputers (including 1 lab available 24 hours and 1 adaptive lab for students with special needs)
Campuswide Network? Yes
Internet Fee? No

EXPENSES/FINANCIAL AID

Tuition Per Credit (Resident/Nonresident): $146/$272

ADMISSIONS INFORMATION

Application Fee: $25
Electronic Application? Yes
Regular Application Deadline: Rolling
Regular Notification: Rolling
Deferment Available? Yes
Length of Deferment: 3 semesters
Non-fall Admissions? Yes
Non-fall Application Deadline(s): Spring, May mini-mester, summer I, summer II
Transfer Students Accepted? Yes
Transfer Policy: Transfer applicants must meet the same university application deadline. Only 6-9 hours may transfer into our program. These hours will be determined by the departmental advisor.

Need-Blind Admissions? No
Number of Applications Received: 324
% of Applicants Accepted: 43
% Accepted Who Enrolled: 60
Average GPA: 2.9
Average GMAT: 560
Other Admissions Factors Considered: GRE scores accepted

INTERNATIONAL STUDENTS

TOEFL Required of International Students? Yes
Minimum TOEFL: 550 (213 computer)

EMPLOYMENT INFORMATION

Placement Office Available? Yes

UNIVERSITY OF NORTHERN IOWA
College of Business Administration

Admissions Contact: Leslie Wilson, Dean
Address: Office of the Dean CBB-325, Cedar Falls, IA 50613-0123
Admissions Phone: 319-273-6243 • **Admissions Fax:** 319-273-2922
Admissions E-mail: cba.info@uni.edu • **Web Address:** www.cba.uni.edu

INSTITUTIONAL INFORMATION

Public/Private: Public
Evening Classes Available? No
Total Faculty: 69
Student/Faculty Ratio: 25:1
Students in Parent Institution: 13,329
Academic Calendar: Semester

PROGRAMS

Degrees Offered: MBA (31 credits, full time or part-time, 10 months to 5.8 years), with concentration in Management

STUDENT INFORMATION

Total Business Students: 118
% Full Time: 37
Average Age: 33

COMPUTER AND RESEARCH FACILITIES

Research Facilities: Donald O. Rod Library; total holdings of 811,000 volumes; 690,512 microforms; 3,033 current periodical subscriptions. CD player(s), online bibliographic retrieval services, online databases
Computer Facilities: Online database
Campuswide Network? No
Internet Fee? No

EXPENSES/FINANCIAL AID

Annual Tuition (Resident/Nonresident): $4,814/$11,238
Room & Board (On/Off Campus): $4,606

ADMISSIONS INFORMATION

Application Fee: $20
Electronic Application? No
Regular Application Deadline: 7/20
Regular Notification: Rolling
Deferment Available? No
Non-fall Admissions? Yes
Non-fall Application Deadline(s): 12/15
Transfer Students Accepted? No

Need-Blind Admissions? No
Number of Applications Received: 87
% of Applicants Accepted: 77
% Accepted Who Enrolled: 61
Other Admissions Factors Considered: For international students: proof of adequate funds, proof of health/immunizations required

INTERNATIONAL STUDENTS

TOEFL Required of International Students? Yes
Minimum TOEFL: 500

EMPLOYMENT INFORMATION

Placement Office Available? Yes

UNIVERSITY OF NOTRE DAME
Mendoza College of Business

Admissions Contact: Hayden Estrada IV, Director of Admissions
Address: 276 Mendoza College of Business, Notre Dame, IN 46556-4656
Admissions Phone: 219-631-8488 • Admissions Fax: 219-631-8800
Admissions E-mail: mba1@nd.edu • Web Address: www.nd.edu/~mba

Would it surprise you to learn that Notre Dame's "small" and "well-rounded" College of Business Administration takes a traditional approach to the MBA? We hope not. Among the academic departments here, finance gets the highest marks among students, and management scores high as well. Students tell us "the people are, without question, the greatest strength of this school. People care about one another and all learning takes place in that context."

INSTITUTIONAL INFORMATION

Public/Private: Private
Evening Classes Available? No
Total Faculty: 112
% Faculty Female: 16
Student/Faculty Ratio: 4:1
Students in Parent Institution: 10,800
Academic Calendar: Semester

PROGRAMS

Degrees Offered: EMBA (2 years), MS in Administration (3 years), MSA (1 year)
Combined Degrees: JD/MBA (4 years), Master of Engineering/MBA (2 years); MS/MBA (2 years)
Study Abroad Options: Instituto Latino Americano de Doctrina y Estudios Sociales (ILADES), Santiago, Chile; Notre Dame London Centre, England

STUDENT INFORMATION

Total Business Students: 332
% Full Time: 100
% Female: 30
% Minority: 5
% International: 30
Average Age: 27

COMPUTER AND RESEARCH FACILITIES

Research Facilities: Irich Angles, Fanning Communication Center, Gigot Center
Computer Facilities: Dial up to NT network
Campuswide Network? Yes

% of MBA Classrooms Wired: 100
Internet Fee? No

EXPENSES/FINANCIAL AID

Annual Tuition: $24,969
Room & Board (On/Off Campus): $4,800
Books and Supplies: $1,300
Average Grant: $14,000
Average Loan: $28,000

ADMISSIONS INFORMATION

Application Fee: $100
Electronic Application? Yes
Early Decision Application Deadline: 11/15
Early Decision Notification: 12/15
Regular Application Deadline: 1/15
Regular Notification: 2/15
Deferment Available? Yes
Length of Deferment: 1 year
Non-fall Admissions? No
Transfer Students Accepted? No
Need-Blind Admissions? Yes
Number of Applications Received: 813
% of Applicants Accepted: 29
% Accepted Who Enrolled: 82
Average GPA: 3.2
GPA Range: 3.1-3.8
Average GMAT: 659
GMAT Range: 610-710
Average Years Experience: 4
Other Admissions Factors Considered: Desire to attend Notre Dame, a track record of community service and leadership
Minority/Disadvantaged Student Recruitment Programs: Ford Review Weekend
Other Schools to Which Students Applied: Northwestern University, University of Michigan, University of Texas—Austin, Vanderbilt University

INTERNATIONAL STUDENTS

TOEFL Required of International Students? Yes
Minimum TOEFL: 600

EMPLOYMENT INFORMATION

Placement Office Available? Yes
% Employed Within 3 Months: 97
Fields Employing Percentage of Grads: Other (2%), Operations (2%), Human Resources (3%), MIS (4%), Strategic Planning (5%), General Management (8%), Consulting (16%), Marketing (20%), Finance (29%)
Frequent Employers: Andersen Consulting, Cap Gemini, Corning, Dell, Deloitte and Touche LLP, Ernst & Young LLC, Ford, Hewlett Packard, IBM, Intel, Pricewaterhouse Coopers LLP, Proctor & Gamble, Sprint
Prominent Alumni: Marc Fields, Raytheon; Justin Johnson, Major League Baseball

UNIVERSITY OF OKLAHOMA
Michael F. Price College of Business

Admissions Contact: Dr. Alice Watkins, Associate Director of Graduate Programs in Business
Address: 307 West Brooks, Adams Hall Room 105-K, Norman, OK 73019-4003
Admissions Phone: 405-325-4107 • Admissions Fax: 405-325-1957
Admissions E-mail: gamundson@ou.edu • Web Address: www.ou.edu/mba/

INSTITUTIONAL INFORMATION

Public/Private: Public
Evening Classes Available? No
Total Faculty: 65
% Faculty Part Time: 26
Students in Parent Institution: 20,026
Academic Calendar: Semester

PROGRAMS

Degrees Offered: MBA (53 credits, 21 months to 6 years), MACC (36-49 credits, 18 months to 6 years), PhD in Business
Combined Degrees: MBA/JD (126 credits, 4-6 years)

STUDENT INFORMATION

Total Business Students: 261
% Full Time: 50
% Female: 34
% Minority: 14
Average Age: 27

COMPUTER AND RESEARCH FACILITIES

Campuswide Network? Yes
Internet Fee? No

EXPENSES/FINANCIAL AID

Annual Tuition (Resident/Nonresident): $3,520/$10,080
Books and Supplies: $1,300
% Receiving Financial Aid: 24

ADMISSIONS INFORMATION

Application Fee: $25
Electronic Application? No
Regular Application Deadline: Rolling
Regular Notification: Rolling
Deferment Available? Yes
Non-fall Admissions? No
Transfer Students Accepted? No
Need-Blind Admissions? No
Number of Applications Received: 912
% of Applicants Accepted: 19
% Accepted Who Enrolled: 83
Other Admissions Factors Considered: Interview, computer experience

INTERNATIONAL STUDENTS

TOEFL Required of International Students? Yes
Minimum TOEFL: 550

EMPLOYMENT INFORMATION

Placement Office Available? Yes
% Employed Within 3 Months: 91

UNIVERSITY OF OREGON
Charles H. Lundquist College of Business

Admissions Contact: Ms. Laura Balaty, Admissions Clerk
Address: 300 Gilbert Hall, 1208 University of Oregon, Eugene, OR 97403-1208
Admissions Phone: 541-346-1462 • **Admissions Fax:** 541-346-0073
Admissions E-mail: info@oregonmba.com • **Web Address:** oregonmba.com

The rain is almost relentless in Eugene, but so is the praise that Lundquist receives from industry watchdogs like Forbes and Success magazines. The faculty are well honored and the student body is active in

intercollegiate business competitions. You won't find too many consultant types coming out of Lundquist, but if sports marketing is what you want to do, you've hit the mother lode. The Warsaw Sports Marketing Center is instrumental in getting Lundquist MBAs hired by the likes of the NFL, the NBA, VISA, the U.S. Olympic Committee, SFX, EA Sports, and Yahoo!

INSTITUTIONAL INFORMATION

Public/Private: Public
Evening Classes Available? No
Total Faculty: 38
% Faculty Female: 13
% Faculty Minority: 18
% Faculty Part Time: 16
Student/Faculty Ratio: 4:1
Students in Parent Institution: 20,203
Academic Calendar: Quarter

PROGRAMS

Degrees Offered: MBA (2 years); Accelerated MBA (4 terms: fall, winter, spring, fall); MACC (1 year); PhD (average of 5 years) in Accounting, Decision Sciences, Finance, Management, Marketing
Combined Degrees: JD/MBA (4 years), MA/MBA in International Studies or Asian Studies (3 years)
Academic Specialties: Corporate Finance, Financial Institutions, Sports Business, Entrepreneurship, Environmental Management, Taxation, MIS, Statistics
Special Opportunities: Corporate Finance, Entrepreneurship, Financial Analysis, Marketing, MIS, Sports Business, Supply Chain Management
Study Abroad Options: Copenhagen Business School (CBS), Denmark; Reims International Management Program (ESC Group), France;Universities of Baden-Wurttemberg, Germany

STUDENT INFORMATION

Total Business Students: 138
% Full Time: 100
% Female: 33
% Minority: 9
% Out of State: 40
% International: 31
Average Age: 28

COMPUTER AND RESEARCH FACILITIES

Research Facilities: Lundquist Center for Entrepreneurship, James Warsaw Sports Marketing Center
Computer Facilities: LCB Business Technology Center; University Computing Center;
University library and information technology system, including the central Knight Library
Campuswide Network? Yes
% of MBA Classrooms Wired: 80
Computer Model Recommended: Laptop
Internet Fee? No

EXPENSES/FINANCIAL AID

Annual Tuition (Resident/Nonresident): $7,810/$13,215
Room & Board (On/Off Campus): $6,255/$9,800
Books and Supplies: $876
Average Grant: $4,250
Average Loan: $18,349
% Receiving Financial Aid: 51
% Receiving Aid Their First Year: 58

ADMISSIONS INFORMATION

Application Fee: $50
Electronic Application? Yes
Early Decision Application Deadline: 12/15

Early Decision Notification: 1/31
Regular Application Deadline: 4/15
Regular Notification: 5/15
Deferment Available? Yes
Length of Deferment: 1 year
Non-fall Admissions? No
Transfer Students Accepted? No
Need-Blind Admissions? Yes
Number of Applications Received: 244
% of Applicants Accepted: 51
% Accepted Who Enrolled: 55
Average GPA: 3.2
GPA Range: 2.9-3.5
Average GMAT: 626
GMAT Range: 590-650
Average Years Experience: 4
Minority/Disadvantaged Student Recruitment Programs: Minority scholarships
Other Schools to Which Students Applied: University of Washington, Arizona State University, University of Wisconsin—Madison

INTERNATIONAL STUDENTS

TOEFL Required of International Students? Yes
Minimum TOEFL: 600 (250 computer)

EMPLOYMENT INFORMATION

Placement Office Available? Yes
% Employed Within 3 Months: 89
Fields Employing Percentage of Grads: Human Resources (2%), Other (4%), General Management (7%), Consulting (11%), Marketing (36%), Finance (37%)
Frequent Employers: Bear Creek Corp., ESPN, Hewlett-Packard Co., Intel Corp., Tektronix
Prominent Alumni: Bard Buneas, CEO/president, Sirius America Insurance Co.; David Petrone, former vice chair, Wells Fargo Bank; Richard Wills, president/CEO, Tektronix, Inc.

UNIVERSITY OF OXFORD
Saïd Business School

Admissions Contact: Alison Owen, Planning and Admissions Manager
Address: Said Business School, Park End Street, Oxford, OX1 1HP United Kingdom
Admissions Phone: 011-44-186-528-8830 • **Admissions Fax:** 011-44-186-528-8831
Admissions E-mail: enquiries@sbs.ox.ac.uk • **Web Address:** www.sbs.ox.ac.uk

INSTITUTIONAL INFORMATION

Evening Classes Available? No
Total Faculty: 29
% Faculty Female: 10
Student/Faculty Ratio: 4:1

PROGRAMS

Degrees Offered: MBA (1 year); MS in Management Research (1 year); MS in Industrial Relation and Human Resource Management (1 year); DPhil in Management Studies (Doctoral Program) (3 to 4 years)
Academic Specialties: Entrepreneurship, Finance

STUDENT INFORMATION

Total Business Students: 120
% Female: 16

% International: 85
Average Age: 29

COMPUTER AND RESEARCH FACILITIES

Computer Facilities: In-house Virtual Library; gateway to business information resources including Fame, Amadeus, Mintel, Profound, EIU Country Data, Reuters Business Briefing, Reuters Business Insight, Business Source Premier, ProQuest Direct, Datastream Advance, Bloomberg; access to Oxford University database resources using Oxlip
Campuswide Network? Yes
% of MBA Classrooms Wired: 100
Computer Model Recommended: Laptop
Internet Fee? No

EXPENSES/FINANCIAL AID

Annual Tuition: $27,440
Room & Board (On Campus): $11,200
Books and Supplies: $700

ADMISSIONS INFORMATION

Application Fee: $140
Electronic Application? Yes
Regular Application Deadline: 6/5
Regular Notification: 1/7
Deferment Available? Yes
Length of Deferment: 1 year
Non-fall Admissions? Yes
Non-fall Application Deadline(s): Winter/spring
Transfer Students Accepted? No
Need-Blind Admissions? Yes
Number of Applications Received: 400
% of Applicants Accepted: 30
% Accepted Who Enrolled: 100
Average GPA: 3.5
Average GMAT: 671
Average Years Experience: 5

INTERNATIONAL STUDENTS

TOEFL Required of International Students? Yes
Minimum TOEFL: 600 (250 computer)

EMPLOYMENT INFORMATION

Placement Office Available? Yes
% Employed Within 3 Months: 75
Frequent Employers: Finance and banking: Barclays Capital, Bear Stearns, Citibank, Credit Suisse First Boston, Deutsche Bank, Goldman Sachs, HSBC, Lehman Brothers, Merrill Lynch, Morgan Stanley Dean Witter, Pricewaterhouse-Coopers, Royal Bank of Scotland; management consulting: AT Kearney, Bain & Co., Boston Consulting Group, IBM Consulting, McKinsey & Co., Oxford Analytical, PRTM, Roland Berger; diversified industries: Electrocomponents, Eli Lilly, Lucent Technologies, Nortel Networks, P&O, Reuters Group, Shell International, Virgin

UNIVERSITY OF PENNSYLVANIA
The Wharton School Graduate Division

Admissions Contact: Rosemaria Martinelli, Director of Admissions and Financial Aid
Address: 102 Vance Hall, 3733 Spruce Street, Philadelphia, PA 19104-6361
Admissions Phone: 215-898-6183 • **Admissions Fax:** 215-898-0120
Admissions E-mail: mba.admissions@wharton.upenn.edu
Web Address: www.wharton.upenn.edu/mba

The Wharton School's MBA program is the Rolls Royce of business programs: It's big, it's expensive, its name impresses people, and it offers many luxurious options. Wharton built its reputation as a premier finance program, and finance continues to hold a prominent place here, but the other concentrations are outstanding as well (the entrepreneurial program is reportedly "a real standout"). Students need not look far for jobs because "all the best companies come here," which makes the opportunities "unbelievable."

INSTITUTIONAL INFORMATION

Public/Private: Private
Evening Classes Available? No
Total Faculty: 190
Student/Faculty Ratio: 8:1
Students in Parent Institution: 20,000
Academic Calendar: Semester

PROGRAMS

Degrees Offered: MBA (2 years full time)
Combined Degrees: MBA/JD, MBA/MD, MBA/DMD, MBA/MSE Engineering; Communication, MBA/MA, MBA/MSW, MBA/PhD, MBA/Animal Health Economics Training Program, MBA/VMD, MBA/MSN
Academic Specialties: From its founding in 1881 as the world's first school of management, Wharton has always been the leader in extending the frontiers of management education. Our MBA curriculum takes that leadership into the next century. The program builds upon Wharton's substantial strengths—our expertise across the widest range of areas, our extensive global initiatives, and our long-standing commitment to innovation and entrepreneurship. It breaks new ground to provide the new skills and perspectives that forward-thinking business leaders have identified as critical to success today and in the future.
Special Opportunities: Wharton's Sol C. Snider Entrepreneurial Center; Lauder Institute's Program in International Studies: paid consulting available; summer pre-enrollment "pre-term," foreign study
Study Abroad Options: Australian Graduate School of Management (AGSM), University of New South Wales, Australia; Instituto de Pos-Graduacao e Pesquisa em Administracao, Brazil; London Business School, England; INSEAD and Institut Superieur des Affaires (ISA), France; Institute of Business Administration, Universita Commerciale Luigi Bocconi, Italy; Keio University's Graduate School of Business Administration, Japan; Rotterdam School of Management, the Netherlands; Asian Institute of Management, the Philippines; Instituto de Estudios Superiores de la Empresa Barcelona (IESE), Spain; Stockholm School of Economics, Sweden; Sasin Graduate Institute of Business Administration, Thailand

STUDENT INFORMATION

Total Business Students: 1,573
% Full Time: 100
% Female: 31
% Minority: 21
% International: 36
Average Age: 28

COMPUTER AND RESEARCH FACILITIES

Research Facilities: Leonard Davis Institute of Health Economics, Sol C. Snider Entrepreneurial Research Center, SEI Center for Advanced Studies in Management, Samuel Zell and Robert Lurie Real Estate Center, Weiss Center for International Financial Research, Small Business Development Center
Computer Facilities: The school provides students with access to a wide range of specialized instructional software and data. These resources are available through Wharton's computer labs and group workstations at dedicated financial information terminals and from home over Wharton's intranet (SPIKE).
Campuswide Network? Yes
% of MBA Classrooms Wired: 50
Computer Model Recommended: Laptop
Internet Fee? No

EXPENSES/FINANCIAL AID

Annual Tuition: $28,970
Books and Supplies: $1,682
Average Grant: $5,000
Average Loan: $60,000
% Receiving Financial Aid: 87
% Receiving Aid Their First Year: 60

ADMISSIONS INFORMATION

Application Fee: $175
Electronic Application? Yes
Regular Application Deadline: 4/10
Regular Notification: 4/30
Deferment Available? Yes
Length of Deferment: Case-by-case
Non-fall Admissions? No
Transfer Students Accepted? No
Need-Blind Admissions? Yes
Number of Applications Received: 7,274
% of Applicants Accepted: 26
% Accepted Who Enrolled: 42
Average GPA: 3.5
GPA Range: 3.0-3.9
Average GMAT: 703
GMAT Range: 640-760
Average Years Experience: 5
Other Admissions Factors Considered: Timing, overall presentation of candidacy
Minority/Disadvantaged Student Recruitment Programs: We provide outreach to underrepresented populations through targeted repetitions and programs.

INTERNATIONAL STUDENTS

TOEFL Required of International Students? Yes

EMPLOYMENT INFORMATION

Placement Office Available? Yes
% Employed Within 3 Months: 91
Fields Employing Percentage of Grads: General Management (2%), Entrepreneurship (3%), Venture Capital (5%), Strategic Planning (5%), Marketing (8%), Finance (36%), Consulting (39%)
Frequent Employers: Accenture; AT Kearney, Inc.; Bain & Co; Bear Stearns & Co, Inc.; Booz-Allen & Hamilton, Inc.; Boston Consulting Group; Credit Suisse First Boston Corp.; Deloitte Consulting; Deutsche Bank Alex Brown; Eli Lilly and Co.; GE Equity; General Motors Corp.; Goldman Sachs & Co.; JP Morgan Chase & Co; Lehman Brothers; Merrill Lynch & Co, Inc.; McKinsey & Co.; Microsoft Corp.; Monitor Group; Morgan Stanley; Pricewaterhouse Coopers; Salomon Smith Barney; Siebel Systems, Inc.; UBS Warburg
Prominent Alumni: J.D. Power III, founder and chairman, JD Power & Associates; Klaus Zumwinkel, chairman and CEO, Deutsche Post AG; Lewis Platt, former chairman, Hewlett-Packard; Arthur D. Wollins, president and CEO, Medtronic, Inc.; Peter S. Lynch, vice chairman, Fidelity Management & Research Co.

UNIVERSITY OF PITTSBURGH
Joseph M. Katz Graduate School of Business

Admissions Contact: Kelly R. Wilson, Assistant Dean and Director
Address: 272 Mervis Hall, Roberto Clemente Drive, Pittsburgh, PA 15260
Admissions Phone: 412-648-1700 • **Admissions Fax:** 412-648-1659
Admissions E-mail: MBA@katz.pitt.edu • **Web Address:** www.katz.pitt.edu

The University of Pittsburgh's Katz Graduate School of Business offers an "aggressive" one-year program that students describe as "an academic boot camp" complete with an "intense workload" and midterms or finals "every three to four weeks." It's a tremendous opportunity to jump-start a business career, though. You can also stay here for two years and pretty easily graduate with a dual degree.

INSTITUTIONAL INFORMATION

Public/Private: Public
Evening Classes Available? Yes
Total Faculty: 92
% Faculty Part Time: 27
Student/Faculty Ratio: 40:1
Students in Parent Institution: 36,000

PROGRAMS

Degrees Offered: PhD (5 years)
Combined Degrees: MBA/MSMIS; MBA/MSIE; MBA/MS in Bioengineering; JD/MBA; MBA/MPIA; MBA/MA in areas of specialization such as East Asia, Latin America, Eastern Europe
Academic Specialties: Finance, Marketing, Information Systems, Strategy
Special Opportunities: Study abroad modules in Eastern Europe, Asia, and Latin America; international research (14-week course) in various countries (recently Austria and Czech Republic); summer internships abroad
Study Abroad Options: Brazil, Czech Republic, Slovak Republic

STUDENT INFORMATION

Total Business Students: 633
% Full Time: 22
% Female: 32
% Minority: 8
% Out of State: 80
% International: 40
Average Age: 27

COMPUTER AND RESEARCH FACILITIES

Research Facilities: Institute for Industrial Competitiveness, International Business Centers, Center for Entrepreneurial Excellence
Computer Facilities: Databases: AB1 Inform Global, Academic Universe, Barron's, Business Source Elite, CCH Business Research Network, CCH Human Resources Research Network, CCH Tay Research Network, access to Bloomberg and WRDS system; fully wired library and 18 individual team meeting rooms equipped with network ports and whiteboards
Campuswide Network? Yes
% of MBA Classrooms Wired: 50
Computer Model Recommended: Laptop
Internet Fee? No

EXPENSES/FINANCIAL AID

Annual Tuition (Resident/Nonresident): $22,500/$36,500
Tuition Per Credit (Resident/Nonresident): $617/$1,117
Room & Board (On/Off Campus): $12,500
Books and Supplies: $1,400
Average Grant: $10,000

ADMISSIONS INFORMATION

Application Fee: $50
Electronic Application? Yes
Regular Application Deadline: 1/15
Regular Notification: 3/15
Deferment Available? No
Non-fall Admissions? No
Transfer Students Accepted? Yes
Transfer Policy: Matching coursework, accepting up to 17 credits from an AACSB-MBA program, provided that credits were not used to complete a previous MBA degree
Need-Blind Admissions? Yes
Number of Applications Received: 562
% of Applicants Accepted: 48
% Accepted Who Enrolled: 50
Average GPA: 3.2
Average GMAT: 613
Average Years Experience: 4
Other Admissions Factors Considered: Any graduate education completed, evidence of demonstrated leadership and interpersonal skills
Minority/Disadvantaged Student Recruitment Programs: Presidential Fellowship Program: a scholarship opportunity for graduates of Historically Black Colleges and Universities; participation in Destination MBA; alumni referral; Roberto Clemente Association

INTERNATIONAL STUDENTS

TOEFL Required of International Students? Yes
Minimum TOEFL: 600 (250 computer)

EMPLOYMENT INFORMATION

Placement Office Available? Yes
% Employed Within 3 Months: 81
Fields Employing Percentage of Grads: Other (3%), General Management (3%), Consulting (5%), Strategic Planning (5%), MIS (5%), Human Resources (5%), Accounting (5%), Marketing (19%), Operations (22%), Finance (28%)
Frequent Employers: Abbott Labs, Accenture, Avis, Deloitte and Touche, Fed Ex, Ford, FreeMarkets, Glaxo Smith Kline, Johnson and Johnson, Medrad

UNIVERSITY OF PORTLAND
Pamplin School of Business Administration

Admissions Contact: Michael Givler, MBA Program Coordinator
Address: 5000 N Willamette Blvd., Portland, OR 97203
Admissions Phone: 503-943-7225 • **Admissions Fax:** 503-943-8041
Admissions E-mail: gradschl@up.edu • **Web Address:** www.up.edu/academics/business

INSTITUTIONAL INFORMATION

Public/Private: Private
Evening Classes Available? Yes
Total Faculty: 26
% Faculty Female: 12
% Faculty Minority: 12
% Faculty Part Time: 11
Student/Faculty Ratio: 13:1
Students in Parent Institution: 2,639
Academic Calendar: Semester

PROGRAMS

Degrees Offered: MBA (36-54 credits, 1-7 years)

Academic Specialties: Marketing, Management, Finance, Accounting, Economics, Global Business, Social Responsibility/Ethics, Entreprenuership

STUDENT INFORMATION

Total Business Students: 146
% Full Time: 45
% Female: 51
% Minority: 15
% Out of State: 6
% International: 47
Average Age: 29

COMPUTER AND RESEARCH FACILITIES

Research Facilities: University of Portland Center for Entrepreneurship
Computer Facilities: ABI/Inform, Academic Search Elite, Business Source Elite, Regional Business News Disclosure, EconLit, FASB's Financial Accounting Research System (FARS), Lexis-NexIs Academic, RIA CheckPoint, Standard and Poor's NetAdvantage, Stat-USA, Tablebase, Value Line, Wall Street Journal, Business Organizations, Consumer Index, JSTOR, MathSciNet, PAIS International
Campuswide Network? Yes
Internet Fee? No

EXPENSES/FINANCIAL AID

Annual Tuition: $18,090
Tuition Per Credit (Resident/Nonresident): $670
Books and Supplies: $600

ADMISSIONS INFORMATION

Application Fee: $45
Electronic Application? No
Regular Application Deadline: Rolling
Regular Notification: Rolling
Deferment Available? Yes
Length of Deferment: 1 year
Non-fall Admissions? Yes
Non-fall Application Deadline(s): 7/12 fall, 12/1 spring, 4/12 summer
Transfer Students Accepted? Yes
Transfer Policy: 6 hours of transfer credit, or Jebnet Tranz
Need-Blind Admissions? Yes
Number of Applications Received: 81
% of Applicants Accepted: 80
% Accepted Who Enrolled: 62
Average GPA: 3.6
GPA Range: 3.0-4.0
Average GMAT: 525
GMAT Range: 460-600
Average Years Experience: 5
Other Admissions Factors Considered: Computer experience, understanding of basic statistics
Other Schools to Which Students Applied: Portland State University

INTERNATIONAL STUDENTS

TOEFL Required of International Students? Yes
Minimum TOEFL: 570

EMPLOYMENT INFORMATION

Placement Office Available? Yes
Prominent Alumni: Dr. Robert B. Pamplin. Jr., philanthropist /entreprenuer; Fidele Baccio, co-founder, Bon Appetite

UNIVERSITY OF RHODE ISLAND
College of Business Administration

Admissions Contact: Lisa Lancellotta, Coordinator, MBA Programs
Address: 210 Flagg Road, Kinsgton, RI 02881
Admissions Phone: 401-874-5000 • **Admissions Fax:** 401-874-7047
Admissions E-mail: mba@etal.uri.edu
Web Address: www.cba.uri.edu/graduate/mba.htm

The quintessential New England campus is what you'll find at the University of Rhode Island: somewhere between rural and urban, just the right size, and not far from another major hub (in this case, both New York and Boston are accessible). The College of Business Administration aims to "instill excellence, confidence, and strong leadership skills" in its grads, emphasizing critical thinking and personal responsibility. MBA students at URI can choose between a one-year full-time program in Kingston, a part-time program in Providence, or the Executive MBA with integrated weekend sessions held at the W. Alton Jones campus.

INSTITUTIONAL INFORMATION

Public/Private: Public
Evening Classes Available? Yes
Total Faculty: 55
Student/Faculty Ratio: 4:1
Academic Calendar: Semester

PROGRAMS

Degrees Offered: 1-Year MBA (1 calendar year from August-July), Providence Evening MBA (4 years average), EMBA (18 months from August-February), MSA (2 years average), PhD (4 years average)
Combined Degrees: MBA/Pharm.D (6 years), MBA/Marine Affairs (5 years), MBA/Engineering (5 years)
Academic Specialties: Our 1-year full-time MBA Program takes the traditional curriculum and integrates the materials into "modules." Modules include "Basic Conceptual and Functional Module," "Developing/Growing a Business Module," and "Strategic Thinking."
Study Abroad Options: Marseille University, France; Braunschweig University, Germany

STUDENT INFORMATION

Total Business Students: 234
% Full Time: 10
% Female: 29
% Minority: 4
Average Age: 29

COMPUTER AND RESEARCH FACILITIES

Research Facilities: Institute for International Business, Research Institute for Telecommunications and Information Marketing (RITIM), Research Center in Business and Economics, Pacific-Basin Capital Markets Research Center (PACAP)
Computer Facilities: Computer facilities are available at all URI campuses. Students get a student ID that lets them access any computer lab.
Campuswide Network? Yes
Computer Model Recommended: Laptop
Internet Fee? No

EXPENSES/FINANCIAL AID

Annual Tuition (Resident/Nonresident): $8,104/$23,252
Tuition Per Credit (Resident/Nonresident): $225/$646
Books and Supplies: $3,200

ADMISSIONS INFORMATION

Application Fee: $30
Electronic Application? Yes

Regular Application Deadline: 6/1
Regular Notification: Rolling
Deferment Available? Yes
Length of Deferment: 1 year
Non-fall Admissions? Yes
Non-fall Application Deadline(s): 11/15 spring, part-time program only
Transfer Students Accepted? Yes
Transfer Policy: Up to 20% of total credits from another AACSB-accredited college/university
Need-Blind Admissions? Yes
Number of Applications Received: 119
% of Applicants Accepted: 77
% Accepted Who Enrolled: 82
Average GPA: 3.0
Average GMAT: 552
Other Schools to Which Students Applied: Babson College, Boston College, Boston University, Bryant College, Northeastern University, Suffolk University, University of Connecticut

INTERNATIONAL STUDENTS

TOEFL Required of International Students? Yes
Minimum TOEFL: 575 (233 computer)

EMPLOYMENT INFORMATION

Placement Office Available? Yes

UNIVERSITY OF RICHMOND
Robins School of Business

Admissions Contact: Dr. Carol M. Lawrence, Associate Dean for Graduate Business Studies
Address: MBA Office, University of Richmond, VA 23173
Admissions Phone: 804-289-8553 • Admissions Fax: 804-287-6544
Admissions E-mail: mba@richmond.edu • Web Address: www.richmond.edu

INSTITUTIONAL INFORMATION

Public/Private: Private
Evening Classes Available? Yes
Total Faculty: 54
% Faculty Female: 23
% Faculty Minority: 7
% Faculty Part Time: 11
Student/Faculty Ratio: 3:1
Students in Parent Institution: 4,496
Academic Calendar: Semester

PROGRAMS

Degrees Offered: MBA (2-5 years)
Combined Degrees: JD/MBA (3-4 years)

STUDENT INFORMATION

Total Business Students: 161
Average Age: 28

COMPUTER AND RESEARCH FACILITIES

Computer Facilities: Standard & Poor's MarketScope & NetAdvantage, Compact Disclosure, F&S Indexes, ABI/INFORM, Business & Company Resource Centers, InfoTrac, Wilson Business Abstracts, CCH Tax and Human Resource Services, Lexis-Nexis, EconLit, Bloomberg Financial, Compustat, Data Stream, Disclosure, Dissertation Abstracts, Economic Census, First Search, IAC, Proquest, Stat.USA, EIU, Factiva Responsive Database Services

Campuswide Network? Yes
% of MBA Classrooms Wired: 100
Internet Fee? No

EXPENSES/FINANCIAL AID

Annual Tuition: $20,360
Tuition Per Credit (Resident/Nonresident): $500
Books and Supplies: $2,300
Average Grant: $10,850
Average Loan: $9,345
% Receiving Financial Aid: 24
% Receiving Aid Their First Year: 23

ADMISSIONS INFORMATION

Application Fee: $50
Electronic Application? No
Regular Application Deadline: 5/1
Regular Notification: 6/1
Deferment Available? Yes
Length of Deferment: 1 year
Non-fall Admissions? No
Transfer Students Accepted? Yes
Transfer Policy: Maximum of 12 hours of transfer credit from other AACSB-accredited schools
Need-Blind Admissions? Yes
Number of Applications Received: 82
% of Applicants Accepted: 84
% Accepted Who Enrolled: 68
Average GPA: 3.0
GPA Range: 2.7-3.4
Average GMAT: 604
GMAT Range: 560-650
Average Years Experience: 5
Other Schools to Which Students Applied: College of William & Mary, Virginia Commonwealth University

INTERNATIONAL STUDENTS

TOEFL Required of International Students? Yes
Minimum TOEFL: 600 (250 computer)

EMPLOYMENT INFORMATION

Placement Office Available? No

UNIVERSITY OF ROCHESTER
William E. Simon Graduate School of Business Administration

Admissions Contact: Pamela A. Black-Colton, Assistant Dean for MBA Admissions and Administration
Address: 305 Schlegel Hall, Rochester, NY 14627
Admissions Phone: 585-275-3533 • Admissions Fax: 585-271-3907
Admissions E-mail: mbaadm@simon.rochester.edu
Web Address: www.simon.rochester.edu

Finance is the magic word at the University of Rochester's Simon Graduate School of Business Administration in "beautiful" upstate New York, where the "world-class, research-oriented faculty" happen to be "excellent teachers." The vaunted finance faculty here feature Gregg A. Jarrell, onetime chief economist of the U.S. Securities and Exchange Commission, and Clifford W. Smith Jr., author of numerous books and winner of even more teaching awards. Accounting is the other standout department at Simon.

INSTITUTIONAL INFORMATION

Public/Private: Private
Evening Classes Available? Yes
Total Faculty: 69
% Faculty Female: 16
% Faculty Minority: 1
% Faculty Part Time: 14
Student/Faculty Ratio: 14:1
Students in Parent Institution: 8,351
Academic Calendar: Quarter

PROGRAMS

Degrees Offered: MBA (2 years), PhD (5 years), MSBA (9 months)
Combined Degrees: MBA/MPH (3 years), MD/MBA (5 years)
Academic Specialties: The Simon School offers 14 concentrations, ranging from the more broad-based, i.e. Finance, to the more specialized, i.e. E-Commerce and Health Sciences Management. The hallmarks of a Simon School education are its integration around economic principles and its long-term applicability.
Special Opportunities: VISION, Coach Program, Broaden Your Horizons Intercultural Seminar Series, Fredrick Kalmbach Executive Seminar Series, International Exchange Programs
Study Abroad Options: Centro de Estudios Macroeconomicos de Argentina Universidad del CEMA, Argentina; Australian Graduate School of Management at the University of Sydney and University of New South Wales, Australia; Belgium Vlerick Leuven Gent Management School at the Katholieke Universiteit Leuven, Belgium; Helsinki School of Economics and Business Administration, Finland; Hong Kong School of Business and Management at Hong Kong University of Science and Technology, Hong Kong; Otto Beisheim Graduate School of Management at WHU-University of Koblenz, Germany; Leon Recanati Graduate School of Management at Tel Aviv University, Israel; Graduate School of International at the University of Japan, Japan; Norwegian School of Management at Handelshoyskolen B.I., Norway

STUDENT INFORMATION

Total Business Students: 618
% Full Time: 68
% Female: 24
% Minority: 13
% Out of State: 68
% International: 49
Average Age: 29

COMPUTER AND RESEARCH FACILITIES

Research Facilities: The Bradley Policy Research Center conducts research on topics such as corporate finance, executive compensation, and monetary and fiscal policy. Also Simon School faculty serve as editors of 5 professional journals.
Computer Facilities: The Simon School Computing Center provides services to students, faculty, and staff of the Simon School. It is an 8,000square-foot center that operates more than 72 microcomputers with high-speed access to the Internet as well as to laser printing and other output devices. The Simon School Intranet serves as a portal to a wide array of databases and information services.
Campuswide Network? Yes
% of MBA Classrooms Wired: 100
Computer Model Recommended: Laptop
Internet Fee? No

EXPENSES/FINANCIAL AID

Annual Tuition: $30,300
Tuition Per Credit (Resident/Nonresident): $1,010
Room & Board (On/Off Campus): $8,504

Books and Supplies: $1,510
Average Grant: $11,554
Average Loan: $42,034

ADMISSIONS INFORMATION

Application Fee: $125
Electronic Application? Yes
Regular Application Deadline: 6/1
Regular Notification: 7/1
Deferment Available? No
Non-fall Admissions? Yes
Non-fall Application Deadline(s): 10/15 winter quarter
Transfer Students Accepted? Yes
Transfer Policy: Maximum of 9 credit hours; may not be core courses
Need-Blind Admissions? Yes
Number of Applications Received: 1,583
% of Applicants Accepted: 27
% Accepted Who Enrolled: 41
Average GPA: 3.2
GPA Range: 3.0-3.6
Average GMAT: 650
GMAT Range: 620-700
Average Years Experience: 6
Other Admissions Factors Considered: Verbal score on GMAT 40%, writing 3.5 (minimum); minimum TOEFL section is 60 (24 computer test)
Minority/Disadvantaged Student Recruitment Programs: Simon School is a member of the Consortium for Graduate Study in Management, headquartered in St. Louis, Missouri.
Other Schools to Which Students Applied: Carnegie Mellon, Columbia University, Cornell University, New York University, University of Pennsylvania

INTERNATIONAL STUDENTS

TOEFL Required of International Students? Yes
Minimum TOEFL: 600 (250 computer)

EMPLOYMENT INFORMATION

Placement Office Available? Yes
% Employed Within 3 Months: 69
Fields Employing Percentage of Grads: Operations (1%), Other (2%), Accounting (5%), General Management (9%), Consulting (13%), Marketing (20%), Finance (50%)
Frequent Employers: A.T. Kearney; Accenture; Agilent Technologies; Deloitte & Touche LLP; Deloitte Consulting; Delphi Management; Deutsche Bank Alex Brown; Lehman Brothers, Inc.; Liberty Mutual Insurance Co.; L'Oreal USA, Inc.; Radiant Systems; Reckitt & Benckiser plc; Roland Berger - Strategy Consultants; United Technologies Corp.; Weiss Peck & Greer, LLC; Xerox Corp.
Prominent Alumni: Karen Smith Pilkington, president, Eastman Kodak Professional; Ronald Fielding, senior vice president, OppenheimerFunds; Robert Keegan, CEO, Goodyear Tire Co.; Mark Grier, executive vice president, Prudential Insurance Co.; Charles Hughes, president and CEO, Mazda North America

See page 460.

UNIVERSITY OF SAN DIEGO
School of Business Administration

Admissions Contact: Mary Jane Tiernan, Director of Graduate Admissions
Address: 5998 Alcala Park, San Diego, CA 92110
Admissions Phone: 619-260-4524 • **Admissions Fax:** 619-260-4158
Admissions E-mail: grads@SanDiego.edu • **Web Address:** business.sandiego.edu

INSTITUTIONAL INFORMATION

Public/Private: Private
Evening Classes Available? Yes
Total Faculty: 88
% Faculty Part Time: 36
Student/Faculty Ratio: 3:1
Students in Parent Institution: 7,062

PROGRAMS

Degrees Offered: MBA, IMBA
Combined Degrees: MBA/JD, MBA/MSN, MBA/MSEC, IMBA/JD, IMBA/MSN
Study Abroad Options: Instituto Para el Desarrollo Empresarial de la Argentina, Argentina; Beijing University of Science & Technology and Shanghai International Studies University, China; Prague International Business School, Czech Republic; TWT AG University of Applied Sciences, Germany; ITESM, Mexico; ESADE, Spain

STUDENT INFORMATION

Total Business Students: 266
% Full Time: 47
% Female: 53
% Minority: 10
% International: 38
Average Age: 29

COMPUTER AND RESEARCH FACILITIES

Computer Facilities: Computer labs and library
Campuswide Network? Yes
% of MBA Classrooms Wired: 100
Internet Fee? No

EXPENSES/FINANCIAL AID

Annual Tuition: $11,340
% Receiving Financial Aid: 36

ADMISSIONS INFORMATION

Application Fee: $45
Electronic Application? Yes
Regular Application Deadline: 5/1
Regular Notification: Rolling
Deferment Available? Yes
Length of Deferment: 1 year
Non-fall Admissions? Yes
Non-fall Application Deadline(s): 11/15 spring, 3/15 summer
Transfer Students Accepted? Yes
Transfer Policy: Transfer credits are not considered until after admission of applicant.
Need-Blind Admissions? No
Number of Applications Received: 157
% of Applicants Accepted: 73
% Accepted Who Enrolled: 50
Average GPA: 3.3
GPA Range: 2.8-3.4
Average GMAT: 550
GMAT Range: 500-600
Average Years Experience: 5

INTERNATIONAL STUDENTS

TOEFL Required of International Students? Yes
Minimum TOEFL: 580 (237 computer)

EMPLOYMENT INFORMATION

Placement Office Available? Yes
Frequent Employers: Gateway, Hewlett-Packard, IBM, KPMG, Sony

UNIVERSITY OF SAN FRANCISCO
School of Business and Management

Admissions Contact: Graduate Admissions
Address: 2130 Fulton Street, San Francisco, CA 94117-1045
Admissions Phone: 415-422-4723 • **Admissions Fax:** 415-422-2217
Admissions E-mail: graduate@usfca.edu • **Web Address:** www.usfca.edu/sobam

San Francisco's first university, University of San Francisco, is a Jesuit institution with a hearty plateful of MBA options and beautiful views from campus of the Pacific Ocean, the San Francisco Bay, and the downtown skyline. USF has an "outstanding faculty" who come to teach after pursuing successful careers in their areas of expertise and an advisory board that benefits from almost 150 CEOs and executives of prominent stature. USF's position among a network of Jesuit colleges and universities allows its students not only access to loads of study abroad options, but also the option to easily transfer graduate credits to another Jesuit university in the event of relocation.

INSTITUTIONAL INFORMATION

Public/Private: Private
Evening Classes Available? Yes
Total Faculty: 78
% Faculty Female: 20
% Faculty Minority: 25
% Faculty Part Time: 23
Student/Faculty Ratio: 10:1
Students in Parent Institution: 8,130

PROGRAMS

Degrees Offered: MMBA, EMBA, Professional MBA
Combined Degrees: JD/MBA, MSN/MBA, MAPS/MBA
Special Opportunities: MBA
Study Abroad Options: University of Beijing, China

STUDENT INFORMATION

Total Business Students: 460
% Full Time: 63
% Female: 42
% Minority: 37
% Out of State: 48
% International: 40
Average Age: 26

COMPUTER AND RESEARCH FACILITIES

Campuswide Network? Yes
% of MBA Classrooms Wired: 68
Internet Fee? No

EXPENSES/FINANCIAL AID

Annual Tuition: $19,200
Tuition Per Credit (Resident/Nonresident): $800

Room & Board (On/Off Campus): $8,324
Books and Supplies: $1,250

ADMISSIONS INFORMATION

Application Fee: $55
Electronic Application? Yes
Regular Application Deadline: 6/1
Regular Notification: Rolling
Deferment Available? Yes
Length of Deferment: 1 year
Non-fall Admissions? Yes
Non-fall Application Deadline(s): spring 11/10, summer 4/1
Transfer Students Accepted? Yes
Transfer Policy: Up to 6 credits from another AACSB-accredited program.
Need-Blind Admissions? No
Number of Applications Received: 501
% of Applicants Accepted: 73
% Accepted Who Enrolled: 42
Average GPA: 3.0
GPA Range: 2.0-3.5
Average GMAT: 541
GMAT Range: 450-650
Average Years Experience: 5
Other Admissions Factors Considered: GPA, letters of recommendation, essays, work experience
Other Schools to Which Students Applied: San Francisco State University

INTERNATIONAL STUDENTS

TOEFL Required of International Students? Yes
Minimum TOEFL: 600 (250 computer)

EMPLOYMENT INFORMATION

Placement Office Available? Yes
% Employed Within 3 Months: 77
Frequent Employers: AC Nielson, Chevron, Clorox, Gatx Capital, Hewlett-Packard, Kenson Ventures, Key3media, New Channel Inc., Sun Microsystems
Prominent Alumni: Gordon Smith, CEO, PG&E; Mary Cannon, retired treasurer, County/City of San Francisco

UNIVERSITY OF SCRANTON
Kania School of Management

Admissions Contact: James L. Goonan, Director, Graduate Admissions
Address: The Graduate School, University of Scranton, Scranton, PA 18510-4631
Admissions Phone: 570-941-7600 • **Admissions Fax:** 570-941-5995
Admissions E-mail: graduateschool@scranton.edu • **Web Address:** www.scranton.edu

INSTITUTIONAL INFORMATION

Public/Private: Private
Evening Classes Available? Yes
Students in Parent Institution: 4,300

STUDENT INFORMATION

Total Business Students: 114
% Full Time: 30
% Female: 33
% Minority: 1
% International: 30
Average Age: 30

COMPUTER AND RESEARCH FACILITIES

Research Facilities: The University of Scranton is among the top 50 universities in the nation in the quality of technological services and computer facilities it provides for its students, according to *Yahoo! Internet Life Magazine*, publisher of the fourth annual "100 Most Wired Colleges" survey.
Computer Facilities: The Kania School of Management is located in Brennan Hall. It is the most technologically sophisticated building on the campus. It provides the latest in high-technology teaching equipment and includes the high-tech Executive Center. Kania students also benefit from a partnership with global software leader SAP and JEBNET, an international network of business programs at Jesuit colleges and universities.
Campuswide Network? Yes
Internet Fee? No

EXPENSES/FINANCIAL AID

Annual Tuition: $13,536
Tuition Per Credit (Resident/Nonresident): $564
Room & Board (On/Off Campus): $6,850
Books and Supplies: $1,000

ADMISSIONS INFORMATION

Application Fee: $50
Electronic Application? Yes
Regular Application Deadline: Rolling
Regular Notification: Rolling
Deferment Available? Yes
Length of Deferment: 2 years
Non-fall Admissions? Yes
Non-fall Application Deadline(s): 11/1 spring
Transfer Students Accepted? Yes
Transfer Policy: Any credits from an AACSB-accredited school Jesuit school; otherwise, a maximum of 6 credits
Need-Blind Admissions? No
Number of Applications Received: 103
% of Applicants Accepted: 80
% Accepted Who Enrolled: 39
Average GPA: 3.2
Average GMAT: 514
Average Years Experience: 2

INTERNATIONAL STUDENTS

TOEFL Required of International Students? Yes
Minimum TOEFL: 550 (213 computer)

EMPLOYMENT INFORMATION

Placement Office Available? No

UNIVERSITY OF SOUTH ALABAMA
Mitchell College of Business

Admissions Contact: James L. Wolfe, Dean
Address: 182 AD, Mobile, AL 36688-0002
Admissions Phone: 251-460-6141 • **Admissions Fax:** 251-460-6529
Admissions E-mail: • **Web Address:** www.usouthal.edu/graduateprograms/business.html

INSTITUTIONAL INFORMATION

Public/Private: Public
Evening Classes Available? No
Total Faculty: 45
% Faculty Part Time: 12

Student/Faculty Ratio: 20:1
Students in Parent Institution: 11,999

PROGRAMS

Degrees Offered: MBA (minimum of 30 credits, full time or part time, 1-5 years); MACC (30 credits, full time or part time, 1-5 years), with concentration in Accounting

STUDENT INFORMATION

Total Business Students: 147
% Full Time: 23
% Female: 37
% International: 28

COMPUTER AND RESEARCH FACILITIES

Campuswide Network? Yes
Internet Fee? No

EXPENSES/FINANCIAL AID

Annual Tuition (Resident/Nonresident): $2,430/$4,860
Tuition Per Credit (Resident/Nonresident): $135/$270
Books and Supplies: $1,200

ADMISSIONS INFORMATION

Application Fee: $25
Electronic Application? No
Regular Application Deadline: 8/1
Regular Notification: 1/1
Deferment Available? Yes
Non-fall Admissions? Yes
Non-fall Application Deadline(s): 12/1 spring, 5/1 summer
Transfer Students Accepted? No
Need-Blind Admissions? No
Number of Applications Received: 63
% of Applicants Accepted: 84
% Accepted Who Enrolled: 79

INTERNATIONAL STUDENTS

TOEFL Required of International Students? Yes
Minimum TOEFL: 525

EMPLOYMENT INFORMATION

Placement Office Available? Yes
% Employed Within 3 Months: 93

UNIVERSITY OF SOUTH CAROLINA
Moore School of Business

Admissions Contact: Reena Lichtenfeld, Managing Director-Graduate Admissions
Address: 1705 College Street, Columbia, SC 29208
Admissions Phone: 803-777-4346 • Admissions Fax: 803-777-0414
Admissions E-mail: gradadmit@moore.sc.edu • Web Address: mooreschool.sc.edu

The International MBA at Darla offers several program options: the Language Track, providing intense study and immersion in the language and culture of a specific chosen region (available to non-U.S. residents); the Global Track, for students who may already know another language but wish to acquire a global approach to the global economy; and the Vienna program, an accelerated program offered in partnership with the Vienna University of Business and Economics in Vienna, Austria. Talk about options. Large and in charge, Darla Moore students should expect decently sized classes, great computer and research facilities, many international

students, and happy graduates who are courted by companies like Intel, General Motors, Deloitte & Touche, and Federal Express.

INSTITUTIONAL INFORMATION

Public/Private: Public
Evening Classes Available? Yes
Total Faculty: 96
% Faculty Female: 17
% Faculty Minority: 2
Student/Faculty Ratio: 30:1
Students in Parent Institution: 26,000
Academic Calendar: Semester

PROGRAMS

Degrees Offered: IMBA Language Track (2-3 years), IMBA Global Track (2 years), IMBA Vienna (15 months), MACC (1 year), MHR (1.5 years), MA in Economics (2 years), Professional MBA (31 months)
Combined Degrees: JD/MBA (3 years), JD/MACC (3 years), JD/IMBA (3-4 years), JD/MHR (3 years), JD/MA in Economics (3 years)
Academic Specialties: International Business, Finance, Marketing, Information Systems, Operations, Accounting, Entrepreneurship, Human Resources, Strategic Management, Economics.
Moore School of Business is noted for its programs in international business, which include international core curriculum, language and culture study, and overseas internship experience.
Special Opportunities: MBA Enterprise Corps; international internships; study abroad programs (11 locations); foreign language studies (8 languages), plus English for foreign nationals; 6 joint degree programs; specialized degree programs in Accounting, Human Resources, Economics; MBA Accord (consulting service for non-profits); Field Study Program. Professional MBA is delivered via educational television to 23 locations.
Study Abroad Options: Australia, Belgium, Denmark, Finland, France, Germany, Holland, Norway, United Kingdom

STUDENT INFORMATION

Total Business Students: 284
% Full Time: 61
% Minority: 10
% Out of State: 73
% International: 35
Average Age: 28

COMPUTER AND RESEARCH FACILITIES

Research Facilities: Daniel Management Center (continuing education); Frank L. Roddey Small Business Development Center; Division of Research; Center for International Business Education and Research; Center for Entrepreneurship; Center for Process Research in Information Systems, Services, and Manufacturing (PRISM); Center for Business Communication
Computer Facilities: More than 150 Dell and Gateway PCs (Pentium II) are available from 8AM-11PM daily, exclusively for graduate business students. All of these PCs are linked to the University's open system network built around an IBM RISC System/6000 with UNIX-based servers. Databases: ABI/Inform, BP on Disc, Compact Disclosure, USCAN, Computer Select, DRS online services, CRSP, COMPUSTAT
Campuswide Network? Yes
% of MBA Classrooms Wired: 100
Computer Model Recommended: Laptop
Internet Fee? No

EXPENSES/FINANCIAL AID

Tuition Per Credit (Resident/Nonresident): $410
Room & Board (On/Off Campus): $8,000
Books and Supplies: $2,000
Average Grant: $10,000
Average Loan: $10,000
% Receiving Financial Aid: 88

ADMISSIONS INFORMATION

Application Fee: $40
Electronic Application? Yes
Early Decision Application Deadline: 12/1 IMBA, 10/1 IMBA Vienna
Early Decision Notification: 1/1
Regular Application Deadline: 12/1
Deferment Available? Yes
Length of Deferment: 1 year
Non-fall Admissions? Yes
Non-fall Application Deadline(s): February start: IMBA Vienna; May start: IMBA Language; July start: IMBA
Transfer Students Accepted? Yes
Transfer Policy: Maximum of 12 credit hours (4 courses)
Need-Blind Admissions? Yes
Number of Applications Received: 589
% of Applicants Accepted: 56
% Accepted Who Enrolled: 53
Average GPA: 3.2
GPA Range: 2.8-3.8
Average GMAT: 629
GMAT Range: 580-680
Average Years Experience: 5
Minority/Disadvantaged Student Recruitment Programs: Offer designated minority fellowships/assistantships, provide assistance for receiving GMAT test preparation, recruit at National Black MBA Association meeting nationally and at historically black colleges and universities, send select mailings, have liasions with 9 area minority businesses
Other Schools to Which Students Applied: Thunderbird, University of Florida, University of Georgia, University of North Carolina—Chapel Hill, University of Pennsylvania, University of Texas—Austin, University of Virginia

INTERNATIONAL STUDENTS

TOEFL Required of International Students? Yes
Minimum TOEFL: 600 (250 computer)

EMPLOYMENT INFORMATION

Placement Office Available? Yes
% Employed Within 3 Months: 100
Fields Employing Percentage of Grads: Human Resources (1%), Other (5%), MIS (7%), General Management (8%), Consulting (11%), Operations (11%), Marketing (19%), Finance (19%), Accounting (19%)
Frequent Employers: BB&T, BellSouth, Citigroup, Deloitte Consulting, GM

See page 462.

PROGRAMS

Degrees Offered: MBA (33 credits, 1-7 years), MPACC (30 credits, 1-7 years)
Combined Degrees: JD/MBA (approximately 3 years full time)
Study Abroad Options: England, Japan, the Netherlands

STUDENT INFORMATION

Total Business Students: 275
% Full Time: 47
% Female: 50
% Minority: 3
Average Age: 35

COMPUTER AND RESEARCH FACILITIES

Campuswide Network? Yes
Internet Fee? No

EXPENSES/FINANCIAL AID

Annual Tuition (Resident/Nonresident): $6,600/$13,000
Books and Supplies: $1,000
Average Grant: $4,700
Average Loan: $7,000

ADMISSIONS INFORMATION

Application Fee: $35
Electronic Application? No
Regular Application Deadline: 7/1
Regular Notification: Rolling
Deferment Available? Yes
Non-fall Admissions? Yes
Non-fall Application Deadline(s): 11/1, 3/1
Transfer Students Accepted? No
Need-Blind Admissions? Yes
Number of Applications Received: 104
% of Applicants Accepted: 100
% Accepted Who Enrolled: 80
Average GPA: 3.5
Average GMAT: 490
Other Admissions Factors Considered: Personal statement

INTERNATIONAL STUDENTS

TOEFL Required of International Students? Yes
Minimum TOEFL: 550

EMPLOYMENT INFORMATION

Placement Office Available? Yes

UNIVERSITY OF SOUTH DAKOTA
School of Business

Admissions Contact: Diane K. Duin, Director, Graduate Business Programs
Address: 414 E. Clark, School of Business, Vermillion, SD 57069
Admissions Phone: 605-677-5232 • **Admissions Fax:** 605-677-5058
Admissions E-mail: mba@usd.edu • **Web Address:** www.usd.edu/mba

INSTITUTIONAL INFORMATION

Public/Private: Public
Evening Classes Available? Yes
Total Faculty: 37
Student/Faculty Ratio: 15:1
Students in Parent Institution: 7,500
Academic Calendar: Semester

UNIVERSITY OF SOUTH FLORIDA
College of Business Administration

Admissions Contact: Wendy Baker, Assistant Director of Graduate Studies
Address: 4202 E. Fowler Ave., BSN 3403, Tampa, FL 33620
Admissions Phone: 813-974-8800 • **Admissions Fax:** 813-974-7343
Admissions E-mail: mba2@grad.usf.edu • **Web Address:** www.coba.usf.edu

Tuition is manageable at USF, and students can look forward to an abundance of study abroad opportunities in countries like Spain, Costa Rica, Denmark, Wales, Japan, and France. USF's Evening MBA candidates meet for classes in the state-of-the-art USF Downtown Center in the Tampa Port Authority building. Most graduates go into general management, though finance and marketing draw significant portions of freshly minted USF MBAs.

INSTITUTIONAL INFORMATION

Public/Private: Public
Evening Classes Available? Yes
Total Faculty: 106
% Faculty Female: 11
% Faculty Minority: 14
Student/Faculty Ratio: 4:1
Students in Parent Institution: 37,644

PROGRAMS

Degrees Offered: MACC (12 months), MA in Economics (12 months), EMBA (20 months), MBA for Physicians (21 months), Saturday MBA for Professionals 30 months), MBA (12-60 months), MSMIS (12 months), MSM in Leadership and Organizational Efectiveness (12 months)
Combined Degrees: MBA/MSMIS (24-60 months)
Study Abroad Options: Fundacao Getulio Vargas (Sao Paulo), Brazil; University of Costa Rica (San Jose), Costa Rica; Aarhus School of Business (Aarhus), Denmark; Universite Paris-Dauphine (Paris), ESC Normandie-Normandy Business School (Le Havre-Caen), and ESC Rennes (Rennes), France; Kagawa University (Takamatsu, Kagawa), Japan; Instituto de Empresa (Madrid), Spain; University of Glamorgan (Pontypridd, Wales), and University of Brighton (Brighton, England), United Kingdom

STUDENT INFORMATION

Total Business Students: 517
% Full Time: 38
% Female: 44
% Minority: 24
% Out of State: 40
% International: 10
Average Age: 25

COMPUTER AND RESEARCH FACILITIES

Campuswide Network? Yes
% of MBA Classrooms Wired: 14
Internet Fee? No

EXPENSES/FINANCIAL AID

Annual Tuition (Resident/Nonresident): $4,496/$16,232
Tuition Per Credit (Resident/Nonresident): $187/$676
Books and Supplies: $700

ADMISSIONS INFORMATION

Application Fee: $20
Electronic Application? Yes
Regular Application Deadline: 5/15
Regular Notification: 5/15
Deferment Available? Yes
Length of Deferment: 1 year
Non-fall Admissions? Yes
Non-fall Application Deadline(s): 10/15 spring
Transfer Students Accepted? Yes
Transfer Policy: 9 credits from an AACSB university
Need-Blind Admissions? Yes
Number of Applications Received: 355
% of Applicants Accepted: 64
% Accepted Who Enrolled: 55
Average GPA: 3.2
GPA Range: 2.9-3.6
Average GMAT: 560
GMAT Range: 510-610
Average Years Experience: 2
Other Schools to Which Students Applied: Florida State University, University of Central Florida, University of Florida

INTERNATIONAL STUDENTS

TOEFL Required of International Students? Yes
Minimum TOEFL: 550 (213 computer)

EMPLOYMENT INFORMATION

Placement Office Available? Yes
Fields Employing Percentage of Grads: Human Resources (2%), Accounting (2%), MIS (4%), Consulting (9%), Operations (9%), Finance (9%), Marketing (13%), General Management (23%)
Frequent Employers: Accenture, Citigroup, Eckerd Corp., First Investors Corp., John Hancock Financial Services, JP Morgan, Raymond James

UNIVERSITY OF SOUTHERN CALIFORNIA
Marshall School of Business

Admissions Contact: A. Keith Vaughn, Director of MBA Admissions
Address: Popovich Hall Room 308, Los Angeles, CA 90089-2633
Admissions Phone: 213-740-7846 • **Admissions Fax:** 213-749-8520
Admissions E-mail: marshallmba@marshall.usc.edu
Web Address: www.marshall.usc.edu

USC's Marshall School of Business boasts "strong academic programs" in an impressive array of areas including finance, marketing, information systems, and entrepreneurship. Students also praise the Pacific Rim Education program here, which consists of a short course covering business practices and management styles on the Pacific Rim and concludes with a field trip to China, Japan, or Mexico. However, students save their highest praise for Marshall's legendary "active and eager" alumni network.

INSTITUTIONAL INFORMATION

Public/Private: Private
Evening Classes Available? Yes
Total Faculty: 177
Student/Faculty Ratio: 8:1
Students in Parent Institution: 28,000
Academic Calendar: Semester

PROGRAMS

Degrees Offered: MBA (2 years full time), MBA PM (3 years evening), MSBA (1 year post-MBA), EMBA (2 years), MACC (1 year), Master of Business Taxation (1 year), International Business Education and Research MBA (1 year), Master of Medical Management (1 year)
Combined Degrees: MBA/DDS, MBA/MA in East Asian Studies, MSG/MBA, MBA/MSISE, MBA/MA in Jewish Studies, JD/MBA, MD/MBA, MBA/MSN, MBA/MPL, PharmD/MBA, MBA/MRED
Academic Specialties: International business in all of its aspects, including coursework in Accounting, Finance, Marketing, Management, Information Systems/Operations Management, Entrepreneurship
Special Opportunities: International Exchange, MBA Enterprise Corps, Entrepreneurship Program, Program in Real Estate. All first-year MBA students in the full-time program travel abroad for 7-10 days to China, Japan, Mexico, Chile, or Indonesia as part of the Pacific Rim Education (PRIME) program. All second-year MBA students in MBA.PM program travel abroad for 7-10 days to China, Japan, Mexico, or Cuba.
Study Abroad Options: Argentina, Australia, Austria, Brazil, Chile, China, Costa Rica, Denmark, France, Germany, Hong Kong, Indonesia, Japan, Korea, Mexico, Phillipines, Singapore, Spain, Switzerland, Taiwan, Thailand, United Kingdom

STUDENT INFORMATION

Total Business Students: 1,477
% Full Time: 39
% Female: 33
% Minority: 10
% Out of State: 50
% International: 23
Average Age: 28

COMPUTER AND RESEARCH FACILITIES

Research Facilities: Center for Effective Organizations, Lloyd Grief Center for Enterpreneurial Studies, Center for Telecommunications Management, Center for International Business Education & Research, Family and Closely Held Business Progam, Experiential Learning Center, Instructional Services Center, Lusk Center for Real Estate, Electronic Economy Research Lab (Ebizlab)

Computer Facilities: Bridge Financial Data, online journals, Corptech, Dow Jones Interactive, Dun & Bradstreet, Lexis-Nexis, Moody's, National Trade Data Bank, SEC Edgar Online, Stat USA.

Campuswide Network? Yes
% of MBA Classrooms Wired: 100
Internet Fee? No

EXPENSES/FINANCIAL AID

Annual Tuition: $28,677
Tuition Per Credit (Resident/Nonresident): $869
Books and Supplies: $2,200
Average Grant: $20,000
Average Loan: $25,000
% Receiving Financial Aid: 95
% Receiving Aid Their First Year: 95

ADMISSIONS INFORMATION

Application Fee: $90
Electronic Application? Yes
Regular Application Deadline: 4/1
Regular Notification: 5/1
Deferment Available? No
Non-fall Admissions? No
Transfer Students Accepted? No
Need-Blind Admissions? Yes
Number of Applications Received: 2,583
% of Applicants Accepted: 25
% Accepted Who Enrolled: 46
Average GPA: 3.3
GPA Range: 3.1-3.5
Average GMAT: 670
GMAT Range: 640-700
Average Years Experience: 4
Other Admissions Factors Considered: Leadership potential, interview (if requested), "fit" with the program
Minority/Disadvantaged Student Recruitment Programs: Marshall is a member of the Consortium for Graduate Study in Management, an alliance of 14 graduate schools of business committed to creating career opportunities for African Americans, Hispanic Americans, and Native Americans. The Consortium provides merit-based full tuition scholarships to enable its Fellows to enroll in MBA programs at its 14 member universities. Marshall also hosts an annual Diversity Weekend during the month of December that is geared toward prospective minority applicants.
Other Schools to Which Students Applied: Duke University, New York University, University of California—Berkeley, University of California—Los Angeles, University of Chicago

INTERNATIONAL STUDENTS

TOEFL Required of International Students? Yes
Minimum TOEFL: 250

EMPLOYMENT INFORMATION

Placement Office Available? Yes
% Employed Within 3 Months: 98
Fields Employing Percentage of Grads: Other (1%), Venture Capital (1%), MIS (2%), Human Resources (2%), Operations (4%), General Management (5%), Consulting (18%), Marketing (28%), Finance (32%)
Frequent Employers: Private firms, corporations, federal judges, government, public-interest non-profits. Private corporations include: American Express, Amgen, Arthur Andersen, Artisan Entertainment, Bank of America Securities, ClickTex.com, ConAgra Grocery Products, Dell, Deloitte & Touche, Ernst & Young, Hewlett Packard, Honeywell, Intel, Kraft Foods, Mattel, Nestle USA, Pricewaterhouse Coopers, Walt Disney Co., Teradyne, Toyota, Wells Fargo, Viant

UNIVERSITY OF SOUTHERN INDIANA
School of Business

Admissions Contact: Dr. Peggy Harrel, Director of Graduate Studies
Address: 8600 University Boulvard, Evansville, IN 47712
Admissions Phone: 812-465-7015 • **Admissions Fax:** 812-464-1956
Admissions E-mail: gssr@usi.edu • **Web Address:** business.usi.edu

INSTITUTIONAL INFORMATION

Public/Private: Public
Evening Classes Available? Yes
Total Faculty: 24
Student/Faculty Ratio: 25:1
Students in Parent Institution: 8,400
Academic Calendar: Semester

PROGRAMS

Degrees Offered: MBA (30, 2.4 to 4 years)

STUDENT INFORMATION

Total Business Students: 113
% Full Time: 4
% Female: 30
% Minority: 5
% International: 2
Average Age: 30

COMPUTER AND RESEARCH FACILITIES

Campuswide Network? Yes
Internet Fee? No

EXPENSES/FINANCIAL AID

Tuition Per Credit (Resident/Nonresident): $166/$333
% Receiving Financial Aid: 2

ADMISSIONS INFORMATION

Application Fee: $25
Electronic Application? Yes
Regular Application Deadline: Rolling
Regular Notification: Rolling
Deferment Available? Yes
Non-fall Admissions? Yes
Non-fall Application Deadline(s): Rolling
Transfer Students Accepted? Yes
Transfer Policy: 12 accepted hours can be transferred into our MBA
Need-Blind Admissions? No
Number of Applications Received: 29

% of Applicants Accepted: 72
% Accepted Who Enrolled: 100
Average GPA: 3.2
Average GMAT: 545

INTERNATIONAL STUDENTS

TOEFL Required of International Students? Yes
Minimum TOEFL: 550 (213 computer)

EMPLOYMENT INFORMATION

Placement Office Available? Yes

UNIVERSITY OF SOUTHERN MAINE
School of Business

Admissions Contact: Alice B. Cash, Graduate Program Manager
Address: PO Box 9300, Portland, ME 04104
Admissions Phone: 207-780-4184 • Admissions Fax: 207-780-4662
Admissions E-mail: mba@usm.maine.edu • Web Address: www.usm.maine.edu/sb

If you're not a Mainah (and not knowing what a Mainah is would mean you aren't), then you might feel like a fish out of water at the University of Southern Maine. A whopping 96 percent of USM students are Maine residents. There's a good reason, too: if you're a resident, you pay about a third of what nonresidents pay. Another stat: Nearly everyone in the MBA program is part time. USM's School of Business greatly boasts its Internship Program, in which many local businesses employ students, eventually hiring them full time after graduation. And it's close to Canada. Go NAFTA.

INSTITUTIONAL INFORMATION

Public/Private: Public
Evening Classes Available? Yes
Total Faculty: 22
% Faculty Female: 32
% Faculty Minority: 5
% Faculty Part Time: 14
Student/Faculty Ratio: 15:1
Students in Parent Institution: 11,382
Academic Calendar: Semester

PROGRAMS

Special Opportunities: MBA, MSA

STUDENT INFORMATION

Total Business Students: 132
% Full Time: 15
% Female: 35
% Out of State: 5
% International: 25
Average Age: 30

COMPUTER AND RESEARCH FACILITIES

Research Facilities: Center for Business and Economic Research
Campuswide Network? Yes
Internet Fee? No

EXPENSES/FINANCIAL AID

Annual Tuition (Resident/Nonresident): $4,800/$13,440
Tuition Per Credit (Resident/Nonresident): $200/$560
Room & Board (On/Off Campus): $6,918

Books and Supplies: $1,000
Average Grant: $1,000
% Receiving Financial Aid: 30

ADMISSIONS INFORMATION

Application Fee: $50
Electronic Application? No
Regular Application Deadline: 8/1
Regular Notification: Rolling
Deferment Available? Yes
Length of Deferment: 1 year
Non-fall Admissions? Yes
Non-fall Application Deadline(s): 12/1 spring
Transfer Students Accepted? Yes
Transfer Policy: Please see catalog: http://usm.maine.edu/catalogs/graduate/
Need-Blind Admissions? Yes
Number of Applications Received: 54
% of Applicants Accepted: 83
% Accepted Who Enrolled: 82
Average GPA: 3.6
GPA Range: 3.4-4.0
Average GMAT: 567
GMAT Range: 510-625
Average Years Experience: 7
Other Admissions Factors Considered: Rigor of the undergraduate field of study, reputation of the institution awarding the baccalaureate degree, academic performance in any previous graduate coursework taken, demonstrated potential for successful completion of the program, qualities likely to enhance the educational environment at USM, demonstrated leadership, performance in outside activities, evidence of creativity and leadership, record of accomplishment in business

INTERNATIONAL STUDENTS

TOEFL Required of International Students? Yes
Minimum TOEFL: 550 (213 computer)

EMPLOYMENT INFORMATION

Placement Office Available? No

UNIVERSITY OF SOUTHERN MISSISSIPPI
College of Business Administration

Admissions Contact: Dianna Ladnier, Assistant Director, Graduate Business Programs
Address: Box 5096, Hattiesburg, MS 39406-5096
Admissions Phone: 601-266-4653 • Admissions Fax: 601-266-5814
Admissions E-mail: mba_mpa@cba.usm.edu • Web Address: www.usmmba.usm.edu

INSTITUTIONAL INFORMATION

Public/Private: Public
Evening Classes Available? Yes
Total Faculty: 62
% Faculty Female: 25
% Faculty Minority: 15
Student/Faculty Ratio: 30:1
Students in Parent Institution: 12,896
Academic Calendar: Semester

PROGRAMS

Degrees Offered: MBA (30 credits, 1-6 years), MPACC (30 credits, 1-6 years)

Combined Degrees: MBA/MPH (69 credits, 2-6 years)
Academic Specialties: Accounting, Marketing, Management, Finance
Special Opportunities: General Business, Accounting
Study Abroad Options: Czech Republic, England, Spain

STUDENT INFORMATION

Total Business Students: 77
% Full Time: 87
% Female: 45
% Minority: 19
% International: 9
Average Age: 26

COMPUTER AND RESEARCH FACILITIES

Research Facilities: Center for Financial Services
Computer Facilities: There are 2 computer labs specifically for business students with a total of 55 PCs. One of the labs is dedicated solely to graduate business students. There is access to numerous online full-text databases on the USM library website from any computer on campus.
Campuswide Network? Yes
% of MBA Classrooms Wired: 100
Internet Fee? No

EXPENSES/FINANCIAL AID

Annual Tuition (Resident/Nonresident): $5,170
Tuition Per Credit (Resident/Nonresident): $216
Room & Board (On/Off Campus): $5,629/$6,500
Books and Supplies: $1,500
Average Grant: $8,690
Average Loan: $2,000
% Receiving Financial Aid: 75

ADMISSIONS INFORMATION

Electronic Application? Yes
Regular Application Deadline: 7/15
Regular Notification: Rolling
Deferment Available? Yes
Length of Deferment: 2 semesters
Non-fall Admissions? Yes
Non-fall Application Deadline(s): 11/15 spring, part time only; 4/15 summer, full time or part time
Transfer Students Accepted? Yes
Transfer Policy: Transfer applicants must fully apply to the program and can transfer a maximum of 6 hours of graduate courses from other accredited institutions. The coursework must be graded (i.e., not pass/fail.).
Need-Blind Admissions? Yes
Number of Applications Received: 132
% of Applicants Accepted: 77
% Accepted Who Enrolled: 26
Average GPA: 3.6
Average GMAT: 535
GMAT Range: 430-660
Average Years Experience: 1
Other Admissions Factors Considered: Resume, work experience

INTERNATIONAL STUDENTS

TOEFL Required of International Students? Yes
Minimum TOEFL: 550 (213 computer)

EMPLOYMENT INFORMATION

Placement Office Available? Yes

UNIVERSITY OF TAMPA
John H. Sykes College of Business

Admissions Contact: Fernando Nolasco, Associate Director, Graduate Studies in Business
Address: 401 W. Kennedy Blvd., Tampa, FL 33606-1490
Admissions Phone: 813-258-7409 • **Admissions Fax:** 813-259-5403
Admissions E-mail: mba@ut.edu • **Web Address:** mba.ut.edu

Located in west central Florida's center of commerce and culture, the University of Tampa has a low student/faculty ratio and claims to house not just professors, but mentors who offer continual personal attention and care to the students. Business events on campus include the Backstage Tour, Executive Luncheon Series, and Executive Tune-Up; students can reap the benefits of these great career-building programs and also attend the meeting where local alumni plan the events for each academic year, providing multiple opportunities to meet future employers and mentors.

INSTITUTIONAL INFORMATION

Public/Private: Private
Evening Classes Available? Yes
Total Faculty: 42
% Faculty Female: 31
Student/Faculty Ratio: 12:1
Students in Parent Institution: 3,957
Academic Calendar: Semester

PROGRAMS

Degrees Offered: MBA (accelerated full time and flex part time), MS in Technology and Innovation Management, MSN
Combined Degrees: MSN/MBA
Academic Specialties: Accounting, Economics, Finance, Information Systems Management
Study Abroad Options: Monterrey Tech, Mexico

STUDENT INFORMATION

Total Business Students: 387
% Full Time: 37
% Female: 41
% Minority: 6
% Out of State: 4
% International: 66
Average Age: 28

COMPUTER AND RESEARCH FACILITIES

Research Facilities: Center for Ethics, Center for Innovation and Knowledge Management, TECO Energy Center for Leadership, Human Resource Institute, Institute for World Commerce Education, Naimoli Institute for Business Strategy, Huizenga Family Foundation Trading Center
Computer Facilities: ABI-Inform, Disclosure, Lexis-Nexis, National Trade Data Bank (NTDB); 1,300 data ports
Campuswide Network? Yes
% of MBA Classrooms Wired: 100
Computer Model Recommended: Laptop
Internet Fee? No

EXPENSES/FINANCIAL AID

Annual Tuition: $8,400
Tuition Per Credit (Resident/Nonresident): $352
Room & Board (On/Off Campus): $5,890
Books and Supplies: $1,000
Average Grant: $9,048
Average Loan: $9,608
% Receiving Financial Aid: 37
% Receiving Aid Their First Year: 32

ADMISSIONS INFORMATION

Application Fee: $35
Electronic Application? Yes
Regular Application Deadline: Rolling
Regular Notification: Rolling
Deferment Available? Yes
Length of Deferment: 1 year
Non-fall Admissions? Yes
Non-fall Application Deadline(s): Rolling
Transfer Students Accepted? Yes
Transfer Policy: Up to 9 hours from an AACSB-accredited schools
Need-Blind Admissions? Yes
Number of Applications Received: 349
% of Applicants Accepted: 43
% Accepted Who Enrolled: 67
Average GPA: 3.4
GPA Range: 2.9-3.9
Average GMAT: 529
GMAT Range: 460-600
Average Years Experience: 4
Other Schools to Which Students Applied: University of Florida, University of South Florida

INTERNATIONAL STUDENTS

TOEFL Required of International Students? Yes
Minimum TOEFL: 577 (230 computer)

EMPLOYMENT INFORMATION

Placement Office Available? Yes
% Employed Within 3 Months: 100
Fields Employing Percentage of Grads: Strategic Planning (4%), Human Resources (4%), Other (7%), Marketing (11%), General Management (22%), Finance (44%)
Frequent Employers: Am South, Franklin Templeton, GATX Capital, Sun Trust, Tampa Electric
Prominent Alumni: Dennis Zank, COO, Raymond James; Lyndon Martin, member, Legislative Assembly, Cayman Islands; Jorgen Adolfsson, Swedish technology entrepreneur

See page 464.

UNIVERSITY OF TENNESSEE— CHATTANOOGA
College of Business Administration

Admissions Contact: Andrea Evans, Graduate Studies Office
Address: Dept. 5305, Siskin Memorial, 615 McCallie Ave., Chattanooga, TN 37403
Admissions Phone: 423-425-4667 • **Admissions Fax:** 423-425-5223
Admissions E-mail: andrea-evans@utc.edu • **Web Address:** www.utc.edu

INSTITUTIONAL INFORMATION

Public/Private: Public
Evening Classes Available? Yes
Total Faculty: 47
% Faculty Part Time: 32
Student/Faculty Ratio: 25:1
Students in Parent Institution: 8,524
Academic Calendar: Semester

PROGRAMS

Degrees Offered: MBA (30-51 credits, 2-6 years), EMBA (30-51 credits, 18 months to 2 years), MACC (30-51 credits, 2-6 years)

STUDENT INFORMATION

Total Business Students: 314
% Full Time: 21
% Female: 45
% Minority: 16
% International: 15
Average Age: 27

COMPUTER AND RESEARCH FACILITIES

Research Facilities: Lupton Library
Computer Facilities: Campuswide computer labs
Campuswide Network? Yes
% of MBA Classrooms Wired: 80
Internet Fee? No

EXPENSES/FINANCIAL AID

Annual Tuition (Resident/Nonresident): $2,214/$5,724
Tuition Per Credit (Resident/Nonresident): $246/$636
Books and Supplies: $650
Average Grant: $550
Average Loan: $2,214

ADMISSIONS INFORMATION

Application Fee: $25
Electronic Application? Yes
Regular Application Deadline: Rolling
Regular Notification: Rolling
Deferment Available? Yes
Length of Deferment: 5 years
Non-fall Admissions? Yes
Non-fall Application Deadline(s): Spring and summer terms
Transfer Students Accepted? Yes
Transfer Policy: A maximum of 9 hours from an accredited school
Need-Blind Admissions? No
Number of Applications Received: 124
% of Applicants Accepted: 90
% Accepted Who Enrolled: 62
Average GPA: 3.1
Average GMAT: 497

INTERNATIONAL STUDENTS

TOEFL Required of International Students? Yes
Minimum TOEFL: 500

EMPLOYMENT INFORMATION

Placement Office Available? Yes
Frequent Employers: BlueCross BlueShield of Tennessee, Erlanger Medical Center, Maytag Corp., McKee Food Corp., Memorial Hospital, Tennessee Valley Authority, UnumProvident

UNIVERSITY OF TENNESSEE— KNOXVILLE
College of Business Administration

Admissions Contact: Donna Potts, Director of Admissions, MBA Program
Address: 527 Stokely Management Center, Knoxville, TN 37996-0552
Admissions Phone: 865-974-5033 • **Admissions Fax:** 865-974-3826
Admissions E-mail: mba@utk.edu • **Web Address:** mba.bus.utk.edu

The small and intimate University of Tennessee College of Business Administrationoffers a "very strong academic program" that students call a "great value for the money." The core curriculum centers on a yearlong case experience in which teams of students run their own businesses, "taking a company from its birth through the entire business cycle." As for Knoxville, "it's a great little city" with "excellent restaurants," and the Smoky Mountains are only a short drive away.

INSTITUTIONAL INFORMATION

Public/Private: Public
Evening Classes Available? No
Total Faculty: 125
% Faculty Female: 18
% Faculty Minority: 6
Student/Faculty Ratio: 15:1
Students in Parent Institution: 26,033
Academic Calendar: Semester

PROGRAMS

Degrees Offered: MBA (17 months, with required internship during summer term)
Combined Degrees: JD/MBA (3.5 to 4 years), MBA/MS in Engineering (2 years and 1/2 summer session)
Academic Specialties: Supply Chain Management, Logistics and Transportation, Operations Management, Marketing, Finance
Special Opportunities: The MBA Symposia, Tennessee Organization of MBAs, Women's Organization of MBAs, Corporate Connections, MBA Marketing Association, Clayton Torch Fund, Haslam Torch Fund; also, 6 national and international case competition teams

STUDENT INFORMATION

Total Business Students: 180
% Full Time: 100
% Female: 26
% Minority: 20
% Out of State: 62
% International: 7
Average Age: 26

COMPUTER AND RESEARCH FACILITIES

Research Facilities: Center for Business and Economic Research, MBA Career Services
Computer Facilities: College of Business computer labs; numerous informational databases; hardware, software, and programming training courses; laptop support center
Campuswide Network? Yes
% of MBA Classrooms Wired: 90
Computer Model Recommended: Laptop
Internet Fee? Yes

EXPENSES/FINANCIAL AID

Annual Tuition (Resident/Nonresident): $5,405/$15,425
Books and Supplies: $1,500
Average Grant: $3,000
Average Loan: $11,353

% Receiving Financial Aid: 50
% Receiving Aid Their First Year: 25

ADMISSIONS INFORMATION

Application Fee: $35
Electronic Application? No
Regular Application Deadline: 3/1
Regular Notification: Rolling
Deferment Available? No
Non-fall Admissions? No
Transfer Students Accepted? No
Need-Blind Admissions? No
Number of Applications Received: 464
% of Applicants Accepted: 37
% Accepted Who Enrolled: 52
Average GPA: 3.3
GPA Range: 2.9-3.8
Average GMAT: 610
GMAT Range: 490-740
Average Years Experience: 4
Minority/Disadvantaged Student Recruitment Programs: THEC Black Graduate Fellowship

INTERNATIONAL STUDENTS

TOEFL Required of International Students? Yes
Minimum TOEFL: 600 (250 computer)

EMPLOYMENT INFORMATION

Placement Office Available? Yes
% Employed Within 3 Months: 55
Fields Employing Percentage of Grads: Consulting (3%), Operations (3%), MIS (5%), Finance (8%), Marketing (14%), Other (23%)
Frequent Employers: Defense Logistics Agency, FedEx, General Electric, Milliken, Pershing, Yoakley& Associates, Procter & Gamble

UNIVERSITY OF TENNESSEE—MARTIN
College of Business and Public Affairs

Admissions Contact: Coordinator of Graduate Programs in Business Administration
Address: 103 Business Administration Building, Martin, TN 38238
Admissions Phone: 731-587-7308 • **Admissions Fax:** 731-587-7241
Admissions E-mail: bagrad@utm.edu • **Web Address:** www.utm.edu/departments/soba/

INSTITUTIONAL INFORMATION

Public/Private: Public
Evening Classes Available? No
Total Faculty: 27
Academic Calendar: Semester

PROGRAMS

Degrees Offered: MBA (30 credits, 9 months to 6 years), MACC (30 credits, 9 months to 6 years)

STUDENT INFORMATION

Total Business Students: 200

COMPUTER AND RESEARCH FACILITIES

Campuswide Network? Yes
Internet Fee? No

EXPENSES/FINANCIAL AID

Annual Tuition (Resident/Nonresident): $2,962/$4,826
Tuition Per Credit (Resident/Nonresident): $165/$434

ADMISSIONS INFORMATION

Application Fee: $25
Electronic Application? No
Regular Application Deadline: Rolling
Regular Notification: Rolling
Deferment Available? Yes
Non-fall Admissions? No
Transfer Students Accepted? No
Need-Blind Admissions? No

INTERNATIONAL STUDENTS

TOEFL Required of International Students? Yes
Minimum TOEFL: 525

EMPLOYMENT INFORMATION

Placement Office Available? Yes

UNIVERSITY OF TEXAS—ARLINGTON
College of Business Administration

Admissions Contact: Davis Hall, Assistant Vice President
Address: Box 19167, Arlington, TX 76019
Admissions Phone: 817-272-2688 • **Admissions Fax:** 817-272-2627
Admissions E-mail: graduate.school@uta.edu • **Web Address:** www2.uta.edu/gradbiz

Chief among the assets of the University of Texas at Arlington's MBA program is its location in the Dallas/Fort Worth Metroplex region, a hub of the active, high-stakes Texas business world. UTA offers flexibility to MBA students, "with most classes held in the evening," and the surrounding area provides a fertile lab for the exploration and pursuit of hundreds of career alternatives. Many of UTA's "hardworking, hard-earning, future-focused" MBA students are part-time and "commuter students."

INSTITUTIONAL INFORMATION

Public/Private: Public
Evening Classes Available? Yes
Total Faculty: 63
% Faculty Female: 17
% Faculty Minority: 25
Student/Faculty Ratio: 20:1
Students in Parent Institution: 23,821
Academic Calendar: Semester

PROGRAMS

Degrees Offered: Online MBA (36 hours of advanced coursework, up to 18 hours of foundation coursework), Accelerated MBA (48 hours), MA in Economics, MSA, MST, MS in Human Resources Management, MS in Marketing Research, MSIS, MS in Real Estate, MPACC, PhD in Business Administration, MSHA
Combined Degrees: May combine any two degrees (usually MBA and specialized program) or a business degree with others, such as Engineering, Architecture, Science, Nursing; can obtain second degree with as few as 18 additional hours. May pursue MBA at University of Texas at Austin with MIM at Thunderbird
Academic Specialties: Finance, Accounting, Information Systems, International Business, Marketing Research, Real Estate, Human Resource Manage-

ment, E-Commerce, Enterprise Resourse Planning
Special Opportunities: Careers Program that includes comprehensive assessment, industry analysis, career exploration and informational interviews, managing in a diverse environment, career-focused academic advising, internships
Study Abroad Options: Royal Melbourne Iinstitute of Technology, Australia; University of North Umbria at Newcastle, England; Ecole Superieure de Commerce, Pau, France; Universitat des Saarlandes, Saarbrucken, Germany; Yonsei University and Sung Kyun Kwan University, Seoul, Korea; ITESM, Mexico; Norwegian School of Management, Olso, Norway

STUDENT INFORMATION

Total Business Students: 587
% Full Time: 31
% Female: 13
% Minority: 5
% International: 14
Average Age: 30

COMPUTER AND RESEARCH FACILITIES

Research Facilities: Center for Information Technologies Management, Center for Research on Organizational and Managerial Excellence, Ryan/Reilly Center for Urban Land Utilization, Center for Marketing Research
Computer Facilities: Visual Basic, JAVA, Microsoft Office Suites, C++, Internet Explorer, Front Page and Publisher, Netscape Web Browser, Windows 2000 Operating System, SAP R/3 version 8i databases
Campuswide Network? Yes
% of MBA Classrooms Wired: 7
Internet Fee? No

EXPENSES/FINANCIAL AID

Annual Tuition (Resident/Nonresident): $2,640/$9,510
Tuition Per Credit (Resident/Nonresident): $88/$317
Books and Supplies: $1,000
Average Grant: $1,460
Average Loan: $8,585
% Receiving Financial Aid: 20
% Receiving Aid Their First Year: 22

ADMISSIONS INFORMATION

Application Fee: $30
Electronic Application? Yes
Early Decision Application Deadline: Rolling
Early Decision Notification: 1/1
Regular Application Deadline: 6/15
Regular Notification: Rolling
Deferment Available? Yes
Length of Deferment: 1 year
Non-fall Admissions? Yes
Non-fall Application Deadline(s): Mid-October spring, mid-March summer
Transfer Students Accepted? Yes
Transfer Policy: Maximum of 9 transferable credits with a grade of B or better from an AACSB-accredited university
Need-Blind Admissions? Yes
Number of Applications Received: 465
% of Applicants Accepted: 57
% Accepted Who Enrolled: 47
Average GPA: 3.2
GPA Range: 3.0-3.5
Average GMAT: 552
GMAT Range: 470-570
Average Years Experience: 5
Other Admissions Factors Considered: Degree held, college/university attended, professional certifications held, professional experience after earning bachelor's degree
Minority/Disadvantaged Student Recruitment Programs: UTA Graduate Business supports activities sponsored by the McNair Scholar Program and

the National Black MBA Association.
TOEFL Required of International Students? Yes
Minimum TOEFL: 550 (213 computer)

EMPLOYMENT INFORMATION

Placement Office Available? Yes
Frequent Employers: Alcon Laboratories; American Airlines; Bank of America; Nokia; Sabre Group Holdings, Inc.
Prominent Alumni: Robert Davis, president and CEO, USAA Insurance Inc.; Brian Chase, executive director, National Space Society

UNIVERSITY OF TEXAS—AUSTIN
McCombs School of Business

Admissions Contact: Dr. Matt Turner, Director of Admission, MBA Programs
Address: Admissions, MBA Program Office, 1 University Station, B6004, Austin, TX 78712
Admissions Phone: 512-471-7612 • **Admissions Fax:** 512-471-4243
Admissions E-mail: McCombsMBA@bus.utexas.edu
Web Address: texasmba.bus.utexas.edu

You can't beat the bang for the buck you get at the University of Texas at Austin's Graduate School of Business. Perks at this "strong quantitative school" include the EDS Financial Trading and Technology Center, a state-of-the-art research facility, and the Austin Technology Incubator, which assists start-up technology entrepreneurs and provides more than 150 students with hands-on entrepreneurial experience. The "beautiful" city of Austin has "a wonderful culture of live music," a vibrant bar scene, and a climate that allows "outdoor sports all year."

INSTITUTIONAL INFORMATION

Public/Private: Public
Evening Classes Available? Yes
Total Faculty: 176
% Faculty Female: 27
Student/Faculty Ratio: 5:1
Students in Parent Institution: 50,000
Academic Calendar: Semester

PROGRAMS

Degrees Offered: McCombs MBA, (2 years), Option II EMBA (2 years), Texas Evening MBA (3 years), EMBA-Mexico City (2 years), EMBA-Dallas (2 years), PhD (5 years), Master of Public Accounting (2 years), Professional Program in Accounting (1 year)
Combined Degrees: MBA/MA in Asian Studies; MBA/MA in Latin American Studies; MBA/MA in Middle Eastern Studies; MBA/MA in Public Affairs; MBA/MA in Russian, Eastern Europe, and Eurasian Studies; MBA/MA in Communications; MBA/MS in Manufacturing and Decision Systems Engineering; MBA/MSN (Most combined degrees are 72-75 credits hours.) MBA/JD (134 credit hours)
Academic Specialties: From the establishment of our latest research centers to the ongoing results of Red McCombs's $50 million donation, the McCombs School continues to offer some of the most exciting innovations in the world of business education. The next few years will be no exception. New for 2002, McCombs introduced the Plus Program, one of our most exciting innovations to date. Through Plus, McCombs students are gaining an edge on the competition, benefiting from a unique curriculum designed to explore the art of business. In team-oriented, non-graded seminars that complement the regular course schedule, McCombs MBAs will explore everything from the arts of sales and negotiation to the complexities of business ethics and global trade. Along the way, they are cultivating the soft skills that recruiters prize and that often spell the difference over the course of a professional career.

Special Opportunities: Plus Program, Spanish Language Track, double-degree programs with 7 schools worldwide, exchange programs with 22 schools worldwide, MOOT Corp,
Masters in Professional Accounting, MBA Investment Fund, Quality Management Consortium, Venture Capital Fellows
Study Abroad Options: Argentina, Australia, Brazil, Canada, Chile, China, Denmark, England, Germany, Finland, France, Hong Kong, Mexico, the Netherlands, Peru, Spain, Switzerland

STUDENT INFORMATION

Total Business Students: 804
% Full Time: 100
% Female: 24
% Minority: 7
% Out of State: 29
% International: 26
Average Age: 28

COMPUTER AND RESEARCH FACILITIES

Research Facilities: AIM Investment Center; Bureau of Business Research; C. Aubrey Smith Center for Auditing Education and Research; Center for Business Measurement and Assurance Services; Center for Business, Technology, and Law; Center for Customer Insight; Center for Energy Finance Education & Research; Center for International Business Education & Research; Center for Manufacturing Systems; Center for Organizations Research; Center for Real Estate Finance; Center for Research in Electronic Commerce; Center for Statistical Sciences; EDS Financial Trading and Technology Center; Hicks, Muse, Tate & Furst Center for Private Equity Finance; Herb Kelleher Center for Entrepreneurship; IC2 Institute; Supply Chain Management Bureau of Business Research
Computer Facilities: McCombs has increased networking capabilities, upgraded servers, increased IT security, and expanded the wireless network for the members of the McCombs Community. In addition, McCombs has added 9 private study rooms equipped with T1 lines, plus a new MBA Leadership Center with Internet connections, a high-tech conference room, and a flat screen television. The Millennium Lab provides a 160-seat, state-of-the-art computer lab for students and is supported by a 100MB switched ethernet.
McCombs is one of the most intensively networked business schools in the country and was one of the first MBA programs to require that every student purchase a standardized laptop. The business school is home to cutting-edge facilities with nearly 900 workstations in 7 different computer labs and an NT lab equipped with 142 state-of-the-art workstations. The school runs a common, wireless operating environment modeled on the highest corporate standards.
Campuswide Network? Yes
% of MBA Classrooms Wired: 100
Computer Model Recommended: Laptop
Internet Fee? No

EXPENSES/FINANCIAL AID

Annual Tuition (Resident/Nonresident): $3,960/$17,040
Room & Board (On/Off Campus): $12,038
Books and Supplies: $1,400
Average Grant: $4,612
Average Loan: $16,000
% Receiving Financial Aid: 70

ADMISSIONS INFORMATION

Application Fee: $125
Electronic Application? Yes
Regular Application Deadline: 3/15
Regular Notification: 5/1
Deferment Available? Yes
Length of Deferment: 1 year
Non-fall Admissions? No
Transfer Students Accepted? No
Need-Blind Admissions? Yes
Number of Applications Received: 2,681
% of Applicants Accepted: 29

% Accepted Who Enrolled: 52
Average GPA: 3.4
GPA Range: 2.9-3.9
Average GMAT: 678
GMAT Range: 630-730
Average Years Experience: 5
Other Admissions Factors Considered: The McCombs School of Business offers an optional interview as part of the application process. The interview offers prospective students an excellent opportunity to determine their potential match with our school and provides an otherwise unavailable avenue to demonstrate their interpersonal skills. In addition, candidates are introduced to a current student or alumnus of the program who can provide personal insight into the assets of the McCombs MBA program. Interviews are entirely optional; they are available on a limited basis. Other factors considered: quality of communication skills displayed in essays as well as diversity of professional skills experiences.
Minority/Disadvantaged Student Recruitment Programs: Consortium for Graduate Study in Management; GMAC Forums; Texas Tour; Top 10 Schools Forum; Toigo Fellowship; National Society for Hispanic MBAs (NSHMBA); National Black MBA; Forte Foundation, a national non-profit organization to increase women in business leadership
Other Schools to Which Students Applied: Indiana University, Northwestern University, Stanford University, University of California—Berkeley, University of California—Los Angeles, University of North Carolina—Chapel Hill, University of Pennsylvania

INTERNATIONAL STUDENTS

TOEFL Required of International Students? Yes
Minimum TOEFL: 620 (260 computer)

EMPLOYMENT INFORMATION

Placement Office Available? Yes
% Employed Within 3 Months: 82
Fields Employing Percentage of Grads: Operations (5%), Consulting (7%), MIS (7%), General Management (12%), Other (19%), Marketing (19%), Finance (31%)
Frequent Employers: AIM, American Airlines, Barclay's Calpine, Campbell, Capital, Citibank, Dell, Deloitte Consulting, Duke, Dynegy, Eli Lilly, El Paso Energy, Frito Lay, General Mills, IBM, Intel, Johnson & Johnson, JP Morgan, Merrill Lynch, Microsoft, Motorola, National Instruments, Reliant Energy, SABRE, The Williams Co.,
Prominent Alumni: Jim Mulva, president, CEO, Conoco Phillips; Bill Gurley, general partner, Benchmark Capital; Don Evans, secretary of commerce, United States; Sara Martinez Tucker, CEO, Hispanic Scholarship Fund; Gerard Arpey, president, COO, American Airlines

PROGRAMS

Degrees Offered: MBA (36-51 credits, 16 months to 6 years), MACC (36-78 credits, 16 months to 6 years)
Combined Degrees: MBA/MPA (60-78 credits, 2-6 years)
Special Opportunities: Internship program
Study Abroad Options: Yes

STUDENT INFORMATION

Total Business Students: 245
% Full Time: 24
% Female: 38
% Minority: 42
% International: 18
Average Age: 32

COMPUTER AND RESEARCH FACILITIES

Computer Facilities: Access to online bibliographic retrieval services and online databases
Campuswide Network? Yes
Internet Fee? No

EXPENSES/FINANCIAL AID

Annual Tuition (Resident/Nonresident): $1,172/$3,035
Tuition Per Credit (Resident/Nonresident): $108/$311

ADMISSIONS INFORMATION

Application Fee: $15
Electronic Application? No
Regular Application Deadline: 7/1
Regular Notification: Rolling
Deferment Available? No
Non-fall Admissions? Yes
Non-fall Application Deadline(s): 11/1 spring, 4/1 summer
Transfer Students Accepted? No
Need-Blind Admissions? No
Number of Applications Received: 65

INTERNATIONAL STUDENTS

TOEFL Required of International Students? Yes
Minimum TOEFL: 600

EMPLOYMENT INFORMATION

Placement Office Available? Yes

UNIVERSITY OF TEXAS—EL PASO
College of Business Administration

Admissions Contact: Yolanda Ruiz, Graduate Advisor
Address: Room 102, El Paso, TX 79968
Admissions Phone: 915-747-5174 • **Admissions Fax:** 915-747-5147
Admissions E-mail: coba@utep.edu. • **Web Address:** www.utep.edu/coba/

INSTITUTIONAL INFORMATION

Public/Private: Public
Evening Classes Available? No
Total Faculty: 59
Students in Parent Institution: 14,500
Academic Calendar: Semester

UNIVERSITY OF TEXAS— PAN AMERICAN
College of Business Administration

Admissions Contact: Dr. Jerry Prock, Director of MBA Programs
Address: 1201 West University, Edinburg, TX 78539-2999
Admissions Phone: 956-381-3313 • **Admissions Fax:** 956-381-2970
Admissions E-mail: mbaprog@panam.edu
Web Address: www.coba.panam.edu/mba/index.htm

The Pan American campus of The University of Texas is only twenty minutes from the Mexican border and a mere 75 miles from the Gulf of Mexico and the South Padre Island resort area. Not bad for a serious-minded business school emphasizing critical thinking and strong leadership skills, eh? The University of Texas—Pan American is in South Texas, a distinctly bicultural locale where many people speak both English and Spanish, providing MBA students with a great place to begin an international business career. UT—Pan American offers the MBA Evening program, the Professional MBA Program, held on Saturdays, and an online MBA program in conjunction with other institutions within the University of Texas system.

INSTITUTIONAL INFORMATION

Public/Private: Public
Evening Classes Available? No
Total Faculty: 17
Students in Parent Institution: 13,640
Academic Calendar: Semester

PROGRAMS

Degrees Offered: MBA (33 credits, 18 months to 7 years), Weekend MBA (33 credits, 2 years)

STUDENT INFORMATION

Total Business Students: 127
% Full Time: 51
% Female: 32
% Minority: 72
% International: 15
Average Age: 31

COMPUTER AND RESEARCH FACILITIES

Research Facilities: CD players
Computer Facilities: Access provided to online bibliographic retrieval services and online databases
Campuswide Network? Yes
Internet Fee? No

EXPENSES/FINANCIAL AID

Annual Tuition (Resident/Nonresident): $1,570/$6,658
Tuition Per Credit (Resident/Nonresident): $54/$248

ADMISSIONS INFORMATION

Electronic Application? No
Regular Application Deadline: 8/1
Regular Notification: Rolling
Deferment Available? No
Non-fall Admissions? Yes
Non-fall Application Deadline(s): 2/1 fall, summer; 9/1 spring
Transfer Students Accepted? No
Need-Blind Admissions? No
Number of Applications Received: 98
% of Applicants Accepted: 31
% Accepted Who Enrolled: 60
Average GPA: 3.0
Average GMAT: 420
Other Admissions Factors Considered: GMAT accepted (minimum 470), interview, personal statement, work experience, letters of recommendation, computer experience

INTERNATIONAL STUDENTS

TOEFL Required of International Students? Yes
Minimum TOEFL: 500 (173 computer)

EMPLOYMENT INFORMATION

Placement Office Available? Yes

UNIVERSITY OF TEXAS—SAN ANTONIO
College of Business

Admissions Contact: Suzette Vallejo, Supervisor, Graduate Admissions
Address: 6900 N. Loop 1604 West, San Antonio, TX 78249-0603
Admissions Phone: 210-458-4330 • **Admissions Fax:** 210-458-4332
Admissions E-mail: graduatestudies@utsa.edu
Web Address: business.utsa.edu/graduate/

The University of Texas at San Antonio offers its students a solid, broad-based education with comprehensive business goals. UTSA provides students with a handful of MBA programs to choose from and opportunities to interact with top local business leaders with programs like the Frost Bank Distinguished Lecture Series and the Business Ethics Symposium. The Executive MBA is a five-semester plan designed for executives and entrepreneurs with significant managerial experience, while the International MBA is designed for students with proficiency in one of the six modern languages, enabling them to study business administration in the context of a global business outlook. The Weekend MBA and Online MBA are also available.

INSTITUTIONAL INFORMATION

Public/Private: Public
Evening Classes Available? Yes
Total Faculty: 87
% Faculty Female: 21
% Faculty Minority: 32
% Faculty Part Time: 13
Student/Faculty Ratio: 24:1
Students in Parent Institution: 22,016
Academic Calendar: Semester

PROGRAMS

Degrees Offered: MBA (33-57 credits, 1-6 years), MBA in International Business (33-63 credits, 1-6 years), MSA (30-60 credits, 1-6 years), MTAX (30-60 credits, 1-6 years), MSMOT (30 credits, 1-6 years), EMBA (42 credits, 21 months), MA in Economics (33-48 credits, 1-6 years), MS in Finance (33-48 credits, 1-6 years), MSIT (33-51 credits, 1-6 years)
Academic Specialties: Our faculty focus their research in a variety of areas supporting the doctoral programs in Accounting, Finance, Management and Organizational Studies, and Information Technology. Faculty in Finance, Economics, and Real Estate are nationally ranked for their quantity and quality of publications in Finance and Real Estate journals. Our Management faculty has received national recognition for their research on human resources and strategies. A new expertise and academic program are being developed in Infrastructure Assurance and Security.
Special Opportunities: Internship program, NAFTA class, Liu Program
Study Abroad Options: Canada; Hong Kong, China; Italy; Guadalajara, Mexico; Prague. New exchange agreements are being developed with Keele University, England; Negocia Académie Commerciale Internationale (ACI), France; Douselldorf University, Germany; and Instituto Tecnologico y de Estudios Superiores de Monterrey—EGADE, Monterrey, Mexico.

STUDENT INFORMATION

Total Business Students: 362
% Full Time: 35
Average Age: 28

COMPUTER AND RESEARCH FACILITIES

Research Facilities: Center for Infrastructure Assurance and Security
Computer Facilities: Access to online bibliographic retrieval services and online databases
Campuswide Network? Yes
Internet Fee? No

EXPENSES/FINANCIAL AID

Annual Tuition (Resident/Nonresident): $3,949/$4,258
Tuition Per Credit (Resident/Nonresident): $132/$400

ADMISSIONS INFORMATION

Application Fee: $25
Electronic Application? Yes
Regular Application Deadline: 7/1
Regular Notification: Rolling
Deferment Available? Yes
Length of Deferment: 3 terms
Non-fall Admissions? Yes
Non-fall Application Deadline(s): 11/1 spring, summer 5/1
Transfer Students Accepted? Yes
Transfer Policy: Please refer to current Graduate Catalog.
Need-Blind Admissions? Yes
Number of Applications Received: 198
% of Applicants Accepted: 70
% Accepted Who Enrolled: 68
Average GPA: 3.1
GPA Range: 2.8-3.5
Average GMAT: 564
GMAT Range: 510-610
Other Admissions Factors Considered: Letters of reference, a current resume, and a personal statement are strongly recommended.

INTERNATIONAL STUDENTS

TOEFL Required of International Students? Yes
Minimum TOEFL: 500 (173 computer)

EMPLOYMENT INFORMATION

Placement Office Available? Yes
Frequent Employers: Dell Computers, HEB Grocery Co.,USAA
Prominent Alumni: Gilbert Gonzalez, undersecretary for rural development, U.S. Department of Agriculture; Ernest Bromley, president and CEO, Bromley & Associates; Susan Evers, general counsel, USAA; William Morrow, president and vice chairman, Grande Communications

UNIVERSITY OF TEXAS—TYLER
School of Business Administration

Admissions Contact: Dr. Mary Fischer, Director of Graduate Programs in Business
Address: 3900 University Boulevard, Tyler, TX 75799
Admissions Phone: 903-566-7363 • **Admissions Fax:** 903-566-7372
Admissions E-mail: gsmith@mail.uttyl.edu • **Web Address:** www.uttyler.edu/cbt/mba.htm

INSTITUTIONAL INFORMATION

Public/Private: Public
Evening Classes Available? No
Total Faculty: 18
% Faculty Part Time: 8
Student/Faculty Ratio: 15:1
Students in Parent Institution: 3,459
Academic Calendar: Semester

PROGRAMS

Degrees Offered: MBA (66 credits, 1-6 years), MBA Health Care Track (66 credits, 1-6 years)
Special Opportunities: General Business
Study Abroad Options: Mexico

STUDENT INFORMATION

Total Business Students: 101
% Full Time: 2
% Female: 41
% Minority: 5
% International: 5
Average Age: 32

COMPUTER AND RESEARCH FACILITIES

Campuswide Network? Yes
Internet Fee? No

EXPENSES/FINANCIAL AID

Tuition Per Credit (Resident/Nonresident): $337/$967

ADMISSIONS INFORMATION

Electronic Application? No
Regular Application Deadline: Rolling
Regular Notification: Rolling
Deferment Available? Yes
Non-fall Admissions? No
Transfer Students Accepted? No
Need-Blind Admissions? No
% Accepted Who Enrolled: 10

INTERNATIONAL STUDENTS

TOEFL Required of International Students? Yes
Minimum TOEFL: 550

EMPLOYMENT INFORMATION

Placement Office Available? Yes

UNIVERSITY OF THE PACIFIC
Eberhardt School of Business

Admissions Contact: Christopher Lozano, ESB Director, Student Recruitment
Address: MBA Program, 3601 Pacific Avenue, Stockton, CA 95211
Admissions Phone: 800-952-3179 • **Admissions Fax:** 209-946-2586
Admissions E-mail: MBA@UOP.EDU • **Web Address:** www.pacific.edu/MBA

The Eberhardt School of Business provides its MBA students with a wagonload of academic options. They begin with numerous study abroad opportunities, including locales like South Korea, Singapore (can you say "Asian Tigers"?) Chile, Malaysia, Spain, Ireland, France, and England. Full-time students with limited prior work experience should participate in an internship between the first and second years. Pacific's tuition is that of a private school, and the student body is small. Most MBA grads go into general management and consulting.

INSTITUTIONAL INFORMATION

Public/Private: Private
Evening Classes Available? Yes
Total Faculty: 12
% Faculty Female: 12
% Faculty Minority: 6
Student/Faculty Ratio: 8:1
Students in Parent Institution: 5,800
Academic Calendar: Semester

PROGRAMS

Degrees Offered: MBA (1 year for business majors and some business minors, 2 years full time for non-business degree holders)
Combined Degrees: MBA/JD (4 years), Peace Corps MBA (4.5 years), PharmD/MBA (5 years)
Academic Specialties: MIS/E-Commerce, Strategy, Commercial Law, Real Estate Law, Residential and Commercial Real Estate, Marketing Research Methods, Consumer Behavior, Small Business Strategy, Entrepreneurship, Production/Operations Management; MBA specializations available in Marketing, Finance
Special Opportunities: Concentrations available in General Management, Entrepreneurship, Finance, Marketing, Management Information Systems
Study Abroad Options: All Peace Corps sites; global study abroad course offered in Lyon, France

STUDENT INFORMATION

Total Business Students: 65
% Full Time: 60
% Female: 40
% Minority: 15
% Out of State: 10
% International: 10
Average Age: 25

COMPUTER AND RESEARCH FACILITIES

Research Facilities: Wireless Internet access is available within the surrounding area of the building.
Computer Facilities: Dow Jones Retrieval, Business Index ASAP; all databases available through Pacificat (about 50-75)
Campuswide Network? Yes
% of MBA Classrooms Wired: 10
Computer Model Recommended: Laptop
Internet Fee? No

EXPENSES/FINANCIAL AID

Annual Tuition: $20,820
Tuition Per Credit (Resident/Nonresident): $694
Room & Board (On/Off Campus): $9,350/$9,000
Books and Supplies: $2,000
Average Grant: $5,000
Average Loan: $18,000
% Receiving Financial Aid: 90
% Receiving Aid Their First Year: 90

ADMISSIONS INFORMATION

Application Fee: $50
Electronic Application? Yes
Regular Application Deadline: 3/1
Regular Notification: Rolling
Deferment Available? Yes
Length of Deferment: 1 year
Non-fall Admissions? Yes
Non-fall Application Deadline(s): 11/1 spring, 2/15 summer
Transfer Students Accepted? Yes
Transfer Policy: Transfer students may waive all first-year courses if they have completed them with a grade of B or better from another AACSB-accredited college. Students may also transfer up to 2 Phase II courses from another AACSB-accredited MBA Program.
Need-Blind Admissions? Yes
Number of Applications Received: 92
% of Applicants Accepted: 46
% Accepted Who Enrolled: 76
Average GPA: 3.4
GPA Range: 3.0-3.7
Average GMAT: 574
GMAT Range: 500-650
Average Years Experience: 2

Other Admissions Factors Considered: Grade trends, formula score (overall GPA × 200 + GMAT ≥ 1200),
Other Schools to Which Students Applied: California Polytechnic State University, San Luis Obispo, California State University—Sacramento, Saint Mary's College of California, Santa Clara University, University of California—Davis, University of California—Berkeley, University of San Francisco

INTERNATIONAL STUDENTS

TOEFL Required of International Students? Yes
Minimum TOEFL: 550 (213 computer)

EMPLOYMENT INFORMATION

Placement Office Available? Yes
% Employed Within 3 Months: 80
Fields Employing Percentage of Grads: Entrepreneurship (5%), Marketing (10%), MIS (12%), Consulting (21%), Finance (21%), General Management (24%)
Frequent Employers: Andersen Consulting, Bank of America, Gallo Winery, Lawrence Livermore National Lab, Pac West Telecommunications
Prominent Alumni: AG Spanos, real estate development; David Gerber, MGM/UA—Film & TV Production; Dave Brubeck, jazz composer/musician; Jaime Lee Curtis, actress; Chris Isaak, rock musician/actor

UNIVERSITY OF TOLEDO
College of Business Administration

Admissions Contact: David Chatfield, Director MBA & EMBA Programs
Address: College of Business Administration, University of Toledo, Toledo, OH 43606-3390
Admissions Phone: 419-530-2775 • **Admissions Fax:** 419-530-7260
Admissions E-mail: mba@utoledo.edu
Web Address: www.business.utoledo.edu/degrees/mba

DaimlerChrysler, General Motors, Ford, and Owens Corning: These are some of the big names that hire UT MBA graduates. The MBA program houses less than 100 students who are mostly male part timers. A multitude of study abroad opportunities are available around the globe, including Australia, the Czech Republic, England, Ireland, Japan, Mexico, and Thailand. The MBA program offers an Executive MBA for mid-career working professionals and the option of a Juris Doctor/MBA dual degree in four years.

INSTITUTIONAL INFORMATION

Public/Private: Public
Evening Classes Available? Yes
Total Faculty: 75
% Faculty Female: 21
% Faculty Part Time: 4
Student/Faculty Ratio: 10:1
Students in Parent Institution: 19,843
Academic Calendar: Semester

PROGRAMS

Degrees Offered: MBA (33-63 credits, 12-24 months), EMBA (42 credits, 15 months), MSA (30 credits, 12-24 months)
Combined Degrees: JD/MBA (3 years)
Study Abroad Options: Australia, Chile, China, Costa Rica, Czech Republic, Denmark, England, France, Germany, Ireland, Israel, Italy, Japan, Mexico, New Zealand, Scotland, Spain, Thailand

STUDENT INFORMATION

Total Business Students: 340
% Full Time: 35

% Female: 39
% Minority: 13
% International: 36
Average Age: 25

COMPUTER AND RESEARCH FACILITIES

Campuswide Network? Yes
% of MBA Classrooms Wired: 80
Computer Model Recommended: Desktop
Internet Fee? No

EXPENSES/FINANCIAL AID

Annual Tuition (Resident/Nonresident): $7,278/$15,731
Tuition Per Credit (Resident/Nonresident): $303/$655
Room & Board (On/Off Campus): $5,830
Books and Supplies: $1,000
Average Grant: $13,564
Average Loan: $18,500

ADMISSIONS INFORMATION

Application Fee: $40
Electronic Application? Yes
Regular Application Deadline: Rolling
Regular Notification: Rolling
Deferment Available? Yes
Length of Deferment: 12 months
Non-fall Admissions? Yes
Non-fall Application Deadline(s): Domestic: 8/1, 4/15, 11/15; international: 5/1, 10/1, 3/1
Transfer Students Accepted? Yes
Transfer Policy: Maximum of 10 credit hours with at least a B from an AACSB-accredited school
Need-Blind Admissions? No
Number of Applications Received: 316
% of Applicants Accepted: 75
% Accepted Who Enrolled: 76
Average GPA: 3.2
Average GMAT: 515
Average Years Experience: 0
Other Admissions Factors Considered: Work, research, and computer experience; type of undergraduate or professional degree
Other Schools to Which Students Applied: Bowling Green State University, University of Findlay, Wayne State University

INTERNATIONAL STUDENTS

TOEFL Required of International Students? Yes
Minimum TOEFL: 550 (213 computer)

EMPLOYMENT INFORMATION

Placement Office Available? No
Frequent Employers: Daimler Chrysler, Dana Commercial Credit, Dana Corp., Eaton Aeroquip, Ford Motor Co., General Motors Corp., Libbey Owens Corning, Owens Illinois, Sun Oil Co.
Prominent Alumni: Edward Kinsey, co-founder, Ariba, Inc.; Ora Alleman, vice president, National City Bank; Michael Durik, executive vice president, The Limited Stores, Inc.; Marvin Herb, CEO, Coca-Cola Bottling Co.; Julie Higgins, exective vice president, The Trust Co. of Toledo

UNIVERSITY OF TORONTO
Joseph L. Rotman School of Management

Admissions Contact: Cheryl Millington, Director of MBA Recruiting and Admissions
Address: 105 St. George Street, Toronto, ON M5S 3E6 Canada
Admissions Phone: 416-978-3499 • **Admissions Fax:** 416-978-5812
Admissions E-mail: mba@rotman.utoronto.ca • **Web Address:** www.rotman.utoronto.ca

The average starting salary of an MBA graduate for the 2001 class of U Toronto's Rotman School of Management was $102,000. Not bad, eh? MBA program options include the Part-Time MBA, the Full-Time MBA, and the Executive MBA, completed in one year. The Joseph L. Rotman School of Management also offers two strong dual degree programs, the Juris Doctor/ MBA and the Master of Nursing/MBA, and both are well regarded in their respective fields. The Rotman MBA also offers opportunities to study in France, the Czech Republic, Israel, Hong Kong, and Singapore, but you'll have to work hard to earn that global advantage, as admission to the study abroad program is pretty selective.

INSTITUTIONAL INFORMATION

Public/Private: Public
Evening Classes Available? Yes
Total Faculty: 84
% Faculty Female: 22
% Faculty Part Time: 15
Student/Faculty Ratio: 7:1
Students in Parent Institution: 55,000
Academic Calendar: September-May

PROGRAMS

Degrees Offered: MBA (2 years full time, 3 years part time), EMBA (13 months), Master of Management & Professional Accounting (27 months)
Combined Degrees: JD/MBA (4 years), BASC/MBA (5 years, 8 months), Master of Nursing/MBA (4 years), MA in Russian and Eastern European Studies/MBA (4 years)
Academic Specialties: Finance, Marketing, Strategic Management
Special Opportunities: International Exchange Program for second-year students
Study Abroad Options: Austria, China, France, Germany, Israel, Mexico, Singapore, Switzerland

STUDENT INFORMATION

Total Business Students: 525
% Full Time: 75
% Female: 35
% International: 39
Average Age: 28

COMPUTER AND RESEARCH FACILITIES

Research Facilities: Bonham Centre for Finance, Business Information Centre (student library), Institute for International Business, Clarkson Centre for Business Ethics, Capital Markets Institute, Centre for Public Management
Computer Facilities: Rotman Web Portal, which provides access to course materials, assignments, study groups, faculty, etc.
Campuswide Network? Yes
% of MBA Classrooms Wired: 100
Computer Model Recommended: Laptop
Internet Fee? No

EXPENSES/FINANCIAL AID

Annual Tuition (Resident/Nonresident): $51,250/$59,450
Room & Board (On/Off Campus): $8,000/$10,000
Books and Supplies: $800
Average Grant: $8,000
Average Loan: $35,000

% Receiving Financial Aid: 65
% Receiving Aid Their First Year: 72

ADMISSIONS INFORMATION

Application Fee: $125
Electronic Application? Yes
Early Decision Application Deadline: 1/15 (domestic students only)
Early Decision Notification: 3/15
Regular Application Deadline: 4/30
Regular Notification: 7/1
Deferment Available? Yes
Length of Deferment: 1 year
Non-fall Admissions? No
Transfer Students Accepted? No
Need-Blind Admissions? Yes
Number of Applications Received: 1,207
% of Applicants Accepted: 32
% Accepted Who Enrolled: 59
Average GPA: 3.7
GPA Range: 3.0-4.0
Average GMAT: 674
GMAT Range: 550-780
Average Years Experience: 5
Other Admissions Factors Considered: Interview when requested by Admissions Committee
Other Schools to Which Students Applied: McGill University, University of Western Ontario, York University

INTERNATIONAL STUDENTS

TOEFL Required of International Students? Yes
Minimum TOEFL: 550 (250 computer)

EMPLOYMENT INFORMATION

Placement Office Available? Yes
% Employed Within 3 Months: 91
Fields Employing Percentage of Grads: General Management (2%), MIS (2%), Marketing (2%), Other (9%), Consulting (13%), Finance (72%)
Frequent Employers: Accenture, A.T. Kearney, Bank of Montreal, CIBC, McKinsey & Co., RBC Dominion Securities, RBC Financial Group, Scotia Capital, TD, UBS Warburg
Prominent Alumni: Joseph L. Rotman, founder and chairman, Clairvest Group Inc.; Ian Locke, general partner, Jefferson Partners,Toronto; Don Morrison, CEO, Research In Motion, Waterloo, Ontario

UNIVERSITY OF TULSA
College of Business Administration

Admissions Contact: Rebecca Holland, Director of Graduate Business Programs
Address: BAH 217, 600 S. College Avenue, Tulsa, OK 74104-3189
Admissions Phone: 918-631-2242 • Admissions Fax: 918-631-2142
Admissions E-mail: graduate-business@utulsa.edu • Web Address: www.cba.utulsa.edu

The UT College of Business Administration offers a private education with a global focus. The low student/faculty ratio allows students to feel immediately "at home" with their professors and in the classroom. UT has multimedia classrooms, several internship opportunities in the Tulsa region, and numerous community service business projects that connect MBA students with the business community. Don't come to Tulsa expecting to globetrot your way through the program, though, as study abroad options are limited to undergraduate students. Frequent employers include PricewaterhouseCoopers, Microsoft, and Boeing.

INSTITUTIONAL INFORMATION

Public/Private: Private
Evening Classes Available? Yes
Total Faculty: 35
% Faculty Female: 14
% Faculty Minority: 8
Student/Faculty Ratio: 7:1
Students in Parent Institution: 4,049
Academic Calendar: Semester

PROGRAMS

Degrees Offered: MTAX (30 hours), MS in Finance (30 hours), MBA (30 hours), Internet-mediated MBA (36 hours, including foundation work)
Combined Degrees: JD/MBA (78 law credits and 24 hours of business courses), JD/MTAX (78 law credits and 24 hours of business courses), MEng/Technology Management (36 hours, 18 engineering and 18 business)
Academic Specialties: Taxation, Management Information Systems, Accounting, Finance (includes Risk Management, Corporate Finance, Investments and Portfolio Management, International Finance options)
Special Opportunities: University Studies Abroad Consortium
Study Abroad Options: Study abroad is available through several programs. Students may take a semester abroad, or they may opt for short programs of 2-6 weeks. Programs at this time are located in Denmark, England, and Italy.

STUDENT INFORMATION

Total Business Students: 138
% Full Time: 32
% Female: 43
% Minority: 7
% Out of State: 11
% International: 18
Average Age: 24

COMPUTER AND RESEARCH FACILITIES

Research Facilities: MIS wireless lab and Williams Risk Management Center located in the College of Business
Computer Facilities: There are computer labs available to students in the College of Business, McFarlin Library (all-campus), Mabee Legal Information Center (law library), Allen Chapman Student Center, and Colleges of Engineering and Arts & Sciences. Databases include Lexis-Nexis, Innopac, Computstat, and a variety of other academic resources.
Campuswide Network? Yes
% of MBA Classrooms Wired: 100
Internet Fee? No

EXPENSES/FINANCIAL AID

Annual Tuition: $10,080
Tuition Per Credit (Resident/Nonresident): $560
Room & Board (On/Off Campus): $5,886/$6,300
Books and Supplies: $1,000
Average Grant: $10,080
Average Loan: $11,687
% Receiving Financial Aid: 20

ADMISSIONS INFORMATION

Application Fee: $30
Electronic Application? Yes
Regular Application Deadline: Rolling
Regular Notification: Rolling
Deferment Available? Yes
Length of Deferment: 1 year
Non-fall Admissions? Yes
Non-fall Application Deadline(s): 1/5 fall, 5/15 spring, 8/15 summer
Transfer Students Accepted? Yes
Transfer Policy: Up to 6 credit hours
Need-Blind Admissions? Yes
Number of Applications Received: 78

% of Applicants Accepted: 56
% Accepted Who Enrolled: 84
Average GPA: 3.3
Average GMAT: 522
GMAT Range: 400-700
Average Years Experience: 2
Other Admissions Factors Considered: Work experience
Minority/Disadvantaged Student Recruitment Programs: GM Minority Scholarship
Other Schools to Which Students Applied: Oklahoma State University, University of Oklahoma

INTERNATIONAL STUDENTS

TOEFL Required of International Students? Yes
Minimum TOEFL: 575 (232 computer)

EMPLOYMENT INFORMATION

Placement Office Available? Yes
% Employed Within 3 Months: 94
Fields Employing Percentage of Grads: Other (5%)
Frequent Employers: Boeing; CITGO; Connect Ship Inc.; Enterprise Rent-A-Car; NESCO; Pricewaterhouse Coopers; Questar, Rooney Engineering; Ross Group; Sabre Corp.; Williams Communications; Williams Energy

UNIVERSITY OF UTAH
David Eccles School of Business

Admissions Contact: Carrie Radmall, Admissions and Scholarship Coordinator
Address: 1645 East Campus Center Drive, Room 101, Salt Lake City, UT 84112-9301
Admissions Phone: 801-581-7785 • **Admissions Fax:** 801-581-3666
Admissions E-mail: masters@business.utah.edu
Web Address: www.business.utah.edu/masters

Utilizing its solid computer and research facilities, the MBA curriculum at the David Eccles School of Business emphasizes the importance of information technology and a deep understanding of the global economy. The MBA program promotes "e-business savvy, a global perspective, an entrepreneurial spirit, and professional integrity," and two powerful joint degrees offered by UT are the MBA/Juris Doctor and the unique MBA/ Master of Architecture. Frequent employers of Utah MBA grads are Accenture, American Express, Intel, IBM, and PricewaterhouseCoopers.

INSTITUTIONAL INFORMATION

Public/Private: Public
Evening Classes Available? Yes
Total Faculty: 60
% Faculty Female: 28
% Faculty Minority: 16
% Faculty Part Time: 25
Student/Faculty Ratio: 5:1
Students in Parent Institution: 25,500
Academic Calendar: Semester

PROGRAMS

Degrees Offered: Accelerated MBA (1 year), EMBA (21 months), Professional MBA (21-32 months), Two-year MBA (21 months), MPACC (9 months), Master of Statistics (9 months minimum), MS in Finance (9 months minimum)
Combined Degrees: MBA/JD (3-4 years, depending on undergraduate degree), MBA/MARCH (3-4 years, depending on undergraduate degree)

Academic Specialties: Information Systems, Corporate Finance, Entrepreneurship and Emerging Business, International Business (We are 1 of only 25 business schools designated as a Center for International Business Education and Research in the country.)
Special Opportunities: MBA study exchange programs
Study Abroad Options: Odense University, Denmark; Pforzheim University, Germany; Vrije University, Holland

STUDENT INFORMATION

Total Business Students: 370
% Full Time: 49
% Female: 31
% Minority: 7
% Out of State: 34
% International: 22
Average Age: 29

COMPUTER AND RESEARCH FACILITIES

Computer Facilities: 65 IBM PC-compatible computers in the computer lab, 50 terminals in the computerized classroom, 20 computers in the technology teaching building. Software includes statisical analysis, database management, spreadsheets, financial modeling, graphics, and word processing. All computers have Internet access. Databases or networks in the field of business include ABI/INFORM, Articles First, On Point, CD Periodical Index, Lexis-Nexis, business periodicals, Moody's, InfoTrak, Axiom Biz, Academic Universe, Business Index ASAP, CCH Internet Tax Network, CIAO, UMI Proquest Direct.
Campuswide Network? Yes
% of MBA Classrooms Wired: 100
Computer Model Recommended: Laptop
Internet Fee? No

EXPENSES/FINANCIAL AID

Annual Tuition (Resident/Nonresident): $4,300/$11,900
Room & Board (On/Off Campus): $6,000/$11,000
Books and Supplies: $1,500
Average Grant: $12,200

ADMISSIONS INFORMATION

Application Fee: $40
Electronic Application? Yes
Regular Application Deadline: 3/15
Regular Notification: 5/10
Deferment Available? No
Non-fall Admissions? Yes
Non-fall Application Deadline(s): 1/15 summer term
Transfer Students Accepted? No
Need-Blind Admissions? Yes
Number of Applications Received: 230
% of Applicants Accepted: 69
% Accepted Who Enrolled: 69
Average GPA: 3.4
GPA Range: 3.1-3.6
Average GMAT: 600
GMAT Range: 560-640
Average Years Experience: 4
Other Admissions Factors Considered: In addition to all factors listed above, we require a TSE score (50 minimum) from international applicants.
Minority/Disadvantaged Student Recruitment Programs: We have several privately donated scholarships reserved for underrepresented groups and to help us build the gender, ethnic, and geographic diversity of our student body.

INTERNATIONAL STUDENTS

TOEFL Required of International Students? Yes
Minimum TOEFL: 600 (250 computer)

EMPLOYMENT INFORMATION

Placement Office Available? Yes
% Employed Within 3 Months: 91
Fields Employing Percentage of Grads: Global Management (2%), Consulting (2%), Operations (2%), General Management (4%), Other (8%), Marketing (12%), Finance (16%), Accounting (23%), MIS (31%)
Frequent Employers: Accenture, American Express, Arthur Andersen, Swloirrw Xonaulrinf, Intermountain Health Care, DMR Consulting, Eaton Corp., IBM, Intel, Iomega, KPMG, Pricewaterhouse Coopers
Prominent Alumni: Stephen Covey, co-founder, vice president, Franklin Covey; Spencer Eccles, chairman, CEO, First Security Corp.; Senator E. Jake Garn, former U.S. senator; J. Willard Marriott, chairman, CEO, president, Marriott Corp.; Geoffrey Wooley, founding partner, Dominion Ventures

UNIVERSITY OF VERMONT
School of Business Administration

Admissions Contact: Ralph Swenson, Director, Graduate College
Address: 333 Waterman Building, Burlington, VT 05405
Admissions Phone: 802-656-0655 • **Admissions Fax:** 802-656-8279
Admissions E-mail: mba@bsad.uvm.edu
Web Address: www.lenny.uvm.edu/Academics/Degree+Programs/MBA/default.htm

INSTITUTIONAL INFORMATION

Public/Private: Public
Evening Classes Available? Yes
Total Faculty: 27
% Faculty Female: 30
% Faculty Part Time: 11
Student/Faculty Ratio: 8:1
Students in Parent Institution: 10,314
Academic Calendar: Semester

PROGRAMS

Degrees Offered: MBA (2 years full time)
Academic Specialties: All functional areas of business
Special Opportunities: Ours is a generalist program. However, students may concentrate in a functional area by selecting elective coursework.
Study Abroad Options: Yaroslavl, Russia; Asia, Europe, South America

STUDENT INFORMATION

Total Business Students: 74
% Full Time: 32
% Female: 30
% Out of State: 35
% International: 35
Average Age: 28

COMPUTER AND RESEARCH FACILITIES

Computer Facilities: Business and Industry, Business and Management Practices, CRSP, Dow Jones Intgeractive, Econ Lit, Expanded Academic ASAP, FIS onLine, Lexis-Nexis Academic, Lexis-Nexis Statistical, National Consumer Survey, Psyc Info, Standard & Poor's Research Insight, Stat USA, Wilson Bus Abstracts, World Dev Indicators
Campuswide Network? Yes
% of MBA Classrooms Wired: 25
Internet Fee? No

EXPENSES/FINANCIAL AID

Annual Tuition (Resident/Nonresident): $8,328/$20,808

Tuition Per Credit (Resident/Nonresident): $347/$867
Books and Supplies: $670
Average Grant: $2,158
Average Loan: $11,503
% Receiving Financial Aid: 12
% Receiving Aid Their First Year: 18

ADMISSIONS INFORMATION

Application Fee: $25
Electronic Application? No
Regular Application Deadline: Rolling
Regular Notification: Rolling
Deferment Available? Yes
Length of Deferment: 1 year
Non-fall Admissions? Yes
Non-fall Application Deadline(s): 12/1 spring
Transfer Students Accepted? No
Need-Blind Admissions? Yes
Number of Applications Received: 75
% of Applicants Accepted: 53
% Accepted Who Enrolled: 70
Average GPA: 3.1
GPA Range: 2.5-3.6
Average GMAT: 602
GMAT Range: 570-640
Other Schools to Which Students Applied: Boston College, Boston University, University of Connecticut, University of Massachusetts—Amherst, University of New Hampshire

INTERNATIONAL STUDENTS

TOEFL Required of International Students? Yes
Minimum TOEFL: 550 (213 computer)

EMPLOYMENT INFORMATION

Placement Office Available? Yes
Frequent Employers: AYCO Co., Bombardier Capital, Farm Credit Bank, International Business Machines (IBM), Macro International
Prominent Alumni: Doug Goldsmith, CFO and vice president, finance and administration, Rock of Ages; Elisabeth Robert, president, CFO, and treasurer, VT Teddy Bear, Inc.; Katherine B. Crosett, principal, Kalex Enterprises, Inc.; Alexander D. Crosett, III, principal, Kalex Enterprises, Inc.

UNIVERSITY OF VIRGINIA
Darden Graduate School
of Business Administration

Admissions Contact: Director of Admissions
Address: PO Box 6550, Charlottesville, VA 22906
Admissions Phone: 804-924-7281 • **Admissions Fax:** 804-924-4859
Admissions E-mail: darden@virginia.edu • **Web Address:** www.darden.virginia.edu

The academics are "certainly rigorous" and the "quality of life is outstanding" at the University of Virginia's "intense but enjoyable and rewarding" Darden School. The administration here does a good job promoting the "Darden community," and students tell us that low tuition, a state-of-the-art facility, and an "incredibly loyal and tight alumni base" round out "an experience beyond expectations."

INSTITUTIONAL INFORMATION

Public/Private: Public

Evening Classes Available? No
Total Faculty: 58
% Faculty Female: 28
% Faculty Minority: 2
% Faculty Part Time: 42
Student/Faculty Ratio: 8:1
Students in Parent Institution: 18,500
Academic Calendar: Semester

PROGRAMS

Degrees Offered: PhD (3 years)
Combined Degrees: MBA/JD (4 years); MBA/MA in Asian Studies (3 years); MBA/MA in Government, Foreign Affairs, or Public Administration (3 years); MBA/ME (3 years); MBA/MSN (3 years), MBA/PhD (4 years)
Academic Specialties: Excellent teachers: most have business experience, more than half have taught overseas, 14% international. Curriculum strengths: general management; case method; integrated, holistic curriculum; required ethic course; teamwork; student-centered learning
Study Abroad Options: Australia; Universite Libre de Bruxelles, Belgium; Canada; Hong Kong University of Science and Technology, China; Finland; International University of Japan, Japan; Mexico; Sweden; Solvay Business School, Belgium; China Europe International Business School, China

STUDENT INFORMATION

Total Business Students: 491
% Full Time: 100
% Female: 30
% Minority: 15
% Out of State: 52
% International: 20
Average Age: 27

COMPUTER AND RESEARCH FACILITIES

Research Facilities: Olsson Center for Applied Ethics, Balten Center for Entreprenuerial Leadership, Taylor Murphy Center for International Business Studies
Computer Facilities: Internet, Dow Jones News/Retrieval, Nexis, Compustat, remote dialing, classroom hookups, etc.
Campuswide Network? No
Internet Fee? No

EXPENSES/FINANCIAL AID

Annual Tuition (Resident/Nonresident): $2,570/$9,115
Books and Supplies: $2,000
Average Grant: $9,050
Average Loan: $17,850
% Receiving Financial Aid: 75
% Receiving Aid Their First Year: 60

ADMISSIONS INFORMATION

Application Fee: $100
Electronic Application? Yes
Regular Application Deadline: 3/15
Regular Notification: 5/1
Deferment Available? No
Non-fall Admissions? Yes
Non-fall Application Deadline(s): 11/2, 12/2, 1/15, 2/15, 3/15
Transfer Students Accepted? No
Need-Blind Admissions? Yes
Number of Applications Received: 3,700
Average GPA: 3.3
Average GMAT: 660
Minority/Disadvantaged Student Recruitment Programs: Consortium for Graduate Study in Management

INTERNATIONAL STUDENTS

TOEFL Required of International Students? Yes

EMPLOYMENT INFORMATION

Placement Office Available? Yes
% Employed Within 3 Months: 100
Fields Employing Percentage of Grads: Operations (2%), Marketing (14%), Consulting (29%), Finance (37%)

UNIVERSITY OF WARWICK
Warwick Business School

Admissions Contact: Jo Mound, MBA Marketing and Recruitment Team
Address: Warwick Business School, Coventry, CV4 7AL United Kingdom
Admissions Phone: 011-44 (0)24 7652 4100 • Admissions Fax: 011-44 (0)24 7657 4400
Admissions E-mail: warwickmba@wbs.ac.uk • Web Address: www.wbs.ac.uk

INSTITUTIONAL INFORMATION

Public/Private: Public
Evening Classes Available? Yes
Total Faculty: 158
% Faculty Part Time: 1
Student/Faculty Ratio: 12:1
Students in Parent Institution: 16,000
Academic Calendar: Trimester

PROGRAMS

Degrees Offered: MBA (12 months full time), Evening MBA (3 years), Modular MBA (3 years), MS in Economics and Finance (12 months), MS in Management Science and Operational Research (1-2 years), MA in Industrial Relations and Personnel Management, MA in Organization Studies (12 months), MA in European Industrial Relations (12 months), Distance-Learning MBA (3-8 years), MS in Financial Mathematics (12 months), MPA (3 years), European MBA (12 months)
Academic Specialties: Marketing, Accounting and Finance, Operations Management
Study Abroad Options: Australia, Austria, Belgium, Canada, Chile, China, Denmark, France, Germany, Holland, Hungary, Israel, Italy, Mexico, Norway, Singapore, South Africa, Spain, Sweden, Switzerland, United States, United Arab Emirates

STUDENT INFORMATION

Total Business Students: 500
% Full Time: 25
% Female: 30
% Minority: 50
% International: 58
Average Age: 30

COMPUTER AND RESEARCH FACILITIES

Research Facilities: The following specialist Research Centres are based within WBS and offer teaching on the Warwick MBA: Corporate Citizenship Unit, Centre for Small and Medium-Sized Enterprises, Local Government Centre, Industrial Relations Research Unit, Financial Options Research Centre
Computer Facilities: MBA student accommodation has Internet access
Campuswide Network? Yes
% of MBA Classrooms Wired: 100
Internet Fee? No

EXPENSES/FINANCIAL AID

Annual Tuition (Resident/Nonresident): $36,000
Room & Board (On/Off Campus): $9,900
Books and Supplies: $9,000

ADMISSIONS INFORMATION

Application Fee: $132
Electronic Application? Yes
Regular Application Deadline: Rolling
Regular Notification: Rolling
Deferment Available? Yes
Length of Deferment: 12 months
Non-fall Admissions? No
Transfer Students Accepted? No
Need-Blind Admissions? No
Number of Applications Received: 1,400
% of Applicants Accepted: 43
% Accepted Who Enrolled: 83
Average GPA: 3.0
Average GMAT: 640
Average Years Experience: 8
Other Admissions Factors Considered: Personal statement, college transcripts, breadth of experience

INTERNATIONAL STUDENTS

TOEFL Required of International Students? Yes
Minimum TOEFL: 620 (260 computer)

EMPLOYMENT INFORMATION

Placement Office Available? Yes
% Employed Within 3 Months: 92

UNIVERSITY OF WASHINGTON
University of Washington Business School

Admissions Contact: Janna Trefren, Assistant Director, MBA Admissions
Address: 110 Mackenzie Hall, Box 353200, Seattle, WA 98195-3200
Admissions Phone: 206-543-4661 • **Admissions Fax:** 206-616-7351
Admissions E-mail: mba@u.washington.edu • **Web Address:** www.mba.washington.edu

The University of Washington's affordable MBA program "has a great reputation," and it boasts "proximity to a high-tech and rapidly growing economy" in "safe," "fun-filled" but expensive Seattle, the capital of the Pacific Northwest. UW draws heavily from the Pacific Rim, a situation agreeable to students from both sides of the Pacific, as "international students add a much needed layer of depth and insight to our education."

INSTITUTIONAL INFORMATION

Public/Private: Public
Evening Classes Available? Yes
Total Faculty: 77
% Faculty Female: 11
% Faculty Minority: 7
Student/Faculty Ratio: 8:1
Students in Parent Institution: 37,971
Academic Calendar: Quarter

PROGRAMS

Degrees Offered: MBA (2 years day time, 2.5 to 3 years evening), PhD (4-5 years)
Combined Degrees: MPAACC (1 year), JD/MBA (4 years), MBA/MAIS (3 years), MBA/MHA (3 years), Program in Engineering and Manufacturing Management (PEMM) (3 years)
Academic Specialties: Finance (corporate finance, investments), Marketing (consumer behavior, direct marketing, Internet marketing), Entrepreneurship,

International Business, E-Business, Accounting, Management, Production Management, Quantitative Methods, Self-Designed Study Plans that include courses in fields outside the business school
Special Opportunities: Program in E-Business, Overseas Study, Global Business Program, Program in Entrepreneurship and Innovation, Business and Economic Development Program, MBA Business Consulting Network, Second-Year MBA Management Field Studies Program
Study Abroad Options: Chile, China, Denmark, England, Finland, France, Germany, India, Japan, Mexico, Singapore, Spain, Switzerland

STUDENT INFORMATION

Total Business Students: 397
% Full Time: 65
% Female: 32
% Minority: 2
% Out of State: 55
% International: 28
Average Age: 29

COMPUTER AND RESEARCH FACILITIES

Research Facilities: Foster Business Library, Center for Technology Entrepreneurship, Center for International Business Education and Research, E-Business Lab
Computer Facilities: All MBA classrooms and facilities have wireless access to the business school network and Internet, computer labs, Special E-Business Lab, Foster Business library online, and database resources such as Lexis-Nexis, Dow Jones, and other systems.
Campuswide Network? Yes
% of MBA Classrooms Wired: 20
Computer Model Recommended: Laptop
Internet Fee? No

EXPENSES/FINANCIAL AID

Annual Tuition (Resident/Nonresident): $8,469/$17,569
Room & Board (On/Off Campus): $8,700/$10,000
Books and Supplies: $1,500
Average Grant: $6,400
Average Loan: $16,750
% Receiving Financial Aid: 70
% Receiving Aid Their First Year: 65

ADMISSIONS INFORMATION

Application Fee: $65
Electronic Application? Yes
Early Decision Application Deadline: 12/1
Early Decision Notification: 1/23
Regular Application Deadline: Rolling
Regular Notification: 4/25
Deferment Available? No
Non-fall Admissions? No
Transfer Students Accepted? Yes
Transfer Policy: Transfer applicants should apply as any other new student. The status of a transfer student is determined on a case-by-case basis, depending on the work completed at another school.
Need-Blind Admissions? Yes
% of Applicants Accepted: 31
% Accepted Who Enrolled: 40
Average GPA: 3.4
GPA Range: 2.9-3.7
Average GMAT: 671
GMAT Range: 630-690
Average Years Experience: 5
Other Admissions Factors Considered: We consider a broad spectrum of factors. No one factors is weighed more heavily than others. We also seek a highly diverse class in terms of academic background, work experience, and personal experience. Applicants from non-business backgrounds and unique backgrounds are encouraged to apply.

Minority/Disadvantaged Student Recruitment Programs: The University of Washington sponsors all-day campus visit programs and receptions for students from underrepresented minority groups. We have scholarships specifically targeting underrepresented minority candidates.

Other Schools to Which Students Applied: Arizona State University, Seattle University, Stanford University, University of California—Berkeley, University of California—Irvine, University of Southern California, University of Texas—Austin

INTERNATIONAL STUDENTS

TOEFL Required of International Students? Yes
Minimum TOEFL: 600 (250 computer)

EMPLOYMENT INFORMATION

Placement Office Available? Yes
% Employed Within 3 Months: 88
Fields Employing Percentage of Grads: Global Management (2%), Other (4%), Consulting (7%), General Management (15%), Marketing (29%), Finance (40%)
Frequent Employers: Alaska Airlines, Amazon.com, ATT Wireless, Bank of America, Capital One, GE Capital, Hewlett Packard, Intel, Lehman Brothers, Microsoft, Nordstrom, Oracle, Paccar, Phillips Medical Systems, Starbucks, Tektronix, Washington Mutual, Wells Fargo Bank
Prominent Alumni: Charles Lillis, former CEO, MediaOne Group; Dan Nordstrom, CEO, Nordstrom.com; Richard Nolan, professor of management technology, Harvard

See page 466.

UNIVERSITY OF WEST FLORIDA
College of Business

Admissions Contact: Dr. W. Timothy O'Keefe, MBA Director
Address: 11000 University Pkwy, Pensacola, FL 32514
Admissions Phone: 850-474-2348 • **Admissions Fax:** 850-474-2716
Admissions E-mail: cob@uwf.edu • **Web Address:** http://uwf.edu/mba/

INSTITUTIONAL INFORMATION

Public/Private: Public
Evening Classes Available? No
Total Faculty: 43
% Faculty Part Time: 8

PROGRAMS

Degrees Offered: MBA (36 credits, minimum of 12 months), with concentrations in Management, Leadership, Finance, marketing, Accounting; MACC (30 credits, minimum of 12 months), with concentration in Accounting

STUDENT INFORMATION

Total Business Students: 260
% Full Time: 22
% Female: 47
% Minority: 14
% International: 5
Average Age: 32

COMPUTER AND RESEARCH FACILITIES

Campuswide Network? No
Internet Fee? No

EXPENSES/FINANCIAL AID

Annual Tuition (Resident/Nonresident): $5,161/$17,660
Tuition Per Credit (Resident/Nonresident): $141/$479

ADMISSIONS INFORMATION

Application Fee: $20
Electronic Application? No
Regular Application Deadline: 4/1
Regular Notification: Rolling
Deferment Available? No
Non-fall Admissions? No
Transfer Students Accepted? No
Need-Blind Admissions? No
Number of Applications Received: 103
% of Applicants Accepted: 88
% Accepted Who Enrolled: 75
Other Admissions Factors Considered: Personal statment, Resume, College Transcripts, Essay

EMPLOYMENT INFORMATION

Placement Office Available? Yes

UNIVERSITY OF WESTERN ONTARIO
Richard Ivey School of Business

Admissions Contact: Larysa Gamula, Director, MBA Program Office
Address: 1151 Richmond Street North, London, ON N6A 3K7 Canada
Admissions Phone: 519-661-3212 • **Admissions Fax:** 519-661-3431
Admissions E-mail: mba@ivey.uwo.ca • **Web Address:** www.ivey.uwo.ca/mba

The workload is heavy and fast-paced and there is a "strong focus on general management" at the University of Western Ontario's Ivey School of Business, which reportedly boasts "the best MBA program in Canada." The average incoming student here is 29 and has five years of work experience, and students describe their "helpful, interesting, and sophisticated" classmates as "diverse in perspectives, experiences, age, and career goals."

INSTITUTIONAL INFORMATION

Evening Classes Available? No
Total Faculty: 70
% Faculty Female: 15
Student/Faculty Ratio: 7:1
Students in Parent Institution: 26,000
Academic Calendar: Semester

PROGRAMS

Degrees Offered: MBA (2 years), Executive MBA (2 years)
Joint Degrees: MBA/Bachelor of Laws (4 years)
Academic Specialties: Global Orientation, General Management, Extensive Exchange Program, Integrated Program, Consulting, E-Business, Globalization
Study Abroad Options: Australia, Austria, Brazil, Chile, China, Denmark, England, France, Germany, Hong Kong, India, Israel, Japan, Korea, Mexico, Netherlands, Philippines, Singapore, South Korea, Spain, Sweden, Switzerland, Thailand

STUDENT INFORMATION

Total Business Students: 600
% Full Time: 100
% Female: 25

% Out of State: 60
% International: 35
Average Age: 29

COMPUTER AND RESEARCH FACILITIES

Research Facilities: Asian Management Institute; Centre for International Business Studies; Institute for Entrepreneurship, Innovation, and Growth; National Centre for Management Research and Development
Computer Facilities: All campus facilities are available to MBA students. The Business Library also has an extensive resource of databases.
Campuswide Network? Yes
% of MBA Classrooms Wired: 100
Computer Model Recommended: Laptop
Internet Fee? No

EXPENSES/FINANCIAL AID

Annual Tuition: $22,000
Room & Board: $6,000
Books and Supplies: $2,000
Average Grant: $2,000

ADMISSIONS INFORMATION

Application Fee: $125
Electronic Application? Yes
Early Decision Application Deadline: Rolling
Regular Application Deadline: 4/1
Regular Notification: Rolling
Deferment Available? Yes
Length of Deferment: 1 year
Non-fall Admissions? No
Transfer Students Accepted? No
Need-Blind Admissions? Yes
Number of Applications Received: 1,100
Average GPA: 3.3
GPA Range: 2.7-3.7
Average GMAT: 660
GMAT Range: 600-710
Minority/Disadvantaged Student Recruitment Programs: Information sessions

INTERNATIONAL STUDENTS

TOEFL Required of International Students? Yes
Minimum TOEFL: 600 (250 computer)

EMPLOYMENT INFORMATION

Placement Office Available? Yes
% Employed Within 3 Months: 96
Frequent Employers: Deloitte & Touche, CAP Gemini Ernst & Young, Salomon Smith Barney, General Motors, Boston Consulting Group, CIBC, Bain and Co., Mercer Management Consulting, Scotiabank, IBM, Credit Suisse First Boston, Manulife Financial, McKinsey and Co., Dell Computer Corp.

UNIVERSITY OF WISCONSIN— EAU CLAIRE
School of Business

Admissions Contact: Ms. Jan Stewart, MBA Program Assistant
Address: 105 Garfield Avenue, Eau Claire, WI 54702-4004
Admissions Phone: 715-836-4733 • **Admissions Fax:** 715-836-2409
Admissions E-mail: admissions@uwec.edu
Web Address: www.uwec.edu/COB/programs/mba/framembahome.htm

INSTITUTIONAL INFORMATION

Public/Private: Public
Evening Classes Available? Yes
Total Faculty: 24
Student/Faculty Ratio: 3:1
Students in Parent Institution: 10,500
Academic Calendar: Semester

PROGRAMS

Degrees Offered: MBA (22 months to 3 years)
Combined Degrees: Partner in the University of Wisconsin Internet Consortium MBA Program

STUDENT INFORMATION

Total Business Students: 100
% Full Time: 5
% Female: 45
% Minority: 8
% International: 10
Average Age: 31

COMPUTER AND RESEARCH FACILITIES

Campuswide Network? Yes
Internet Fee? No

EXPENSES/FINANCIAL AID

Annual Tuition (Resident/Nonresident): $5,380/$16,014
Tuition Per Credit (Resident/Nonresident): $300/$890
Room & Board (On/Off Campus): $3,560
Books and Supplies: $1,000

ADMISSIONS INFORMATION

Application Fee: $45
Electronic Application? Yes
Regular Application Deadline: Rolling
Regular Notification: Rolling
Deferment Available? Yes
Length of Deferment: 1 year
Non-fall Admissions? Yes
Non-fall Application Deadline(s): Rolling: spring, summer
Transfer Students Accepted? Yes
Transfer Policy: Must be from other AACSB-accredited schools
Need-Blind Admissions? Yes
Average GPA: 3.2
Average GMAT: 525
Average Years Experience: 9
Minority/Disadvantaged Student Recruitment Programs: Qualified students should apply.

INTERNATIONAL STUDENTS

TOEFL Required of International Students? Yes
Minimum TOEFL: 550 (213 computer)

EMPLOYMENT INFORMATION

Placement Office Available? Yes
% Employed Within 3 Months: 100

UNIVERSITY OF WISCONSIN— LA CROSSE

College of Business Administration

Admissions Contact: Tim Lewis, Director
Address: 1725 State Street, La Crosse, WI 54601
Admissions Phone: 608-785-8067 • **Admissions Fax:** 608-785-6695
Admissions E-mail: admissions@uwlax.edu • **Web Address:** www.uwlax.edu

INSTITUTIONAL INFORMATION

Public/Private: Public
Evening Classes Available? Yes
Total Faculty: 43
% Faculty Female: 28
% Faculty Minority: 22
Student/Faculty Ratio: 30:1
Students in Parent Institution: 8,700
Academic Calendar: Semester

PROGRAMS

Degrees Offered: MBA (18-36 months)
Academic Specialties: New curriculum started Fall 2002: Team-taught, integrated core organized around themes in changing technological environment, globalization, social and environmental responsibility

STUDENT INFORMATION

Total Business Students: 65
% Full Time: 18
% Female: 37
% Minority: 12
% International: 6
Average Age: 29

COMPUTER AND RESEARCH FACILITIES

Research Facilities: Business Development Center
Computer Facilities: University of Wisconsin System libraries
Campuswide Network? Yes
% of MBA Classrooms Wired: 50
Internet Fee? No

EXPENSES/FINANCIAL AID

Annual Tuition (Resident/Nonresident): $5,570/$16,200
Tuition Per Credit (Resident/Nonresident): $290/$770
Room & Board (On/Off Campus): $6,000
Books and Supplies: $500
% Receiving Financial Aid: 15

ADMISSIONS INFORMATION

Application Fee: $48
Electronic Application? Yes
Regular Application Deadline: Rolling
Regular Notification: Rolling
Deferment Available? Yes
Length of Deferment: Rolling
Non-fall Admissions? Yes
Non-fall Application Deadline(s): 30 days

Transfer Students Accepted? Yes
Transfer Policy: Maximum of 9 credits may be transferrable
Need-Blind Admissions? Yes
Number of Applications Received: 44
% of Applicants Accepted: 80
% Accepted Who Enrolled: 54
Average GPA: 3.0
Average GMAT: 520
Average Years Experience: 4

INTERNATIONAL STUDENTS

TOEFL Required of International Students? Yes
Minimum TOEFL: 550

EMPLOYMENT INFORMATION

Placement Office Available? Yes

UNIVERSITY OF WISCONSIN— MADISON

School of Business

Admissions Contact: Betsy Kacizak, Director of Admissions and Financial Aid
Address: 3150 Grainger Hall, 975 University Avenue, Madison, WI 53706
Admissions Phone: 608-262-4000 • **Admissions Fax:** 608-265-4192
Admissions E-mail: uwmadmba@bus.wisc.edu
Web Address: www.bus.wisc.edu/graduateprograms

The placement office bends over backward for students, and there are many "high-quality specialty/niche programs" at the University of Wisconsin—Madison's School of Business. Among the best of these is the one and only AC Neilsen Center for Market Research, "which provides top-notch training" and "great connections to the industry." After class, "Madison is a wonderful place to be a student—what with its "plethora of restaurants, bars, and arts activities"—and "the city is great for outdoor enthusiasts."

INSTITUTIONAL INFORMATION

Public/Private: Public
Evening Classes Available? Yes
Total Faculty: 83
% Faculty Female: 19
Student/Faculty Ratio: 6:1
Academic Calendar: Semester

PROGRAMS

Degrees Offered: MBA (2 years), MSB (2 years), MAB (2 years)
Combined Degrees: JD/MBA (4 years)
Academic Specialties: Faculty are strong in all areas of teaching and research. Seven-week modules combined with semester courses allows for the best mix of core courses and electives. The shorter segments allow material to be more current and tailored to the individual needs. Schedule also allows greater opportunity for students to take electives in their majors, both inside and outside of the Business School.
Special Opportunities: UW—Madison is known for its specialty programs and centers such as the A.C. Nielsen Center for Marketing Research, the Applied Corporate Finance (ACFIN) Program, the Bolz Center for Arts Administration, the Center for Product Management, the Center for Urban Land Economics Research, the Erdman Center for Manufacturing and Technology Management, the Grainger Center for Supply Chain Management, Stephen L. Hawk Center for Applied Security Analysis, and the Weinert Center for Entrepreneurship.

Study Abroad Options: Wirtschaftsuniversitat, Vienna, Austria; Pontifica Universidad Catolica, Santiago, Chile; University of International Business and Economics, Beijing, China; Copenhagen Business School, Copenhagen, Denmark; ESCP-EAP, Paris, France; Universita Bocconi, Milan, Italy; Monterrey Tech, Monterrey, Mexico; Norwegian School of Management-BI, Oslo, Norway; National University, Singapore; annual study tour led by a UW—location changes every year

STUDENT INFORMATION

Total Business Students: 470
% Full Time: 76
% Female: 30
% Minority: 13
% International: 32
Average Age: 28

COMPUTER AND RESEARCH FACILITIES

Research Facilities: A.C. Nielsen Center for Marketing Research, Applied Corporate Finance (ACFIN) Program, Bolz Center for Arts Administration, Center for Product Management, Center for Urban Land Economics Research, Erdman Center for Manufacturing and Technology Management, Grainger Center for Supply Chain Management, Stephen L. Hawk Center for Applied Security Analysis, Weinert Center for Entrepreneurship
Computer Facilities: Graduate students have their own computer lab in Grainger Hall and can use the school's general computer lab or any of the 1000-plus other public computers on campus. Full Internet access and e-mail connections are available in Grainger Hall and in dorm rooms. The library has many research databases available such as Lexis-Nexis, Dow Jones, ABI Inform, etc.
Campuswide Network? Yes
% of MBA Classrooms Wired: 100
Computer Model Recommended: Laptop
Internet Fee? No

EXPENSES/FINANCIAL AID

Annual Tuition (Resident/Nonresident): $8,336/$23,774
Books and Supplies: $690
Average Grant: $3,386
Average Loan: $12,761
% Receiving Financial Aid: 78
% Receiving Aid Their First Year: 49

ADMISSIONS INFORMATION

Application Fee: $45
Electronic Application? Yes
Regular Application Deadline: 4/10
Regular Notification: Rolling
Deferment Available? No
Non-fall Admissions? No
Transfer Students Accepted? Yes
Transfer Policy: Students may transfer up to 6 credits of advanced/core courses taken within the last 2 years. Students must have earned a grade of B or better in all transfer courses. Students may also waive up to 13 credits of foundation courses.
Need-Blind Admissions? Yes
Number of Applications Received: 1,123
% of Applicants Accepted: 27
% Accepted Who Enrolled: 55
Average GPA: 3.3
Average GMAT: 631
Average Years Experience: 5
Minority/Disadvantaged Student Recruitment Programs: Consortium for Graduate Study in Management, Minority Fellowship Program, advanced opportunity fellowships, Wisconsin Investment Scholars Program

INTERNATIONAL STUDENTS

TOEFL Required of International Students? Yes
Minimum TOEFL: 600 (250 computer)

EMPLOYMENT INFORMATION

Placement Office Available? Yes
% Employed Within 3 Months: 72
Fields Employing Percentage of Grads: Human Resources (1%), Operations (2%), Accounting (2%), Consulting (3%), MIS (5%), General Management (11%), Finance (20%), Marketing (27%), Other (29%)
Frequent Employers: American Family Insurance; Clorox Co.; Deloitte Consulting; General Mills, Inc.; Grainger, Inc.; Guidant Corp.; Kraft Foods, Inc; Lands' End, Inc.; Phillip Morris USA; Samsung Electronics
Prominent Alumni: John P. Morgridge, chairman of the board, Cisco Systems, Inc.; Tom Falk, CEO, Kimberly-Clark; Melinda Mount, executive vice president and managing director, AOL UK; Arthur C. Nielsen, Jr., former chairman and CEO, AC Nielsen Co.; Paul J. Collins, vice chairman, Citigroup

UNIVERSITY OF WISCONSIN— MILWAUKEE
School of Business Administration

Admissions Contact: Sarah M. Sandin, MBA/MS Program Manager
Address: PO Box 742, Milwaukee, WI 53201-0742
Admissions Phone: 414-229-5403 • **Admissions Fax:** 414-229-2372
Admissions E-mail: uwmbusmasters@uwm.edu
Web Address: www.uwm.edu/Dept/Business/SBA

Available for the business-minded at UW—Milwaukee, near the shores of beautiful Lake Michigan, are the standard MBA, a dynamic and flexible program with more than 10 elective tracks, and the MS/MBA Coordinated Degree program, which prepares its grads for managerial positions in information technology and related fields.

INSTITUTIONAL INFORMATION

Public/Private: Public
Evening Classes Available? Yes
Total Faculty: 42
% Faculty Female: 24
% Faculty Minority: 33
% Faculty Part Time: 14
Student/Faculty Ratio: 13:1
Students in Parent Institution: 24,344
Academic Calendar: Semester

PROGRAMS

Degrees Offered: MBA (2-7 years), EMBA (22 months), MSM (2-7 years)
Combined Degrees: Master of Human Resources and Labor Relations (2-7 years), Engineering Management Master's Program (17 months), MPA Non-Profit Management (2-7 years), MBA/MSN (3-7 years)
Academic Specialties: Management Information Systems, E-Business, Taxation, Management
Study Abroad Options: Chile; England; ESSEC, France; Ireland

STUDENT INFORMATION

Total Business Students: 295
% Full Time: 18
% Female: 38
% Minority: 7

% International: 17
Average Age: 28

COMPUTER AND RESEARCH FACILITIES

Research Facilities: Bostrom Center for Business Competitiveness, Innovation and Entrepreneurship; School of Business Administration Center for Technology Innovation; Deloitte & Touche Center for Multistate Taxation; Helen Bader Institute for Nonprofit Management; International Business Center; Low-Income Taxpayer Clinic; Minority Entrepreneurship Program; Institute For Global Studies
Computer Facilities: Disclosure (Thomson Financial); CRSP and Compustat through Wharton Research Data Services (WRDS)
Campuswide Network? Yes
Internet Fee? No

EXPENSES/FINANCIAL AID

Annual Tuition (Resident/Nonresident): $8,046/$22,482
Tuition Per Credit (Resident/Nonresident): $657/$1,559
Room & Board (On/Off Campus): $6,000/$5,132
Books and Supplies: $800
Average Grant: $8,061
Average Loan: $11,312
% Receiving Financial Aid: 25
% Receiving Aid Their First Year: 47

ADMISSIONS INFORMATION

Application Fee: $45
Electronic Application? Yes
Regular Application Deadline: Rolling
Regular Notification: Rolling
Deferment Available? Yes
Length of Deferment: 1 year
Non-fall Admissions? Yes
Non-fall Application Deadline(s): Rolling
Transfer Students Accepted? Yes
Transfer Policy: The application process is the same for all applicants.
Need-Blind Admissions? Yes
Number of Applications Received: 183
% of Applicants Accepted: 63
% Accepted Who Enrolled: 56
Average GPA: 3.0
GPA Range: 2.0-4.0
Average GMAT: 540
Average Years Experience: 4
Other Admissions Factors Considered: GMAT and GRE scores accepted for MS program
Minority/Disadvantaged Student Recruitment Programs: The UWM Graduate School offers an Advanced Opportunity Program (AOP) fellowship.
Other Schools to Which Students Applied: Marquette University, University of Wisconsin—Madison, University of Wisconsin—Whitewater

INTERNATIONAL STUDENTS

TOEFL Required of International Students? Yes
Minimum TOEFL: 550 (213 computer)

EMPLOYMENT INFORMATION

Placement Office Available? Yes
% Employed Within 3 Months: 85
Frequent Employers: Deloitte & Touche, Kohler Co., Northwestern Mutual,

UNIVERSITY OF WISCONSIN— OSHKOSH
College of Business Administration

Admissions Contact: Lynn Grancorbitz, MBA/MSIS Programs Assistant Director and Advisor
Address: Clow Classroom 151, 800 Algoma Blvd, Oshkosh, WI 54901
Admissions Phone: 800-633-1430 • **Admissions Fax:** 920-424-7413
Admissions E-mail: mba@uwosh.edu • **Web Address:** www.uwosh.edu/coba/

INSTITUTIONAL INFORMATION

Public/Private: Public
Evening Classes Available? Yes
Total Faculty: 44
Student/Faculty Ratio: 11:1
Students in Parent Institution: 10,528
Academic Calendar: Semester

PROGRAMS

Degrees Offered: MBA (1-7 years)

STUDENT INFORMATION

Total Business Students: 525
% Full Time: 5
% Female: 60
% Minority: 2
% International: 3

COMPUTER AND RESEARCH FACILITIES

Campuswide Network? Yes
Internet Fee? No

EXPENSES/FINANCIAL AID

Annual Tuition (Resident/Nonresident): $4,664/$13,622
Tuition Per Credit (Resident/Nonresident): $200/$600

ADMISSIONS INFORMATION

Application Fee: $45
Electronic Application? No
Regular Application Deadline: 7/1
Regular Notification: Rolling
Deferment Available? Yes
Non-fall Admissions? Yes
Non-fall Application Deadline(s): 12/1 spring, 4/1 summer
Transfer Students Accepted? No
Need-Blind Admissions? No
Number of Applications Received: 220
% of Applicants Accepted: 91
% Accepted Who Enrolled: 50
Other Admissions Factors Considered: Work and computer experience
Other Schools to Which Students Applied: University of California—Berkeley, University of California—Los Angeles, University of Chicago, St. John's University, Rensselaer Polytechnic Institute

INTERNATIONAL STUDENTS

TOEFL Required of International Students? Yes
Minimum TOEFL: 550

EMPLOYMENT INFORMATION

Placement Office Available? Yes
% Employed Within 3 Months: 98

UNIVERSITY OF WISCONSIN—PARKSIDE

School of Business and Technology

Admissions Contact: Brad Piazza, Assistant Dean
Address: 900 Wood Road, Box 2000, Kenosha, WI 53141-2000
Admissions Phone: 262-595-2046 • **Admissions Fax:** 262-595-2680
Admissions E-mail: piazza@uwp.edu
Web Address: www.uwp.edu/academic/business.technology

INSTITUTIONAL INFORMATION

Public/Private: Public
Evening Classes Available? Yes
Total Faculty: 16
% Faculty Female: 33
% Faculty Minority: 26
Student/Faculty Ratio: 6:1
Students in Parent Institution: 4,950
Academic Calendar: Semester

PROGRAMS

Degrees Offered: MBA (minimum of 2 semesters full time if starting in fall semester; minimum of 4 semesters part time)
Academic Specialties: Our MBA program is elective-driven. Of the 32 degree credits that must be earned, 14 of them are electives.

STUDENT INFORMATION

Total Business Students: 93
% Full Time: 10
% Female: 55
% Minority: 22
% International: 22

COMPUTER AND RESEARCH FACILITIES

Campuswide Network? Yes
% of MBA Classrooms Wired: 100
Internet Fee? No

EXPENSES/FINANCIAL AID

Annual Tuition (Resident/Nonresident): $4,540/$14,364
Tuition Per Credit (Resident/Nonresident): $264/$810
Books and Supplies: $300

ADMISSIONS INFORMATION

Application Fee: $45
Electronic Application? Yes
Regular Application Deadline: 8/1
Regular Notification: Rolling
Deferment Available? Yes
Length of Deferment: 12 months
Non-fall Admissions? Yes
Non-fall Application Deadline(s): 12/15, 4/15
Transfer Students Accepted? Yes
Transfer Policy: Must be accepted into the program; maximum of 12 credits may transfer
Need-Blind Admissions? Yes
Number of Applications Received: 32
% of Applicants Accepted: 84
Average GPA: 3.0
GPA Range: 2.5-3.9
Average GMAT: 500
GMAT Range: 400-700
Average Years Experience: 3
Other Admissions Factors Considered: Advanced Opportunity Program (AOP) scholarships

INTERNATIONAL STUDENTS

TOEFL Required of International Students? Yes
Minimum TOEFL: 550 (213 computer)

EMPLOYMENT INFORMATION

Placement Office Available? Yes

UNIVERSITY OF WISCONSIN—WHITEWATER

College of Business and Economics

Admissions Contact: Donald K. Zahn, Associate Dean
Address: 800 West Main Street, Whitewater, WI 53190
Admissions Phone: 262-472-1945 • **Admissions Fax:** 262-472-4863
Admissions E-mail: zahnd@uww.edu • **Web Address:** www.uww.edu

UW—Whitewater is known mostly for its degree programs in accounting, but its management programs are starting to gain recognition. Daytime or evening and part-time or full-time students can take advantage of UW—Whitewater's MBA programs, and students anywhere in the world can obtain an MBA in marketing, finance, management, or international business via the Internet with the AACSB-accredited Online MBA.

INSTITUTIONAL INFORMATION

Public/Private: Public
Evening Classes Available? Yes
Total Faculty: 62
% Faculty Female: 20
% Faculty Minority: 5
Student/Faculty Ratio: 28:1
Students in Parent Institution: 10,521
Academic Calendar: Semester

PROGRAMS

Degrees Offered: MBA (36-51 credits, minimum of 18 months full time or part time), with concentrations in Accounting, Decision Support Systems, Finance, Human Resource Management, International Business, IT Management, Management, Marketing, Technology and Training, Operations and Supply Chain Management; MS in CIS (36 credits, 3 years full time or part time); MPACC (30-60 credits, 1-2 years full time or part time)
Study Abroad Options: Australia, Czech Republic, England, France, Mexico, Netherlands, Russia, Sweden, Switzerland

STUDENT INFORMATION

Total Business Students: 405
% Full Time: 21
% Female: 60
% Minority: 1
% Out of State: 5
% International: 75
Average Age: 30

COMPUTER AND RESEARCH FACILITIES

Campuswide Network? Yes
Internet Fee? No

EXPENSES/FINANCIAL AID

Annual Tuition (Resident/Nonresident): $5,424/$16,060
Tuition Per Credit (Resident/Nonresident): $301/$892
Room & Board (On/Off Campus): $4,100

Books and Supplies: $2,400
Average Grant: $500

ADMISSIONS INFORMATION

Application Fee: $45
Electronic Application? Yes
Regular Application Deadline: Rolling
Regular Notification: Rolling
Deferment Available? Yes
Length of Deferment: 1 year
Non-fall Admissions? Yes
Non-fall Application Deadline(s): Rolling; for international students: 6/1 fall, 10/1 spring
Transfer Students Accepted? Yes
Transfer Policy: Transfer applicants must meet the same requirements as a non-transfer student. Nine credits may be transferred into the program.
Need-Blind Admissions? No
Number of Applications Received: 111
% of Applicants Accepted: 93
% Accepted Who Enrolled: 100
Average GPA: 3.1
GPA Range: 2.1-3.9
Average GMAT: 523
GMAT Range: 320-720
Average Years Experience: 5
Other Admissions Factors Considered: A resume, work experience, and computer experiences are all recommended for application.
Other Schools to Which Students Applied: Marquette University, University of Wisconsin—Madison, University of Wisconsin—Milwaukee, University of Wisconsin—Oshkosh, University of Wisconsin—Parkside

INTERNATIONAL STUDENTS

TOEFL Required of International Students? Yes
Minimum TOEFL: 550 (213 computer)

EMPLOYMENT INFORMATION

Placement Office Available? Yes
% Employed Within 3 Months: 88

UNIVERSITY OF WYOMING
College of Business

Admissions Contact: Terri L. Rittenburg, Director of MBA Program
Address: PO Box 3275, Laramie, WY 82071
Admissions Phone: 307-766-2449 • **Admissions Fax:** 307-766-4028
Admissions E-mail: mba@uwyo.edu • **Web Address:** business.uwyo.edu/mba

Anyone possessing an undergraduate degree, including a student with no previous formal business experience, is invited to apply to the University of Wyoming's MBA program. Students should expect to receive a formidable education, stressing effective communication and writing, presentations, and teamwork.

INSTITUTIONAL INFORMATION

Public/Private: Public
Evening Classes Available? Yes
Student/Faculty Ratio: 3:1
Students in Parent Institution: 11,904
Academic Calendar: Semester

PROGRAMS

Degrees Offered: MBA (11 months without foundation year; 23 months if foundation year is necessary)
Academic Specialties: Strengths of faculty and curriculum in solving business problems, decision-making, interpersonal skills, balancing human and quantitative management tools
Study Abroad Options: Ecole Superieure de commerce (ESC) Tours, France

STUDENT INFORMATION

Total Business Students: 63
% Full Time: 52
% Female: 36
% International: 18
Average Age: 28

COMPUTER AND RESEARCH FACILITIES

Campuswide Network? Yes
% of MBA Classrooms Wired: 12
Internet Fee? No

EXPENSES/FINANCIAL AID

Annual Tuition (Resident/Nonresident): $2,988/$8,676
Tuition Per Credit (Resident/Nonresident): $161/$166
Room & Board (On/Off Campus): $6,212
Books and Supplies: $300

ADMISSIONS INFORMATION

Application Fee: $40
Electronic Application? Yes
Regular Application Deadline: 2/1
Regular Notification: Rolling
Deferment Available? Yes
Length of Deferment: 1 year
Non-fall Admissions? No
Transfer Students Accepted? Yes
Transfer Policy: Maximum of 9 credits with a minimum grade of B from an AACSB-accredited school
Need-Blind Admissions? Yes
Average GPA: 3.2
Average GMAT: 558

INTERNATIONAL STUDENTS

TOEFL Required of International Students? Yes
Minimum TOEFL: 525 (197 computer)

EMPLOYMENT INFORMATION

Placement Office Available? Yes

UTAH STATE UNIVERSITY
College of Business

Admissions Contact: School of Graduate Studies, Admissions Officer
Address: 900 Old Main Hill, Logan, UT 84322-0900
Admissions Phone: 435-797-1189 • **Admissions Fax:** 435-797-1192
Admissions E-mail: gradsch@cc.usu.edu • **Web Address:** www.usu.edu

Utah recently evaluated its offerings in comparison to other fully accredited schools, establishing an accelerated team-oriented business core and a choice of nine specializations. It introduced "intrasessions," nonacademic courses intended to "develop personal skills related to employment and the 'corporate culture.'" Utah State's Partners in Business program draws local, national, and international leaders to campus for seven featured programs each year, as well as the Shingo Prize competition, giving MBAs access to a multitude of business personalities and the chance to evaluate real corporate proposals.

INSTITUTIONAL INFORMATION

Public/Private: Public
Evening Classes Available? No
Total Faculty: 81
% Faculty Part Time: 8
Student/Faculty Ratio: 30:1
Students in Parent Institution: 20,808
Academic Calendar: Semester

PROGRAMS

Degrees Offered: MACC (2 years), MS in Business Information Systems and Education (2 years), MS in Economics/MBA (2 years), MSS in Human Resource Management (2 years)
Study Abroad Options: Italy Consortium; the Netherlands; Oslo, Norway

STUDENT INFORMATION

Total Business Students: 370
% Full Time: 39
% Female: 27
% Minority: 4
% International: 20
Average Age: 30

COMPUTER AND RESEARCH FACILITIES

Research Facilities: Center for E-Commerce
Computer Facilities: Learning Resource Center provides access to online databases and bibliographies.
Campuswide Network? Yes
% of MBA Classrooms Wired: 100
Internet Fee? No

EXPENSES/FINANCIAL AID

Annual Tuition (Resident/Nonresident): $2,426/$7,438
Average Grant: $2,800
Average Loan: $3,000
% Receiving Financial Aid: 5
% Receiving Aid Their First Year: 5

ADMISSIONS INFORMATION

Application Fee: $50
Electronic Application? Yes
Regular Application Deadline: Rolling
Regular Notification: Rolling
Deferment Available? Yes
Length of Deferment: 1 year
Non-fall Admissions? No
Transfer Students Accepted? No
Need-Blind Admissions? No
Number of Applications Received: 105
% of Applicants Accepted: 81
% Accepted Who Enrolled: 94
Average GPA: 3.5
GPA Range: 3.0-4.0
Average GMAT: 590
GMAT Range: 500-720
Average Years Experience: 10
Other Schools to Which Students Applied: Brigham Young University, University of Utah, Weber State University

INTERNATIONAL STUDENTS

TOEFL Required of International Students? Yes
Minimum TOEFL: 550

EMPLOYMENT INFORMATION

Placement Office Available? Yes
% Employed Within 3 Months: 80
Fields Employing Percentage of Grads: General Management (10%), MIS (10%), Human Resources (10%), Finance (20%), Accounting (50%)
Frequent Employers: Allegiance Health Care, Ernst & Young, Hewlett Packard, Micron

VALDOSTA STATE UNIVERSITY
Langdale College of Business Administration

Admissions Contact: Teresa Williams, Graduate School
Address: 903 N. Patterson Street, Valdosta, GA 31698-0005
Admissions Phone: 229-333-5694 • **Admissions Fax:** 229-245-3853
Admissions E-mail: mba@valdosta.edu • **Web Address:** www.valdosta.edu/coba/grad

INSTITUTIONAL INFORMATION

Public/Private: Public
Evening Classes Available? No
Total Faculty: 10
% Faculty Female: 20
Student/Faculty Ratio: 5:1
Academic Calendar: Semester

PROGRAMS

Degrees Offered: MBA (30 credits, 2-7 years)

STUDENT INFORMATION

Total Business Students: 50
% Female: 44
% Minority: 20
% International: 12
Average Age: 30

COMPUTER AND RESEARCH FACILITIES

Computer Facilities: On-campus computer lab
Campuswide Network? Yes
% of MBA Classrooms Wired: 100
Internet Fee? No

EXPENSES/FINANCIAL AID

Annual Tuition (Resident/Nonresident): $4,395/$13,095
Room & Board (On/Off Campus): $2,200/$2,500
Books and Supplies: $800

ADMISSIONS INFORMATION

Application Fee: $25
Electronic Application? Yes
Regular Application Deadline: Rolling
Regular Notification: Rolling
Deferment Available? Yes
Length of Deferment: 1 semester
Non-fall Admissions? Yes
Non-fall Application Deadline(s): spring, summer, fall
Transfer Students Accepted? No

Need-Blind Admissions? No
Number of Applications Received: 50
% of Applicants Accepted: 60
% Accepted Who Enrolled: 63
Average GPA: 3.3
Average GMAT: 512
Average Years Experience: 4
Other Admissions Factors Considered: GMAT, GPA, work experience, computer experience

INTERNATIONAL STUDENTS

TOEFL Required of International Students? Yes
Minimum TOEFL: 550 (213 computer)

EMPLOYMENT INFORMATION

Placement Office Available? Yes
% Employed Within 3 Months: 100

VANDERBILT UNIVERSITY
Owen Graduate School of Management

Admissions Contact: Todd Reale, Director, MBA Admissions and Marketing
Address: 401 21st Avenue South, Nashville, TN 37203
Admissions Phone: 615-322-6469 • **Admissions Fax:** 615-343-1175
Admissions E-mail: admissions@owen.vanderbilt.edu • **Web Address:** mba.vanderbilt.edu

An intimate setting, innovative programs, and a top-flight faculty are the distinguishing characteristics of the Owen Graduate School of Management at Vanderbilt University. There is also a "unique" electronic commerce program here, and students say they really benefit from Vanderbilt's genial, laid-back southern setting. Additional amenities of the Vanderbilt experience include a "great gym," low cost of living, and nightlife that is reportedly "a blast."

INSTITUTIONAL INFORMATION

Public/Private: Private
Evening Classes Available? No
Total Faculty: 65
% Faculty Female: 17
% Faculty Minority: 11
% Faculty Part Time: 35
Student/Faculty Ratio: 10:1
Students in Parent Institution: 10,496
Academic Calendar: Semester

PROGRAMS

Degrees Offered: MBA (2 years full time), EMBA (2 years), PhD (4-plus years)
Combined Degrees: MBA/JD (4 years), MBA/MD (5 years), MBA/MSN (5 semesters) MBA/ME (5 semesters), MBA/MLAS (3 years), MBA/BA or MBA/BS (5 years)
Academic Specialties: Accounting, Brand Management, E-Commerce, Entrepreneurship, Environmental Management, Finance, General Management, Health Care, Human and Organizational Performance, Information Technology, International Business, Law and Business, Marketing, Operations Management, Strategy. Only about one-third of the modular curriculum is required, after which students can choose from more than 150 electives, including project-based and independent study coursework.
Special Opportunities: Individually arranged exchange experiences are available through Owen@Vanderbilt. Internship opportunities may be included with a number of our exchange programs. Up to 15 credits of the 60 required

for the MBA degree may be earned at another Vanderbilt graduate or professional school, or at one of the international exchange partners.
Study Abroad Options: Austria, Brazil, Chile, China, Costa Rica, France, Germany, Japan, Mexico, Norway, South Africa, Spain, Venezuela, United Kingdom

STUDENT INFORMATION

Total Business Students: 449
% Full Time: 100
% Female: 24
% Minority: 9
% Out of State: 75
% International: 27
Average Age: 28

COMPUTER AND RESEARCH FACILITIES

Research Facilities: Financial Markets Research Center, eLab, Owen Entrepreneurship Center, Vanderbilt Center for Environmental Studies
Computer Facilities: Wireless computer network throughout Management Hall; Internet connections from on-campus and off-campus residences and other remote locations; extensive Intranet resources; dozens of online databases including Dow Jones, Hoover's, Lexis-Nexis, and ProQuest
Campuswide Network? Yes
% of MBA Classrooms Wired: 100
Computer Model Recommended: Laptop
Internet Fee? No

EXPENSES/FINANCIAL AID

Annual Tuition: $28,900
Room & Board (On/Off Campus): $8,780
Books and Supplies: $1,256
Average Grant: $17,000
Average Loan: $38,480
% Receiving Financial Aid: 60

ADMISSIONS INFORMATION

Application Fee: $100
Electronic Application? Yes
Regular Application Deadline: 4/15
Regular Notification: 5/31
Deferment Available? No
Non-fall Admissions? No
Transfer Students Accepted? No
Need-Blind Admissions? Yes
Number of Applications Received: 1,024
% of Applicants Accepted: 47
% Accepted Who Enrolled: 46
Average GPA: 3.3
GPA Range: 3.0-3.5
Average GMAT: 648
GMAT Range: 610-670
Average Years Experience: 5
Other Admissions Factors Considered: Caliber of undergraduate institution; difficulty of major; quality and duration of prior work experience; professional responsibilities and accomplishments; career progression/advancement; well-defined career goals; extracurricular, professional, and community involvement; leadership potential; interpersonal skills; communication skills; team orientation; diversity (gender, ethnic, cultural, geographic, academic, professional, etc.); cross-cultural awareness, understanding, experience, appreciation
Minority/Disadvantaged Student Recruitment Programs: Diversity Weekend (mid-January) is specially targeted to prospective female, U.S. minority, and international students. Featuring presentations, discussions, workshops, tours, meals and social activities, Diversity Weekend helps candidates learn about the Vanderbilt MBA curriculum, admission requirements, financial aid, career management, and Owen@Vanderbilt's supportive community. Diversity Weekend begins with an optional reception on Friday evening and runs

all day Saturday into the evening, concluding with another social event. Admission interviews may be available and must be scheduled in advance.

Other Schools to Which Students Applied: Duke University, Emory University, Georgetown University, Indiana University, University of North Carolina—Chapel Hill, University of Texas—Austin, University of Virginia

INTERNATIONAL STUDENTS

TOEFL Required of International Students? Yes
Minimum TOEFL: 600 (250 computer)

EMPLOYMENT INFORMATION

Placement Office Available? Yes
% Employed Within 3 Months: 80
Fields Employing Percentage of Grads: Human Resources (2%), Other (3%), MIS (3%), Operations (4%), Consulting (5%), General Management (17%), Marketing (25%), Finance (41%)
Frequent Employers: A.T. Kearney; AT&T; Banc of America; Bear Stearns & Co.; Eli Lilly & Co.; Emerson Electric; FedEx; Ford Motor Co.; Gaylord Entertainment; Investment Scorecard; JP Morgan/Chase; Jeffries & Co.; Johnson & Johnson; Reliant Energy; Robertson Stephens; Saks, Inc.; SAP America; Scott, Madden & Associates; Unilever; Wachovia Securities.
Prominent Alumni: David Farr, CEO, Emerson Electric; David Ingram, chairman and president, Ingram Entertainment; Brad Martin, chairman and CEO, Saks, Inc.

See page 468.

VILLANOVA UNIVERSITY
College of Commerce and Finance

Admissions Contact: Ms. Elizabeth Eshleman, Corporate Liaison
Address: 800 Lancaster Avenue, Bartley Hall Suite 1054, Villanova, PA 19085
Admissions Phone: 610-519-4336 • **Admissions Fax:** 610-519-6273
Admissions E-mail: mba@villanova.edu • **Web Address:** www.mba.villanova.edu

Villanova features a unique pass/fail three-day "orientation" called the Leadership Skills Lab, where students get a taste of what is expected of them while they focus on communication and negotiation in a "cohesive team atmosphere." Villanova's broad-based MBA curriculum was recently revamped to increase emphasis on technology integration, cross-functional solutions, teamwork, and strategic decision-making. Villanova makes the claim that "we align our program with work and life realities," so expect the program to practice flexibility regarding obligations that exist outside the classroom.

INSTITUTIONAL INFORMATION

Public/Private: Private
Evening Classes Available? Yes
Total Faculty: 93
Student/Faculty Ratio: 12:1
Students in Parent Institution: 10,396
Academic Calendar: Semester

PROGRAMS

Degrees Offered: MBA, EMBA, FTE MBA (24 months), MTAX, Master of Accounting and Professional Consultancy
Combined Degrees: JD/MBA
Study Abroad Options: East China Normal University, China; Universidad Catolica De Valparaio, Costa Rica; European Business School, Germany; University of Warsaw, Poland; Nizhny Novgorod State University, Russia

STUDENT INFORMATION

Total Business Students: 622
% Full Time: 10
% Female: 35
% Minority: 2
% Out of State: 3
% International: 5
Average Age: 28

COMPUTER AND RESEARCH FACILITIES

Campuswide Network? Yes
% of MBA Classrooms Wired: 100
Computer Model Recommended: Laptop
Internet Fee? No

EXPENSES/FINANCIAL AID

Annual Tuition: $13,800
Tuition Per Credit (Resident/Nonresident): $575
Books and Supplies: $800
Average Grant: $27,000

ADMISSIONS INFORMATION

Application Fee: $40
Electronic Application? Yes
Regular Application Deadline: 6/30
Regular Notification: Rolling
Deferment Available? Yes
Length of Deferment: 1 year
Non-fall Admissions? Yes
Non-fall Application Deadline(s): 11/15 spring, 3/31 summer
Transfer Students Accepted? Yes
Transfer Policy: Maximum of 9 credits from AACSB-accredited MBA program
Need-Blind Admissions? Yes
Number of Applications Received: 453
% of Applicants Accepted: 70
% Accepted Who Enrolled: 67
Average GPA: 3.2
GPA Range: 2.6-3.4
Average GMAT: 586
GMAT Range: 540-620
Average Years Experience: 5
Other Schools to Which Students Applied: Drexel University, Temple University

INTERNATIONAL STUDENTS

TOEFL Required of International Students? Yes
Minimum TOEFL: 600 (250 computer)

EMPLOYMENT INFORMATION

Placement Office Available? Yes
% Employed Within 3 Months: 98

VIRGINIA COMMONWEALTH UNIVERSITY
School of Business

Admissions Contact: Tracy S. Green, Director of Graduate Programs
Address: 1015 Floyd Ave., PO Box 844000, Richmond, VA 23284-4000
Admissions Phone: 804-828-4622 • **Admissions Fax:** 804-828-7174
Admissions E-mail: gsib@vcu.edu • **Web Address:** www.bus.vcu.edu/gsib

The Virginia Commonwealth University owns a suite of great historical buildings; one is the Ritter-Hickok House, in which spies were imprisoned during the Civil War. There's more to this school than a full-flavored southern history, though: VCU recently turned its Classic MBA into a Technology-Focused MBA with the help of its information systems faculty. The Fast-Track MBA is also available for the instruction of professionals with six or seven years of experience.

INSTITUTIONAL INFORMATION

Public/Private: Public
Evening Classes Available? Yes
Total Faculty: 93
Student/Faculty Ratio: 20:1
Academic Calendar: Semester

PROGRAMS

Degrees Offered: MBA (2 years), MS in Business with multiple concentration choices (2 years), MACC (2 years), MTAX (2 years), MA in Economics (2 years), MSIS (2 years), PhD (5 years)
Combined Degrees: BS/MACC (5 years for entering undergraduate students), BS in Engineering/MBA, PharmD/MBA
Special Opportunities: Focused MS degrees and MBA concentrations in Decision Sciences, Finance, Global Marketing Management, Human Resource Management and Industrial Relations, Real Estate Valuation
Study Abroad Options: Italy; exchange with Ecole Superieure de Commerce Marseille-Provence, France

STUDENT INFORMATION

Total Business Students: 253
% Full Time: 24
% Female: 39
% Minority: 11
Average Age: 29

COMPUTER AND RESEARCH FACILITIES

Research Facilities: Alfred L. Blake Chair of Real Estate, Center for Corporate Education, Employment Support Institute, Family Business Forum, Information Systems Research Institute, Insurance Studies Center, Philip Morris Chair in International Business, VCU Center for Economic Education, Virginia Council for Economic Education, Virginia Real Estate Research Center, Virginia Labor Studies Center
Computer Facilities: University Library Services maintains all database access.
Campuswide Network? Yes
% of MBA Classrooms Wired: 50
Internet Fee? Yes

EXPENSES/FINANCIAL AID

Annual Tuition (Resident/Nonresident): $6,404/$15,472
Books and Supplies: $600
Average Grant: $8,375
Average Loan: $12,000

ADMISSIONS INFORMATION

Application Fee: $30

Electronic Application? No
Early Decision Application Deadline: 4/1 fall
Early Decision Notification: 5/1
Regular Application Deadline: 6/1
Regular Notification: 7/1
Deferment Available? Yes
Length of Deferment: 1 year
Non-fall Admissions? Yes
Non-fall Application Deadline(s): 11/1 spring, 3/1 summer
Transfer Students Accepted? Yes
Transfer Policy: Students who were admitted to and completed coursework at other AACSB-accredited institutions may apply to VCU and seek transfer of up to 6 semester hours of work toward the VCU graduate degree. Students must have earned no less than a B in each class to be transferred. The decision to transfer courses is left to the discretion of the director of graduate programs.
Need-Blind Admissions? Yes
Number of Applications Received: 118
% of Applicants Accepted: 74
% Accepted Who Enrolled: 78
Average GPA: 3.1
Average GMAT: 527
Other Admissions Factors Considered: Full-time employment beyond earning the undergraduate degree
Other Schools to Which Students Applied: University of Richmond, James Madison University, College of William & Mary

INTERNATIONAL STUDENTS

TOEFL Required of International Students? Yes
Minimum TOEFL: 600 (250 computer)

EMPLOYMENT INFORMATION

Placement Office Available? Yes

VIRGINIA POLYTECHNIC INSTITUTE AND STATE UNIVERSITY
Pamplin College of Business

Admissions Contact: Susan Vest, Enrollment Coordinator
Address: 1044 Pamplin Hall, Virginia Tech, Blacksburg, VA 24061
Admissions Phone: 540-231-6152 • **Admissions Fax:** 540-231-4487
Admissions E-mail: mba_info@vt.edu • **Web Address:** www.mba.vt.edu

Students are enthusiastic about Pamplin's growing reputation. Active student participation is a distinguishing factor of Pamplin's MBA education, which focuses on "the interrelationships among the various functions within a firm" and is available on a full-time or part-time basis. Upon graduation, students will "bask in the reputation" of the program, as recent grads have been hired by a long list of companies that includes Lucent Technologies, Pfizer pharmaceuticals, and Ford Motor Company.

INSTITUTIONAL INFORMATION

Public/Private: Public
Evening Classes Available? Yes
Total Faculty: 116
Students in Parent Institution: 27,800

PROGRAMS

Degrees Offered: Accounting and Information Systems: MACC (30 semester hours), PhD; PhD in Finance, Insurance, and Business Law; PhD in Management; PhD in Business Information Technology; PhD in Marketing; MBA (48 credit hours), with concentrations in Information Systems Technology, Systems Engineering Management, E-Commerce, Executive Leadership, Human Resources, Investment and Financial Services Management, Corporate Financial Management, Financial Risk Management, Global Business, Marketing in High Technology Industries

Combined Degrees: MBA/MIM (33 semester hours in the Pamplin MBA Program and 30 trimester hours at Thunderbird)

Study Abroad Options: Short programs: INTOP III, Austria; International Business Consulting, Slovenia. Semester abroad: CIU Spring Semester in Europe, Italy; Fall Semester in Europe, Switzerland). Summer abroad: Global Workplace, Eastern Europe; European Integration: Business and Accounting Issues, Western and Central Europe; International Electronic Commerce, Austria; London Internships, England; Marketing in the EU, France; Business in the EU, Germany; Managerial and Ethical Challenges in the Global Marketplace, Asia; China/Hong Kong/Vietnam Program in Finance and China/Hong Kong/Vietnam Program in Marketing, China, Hong Kong, and Vietnam

STUDENT INFORMATION

Total Business Students: 203
% Full Time: 35
% Female: 34
% Minority: 2
% International: 42
Average Age: 23

COMPUTER AND RESEARCH FACILITIES

Campuswide Network? Yes
% of MBA Classrooms Wired: 100
Computer Model Recommended: Laptop
Internet Fee? No

EXPENSES/FINANCIAL AID

Annual Tuition (Resident/Nonresident): $2,370
Tuition Per Credit (Resident/Nonresident): $296/$479
Books and Supplies: $8,200
Average Grant: $2,000
% Receiving Financial Aid: 15
% Receiving Aid Their First Year: 15

ADMISSIONS INFORMATION

Application Fee: $45
Electronic Application? Yes
Regular Application Deadline: 2/2
Regular Notification: Rolling
Deferment Available? Yes
Length of Deferment: 1 year
Non-fall Admissions? No
Transfer Students Accepted? No
Need-Blind Admissions? Yes
Number of Applications Received: 221
% of Applicants Accepted: 67
% Accepted Who Enrolled: 64
Average GPA: 3.3
GPA Range: 3.0-3.6
Average GMAT: 638
GMAT Range: 610-672
Average Years Experience: 4

INTERNATIONAL STUDENTS

TOEFL Required of International Students? Yes
Minimum TOEFL: 550 (213 computer)

EMPLOYMENT INFORMATION

Placement Office Available? No
% Employed Within 3 Months: 29
Fields Employing Percentage of Grads: Consulting (1%), Other (3%), Operations (3%), MIS (3%), Finance (4%)

Frequent Employers: Accenture, CapGemini Ernst & Young, Corning Cable Systems, Deloitte & Touche, Eastman Chemical, FedEx, First USA, Free Markets, GMAC, Lockhead Martin, Lucent Technologies, Norfolk Southern, National Basketball Association, Princewaterhouse Coopers

WAKE FOREST UNIVERSITY
FAST-TRACK EXECUTIVE MBA

Admissions Contact: Jamie Barnes, Director, Evening & Fast-Track Executive Programs
Address: PO Box 7368, Winston-Salem, NC 27109-7368
Admissions Phone: 336-758-4584 • **Admissions Fax:** 336-758-5830
Admissions E-mail: evening.exec@mba.wfu.edu • **Web Address:** www.mba.wfu.edu

INSTITUTIONAL INFORMATION

Public/Private: Private
Evening Classes Available? Yes
Total Faculty: 52
% Faculty Female: 14
% Faculty Minority: 15
% Faculty Part Time: 21
Student/Faculty Ratio: 12:1
Students in Parent Institution: 6,323
Academic Calendar: Semester

PROGRAMS

Degrees Offered: MBA (21 months full time), Winston-Salem Evening MBA (24 months), Winston-Salem Fast-Track EMBA (17 months), Charlotte Evening MBA (24 months), Charlotte Saturday MBA (24 months)

Combined Degrees: JD/MBA (4 years), MD/MBA (5 years), PhD/MBA (5 years), MSA/MBA (6 years)

Academic Specialties: The curriculum is designed so that the sequence of courses maximizes the educational experience. Tools, skills, concepts, and principles build upon one another in a logical sequence as students progress. This approach enhances the understanding of the complex relationships found in today's organizations. After completion of the core courses throughout the first 5 semesters, students enroll in elective courses in the final semester.

Special Opportunities: Babcock Leadership Series, Elevator Case Competition

Study Abroad Options: Wirtschafts Universitaet, Wien, Austria; Groupe ESC Bordeaux, France; University of Kaiserslautern, the Otto Blesheim Graduate School of Management-WHU—Koblenz, and the Stuttgart Institute of Management and Technology, Germany; Institute of Business Studies, Moscow, Russia. Summer study: Austria; China; Oxford University, England; France; Japan

STUDENT INFORMATION

Total Business Students: 630
% Full Time: 37
% Female: 23
% Minority: 10
% Out of State: 67
% International: 30
Average Age: 29

COMPUTER AND RESEARCH FACILITIES

Research Facilities: Flow Institute for International Studies, MBA House for International Students, Angell Center for Entrepreneurship, Family Business Center, Babcock Demon Incubator (new business/venture capital incubator), Capital Markets Training Center, Future Focus 2020

Computer Facilities: All classrooms are outfitted with integrated computer and audio-visual equipment. The MBA students have a dedicated computer lab equipped with Dell PCs, which are networked to high-quality laser printers. Students have access to numerous Web-based information systems such as Bloomberg, Lexis-Nexis, ProQuest, Primark, Investext, and Standard and Poor's. They also have access to Dow Jones and Dialog information services.

Campuswide Network? Yes
% of MBA Classrooms Wired: 100
Internet Fee? No

EXPENSES/FINANCIAL AID

Annual Tuition: $25,000
Tuition Per Credit (Resident/Nonresident): $1,010
Books and Supplies: $1,500
Average Grant: $3,440
Average Loan: $19,097
% Receiving Aid Their First Year: 61

ADMISSIONS INFORMATION

Application Fee: $75
Electronic Application? Yes
Regular Application Deadline: Rolling
Regular Notification: Rolling
Deferment Available? Yes
Length of Deferment: 1 year
Non-fall Admissions? No
Transfer Students Accepted? No
Need-Blind Admissions? Yes
Number of Applications Received: 96
% of Applicants Accepted: 93
% Accepted Who Enrolled: 69
Average GPA: 3.2
GPA Range: 2.7-3.5
Average GMAT: 570
GMAT Range: 510-640
Average Years Experience: 6
Other Schools to Which Students Applied: Duke University, University of North Carolina—Chapel Hill, University of North Carolina—Greensboro

WAKE FOREST UNIVERSITY BABCOCK GRADUATE SCHOOL OF MANAGEMENT, FULL-TIME PROGRAM

Admissions Contact: Mary Goss, Director of Admissions & Student Affairs
Address: PO Box 7659, Winston-Salem, NC 27109
Admissions Phone: 336-758-5422 • **Admissions Fax:** 336-758-5830
Admissions E-mail: admissions@mba.wfu.edu • **Web Address:** www.mba.wfu.edu

The campus is gorgeous, the "brilliant" professors are "real people" who are "fun to go to lunch with," and there are some of "the smallest section sizes of any major MBA program" in the country at Wake Forest University's Babcock School of Management. "Students get to know each other pretty well," which creates "an environment of free interaction" and "a genuine sense of community here that extends to faculty, staff, students, and their families."

INSTITUTIONAL INFORMATION

Public/Private: Private
Evening Classes Available? Yes
Total Faculty: 52

% Faculty Female: 14
% Faculty Minority: 15
% Faculty Part Time: 21
Student/Faculty Ratio: 12:1
Students in Parent Institution: 6,323
Academic Calendar: Semester

PROGRAMS

Degrees Offered: MBA (21 months, full time), Winston-Salem Evening MBA (24 months), Winston-Salem Fast-Track EMBA (17 months), Charlotte Evening MBA (24 months), Charlotte Saturday MBA (24 months)
Combined Degrees: JD/MBA (4 years), MD/MBA (5 years), PhD/MBA (5 years), MSA/MBA (6 years)
Academic Specialties: Integrated curriculum in the first year with functional area tracks offered in the second year. First year: Intergrated curriculum taught in 3 modules—business foundations, functional and cross-functional applications, and strategic and international perspectives. Second year: 16 tracks offered within the following disciplines: Finance, Marketing, O, consulting, Enterpreneurship, Information Technology Management
Special Opportunities: Babcock Leadership Series, Mentor Program, Management Consulting Practicum, Marketing Case Competition, Elevator Case Competition, KACE Competition (case-writing competition)
Study Abroad Options: Wirtschafts Universitaet, Wien, Austria; Groupe ESC Bordeaux, France; University of Kaiserslautern, the Otto Blesheim Graduate School of Management-WHU—Koblenz, and the Stuttgart Institute of Management and Technology, Germany; Institute of Business Studies, Moscow, Russia. Summer study: Austria; China; Oxford University, England; France, Japan

STUDENT INFORMATION

Total Business Students: 630
% Full Time: 37
% Female: 23
% Minority: 10
% Out of State: 67
% International: 30
Average Age: 27

COMPUTER AND RESEARCH FACILITIES

Research Facilities: Flow Institute for International Studies, MBA House for International Students, Angell Center for Enterpreneurship, Family Business Center, Babcock Demon Incubator (new business/venture capital incubator), Capital Markets Training Center, Future Focus 2020
Computer Facilities: All students are provided with an IBM ThinkPad laptop computer as part of tuition. All classrooms are outfitted with integrated computer and audio-visual equipment. The MBA students have a dedicated computer lab equipped with Dell PCs, which are networked to high-quality laser printers. Students have access to numerous web-based information systems such as Bloomberg, Lexis-Nexis, ProQuest, Primark, Investext, and Standard and Poor's. They also have access to Dow Jones and Dialog information services.
Campuswide Network? Yes
% of MBA Classrooms Wired: 100
Computer Model Recommended: Laptop
Internet Fee? No

EXPENSES/FINANCIAL AID

Annual Tuition: $25,000
Tuition Per Credit (Resident/Nonresident): $958
Room & Board (On/Off Campus): $5,600
Books and Supplies: $1,500
Average Grant: $11,727
Average Loan: $26,028
% Receiving Financial Aid: 79
% Receiving Aid Their First Year: 82

ADMISSIONS INFORMATION

Application Fee: $50
Electronic Application? Yes
Early Decision Application Deadline: 12/1
Early Decision Notification: 12/25
Regular Application Deadline: 4/1
Regular Notification: Rolling
Deferment Available? Yes
Length of Deferment: 1 year
Non-fall Admissions? No
Transfer Students Accepted? No
Need-Blind Admissions? Yes
Number of Applications Received: 577
% of Applicants Accepted: 47
% Accepted Who Enrolled: 44
Average GPA: 3.2
GPA Range: 2.9-3.6
Average GMAT: 639
GMAT Range: 610-670
Average Years Experience: 4
Other Admissions Factors Considered: Demonstrated potential for management careers through academic achievement, professional experience, and community involvement
Minority/Disadvantaged Student Recruitment Programs: Babcock offers Diversity Day, an event for prospective minority students, and we participate in the National Black MBA Association and the National Hispanic Society of MBA's Career Forums.
Other Schools to Which Students Applied: Duke University, Emory University, Indiana University, University of Maryland—College Park, University of North Carolina—Chapel Hill, Vanderbilt University, Washington University in St. Louis

INTERNATIONAL STUDENTS

TOEFL Required of International Students? Yes
Minimum TOEFL: 600 (250 computer)

EMPLOYMENT INFORMATION

Placement Office Available? Yes
% Employed Within 3 Months: 88
Fields Employing Percentage of Grads: Strategic Planning (2%), Consulting (6%), General Management (7%), Operations (7%), MIS (7%), Marketing (20%), Finance (51%)
Frequent Employers: Citigroup, Inc.; BB&T Corp.; Emerson Electric Co.; Ingersoll Rand Co.; Northstar Travel Media; Philip Morris; Progress Enery Inc.; R.J. Reynolds Tobacco Co.; Sara Lee Corp.; Wachovia Corp.
Prominent Alumni: Charles W. Ergen, CEO, EchoStar Communications Corp.; G. Kennedy Thompson, president and CEO, Wachovia Corp.; William G. Taylor, president, The Springs Co.; Charles L. Nesbit, Jr., president and CEO, Sara Lee Intimate Apparel; John K. Medica, vice president, Dell Computer Corp.

WASHINGTON STATE UNIVERSITY
College of Business and Economics

Admissions Contact: Anita Young or Kristin Barton
Address: PO Box 644744, Pullman, WA 99164-4744
Admissions Phone: 509-335-7617 • **Admissions Fax:** 509-335-4735
Admissions E-mail: mba@wsu.edu • **Web Address:** www.cbe.wsu.edu/graduate

MBA students at Washington University's Olin School of Business tell us that its intimate size, flexible curriculum, and faculty composed of "heavy

hitters" make it a worthwhile choice. Experiential learning is another major focal point of the Olin approach. Practicum allows students to consult for area companies on matters ranging from marketing to strategy. Thus far, a slew of firms, including Enterprise Rent-A-Car, Ford Motor Company, PricewaterhouseCoopers, Ralston Purina, and Monsanto, have asked Olin students for their advice.

INSTITUTIONAL INFORMATION

Public/Private: Public
Evening Classes Available? No
Student/Faculty Ratio: 25:1
Students in Parent Institution: 17,000

PROGRAMS

Degrees Offered: PhD in Business Administration (4 years), MBA (1-2 years), MACC (2 years)
Combined Degrees: JD/MBA (4 years)
Academic Specialties: Management Information Systems, Finance and Investments, Hotel and Restaurant Administration

STUDENT INFORMATION

Total Business Students: 119
% Full Time: 94
% Female: 43
% Minority: 7
% Out of State: 42
% International: 37
Average Age: 27

COMPUTER AND RESEARCH FACILITIES

Campuswide Network? Yes
% of MBA Classrooms Wired: 9
Internet Fee? No

EXPENSES/FINANCIAL AID

Books and Supplies: $1,000
Average Grant: $4,000
Average Loan: $10,000
% Receiving Financial Aid: 40
% Receiving Aid Their First Year: 15

ADMISSIONS INFORMATION

Electronic Application? Yes
Regular Application Deadline: Rolling
Regular Notification: Rolling
Deferment Available? No
Non-fall Admissions? Yes
Non-fall Application Deadline(s): Rolling
Transfer Students Accepted? No
Need-Blind Admissions? Yes
Number of Applications Received: 221
% of Applicants Accepted: 43
% Accepted Who Enrolled: 60
Average Years Experience: 2
Other Schools to Which Students Applied: Brigham Young University, University of Washington, Gonzaga University, Oregon State University

INTERNATIONAL STUDENTS

TOEFL Required of International Students? Yes
Minimum TOEFL: 580

EMPLOYMENT INFORMATION

Placement Office Available? No

WASHINGTON UNIVERSITY IN ST. LOUIS

John M. Olin School of Business

Admissions Contact: Brad Pearson, Director of MBA Admissions
Address: Campus Box 1133, One Brookings Drive, St. Louis, MO 63130
Admissions Phone: 314-935-7301 • **Admissions Fax:** 314-935-6309
Admissions E-mail: mba@olin.wustl.edu • **Web Address:** www.olin.wustl.edu

INSTITUTIONAL INFORMATION

Public/Private: Private
Evening Classes Available? Yes
Total Faculty: 72
% Faculty Female: 18
% Faculty Minority: 3
% Faculty Part Time: 37
Student/Faculty Ratio: 14:1
Students in Parent Institution: 11,606
Academic Calendar: Semester

PROGRAMS

Degrees Offered: MBA (22 months full time), EMBA (18 months), Professional MBA (3 years part time), PhD (5 years)
Combined Degrees: MBA/MHA (3 years), MBA/MARCH (3 years), MBA/MA in East Asian Studies (3 years), MBA/MSW (3 years), MBA/MA in International Affairs (3 years), MBA/JD (4 years)
Academic Specialties: Faculty specialize in all business disciplines. Faculty recently joined with expertise in health economics and technology management. Olin's curriculum is designed to focus on the individual student. Courses are offered on a mini-semester basis to give students more choice in electives. All students participate in Professional Development Planning, a self-assessment program through which students identify their skills, weaknesses, and career aspirations. They then craft an individualized program of study, including courses, extracurricular activities, and experiential learning.
Special Opportunities: Experiential learning through corporate (Practicum) and non-profit (Taylor Community Consulting Program) management consulting; business plan development for entrepreneurs (Hatchery); hands-on investment management and global fund activities (Investment Praxis); global management studies, including a 2-week in-country immersion experience, using total quality management techniques (Total Quality Schools), MBA Enterprise Corps, foreign study
Study Abroad Options: Manchester Business School, England; University of Paris-Dauphine, France; Otto Beisheim Graduate School of Management, WHU-Koblenz, Germany; ESADE, Spain; IESA, Venezuela

STUDENT INFORMATION

Total Business Students: 662
% Full Time: 47
% Female: 20
% Minority: 16
% Out of State: 90
% International: 35
Average Age: 28

COMPUTER AND RESEARCH FACILITIES

Research Facilities: Business, Law, and Economics Center; Boeing Center for Technology, Information, and Manufacturing
Computer Facilities: 60-unit computer lab in Simon Hall, home to the Olin School; an "Express Lab" for checking e-mail and printing papers between classes. This year a new computer lab was created exclusively for laptop users. All classroom seats now have power outlets and 100 Mb/sec network connections. The network "backbone" is fiber optic at 1 Gb/sec. Our wireless LAN was upgraded this year and now provides coverage to all student-accessible public areas such as student lounges, the library, study rooms, May Auditorium, and the Lopata Courtyard. Prometheus e-learning courseware (now part of Blackboard, Inc.) was introduced last year and is now available to all students and their professors. Each year, approximately one-third of the student computer-lab PCs are replaced with "leading edge" systems. This year, our new machines were Dell computers with 2.26 Ghz Pentium 4 processors, 256 MB RAM, 19-inch color monitors, and read/writeable CD drives. We have added a new HP 20-ppm duplex color laser printer. The lab also has several high-speed laser printers and scanners. Available databases: Bridge Data Systems, Dow Jones Interactive, Nexis, RDS Business Reference Suite, Proquest Direct (ABI), Infotrac, Disclosure Global Access, Dun & Bradstreet, ISI Emerging Markets, Hoover Online Buisness Network, FIS Online (Moody's), Info USA, Standard & Poors Net Advantage, Zacks Research.
Campuswide Network? Yes
% of MBA Classrooms Wired: 100
Computer Model Recommended: Laptop
Internet Fee? No

EXPENSES/FINANCIAL AID

Annual Tuition: $29,700
Tuition Per Credit (Resident/Nonresident): $850
Room & Board (On/Off Campus): $12,500
Books and Supplies: $2,500
Average Grant: $11,524
Average Loan: $26,086
% Receiving Financial Aid: 70
% Receiving Aid Their First Year: 71

ADMISSIONS INFORMATION

Application Fee: $100
Electronic Application? Yes
Regular Application Deadline: 4/25
Regular Notification: 6/20
Deferment Available? No
Non-fall Admissions? No
Transfer Students Accepted? Yes
Transfer Policy: Maximum of 9 credits from an AACSB-accredited graduate program
Need-Blind Admissions? Yes
Number of Applications Received: 1,083
% of Applicants Accepted: 35
% Accepted Who Enrolled: 44
Average GPA: 3.3
GPA Range: 3.0-3.6
Average GMAT: 651
GMAT Range: 620-690
Average Years Experience: 6
Other Admissions Factors Considered: Community service, leadership experience, individual character
Minority/Disadvantaged Student Recruitment Programs: Consortium for Graduate Study in Management (funds fellowships for talented minorities)
Other Schools to Which Students Applied: Emory University, Harvard University, Northwestern University, University of Chicago, University of Michigan, University of North Carolina—Chapel Hill, Vanderbilt University

INTERNATIONAL STUDENTS

TOEFL Required of International Students? Yes
Minimum TOEFL: 590 (243 computer)

EMPLOYMENT INFORMATION

Placement Office Available? Yes
% Employed Within 3 Months: 70
Fields Employing Percentage of Grads: Operations (3%), Other (4%), General Management (5%), Consulting (17%), Marketing (18%), Finance (36%)
Frequent Employers: American Airlines, Anheuser-Busch, AT Kearney, Bank of America, Bear Stearns, Capital One, Citibank, Emerson, ExxonMobil, GE Capital, Guidant, Noble International Ltd., SBC Communications, 3M, Wells Fargo

Prominent Alumni: Priscilla L. Hill-Ardoin, senior vice president—FCC, SBC Communications, Inc.; Steve Fossett, chairman, Larkspur Securities Inc.; James H. Hance, Jr., vice chairman and CFO, Bank of America; W. Patrick McGinnis, President and CEO, Nestle Purina Pet Care; William J. Shaw, President & COO, Marriott International

See page 470.

WAYNE STATE UNIVERSITY
School of Business Administration

Admissions Contact: Linda S. Zaddach, Assistant Dean of Student Affairs
Address: Office of Student Services, 5201 Cass, Room 200, Detroit, MI 48202
Admissions Phone: 313-577-4505 • **Admissions Fax:** 313-577-5299
Admissions E-mail: l.s.zaddach@wayne.edu • **Web Address:** www.busadm.wayne.edu

INSTITUTIONAL INFORMATION
Public/Private: Public
Evening Classes Available? Yes
Total Faculty: 94
% Faculty Part Time: 40
Student/Faculty Ratio: 35:1
Students in Parent Institution: 31,168
Academic Calendar: Semester

PROGRAMS
Degrees Offered: MBA (36 credits, 1-6 years), MST (36 credits, 1-6 years)

STUDENT INFORMATION
Total Business Students: 1,379
% Full Time: 10
% Female: 42
Average Age: 28

COMPUTER AND RESEARCH FACILITIES
Campuswide Network? Yes
Internet Fee? No

EXPENSES/FINANCIAL AID
Annual Tuition (Resident/Nonresident): $5,733/$12,663
Tuition Per Credit (Resident/Nonresident): $239/$530

ADMISSIONS INFORMATION
Application Fee: $20
Electronic Application? Yes
Regular Application Deadline: 8/1
Regular Notification: Rolling
Deferment Available? No
Non-fall Admissions? Yes
Non-fall Application Deadline(s): 12/1, 4/1
Transfer Students Accepted? No
Need-Blind Admissions? No
Number of Applications Received: 543
% of Applicants Accepted: 76
% Accepted Who Enrolled: 71
Average GPA: 3.1
Average GMAT: 515
Other Admissions Factors Considered: GMAT, GPA

INTERNATIONAL STUDENTS
TOEFL Required of International Students? Yes
Minimum TOEFL: 550

EMPLOYMENT INFORMATION
Placement Office Available? Yes
% Employed Within 3 Months: 95

WEBER STATE UNIVERSITY
John B. Goddard School of Business and Economics

Admissions Contact: Dr. Mark A. Stevenson, MBA Enrollment Director
Address: 3806 University Circle, Ogden, UT 84408-3806
Admissions Phone: 801-626-7545 • **Admissions Fax:** 801-626-7423
Admissions E-mail: mba@weber.edu • **Web Address:** goddard.weber.edu/dp/mba

Weber State's MBA programs are only a couple of years old, but they are already reputedly "personalized, flexible, and thought-provoking." Classes (called "hybrid courses" because they combine traditional face-to-face instruction with online course work) are taught at night at the WSU—Davis campus in Layton. The program accepts applicants with undergraduate degrees in any discipline, whereas only business undergraduates need apply to the Fast-Track MBA, completed in as little as 56 weeks. Goddard's MBA students have, on average, four years of work experience, and are split about 50-50 between the two available programs.

INSTITUTIONAL INFORMATION
Public/Private: Public
Evening Classes Available? Yes
Total Faculty: 18
% Faculty Female: 38
Student/Faculty Ratio: 5:1
Students in Parent Institution: 16,800

PROGRAMS
Degrees Offered: MBA, MPACC
Academic Specialties: The John B. Goddard School of Business & Economics MBA degree is fully accredited by AACSB International. The Goddard School MBA is designed to meet the needs of working professionals who wish to advance in their careers. MBA courses are taught in the evenings at the WSU—Davis campus in Layton. Our general management graduate curriculum consists of "hybrid courses" that blend the best of traditional classroom instruction with online educational tools and the power of the Internet.
Special Opportunities: The Goddard School MBA Program offers two different tracks: The Fast-Track MBA program is open only to students who have completed an undergraduate business degree from an AACSB-accredited school within the past 10 years. Students eligible for this option complete 36 credit hours of MBA coursework. Full-time students who pursue this option can complete the Fast-Track program in as little as 56 weeks. The Non-Business Major Track is for those who have undergraduate degrees in fields other than business. Half of our current students fall into this category. The Non-Business Major Track is a 55-credit-hour MBA Program that can be completed in 2 years of full-time study. We have designed a set of foundations courses to prepare these students to move into the advanced MBA curriculum.

STUDENT INFORMATION
Total Business Students: 75
% Full Time: 75
% Female: 32
% Minority: 4
% International: 9
Average Age: 31

COMPUTER AND RESEARCH FACILITIES

Campuswide Network? Yes
Internet Fee? No

EXPENSES/FINANCIAL AID

Annual Tuition (Resident/Nonresident): $6,000/$13,000
Books and Supplies: $2,000
Average Grant: $3,145
Average Loan: $6,000

ADMISSIONS INFORMATION

Application Fee: $30
Electronic Application? Yes
Regular Application Deadline: 6/1
Regular Notification: Rolling
Deferment Available? Yes
Length of Deferment: 1 year
Non-fall Admissions? Yes
Non-fall Application Deadline(s): 11/1 spring
Transfer Students Accepted? Yes
Transfer Policy: Transfer credits from AACSB-accredited programs accepted
Need-Blind Admissions? Yes
Number of Applications Received: 63
% of Applicants Accepted: 75
% Accepted Who Enrolled: 94
Average GPA: 3.4
GPA Range: 3.1-3.7
Average GMAT: 571
GMAT Range: 530-620
Average Years Experience: 5
Other Admissions Factors Considered: Candidates from non-English-speaking countries are required to take the Test of English as a Foreign Language (TOEFL), unless they received their bachelor's degree from a university in which the language of instruction was English. Transcript evaluations are also required for international applicants.
Other Schools to Which Students Applied: Utah State University, University of Utah

INTERNATIONAL STUDENTS

TOEFL Required of International Students? Yes
Minimum TOEFL: 550 (213 computer)

EMPLOYMENT INFORMATION

Placement Office Available? Yes

WEST VIRGINIA UNIVERSITY
College of Business and Economics

Admissions Contact: Jennifer Butler, Associate Director
Address: PO Box 6025, Morgantown, WV 26506-6025
Admissions Phone: 304-293-5408 • **Admissions Fax:** 304-293-2385
Admissions E-mail: mba@wvu.edu • **Web Address:** www.be.wvu.edu

Touted as a great educational buy, West Virginia University offers a business education that covers all bases. Whether you're an executive looking for additional theoretical grounding or a beginner with an undergrad degree and a curiosity about the backbone of business, WVU has a program catered to your needs and schedule.

INSTITUTIONAL INFORMATION

Public/Private: Public
Evening Classes Available? Yes
Total Faculty: 65
% Faculty Female: 18
% Faculty Minority: 2
% Faculty Part Time: 6
Student/Faculty Ratio: 18:1
Students in Parent Institution: 22,000
Academic Calendar: Semester

PROGRAMS

Degrees Offered: MBA (1 year), EMBA (2 year), IMBA (1 year accelerated), MSIR (1 year), MPACC (2 years), PhD in Economics
Combined Degrees: MBA/JD
Academic Specialties: AACSB accredited; WVU is a Carnegie research-extensive institution.
Study Abroad Options: Germany; Italy; selected destinations in MBA International Business trip

STUDENT INFORMATION

Total Business Students: 187
% Full Time: 18
% Female: 42
% Minority: 6
% Out of State: 73
% International: 36
Average Age: 30

COMPUTER AND RESEARCH FACILITIES

Campuswide Network? Yes
% of MBA Classrooms Wired: 100
Computer Model Recommended: Laptop
Internet Fee? No

EXPENSES/FINANCIAL AID

Annual Tuition (Resident/Nonresident): $11,300/$30,800
Tuition Per Credit (Resident/Nonresident): $383/$804
Books and Supplies: $1,500

ADMISSIONS INFORMATION

Application Fee: $50
Electronic Application? Yes
Regular Application Deadline: 3/1
Regular Notification: 3/31
Deferment Available? Yes
Length of Deferment: 1 year
Non-fall Admissions? Yes
Non-fall Application Deadline(s): July
Transfer Students Accepted? No
Need-Blind Admissions? Yes
Number of Applications Received: 156
% of Applicants Accepted: 24
% Accepted Who Enrolled: 89
Average GPA: 3.3
GPA Range: 3.0-3.7
Average GMAT: 560
GMAT Range: 520-630
Average Years Experience: 7
Other Schools to Which Students Applied: Marshall University, Pennsylvania State University, Syracuse University, Temple University, University of Kentucky, University of Pittsburgh, Virginia Polytechnic Institute and State University

INTERNATIONAL STUDENTS

TOEFL Required of International Students? Yes
Minimum TOEFL: 580

EMPLOYMENT INFORMATION

Placement Office Available? Yes
% Employed Within 3 Months: 98
Prominent Alumni: John Chambers, CEO, Cisco Systems; Glen Hiner, CEO, Owens Corning; Homer Hickam, author; Ray Lane, former president and COO, Oracle; Jerry West, general manager, Los Angeles Lakers

WESTERN CAROLINA UNIVERSITY
College of Business

Admissions Contact: Philip Little, Director of MBA Program
Address: 112 Forsyth Building, Cullowhee, NC 28723
Admissions Phone: (828) 227-7402 • **Admissions Fax:** (828) 227-7414
Admissions E-mail: fdeitz@email.wcu.edu
Web Address: www.wcu.edu/cob/graduate/index.htm

Located "in a rural valley between the Blue Ridge and Great Smoky Mountains," Western Carolina University's main campus in Cullowhee is a beautiful wooded area with all of the modern amenities a prospective b-school student could want: great academic, residential, and recreational facilities and a spot on Yahoo! Internet Life magazine's "100 Most Wired Campuses" list. Class sizes are small, and professors use a mixture of teaching methods to best "balance theory with practical application" and prepare students to "handle the business complexities of the global marketplace."

INSTITUTIONAL INFORMATION

Public/Private: Public
Evening Classes Available? Yes
Total Faculty: 41
% Faculty Female: 29
% Faculty Minority: 5
Student/Faculty Ratio: 3:1
Students in Parent Institution: 7,033
Academic Calendar: Semester

PROGRAMS

Degrees Offered: MBA (1.5 years full time), MACC (1.5 years full time), Master of Project Management (2 years online)
Academic Specialties: The graduate faculty have PhD degrees in all areas of business; combined with real world experience, they provide students with a broad knowledge of the business world.

STUDENT INFORMATION

Total Business Students: 132
% Full Time: 52
% Female: 32
% Minority: 6
% International: 20
Average Age: 27

COMPUTER AND RESEARCH FACILITIES

Computer Facilities: All resources in library, career, and placement centers are available.
Campuswide Network? Yes
% of MBA Classrooms Wired: 100
Internet Fee? No

EXPENSES/FINANCIAL AID

Annual Tuition (Resident/Nonresident): $1,414/$9,482
Books and Supplies: $4,480

Average Grant: $3,201
Average Loan: $10,237
% Receiving Financial Aid: 50
% Receiving Aid Their First Year: 63

ADMISSIONS INFORMATION

Application Fee: $40
Electronic Application? No
Regular Application Deadline: Rolling
Regular Notification: Rolling
Deferment Available? Yes
Length of Deferment: 1 year
Non-fall Admissions? Yes
Non-fall Application Deadline(s): Rolling admission: spring, summer terms
Transfer Students Accepted? Yes
Transfer Policy: Up to 6 hours of graduate credit
Need-Blind Admissions? Yes
Number of Applications Received: 106
% of Applicants Accepted: 92
% Accepted Who Enrolled: 53
Average GPA: 3.0
GPA Range: 2.0-3.0
Average GMAT: 500
GMAT Range: 430-540
Average Years Experience: 6
Other Admissions Factors Considered: Computer experience

INTERNATIONAL STUDENTS

TOEFL Required of International Students? Yes
Minimum TOEFL: 550 (213 computer)

EMPLOYMENT INFORMATION

Placement Office Available? Yes

WESTERN ILLINOIS UNIVERSITY
College of Business and Technology

Admissions Contact: Director of MBA Program
Address: 1 University Circle, 115 Sherman Hall, Macomb, IL 61455
Admissions Phone: 309-298-3157 • **Admissions Fax:** 309-298-3111
Admissions E-mail: Admissions@wiu.edu • **Web Address:** www.wiu.edu/users/micobtd/

INSTITUTIONAL INFORMATION

Public/Private: Public
Evening Classes Available? No
Total Faculty: 79
Students in Parent Institution: 132
Academic Calendar: Semester

PROGRAMS

Degrees Offered: Accounting, Decision Sciences, Economics, Entrepreneurship, Finance, Human Resources, Information Management, International Business, Management, Management Information Systems, Marketing, Project Management, Taxation, Logistics

STUDENT INFORMATION

Total Business Students: 132
% Full Time: 64
% Female: 42
% Minority: 1
% Out of State: 1

% International: 15
Average Age: 24

COMPUTER AND RESEARCH FACILITIES

Research Facilities: University Library plus 3 additional on-campus libraries, with total holdings of 1,000,000 volumes; 200,00 microforms; 3,500 current periodical subscriptions. CD player(s) available for graduate student use; access provided to online biblioraphic retrieval services
Campuswide Network? No
Internet Fee? No

EXPENSES/FINANCIAL AID

Annual Tuition (Resident/Nonresident): $4,608/$7,974
% Receiving Financial Aid: 34

ADMISSIONS INFORMATION

Application Fee: $1
Electronic Application? No
Regular Application Deadline: Rolling
Regular Notification: Rolling
Deferment Available? Yes
Length of Deferment: 1
Non-fall Admissions? Yes
Non-fall Application Deadline(s): Rolling
Transfer Students Accepted? No
Need-Blind Admissions? No
Number of Applications Received: 250
% of Applicants Accepted: 50
% Accepted Who Enrolled: 60
Other Admissions Factors Considered: Bachelor's degree, minimum GPA of 2.5, college transcripts, minimum GMAT of 450

INTERNATIONAL STUDENTS

TOEFL Required of International Students? Yes
Minimum TOEFL: 550

EMPLOYMENT INFORMATION

Placement Office Available? No

Study Abroad Options: International exchange programs in Germany, Japan, Mexico

STUDENT INFORMATION

Average Age: 29

COMPUTER AND RESEARCH FACILITIES

Research Facilities: Waldo Library plus 3 additional on campus libariries, with total holdings of 1,649,454 volumes; 609,529 microforms; 5,444 current periodicals. CD players available for graduate students; access provided to online biblographic retrievel services; alumni network, career counsling/planning, career fairs, career library, career placement, electronic job bank, job interviews arranged, resume, referral to employers, resume preparation
Campuswide Network? Yes
Internet Fee? No

EXPENSES/FINANCIAL AID

Tuition Per Credit (Resident/Nonresident): $154/$372

ADMISSIONS INFORMATION

Application Fee: $25
Electronic Application? No
Regular Application Deadline: 7/1
Regular Notification: 1/1
Deferment Available? Yes
Non-fall Admissions? Yes
Non-fall Application Deadline(s): 11/1, 3/15
Transfer Students Accepted? No
Need-Blind Admissions? No
Number of Applications Received: 400
% of Applicants Accepted: 69
% Accepted Who Enrolled: 73

INTERNATIONAL STUDENTS

TOEFL Required of International Students? Yes
Minimum TOEFL: 550

EMPLOYMENT INFORMATION

Placement Office Available? No

WESTERN MICHIGAN UNIVERSITY
Haworth College of Business

Admissions Contact: David A. Burnie, Associate Dean and Director of Graduate Programs
Address: 2240 Seibert Administration Building, Kalamazoo, MI 49008-5211
Admissions Phone: 269-387-2000 • **Admissions Fax:** 269-387-2096
Admissions E-mail: ask-wmu@wmich.edu • **Web Address:** www.hcob.wmich.edu

INSTITUTIONAL INFORMATION

Public/Private: Public
Evening Classes Available? Yes
Total Faculty: 100
Academic Calendar: Semester

PROGRAMS

Degrees Offered: MBA (15 months), with concentrations in Accounting, Economics, Management, Management Information Systems, Marketing, Finance; MSA (18 months); Professional MBA (1-3 years)
Academic Specialties: Case study, computer-aided instruction, computer simulations, faculty seminars, group discussion, lecture, research, simulations, student presentations, study groups, team projects

---

WESTERN WASHINGTON UNIVERSITY
College of Business and Economics

Admissions Contact: Juliet A. H. Barnes, Program Manager
Address: 516 High St., Parks Hall 419, Bellingham, WA 98225-9072
Admissions Phone: 360-650-3898 • **Admissions Fax:** 360-650-4844
Admissions E-mail: MBA@wwu.edu • **Web Address:** www.cbe.wwu.edu/mba

INSTITUTIONAL INFORMATION

Public/Private: Public
Evening Classes Available? Yes
Total Faculty: 42
% Faculty Female: 17
Students in Parent Institution: 12,500

PROGRAMS

Degrees Offered: MBA (92 quarter credits, 7 quarters), Accelerated-Track MBA (60 quarter credits, 5 quarters), Evening-Track MBA (72 quarter credits, 9 quarters part time)

STUDENT INFORMATION

Total Business Students: 62

% Full Time: 73
% Female: 36
% Minority: 7
% International: 24
Average Age: 30

COMPUTER AND RESEARCH FACILITIES

Research Facilities: Centers for economic business research, international business, small business development
Computer Facilities: On-campus Internet access, laser printers, scanners, financial/academic/periodic journals and databases
Campuswide Network? Yes
Internet Fee? No

EXPENSES/FINANCIAL AID

Annual Tuition (Resident/Nonresident): $4,983/$15,201
Tuition Per Credit (Resident/Nonresident): $166/$507
Books and Supplies: $1,500

ADMISSIONS INFORMATION

Application Fee: $35
Electronic Application? No
Regular Application Deadline: 5/1
Regular Notification: 6/1
Deferment Available? No
Non-fall Admissions? Yes
Non-fall Application Deadline(s): 5/1
Transfer Students Accepted? No
Need-Blind Admissions? No
Number of Applications Received: 89
% of Applicants Accepted: 69
% Accepted Who Enrolled: 77
Average GPA: 3.3
Average GMAT: 544
Average Years Experience: 7

INTERNATIONAL STUDENTS

TOEFL Required of International Students? Yes
Minimum TOEFL: 567 (227 computer)

EMPLOYMENT INFORMATION

Placement Office Available? Yes

WICHITA STATE UNIVERSITY
Barton School of Business

Admissions Contact: Dorothy Harpool, Director of MBA Programs
Address: 1845 N. Fairmount, Wichita, KS 67260-0048
Admissions Phone: 316-978-3230 • **Admissions Fax:** 316-978-3767
Admissions E-mail: grad.business@wichita.edu • **Web Address:** business.twsu.edu

Entrepreneurship is a major focus at the Barton School of Business, and Wichita is the birthplace of some top-flight companies, including Cessna, Beech, Coleman, Learjet aircraft companies, and Koch Industries. You can find the original Pizza Hut building on the Wichita State campus, since two of Barton's alumni, Dan and Frank Carney, started the business in Wichita in 1958 with $600 and some used equipment. Barton's "traditional, managed-based" MBA focuses on perceiving an organization as an integrated system and offers "a unique blend of cutting-edge classroom instruction and practical business application" to its students.

INSTITUTIONAL INFORMATION

Public/Private: Public
Evening Classes Available? Yes
Total Faculty: 45
% Faculty Female: 16
% Faculty Minority: 18
Student/Faculty Ratio: 5:1
Academic Calendar: Semester

PROGRAMS

Degrees Offered: MBA (2 years), EMBA (22 months), MBA/MSN (4 years)
Combined Degrees: MBA/MSN (MBA: 30 hours; nursing: 36 hours)

STUDENT INFORMATION

Total Business Students: 255
% Full Time: 26
% Female: 45
% Minority: 8
% International: 38
Average Age: 26

COMPUTER AND RESEARCH FACILITIES

Research Facilities: Ablah Library, with total holdings of 938,817 volumes; 907,837 microforms; 6,319 current periodical subscriptions. CD player(s) available
Campuswide Network? Yes
% of MBA Classrooms Wired: 75
Internet Fee? No

EXPENSES/FINANCIAL AID

Annual Tuition (Resident/Nonresident): $3,315/$9,075
Tuition Per Credit (Resident/Nonresident): $138/$378
Books and Supplies: $800
Average Grant: $6,000
Average Loan: $2,000

ADMISSIONS INFORMATION

Application Fee: $35
Electronic Application? Yes
Regular Application Deadline: 6/1
Regular Notification: 6/15
Deferment Available? Yes
Length of Deferment: 1 year
Non-fall Admissions? Yes
Non-fall Application Deadline(s): 12/1 spring
Transfer Students Accepted? Yes
Transfer Policy: Only AACSB-accredited classes may be transferred in.
Need-Blind Admissions? Yes
Number of Applications Received: 183
% of Applicants Accepted: 63
% Accepted Who Enrolled: 88
Average GPA: 3.3
Average GMAT: 530
Average Years Experience: 3

INTERNATIONAL STUDENTS

TOEFL Required of International Students? Yes
Minimum TOEFL: 550 (213 computer)

EMPLOYMENT INFORMATION

Placement Office Available? Yes

WIDENER UNIVERSITY
School of Business Administration

Admissions Contact: Lisa Bussom, Assistant Dean
Address: 1 University Place, Chester, PA 19013
Admissions Phone: 610-499-4305 • **Admissions Fax:** 610-499-4615
Admissions E-mail: gradbus.advise@widener.edu • **Web Address:** www.sba.widener.edu

"We take your education personally" is the credo of Widener University, where the student/faculty relationship is based on personal attention. Widener has recently revamped its MBA program to offer students a modern ethical, global, and technological approach to business education.

INSTITUTIONAL INFORMATION

Public/Private: Private
Evening Classes Available? Yes
Total Faculty: 46
% Faculty Female: 33
% Faculty Part Time: 26
Student/Faculty Ratio: 6:1
Students in Parent Institution: 6,700
Academic Calendar: Semester

PROGRAMS

Degrees Offered: MBA (36-54 credits, 1.5 to 7 years, average of 4 years part time), MBA with Health and Medical Services concentration (40-59 credits, 1.5 to 7 years, average of 4 years part time), MSAIS (33 credits), MST (33 credits), MS in Human Resources Management (33 credits), MSIS (33 credits), MS in Management and Technology (36 credits)
Combined Degrees: MBA/JD (3 years full time, 4 years part time), MBA/ME (2 years full time, 5 years part time), MBA/Doctor of Clinical Psychology (5 years full time), MBA in Health and Medical Services Administration/Doctor of Clinical Psychology (5 years full time)
Academic Specialties: Financial Planning, Technology Management, Information Systems, Health Administration
Special Opportunities: Internship program is available.

STUDENT INFORMATION

Total Business Students: 201
% Full Time: 11
% Female: 38
% Minority: 10
% International: 5
Average Age: 30

COMPUTER AND RESEARCH FACILITIES

Research Facilities: MBA students have access to all computer facilities on the main campus in Chester and the Delaware Campus. Students can search databases from home through library website. Specialized computer lab for MIS/IS courses, including SAP software, is available.
Computer Facilities: MBA students have full access to the Law Library.
Campuswide Network? Yes
% of MBA Classrooms Wired: 100
Internet Fee? No

EXPENSES/FINANCIAL AID

Annual Tuition: $13,680
Tuition Per Credit (Resident/Nonresident): $570
Books and Supplies: $900
% Receiving Financial Aid: 35

ADMISSIONS INFORMATION

Application Fee: $25
Electronic Application? Yes
Regular Application Deadline: 8/1
Regular Notification: Rolling
Deferment Available? Yes
Length of Deferment: 1 year
Non-fall Admissions? Yes
Non-fall Application Deadline(s): 12/1 spring, 4/1 summer
Transfer Students Accepted? No
Need-Blind Admissions? Yes
Number of Applications Received: 206
% of Applicants Accepted: 44
% Accepted Who Enrolled: 44
Average GPA: 3.0
GPA Range: 2.7-3.3
Average GMAT: 501
GMAT Range: 460-530
Average Years Experience: 8
Other Admissions Factors Considered: Work experience
Other Schools to Which Students Applied: Drexel University, La Salle University, Pennsylvania State University—Great Valley Campus, Temple University, University of Delaware, Villanova University

INTERNATIONAL STUDENTS

TOEFL Required of International Students? Yes
Minimum TOEFL: 550 (213 computer)

EMPLOYMENT INFORMATION

Placement Office Available? Yes
Frequent Employers: The MBA program is part-time with more than 85% of our students working full time while earning their degree. Employers of our students include: Boeing Co., DuPont, First Union, MBNA, and PFPC.
Prominent Alumni: Leslie C. Quick, founder, Quick & Reilly; H. Edward Hanway, CEO, Cigna Corp.; Paul Biederman, chairman, Mellon Mid-Atlantic; Mary McKenney, CEO, ManageMyProperty.com

WILLAMETTE UNIVERSITY
Atkinson Graduate School of Management

Admissions Contact: Judy O'Neill, Assistant Dean/Director of Admission
Address: 900 State Street, Salem, OR 97301
Admissions Phone: 503-370-6167 • **Admissions Fax:** 503-370-3011
Admissions E-mail: agsm-admission@williamette.edu
Web Address: www.willamette.edu/agsm

The Atkinson School has the only graduate management program in the nation accredited for both business administration and public administration. Accordingly, its MBA for business, government, and not-for-profit management is the only degree that grants its recipients the benefits of an MBA and an MPA. Atkinson has a progressive outlook, claiming that the school "goes far beyond existing ideas of management education," providing programs "that redefine real-world experience" and enabling students to "receive an unprecedented multi-sector, multi-opportunity education."

INSTITUTIONAL INFORMATION

Public/Private: Private
Evening Classes Available? No
Total Faculty: 12
% Faculty Female: 17
Student/Faculty Ratio: 14:1

Students in Parent Institution: 2,261
Academic Calendar: Semester

PROGRAMS

Degrees Offered: MBA for Business, Government, and Not-for-Profit Management (2 years full time, 4-6 years part time, 1 year accelerated full time)
Combined Degrees: MBA/JD (4 years)
Academic Specialties: General Business, Goverment and Not-for-Profit Management; Accounting; Finance; Human Resources; Marketing; Organizational Analysis; Public Management; Management Science; Negotiation/Dispute Resolution
Curriculum stresses the practical application of management theory to real-world organizations. Real-world experiences include the Atkinson School PaCE Project, in which students create and run a real enterprise; internships; class consulting projects; case studies; simulations, etc. We offer the only MBA program dually accredited for business by AACSB International and public administration by NASPAA.
Study Abroad Options: University of Southern Denmark, Denmark; Linkoping University, Sweden

STUDENT INFORMATION

Total Business Students: 173
% Full Time: 90
% Female: 43
% Minority: 10
% Out of State: 58
% International: 30
Average Age: 27

COMPUTER AND RESEARCH FACILITIES

Research Facilities: Willamette University Center for Public Policy Research, Willamette University Center for Dispute Resolution
Computer Facilities: The Atkinson School has a wireless computing environment. Library databases include: online card catalog, Academic Search Elite, Academic Universe, Business Dateline, Business Source Elite, Ingenta Uncover, Congressional Universe, EconLit, PAIS, Newspaper Source, Presidential Papers, Psych Info, Standard & Poors NetAdvantage, State Capital Universe, Statistical Universe, Stat USA, Web of Science/Social Science, Wilson Business Abstracts.
Campuswide Network? Yes
% of MBA Classrooms Wired: 40
Computer Model Recommended: Laptop
Internet Fee? No

EXPENSES/FINANCIAL AID

Annual Tuition: $18,050
Tuition Per Credit (Resident/Nonresident): $602
Books and Supplies: $1,200
Average Grant: $8,165
Average Loan: $17,712
% Receiving Financial Aid: 71
% Receiving Aid Their First Year: 71

ADMISSIONS INFORMATION

Application Fee: $50
Electronic Application? Yes
Regular Application Deadline: Rolling
Regular Notification: Rolling
Deferment Available? Yes
Length of Deferment: 1 year
Non-fall Admissions? No
Transfer Students Accepted? Yes
Transfer Policy: May transfer up to 6 credits of appropriate graduate-level management coursework with the approval of the dean
Need-Blind Admissions? Yes
Number of Applications Received: 174
% of Applicants Accepted: 74

% Accepted Who Enrolled: 57
Average GPA: 3.0
GPA Range: 2.9-3.5
Average GMAT: 550
GMAT Range: 480-590
Average Years Experience: 3
Minority/Disadvantaged Student Recruitment Programs: University-endowed scholarship programs
Other Schools to Which Students Applied: Arizona State University, Oregon State University, Portland State University, University of Oregon, University of Portland, University of Washington, Washington State University

INTERNATIONAL STUDENTS

TOEFL Required of International Students? Yes
Minimum TOEFL: 570 (230 computer)

EMPLOYMENT INFORMATION

Placement Office Available? Yes
% Employed Within 3 Months: 76
Fields Employing Percentage of Grads: MIS (3%), Entrepreneurship (6%), Consulting (6%), Accounting (6%), General Management (8%), Operations (8%), Human Resources (8%), Other (10%), Marketing (14%), Finance (25%)
Frequent Employers: Andersen, Bonneville Power Administration, Deloitte & Touche, Hewlett-Packard Co., Intel Corp., Nike Inc., Planar Systems, State of Oregon, Tektronix Inc., U.S. Government, Xerox
Prominent Alumni: Marcus Robins, investments; Grace Crunican, government; Tom Hoover, marketing research; Ann Jackson, not-for-profit management; Tom Neilsen, general management

See page 472.

WINTHROP UNIVERSITY
College of Business Administration

Admissions Contact: Director of Graduate Studies
Address: 209 Tillman Hall, Rock Hill, SC 29733
Admissions Phone: 803-323-2204 • **Admissions Fax:** 803-323-2292
Admissions E-mail: graduatestudies@winthrop.edu • **Web Address:** cba.winthrop.edu

INSTITUTIONAL INFORMATION

Public/Private: Public
Evening Classes Available? No
Total Faculty: 44
Students in Parent Institution: 5,304
Academic Calendar: Semester

PROGRAMS

Degrees Offered: MBA (39 credits, minimum 18 months), MBA in Accounting (33 credits, minimum 18 months), EMBA (51 credits, minimum 2 years)

STUDENT INFORMATION

Total Business Students: 250
% Full Time: 40
Average Age: 34

COMPUTER AND RESEARCH FACILITIES

Campuswide Network? Yes
Internet Fee? No

EXPENSES/FINANCIAL AID

Annual Tuition (Resident/Nonresident): $2,370/$4,360
Tuition Per Credit (Resident/Nonresident): $199/$365

ADMISSIONS INFORMATION

Application Fee: $35
Electronic Application? No
Regular Application Deadline: 7/15
Regular Notification: Rolling
Deferment Available? Yes
Non-fall Admissions? Yes
Non-fall Application Deadline(s): 12/1 spring, 5/1 summer
Transfer Students Accepted? No
Need-Blind Admissions? No
Other Admissions Factors Considered: Letter of recommendation, interview, essay, work experience, personal statement, computer experience

INTERNATIONAL STUDENTS

TOEFL Required of International Students? Yes
Minimum TOEFL: 550

EMPLOYMENT INFORMATION

Placement Office Available? Yes
% Employed Within 3 Months: 85

WORCESTER POLYTECHNIC INSTITUTE
Department of Management

Admissions Contact: Norm Wilkinson, Director of Graduate Management Programs
Address: 100 Institute Road Worcester, MA 01609
Admissions Phone: 508-831-5218 • **Admissions Fax:** 508-831-5720
Admissions E-mail: gmp@wpi.edu • **Web Address:** www.mgt.wpi.edu

In addition to the main campus in Worcester, New England's third largest city, Worcester Polytechnic Institute has campuses in Waltham and Southborough, not to mention the extensive programs offered anytime, anywhere through distance learning. Entrepreneurs will be nurtured and challenged here through course work, competitions, organizations, and awards. With management and technology at the core of WPI's 24-year old MBA program, students can focus on one of six concentrations and choose from more than 100 graduate electives. And what a payoff: the MBA program boasts that, on average, students see a 63 percent increase in their salaries from the time they matriculate to the time they graduate.

INSTITUTIONAL INFORMATION

Public/Private: Private
Evening Classes Available? Yes
Total Faculty: 23
% Faculty Female: 39
% Faculty Minority: 0
% Faculty Part Time: 9
Student/Faculty Ratio: 11:1
Students in Parent Institution: 3,700
Academic Calendar: Semester

PROGRAMS

Degrees Offered: MBA (2 years); MS in Marketing and Technological Innovation (1.5 years); MS in Operations and Information Technology (1.5 years)
Combined Degrees: BS/MBA (5 years)

STUDENT INFORMATION

Total Business Students: 250
% Full Time: 10
% Female: 41

% Minority: 0
% International: 85
Average Age: 34

COMPUTER AND RESEARCH FACILITIES

Campuswide Network? Yes
% of MBA Classrooms Wired: 0
Computer Model Recommended: No prefrence
Internet Fee? No

EXPENSES/FINANCIAL AID

Annual Tuition: $20,592
Tuition Per Credit (Resident/Nonresident): $858
Room & Board (Off Campus): $8,100
Books and Supplies: $1,100
% Receiving Financial Aid: 50
% Receiving Aid Their First Year: 35

ADMISSIONS INFORMATION

Application Fee: $70
Electronic Application? Yes
Regular Application Deadline: 6/1
Regular Notification: Rolling
Deferment Available? Yes
Length of Deferment: 1 year
Non-fall Admissions? Yes
Non-fall Application Deadline(s): 10/1 Spring
Transfer Students Accepted? Yes
Transfer Policy: 9 credits maximum
Need-Blind Admissions? Yes
Number of Applications Received: 58
% of Applicants Accepted: 66
% Accepted Who Enrolled: 53
Average GPA: 3.4
Average GMAT: 620
GMAT Range: 560-670
Average Years Experience: 8
Other Admissions Factors Considered: Leadership positions held
Other Schools to Which Students Applied: Babson College, Bentley College, Boston University, Northeastern University

INTERNATIONAL STUDENTS

TOEFL Required of International Students? Yes
Minimum TOEFL: 500 (213 computer)

EMPLOYMENT INFORMATION

Placement Office Available? Yes
% Employed Within 3 Months: 90
Fields Employing Percentage of Grads: Human Resources (2%), MIS (60%), Marketing (13%), Consulting (20%), Entrepreneurship (18%)
Frequent Employers: Raytheon, Fidelity, Textron, GE, Teradyne, BAE Systems, EMC

WRIGHT STATE UNIVERSITY
Raj Soin College of Business

Admissions Contact: Director of MBA Programs
Address: 110 Rike Hall, Dayton, OH 45435-0001
Admissions Phone: 937-775-2437 • **Admissions Fax:** 937-775-3545
Admissions E-mail: rscob-admin@wright.edu • **Web Address:** www.wright.edu/business

Thankfully, voters decided to name the school Wright State University in '65 to honor Dayton's Wright Brothers instead of other title suggestions, such as Whatsamatta U. The MBA program offered at the Raj Soin School of Business has an incredibly flexible curriculum, so if you're totally unsure about what you'll be doing over the next year or more between your job, kids, and school, Wright State may very well be a fit for you. Students can choose from nine concentrations in order to gain specialized knowledge as their business talents mature in the program, and they can earn the degree in as little as 11 months or stretch it out for five years.

INSTITUTIONAL INFORMATION

Public/Private: Public
Evening Classes Available? Yes
Total Faculty: 66
% Faculty Female: 24
Student/Faculty Ratio: 8:1
Academic Calendar: Quarter

PROGRAMS

Degrees Offered: MBA (1-5 years), MS in Social and Applied Economics (1-5 years), MACC (1-5 years)
Combined Degrees: MBA/MSN (2-5 years), MBA/MS in Social and Applied Economics (2-5 years)
Special Opportunities: CIS or MIS, E-Business (includes E-Commerce), Economics, Finance (includes Banking), International Business, Management, Marketing, Other, Production/Operations Management/Managerial Economics, Supply Chain Management/Transportation/Logistics

STUDENT INFORMATION

Total Business Students: 411
% Full Time: 33
% Female: 46
Average Age: 28

COMPUTER AND RESEARCH FACILITIES

Campuswide Network? Yes
Internet Fee? No

EXPENSES/FINANCIAL AID

Annual Tuition (Resident/Nonresident): $5,847/$10,182
Tuition Per Credit (Resident/Nonresident): $184/$318

ADMISSIONS INFORMATION

Application Fee: $25
Electronic Application? Yes
Regular Application Deadline: 1/1
Regular Notification: 1/1
Deferment Available? Yes
Length of Deferment: 4 quarters
Non-fall Admissions? Yes
Non-fall Application Deadline(s): 1/1
Transfer Students Accepted? Yes
Transfer Policy: Transfer applicants must meet WSU admissions requirements and can transfer up to 4 classes, with faculty approval.
Need-Blind Admissions? Yes
Number of Applications Received: 241

% of Applicants Accepted: 46
% Accepted Who Enrolled: 59
Average Years Experience: 5

INTERNATIONAL STUDENTS

TOEFL Required of International Students? Yes
Minimum TOEFL: 550

EMPLOYMENT INFORMATION

Placement Office Available? No

XAVIER UNIVERSITY
Williams College of Business

Admissions Contact: Jennifer Bush, Director, MBA Enrollment Services
Address: 3800 Victory Parkway, Cincinnati, OH 45207
Admissions Phone: 513-745-3525 • **Admissions Fax:** 513-745-2929
Admissions E-mail: XUMBA@xu.edu • **Web Address:** www.xavier.edu/mba

The Xavier MBA has a team-based curriculum that "emphasizes the dynamic nature of business and teaches the skills to grow and change with it." Students may cater the broad-based On-Site MBA program to their specific goals and interests by choosing from nine concentrations. Experienced professionals who can make it to class once a week will be able to earn an Executive MBA in just 19 months. Xavier is a Jesuit university, so the curriculum has roots in Jesuit philosophy, stressing ethical and moral issues while encouraging the development of the whole person.

INSTITUTIONAL INFORMATION

Public/Private: Private
Evening Classes Available? Yes
Total Faculty: 57
% Faculty Female: 32
% Faculty Part Time: 50
Student/Faculty Ratio: 16:1
Students in Parent Institution: 6,499
Academic Calendar: Semester

PROGRAMS

Degrees Offered: Add-on concentration for Post-MBA graduates in 8 areas (approximately 2 semesters)
Combined Degrees: Master of Health Services Administration/MBA (approximately 3 years); MSN/MBA (approximately 3 years)
Academic Specialties: 8 areas of concentration available: Accounting, E-Business, Finance, General Business, Human Resources, Information Systems, International Business, Marketing; Weekend (Saturday) MBA, EMBA, and On-Site MBA programs available
Study Abroad Options: Beijing International MBA at Peking University, China; ESC-Bordeaux, France; annual summer study trips to Asia, Europe, and South America. Through Jesuit Business School Network agreement, students have access to study abroad trips with 23 other Jesuit AACSB-accredited MBA schools.

STUDENT INFORMATION

Total Business Students: 903
% Full Time: 17
% Female: 21
% Minority: 9
% Out of State: 9
% International: 10
Average Age: 28

COMPUTER AND RESEARCH FACILITIES

Research Facilities: Xavier University Entrepreneurial Center, Xavier University Center for Business Ethics
Computer Facilities: Business and Company Resource Center, CCH Tax Research Network, Business and Industry, Business and Management Practices, Business Dateline, Comppustat, E-Marketer Reports, Econ Lit, Infotrac General Business File, Lexis-Nexis Academic Universe, Stat-USA, Business Source Premier, Mergent OnLine, Investext Plus, ValueLine, Thompson Research, Social Sciences Citation Index
Campuswide Network? Yes
% of MBA Classrooms Wired: 50
Internet Fee? No

EXPENSES/FINANCIAL AID

Annual Tuition: $8,370
Tuition Per Credit (Resident/Nonresident): $465
Books and Supplies: $600
Average Grant: $708

ADMISSIONS INFORMATION

Application Fee: $35
Electronic Application? Yes
Regular Application Deadline: Rolling
Regular Notification: Rolling
Deferment Available? Yes
Length of Deferment: 1 year
Non-fall Admissions? Yes
Non-fall Application Deadline(s): Rolling
Transfer Students Accepted? Yes
Transfer Policy: 6 hours of core curriculum from AACSB-accredited programs only; up to 18 hours of core curriculum form AACSB-accredited Jesuit MBA Network schools
Need-Blind Admissions? Yes
Number of Applications Received: 336
% of Applicants Accepted: 69
Average GPA: 3.2
GPA Range: 2.9-3.5
Average GMAT: 550
GMAT Range: 500-590
Average Years Experience: 7
Other Schools to Which Students Applied: Northern Kentucky University, University of Cincinnati

INTERNATIONAL STUDENTS

TOEFL Required of International Students? Yes
Minimum TOEFL: 550 (213 computer)

EMPLOYMENT INFORMATION

Placement Office Available? Yes
% Employed Within 3 Months: 24
Fields Employing Percentage of Grads: Other (5%), MIS (8%), Human Resources (8%), Finance (15%), Accounting (15%), General Management (19%), Marketing (30%)
Prominent Alumni: George Schaefer, president/CEO, Fifth Third Bancorp; Robert J. Kohlhepp, CEO, Cintas Corp.; Ken Lucas, U.S. congressman; Carlos Alcantara, president, International Penzoil-Quaker State; Lloyd Ward, president, U.S. Olympic Committee

YALE UNIVERSITY
Yale School of Management

Admissions Contact: James R. Stevens, Director of Admissions
Address: 135 Prospect Street, PO Box 208200, New Haven, CT 06520-8200
Admissions Phone: 203-432-5932 • **Admissions Fax:** 203-432-7004
Admissions E-mail: mba.admissions@yale.edu • **Web Address:** www.mba.yale.edu

Where do "the best, brightest, and most diverse management students" go for their MBAs? Yale, of course, where "brilliant, accomplished," and "innovative" professors are "well published" and "100 percent accessible." Yale's nontraditional (i.e., "noncompetitive") grading system "encourages students to take risks with difficult course work," and while students report a fair amount of academic pressure, they say it "varies because it's self-imposed."

INSTITUTIONAL INFORMATION

Public/Private: Private
Evening Classes Available? No
Total Faculty: 82
% Faculty Female: 12
% Faculty Part Time: 39
Student/Faculty Ratio: 8:1
Students in Parent Institution: 11,270
Academic Calendar: Semester

PROGRAMS

Degrees Offered: MBA (2 years full time), PhD in Management
Combined Degrees: MBA/JD with Yale Law School (4 years), MBD/MD with Yale Medical School (5 years), MBA/MARCH with Yale School of Architecture (4 years), MBA/MFA with Yale School of Drama (4 years), MBA/MSN with Yale Nursing School (3 years), MBA/MDIV or MAR with Yale Divinity School (3 years), MBA/MEM or MF in Environment with Yale School of Forestry and Environmental Studies (3 years), MBA/MPH with Yale School of Public Health (EPH) (3 years), MBA/MA in East Asian Studies, International Development Economics, International Relations, or Russia and East European Studies with Yale Graduate School of Arts and Sciences (3 years)
Academic Specialties: Finance, Accounting, Strategy, and overall, International and General Management
Special Opportunities: The Yale SOM-Goldman Sachs Foundation Partnership on Nonprofit Ventures is a new initiative at the Yale School of Management (SOM) that will launch a pioneering business plan competition for nonprofits (http://ventures.yale.edu/). The Yale School of Management Leaders Forum is one of the most prestigious speakers programs in a university setting (http://www.mba.yale.edu/mba_admissions/advisors/speakers2002-2003.asp). Sachem Ventures, LLC, is a new $1.5 million MBA-managed venture capital fund that is unique to the business school arena. Forty students—10% of the school—help manage the fund (http://www.sachemventures.com/). Y50K Entrepreneurship Competition: Sponsored by the Yale Entrepreneurial Society (YES), the competition awards a total of $100,000 to Yale students (http://www.yes.yale.edu/y50k.asp). Summer Internship Program in Entrepreneurship: The summer internship program enables students, under the guidance of faculty, to work on local entrepreneurial ventures. Students do in-depth market, product, and competitor research; create viable business strategies; write business plans; and find the initial human and financial resources needed to launch the business. The Connecticut Venture Group: This group supports investment in the state by providing a network and forum for those involved in creating high-growth enterprises. CVG also holds a business plan competition for graduate students. Yale SOM Outreach: This is a student-run group providing professional quality pro bono consulting assistance to a variety of nonprofit, public, and private organizations in the greater New Haven area (http://students.som.yale.edu/sigs/outreach/default.htm). Internship Fund: The first of its kind among the nation's business schools, the Internship Fund

provides financial support to students who pursue summer internships in the public and non-profit sector.

Study Abroad Options: Student accessibility to summer internships at leading organizations throughout the world. Summer internships are mandatory and the duration is approximately 3 months.

STUDENT INFORMATION

Total Business Students: 481
% Full Time: 100
% Female: 30
% Minority: 10
% International: 38
Average Age: 28

COMPUTER AND RESEARCH FACILITIES

Research Facilities: International Center for Finance (ICF) (http://icf.som.yale.edu/), International Institute for Corporate Governance (IICG) (http://iicg.som.yale.edu/), Partnership on Nonprofit Ventures (http://ventures.yale.edu/), Chief Executive Leadership Institute (CELI) (www.ceoleadership.com), Sachem Venture Capital Fund (www.sachemventures.com/)
Computer Facilities: See our website: www.som.yale.edu/ssl.
Campuswide Network? Yes
% of MBA Classrooms Wired: 100
Computer Model Recommended: Laptop
Internet Fee? No

EXPENSES/FINANCIAL AID

Annual Tuition: $32,500
Room & Board (On/Off Campus): $14,850
Books and Supplies: $1,650
Average Grant: $10,000
Average Loan: $44,128
% Receiving Financial Aid: 78

ADMISSIONS INFORMATION

Application Fee: $180
Electronic Application? Yes
Regular Application Deadline: 3/15
Regular Notification: 5/31
Deferment Available? Yes
Length of Deferment: 1 year
Non-fall Admissions? No
Transfer Students Accepted? No
Need-Blind Admissions? No
Number of Applications Received: 2,517
% of Applicants Accepted: 15
% Accepted Who Enrolled: 63
Average GPA: 3.5
GPA Range: 3.3-3.7
Average GMAT: 698
Average Years Experience: 5
Other Admissions Factors Considered: Academic potential, professional accomplishments, leadership qualities, entrepreneurial skills, personal values and goals
Minority/Disadvantaged Student Recruitment Programs: Minority recruitment is a vitally important priority for the Yale School of Management's admissions office. The school's comprehensive recruitment program includes: Minority MBA Workshops held in major cities nationwide; pre-MBA prep programs; scholarships; annual minority student receptions; Minority Student Weekend; participation in Destination MBA; the National Black MBA Association; the National Society of Hispanic MBAs Conference; Management Leadership for Tomorrow's mentoring program; collaboration with Yale SOM Black Business Alliance and Hispanic MBA Advisory Council, active student interest groups. Applicants are encouraged to visit the Minorities@YaleSOM section at http://mba.yale.edu for more information on these programs or to contact the school's Associate Director of Minority and Student Affairs.

Other Schools to Which Students Applied: Columbia University, Cornell University, Harvard University, New York University, Northwestern University, Stanford University, University of Pennsylvania

INTERNATIONAL STUDENTS

TOEFL Required of International Students? Yes
Minimum TOEFL: 600 (250 computer)

EMPLOYMENT INFORMATION

Placement Office Available? Yes
% Employed Within 3 Months: 76
Fields Employing Percentage of Grads: MIS (1%), Operations (2%), General Management (5%), Marketing (9%), Other (13%), Consulting (25%), Finance (45%)
Frequent Employers: American Express, Booz Allen & Hamilton, Credit Suisse First Boston, Deutsche Bank, General Electric, Goldman Sachs & Co., IBM, McKinsey & Co., Pricewaterhouse Coopers LLP, Standard & Poors
Prominent Alumni: John Thornton, Co-COO and president, Goldman Sachs; Nancy Peretsman, executive vice president and managing director, Allen & Co.; Indra Nooyi, president and CFO, PepsiCo Inc.; Fred Terrell, managing partner and CEO, Provender Capital Group; Thomas Krens, director, Solomon R. Guggenheim Foundation

See page 474.

Part IV

School Says . . .

In this section you'll find schools with extended listings describing admissions, curriculum, internships, and much more. This is your chance to get in-depth information on programs that interest you. The Princeton Review charges each school a small fee to be listed, and the editorial responsibility is solely that of the university.

AMERICAN UNIVERSITY

AT A GLANCE

Recognized by *BusinessWeek* in its rankings of top business schools, Kogod is positioning itself squarely in the upper echelons of America's finest business schools. Led by a new dean with a new vision, Kogod is recognized for special assets. These include a faculty with outstanding expertise in international business, well-placed graduates around the world, a leadership position in business information technology, and the competitive advantage of direct access to the financial and policy-making power of Washington, DC.

Theory and practice exist side by side in our classrooms. Our programs are enhanced with a range of unique business and academic partnerships. As a result, Kogod students become well-informed, highly skilled professionals, ready to compete and succeed in the global marketplace.

Five fundamental tenets are woven into every course, every activity, and every element of the Kogod degree programs. These are the promotion of a global orientation, the effective use of technology in business management, the integration of real-world business perspectives, a focus on professional skills, and an emphasis on the individual and community.

Combined with our traditional strengths, these attributes ensure that all graduate and undergraduate programs at Kogod track with contemporary business realities to produce effective business leaders for the next century.

LOCATION & ENVIRONMENT

The Kogod School of Business at American University is situated on a beautiful, 76-acre campus in one of the most desirable residential neighborhoods of Northwest Washington, DC. There are 37 buildings on campus, including the library, administration buildings, classroom buildings, residence halls, interdenominational religious center, and sports center. The campus boasts a luxurious, grassy quad, surrounded by well-landscaped natural areas, and distinguished buildings of notable architecture, many of which have been recently renovated.

There is a 24-hour computer center, plus 11 computer labs on campus, including the Kogod Computer Lab. Computers are loaded with business standard, as well as course- specific, software applications and provide high-speed Internet access. All labs are equipped with scanners and laser printers. Every dorm room has high-speed Internet access, as well. The campus has radio and TV studios, science labs, art studios, recital halls, and a theatre. The new home for the Kogod School of Business, located in the center of campus, opened in October 1999.

American University offers a unique access to our seat of government, foreign embassies, corporate headquarters, national and international institutions, museums, galleries, theatres, and parks. International business and political leaders often lecture at the university, and in many instances curricula are specifically designed to maximize our "Washington as global business and policy center" advantage.

PROGRAMS & CURRICULUM

The Kogod MBA program is a flexible, student-centered program. It provides a solid grounding in theory combined with the specific skills needed to manage in an environment of rapid technological development and tightly integrated international markets.

At Kogod, we prepare students for the realities of today's business world. Our graduates can meet the increasingly complex demands of employers. In particular, our MBA focuses on the managerial aspects of information technology and global business practices. Our redesigned graduate programs empower students to pursue two concentration programs.

First and Second Years

During the first year, students master the basics of each business function. They acquire analytical skills and optimize cross-functional understanding. Students meet regularly with professors to coordinate the content and assignments in the core curriculum modules, and to ensure that they possess the skills necessary to move forward.

In the second year, the focus shifts to the particulars of the selected concentration(s). Course work will investigate societal and ethical standards, as well as the legal and ethical issues confronting global business managers.

Capstone Course Work

The capstone course—"Applied Strategic Management in a Global Environment" (MGMT 624)—provides the opportunity to work in a small team to analyze a real company's external environment, perform an internal strategic management audit, and develop a strategic plan for operating in a competitive global environment.

In the final semester, students have the opportunity to expand upon the classroom experience with an extended field practicum. This practicum is a consulting team project arranged and supervised by a faculty advisor.

As part of a cross-functional team, students apply their expertise and creativity to a real-world problem for a local, national, or international business. Together with a team, they meet with company managers, identify key issues, develop solutions, and recommend actions.

Teamwork

Teamwork shapes graduate studies at Kogod. Students develop a strong sense of camaraderie with classmates. The MBA program is diverse in educational background, profession, and culture. The diverse perspectives of classmates provide valuable insights into the realities of today's global marketplace.

The Kogod MBA is a 51-credit-hour program, including 31.5 credit hours of required courses, and 19.5 credit hours of electives. Students entering the full-time program in the fall semester should complete the curriculum in 21 months.

Up to nine credit hours of course work from economics, accounting, organizational behavior, and statistics may be waived if students have taken equivalent course work at the undergraduate level in the past seven years and received grades of B or better.

Up to nine credit hours of course work may be transferred from an AACSB-accredited MBA program. These courses must have been completed in the past seven years with a grade of B or better.

The 19.5-elective credit hours allow students to declare up to two concentrations. Concentrations may be designed from course work taken through other academic units of American University. However, no more than 12 credit hours may be taken in any one area of concentration, and no more than 9 credit hours may be taken outside of the Kogod School of Business (with the exception of dual or joint degree programs).

MBA students may take a maximum of six credit hours in 500-level courses or graduate courses that meet concurrently with undergraduate courses.

Intensive Writing Requirement

Students must earn a grade of B or better in six credits from a combination of the following courses:

MGMT-624 Applied Strategic Management in a Global Environment (3)

MGMT-622 Business, Ethics, and Society (3) or ACCT-623 Business Law (3)

IBUS-618 Manager in the International Economy (3)

FACILITIES & EQUIPMENT

Premier schools require premier facilities. We are proud to unveil such a facility at Kogod.

The Kogod School of Business is situated in the center of American University's beautiful 76-acre campus. This modern, state-of-the-art business education center is worthy of the programs it houses.

Top Technology

The Kogod building is specially designed for easy interaction between students and faculty. It features tiered, executive style classrooms, and high-tech team conference rooms. Seminar rooms and meeting spaces, as well as classrooms, are fully wired for all telecommunications needs, including teleconferencing events.

The Kogod building reflects the school's commitment to quality. It incorporates cutting- edge information technology applications for the fields of accounting, human resources, entrepreneurship, and marketing and management strategy. Not only does it consolidate all Kogod business programs under one roof for the first time, but it also enables Kogod to provide an appealing classroom environment for students and faculty.

Kogod College of Business Administration

The First-Floor Plan

The plans for the building provide opportunities for expanded executive education programs and business partnerships. The executive training classroom has multimedia and telecommunications equipment for high-quality presentations, and future technological improvements, including video teleconferencing. Events and seminars —e.g., the Family Business Forum and Personal Investing Series— will be significantly enhanced because of these special rooms.

The executive-style lounge, reception hall, and Graduate Placement Center Office all provide a highly professional environment for corporate recruitment, interviews, and VIP functions.

The Second-Floor Plan

The dean's reception area and office suite, including administrative support areas and program offices, are housed on this floor. Corporate partners, business and government leaders, and alumni will be very comfortable working with the dean, program directors, Kogod faculty, and staff in these surroundings.

The Terrace Floor Plan

Each year Kogod students participate in the Kogod Case Competition, assisting Washington area businesses with evolving management issues. The terrace level includes an MBA case study room. This room is used for presentations during the competition, and by the businesses that benefit from the students' analyses. The case study room also functions as a seminar room.

The terrace level also provides a student lounge, additional breakout conference rooms, and faculty offices. Because Kogod is committed to enhancing students' interaction with faculty, the design of this level puts faculty offices near classrooms and aligns the student lounge with student government offices.

The Kogod School of Business provides students, faculty, administrators, alumni, and business partners with the best academic business facility in Washington, DC.

EXPENSES & FINANCIAL AID

Costs 2003–2004

The tuition fee for students enrolled in the MBA program of Kogod School of Business of American University is $12,154 per semester for full-time students, $899 per credit hour for 9-13 credit hours, and $877 per credit hour for fewer than 9 credits.

Graduate Student Fees

- Student Activity fee (all students): $25 per semester
- Sports Center fee (full-time students): $65 per semester
- Sports Center fee (part-time students): $30 per semester
- Technology fee (full-time students) $55 per semester
- Technology fee (part-time students) $20 per semester

Living and Housing Costs

Although many graduate students live off campus, the University provides graduate dormitory rooms and apartments. The Off-Campus Housing Office maintains a referral file of rooms and apartments.

Financial Aid

The Kogod School of Business and American University offer a wide range of financial assistance programs. In fact, more than 25 percent of full-time AU graduate students receive merit-based fellowships and assistantships. We are also proud of the exceptional number of scholarships awarded to international students.

Graduate study scholarships and graduate assistantships are available to full-time students. Special opportunity awards for members of U.S. minority groups parallel the regular honor awards and take the form of assistantships and scholarships.

FACULTY

Kogod's reputation is greatly enhanced by our faculty of internationally recognized scholars. Like our student population, this distinguished group represents virtually every corner of the world.

These full-time scholars possess superior academic credentials. They are universally committed to upholding high standards of teaching and to supporting students in developing state-of-the-art solutions to real problems facing industry today.

Many of our faculty members serve as consultants to major corporations around the world; others consult with various sectors of government or are actively engaged in research.

STUDENTS

Today's business environment is much more demanding than ever before. To succeed requires not only exceptional academic skills, but also a well-developed business acumen and substantial leadership experience. The Kogod School of Business gives all students the opportunity to get involved, become effective leaders, and recognize individual and organizational achievements.

Kogod offers many organizations and clubs that stress student empowerment and involvement. These organizations make the graduate school experience more rewarding. Whether students choose to run for office in the Graduate Business Association (GBA), chair a student-run committee, or just become a member of a club that suits their interests, there is definitely something for everyone.

Remember that life at Kogod is what you make it. Aside from the rigorous academic program, students should take the opportunity to network with alumni and potential employers, interact with fellow students outside the classroom, and prepare themselves for a rewarding career.

ADMISSIONS

The application for the Kogod School of Business is an electronic process. An online application can be completed at www.kogod.american.edu. In addition to this online application for graduate admission, applicants also need to send a personal statement, two letters of recommendation, official transcripts from all undergraduate and graduate institutions in sealed envelopes, Personal and Immigration Request Form (international applicants only) along with financial documentation, and $60 (U.S.) application fee (do not send cash). Applications without fees will not be processed, and there are no fee waivers. In addition, the official Educational Testing Service copy of test scores should be sent to American University (ETS code 5007). Resumes can be sent via U.S. mail or email to mbakogod@american.edu.

ADDITIONAL INFORMATION

Like many MBA programs, American University boasts an emphasis on the hot topics in today's MBA market—global business and information technology. But with its prime Washington, DC location, and proximity to tech powerhouses in Virginia and Maryland such as AOL, American is well positioned to deliver on that promise. Come ready for cultural interaction—more than 40 percent of the student body is international—and leadership opportunities galore. In an unusual democratic twist, American expects its students to contribute to the running of the program.

CAREER SERVICES & PLACEMENT

Preparation for life after graduation begins on the first day at Kogod, and we offer a number of services to help make our graduates' employment search as successful as possible. Our services include the following:

- One-on-one career counseling
- Professional development workshops
- Corporate presentations and on-campus recruitment
- Career fairs
- gradSOURCE, a Web-based career management database
- Industry and career panels
- Alumni career networking events
- Mock interview program and self-assessment tools
- Corporate site visits
- Executive mentoring program
- Internship program

ARIZONA STATE UNIVERSITY

AT A GLANCE

Today's managers face an increasingly global landscape that is continuously transformed by technology. This dynamic environment presents opportunity, but also challenge, as managers grapple with the demands of efficiency, quality, and profit. The W. P. Carey MBA at Arizona State University (ASU) prepares students for this exciting world by grounding with business essentials and teaching MBA candidates to develop specialized knowledge based on career goals.

The intensive first year of the W. P. Carey MBA is an integrated academic experience that builds advanced managerial knowledge and skills, essential for a successful career. The second year specializations, with their elective options, fill the immediate need for value-added expertise that students can offer an employer upon graduation. The W. P. Carey MBA emphasizes experiential, applied knowledge, and best practices from a faculty with a wealth of cumulative experience and scholarship.

Alumni of the W. P. Carey MBA program repeatedly say that they were well prepared for their next step after graduation, and that the training they received at W. P. Carey has continued to fuel professional advancement years later.

In January 2003, ASU's School of Business received a gift of $50 million, endowing the W. P. Carey School of Business. This endowment—the second largest single gift to any U.S. business school—is validation of the W. P. Carey School's consistent record of excellence in business education and research. Benefit from this vibrant academic institution located in one of the largest urban centers in the U.S.

LOCATION & ENVIRONMENT

The main campus is located in the metropolitan Phoenix area, one of the fastest-growing population centers in the country. A mix of leading high technology firms, a robust real estate and financial sector, and services for business and consumers characterizes the local economy. The sun shines more than 300 days of the year, and the area is known as a world-class destination for tourists seeking a combination of business and recreation. Phoenix also serves as a gateway to many unique geographical and outdoor opportunities in the "four-corner states" and California. Students can experience the Grand Canyon, Colorado River, southern Utah's Bryce and Zion National Parks, skiing, hiking, mountain biking, and rock climbing, among many other activities. ASU is one of the nation's ten largest universities.

With nearly 50,000 students from all states and more than 120 countries, ASU is a diverse scholarly environment, and a center for cultural and social activities.

W. P. Carey School of Business

Within the past decade, the school of business at ASU has emerged as one of the leading public business schools in the country. The school's recent endowment of $50 million from New York real estate investment banker, Wm. Polk Carey, is an indisputable endorsement of its consistent track record of innovation and excellence.

The W. P. Carey School of Business has been accredited for more than 40 years by AACSB International—The Association to Advance Collegiate Schools of Business. It offers highly ranked undergraduate degrees, doctoral degrees, and professional master's degrees, including the internationally respected W. P. Carey MBA.

The W. P. Carey MBA has been consistently recognized by such publications as *U.S. News & World Report*, *BusinessWeek* and *Financial Times*. There are more that 1,000 students pursuing the W. P. Carey MBA degree.

DEGREES OFFERED

The W. P. Carey School of Business offers the Master of Business Administration degree with the option to focus on one area of specialization or dual degree.

U.S. News & World Report ranks three W. P. Carey MBA programs in the top 25 nationally—supply chain management is 5th, with information systems at 17th, and accounting at 20th.

Specialization and dual degree choices include:

Supply Chain Management: W. P. Carey is a recognized global leader in a field that provides deep experience and expertise in the strategic planning and integration of global information and processes across all functions.

Financial Management and Markets: Builds skills in the management of business and financial risk, investment decisions, and resource allocation for the most positive impact on shareholder value—all with a primary focus on corporate finance

Services Marketing and Management: An internationally renowned specialization that promotes profitable market advantage through enhanced management of customer relationships, and the quality of services provided

Sports Business: Delivers practical experience, advanced business skills, and an understanding of industry dynamics required to finance, manage, and market a broad range of sports products and services

Information Management: A dual degree choice from a global leader in strategic technology management that consistently ranks among the leaders in e-business strategy and leveraged technology

Health Services Administration: A dual degree program that bundles together the benefits of the W. P. Carey MBA core with a health administration curriculum, plus a second year specialization

Other Dual Degrees: Students may also take advantage of our additional dual degree options. In most cases, requirements for both degrees can be completed in two years. Options include Master of International Management, in cooperation with Thunderbird—The American Graduate School of International Management; Master of Science in Economics; Master of Accountancy and Information Systems; Master of Taxation; Master of Architecture; and Juris Doctorate

PROGRAMS & CURRICULUM

The W. P. Carey MBA is an enriching educational experience, providing lifelong value. The program builds and strengthens knowledge, skills, and managerial abilities by means of technical, analytical, and case materials that inform about the functional areas of business.

Integrated, flexible, and wide-breadth characterize the objectives of the W. P. Carey MBA curriculum. Students benefit increasingly from greater cross-disciplinary opportunities, while the depth of specialization course work is maintained.

During the first year, students acquire fundamental business management knowledge. The core curriculum stresses collaboration and teamwork, analysis, ethical decision- making, and written and oral communication. Workshop series held in the first year are designed to ensure class-wide mastery of requisite business skills, allowing subsequent courses to begin at a more advanced level. Other courses prepare students to recognize and appreciate the relationships among the business disciplines taught in required core courses.

In the second year, students prepare for careers in pivotal fields such as services marketing and management, supply chain management, financial management and markets, and sports business. Others take advantage of dual degree opportunities including information management, health services administration, economics, accountancy and taxation.

W. P. Carey MBA students tailor their specialization or dual degree with elective hours that complement their career aspirations. The W. P. Carey MBA curriculum is delivered in four eight-week terms per academic year, allowing students more flexibility for elective course work.

Students put their new knowledge into practice through applied projects, business presentations and case competitions. W. P. Carey MBAs participate in two major case competitions each year. First and second year students, with diverse work experience as well as cross-disciplinary career interests, team together creating an effective incubator for real-world project experience, and allowing students to develop leadership skills.

Between the first and second years of the program, students are strongly encouraged to complete a summer internship. An internship opportunity not only allows students to apply their new skills, but internships can play a large part in retaining full-time employment after graduation.

FACILITIES & EQUIPMENT

The W. P. Carey School of Business is housed in two buildings that contain an

W. P. Carey School of Business

auditorium, lecture halls, seminar rooms, faculty, administrative, and graduate offices, several computer resource centers, and a coffee house.

As a longstanding leader in developing technological facilities, the W. P. Carey School completed a $6.9 million renovation project in 2001. The business complex is now equipped with wireless access points throughout its two buildings, including the external patio and fountain areas. Citrix Thin Client servers allow students to use complex software programs wirelessly, as well as remotely, from home or office.

The renovation also included upgrades to the Ford Graduate Suite. A dedicated resource for graduate business students, the graduate suite includes a student center, eight fully mediated team rooms, two computer labs, open study areas with data ports for laptops, and student organization offices.

The school of business is home to the L. William Seidman Research Institute, whose affiliated centers and programs conduct specialized research on business topics such as entrepreneurship, economics, finance, quality, and knowledge management. The institute is an instrumental student resource for current research in the pivotal business disciplines of the twenty-first century.

Close to the business complex is ASU's Charles Trumbull Hayden Library. One of the largest research libraries in North America, Hayden Library contains more than 2.9 million volumes, including many in business and economics, and the specialized Arthur C. Young Tax Collection. The school of business is strategically located next to the Student Recreation Center (SRC), which consists of 135,000 square feet of indoor activity space, various outdoor fields and court space, and two pools.

EXPENSES & FINANCIAL AID

Estimated tuition and fees for 2003–2004 are $13,295 for Arizona residents and $21,815 for nonresidents. Books and supplies average $2,100 per year. Most W. P. Carey MBA students live off-campus in nearby apartment complexes, and married couples find suitable housing in the local community. Average rents for apartments range from $550 to $800 (one to two bedrooms) per month. On-campus residential facilities are available on a limited basis for graduate students, and cost from $3,500-$4,300 annually.

The W. P. Carey MBA is fortunate to have a well-endowed array of financial resources. These include grants, fellowships, scholarships, assistantships and out-of-state tuition waivers available to students based on various criteria, including need and merit. Approximately 95 percent of last year's entering class received at least one scholarship award. The PepsiCo Scholarship is a "full ride" award for under represented students.

FACULTY

There are more than 179 full-time faculty that are members of the W. P. Carey School of Business.

Faculty travel the globe to present research in leading conferences. These scholars also develop new knowledge through research, consulting, and other interactions with major corporations. They bring their intellectual energy and real-world research experiences to bear on the school's business curriculum and student experience—shaping new business and community leaders.

Their efforts have helped ASU to earn the highest research designation awarded by the Carnegie Foundation's Classification of Institutions of Higher Education.

STUDENTS

Students attending the W. P. Carey MBA have diverse academic and geographic backgrounds. In the fall of 2002 entering class, the average age is 28, with 4.4 years of professional, post-baccalaureate work experience. Most incoming students hold a bachelor's degree in either business or science.

Students may join an array of organizations in order to develop a network of peers. All students are members of the W. P. Carey MBA Association. In addition, students may belong to other W. P. Carey MBA organizations such as the Admissions Committee, Black Student Association, Entrepreneurs Club, Finance Association, Graduate Latin Business Exchange, Graduate Women In Business, International Business Association, Investment Management Fund, Managers of Information Technology and E-Business, Masters Consulting Group, MBAsia, Student Ambassadors, Supply Chain Management Association, and the Volunteer Council. Other important aspects of the program include working on field projects and summer internships.

ADMISSIONS

To better meet the logistical challenges of our worldwide applicant pool, the W. P. Carey MBA accepts applications only through its web-based ASU Graduate College online application. For information or to begin an application, go to wpcareymba.asu.edu/apply.

Application submission target dates are January 1, February 1 (for international applicants) and May 1. The W. P. Carey MBA is on rolling admissions and will review applications until all seats are filled. Admission is for the fall term only.

Application to the W. P. Carey MBA is open to individuals with at least two years of full-time work experience who hold a bachelor's degree, or its equivalent, in any discipline from an accredited college or university.

The W. P. Carey MBA Admissions Committee looks for well-rounded individuals with leadership skills, strong academic credentials, managerial experience or potential, and the ability to contribute to the diversity of the class. Transcripts, GMAT scores, TOEFL scores (for international students), work history, essay questions, letters of recommendation, and a required interview all influence the admission decision.

In the fall 2002 entering class, the average age was 28, with 4.4 years of professional, post-baccalaureate work experience. The class averaged a GPA of 3.42 on a 4.0 scale, a GMAT score of 654 and a TOEFL score of 630 (paper based)/276 (computer based).

Due to the high volume of applications and the limited size of the entering class, students are strongly encouraged to apply as early as possible.

ADDITIONAL INFORMATION

Students may combine the globally recognized W. P. Carey MBA core curriculum with specialized training in international management during their second year of study.

The W. P. Carey School has developed several partnerships with outstanding institutions abroad. These include:

- ESC Toulouse, Toulouse, France
- Universidad Carlos III de Madrid, Madrid, Spain
- Instituto Technologico Y De Estudios Superiores De Monterrey, Campus Estado de Mexico (ITESM-CEM), Mexico City, Mexico
- Escuela de Administracion de Negocios Para Graduados, Lima, Peru

The "very quick" trimester academic calendar at Arizona State University makes the MBA program a bit hectic, but "an enormous number of companies recruit here"—especially from the Southwest—and students leave "well-equipped to work with top level executives, as well as loading dock or field representatives." Also, "living in Phoenix is great," and Computerworld recently ranked ASU's joint degree program in information management at 15th in the nation.

CAREER SERVICES & PLACEMENT

Despite the downturn in the economy, 2002 W. P. Carey MBA graduates did extremely well, attaining an employment rate of 85 percent by three months after graduation.

Students partner with the Graduate Career Management Center at the W. P. Carey School of Business to learn how to develop a personalized career management plan, expand effective self marketing skills, investigate and interact with prospective employers, and manage their own job search.

The Graduate Career Management Center and ASU Career Services partner with more than 100 companies that schedule on-campus interviews annually. Resources offered by the Graduate Career Management Center to help students compete successfully in the employment marketplace include individual career consulting, professional development seminars, and networking opportunities with regional business professionals. In 2002, the average salary of the W. P. Carey MBA graduate was $74,518.

BABSON COLLEGE

AT A GLANCE

Educating The World's Future Entrepreneurial Leaders

The Franklin W. Olin Graduate School of Business at Babson College is committed to educating entrepreneurial leaders. Entrepreneurial leadership is a way of thinking and acting to create opportunities. Recognized as the world leader in entrepreneurial education, and as a leader in integrated curriculum design, Babson is a very special place to study. Students are noted for their creativity, teamwork, and ability to see business problems from a holistic perspective. I know that as you read more about Babson, you will want to become a part of this unique educational community.

— Mark P. Rice, The Murata Dean

LOCATION & ENVIRONMENT

Babson College, founded in 1919 by financier and entrepreneur Roger W. Babson, is located on a 450-acre wooded site in Wellesley, Massachusetts—just 12 miles from Boston. Boston and the surrounding region offer a pleasing and exciting environment with a rich artistic, historic, and intellectual life.

DEGREES OFFERED

Babson offers a Master of Business Administration degree.

PROGRAMS & CURRICULUM

All programs emphasize the global aspects of business and the value of the entrepreneurial spirit.

The Two-Year MBA program is an integrated curriculum stressing opportunity recognition, innovation, and creative problem solving. With an emphasis on teamwork, first year course work and activities take students through each step of the business development cycle, while using varied approaches to address innovation as a strategic tool, entrepreneurial thinking, quality as a competitive advantage, the importance of having a global advantage, and the value of leadership. The highlight of the first year is the Babson Consulting Alliance Program, which assigns student teams to year-long projects with local businesses. The second year (30 credit hours) is designed to build upon the first-year course work, allowing students to focus their interests with elective courses.

The one-year MBA is an accelerated program that allows students with an undergraduate business degree to complete their MBA in three rigorous full-time semesters. Beginning each May, students enroll in a series of integrated modules during the first semester, and then join the second year MBA students to complete the equivalent of fifteen courses in one calendar year. Candidates who work in the Boston area may complete the summer modules full-time, return to work in September, and finish the remainder of the program on a part-time basis in two years.

For working professionals, the redesigned Evening MBA program begins each fall and spring, and builds on a more compact core of eight courses, four of which are fully integrated. These integrated courses feature a cross-disciplinary approach designed to encourage students to analyze how management works. The new Evening MBA program not only provides increased flexibility, but also enables students to complete the degree in approximately three years.

The new Fast-Track MBA program is a hybrid format MBA program that enables students to earn their MBA in 27 months while remaining on the job. Blending in-person and online instruction, the course work and activities trace the business development cycle—from recognizing and assessing a business opportunity and formulating a strategy, to creating and implementing the delivery system, and finally, to evolving the strategy and systems as conditions change over time.

FACILITIES & EQUIPMENT

Babson students have access to an extensive business collection of print, media, and electronic resources. A staff of professionals is available to help students find the information they need and to offer instruction in the use of those databases on which business practitioners rely.

Some of the information resources available electronically include newspapers, trade journals, investment analysis reports, corporate financials and directories, and international business information. The following are just a few of the electronic services available: Dow Jones/Factiva, FirstSearch, Infotrac, Lexis-Nexis, ProQuest, and Bloomberg.

The library also has a collection of books on business and liberal arts topics, daily business and general newspapers, and magazines and academic journals covering the full range of business activity. These resources are complemented by other media items and a room within the library where they can be viewed and heard. Students seeking rooms where they can work individually or in groups can use the study rooms equipped with projection or plasma screen units, desktop computers, white boards, and speaker telephones. Throughout the library, students can connect to library resources and the Babson network with wireless laptop connections.

The library also houses the Stephen D. Cutler Investment Management Center, where fifteen computer workstations are equipped with state-of-the-art investment software. Bloomberg, SDC Platinum, Datastream, and Compustat Research Insight are a few of the electronic services that provide market information to Babson students, just as they do to investment professionals. The center is used continuously throughout the day by individual students, groups of students, entire classes, and faculty members.

The Horn Computer Center is equipped with 150 computer workstations that run a diversified library of business-oriented programs in a Windows environment. The Horn center operates a 24-hour computer lab. A wireless network is in place in the Horn Library and Olin Hall. Most classrooms are equipped with computer projection hardware. Babson expects that entering students are comfortable with basic spreadsheet and word processing operations.

EXPENSES & FINANCIAL AID

Nine-month academic year cost estimates for 2003–2004 for the Two-Year MBA program are $28,344 for tuition, $1900 for books and supplies, and $15,004 for living expenses.

Tuition for the One-Year MBA program is $39,672. Per credit tuition for the Evening MBA program is $856. The pre-MBA for international students costs $1,000. Merit programs that award scholarships include Babson Fellows, Olin Fellows, Babson Fellowships for Students of Color, Olin Scholarships, and Babson Scholars.

FACULTY

Babson's faculty is an internationally and professionally diverse group, representing nations in Asia, Australia, Europe, and North and South America, and with backgrounds in pharmaceutical, banking, high technology, retailing, and other industries. They are practitioners and scholars, executives and teachers, and researchers and consultants who have lived and worked in international settings.

F.W. Olin Graduate School of Business

STUDENTS

Students in the Two-Year MBA program are, on average, 28 years old and have about five years of work experience. GMAT scores range from 550-770. Women comprise 23 percent of the class. Students come from such diverse industries as banking and investment institutions to advertising, biotechnology, publishing, telecommunications, and high technology.

International students compose 30 percent of MBA enrollment. The pre-MBA orientation for international students begins two weeks before Module I classes. This intensive program consists of familiarization with the campus, library, computer center, and other services and workshops. Also, Babson faculty members present a basic introduction to economics, marketing, and the case method. Recreational and social events are scheduled. International students may apply for a U.S. internship and are eligible for the Global Management Program.

ADMISSIONS

Students are admitted to the program based on a careful evaluation of academic records, professional qualifications, GMAT scores, and personal attributes. Interviews are required for admission to full-time MBA programs. The current class has GMAT scores in the 550-770 range, and the average undergraduate GPA is 3.1. International students must submit TOEFL results and official English translations of all academic documents. All candidates should have strong mathematics, computer, economics, and business writing skills.

Application deadlines for the Two-Year MBA program are November 30, January 31, March 15, and April 15; for the One-Year MBA program, October 31, November 30 and January 31; and for the Evening MBA program, October 15 and November 15 for spring admission, and May 15, June 15, and July 15 for fall admission. Decisions are mailed four to six weeks after each deadline.

For more information, applicants should contact:

Office of Graduate Admission
F. W. Olin Graduate School of Business
Babson Park, Massachusetts 02157- 0310
Telephone: 781-239-4317
800-488-4512 (toll-free within the U.S.)
Fax: 781-239-4194
E-mail: mbaadmission@babson.edu
World Wide Web: www.babson.edu/mba

ADDITIONAL INFORMATION

Global business perspectives are not new at Babson. An international concentration is available and requires bilingualism, participation in a Global Management Program, and completion of required and elective international courses. The Global Management Program places students in structured field consulting projects with corporations in Asia, Australia, Europe, and South America. International electives combine intensive classroom experience with industry-based projects in international settings. International internships, electives, and study abroad opportunities satisfy the Two-Year MBA program's cross cultural requirement and are open to students in all Babson MBA programs.

Babson fosters the entrepreneurial spirit through a variety of activities and opportunities. These include electives, endowed chairs in entrepreneurship, induction of innovative business people into the Academy of Distinguished Entrepreneurs on Founder's Day, the Douglass Foundation Entrepreneurial Prizes, and the Babson Entrepreneurial Exchange—a student-run network of current and future entrepreneurs who exchange information about business development and venture opportunities.

Successful business partnerships have always been a major component of Babson programs. First year student teams consult with Boston area organizations through the year-long Babson Consulting Alliance Program. The Management Consulting Field Experience offers a variety of second year consulting projects.

Babson College enjoys a reputation of being synonymous with entrepreneurial studies. Budding capitalists here enjoy "outstanding" course offerings, abundant opportunities for "in-the-field" learning, and access to the many perks of the "entrepreneurial incubator space" in newly built Olin Hall. Other highlights include a "tough, fun," and "committed" faculty, and a Business Mentor Program, which allows students to work as consultants for companies in the Boston area.

CAREER SERVICES & PLACEMENT

Made up of a staff of six professionals, the Center for Career Development offers a career management curriculum that is integrated into the first year course work, and is required for all full-time students; an online professional development survey of work experience and interests, allowing the staff to direct students to internship and employment opportunities; internships offering either stipends or course credit; job fairs; and online alumni and employer databases.

BARUCH COLLEGE/CITY UNIVERSITY OF NEW YORK

AT A GLANCE

The Zicklin School of Business is the largest collegiate school of business in the nation and the only CUNY unit that offers business programs accredited by the AACSB—International Association for Management Education. The Zicklin School offers degree programs leading to the BBA, MBA, Executive MBA, MS, Executive MS in Finance, and the Baruch/Mt. Sinai MBA in Health Care Administration, which is accredited by the Accrediting Commission on Education for Health Care Administration (ACEHSA). Among its exciting new initiatives are the Zicklin Full-Time MBA program, which enrolls a select group of candidates, whose credentials and average GMAT scores of 647 place them among the top students in the nation. Its combined five-year undergraduate/MS degree program in accountancy meets the latest education requirements for the CPA exam. The Zicklin School houses City University's PhD in Business, and offers a joint degree program leading to the JD/MBA degrees in conjunction with both Brooklyn Law School and The New York Law School.

In 1998, the Zicklin School of Business was named in appreciation for a generous endowment from alumnus and financier, Lawrence Zicklin, class of 1957.

LOCATION & ENVIRONMENT

With a prime location in Manhattan's historic Gramercy Park neighborhood, and the leading edge Flatiron District, Baruch is at the heart of one of the world's most dynamic business and cultural centers—within easy reach of Wall Street, "Silicon Alley," and the headquarters of major business, financial firms, and non-profit organizations. This real-world environment adds immeasurably to the value of a Baruch education, and offers unparalleled internship and career opportunities. The campus extends from East 22nd Street to East 26th Street (Madison and Third Avenues), and is surrounded by a variety of ethnic restaurants and stores of all kinds. All of New York City's museums, theaters, concert halls, clubs, sports arenas, and beaches are easily accessible by public transportation.

DEGREES OFFERED

The Zicklin School offers degree programs leading to the BBA, MBA, Executive MBA, MS, Executive MS in Finance, and the Baruch/Mt. Sinai MBA in Health Care Administration, which is accredited by the Accrediting Commission on Education for Health Care Administration (ACEHSA).

PROGRAMS & CURRICULUM

Zicklin's premier program is the full-time Honors MBA, a very selective honors format that evolved from the successful Jack Nash Honors MBA program. The MBA is also offered in an accelerated part-time format for those who wish to complete their degree in 28 months while continuing to work, and the flex-time format for full- or part-time students who need a wider range of options in scheduling their graduate study. Twenty courses (57 credits) are required. The 12-course core curriculum is designed to provide students with an understanding of the basic principles of both management, and the environment in which managerial decisions are made. Courses include accountancy, economics, finance, behavioral sciences, quantitative methods, statistics, information systems, production, and marketing.

Supplementing the core are 12 credits of elective courses, including one international elective. Beyond the core, students can specialize in accountancy, computer information systems, economics, entrepreneurship, finance and investments, health care administration, industrial/organizational psychology, international business, management, marketing, operations research, statistics, or taxation.

Those who wish to design their own MBA programs can select unique, cross-disciplinary combinations of courses to fulfill the 12-credit specialization requirement. These combinations are useful for students interested in careers in such fields as marketing in financial institutions or banking operations. A few examples of the many specialization courses available to students are Futures and Forwards Markets, Options Markets, Mergers and Acquisitions, International Trade and Investment Law, International Commodity Trading, International Corporate Finance, Computer Simulation for Solving Business Problems, Product Planning and Development, and Entrepreneurial Ventures.

Students who wish to do a double major can add one additional elective course to create a second four-course major. The Zicklin School also offers a strategic management Executive MBA, as well as Executive MS programs in finance and industrial, and labor relations.

FACILITIES & EQUIPMENT

The College has just moved into a 17 floor academic complex that is now the home of the Zicklin School. The award winning design encloses modern, multimedia equipped classrooms, all faculty offices, two large production level theaters, a fitness center with a gym and swimming pool, a television studio, and an enhanced Center for Student Life.

Baruch's Information and Technology Building, which opened on East 25th Street in 1994, houses The William and Anita Newman Library, the Baruch Computing and Technology Center (which includes 400 computer workstations in an open access lab), student and administrative offices, and a state-of-the-art multimedia center.

More than three times the size of its predecessor, the 1,450-seat library has local area networks that provide access to a wide variety of electronic information resources. Students and faculty members can access the Internet and hundreds of online databases through the Dow Jones News/Retrieval, Lexis-Nexis, and Dialog services, in addition to its traditional holdings. The Baruch community also has access to the 4.5 million volumes in the CUNY library system and to the collections of the New York Public Library.

In March 2000, Baruch opened the Subotnick Financial Services Center/Bert W. and Sandra Wasserman Trading Floor, a unique educational facility for students and the financial community that features a fully equipped, simulated trading environment with continuous live data feeds by Reuters, integrating financial services practice into the MBA curriculum.

EXPENSES & FINANCIAL AID

Tuition for New York State residents for the fall 2003 term was $3,750 per semester for full-time, and $330 per credit for part-time MBA study; $2,720 per semester for full-time and $230 per credit for part-time MS study.

For out-of-state residents and international students, tuition was $555 per credit for full or part-time MBA study, and $425 per credit for full or part-time MS study. Tuition and fees are subject to change without notice. Average estimated annual cost for books, supplies, transportation, and personal expenses is $13,000 per year.

Financial aid is available and is merit-based. Honors MBA tuition scholarships of $2,000 to $4,000 per year are awarded to 20-25 of the most qualified students in the full-time Honors MBA program. Graduate assistantships require 12 hours of work for a faculty member or administrative area each week for a $5,000 annual stipend. They are awarded primarily to honors students, and do not include a tuition waiver. International students are eligible for both Honors scholarships and graduate assistantships.

In the fall, the Mitsui USA Foundation awards two annual scholarships of $5,000 each to newly admitted full-time students pursuing an MBA degree in international business. Applicants for the Mitsui Scholarships must be United States citizens or permanent residents. The Carl Spielvogel Scholarship offers an annual award of $5,000 in the fall to newly admitted full-time students pursuing an MBA degree in international marketing.

Financial aid is also available to graduate students through other sources, including various state, federal, and college programs. International students are not eligible for most of these programs.

Zicklin School of Business

FACULTY

The faculty of the Zicklin School of Business is large, distinguished, and diverse. They include noted scholars, authors, sought after consultants, and master teachers. They hold advanced degrees from such prestigious institutions as Harvard, MIT, Columbia, Stanford, Northwestern, Chicago, New York University, Cornell, Berkeley, Yale, Dartmouth, Michigan, UCLA, Indiana, Texas, Oxford, Princeton, Cal Tech, Duke, Georgetown, and other world class universities.

Through their important work, the Zicklin School provides ideas and solutions for a rapidly changing global business environment. Among the many who are internationally recognized authorities in their fields, the Zicklin faculty include:

- S. Prakash Sethi, University Distinguished Professor of Management, who serves as a consultant for Mattel Inc. and helped the company establish a worldwide code of conduct and monitoring plan

- Robert A. Schwartz, University Distinguished Professor of Economics and Finance, an expert in securities markets, microstructure, and the electronic call auction

- Yoshihiro Tsurumi, a scholar in the fields of industrial policy, international transfer of technology, and global business, and a leading consultant to many government and multinational firms and the International Monetary Fund

- June O'Neill, the Wollman Professor of Economics and Director of the Center for the Study of Business and Government at Baruch, who served as the director of the U.S. Congressional Budget Office from 1995-1999

Many faculty members are regularly called upon for expert commentary by such media outlets as the *Wall Street Journal*, the *Washington Post, Crain's New York Business, USA Today,* CNBC, and CNN.

See our website at http://aux.zicklin.baruch.cuny.edu/hires/for the bios of our newest faculty members.

STUDENTS

Baruch's reputation for excellence extends to all parts of the world, attracting students from New York, neighboring states, and abroad. The cohort style MBA program offers students the option of full-time or part-time study. Full-time students complete the degree program in two years; part-time students average four years. The diverse group of men and women doing graduate work at Baruch hold undergraduate degrees from more than 200 colleges and universities. There are more than 400 international graduate students, who represent approximately 50 countries.

The average graduate student is 28 years old. At least two years of full-time work experience before applying is strongly encouraged. Many MBA students at Baruch have undergraduate degrees in business, but the majority have majored in liberal arts, the sciences, or engineering. Professional experience varies widely. Forty percent of the students are women, while members of minority groups represent almost 30 percent of the student body. International students make up close to 50 percent of the full-time MBA student population.

The Baruch degree is highly valued. Graduates may be found at all levels in business, industry, and public life. Notable graduates include Laura Altschuler, President, New York City League of Women Voters; the Honorable Abraham D. Beame, former Mayor of the City of New York; Lawrence Zicklin, Chairman of the Board, Neuberger Berman Inc.; Matthew Blank, Chairman of the Board and CEO, Showtime Networks; Irving Schneider, Vice Chairman, Helmsley Spear; and Sally Guido, CEO, Lee Myles.

ADMISSIONS

Applicants for any program must take the GMAT. The average student admitted into the program in 2002–2003 had a GMAT score of 607 and an undergraduate grade point average of 3.2. For the full-time Honors MBA program, the average GMAT is 644 and the GPA is 3.4. International students whose native language is not English must take the Test of English as a Foreign Language (TOEFL) and the Test of Written English (TWE). In addition to test scores, applicants must submit application forms, an essay, a resume, official transcripts from every college or university attended, two letters of recommendation, and a nonrefundable application fee of $50.

Application deadlines for fall admission are April 30 for full-time Honors MBA students, the accelerated part-time MBA students, and all international flex-time students, and May 31 for domestic flex-time students. For spring admission, the deadline is October 31 for all flex-time students. There is no admission into the full-time Honors MBA or the accelerated part-time MBA programs in the spring. Applicants are encouraged to submit their applications as early as possible.

Application materials can be obtained from our website at www.zicklin.baruch.cuny.edu/admissions/graduate.html#theapplication. For additional information applicants should contact:

Zicklin School of Business Office of Graduate Admissions
Baruch College of the City
University of New York
One Bernard Baruch Way, Box H-0820
New York, NY 10010-5518
Telephone: 646-312-1300
Fax: 646-312-1301
E-mail: ZicklinGradAdmissions@baruch.cuny.edu
World Wide Web: www.zicklin.baruch.cuny.edu

For Executive Programs information, applicants should contact:

Zicklin School Executive Programs
Baruch College of the City
University of New York
One Bernard Baruch Way, Box B13-282
New York, NY 10010-5518
Telephone: 646-312-3100
Fax: 646-312-3101
E-mail: ExProgBus@baruch.cuny.edu
World Wide Web: www.zicklin.baruch.cuny.edu

ADDITIONAL INFORMATION

In addition to our regular MBA programs, the Zicklin School also offers a joint JD/MBA in conjunction with New York Law School or Brooklyn Law School, MS degrees in a variety of business areas, an Executive MBA, Executive MS in Finance, and Executive MS in Industrial and Labor Relations. Executive MS Programs in Finance and Marketing are currently offered, or are being planned, in the following locations: China—Shenzhen, Beijing, Shanghai, Guangzhou, Israel—College for Management, Rishon Le'Tzion, Taiwan—Taipei, Technology Park Hong Kong.

The Baruch/Mt. Sinai Graduate MBA Program in Health Care Administration is dedicated to the graduate business education of practicing professionals in the health care industry. It is expected that MBA Program graduates will attain senior positions within the field and will work in a wide range of health care organizations that reflect the diversity of the field, and the diversity of populations to be served.

CAREER SERVICES & PLACEMENT

The Graduate Career Services office offers students a range of job search services. A core curriculum of workshops is offered to all students and covers topics such as job search strategies, resume writing, interviewing techniques, networking strategies, and job search correspondence. Individual career counseling and consultation are also available. On-campus recruiting is held throughout the year, and career fairs are held as the market warrants. Students have unlimited access to the various full-time and internship position openings that are posted regularly on E-Recruiting and in the Office Resource Center. Special events, such as career seminars, company information sessions, and other networking opportunities, are also held throughout the year.

BAYLOR UNIVERSITY

AT A GLANCE

Baylor University's MBA program provides students with the kind of personal, in-depth, hands-on learning that best equips students for success in today's business world. Unlike traditional curricula, which simply move students through one business course after another, Baylor's MBA program integrates its core MBA courses across functional areas, giving students the opportunity to study business the way people do business.

Each semester, a focus firm is selected and analyzed across the core MBA curriculum, giving students the chance to solve real-world business problems from several aspects at once, just as they will on the job. Students learn to work cooperatively in teams, resolve conflicts, foster personal relationships, and hone communication skills—all competencies cited by managers as critical in today's workplace.

Students work within a diverse population led by some of America's most highly regarded business professors as they sharpen collaborative, technical, leadership, and communication skills. Three lockstep semesters and one summer semester make up the 16-month program. Students move through the semesters as a unit, creating a team approach to learning, and camaraderie among class members.

Small classes, hosted at the University's state-of-the-art Hankamer School of Business in Waco, Texas, set the stage for an integrated learning experience that balances leading edge business theory with practical, hands-on, real-world challenges.

For students new to business education, Baylor offers the Integrated Management Seminar (IMS), a unique semester designed specifically for students without an undergraduate business degree.

LOCATION & ENVIRONMENT

A facility that fosters success, the Hankamer School of Business is housed in one of the newest buildings on the Baylor campus. Features such as wireless networking, seminar style classrooms, a 75-seat video conferencing room and the Graduate Center maximize discussion and interaction between students and faculty. Wireless network access for notebook computers is provided throughout Hankamer and the main Baylor campus, offering the latest in technological education. The 150,000 square-foot McLane Student Life Center is the centerpiece of the 60-acre Student Life Complex.

The heart of Texas welcomes our students. With an area population of 208,000, the 550-acre main campus in Waco, Texas is centrally located in the Lone Star State, within 150 miles of four major metropolitan cities—Dallas, Houston, Austin and San Antonio. Baylor is a private, co-educational Baptist institution, chartered in 1845 by the Republic of Texas. It is the oldest continuously operated university in the state, and the largest Baptist university in the world.

DEGREES OFFERED

The Hankamer School of Business offers 12 graduate programs, including two joint programs with Baylor Law School. The largest program in Baylor Business is the full-time MBA. For students new to business education, Baylor offers the Integrated Management Seminar (IMS), designed specifically for students wanting to enter Baylor's MBA or MSIS program, but needing business prerequisites. Once students pass the intensive one semester IMS, they enter the first semester of the MBA or MSIS program. Programs include: Master of Business Administration (MBA), Executive MBA program in Dallas (EMBA), Executive MBA program in Austin-Waco (EMBA), MBA-International Management (MBA-IM), MBA-Information Systems Management (MBA-ISM), MBA/Master of Science in Information Systems (MBA/MSIS), Master of Science in Information Systems (MSIS), Master of Accountancy (MACC), Master of Taxation (MTAX), Master of Science in Economics (MS-ECO), Juris Doctorate/MBA (JD/MBA), and Juris Doctorate/MTAX (JD/MTAX).

PROGRAMS & CURRICULUM

MBA Program

The design of the MBA core courses center around the business cycle of planning, implementation, and evaluation. Choose from a wide range of elective courses that allow the opportunity to specialize or generalize, including health care administration, information systems, and entrepreneurship. In as little as 16 months, students build the solid, overall business foundation needed for career expansion. During the summer semester, students can work in an internship, study abroad through an international exchange program, or take elective courses on campus.

MBA with a Specialization in Health Care Administration

In response to a growing need in the medical world for people who can effectively manage complex medical systems, Baylor offers a specialization within its MBA program.

MBA-International Management (MBA-IM)

For students interested in careers overseas or with international divisions of domestic corporations, Baylor's MBA-IM International Business degree gives an in-depth understanding of business enterprises in a global market.

MBA-Information Systems Management (MBA-ISM)

Demand for technological knowledge and skills makes Baylor's information systems degree extremely marketable. The MBA-ISM is designed to provide students with technical skills in information systems within the integrative MBA curriculum. An undergraduate degree in information systems or computer science is required.

MBA/Master of Science in Information Systems (MBA/MSIS)

The MBA/MSIS program gives students an in-depth study of management while training in all aspects of Information Systems.

Master of Science in Information Systems (MSIS)

For students choosing to develop expertise in the rapidly growing field of information systems, the MSIS program leads to careers in systems analysis, systems design, client/server applications development, system implementation, systems integration, global information systems, telecommunications and networks, and business process re-engineering.

Master of Accountancy (MAcc)

Following the national trend shifting the focus of accounting education toward the graduate level, the MAcc provides students with the technical background and complementary professional skills necessary for careers in public accounting.

Master of Science in Economics (MSEc)

Whether seeking full-time employment or planning to pursue a doctorate in economics, the MSEc is a viable degree. Students learn to apply theory to business and government problems, and significantly expand analytical skills.

FACILITIES & EQUIPMENT

One of the strategic objectives of the Hankamer School of Business is to provide students with the tools to succeed in today's technology fueled business environment. All Baylor business students take advantage of the wireless networking environment throughout the Baylor campus. MBA and MSIS students are required to purchase a notebook computer, and they use the computers extensively during their program. The central libraries, special libraries and resource centers of Baylor house more than 1.6 million bound volumes, more than 2.8 million microforms and government document pieces, and thousands of electronic resources, audiovisual items, maps, charts and photographs.

EXPENSES & FINANCIAL AID

Dollar for dollar, students get more from a Baylor graduate business education than almost anywhere in the country. *Money* magazine consistently ranks Baylor among the best values in the country. Our tuition is among the lowest of any major private university in the Southwest and one of the least expensive in the nation.

Dean's Scholars

Ten scholarships of 100 percent tuition remission are awarded to our most outstanding students. Applications are measured by professional work experience, GMAT scores, leadership skills, community involvement, and undergraduate GPAs.

International Fellowships

All MBA students are considered for these awards, given on the basis of international experiences, travel, and multicultural exposure. They are awarded 75–100 percent tuition remission, plus a monthly stipend in exchange for 15 hours work per week for a professor or department on campus.

Baylor Express Fellowships

A few fellowships are reserved for students entering the MBA program directly after their undergraduate studies. They are awarded 50 percent tuition remission, plus a monthly stipend in exchange for 15 hours work per week for a professor or department on campus.

Hankamer School of Business

Graduate Assistantships
Assistantships are awarded ranging from 50-100 percent tuition remission, plus monthly stipends. Applications should be filed no later than 60 days prior to enrollment.

FACULTY
We believe a strong student-professor relationship can have dynamic, lifelong benefits. As a result, close mentoring relationships with faculty are a reality at Baylor. While it is possible at many large MBA programs for students to get lost in the shuffle, at Baylor students work with faculty members on academic and nonacademic projects. While Baylor is known for its teaching excellence, the Hankamer School of Business' recognized strength as an AACSB–accredited school draws upon the expertise of the faculty as consultants and noted scholars.

STUDENTS
Baylor offers a diverse community of people from around the world, including MBA students from a wide variety of states and many countries. International students comprise 25 percent of Baylor's MBA enrollment. This culturally diverse learning environment gives students the global perspective necessary to succeed in today's world market.

ADMISSIONS
Admission to Baylor Business is competitive. The ideal candidates for the MBA program are individuals with professional work experience, outstanding scholarship, a commitment to community service, and a motivation to pursue an intense graduate business program. MBA candidates should have strong analytical capabilities and communication skills. For programs other than the MBA, Baylor Business looks for similar qualities.

Students are required to have a bachelor's degree from an accredited institution in the United States, or proof of equivalent training at a foreign university.

Personal Essays and Resume
The personal essays are an opportunity to express unique qualifications, experiences, and reasons for applying to a graduate business program at Baylor. A current resume is requested, specifically describing those activities, honors, or awards believed to be helpful in ensuring success in a graduate business program at Baylor.

Transcripts
It is the applicant's responsibility to secure and submit transcripts from each university attended for all undergraduate and graduate course work. The transcripts should be sent in a sealed envelope to the Graduate School. All international transcripts must be translated into English. Unofficial transcripts and test scores can be submitted for the review process. If Baylor Business recommends the applicant be approved for admission, official transcripts and official test scores must be submitted to complete the application.

Standardized Tests
If applying for an MBA, MAcc or MTax program, Graduate Management Admission Test (GMAT) scores must be submitted. If are applying to the MSEco or MSIS program, either the GMAT or the Graduate Record Examination (GRE) scores should be submitted. Please request the official scores for either the GMAT or GRE be sent to Baylor University, code 6032.

TOEFL Test
International students are required to take the Test of English as a Foreign Language (TOEFL) unless the applicant has a degree conferred by a U.S. accredited higher education institution. A minimum cumulative score of 600 (paper) or 250 (computer) is required. Request official TOEFL scores to be sent to Baylor University.

Letters of Recommendation
Letters of recommendation provide additional information regarding abilities, and should be obtained from individuals who know the applicant well and can present balanced evaluations and assessments. Two recommendations are required. Recommendation Forms can be downloaded from our website.

Application Fee
The application requires a $50, nonrefundable fee, payable by credit card or by check to Baylor University.

Interview
Applicants for the MBA program are encouraged to contact the Graduate Programs Office to schedule an interview. Interviews are not required but can help applicants present key aspects of background, career goals, and motivation not easily demonstrated in a written application. Applicants who are able to travel to campus for an interview can also arrange to visit an MBA class and to meet current students and faculty.

Application Deadlines
Baylor Business has a rolling admissions process. Decisions are made as applications are reviewed. Early deadlines are suggested for students interested in applying for graduate assistantship awards. General deadlines are for all applications.

For admission in spring, 2004, early deadline is September 1, and general deadline is November 1. For admission in summer, 2004, early deadline is February 1, and general deadline is April 1. For admission in fall 2004, early deadline is March 15, and general deadline is June 15.

ADDITIONAL INFORMATION
Each semester, MBA students analyze a "focus firm" inside and out, giving students "the chance to solve real-world business problems from several aspects at once." The focus firm is a corporate alliance project involving one company each semester. Interaction with the firm's executives gives students and faculty the opportunity to explore the company's current core issues, making it the centerpiece of the MBA curriculum for the semester. In fall 1998, Baylor's focus firm was Dell Computers, headquartered in (relatively) nearby Austin.

The Mentoring Program is designed to help students gain access to a trusted and familiar advisor, and insight into the day-to-day life of a mentor, while transitioning from school to career. It fosters relationships among current Baylor students and graduate business alumni.

Baylor Business
Our commitment to the personal, as well as professional, development of our students is distinctive. Values based guidance of faculty mentors, and innovative program design allows students to take their career—and life—wherever they want to go. Baylor's graduate business programs provide the comprehensive learning experience needed to achieve career objectives, within the context of greater personal development goals designed to serve our students for life.

Personal Development
While establishing solid business principles expected of a graduate business student, Baylor also gives students the chance to master competencies that are above and beyond the traditional business degree.

Global Perspective
As new global markets open, international perspective becomes ever more crucial. International business curricula, an active international student body, and international summer exchange programs broaden horizons and encourage students to view the "bigger picture."

Teamwork
Emphasis on teamwork creates an environment of cooperation within degree programs and within individual classes at Baylor Business. Students will share expertise with classmates, form small study groups, and establish a network of relationships that can last far beyond graduate studies at Baylor.

CAREER SERVICES & PLACEMENT
Hundreds of employers consult Baylor's Career Services Center annually for potential Baylor graduate employees. One of the country's most sophisticated automation systems affords firms easy access to students' credentials. Graduate business students will benefit from the individual attention of the associate director of MBA Career Services, who helps match candidates with potential employers for both full-time positions and internships.

CASE WESTERN RESERVE UNIVERSITY

AT A GLANCE

The Weatherhead School of Management at Case Western Reserve University is proud to play a leading role in the evolution of management education. This is achieved by integrating the fundamentals of business with ideas and practices that are transforming individuals, organizations and society. This passionate support of innovation has built our international reputation for producing MBA graduates that help organizations achieve sustainable competitive advantage.

Weatherhead's unique teaching approach features a blend of functional and interpersonal skills that organizations increasingly need. As a result, our MBAs are strong candidates in a business world that demands individuals who make an impact from day one. The input we ask for, and receive, from local, national and international businesses, as well as our extensive alumni network, is critical to designing our curriculum and advancing our graduates' careers.

The Most Advanced Business Learning Facility in the World
The Weatherhead School entered an exciting new phase of growth with the opening of the Peter B. Lewis Building in October 2002. The Lewis Building reflects our innovative approach and clearly places Weatherhead in the vanguard of business education.

The Weatherhead MBA is a distinctive, challenging, and provocative education that will prepare graduates for a rewarding career in a dynamic, complex, and global business environment. Our graduates are redefining business leadership for the twenty-first century.

The University Setting
Case Western Reserve University (CWRU) is a nationally recognized, independent university that traces its heritage to the founding of Western Reserve University in 1826 and Case Institute of Technology in 1880, culminating in their federation in 1967. Nearly 9,600 students are enrolled, with approximately 6,000 making up the graduate student body. More than 100 different countries are represented, providing a contemporary international perspective.

LOCATION & ENVIRONMENT

A dynamic center of industry, wealth, population and culture, Greater Cleveland offers a variety of advantages to Weatherhead MBA students. With its prime location on the shore of Lake Erie, Cleveland is a thriving international port as well as home to more than two dozen Fortune 500 corporations, offices of all leading accounting firms, the fourth district Federal Reserve Bank, world-class health care organizations, and a flourishing entrepreneurial community.

One-third of Weatherhead's MBA courses involve field projects in Cleveland's diverse management community, which spans the manufacturing, banking, health care, aerospace/defense, automotive, and consumer goods industries as well as the nonprofit sector. The executives and managers who participate in Weatherhead's MBA Mentor Program reflect the high quality and diversity of Cleveland's management community.

Along with its professional advantages, Cleveland offers outstanding recreation and entertainment opportunities.

DEGREES OFFERED

The Weatherhead School offers a number of graduate business program options—a traditional two-year, full-time MBA; a one year, accelerated full-time MBA for those with undergraduate business degrees; and an evening part-time MBA program for the working professional. All programs offer the same faculty and opportunity to concentrate in any of our 18 areas of concentration.

In addition, we offer a number of joint degree options for those with interest in law, medicine, or other areas of business, such as MBA/JD, MBA/Master of Science in Nursing, MBA/MD, MBA/Master of International Management (with Thunderbird—American Graduate School of International Management), MBA/Master of Science in Social Administration, MBA/Master of Public Health, MBA/Master of Science in Management in Operations Research, MBA/Master of Science in Management in Supply Chain Management, and MBA/Master of Accountancy.

PROGRAMS & CURRICULUM

The Weatherhead School of Management's integrative MBA curriculum enhances the potential of each student to create value by drawing from different perspectives to identify, analyze, and resolve complex problems. The program is designed to meet today's challenging business environment by producing a new generation of leaders who possess the skills and insights that organizations need in order to prosper. Our strength is the product of a dynamic community of students, faculty, business partners and alumni. These groups—representing true global diversity—interact in a collaborative setting that promotes a vibrant exchange of ideas and constant exploration of new ways to work together.

Being creative and agile in designing systems and adapting to change

- Strategic Issues and Applications, a first year introduction to organizations and management
- Integrative functional core courses
- Expanded international study opportunities

Developing and enhancing organizational leadership

- Development of managerial and career skills
- Guest lecturers from local, regional, national, and international organizations

Making a personal commitment to lifelong learning

- Expansion of leadership assessment and development throughout the MBA program

Adding value in a special area of expertise

- A wider selection of advanced elective courses

Contributing to the betterment of communities and society

- Increased emphasis on community service
- Student run conferences on current issues in management

Advanced Electives in 18 Areas
Students select a sequence of elective courses to develop depth and diversity in an area of special interest, or to design a sequence in general management. A minimum of three elective courses is required to establish an area of specialization from the following list: accountancy, financial reporting and management control; banking and finance; bioscience entrepreneurship (new for fall 2003); e-business; economics; entrepreneurship; health systems management; international management; labor and human resource policy; management information systems; management of technology; management policy; marketing; nonprofit management; operations management; operations research; organizational behavior; and supply chain management.

FACILITIES & EQUIPMENT

The Peter B. Lewis Building, opened in the fall of 2002, is the culmination of the vision of the Weatherhead community. Designed by renowned architect Frank Gehry, the Lewis Building gives the Weatherhead School a striking physical identity within Case Western Reserve University. Inside is a truly unique architectural and technological infrastructure that opens new learning possibilities and gives students the resources they need to compete at the highest levels of business.

State-of-the-Art Learning Environment
The classrooms in the building are acoustically designed to foster active learning, and ensure that every student can be seen and heard comfortably by the rest of the class. The main classroom is a tiered, oval room that places the instructor and up to 60 students in an interactive setting featuring white boards around the full perimeter of the room, allowing any student to take the lead during class discussions. Outside the classroom, students have access to 14 group study rooms, numerous open meeting areas, a student lounge with meeting space, and a large reading room for quiet study.

Powerful Technology
The Lewis Building is the most technologically advanced business education facility in the world today. With an all-building switched gigabit network, as well as a broadband network, Weatherhead boasts connections 10-100 times faster than other business schools. This robust infrastructure enables multimedia and video conferencing with schools and organizations across the globe from every classroom. Each individual classroom seat has ample power and data connections to the Internet and CWRUnet, the University's fiber optic network.

Weatherhead School of Management

EXPENSES & FINANCIAL AID

For the academic year 2004 (beginning fall 2004), tuition for full-time, two-year students is estimated at $14,790 per semester. Students in the traditional two-year program will pay tuition of $29,580 for the first year and can expect a four to seven percent increase for the second year of tuition.

Full-time students can expect to spend approximately $2,500 for the required laptop computer and $900-$1,200 for rent, food, and living expenses per month in the program. Books will cost approximately $500 per semester.

Students in the evening, part-time MBA program pay tuition based upon a per credit hour fee. Tuition for 2003-2004 is $1,185 per credit hour, or $3,555 per three credit course. Tuition is estimated to increase by four to seven percent for the 2004-2005 academic year.

The Weatherhead School offers merit-based scholarships to approximately 45 percent of the incoming full-time class.

FACULTY

Weatherhead's internationally known faculty is known for their ability to integrate cutting-edge research with real-world business applications. Weatherhead's 92 full-time faculty provide teaching and research strength in the most up to date and creative areas of management knowledge and teaching techniques. For more information on specific research and areas of specialty of our faculty, please visit our website at www.weatherhead.cwru.edu/wsom/profiles/main.htm.

STUDENTS

Weatherhead students are a very diverse group in terms of ethnicity, nationality, educational background, and work experience. Approximately 40 percent of our students are international, representing, on average, 20–25 different countries. As you can see from the list below, our students bring a strong academic grounding and a wealth of experiences to the program, which is beneficial to all they share with during the MBA experience.

Undergraduate Majors

Most students in the fall 2003 entering class hold undergraduate degrees in either business administration (31 percent) or science/math/engineering (31 percent). Other degrees held are in economics (5 percent), and humanities/social sciences (30 percent).

Professional Backgrounds

The most common backgrounds are in financial services (10 percent) and manufacturing/operations (17 percent).

Community Service

The School believes the contribution of knowledge, skills, and energy to the community is a sound investment for all future leaders. MBA students may participate in a high school student advisory group, through which they counsel local high school students on career and educational goals, resume writing, and interviewing skills.

Student Organizations

The Graduate Business Student Association (GBSA) was formed by Weatherhead MBA students to serve as a liaison with WSOM faculty and staff on issues pertaining to student life. The primary focus of the Association is to enhance each student's MBA experience in the areas of professional development, academic achievement, and community involvement. Weatherhead offers dozens of additional professional organizations and special interest groups.

ADMISSIONS

The Weatherhead MBA program admission policy has been developed to ensure that incoming classes will be composed of highly qualified individuals representing diverse academic, professional, and cultural backgrounds and accomplishments. The MBA program is open to graduates of accredited, four-year colleges and universities. Individuals who have already earned an MBA degree (whether in the U.S. or another country) are not eligible to apply for admission to our MBA program. We offer a number of specialized degrees or certificate programs for individuals who already hold an MBA degree.

Full-time candidates, to the traditional two-year program are admitted for fall semester only. The one year accelerated program begins with the summer semester (late May) only. Deadlines for both programs are as follows: first round—January 30, second round—March 19. Applicants to the evening, part-time program can begin the program at the fall, spring or summer semester. Application deadlines are approximately 1 1/2 months before the start of the semester. Application for entry into the June 2004 class is based on the "stage" admission system.

The preferred method of application is online for either the full or part-time programs. Access the online application feature at:

https://apply.embark.com/MBAEdge/CWRU/15/. Application materials can also be downloaded from our website.

ADDITIONAL INFORMATION

Accelerated MBA curriculum for undergraduate business majors

Students who have completed an undergraduate degree in business within the last 10 years may qualify for our accelerated one-year MBA program. Beginning in late May of each year, a select group of up to 45 students completes their studies by the following May. The program offers the same academic options as the traditional two-year program.

International Management Specialization

In addition to MBA electives, students may take designated elective courses in other schools and departments of CWRU, including anthropology, history, political science, modern languages, and law.

Joint MBA/MIM Program

In conjunction with the American Graduate School of International Management (Thunderbird) in Glendale, Arizona, students can earn a joint MBA/Master of International Management degree. Students earn both degrees in two years, including summer terms.

International Opportunities

To broaden the MBA experience, the Weatherhead School offers a variety of international study opportunities for full- and part-time MBA students. MBA students may choose a specialization in international management.

The Weatherhead School participates in fall semester MBA exchange programs with leading management schools around the world. Students have the opportunity to study in England, Denmark, Norway, Germany, France, Austria, Spain, Israel, Mexico, Costa Rica, and the Philippines.

The International Institutes were developed to provide intensive, short term, opportunities for both evening and full-time MBA students. This includes the study of critical issues and opportunities within the rapidly changing economies, and cultural and business environments around the world. Current institutes travel to France, Germany, Hungary, South Africa, England, Belgium, the Czech Republic, Slovakia, Austria, and Australia.

The MBA Enterprise Corps

As one of the top 35 U.S. schools invited to participate in the MBA Enterprise Corps, the Weatherhead School offers an exciting international opportunity to MBA graduates. Through the MBA Enterprise Corps, recent graduates assist private enterprises in former socialist countries in Eastern Europe, spending one to two years transferring knowledge and skills to managers of emerging businesses.

For more information, please visit our homepage www.weatherhead.cwru.edu—learn more about our programs, request a brochure, or sign up for an on-campus visit.

CAREER SERVICES & PLACEMENT

The School offers students many powerful advantages in planning a dynamic career path and managing the challenges and rewards of the professional marketplace. Weatherhead MBA students have the special advantage of the individualized career counseling, direct referral system, and networking opportunities available only in a small, personalized MBA program. Strategic career planning begins with a required, first semester program including seminars in presentation skills, networking, resume writing, and interview skills. The Weatherhead School's one of a kind MBA Mentor Program matches interested students with executive mentors according to students' individual career interests.

CHINESE UNIVERSITY OF HONG KONG

AT A GLANCE

The Chinese University of Hong Kong (CUHK) is a pioneer in business education in Hong Kong and the first university to establish a full-time MBA degree program in Hong Kong. The Faculty of Business Administration of CUHK was one of the first two business schools in Asia accredited by AACSB International. We are also the first business school outside North America to establish the CUHK Chapter of Beta Gamma Sigma, the international honor society for business and management programs.

The MBA programs were ranked No. 1 in the Asia Pacific (*Asia Inc*, August 2002). Our commitment to innovation was the key to its No. 1 place. The Executive MBA Program was also ranked No. 1 in Asia by *Financial Times* in 2002 and *BusinessWeek* in 2001. An uncompromising insistence on quality and innovation continues to strengthen our status as one of the leading business schools in Asia. Our achievement is also reflected in our 2,800 graduates, who are very successful businessmen and women and entrepreneurs, and who hold prominent management positions in local and overseas corporations.

LOCATION & ENVIRONMENT

The University is situated north of Shatin in the New Territories. It overlooks the beautiful Tolo Harbour to the north and the Tide Cove to the east. Majestic mountains rising to more than 900 meters are in view from any direction.

The administration and faculty offices of the MBA programs are housed in the Leung Kau Kui Building on the central campus, where both the Full-time MBA Program and the MBA Program (Weekend Mode) classes are held. At this site we are able to provide a first-class learning environment with modern classrooms and leading-edge technology and computing support.

DEGREES OFFERED

Full-time MBA Program, Part-time MBA Program (Weekend Mode), Part-time MBA Program (Evening Mode), EMBA Program, OneMBA Global Program, MBA Program in Health Care, MBA Program in Finance, MS in Finance, Master of Philosophy in Business Administration, PhD of Philosophy in Business Administration, Master of Accountancy, MS in Global Business Program, MS in Information and Technology Management Program, MS in Business Economics Program, MS in E-Business Program, MS in Marketing Program

PROGRAMS & CURRICULUM

The MBA programs offer five types of program that lead to the degree of Master of Business Administration (MBA): the Full-time MBA Program, the MBA Program (Evening Mode), the MBA Program (Weekend Mode), MBA Program in Health Care, and the OneMBA Global Program.

Full-Time MBA Program

The curriculum is designed with the principles of integration and sequential modules so that students can understand when and how business concepts from various business disciplines can be applied in a business life cycle. The program consists of Pre-core Courses, Integrated Core Course, Advanced Required Courses, Capstone Courses, and Electives totaling 51 units.

Completion of the curriculum will take 18 months of full-time study. Classes are held on campus.

MBA Program (Evening Mode)

This program consists of Core Courses and Electives totaling 48 units. Students are required to participate in Business Field Study—Mainland China for graduation requirement.

The completion of the entire program will normally take two years. Under special circumstances and with the approval of the Director of MBA Programs, students can extend their period of study to more than three years, but they are required to complete the 48 units within five consecutive years in order to qualify for the MBA degree.

MBA Program (Weekend Mode)

This MBA program is for non-Business Administration graduates only. The program also consists of Core Courses and Electives totaling 48 units. Students are required to participate in Business Field Study—Mainland China for graduation requirement.

The completion of the entire program will normally take two years. Under special circumstances and with the approval of the Director of MBA Programs, students can extend their period of study to more than three years, but they are required to complete the 48 units within five consecutive years in order to qualify for the MBA degree. Those who need to complete the program in more than two years will take elective courses in the evenings, which are offered by the MBA Program (Evening Mode).

FACILITIES & EQUIPMENT

MBA Town Centre

The new MBA Town Centre, a state-of-art learning environment for business professionals of the twenty-first century, covers nearly 900 square meters. The Centre is equipped with the latest audiovisual facilities. The computers in the Centre are connected in a local area network so that software and printers can be shared, and the Centre's server is connected to the CUHK campus and to the Internet, so students can check email and conduct web searches. The MBA Town Centre with its location in Central enables the busy part-time MBA students to attend classes in comfort and with top-class learning technology.

A First-Class Library

The University Library System consists of the main library and branch libraries, including the college libraries and a medical library. It houses a collection of more than 1,614,000 bound volumes of books and periodicals. The entire catalogue is computerized so that search and access is greatly facilitated. There is a large collection of books and periodicals related to business and management, which provides useful resources for the study and research needs of the students and staff.

Universities Service Centre for China Studies

The Universities Service Centre provides a comprehensive, user-friendly collection of original source materials on contemporary China for scholars all over the world. The Centre's library on post-1949 China is incomparable in its coverage: complete runs from the early 1950s up to the present of most of China's provincial and national newspapers; a collection of provincial yearbooks; many hundreds of county gazetteers; and a judiciously chosen collection of the most valuable books available on the mainland, many of which are unavailable elsewhere in the world. Currently the Centre subscribes to 2,000 magazines in Chinese and more than 80 in English, and to more than 400 Chinese newspapers.

The Centre's collection provides an unmatched support for China-related research and is frequently used by MBA faculty members and students in their China-related business research.

State-of-the-Art Computing Facilities

The University's computer facilities are coordinated and networked at the University Information Technology Service Centre (ITSC), offering a vast array of personal computer laboratory services to the academic, research, and administrative communities of the University. To cope with these different dimensions of services, ITSC has multiplexed its computer facility in recent years. This system is fully networked—institutionally, locally, and internationally—and incorporates both high-powered mainframe computers as well as local area and personal computer systems. ITSC has recently established special-purpose laboratories furnished with high-tech facilities for multimedia development, optical mark scanning, color laser printing, image scanning, data visualization, and even user self-paced learning. Most of these facilities are accessible to the end user via the campus gigabit Ethernet backbone network.

Additional Computer Facilities for MBA Students

In addition to making the most of the general computing facilities of the University, the Faculty of Business Administration has also installed more than 100 microcomputers in a local area network (LAN) environment. These computing facilities are installed at the Personal Computer Laboratory of Fung King Hey Building for the use of faculty, students, and staff. On top of the many applications provided by the faculty, users of the PC Lab can also access all campuswide as well as Internet applications through the University's campuswide backbone network provided by the ITSC.

A LAN of Pentium-based PCs has also been installed at the Central MBA Town Centre for the use of the MBA and Executive MBA students. The PCs in the lecture rooms are integrated with contemporary Audio/Video systems to facilitate multimedia teaching. Access to the Internet and is also made available through a designated leased line.

MBA Programs

EXPENSES & FINANCIAL AID

Full-Time MBA Program (2003–2004)

Admission fee: $25

Tuition fee for whole program: $17,135

Estimated room and board per academic year: $3,000 on campus; $18,460 off campus

Estimated cost of books and other academic expenses per academic year (full-time students only): $10,974

Financial aid: Annual scholarship/grant aid awarded to MBA students receiving scholarships/grants ranges from $130 to $6,400.

Average (annual) loans aid to MBA students receiving loans: $1,282

FACULTY

The Faculty of Business Administration of The Chinese University of Hong Kong is accredited by AACSB International. We are the first business school outside North America to establish a chapter of Beta Gamma Sigma, an international honor society for business and management programs accredited by AACSB International. In addition, we are a member of PIM (Program in International Management), an international consortium of outstanding higher education institutions that deliver graduate-equivalent degrees in management.

There are two schools and four departments in the faculty, which include the School of Accountancy and the School of Hotel and Tourism Management, and the Departments of Decision Sciences and Managerial Economics, Finance, Management, and Marketing. All departments and the School of Accountancy deliver courses in the MBA programs.

The International CUMBA Faculty

A key strength of the MBA programs is a team of international faculty from Australia, Hong Kong, Europe, India, Japan, Korea, New Zealand, the People's Republic of China, Southeast Asia, Taiwan, and the United States. Distinguished visiting scholars share research and consultancy experiences during seminars and forums throughout the year, bringing with them the perspectives of business issues and practices from their home countries as well as from other countries where they have taught.

STUDENTS

Full-Time MBA Program

> **Number of students:** 65
> **Average age:** 29
> **Average years of work experience:** 4–5 years
> **Percent women:** 53%
> **International students:** 30%

Part-Time MBA Program

> **Number of students:** 279
> **Average age:** 31
> **Average years of work experience:** 6–8 years
> **Percent women:** 39%
> **International students:** 15%

ADMISSIONS

Academic Requirements

Admission to the Full-time MBA Program, the MBA Program (Evening Mode), and the MBA Program (Weekend Mode) is open to graduates of recognized colleges and universities who have a bachelor's degree, normally with honors not lower than Second Class Lower Division or with an average grade "B" or better.

Applicants who have recognized professional qualifications equivalent to an honors degree may also be considered for admission. Those applying to the evening and weekend programs are required to have at least three years of full-time work experience after obtaining their bachelor's degrees or recognized professional qualifications.

GMAT Requirement

In addition to possessing outstanding records, the MBA programs require all applicants to take the GMAT. For our admission purpose, the scores of GMAT tests taken more than three years prior to the admission year are not considered.

The GMAT scores of applicants are considered only if they are received by our Admissions Office by the end of February prior to the September admission date. Applicants should arrange to send the official GMAT scores to the MBA Programs of The Chinese University of Hong Kong. (The code is 0812).

English Language Proficiency Requirement

All applicants must satisfy this requirement before being admitted to the MBA programs. The verbal score on the GMAT is assessed to determine if an applicant has met this requirement.

Admission Procedures

Admission dates start from the beginning of December to the end of February for each academic year. Applicants may submit online applications at https://mbaonline.baf.cuhk.edu.hk. Two copies of the most updated official transcripts of all undergraduate work must be sent directly to the Admissions Office by the registrar(s) of the institution(s) at which the applicant did undergraduate work. Students in their final year of their undergraduate courses are required to send in their final transcripts as soon as they are available. In addition, two recommendation forms must also be completed by the referees and directly sent by them to the MBA programs.

After reviewing the application files, the Admissions Office will invite shortlisted candidates to an interview with faculty members of the MBA programs. The interview provides an opportunity for the faculty members to evaluate the applicants' analytical and interpersonal abilities, as well as their managerial and leadership potential. Admission interviews are held in April in Hong Kong. The final acceptance result will be sent to each candidate shortly after the interviews. Admitted candidates are required to register by the end of May.

Students from Overseas

The MBA programs welcome applications from overseas students who live or work abroad. The application deadline is the end of January. Interviews for selected applicants will be conducted via telephone or in person by CUMBA representatives.

Admitted overseas students must obtain a student visa in order to study in Hong Kong. Applicants must also name a resident in Hong Kong, aged over 21, to act as a sponsor. Those who are unable to get a sponsor may apply to the Graduate School Secretariat to act in this capacity.

ADDITIONAL INFORMATION

Reciprocal Recognition of Credits between CUHK and HEC

Full-time MBA students may participate in a cooperative program that has been co-organized by CUHK and the HEC School of Management in Paris. Participating CUHK students will complete the required first-year MBA courses at CUHK and study at HEC in their second year.

OneMBA Global Program

The Faculty of Business Administration at The Chinese University of Hong Kong has joined forces with four partner institutions: Erasmus University's Rotterdam School of Management, The Netherlands; the Kenan-Flagler Business School at the University of North Carolina at Chapel Hill; Tec de Monterrey's Graduate School of Business Administration and Leadership, Mexico; and the Fundacao Getulio Vargas Escola de Administracao de Empresas de Sao Paulo, Brazil, to launch the OneMBA Global Program, perhaps the world's first Executive MBA with a truly international focus.

More than mere window dressing, the global elements of the 21-month OneMBA Global Program run from a jointly developed curriculum, to an international faculty, to a series of global residencies on four continents. Fully one-third of the course work is done overseas, with a focus on gaining experiences and developing professional networks, rather than merely sitting in a classroom. For many, building an international network while honing their managerial skills is crucial to their continued success.

CAREER SERVICES & PLACEMENT

We have established a CUMBA Online Career Centre (http://mbacareer.baf.cuhk.edu.hk). It serves as a job agent to cater for the needs of the students and potential employers. Having acquired a balanced management education in theory and practice, our graduating students are well equipped. They have learned to be strategic in their approach and implementation of business and management processes.

CLAREMONT GRADUATE UNIVERSITY

AT A GLANCE

The Drucker School of Management, located in beautiful Claremont, California, is a unique management school dedicated to training people to become effective and ethical leaders and managers, in whatever industries they serve. This focus stems from our belief that management is a liberal art, a human enterprise encompassing perspectives from the social and behavioral sciences. Named after one of the most prominent management thinkers of the 20th century, Peter F. Drucker, the Drucker MBA program offers a high quality, interactive educational experience. Drucker classes are small—averaging 25 students per class—and instruction is given from world-renowned professors. Approximately 70 percent of our classroom instruction is either in discussion or case analysis format, and we incorporate team building in classroom projects and presentations. Additionally, we are ranked 20th by the 2003 *U.S. News & World Report* survey in General Management.

LOCATION & ENVIRONMENT

Claremont is located approximately 25 miles east of the City of Los Angeles, and 6 miles west of Ontario International Airport. It is a small suburban college town community with a population of 34,000. Claremont consists of 14 square miles at an elevation of between 1,100 and 1,800 feet above sea level. The average yearly temperature is 63 degrees with average annual rainfall of 17 inches.

Nestled in the foothills of the San Gabriel Mountains, this charming community is famous for its tree lined streets, world renowned colleges, and charming "old town" restaurants and shops. Claremont provides the atmosphere of a New England college town within comfortable driving distance of major Southern California attractions and sports stadiums.

DEGREES OFFERED

The Drucker School of Management offers the MBA degree.

MBA Program

Consistent with our vision, we attract students who already exhibit strong leadership and achievement skills, or who clearly show the potential to develop such skills. These students typically wish to develop themselves both as individuals and as professional executives fully competent in the complex, globally connected economy. Students recognize our focus on strategy, leadership, and risk management, and our philosophy of management as a liberal art. The effectiveness of this positioning strategy is confirmed by the fact the Drucker School's MBA program was ranked 20th nationally by *U.S. News & World Report* in the General Management category of the 2003 rankings.

Curriculum

The Drucker MBA curriculum is designed in a layered yet integrated fashion, allowing the student to sequentially build knowledge and develop professional skills. Core courses or foundation level courses provide candidates with an understanding of the fundamental disciplines of management. Advanced core courses are geared to help students integrate key concepts and skills necessary for strategic or general management. Elective courses enable students to specialize in a particular field of interest.

Our flexible MBA curriculum allows both full-time and part-time students to select an area of emphasis in strategic management, risk management/finance, leadership, marketing, information sciences, and human resources. Students are also able to take courses outside of the management program in the areas of psychology, politics and policy, economics, and biosciences. Other disciplines are also available to our students through the various schools in the Claremont Graduate University and the Claremont College Consortium that consists of Claremont McKenna College, Pomona College, Harvey Mudd College, Scripps College, Pitzer College, and the Keck Graduate Institute of Applied Life Sciences.

We offer courses overseas and have several semester exchange programs. Our overseas courses are:

- Global Operations Management (1 week in Monterrey, Mexico)
- GStrategic Risk Management in an Emerging Economy (1 week in Mexico City)
- GGlobal Strategy and Trade (2 weeks at Oxford University)

Semester exchanges:
- GTheseus Institute (Nice, France)
- GSt. Gallens University (Switzerland)
- Hitotsubashi University (Tokyo, Japan)

Peter F. Drucker sets the standard for a faculty whose teaching and research is consistently influencing management practice. Our globally renowned faculty writes groundbreaking books and serve as consultants to organizations worldwide. A professor may counsel a Fortune 100 CEO in the morning, and share the insights with a class that evening. Being a teaching university—as opposed to a research university—our faculty has time outside of class to meet with students, and have time outside of school to maintain their own consulting practices.

Professors such as Mihaly Csikszentmihalyi, Vijay Sathe, Richard Smith, Jean Lipman-Blumen, and Richard Ellsworth comprise the core faculty who are globally renowned in their respective areas of research and interest.

Special Programs

Dual Degree: Dual degrees allow students to obtain two degrees in an accelerated period of time. The dual degrees Drucker School offers are MBA/MSMIS, MBA/MSFE, MBA/MSHRD, MBA/MS, and MBA/MA.

Course Auditing: Students taking 12 or more credits are allowed to audit a course of their choice, at no cost, at any of our seven colleges within the Claremont College Consortium. The audited course will appear on the transcript as an audit course, but will not count for credit.

IF Program: The International Fellows Program helps students adapt quickly to learning in a different culture, build the level of confidence needed for success in the classroom and beyond, and develop sophisticated spoken and written English skills for academic and professional purposes.

Alumni Mentoring Program: Each admitted student is assigned an alumnus to share the Drucker School experience. This program also enables students to benefit from the life experience and opportunities of a Drucker School alumnus.

Student Mentoring Program: Each admitted student is assigned a current student as a mentor from the moment he/she is admitted to the moment he/she is enrolled.

Drucker Board-Student Mentoring Program: The Drucker Board of Visitors Mentoring Program rewards the top 10 percent of our students. This mentoring program connects top students, one-on-one, with board members who are high ranking executives from companies such as JP Morgan Chase, McKinsey & Co., Bain & Co., Wells Fargo Bank, Edward D. Jones, Deloitte and Touche, Dimensional Fund Advisors, and Forbes. These mentoring programs assist students with anything ranging from course selection and student associations to internship opportunities, and hold the possibility for full-time job offers.

CAREER SERVICES & PLACEMENT

The ultimate objective of any successful career services function within a business school is the successful transition of students out of the classroom and into the working world, with job and career opportunities closely aligned with the graduates' interests and capabilities. The career services provided to students at the Peter F. Drucker Graduate School of Management are designed to provide the tools needed to successfully navigate a course into the working world and beyond. While the department has brought some of the major U.S. corporations on campus to interview—companies such as GE Capital, Deloitte & Touche, Johnson & Johnson, Wedbush Morgan Securities—our strength has been in training students to successfully conduct a significant portion of their own job and

Peter F. Drucker Graduate School of Management

career search. Students have available to them a ready arsenal of programs, workshops, and company information sessions to help them define their short and long term objectives, while providing significant information about companies, industries, and career paths. We invite you to learn more about our capabilities and programs by visiting our website http://careers.cgu.edu.

EXPENSES & FINANCIAL AID

- Tuition: $17,021 full-time (16 credits); $1,099 per credit part-time
- Fees: $80
- Books and supplies: $400
- Health insurance: $225
- Average rent: $600–$700/month (not including meals)°
- Expenses: Expected expenses are approximately $12,000 per year, including housing, meals and entertainment

°*We have on-campus graduate apartments (first come first serve) and numerous off-campus housing resources/assistance.*

Financial Aid

Merit and need based scholarships are available for U.S. and international students alike. Institutional financial aid is based on professional work experience, academic qualifications, and GMAT score. To be considered, applicants must complete the Application for Institutional Financial Aid, and submit their completed application with all accompanying materials by the financial aid deadline. Government loans (FAFSA—for U.S. citizens and permanent residents) and International Student loans are also available. For more information, please contact Rosie Ruiz at rosie.ruiz@cgu.edu.

STUDENTS

The Peter F. Drucker Graduate School of Management at Claremont Graduate University, located in beautiful Claremont, California, is a unique management school dedicated to training people to become effective and ethical leaders, strategists, and visionaries in whatever organization they serve. Our focus stems from the belief that management is a liberal art, a human enterprise encompassing perspectives from the social and behavioral sciences. This positions Drucker as a "different school of thought," and not just another business school.

In his book, *The New Realities,* Peter Drucker explains why management is a liberal art:

> Management is thus what tradition used to call a liberal art—'liberal' because it deals with the fundamentals of knowledge, self-knowledge, wisdom, and leadership; 'art' because it is practice and application. Managers draw on all the knowledge and insights of the humanities and the social sciences—on psychology and philosophy, on economics and history, on the physical sciences and ethics. But they have to focus this knowledge on effectiveness and results—on healing a sick patient, teaching a student, building a bridge, designing and selling a user friendly software program.

Named after the most prominent management thinker of the twentieth century, Peter F. Drucker, the Drucker MBA program offers a high quality interactive educational experience: small classes averaging 25 students per class and instruction from world-renowned professors. Approximately 70 percent of our classroom instruction is either in discussion or case analysis format, and we incorporate team building in classroom projects and presentations. In a nutshell, our classes are highly interactive. Additionally, we are ranked 20th nationally in the 2003 General Management category by *U.S. News & World Report.*

Student life at the Drucker School is busy and diverse. In addition to challenging academic programs, students can also participate in a number of special interest clubs designed to further both academic and career interest. Clubs include the Consulting Club, the Finance Club, the Marketing Club, Professional Women's Networking Club, Net Impact, and Business Entertainment Association among others.

The Drucker School Student Association is the student-run governance body that works with the Dean and his staff to ensure that student interests and needs are being addressed. Student study rooms, computer labs, and common areas give our students places to gather to exchange ideas and develop friendships.

Most of our students live near the campus, many within walking distance. The variety of events taking place both at the Claremont Colleges and around the Los Angeles basin give students a tremendous range of social, cultural, and sports activities from which to choose.

The Drucker School prides itself on its diverse, talented, and proactive student population. Drawn from a pool of exceptional people, the Drucker MBA students have a wide range of interests, besides the usual rigors of academia. Students are involved in many activities within the program and the university.

There are numerous opportunities for Drucker MBAs to be associated with leadership roles through the various student organizations and clubs. Most clubs and student organizations are elected and run by students based on the mission of that particular organization.

ADMISSIONS

The Peter F. Drucker Graduate School of Management at Claremont Graduate University prides itself in being "A Different School of Thought." Our student body is academically, professional, racially, and geographically diverse, and we do not require an undergraduate background in business or economics. Our aim is to create an environment that more realistically reflects the world around us.

We do not have minimum cut-offs for the GMAT and GPA, as we attempt to individualize each application by evaluating the "whole person."

In order for an application to be complete, applicants must submit the following:

- Application
- Student profile sheet and application for institutional financial aid (if applicable)
- Three letters of reference (recommendation letters)
- Official transcripts from every college/university attended
- Personal statement (three to five pages, double-spaced)
- Current resume
- GMAT score
- TOEFL score (for international students)
- $50 application fee
- A personal interview is highly recommended

Application Deadlines
- Fall semester (financial aid applicants): February 15
- Fall semester (regular applicants): May 1
- Spring semester (international and financial aid applicants): October 1
- Spring semester (regular applicants): November 15

If applying for financial aid, all documents must be in by the above dates. We also have rolling admissions based on space availability.

ADDITIONAL INFORMATION

The chief draw of the Peter F. Drucker Graduate Management Center is the school's namesake. Mr. Drucker wrote *The Practice of Management,* the sacred writ of MBAs the world over, and the first book to recognize management as a distinct and important business skill. Students tell us there is a real "family atmosphere" here and a "super high emphasis on hands-on learning," and "if you plan carefully, you can assemble a schedule of world class professors."

CAREER SERVICES & PLACEMENT

For information on career services and placement, visit http://careers.cgu.edu/.

COLLEGE OF WILLIAM AND MARY

LOCATION & ENVIRONMENT

While many MBA courses encompass a global perspective, the student body (approximately 38 percent international) provides additional insight into global business issues. Several options for further internationalizing the William and Mary MBA are available, including course work that features hands-on study tours to international locations and exchange partnerships that offer international immersion experiences. These include ESCP-EAP, the European School of Management in France; INCAE in Costa Rica; the Norwegian School of Economics and Business Administration; and the Otto Beisheim Graduate School in Germany.

The College of William and Mary works to help students clarify their goals, and recognize their expectation to achieve a challenging professional position with excellent compensation following the academic rigor of the MBA program. The MBA Career Services Office, in partnership with alumni and corporate leaders, provides exposure and access to Fortune 500 recruiters through a comprehensive Career Management Program. This Program includes participation in MBA Consortium events in Atlanta, New York City, Washington, DC, and the Silicon Valley, as well as a full range of on- and off-campus recruiting activities. Career forums bring corporate representatives to campus for panel discussions; and alumni encourage networking, provide mock interviews, resume reviews, and mentoring relationships. SERC members work closely with the MBA Career Services team to provide corporate contacts and expert guidance on professional opportunities. Current placement profiles and recruiter lists can be found online at http://business.wm.edu.

A modern graduate housing complex designed specifically for graduate students offers two, three, or four bedroom apartments within walking distance to the School of Business Administration. Early applications for on-campus housing are encouraged. Students living off-campus can choose from a variety of privately managed living options in Williamsburg, or commute from neighboring cities.

Entering full-time MBA students are required to bring a laptop computer. Minimum specification requirements can be found online at http://business.wm.edu. Each classroom seat is equipped with power and network hookups, with wireless technology available in some areas. The School of Business facilities include modern, executive style classrooms, a computer lab, and team study and conference rooms housed within the historic section of the William and Mary campus.

PROGRAMS & CURRICULUM

The College of William and Mary offers the MBA degree in three formats: full-time, evening, and executive. William and Mary provides a broad management education that offers immediate access to faculty, and one-on-one interaction with some of today's most intriguing corporate leaders and risk taking entrepreneurs. The MBA curriculum reflects the complexities of the business world, where everyday problems are not separated into academic disciplines.

In the full-time MBA program, the first year provides a thorough grounding in management theory and practice. Proceeding through a uniquely integrated curriculum, MBA candidates examine business problems from every possible angle until a comprehensive understanding is achieved. This method requires intense collaboration among faculty, as well as a flexible schedule that changes to accommodate topic modules and to allow for interaction with visiting business executives. Second year MBA candidates return from internships having mastered the fundamentals, and pursue specialized study in accounting, finance, economics, marketing, information technology, operations, organizational behavior and human resource management, or general management.

Joint degree programs that combine the MBA with law (MBA/JD) or public policy (MBA/MPP) are offered cooperatively with William and Mary's Marshall-Wythe School of Law and the Thomas Jefferson Program in Public Policy.

To meet the needs of working professionals, the evening and executive MBA programs offer the same high quality education available to full-time students. Through the evening program, students pursue the MBA during the evening hours over three to four years in the centrally located Peninsula Center in Newport News, Virginia. The Executive MBA is an intensive program, meeting on alternate Fridays and Saturdays with four residency periods over 20 months.

Accessibility to faculty makes the William and Mary MBA experience truly exceptional. William and Mary MBA students benefit from engaged faculty who are extraordinary educators. They are practitioners who are recognized for outstanding achievements within their chosen fields, and award winners who are committed to delivering graduate management programs that are superior on every level. Due to the carefully crafted size of the MBA programs, faculty members are attentive to the aspirations of each student and are easily accessible for consultation. They challenge students to reframe business concepts and processes in the context of currently developing corporate strategy. This approach is the backbone of a quality MBA education, and one of the many reasons why William and Mary graduates excel.

The MBA Association is the representative organization for graduate business students. The Association maintains a committee structure, representing all facets of business, which allows students with common academic and professional goals to come together with faculty and experienced business executives in a focused, team-based environment.

The opportunity to learn about business trends straight from the trendsetters themselves enhances the MBA programs at William and Mary. The MBA Executive Speaker Series brings corporate leaders into the classroom and small discussion group settings for one-on-one interaction with students.

Another unique aspect is the Senior Executive Resource Corps (SERC), a network of experienced executives with senior level expertise, representing 22 different industries. The members of this volunteer group serve as mentors to William and Mary MBAs and share their considerable business acumen as real-world resources. SERC members collaborate with faculty to advise student teams during the Field Studies consulting projects, conducted by second year, full-time MBA students. The Field Studies program requires students to apply the knowledge and skills gained from the first year and internship experiences in identifying, researching, and proposing solutions for real business problems faced by national and regional clients. Additional information can be found online at http://business.wm.edu/corporate.

EXPENSES & FINANCIAL AID

William and Mary provides exceptional academic programs with comparatively low tuition and fees. Considering the success of our graduates, our programs offer a compelling return on investment. Full-time MBA students will find some resources made available through scholarships, loans, and graduate assistantships. Scholarship and graduate assistantship awards are based solely on merit. Loan eligibility is based on need as determined by filing the U.S. Department of Education's Free Application for Federal Student Aid (FAFSA). Although participation in some loan programs is limited to U.S. citizens and permanent residents, international students may be eligible for private or alternative loans.

The total annual, full-time, in state student budget for 2002–2003 is $25,808, including tuition and fees of $9,978, room and board of $8,330, computer and software totaling $3,500, miscellaneous expenses of $3,000, and books and supplies totaling $1,000. The total annual, full-time, out-of-state and international student budget for 2002–2003 is $37,088. This includes tuition and fees of $21,258, room and board of $8,330, computer and software totaling $3,500, miscellaneous expenses of $3,000, and books and supplies totaling $1,000.

Graduate School of Business

Evening MBA tuition and fees for 2002–2003 are $306 per credit hour (in state) and $620 per credit hour (out-of-state), up to eight credit hours per semester.

STUDENTS

"The blend of opportunities afforded by the William and Mary School of Business is unmatched; the College is within easy reach of some of the world's most vibrant business centers, the MBA program's small size fosters interaction, and the school's passionate faculty is dedicated to facilitating an MBA experience based on partnerships. Ours is a cutting-edge approach to global business education; we provide a real-world perspective, impressive corporate connections, and unfettered access to some of the sharpest minds teaching business today. We invite you to preview our MBA program; one of the most challenging and intimate graduate business educations offered."

—Lawrence B. Pulley, Dean and
Elizabeth Clarke Professor of Business Administration

Founded in 1693, The College of William and Mary is the second oldest educational institution in the U.S. and has educated four U.S. Presidents: George Washington, Thomas Jefferson, James Monroe, and John Tyler. Other alumni range from American luminaries like John Marshall to modern business trailblazers such as Mark McCormack, Founder, Chairman, and CEO of IMG. The striking architecture of the William and Mary campus provides a tour through three hundred years of history and tradition located in the heart of colonial Williamsburg, Virginia. Although it retains its traditional title of "College," William and Mary is in reality a small public university with approximately 5,500 undergraduate and 2,000 graduate students. The College is just a 45-minute drive from Virginia Beach, Norfolk, or Richmond, which are home to a broad array of industries; just over two hours from Washington, D.C.; and half a day from New York City.

The William and Mary student body exhibits diverse academic and professional achievements, which adds great richness to the environment. The small class size, usually two sections of 50 students each, facilitates a fellowship among students, faculty, alumni, and corporate leaders. The average entering full-time student is 28 years old with approximately five years of post-undergraduate work experience. Thirty-seven percent of the class is women, 33 percent is international, and U.S. minority students comprise 10 percent of the class.

The program emphasizes teamwork. Student teams designed to link MBA candidates with varying strengths provide a preview of the cross-functional work groups they will encounter in professional settings. Through live case studies, students analyze trends as they develop in the business world. Students and faculty manage information as it unfolds, and participate together in examining the complexities of alternative scenarios. This immersion in teamwork and collaboration prepares William and Mary MBAs to develop comprehensive business solutions in the classroom and the real world.

ADMISSIONS

The full-time and evening MBA programs are small by design. The effectiveness of these programs depends on the relationships developed within student teams, and those forged between students and faculty. While some MBA candidates enter the program with business related degrees or experience, many students enter from an array of different academic and professional disciplines. Admission decisions are based on academic record, professional experience, GMAT scores, recommendations, interview, essays, and other indicators of aptitude for graduate study in business. Applicants are encouraged to apply online at http://business.wm.edu/mba.

Admission to the full-time MBA program is granted for the fall term only. There are three formal application review periods, followed by a rolling admission process. Applicants for fall 2003 who apply by November 15 are notified by February 1; January 15 applicants are notified by March 15; March 15 applicants are notified by May 1; April 15 applicants are notified by June 1; May 15 applicants are notified by July 1. Those who apply after May 15 are notified on a rolling basis. Applicants are encouraged to apply early for full scholarship consideration.

Admission to the evening MBA program is offered for both the fall and spring semesters on a rolling basis. Applicants who apply for spring 2003 admission by November 15 are notified by December 15. Those who apply for fall 2003 admission by July 1 are notified by August 1. Interested students should contact:

Office of MBA Admissions
School of Business Administration
The College of William and Mary
PO Box 8795
Williamsburg, VA 23187-8795
Phone: 757-221-2900
Toll free (U.S. only): 888-203-6994
Fax: 757-221-2958
E-mail: admissions@business.wm.edu
Web: http://business.wm.edu/mba

ADDITIONAL INFORMATION

A "smaller program," "non-competitive attitude," and state school prices attract MBAs to the College of William and Mary Graduate School of Business, where "very enthusiastic, very capable," and "very tough" professors offer "a great deal of personal attention." Incoming students here participate in an Outward Bound style orientation week, during which they divide into teams and compete in, among other things, a high ropes course and a raft building exercise.

COLLEGE OF WILLIAM AND MARY MAC PROGRAM

"The current climate in the accounting profession and the recent passage of the Sarbanes-Oxley Act of 2002 and other measures have focused attention on the need for accounting professionals to have an advanced understanding of their field and high ethical standards. In fact, students from a variety of academic and business backgrounds would benefit from William & Mary's one-year Master of Accounting (MAC) Program. The program is designed to ensure that students obtain the academic, professional, and ethical training they need to function effectively in today's rapidly changing business environment. The dedicated and scholarly MAC faculty has designed a rigorous program for accounting and nonaccounting undergraduate majors alike. I invite you to take a closer look at our program; you will find that it is one of the best around."

—Lawrence B. Pulley
Dean and T.C. and Elizabeth Clarke
Professor of Business Administration

THE SCHOOL AT A GLANCE

The College of William & Mary, founded in 1693, is the second oldest educational institution in the United States. Alma mater of three presidents and countless other Early Republic luminaries, the College offered its first business-oriented class in 1798: Political Economy. One-hundred and twenty-four years later in 1922, William & Mary undergraduates had the opportunity to pursue a full course of study in accounting through the College's first School of Business Administration.

Today approximately 5,500 undergraduates and 2,000 graduate students study a wide variety of subjects on the beautiful William & Mary campus located in the heart of Colonial Williamsburg, Virginia. Williamsburg's close proximity to Virginia Beach, Norfolk, and Richmond and relative proximity to Washington, D.C. and New York City allow students to partake in a vibrant business, political, and cultural life.

STUDENTS

Small by design, the Master of Accounting (MAC) Program enrolls approximately 30 individuals each fall. The entering Class of 2004 draws students from around the world and across the mid-Atlantic region. Thirty-two percent of the class is male and the average age is 24.7 years old. The majority of the students are entering the program directly from their undergraduate studies, where they pursued majors in accounting, finance, and business administration. For the 39 percent with post-graduate work experience, their undergraduate majors also included international studies, economics, agricultural business, and math. A small number of enrolling students already hold master's degrees in economics, finance, and computer science. The average GMAT score is 630, while the average undergraduate GPA is approximately 3.33.

ACADEMICS

Flexibility and academic rigor are the hallmarks of the William & Mary MAC Program. Believing in the value that people from diverse academic backgrounds bring to the accounting profession, the award-winning faculty created the full-time, two-semester, 30-credit-hour MAC Program to attract both accounting and nonaccounting undergraduate majors.

Core Curriculum

All MAC students benefit from the same 15-credit-hour core curriculum designed to strengthen their knowledge of financial reporting and accounting information systems, finance, and the art of effective business communication. The core includes:

BUAD 502 Professional Accounting I (3)

BUAD 503 Professional Accounting II (3)

BUAD 504 Financial Markets and Valuation (3)

BUAD 505 Accounting Information System Design & Management (3)

BUAD 506 Analytical Tools for Financial Modeling (1.5)

BUAD 507 Communications & Professional Development (1.5)

For nonaccounting majors or those accounting majors who might not have had classes in auditing, taxation, and/or cost accounting, the core curriculum expands to include:

BUAD 509 Professional Auditing & Assurance Services (3)

BUAD 514 Strategic Cost Management (3)

BUAD 515 Influence of Taxation on Business Decisions (3)

Electives

Students round out their MAC course of study by selecting electives from the College's Master of Business Administration (MBA) Program that complement their career objectives. Accounting undergraduates typically select 15 credit hours (five classes) while nonaccounting majors take six credit hours of electives (two classes). The wide variety of MBA electives includes, but is not limited to:

BUAD 514 Cost Administration/Financial Control Systems

BUAD 516 Tax Research & Advanced Business Entity Tax

BUAD 527 Database Management

BUAD 529 Electronic Commerce

BUAD 532 Corporate Financial Policy

BUAD 536 Portfolio Management

BUAD 542 Marketing Strategy

BUAD 557 Leadership & Planned Change

BUAD 574 Principles of Negotiation

BUAD 577 Management Science

BUAD 583 Non-Profit Organizations

BUAD 595 Business Law

BUAD 595 Business Research Seminar in Internet Law

BUAD 595 Stock Market Trends

Opportunities exist for those students with an undergraduate course in taxation to take electives in the Law School with instructor permission. In fact, MAC students interested in tax can pursue that specialty by taking up to 12 credit hours of taxation. Other nonbusiness electives in law and computer science are available to MAC students with instructor approval.

FACULTY

The dedicated faculty of the Graduate School of Business are proud of the personalized attention they are able to provide the students.

The intimate size of the MAC Program allows students to interact with these outstanding scholars and enthusiastic educators both in and out of the classroom.

The core MAC faculty brings a diverse array of specialties and research interests to their teaching:

Julie Agnew, PhD, Boston College

  Personal Investing in 401(k) Plans, Behavioral Finance

Audra Boone, PhD, Pennsylvania State University

  Divestitures, Mergers & Acquisitions, Equity Offerings

Ted Boone, MS, Pennsylvania State University

  Information Technology Utilization, Supply Chain Management

Denise Jones, PhD, University of Colorado

  Voluntary Disclosure, Valuation of Intangibles

Aamer Sheikh, PhD, University of Georgia

  Earnings Management, Executive Compensation

James Smith, PhD, University of Arizona

  Taxation of Property Transactions & Business Entities

Kimberly Smith, PhD, University of Maryland

  Executive Compensation, Capital Investments

Robert Stowers, EdD, Rutgers University

  Effective Presentations, Business Writing

G. Thomas White, PhD, Virginia Tech

  Financial Reporting, Regulation of Accounting Services

CAMPUS LIFE

William & Mary with its ivy-covered brick buildings and seventeenth-century Wren Building looks like the quintessential college campus. Students delight in throwing Frisbees in the tree-lined Sunken Garden as much as they enjoy attending lectures by such public figures as Kofi Annan, Secretary General of the United Nations, and former William & Mary Chancellor Margaret Thatcher.

Many cultural and social opportunities exist in Williamsburg, from the Muscarelle Museum of Art's recent exhibit on Georgia O'Keefe to the live music performances at The Green Leafe Café—a taphouse tradition among students. A short drive to Virginia Beach or Richmond brings students even more cultural and entertainment opportunities.

Students may elect to live on campus in the modern, apartment-style graduate student complex. The complex, located within walking distance of the Graduate School of Business, sits next to the indoor tennis courts and the Law School.

COSTS

The Master of Accounting Program provides an excellent education at a reasonable cost. The cost becomes even more reasonable when one looks at the placement and starting salaries of the graduates.

The MAC Program boasts alumni in the big four accounting firms at offices nationwide, the top regional and local firms, prominent companies in the private sector, and the federal government.

Tuition and fees for 2003–2004 for in-state students total $10,000 and for out-of-state students total $20,340. Both in-state and out-of-state students are required to have a specially configured laptop and should allocate a maximum amount of $3,500 for its purchase if they do not already own one. Additionally, students should budget approximately $8,500 for room and board, $3,000 for miscellaneous expenses, and $1,000 for books and supplies.

Scholarships and graduate assistantships are available on a competitive basis. Total awards typically range from $500 to $16,000. Seventy-five percent of the entering Class of 2004 received some amount of merit aid. U.S. citizens and permanent residents can apply for need-based student loans through the Federal Student Loan Program. For more information on the program, go to www.fafsa.ed.gov/.

ADMISSIONS

Prerequisites

To ensure student success, MAC applicants are required to have successfully completed Principles of Accounting, Intermediate Accounting I, Financial Management, Statistics, and Introduction to Information Technology. Recognizing that some nonaccounting majors might not have taken Intermediate Accounting I, the program offers an intensive 14-day course in August prior to the start of classes.

Application Deadlines

Offers of admission are made on a revolving basis until the class is full. For priority merit aid consideration, all applicants are encouraged to apply before March 15. International applicants are strongly encouraged to apply by February 1 to allow sufficient time for visa processing. Applications from international applicants who are not currently residing in the U.S. on a valid visa will not be accepted after March 15. Notification of admission decisions will occur within two weeks of the receipt of a complete application and interview. Please apply online at http://business.wm.edu/mac.

Evaluation of Applications

Admissions decisions are based upon the applicant's academic record, GMAT score, TOEFL score (for non-native speakers of English), essay, recommendations, interview, and other indicators of aptitude for graduate study of accounting and business. International applicants are also required to submit a "Course by Course" evaluation of their transcripts performed by World Education Services (WES).

The Original College Building: The Sir Christopher Wren Building

Admissions Contact: Aimee Turner Keeney
Coordinator of Students Services, Master of Accounting Program
Tyler Hall, Room 235, Williamsburg, VA 23187
Phone: 757-221-2875
Fax: 757-221-2937
E-mail: MAC@business.wm.edu
Web Address: www.business.wm.edu/mac

ERASMUS GRADUATE SCHOOL OF BUSINESS

AT A GLANCE

Rotterdam School of Management (RSM) is at the forefront of new developments. Technological breakthroughs are changing the business scene at tremendous speed. Business leaders must be able to deal with the new technologies and the way in which they affect our businesses, and even our lives. RSM aims to provide the MBA participants with the knowledge and skills required to effectively deal with the changes our new era brings, and to prepare them for the challenges ahead.

"The ability to innovate and to remain at the leading edge of developments in management theory and practice are critical for the success of MBA participants and of MBA programs. The Rotterdam School of Management continuously strives to build upon the success we have achieved through a continuous focus on issues of international business, information technology, and soft management skills. These features complement an in-depth, integrated MBA curriculum aimed at creating managers capable of leading global companies."

—Kai Peters, Dean

CAMPUS & LOCATION

The Rotterdam School of Management is a foundation of Erasmus University Rotterdam, which is renowned for its business orientation. The University was founded in 1913 by Rotterdam entrepreneurs, and named after Erasmus Desiderius Roterodamus. Erasmus was born in Rotterdam in the late fifteenth century. He was a leader of the liberal reform movement in Europe, and dreamed of democracy of the intellect and correct use of free will. It is this humanist tradition that still lives on in the University, which today has more than 16,000 students, of whom some 1,600 are enrolled in postgraduate studies.

Rotterdam School of Management is located on the Woudestein Campus of the Erasmus University. The University campus is situated close to the center of Rotterdam. RSM offers housing services for all international students near the University campus. The language laboratory, sports center, libraries, restaurant, shops, and information services at Erasmus University are available to RSM students.

The dedicated RSM building on the Erasmus Woudestein campus officially opened in March 2000. The facilities include eight large theater style classrooms, breakout rooms, student lounges, a cafeteria, and staff offices.

RSM provides an online library for students. Erasmus University library databases and catalogues, along with online content providers such as Hoovers.com, and Lexis-Nexis Academic Universe form RSM's online library facilities. RSM is continually updating the online library content with information relevant to business students and, in fact, is the first European business school to offer the Lexis-Nexis Academic Universe to students.

The RSM Career Management Center (CMC) is dedicated to helping students make sound career choices. They provide guidance, training, and support. The CMC also supports, coordinates, and facilitates company presentations and other recruitment events for many top international firms to provide opportunities to meet as many companies as possible on campus.

DEGREES OFFERED

In addition to a general management education that combines the highest academic quality with real-world relevance, the full-time International MBA and MBA/MBI programs focus on the management of information technology (MBA/MBI), finance, marketing, strategy, and entrepreneurship.

The two-year, part-time weekend Executive MBA (EMBA) program combines general management orientation with an emphasis on the key drivers that transform our fast moving business environment.

The modular Executive OneMBA program is designed for achievement-oriented executives with increasing international responsibilities. Through a partnership of five top schools, OneMBA connects a globally diverse network of executives from four continents.

The Master's in Financial Management (MFM) program prepares young professionals for international finance careers. Taking a decision-oriented approach, the comprehensive curriculum design ensures that theoretical insights are grounded in practical application.

The Master's in HR (MHR) program is designed for HR professionals aiming to build a solid HR knowledge base. The MHR program not only explains the qualities of leadership, but it develops participants into HR business leaders.

RSM offers the following Dutch language open enrollment executive education programs: Interim Management, Business Valuation, International Account Management, and The Executive Gateway Series (TEG).

RSM also creates executive education programs specifically tailored to the needs of your company.

PROGRAMS & CURRICULUM

The full-time International MBA and MBA/MBI programs commence in October each year, bringing together over 150 students from more than 50 countries for an intensive 15 month, hands-on approach to management. In addition to a general management education that combines the highest academic quality with real-world relevance, participants can focus on the management of information technology (MBA/MBI), finance, marketing, strategy, and entrepreneurship. The curriculum includes an internship, electives, and the possibility to spend an exchange semester abroad.

The curriculum of the full-time International MBA and MBA/MBI programs covers all major aspects of general management. During the first year, students are provided with the management basics and an understanding of business disciplines of organizations. Running parallel to these core courses are career management and communication workshops.

The second year allows students to tailor their studies to areas of their interest. Through electives and mini courses, they can focus on areas such as corporate finance, marketing, entrepreneurship, or IT. Students also have the opportunity to participate in an exchange program with top business schools worldwide.

In addition to an international focus throughout the program, RSM maintains student exchange programs with international business schools on different continents. These schools are leading institutions in management education. During the fourth semester, approximately 30 percent of our students are selected to go on exchange to United States, Canadian, Asian, European or African business schools. The objective of the exchange program is to give students increased exposure to cultures other than their own.

Rotterdam School of Management

The International MBA/MBI program is designed for students who, in addition to a general management education, wish to spend further time concentrating on the managerial aspects of information technology (IT). The MBA/MBI program is largely identical to the MBA program during the first and second semester. During the third semester they will have an MBI exclusive eight-week summer program of required courses, and an internship focusing on issues such as telecom, media, and technology. In the fourth semester, students complete one additional MBI elective and a range of MBA electives, or they can choose to participate in the Exchange Program.

The academic faculty represents a mix of professors from RSM and Erasmus University, visiting faculty members of prestigious international universities, and consultants and managers active in various industries. Faculty members are international professionals who bring up to date management techniques and practices into the classroom. They are committed to a wide range of teaching methods such as lectures, case studies, field trips, group work, management games, and real life projects.

The RSM Alumni Network is a very international network of all RSM graduates. Alumni are closely involved in the School's activities and are always pleased to meet potential students and discuss their experiences at RSM with them.

RSM was founded with the support of major Dutch multinationals, and has since developed close ties with the international business community. Companies such as Citibank, Arthur D. Little, and ABN AMRO Bank actively take part in the curriculum of the MBA program.

The RSM is consistently ranked as one of Europe's top business schools. *The Economist's* "Which MBA?" describes the RSM as innovative, interesting, friendly, and representing excellent value.

FACILITIES

The new RSM building on the Erasmus Woudstein campus officially opened in March 2000. Dedicated facilities include eight large theatre style classrooms, breakout rooms, student lounges, a business library, a cafeteria, and staff offices. Facilities in the RSM building also include three computer labs available for students participating in any of the RSM degree programs, one desktop lab with 66 desktops connected to the local area network, and two laptop labs where 55 student-owned laptops can be connected. The main theater style classrooms are equipped with professional and state-of-the-art audiovisual and multimedia facilities, including high speed video conferencing, cable television, and laptop plug ins. Each student receives an account to access the Internet from home. The network supports numerous Windows NT applications, including Microsoft Office 2000, online databases, Internet access, and specialized business programs.

The Eneco Trading Room provides state-of-the-art trading room technology in a high-tech educational environment. As the first business school on the continent to house a trading room, RSM uses this facility to add value to its present portfolio of finance courses and executive programs. The trading room is used in the second semester of every MBA program. It is also used to create customized programs on trading and risk management. In this way, the ENECO Trading Room at RSM is a vehicle to provide in-depth knowledge to professionals, as well as introduce finance to nonfinance professionals.

The Business Information Center (BIC) specifically selects books and annual reports, directories and periodicals to support the MBA and MBA/MBI curriculum. Furthermore, the BIC has access to all relevant online and CD-Rom databases. RSM students have free access to all books, reports, magazines, databases, and business periodicals online.

Students can also make use of the library and information services available from the Erasmus University. The University Library possesses more than 800,000 volumes and subscribes to about 8,000 periodicals. The fields of study are general economics, business economics, management, law, social sciences, history, arts, and philosophy. Many publications are available on microfiche, microfilm, videotape and compact disc. The library also has access to various external databases through online and CD-Rom databases.

EXPENSES & FINANCIAL AID

Tuition fees are as follows:

EMBA: $38,500

MFM: $22,500

MHR: $30,000

OneMBA: $48,000

MBA: $34,000

MBA/MBI: $37,000

STUDENTS

The Rotterdam School of Management is a business school that attracts students from all over the world. Approximately 50 different nationalities are represented in the current student population of 360 (180 incoming students per year). Only four percent of the students are Dutch; the remaining 96 percent are international. Students come from a wide variety of academic backgrounds. An average breakdown is 30 percent engineering, 25 percent business, 20 percent science and medicine, 20 percent humanities and social sciences, and 5 percent law. The average age of students is 29, and the average years of work experience is five.

Working in groups is an essential element of the MBA programs. The emphasis on teamwork provides a realistic model for the way in which management issues are handled in the business world. Students learn the vital significance of teamwork and the value of cooperation when they are confronted with a wide range of approaches to a single problem. By forming teams of students with different cultural and educational backgrounds, various problem-solving techniques are recognized and appreciated. This enriches the learning experience of all students.

All RSM activities are international by definition, as the student body represents so many nationalities. Students can receive assistance with applications for visa and housing matters.

ADMISSIONS

RSM welcomes applications from outstanding individuals whose intellectual ability, management potential, and personal qualities indicate that they will benefit from, and contribute to, the learning environment. Eligibility requirements include a recognized university degree, GMAT score, two letters of recommendation (academic and/or professional), relevant (full-time, post-graduate) work experience, proficiency in English, and a personal interview.

The 2003 application deadline is June 15 for the MBA, OneMBA, and MFM programs, and May 12, July 14, September 15, October 20, November 17, and December 8 for the EMBA program. Applications are processed on a continuous basis in order of receipt. Late applicants are placed on a waiting list. For more information, contact:

Ms. Suzanne Whyte or Ms. Vicky Debbage
Garcia Marketing & Admissions Managers
Rotterdam School of Management
Erasmus Graduate School of Business
J-Building Burgemeester Oudlaan 50 3062 PA Rotterdam The Netherlands
Phone: + 31 10 408 2222
Fax: + 31 10 452 2126/9509
www.rsm.nl
www.OneMBA.com/Europe

Global Executive MBA

International MBA

An electronic, executive education experience

At the international crossroads of the Americas

The Alvah H. Chapman, Jr., Graduate School of Business is accredited by the AACSB International—The Association to Advance Collegiate Schools of Business. Florida International University is an equal opportunity/equal access employer and institution.

GOLDEN GATE UNIVERSITY

AT A GLANCE

Golden Gate University traces its origins to the founding of the San Francisco YMCA in 1853. It is a fully accredited, nonprofit, private university. A pioneer in the case study method of instruction, GGU is recognized for practical, professional education. The University provides instruction for more than 6,000 students in California, at sites in San Francisco, Silicon Valley, Sacramento, Monterey Bay, and Los Angeles. Programs are also offered in Seattle and online via CyberCampus.

At Golden Gate University, students explore the global business environment and launch their futures in the graduate business program. Students are surrounded by motivated, experienced classmates who bring as much richness to the learning environment as the professors. Students apply what they learn before they graduate, and the skills they learn work for them as they pursue their studies.

DEGREES OFFERED

GGU offers MBA degrees with concentrations in accounting, computer information systems, electronic business, finance, human resource management, international business, management, marketing, operations and supply chain management, and telecommunications management. GGU also offers the Executive Master of Business Administration (EMBA).

Other degrees offered are:

- Master of Accountancy
- MA in Applied Psychology with a concentration in counseling or industrial/ organizational psychology
- MA in Psychology with a concentration in marriage, family and child counseling
- Master of Business Administration (MBA) with a general course of study
- MS in Computer Information Systems
- MS in Database Development and Administration
- MS in Digital Security
- MS in Electronic Business Systems and Technologies
- MS in Enterprise Information Technology
- MS in Finance
- MS in Financial Planning
- MS in Human Resource Management
- MS in Integrated Marketing Communications
- MS in Management of Technology MS in Marketing
- MS in Software Engineering
- MS in Taxation
- MS in Telecommunications Management
- MS in Web Design and Development
- Doctor of Business Administration

PROGRAMS AND CURRICULUM

The skilled staff in the Career Services Center works closely with students and employers. Students benefit from professional career counseling, job search workshops and programs, computerized skills assessment, placement services, networking opportunities, and annual career fairs that feature on-campus recruiting by major corporations. In addition, students are encouraged to participate in internships as an integral part of the program, which allows for exploration of new career areas and opportunities to see the inside workings of a target company.

EXPENSES & FINANCIAL AID

Golden Gate University is one of the most affordable private universities in Northern California. Tuition includes all standard fees and is the same for California residents and nonresidents. Tuition is charged by the course (most courses are three units), and costs vary by program. Graduate tuition for 2002–2003 was $1,656 per course. Books, supplies, and living expenses are additional.

Edward S. Ageno School of Business

STUDENTS

Students are one of GGU's finest resources. The students accepted into the program are mature and self-directed. They take their education seriously. Working students in the School of Business represent a wide variety of occupations and companies. They are often the nexus of an invaluable network of professional contacts for their classmates.

The student population at GGU is known for its diversity in culture, ethnicity, age, and work experience. Through working and studying with a variety of different people, students gain an edge in the international business world of today. This makes for an enriching classroom environment, where discussions are challenging and informative on many levels.

Approximately 16 percent of Golden Gate University students are from outside the United States. They come from countries in Asia, the Pacific Rim, and elsewhere throughout the world. Many international students bring with them working experience from their countries, creating a dynamic global learning environment.

ADMISSIONS

Applicants to the master's program must have a bachelor's degree from a regionally accredited college or university in the United States or the equivalent from a recognized international institution. Students must also satisfy basic mathematics, writing, and computer proficiency requirements.

Applicants to the MBA program must submit an official score report from the GMAT, official transcripts from all schools previously attended, a statement of purpose, and a completed graduate application form, along with the appropriate application fee (some applicants are not required to provide a GMAT score). Applicants whose native language is not English are required to meet the English language proficiency requirement by submitting TOEFL scores. University admissions information and online applications can be found on the GGU website at www.ggu.edu.

GGU accepts applications on a rolling admissions basis, beginning up to one year prior to enrollment, and applications are reviewed as they become complete. International students should apply by the following dates: June 1 for fall trimester, October 1 for spring trimester, and February 1 for summer trimester. For more information, students should contact:

Office of Admissions
Golden Gate University
536 Mission Street
San Francisco, CA 94105-2968
Telephone: 415-442-7800 (San Francisco campus)
800-GGU-4YOU (toll-free for any campus within the U.S.)
Fax: 415-442-7807 (San Francisco campus)
E-mail: info@ggu.edu
World Wide Web: www.ggu.edu

MONMOUTH UNIVERSITY

AT A GLANCE

Monmouth University was founded in 1933 with federal assistance, largely to provide opportunity for higher education for area high school graduates who—in those Depression days—could not afford to go away to college. It was a two-year institution, holding classes only in the evening. For a time, it appeared uncertain whether the College would have adequate funds to continue. With support from students and the community, however, the fledgling College survived the economic crisis and quickly assumed its present private status. In 1956, it was renamed Monmouth College and accredited by the state to offer four-year programs leading to the baccalaureate degree. Less than a decade later, it was authorized to offer master's degree programs. In 1995, the New Jersey Commission on Higher Education designated Monmouth a teaching university.

Monmouth University, as described in its Mission Statement, is an independent, comprehensive institution of higher learning emphasizing teaching and scholarship at the undergraduate and graduate levels. The University is dedicated to service in the public interest and, in particular, to the enhancement of the quality of life. Monmouth University is committed to providing a learning environment that enables men and women to pursue their educational goals, to reach their full potential, to determine the direction of their lives, and to contribute actively to their community and society.

The mission of the School of Business Administration is to excel in educating business students by integrating scholarship and business experience in academic programs that are subject to continuous review and improvement. The School of Business Administration is accredited by the AACSB—The Association to Advance Collegiate Schools of Business. The primary purpose of our programs is to enable graduates to acquire the knowledge, skills, and practical judgment necessary for responsible and rewarding careers in business. The School of Business Administration prepares its graduates for positions of leadership in both the private and public sectors. Faculty with strong academic and business experience has developed curricula that stress critical thinking, sophisticated communications skills, and a flexible managerial perspective.

Seven schools within the University—the School of Business Administration; the Edward G. Schlaefer School; the School of Education; the Graduate School; the Marjorie K. Unterberg School of Nursing and Health Studies; the School of Science, Technology, and Engineering; and the Wayne D. McMurray School of Humanities and Social Sciences—provide a wide variety of academic programs at both the undergraduate and graduate levels. Today Monmouth offers more than 50 undergraduate and numerous graduate degree programs and concentrations. More than 1,600 undergraduates are resident students.

LOCATION & ENVIRONMENT

The University is located in a quiet, residential area of an attractive community near the Atlantic Ocean, about an hour and a half from the metropolitan attractions of New York City and Philadelphia. Monmouth enjoys the advantage of proximity to many high-technology firms and financial institutions, and a thriving business-industrial sector. These provide employment possibilities for Monmouth University graduates.

The University's 151-acre campus, considered one of the most beautiful in New Jersey, includes, among nearly 50 buildings, a harmonious blend of historic and contemporary architectural styles. Bey Hall, the School of Business Administration building—which contains case study classrooms, seminar rooms, and computer laboratories—houses the MBA program.

PROGRAMS & CURRICULUM

Monmouth University School of Business Administration offers the MBA, the MBA with track in Accounting, and the MBA with concentration in health care management. The purpose of the MBA program is to serve well-qualified graduate students who are committed to the pursuit of more demanding and extensive responsibilities, the enhancement of their competencies, and an improvement in their value to the organizations they serve. The graduate program combines theory and practice of management, and concentrates on contemporary managerial responsibilities. The curriculum underscores the complexity and diversity of managerial decisions in both the national and international economy. The MBA student learns in small classes that promote close interaction with our business faculty, and benefits from special contributions by visiting lecturers. In addition, Monmouth's $6.5 million business administration building, Bey Hall (which opened in 1991), provides business students with a contemporary learning environment.

A student must complete a minimum of 30–36 credits, which include Core Courses, Beyond the Core Courses, the Integrative Capstone Course, and Elective Courses, where applicable. After admission, permission is required to take courses at another institution. Non-matriculated students are prohibited from enrolling in graduate business courses.

MBA Requirements

To earn an MBA requires 30–48 credits, depending on previous course work. The specific requirements are as follows:

- Core Courses (0–18 credits): BE501, BM502, BA503, BM506, BM507, and BK509. Core Course(s) may be waived if equivalent undergraduate or graduate course(s) were completed within seven years with a grade of B or better.

- Beyond the Core Courses (30 credits°): BF511, BM515, BA541, BM563 or BK535, BM590, a technology course (BM520 or 565), a business environment course (BE561 or 571 or 572 or 575 or BF517 or an elective°°), a behavioral course (BM525 or an elective°°), a marketing course (BK533 or 535 or 539 or 540 or 541 or an elective°°), and a quantitative course (BM549 or 556 or an elective°°).

  ° In courses beyond the Core, excluding BM515, 520, 563, 565, and 590, there cannot be more than two BA, BE, BF, BM, or BK courses.

  °° Indicates that an elective may be taken instead of one of the specified courses if the student has completed a related Core Course at Monmouth University as follows: BE501 is related to the business environment course requirement; BM502 is related to the behavioral course requirement; BK509 is related to the marketing course requirement; and BM506 is related to the quantitative course requirement.

MBA Health Care Management Requirements

To earn the MBA with a concentration in health care management requires 33-54 credits, depending on previous course work. The specific requirements are as follows:

- Core Courses (0–18 credits): BE501, BM502, BA503, BM506, BM507, and BK509. Core Course(s) may be waived if equivalent undergraduate or graduate course(s) were completed within seven years with a grade of B or better.

- Beyond the Core Courses (21 credits): BM515, BA541, BF511, BM590, an international course (BM563 or 535), a technology course (BM520 or 565), a marketing course (BK533 or 535 or 539 or 540 or 541, or a related elective). An Elective may be taken in place of the required course if the related course was completed at Monmouth University.

- Concentration in health care management (12–15 credits): BH571, BH572, BH573, BH574, and BH575 (course may be waived with sufficient relevant health care experience).

School of Business Administration

EXPENSES & FINANCIAL AID

For 2002–2003, the cost is $549 per credit, and the comprehensive fee is $284 per semester.

FACULTY

The graduate faculty provides the core of instruction in the graduate program at Monmouth University. Recognized for their scholarly achievements by peers in their fields, members of the faculty provide a challenging classroom environment. The mission of the faculty is to ensure that Monmouth graduates leave the University ready to exercise socially responsible leadership in their professions and the community. The faculty brings the insight from research and professional experience into the classroom. Graduate students are drawn into the ongoing, creative work of the faculty through classroom demonstration, as research assistants, and through attendance at professional meetings. The graduate faculty also serves as advisors and mentors to students—in many cases not only during the course of their studies, but also after they graduate from the University.

Working directly with senior faculty who are engaged in research is a key element in graduate-level study. In recent interviews, a group of student leaders on campus unanimously agreed that the opportunity to work closely with faculty is the greatest single benefit of Monmouth's small class size and engaged faculty. Students are able to achieve a comfortable rapport with the professors.

Within the School of Business Administration is the Kvernland Chair in Philosophy and Corporate Social Policy, which has been endowed through generous gifts in the name of Jack T. Kvernland, a late trustee of the College. Professor Guy Oakes, of the Department of Management, currently occupies this chair. Professor Oakes is studying problems concerning the relationship between corporate, public, and private values in American life. The School also administers the Real Estate Institute, which is directed by Professor Donald Moliver, of the Department of Economics and Finance.

STUDENTS

Now, more than ever, an advanced degree is key to success in the business world. At Monmouth University, we educate business students by integrating scholarship and real-world experience in academic programs that are continuously reviewed and improved. If you seek to acquire the knowledge, skills, and practical judgment necessary for a rewarding career in business, consider our graduate programs.

Whether breaking into a new career or moving up the administrative ladder, an advanced degree in business from Monmouth University is what you need.

- Learn directly from highly qualified faculty, gaining insight from their years of business experience.
- Make contacts that will last a lifetime as classes are attended with other business professionals seeking advancement.
- Gain expertise in business administration in a wide array of topics including management, accounting, finance, and marketing. Explore international and technological dimensions.
- With an MBA, stand out from your peers as a sought-after professional in the business world.

ADMISSIONS

The School of Business Administration requires candidates for admission to the MBA programs to take the Graduate Management Admission Test (GMAT) prior to admission, achieving a score of at least 450. A total minimum score of 1000—comprising the sum of the baccalaureate GPA multiplied by 200, plus the GMAT total score—and a four-year baccalaureate degree are required for admission. The exceptions to the general rule above are as follows:

- A four-year baccalaureate degree and a minimum GMAT total score of 500.
- A recipient of a baccalaureate degree more than eight years ago; adequate business experience at the managerial level; completion of the GMAT with a minimum score of 450; and two letters of recommendation. The student must submit an autobiographical resume detailing his or her work experience to date.
- A master's degree or a doctorate degree (PhD, EdD, MD, or JD).
- A four-year baccalaureate degree and CPA or CFA licensure.

Conditional admission will be granted to a small number of qualified applicants. The MBA Program Director should be consulted for specific criteria.

ADDITIONAL INFORMATION

Monmouth University is licensed by the New Jersey Commission on Higher Education, and accredited by the Middle States Association of Colleges and Schools. In addition, the Chemistry program is on the Approved List of the American Chemical Society (ACS); the Nursing program is accredited by the National League for Nursing (NLN); the Social Work undergraduate program is accredited by the Council on Social Work Education (CSWE); and the School of Business Administration and its MBA program are accredited by AACSB—The Association for the Advancement of Collegiate Schools of Business.

Contact the Office of Graduate Admissions, Director: Kevin Roane, at 732-571-3452 or 800-320-7754.

NORTH CAROLINA STATE UNIVERSITY

AT A GLANCE

At NC State, we've created an MBA with focus. Our emphasis on technology and business sets us apart. The curriculum revolves around the role of technology in business, and the ways technology can improve business processes in all kinds of industries. From new e-commerce ventures to more traditional manufacturing and consumer services, the intelligent use of technology is making the difference for successful organizations. The NC State MBA program will help students develop a keen understanding of general business and management principles. A concentrated study of a technology-oriented business process or function gives students an edge in the marketplace.

Our focus on outstanding MBA education is illustrated by a full-time program, plus an evening option for working professionals; a reputation for excellence in technology management; interdisciplinary programs within NC State's vast network; an innovative faculty with cutting-edge teaching and research; quality students from diverse backgrounds; and unmatched value in management education.

LOCATION & ENVIRONMENT

NC State was founded in 1889 as a land-grant institution that, within 100 years, has become one of the nation's leading research universities. Located in the Research Triangle, a world-renowned center of research, industry, technology, and education, the College of Management is housed on the 623-acre main campus of NC State, which lies just west of downtown Raleigh, the state capital. NC State comprises eleven colleges and schools, serving a total student population of 27,000. More than 5,000 of those students are in graduate programs.

DEGREES OFFERED

MBA—Master of Business Administration: Full-time (51 credit hours) and part-time (45 credit hours) programs; concentrations in electronic commerce, financial management, information technology management, operations and supply chain management, product innovation management, marketing management, and technology commercialization.

PROGRAMS & CURRICULUM

The NC State MBA curriculum was designed to prepare students for management careers, and to provide unique offerings of technology-oriented courses and concentrations. In this program, students will develop a clear understanding of the business functions, such as marketing and finance that make a typical firm tick. But, students will also gain knowledge and hands-on skills in technology-related fields. This approach will make acquired skills and knowledge adaptable to a variety of industries, functions, and work environments. Our alumni have built successful management careers, often in technology-oriented firms and the technical areas of traditional companies.

The curriculum is built around core classes in the basics of management, a specialized concentration, and open electives. Many of the MBA concentrations emphasize business processes—such as new product development—while others focus on traditional organizational functions, such as finance or operations. The concentration requirement ensures that our graduates have depth in one area that will distinguish them from MBA graduates with a general management orientation.

Introductory courses in accounting, economics, finance, marketing, management, operations, and strategy lay a foundation in the business basics. In concentration and elective courses, students will begin to integrate the functions as specialized business processes are explored in depth.

Our faculty has created an integrated curriculum that incorporates technology, global perspectives, and real-world business problems into each class. The interdisciplinary courses and concentrations help students get the most out of their MBA experience. Students gain valuable experience as they work in teams to solve business problems.

Students will be surrounded by classmates with a wide range of experience—from electrical engineers and bench chemists to sales representatives and project managers. In some of the technical courses, students work on projects with other students from NC State's highly regarded graduate programs in computer science, engineering, design, and the sciences. Faculty from other NC State colleges, such as engineering and design, often participate in instructor-led practicum experiences.

An MBA concentration gives students an opportunity to focus studies on a specialized technology process or critical business function. Each concentration includes some required courses and a choice among electives in that field. Most concentrations require students to complete a semester-long team project by working closely with a corporate client to solve a relevant business problem.

FACILITIES & EQUIPMENT

The College of Management is headquartered in Nelson Hall, which houses classrooms, computer labs, and the offices of the faculty members and students. Classrooms have been completely remodeled with tiered seating, laptop connections, and complete multimedia facilities. The College of Management's computer lab houses 100 microcomputers connected to a campus-wide network. Students have access to a wide range of spreadsheet, word processing, database, statistical, and econometric software, along with several large databases. D.H. Hill Library, located near the center of campus, offers access to millions of volumes of books and journals, and an extensive and growing collection of CD-ROM and electronic databases. Graduate students also have borrowing privileges at Duke, UNC—Chapel Hill, and NC Central.

EXPENSES & FINANCIAL AID

The 2004-2005 budget for MBA students depends on the number of credit hours the student takes and the student's residency status.

The estimated annual tuition for the 2004–2005 school year is $9,036 for North Carolina residents in the full-time program, and $6,279 for North Carolina residents in the part-time program. The estimated annual tuition for the 2004–2005 school year is $20,685 for nonresidents in the full-time program, and $15,016 for nonresidents in the part-time program.

Graduate assistantships are available to full-time students through the College of Management. Grants and loan programs are available through the Graduate School and the University's Financial Aid Office.

College of Management

FACULTY

The College of Management has built a faculty rich in technology-related business expertise, management experience, and practical research. Our professors also have a passion for teaching and a commitment to working closely with industry to solve real-world problems. It's an energetic group focused not on yesterday's business trends, but on the future of the marketplace and workplace.

MBA faculty has been selected for a number of college and university teaching awards. Their recognition has honored not only their classroom proficiency, but also their innovative use of technology-enhanced teaching tools, and their integration of real business applications with the management curriculum.

With help from other professors in NC State's technical programs, the faculty has a strong commitment to breaking down organizational barriers to teaching and research. The college's own entrepreneurial spirit has inspired a number of faculty to seek on- and off-campus partnerships with scholars and teachers in other academic areas—particularly in engineering, design, and computer science.

Our faculty excel in both traditional scholarly pursuits and practical, corporate-sponsored research. We are home to a number of extensively published scholars, and editors and editorial board members of prestigious research journals in accounting, finance, marketing, strategy and operations management. Corporate partnerships and federal grants have jumpstarted some of the college's most high-profile research programs, many of which include both faculty and student research projects.

STUDENTS

Almost all MBA students have professional work experience, many in high-technology industries, such as telecommunications or software; others in industries, such as health care or financial services, where technology is the key to a competitive advantage. A technical background is not essential for the MBA, but all students must be willing to learn about technology and the management challenges it creates. More than 60 percent of MBA students have undergraduate degrees in science, computer science, or engineering. Another 24 percent were business majors. The rest come from a variety of fields, including the social sciences and humanities.

The average MBA student has six years of work experience. The age range of students is between 22 and 45. Women comprise approximately 28 percent of each entering class; members of minority groups, approximately 3 percent; and international students, 9 percent.

ADMISSIONS

MBA students must have a baccalaureate degree from an accredited college or university and are strongly encouraged to have had courses in calculus, statistics, and economics. Admissions decisions are based on previous academic performance, GMAT scores (a 625 average), two essays, letters of reference, and previous work and volunteer experience. Applicants whose native language is other than English, regardless of citizenship, must also submit TOEFL scores of at least 260 (computer-based test). Interviews are not required for part-time applicants.

ADDITIONAL INFORMATION

The curriculum in electronic commerce is projected to encompass four three-unit courses: Introduction to the Digital Economy, EC Network Infrastructure and Software Tools, an EC elective, and EC Practicum—a project-based course that focuses on the practical aspects of creating and running an e-commerce enterprise. Students work with businesses, such as IBM, to examine how electronic commerce can best be put to practice.

The Technology, Education, and Commercialization (TEC) program within the MBA is designed to promote both educational and technology transfer objectives. Supported by the National Science Foundation, graduate students and faculty members in the College of Management work closely in teams with their counterparts in the science and engineering disciplines to identify, evaluate, and commercialize promising technologies.

CAREER SERVICES & PLACEMENT

An MBA degree gives students skills that are highly valued by employers. The College's students have access to a wide range of programs and services to enhance their marketability. Professional career counseling is available. The MBA program provides workshops on resume writing and cover letters, interviewing skills; and job search strategies. In addition to on-campus recruiting for permanent jobs and internships, the RedWall Career Center maintains an online resume referral and job posting service, hosts job fairs, and maintains a library of information about career opportunities with specific companies.

RENSSELAER POLYTECHNIC INSTITUTE

AT A GLANCE

Rensselaer's Lally School develops tech-savvy, versatile business leaders adept at advancing business through innovation. The school's graduates are entrepreneurial managers who understand how to create business value through the application of technology across business functions. Along with starting their own ventures, our MBAs are employed by a broad array of the world's leading technology-based product and services corporations. The Lally School of Management and Technology is nationally accredited by AACSB International.

LOCATION & ENVIRONMENT

While quiet and park-like, Rensselaer's 260-acre campus has all the conveniences of a self-contained city. The campus setting is a blend of modern style and classic charm. Built into a hillside, the campus overlooks the historic city of Troy and the Hudson River. With red brick buildings dating from the early 1900s adjacent to state-of-the-art research and teaching facilities, Rensselaer's campus reflects a majestic past and exciting future.

The Troy, NY, campus is only 10 minutes from Albany, the capital city of New York, and a 2 1/2-hour commute to New York City. It is easily accessible to Boston and Montreal. Boating, skiing, and hiking are close by in the Adirondack, Catskill, Berkshire, and Green mountains. Amtrak and the Albany International Airport offer newly renovated facilities. The Capital Region is a major center for government, industry, research, and academic life. Rensselaer's commitment to innovation and technological entrepreneurship complements ongoing efforts to transform the Capital Region into a "tech valley," which is rapidly becoming one of the country's leading-edge hubs for research and technology.

DEGREES OFFERED

Rensselaer's Lally School offers three graduate degree programs: Master of Science in Management; Master of Business Administration; and Doctor of Philosophy in Management and Technology, which offers a research-oriented program for those pursuing a career path in either academia or research.

Master of Business Administration

Lally's premiere degree program is the MBA. The MBA curriculum provides students with the opportunities, knowledge, and support to become "masters of business innovation" through hands-on projects and teamwork. Areas of concentration in the Lally MBA include:

- Strategy and technological entrepreneurship
- Management of information systems (MIS)
- Finance
- New product development and marketing
- Production and operations management
- Environmental management and policy

Students also may customize a management and technology concentration.

In addition to the mainstay MBA program, the Lally School offers three additional tracks. The Executive MBA is a two-year, weekend-based, intensive course of study for working professionals. The Sino-U.S. MBA addresses the needs of companies establishing and expanding businesses in China. The JD-MBA allows students with a strong interest in intellectual property issues to pursue a law degree and an MBA degree simultaneously.

Lally students also can obtain a dual degree by combining their MBA with an MS in information technology or an MS from one of the other Rensselaer schools (72 credit hours total). This option allows students to add business acumen to a depth of technical knowledge in established or emerging technologies.

PROGRAMS & CURRICULUM

The Lally MBA program includes 20 courses (or 60 credit hours total) and two seminars. Within this curriculum is Lally's flagship course: Design, Manufacturing, and Marketing (DMM). In a yearlong process, students navigate their way through new product development—from conceptualization to commercialization. Taught by a cross-functional team of four faculty, student teams conduct field based market research, generate multiple new product concepts, test and finalize concept selection, navigate the design process, create a manufacturing plan, launch a marketing plan, and analyze associated infrastructure costs to support their recommendations.

A second unique course offering is Commercializing Advanced Technologies. This course is based on Lally's cutting-edge radical innovation research program. Students select a piece of "intellectual property" from Rensselaer's patent portfolio, research and propose potential market applications, develop a business model, and draft a licensing agreement or a full business plan. Work involves interviewing inventors and conducting extensive market research. Students work with Rensselaer's Office of Technology Commercialization and the Albany Law School as a part of this course. Student projects from this class and DMM often become the seed of a new incubator business, or re-emerge as presentations in venture capital competitions.

During the first year of the MBA program, the incoming students have a set curriculum and take all of their courses together as a cohort. The cohort structure fosters a sense of community among members, and cultivates learning, information sharing, partnering, and long-term business relationships. The second year of the MBA program includes three required courses: strategy, ethics, and international business. Seven additional elective courses round out the student's degree program.

Entrepreneurship is a mainstream activity of the Lally School. *Entrepreneur* magazine ranks Rensselaer's Lally School of Management and Technology in the top 25 for entrepreneurial programs nationally. The Paul J. '69 and Kathleen M. Severino Center for Technological Entrepreneurship leads this mission by encouraging students to consider the benefits of creating new privately-owned companies or corporations. Activities include business forums on technology incubation, high-tech entrepreneurship, and venture capital funding; the Rensselaer Entrepreneurship Interns Program; an annual Women in Entrepreneurship seminar; and a regional Tech Valley Collegiate Business Plan Competition. Student teams from area colleges enter the annual business plan competition seeking an award of seed-stage capital, plus the opportunity to present their proposals to venture capitalists in Boston, New York, and California.

The Lally School has also received national recognition for its MIS concentration. The MIS concentration integrates Lally's historical strengths in operations research and statistics with Rensselaer's technological pre-eminence in information technology and computer science. Students have an opportunity to work with faculty across the Rensselaer campus as they learn about the strategic uses of information technology in such contexts as supply-chain management, outsourcing, enterprise re-engineering, and eBusiness.

FACILITIES & EQUIPMENT

The Lally School is housed in the Pittsburgh Building, a 43,000 square-foot teaching and research facility. Recently modernized, the building provides technology-intensive multimedia classrooms, distance-learning facilities, and student lounges with laptop connectivity. Management students are encouraged to build their own online systems (inventory, enterprise portals, e-commerce applications, order processing, etc.). To this end, the Lally tech center provides enterprise databases, Web servers, portals, commerce servers, and a host of other programs to assist students. Additionally, the Folsom Library provides more than 60 online databases including ABI/INFORM Global, Forrester Research, and Standard & Poor's NetAdvantage for student research.

Lally School of Management and Technology

EXPENSES & FINANCIAL AID

Rensselaer is committed to supporting full-time graduate students with tuition support combined with a stipend awarded on a competitive basis, and based on merit. Additional fellowships and other financial support may also be available. Expenses for the 2003–2004 academic year are estimated at $39,717 for full-time students. This includes a flat rate of $27,700 for tuition, $9,000 for estimated living expenses, expenses for books, health and dental services and insurance, and miscellaneous fees. International students should contact Graduate Admissions, admissions@rpi.edu or 518-276-6216 for financial aid information.

FACULTY

Lally faculty is recruited for their world-class capabilities in teaching and research. Strong emphasis is placed on the delivery of the MBA and PhD instructional programs. These programs build upon Lally's state-of-the-art research in the areas of technological entrepreneurship; new product development and radical innovation; management information systems; financial technology; global management of technology; and biotech entrepreneurship, an emerging focus at the Lally School. Many full-time faculty members have substantial managerial experience in business or government.

STUDENTS

Aspiring business leaders must be both managerially and technologically astute. Select admissions criteria result in a highly qualified MBA class, and provide added value for students who choose to study at Rensselaer to develop these management tools.

Seminars offer a rigorous academic environment and personal interaction between students, faculty members, and guest speakers. Students may participate in cutting-edge research, such as our Radical Innovation Project (featured in *BusinessWeek*), studying the commercialization of next-generation products and services by established firms.

Lally's diverse student population offers a variety of cultural, educational, and business perspectives. An active Graduate Management Student Association sponsors social, career, and recreational activities, intramural sports, and community service.

Students may work on projects or cooperative work experiences with companies at the Rensselaer Incubator Center, the Rensselaer Technology Park, or area firms that include GE, Lockheed Martin, Allied Signal, Albany International, First Albany, and a host of smaller companies. Companies at the Rensselaer Technology Park represent technologies ranging from electronic to physics research, from biotechnology to software. Our nationally acclaimed Incubator Center provides even more opportunity. Founded in 1980 as the first university-based incubator in the nation, the Incubator Center provides a unique entrepreneurial environment—harnessing academic, research, and community resources to assist technology start-up enterprises.

ADMISSIONS

Applicants should possess quantitative skills, a strong interest in technology, and significant work experience. Many students hold a degree in science or engineering. However, it is not a requirement. Each year, a select number of recent college graduates are also considered for admission. The Graduate Management Admissions Test (GMAT) is mandatory for all students. International students are required to take the TOEFL, and must obtain a minimum score of 600. Immigration documents will be issued after admission. The Lally School values a culturally diverse student body. Faculty and staff are committed to the professional development of women and minorities, and seek a strong international representation.

Applications are accepted year-round, and admission decisions are made on a rolling basis. Early submission is strongly encouraged, preferably by January 15 for tuition support and stipend consideration. The academic year runs from late August through mid-May. A full-time program can be completed in two years. A summer session allows for additional flexibility in terms of course work and internships with area companies. Working professionals can custom-tailor an MBA or MS in Management through evening courses as well.

Visit our website http://lallymba.mgmt.rpi.edu for an online application and program information. To request additional information or to schedule a visit, contact:

Director of Graduate Admissions
Lally School MBA/Master's Programs
Rensselaer Polytechnic Institute
110 8th Street Pittsburgh Building
Troy, New York 12180-3590
Tel.: 518-276-6586
Fax: 518-276-2665
E-mail: lallymba@rpi.edu

ADDITIONAL INFORMATION

A distinguished speaker series is conducted throughout the year, bringing senior executives to speak and interact with students in an intimate venue on a variety of strategic management issues.

Rensselaer's intimate Lally School of Management and Technology is not for technophobes or the faint-hearted. Nearly everyone here has an extensive background in computers and engineering, and the "friendly but busy" students study like crazy. RPI boasts small classes, great computing facilities, and a lot of student/faculty interaction. RPI's "top-notch" professors "have a wealth of both academic and professional experience."

Business students can access Rensselaer's rich array of campus-wide programs and resources to fully leverage the Institute's strengths in management and technology. Additionally, through its corporate partners' network, Lally faculty and staff ensure that the curriculum is aligned to the needs of hiring managers, and cultivate and maintain high-level networking opportunities for business students. Students meet with alumni for mentoring and career advice, and classes feature guest speakers, senior managers, and policy makers.

CAREER SERVICES & PLACEMENT

The Lally Career Resources Office works with all Lally students to clarify their strengths and goals, and assist in developing job search strategies. The office provides a full range of services including on-campus corporate interviews, career fairs, alumni mentoring and networking, situation-specific interviewing skills, and resume books for distribution to corporate recruiters. All MBA students participate in the Gary Craig '68 Career Seminar to develop the skills needed to successfully compete in today's job market. The Seminar uses corporate executives, experienced recruiters, videotaped mock interviews, and experiential activities such as a business etiquette dinner. Students have access to both the Lally JobBank and Rensselaer's Career Development Center's (CDC) databases. Rensselaer's campus-wide CDC and the Archer Center for Leadership Development complement the Lally services by offering corporate career days, executive roundtable discussions, a Cooperative Job-Educational Program (co-op), and professional development seminars.

RICE UNIVERSITY

AT A GLANCE

"Classroom learning is only one aspect of a complete business education. In this era of rapid globalization, change is the only constant, and companies want more than good managers—they want great leaders who can resolve issues with a multidisciplinary approach.

"While many business schools continue to emphasize theory, the Jones School curriculum builds on theory with an experiential learning process we call Action Learning. We're one of two business schools that require all our students to take their classroom knowledge into real business settings.

"We've applied this philosophy of change as the only constant to ourselves as well. After seeking input from our faculty, students, and industry leaders—including top management at major corporations to determine which skills they consider most valuable—we've designed an innovative course of study that provides all you'll need to excel in the global business environment. Our focus on leadership has been widely recognized, including by the Wall Street Journal."

—Gilbert R. Whitaker, Jr., Dean

Ranked nationally as the number one Finance program (second in the world) by *The Economist* in 2003, the Rice MBA program at the Jesse H. Jones Graduate School of Management of Rice University has risen quickly from its founding in 1974. Other recent rankings include:

Ranked at number one, nationally, in Career Progress (sixth in world) by *The Financial Times;* number two in U.S. (eighth in world) for Marketing by *The Economist;* number two in U.S. (seventh in world) for Economics by *The Economist;* number three in U.S. (fourth in world) for Faculty Quality by *The Economist;* number 31 overall by *U.S. News & World Report.*

The small class size of 180 students provides an intimate, dynamic learning environment in the new state-of-the-art facility. Close connections with the faculty and alumni opens a world of opportunity, as does the location—Houston—home to the second largest concentration of Fortune 500 headquarters. Whether interested in staying in Texas, working elsewhere in the U.S., or relocating internationally, students can achieve their goals with a Rice MBA.

Additional information and a full list of media mentions are available through our website: www.jonesgsm.rice.edu.

LOCATION & ENVIRONMENT

Rice University is located on a beautiful, wooded, 300-acre campus in central Houston, minutes from the downtown business district and the city's world-class theater district. The campus is located across the street from the renowned Texas Medical Center, and within walking distance to the museum district, Houston Zoological Gardens, and Hermann Park. The surrounding neighborhood is one of Houston's most attractive. The new light rail line will connect Rice to Downtown, Minute Maid Park (home of the MLB Astros), and Reliant Stadium (home to the NFL Texans), beginning in 2004.

DEGREES OFFERED

The Jones School focuses all of its energy on graduate business education. Available degrees include the MBA, MBA for Executives, MBA/Master's in Engineering with the George R. Brown College of Engineering at Rice, and MBA/MD in conjunction with Baylor College of Medicine.

PROGRAMS & CURRICULUM

Why Rice?

Choosing the right graduate business program is a decision with lasting implications. People who choose the Jones School can do well anywhere. Here are the top reasons alumni and students are glad they chose the Rice MBA program:

Personal Attention

One of the hallmarks of Rice University's Jones School is its moderate class size, which creates a highly unusual learning environment that differentiates it from other top-tier business schools. This allows close working relationships between students and our outstanding faculty. Even outside the classroom, *BusinessWeek*

says, "Rice scores among the leaders for having faculty who are accessible to students."

Leading-Edge Curriculum

The Jones School action-learning curriculum is at the forefront of management education. The methodology and modular structure are designed to help students develop crucial leadership and managerial skills, such as negotiating effectively and learning when to partner, and when to compete. In an action-learning project toward the end of the first year, students integrate these tools with a team of classmates, consulting full-time with a company to solve a specific problem. The required second-year entrepreneurship course—one of the few required courses of its kind in the nation—and numerous experiential learning-based electives will provide additional opportunities to put acquired knowledge to work. When it comes to getting a summer internship between first and second years, students have found that the action-learning project is regarded as an internship, giving them an advantage in securing an interesting summer internship. Our students have twice as much internship experience as most MBA graduates when exploring job options in their second year.

Reputation

Rice University is consistently ranked as one of America's best teaching and research universities. It has the fifth largest endowment per student among American universities. The Jones School is among the world's best business schools. In 2002, the *Financial Times* ranks the Jones School among the top 25 business schools in the U.S., and top 40 in the world. In 2002, *The Economist* ranked our faculty third best in the U.S. and fourth best in the world. Our finance program was ranked as the best in the U.S, and tied for the second best in the world by *The Economist*, and ranked in the top ten by the *Financial Times* in 2002. Our marketing program was ranked second in the U.S., and tied for eighth in the world by *The Economist*. Employers also recognize the quality of our graduates—the Jones School is ranked among the top ten by *U.S. News* for employment at three months in 2002. *BusinessWeek* named Professor Ed Williams as one of the two best entrepreneurial instructors in the U.S. Faculty in other areas have also been honored as leaders in their fields. The Jones School has been singled out for its support of women and minority students by *The Economist*, the *Financial Times*, and *Time* magazine.

First-Class Facilities

The Jones School moved into its new home in August 2002. The 167,000 square-foot building offers state-of-the-art facilities, including the best, broadest, and most in-depth finance center of any business school. Most school finance centers are basically equity desks. Rice's El Paso Finance Center is designed to bring the markets to students, and the students to the markets, and will have four desks: energy, equity, fixed income, and currency. Other facilities include a 14,000-square-foot Business Information Center providing students with everything from periodicals and annual reports to online access retrieval of the latest financial information; tiered classrooms to enhance case-study method instruction; behavioral research and observation rooms for focus group research and interviews; comfortable breakout rooms for group study and discussion; a 425 seat auditorium where students and faculty can gather together as a group; a "cyber-commons" where students and faculty can meet with both coffee and ports for computer and network connectivity; and a career planning suite, where advisors can help students develop their interviewing and job search skills, and where corporations can interview students for internships or permanent positions. Student are given fully loaded laptops as part of their tuition, and the new building is equipped to make the most sophisticated use of electronic access.

Business Connections

Houston is second only to New York in Fortune 500 corporate headquarters, and is also an operating center for more than half of the world's largest internationally based, corporations. *BusinessWeek*'s most recent edition of The Best Business Schools rated the Jones School at 11 of 61 for providing graduates with "useful contact with outside business professionals."

Jesse H. Jones Graduate School of Management

Multiple Approaches to Learning

In every course, students have an unparalleled opportunity to work one-on-one with an accessible, involved, and energetic faculty. In 2002, 24 members of our faculty were nominated by the Classes of 2000 and 1997 for outstanding teaching awards. It speaks well for the school that so many faculty were judged to have had lasting impact on students they taught two and five years ago, respectively.

Curriculum Profile

A comprehensive core curriculum focuses on managerial and leadership skills, ethics, information technology, and communication skills in addition to the functional areas. An Action Learning Project in the first year gives students the opportunity to learn how to integrate disciplines and turn knowledge into action. A modular format promotes flexibility in course structure. A core entrepreneurship course in the second year further refines integration of business disciplines. Students take 25 credit hours of electives in their second year, which allows them to custom design their curriculum to suit career goals.

Personalized Career Planning

The Jones School's Career Planning Center (CPC) is an extremely valuable advocate for the future of its students. The CPC offers more campus interviews per student and more personalized service than any "top 10" MBA program in the U.S. In April 2002, *U.S. News & World Report*, ranked the Jones School one of the top 10 business schools for graduates employed at three months, along with Stanford, Harvard, and Yale. Rice MBA graduates are consistently among the top 20 business schools for total compensation offers.

FACILITIES & EQUIPMENT

In August 2002, the Jones School occupied its new home of 167,000 square feet. The new building offers three times the space of Herring Hall (the previous home of the Jones School) and houses everything from the dean's office to the Business Information Center to the Career Planning Center. Wired and wireless technology is in place to assist in research and information gathering.

Some of the highlights of the new building include the El Paso Corporation Finance Center, behavioral research and observation rooms, a 450 seat two-tiered auditorium, the 14,000 square-foot Business Information Center, a cyber-commons, a dining hall, 13 classrooms of various size and design, and more than 40 team meeting rooms—all for a class of 180 students! Since the Jones School focuses solely on MBA education, access to facilities is never a problem.

Additional information and photos of the new facility can be reviewed at www.jonesgsm.rice.edu/jonesgsm/The_New_Building_Home.asp

EXPENSES & FINANCIAL AID

Application fee: $100

Tuition: $28,000 per year for the class entering in fall 2003. Laptop computer, hardware and software are included in this price.

Total estimated expenses: Approximately $49,000 per year

Financial aid: About 65 percent of each class receives financial aid from the school. We offer a limited amount of aid to international students. An independent association, RICE-TMS, funds minority scholarships for Jones School students.

FACULTY

The Jones School's faculty is consistently recognized for their knowledge, research, teaching ability, and student focus. Each member of the Jones faculty maintains a balance between teaching and research, ensuring that students receive the most current, leading-edge education.

In fact, in the 13th edition of its guide to business schools around the world, "Which MBA?" *The Economist* ranked the Jones School fourth in the world and third in the U.S. for faculty quality.

STUDENTS

Class of 2003 Profile

The Class of 2003 represents 35 different nationalities. The break down of international students is Europe, 6 percent; North America, 71 percent; Latin America, 5 percent; Asia, 16 percent; Africa, 1 percent; Middle East, 1 percent. The average age is 27years, with a range of 22 to 43 years. Thirty-nine percent have more the 5 years of work experience, 38 percent have 3-5 years of work experience, 22 percent have 1-3 years of work experience; and 1 percent have less than one year of work experience. Forty percent have degrees in business and economics; 40 percent in engineering, science, and math; and 20 percent in liberal arts.

ADMISSIONS

Admission requirements are a bachelor's degree; GMAT (no minimum; average scores are 630-660); TOEFL for international applicants (minimum score of 600); no work experience is required of exceptionally qualified students (up to 5 percent of the class).

Academic Background

Applicants must have a four-year undergraduate degree from an accredited college or university if education was received in the United States. International applicants must have the equivalent of a U.S. four-year degree. Applicants who have completed a three-year Bachelor of Commerce (BCom) degree are also required to have a two-year Master of Commerce (MCom) degree. Undergraduate and graduate GPAs, GMAT scores (or GRE scores if applying to the joint MBA/ME degree program, or MCAT scores if applying to the MBA/MD program), choice of major, electives, course load, and grade patterns are all considered. Interviews are by invitation.

Leadership Potential

Demonstrated leadership and management experiences, both on the job and through extracurricular activities, will help us assess an applicant's leadership potential.

Confidential Evaluations

Evaluations from employers and/or professors shed perspective on an applicant's capabilities, enabling us to assess qualifications more accurately.

A Personal Statement

Three essays that articulate career goals, work experience, and reasons for choosing Rice University's Jones School are a crucial component of the application. Use them to convey intangibles: Why are you pursuing an MBA? How have you benefited from your academic, professional, and personal opportunities? What qualities will you bring to the Jones School, and what will you seek from us?

Electronic applications are available—please visit our website.

CAREER SERVICES & PLACEMENT

According to *The Financial Times* in 2003, the Jones School received the highest ranking among U.S. business schools for Career Progress, defined as "the degree to which alumni have moved up the career ladder three years after graduating. Progression is measured through changes in level of seniority and the size of the company in which they are employed." It was ranked sixth in the world in this category.

The Career Planning Center (CPC) is housed within the Jones School building, and works only with Rice MBA students and alumni. Rice also participates in the MBA Consortium, allowing students to meet and interview with companies not currently recruiting on campus. The efforts of the CPC coupled with student talent and hard work, the Action Learning Project, and Jones curriculum resulted in 100 percent internship placement for the class of 2003—a rare result given the economic conditions.

ST. JOHN'S UNIVERSITY

AT A GLANCE

The Tobin College of Business: Business Leadership. For Life.

For nearly 75 years, the Tobin College of Business has offered future business leaders a strong foundation in management education with a focus on developing individuals for the most senior corporate positions in the world. The importance that we attach to practical business knowledge and technology, globalization as reflected in our being a first mover among American business schools in establishing a campus abroad, and a deep appreciation for the special ethical challenges of business practice in our contemporary environment, enable the College to offer unique opportunities for students who are committed to excellence. These features, combined with our network of over 35,000 alumni worldwide, our talented and dedicated faculty, outstanding resources, and commitment to a values-based business education, all make the College unique in providing business leadership skills for life.

LOCATION & ENVIRONMENT

The Peter J. Tobin College of Business (TCB) has three residential campuses in exciting New York City, and one campus in Rome, Italy. The park-like Queens and Staten Island campuses are minutes from Manhattan. The 10-story building that makes up the Manhattan campus stands in the heart of New York's Financial Center. The campus in Rome, Italy reflects the broad reach and international focus maintained by the Tobin College of Business.

Campus Overviews:
Queens Campus
8000 Utopia Parkway
Jamaica, NY 11439
Phone: 718-990-2600

One of the city's most recognized campuses, St. John's 105-acre Queens campus has rolling lawns, imposing stone buildings, and magnificent new student residence halls.

The Queens campus is in a quiet neighborhood of tree-lined streets and handsome private homes. Yet a quick ride by car, bus, or subway takes students into exciting New York City. Students can ride into Manhattan to catch a Broadway play, root for the Knicks, visit a museum, or sip coffee at a Greenwich Village cafe.

Staten Island Campus
300 Howard Avenue
Staten Island, NY 10301
Phone: 718-390-4500

High on a wooded bluff overlooking New York harbor, St. John's University's charming Staten Island campus is located on the site of a 19th century estate. Though the campus is in New York City's most suburban borough, the excitement of Manhattan is easily accessible by car, bus, or a scenic ferry ride across the harbor.

The 18-acre Staten Island campus features broad lawns, winding paths, and red brick, neo-Georgian buildings. There also are strikingly modern facilities, including the new Kelleher Center.

Students at our Staten Island campus enjoy apartment-style housing. The three-story residences are clustered around a central lawn adjacent to campus, so students can easily walk to class from their rooms.

Manhattan Campus
101 Murray Street
New York, NY 10007
Phone: 212-277-5113

This 10-story building in lower Manhattan is just a few blocks from Wall Street, Battery Park City, and the city's Financial Center.

Ideally located at Murray Street and the West Side Highway, the distinctive, ziggurat-shaped building features high-tech classrooms, athletic facilities, a cafeteria, and a library with one of the world's largest collections of insurance-related texts. The campus is close to many of Manhattan's other attractions, including Greenwich Village, SoHo, Little Italy, Chinatown, and the renovated Chelsea recreational piers dotting the Hudson River.

There are a limited number of student residences available at our Manhattan campus. Due to high demand, the residences are available on a first come, first served basis. As with St. John's other New York campuses, residence life at the Manhattan campus fosters a friendly, supportive atmosphere with a dedicated and well-trained residence life staff.

Rome Campus
Rome Graduate Center
Via Santa Maria
Mediatrice 24 Rome, Italy 00165
Phone: 011-39-06-393-842

Global in outlook, St. John's University prepares students for success in an increasingly international marketplace. The Graduate Center in Rome plays an important role in this mission.

Located at the historic Pontificio Oratorio San Pietro, just off the Via Aurelia on Via Santa Maria Mediatrice, the Rome Campus offers St. John's first overseas MBA program. The program, launched in fall 1995, is designed to provide students with access to the professional expertise of international corporate leaders. A master's program in International Relations also is offered at the Graduate Center.

DEGREES OFFERED

The MBA degree is offered with specializations in accounting, taxation, decision sciences, executive management, finance, financial services, international business, international finance, marketing management, insurance, actuarial sciences, risk management, and computer information systems for managers. Successful completion requires a minimum of 36 credit hours. Additional credits may be required, depending on previous course work that has been completed in business and economics. Individual plans of study are developed for each student in consultation with advisers and faculty members in the College. The degree may be completed on either a part-time or full-time basis, and includes study in the MBA core, specialization courses, and electives. The Master of Science (MS) degree is offered in taxation, accounting and in risk and insurance. Advanced Professional Certificates (APCs) are available to individuals who have completed the MBA degree, and are designed to enable such students to accrue additional knowledge or skills in another field or update and enhance skills in their current field. Eighteen credits are required for completion of the APC.

The Rome campus offers the MBA degree in international finance and marketing.

PROGRAMS & CURRICULUM

The Tobin College has a long history of providing a strong educational foundation to individuals who have risen to senior executive positions all over the world. The educational philosophy is grounded in the importance of not just conveying business knowledge and skills, but also developing leaders who appreciate the need to think, and often act, globally, and who realize and appreciate the role that ethics and social responsibility plays in successful business practice.

St. John's early recognition of the important role that the globalization of business holds for future business leaders is represented by its having been one of the first American business schools to establish a real presence beyond U.S. shores in Rome, Italy. Today, the campus there is a thriving center for students interested primarily in the intersection of business and international markets.

The Tobin College is fully accredited by AACSB International—The Association to Advance Collegiate Schools of Business.

Peter J. Tobin College of Business

FACILITIES & EQUIPMENT

The Main Library of the University is in St. Augustine Hall, located on the Queens campus. Together with the collections of the Loretto Memorial Library on the Staten Island campus, the Law School Library, the Oakdale Campus Library, the Kathryn and Shelby Cullom Davis Library in Manhattan, and the Rome campus library, the total University library collection numbers 1.7 million volumes and includes more than 6,000 periodic subscriptions. These materials support course offerings as well as students' cultural and recreational interests. The collection includes government documents and audiovisual materials.

Specific support for the study of business is provided by a collection of more than 63,422 book titles and 648 business periodical subscriptions. There is also an extensive collection of indexes, abstracts, and full-text databases; these include ABI/INFORM available through UMI/Proquest, EBSCO, Lexis-Nexis, and OCLC First Search. The library houses specialized services, both in print and electronic formats, from Commerce Clearing House, Research Institute of America, Standard & Poor's, Dun & Bradstreet, and Value Line.

Extensive computer facilities include over 90 multimedia classrooms and more than 2,000 computers available for student use. A special graduate commons area in the main library is reserved for the use of MBA students.

EXPENSES & FINANCIAL AID

Tuition in 2003–2004 is $685 per credit. An additional $75 general fee per term is due at the time of registration. A limited number of graduate assistantships are awarded, based on academic merit.

Living expenses in the New York metropolitan area vary widely, depending on housing and lifestyle. St. John's offers students a variety of housing opportunities. Through the Office of Residence Life, graduate students can secure on-campus housing (subject to availability). To be considered for on-campus housing, students should submit their request to the Office of Admission. Through the University's Housing Service, students can find comfortable and convenient off-campus housing in surrounding neighborhoods. All inquiries concerning off-campus housing should be directed to the Office of Student Life at 718-990-6257.

FACULTY

The faculty at the Tobin College of Business is drawn from leading institutions all over the world. Our full-time faculty number 101, and this group is complemented by business practitioners who regularly serve as adjunct instructors or co-teachers of courses.

Tobin College faculty members are selected for their commitment to teaching and their understanding of the real world of business. Ninety percent of the faculty members hold the highest terminal degree in the field, and together they possess an internationally diverse portfolio of business experience. Six members of the faculty are internationally recognized Fulbright Scholars, and numerous others are frequent consultants to businesses and the business news media.

STUDENTS

With a student enrollment that reflects the cultural diversity present within actual business settings, and the very special business center that is Manhattan in close proximity, the Tobin College has succeeded in launching the careers of more than 35,000 business leaders worldwide. Currently, there are over 700 students enrolled at the Tobin College Graduate Division. Special opportunities exist for students to network with alumni of the College for the purposes of career information and development, and internships.

As of fall 2002, Tobin College has 232 first-time graduate students, with a total of 746 graduate students enrolled. Women make up 43 percent, and men make up 57 percent of the student population. The average age is 29. Most are from New York—68 percent— and the remaining 32 percent are from other states and countries. The average GMAT score is 530, and average GPA is 3.25.

ADMISSIONS

Admission to the Tobin College has become increasingly competitive in recent years, and prospective students are encouraged to begin the process early. Students are evaluated using the full portfolio of materials requested by the College.

All applicants must possess a baccalaureate degree from an accredited institution, or the international equivalent. The candidate should submit, in addition to the $40 nonrefundable application fee, official transcripts from all undergraduate, graduate, and professional schools attended. In addition, results of the GMAT (Graduate Management Admission Test) taken within the last five years, a resume, letters of recommendation, and a personal statement should be submitted with the application. Details of these requirements may be obtained from the Office of Admissions of Tobin College or from the College's website. Applicants whose native language in not English must also submit the results of the TOEFL.

ADDITIONAL INFORMATION

In addition to extensive opportunities to study abroad, selected students may participate in the Executive-in-Residence program, which provides with students with special opportunities to serve as consultants in partnership with senior corporate executives in solving business challenges. The program is designed to help students develop a deeper understanding of corporate leadership and the complexities of organizational decision-making.

Recently, an alumni-funded Student Investment Fund was established to enable students to obtain hands-on investing experience under the guidance of seasoned faculty members and alumni with vast Wall Street experience. Students invest real money in real markets and in real-time to full develop their portfolio management skills.

Service learning projects offer students opportunities to both learn and serve their communities simultaneously. Generally focused on nonprofit organizations in need of business expertise, these projects are supervised by senior faculty and provide consulting services of varying types to subject organizations on a pro bono basis.

One of the greatest strengths of Tobin College is its extensive and loyal network of more than 35,000 alumni worldwide, many of whom hold the most senior executive positions in major business and nonprofit organizations. There is a strong partnership with business, both within and outside of the U.S., and events bring together distinguished speakers, business leaders, faculty members, and students for discussions that are of concern in today's global economy. The Henry George Lecture Series is a semi-annual event that features a leading expert in economic affairs. The Dean's Advisory Board is a regular presence at the College and is comprised of alumni and non-alumni who provide their insights and expertise to students and faculty members alike. Among the members of this board are Jim Schiro, CEO of Zurich Financial Services; Eugene Sullivan, former CEO of Borden, Inc.; and Patrick Purcell, publisher of the Boston Herald.

CAREER SERVICES & PLACEMENT

The Career Center's professional placement programs offer a wide variety of services designed to give each graduate student and alumnus the competitive edge. Services and resources include career advisement, on-campus interviews, full-time and part-time employment opportunities, a career resource library, resume preparation and interview techniques, a videotape library, and mock interview sessions. Owing largely to these services and the extensive network of successful alumni, Tobin College has consistently enjoyed a high rate of job placement for MBA students within three months of graduation—most recently over 80 percent.

SAN JOSE STATE UNIVERSITY

LOCATION & ENVIRONMENT

The main campus is comprised of 10 closed city blocks adjacent to downtown San Jose. The buildings are a mix of "Old Spanish" and "Modern Government" architecture separated by many fountains, trees, and spacious lawns.

Business classes are held in the newly renovated Boccardo Business Education Center. All rooms in the 82,000 square-foot building are now wired for computer access. In addition, 18 of the 46 classrooms are equipped with "smart podia" containing Internet and television access, document cameras, and VCRs. Each room is also fully American Disabilities Act compliant, with wheelchair stations and a public address system that accommodates hearing-impaired students.

The Clark Library and special collection libraries on campus house almost a million volumes and approximately 3,500 periodical titles. Clark Library serves as a federal and state repository. Special interest libraries include the Steinbeck Center, Beethoven Center, and the Chicano Library Resource Center. A collaborative effort between the City of San Jose and San Jose State University (SJSU) has resulted in the construction of a new joint library, the Dr. Martin Luther King Jr. Library, scheduled to open in fall 2003.

The off-campus location at Rose Orchard Technology Center is approximately 12 miles from the main campus. The Rose Orchard site is located in a technology park setting in the heart of the Silicon Valley high-tech corridor, making it convenient to many working adults.

Staffed by 15 full-time professionals, SJSU's Career Center offers a range of resources to help students and recent graduates meet with success in the search for employment. Services include career advising and assistance, with resume preparation and interview skills. The Center maintains a resource library, a career lab with workstations and career guidance software, and a job bank with more than 100,000 listings. Graduate employment reports, containing information on the job placement rate of SJSU graduates, and average starting salaries, are also available. On-campus recruiting and job fairs are organized by the Center, putting students and recent graduates in touch with potential employers.

PROGRAMS & CURRICULUM

The evening on-campus MBA program consists of 13-16 three-unit courses, each 15 weeks long. This program is designed for students who prefer the University educational atmosphere, or who are attending graduate school full-time.

The evening off-campus MBA program delivers the same courses in eight-week modules throughout the calendar year. This format allows students to complete six courses per year. Courses are held at the College of Business off-campus site, located in the heart of Silicon Valley's high-tech corridor.

The MBA-One is a one-year, full-time daytime MBA program designed for non-working individuals who prefer an executive cohort style of learning. The lockstep program design allows the completion of the MBA degree in one year.

The MBA programs are open to individuals from all undergraduate disciplines.

The daytime Master of Science in Accountancy (MSA) degree program is for full-time students with non-business baccalaureate degrees. This is an 11-month, lock-step program that begins in June of each year. The program includes a professional, paid internship component.

The evening Master of Science in Taxation (MST) degree program is designed to provide tax professionals with conceptual understanding and technical knowledge to compete in the dynamic tax world. This program is offered in modules to accommodate full-time professionals. A full-time student who has earned an undergraduate degree in business, or passed the CPA exam, can complete the MST in 11 months.

The accelerated evening Master of Science in Transportation Management (MSTM) degree program is designed to meet the career education needs of working transportation professionals by using "distance learning" technology.

The MBA/MSE off-campus accelerated evening dual degree program is a combined program for engineering professionals who wish to pursue technical and executive management positions.

All business graduate programs are accredited by the AACSB International—The Association to Advance Collegiate Schools of Business—and the Western Association of Schools and Colleges.

College of Business

EXPENSES & FINANCIAL AID

Fees for in-state residents enrolled in the on-campus program are $747 for one to six units per semester. Resident students enrolled for more than six units pay $1,110 per semester. Nonresidents pay an additional $282 per unit. Students in the off-campus program pay fees of $1,410 per course. The program fee for the MBA-One is $22,560.

Financial aid eligibility for U.S. residents is determined after completing the Free Application for Federal Student Aid (FAFSA), available from the University Financial Aid Office.

FACULTY

The College of Business has over 100 full-time equivalent faculty positions, and takes advantage of its Silicon Valley location by hiring local area professionals to teach part-time. Full-time faculty are encouraged to establish industry connections to inform their teaching and research, most of which is applied. Faculty is evaluated on their teaching performance, and take pride in teaching well. They assign classroom projects that enable students to make Silicon Valley connections and work one-on-one with interested students on research and teaching projects. No courses are taught by teaching assistants.

STUDENTS

San Jose State University is California's oldest institution of public higher education. Founded in 1857 in San Francisco as a teacher training school, it was named the California State Normal School in 1862 and moved to San Jose in 1871. Today, SJSU is a large university serving more than 27,000 students.

SJSU's scope has changed to meet the needs of today's society, but its long tradition of excellence in teaching remains. The early-day teacher's training school became San Jose State College in 1935, and a member of the California State system in 1961. It began awarding master's degrees in 1949, and achieved university status in 1972.

As the Santa Clara Valley evolved from a rich agricultural region into Silicon Valley, an internationally known high-technology research and development center, the University's mission expanded to fill the ever widening educational needs.

Today, the multicultural student body prepares for careers in business, social work, engineering, science, technology, education, social sciences, arts, and humanities. The University offers degrees and professional credentials in more than 150 disciplines.

The mission of the College of Business graduate programs is to provide advanced business and professional education to high-potential individuals with diverse backgrounds and work experiences. Graduates are prepared to make decisions that are socially and fiscally responsible, personally enriching, and professionally advantageous. We offer a choice of academically challenging, multidisciplinary programs—each of which continuously improves to keep pace with a dynamic environment.

SJSU has an active MBA Association. The MBA Association is a student organization that exists for three reasons: to increase and enhance networking among students; to aid in the dissemination of information among the students and the MBA program; and to strengthen the links between the students and the business community. The group hosts many social and academic events each year, including new student orientation, Silicon Valley speakers, and career events.

ADMISSIONS

Prospective business graduate students must complete and submit an application, the application fee, and one official transcript from every post-secondary school attended. Application due dates for U.S. residents are May 1 for the fall semester and September 15 for the spring semester. International students must apply by March 1 for the fall semester and by August 31 for the spring semester. San José State requires international applicants, for whom English was not the medium of instruction, to take the TOEFL exam. Scores required are 213 computer-based, or 550 paper-based. The Business Graduate Programs Office requires applicants to have a GMAT score of 500, with both verbal and quantitative scores in the 50th percentile. A GPA of 3.0 is also required.

For more information, contact:

San José State University
Business Graduate Programs
One Washington Square
San José, CA 95192-0162
Telephone: 408-924-3420
Fax: 408-924-3426
E-mail: mba@cob.sjsu.edu
World Wide Web: www.cob.sjsu.edu/graduate

SOUTHERN METHODIST UNIVERSITY

AT A GLANCE

The Cox School of Business at Southern Methodist University (SMU) is committed to transforming the world of business—one person at a time. Toward that end, we bring students, professors, business practitioners, and executive mentors together in an engaging, close-knit environment that promotes the free exchange of ideas, rigorous scholarship, and practical application. The result is a robust educational experience that enables students to achieve their professional goals.

One of the Cox School's distinct advantages is our location in the heart of Dallas—a metropolitan city with a thriving and diverse economy; thousands of corporate headquarters; a warm-weather climate; and a high quality, low cost of living. Many of our enrichment programs and activities are designed to allow students to connect with the city's leading companies and learn valuable lessons from experienced business leaders.

At Cox, students have ample opportunity to enhance what is learned in the classroom through pioneering programs, innovative enrichment activities, and specialized institutes and centers of expertise—all supported by state-of-the-art resources and facilities.

Key Benefits and Features

- Access to accomplished business leaders, and leadership training through the Business Leadership Center and the Associate Board Executive Mentor Program.

- Connections to many of Dallas's most prominent executives and successful companies, along with convenient access to the city's many cultural and recreational opportunities.

- Exposure to, and immersion in, foreign economies, businesses, and cultures through the American Airlines Global Leadership Program.

- Close interaction with classmates, faculty, staff, business practitioners, and executive mentors afforded by the school's small size.

- Lifelong affiliation with an internationally recognized program, and an alumni network comprising more than 26,000 people worldwide.

LOCATION & ENVIRONMENT

SMU, established in 1911, has six different schools and graduate programs, in addition to its undergraduate program. The total undergraduate and graduate population is approximately 10,500 students. The University's location in one of the world's major centers of commerce gives students an excellent advantage. The city of Dallas ranks third in the United States as a site of major corporate headquarters, and sixth in the world for multinational corporate headquarters. Dallas offers a wide variety of cultural events and opportunities, from national league sports to the nationally renowned Myerson Symphony Center and the Dallas Museum of Art.

From state-of-the-art classrooms to the Business Information Center, the Cox School offers the latest in business technologies. Beginning the fall 2003, all Cox MBA students are required to own or have access to a laptop computer. The Cox School offers 802.11b Wireless Networking. This technology allows students to use their own laptop computer on the network from a classroom. After class, students can walk from a classroom to a study room and continue to use the Internet from their computer on the network. Students use an in-house network (accessible from home) to communicate with other students and faculty members, connect with the Internet to conduct classroom assignments, and access numerous business databases and research tools.

The MBA Career Management Center (CMC) partners with students to help develop and implement successful career strategies. Students participate in the Career Management Training Program and receive individualized career counseling sessions year-round.

DEGREES OFFERED

Cox MBA full-time program; Cox Professional MBA (evening/weekend, fully employed program); and Cox Executive MBA program (weekend, fully employed program).

Joint Degrees: JD (Juris Doctor), and Cox MBA MA (Master of Arts in Arts Administration and Cox MBA Master of Science in Accounting).

PROGRAMS & CURRICULUM

The Cox MBA program provides an integrated curriculum that helps students establish a solid foundation for success in business. The small class size encourages students to work closely with the faculty and individualize their MBA experience. Located in Dallas, a national and international business center, the Cox School MBA program offers nationally recognized faculty members, a global focus, and close ties with the business community. At Cox, MBAs gain much more than a business education—they gain a personalized business experience.

The two-year MBA curriculum is composed of 60 credit hours that include a global experience and a modular curriculum. The Cox School's program builds a strong portfolio of diverse international perspectives and course offerings for the Cox MBA student who is graduating in the twenty-first century.

First year students complete 10 core courses, the Global Leadership Program (GLP), and 2 short courses in Managing Your Career and Managerial Communication Skills. In addition, there is an opportunity to complete several business elective courses. Students commence their summer internships after they return from the GLP travel abroad experience. Second year students focus on electives and completion of a concentration. The modular curriculum allows students to take an increased number of electives each spring and fall. Module courses are 7-week, short courses scheduled within the traditional semester. Some of these courses are closely integrated, while others are short, stand-alone courses. This design provides students with greater curriculum flexibility, which allows students to build depth in an area of emphasis, or create breadth for a broader perspective of business. Cox MBA students are required to select and complete a concentration in one of the following areas: accounting, financial consulting, finance (corporate or investments), information technologies and operations management, e-business/telecommunications, general management, strategic leadership, marketing (marketing consulting or product and brand management), or strategy and entrepreneurship.

Joint degree programs are offered in conjunction with the law school for a Juris Doctor/MBA (4.5 years), and with the Meadows School of Arts for a Master of Arts in Administration/MBA (6 semesters).

American Airlines Global Leadership Program

Today's business leaders must be global thinkers. At Cox, global thinking is incorporated into the MBA curriculum. The Global Leadership Program is a mandatory, two-week, travel abroad course. All first year students travel to one of three regions of the world—Asia, Europe, or Latin America—to meet with business and government leaders. The goal is to allow students to experience how business is conducted globally. In addition, the Cox School's location—at the gateway to NAFTA and Latin America—is well positioned for enhancing international perspectives.

Business Leadership Center

Cox's distinguished Business Leadership Center (BLC) complements the classroom curriculum throughout the two-year period. The BLC's innovative program is designed to help students develop effective management skills through seminars that center on interpersonal and communication skills, team building, and negotiation skills. Courses are organized by business leaders, and taught by outside consultants from some of today's most progressive corporations.

International Exchange Programs

An international exchange program allows select students to experience their international business education first-hand by studying abroad. Cox has relationships with schools in Australia, Belgium, Brazil, China, Denmark, England, France, Germany, Japan, Mexico, Singapore, Spain, and Venezuela.

Other Programs

In addition to the full-time, two-year MBA program, Cox offers a part-time, three-year professional MBA program developed for working professionals, and a 21-month executive MBA program for candidates with significant managerial experience. Cox also offers a one-year Master of Science in Accountancy program.

FACILITIES & EQUIPMENT

Facilities at Cox are some of the most technologically advanced. There is wireless Internet access for the more than 1,500 students who are enrolled in the Cox School working toward a BBA, MBA, or Executive MBA.

Cox School of Business

The building that housed the original School of Business Administration was established in 1952 as the Joseph Wylie Fincher Memorial Building. It was joined in 1987 by the Cary M. Maguire Building and the Trammell Crow Building. Today, the Fincher Building houses administrative and faculty offices, while the Maguire and Crow Buildings house classrooms, computer labs, and student study rooms. Included in the Cox School complex is the Business Information Center (BIC), combining traditional features of a university library with the technological advancements of online databases and other resources.

The James M. Collins Executive Education Center is a state-of-the-art teaching and conference facility designed to meet the evolving needs of business executives, managers, and professionals. The Collins Center will house the Cox School's Division of Executive and Management Development and Executive MBA program. It is scheduled to open in fall 2004.

EXPENSES & FINANCIAL AID

A graduate management education is one of the most important investments you will ever make. The returns can be measured in enhanced job opportunities, self-confidence, and post-MBA success. In addition to helping maximize your career potential, the Cox School also does everything possible to make graduate management education affordable.

The cost of tuition and fees for 2003–2004 is $29,462. Books and supplies are approximately $1,650. Off-campus housing generally costs between $600 and $1,200 per month.

Merit scholarships are awarded to students each year based on individual merit and achievement. Recipients are selected on the basis of demonstrated academic achievement, managerial experience, and managerial potential. A variety of named scholarships and awards are available. Scholarships are awarded for the entire two-year period, subject to satisfactory academic performance. Approximately 70 percent of Cox MBA students receive some form of merit scholarship.

FACULTY

Comprising graduates from Wharton, Stanford, University of Chicago, and other top-tier business schools, the Cox faculty has a strong national reputation. By combining research and teaching expertise in such areas as business leadership and ethics, management, and finance with corporate and consulting experience, our professors help students ground business theory in relevant, real-world case studies. Ninety-four percent of our faculty members have a PhD, higher than the national average for business school faculties.

But what sets our faculty members apart is their passion for teaching. Students find the classroom environment engaging, challenging, and rewarding. Outside the classroom, students interact with professors in their offices as well as at social events, lecture series, club meetings, and even SMU sporting events. All this translates into more opportunities for students to interact with top scholars in their respective disciplines.

STUDENTS

Cox MBA students come from all regions of the United States and the world. Each fall, Cox enrolls approximately 120 new students into the full-time MBA program and joint degree programs (Juris Doctor/MBA, and Master of Arts in Arts Administration/MBA). Students have a wide variety of academic disciplines and professional experiences. The average amount of work experience prior to entering the MBA program is five years, and the average age is 28 years old. Women comprise more than 30 percent of the student population, and minorities account for 17 percent of the domestic student body.

Cox's small size not only promotes collaboration among students, it also creates a close and supportive environment for students, the faculty, and the staff. The small size also gives students significant opportunities to assume leadership roles in MBA student organizations and advisory groups.

At Cox, students can speak many languages—Japanese, Italian, Spanish, Chinese, Korean, Hindi, German, Marathi, Punjabi, Ibo, Yoruba, Hausa, Bulgarian, Russian, French, Taiwanese, and Latvian, to name a few.

At Cox, professional backgrounds of the students are: investment bankers, market managers, school teachers, engineers, pharmaceutical salespeople, White House staff, former Marines, missionaries, CEOs, programmers, consultants, and territory managers as a sample list.

At Cox, the student population includes a ski instructor, a former pro tennis player, a cruise director, a professional golfer, a triathlete, a singer in a rock band, scuba divers, and cricket players.

ADMISSIONS

Admission to the Cox School MBA program is highly selective. The Cox MBA Admissions Committee seeks a diverse group of candidates demonstrating significant professional and life experiences, strong academic capabilities, leadership potential, interpersonal and communication skills, and personal qualities such as maturity, self-confidence, and motivation. Finally, and most importantly, candidates should possess a strong commitment to learning and achievement.

Successful applicants have several years of full-time work experience, a strong undergraduate academic record, and competitive scores on the Graduate Management Admissions Test (GMAT). Although not required, we strongly recommend that applicants also have a working knowledge of accounting, statistics, and microeconomics.

Students enter the full-time program in the fall semester only (orientation is held mid-August). Application deadlines for all applicants to the full-time MBA program are as follows: December 3, January 28, March 10, and April 30. To be considered for scholarships, students should apply by March 10. International students should apply by March 10. After May 1, admission decisions are made on a space-available basis.

Students enter the part-time program in the fall (orientation is held in August) and spring (orientation is held in January). The application deadline for fall admission is May 30; for spring admission, November 1. For more information, contact the Admissions Office.

ADDITIONAL INFORMATION

American Airlines Global Leadership Program

Imagine it is May 7, 2004. You are in Sao Paulo, Brazil, preparing to join fellow Cox MBA Class of 2005 teammates for a full day of corporate visits. At 8:15 a.m. the bus will depart for your first meeting at Embraer, one of the world's largest aircraft manufacturers. You spent a late evening networking with Sao Paulo alumni, you're a bit tired but excited about the day ahead. After an insightful morning touring the plant and learning about the company, you are off to have lunch with senior management at PricewaterhouseCoopers. Your afternoon takes you to ABN AMRO where you meet with Fabio Okamoto, Vice President (Cox MBA Class of 1995). After dinner and engaging conversation with company representatives, you call it an early evening. Tomorrow is a free day to learn more about the culture of Sao Paulo with a group of your classmates. After that, off to Buenos Aires, Argentina to explore other multinational corporations such as Frito Lay, Repsol YPF, and Arcor.

The American Airlines Global Leadership Program is one of the hallmarks of the Cox MBA program. The ten-day international immersion experience allows first year students to explore cultures and businesses in other regions of the world. No need to worry about planning or financing the trip—Cox takes care of all the details!

This is a sample itinerary, including previously visited countries and companies. Dates, locations, and company visits are subject to change.

CAREER SERVICES & PLACEMENT

The Cox MBA Career Management Center (CMC) is committed to helping students obtain an ideal career position. CMC staff work closely with students from the first day of the MBA program to create and implement an individualized Career Development Plan tailored to job search needs and professional goals.

Through the CMC, students can tap into a range of services, materials, and resources: one-on-one counseling sessions; job-search workshops; company information sessions and on-campus interviews; mock interviews; roundtable events; career fairs; networking breakfasts; career panels; consortium events; eRecruiting; and CMC newsletter, website, and library.

TCU

AT A GLANCE

The Neeley MBA Program at TCU brings together the right combination of what matters most in graduate business education:

Broad-based, integrated curriculum that fosters strategic thinking . . .
The Neeley curriculum prepares students to assimilate and evaluate information across functional areas, look for broader opportunities, and make decisions that will open doors for the company. Neeley students will have the tools and models to thoroughly examine the options, and the strategic framework to find creative solutions.

Delivered in a dynamic, hands-on learning environment . . .
The small program size, nationally acclaimed faculty, and highly interactive environment allow students to learn from those around them, some of business' best and brightest.

With innovative programs to enhance highly valued professional skills . . .
Neeley offers a comprehensive Professional Development Program of individualized assessments, one-on-one coaching, and workshops to sharpen leadership, teamwork, and communication skills, making our students a more valuable asset to any organization.

And expand career options . . .
Neeley offers everything students need to take their career to the next level: access to our extensive ties to top employers, an international network of alumni, numerous opportunities to meet executives from leading firms, and an interactive MBA Mentor Program.

In one of the nation's most exciting and fastest growing business environments . . .
Home to the corporate headquarters and branch operations of many of the country's leading firms, the Dallas-Fort Worth Metroplex provides students with enhanced opportunities to interact with leading companies, add new experiences to their résumés, and expand their professional network.

At an exceptional value in private education . . .
Neeley offers competitively priced tuition for a hands-on, challenging program that holds its own with the nation's best.

Through an aggressive scholarship program to attract the best and brightest, almost 70 percent of Neeley students receive merit-based scholarships and graduate assistant awards.

LOCATION & ENVIRONMENT

The Dallas-Fort Worth Metroplex is an ideal setting in which to study business. Because of the area's central U.S. location, access to major transportation hubs, pleasant climate, and relatively low cost of living, DFW is consistently cited as one of the best places to conduct business in the United States. In addition to serving as home to the corporate headquarters and branch operations of many leading firms, DFW is a hotbed of entrepreneurial activity.

Fort Worth is home to the world headquarters of Radio Shack, Burlington Northern Santa Fe, American Airlines, Bell Helicopter Textron, Pier 1, Alcon Laboratories, and a host of other cutting-edge corporations. Many of these companies share close ties with TCU, with company executives visiting campus regularly, mentoring students, and providing invaluable input and guidance to keep Neeley's programs and graduates at the top of their game. Additionally, these companies frequently look to TCU for new hires, giving Neeley students the inside track for some of the best career opportunities in the country.

Fort Worth is also a great place to live, with fabulous Sun Belt weather and some of the nation's best entertainment, cultural attractions, dining, shopping, sports, and much more. The TCU campus is located in a charming residential area on a 260-acre, beautifully landscaped campus just five minutes from downtown and near the city's world-class museums, zoo, botanical gardens, and riverside parks.

DEGREES OFFERED

The Neeley Schools offers the following degree options:

MBA (full-time)—21 months

Accelerated MBA (full-time)—12 months for applicants with a BBA, at least 3 years of postgraduate work experience, and minimum GMAT of 620

Professional MBA (part-time, evenings)—28-33 months

Executive MBA—21 months

MAc (Master of Accounting)—21 months

MIM (Master of International Management)—21 months split between TCU and Universidad de las Américas (UDLA) in Mexico

PROGRAMS & CURRICULUM

The curriculum is designed to help students develop the conceptual framework and analytical tools needed to understand complex business issues from a broader, top-level perspective. The academic program is much more than a collection of courses. It is a well-integrated experience in which projects, cases, and speakers cross disciplinary lines and prepare students to develop creative solutions.

The Neeley School is not a place where students listen and observe. It's a place for students to discuss, challenge, debate, and act. Classes are small, allowing for individual attention and access to the nationally acclaimed faculty.

The high-energy environment constantly challenges students to integrate and apply what they learn through frequent team projects and case studies, as well as several innovative programs for experiential learning.

FACILITIES & EQUIPMENT

In February 2003, the Neeley School opened the new Steve and Sarah Smith Entrepreneurs Hall, a 50,000-square-foot facility that provides state-of-the-art classrooms, a new student lounge, and more than 20 team rooms for MBA students. Additionally, the facility is home to the Ryffel Center for Entrepreneurial Studies and an expanded Graduate Career Services Center. Smith Hall is the third building in the Neeley School complex, and increased the capacity of the School in excess of 50 percent.

EXPENSES & FINANCIAL AID

The Neeley MBA Program is competitively priced for an exceptional, private university. Significant scholarship and financial aid resources are available on a competitive basis to assist students in the transition back to school. About 70 percent of all full-time Neeley MBA students typically receive scholarships or graduate assistant awards based on merit, with awards ranging from $2,000 to $25,000 per year. These awards are available to students of all nationalities. Also noteworthy is the Martin Luther King/Henry B. Gonzalez Scholarship made available to Neeley MBA students by the PepsiCo Foundation.

FACULTY

At the Neeley School, students have access to a faculty comprised of talented, caring individuals who are leading experts in their respective fields. They are respected scholars, frequently published in leading business journals and as textbook authors. Many are sought-after business consultants, sit on corporate boards, have owned their own businesses, or have themselves held influential positions with leading companies. They maintain close ties with top professionals in their fields of expertise, many who regularly visit MBA classes to share inside stories about some of business' most exciting moments. Most important, Neeley faculty members are top-notch teachers, able to help students discover new ways of looking at business issues.

With the program's relatively small size, Neeley faculty members come to know students personally, taking time to challenge, engage, and inspire each class member. These relationships are genuine and lasting, with faculty often serving as professional resources long after students go on to successful careers. Neeley faculty members also are trusted mentors, providing the behind-the-scenes guidance and encouragement that can make a real difference in the careers of Neeley students.

M. J. Neeley School of Business

STUDENTS

Neeley MBA students are in good company, interacting with other highly motivated, rising professionals who have a variety of academic and career successes under their belts. Purposefully selected to create a broad cross-section of industry experience, academic credentials, and geographic backgrounds, Neeley's rich mix of students invariably produces a lively give-and-take in the classroom and the opportunity to evaluate issues from many different perspectives.

A typical entering class is made up of a select group of about 70 students. Neeley students challenge yet support one another. Progressing through the curriculum as a cohort group, Neeley students quickly develop close working relationships that often lead to lifelong friendships and extremely valuable long-term professional networks.

ADMISSIONS

The Neeley School at TCU seeks to bring together highly motivated and academically talented students from a broad range of backgrounds. Admission is competitive and seeks excellence. Candidates should be proactive individuals who can contribute in a highly interactive, team-based learning environment and who have meaningful life and professional experiences upon which to draw. Most of all, the Neeley School seeks bright, motivated students who are dedicated to success.

ADDITIONAL INFORMATION

Professional Development Program

To give students the skills that employers value most, Neeley offers the Professional Development Program (PDP), a collection of assessments, one-on-one coaching, workshops, and formal certification covering five key areas: leadership, communication, team building, global perspective, and career management. While other top schools may offer some training in these areas, Neeley's PDP is unique in that it offers a true assessment approach to targeting individual needs. Extensive use of proven assessment tools helps identify a student's strengths and weaknesses, providing the basis for consultation with a professional counselor to develop an individual action plan for improvement.

Experiential Learning

Experiential learning is an integral part of the Neeley MBA experience. Students participating in the Educational Investment Fund (EIF) manage an investment portfolio valued in excess of $1.5 million. The learning experience is invaluable, as is the chance for students to add investment experience to their résumés and gain access to successful EIF alumni now managing money around the world. Through the Student Enterprise Projects, corporate clients hire student teams as paid consultants. Because the companies are charged a significant fee for the team's services, the consultant-client relationship is very real. The clients expect results and challenge students to provide meaningful, real-world solutions. At the end of the first two semesters, students participate in an Integrative Project that requires them to pull together all that they have learned to date and effectively pitch their case solution to a panel of business professors and visiting executives. Along with professional summer internships, these unique programs allow students to gain new experiences and showcase their abilities to prospective employers.

International Experience Electives

Neeley students acquire firsthand experience with global business practices through several international electives taught abroad, in English, by TCU faculty members. To make the time and travel commitment more convenient, the courses are offered in one- to three-week mini-semesters between regular semesters or over breaks. Class locations and subjects may vary by academic year. Recent offerings include Legal and Financial Considerations of the European Union (Rome and Florence, Italy) and International Transactions and Entrepreneurship (London, England, and Cologne, Germany).

Corporate Perspective

Through the Industry-Led Perspective Series, students learn from senior-level executives, frequently prominent Neeley alumni, in an intimate seminar setting. Visiting executives share their insights on the current challenges faced by their firms, giving students an inside look at the critical decisions that have shaped the direction of a company. Recent speakers have included: Nick Giachino (TCU '77), senior vice president, Pepsi-Cola USA; Trip Tripathy (TCU '87), CFO, The Limited; and Pam Bledsoe Noble (TCU '91), portfolio manager, USAA Investment Management Company. Neeley students have the opportunity to develop a broader dialogue with executives through the MBA Mentor Program, which matches second-year MBA students with local alumni and/or community business leaders.

Centers of Excellence

In only its third year of existence, the Ryffel Center for Entrepreneurial Studies was recognized by *Entrepreneur Magazine* as one of the Top 40 Entrepreneurship Programs in the United States. The Center has helped the Neeley School attract some of the top entrepreneurship faculty in the country and offers a variety of programs to enhance the learning experience of graduate students. The Supply and Value Chain Center offers educational and research programs for students and business leaders to help them develop a strategic approach to building better integrated, more effective supply chains. The Luther King Capital Management Center for Financial Studies provides state-of the-art technology and other scholarly resources to support faculty and student research in the field of finance. The Center for Professional Communication dedicates a hi-tech facility and professional staff to assist students in developing more effective communication skills through assessment, workshops, and individual coaching.

Thanks to its prime location in the Dallas-Fort Worth Metroplex, students at TCU's very affordable Neeley School of Business have "great connections" all over the region. Neeley also offers a unique finance elective that allows students to manage the $1.3 million William C. Connor Educational Investment Fund. If you are looking for an affordable place to get your MBA, you will be hard-pressed to beat Neeley, especially if you want a career in Dallas.

CAREER SERVICES & PLACEMENT

The Neeley School offers everything students need to take their career to the next level: access to extensive ties to top employers, an international network of alumni, numerous opportunities to meet executives from leading firms, and an interactive MBA Mentor Program. Throughout the process, the Graduate Career Services Center provides individual coaching and frequent workshops—typically led by visiting executives and alumni—to assist in career exploration and expand career management skills.

UNION COLLEGE

AT A GLANCE

Graduate study at Union is a very special experience. Union's first-rate faculty delivers a relevant, accredited curriculum within a "small college" environment. Faculty at the MBA program have distinguished careers in teaching, consulting, and research. It is Union's high-quality academic program, small size, and careful attention to the individual needs of each student that make graduate study at the college such a rewarding experience.

Small classes (average size: 15) ensure that your Union education is not a "spectator sport." It is virtually impossible to become "lost" at the MBA program. Faculty are routinely accessible outside of class for individual student questions and conversation. Almost all classes meet in the evening, enabling Union to bring full- and part-time students together in an exciting and educationally valuable way.

LOCATION & ENVIRONMENT

Founded in 1795, Union College is located in Schenectady, New York, part of a metropolitan area of 850,000 centered in Albany, the state capital. The Capital District is a major education center with 55,000 students at a dozen colleges and universities, and the area's large array of businesses and government agencies offer extensive internship and career possibilities. Schenectady is three hours from both New York City and Boston, and four hours from Montreal, and the city is served by Albany International Airport and Amtrak. The 100-acre campus is the first united campus plan in America and combines classical architecture with modern academic facilities.

Numerous facilities, resources, and services are at the disposal of Union students. Schaffer Library holds more than 50,000 volumes; approximately 2,000 current serials; government documents; a periodicals reading room; faculty studies; and more than 500 individual study spaces. A major renovation and expansion of the Library was finished in 1998. The F.W. Olin Center, a $9 million high-technology classroom and laboratory building, is another major addition to the College. The Science and Engineering Center contains a number of specialized research tools available for student use. The Arts Center has been extensively renovated, and the Morton and Helen Yulman Theater greatly enhances the art program.

Union's central computer facility consist of several multiuser servers on a campuswide fiber-optic-based network that includes UNIX, Windows T2000, and Apple Macintosh servers. The center hosts the College's main web server and its library automation system. Connected to the network are more than 1,200 College-owned personal computers and workstations. More than 20 electronic classrooms are used to enhance the integration of technology and academic studies. Laboratories with Windows and Apple Macintosh computers and UNIX workstations are available for student use. Each residence hall room is wired (one Ethernet connection per resident), providing access to the College's computing resources and the World Wide Web.

The Murray and Ruth Reamer Campus Center provides space for social and community activities and services for the entire campus. Dining facilities, a pub, an auditorium, a radio station, and multiple student activities spaces are important parts of the building. The historic Nott Memorial has been renovated to become a display and discussion center. Highlights among the athletic facilities are the Alumni Gymnasium with an eight-lane swimming/diving pool and squash and racquetball courts; a 3,000-seat ice rink; an Astroturf field; and an all-weather track. A $10 million project to revitalize the neighborhood to the immediate west of campus was just completed. Key elements include apartment-style housing for 160 students, a security center, and a community center.

DEGREES OFFERED

The Master of Business Administration Program prepares students for functional, managerial, and executive-level positions in a wide variety of manufacturing, service, and public policy enterprises. The design and delivery of the curriculum emphasize a broad exposure to core business disciplines; the building of analytical, computer, and human resource skills; and the development of an ethical, systems-oriented, cross-functional view of management. Classes incorporate a global business perspective. Union graduates understand international business practices; many have experience working and living abroad, and all learn how to communicate cross-culturally. The Master of Business Administration is accredited by the AACSB International—The Association to Advance Collegiate Schools of Business. It is one of only 28 "graduate only" accredited MBA programs in the world.

The MBA in Health Systems Administration prepares graduates for careers as administrators and analysts in health care, governmental, and private-sector organizations with strong health care interests. Typical organizations hiring health systems graduates include hospitals, clinics, health maintenance organizations, consulting firms, planning and regulatory agencies, and research firms. The curriculum is designed to help students understand the complexities of the health care system and to provide the skills necessary to allocate resources, execute programs, and manage health and health-related facilities more effectively.

The program is accredited by both the Accrediting Commission on Education for Health Services Administration (ACEHSA) and AACSB International. It is one of only 21 prestigious dually accredited health administration programs worldwide.

Union offers three joint degree programs. In cooperation with Albany Law School, students can obtain a JD and MBA; in cooperation with Albany College of Pharmacy, Union offers a joint pharmacy degree. Union undergraduates may also pursue a joint degree program that leads to a bachelor's degree and MBA.

PROGRAMS & CURRICULUM

MBA Curriculum

The MBA curriculum at Union consists of classes that incorporate a global business perspective. At a time when multinational corporations dominate the world's financial markets and e-commerce brings products and services to consumers across the globe, leaders in business and industry must possess both business acumen and an understanding of the peoples and customs of the world. At Union, we prepare students to succeed in the intensely competitive global environment.

Students must complete 20 courses (10 core courses and 10 electives) to fulfill MBA degree requirements. Course work is required in two areas: MBA Core courses and electives. Typically, requirements are completed in two years of full-time study or four years of part-time study. Course waivers are dependent on prior course work and require approval of the program director. The MBA programs may accept student requests for course waivers or course transfers up to a limit of eight courses.

MBA Core courses (all students complete these required courses) are Managing Ethically in a Global Environment, Mathematics of Management (1/2), Introduction to Probability (1/2), Statistical Modeling in Management, Financial Accounting, Financial Analysis & Decision-making, Principles of Economics, Marketing Management and Strategy, Operations Management, Managing People & Teams in Organizations, and Legal Principles of Business.

Students are able to build a focus depending on their interests and career goals. Students take one course in each of the following focus areas and three in the area(s) of their choice.

- Finance Courses: Advanced Concepts of Financial Reporting I, Financial Management, Money & Banking, International Finance, Income Tax Accounting, Cost Accounting, Investments

- Economics Courses: Managerial Economics, International Economics, Monetary Economics, Efficient Management of Technology, Seminar in International Finance

- Marketing Courses: E-Commerce, Marketing Research Techniques, Industrial Marketing, International Marketing Management

- Operations/Management Science Courses: Quality Systems Management, Simulation, Lean Production Management, Statistical Methods

- Management Courses: Management for Information Systems, Organizational Theory, Organizational Development & Transformation, Human Resource Management, High Performance Leadership

MBA @ Union

- International Courses: International Economics, International Finance, Seminar in International Finance, International Marketing Management, International Business & Competitive Theory
- Capstone (all students take this course): Strategic Planning and Policy

MBA Health Systems Curriculum

Faculty believe that in order for students to derive maximum benefit from the curriculum, the theoretical insights generated during in-class discussion must be supplemented by practical, "hands-on" experience in the field. Consequently, a full-time internship is a program requirement. Normally, the internship is completed during the summer between the first and second years of study. This approach enables students to integrate practical work experience into the advanced portion of the academic program. Most students complete the internship within a health care institution.

Students must complete 20 courses (18 required and 2 elective) and an internship to fulfill MBA in Health Systems Administration degree requirements. Course work is required in three areas: MBA Core courses, MBA Health Systems courses, and electives. Typically, requirements are completed in two academic years of full-time study or four years of part-time study. Course waivers are dependent on prior course work and require approval of the program director.

- Required Core Courses (students must take each of these courses): Managing Ethically in a Global Environment, Introduction to Health Systems, Mathematics of Management (1/2), Introduction to Probability (1/2), Statistical Modeling in Management, Financial Accounting, Financial Analysis & Decision-making, Principles of Economics, Marketing Management & Strategy, and Operations Management
- Required Advanced Courses (students must take each of these courses): Health Care Finance, Health Economics, Health Systems Marketing and Planning, Structural Dynamics in Health Systems, Legal Aspects of Health Care, Health Policy and Information Systems, Strategic Issues for Health Care Organizations
- Elective Courses (students must take any three): Advanced Concepts in Financial Reporting, Money and Banking, International Finance, Industrial Marketing, E-Commerce, International Marketing Management, Quality Systems Management, Management Science, Organizational Development and Transformation, Management for Information Systems, High Performance Leadership, Human Resource Management, Group Practice Management, Issues in Long Term Care

EXPENSES & FINANCIAL AID

Tuition for the MBA program for the academic year is $16,200. Program fees are $150. There is no on-campus housing for graduate students. Off-campus housing costs for room and board are approximately $8,800 per year.

Merit-based assistance is available to both U.S. and non-U.S. citizens. Competitive scholarships are awarded. Graduate student loans, co-op opportunities, part-time employment, and affordable graduate housing are available.

Graduate scholarships in the form of tuition waivers are available to full-time students. Students are selected for these competitive awards on the basis of prior academic performance, professional experience, and managerial potential. Student loans are available to both full- and part-time matriculated students.

FACULTY

Union's distinguished faculty are readily accessible to students outside the classroom. With an average class size of 15, classes include open discussion and intensive feedback. Union faculty have consulted and lectured in places such as Australia, Belgium, India, China, Japan, Latvia, Tajikistan, Scandinavia, and the British Isles.

STUDENTS

Union MBA students are a very diverse group. There is almost an even number of full- and part-time students, ranging from accelerated undergraduates to CEOs, doctors, lawyers, and entrepreneurs. Nineteen percent are international students. The program is designed for students ranging from those with no management background to those with years of experience. It is our philosophy that these diverse student populations experience a more rewarding and higher quality education when learning in a mixed environment. Thus, student populations are integrated in the same class and not taught separately.

ADMISSIONS

Applicants may seek admission to the MBA programs as matriculated graduate students throughout the year. Notification of an admissions decision is made within two weeks of receipt of a completed application. Students may begin their study in any term. Applications for admission are accepted on a rolling basis. International students whose native language is not English must take the TOFEL exam.

Criteria for admission to the MBA programs include a student's postsecondary academic record, career objectives, personal recommendations, and standardized test scores. Course waivers and transfer credit may be approved up to a maximum of eight courses. In general, a minimum GPA of 3.0 is expected in previous academic work. Applicants must submit a $50 application fee, essays, three letters of recommendation, official GMAT test scores, and official transcripts of all previous academic work.

ADDITIONAL INFORMATION

Internships are a crucial part of the Union MBA program. Through contacts in major businesses all over the world, we are able to help students find an internship in the industry and country of their choosing. Union students have interned at General Electric, Bank of America, Orion Consulting, PricewaterhouseCoopers, Morgan Stanley Dean Witter, Nestle, and other corporations. Often these experiences lead to full-time employment opportunities after graduation.

CAREER SERVICES & PLACEMENT

MBA faculty, the Associate Director for Career Placement, and Union's Career Development Center offer a variety of opportunities for GMI students and alumni to explore career paths and learn the job search and career development skills needed to advance in their long-term careers. Services and resources include one-on-one career counseling, self-assessment, workshops, videotaped mock interviews, resume development and critique, an online resume referral services, on-campus recruiting, "U-CAN" (The Union Carrer Advisory Network, a database of over 1,100 Union alumni representing 16 major career fields), an on-campus Career Festival, employer literature, and credential files.

Career advising and placement services are available to all matriculated full- and part-time graduate students. All MBA students are routinely apprised of upcoming events, workshops, and job opportunities.

Sampling of organizations employing recent GMI graduates: Albany International Corp., Albany Medical Center Hospital, Albany Memorial Hospital, Bank of New York, Blue Cross/Blue Shield, Ellis Hospital, Ernst & Young, General Electric, Health Association of New York State, KPMG, Moody's Investors Service, Morgan Stanley Dean Witter, New York State Department of Health, Nickelodeon, Novalis Corporation, PricewaterhouseCoopers, St. Claire's Hospital, SONY Music, and Wells Fargo

UNIVERSITY OF ARKANSAS—FAYETTEVILLE

AT A GLANCE

The University of Arkansas—Fayetteville serves as the major center of liberal and professional education and as the primary land-grant campus for the state. The University offers graduate education leading to the master's degree in more than 82 fields and to the doctoral degree in more than 30 carefully selected areas.

The MBA program at the Walton College is a 38 credit-hour program, providing a balanced mix of case studies and lectures as well as individual work and team projects in an AACSB International-approved curriculum. Redesigned in 2000, the lock-step program begins around July 1 of each year and ends around June 30 of the following year. In addition to a Strategic Retail Alliances concentration, you may also choose such traditional degree concentrations as finance, global business, or entrepreneurship. With the unique advantages described above, you can be sure that you are receiving a quality degree that will be respected by your peers and will equip you with the skills you need to build a successful career.

Location, Location, Location

Part of the larger University of Arkansas system, the Walton College is located in Fayetteville, Arkansas. In recent years, Northwest Arkansas has emerged as a global hub for retailing. The area is home to Wal-Mart, Tyson Foods, and JB Hunt, as well as the major offices of over 150 Fortune 500 companies such as Procter & Gamble, Unilever, Coca-Cola, Clorox, Levi Strauss, and many others. In 2002, the area was named by *BusinessWeek* as one of the "Dazzling Dozen," 12 areas of the country seemingly untouched by national economic conditions, and ranked by *Forbes Magazine* as the number 23 place in the United States to "Build Your Business."

The Right Tools

Through partnerships with AC Nielsen, IRI, and Spectra, MBA students at the University of Arkansas gain hands-on experience with the leading market research tools and category management tools in the consumer packaged goods industry, the only MBA program in the United States to have all three systems available.

Real-World Experience

Our MBA students tackle real-world issues by taking leadership roles in consulting projects with Fortune 500 firms such as Procter & Gamble, Wal-Mart, FujiFilm, JB Hunt, Alltel Communications, and others.

ROI

Our Accelerated MBA Program gets you back into the working world fast and provides a superior return on investment. The opportunity cost in terms of lost income and the actual expenses in terms of tuition and fees are substantially lower than those of two-year MBA programs, which means that you will reach the break-even point much more quickly on your investment, and your annualized rate of return will be much higher.

The Strength of Resources

In what was then the largest gift to a public college of business, the Walton Family Charitable Support Foundation in 1998 gave $50 million to the College of Business. The college was subsequently renamed in honor of the late Sam M. Walton. This gift provided the springboard to catapult the undergraduate program to 28th in the nation according to *U.S. News & World Report*. It has had a similar effect on the quality of our MBA program, which was completely revised in 2000. Further, the Campaign for the 21st Century, a $900 million University-wide campaign has raised more than $600 million to continue to make even greater strides throughout the University of Arkansas.

LOCATION & ENVIRONMENT

Part of the larger University of Arkansas system, the Walton College is located in Fayetteville, Arkansas. Situated in the heart of the Ozark Mountains, this community of 60,000 residents is situated in the northwestern corner of the state and is a two-hour drive from Tulsa, four hours from Kansas City, and five hours from Dallas and St. Louis. A regional airport offering daily flights to Atlanta, Chicago, Dallas, Memphis, New York, and St. Louis services the area.

PROGRAMS & CURRICULUM

The MBA program at the Sam M. Walton College of Business has a strategic advantage over other MBA programs in the field of retail marketing. Our concentration in Strategic Retail Alliances prepares you like no other program for a successful career in the consumer packaged goods industry in the rapidly growing mass retail sector.

Retail Focus

The Center for Retailing Excellence is emerging as a leader in supporting research in the issues facing the retailing industry. The CRE annual conference and symposium, "Understanding the Mass Retail Shopper," was attended by more than 350 retailing executives, who came to hear speakers such as Bob Flaherty, vice president, Nestlé's, and Todd Hale, a senior vice president with AC Nielsen's Homescan Consumer Insights Sales and Service.

The accelerated, one-year MBA program at the Walton College is a 38 credit-hour program, providing a balanced mix of case studies and lectures as well as individual work and team projects in an AACSB International-approved curriculum. In addition to a Strategic Retail Alliances concentration, you may also choose such traditional degree concentrations as finance, global business, or entrepreneurship.

EXPENSES & FINANCIAL AID

Tuition and fees for one semester of the 2001–2002 academic year were $3,175 for Arkansas residents and $6,520 for nonresidents for 12 hours of graduate-level studies. In addition, students enrolled in six or more hours are assessed $200 for health, activity, technology, recreation, transportation, and facilities fees. International students must show proof of health insurance and are required to pay a nonimmigrant student service fee of $40 per semester.

Fayetteville consistently has been selected as one of the best cities in which to live in the United States. The area has a relatively low cost of living; students can expect to pay approximately $9,200 a year for living expenses, including room, board, books, supplies, and personal expenses.

Students may apply for graduate assistantships, which currently offer a tuition waiver and pay a stipend of $6,500 for 12 months. Students who are awarded graduate assistantships are required to work 12 hours per week to support the instructional or research needs of the faculty in the Sam M. Walton College of Business.

Sam M. Walton College of Business Administration

STUDENTS

The entire UA population is composed of approximately 15,000 students. The Sam M. Walton College of Business enrolls approximately 2,500 undergraduate students and approximately 200 graduate students.

The UA MBA experience is different from the experience found in large MBA programs. Arkansas's small program size allows frequent and substantial contact among students and between students and faculty members. A very active graduate business student association plans and carries out community outreach work, professional development activities, and social functions.

Arkansas MBA students have widely varying backgrounds. More than 13 states and 20 countries are represented in the MBA student body. Students average 26 years of age and possess, on average, two years of professional work experience prior to joining the program. Approximately 42 percent of students are women, 16 percent are members of minority groups, and 26 percent are international students.

The MBA program is open to any undergraduate degree student. Nearly 20 percent of students possess undergraduate degrees and work experience in chemical, civil, electrical, industrial, or mechanical engineering. Other majors include business, biology, history, liberal arts, political science, psychology, and other social sciences.

ADMISSIONS

Admission to the Master of Business Administration program is competitive and limited. Successful applicants are expected to rank in the 80th percentile on the GMAT and possess a cumulative undergraduate grade point average of 3.4. International applicants must score a minimum of 550 on the Test of English as a Foreign Language (TOEFL), and a TOEFL score of 600 is strongly recommended.

Although work experience is not required for the full-time program, applicants with a minimum of two years of professional work experience are given preference. Applicants to the managerial program must possess two years of full-time work experience prior to graduation. Letters of recommendation from those familiar with the applicant's aptitude for graduate-level work in business and essays from the applicant are weighted heavily in admission decisions.

International applicants, all applicants without an undergraduate business degree, and applicants who completed an undergraduate degree in business more than three years ago should submit their completed application materials by November 15. Admission decisions for early applicants are made by December 15, giving the successful applicant sufficient time to complete the preparatory work prior to matriculation in the summer. Preference in admission and financial aid is given to applicants who submit their application prior to February 15. All applications received after February 15 are processed on a space-available basis. In no case is an applicant admitted after May 15.

For additional information, students should contact:

MBA Director
Graduate School of Business
CBA Suite 475
Sam M. Walton College of Business
University of Arkansas
Fayetteville, Arkansas 72701
Phone: 501-575-2851
Fax: 501-575-8721
Email: gsb@walton.uark.edu
Website: www.uark.edu/depts/mba/public_html/

ADDITIONAL INFORMATION

The MBA program at the Sam M. Walton College of Business has a strategic advantage over other MBA programs in the field of retail marketing. Our concentration in Strategic Retail Alliances prepares you like no other program for a successful career in the consumer packaged goods industry in the rapidly growing mass retail sector.

CAREER SERVICES & PLACEMENT

The Walton College has a dedicated Career Development Center with a network of alumni in nearly every major local company, including Wal-Mart, Procter & Gamble, JB Hunt, Acxiom, FujiFilm, Kraft Foods, Unilever, Tyson Foods, IBM, and others.

Services that are provided include resume preparation, counseling, career workshops, employer information services, and employment search assistance. UA MBA graduates have been successful in finding jobs with partnering firms and with Fortune 500 companies. To help students get connected, the Graduate School of Business hosts frequent MBA alumni networking events.

UNIVERSITY OF CALIFORNIA—BERKELEY

FINANCIAL ENGINEERING EDUCATION AT UC BERKELEY

The Master's in Financial Engineering (MFE) Program provides students with a graduate degree from UC Berkeley's Haas School of Business. Instruction is led by world-renowned faculty from Haas, UCLA's Anderson School, and UC Irvine's School of Management.

Students in the MFE program learn to employ theoretical finance and computer modeling skills to make pricing, hedging, trading, and portfolio management decisions. Courses and projects emphasize the practical applications of these skills.

Admission to this full-time program is offered on a rolling basis. The one-year program begins every March and ends the following April.

Graduates of the Master's in Financial Engineering Program are prepared for careers in Investment Banking, Corporate Strategic Planning, Risk Management, Primary and Derivative Securities Valuation, Financial Information Systems Management, Portfolio Management, and Securities Trading.

CAMPUS & LOCATION

Only a handful of universities in the world can match the reputation of the University of California at Berkeley. Its graduate programs are consistently ranked among the best in the world. The business school was founded in 1898, making it the second oldest collegiate business school in the United States and the first at a public university. The Haas School is widely known for its diverse and talented faculty, staff, students and alumni. The school's programs benefit significantly from the university's practice of interdisciplinary research and teaching, and the school's strong connections to nearby San Francisco and Silicon Valley.

PROGRAMS & CURRICULUM

MFE courses are designed exclusively for MFE students and are seamlessly integrated with one another. This cooperation between course material allows the mathematical, statistical, and computer science methods to be integrated with the theoretical framework and institutional settings in which they are applied. In addition to course work, students attend weekly discussions held by finance practitioners through the Financial Practice Seminar Series. Internships are also encouraged during the fall break from mid-October to mid-January.

Course Listing: Fundamentals of Investments, Fundamentals of Corporate Finance, Introduction to Financial Programming, Introduction to Stochastic Calculus, Derivatives: Economic Concepts, Derivatives: Quantitative Methods, Fixed Income Markets, Credit Risk Modeling, Equity & Currency Markets, Financial Risk Measurement and Management, Empirical Methods in Finance, Advanced Computational Finance, Success and Failure in Financial Innovation, The Design of Securities for Corporate Financing, Accounting for Derivatives, Real Options & Commodity Derivatives, Asset-Backed Security Markets, Dynamic Asset Management, Behavioral Finance, and Applied Finance Project.

EXPENSES & FINANCIAL AID

MFE Tuition 2004–2005: $38,000

Estimated Living Expenses 2004–2005: $27,693

The MFE Program does not offer scholarships or grants. All assistance is in the form of loans, which must be repaid after graduation or dropping below six units. Federal financial aid in the form of loans is available for students who are citizens or permanent residents of the United States. International students can only apply for private loans with a U.S. citizen or U.S. permanent resident as a co-signer. Full information about financial aid is available at: http://www.haas.berkeley.edu/MFE/faid.html

FACULTY

The MFE faculty is comprised of distinguished finance instructors from the Haas School of Business at UC Berkeley, the Anderson Graduate School of Management at UCLA, and UC Irvine's School of Management. The MFE Faculty performs preeminent research in quantitative finance—research that feeds directly into the MFE curriculum. Many of these scholars also have practical experience in the creation of financial instruments and software and the implementation of innovative financial strategies. Their expertise is widely recognized and respected. Noteworthy: Professor Mark Rubinstein (Haas), Winner of nine prizes for papers in financial economics; 1995 Financial Engineer of the Year and Professor Francis Longstaff (UCLA), former Head of Fixed Income Derivative Research, Salomon Brothers Inc.

Haas School of Business
Master of Financial Engineering Program

STUDENTS

Profile Class of 2003–2004

Average Age at Enrollment: 29

Average Years of Post-University Experience: 3.7

Average Undergraduate GPA: 3.50

Average GMAT/GRE Q Score: 93%

Average GMAT/GRE V Score: 74%

Average GMAT/GRE A Score: 67%

Prior Degrees

Bachelor's: 63%

Master's: 29%

PhD: 8%

PhD Candidates: 2%

Prior Majors

Engineering: 34%

Mathematics: 20%

Economics: 19%

Finance: 6.5%

Natural Sciences: 12%

Computer Science: 6.5%

Business: 2%

Prior Employment

Engineering: 17%

Marketing/Sales: 2%

Information Systems: 9%

Finance: 25%

Research & Development: 18%

Project Management: 8%

Consulting/Management Services: 15 %

Other: 6%

ADMISSIONS

Applications Received: 390

Number of Admits: 92 (24%)

Enrolled Students: 59

The 60 students who are enrolled each year to the MFE program have a high level of intellectual curiosity, a strong interest in finance, and strong analytical skills. Though there is no specific degree requirement, most students will have backgrounds in quantitative disciplines such as mathematics, statistics, the physical sciences, engineering, operations research, computer science, finance, or economics. It is also expected, though not required, that applicants have work or research experience in which they have applied quantitative skills creatively. In order to screen for candidates that have the ability to succeed in the program, the admissions committee carefully reviews all parts of a student's application, including grades, test scores, recommendations, and essays.

Requirements:

Valid degree from an accredited institution, comparable to the four-year bachelor's degree from Berkeley, and sufficient training to undertake graduate study in finance

A satisfactory scholastic average, usually a minimum of 3.0 in upper division work

Graduate Management Admission Test (GMAT) or the Graduate Record Examinations (GRE) General Test

A strong quantitative background including linear algebra, multivariate calculus, differential equations, numerical analysis, and advanced statistics and probability

Prior experience in computer programming (C, C++) and familiarity with computers as a computational and management tool

Excellent writing, speaking, and presentation skills (in English)

International applicants: Please refer to the application packet for full requirements

ADDITIONAL INFORMATION

The Haas MFE Program is the only degree program in financial engineering offered solely under the auspices of a business school. Most financial engineering programs are taught in mathematics, engineering, or operations research departments. As a result, MFE students learn about computational finance within the context of business and economic principles, and enjoy the additional advantages of the business school's career services, corporate contacts, and orientation toward business applications. The MFE program is also the only financial engineering program that includes a ten-week, mid-program, optional winter internship as part of the curriculum.

CAREER SERVICES & PLACEMENT

Students in the MFE Program primarily obtain internships and full-time positions through recruiting events and on-campus interviews coordinated by the MFE office. Presentation workshops, mock interviewing, resume and proposal writing assistance, and career counseling are available through the program office. Students may also take advantage of services and tools provided by the Chetkovich Career Center at Haas. Students may attend corporate presentations and career workshops, and make full use of the Center's online company research databases. MFE students may also participate in resume drops for on-campus interviewing opportunities posted on the Haas Career Center website. Employment statistics for MFE graduating classes are available on the MFE website.

UNIVERSITY OF CALIFORNIA—DAVIS

AT A GLANCE

The UC—Davis MBA program encourages students to think creatively and integrate the many disciplines of business management into the "big picture." At the UC—Davis Graduate School of Management, we offer a supportive, cooperative learning environment that encourages you to stretch intellectually. Your classmates at UC—Davis will be a select group of today's brightest, most energetic students. Classes are small, and you will have close interactions with faculty members who are internationally renowned experts. This is an exciting time to be at UC—Davis and an opportunity for you to grow at one of the best business schools and universities in the country.

—Nicole Woolsey Biggart, Dean

LOCATION & ENVIRONMENT

With students comprising nearly half of the city's population, Davis is truly one of the few remaining "college towns" in this state or nation. As one of the country's great research universities and the most academically diverse of all the University of California campuses, UC—Davis is home to scholars of worldwide reputation in more than 100 academic fields. They have found that UC—Davis is an adventurous academic environment that is nurtured by dynamic interdisciplinary cooperation, entrepreneurial public-private partnerships, and a caring spirit. As progressive as the University's academic programs are, UC—Davis has preserved the values of friendliness, openness, and cooperation.

The city of Davis is surrounded by some of the most economically vital, naturally magnificent communities in California. Close by, the state capital of Sacramento affords all the amenities expected in a metropolitan area and is home to the state legislature, an expanding high-technology manufacturing industry, and a community of data processing enterprises. A short distance to the southwest is the cosmopolitan San Francisco Bay Area and Silicon Valley. An hour's drive west is the beautiful Napa Valley wine country, and two hours east lies stunning Lake Tahoe.

Academic resources include a library of over 3.1 million volumes, ranked among the top research libraries in North America. A full-time Business Reference Librarian is available to assist students with the latest information-gathering strategies, including some of the most comprehensive online databases available today and access to over 1,000 scholarly and trade journals in business, management, finance, and economics. The School's newly remodeled classrooms feature state-of-the-art multimedia instructional support.

The School maintains a 24-hour computer lab with access to the University's high-speed network, the latest business software, networking to extensive library services, and the Internet and intranet. Access to the network within the Business School facility is wireless. Each student is issued a University computer account, which includes email.

Prior to starting classes, the Career Services Center begins connecting with each student, offering support and personal guidance. Through workshops, on-campus recruiting, mock interviews, and an emphasis on internships, the Career Services Center provides students with the tools needed to build long-term relationships with the corporate community. In addition to an online application and job posting system, MBA students participate in on-campus interviewing for career and internship positions, career fairs, company information sessions, and on-site company tours. Approximately 39 percent of UC—Davis's MBA students were placed in the high-tech industry, including positions in finance, marketing, consulting, and technology management. Over the past few years, an average of 92 percent of the School's students have been placed in internship positions after their first year in the program. The total compensation package for students graduating from the UC—Davis GSM has averaged $86,500.

DEGREES OFFERED

MBA, MBA/JD, MBA/Master of Engineering, MBA/MS Agricultural & Resource Economics, MBA/MD, Corporate Environmental Management Self-Directed Interdisciplinary Program

PROGRAMS & CURRICULUM

The UC—Davis Graduate School of Management has accomplished what many in academic circles felt was impossible for such a small and young MBA program; it is being ranked among the Top 50 in the nation. Conceived just over 20 years ago, the program is recognized for the high quality of its graduates, its world-class faculty, and the excellence of its overall program.

The UC—Davis MBA program cultivates each student's ability to deal successfully with the challenges of a continually changing, increasingly complex global business environment. The program's strengths come from:

* A managerial approach to the basic business disciplines
* A student/faculty ratio of 10:1
* A curriculum that integrates the technological, social, political, economic, and ethical aspects of business
* A variety of teaching methodologies, including case studies, lectures, class discussions, computer simulations, team projects, and "real world" applications

The program is comprised of 24 classes (72 quarter units). Joint degrees are available in law (MBA/JD), engineering (MBA/MEng), medicine (MBA/MD), and agricultural management (MBA/MS). All students spend their first year in "core" classes mastering the curriculum, which provides a common foundation of fundamental management knowledge and skill. Elective concentrations available in the full-time day program or in the evening MBA Program for Working Professionals are accounting, corporate environmental management, e-commerce, environmental and natural resource management, finance, health services management, information technology, international management, marketing, not-for-profit management, technology management, and general management. Students can also design a customized concentration.

UC—Davis encourages students to take advantage of the many opportunities to participate in exchange programs with universities abroad. The invaluable experience at another university gives students a first-hand look at how companies are affected by fluctuations in the global marketplace. Students emerge from this experience with a comprehensive understanding of the "big picture."

As more students of diverse interests and backgrounds engage in MBA education, UC—Davis is striving to expand the opportunities for students to study abroad. UC—Davis has established student exchange programs with 11 renowned international universities. Students can also take advantage of a "one-way" exchange with a number of other universities abroad. Established student exchange programs include Hong Kong University of Science and Technology; Instituto Tenologico Antonomo de Mexico (ITAM); Pontifica Universidad Catolica de Chile in Santiago, Chile; Erasmus University in Rotterdam, Holland; Heinrich Heine Universitat Dusseldorf, Germany; Fundacao Getulio Vargas in Sao Paulo, Brazil; Helsinki School of Economics and Business Administration in Helsinki, Finland; Groupe HEC, Institut Superieur des Affaires (ISA), France; Manchester Business School, England; Australian Graduate School of Management (AGSM); and Jonkoping International Business School (JIBS) in Sweden.

To enhance preparation for the job market, the School requires students to participate in a videotaped mock interview with one of several executives drawn from both the public and private sector. This program gives students a unique chance to meet top executives face to face as well as to dramatically improve interviewing skills.

Graduate School of Management

The annual Alumni Day gives current students the "inside track" on up-to-date industry information and career opportunities from alumni and also provides a valuable networking activity.

The School encourages prospective students to take advantage of the Visitation Program. While visiting the School, prospective students are able to talk one on one with current students and professors and can attend a class.

To enhance each student's learning and networking experience, the School has developed close ties with leaders throughout business and government. They are frequent visitors to campus, serving as guest lecturers in classes, as interviewers in the mock interview program, and as speakers at frequent School-sponsored events. Through these important contacts, students gain access to high-profile companies and establish relationships with potential employers.

The Executive-in-Residence program gives students and faculty members alike a unique opportunity to work closely with a top business leader during the executive's quarter-long visit to the School.

The Dean's Advisory Council, made up of many of California's top business leaders, provides the School with one of its strongest connections to the business community. The School's Business Partnership Program also provides an important avenue for top regional organizations to become involved with UC—Davis MBAs. Students are invited to network with these corporate executives at breakfast meetings and special lectures.

EXPENSES & FINANCIAL AID

The estimated fees for the 2003–2004 year for full-time study are $15,065 for California residents and $26,642 for nonresidents. These fees are subject to change. The 2003–2004 cost of the MBA Program for Working Professionals is $1,660 per class. Many reasonably priced apartments are within biking distance. Monthly rents range from $650 for a studio to $1,800 for a three-bedroom apartment. Books and supplies are approximately $1,600 for the academic year. Need-based grants, loans, and fee offsets are available, as is the merit-based GSM Scholar's Grant.

Financial aid eligibility at any school is based on the program's cost of attendance, a standard figure reflecting not only fees or tuition, but also basic expenses students incur during the academic year. Both the University of California and the Graduate School of Management have financial aid available for students, including grant funding. More than 90 percent of GSM students who apply for financial assistance receive some type of support. The UC—Davis Graduate Financial Aid Office administers loans, grants, funds, and work-study employment that are available to all graduate and professional students. The Office also offers short-term and emergency loans designed to help students with unexpected expenses. The Graduate Financial Aid staff in that office can guide students in applying and qualifying for University grants, loans, work-study, and other financial support.

FACULTY

The faculty of the UC—Davis Graduate School of Management represent doctoral preparation from many of the most prestigious schools in the country and excel both as teachers and researchers. Their current consulting projects keep them in touch with managerial concerns of leading U.S. corporations as well as federal and state agencies. But one of the most distinctive features of this faculty is the close relationship they forge with students. The School recognizes the academic value students receive when given the opportunity to work closely and individually with faculty members, and offers many formal and informal chances to do so. The student/faculty ratio is 10:1.

STUDENTS

UC—Davis MBA students bring to the School a wide variety of academic and work experiences, and the School's personalized focus and "hands-on" teaching approach are augmented by this diversity. Because of the strong emphasis on technology management, the School is very attractive to students with backgrounds in engineering and the sciences as well as those with business and economics degrees. More than 32 percent of the fall 2003 entering class will come from undergraduate majors in the humanities and social sciences. The most recently admitted class represents 49 undergraduate institutions.

The average full-time student is 29 years old and has five years of full-time work experience. Women make up 34 percent of the student population, and international students make up 16 percent.

The School encourages applications from international students. To be eligible for admission to the program, international students must take the TOEFL and earn a score of 250 or better on the computer-based test or 600 or better on the paper-based test. If admitted, international students must provide a Statement of Finances for visa purposes, showing at least $41,650 available to cover tuition and fees for their first year.

ADMISSIONS

Admission to the UC—Davis Graduate School of Management is highly selective. Applicants are evaluated on the basis of demonstrated academic achievement, performance on the Graduate Management Admission Test (GMAT), and interest in professional management. Full-time business experience is considered an asset. No particular area of undergraduate preparation is required, but the University requires the completion of a bachelor's degree from an accredited college or university. The 2003 entering class has an average GMAT score of 679 and an average undergraduate GPA of 3.4.

Fall application deadlines for domestic applicants are December 1, February 1, and April 1. Deadlines for international applicants are December 1 and February 1. The deadline for the MBA Program for Working Professionals is April 1.

UNIVERSITY OF DENVER

THE COLLEGE AT A GLANCE

"At the Daniels College of Business, we are committed to your success—as a highly competent professional, a team builder and leader, and a valued member of your community. Founded in 1908, the Daniels College of Business is the nation's eighth-oldest accredited collegiate business school and a leader in management education. With one of the nation's premier MBA programs, we put you at the cutting edge of knowledge, present an educational experience that prepares you for a lifetime of leadership, and provide our commitment to your career placement and development. We do all this in a classic campus setting located in Denver, a wonderful city that symbolizes the dynamic business environment of the Rocky Mountain West."

—James R. Griesemer, Dean

LOCATION & ENVIRONMENT

The University of Denver is the largest independent, private university in the Rocky Mountain Region, with more than 8,800 students from more than 80 countries. Founded in 1864 by John Evans, the Colorado Territory Governor for Abraham Lincoln, the 125-acre University of Denver campus is located in a quiet neighborhood in Denver, Colorado, providing students an academic atmosphere with access to the cosmopolitan population, activities, and lifestyle of Denver, with the Rocky Mountains nearby.

In September 1999, the $25 million Daniels College of Business Building opened. One of the nation's most technologically advanced business school facilities, the building has more than 3,000 data ports for instant access to the Internet. It houses the Advanced Technology Center, a state-of-the-art laboratory with more than $1 million worth of the latest software and hardware.

Computer facilities include labs with 125 networked PCs that support word processing, spreadsheet, and visual presentation software; UNIX mainframes that provide statistical packages; and Internet and information research database access.

The Daniels Career Placement Center helps students assess career choices and develop effective career strategies using a wide range of resources. Workshops and personal counseling are available to help students enhance job search skills, techniques, and knowledge. Career forums, job fairs, alumni networking events, regional consortium events, computerized job and internship listing databases, a research library, and an alumni mentor program provide access to employers from around the nation.

PROGRAMS & CURRICULUM

The Daniels College of Business MBA program presents a forward-thinking curriculum that challenges students through an active learning environment. The new core curriculum incorporates experiential elements in leadership, career management, technology, and group work in addition to traditional methods of learning. Through this exciting experience, students learn technical business knowledge, refine skills that are key to managerial excellence, and gain an appreciation for values-based leadership.

Mirroring the cross-functional involvement of management decision-making, the courses combine the business technical fundamentals and management skills into a more applications-oriented format from which students develop a comprehensive view of business the way it actually operates. Included in the experience are an outdoor leadership and team-building program, opportunities for volunteer participation, and a team field-study project in which students work with Denver-based organizations.

Students move through the core into elective or specialization courses that provide focus to their degree. Specializations in accounting, construction management, electronic commerce, entrepreneurship, finance, information technology, marketing, real estate, and resort and tourism management are available, or students may create their own specializations from courses offered at the University.

A part-time MBA program is available. Other options include an MBA/JD joint-degree program and a flexible dual-degree program that allows students to combine their MBA degree with programs from other schools and departments within the University of Denver.

The Executive MBA program is an 18-month program designed to strengthen the management skills and leadership abilities of middle- and upper-level managers and managing professionals. Intensive course work, creative problem-solving, and an international cultural travel seminar provide firsthand knowledge of management, international, and emerging business opportunities.

The Accelerated MBA is a cutting-edge graduate study program designed for high-potential men and women with at least two years of management experience who want to strengthen technical business skills and enhance leadership abilities.

The integrated curriculum helps develop creative critical thinking and decision-making through courses that focus on applying business tools in an interrelated format. Exciting core courses have replaced traditional individual function courses to combine tools and skills as students use them.

A three-day outdoor leadership experience provides an arena for students to learn key elements of communication skills, team building, and consensus problem-solving. Added to the managerial excellence focus are negotiation skills and Myers-Briggs testing.

The Daniels College of Business' 83 full-time faculty members have a balance of industry experience and academic dedication, providing a classroom environment that is diverse and exciting. They have developed the curriculum with outside business leaders and continue to refine the program as well as maintain their excellence in teaching, research, and consulting. They are recognized worldwide for their industry knowledge and work with educational organizations such as the Fulbright Foundation.

The Daniels College of Business' MBA program emphasizes international business and a global understanding of cultures and perspectives. Core courses focus on global perspectives, and elective courses include international marketing, comparative management, and multinational finance. In addition, courses in international politics, economics, and policy analysis are available from the University's Graduate School of International Studies.

Daniels College of Business

The Daniels College of Business works with corporate advisors in a multitude of program areas. The curriculum continues to be shaped by faculty members and corporate advisors. The Career Placement Center works with executives in operations and panel discussions, and the team field study course, Integrative Challenge, is a partnership with Denver-area corporations and businesses that utilize Daniels students to address management problems. In addition, the Career Placement Center alumni mentor program provides contacts with alumni in a wide range of industries and positions for placement counseling and assistance.

EXPENSES & FINANCIAL AID

For the academic year 2002–2003, tuition for full-time students attending three quarters was $22,680. Expenses for books, supplies, fees, housing, and meals vary, depending on the number of courses taken per quarter and extracurricular activities. Even though Denver is the largest city in the Rocky Mountain region, the cost of living is well below other major U.S. cities.

STUDENTS

Daniels College of Business students have a wide range of academic and professional backgrounds and represent more than 30 countries around the world. Insights and skills from an average of more than six years of professional experience and undergraduate majors, including business, engineering, international studies, history, and economics, provide diverse perspectives that add to dynamic classroom environments and group projects. Of the approximately 560 MBA students in the Evening, Accelerated, and Executive MBA programs, 51 percent are working professionals, 34 percent are women, and 15 percent are international students.

Prominent alumni include James Unruh, chairman and CEO, Unisys; Peter Coors, CEO, Coors Brewing Company; June Travis, executive vice president, National Cable Television Association; Andy Daly, president, Vail Associates; Thomas Marsico, CEO, Marsico Capital Management; and David Bailey, CEO (retired), Wells Fargo Bank West.

ADMISSIONS

The Daniels College of Business enrolls students in September and March. Applications are reviewed on a rolling basis through a comprehensive process that evaluates previous academic performance and completion of an undergraduate degree from an accredited college or university, results of the GMAT, professional work experience, responses to essay questions, two letters of recommendation, and a completed application form. International students whose primary language is not English or who graduated from an institution where English is not the primary language of instruction are required to submit TOEFL results. Interviews are not always required.

Applications are evaluated on a rolling basis as they are received and completed, with a decision response within five weeks of completion. The deadline for September enrollment is May 1, and the deadline for March enrollment is January 1. Applications received after these dates are reviewed on a space-available basis. For inquiries, students should contact:

Rifkin Center for Student Services
Daniels College of Business
University of Denver
2101 South University Boulevard
Denver, CO 80208
Phone: 303-871-3416; 800-622-4723 (toll-free)
Fax: 303-871-4466
Email: daniels@du.edu
Website: www.daniels.du.edu

ADDITIONAL INFORMATION

A "great city, great mountains," and "great outdoor life" are a few of the perks available at the University of Denver's Daniels College of Business, "one of the nation's most technologically advanced business schools" and home to a sizable international student contingent. Scheduling is "flexible" and the range of courses is broad, though the academic pressure can be "intense" thanks largely to a "hectic" quarter system.

UNIVERSITY OF FLORIDA

For more than 50 years, the University of Florida has developed successful leaders and managers to meet the challenges of a rapidly changing business environment. We are committed to promoting academic excellence, creating innovative programs, and fostering a collegial environment. Innovative new programs and curricular enhancements provide improved accessibility and greater flexibility for all students. Small class sizes, a low student/faculty ratio, and an expanded program staff ensure that individual needs are met throughout the program. Tremendous value results from the combination of our nationally recognized MBA program, the comparatively low cost of attendance, and Gainesville's high quality of life. We look toward a bright future with renewed focus, ambition, and spirit. We invite you to join the dynamic Florida MBA community.

—John Kraft, Dean

LOCATION & ENVIRONMENT

The University of Florida is a comprehensive, public research university that was founded in 1853. With more than 46,000 students, it is the sixth largest university in the nation. It is the only public university in the Southeast that is a member of the prestigious Association of American Universities. The University of Florida has established a place for itself among the country's elite institutions of higher learning.

Florida's Business School is located in the northeast corner of campus, in an area known as the "Business Triangle." It is adjacent to the University's administration building and the main library facilities. Bryan Hall contains a computer lab and a study lounge (exclusively for MBA students), along with a student information center and offices for the MBA program staff members. Classrooms, faculty offices, and academic research centers are housed in Stuzin and Matherly Halls, the other two buildings that comprise the Business Triangle. Florida's 2,000-acre campus features athletic facilities that are among the nation's finest—including two state-of-the-art fitness centers and a championship golf course. The campus also has a performing arts center, a wildlife sanctuary, and several museums for students to enjoy.

The classrooms and study areas utilized by the MBA program are all linked to the Business School's computer network. MBA students are required to have a notebook computer in order to be able to participate in this interactive learning environment.

Florida features a staff of dedicated career services professionals who assist MBA students with their career development. The staff uses a series of skill assessments and other activities to help students develop comprehensive career plans. These tools include workshops for creating effective resumes and improving interview skills. The staff also develops and maintains working relationships with corporate recruiters, coordinates recruiting events, and maintains an extensive list of job postings for positions in major cities. MBA students also may utilize the University's Career Resource Center, widely regarded as one of the nation's best.

PROGRAMS & CURRICULUM

The University of Florida is nationally recognized for the academic excellence of its MBA programs and for the exceptional value that it provides. The MBA experience at Florida is unique in that it empowers students to tailor their education according to their individual needs. The University offers 9 distinct MBA program options, 15 academic concentrations, 6 certificate programs, 7 joint degree programs, and a dual-degree program.

Eligible students who desire to attend school full-time may apply for one of our traditional programs and complete their degree in one or two years regardless of their undergraduate degree. Florida's unique one-year program (Option A) allows students from a nonbusiness undergraduate degree to earn their degree within 12 months, enabling them to return to the work force sooner. In addition, all students who enroll in this program automatically earn a one-third tuition waiver. Students who received an undergraduate degree in business within the past seven years may enroll in the Option B one-year MBA. This program allows students to earn their degree in nine months while focusing on their specific field of study. All traditional programs are delivered in a modular format composed of eight-week quarters. Students can focus their studies in one or more of the following areas: finance, competitive strategy, marketing, entrepreneurship, security analysis, decision and information sciences, arts administration, general business, global management, international studies, human resources management, Latin American business, management, real estate, and sports administration.

Florida also provides an opportunity for its students to dedicate themselves to a more intensive course of study. The program awards certificates to students who allocate a large majority of their elective hours toward the study of one of the following functional areas: financial services, supply chain management, entrepreneurship and technology management, decision and information sciences, electronic commerce, and global management. Seven joint degree programs enable students to combine the MBA with a UF degree in law, engineering, exercise and sport sciences, biotechnology, medical sciences, pharmacy, or medicine.

Busy professionals who want to earn the MBA degree without interrupting a successful career may elect to enroll in one of Florida's programs for working professionals. Students in the Executive MBA Program and MBA for Working Professionals Programs (two-year and one-year options) meet on campus just one weekend per month. Our newest professional program, the MBA for Engineers and Scientists, was tailor-made for people with technical backgrounds and follows the same weekend format as our MBA for Working Professionals.

Florida also offers an Internet MBA in two-year and one-year options. The Internet MBA utilizes leading-edge interactive technology to deliver a high caliber graduate degree via flexible distance learning. The program requires only occasional visits to the campus: for orientation and one weekend at the end of each term. MBA students have the opportunity to study abroad via one of 16 international exchange programs. In addition, they have the option to pursue a dual degree— the MBA/Master of International Management (MIM), offered in conjunction with Thunderbird, The American Graduate School of International Management.

Corporate Partnerships

Corporate leaders are an integral part of Florida's business school community. The program is supported largely by the contributions of its executive advisory board, corporate recruiters, and alumni. Prominent business leaders routinely visit the University to speak to students via the Distinguished Speaker Series or by invitation from various professors. Recent speakers include Craig R. Barrett, CEO, Intel Corporation; Warren Buffet, chairman, Berkshire Hathaway; Richard Teerlink, former chairman of the board, Harley Davidson; and Mary Alice Taylor, chairperson and CEO, HomeGrocer.com.

Warrington College of Business

EXPENSES & FINANCIAL AID

The Florida MBA is consistently rated as one of the best buys in business education. Nationally ranked academic programs, low cost of attendance, and Gainesville's high quality of life combine to provide students with tremendous value. A limited number of merit-based MBA fellowships and graduate assistantships are available to help traditional students reduce their educational expenses.

FACULTY

Florida's MBA faculty members possess exceptional credentials and are recognized by industry leaders and their peers for contributions to various areas of expertise. With small average class sizes for electives, students have maximum access to these top-notch instructors. The Departments of Accounting, Marketing, Finance, and Management are consistently ranked among the Top 25 in the country. Individual faculty members have been honored with national awards for their excellence in research. Members of the faculty serve as editors for major journals of marketing, finance, accounting, management, and business law. They also direct 13 research centers, which explore emerging trends in a wide array of business disciplines. These faculty members are not just preeminent researchers; they are outstanding teachers as well.

STUDENTS

Florida's programs integrate distinguished faculty, talented students, a dedicated staff, and successful alumni to form a cooperative and supportive community. Florida MBA students come from diverse backgrounds and average approximately five years of work experience. They come from a variety of academic backgrounds, ranging from philosophy to engineering. Traditional MBA students benefit from involvement in various extracurricular activities, including student organizations such as the MBA Association, MBA Ambassadors, the Investment Club, Graduate Women in Business, and the International Business Association.

Prominent Alumni

Prominent alumni include John Dasburg, CEO, Burger King; Hal Steinbrenner, general partner, New York Yankees; Allen Lastinger, former president/COO, Barnett Banks; Jonathan Root, general partner, US Venture Partners; Bill Gurley, general partner, Benchmark Capital; Manny Fernandez, UF Board of Trustees; Judith Rosenblum, chief learning officer, Coca-Cola; Chris Verlander, president and COO, American Heritage Life; and Randall P. Bast, cofounder of Innovex Group.

ADMISSIONS

Candidates are evaluated based on their academic achievement and aptitude, professional experience, and personal character. All applicants must have a bachelor's degree from an accredited U.S. institution or its international equivalent. Additional requirements include at least two years of significant, full-time, post-baccalaureate work experience; official GMAT scores; official transcripts; two letters of recommendation; four essays; and completed application forms. All one-year program options, with the exception of the traditional one-year MBA—Option A, require an acceptable undergraduate business degree. Official TOEFL scores are required for applicants whose native language is not English. Other requirements vary by program. Students should refer to the application packet for details. The Traditional MBA Program (one-year MBA—Option B

and two-year option), the MBA for Professionals (one-and two-year options), and the Executive MBA Program begin each August; the Internet MBA Programs (one- and two-year options) and the MBA for Engineers and Scientists Programs begin each January; and the Traditional MBA Program (one-year Option A) commences in April. Prospective students should refer to the application packet or the Florida MBA Programs' website for specific application deadlines, program calendars, and budgets. An online inquiry and application system is available through the website as well.

Admissions Contact:
Admissions Coordinator
134 Bryan Hall, PO Box 117152
Gainesville, FL 32611-7152
Phone: 352-392-7992
Fax: 352-392-8791
Email: floridamba@notes.cba.ufl.edu
Website: www.floridamba.ufl.edu

Strong programs in entrepreneurship and finance, diverse course offerings, and a paradise-like atmosphere draw future MBAs to the practical University of Florida Graduate School of Business. It's also "a bargain financially"—particularly for in-staters—and the sweltering, hopping, activity-laden college town of Gainesville "is probably unparalleled socially."

ADDITIONAL INFORMATION

Did you know that with an undergraduate degree in business, you have the opportunity to complete your MBA in just 11 months from one of the top MBA programs in the nation?

You begin at UF during the summer with a review of the basics, then start your MBA elective courses during the fall and spring semesters. You graduate in May—just 11 months after starting your program. Courses are taken in eight-week modules that allow you to select more electives than you could under the conventional semester system. With more than 60 electives from which to choose, you can maximize your learning and customize your MBA by earning certificates or concentrations in subjects such as finance, supply chain management, entrepreneurship, decision and information sciences, global management, and many other topics that are in demand in today's competitive job market.

Florida's MBA program is nationally recognized by *U.S. News & World Report* and *BusinessWeek,* both of which rank our traditional MBA program among the Top 50 in the nation. Our academic Departments of Marketing, Finance, and Accounting receive high marks from *U.S. News & World Report*—all are ranked among the Top 25 in the nation. In addition, our MBA faculty possess the unique combination of being exceptional in their fields as well as student-friendly. With small average class sizes for electives, you have maximum access to these top-notch instructors.

After investing only 11 months, you will have the professional knowledge and credentials you need to take your career to the next level. Don't let this opportunity pass you by. Apply now, online via our website, at www.floridamba.ufl.edu. We look forward to receiving your application!

UNIVERSITY OF IOWA

AT A GLANCE

The University of Iowa's Henry B. Tippie School of Management offers a Master of Business Administration (MBA) degree that consistently ranks in the Top 50 MBA programs in the world. There are many characteristics that contribute to the quality of the Tippie MBA including a flexible curriculum and great placement results. But, here are a few of the attributes that set Tippie apart from other programs.

A Personal Touch

At Tippie, our students are never just a face in the crowd. They form relationships with classmates, faculty, and staff that continue long after the formal program is complete. In fact, our students are on a first-name basis with the Dean. By limiting class size, we provide a program that meets individual needs.

Reputation

The Tippie School of Management is nationally and internationally recognized for its quality. We attract the best and brightest students from around the world to our program. While at Tippie, students enhance their knowledge of business fundamentals, develop leadership experience, and advance their professional development. Consistently, we produce graduates that go on to business success across the country and around the world.

Environment

Iowa City has a cosmopolitan atmosphere and rich culture, which contributed to the city's selection as one of the nation's best small cities by *Forbes Magazine*. Enjoy Big 10 athletics, world-class cultural events, theaters, museums, ethnic restaurants, and parks while being within easy driving distance of several major metropolitan areas such as Chicago, Minneapolis, St. Louis, and Kansas City.

The Tippie MBA is one-of-a-kind. Students thrive in our internationally ranked program that provides a personalized business education. Taught by world-class faculty in a dynamic, Big 10 town, the Tippie MBA is an outstanding value.

LOCATION & ENVIRONMENT

Iowa City is a diverse, highly cosmopolitan community of 60,000 set in the natural scenic beauty of Iowa's rolling hills and woods.

As a place to live, our town keeps winning awards and accolades:

- Ranked number two in *Forbes Magazine's* 2002 list of the 96 Best Small Metropolitan Areas in the U.S.
- Selected the number-one place to live in the nation by *Editor & Publisher Magazine*
- Named 1 of the 10 Most Enlightened Towns in the country by *Utne Reader*
- Listed in the book *The 100 Best Small Art Towns in America*

Iowa City has all the art galleries, ethnic foods, historic architecture, and vibrant atmosphere of a much larger city but with the compactness and friendly feeling of a small town.

The University of Iowa campus is seamlessly integrated with the Iowa City community. The 1,900-acre campus is located along both sides of the Iowa River. The campus community provides a rich variety of activities and resources for students including Big 10 athletics, natural history and art museums, Hancher Auditorium, and the UI Hospitals and Clinics.

Business programs are housed in the 187,000-square-foot John Pappajohn Business Building. The building integrates multimedia capabilities and instructional technology throughout the classrooms and facilities. In addition to the largest computer laboratory on campus, a wireless LAN provides students access to a full range of technology services.

PROGRAMS & CURRICULUM

The Tippie MBA program emphasizes applied business learning in a collaborative, team-based environment. The curriculum is founded on a core of courses that includes key functional areas of finance, marketing, accounting, statistics, organizational behavior, operations management, economics, and strategic management. Students select a concentration from one of the following areas: accounting, entrepreneurship, finance, strategic management and consulting, management information systems, marketing, or operations management. An individually designed concentration is also an option for those with more specific interests.

FACILITIES & EQUIPMENT

The state-of-the-art facilities of the John Pappajohn Business Building provide a comfortable arena for learning. The Tippie School of Management uses the latest communication and course delivery technology to help MBA classes network effectively. The Internet conferencing system allows students to work in real time on a project. For example, study group members can log on and work on a spreadsheet project simultaneously.

Some of the building highlights:

- The Marvin A. Pomerantz Business Library provides a 30,000-volume resource area with electronic access to libraries around the world.
- Laptop computers are available for checkout from the library for use throughout the building.
- A wireless LAN provides Internet access to any student with a network-enabled laptop.
- Students may take advantage of the Tippie College's purchase plan for a Dell laptop computer.
- Our Instructional Technology Center features 100 computer workstations (the largest on campus), two 32-seat computer classrooms, and a computerized operations/behavioral laboratory.
- The latest technology in the classrooms greatly enhances student learning experiences.

EXPENSES & FINANCIAL AID

The Tippie MBA provides one of the best returns on investment available. This nationally accredited program provides a top-notch education that can help students take their career to the next level.

2003–2004 Academic Year Tuition and Fees

Annual tuition (resident/nonresident): $10,050/$18,362

Computer fees: $188

Health fees: $169

Student union, activities, and service fees: $175

Building fee: $119

Total tuition and fees (resident/nonresident): $10,701/$19,013

Henry B. Tippie School of Management

Merit-Based Financial Aid

Merit-based financial aid is offered to outstanding candidates each year. The criteria for these awards mirror those for admission—academic record, work history, leadership experience, test scores—although only those with the highest qualifications receive offers for aid. Both domestic and international applicants are eligible for awards. Awards may consist of a scholarship, a graduate assistantship, or both. Most scholarships vary from $1,000 to $4,000. Graduate assistantships provide a salary of approximately $8,000, a contribution toward health insurance costs, and resident tuition status for non-Iowa residents.

FACULTY

Tippie MBA faculty members hold doctoral degrees from some of the world's top educational institutions, and all bring practical experience into the classroom. They combine theoretical frameworks, case studies, and real projects to impart a complete understanding of business problems. The MBA faculty take personal interest in their students, taking the time to get to know them outside the classroom.

STUDENTS

Tippie MBAs are not passive recipients of education but active players in determining the type of MBA experience delivered. Student organizations offer students an opportunity to develop their leadership potential and team-building skills. Student clubs organize professional development events, career networking opportunities, social events, and many other activities that enhance the Tippie MBA experience.

The entering class in the full-time MBA program averages more than three years of work experience, a grade point average (GPA) of approximately 3.3 (4.0 scale), and a GMAT score of 640.

ADMISSIONS

The Tippie MBA is seeking candidates who have clearly demonstrated the ability to complete a rigorous academic program and the potential for success in a professional environment. Numerous factors are important in the admission review process.

Academic Background

In addition to cumulative GPA, we consider the difficulty of the major completed and the reputation of the institution. We do not require a specific minimum GPA. However, last year's class average was 3.3. We do not attempt to translate results from institutions that do not use a 4.0 scale into a 4.0 scale "equivalent." Rather, we consider the results within the context of the institution and the country's educational system.

Standardized Tests

GMAT: All candidates must submit a GMAT score. We do not require a specific minimum score; however, the class average is approximately 640.

TOEFL: Candidates from countries where English is not the native language must submit a TOEFL score. The minimum acceptable score is 250 (computer test) or 600 (paper test).

Work Experience

Professional work experience is required. A minimum of two years of full-time work experience after completion of the bachelor's degree is recommended. Successful applicants typically have three to five years of work experience.

Leadership

Evidence of leadership ability is important in demonstrating the candidate's potential for contributing to the learning environment. Ideal candidates have clear records of leadership in school, work, and the community.

Admission Interview

An interview is required before an admission offer is made. An admission interview is included in your campus visit. For those who are not able to visit Iowa City, an alternate format, usually a telephone interview, is arranged. Interviews are also available with Tippie representatives who may be traveling to your city.

Campus visits may be scheduled at any time regardless of where you are in the application process.

Candidates not participating in a campus visit are invited to participate in an interview only after a preliminary review of the application is completed.

ADDITIONAL INFORMATION

The "immensely talented and cooperative" students at the University of Iowa School of Management say theirs is "an MBA program on the rise." Iowa boasts an "incredibly advanced" facility complete "with the latest multimedia," a "fantastic" administration, and an "ever-improving atmosphere." Finance is probably the strongest discipline here, thanks to innovative programs like "the Applied Securities Management program, which allows students to apply classroom ideas to manage real portfolios."

UNIVERSITY OF KENTUCKY

AT A GLANCE

The Gatton MBA Program is defined by three important qualities that set us apart:

Value

Ours is a small program by most standards. But the advantage of small size becomes obvious when considering the numerous factors that drive the quality of the program. For starters, our program affords closer interaction with our world-class faculty, greater cohesion among MBA students, and tighter networking opportunities with employers, alumni, and visiting executives. Also, value is also a function of our highly competitive tuition rates, which creates a higher rate of return (the overall cost of the MBA versus post-MBA starting salary) on your educational investment.

Experience-Enhancing

Whether you enter the program as a highly experienced, seasoned manager, an early career corporate fast-tracker, or a relatively inexperienced, yet energetic executive-to-be hopeful, our curriculum features many experience-enhancing activities, exercises, and simulations that are real-world, real-time, and hands-on. Each is designed to build your skills set, broaden your perspectives, and challenge and test your capabilities.

Expedience

Our 36-hour program enables most students to earn their degrees in three semesters (beyond the program prerequisites). Though expedient, the program doesn't sacrifice quality. Our program is rigorous, intense, and fast-paced. Simply put, it gets you prepared for the job market sooner, thus further enhancing the value of the Gatton MBA.

The Gatton MBA is fully accredited by the AACSB International (The Association to Advance Collegiate Schools of Business).

LOCATION & ENVIRONMENT

The UK campus and the Gatton College of Business and Economics are close to the heart of downtown Lexington, a city with a population of 243,000, where many of the cultural and recreational amenities of a large city are combined with the charm and traditions of a small town. Famed for its horse farms, Lexington lies within a 500-mile radius of nearly three-fourths of the manufacturing, employment, retail sales, and population of the United States. Established in 1865, the University of Kentucky has more than 23,000 students, of whom approximately 6,200 are graduate students. Founded in 1925 as the College of Commerce, the Gatton College of Business and Economics occupies a modern building with all the facilities needed to fulfill the mission of excellence in teaching, research, and service.

As befits a Carnegie Foundation Research University of the first class, the University of Kentucky has excellent facilities. The $58 million William T. Young Library, which opened in spring 1998, contains more than 2.5 million volumes and receives more than 27,000 periodical and serial titles. The M. I. King Library houses several special and rare books collections. The Computing Center has several high-level systems supporting research and networking needs. Within the College are the electronic Business Information Center for state-of-the-art business database access and seven centers of research that serve as resources to the state, local, and international business community. At sites throughout the campus, computer workstations cater to the computing needs of all students.

Major corporations, such as Procter & Gamble, National City, Cinergy, Brown & Williamson, Aegon, Humana, Accenture, and Eli Lilly are among several that recruit graduates of the University of Kentucky's Master of Business Administration program. Seventy percent of the graduates of the MBA program choose to stay in the Kentucky/Ohio region due to career opportunities and the low cost of living. The average compensation for the 2001–2002 graduates was $65,000, which would be equivalent to $203,000 in New York; $131,000 in Chicago; $99,000 in Los Angeles; and $90,000 in Atlanta. Janie Thomas, MBA Director of Recruitment and Placement, provides many employment opportunities for students through the MBA Center, Business Career Fair, Career Center, and professional organizations. She also provides assistance in resume writing, interviewing, and all aspects of job search through both seminars and one-on-one consultations.

The College's University of Kentucky Business Partnership Foundation consists of prominent individuals in the business and academic communities. The Board of Directors of the Foundation fulfills an important role in assessing the present and future needs of the business world and in advising the College on how to provide the education necessary to meet those needs in a manner consistent with the College's missions of excellence in teaching, research, and service. Local businesses provide scholarships and internships for MBA students. Guest speakers from the business community visit the college on a regular basis throughout the year.

DEGREES OFFERED

MBA (1.5 years), MS Accounting (1 year), MS Economics (1.5 years), PhD in Business Administration (4-plus years), PhD in Economics (4-plus years)

PROGRAMS & CURRICULUM

The Gatton MBA offers two distinct tracts. The Business Track is for students who hold an undergraduate degree in business and seek a course of study designed to develop more advanced skills across a wide range of business functions or focused within a particular functional area of business.

The Non-Business Track is for students who seek a course of study that will provide broad-based management training but who do not have an undergraduate degree in business (often possess a degree in engineering, computer science, or a liberal arts degree).

Both programs require a minimum of 36 hours after the completion of all prerequisites and have a basic core of six courses. For the business undergraduate, the remaining six courses are electives that reflect the student's individual career interests or a specific area of study.

For nonbusiness undergraduates, four additional courses beyond the core focus on organizational behavior, production management, marketing, and finance. The remaining two courses are electives.

The MBA curriculum also includes three "experiential learning modules" (ELMs) designed to expose both Business Track and Non-Business Track students to a set of complex, real-world managerial challenges designed to enhance the skills, perspective, and understanding gained through MBA class work.

1. Lean Manufacturing and Business Systems Simulation

   MBAs will participate in a variant of UK's world-class lean manufacturing simulation to gain first-hand experience of the managerial skills necessary to create a lean, effective, and profitable organization. More than just mastering "manufacturing" competence, achieving a lean organization requires managers to develop and integrate a broad mix of leadership skills, strong unit culture, technology, planning and control systems, and attitude.

2. Leadership, Strategic Planning, and Tactical Execution Exercise

   Drawing from a rich set of military-to-business concepts, MBA students will utilize the key features of the U.S. Army's military decision-making and tactical execution processes to reconnoiter, plan, and execute an assault [paintball battle] against the "enemy" in a real-time, high-intensity, yet fun competitive context.

3. MBA Case Competition

   Drawing from their course work, prior experience, teamwork, and intuition, teams of MBA students present a consulting-quality analysis and detailed recommendations (to an executive and faculty judging panel) that address the key competitive challenges and issues that confronts the particular company selected for the focus of the competition. Teams delivering the best presentations are invited to the competition's "final four"—a final round of presentations where the winning team is chosen.

Gatton College of Business and Economics

Qualified students are also able to participate in a growing number of independent field study projects for 1–6 credit hours. Some field studies are centered on a research project facilitated by one-on-one interaction between a particular MBA faculty member and a student. Such projects might involve, for example, the development and administration of a large-sample employee skills, job satisfaction, and salary survey.

Other projects involve participation on a small team of MBA students that works with a local company to, for example, develop and conduct a market viability analysis for a new product concept, etc. UK MBA teams have and continue to participate in field study projects with a wide range of companies—from small biotech start-ups like ChipRx, to Fortune 500 companies that include Valvoline, Lexmark, Kellogg's, to nonprofit organizations like Habitat for Humanity.

EXPENSES & FINANCIAL AID

The College and Graduate School offer merit-based scholarships and fellowships. Approximately 21 percent of the fall 2001 entering class received some form of College-based aid, including scholarships for members of minority groups and disadvantaged students. Students of outstanding merit are nominated for Graduate School Fellowships. Eligible students may also obtain on-campus employment through the UK STEPS service and the UK work-study program.

The University of Kentucky operates on the semester system. For 2003–2004, in-state graduate tuition for a full-time student is $2,871 per semester. Part-time in-state students paid $244 per credit hour. Nonresident full-time graduate tuition was $7,393 per semester. Part-time nonresident tuition was $646 per credit hour. The registration fee for full-time students was $232 per semester. Part-time students paid $12 per credit hour. A full-time nonresident student can expect to pay approximately $19,000 per academic year for tuition, fees, books, supplies, room, meals, and health insurance. On-campus housing rents range from $403 to $635 per month.

STUDENTS

In fall 2002, the College enrolled 106 new MBA students. Of this new class, women represented 44 percent, international students 9 percent, and members of minority groups 11 percent of the student body. Thirty-nine percent of the students were part-time. The average age of students was 26, the average work experience was about 3 years, and the average GMAT score was 608.

There are more than 1,300 MBA alumni in all 50 states and in 22 other countries. Prominent alumni of the College include the presidents and CEOs of numerous corporations including public companies listed on the NYSE. Inductees into the College's Hall of Fame include, but are not limited to, the CEO of Bearning Point (formerly KPMG) Consulting; Edward T. Breathitt, former Kentucky State Governor; Carl F. Pollard, former chairman and CEO, Columbia Healthcare, Inc.; James E. Rogers, chairman, president, and CEO, PSI Holdings, Inc.; Warren W. Rosenthal; Chris Sullivan, CEO, Outback Steakhouse; and Paul Chellgren, CEO, Ashland Oil, Inc.

ADMISSIONS

Admission to the full- and part-time programs are for the fall semester only. An undergraduate degree with a minimum GPA of 2.75 is required, together with the following course work: two principles of accounting courses (financial, managerial), two principles of economics courses (micro, macro), a course in statistics and probability, and an elementary calculus course. All prerequisite courses should be equivalent to at least three semester hours. Applicants must also submit a GMAT score, and international applicants must also present a minimum TOEFL score of 550 (paper-based) or 213 (computer-based) overall and a minimum Test of Written English (TWE) score of 4.5. Academic background, GMAT score, personal recommendations, and the applicant's statement of purpose are all considered in the evaluation for admission. Demonstrated academic ability and potential for subsequent success in the business world are qualities that are looked for in applicants.

Admission to the College's graduate business programs is achieved by applying to both the Graduate School and the MBA program. The MBA program accepts applicants for the fall semester only. Deadlines for applying are as follows: for international students, February 1; priority deadline for domestic students and financial aid consideration for full-time students, April 1; final deadline for completed applications to be submitted for consideration, July 15.

Successful applicants are usually notified two to four weeks after the receipt of all required documentation. For information, applicants should visit our website at http://gatton.uky.edu.

ADDITIONAL INFORMATION

The Gatton MBA currently offers five joint/dual degree opportunities.

The MBA/BS Engineering Program is a fully integrated five-year program culminating with the awarding of both the Bachelor of Engineering and Master of Business Administration (MBA) degrees. The program includes a mandatory study abroad experience. It is a very selective program limited to 25 students per year.

Because some aspects of business and law are interrelated, students can obtain the joint MBA and Juris Doctor (JD) degrees in only four years instead of the five required if the degrees were pursued separately. As a result, students gain marketable skills and specialized employment opportunities in less time than might otherwise be required.

The Gatton College of Business and Economics also offers dual degree programs with the College of Pharmacy and the College of Medicine. Each of these programs will require that students apply formally and independently to each program and meet the admission requirements of each. Upon completion of both programs, graduates will receive the MD and MBA degrees, or the PharmD and MBA degrees.

Never before has the confluence of economic globalization, international relations, diplomacy, and national/regional security issues become such a priority on the national agenda. In response, the Gatton College of Business and Economics and the Patterson School of Diplomacy and International Commerce offer the opportunity for students to concurrently pursue both the MBA and the MA (in International Commerce, Foreign Relations, etc.) degrees. MBA/Patterson students are able to complete both degree programs in five semesters.

The MBA program at the University of Kentucky offers two distinct tracks: a business track for students with undergraduate business degrees and a nonbusiness track for everybody else. Both can be completed in three semesters, but the business track is a lot more flexible. Students here say one of the main advantages of UK is its location: a "safe" college town in a region of strong economic growth. When monotony sets in, more metropolitan Louisville is a short drive away.

CAREER SERVICES & PLACEMENT

The Gatton MBA program career services activities and resources include:

- Regular recruiting visits by companies, government organizations, and nonprofits big and small—from Fortune 500 companies, like Procter & Gamble and Bearing Point (formerly KPMG) Consulting, to small biotech start-ups, like ChipRx, to the federal government's General Accounting Office

- Regular recruiting fairs for manufacturers, financial and information services, agribusiness companies, and health service companies

- A sophisticated online system to for searching job listings, posting student resumes, reserving interview slots, etc.

- Top-ranked Career Center facilities, including professionally appointed meeting/interview rooms, video-equipped mock interview rooms, career resource library, etc.

UNIVERSITY OF ROCHESTER

PROGRAMS & CURRICULUM

The Simon School's MBA programs are designed to train individuals to solve management problems as team members in a study-team structure. It is a place where thinkers become leaders! The curriculum emphasizes learning the principles of economics and effective decision-making through a mix of lecture, case study, and project courses. The degree program requires 67 hours (20 quarter courses) and can be completed in six quarters of full-time study. Four core courses are required in the underlying disciplines of economics, applied statistics, accounting, and computers and information systems. One course must be taken in each of the functional areas of finance, marketing, operations management, and organization theory. A 3-credit course over two quarters in business communications is required of all full-time students. Twelve elective courses are required, of which five or more may form a sequence of concentration, although a concentration is not required for graduation. The 14 areas of concentration offered are corporate accounting, public accounting, accounting and information systems, business environment and public policy, computers and information systems, e-commerce, entrepreneurship, finance, health sciences management, international management, marketing, operations management-manufacturing, operations management-services, and competitive and organizational strategy. Students may select an individualized double-concentration to customize their course of study in preparation for specific career objectives.

FACILITIES & EQUIPMENT

Schlegel Hall, opened in 1991, is the Simon School's classroom and student services building. It contains case-style classrooms equipped with state-of-the-art technology and rear projection equipment, study rooms, a student lounge, and its own Computing Center. The center supports student-accessible IBM-compatible computers linked for data sharing and laser printing via local area networks and access to several external data sources, such as Bloomberg Business News, as well as email services on the Internet. An extensive wireless LAN network makes Internet access even easier. James S. Gleason Hall, a 38,000-square-foot addition, was completed in October 2001. On-campus graduate housing, both high-rise apartments and townhouses, is available to Simon students. Off-campus housing is also available.

EXPENSES & FINANCIAL AID

In addition to the $125 application fee, tuition was $1,010 per credit hour, or $30,300 per year, for 2002–2003. The cost of books and supplies averages $1,300 a year, and living expenses (rent, food supplies, personal expenses, and health insurance) were estimated at less than $10,000 for the 2002–2003 academic year. Both U.S. and international applicants are eligible for merit awards. The deadline for applying for merit-scholarship assistance is February 1 for September applicants and August 1 for January applicants.

FACULTY

The Simon School faculty is known internationally for leading scholarship in management education. There is a long tradition at Simon of coordinating teaching and research, as well as integrating knowledge from all of the functional areas into the curriculum. Faculty accessibility is a specific benefit of a Simon education. Teaching awards for the best teachers are presented annually by each MBA class, and teaching is improved continuously through a formal faculty peer-review. Leading-edge research is intrinsic to teaching the basic scientific principles of management. Many research findings used by the Simon faculty in classroom study have served as foundations for corporate practices in use today. Simon faculty members serve as editors on five major academic journals, and recent studies of research productivity rank them among the top five faculties in the United States.

William E. Simon Graduate School of Business Administration

STUDENTS

Each September approximately 180 students enter the Simon community as members of four cohorts (class teams). Another 50 students join their classmates in January as cohort number five. Each cohort takes all core classes together. September entrants complete the first-year core courses during the fall, winter, and spring quarters; the majority of January entrants complete core courses during the winter, spring, and summer quarters. Within each cohort, students are assigned to a study team of four or five members. Due to the large number of students from outside the United States (40 percent), the study-team structure at the Simon School takes on special significance. Each team always includes representatives from at least two countries.

Simon students enter the program with a wide range of educational, professional, and geographic backgrounds. In the class of 2004, 115 undergraduate institutions and 30 countries are represented. Undergraduate majors include economics, humanities, social sciences, business and commerce, engineering, and math and science. Prior full-time work experience averages 5.8 years, and the average age is 29. Women comprise 23 percent of the class. Twenty-four percent of Simon students are members of American minority groups.

ADMISSIONS

A Simon School Admissions Committee reads each application individually and evaluates recommendations, teamwork and communication skills, the nature and scope of prior work experience, the undergraduate academic record, GMAT scores, TOEFL scores as an indicator of English-language skills, evidence of leadership and maturity, and career focus. English language proficiency is critically important for successful interaction in the Simon School's geographically diversified study-team structure. Potential contributions to Simon classmates and to the world's business community are carefully considered. All undergraduate majors are represented in the program.

ADDITIONAL INFORMATION

The Pre-term Program is another way in which Simon strives to instill a thirst for leadership in each student. In addition to welcoming students into the program, the Pre-term is an excellent opportunity to jump-start the career planning process. During the two-week Pre-term period, students participate in a statistics review workshop, self-assessment exercises, personal selling and communication skills instruction, corporate leadership training, and one-on-one career counseling. The goals of the Pre-term include acclimating students to campus life, assessing and building on specific skills, and introducing the valuable programs of the Career Management Center. In addition, students participate in several Vision Modules (the student-managed portion of a Simon MBA) designed to enhance leadership skills in the areas of team building, training in diversity issues, ethical decision-making, and social responsibility.

To ensure that Simon School graduates possess effective oral and written communication skills, so important in leadership, they are required to complete a management-communication sequence comprising two courses, Interpersonal Communication Strategy and Management Communication.

Finance is the magic word at the University of Rochester's Simon Graduate School of Business Administration in "beautiful" upstate New York, where the "world-class, research-oriented faculty" happens to be composed of "excellent teachers." The vaunted finance faculty here features Gregg A. Jarrell, one-time chief economist of the U.S. Securities and Exchange Commission, and Clifford W. Smith Jr., author of numerous books and winner of even more teaching awards. Accounting is the other standout department at Simon.

CAREER SERVICES & PLACEMENT

The Career Management Center is committed to Simon students' success! Through one-on-one career counseling, targeted education, and the development of a personalized job search strategy, Simon students are poised to secure meaningful internships and full-time opportunities in investment banking, finance, consulting, marketing, technology, e-commerce, and operations. Aggressive corporate outreach and long-standing recruiting relationships account for 71 percent of the full-time hires for the Class of 2002.

UNIVERSITY OF SOUTH CAROLINA

AT A GLANCE

Moore School of Business is known for its expertise and experience in international business. Top-ranked in national and international surveys, Moore School's undergraduate and graduate programs offer students opportunities to learn and work in a global business environment.

Moore School of Business is a comprehensive business school offering a full range of options for business education, including degree programs at the undergraduate, master's, and doctoral levels, plus executive education, distance education, research centers, and outreach support.

The 2,600 undergraduate and 800 graduate students are taught by 96 full-time faculty plus qualified full-time lecturers in specialty areas of business and technology. The school is housed in a modern nine-story building that contains offices, research labs and centers, classrooms, presentation and seminar rooms, television classrooms, computer labs, and a full business library. Offices and classrooms are connected by the campus digital and/or video network.

In March of 1998, Moore School of Business became the first major business school named for a woman, honoring University of South Carolina alumna and business executive Darla Moore. The school builds on its long history of innovation and achievement, serving as an asset to South Carolina by being part of the global network of business.

LOCATION & ENVIRONMENT

Moore School of Business has an urban campus with green space and gardens, historic buildings, and easy access to recreation and cultural events. With its location in the heart of Columbia, the capital of South Carolina, students can take advantage of water sports on the nearby rivers and lakes, hiking and skiing in the mountains, and fishing and sailing on the Atlantic Coast. In town, the Columbia Museum of Art provides traveling exhibitions and a substantial permanent collection. The Town Theatre, the Workshop Theatre, and the Koger Center are among the many venues offering theater beyond the very active University performances. Columbia is home to the world-class Riverbanks Zoo and Botanical Garden and the historic State Museum. Nightlife abounds around campus, with live bands performing rock, jazz, and blues, and the area is the origin of popular groups such as Hootie and the Blowfish. The gentle southern climate makes outdoor sports and recreation a year-round pursuit.

DEGREES OFFERED

Bachelor of Science in Business Administration

International Master of Business Administration

Master of Business Administration

Master of Human Resources

Master of Accountancy

Master of Arts in Economics

Doctor of Philosophy in Business Administration

Doctor of Philosophy in Economics

PROGRAMS & CURRICULUM

A global perspective on business is woven into the programs at Moore School of Business on both the undergraduate and graduate level.

The school is noted for its innovative International Master of Business Administration (IMBA), which now offers more flexibility in curriculum and length of program. IMBA provides three options: Language Track, with its emphasis on intensive language study, overseas internship, and geopolitical studies; Global Track, with a focus on the political, economic, and business factors affecting the investment climate of various regions throughout the world, and which includes the international internship; and the IMBA Vienna Program, an all-English-language, 15-month joint venture with Vienna's leading business school, the Wirtschaftsuniversität Wien.

Specialized master's degree programs provide additional options—in accounting through the Master of Accountancy (MACC) with tracks in Business Measurement Assurance and Taxation; in human relations through the Master of Human Relations (MHR); and in economics with the Master of Arts in Economics (MA). These offer targeted programs with high placement rates for students with specific career goals. The school offers two doctoral degrees, the PhD in Business Administration and the PhD in Economics for people interested in academic, public service, and research careers.

Moore School's International Business specialty has been ranked first or second for 14 consecutive years in *U.S. News & World Report's* survey of America's Best Graduate Schools. The *Financial Times* of London ranked the school's MBA programs 45th in competition with the world's best MBA programs, keeping it in the Top 100 for four consecutive years. The school has also been included in *BusinessWeek's* Top 50 and Top 100 Business Schools listing in various years. *The Economist* has included Moore's graduate programs in its Top 100 Business Schools Worldwide and in the Top 50 U.S. Business Schools.

The undergraduate curriculum has been designed to integrate the recurring themes of business throughout the student's four-year experience. Accounting, computer applications, business communication, business law and ethics, economics, entrepreneurship, and international business are part of an integrated core. A strong emphasis on liberal arts, a flexible curriculum, and the option to study abroad rank this program's International Business specialization number one in *U.S. News & World Report's* survey of America's Best Colleges for the last four years.

FACILITIES & EQUIPMENT

Moore School of Business at the University of South Carolina is housed in a nine-story building with offices and classrooms in close proximity to foster interaction between students and faculty.

Facilities include the Elliott White Springs Business Library, Japan Business Library, Center for Entrepreneurship, James C. Self Computer Lab, Center for Business Communication, auditoriums, media classrooms, TV studio classrooms, meeting rooms, and teleconference facilities.

The computer network provides wireless connection to the Internet and permanent email options to students and alumni.

Darla Moore School of Business

EXPENSES & FINANCIAL AID

Moore School of Business has been rated a "best buy" and best "ROI" at various times by *Forbes* and *BusinessWeek*. A set program fee for each program in lieu of tuition, and strong merit-based financial aid packages and work grants make Moore attractive to talented students.

IMBA Language and Global Track program fees are $26,500 for South Carolina residents and $44,400 for nonresident students. IMBA Vienna Program fee is $29,000 for either resident or nonresident.

The Darla Moore Fellowships award $10,000 per year for two years in the IMBA Language and Global Tracks, and $10,000 for the IMBA Vienna Program. For the 2002–2003 academic year, 31 students accepted the fellowships. Some of these students also received substantial fee reductions and work grants.

Other fellowships offered to incoming IMBA students include the Fluor Daniel International Business Fellowship of $15,000 per year for two years. Also the Liberty Corporation of Greenville, South Carolina, established an endowment that provides fellowships ranging from $5,000 per year to $8,000 per year for two years. The J. Willis Cantey Memorial Fellowship of $12,000 per year for two years is open to South Carolina residents.

Fee reductions are offered in conjunction with work grants and range from $5,000 to $20,000. Work grants pay $1,000 per semester in salary for working 10 hours a week with faculty and staff in the Moore School of Business.

Cost of living in Columbia, South Carolina, is relatively low. Housing can be found around campus for an average of $550/month for a two-person apartment.

FACULTY

Moore School of Business has 14 endowed chairs and named professorships plus 24 fellowships. Many of the faculty have lived and worked in other countries and all have professional or doctoral-level degrees. Many professors are members or directors of academic or professional boards, and are contributors to, or editors of, professional journals. Core graduate courses are taught exclusively by professors. Currently Moore has 96 tenure track professors and 10 teaching lecturers.

STUDENTS

Students in the IMBA program tend to be about 26–30 years old (28 years average), with two to seven years of work experience. Thirty percent of the students are women, and 35 percent of the students are foreign nationals. About 30 percent of the students have an undergraduate major of Business, but majors also include Economics, Engineering, International Studies, Political Science, Languages, and Liberal Arts. The diverse student population draws students from South America, Western and Eastern Europe, Asia, Africa, and Australia in addition to the U.S. population.

IMBA students have an average GMAT of 630 and an average GPA of 3.21 for undergraduate studies.

ADMISSIONS

GMAT scores, undergraduate GPA, work experience, and essays are the most important elements of a graduate application portfolio. Depending on the competitiveness of the program to which the student is applying, the GMAT should be between 540 and 680, the TOEFL has a minimum requirement of 600, and the undergraduate GPA should be about 3.22 or higher. Graduate programs prefer students with two or more years work experience. The application deadline for the IMBA is December 1 for best consideration and financial aid (October 1 for IMBA Vienna). Application may be made online (see http://mooreschool.sc.edu).

Admissions Contact: Ms. Reena Lichtenfeld, Managing Director-Graduate Admissions

Graduate Admissions, Room 520
Columbia, SC 29208
Phone: 803-777-4346
Fax: 803-777-0414
Email: gradadmit@moore.sc.edu
Website: mooreschool.sc.edu

ADDITIONAL INFORMATION

Moore School of Business offers specialized master's degrees in accounting (Master of Accountancy, economics (MA in Economics), and human resources (Master of Human Resources).

Also offered is an MBA for working professionals, the Professional MBA, distributed by satellite to 23 receiving locations throughout South Carolina. This program has been on-going for more than 30 years and features professors teaching by live television with interactive audio. Students in the various locations can interact with the professor and each other. Classes are offered in the evenings and some Saturdays throughout the semester.

Flexibility of start date, class time, curriculum, and location attracts working professionals in business, engineering, and accounting who want to enhance their careers by earning an MBA from an accredited university.

The Moore School of Business has revised and improved its world-renowned international graduate business program. The updated International Master of Business Administration (IMBA) Program has garnered its number-two ranking for international business by providing guaranteed overseas internships, a comprehensive international core curriculum, and concentration in an area of specialization. Students choosing the IMBA program must select one of three options:

- Language Track: Spanish, Portuguese, French, German, Italian, Chinese, or Japanese
- Global Track
- Vienna Program with joint partner in Vienna, Austria, the Wirstchaftuniversitat Wein (WU-Wein)

No matter the option, the international program at the Moore School of Business is so unique and robust that it simply cannot be compared to any other international program. It stands alone in its class.

CAREER SERVICES & PLACEMENT

Moore School of Business Graduate Career Management Office partners with students to achieve their career goals. A highly structured Career Development Curriculum prepares students for their job search soon after they come to campus. The Graduate Career Management Office uses the Birkman Method as an assessment instrument to advise students on programs of study, internship opportunities, and job search plans.

More than 150 companies come to USC to recruit students each year. Top recruiters include Citigroup, General Motors, BB&T, BMW, Deloitte Consulting, and BellSouth. Students use online resume services and videoconference facilities for contacts and interviews worldwide.

The placement rate of those for whom we have data averages 70 percent at graduation, and 100 percent within six months, with some programs having a consistent 100 percent placement rate within three months. The average starting salary is in the $58,000 to $70,000 range depending on field.

UNIVERSITY OF TAMPA

AT A GLANCE

Congratulations! By exploring our MBA program you've recognized that a leading twenty-first-century enterprise requires rethinking of yourself and your career. Technological, environmental, demographic, and political changes are transforming the world, creating new demands for performance. Our goal is to provide you with perspective, skills, mentoring, and lots of opportunities for fully expressing your potential and meeting those demands.

We can help you prepare you for leadership responsibilities in a technically sophisticated, diverse global environment where change rules. We're part of one of the nation's most vibrant regional economies. Whether it's the Internet, computer technology, financial services, telecommunications, international trade and tourism, or one of a dozen other industries, we have experience and contacts.

The John H. Sykes College of Business is accredited by AACSB International—The Association to Advance Collegiate Schools of Business. The University is also accredited by Southern Association of Colleges and Schools to award associate, baccalaureate, and master's degrees.

LOCATION & ENVIRONMENT

The 90-acre University of Tampa campus offers a full-service educational setting that includes a comprehensive library, a broad range of technology and support, an active Career Services and Placement Center, and many student programs. Tampa Bay is among the Top 10 fastest growing areas in the United States and a great place to be for career building.

When it comes to technology, the John H. Sykes College of Business is keeping pace. The new 80,000-square-foot facility boasts more than 1,300 data ports for high-speed networking and access to the Internet. You can log onto the information highway in all 30 classrooms, student break-out rooms, 3 computer labs, and even in the hallways and vending area. Use these to communicate with your professors, classmates, and students here and around the world.

The Huizenga Family Foundation Trading Center is one of the technological centerpieces of the building, providing a significant hands-on dimension to finance education. The Trading Center offers Bloomberg Professional real-time trading information on large plasma screens and workstations.

DEGREES OFFERED

The MBA program is requires between 39.5 and 51.5 credit hours to complete depending upon the undergraduate background. Full-time students can complete the entire program in as little as 16 months in the Acclerated Full-time Day Program. Students who work full-time can complete the course work in less than three years in the Flex Part-time Evening Program.

The Master of Science in Technology and Innovation Management program focuses on developing managers to lead the process of innovation in all types of business, and takes the global perspective necessary to compete successfully through technology innovation. The program has been extensively benchmarked against similar degrees offered by leading business schools around the world. The courses are specific to technology companies and industry, focused on actual issues that are particularly acute in technology companies. The MS-TIM is offered part-time in the evenings and requires 34 credit hours.

The University also offers an MBA/MSN program.

PROGRAMS & CURRICULUM

The Fast Start Workshop is a two-and-a-half-day weekend program that includes a team-based business simulation that demonstrates essential business concepts and perspectives, how to work in and lead a team, and how to make effective oral and written presentations.

The Leadership Development Program has several program elements that improve the student's leadership capacity after graduation. Some elements include Leading for Performance, Executive Coaches for students, and the online Leadership Resource Guide.

The Leading for Performance course utilizes an experiential learning process to increase self-awareness as a high-performance leader and to focus on the role of the leader to align people with the goals of an organization. In this initial course, students have the opportunity to work with a skilled faculty team with expertise in management, exercise science, psychology, and nutrition. The result is a Personal Commitment Plan that sets personal and leadership goals to implement during your MBA program. It is all designed to achieve an effective work-life balance that can support sustained high performance throughout the student's career.

In Executive Coaching and Mentoring, students work one-on-one with business executives from the local community and our MBA alumni and faculty to develop leadership and interpersonal skills. Faculty continuously mentor students throughout their programs.

In the Capstone Experience, students work in teams to perform a strategic business assessment and create an oral and written presentation for the top leadership of an actual company. Student teams have helped take companies into new international markets, redirect marketing and financial strategies, and restructure entire organizations—well beyond textbook case studies and solutions.

Program Requirements

Because it is important that every admitted student have a strong knowledge and understanding of key business quantitative skills from the beginning and to fully benefit from and contribute to the program, you will be required to complete Developing Software Competencies, Analytic Skills, and/or the Foundation Course Sequence prior to enrolling in the Integrated Core. Also note that students required to take Professional Writing and Research Techniques are required to complete this class during the first semester of enrollment. Some students qualify for a waiver of some of these requirements.

The Integrated Core is a series of 12 intellectually challenging half-semester course modules designed to develop the practical hands-on business knowledge and tools required to lead the value creation process. Students also deepen business knowledge of specific topics by taking 12 credits in any one of seven MBA concentrations.

FACILITIES & EQUIPMENT

When it comes to technology, the John H. Sykes College of Business is keeping pace! The new 80,000-square-foot facility boasts more than 1,300 data ports for high-speed networking and access to the Internet. You can log onto the information highway in all 30 classrooms, student break-out rooms, 3 computer labs, and even in the hallways and vending area. Use these to communicate with your professors, classmates, and students here and around the world.

The Macdonald-Kelce Library provides complete research and study aids in convenient, comfortable, and quiet surroundings. UTOPIA, our online catalog, provides Web access to Library holdings and links to e-books and databases. Using E-Search, students can remotely access online databases such as Business Source Premier, ABI-INFORM, DISCLOSURE, and Investext. The Library staff will assist you in accessing these information sources. You may obtain materials from other area, regional, and national libraries through Interlibrary Loan. Also available through UTOPIA are U.S. government documents, and many are available both on and off campus. Documents include publications such as STAT-USA and USA Trade Online. While in the Library, you may connect through the Library's wireless network.

EXPENSES & FINANCIAL AID

Tuition for 2003–2004 is $370 per credit hour. Tuition is payable at registration each semester. In addition, a $35 student services fee is required each term. The cost of books, supplies, health insurance, and personal expenses is additional.

Graduate assistantships are available each academic year. Assistantships provide tuition waiver for up to six classes per year plus a $3,000 stipend. Recipients must be full-time students and work 20 hours per week. The University offers a variety of financial aid programs. Graduate students who are not currently employed may apply for a noncredit internship with a local business.

FACULTY

All of the MBA faculty members have PhDs. More than half of our graduate faculty have won awards for teaching and professional excellence. Many of our

John H. Sykes College of Business

faculty have owned their own businesses, have helped lead and build major companies, or are engaged in consulting at the highest leadership levels.

STUDENTS

Students bring unique cultural practices and perspectives on business, providing an environment in which alternative ideas and ways of thinking are freely exchanged. When international students graduate, they take with them cutting-edge business practices and techniques that make them successful wherever they go. The cultural and educational exchanges that occur at UT provide a perfect training ground for both international and American students.

MBA Part-Time Student Admissions Profile, Fall 2002

Average GMAT: 530
Average GPA: 3.3
Years of full-time work experience: 6
Average TOEFL: 590
Average age: 31

MBA Full-Time Student Admissions Profile, Fall 2002

Average GMAT: 515
Average GPA: 3.3
Years of full-time work experience: 2
Average TOEFL: 604
Average age: 26

MBA Student Population by Geographic Area, Fall 2002: Mid-Atlantic 7%; Midwest 1%; Northeast 3%; South 56%; Southwest 6%; West 4%; International 23%

MBA Student Concentrations, Fall 2002: Accounting 4%; Entrepreneurship 1%; Finance 18%; General 28%; Information Systems Management 18%; International Business 11%; Management 8%; Marketing 12%

MBA Student Undergraduate Majors, Fall 2002: Business: 54%; Economics 5%; Engineering 7%; Humanities 10%; Liberal Arts 7%; Math and Science 8%; Social Sciences 9%

MBA Student Current Employment by Industry, Fall 2002: Communication/Utilities 12%; Consulting/Professional Services 11%; Financial Services 28%; Government/Nonprofit 6%; Health Care 7%; High-tech 9%; Information Services 5%; Manufacturing/Service 22%

ADMISSIONS

Applications are processed on a rolling basis, and students are admitted for the fall, spring, or, on a limited basis, in the summer sessions. Individual interviews are encouraged but not required. All students admitted to the MBA program must have earned four-year undergraduate degrees. A specific undergraduate degree is not required.

Students entering the MBA program are expected to be competent in mathematics, have strong communications skills (both written and oral), and be competent with use of computers.

To be considered for graduate admissions, applicants must submit a completed application, $35 application fee, official transcripts of all previous college work (must be received directly from each institution), GMAT or GRE score report, two letters of recommendation from professionals (e.g., employers or professors) familiar with the applicant's academic potential, and a TOEFL score report for those who are international applicants.

CONCENTRATIONS

Accounting

The UT accounting concentration may be completed in either of two ways:

- The public accounting track provides for completion of the MBA in addition to meeting the requirements to sit for the CPA examination. Successful candidates grow the skills both to advance as valued members of management teams and to master demanding technical examinations like the CPA.

- The CFO/controller track prepares the student to function as a business executive with a wide-ranging knowledge of total business operations, best practices, and corporate strategy. In addition to understanding the development, dissemination, and application of financial data, management skills focused on adding value to an organization are emphasized.

Entrepreneurship

In all industrialized countries, new businesses create the majority of net new jobs, yet most entrepreneurs have no formalized instruction in how to launch a new business. This concentration prepares students for the intricacies of planning, launching, and leading a new business. The curriculum is designed around two themes: screening and recognizing opportunities to create value, and personal innovation despite scarce organizational resources.

Finance

Business professionals adept at applying complex economic and accounting concepts in decision-making are in great demand. Managerial decisions in organizations, as well as timely analyses of investment alternatives, require input from financially educated professionals. A finance concentration may be completed in any of three ways:

- The investment analysis and management track emphasizes the complex analysis of equities, fixed income securities, and derivatives.

- The corporate financial strategy and management track emphasizes decision-making in the corporate managerial arena.

- The finance student may also complete a nonspecific General Finance track. The student obtains exposure in both the managerial and investment areas. Additional finance electives are at the student's option.

Information Systems Management

The information systems management concentration deals with managing information as a strategic corporate asset and resource. Students are prepared with the knowledge and tools needed to integrate people, hardware, software, and data for optimal planning, decision-making, and problem-solving. The curriculum is designed to empower leaders with an understanding of how information systems and technologies may be used to achieve the corporation's mission and vision.

International Business

The international business concentration provides the student a broad-based business background; develops an understanding and appreciation for the strategic, operational, and behavioral aspects of managing across cultures; investigates the development and implementation of marketing techniques and programs on an international scale; and emphasizes the special risks and problems encountered by multinational managers.

Management

Professional managers must know how to ethically manage businesses with attention to customer value, returns to stakeholders, and satisfaction in personal and corporate employee development. The UT management concentration involves students in business consulting exercises, working to solve problems of real companies.

Marketing

The marketing concentration provides students with a broad-based education in what it means for an organization to be truly "market-driven." Class projects involve students in making decisions about product development, pricing, promotion, marketing research, sales compensation, cost containment, and production scheduling.

Career Services & Placement

Graduate students can expect individualized attention from the professional staff of the Career Services Center. Typical graduate services include resume critique, design and referral, personal career advising, interview skills refreshers, on-campus company interview opportunities, and informational interviews with other professionals from the greater Tampa Bay area. Also, with its combination of a resume database, internships, online employer access to resume books and job listings, the HIRE-UT system is the epitome of online career services, perfectly suited for today's busy professionals.

UNIVERSITY OF WASHINGTON

AT A GLANCE

MBA students at the University of Washington tailor their education for a future they define. They build on a first-year integrated curriculum that focuses on core business concepts with special programs and summer internships at local companies like Microsoft or Starbucks. Students customize the MBA program with a broad range of electives, choosing from certificate programs such as Entrepreneurship and Innovation, or clusters of courses organized around an area of special interest such as world trade. Other students augment their programs with classes from other colleges and schools, or pursue dual degrees.

The University of Washington enjoys a long-standing reputation for excellence in education and research, receiving more government research funding over the past 26 years than any other public university in the nation. MBA candidates benefit from the opportunity to study with faculty who guide them to the frontiers of knowledge. The low faculty/student ratio and collaborative culture create a dynamic entrepreneurial learning community where connections are easily made. Study teams, networking, mentoring, and internships provide MBA students with key connections. Through the Business Connections Center, students also have access to more than 40,000 alumni and other critical career resources.

LOCATION & ENVIRONMENT

The University of Washington achieves international recognition in both teaching and research. Since 1975, the University has ranked first among public institutions in the number of federal grants and contracts awarded to its faculty members. Its 16 schools and colleges provide education to 34,000 students, who can choose from more than 100 academic disciplines and 5,000 courses.

The University's prominence is assisted by its Seattle location, home to major companies in aerospace, technology, biotechnology, medical equipment, and engineering. Seattle has a unique connection to Asia and the largest port in the Northwest. Executives from many local companies maintain close connections with the UW Business School, serving on advisory boards, appearing as guest speakers in the classroom, and mentoring MBA students.

DEGREES OFFERED

The UW Business School offers an undergraduate degree and a full range of graduate degrees. Offerings include:

- BA
- MBA
- Evening MBA
- Executive MBA
- Global Executive MBA
- Technology Management MBA
- Master of Science in Information Systems
- Master of Professional Accounting
- PhD

PROGRAMS & CURRICULUM

MBA Program

In the first year, the UW MBA Program focuses on an integrated study of major business functions: fundamentals in accounting, finance, marketing, ethics, operations management, and information systems are woven into modules of varying length. In the spring quarter of Year One, students select bridge electives to gain exposure to topics available in Year Two and develop skills that can be applied in optional summer internships.

Year Two presents an open-ended opportunity to individualize the program of study. Students can follow a traditional concentration with courses across 11 disciplines, customize a concentration of classes, or choose a special certificate program. Some students also opt for a dual degree.

Special Programs

- Center for Technology Entrepreneurship: Teaming with graduate students in engineering and the medical school, MBA students gain access to "next-generation" technologies, experts in intellectual property management, and venture capitalists.

- The Global Business Program: Students explore the complexities of working in a globally connected marketplace through this program ranked by *U.S. News & World Report* as one of the Top International Business Graduate Programs in the country.

- E-Business: Students prepare to think creatively, aggressively, and critically about the strategic use of information in creating shareholder value.

- Business and Economic Development: Students learn about inner city development and small business management while providing entrepreneurs assistance to help grow their companies.

- Multiple Degree Programs: Students complete a second graduate degree in engineering, law, international studies, public health, or accounting.

Business School

EXPENSES & FINANCIAL AID

The UW Business School MBA Program offers a very good value. Out-of-state tuition is $5,868 per quarter; Washington residents pay $2,835. Other annual expenses are estimated at about $16,990. Here is a breakdown:

Room and board: $10,000

Books, computers, and supplies: $3,000

Local transportation: $1,200

Personal expenses: $2,400

MBA Association dues (for two years): $190

MBA Club dues: $200

Financial Aid

Financial aid is available from the University of Washington and the UW Business School in the form of loans, work-study, fellowships and scholarships, and academic employment.

All admitted applicants are considered for merit-based scholarships. Once admitted, each student may also apply for other Business School scholarships. An application for these is included with the letter of admission.

Loans

Domestic applicants may obtain federal loan application forms at www.fafsa.ed.gov. For more information contact the Office of Student Financial Aid at UW at osfa@u.washington.edu.

FACULTY

The UW Business School philosophy emphasizes a partnership between students and faculty members. Professors at the UW Business School have achieved recognition for both teaching and research. MBAs praise the faculty's active involvement in student learning and their integration of research and teaching. Professors take a personal interest in their students and, in return, they demand a high level of student effort and commitment.

STUDENTS

Class size for each entering MBA cohort at the UW Business School is no more than 150 students. Ninety percent of students' undergraduate degrees are distributed almost equally among liberal arts, business, and science. The average student in last year's class was 29 years old and had more than 5 years of work experience. International students made up about 28 percent of the class and represented 17 different countries. The class that entered in 2002 had an average GPA of 3.46 and an average GMAT score of 671.

The UW Business School strives to create an environment that is representative of society as a whole—age, racial or ethnic origin, cultural background, activities and accomplishments, goals, previous study, and life experiences of individuals contribute to the creation of such an environment.

Students find highly individualized course concentrations, a personal study plan, and an emphasis on teamwork that stresses collaboration over competition. Most participate in at least two student organizations in which they can acquire leadership skills and pursue special interests. A sampling of clubs and associations includes Speak Easy, where students can improve presentation skills; the Consulting Club, where alumni train students for consulting-firm interviews; and the Global Business Association, which develops three international study tours a year.

ADMISSIONS

The UW Business School believes that personal connections are essential to business education, just as they are to business. Advance counseling is strongly advised for anyone considering an MBA program. The MBA program encourages campus visits to meet face-to-face with admissions staff or attend a reception held in cities nationwide. Prospective students are strongly encouraged to schedule an interview after completing the GMAT and arrange for classroom visits as desired.

Each fall, the UW Business School admits up to 150 men and women with the highest potential for achievement in management. The MBA program seeks individuals who have demonstrated high-quality academic work and who will contribute to the diversity of both the student body and the ranks of professional management.

Applicants must:

- Complete the equivalent of a four-year U.S. bachelor's degree from an accredited college or university
- Meet a quantitative analysis requirement and possess minimum English language skills
- Take the GMAT
- Apply to each school, college, or department of interest if pursuing concurrent degrees
- Complete preparatory course work

ADDITIONAL INFORMATION

The University of Washington's affordable MBA program "has a great reputation," and it boasts "proximity to a high-tech and rapidly growing economy" in "safe," "fun-filled," but expensive Seattle, the capital of the Pacific Northwest. UW draws heavily from the Pacific Rim, a situation agreeable to students from both sides of the Pacific as "international students add a much needed layer of depth and insight to our education."

VANDERBILT UNIVERSITY

AT A GLANCE

Complexity, change, innovativeness, competition—these are the constants in the new economy. Vanderbilt University's Owen Graduate School of Management stands apart among leading business schools in preparing individuals to succeed in this challenging world. Owen@Vanderbilt is a young, dynamic, and progressive institution dedicated to setting a new standard in business education. A Vanderbilt MBA degree signals resourceful, creative thinking and tested leadership skills. Innovators and leaders are forged by Owen@Vanderbilt in a rigorous program that encompasses a unique combination of attributes:

- Excellence in key academic areas that speak to the core of the global economy—among them Finance, Marketing, Operations, Electronic Commerce, Information Technology, Human and Organizational Performance, and Strategy. Owen@Vanderbilt also creates competent leaders in highly specialized fields such as Entrepreneurship, International Business, Brand Management, Law and Business, Health Care, and Environmental Management.

- A world-class faculty rich in research, steeped in the realities of business, and reflective of Owen@Vanderbilt's international reputation for excellence. The University, its business school and many of its graduate and professional schools are consistently rated among the nation's finest.

- A collegial, team-oriented culture in which students can truly flourish—developing, applying, and testing their ideas, knowledge, and leadership skills. We bring together in one of the smallest top business schools a highly select group of individuals from around the world, representing a great diversity of academic, professional, and cultural backgrounds. Academic rigor is matched by ceaseless opportunities for students to interact in a friendly, productive way with other students, faculty, alumni, and business leaders, becoming an integral part of Owen@Vanderbilt's expanding global community.

- The Nashville metropolis. One of the Southeast's booming and most vibrant, sophisticated, and livable cities, Nashville is enthusiastically touted by the Vanderbilt community as an ideal place to go to school.

LOCATION & ENVIRONMENT

Vanderbilt University is located in Nashville, Tennessee. A major southeastern city and the Tennessee state capital, Nashville has a population of 1.2 million and lies within 600 miles of 50 percent of the population of the continental United States. A center for publishing, health care, entertainment, banking, finance, insurance, and automobile manufacturing, Nashville is home base for many international corporations. Nashville's mild weather, acres of green space, sense of history, and dynamic business climate create an ideal environment for learning and recreation.

Founded in 1873, Vanderbilt University is one of a few independent universities with both a quality undergraduate program and a full range of graduate and professional programs. It has a strong faculty of more than 1,800 full-time members and a diverse student body of about 10,000. The 316-acre campus is less than two miles from Nashville's downtown business district, combining the advantages of an urban location with a peaceful, park-like setting of broad lawns, shaded paths, and quiet plazas.

Vanderbilt University's Graduate School of Management opened its doors in 1969 to 10 students and 10 faculty members. Today, as one of the world's leading business schools, Vanderbilt's Owen Graduate School of Management still retains one of the nation's best student/faculty ratios of 10:1. Owen@Vanderbilt is also known for the spirit of teamwork, challenging academics, and stimulating research environment that fuel its appeal to students from nearly 40 countries and to faculty, staff, alumni, and corporate recruiters.

DEGREES OFFERED

Vanderbilt University offers five dual degree programs that allow multidisciplinary study in management and another graduate or professional program. Dual degree students earn both the MBA degree and a second degree in less time than it would normally take to complete the degrees separately. Dual degree programs are available with Vanderbilt's nationally recognized programs in Law, Medicine, Nursing, Engineering, and Latin American Studies.

The Owen Graduate School of Management offers a variety of nondegree programs and seminars, including open-enrollment and custom executive education programs. For more information and a complete list of offerings, please call 615-322-2513, send an email to execed@owen.vanderbilt.edu, or visit http://mba.vanderbilt.edu/execprog/index.cfm.

PROGRAMS & CURRICULUM

Each August, a diverse group of 220–225 talented students from around the world enrolls in Owen@Vanderbilt's full-time MBA program. Nearly 40 countries are represented in the program, and many students have spent time living, working, studying, and traveling in countries other than their own. Students come from a wide variety of academic, professional, and personal backgrounds.

An important feature of Owen@Vanderbilt's modular curriculum is its flexibility. Each semester is divided into two seven-week modules in which students typically take three or four 2-credit courses. Students complete most of the 22 credits in the core curriculum during the fall semester of the first year. The remaining core courses are taken in the spring semester of the first year, when students also begin taking elective courses toward the total of 60 credits required for graduation. The entire second year is open to elective courses, of which there are more than 150 from which to choose. Students can earn up to 15 credits of their MBA degree outside of Owen@Vanderbilt by taking classes in another graduate or professional school at the University or by spending a semester abroad at one of 17 different international exchange partners.

Students are required to specify a primary area of concentration in accounting, electronic commerce, finance, general management, human and organizational performance, information technology, law and business, marketing, operations, or strategy. Each concentration requires 12 credits of elective study beyond the core curriculum. In addition, students may pursue an emphasis in brand management, entrepreneurship, environmental management, health care, or international business, all of which require 8 credits beyond the core. Given the minimal number of core courses, flexibility of the modular curriculum, and wide selection of electives, it is possible for students to complete more than one area of concentration and/or emphasis.

In addition to significant international content in the curriculum and several student organizations with a global focus, international exchange programs are available with 17 institutions around the world. These include programs in Austria, Brazil, Chile, China, Costa Rica, England, France, Germany, Japan, Mexico, Norway, Spain, South Africa, and Venezuela. Participating students typically spend the fall semester of their second year studying abroad.

Faculty at Owen use a variety of teaching methods, including lecture, case study, class discussion, group projects, and independent study. The overall academic atmosphere and culture of the School is team-oriented, cooperative, and supportive so that students are able to maximize their opportunities for personal and professional development.

FACILITIES & EQUIPMENT

Beginning with the fall 2000 entering class, Owen@Vanderbilt implemented a pioneering wireless computer network that enables students, faculty, and staff to collaborate and communicate more efficiently. IBM Thinkpads with wireless capabilities are required for all incoming students as part of Owen@Vanderbilt's commitment to the practical use of new technologies. The school has state-of-the-art facilities running Pentium-based PCs with a fast processor, substantial memory, CD-ROM drive, large monitor, and Microsoft Office. All computers are networked for file-sharing, email, electronic information resource, and Internet access for faculty, staff, and students.

eLab, the first research center for electronic commerce at a business school, was established in 1994. This renowned center is directed by two of the world's leading scholars in electronic commerce. Recently, the center received $1 million in funding from Vanderbilt University to expand its infrastructure, hire additional staff, and conduct cutting-edge academic research in an online environment.

Owen@Vanderbilt established the first electronic commerce research center at a major business school. The School's broad curriculum and innovative research in

Owen Graduate School of Management

electronic commerce earned it recognition as a Top 10 MBA program in this field. Owen@Vanderbilt's concentrations in electronic commerce and information technology provide more than 20 elective options.

EXPENSES & FINANCIAL AID

All admitted applicants are considered for merit-based scholarships, which range from $4,000 per year to full tuition and the prestigious Dean's Scholar award, the highest honor for an incoming student that includes an additional $10,000 stipend ($5,000 per year). Merit-based awards are typically reserved for the top 35–40 percent of the incoming class, and the selection process is very competitive. Scholarships and fellowships are offered in each round of admission, but candidates are encouraged to apply as early as possible because funding is limited.

More information about financial aid is available at http://mba.vanderbilt.edu/mba/finanaid.cfm.

STUDENTS

The Owen Graduate School of Management recruits extensively in Europe, Asia, Latin America, the Middle East, and North America. Given the School's strong international reputation, Owen attracts students from nearly 40 countries. Approximately 25–30 percent of full-time MBA students are citizens of countries other than the United States.

There are numerous student organizations and extracurricular activities, including 100 Percent Owen (community service), *The Bottom Line* (student newspaper), Christian Business Association, Distinguished Speaker Series, Electronic Commerce Club, Entrepreneurship Club, Finance Association, Global Business Club, Health Care Club, Human and Organizational Performance Association (HOPA), Just Do It—Right, Latin Business Association, Management Consulting Association, Marketing Association, Marketspace, Max Adler Student Investment Fund, Operations Club, Outdoor Adventures Club, Owen Black Student Association (OBSA), Owen Consulting Services, Owen School Student Association (OSSA), Rugby Team, Soccer Team, Spouses and Significant Others of Owen Students (SOS), and the Women's Business Association.

The Owen experience extends beyond two years of course work. Students form friendships and professional ties that last a lifetime. Owen graduates are instantly recognized by their alumni peers and have a unique bond. They benefit immensely from the networking opportunities and wealth of knowledge of their fellow alums by sharing expertise from many fields to make each better at their own jobs. Please visit http://mba.vanderbilt.edu/alumdev/index.cfm for more information.

The Alumni Board of Directors is a group of accomplished executives who invest their personal time and considerable energy to keep the Owen School moving forward. In addition to local alumni clubs across the United States and around the world, the Owen Graduate School of Management has the largest online club of any business school on *Yahoo!* Please visit http://clubs.yahoo.com/clubs/owengsm for more information.

ADMISSIONS

The Admissions Committee evaluates applicants on the basis of academic ability, professional experience, personal qualities, and leadership potential. A strong record of achievement and potential for future success in each of these areas is highly desirable. While there is no minimum requirement for prior work experience, almost 90 percent of recent incoming classes had three or more years of experience.

Attributes Owen seeks in its students include: demonstrated achievement in academic, professional, and community activities; well-defined career goals; interpersonal skills; professional presence; maturity and sound judgment; critical thinking and analytical skills; initiative and motivation; team skills; knowledge of and interest in the Vanderbilt MBA program.

The Vanderbilt MBA application consists of data forms, a resume, detailed work history, essays, recommendations, official test scores, official transcripts, the application fee, and for international candidates, a financial support document. Completed applications are screened, and qualified individuals are invited to interview with an admissions officer, either in person or by telephone, if they haven't already completed an interview. The interview is required of all qualified candidates prior to admission. All admitted applicants, domestic and international, are automatically considered for merit-based scholarships and fellowships. Candidates are notified of merit-based awards, if any, at the same time an offer of admission is extended.

Current application materials for the fall incoming class are usually available by early September. Almost 90 percent of all candidates choose to apply online at http://mba.vanderbilt.edu/admissions/. Paper-based applications are acceptable and may be printed at http://mba.vanderbilt.edu/mba/app_forms.cfm. Application deadlines are November 30, January 31, March 15 (last deadline for international applicants), and April 15 for admission to the class starting in August of each year. After the first round, admission decisions are made on a rolling basis, and letters are usually mailed within 8–10 weeks of the corresponding deadline.

You may contact the MBA Admissions Office with any questions you may have about the Vanderbilt MBA program. The following links will provide most of the information you need and the quickest service:

Owen@Vanderbilt Website: http://mba.vanderbilt.edu
Request Materials: http://mba.vanderbilt.edu/admissions/
Apply Online: http://mba.vanderbilt.edu/admissions/
Visits and Events: http://mba.vanderbilt.edu/admissions
Admissions Calendar: http://mba.vanderbilt.edu/mba/adm_calendar.cfm

All other inquiries should be directed to admissions@owen.vanderbilt.edu.

ADDITIONAL INFORMATION

The Owen Graduate School of Management participates in most major recruiting events around the world. Owen@Vanderbilt also hosts numerous information sessions and receptions in North America, as well as several weekend events on campus throughout the year. A calendar of upcoming events is located at http://mba.vanderbilt.edu/admissions.

The Vanderbilt MBA program also welcomes and encourages visits to campus any time during the year but especially when classes are in session. Owen@Vanderbilt's Campus Visit Program provides an individual itinerary for each prospective student that includes a visit to class and lunch with a student host, an informational or evaluative interview with an admissions officer, and a small group meeting with a member of the career management staff. A campus visit can be requested online at http://mba.vanderbilt.edu/admissions.

Prospective students who are visiting campus may schedule either an informative or evaluative interview with an admissions officer regardless of their status in the admissions process. Otherwise, candidates must submit a completed application before being invited to schedule an interview, which may be conducted in person or by telephone. Both options are given equal consideration in the evaluation process, but a campus visit is strongly recommended whenever possible. Appropriate business attire is recommended, unless specified otherwise. Please bring a copy of your current resume to the interview.

CAREER SERVICES & PLACEMENT

What distinguishes Owen@Vanderbilt from other business schools is its highly personal approach to career management, which ensures that each student receives the individual attention they desire. By partnering with students, the Career Management Center (CMC) supports the professional development of all students by providing a weekly newsletter, one-on-one counseling sessions, career skills workshops, industry-related seminars, company information sessions, on-campus interviews, recruiter feedback, networking trips, off-campus career consortia, and more.

Throughout the Owen@Vanderbilt experience, the CMC acts as a personal team of career coaches—helping evaluate the right fit between your goals and opportunities in the global marketplace. You'll receive individual assistance in defining your career goals, executing your strategy, and negotiating job offers. Salaries, signing bonuses, and even stock options for graduating Owen@Vanderbilt MBAs are highly competitive with other top business schools, and Owen MBAs accept jobs in highly diverse geographic locations.

For more information visit www.mba.vanderbilt.edu/cmc/prostudent.cfm.

WASHINGTON UNIVERSITY IN ST. LOUIS

AT A GLANCE

At Olin, you'll find a supportive community where each person's interests and ideas make a difference. With approximately 160 MBA students in a class, you're assured of receiving individual attention from our faculty and staff. And it's likely that you'll get to know our dean, Stuart Greenbaum.

Olin's curriculum is based on the understanding that no two students are identical—therefore, no single, prescribed curriculum is expected to meet everyone's needs. That's what makes the Olin curriculum different: it's flexible, it's based on a relatively small set of required classes and a large number of electives, and it acknowledges students' individual strengths and career aspirations.

Experiential learning is an important element in your learning strategy. We offer a broad and innovative menu of hands-on learning opportunities that enable you to apply your classroom knowledge to real-life business situations. These programs help you develop confidence in your leadership ability, gain consulting experience, and hone your communication and teamwork skills.

LOCATION & ENVIRONMENT

Founded in 1853, Washington University is recognized among the Top 20 universities in the United States, according to *U.S. News & World Report*. The University is located in a picturesque suburban setting and is within walking distance of Forest Park. The Hilltop Campus, where Olin is situated, is seven miles west of the Mississippi Riverfront and the St. Louis Arch. Learning takes place in the supportive, comfortable atmosphere of a small college with the resources and amenities of a larger university. St. Louis is a thriving metropolitan center with notable art galleries, museums, theater, sporting events, and bustling ethnic neighborhoods. It is home to a dynamic corporate community that fosters projects, internships, and mentoring programs for Olin MBAs.

John E. Simon Hall

Opened in 1986, the Olin School occupies John E. Simon Hall. The 80,000-square-foot building houses modern classrooms and study areas, an extensive library with online computer linkups to all major data systems, modern faculty and administrative offices, and a 70-unit computer lab for student use.

Charles F. Knight Executive Education Center

The Knight Center, Olin's new executive residential living and learning facility, reflects Washington University's tradition of world-class scholarship and research, as well as the Olin School's philosophy of education for a lifetime of achievement. The 135,000-square-foot building includes classrooms, breakout rooms, lounges, a dining area, 66 bedrooms, administrative offices, a fitness center, and a pub.

DEGREES OFFERED

The following degrees are offered:

BSBA

MSBA

MBA (full-time)

MBA (part-time)

Executive degree programs

PhD

FACULTY

Approximately 26 tenured professors, 37 additional tenure-track professors, 2 visiting professors, and 26 part-time professors who are world-class scholars serve on Olin's faculty. They hold positions on editorial boards, publish articles in top journals, and earn distinction as exemplary teachers and strong community builders who advance the vision of the Olin School. They are instrumental in developing the curriculum to reflect state-of-the-art business practices. Six adjunct faculty members who are leaders in the business community bring to the classroom a passion for merging business theory with cutting-edge business practices.

John M. Olin School of Business

STUDENTS

The full-time MBA program enrolls approximately 150 new students each year. They have diverse undergraduate backgrounds ranging from business and the humanities to engineering and the sciences. On average, an entering class includes students from more than 30 states and as many as 26 foreign countries. Students also have the opportunity to participate in one or more of Olin's 24 student organizations. These organizations allow students to further expand their professional network and hone leadership skills. A student-administered honor code designed to govern full-time MBA students represents Olin MBAs' commitment to excellence in the classroom and sends a direct message to future employers: students are graduating from a community that actively practices an exemplary standard of integrity.

ADMISSIONS

Admission to Olin is selective. The Olin Admissions Committee reviews applications based on a series of four deadlines with the earliest falling in mid-November. Qualified full-time MBA students are admitted to start in the fall semester only. The committee reviews all information in the application to determine a candidate's ability to perform in an intensely rigorous academic environment. The committee also seeks to identify students who will add significantly to the academic, cultural, and social character of the School. Prospective students must submit an Olin application in hard copy, online, or through MBA Multi-App interactive software. The committee also requires a current GMAT score, results of the TOEFL exam (if applicable), official transcripts from each university previously attended, a work history form, essays, a resume, and two letters of recommendation. Interviews are strongly encouraged.

ADDITIONAL INFORMATION

Olin offers a wide range of opportunities to incorporate global perspectives and experiences into the MBA program. A variety of international business electives in finance, marketing, and strategy are available. Students also may take courses in other graduate programs at Washington University such as East Asian Studies, International Affairs, Law, and Health Administration. Other options include the Global Management Studies course, where students help select the international destination; research the country's history, social customs, and business practices; and consult on country-specific projects for corporate clients. The course ends with a two-week trip to the selected country. One-semester exchange programs are also offered with institutions in England, France, Germany, and Venezuela, as well as a two-week summer program in London. Additionally Olin is a member of the MBA Enterprise Corps, a consortium of leading business schools that enables students to work in newly privatized companies in emerging markets.

MBA students at Washington University's Olin School of Business tell us that its intimate size, flexible curriculum, and faculty composed of "heavy hitters" make it a worthwhile choice. Experiential learning is another major focal point of the Olin approach. Practicum allows students to consult for area companies on matters ranging from marketing to strategy. Thus far, a slew of firms, including Enterprise Rent-A-Car, Ford Motor Company, PricewaterhouseCoopers, Ralston Purina, and Monsanto, have asked Olin students for their advice.

CAREER SERVICES & PLACEMENT

Through an aggressive program targeting the needs of students and employers, Olin's Weston Career Resources Center (WCRC) actively assists all MBA students in developing and sustaining their self-managed career goals. The center boasts a highly successful recruiting record that is attributable to extensive student involvement, a vital alumni network, cutting-edge information systems, and dynamic corporate partnerships. Over 150 companies request interviews and hire Olin students each year. In addition to sponsoring several road shows—student-organized visits to targeted regions and companies—the WCRC also participates in "Managing Your Career Strategy," a required course for first-year MBAs and provides workshops on job search techniques, interviewing, and salary negotiations.

WILLAMETTE UNIVERSITY

AT A GLANCE

Willamette University's Atkinson Graduate School of Management offers the only MBA program in the nation accredited by the two most prestigious organizations governing management education: AACSB International (business) and NASPAA (public administration). The distinctive dual accreditation provides professional recognition and respect in all sectors and prepares students for careers in entrepreneurial, business, consulting, government, and not-for-profit organizations. The School has also been recognized as one of the country's best business schools by *BusinessWeek* and *U.S. News & World Report*.

The learning environment emphasizes excellent teaching, teamwork, and the practical application of management theory to managerial decision-making. From the first day of class, Atkinson students apply what they learn to real organizations. The Atkinson School PaCE Project (where teams of students create and run a real enterprise), case studies, internships, simulations, and consulting projects provide multiple opportunities to "learn by doing" and build the professional work experience employers value.

The Atkinson School is part of Willamette University. Willamette University is widely recognized for the excellence of its academic programs, the quality of its students, the dedication of its faculty, and the success of its alumni. The University offers 34 undergraduate majors and three graduate professional degrees: the MBA (Master of Business Administration for Business, Government, and Not-for-Profit Management), the MAT (Master of Arts in Teaching), and the JD (Doctor of Jurisprudence).

LOCATION & ENVIRONMENT

Willamette University is located in Salem, Oregon. The University's campus is spacious and one of the most beautiful college campuses in the United States. Salem has been twice honored as an "All American City" and offers a lifestyle that is friendly, uncomplicated, and inexpensive compared to the larger cities of the West.

The downtown area is a short walk from the Atkinson School, offering major department stores linked with sky-bridges, traditional and ethnic restaurants, coffeehouses, and movie theaters. Salem is home to many historic sites, 96 city parks, indoor and outdoor concerts featuring international performers, art and wine festivals, bike paths, running trails, and the Oregon State Fair.

Seventy percent of Atkinson alumni choose to live and work in the Pacific Northwest after graduation. The Salem-Portland I-5 corridor is home to a multitude of businesses (including Northwest legends Nike, Intel, and Tektronix) and hosts a large variety of government and not-for-profit organizations.

A note about the weather: Don't believe what you hear—one way or the other. It doesn't rain all the time. The summers are mainly warm and sunny; the fall is usually clear and beautiful; the spring is a little bit of everything. In the winter it's fine library weather.

Student organizations include Atkinson Student Association (student government), Atkinson Management Society (alumni association), Atkinson Marketing Association, Atkinson Public Management Association, International Graduate Student Association, Joint Degree Association, and the Society for Human Resource Management.

DEGREES OFFERED

Willamette University's Atkinson Graduate School of Management offers the MBA for Business, Government, and Not-for-Profit Management. The Atkinson School degree is the first and only MBA program accredited for both business (AACSB International) and public administration (NASPAA). It is a multisector, multi-opportunity degree that prepares students for the business of management—whether it is managing the business of business, the business of government, or the business of not-for-profit organizations.

Students may also pursue a joint degree in management and law (MBA/JD) through a cooperative agreement between Willamette University's College of Law and Atkinson Graduate School of Management. Candidates for the MBA/JD joint degree program must apply and be admitted to both the College of Law and the Atkinson School.

PROGRAMS & CURRICULUM

The Two-Year MBA Program

The traditional two-year Atkinson School MBA Program is designed for full-time students who have a bachelor's degree in the liberal arts, engineering, or other areas of study. It is also designed for full-time students who have a major in business from a college of liberal arts or a business program that is not accredited for business administration by AACSB International (note: less than 50 percent of business programs in the United States are accredited by AACSB International) or students with a business degree who are not eligible for the accelerated program.

During the first year of study, students complete the required core curriculum, a set of 10 courses where students learn the financial, marketing, accounting, human resource, international, organizational, statistical, economic, quantitative, and information technology tools that support managerial decision-making. Students immediately apply what they learn through the unique Private, Public, and Community Enterprise Project (PaCE)—an extensive hands-on management project in which teams of students create a business, make a profit, close the business, and donate their profits to a local not-for-profit organization. The PaCE project and the core curriculum are carefully planned to provide a cross-functional learning experience that offers the powerful combination of a wealth of new skills and the opportunity to put those skills to the test in a real organization.

Fall Semester Core Courses are Managing Organizations, Managing Exchange, PaCE Project, Finance, Management Controls, and Foundations of Quantitative Analysis.

Spring Semester Core Courses are Managing Organizations, Managing Exchange, PaCE Project, Economics, Management Information Technology, and Statistical Inference and Model Formulation.

During the second year of study, students use the elective curriculum to design a program that meets their individual career goals. Students may choose to pursue a broad background in general management or develop greater depth of knowledge in one or more career areas of interest. Elective courses include classes that involve projects and consulting for organizations, internships, independent study, industry analysis, case studies, research, study abroad programs, and traditional management classes.

The Accelerated Option

The accelerated option of the Atkinson School MBA for Business, Government, and Not-for-Profit Management is designed for people who have a strong background in the academic study of business as well as professional work experience. Through this program, admitted students may be eligible to waive up to 30 credits of the required core curriculum and complete the Atkinson School MBA in approximately one academic year of full-time study (or longer as a part-time student).

Admission to the accelerated program is selective and determined by a complete review of all application materials. To qualify to apply for the accelerated option, applicants must have:

- Completed a bachelor's degree in business from a program accredited by AACSB International within seven years of entering the Atkinson School
- Earned a cumulative undergraduate grade point average of 3.2 or better in the business degree
- Completed at least two years of professional work experience

Students admitted to the accelerated program focus their studies in the Atkinson School elective curriculum. Career areas of interest include accounting, finance, human resources, information technology, international management, marketing, organizational analysis, public management, and quantitative analysis/management science.

FACILITIES & EQUIPMENT

Willamette University facilities include two libraries, several computer labs, state-of-the art classrooms, recreational and fitness facilities, dining centers, a concert hall, an art museum, student apartments, and more.

Atkinson students have 24-hour-a-day wireless access to the Internet, email, and local network software and printing services. Students are required to have a laptop computer with wireless LAN capability and a standard suite of software for word processing, spreadsheets, and presentations.

The University's Mark O. Hatfield Library and the J.W. Long Law Library support the research needs of Atkinson students. Services include a Management/Economics Librarian who assists students and faculty; electronic databases; books;

Atkinson Graduate School of Management

periodicals; journals; newspapers; specialized materials; and programs that provide access to more than 4 million books, journals, and library resources.

EXPENSES & FINANCIAL AID

Willamette University's Atkinson School provides a nationally recognized MBA education at a reasonable and manageable cost. Atkinson School tuition for full-time students enrolled in 12 to 18 semester credits of course work is $9,510 per semester or $19,020 for the 2003–2004 academic year. Tuition for part-time students is $634 per semester credit. The student body fee is $50, and estimated living expenses are $7,550–$11,350.

The budget for full-time Atkinson School students includes the estimated costs of tuition, books, fees, and living expenses (living expenses include room, board, and personal expenses). Tuition, books, and fees are common costs among students. Living expenses vary with the needs and choices of individuals. Students are also required to have a laptop computer with 802.11b wireless LAN capability and a standard suite of software. If you need to purchase a laptop, the cost to purchase the required laptop can be included in your financial aid budget. For planning purposes, students should assume an annual tuition increase of 4 percent to 5 percent for the following academic year.

Willamette University offers a variety of programs to make your Atkinson School MBA as affordable as possible. Atkinson students finance their education with the help of loans, scholarships, family resources, income from work, and Tuition Management Systems payment program.

Full-time students may be eligible for Atkinson School scholarships. Scholarships are awarded on the basis of merit as measured by GMAT or GRE scores, undergraduate grade point average, and experience. Scholarships range in value from 25 percent to 100 percent of tuition.

U.S. citizens and permanent residents may be eligible to borrow up to $18,500 per year through the Federal Stafford Loan Programs. Eligibility for the Stafford Loan Programs is determined by submission and analysis of the FAFSA (Free Application for Federal Student Aid). U.S. citizens and permanent residents may also be eligible for private credit-based educational loans and campus work programs.

International students may be eligible for Atkinson School merit-based scholarships and for private credit-based educational loans if they have a cosigner who is a U.S. citizen or permanent resident. However, international applicants and/or their sponsor should be prepared to fund the entire cost of educational and living expenses for the two-year program.

FACULTY

The Atkinson School faculty are excellent teachers who share an intense commitment to the academic and professional successes of their students. In addition to being excellent teachers, the Atkinson faculty are leaders of community and professional organizations; authors of books, articles, and software packages; editors and reviewers of professional journals; entrepreneurs; consultants to business, government, and not-for-profit organizations; and members of national and regional boards that make important decisions about management education in America. What sets the Atkinson faculty apart from other programs is the faculty's commitment to individual student achievement. One hundred percent of Atkinson faculty have a doctorate degree.

Research interests of faculty include corporate capital structure and dividend policy, public budgeting, managerial value systems and decision styles, organizational change, financial derivatives, risk management, financial markets and institutions, market efficiency, business process design and reengineering, critical success factors of implementing integrated systems, decision-making in small business, value-chain analysis, statistical computing, resampling methods, applied forecasting, conflict management, negotiation, acquisition and dissemination of market information, public policy analysis, global human resources, corporate responsibility, global teams, global leadership, economics of information, international strategy, foreign market entry, and government promotion of international business.

STUDENTS

The Atkinson student profile is characterized by the same diversity of age and experience that is common to the work environment of most organizations. Students come to the Atkinson School with a variety of academic backgrounds and work experience. Some have years of management experience and are pursuing career advancement or change. Others have recently completed their bachelor's degree and are preparing for entry-level management positions.

Atkinson students excel as individuals and as team members. They have received national, regional, and local awards for the quality of their work and have been selected for prestigious fellowship and internship programs.

ADMISSIONS

Admission to the Atkinson School is based on academic ability and managerial potential. Academic ability is evaluated by the applicant's past academic performance, recommendations, and performance on the GMAT or GRE. Managerial potential is evaluated by the applicant's general experience, work experience, motivation, leadership, involvement in organizational or community activities, communication skills, and commitment to attain a graduate management education. These characteristics are evaluated through information provided on the Application for Admission, letters of recommendation, personal statement of experience/goals, and, often, an interview with the applicant. Candidates are also evaluated on their potential to contribute to and benefit from the learning environment of the Atkinson School.

Each applicant is evaluated individually. Applicants must have a baccalaureate degree from an accredited college or university in the United States or an equivalent degree from another country. There are no specific course prerequisites for admission, but students should have an understanding of mathematical principles and well-developed writing skills. Experience with word processing and spreadsheet applications is also helpful.

Applicants requesting admission to the Atkinson School must submit the following materials to the Atkinson School Admission Office: application for admission (paper or online), personal statement of experiences and professional goals, two letters of evaluation, official transcripts of all undergraduate and graduate course work, official GMAT or GRE scores, and a $50 nonrefundable application fee.

In addition to the documents listed above, international applicants must submit the following: English translation of academic records and transcripts, Statement of Financial Responsibility and official bank verification showing sufficient resources to cover 2 years of educational and personal expenses, and a photocopy of the name page of their passport showing the exact spelling of their name as it appears on their passport. International students for whom English is not the first language must also submit a TOEFL score of 230 or higher on the computer-based test.

The Atkinson School has a rolling admission process and reviews applications throughout the year. Applications completed by March 31 receive priority in admission and scholarship decisions. Applications submitted after March 31 may also receive consideration for admission and scholarship assistance.

Applicants will be notified of the admission decision within three weeks of completion of the application process.

Applicants are always welcome to contact the Atkinson School Admission Office at agsm-admission@willamette.edu or 503-370-6167 to check on the status of the application and communicate with members of the admission staff.

We encourage you to contact us for more information. Email agsm-admission@willamette.edu, call 503-370-6167, or visit our website at www.willamette.edu/agsm.

CAREER SERVICES & PLACEMENT

The Atkinson School works with students and employers to provide a complete program of services connecting students and alumni with employment opportunities. Career service programs help students develop strategic career management skills, improve job search skills, and obtain internships and employment. Services include workshops, internship programs, on-campus interviews, employment opportunity postings, national employment databases, individual counseling, mentoring programs, and career/networking fairs.

YaleMBA

Why You Should Come to Yale

■ **You will be taught by some of the world's best faculty**, who all teach in the MBA program.

■ **You will be a member of a group of outstanding students** from business, government and nonprofit backgrounds, and 40 countries. The relationships you develop at Yale will introduce you to a rewarding network of Yale scholars, advisors, and alumni that you will have for life.

■ **You will be part of the Yale tradition** wherein learning takes place in small, intimate settings that combine exceptional teaching with unequaled access to world-class faculty.

■ **You will be immersed in a rich and exciting learning environment.** We provide a solid framework of hard-edged business skills and special courses taught by former CEOs and other international leaders.

■ **You will have access to all of Yale University**, one of the world's great centers of learning. Students are encouraged to take advantage of classes and degrees offered throughout Yale.

You will have a once-in-a-life-time opportunity to interact personally with the men and women who are leading major global organizations through our Leaders Forum speakers program.

**Admissions Profile
Class of 2004**
Average GMAT Score: 698
Average College GPA: 3.5

Class Size

The smallest classes of any top MBA program.

Top Ten

An Ivy-League education ranked in the top ten by The Wall Street Journal, Forbes, The Economist, and the Financial Times.

Employment

Finance **43%**

Consulting **18%**

Technology/Other **19%**

Manufacturing **15%**

Nonprofit/Public **6%**

ADDITIONAL B-SCHOOLS

In this section, you'll find detailed profiles of a few business schools that are not yet accredited by the AACSB, with information about their programs, faculty, facilities, and admissions. The Princeton Review charges each school a small fee to be listed, and the editorial responsibility is solely that of the college.

Brandeis University

INTERNATIONAL BUSINESS SCHOOL

Pioneers in Global Markets

The Brandeis International Business School (IBS) is a pioneering school dedicated to preparing students for the careers of the global economy in international business, finance and economics. We teach state-of-the-art theory, immerse students in international experiences, and connect them to best practice in business and policy.

International to the Core

We are truly focused on the global economy. From a course on the global economic environment to advanced electives, the IBS experience is thoroughly international. More than half of our students come from Europe, Asia, Africa and Latin America—54 countries in all this year—and international experiences are built into our programs in partnership with major foreign schools and companies.

Boston: A Great Place to Live and Study

Brandeis is in Greater Boston, home to eight major research universities and to 250,000 students. IBS students are able to cross-register for courses at a number of these institutions. The region is a vibrant center for the financial services, high technology and consultancy industries, providing many career opportunities for our graduates. Deeply historic and dynamically modern, the area offers one of the most livable and stimulating environments in the United States.

Our Degree Programs

We have four degree programs offering a wide range of skills for careers:

- **MBA International** – managerial and analytical skills for international investments and businesses

- **Master of Arts in International Economics and Finance** – analytical and technical skills for business and policy decisions in global markets

- **Ph.D.** – advanced preparation in theory, institutions and empirical analysis

- **Master of Science in Finance** (part-time) – applied financial theory and analysis for mid-career professionals

Our courses are highly flexible, offering a choice of concentrations and more than 50 electives, a high proportion of which are new each year, reflecting developments in the world's economy. Global theory and practice are integrated into every course.

IBS

Connected to Business

Many senior executives visit the School each semester through our CEO, Entrepreneurs, Corporate Responsibility and Real Estate forums. Students also have opportunities for informal interaction with them in classes. Speakers at the forums have included Sumner Redstone of Viacom, former US Trade Representative Charlene Barshefsky, Roger Berkowitz of Legal Seafoods, Hardwick Simmons of the NASDAQ Stock Market, and Thomas Friedman of the New York Times.

Employment

IBS has a strong record of placing its students in leading corporations and public sector institutions across the globe. Recent graduates have secured positions at Lehman Brothers, JP Morgan Chase, GE Asset Management, Standard and Poor's, McKinsey and Co, Goldman Sachs, National Economic Research Associates (NERA), Ernst and Young, and the World Bank. Our career development effort is highly personalized and tightly focused on individual career objectives. Early on in their time at Brandeis, students are introduced to a process designed to hone their job-seeking skills and bring them into direct contact with companies and other potential employers.

International Experience

International experience is an integral part of the IBS education. For many students this takes the form of a semester abroad at one of our 19 prestigious partner institutions around the globe, or a period working for a company outside the United States. And by graduation, all our students are able to do business in more than one language.

Admission Profile:

Average GMAT – 600
Average Undergraduate GPA – 3.4
Average Work Experience – 4 years
Total Enrollment for 2003/4 – 252
Countries Represented – 54

Contact

Brandeis International Business School
Sachar International Center, MS 032
415 South Street
Waltham, MA 02454-9110

Tel: 781-736-2252
    800-878-8866 (toll-free)

E-mail: admission@lemberg.brandeis.edu

www.brandeis.edu/global

CHINA EUROPE INTERNATIONAL BUSINESS SCHOOL

AT A GLANCE

The China Europe International Business School (CEIBS) is a nonprofit, 50-50 joint venture established in November 1994 under an agreement between MOFTEC and the European Commission, with funding from the European Union and Shanghai Municipal Government. Its joint venture partners are the European Foundation for Management Development (EFMD) and Shanghai Jiaotong University. The school has its main campus in Shanghai, a representative office in Beijing, and a liaison office in Shenzhen.

CEIBS is a business school of international caliber and the first one to offer a full-time MBA program, an Executive MBA program, and a wide array of Executive Education programs in Mainland China. In its first eight years, CEIBS has become the leading business school in China. Its MBA program, Executive MBA program, and custom programs of executive education have all been ranked among top 100 globally by UK-based *Financial Times*.

CAMPUS & LOCATION

Occupying a site of four hectares, the CEIBS campus in Pudong, Shanghai, was designed by the internationally renowned Pei Cobb Freed & Partners. It was inaugurated in October 1999 when Phase I—which is comprised of a well-appointed and aesthetic set of academic, administrative, and accommodation facilities, beautifully set in a landscaped courtyard formation—was completed. Doubling the Shanghai campus capacity, the construction of Phase II will be finished by the end of 2003.

In addition to its main campus in Shanghai, CEIBS also has a representative office in Beijing, and a liaison office in Shenzhen.

DEGREES OFFERED

CEIBS offers the MBA (Master of Business Administration), and the EMBA (Executive Master of Business Administration).

PROGRAMS & CURRICULUM

At CEIBS, our aim is to provide students with the necessary skills to be a global business leader with our 17-month, intensive, full-time program. The curriculum consists of 18 core units and 8 elective units.

The Basic Functions

The first phase of the program consists of 15 core units to provide our students with basic management skills, and an understanding of various business functions of an organization. Subjects include major disciplines such as financial management, economics, statistics, human resource management, organizational behavior, marketing management, information technology, commercial law, and business ethics.

The Advancement Modules

The second phase consists of two blocks of diverse electives that permits our students to tailor the MBA program according to their interest and career goals, as well as the opportunity to understand the interdependence between functional areas of a business organization through utilizing the skills acquired in phase one of the program.

Final Integration

In the final phase of the curriculum, our students will undertake four final units that encompass skills gained throughout the last 14 months of the program. Our students will have the opportunity to participate in an intense, hands-on business simulation program developed internally by CEIBS.

FACILITIES

Occupying a site of four hectares, the CEIBS campus in Pudong, Shanghai, was designed by the internationally renowned Pei Cobb Freed & Partners. The campus is both very modern, while at the same time providing an aesthetic setting for reflection and study.

The three-level Academic Center is surrounded by a paved and landscaped courtyard. This facility houses six lecture theatres, twelve discussion rooms, three lecture rooms, and dozens of faculty and administration offices. All lecture theatres and rooms facilitate participation, discussion, and debate. There are also ample discussion rooms next to lecture theatres for case discussion.

The auditorium immediately adjacent to the Academic Center is our 317 tier seated Shanghai Petrochemical Auditorium. Equipped with a wireless system of simultaneous interpretation, the Auditorium provides an ideal venue for large-scale activities involving an international audience.

The Global Sources Information Center (library) provides more than 2,000 electronic journals and databases covering every aspect of business and management, in addition to the traditional printed books and journals. E-databases include UMI's business and management journals, *Dow Jones' Business News*, China business information from EIU and ISI, *Wanfang's Company Directory*, and *OCLC's Union Catalogue* of around 35,000 worldwide libraries.

There are a total of 130 units in the two dormitories that provide a total capacity for 260 students. However, a number of new dormitories are currently under construction. Every unit is equipped with a telephone, a computer connection, satellite TV hook ups and a private bathroom.

The construction of Phase II, which will double the Shanghai campus capacities, will be finished by the end of 2003. It includes two academic centers, one student center, one gymnasium, two student dormitories, and one faculty residence.

EXPENSES & FINANCIAL AID

The application fee: Mainland Chinese applicants: RMB 500

Overseas applicants: $80 (U.S. Dollars)

The tuition fee for the 17-month program for the class entering in June 2004 is:

Mainland Chinese students: RMB 138,000

Overseas students: $25,000 (U.S. Dollars)

CEIBS provides a large amount of scholarships to first and second year MBA students. They include:

- EU Scholarship: 10 full tuition, and 10 half tuition, scholarships to first year mainland Chinese MBA students

- L'Oral China Scholarship: At least one full tuition scholarship to a first year MBA student

- CEIBS International Scholarship: Two scholarships of $5,000 (U.S. Dollars) each, and six scholarships of $2,500 (U.S. Dollars) each to first year overseas students

- Emerson Scholarship: Two scholarships of RMB 20,000 each to second year MBA students

- Baosteel Scholarship: Three scholarships of RMB 3,000 each to second year Chinese MBA students

- Internship Scholarship: EURO 2,500 each to second year MBA students going to Europe for internship

- Exchange Student Scholarship: Scholarship will be provided to students going to Europe for exchange to the extent possible

Bank loans are available for Mainland Chinese students only. Students meeting the criteria set out by the bank can borrow a maximum RMB 110,000 for three years.

FACULTY

The increased reputation of the CEIBS MBA program is largely a result of the commitment and excellent research demonstrated by our faculty. Along with the growth of the CEIBS MBA program, core faculty members have grown substantially in size and diversification in recent years.

In addition to its permanent faculty, the CEIBS MBA program also invites many visiting professors from top universities and business schools around the world to teach MBA classes. Most of these visitors are regulars that come repeatedly to CEIBS. These visiting faculty possess a track record of teaching excellence at CEIBS, and have a genuine interest in the school and China.

STUDENTS

Students at CEIBS are selected from a large and diverse pool of candidates based on their academic capabilities, managerial potential, and interpersonal skills. Students at CEIBS are highly motivated individuals who are capable of bringing new insights and knowledge to a broad range of business situations and problems.

There are 112 students enrolled in the 2003 MBA class. The average age is 29.7 years. Of those students, 33 percent are female. Average GMAT score for the class is 665, with the middle 80 percent falling in the range of 610-730.

ADMISSIONS

The CEIBS MBA admission process is highly competitive, as places are limited to only 124 seats per incoming class. To keep the high quality of CEIBS MBA program, all candidates are expected to meet the following requirements:

- A bachelor's degree, or its equivalent

- A minimum of two years full-time work experience

- A balanced GMAT score: successful applicants usually score in excess of 600

- Proficiency in English: TOEFL or IELTS is recommended to applicants whose native language is not English

Applicants should manage time carefully to make sure that all the necessary information is collected prior to submitting an application. The admissions process will begin only when a complete portfolio of documents is submitted for evaluation.

The application deadline for prospective mainland candidates for the 2004 class is January 25, 2004; the deadline for international applicants is February 29, 2004. As the program is highly competitive in nature, applicants are encouraged to apply in the first, second, and third stages. Spaces offered in the fourth and fifth stage are likely to be limited. Please go to our website for details about application stages.

Application

Beginning in 2003, two channels will be offered for application to the CEIBS MBA program. One is to fill out the paper application form, and the other is to complete the CEIBS online application form (www.ceibs.edu/mba/onlineapp.html). No preference will be given to applicants using either form.

CAREER SERVICES & PLACEMENT

At CEIBS, we believe in providing lifelong learning skills to students that can be transferred and applied in both social and professional settings. Being the best business school in Mainland China, CEIBS is widely recognized by the corporate world as a great source of individuals with proven academic excellence and managerial potential. In 2003, the *Financial Times* ranked the CEIBS MBA program globally as the number one school for procuring employment within three months after graduation.

The CEIBS Career Development Center assists students in effectively managing their careers. The Center's services include organizing the on-campus presentation for recruitment, organizing the job fair, assisting to post job openings, assisting to arrange the on- and off-campus interviews, organizing workshops and seminars on job searching skills and career development, providing individual career counseling services, and assisting with CV writing.

Major Employers (For MBA Students Graduating in 2002)

Some well-known companies hiring our 2002 graduates are Bearingpoint, Eli Lilly, Michelin China, Philips Consumer Electronics (China), BP China Ltd., Nike, Bekaert Asia Shanghai Office, Bosch (China) Investment Ltd., Honeywell, LVMH Fashion Group, Shanghai Cognis Oleochemical Co., Ltd., Siemens China, and A.T. Kearney Shanghai.

INDIAN SCHOOL OF BUSINESS

AT A GLANCE

The Indian School of Business (ISB) is about creating business leaders who are ready to take charge. Our post-graduate program in management offers extraordinary learning opportunities that combine basic business fundamentals with the advanced learning necessary to be successful business leaders.

ISB is born of a partnership of eminent business leaders, entrepreneurs, and academics from around the world. This corporate-academia partnership has ensured that the content of our program is relevant, international in perspective, and delivered at world-class standards.

We have formal affiliations with three of the world's leading business schools—Kellogg School of Management at Northwestern University, The Wharton School at the University of Pennsylvania, and London Business School.

Our world-class programs are offered at highly competitive fees, on a futuristic campus situated in the hi-tech city of Hyderabad.

LOCATION & ENVIRONMENT

Spread over a scenic expanse of 250 acres, the ISB campus is situated on the outskirts of Hyderabad, 45 minutes away from the international airport.

Experiencing India

Few countries on earth have the prodigious diversity that India offers. From north to south and east to west, the people, the languages, the customs, the cuisines, and the landscape are astonishingly different. Hyderabad is located centrally in India, a city that is a fusion of the traditional and the modern.

A fusion of heritage and hi-tech, Hyderabad is a vibrant, 400 year old city with an interesting history, famous for its architecture, pearls, and rich cuisine. But of late, Hyderabad has also emerged as India's Silicon Valley, and the preferred destination for new business, both Indian and international. The city has been attracting worldwide attention as the crucible in which India's IT revolution is taking place, and the site where global technology companies such as Motorola, Oracle, Citicorp, and Microsoft have chosen to establish their offices.

DEGREES OFFERED

We offer a one-year, post-graduate program (comparable to an MBA), and short-term open and customized executive programs.

Contemporary Curriculum

Our curriculum has been developed with the help of an International Academic Council comprised of faculty members from ISB and top-ranked business schools such as the University of Chicago, Harvard, Kellogg, Stanford, and Wharton.

Our program brings a cutting-edge focus on analytical finance, entrepreneurship, technology, marketing, managing in emerging markets, and leadership and change management—all areas of tremendous relevance in grooming tomorrow's business leaders. The core and elective courses provide the fundamentals of management education with the flexibility of individual exploration in the chosen areas of interest.

In addition, students have the option of taking up independent studies. Expert modules are a series of lectures by renowned professors in their area of expertise. They offer students a chance to meet and talk to some of the world's best management thinkers. The courses offered in the post-graduate program are categorized into nine areas: finance, economics and public policy, accounting, entrepreneurship, strategy, organizational behavior, marketing, operations, and information systems.

Leadership Development Program

The Leadership Development Program (LDP) is unique to ISB. Through a series of lectures, discussions, group practice sessions, and workshops, it aims to inculcate in the students the skills required to become tomorrow's business leaders.

Corporate Interaction

Corporate involvement is one of the key features that set ISB apart from most other business schools. We engage business leaders and entrepreneurs throughout the academic year, through visits and workshops, to give the students a 'practitioner's' perspective.

International Student Exchange Programs

We sponsor student exchange programs, giving students the opportunity to study for two terms at a leading business school in another country. Our current partners for this program are the Kellogg School of Management and London Business School.

FACILITIES & EQUIPMENT

ISB offers a wide range of facilities on campus to ensure a students life is hassle-free and enriching. The heart of the ISB community is the Academic Center. This is equipped with state-of-the-art facilities—in particular, a broadband communications network that ensures instant global connectivity. ISB students work and live in a wired and wireless environment. Students can interact by computer or video link with faculty, business leaders, and students anywhere in the world during their courses, projects, and research studies.

The Learning Resource Center (LRC), towering in the middle of the Academic Center, hosts the library. Aimed at being the most comprehensive business library in Asia, the LRC has over 1,500 periodicals, an extensive collection of books, and databases covering all aspects of management and business. The databases that the LRC has subscribed to include ABI-Inform Global, Economist Intelligence Unit, ISI Emerging Market, Prowess, and Vans Electronic Library, among others.

EXPENSES & FINANCIAL AID

Estimated expenses for 2004-2005: Cost in INR for Indian nationals is 7,50,000 for tuition, 1,75,000 for accommodation in a four-bedroom apartment, 2,35,000 for accommodation in a studio apartment, 37,500 for the student activities fee, and 40,000 for miscellaneous expenses such as textbooks, business calculator, laundry, and food.

Cost in U.S. dollars for international students is $15,000 for tuition, $3,500 for accommodation in a four-bedroom apartment, $4,700 for accommodation in a studio apartment, $750 for the student activities fee, and $800 for miscellaneous expenses such as textbooks, business calculator, laundry, and food.

Every student is required to have a laptop computer. These can be leased through the school, or students can bring their own according to specifications given by ISB. Students admitted to the program will be sent these specifications along with their welcome pack.

Financial Aid

Financial aid is available for the entire program in the form of loans and scholarships. Educational loans covering up to 90 percent of the costs, at discounted rates, are offered by various banks subject to meeting their loan requirements. Scholarships are merit- based. The details of terms and requirements of loans are available on the ISB website. ISB helps loan applicants in the processing and disbursement of the loans. In 2003–2004, about 100 students availed of loans.

ISB and several companies offer scholarships to qualified students.

ADMISSIONS

Admission Criteria

To be eligible for admission, students must possess: a bachelor's degree in any discipline, preferably a minimum of two years full-time work experience, and GMAT scores; international students from countries where English is not the primary language of instruction must take the TOEFL.

The Admissions Committee will evaluate all applications. Short-listed candidates will be interviewed as a part of the selection process.

We employ the following criteria for admission assessment:

- *Leadership Potential:* Preference is given to students who have demonstrated leadership qualities in their work and/or academic life. This is assessed primarily through the recommendations included in the application form. Hence, students must include recommendations from their workplace, preferably from their direct supervisor. While most applicants may not have had a chance to demonstrate leadership skills at a public level, initiatives at work or in their personal life will help the Committee assess the candidate's potential.

- *Diversity:* We believe that student diversity is a very important element of an international education. Applicants are encouraged to describe their backgrounds and provide details about what and how they can contribute to the student community. Diversity can be in the form of educational background, work experience, nationality, or personal experiences and goals.

- *Academic Background:* The program is rigorous. Since its short duration makes it even more challenging, students must possess a convincing academic record. While evaluating this performance, we consider the quality of the applicant's undergraduate institute, as well as the marks obtained (percentage, division, grade point average (GPA), class rank, etc.). However, there is no cut-off score.

- *Work Experience:* The diverse professional experience of students contributes to the rich and stimulating experience of the ISB program. Applicants are not distinguished according to industry or job function. However, we are specifically interested in how an applicant has contributed to an organization. Successful applicants must demonstrate managerial and leadership potential, maturity, drive, and focus.

- *The Sponsorship Program:* This program allows corporations to plan the career paths of highly successful employees by grooming them for senior management positions within the company. Organizations that have sponsored students include Citibank, Intel Corporation, Hindustan Lever Limited, the Standard Chartered Group, and Dr. Reddy's Labs. Sponsored candidates have to meet the ISB admission requirements.

Application Process
To apply to ISB, all applicants must:

- Appear for the GMAT. More information about the GMAT is available at www.gmat.com. ISB's GMAT school code is 7010. Indian applicants may contact the ETS representative office at: Phone: 011-651-1649. Fax: 011-609-7103.

- Submit their TOEFL score, if applicable. This applies only to applicants from countries where English is not the primary language. For more information on TOEFL, visit www.toefl.org. The ISB's TOEFL school code is 9047.

- Complete the application form, including essays, transcripts, evaluations, and GMAT scores.

- Send the completed application form along with the nonrefundable application fee of U.S. $100 or Rs. 5,000 to the Admissions Office.

For further information on admissions, please contact:

The Admissions Office
Indian School of Business
The ISB Campus Gachibowli
Hyderabad 500 019 INDIA
Phone: +91 (40) 2300 7000
Fax: +91 (40) 2300 7099
Email: admissions@isb.edu
Website: www.isb.edu/pgp

Foreign students who are admitted must seek a student visa from the Indian Embassy in their country.

ADDITIONAL INFORMATION
We believe research will make ISB truly distinctive. To achieve this, we are setting up six Centers of Excellence in the research areas of leadership and change management, entrepreneurship, technology in emerging markets, strategic marketing, and analytical finance. These Centers will undertake research, teaching, and networking activities in their areas, with a focus on emerging economies.

The Centers will imbue future generations of business leaders with the entrepreneurial spirit and expertise they need to succeed in a business environment that is changing faster than ever before. They will equip them with the capability to successfully lead organizations at the forefront of technological change, and inculcate in them the skills they need to help companies manage the transition from emerging to developed economies. The first of these, the Wadhwani Center for Entrepreneurial Development has already been set up.

Global Consulting Practicum
The Global Consulting Practicum (GCP), offered in collaboration with The Wharton School, is a cross-functional, globally oriented program that educates students in the problems of international business and the skills of consulting. In the GCP, two teams from Wharton and ISB jointly help clients to enter, or enhance, their positions in the North American market.

Marketing Strategy Competition
The Goizueta Marketing Strategy Competition (GMSC) provides students with a hands-on approach to solving the marketing strategy problems that organizations face. Goizueta Business School at Emory University partners with three business schools on this competition: HEC in Paris, ITAM in Mexico, and ISB in India. Teams of students work with U.S. companies and compete for cash prizes.

CAREER SERVICES & PLACEMENT
ISB continues it's impressive placement record with an outstanding placement season for the second graduating class of the post-graduate program in management. The Class of 2003 received 222 offers extending across various industries—consulting, finance, marketing, to name a few. The Indian salary average was INR 8.3 lakhs, while the highest offer received was INR 18 lakhs. Offers for international positions were spread across the U.S., Middle East, and Asia, with the highest offer being U.S. $103,333.

ISB's comprehensive Career Development Program helped students explore a wide range of career opportunities. Our distinctive focus on lateral placements translated into 180 offers for lateral positions, with a noteworthy 83 percent of the class receiving lateral offers.

Students enhanced their careers through their interaction with faculty, their peer group, and the career opportunities provided by ISB with more than 50 percent of the class of 2003 making career shifts this year.

Career Services
ISB has a dedicated Career & Alumni Services (CAS) Office that assists students in the pursuit of their career goals. The CAS provides career counseling, career information services, and conducts skill development workshops.

Rolling Placement Process
The ISB follows a unique rolling placement process, which is recruiter-friendly. Evaluation of students for short-lists and subsequent interviews are scheduled in two cycles between January and April, based on the recruiter's convenience.

The placement process is comprised of four steps:

- *Pre-Placement Talks (PPTs):* Pre-placement talks facilitate recruiter-student interaction while providing students an opportunity to learn more about the organization and any position on offer.

- *Expressions of Interest and Short-lists:* Based on information provided by various organizations during the PPTs, or through their job postings on the ISB Placement Website, students submit applications that help recruiters develop a student short-list for further assessment.

- *Interviews:* Interviews may be conducted on- or off-campus and are scheduled to facilitate multiple recruiting patterns.

- *Job Offers & Acceptances:* Recruiters and students have clearly defined deadlines within which job offers may be made by the recruiter, and either rejected or accepted by the student.

Lateral Hiring at ISB
ISB's Rolling Placement Process is designed to augment lateral hiring into companies, a concept successfully pioneered by ISB in India. A lateral hire is described as any recruitment excluding entry-level positions. The objective of lateral recruitment is to ensure that students with extensive work experience are placed at positions that fully leverage their expertise and professionalism.

A measure of the success of ISB's lateral placement process is the 180 lateral offers made by recruiters this year. Eighty-three percent of the placements for the Class of 2003 were for lateral positions distributed across various functions in middle and senior management, including the position of Chief Executive Officer. Several students made career shifts this year, moving across consulting, financial services, manufacturing, IT, telecom, and media.

PENN STATE UNIVERSITY—GREAT VALLEY CAMPUS

AT A GLANCE

Penn State—Great Valley is dedicated to meeting the needs of working adults. Master's degree programs may be completed on a part-time basis, through evening and Saturday classes, in two to three years. We also offer an accelerated, daytime MBA that may be completed in one year.

Master's degree programs are offered in education, engineering, information science, management, and software engineering. In education, programs include: curriculum and instruction, special education, instructional systems, and principal certification.

The Management Department offers a Master's of Business Administration with three tracks: business administration, new ventures and entrepreneurial studies, and biotechnology and health industry management. Post-master's certificates in finance, health industry management, human resources management, management information systems, marketing, and new ventures are also offered.

The Engineering Department offers the Master of Engineering in Systems Engineering, Master of Software Engineering, and a Master of Science in Information Science, as well as a minor in bioinformatics for all programs.

Over 1,600 graduate students are enrolled on a part-time basis at Great Valley.

LOCATION & ENVIRONMENT

The campus is located in the western suburbs of Philadelphia in the Great Valley Corporate Center, just off Route 202 between King of Prussia and West Chester. We are easily accessible to the Pennsylvania Turnpike, Schuylkill Expressway, Route 422, and Route 30.

Penn State—Great Valley is a full-service, state-of-the-art campus with extensive computing resources and a research library.

DEGREES OFFERED

Degrees offered at Penn State Great Valley:

Business and Management

MBA, with options in business administration, new ventures and entrepreneurial studies, and biotechnology and health industry management

Education

Master of Education in Curriculum and Instruction; Master of Education in Instructional Systems, with emphases in Leadership in Technology Integration (for educators) and Training Design and Development (for training professionals); Master of Science in Instructional Systems, Training Design and Development emphasis; Master of Education in Special Education; and Master of Science in Special Education

Engineering

Master of Engineering in Systems Engineering; Master of Science in Information Science; Master of Software Engineering; and Minor in Bioinformatics

Certificate Programs

Principal Certification Special Education—Instructional I and Supervisory; Certification Bioinformatics; Post-Master's certificates in Business Administration

PROGRAMS & CURRICULUM

Education

Curriculum and Instruction (MEd); Instructional Leadership Instructional Systems (MEd and MS); Leadership in Technology Integration (for educators); Training Design and Development; Special Education (MEd and MS); Instructional I and Supervisory Certification in Special Education; Principal Certification

Engineering

Software Engineering (MSE); Systems Engineering (MEng); Optional Minor for both programs in Bioinformatics

Information Science (MSIS)

Business and Management

Master of Business Administration (MBA); Biotechnology and Health Industry Management; Business New Ventures and Entrepreneurial Studies

Post-Master's Certificates

Biotechnology and Health Industry Management; Finance; Human Resources Management; Management Information Systems; Marketing and New Ventures; and Entrepreneurial Studies

School of Graduate Professional Studies

FACILITIES & EQUIPMENT

Penn State—Great Valley is a full-service campus with state-of-the-art facilities. The learning environment includes state-of-the art computing resources; modern, comfortable corporate style classrooms; and instruction focused on the adult professional. Online databases and full-text resources are available in the Penn State—Great Valley library. The library houses 26,000 books, 380 current professional, trade, and popular periodicals, a collection of government publications, microfiche, CD-ROMs, and books on audiotape. Drawing on the resources of the entire University, the library is part of the University Libraries system—one of the leading academic research library organizations in the nation.

Computing Services

Penn State—Great Valley's Computing Services offers advanced technological equipment and resources, supporting learning and research. We provide laboratories and classroom networks with more than 150 Pentium-class microcomputer workstations. These workstations offer a wide variety of software applications, and are connected to the University's WAN. Additionally, we offer two-way video conferencing and other educational services using compressed video technology.

EXPENSES & FINANCIAL AID

Many part-time adult graduate students benefit from tuition reimbursement plans offered by their employers, or draw on personal savings. In addition to student loans, Penn State—Great Valley offers an Employer Assisted Tuition Deferred Payment Plan. Students who are employed by an organization that maintains a qualified tuition reimbursement program are eligible for this plan, which allows them to defer payment until the fourth week of the next semester. For more information on this, and other payment plans, contact the Bursar's Office at 610-648-3238.

A student aid counselor can provide information about a range of financial aid options to supplement those resources, including loans, grants, work-study, fellowships, graduate assistantships, and scholarships. For more information, contact the financial aid office at 610-648-3216.

Tuition

During the 2002–2003 school year, in-state tuition was $471 per credit; out-of-state tuition was $832 per credit.

FACULTY

Penn State—Great Valley's faculty has established reputations as scholars, consultants, researchers, and practitioners. Our faculty is made up of both full-time professors and part-time instructors, combining top academic credentials with a firm grasp of real-world issues, helping students sharpen problem-solving skills and techniques critical to career success. They offer different, balanced perspectives and work together with professionals in business and industry giving students a hands-on approach to learning. It is easy to build relationships with our faculty, who also serve as advisors and mentors.

STUDENTS

Penn State—Great Valley students are working adults attending courses in the evenings or on Saturdays on a part-time basis. The average age of our students is early 30's. Students have, on average, six years of work experience. More than 1,600 students are enrolled at Penn State—Great Valley.

ADMISSIONS

To receive admission consideration, applicants for admission must hold a bachelor's degree from a regionally accredited U.S. institution, or a comparable degree from a recognized college or university outside of the United States. There are additional admission requirements for each program. Detailed program information, specific admission requirements, and application packets are available from the Admissions Office at Penn State—Great Valley.

For more information, contact Penn State—Great Valley at 610-648-3200 or www.gv.psu.edu.

CAREER SERVICES & PLACEMENT

The Career Advancement Center provides self-assessment instruments, resources, and workshops. A career counselor is available to work one-on-one with students to plot an appropriate career strategy. For more information, contact Michele Auciello at 610-648-3212.

UNIVERSITY OF BRITISH COLUMBIA

AT A GLANCE

The University of British Columbia (UBC) MBA is a rigorous 15-month program built around a challenging and results-focused curriculum that prepares students for business leadership. Students can choose either to enhance the depth of their specialization or to broaden their skill set through a range of more than 80 elective modules in 14 different subject areas. Central to the UBC MBA is an innovative, award-winning 4-month Core Program integrating seven key business disciplines into one foundation course.

The UBC MBA program commences annually in September, with optional preparatory course work (ISP and Pre-Core) starting in late July.

CAMPUS & LOCATION

The University of British Columbia, located in Vancouver, boasts to be one of Canada's most beautiful university campuses. It was established in 1915 and is the nation's third largest university, with an enrolment of more than 38,000 students from around the world. The Sauder School of Business is Canada's premier research business school with internationally renowned faculty who are at the forefront of management thinking.

The UBC campus sits on 40 park-like hectares bordered by forest and beach, and is easily accessible by car, bicycle, and public transit. On-campus housing and nearby residential neighborhoods provide a variety of accommodation options. The campus has a number of recreational facilities, including swimming pools, weight rooms, fitness centers, hockey and curling rinks, and dance and martial arts studios. UBC is also home to the Museum of Anthropology and the Chan Centre for Performing Arts.

UBC is located only 20 minutes from downtown Vancouver, a city of 2 million people situated between the Pacific Ocean and the magnificent coastal mountain range. Vancouver is consistently ranked as one of the world's most liveable cities and is notable for incredible outdoor activities, fine dining, and a vibrant cultural scene. Vancouver is a clean, safe, and cosmopolitan city with a desirable year-round temperate climate. The city's port position on the Pacific Rim ensures strong linkages with international markets.

DEGREES OFFERED

MBA, IMBA, LLB/MBA, MA/MBA, MM, MSc, PhD, BCom

PROGRAMS & CURRICULUM

The key components of the UBC MBA program curriculum are: the Integrated Core Program; Post-Core specialization studies; the Professional Development Program; internships/industry projects; and international exchange opportunities.

The Integrated Core provides an intensive foundation in finance, marketing, accounting, human resources, statistics, managerial economics, and information systems. It is team taught as one comprehensive course to mirror the complexity of the global business environment. Individual subject areas are taught separately and from an integrative perspective to help develop students' understanding of the true multidimensional nature of business. Students develop a broad-based, senior-level strategic approach to business decision-making, as well as collaborative and leadership skills.

Following the Integrated Core, students can enhance their marketability by developing expertise in one of five areas of specialization: finance, information technology management, marketing, strategic management, or supply chain management. Sub-specializations are also offered in e-business and international business. Each specialization consists of required and elective modules.

Students also have the opportunity to apply their knowledge through either a three-month internship with an organization or an industry project supervised by a faculty member related to their area of specialization.

The Professional Development Program (PDP) is dedicated to enhancing students' personal effectiveness through seminars, workshops, guest speakers, discussion groups, networking events, career coaching, and self-directed activities. Valuable skills taught during PDP include time and meeting management, presentation skills, managing multicultural teams, conflict resolution, as well as career management tools.

The UBC MBA program offers students a global perspective through specialized international courses, interaction with the multicultural student body and faculty, and participation in one of the many MBA exchanges. UBC exchanges with an impressive list of 21 leading business schools in 16 countries around the world.

FACILITIES

The Henry Angus Building is the primary home of the Sauder School of Business, though some Executive Education seminars take place in downtown Vancouver at UBC Robson Square.

The David Lam Management Research Library houses a collection of print and electronic materials covering all facets of business management and acts as a resource for students and academic researchers as well as members of the business community.

The Sauder School of Business Technological Services supports the academic and research activities of the Business School. Students have access to campus wireless network facilities and a number of computer labs in the Business School.

EXPENSES & FINANCIAL AID

Tuition fees for the 15-month MBA program are $36,000 CAD for both domestic and international students. Participants can expect to spend another $15,000 to $20,000 CAD for books, materials, and living expenses during the program.

All domestic and international students admissible to the program are eligible for merit-based awards in amounts ranging from $1,000 to $18,000 CAD. Application to the UBC MBA serves as application to these awards, and it is to the applicant's advantage to apply early to be considered for scholarships. UBC MBA students also have access to an institutionally negotiated loan package to financially support their studies.

MBA students are not encouraged to work part time during the program. However, most students earn an average salary of $3,000 CAD per month during their summer internships. Some students are also asked to provide marking or exam invigilation assistance to Business School subjects during their program of studies. A number of performance-based scholarships are available to recognize top students in the MBA program.

Sauder School of Business

FACULTY

The Sauder School of Business has 103 faculty members with impressive backgrounds and achievements. For a current list of faculty and their academic and research profiles, please visit our website.

STUDENTS

Honored by the University's Campus Advisory Board on Student Development for having "a significant positive impact on student life and student development," the UBC MBA program experience fosters a spirit of cooperation and teamwork evident from study groups to social events. Beyond the rich educational experience, the reward is a lifetime network of international friends and business contacts. The Business School network links 15,000 alumni in 56 countries around the world.

Typical Class Profile

Average age: 31 years

Average work experience: 7 years

Average GMAT score: 640

Male/Female ratio: 65/35

Domestic/International visa ratio: 70/30

ADMISSIONS

Applicants must have a four-year bachelor's degree or recognized equivalent from an accredited institution, with a solid academic record and a competitive GMAT score to be eligible for admission to the UBC MBA program. Candidates with diverse academic and professional backgrounds are encouraged to apply. Applicants with less than three years of work experience are admitted to the program only under exceptional circumstances. Successful candidates possess managerial and leadership potential, maturity, ambition, drive, and a clear sense of purpose, demonstrated by professional experience, extracurricular activities, personal interests, and written submissions.

Individuals applying to the MBA program may do so via the online application form. Applicants must ensure that all supporting documents are received by the MBA Programs Office at the Sauder School of Business within two weeks of completing the online application. Documents must include official transcripts and test scores, references, current resume, and a nonrefundable $125 CAD application fee, which is required prior to the application being processed. Applicants who completed their degree in a language other than English must submit acceptable IELTS or TOEFL test scores to demonstrate English language proficiency.

The application deadline for the MBA program is February 28, with the program commencing annually in September. The UBC MBA program uses rolling admissions, so it is to the applicant's advantage to submit completed applications as early as possible before the deadline.

SPECIAL PROGRAMS

UBC offers a joint LLB/MBA degree, which is a four-year program administered jointly by the Business School and the Law School. Applicants are required to apply directly to both schools indicating their desire to be considered for the joint program; enrollment is limited to students who demonstrate academic excellence. Students must complete 86 credits in Law and 45 credits in the MBA through a program of study approved by the Joint Degrees Committee.

The UBC MBA is offered on a part-time basis through the School's downtown campus. The MBA Part-time Program is 51 credits and takes 28 months to complete.

Those seeking a highly specialized and technical business degree may be more suitable for the MM (Master of Management) in Operations Research, Management Information Systems, or Transportation & Logistics at the Sauder School of Business.

CAREER SERVICES & PLACEMENT

The Sauder School of Business Career Centre offers personal consultation and a structured program to assist in identifying, developing, and achieving career goals. Program participants complete a web-based self-assessment test prior to beginning classes in order to clarify career direction. During the period of study, MBA students receive one-on-one career coaching and skills training in areas such as resume building, personal presentation, business etiquette, interviewing, and networking.

The Career Centre actively promotes MBA graduates to the business community locally, nationally, and internationally through its extensive network of corporate contacts. Participants' resumes are published in the UBC MBA Resume Book and distributed both in print and online. Many corporate recruiters host information sessions to interview graduates for post-graduate employment and internships each year.

Employment Statistics for 2002 UBC MBA Graduates:

% Employed at graduation: 89

% Employed in Canada: 84

% Employed internationally: 16

Average salary: $78,000 CAD

Average signing bonus: $14,000 CAD

UNIVERSITY OF DUBLIN

AT A GLANCE

The "College of the Most Holy and Undivided Trinity of Queen Elizabeth near Dublin" was established by the citizens of Dublin under a charter of Queen Elizabeth I in 1592. It is the oldest university in Ireland and one of the oldest in Europe. It combines great traditions of scholarship, independence of thought, and breath of vision with an international reputation for excellence at the cutting edge of science, technology, the arts, and social sciences.

The campus is located on an exceptional city center site that provides immediate access to the heart of Ireland's bustling and growing capital, while retaining within the college grounds a calm and scholarly environment for reflection and learning.

The School of Business Studies is located in the Faculty of Business Economics and Social Studies. The faculty is one of six in the College, the others being Humanities, Letters, Science, Engineering & Systems Sciences, and Health Sciences. The School of Business Studies is unusual among business schools in that it is fully integrated into the University, able to draw on Trinity's strengths in disciplines such as economics, law, and technology to complement the School's own faculty.

The School has an international teaching faculty with links to more than 50 universities in all parts of the world. The educational objectives of the school encourage students to develop their analytical and problem-solving abilities in an environment of creativity and reflection. There is a strong emphasis on effective individual and team performance and on general/strategic management in the global context.

CAMPUS & LOCATION

Situated on the East Coast adjacent to the Irish Sea, Dublin is Ireland's economic political, social, and cultural nerve center. It offers a unique combination of compact city combined with close proximity to mountains and sea. Within half an hour of the bustling city center you can be in the heart of a tranquil and beautiful countryside or strolling a magnificent shoreline. More than 1,000 years old, the rich traditions and turbulent history of the city have inspired writers, artists, and musicians through the ages. Today, the city has become a thriving center of culture and enjoyment. It is also of course the capital of a dynamic economy, hosting numerous world-leading businesses, particularly in the e-business, information and communications technology, chemical and pharmaceutical, and financial services sectors, and enjoying world-record levels of growth.

Situated in the center of the city, Trinity College is intimately associated with Dublin's history and its contemporary business and cultural life, and its faculty are closely associated with Irish and global businesses.

Degrees Offered

Undergraduate Degrees in Business Taught Master's programs: full-time Masters in Business Administration (MBA), part-time MSc (Management), master's and doctoral studies by research.

PROGRAMS & CURRICULUM

Trinity MBA Program 2004

The Trinity MBA is a one-year, full-time program, organized as a set of five modules, each with a different theme, and a Program Preliminary Week. These themes are keyed to the structure of the Company Project, which represents the "capstone" of the program.

Module Theme

Module themes are linked explicitly to the stages of the Company Project. As such, the theme for Module 2 supports the Industry Analysis Stage of the Project; that for Module 3 supports the Company Analysis Stage; that for Module 4 supports the Issue Identification and Analysis Stages. This support is derived from the integration of the courses taught during the Modules, both with each other and with the needs of the Project Stages. Please note that the program is constantly evolving in a process of continuous improvement, thus some details may be subject to change

The objective of Module 1 is to introduce the participants to the program, to the College, and to each other. These objectives are achieved through a series of classroom and group activities that address both the substance of the program and the fundamental learning skills needed to benefit from the program.

The course work in Modules 2–5 can be grouped into five streams: core areas of business; the environment of business; fundamental skills; career management and personal development; and the Company Project. Full details of course content, reading, case studies, etc., will be issued prior to the commencement of each module.

FACILITIES

Students in the Trinity MBA program enjoy a dedicated classroom and a suite of offices and common rooms. All are equipped with individual data points for access to the MBA intranet, college network, and World Wide Web. Students have access to Trinity's world-famous libraries and extensive data bases.

Life in College can be as exciting and as enriching as you wish (or have time!) to make it. There is a wide range of activities to suit all tastes, including student societies, sports clubs, staff and student representation, and student publications. Full details can be found on the college website, www.tcd.ie.

EXPENSES & FINANCIAL AID

The fee for the Trinity MBA is ¤20,500.

FACULTY

The Trinity School of Business Studies has a full-time faculty of 28.

Research is a fundamental basis of the School's work. All staff are active researchers with varied interests in subject matter and methodological terms. All share an interest in interdisciplinary study and in research that pushes the boundary of theory and understanding, while at the same time illuminating practice for the professional manager.

STUDENTS

The Trinity experience is certainly not that of an "MBA factory." The small class size and accessible teaching staff ensure the unique and very personalized learning experience.

The Trinity MBA is characterized by its small class size; the Class of 2003, for example, comprises 32 students. This class size is small enough for everyone to feature as an individual and to encourage close relationships between students themselves and with the teaching staff. On the other hand, the mix of nationalities—there are 12 nationalities represented in the Class of 2003—professions, and managerial backgrounds promotes healthy tension and the discovery of new perspectives.

The following profiles of recent graduates give a flavor of the mix of people in the Trinity MBA program:

Student Profiles

Brendan Cannon, Intel Ireland: "The TCD MBA was the perfect combination for my needs"

Having graduated from Trinity College with a degree in Business Studies, Brendan worked in management positions in Japan, the United Kingdom, and the United States.

"To draw together these different strands of management experience, I sought out an MBA program that would focus on general management skills, a cooperative atmosphere, and international focus.

"The TCD MBA, with its focus on providing a suite of 'state-of-the-art' business disciplines while cultivating vital interpersonal skills, was the perfect combination for my needs. Trinity's selection procedure ensures a mix of students from diverse background who are highly motivated and committed to success. I enjoyed the Trinity learning experience, the personal journey that it facilitated, and the lasting friendships that were forged over the year. All in all, the Trinity MBA has proven to be excellent value for money."

On graduation from the TCD MBA, Brendan joined Intel Ireland where he is finance manager for the New Business Development Group. "In an exciting incubator environment, we chart emerging opportunities and work to develop new businesses. Working in the rapidly changing business environment of today, where

Trinity College School of Business Studies

the component parts change with each development in technology while the business fundamentals remain the same, my MBA has proven to be a vital management tool."

Natalia Alviar, Accenture: Having gained her degree in Information Systems Engineering, Natalia, from Bogota, Colombia, worked in IT Management and consulting before deciding that it was time to broaden her knowledge through an international MBA program.

"After gathering a lot of information and comparing many programs, I made my decision for the Trinity MBA based on several factors, including the small size of the group; the Company Project; the strong emphasis on team work as a critical managerial skill; the one-year duration of the program; and finally, the well-rounded business program, which would be a good complement to my specialized and technical background. The program offered for me the best value for money I could find."

Summing up her experience of her year at Trinity, she says, "All my expectations were met and exceeded. The program gave me the opportunity to meet and become friends with extraordinary people in professional and personal terms, from many different countries. The mix of cultures and different ways of thinking made the program an extraordinary and challenging one-time-in-a-life experience. The program and Trinity's faculty put the MBA class members in contact with several important Irish and multinational companies to continue our professional career. As result of this contact, I joined Andersen Consulting (now Accenture) where my professional growth continues."

Olga Gusak AIB Group plc.: Having worked for eight years in project management and raising finance for major aviation and public infrastructure projects in Eastern Europe and CIS, Olga—originally from Lyiv, Ukraine—decided to broaden her understanding of strategic business development and financial management.

"I chose the Trinity MBA because it offered a combination of a one-year intensive program, group-work, and real-life company-project experience in a well-rounded business program focused on strategic business management. Such a combination definitely is money well spent.

"Despite a relatively small size of the Trinity MBA class, it was a truly international experience—people from 15 countries, and an almost 50:50 male/female split.

"The Trinity MBA provided us with valuable project experience in domestic and international companies based in Ireland, all of which are part of the Celtic Tiger success story. Furthermore, in my case, the Company Project led to a future job—I was hired as a strategy consultant by AIB Group in Ireland and after less than a year offered a job in its Polish division as director, Corporate Banking."

ADMISSIONS

Each MBA class is selected not only on the grounds of the academic and professional experience of the individual but also with a view to providing a stimulating balance of basic disciplinary training, work experience, and international background.

Admission is by a competitive process. Early application is strongly advised, ideally before January 31 and not later than June 30. Later applications from well-qualified applicants may be considered, provided all the places on the program have not been allocated. Applications will be reviewed on an ongoing basis throughout the year but will only be considered for the next MBA class for which vacancies exist at the time of the application.

Applications should be addressed to:

Kate Morris, Program Administrator
Trinity MBA Program
School of Business Studies
Trinity College
Dublin 2, Ireland

Applicants whose applications have been accepted by the School of Business Studies will receive formal notification of admission from the Dean of Graduate Studies.

Applicants should hold a university degree or its equivalent and should have a minimum of three years work experience. Mature applicants may be considered on the basis of a sustained, exceptional record of achievement in employment. The preferred age range is 25–35 years. Each candidate is required to present a satisfactory result in the Graduate Management Admissions Test (GMAT).

Applications are assessed on the basis of their completed application form, their references, their GMAT score, and their TOEFL score for those for whom English is not their first language. In some cases interviews are required.

ADDITIONAL INFORMATION

Trinity College was one of the first European universities to offer an MBA program, in 1964, and the Trinity MBA has developed continuously since then. In 1999 it became the first Irish MBA program to receive the prestigious international accreditation of the Association of MBAs (AMBA).

General Management Perspective

The program provides an integrated and integrative view of management and emphasizes the perspective and skills of the general manager. Only individuals of high caliber are accepted, and students are individually challenged to attain the highest standards of personal excellence. We expect our graduates to make their mark in their chosen fields, following in the footsteps of generations of Trinity graduates.

The Company Project

The Company Project is at the heart of the Trinity MBA. As one of a group of five to six participants you are assigned to work on issues of major strategic concern to participating companies, varying from entrepreneurial start-ups to established international brand names. Here you integrate your learning as a team member, apply your growing competence to real-world situations, and report regularly to the top management of the company.

As well as providing a challenging context in which to practice what you have learned, the Company Project acts as a bridge from study back to the world of management as an MBA graduate.

"The Trinity MBA Company Project is a world-class experiential learning opportunity in high-level management practice. With the excellent support offered by tutors and other faculty throughout the execution of the program, students leapfrog more pedestrian approaches to the development of management skills and participate fully in the arena of senior management decision-making.

To reach this level in a one-year program is remarkable and an outcome that makes the Trinity Program a truly exceptional value among MBA programs worldwide."

—Professor Paul Bishop, Magna International Professor,
Richard Ivey School of Business, University of Western Ontario;
External Examiner, Trinity MBA Program

CAREER SERVICES & PLACEMENT

Trinity MBA students are actively assisted in their career choices during their time at Trinity. Support and advice for career management is available throughout the year from the College Careers Advisory Service and from the faculty of the Business School.

A stream of classes, events, and activities, extending across the five modules of the program, integrate the themes of Career Management and Personal Development. They include coaching on key managerial skills, team working, preparation of a curriculum vitae (CV) in response to an advertisement for a position of interest, practice interviews by professional recruiters, and networking opportunities with the Trinity Business Alumni. Students work on the publication of a directory of class resumes that will be widely distributed to major companies and agencies.

The Director of the College Careers Advisory Service and an experienced Human Resource Management Consultant work with individual students throughout the year, providing guidance and advice on their career-planning and job search strategies.

Schulich
School of Business
York University

Leading
IN A world of change

The Schulich School of Business is the highest ever ranked Canadian school and one of the top 10 non-US schools in the world. Schulich offers flexible, year-round studies and one of the broadest ranges of business degrees and degree specializations of any business school in North America.

Highest Ever Ranked Canadian Business School

The Economist Intelligence Unit, a division of the prestigious business publication *The Economist*, ranked Schulich 17th in the world among leading business schools in its 2002 global survey. It was the highest global ranking ever achieved by a Canadian business school. The ranking measured the ability of business schools to provide new career opportunities, personal development and educational experience, increased salary, and networking opportunities.

A WORLD OF Choice

Choose the Degree That's Right for You

- MBA
  Full-Time
  Part-Time
  Accelerated
  Executive
- MBA/LLB
- MBA/MFA/MA
- IMBA (International MBA)
- MPA

REAL-WORLD Relevance

One of the hallmarks of management education at Schulich is real-world learning. The strategy field study takes students far beyond the case method into a real-time, real-world business for one of the richest and most intense learning experiences they will ever have.

A WORLD OF Opportunity

Some of the many leading world-class companies that recruit Schulich MBAs:

Asian Development Bank	CDC IXIS Capital Markets	L'Oréal	Samsung
American Express	Celestica	Manulife Financial	Scotiabank
Aventis Pasteur Limited	CIBC World Markets	Nestlé	Siemens
Bayer	Citigroup	Quebecor World Europe	Visa International
BMW	DBS Bank	RBC Financial	
Bombardier Transportation	Goldfarb Consultants	Saatchi & Saatchi	

The new Schulich School of Business and Executive Learning Centre, completed in September 2003, was designed following intensive study of the best features of the world's top business schools. Attributes such as technology-enhanced classrooms, state-of-the-art library and computer facilities, wireless Internet cafes, courtyards and a 300-seat auditorium will greatly enhance teaching, learning and research at Schulich.

Profile of the Schulich MBA Class of 2002

- Average age: **30**
- Average years' work experience: **7**
- Average GMAT: **647**
- GMAT range: **550-790**
- Average GPA: **3.3/4.0 (B+)**
- Male: **60%**
- Female: **40%**
- International students: **59%**

GLOBAL Reach

As Canada's Global Business School™, Schulich has one of the strongest international networks of any school in the world. MBA students at Schulich have the opportunity to pursue academic exchanges with more than 50 of the best business schools from around the world, as well as placement and internship opportunities with 150 global corporations in more than 50 countries.

In addition to its International MBA (IMBA) program, Schulich offers MBA students a broad range of international study options.

The Schulich alumni network of 16,000 members is served by 23 chapters world wide.

Schulich's World-Class Faculty

Schulich's highly diverse and international faculty members are among the most distinguished academics in their various fields. Research conducted by the School's faculty members provides a strong balance between academic rigour and research and real-world relevance. Faculty are highly sought after by the media and the private sector as expert consultants and commentators on a wide range of business issues.

INFORMATION AND INQUIRIES

The Division of Student Services and International Relations
Schulich School of Business
York University
4700 Keele Street
Toronto, Ontario, Canada M3J 1P3

DOMESTIC ADMISSIONS

Tel: (416) 736-5060
Fax: (416) 650-8174
E-mail: admissions@schulich.yorku.ca

INTERNATIONAL ADMISSIONS

Tel: (416) 736-5059
Fax: (416) 650-8174
E-mail: intladmissions@schulich.yorku.ca

www.schulich.yorku.ca

INDEXES

ALPHABETICAL LIST OF SCHOOLS

A

B

C

D

E

F

G

H

I

J

Jackson State University — 196
Jacksonville State University — 197
James Madison University — 197
John Carroll University — 198

K

Kansas State University — 198
Kennesaw State University — 199
Kent State University — 200

L

La Salle University — 201
Lamar University — 201
Lehigh University — 202
Louisiana State University — 203
Louisiana State University—Shreveport — 204
Louisiana Tech University — 204
Loyola College in Maryland — 205
Loyola Marymount University — 205
Loyola University Chicago — 206
Loyola University New Orleans — 207

M

Marquette University — 208
Marshall University — 208
Massachusetts Institute of Technology — 209
McNeese State University — 210
Miami University — 211
Michigan State University — 211
Milsaps College — 212
Mississippi State University — 213
Monmouth University — 214, 428
Montana State University — 215
Montclair State University — 215
Morgan State University — 216
Murray State University — 216

N

National University of Singapore — 217
New Jersey Institute of Technology — 217
New Mexico State University — 218
New York University Leonard N. Stern School of Business — 219
New York University Stern Executive MBA Program — 220

Nicholls State University — 220
North Carolina State University — 221, 430
North Dakota State University — 221
Northeastern University — 222
Northern Arizona University — 222
Northern Illinois University — 223
Northern Kentucky University — 224
Northwestern University — 224

O

Oakland University — 225
Ohio State University — 226
Ohio University — 227
Oklahoma State University — 227
Old Dominion University — 228
Oregon State University — 229

P

Pace University — 229
Pacific Lutheran University — 230
Penn State University—Great Valley Campus — 484
Pennsylvania State University IMBA — 231
Pennsylvania State University — 231
Pennsylvania State University—Erie, The Behrend College — 232
Pennsylvania State University— Harrisburg Campus — 233
Pepperdine University — 234
Pittsburg State University — 235
Portland State University — 236
Purdue University—Calumet — 237
Purdue University—West Lafayette — 237

Q

Queen's University — 238

R

Radford University — 239
Rensselaer Polytechnic Institute — 240, 432
Rice University — 241, 434
Rider University — 242
Rochester Institute of Technology — 242
Rollins College — 243
Rutgers/The State University of New Jersey — 244
Rutgers/The State University of New Jersey—Camden — 245

S

Saginaw Valley State University — 246
St. Cloud State University — 246
St. John's University — 247, 436
Saint Joseph's University — 248
Saint Louis University — 249
Saint Mary's University, Canada — 249
Saint Mary's University, San Antonio — 250
St. Mary's University of Minnesota — 251
Salisbury University — 251
Sam Houston State University — 252
Samford University — 252
San Diego State University — 253
San Francisco State University — 254
San Jose State University — 254, 438
Santa Clara University — 255
Seattle Pacific University — 256
Seattle University — 256
Seton Hall University — 257
Simmons College — 258
Southeast Missouri State University — 259
Southeastern Louisiana University — 260
Southern Illinois University— Carbondale — 260
Southern Illinois University— Edwardsville — 261
Southern Methodist University — 262, 440
Southwest Missouri State University — 263
Southwest Texas State University — 264
Stanford University — 264
State University of West Georgia — 265
Stephen F. Austin State University — 266
Stetson University — 267
Suffolk University — 267
Syracuse University — 268

T

TCU — 269, 442
Tel Aviv University — 270
Temple University — 271
Tennessee State University — 272
Tennessee Technological University — 272
Texas A&M University—College Station — 273
Texas A&M University—Commerce — 274
Texas A&M University—Corpus Christi — 275
Texas Tech University — 275
Thunderbird — 276
Truman State University — 277
Tulane University — 278

U

Union College — 279, 444
Universidad Panamericana — 280
Universite Laval — 281

BUSINESS PROGRAM NAME

Location
USA
Alabama

Alaska

Arizona

Arkansas

California

Colorado

Connecticut

Delaware

District of Columbia

Florida

Georgia

Hawaii

Idaho

Illinois

Ireland

Israel

Mexico

The Netherlands

Singapore

Spain

Switzerland

United Kingdom

ABOUT THE AUTHOR

Nedda Gilbert is a graduate of the University of Pennsylvania and holds a master's degree from Columbia University. She has worked for The Princeton Review since 1985. In 1987, she created The Princeton Review corporate test preparation service, which provides Wall Street firms and premier companies tailored educational programs for their employees. She currently resides in New Jersey.

Notes

Notes

www.PrincetonReview.com

The Princeton Review
Admissions Services

At The Princeton Review, we care about your ability to get accepted to the best school for you. But, we all know getting accepting involves much more than just doing well on standardized tests. That's why, in addition to our test preparation services, we also offer free admissions services to students looking to enter college or graduate school. You can find these services on our website, *www.PrincetonReview.com*, the best online resource for researching, applying to, and learning how to pay for the right school for you.

No matter what type of program you're applying to—undergraduate, graduate, law, business, or medical—**PrincetonReview.com has the free tools, services, and advice you need to navigate the admissions process.** Read on to learn more about the services we offer.

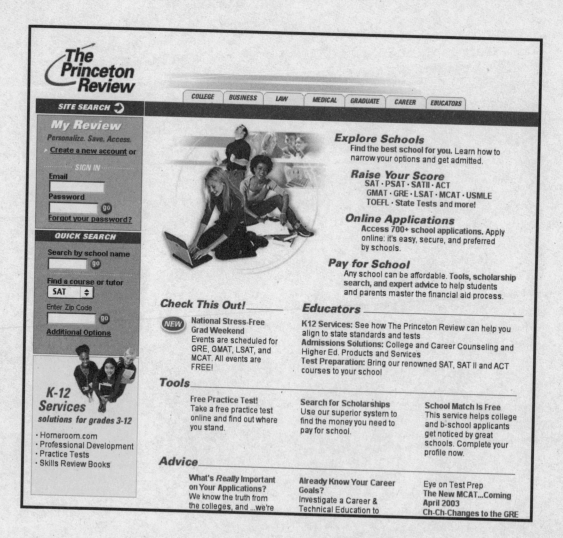

Research Schools
www.PrincetonReview.com/Research

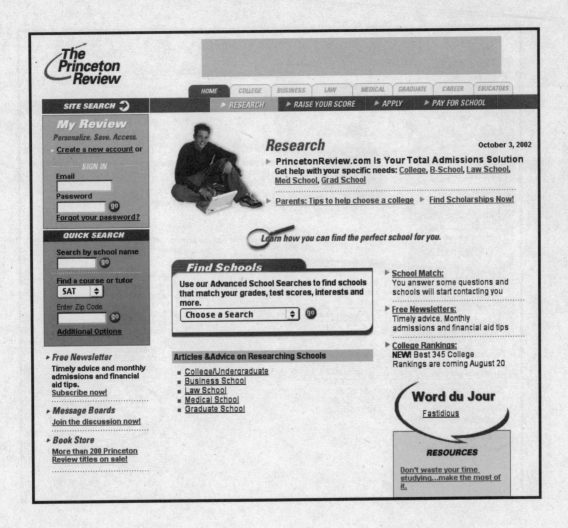

PrincetonReview.com features an interactive tool called **Advanced School Search.** When you use this tool, you enter stats and information about yourself to find a list of schools that fit your needs. From there you can read statistical and editorial information about every accredited business school, law school, medical school, and graduate school.

If you are applying to business school, make sure to use **School Match**. You tell us your scores, interests, and preferences and Princeton Review partner schools will contact you.

No matter what type of school or specialized program you are considering, **PrincetonReview.com has free articles and advice, in addition to our tools, to help you make the right choice.**

Apply to School
www.PrincetonReview.com/Apply

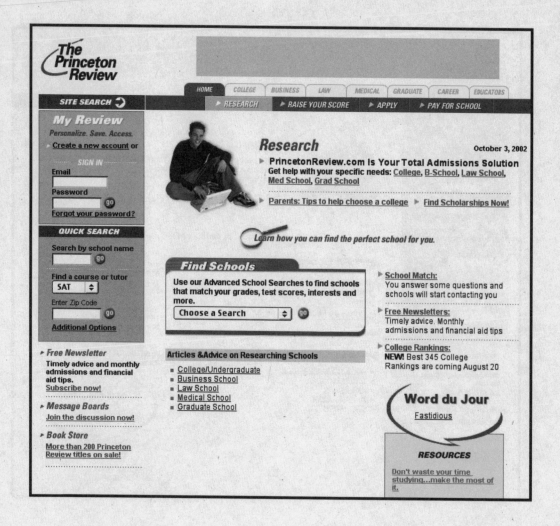

For most students, completing the school application is the most stressful part of the admissions process. PrincetonReview.com's powerful **Online School Application Engine** makes it easy to apply.

Paper applications are mostly a thing of the past. And, our hundreds of partner schools tell us they prefer to receive your applications online.

Using our online application service is simple:

- Enter information once and the common data automatically transfers onto each application.
- Save your applications and access them at any time to edit and perfect.
- Submit electronically or print and mail in.
- Pay your application fee online, using an e-check, or mail the school a check.

Our powerful application engine is built to accommodate all your needs.

Pay for School
www.PrincetonReview.com/Finance

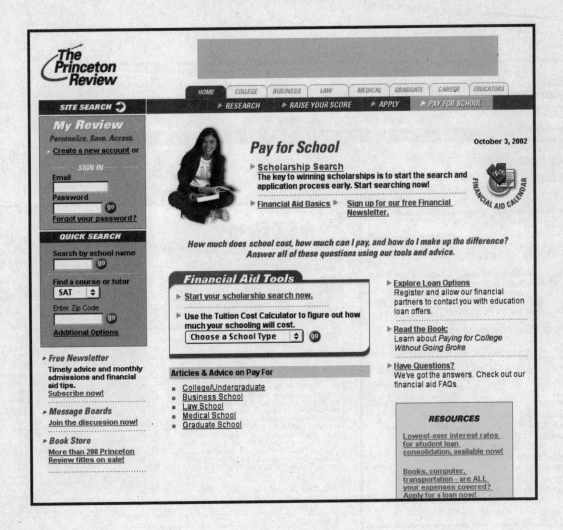

The financial aid process is confusing for everyone. But don't worry. Our free online tools, services, and advice can help you plan for the future and get the money you need to pay for school.

Our **Scholarship Search** engine will help you find free money, although often scholarships alone won't cover the cost of high tuitions. So, we offer other tools and resources to help you navigate the entire process.

Filling out the FAFSA and CSS Profile can be a daunting process, use our **Strategies for both forms** to make sure you answer the questions correctly the first time.

If scholarships and government aid aren't enough to swing the cost of tuition, we'll help you secure student loans. The Princeton Review has partnered with a select group of reputable financial institutions who will help **explore all your loans options**.

If you know how to work the financial aid process, you'll learn you don't have to **eliminate a school based on tuition.**

Be a Part of the PrincetonReview.com Community

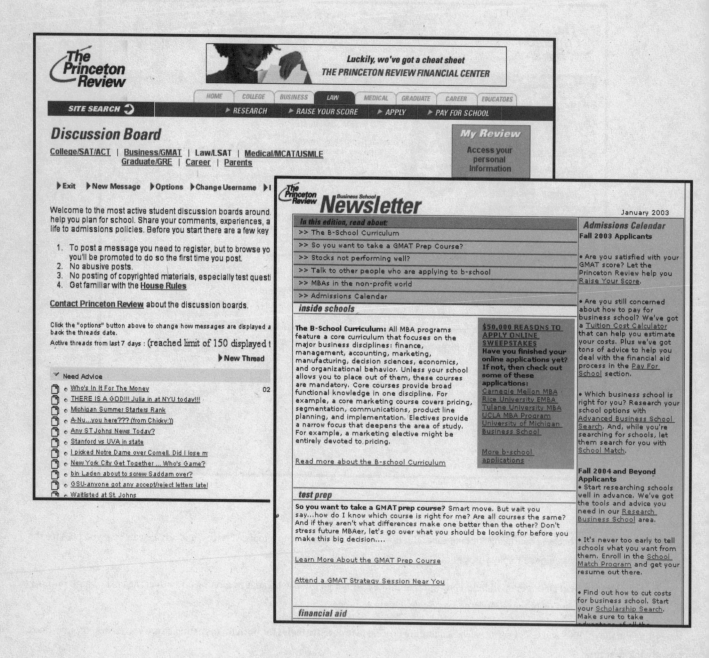

PrincetonReview.com's **Discussion Boards** and **Free Newsletters** are additional services to help you to get information about the admissions process from your peers and from The Princeton Review experts.

Book Store
www.PrincetonReview.com/college/Bookstore.asp

In addition to this book, we publish hundreds of other titles, including guidebooks that highlight life on campus, student opinion, and all the statistical data that you need to know about any school you are considering. Just a few of the titles that we offer are:

- Complete Book of Business Schools
- Complete Book of Law Schools
- Complete Book of Medical Schools
- The Best 351 Colleges
- The K&W Guide to Colleges for Students with Learning Disabilities or Attention Deficit Disorder
- Guide to College Majors
- Paying for College Without Going Broke

For a complete listing of all of our titles, visit our **online book store**:

www.princetonreview.com/college/bookstore.asp

More expert advice from  The Princeton Review

G ive yourself the best chances for getting into the business school of your choice with The Princeton Review. We can help you get higher test scores, make the most informed choices, and make the most of your experience once you get there. We can also help you make the career move that will let you use your skills and education to their best advantage.